C000020674

1,000,000 Books

are available to read at

Forgotten Books

---◆---

www.ForgottenBooks.com

---◆---

Read online
Download PDF
Purchase in print

ISBN 978-1-5285-3534-2
PIBN 10917129

This book is a reproduction of an important historical work. Forgotten Books uses
state-of-the-art technology to digitally reconstruct the work, preserving the original format
whilst repairing imperfections present in the aged copy. In rare cases, an imperfection in
the original, such as a blemish or missing page, may be replicated in our edition. We do,
however, repair the vast majority of imperfections successfully; any imperfections that
remain are intentionally left to preserve the state of such historical works.

Forgotten Books is a registered trademark of FB &c Ltd.
Copyright © 2018 FB &c Ltd.
FB &c Ltd, Dalton House, 60 Windsor Avenue, London, SW19 2RR.
Company number 08720141. Registered in England and Wales.

For support please visit www.forgottenbooks.com

1 MONTH OF
FREE
READING

at

www.ForgottenBooks.com

By purchasing this book you are eligible for one month membership to ForgottenBooks.com, giving you unlimited access to our entire collection of over 1,000,000 titles via our web site and mobile apps.

To claim your free month visit:
www.forgottenbooks.com/free917129

* Offer is valid for 45 days from date of purchase. Terms and conditions apply.

English
Français
Deutsche
Italiano
Español
Português

www.forgottenbooks.com

Mythology Photography **Fiction**
Fishing Christianity **Art** Cooking
Essays Buddhism Freemasonry
Medicine **Biology** Music **Ancient**
Egypt Evolution Carpentry Physics
Dance Geology **Mathematics** Fitness
Shakespeare **Folklore** Yoga Marketing
Confidence Immortality Biographies
Poetry **Psychology** Witchcraft
Electronics Chemistry History **Law**
Accounting **Philosophy** Anthropology
Alchemy Drama Quantum Mechanics
Atheism Sexual Health **Ancient History**
Entrepreneurship Languages Sport
Paleontology Needlework Islam
Metaphysics Investment Archaeology
Parenting Statistics Criminology
Motivational

LAWS

OF THE

STATE OF NEW YORK,

PASSED AT THE

ONE HUNDRED AND THIRTY-SIXTH SESSION

OF THE

LEGISLATURE,

BEGUN JANUARY FIRST, 1913, AND ENDED MAY
THIRD, 1913,

ALSO CHAPTERS 794–800 PASSED AT THE EXTRAORDI-
NARY SESSION, BEGUN JUNE 16, 1913,

AT THE CITY OF ALBANY,

AND ALSO OTHER MATTERS REQUIRED BY LAW TO
BE PUBLISHED WITH THE SESSION LAWS.

For chapters 801–810, passed at the extraordinary
session, see end of volume 3.

ALBANY
J. B. LYON COMPANY, STATE PRINTERS
1913

189415

STANFORD LIBRARY

TABLE OF CONTENTS.

[iii]

For chapters 801-810, passed at the extraordinary session, see end of volume 3.

CERTIFICATE.

STATE OF NEW YORK,

OFFICE OF THE SECRETARY OF STATE,

ALBANY, *September* 10, 1913.

Pursuant to the directions of chapter 37, laws of 1909, entitled legislative law, I hereby certify that the following volume of the laws of this state was printed under my direction.

MITCHELL MAY,
Secretary of State.

In this volume, every act which received the assent of a majority of all the members of the legislature, three-fifths of all the members elected to either house thereof being present, pursuant to section 25 of article 3 of the constitution of this state, is designated under its title by the words " passed, three-fifths being present." And every act which received the assent of a majority of all the members elected to each branch of the legislature, pursuant to section 15 of article 3 of the constitution of this state, is designated under its title by the words " passed, a majority being present." And every act which received the assent of two-thirds of all the members elected to each branch of the legislature, pursuant to section 20 of article 3 of the constitution of this state, is designated under its title by the words " passed by a two-thirds vote." (See legislative law, laws of 1909, chapter 37, section 44.)

[v]

PUBLICATION OF SESSION LAWS.

§ 45. **Publication of session laws; contents of published volumes of session laws.** The secretary of state shall annually cause the session laws to be published as soon as possible after the adjournment of the legislature. Such volumes shall contain:

1. A statement of the names and residences of the governor, lieutenant-governor, senators and members of assembly, the presiding officers and clerks of both houses in office during each session.

2. The laws and concurrent resolutions passed at each session.

3. Amendments to the state constitution approved and ratified by the people at the last preceding general election.

4. Tables showing the laws and parts thereof amended or repealed by such laws.

5. Indexes of the laws and concurrent resolutions contained in such volumes.

6. Such other matters as are required by law to be published in such volumes.

Such laws, concurrent resolutions, tables, indexes and other matters so required to be published shall be prepared for publication in the state library under the supervision of the director thereof. Side notes or section headings shall be inserted indicating the subject-matter of the several sections of the laws and concurrent resolutions. Suitable references to existing general or consolidated laws, codes, or special or local laws may be made in foot notes or otherwise. The said director may submit to the state printing board changes in the style of execution as to type and paper, which, when approved by such board, shall be the style of execution to be thereafter followed in the publication of session laws. All contracts hereafter entered into for the printing of session laws shall be for terms of two years, and shall provide for the printing thereof in the style as so approved, and with

the notes and references and in the form, and containing the
matter, herein authorized or required. Each volume printed for
the state shall contain the certificate of the secretary of state that
it was printed under his direction. (Legislative law, L. 1909,
ch. 37, § 45, as amended by L. 1911, ch. 272.)

List of Officers and Members of the Legislature.

1913.

NAMES AND RESIDENCES

Of the Governor, Lieutenant-Governor, Senators and Members of Assembly, the Presiding Officers and Clerks of Both Houses of the Legislature of the State of New York at the Time of the Passage of the Laws Contained in this Volume.

GOVERNOR.

WILLIAM SULZER..........................New York, New York County.

LIEUTENANT-GOVERNOR.

MARTIN H. GLYNN............................Albany, Albany County.

CLERK OF THE SENATE.

PATRICK E. McCABE..........................Albany, Albany County.

SENATORS.

District.	NAME.	County.	Address.
1..	Thomas H. O'Keefe.........	Nassau..............	Oyster Bay.
2..	Bernard M. Patten..........	Queens..............	Long Island City.
3..	Thomas H. Cullen...........	Kings...............	Brooklyn.
4..	Henry P. Velte.............	Kings...............	Brooklyn.
5..	William J. Heffernan........	Kings...............	Brooklyn.
6..	William B. Carswell.........	Kings...............	Brooklyn.
7..	Daniel J. Carroll............	Kings...............	Brooklyn.
8..	James F. Duhamel..........	Kings...............	Brooklyn.
9..	Felix J. Sanner.............	Kings...............	Brooklyn.
10..	Herman H. Torborg.........	Kings...............	Brooklyn.
11..	Christopher D. Sullivan.....	New York...........	New York city.
12..	John C. Fitzgerald..........	New York...........	New York city.
13..	James D. McClelland.......	New York...........	New York city.
14..	James A. Foley.............	New York...........	New York city.
15..	John J. Boylan.............	New York...........	New York city.
16..	[1]Robert F. Wagner..........	New York...........	New York city.
17..	Walter R. Herrick..........	New York...........	New York city.
18..	Henry W. Pollock..........	New York...........	New York city.

[1] Temporary president.

ix

SENATORS—(Concluded).

District.	NAME.	County.	Address.
19..	¹George W. Simpson.........	New York............	New York city.
20..	James J. Frawley............	New York............	New York city.
21..	¹Stephen J. Stilwell..........	New York............	New York city.
22..	¹Anthony J. Griffen..........	New York............	New York city.
23..	¹George A. Blauvelt.........	Rockland............	Monsey.
24..	John F. Healy..............	Westchester.........	New Rochelle.
25..	John D. Stivers.............	Orange..............	Middletown.
26..	⁴Franklin D. Roosevelt......	Dutchess............	Hyde Park.
27..	Abraham J. Palmer.........	Ulster..............	Milton.
28..	Henry M. Sage.............	Albany..............	Menands.
29..	John W. McKnight.........	Rensselaer..........	Castleton.
30..	George H. Whitney.........	Saratoga............	Mechanicville.
31..	Loren H. White............	Schenectady.........	Delanson.
32..	Seth G. Heacock...........	Herkimer...........	Ilion.
33..	James A. Emerson..........	Warren.............	Warrensburg.
34..	Herbert P. Coats...........	Franklin............	Saranac Lake.
35..	Elon R. Brown.............	Jefferson...........	Watertown.
36..	William D. Peckham........	Oneida.............	Utica.
37..	Ralph W. Thomas...........	Madison............	Hamilton.
38..	J. Henry Walters...........	Onondaga...........	Syracuse.
39..	Clayton L. Wheeler.........	Delaware...........	Hancock.
40..	Charles J. Hewitt..........	Cayuga.............	Locke.
41..	John F. Murtaugh..........	Chemung...........	Elmira.
42..	Thomas B. Wilson..........	Ontario.............	Hall.
43..	John Seeley...............	Steuben............	Woodhull.
44..	Thomas H. Bussey.........	Wyoming...........	Perry.
45..	George F. Argetsinger......	Monroe.............	Rochester.
46..	William L. Ormrod.........	Monroe.............	Churchville.
47..	George F. Thompson.......	Niagara............	Middleport.
48..	John F. Malone............	Erie................	Buffalo.
49..	Samuel J. Ramsperger......	Erie................	Buffalo.
50..	Gottfried H. Wende........	Erie................	Buffalo.
51..	Frank N. Godfrey..........	Cattaraugus........	Olean.

² Vice Henry Salant, originally seated on the face of the returns. A recount of the vote showed a plurality for Simpson, who was accordingly seated by the senate April 26, 1913.

³ Removed from office May 24, 1913.

⁴ Resigned March 17, 1913. Appointed assistant secretary of the navy.

SPEAKER OF THE ASSEMBLY.

ALFRED E. SMITH..........................New York, New York County.

CLERK OF THE ASSEMBLY.

GEORGE R. VAN NAMEE.......................Watertown, Jefferson County.

MEMBERS OF ASSEMBLY.

District.	NAME.	County.	Address.
1..	Harold J. Hinman..........	Albany...............	Albany.
2..	John G. Malone..........	Albany...............	Albany.
3..	William C. Baxter..........	Albany...............	Watervliet.
	Ransom L. Richardson......	Allegany............	Fillmore.
	Mortimer B. Edwards......	Broome............	Lisle.
	Clare Willard..............	Cattaraugus.........	Allegany.
	Michael Grace............	Cayuga............	Weedsport.
1..	George W. Jude............	Chautauqua.........	Jamestown.
2..	John Leo Sullivan..........	Chautauqua.........	Dunkirk.
	Robert P. Bush...........	Chemung............	Horseheads.
	Walter A. Shepardson......	Chenango............	Norwich.
	Charles J. Vert............	Clinton............	Plattsburgh.
	Alexander W. Hover.......	Columbia............	Germantown.
	Niles Freeland Webb.......	Cortland............	Cortland, R. F. D. 4.
	John W. Telford..........	Delaware............	Margaretville.
1..	Myron Smith.............	Dutchess............	Millbrook.
2..	John Augustus Kelly......	Dutchess............	Poughkeepsie.
1..	George Frederick Small......	Erie...............	Buffalo.
2..	Clinton T. Horton..........	Erie...............	Buffalo.
3..	Albert F. Geyer..........	Erie...............	Buffalo.
4..	Edward D. Jackson........	Erie...............	Buffalo.
5..	Richard F. Hearn..........	Erie...............	Buffalo.
6..	James M. Rozan..........	Erie...............	Buffalo.
7..	Joseph Vincent Fitzgerald....	Erie...............	Lancaster.
8..	George Geoghan..........	Erie...............	Buffalo.
9..	John Dorst, Jr............	Erie...............	Akron.
	Spencer G. Prime, 2d.......	Essex...............	Upper Jay.
	Alexander Macdonald......	Franklin............	St. Regis Falls.
	James H. Wood...........	Fulton and Hamilton..	Gloversville.
	Clarence Bryant..........	Genesee............	LeRoy.
	J. L. Patrie..............	Greene......,.....	Catskill.
	E. Bert Pullman..........	Herkimer............	Fulton Chain.
1..	H. Edmund Machold........	Jefferson............	Ellisburg.
2..	John G. Jones............	Jefferson............	Carthage.
1..	John Joseph Kelly.........	Kings...............	Brooklyn.
2..	William J. Gillen..........	Kings...............	Brooklyn.
3..	Frank J. Taylor..........	Kings...............	Brooklyn.
4..	Harry W. Kornobis........	Kings...............	Brooklyn.
5..	Vincent A. O'Connor.......	Kings...............	Brooklyn.
6..	Lester D. Volk...........	Kings...............	Brooklyn.
7..	Daniel F. Farrell..........	Kings...............	Brooklyn.
8..	John J. McKeon..........	Kings...............	Brooklyn.
9..	Frederick S. Burr.........	Kings...............	Brooklyn.
10..	George E. Dennen..........	Kings...............	Brooklyn.
1..	Karl Soden Deits..........	Kings...............	Brooklyn.

LIST OF OFFICERS.

MEMBERS OF ASSEMBLY—(Continued).

District.	NAME.	County.	Address.
12.	Wm. Pinkney Hamilton, Jr...	Kings................	Brooklyn.
13.	James H. Finnigan...........	Kings................	Brooklyn.
14.	James J. Garvey............	Kings........:.....	Brooklyn.
15.	Thomas E. Willmott.........	Kings................	Brooklyn.
16.	Jesse P. Larrimer..........	Kings................	Brooklyn.
17.	Frederick Ulrich...........	Kings................	Brooklyn.
18.	Joseph Henry Esquirol......	Kings................	Brooklyn.
19.	Jacob Schifferdecker.......	Kings................	Brooklyn.
20.	Cornelius J. Cronin.........	Kings................	Brooklyn.
21.	Harry Heyman..............	Kings................	Brooklyn.
22.	Joseph J. Monahan.........	Kings................	Brooklyn.
23.	Thomas L. Ingram..........	Kings................	Brooklyn.
	James B. Van Woert.......	Lewis................	Greig.
	Edward M. Magee..........	Livingston...........	Groveland Station.
	Morrell E. Tallett.........	Madison..............	DeRuyter.
1.	Jared W. Hopkins..........	Monroe..............	Pittsford.
2.	Simon Louis Adler.........	Monroe..............	Rochester.
3.	August V. Pappert.........	Monroe..............	Rochester.
4.	Cyrus W. Phillips.........	Monroe..............	Rochester.
5.	Charles H. Gallup.........	Monroe..............	Adams Basin.
	Walter A. Gage............	Montgomery.........	Canajoharie.
	Thomas B. Maloney........	Nassau..............	Great Neck Sta., L. I.
1.	Thomas Byron Caughlan.....	New York...........	New York city.
2.	Alfred E. Smith............	New York...........	New York city.
3.	Harry E. Oxford...........	New York...........	New York city.
4.	Aaron J. Levy.............	New York...........	New York city.
5.	James J. Walker..........	New York...........	New York city.
6.	Jacob Silverstein..........	New York...........	New York city.
7.	Peter P. McElligott........	New York...........	New York city.
8.	Solomon Sufrin............	New York...........	New York city.
9.	Charles D. Donohue........	New York...........	New York city.
10.	[a]Maxim Birnkrant........	New York...........	New York city.
11.	John Kerrigan.............	New York...........	New York city.
12.	Joseph D. Kelly...........	New York...........	New York city.
13.	James C. Campbell.........	New York...........	New York city.
14.	Robert Lee Tudor..........	New York...........	New York city.
15.	Theodore Hackett Ward.....	New York...........	New York city.
16.	Martin G. McCue..........	New York...........	New York city.
17.	Mark Eisner..............	New York...........	New York city.
18.	Mark Goldberg............	New York...........	New York city.
19.	Thomas F. Denney.........	New York...........	New York city.
20.	Patrick J. McGrath........	New York...........	New York city.
21.	Thomas Kane..............	New York...........	New York city.
22.	Edward Weil..............	New York...........	New York city.
23.	David Chester Lewis.......	New York...........	New York city.
24.	Owen M. Kiernan..........	New York...........	New York city.
25.	David H. Knott...........	New York...........	New York city.
26.	Abraham Greenberg........	New York...........	New York city.
27.	[b]Raymond B. Carver......	New York...........	New York city.
28.	Salvatore A. Cotillo.......	New York...........	New York city.
29.	Charles Joseph Carroll.....	New York...........	New York city.
30.	Louis A. Cuvillier........	New York...........	New York city.
31.	Michael Schaap...........	New York...........	New York city.

[a] Vice Meyer Greenberg who resigned February 21, 1913. A recount of the vote showed a plurality for Birnkrant who was seated by the assembly, March 10, 1913.
[b] Resigned August 19, 1913.

MEMBERS OF ASSEMBLY—(Concluded).

District.	NAME.	County.	Address.
32	Louis D. Gibbs	New York	New York city.
33	Thomas John Lane	New York	New York city.
34	Patrick Joseph McMahon	New York	New York city.
35	Ernest E. L. Hammer	New York	New York city.
1	Eugene A. McCollum	Niagara	Lockport.
2	Frank Mead Bradley	Niagara	Barker.
1	Fred Frank Emden	Oneida	Utica.
2	Herbert Erwin Allen	Oneida	Clinton.
3	John Brayton Fuller	Oneida	Marcy.
1	Patrick J. Kelly	Onondaga	Marcellus.
2	Stephen Gay Daley	Onondaga	Syracuse.
3	Thomas K. Smith	Onondaga	Syracuse.
	Herman Ferdinand Schnirel	Ontario	Geneva.
1	Caleb H. Baumes	Orange	Newburgh.
2	William Thomas Doty	Orange	Circleville.
	Marc Wheeler Cole	Orleans	Albion.
	Thaddeus C. Sweet	Oswego	Phoenix.
	LaVern P. Butts	Otsego	Oneonta.
	John R. Yale	Putnam	Brewster.
1	Samuel J. Burden	Queens	Long Island City.
2	[7]Alfred J. Kennedy	Queens	Whitestone.
3	Albert C. Benninger	Queens	Ridgewood.
4	[8]Howard Sutphin	Queens	Jamaica.
1	C. Frederick Schwarz	Rensselaer	Troy.
2	Tracey D. Taylor	Rensselaer	Berlin.
	Ralph Rappé McKee	Richmond	Tompkinsville.
	Frederick George Grimme	Rockland	Sparkill.
1	Frank L. Seaker	St. Lawrence	Gouverneur.
2	John A. Smith	St. Lawrence	North Lawrence.
	Gilbert Thompson Seelye	Saratoga	Burnt Hills.
	Arthur Porter Squire	Schenectady	Rotterdam Junction.
	Edward A. Dox	Schoharie	Richmondville.
	John W. Gurnett	Schuyler	Watkins.
	Augustus S. Hughes	Seneca	Seneca Falls.
1	Charles A. Brewster	Steuben	Addison.
2	James L. Seely, Jr	Steuben	Canisteo.
1	Stephen A. Fallon	Suffolk	Setauket.
2	John J. Robinson	Suffolk	Centerport.
	John K. Evans	Sullivan	Bloomingburg.
	John Gilbert Pembleton	Tioga	Tioga Center.
	Minor McDaniels	Tompkins	Ithaca.
1	Lawrence M. Kenney	Ulster	Saugerties.
2	Eldridge M. Gathright	Ulster	Marlborough.
	Henry E. H. Brereton	Warren	Diamond Point, Lake George.
	Eugene R. Norton	Washington	Granville.
	Albert Yeomans	Wayne	Walworth.
1	Tracy P. Madden	Westchester	Yonkers.
2	Verne Morgan Bovie	Westchester	New Rochelle.
3	Wilson Randolph Yard	Westchester	Pleasantville.
4	Mortimer Charles O'Brien	Westchester	White Plains.
	John Knight	Wyoming	Arcade.
	Edward C. Gillett	Yates	Penn Yan.

[1] Resigned May 10, 1913.
[2] Resigned August 13, 1913.

LAWS OF THE STATE OF NEW YORK.

PASSED AT THE 136TH REGULAR SESSION OF THE LEGISLATURE, BEGUN JANUARY 1, 1913, AND ENDED MAY 3, 1913, AT THE CITY OF ALBANY, AND INCLUDING CHAPTERS 794-800 PASSED AT THE EXTRAORDINARY SESSION, BEGUN JUNE 16, 1913.

VOLUME I.

Chap. 1.

AN ACT to amend the highway law, in relation to the punishment for violation thereof in the operation of motor vehicles.

Became a law January 16, 1913, with the approval of the Governor. Passed, three-fifths being present.

The People of the State of New York, represented in Senate and Assembly, do enact as follows:

Section 1. Subdivision nine of section two hundred and ninety of chapter thirty of the laws of nineteen hundred and nine, entitled "An act relating to highways, constituting chapter twenty-five of the consolidated laws," as added by chapter three hundred and seventy-four of the laws of nineteen hundred and ten, is hereby amended to read as follows:

9. Any person violating any of the provisions of any section of this article, which violation is stated separately to be a misdemeanor, is punishable by imprisonment for not more than one year or by a fine of not more than five hundred dollars, or by both. and for a violation of any other provision of this article,[1] for which violation no punishment has been specified, shall be guilty of a misdemeanor punishable by a fine of not exceeding twenty-five dollars.

§ 2. Subdivision eleven of section two hundred and ninety of said chapter as added by chapter three hundred and seventy-four

(margin notes: 1909, ch. 30, § 290, subd. 9, as added by L. 1910, ch. 374, amended. — Penalties for violations of provisions relative to operation of motor vehicles. — § 290, subd. 11, as added by L. 1910, ch. 374, amended.)

[1] Words "which violation is stated separately to be a misdemeanor, is punishable by imprisonment for not more than one year or by a fine of not more than five hundred dollars, or by both, and for a violation of any other provision of this article," new.

of the laws of nineteen hundred and ten, is hereby amended to
read as follows:

11. **Release from custody, bail, et cetera.** In case any person
shall be taken into custody charged with a violation of any of the
provisions of this article, he shall forthwith be taken before the
nearest magistrate, captain, lieutenant, clerk of the court or
acting lieutenant who shall have the power of a magistrate and
be entitled to an immediate hearing or admission to bail, and if
such hearing cannot then be had, be released from custody on
giving a bond or undertaking, executed by a fidelity or surety company authorized to do business in this state, or other bail in the
form provided by section five hundred and sixty-eight of the code
of criminal procedure, such bond or undertaking to be in an
amount not exceeding one hundred dollars, if the charge be for
a misdemeanor, except as herein provided where the charge is a
violation of subdivision three of section two hundred and ninety
of this article,[2] for his appearance to answer for such violation
at such time and place as shall then be indicated. In case a person
is taken into custody charged with being guilty of a felony in
violation of any of the provisions of this article, such bond or
undertaking shall be in an amount not less than one thousand
dollars. On giving his personal undertaking to appear to answer
any such violation at such time and place as shall then be indicated, secured by the deposit of a sum of money equal to the
amount of such bond or undertaking, or in lieu thereof, in case
the person taken into custody is the owner, by leaving the motor
vehicle, or in case such person taken into custody is not the owner,
by leaving the motor vehicle as herein provided with a written
consent given at the time by the owner who must be present,
with such officer; or in case such person is taken into custody
because of a violation of any of the provisions of this article other
than on a charge of violating any of the provisions of subdivision
three of section two hundred and ninety and such officer is not
accessible, be forthwith released from custody on giving his name
and address to the person making the arrest and depositing with
such arresting officer the sum of one hundred dollars, or in lieu
thereof, in case the person taken into custody is the owner, by
leaving the motor vehicle, or, in case such person taken into custody is not the owner, by leaving the motor vehicle with a written

---

[2] Words "except as herein provided where the charge is a violation of
subdivision three of section two hundred and ninety of this article," new.

consent at the time by the owner who must be present; provided
that, in any such case, the officer making the arrest shall give a
receipt in writing for such sum or vehicle deposited and notify
such person to appear before the most accessible magistrate, describing him, and specifying the place and hour.   In case such
bond or undertaking shall not be given or deposit made by the
owner or other person taken into custody, the provisions of law
in reference to bail, in case of misdemeanor, shall apply, where
the charge is a violation of subdivision three of section two hundred and ninety of this article, the provisions of law in reference
to bail in cases of a misdemeanor or a felony as the case may be
shall apply exclusively.

§ 3. This act shall take effect immediately.

Chap. 2.

AN ACT making an appropriation to provide for the compensation and expenses of persons appointed by the governor to examine and investigate departments, boards, bureaus and commissions of the state.

Became a law January 21, 1913, with the approval of the Governor. Passed,
three-fifths being present.

*The People of the State of New York, represented in Senate
and Assembly, do enact as follows:*

Section 1. The sum of fifty thousand dollars ($50,000), or so
much thereof as may be necessary, is hereby appropriated out
of any moneys in the treasury not otherwise appropriated, for
the compensation of persons appointed by the governor to examine and investigate departments, boards, bureaus and commissions of the state, and for expenses necessarily incurred in the
examinations or investigations of such departments, boards,
bureaus and commissions, including services of assistants and
stenographers, pursuant to section eight of the executive law.

§ 2. This act shall take effect immediately.

Chap. 3.

AN ACT to amend the military law, in relation to the adjutant-
general of the state.

**Became a law January 29, 1913, with the approval of the Governor. Passed,
three-fifths being present.**

*The People of the State of New York, represented in Senate
and Assembly, do enact as follows:*

L. 1909, ch.
41, § 18, as
amended by
L. 1911,
ch. 281,
amended.

Section 1. Section eighteen of chapter forty-one of the laws of
nineteen hundred and nine, entitled "An act in relation to the
militia, constituting chapter thirty-six of the consolidated laws,"
as amended by chapter two hundred and eighty-one of the laws
of nineteen hundred and eleven, is hereby amended to read as
follows:[1]

§ 18. **The adjutant-general of the state, his pay, assistants and
employees.** The adjutant-general of the state shall have such
assistants, and such clerks, employees and laborers as may be
necessary from time to time who shall be appointed and shall be
removed by him at his discretion, and any officer, who is such an
assistant, may be rendered supernumerary by the governor at any
time. He may by a writing filed in his office designate any one
of his assistants to act as the adjutant-general of the state in the
absence of the latter from the capital city of the state or in case
of his inability to perform the duties of his office. There will be
allowed to the adjutant-general of the state for his salary five
thousand five hundred dollars annually. There shall be allowed
annually fifteen thousand three hundred dollars or so much thereof
as may be necessary for the salaries of the assistants. Necessary
traveling expenses and subsistence of the adjutant-general of the
state and his assistants when traveling on duty and under orders
as well as the office expenses, clerical services and labor will also
be allowed. The adjutant-general of the state may require his
assistants or any of them to give bonds with sufficient surety in
not exceeding fifteen thousand dollars each to the people of the
state conditioned for the faithful discharge of their duties, such
bonds to be approved by the governor and comptroller and filed
in the latter's office.

§ 2. All acts or parts of acts inconsistent with this act are
hereby repealed.

§ 3. This act shall take effect immediately.

---

[1] Section materially amended.

Chap. 4.

AN ACT to incorporate the Harriman Research Laboratory.

Became a law January 30, 1913, with the approval of the Governor. Passed, three-fifths being present.

The People of the State of New York, represented in Senate and Assembly, do enact as follows:

Section 1. William G. Lyle, M. D., Lewis R. Morris, M. D., Corpora-tors.
Mary W. Harriman, Wirt Howe, Robert L. Gerry, and such other persons as may hereafter be associated with them and their successors, are hereby constituted a body corporate by the name of Corporate name.
The Harriman Research Laboratory for the purpose of conducting, assisting and encouraging scientific investigation, experimen- Purpose.
tation, and research in the sciences and arts of hygiene, medicine and surgery, physics, chemistry, bacteriology and allied subjects, in the nature and causes of disease and the methods of its prevention and treatment and making knowledge relating to these various subjects available to the public. It shall be within the purposes of said corporation to use any means to those ends which from time to time shall seem to it expedient, including research, publication, education.

§ 2. The corporation hereby formed shall have the power to Powers as, to property,
take and hold by bequest, devise, gift, purchase, lease or otherwise, and income
either absolutely, or in trust, for any of its purposes any property, real or personal, without limitation as to amount or value, except such limitation, if any, as the legislature shall hereafter impose; to convey such property and to invest and re-invest any principal and deal with and expend the income of the corporation in such manner as in the judgment of the trustees shall best promote its objects. It shall have the powers and be subject to Application of member-
all the restrictions which now appertain by law to membership ship cor-poration
corporations so far as the same are applicable thereto, and are laws.
not inconsistent with the provisions of this act. By the way of amplification and not by the way of limitation of its powers, it Further specific
shall further have power to build, purchase, improve, enlarge, powers.
equip and maintain laboratories and other buildings in the city of New York and elsewhere necessary or appropriate for its work, to own and operate land and buildings for the breeding, raising and keeping of plants and animals to be used for the purposes; to furnish treatment for diseases of man and of animals, and to

provide and maintain all necessary equipment therefor; to conduct and assist such scientific experiments or investigations upon plants or animals as may be necessary or proper for carrying on its work of research; to appoint committees of experts to direct special lines of research, to aid, co-operate with other associations or corporations engaged in similar work within the United States of America, or elsewhere; to aid and co-operate with investigators, in its own laboratories or elsewhere; to collect statistics and information, and to publish and distribute documents, reports and periodicals; to carry on such educational work along the lines of its corporate purposes as it may deem wise; to provide for such and furnish public instruction in hygiene, sanitation and the laws of health, to conduct lectures and hold meetings; to acquire and maintain a library, and in general to do and perform all things necessary or convenient for the promotion of the objects of the corporation or any of them. The persons named in the first section of this act, or a majority of them, shall hold a meeting and organize the corporation and adopt by-laws, not inconsistent with the constitution or laws of this state, which shall prescribe the qualifications of members, the number of members who shall constitute a quorum for the transaction of business at meetings, the number of directors by whom the affairs of the corporation shall be managed, the qualifications, powers, and manner of selection of the directors and officers of the corporation and any other provisions for the management and disposition of the property and regulation of the affairs of the corporation which may be deemed expedient. The corporation shall have power by by-laws or contract to create a board of trustees, to which it may delegate such of the powers, duties and obligations of the members or directors of such corporation as it may deem wise, including the power to choose directors and to have the care, custody and management of its property, subject to such provisions and limitations as may be therein prescribed; and the number of such trustees may be fixed and altered and their appointment may be made in such manner, at such times, and by such persons, boards or corporations, whether members of this corporation or not as may be therein provided.

§ 3. No officer, member, trustee, director, or employee of said corporation shall be entitled to receive any pecuniary profit from the operation thereof, except reasonable compensation for services in effecting one or more of its corporate purposes.

§ 4. This act shall take effect immediately.

Marginal notes: Organization. By-laws. Members. Directors. Board of trustees; powers, duties, number. Pecuniary profit prohibited; compensations.

Chap. 5.

AN ACT making an appropriation for the investigation, care, maintenance and improvement of the state reservation at Saratoga Springs.

Became a law February 6, 1913, with the approval of the Governor. Passed, three-fifths being present.

The People of the State of New York, represented in Senate and Assembly, do enact as follows:

Section 1. The sum of seven thousand five hundred dollars ($7,500) is hereby appropriated from any moneys in the treasury not otherwise appropriated, for the investigation, care, maintenance and improvement of the state reservation at Saratoga Springs by the commissioners of said reservation to be paid by the treasurer on the warrant of the comptroller upon vouchers approved by the said commissioners.

§ 2. This act shall take effect immediately.

Chap. 6.

AN ACT making appropriations for certain immediate expenses of the legislature, and providing for deficiencies in former appropriations therefor.

Became a law February 7, 1913, with the approval of the Governor. Passed by a two-thirds vote.

The People of the State of New York, represented in Senate and Assembly, do enact as follows:

Section 1. The several sums hereinafter named, or so much thereof as may be necessary, are hereby appropriated out of any money in the treasury, not otherwise appropriated, payable by the treasurer on the warrant of the comptroller for the purposes and in the manner hereinafter provided:

FROM THE GENERAL FUND.

LEGISLATIVE.

For deficiency for expenses of legislative committees, including compensation of witnesses; for indexing the bills, journals and Miscellaneous expenses.

documents of the senate and assembly; for indexing the executive journals of the senate and for preparation of supplementary indices to senate and assembly bills, journals and documents, to be paid upon the certificate of the temporary president of the senate or the speaker of the assembly, respectively; for postage and transportation of letters, reports, documents and other matter sent by express or freight, including boxes and coverings for the same, for printing and furnishing the legislative manual and clerk's manual; for law and reference books and publications for the senate and assembly libraries, committees and legislature; for legislative indices to senate and assembly bills, journals and documents; for extra clerical services and engrossing; for furniture, alteration and repairs to legislative rooms, and for other contingent expenses of the legislature, to be paid upon the certificate of the clerk of the senate or assembly, respectively, fifty thousand dollars ($50,000), or so much thereof as may be necessary.

For deficiency for the advances by the comptroller to the clerks of the senate and assembly for the clergymen officiating as chaplains, to be paid at the rate of five dollars for each day of attendance; for printing, stationery, supplies, file boards and record books; for preparation, proof reading and comparison of journals and financial reports; clerical and stenographic services; for engrossing resolutions; for books and blanks; for care of bills, documents and library; for law books and binding of books and records; for steel cases, furniture and appurtenances; for expenses for receiving reports and printed documents, storing, addressing and forwarding the same; for extra clerical service; and for other contingent expenses, fifty thousand dollars ($50,-000), or so much thereof as may be necessary.

Bill draft ing de- partment. For the compensation of additional assistants in the legislative bill drafting department and for additional necessary incidental office expenses during the legislative session, for the purpose of increasing the efficiency of the department, to be paid upon the certificate of the temporary president of the senate and the speaker of the assembly, twelve thousand dollars ($12,000), or so much thereof as may be necessary.

§ 2. This act shall take effect immediately.

Chap. 7.

AN ACT to amend the insurance law, in relation to agents.

Became a law February 10, 1913, with the approval of the Governor. Passed, three-fifths being present.

The People of the State of New York, represented in Senate and Assembly, do enact as follows:

Section 1. Section one hundred and forty-two of chapter thirty-three of the laws of nineteen hundred and nine, entitled "An act in relation to insurance corporations, constituting chapter twenty-eight of the consolidated laws," as added by chapter seven hundred and forty-eight of the laws of nineteen hundred and eleven, and amended by chapters one and one hundred and seventy-two of the laws of nineteen hundred and twelve, is hereby repealed. *L. 1909, ch. 33, § 142, as added by L. 1911, ch. 748, and amended by L. 1912, cha. s. 1, 172,ᵖ re-pealed.*

§ 2. Such chapter is hereby amended by inserting therein a new section to be section one hundred and forty-two thereof to read as follows: *New § 142 added.*

§ 142. **Agent's certificate of authority.** The term "agent" in this section shall include an acknowledged agent or any person, partnership, association or corporation who shall in any manner aid in transacting the insurance business of any underwriter, incorporated or unincorporated, by negotiating for or placing risks or delivering policies or collecting premiums, but shall not include the officers and salaried employees of any such underwriter, who do not receive commissions. Every underwriter, incorporated or unincorporated, engaged in the transaction of any business of insurance within this state, upon the employment or termination of the employment of any person, partnership, association or corporation to act as its agent within this state, shall certify such fact together with the name and address of such agent to the superintendent of insurance; and shall also annually during the month of January, in such form as the superintendent of insurance shall prescribe, file with him a list of the names and addresses of all its agents authorized to act as such within the state. No person, partnership, association or corporation shall as agent act for any such underwriter in this state, unless such underwriter shall have fully complied with the provisions of this chapter nor unless such agent shall have procured an agent's certificate of authority from the superintendent of insurance. The superintendent of insurance shall file in his office evidence of the issuance of every such certificate to an agent, together with evidence of such agent's authority from each underwriter for whom he is to act. An agent's certificate of authority shall be issued only upon application filed with the superintendent of insurance, in such form as the superintendent of insurance shall prescribe. Every such certificate shall expire on the thirty-first day of December of the calendar year in which the same shall have been issued, but if the application for the renewal of any such certificate shall have been filed with the superintendent of insurance before January first of any year such agent may continue to act as such under such expired certificate until the issuance to him by the superintendent of insurance of a new certificate or until five days after the superintendent of insurance shall have refused to renew such certificate and shall have served notice of such refusal on such agent. Service of such notice may be made either personally or by mail, and, if by mail, shall be deemed complete if such notice is deposited in the post office, postage prepaid, directed to the applicant at the place of residence or business specified in his application. An underwriter, authorized to transact the insurance business within this state, who shall employ as agent any person, partnership, association or corporation not having an agent's certificate of authority from the superintendent of insurance authorizing him to act as agent shall not authorize or permit such agent under his contract of employment to solicit insurance or issue policies for such underwriter until such agent shall have procured a certificate of authority as required by this section. An agent's certificate of authority shall be revoked by the superintendent of insurance if, after due investigation and a hearing either before himself or before any salaried employee of the insurance department designated by him whose report he may adopt, he determines that the holder of such certificate has violated any provision of this chapter, or has been guilty of fraudulent practices. No individual, corporation, partnership or association whose certificate of authority is so revoked, nor any partnership, or association of which such individual is a member, nor any corporation of which he is an officer, shall be entitled to any certificate of authority under this section for one year after such revocation, or, if such revocation be reviewed by certiorari proceedings, for one year after the final determination thereof affirming the action of the superintendent in revoking such certificate.

If any such certificate held by a partnership, association or corporation be so revoked, no member of the partnership or association or officer of the corporation shall be entitled to any such certificate for the same period of time, if the superintendent of insurance determine that such member or officer was personally at fault in the matter on account of which the certificate was revoked. The action of the superintendent of insurance in granting or refusing to grant or renew a certificate of authority or in revoking or refusing to revoke such certificate under this section shall be subject to review by writ of certiorari, at the instance of the applicant for such certificate, the holder of a certificate so revoked or the holder of any certificate or the person aggrieved. If the superintendent of insurance shall revoke or shall refuse to renew the certificate of authority of any agent issued under this section and such agent shall apply for a writ of certiorari to review such action, the certificate of authority of such agent shall be deemed to be in full force and effect for all purposes including the right to renewal until the final determination of such certiorari proceedings and all appeals therefrom.

This section shall not apply to any contract of life insurance, nor to any contract of insurance upon or in connection with marine or transportation risks or hazards other than contracts for automobile insurance, nor to contracts of insurance upon property located without this state, nor to contracts made by persons, partnerships, associations or corporations authorized to do business under articles five, six, seven and nine of this chapter.

Any person, partnership, association or corporation violating any provision of this section shall, in addition to any other penalty in this chapter provided, forfeit to the people of the state five hundred dollars.

Nothing in this chapter shall be so construed as to prevent any underwriter authorized to do business within this state from authorizing a broker to whom a certificate of authority has been issued under this chapter to act as agent of such underwriter for the collection of premiums.

§ 3. This act shall take effect twenty days after it becomes a law.

In effect after 20 days.

Chap. 8.

AN ACT to amend chapter four hundred and seventy-seven of the laws of nineteen hundred and six, entitled "An act to revise the charter of the city of Elmira," relating to limitation of moneys to be raised for defraying city expenses.

Became a law February 11, 1913, with the approval of the Governor. Passed, three-fifths being present.

Accepted by the City.

The People of the State of New York, represented in Senate and Assembly, do enact as follows:

L. 1906, ch. 477, § 32, subd. h, as amended by L. 1911, ch. 674, amended.

Section 1. Subdivision "h" of section thirty-two of chapter four hundred and seventy-seven of the laws of nineteen hundred and six, entitled "An act to revise the charter of the city of Elmira," as amended by chapter six hundred and seventy-four of the laws of nineteen hundred and eleven, is hereby amended to read as follows:

Estimates for fire department.

h. A sum necessary for supplying and keeping in good condition and repair fire engines, engine houses, fire alarm, telegraph, teams and other things, deemed necessary for the extinguishment of fires and for paying the salaries and wages of the officers and employees of the fire department, and to procure a supply of water for the extinguishment of fires, to be designated "fire department fund." Provided, that for all the purposes in this section above stated, the said estimate exclusive of indirect revenue and the sum voted therefor in pursuance of section fifty-one[1] of this act, shall not exceed [2]one per centum of the assessed valuation of all taxable property in said city based upon the last preceding state and county tax roll. In case there remain any unexpended balance of the appropriation made for any of said funds for the previous year, the mayor shall show in his said estimate (1) the probable total amount needed for the purpose of any such fund; (2) the amount of any such unexpended balance as above mentioned; and (3) the difference between items (1) and (2) being the amount necessary to be levied in the city tax.

§ 2. This act shall take effect immediately.

---

[1] As amended by L. 1910, ch. 602.
[2] Remainder of sentence formerly read: "two hundred thousand dollars."

Chap. 9.

AN ACT to amend the insurance law, in relation to the revocation of the certificate of authority of a foreign insurance corporation.

Became a law February 12, 1913, with the approval of the Governor. Passed, three-fifths being present.

The People of the State of New York, represented in Senate and Assembly, do enact as follows:

Section 1. Section thirty-two of chapter thirty-three of the laws of nineteen hundred and nine, entitled "An act in relation to insurance corporations, constituting chapter twenty-eight of the consolidated laws," as amended by chapter three hundred and one of the laws of nineteen hundred and nine, is hereby amended to read as follows:

§ 32. **Renewal of certificate of authority; revocation.**[1] The certificate of authority granted by the superintendent of insurance, pursuant to the provisions of this chapter, to a foreign insurance corporation to do business in this state, shall not remain in force for a longer period than one year, and all such certificates shall expire on the thirtieth day of April of the year next following the date of issue. The statements and evidences of investment required by this chapter to be filed in the office of the superintendent before a certificate of authority is granted to a foreign corporation, shall be renewed from year to year, in such manner and form as the superintendent may require, with an additional statement of the amount of premiums received and losses sustained in this state during the preceding year so long as such authority continues. If the superintendent is satisfied that the capital, securities and investments remain secure, and that it may be safely intrusted with a continuance of its authority to do business, he shall grant a renewal of such certificate of authority. [2]Whenever in the judgment of the superintendent of insurance it will best promote the interests of the people of this state, he may, after a hearing on notice, revoke the certificate of authority of a foreign corporation to do business in this state, prior to its expiration under this section. The action of the superintendent of insurance in revoking the certificate of authority of a foreign corporation shall be subject to review by writ of certiorari.

§ 2. This act shall take effect immediately.

Marginal notes: L. 1909, ch. 33, § 32, as amended by L. 1909, ch. 301, amended.

---

1 Word "revocation" new.
2 Remainder of section new.

Chap. 10.

AN ACT to amend the code of civil procedure, in relation to distributive shares of infants.

Became a law February 12, 1913, with the approval of the Governor. Passed, three-fifths being present.

The People of the State of New York, represented in Senate and Assembly, do enact as follows:

§ 2746
amended.

Section 1. Section twenty-seven hundred and forty-six of the code of civil procedure, is hereby amended to read as follows:

§ 2746. Idem; share of infant. When a legacy or distributive share is payable to an infant, the decree may, in the discretion of the surrogate's court, direct it, or so much of it as may be necessary, to be paid to his general guardian, to be applied to his support and education; or when it does not exceed two hundred and[1] fifty dollars, the decree may order it to be paid to his father or to his mother or to some competent person with whom the infant resides or who has some interest in his welfare, for the use and benefit of such infant. Said court may, in its discretion, by its decree, direct any legacy or distributive share, or part of a legacy or distributive share, not paid or applied as aforesaid, which is payable to an infant, to be paid to the general guardian of such infant, upon his executing and depositing with the surrogate in his office, a bond running to such infant, with two or more sufficient sureties duly acknowledged and approved by the surrogate, in double the amount of such legacy or distributive share, conditioned that such general guardian shall faithfully apply such legacy or distributive share, and render a true and just account of the application thereof, in all respects, to any court having cognizance thereof, when thereunto required, the sureties in which bond shall justify as required in this act, unless the surrogate shall determine that the general bond given by the guardian is ample and of sufficient amount to cover such legacy or distributive share. The said court may, in its discretion, from time to time, authorize or direct such general guardian to expend such part of such legacy or distributive share, in the support, maintenance and education of such infant as it deems necessary. On such infant's coming twenty-one years of age, he shall be entitled to receive, and his general guardian shall pay or deliver to him,

---

[1] Words "two hundred and" new.

under the direction of the surrogate's court, the securities so taken, and the interest or other moneys that may have been paid to or received by such general guardian, after deducting therefrom such amounts as have been paid or expended in pursuance of the orders and decrees of said court, so made as aforesaid, and the legal commissions of such guardian; and the said general guardian shall be liable to account in and under the direction of the surrogate's court, to his ward, for the same; in case of the death of said infant, before coming of age, the said securities and moneys, after making the deductions aforesaid, shall go to his executors or administrators, to be applied and distributed according to law, and the general guardian shall in like manner be liable to account to such administrator or executor. If there be no general guardian, or if the surrogate's court do not order or decree the payment or disposition of the legacy or distributive share in some of the ways above described, then the legacy or distributive share, or part of the same not disposed of as aforesaid, whether the same consists of money or securities, shall, by the order or decree of the surrogate's court be paid and delivered to and deposited in said court, by paying and delivering the same to and depositing it with the county treasurer of the county, to be held, managed, invested, collected, reinvested and disposed of by him, as prescribed and required by section two thousand five hundred and thirty-seven of this act. The regulations contained in the general rules of practice, as specified in subdivision eight of section four of the state finance law, and the provisions of title three of chapter eight of this act apply to money, legacies and distributive shares paid to and securities deposited with the county treasurer, as prescribed in this section; except that the surrogate's court exercises with respect thereto, or with respect to a security in which any of the money has been invested, or upon which it has been loaned, the power and authority conferred upon the supreme court by section seven hundred and forty-seven of this act.

§ 2. This act shall take effect September first, nineteen hundred and thirteen. In effect Sept. 1, 1913.

Chap. 11.

AN ACT to amend the benevolent orders law, in relation to powers
of joint corporations.

Became a law February 12, 1913, with the approval of the Governor. Passed,
three-fifths being present.

*The People of the State of New York, represented in Senate
and Assembly, do enact as follows:*

L. 1909,
ch. 11. § 9
amended.

Section 1. Section nine of chapter eleven of the laws of nineteen
hundred and nine, entitled "An act relating to benevolent orders,
constituting chapter three of the consolidated laws," is hereby
amended to read as follows:

§ 9. **Powers of joint corporations.** Such corporation may acquire real property in the town, village or city in which such hall,
home, temple or building is or is to be located, and erect such building or buildings thereupon for the uses and purposes of the corporation, as the trustees may deem necessary, or repair, rebuild or
reconstruct any building or buildings that may be thereupon
and furnish and complete such rooms therein as may appear
necessary for the use of such bodies or for any other purpose
for which the corporation is formed; and may rent to other
persons[1] any portion of such building or[2] real property for
business or other purposes.[3] Until such real property shall be
acquired or such building erected or made ready for use,
the corporation may rent and sublet such rooms or apartments in
such town, village or city as may be suitable or convenient for the
use of the bodies mentioned in such certificate, or of such other
bodies as may desire to use them, and the board of trustees may
determine the terms and conditions on which rooms and apartments in such building or buildings, when erected, or which may be
leased, shall be used and occupied. Before such corporation composed of not more than thirty bodies shall purchase or sell any real
property, or erect or repair any building or buildings thereupon,
and before it shall purchase any building or part of a building for
the use of a corporation, it shall submit to the bodies constituting
the corporation, the proposition to make such sale or purchase, or
to erect or repair any such building or buildings, or to rent any

---

[1] Words " any room in such building or," omitted.
[2] Words " building or," new.
[3] Words " for business or other purposes," new.

building or part thereof; for the use of the corporation; and unless such proposition receives the approval of two-thirds of the bodies constituting the corporation, such proposition shall not be carried into effect. The evidence of the approval of such proposition by any such body shall be a certificate to that effect signed by the presiding officer and secretary of the body, or the officers discharging duties corresponding to those of the presiding officer and secretary, under the seal of such body. But where land is purchased for the purpose of erecting a hall, home or temple thereon, the buildings upon such land at the time of such purchase may be sold by the trustees without such consent. The powers of the board of trustees of every corporation created hereunder and composed of more than thirty bodies, respecting sales, purchases and repairs, shall be fixed by the by-laws adopted by the representatives of the various bodies composing such corporation, or shall be determined by such representatives when assembled in annual session. Every corporation created hereunder shall have power to enforce, at law or in equity, any legal contract which it may make with any of the bodies composing it respecting the care and maintenance of members or other dependents of such body, the same as if such body or bodies were not members of the corporation. Any corporation created hereunder shall have power to take and hold real and personal estate by purchase, gift, devise or bequest subject to the provisions of law relating to devises and bequests by last will and testament or otherwise.

§ 2. This act shall take effect immediately.

Chap. 12.

AN ACT to amend the insurance law, in relation to brokers.

Became a law February 13, 1913, with the approval of the Governor. Passed, three-fifths being present.

The People of the State of New York, represented in Senate and Assembly, do enact as follows:

Section 1. Chapter thirty-three of the laws of nineteen hundred and nine, entitled "An act in relation to insurance corporations, constituting chapter twenty-eight of the consolidated laws," is hereby amended by inserting therein a new section, to be section one hundred and forty-three thereof, to read as follows:

New § 143 added to L. 1909, ch. 33.

§ 143. Brokers' certificate of authority. The term " broker "
in this section shall include any person, partnership, association
or corporation who, for money, commission or anything of value,
acts or aids in any manner on behalf of the insured in negotiating
contracts of insurance or placing risks or taking out insurances,
including surety bonds. No underwriter, authorized or permitted
to do business in this state, or agent thereof, shall pay any money
or commission or give or allow anything of value to any person,
partnership, association or corporation not a duly authorized agent
of such underwriter for or because of his or its negotiating a contract of insurance or placing a risk or taking out insurance or a
surety bond, unless such person, partnership, association or corporation is authorized to act as a broker. No person, partnership,
association or corporation shall, after July first, nineteen hundred
and thirteen, act as broker in the solicitation or procurement of
applications for insurance or receive for or because of negotiating
a contract of insurance or placing a risk or taking out insurance
including a surety bond any money or commission or other thing
of value from any underwriter authorized or permitted to do an
insurance business in this state, or from an agent of any such
underwriter, without first procuring a certificate of authority so
to act from the superintendent of insurance.

The superintendent of insurance shall issue such broker's certificate of authority to a person, partnership, association or corporation, applying therefor, who is trustworthy and is competent to
transact an insurance brokerage business in such manner as to
safeguard the interests of the insured.

A certificate of authority issued to a corporation, partnership
or association shall authorize only the officers and directors of the
corporation, or the members of the partnership or association,
specified in the certificate, each of whom must be qualified to
obtain a certificate to act as brokers. The fee to be paid to the
superintendent of insurance by the applicant for such broker's
certificate at the time the application is made, and annually for
the renewal thereof, shall be ten dollars, if the applicant's principal place of business is in a city and two dollars if not in a city.
If the applicant be a corporation, partnership or association such
fee shall be paid for each person specified in the certificate.

Every broker's certificate of authority shall expire on the thirty-
first day of December of the calendar year in which the same shall
have been issued, but if an application for the renewal of any

such certificate shall have been filed with the superintendent of insurance before January first of any year the certificate of authority sought to be renewed shall continue in full force and effect until the issuance by the superintendent of insurance of the new certificate applied for or until five days after the superintendent of insurance shall have refused to issue such new certificate and shall have served notice of such refusal on the applicant therefor. Service of such notice may be made either personally or by mail, and, if by mail, shall be deemed complete if such notice is deposited in the post-office postage prepaid, directed to the applicant at the place of business specified in the application.

Before any broker's certificate of authority shall be issued by the superintendent of insurance there must be filed in his office a written application therefor. Such application shall be in the form or forms and supplements thereof prescribed by the superintendent of insurance and must set forth (1) the name and address of the applicant, and if the applicant be a partnership or association, the name and address of each member thereof, and if the applicant be a corporation, the name and address of each of its officers and directors; (2) whether any certificate of authority as agent or broker has been issued theretofore by the superintendent of insurance to the applicant, and, if the applicant be an individual, whether any such certificate has been issued theretofore to any partnership or association of which he was or is a member or to any corporation of which he was or is an officer or director, and, if the applicant be a partnership or association whether any such certificate has been issued theretofore to any member thereof, and, if the applicant be a corporation, whether any such certificate has been issued theretofore to any officer or director of such corporation; (3) the business in which the applicant has been engaged for the year next preceding the date of the application, and, if employed by another, the name or names and address or addresses of such employer or employers; (4) such information as the superintendent of insurance may require of applicants to enable him to determine their trustworthiness and competency to transact the insurance brokerage business in such manner as to safeguard the interests of the assured.

An application for a broker's certificate of authority must be signed and verified by the applicant and, if made by a partnership or association, by each member thereof and if made by a corporation by each officer and director thereof to be authorized thereby to act as a broker.

If an application for a certificate of authority under this section be filed in the year nineteen hundred and thirteen within sixty days after this section takes effect the applicant and the persons named in the application may, notwithstanding the provisions of this section, act as brokers until notice of rejection of the application shall have been served as herein provided with respect to renewal applications.

A corporation, association or partnership to whom a certificate of authority shall have been issued by the superintendent of insurance under this section may at any time make an application to the superintendent of insurance for the issuance of a supplemental certificate of authority authorizing additional officers or directors of the corporation or members of the partnership or association to act as brokers, and the superintendent of insurance may thereupon issue to such corporation, association or partnership a supplemental certificate accordingly upon the payment of an additional fee for each member or officer or director thereby authorized to act as a broker.

A certificate issued under this section shall be revoked by the superintendent, if after due investigation and a hearing either before him or before any salaried employee of the insurance department designated by him whose report he may adopt, he determines that the holder of such certificate (1) has violated any provision of the chapter by any act or thing done in respect to insurance for which such certificate is required; or (2) has made a material misstatement in the application for such certificate; or (3) has been guilty of fraudulent practices; or (4) has demonstrated his incompetency or untrustworthiness to transact the insurance brokerage business for which such certificate of authority shall have been granted by reason of anything done or omitted in or about such business under the authority of such certificate.

No individual, partnership, association or corporation whose certificate of authority is so revoked nor any partnership or association of which such individual is a member, nor any corporation of which he is an officer or director shall be entitled to any certificate of authority under this section for a period of one year after such revocation, or, if such revocation be reviewed by certiorari proceedings, for one year after the final determination thereof affirming the action of the superintendent in revoking such certificate. If any such certificate held by a partnership, association or corporation be so revoked, no member of the partnership or association or officer or director of the corporation shall be entitled to such a certificate for the same period of time, if the superintendent of insurance determines and finds that such member or officer or director was personally at fault in the matter on account of which the certificate was revoked. The holder of any such certificate or any person aggrieved may file with the superintendent of insurance a verified complaint setting forth facts from which it shall appear that any such certificate ought to be revoked. The superintendent must thereupon, after investigation and a hearing as herein provided, determine whether such certificate shall be revoked.

If an application for a certificate of authority under this section be rejected or such a certificate be revoked by the superintendent of insurance notice thereof shall forthwith be served on the applicant or on the holder of such certificate either personally or by mail, and, if by mail, such service shall be complete if such notice be deposited in the post-office postage prepaid, directed to the applicant or the holder of such certificate, as the case may be, at the place of business specified in the application or certificate.

The action of the superintendent of insurance in granting or refusing to grant or to renew a certificate of authority or in revoking or refusing to revoke such a certificate shall be subject to review by writ of certiorari, at the instance of the applicant for such certificate, the holder of a certificate so revoked or the holder of any such certificate or the person aggrieved. If the superintendent of insurance shall revoke or shall refuse to renew the certificate of authority of any broker issued under this section and such broker shall apply for a writ of certiorari to review such action, the certificate of authority of such broker shall be deemed to be in full force and effect for all purposes, including the right to renewal, until the final determination of such certiorari proceedings and all appeals therefrom, provided the fee for such certificate be paid.

This section shall not apply to any contract of life insurance nor to any contract of insurance upon or in connection with marine or transportation risks or hazards other than contracts for automobile insurance, nor to contracts of insurance upon property located without this state, nor to contracts made by persons, partnerships, associations or corporations authorized to do business under articles five, six, seven and nine of this chapter.

Any person, partnership, association or corporation violating any of the provisions of this section shall, in addition to any other penalty in this chapter provided, forfeit to the people of the state five hundred dollars.

In effect
after 20
days.

§ 2. This act shall take effect twenty days after it becomes a law.

Chap. 13.

AN ACT to amend chapter one hundred and five of the laws of eighteen hundred and ninety-one, entitled "An act to revise the charter of the city of Buffalo," as amended by chapter three hundred and forty-five of the laws of eighteen hundred and ninety-three and by chapter five hundred and eighty-six of the laws of eighteen hundred and ninety-nine, authorizing said city to borrow money by the sale and issue of its bonds for the acquisition of lands and the construction, equipment and furnishing of buildings for school purposes.

Became a law February 13, 1913, with the approval of the Governor. Passed, three-fifths being present.

Accepted by the City.

The People of the State of New York, represented in Senate and Assembly, do enact as follows:

L. 1891,
ch. 105,
§ 329, as
amended by
L. 1893, ch.
345, and L.
1899, ch.
586,
amended.

Section 1. Section three hundred and twenty-nine of chapter one hundred and five of the laws of eighteen hundred and ninety-one, entitled "An act to revise the charter of the city of Buffalo," as amended by chapter three hundred and forty-five of the laws of eighteen hundred and ninety-three and by chapter five hundred and eighty-six of the laws of eighteen hundred and ninety-nine, is hereby further amended so as to read as follows:

Expenses
of school
department.

Purchase
of school
lots; school
buildings.

§ 329. All expenses of the school department shall be included in and paid out of the general fund. The comptroller is hereby authorized to embrace in his estimates a sum not exceeding two hundred and fifty thousand dollars annually, which shall be used solely for the purchase of school lots and the erection, enlargement, repairs and furnishing of school buildings. [1]It shall be law-

---

1 Remainder of section materially amended.

ful for the city to purchase or acquire lands for school purposes and to erect, equip and furnish buildings thereon and to raise money for either or any of such purposes by issuing the bonds of the city in such amounts and payable at such times and places and bearing such rate of interest as the common council shall, from time to time, determine by resolution adopted by a vote of two-thirds of the members elected to each of the boards composing said common council; said bonds, however, to be due in not more than fifty years from their date and to be sold at not less than their par value and the accrued interest thereon. Bond issues.

§ 2. This act shall take effect immediately.

Chap. 14.

AN ACT to amend chapter one hundred and forty-eight of the laws of nineteen hundred and five, entitled "An act to authorize the board of trustees of the village of White Plains to acquire lands for the site of a public library and to maintain a public library, and issue bonds therefor," in relation to the amount to be raised by taxation and expended, annually, for maintaining said library.

Became a law February 13, 1913, with the approval of the Governor. Passed, three-fifths being present.

The People of the State of New York, represented in Senate and Assembly, do enact as follows:

Section 1. Section three of chapter one hundred and forty-eight of the laws of nineteen hundred and five, entitled "An act to authorize the board of trustees of the village of White Plains to acquire lands for the site of a public library and to maintain a public library, and issue bonds therefor," as amended by chapter forty-three of the laws of nineteen hundred and six and chapter three hundred and six of the laws of nineteen hundred and eleven, is hereby amended to read as follows: L. 1905, ch. 148, § 3, as amended by L. 1906, ch. 43, and L. 1911, ch. 306, amended.

§ 3. The board of trustees is hereby authorized and empowered with the proceeds of the sale of said bonds or any part thereof to purchase lands for a library site, and the said board is hereby authorized and empowered to acquire by purchase any lands, rights or easements necessary or requisite for the purpose of carrying Acquisition of site.

out the provisions or purposes of this act, at such price or prices
as they shall deem fair and reasonable, and if unable to acquire
the same by private purchase, the board of trustees shall have the
power to acquire such lands, rights or easements on behalf of said
village by condemnation, under the condemnation law.[1] The said
Mainte-
nance,
provision
for.
board of trustees of the village of White Plains is also authorized
annually to raise a sum not to exceed eight[2] thousand dollars,
for the purpose of maintaining, supporting and improving a
public library in and for said village, said sum to be raised, in
the same manner that all of the village taxes are now raised,
in said village. The board of education of the joint union free
school district number one of the towns of White Plains and
Harrison shall pay all sums of money raised by taxation in
such school district for the purpose of maintaining a public library
over to the board of trustees of the village of White Plains. The
said funds so received by said board shall be used towards the
maintenance of said library. The aggregate amount to be expended for the maintenance and improvement of said library shall
not exceed the sum of eight[2] thousand dollars, in any one year.

§ 2. This act shall take effect immediately.

Chap. 15.

AN ACT to repeal certain local laws relating to Washington
county.

Became a law February 13, 1913, with the approval of the Governor. Passed,
three-fifths being present.

*The People of the State of New York, represented in Senate
and Assembly, do enact as follows:*

L. 1819,
ch. 66
repealed.
Section 1. An act entitled "An act relative to jury districts in
the county of Washington," being chapter sixty-six of the laws of
eighteen hundred and nineteen as amended by chapter two hundred and thirty-two of the laws of eighteen hundred and
twenty-two and chapter one hundred and ninety-seven of the laws
of eighteen hundred and fifty-three is hereby repealed.

§ 2. This act shall take effect immediately.

---

[1] Code of civil procedure, §§ 3357-3384.
[2] Formerly " five."

Chap. 16.

AN ACT to amend the penal law, in relation to processions on Sunday in cities.

Became a law February 14, 1913, with the approval of the Governor. Passed, three-fifths being present.

The People of the State of New York, represented in Senate and Assembly, do enact as follows:

Section 1. Section twenty-one hundred and fifty-one of chapter eighty-eight of the laws of nineteen hundred and nine, entitled "An act providing for the punishment of crime, constituting chapter forty of the consolidated laws," as amended by chapter one hundred and forty-seven of the laws of nineteen hundred and eleven, is hereby amended to read as follows:

L. 1909, ch. 88,
§ 2151 as amended
by L. 1911, ch. 147, amended.

§ 2151. **Processions and parades on Sunday.** All processions and parades on Sunday in any city, excepting only funeral processions for the actual burial of the dead, and processions to and from a place of worship in connection with a religious service there celebrated, are forbidden; and in such excepted cases there shall be no music, fireworks, discharge of cannon or firearms, or other disturbing noise. At a military funeral, or at the funeral of a United States soldier, sailor or marine, or of a national guardsman, or of a deceased member of an association of veteran soldiers, sailors or marines, or of a disbanded militia regiment, or of a secret fraternal society, music may be played while escorting the body; also in patriotic military processions on Sunday previous to Decoration day, known as Memorial Sunday, to cemeteries or other places where memorial services are held, and also by organizations of the national guard or naval militia attending religious service on Sunday;[1] but in no case within one block of a place of worship where service is then being celebrated. A person willfully violating any provision of this section is punishable by a fine not exceeding twenty dollars or imprisonment not exceeding ten days, or by both.

§ 2. This act shall take effect immediately.

---

[1] Words " and also by organizations of the national guard or naval militia attending religious service on Sunday," new.

Chap. 17.

AN ACT to amend the town law, in relation to the compensation of town auditors.

Became a law February 14, 1913, with the approval of the Governor. Passed, three-fifths being present.

The People of the State of New York, represented in Senate and Assembly, do enact as follows:

L. 1909,
ch. 63,
§ 154, as
amended
by L. 1910,
ch. 24, and
L. 1912,
chaps. 72,
258,
amended.

Section 1. Section one hundred and fifty-four of chapter sixty-three of the laws of nineteen hundred and nine, entitled "An act relating to towns, constituting chapter sixty-two of the consolidated laws," as amended by chapter twenty-four of the laws of nineteen hundred and ten and chapters seventy-two and two hundred and fifty-eight of the laws of nineteen hundred and twelve, is hereby amended to read as follows:

§ 154. **Meetings and compensation of town auditors.** The board of town auditors, or town board where no regular town board of audit has been chosen, in a town having a population of four thousand and upwards, may meet quarterly in each year on the first Mondays of February, May, August and November, for the purpose of auditing, allowing or rejecting all charges, claims and demands against the town. Each town auditor shall be entitled to receive for his services three dollars for each day, not exceeding in the aggregate twelve days in any one year, except in towns having a population of twelve thousand and upwards, in which towns each of such town auditors shall be entitled to receive for his services three dollars for each day, but not to exceed thirty days in any one year and except that in towns having a population of twenty thousand and upwards, in which towns each of such town auditors shall be entitled to receive for his services such compensation as shall be fixed by the town board of such town, and not less than[1] three nor more than five[2] dollars for each day, but not to exceed sixty days in any one year, actually and necessarily devoted by him to the service of the town, in the duties of said office.

§ 2. This act shall take effect immediately.

---

[1] Words "such compensation as shall be fixed by the town board of such town, and not less than," new.
[2] Words "nor more than five," new.

Chap. 18.

AN ACT to amend section two of the state law, in relation to boundary lines between the state of New York and the state of Connecticut.

Became a law February 14, 1913, with the approval of the Governor. Passed, three-fifths being present.

The People of the State of New York, represented in Senate and Assembly, do enact as follows:

Section 1. Section two of chapter fifty-nine of the laws of nineteen hundred and nine, entitled "An act in relation to the sovereignty, boundaries, survey, great seal and arms of the state, congressional districts, senate districts, and apportionment of the members of assembly of this state, and enumeration of the inhabitants of the state, constituting chapter fifty-seven of the consolidated laws," as amended by chapter three hundred and fifty-two of the laws of nineteen hundred and twelve, is hereby amended to read as follows:

§ 2. **Connecticut boundary line.** The boundary line between the states of New York and Connecticut is as follows:

Commencing at a granite monument (No. 1), at the northwest corner of the state of Connecticut, marking the corner of Massachusetts, New York and Connecticut, in latitude 42° 02' 58" .427 and longitude 73° 29' 15" .959; thence south 2° 42' 30" west 30,569 feet to a granite monument (No. 12) 470 feet south of the Bird Hill road between Millerton and Ore Hill in latitude 41° 57' 56" .772 and longitude 73° 29' 35" .078; thence south 3° 53' 44" west 15,846 feet to a monument (No. 18) in the south side of the highway from Millerton to Sharon along the north shore of Indian pond in latitude 41° 55' 20" .586 and longitude 73° 29' 49" .318;[1] thence south 2° 47' 51" west 10,681 feet to a monument (No. 21) on the cliff north of Webatuck creek in latitude 41° 53' 35" .190 and longitude 73° 29' 56" .210; thence south 4° 39' 01" west 10,683 feet to a monument (No. 24) in the rear of R. E. Randall's house on the east road from Sharon Valley to Leedsville in latitude 41° 51' 49" .995 and longitude 73° 30' 07" .652; thence south 3° 49' 10" west 26,405 feet to a monument (No. 32) on the westerly slope of a rocky hillside at the corner of the towns of Sharon

L. 1909, ch. 59, § 2, as amended by L. 1912, ch. 353, amended.

---

[1] Formerly ".316."

and Kent in latitude 41° 47′ 29″ .709 and longitude 73° 30′ 30″ .871; thence south 3° 52′ 35″ west 10,457 feet to a monument (No. 35) on the shoulder of a mountain northeast of Bog Hollow, in latitude 41° 45′ 46″ .637 and longitude 73° 30′ 40″ .199; thence south 3° 06′ 18″ west 16,045 feet to a monument (No. 41) at the easterly edge of a large pasture north of Preston mountain, known as the Chapel lots, in latitude 41° 43′ 08″ .354 and longitude 73° 30′ 51″ .658; thence south 3° 57′ 03″ west 10,657 feet to a monument (No. 45) at the southerly end of Schaghticoke mountain in latitude 41° 41′ 23″ .320 and longitude 73° 31′ 01″ .335;[2] thence south 2° 41′ 41″ west 10,534 feet to a monument (No. 48) on the northwesterly slope of Ten-Mile hill in latitude 41° 39′ 39″ .359 and longitude 73° 31′ 07″ .860; thence south 3° 31′ 33″[3] west 21,140 feet to a monument (No. 55) at the northerly end of a rocky hill about a mile south of the northeast corner of the town of Pawling, New York, in latitude 41° 36′ 10″ .894 and longitude 73° 31′ 24″ .972; thence south 4° 24′ 52″ west 10,785 feet to a monument (No. 59) in a field east of a right angle in the road from Quaker Hill to Sherman in latitude 41° 34′ 24″ .659 and longitude 73° 31′ 35″ .893; thence south 3° 52′ 52″ west 10,520 feet to a monument (No. 64) on a ledge falling southwest to a brook in the southwestern part of the town of Sherman in latitude 41° 32′ 40″ .963 and longitude 73° 31′ 45″ .257; thence south 4° 28′ 48″ west 10,410 feet to a monument (No. 68) on Cranberry mountain in latitude 41° 30′ 58″ .424 and longitude 73° 31′ 55″ .946; thence south 2° 24′ 38″ west 10,617 feet to a monument (No. 72) on the northerly slope of a hill a mile south of Haviland Hollow in latitude 41° 29′ 13″ .627 and longitude 73° 32′ 01″ .813; thence south 3° 03′ 12″ west 20,731 feet to a monument (No. 80) in a mowed field southeast of an angle in the road from Brewster to Ball pond in latitude 41° 25′ 49″ .108 and longitude 73° 32′ 16″ .309; thence south 4° 53′ 12″ west 10,279 feet to a monument (No. 84) on the northerly side of a rocky summit northwest of Mill Plain in latitude 41° 24′ 07″ .915 and longitude 73° 32′ 27″ .798; thence south 2° 45′ 48″ west 10,527 feet to a monument (No. 89) in a swampy pasture south of a right angle in a back road which runs along the line between the towns of Danbury and

---

[2] Formerly ".535."
[3] Formerly " 35"."

Ridgefield in latitude 41° 22' 24" .030 and longitude 73° 32' 34"
.456; thence south 4° 36' 39" west 10,878 feet to a monument
(No. 91) in a swamp near Mopus brook in latitude 41° 20' 36"
.900 and longitude 73° 32' 45" .920; thence south 4° 12' 16"
west 10,493 feet to a monument (No. 96) south of a ledge on
Titicus mountain in latitude 41° 18' 53" .507 and longitude
73° 32' 56" .001; thence south 6° 32' 21" west 7,214 feet to a
monument (No. 98) known as the Ridgefield angle on a steep
side hill sloping toward South pond in latitude 41° 17' 42" .690
and longitude 73° 33' 06" .764; thence south 32° 46' 06" east
14,109 feet to a monument (No. 103) in a swamp near a small
brook in latitude 41° 15' 45" .460 and longitude 73° 31' 26"
.775; thence south 32° 41' 46" east 10,443 feet to a monument
(No. 106) at the westerly side of a rocky ridge near the southwest corner of Ridgefield in latitude 41° 14' 18" .626 and longitude 73° 30' 12" .940; thence south 32° 02' 28" east 11,047
feet to a monument (No. 109) known as the Wilton angle in
woodland northwest of Bald Hill in latitude 41° 12' 46" .101
and longitude 73° 28' 56" .263; thence south 59° 59' 58" west
9,588 feet to a monument (No. 112) on the south side of a short
cross road leading west from the Vista road in latitude 41° 11'
58" .721 and longitude 73° 30' 44" .877; thence south 57° 58'
49" west 6,002 feet to a monument (No. 115) on the northeasterly slope of a low, wooded hill one-half mile west of Mud pond
and northeast of Sellick's Corners in latitude 41° 11' 27" .272
and longitude 73° 31' 51" .438; thence south 59° 09' 58" west
15,983 feet to a monument (No. 120) on the summit of a rocky
ridge half way between two large swamps, northeast of long ridge
in latitude 41° 10' 06" .294 and longitude 73° 34' 50" .871;
thence south 58° 56' 22" west 21,193 feet to a monument (No.
127) in level woodland west of a low hill west of Banksville in
latitude 41° 08' 18" .189 and longitude 73° 38' 48" .129; thence
south 58° 32' 47" west 26,355 feet to a rough granite monument
(No. 140) known as the Duke's Trees angle, set in concrete with
its top below the roadway called King street in latitude 41° 06'
02" .205 and longitude 73° 43' 41" .778; thence south 31° 29'
41" east 11,440 feet to a monument (No. 148) 300 feet north
of the road leading west from King street south of Rye lake in
latitude 41° 04' 25" .814 and longitude 73° 42' 23" .747; thence
south 32° 10' 57" east 14,975 feet to a monument (No. 153)
at the east side of King street 1,000 feet north of Ridge street

in latitude 41° 02′ 20″ .570 and longitude 73° 40′ 39″ .666; thence south 32° 07′ 30″ east 11,401 feet to a granite monument (No. 158) set at the north side of Byram bridge in a concrete pier on a granite ledge known since 1684 as the Great Stone at the wading place in latitude 41° 00′ 44″ .662 and longitude 73° 39′ 20″ .172; thence south 9° 53′ 43″ west 835 feet to a brass bolt and plate (No. 159) set in the top of a large boulder in Byram river in latitude 41° 00′ 36″ .535 and longitude 73° 39′ 22″ .044; thence south 18° 56′ 41″ west 3,735 feet to angle No. 161 in Byram river in latitude 41° 00′ 1″ .626 and longitude 73° 39′ 37″ .863, this tangent being produced and referenced on the shore by a brass bolt and plate leaded into the rock on a steep hill; thence south 12° 57′ 02″ east 965 feet to angle No. 162 in Byram river in latitude 40° 59′ 52″ .335 and longitude 73° 39′ 35″ .044, the line being produced and referenced by a bolt and plate in the rock on a hill east of the river; thence south 5° 14′ 08″ west 950 feet to angle No. 163 in Byram river in latitude 40° 59′ 42″ .995 and longitude 73° 39′ 36″ .173, the line being produced and referenced by a bolt and plate in the ledge on the west shore of the river; thence south 9° 10′ 19″ east 692 feet to angle No. 164 in Byram river in latitude 40° 59′ 36″ .249 and longitude 73° 39′ 34″ .736, the line being produced and referenced by a bolt and plate in the shore; thence south 34° 35′ 04″ east 684 feet to angle No. 165 in Byram river in latitude 40° 59′ 30″ .682 and longitude 73° 39′ 29″ .671, both ends of this and the three subsequent tangents being produced and referenced by brass bolts and plates set in the ledge on the shore of the river; thence south 26° 00′ 02″ east 229 feet to angle No. 166 in latitude 40° 59′ 28″ .646 and longitude 73° 39′ 28″ .360; thence south 5° 26′ 38″ west 402 feet to angle No. 167 in latitude 40° 59′ 24″ .694 and longitude 73° 39′ 28″ .857; thence south 50° 49′ 51″ west 815 feet to angle No. 168 in latitude 40° 59′ 19″ .608 and longitude 73° 39′ 37″ .096; thence south 30° 01′ 41″ east 1,924 feet to angle No. 169, a point in the center of the channel in line with the breakwater at Lyon's or Byram point in latitude 40° 59′ 03″ .152 and longitude 73° 39′ 24″ .546, the northerly end of this tangent being produced back and referenced by a brass bolt and plate in the ledge overlooking the harbor; thence south 45° east 17,160 feet or three and one-quarter miles to angle No. 170 in latitude 40° 57′ 03″ .228 and longitude 73° 36′ 46″ .418, the first angle point in Long Island sound described by the joint commissioners of

New York and Connecticut by a memorandum of agreement dated December eighth, eighteen hundred and seventy-nine; thence in a straight line (the arc of a great circle) north 74° 32′ 32″ east 434,394 feet to a point (No. 171) in latitude 41° 15′ 31″ .321 and longitude 72° 05′ 24″ .685, four statute miles true south of New London lighthouse; thence north 58° 58′ 43″ east 22,604 feet to a point (No. 172) in latitude 41° 17′ 26″ .341 and longitude 72° 01′ 10″ .937, marked on the United States coast survey chart of Fisher's Island sound annexed to said memorandum,— which point is on the long east ¾ north sailing course drawn on said map 1,000 feet true north from the Hammock or North Dumpling lighthouse; thence following said east ¾ north sailing course north 73° 37′ 42″ east 25,717 feet to a point (No. 173) in latitude 41° 18′ 37″ .835 and longitude 71° 55′ 47″ .626, marked No. 2 on said map; thence south 70° 07′ 26″ east 6,424 feet toward a point marked No. 3 on said map until said line intersects the westerly boundary of Rhode Island at a point (No. 174) in latitude 41° 18′ 16″ .249 and longitude 71° 54′ 28″ .477 as determined by the joint commissioners of Connecticut and Rhode Island by a memorandum of agreement dated March twenty-fifth, eighteen hundred and eighty-seven.

The geodetic positions given in this description are based on Clark's spheroid of eighteen hundred and sixty-six and the astronomical data adopted by the United States coast and geodetic survey in eighteen hundred and eighty and are computed from data given in appendix number eight to the report of the said survey for eighteen hundred and eighty-eight, entitled " Geographical Positions in the State of Connecticut."

The boundary line hereinbefore described and determined which has been located and defined as, and in the manner, provided by section eight of this chapter is fully and accurately laid down on duplicate maps, one copy of which has been deposited with the secretary of state of the state of New York and the other copy thereof with the secretary of state of the state of Connecticut.

Nothing herein contained shall be construed to affect any existing titles to property, corporeal or incorporeal, held under grants heretofore made by either of said states, nor to affect existing rights which said states or either of them or which the citizens of either of said states may have by grant, letters-patent or prescription of fishing in the waters of said sound, whether for shell or floating fish irrespective of the boundary line hereby estab-

lished, it not being the purpose hereof to define, limit or interfere with any such right, rights or privileges whatever the same
may be.

Trans-
mission to
governor
of Con-
necticut. The governor is authorized and requested to transmit a copy
of this act to the governor of the state of Connecticut, and upon
receiving acknowledgment of its receipt by the state of Connecticut the governor of this state shall cause such acknowledgment
to be filed in the office of the secretary of state.

Request
for ap-
proval of
congress. The governor of this state is authorized in concurrence with
the governor of the state of Connecticut to communicate to con-
gress the action of the two states on this subject and to request
the approval of congress of the boundaries thus established and
monumented.

§ 2. This act shall take effect immediately.

Chap. 19.

AN ACT to amend the village law, in relation to powers of village trustees to provide for band concerts.

Became a law February 14, 1913, with the approval of the Governor. Passed,
three-fifths being present.

*The People of the State of New York, represented in Senate
and Assembly, do enact as follows:*

L. 1909,
ch. 64,
§ 88,
subd. 22a,
as added by
L. 1911,
ch. 519,
made § 89,
subd. 22a,
and
amended. Section 1. Subdivision twenty-two-a of section eighty-eight of
chapter sixty-four of the laws of nineteen hundred and nine, en-
titled "An act relating to villages, constituting chapter sixty-four
of the consolidated laws," as added by chapter five hundred and
nineteen of the laws of nineteen hundred and eleven is hereby
transferred to and inserted in section eighty-nine of such chapter
and made subdivision twenty-two-a of section eighty-nine, instead of section eighty-eight, to which it was erroneously added,
and is hereby amended to read as follows:

22-a. Band concerts. May[1] provide for public band concerts
within the village, annually between June first and September
fifteenth, but only after a proposition therefor, the submission
whereof is hereby authorized, shall have been duly adopted at a
village election, which proposition shall state the maximum
amount to be expended for such purpose in any one year.

§ 2. This act shall take effect immediately.

---

[1] Words " if a village of the third class," omitted.

Chap. 20.

AN ACT to amend chapter one hundred and fifty-seven of the laws of eighteen hundred and forty-four, entitled "An act to incorporate the village of Mohawk," in relation to the creation of a board of commissioners for the Weller library in the village of Mohawk, and defining its powers and duties.

Became a law February 18, 1913, with the approval of the Governor. Passed, three-fifths being present.

The People of the State of New York, represented in Senate and Assembly, do enact as follows:

Section 1. Section seventeen of chapter one hundred and fifty-seven of the laws of eighteen hundred and forty-four, entitled "An act to incorporate the village of Mohawk," is hereby amended by adding at the end thereof a new subdivision to be subdivision twenty-five,[1] to read as follows:

25. (a) To appoint six commissioners who shall constitute a separate board of commissioners, vested with the care, management and control of the real and personal property devised and bequeathed to the village of Mohawk by the last will and testament of Frederick U. Weller and Helen Weller, both deceased, late of Mohawk, New York, which board so created shall be hereafter styled "Weller library commission." Each of the commissioners so appointed shall be at the time of his appointment and during his term of office a resident of the village and a taxpayer and qualified elector therein; and they shall be so appointed that not more than three of such commissioners in office at any one time shall be members of the same political party. They shall hold office from the date of their appointment, or as soon thereafter as they shall have qualified, respectively, until the first day of January next ensuing and for one, two, three, four, and five years thereafter, and their respective terms of office shall be designated by the board of trustees at the time of making such appointments. Thereafter it shall be the duty of the board of the Weller library commission to appoint, during the month of December of each year, a commissioner to succeed the one whose term of office expires on the first day of January following, and such appointee shall hold office for the term of five years from the first day of

Marginal notes: Subd. 25 added to L. 1844, ch. 157, § 27. — Village trustees to appoint Weller library commission. — Qualifications of commissioners. — Terms. — Appointment of successors.

---

[1] Subd. 25 is amended by L. 1913, ch. 255, post.

2

Holdovers. January next ensuing his appointment; provided, however, that if the board of the Weller library commission fail to so appoint before the first day of January, the commissioner whose term of office then expires shall continue to hold office until his successor is appointed and has qualified, but the office shall be deemed vacant for the purpose of appointing his successor, and such appointment may be made at any time thereafter for the balance of the unexpired term.

Oath of office. (b) Every commissioner, before entering upon the duties of his office, shall take and file with the village clerk the oath of office prescribed by the constitution[2] of the state.

Organization. (c) Within thirty days after their appointment as hereinbefore provided, such commissioners shall meet at the Weller library in said village and proceed to organize as the Weller library com-

President. mission. They shall, at such meeting, designate one of their number to be president of the commission whose duty it shall be to preside at the meetings at which he is present, to call special meetings of the commission upon the request of any two other commissioners, or of his own motion whenever in his discretion he may deem it necessary. In the absence of the president, the commissioner having the shortest term to serve shall preside. Any

Quorum. four of said commissioners shall constitute a quorum for the transaction of business, and the concurrence of at least four commissioners shall be necessary for the transaction of any business and no resolution shall be adopted or other action taken unless four commissioners present at the meeting shall vote affirmatively

Secretary. therefor. They shall also designate at such first meeting one of their number to be secretary of the commission whose duty it shall be to keep accurate and correct minutes of all the proceedings of the commission, to keep in his custody and properly preserve all books, records, maps and papers appertaining to the business

Treasurer. and proceedings of the commission. They shall also designate at said first meeting one of their number to be the treasurer of the commission to receive and collect all moneys paid, turned over or to be paid or turned over to said commission and to keep an accurate statement of all receipts and disbursements of the com-

Annual financial report. mission. Said Weller library commission shall on December thirty-first of each year make and file with the village clerk of Mohawk a report of its receipts and disbursements which shall

---

[2] See constitution, art. 13, § 1; public officers law (L. 1909, ch. 51), § 10, as amended by L. 1913, ch. 59, post.

be published in the official newspaper in conjunction with the
annual village report. The treasurer shall, before entering upon Bond of
the duties of his office, execute and file with the village clerk a
bond with one or two sureties approved by the board of trustees
of the village, in the sum of fifty thousand dollars and conditioned
upon his promptly turning over all village funds which shall come
into his hands and faithfully performing the duties of his office.
The commissioners so appointed, when they shall have organ- Powers of
ized as the Weller library commission, shall be vested with the sioners
control, management and supervision of the property, real and property.
personal devised and bequeathed to the village of Mohawk by the
last will and testament of Frederick U. Weller and Helen Weller,
respectively, and they shall hold legal title to all such property
in trust for said village for the uses and purposes as set forth and
described in said wills of Frederick U. Weller and Helen Weller.

(d) The Weller library commission shall accept, receive and Acceptance
maintain in trust as aforesaid, the house and grounds surrounding tenance of
and connected with said house situate in the village of Mohawk library.
which was occupied by Frederick U. Weller at the time of his
death for the sole purposes and to be used solely for a free public
library for said village to be named and known as the "Weller Name of
Library." Said library shall be open at least two days in each When open:
week and more if deemed necessary or beneficial and shall be free free to into all of the inhabitants of said village; all as prescribed in the
fourth clause of said will. The Weller library commission shall Acceptance
accept and receive in trust all the rest and residue of the property of property
which passed to said village under the sixth clause of said will of will of
Frederick U. Weller to be collected and sold and converted into U. Weller.
money and the proceeds thereof to be invested in United States
government bonds and the interest and income therefrom to be
used and devoted as follows: To keep and maintain in good repair Purpose
and order the burial lot and vault of Weller and Morgan in the devoted.
cemetery at Mohawk; to keep in order the grounds devised for
the use of the library and to rebuild and remodel the buildings on
said grounds making them suitable for a library and to keep the
same in proper repair; and to purchase books for and to care for,
support and maintain the library in a proper manner. If, at any Sale of
time, it shall be deemed necessary by the Weller library commis- grounds
sion for the benefit and the proper support and maintenance of income.
said library to have more income than above provided, the commission is hereby authorized and directed, as provided in the

seventh clause of said will, to dispose of, sell and convey so much
of the grounds above devised for the purposes of a library, as
shall not be necessary for the proper use and convenience of such
library and in case of such sale of any of said grounds, the proceeds thereof shall be invested in United States government bonds,
the income therefrom to be used and devoted the same as the interest and income from the other property devised and bequeathed
to the said village as provided in said will. The Weller library
commission shall accept and receive in trust for said village all the
property, bequeathed and devised to the village of Mohawk by
the third clause of the will of Helen Weller, to be invested in
United States government bonds and the interest and income therefrom to be used and devoted as follows: To keep and maintain in
good repair and order the burial lot and vault of Weller and
Morgan in the cemetery at Mohawk; pursuant to the second subdivision of the third clause of said will, to rebuild and remodel
the buildings suitable for a library and keep the same in repair;
to purchase books and support, and maintain the public library
for the village of Mohawk as provided for in the last will and
testament of her husband Frederick U. Weller. The said commission may receive and hold in trust for said village any gift,
devise or bequest of money or other property for the purpose of
using the avails and earnings thereof in caring for and maintaining said Weller library and grounds or fulfilling the purpose
of said gift, devise or bequest. Any vacancy which may at any
time occur in said board of commissioners through death, resignation or any other cause shall be filled by the remaining commissioners. The commissioners may make and adopt all necessary
and reasonable rules and regulations for the use, care, management
and protection of said Weller library, and to provide for the conduct of persons while within the said library building and grounds
and the exclusion therefrom of improper persons or assemblages,
and jointly to enact all such rules, by-laws and regulations, and to
alter the same, as may be reasonable and essential to the proper
conduct and care of said Weller library and grounds. All such
rules and regulations shall be plainly printed and posted in conspicuous places throughout the library building and grounds and
when so posted shall be deemed to be brought to the notice of all
persons and to become forthwith in full force and effect, and the
commission may prescribe penalties for the violation of any rule,
regulation or ordinance not to exceed twenty-five dollars for each

Acceptance in trust of property under will of Helen Weller.

Purposes to which devoted.

Acceptance of gifts, etc.

Vacancies in commission.

Rules for care and management of library.

Posting of rules.

Penalties for violations.

violation to be recovered in an action brought by them in the name
of the village against the persons who have been guilty of such vio-
lations. No commissioner appointed hereunder shall be interested Commis-
sioners
not to be
interested
directly or indirectly in any contract, claim or account for or
relating to any work done or material furnished for or on account in work
done or
material
furnished.
of any matter under the control of the commission; nor shall any
commissioner receive any compensation for his services except for No com-
pensation.
actual disbursements made or expenses incurred by him by the
express direction of the commission. It shall be the duty of the Commis-
sion, when
to be
appointed.
board of trustees of the village of Mohawk to appoint said commis-
sioners within twenty days after this act goes into effect. Upon
the organization of the Weller library commission it shall be the Property,
when to be
turned
over.
duty of the board of village trustees to immediately turn
over to said commissioners all property of every description pertaining and relating to the Weller library. All
funds received by the treasurer of said commission shall be kept Weller
library
fund.
and set aside as a separate and distinct Weller library fund which
shall thereafter be withdrawn and paid out only by said treasurer Payments
therefrom,
how made.
upon the audit and order of said commissioners, certified to him
by a written order signed by the secretary of the commission and
countersigned by its president, which shall specify the names of
the persons to whom and the amount of money to be paid, together
with a statement of the purposes for which such payment is made,
and it shall be the duty of said treasurer upon the audit and order
of said commissioners to pay to the persons as in the order directed the sum of money specified. All moneys in any way Deposi-
tories.
acquired by said commission for the purposes of said Weller library shall be deposited by the treasurer of the commission
in such bank or place of deposit as the Weller library commis-
sioners shall direct. The commission shall provide suitable books Books for
secretary
and
treasurer.
for the secretary and treasurer for the entry of all items of re-
ceipts and disbursements and for the recording of all transactions
affecting the powers and duties of the commission. The com- Employees.
mission shall have power to appoint, employ and discharge agents
or subordinates and other employees and to fix their compensation.
The by-laws shall prescribe regular meetings for the commission Amend-
ment of
by-laws
and rules.
and the by-laws, rules and regulations shall be subject to alter-
ation, revision or amendment only at regular meetings or at a
meeting called for such purpose, provided that ten days' written
notice be given either personally or by mail, of the proposed
change.

§ 2. This act shall take effect immediately.

Chap. 21.

AN ACT to amend the insurance law, in relation to organizations
in assisting in establishing insurance rates.

Became a law February 19, 1913, with the approval of the Governor. Passed,
three-fifths being present.

*The People of the State of New York, represented in Senate
and Assembly, do enact as follows:*

New § 140
added to
L. 1909,
ch. 33.

Section 1. Chapter thirty-three of the laws of nineteen hundred
and nine, entitled "An act in relation to insurance corporations
constituting chapter twenty-eight of the consolidated laws," is
hereby amended by inserting a new section to be one hundred and
forty and to read as follows:

§ 140. **Organizations for assisting in establishing insurance
rates.** Every corporation, association, bureau or board which now
exists or hereafter may be formed, and every person who maintains
or hereafter may maintain a bureau or office, for the purpose of
assisting any underwriting corporation, association, bureau or person in formulating, fixing, promulgating, applying or maintaining
a rate on property or risks of any kind located in this state, shall
file with the superintendent of insurance a copy of the articles of
agreement, association or incorporation and the by-laws and all
amendments thereto under which such person, association, bureau
or board operates or proposes to operate, together with his or its
business address, as well as such other information concerning
such organization and its operations as may be required by the superintendent. Every such person, corporation, association, bureau or board, whether before or
after filing of the information specified in the last preceding
paragraph, shall be subject to the visitation, supervision and examination of the superintendent of insurance, who shall cause to
be made an examination thereof as often as he deems it expedient.
For this purpose he may appoint as examiners one or more competent persons, and upon such examination, he, his deputy or any
examiner authorized by him shall have all the powers given to the
superintendent, his deputy or any examiner authorized by him by
section thirty-nine of this chapter, including the power to examine
under oath the officers or agents and all persons deemed to have
material information regarding the business of or manner of
operation of every such person, corporation, association, bureau
or board.

This section shall not apply to any contract of life insurance, nor to any contract of insurance upon or in connection with marine or transportation risks or hazards other than contracts for automobile insurance, nor to contracts of insurance upon property or risks located without this state, nor to contracts made by persons, partnerships, associations or corporations authorized to do business under articles five, six, seven and nine of this chapter, but it shall apply to all other forms of insurance mentioned in any article of this chapter.

§ 2. This act shall take effect immediately.

Chap. 22.

AN ACT to amend the insurance law, in relation to requiring adjusters of loss or damage by fire to procure a certificate of authority from the superintendent of insurance.

Became a law February 19, 1913, with the approval of the Governor. Passed, three-fifths being present.

The People of the State of New York, represented in Senate and Assembly, do enact as follows:

Section 1. Chapter thirty-three of the laws of nineteen hundred and nine, entitled "An act in relation to insurance corporations, constituting chapter twenty-eight of the consolidated laws," is hereby amended by inserting therein a new section, to be section one hundred and thirty-eight-a,[1] to read as follows:

§ 138-a. **Public adjusters; certificate of authority.** No person, partnership, association or corporation shall, after July first, nineteen hundred and thirteen, engage in the business of adjusting loss or damage by fire under a policy or policies of insurance upon property within this state, or advertise, solicit business or hold himself out to the public as such an adjuster, without first procuring a certificate of authority so to act from the superintendent of insurance.

The superintendent of insurance shall issue such adjuster's certificate of authority to a person, partnership, association or corporation, applying therefor, who is trustworthy and is competent to transact such business in such manner as to safeguard the interests of the public.

A certificate of authority issued to a corporation, partnership

§ 138a added to L. 1909, ch. 33.

1 Section 138a is amended by L. 1913, ch. 522, post.

or association shall authorize only the officers and directors of the corporation, or the members of the partnership or association, specified in the certificate, each of whom must be qualified to obtain a certificate to act as adjusters. The fee to be paid to the superintendent of insurance by the applicant for such adjuster's certificate at the time the application is made, and annually for the renewal thereof, shall be twenty-five dollars. If the applicant be a corporation, partnership or association such fee shall be paid for each person specified in the certificate.

Every adjuster's certificate of authority shall expire on the thirty-first day of December of the calendar year in which the same shall have been issued, but if an application for the renewal of any such certificate shall have been filed with the superintendent of insurance before January first of any year the certificate of authority sought to be renewed shall continue in full force and effect until the issuance by the superintendent of insurance of the new certificate applied for or until five days after the superintendent of insurance shall have refused to issue such new certificate and shall have served notice of such refusal on the applicant therefor. Service of such notice may be made either personally or by mail, and, if by mail, shall be deemed complete if such notice is deposited in the post-office postage prepaid, directed to the applicant at the place of business specified in the application.

Before any adjuster's certificate of authority shall be issued by the superintendent of insurance there must be filed in his office a written application therefor. Such application shall be in the form or forms and supplements thereof prescribed by the superintendent of insurance and must set forth (1) the name and address of the applicant, and if the applicant be a partnership or association, the name and address of each member thereof, and if the applicant be a corporation, the name and address of each of its officers and directors; (2) whether any certificate of authority as agent, broker or adjuster has been issued theretofore by the superintendent of insurance to the applicant, and, if the applicant be an individual, whether any such certificate has been issued theretofore to any partnership or association of which he was or is a member or to any corporation of which he was or is an officer or director, and, if the applicant be a partnership or association, whether any such certificate has been issued theretofore to any member thereof, and, if the applicant be a corporation, whether any such certificate has been issued theretofore to any officer or director of such corporation; (3) the business in which the applicant has been engaged for the year next preceding the date of the application, and, if employed by another, the name or names and address or addresses of such employer or employers; (4) such information as the superintendent of insurance may require of applicants to enable him to determine their trustworthiness and competency to transact the business of adjuster in such manner as to safeguard the interests of the public.

An application for an adjuster's certificate of authority must be signed and verified by the applicant and, if made by a partnership or association, by each member thereof and if made by a corporation by each officer and director thereof to be authorized thereby to act as an adjuster.

If an application for a certificate of authority under this section be filed in the year nineteen hundred and thirteen within sixty days after this section takes effect the applicant and the persons named in the application may, notwithstanding the provisions of this section, act as public adjuster until notice of rejection of the application shall have been served as herein provided with respect to renewal applications.

A corporation, association or partnership to whom a certificate of authority shall have been issued by the superintendent of insurance under this section may at any time make an application to the superintendent of insurance for the issuance of a supplemental certificate of authority authorizing additional officers or directors of the corporation or members of the partnership or association to act as adjusters, and the superintendent of insurance may thereupon issue to such corporation, association or partnership a supplemental certificate accordingly upon the payment of an additional fee for each member or officer or director thereby authorized to act as an adjuster.

A certificate issued under this section shall be revoked by the superintendent, if after due investigation and a hearing either before him or before any salaried employee of the insurance department designated by him whose report he may adopt, he determines that the holder of such certificate (1) has violated any provision of the chapter by any act or thing done in respect to insurance for which such certificate is required; or (2) has made a material misstatement in the application for such certificate; or (3) has been guilty of fraudulent practices; or (4) has demonstrated his incompetency or untrustworthiness to transact the business for which such certificate of authority shall have been granted by reason of anything done or omitted in or about such business under the authority of such certificate.

No individual, partnership, association or corporation whose certificate of authority is so revoked nor any partnership or association of which such individual is a member, nor any corporation of which he is an officer or director shall be entitled to any certificate of authority under this section for a period of one year after such revocation, or, if such revocation be reviewed by certiorari proceedings, for one year after the final determination thereof affirming the action of the superintendent in revoking such certificate. If any such certificate held by a partnership, association or corporation be so revoked, no member of the partnership or association or officer or director of the corporation shall be entitled to such a certificate for the same period of time, if the superintendent of insurance determines and finds that such member or officer or director was personally at fault in the matter on account of which the certificate was revoked. The holder of any such certificate or any person aggrieved may file with the superintendent of insurance a verified complaint setting forth facts from which it shall appear that any such certificate ought to be revoked. The superintendent must thereupon, after investigation and a hearing as herein provided, determine whether such certificate shall be revoked.

If an application for a certificate of authority under this section be rejected or such a certificate be revoked by the superintendent of insurance notice thereof shall forthwith be served on the applicant or on the holder of such certificate either personally or by mail, and, if by mail, such service shall be complete if such notice be deposited in the post-office postage prepaid, directed to the applicant or the holder of such certificate, as the case may be, at the place of business specified in the application or certificate.

The action of the superintendent of insurance in granting or refusing to grant or to renew a certificate of authority or in revoking or refusing to revoke such a certificate shall be subject to review by writ of certiorari, at the instance of the applicant for such certificate, the holder of a certificate so revoked or the holder of any such certificate or the person aggrieved. If the superintendent of insurance shall revoke or shall refuse to renew the certificate of authority of any adjuster issued under this section and such adjuster shall apply for a writ of certiorari to review such action, the certificate of authority of such adjuster shall be deemed to be in full force and effect for all purposes, including the right to renewal, until the final determination of such certiorari proceedings and all appeals therefrom, provided the fee for such certificate be paid.

This section shall not apply to an agent or employee of an underwriter by whom a policy of insurance against loss or damage by fire shall have been written upon property within this state, in adjusting loss or damage under such policy nor to a broker acting as adjuster without compensation for a client for whom he is acting as broker, nor to contracts made by persons, partnerships, associations or corporations authorized to do business under article nine of this chapter.

Any person, partnership, association or corporation violating any of the provisions of this section shall, in addition to any other penalty in this chapter provided, forfeit to the people of the state five hundred dollars.

§ 2. This act shall take effect twenty days after it becomes a law. In effect after 20 days.

Chap. 23.

AN ACT to amend the insurance law, in relation to organizations for assisting underwriters in insurance business generally.

Became a law February 19, 1913, with the approval of the Governor. Passed, three-fifths being present.

The People of the State of New York, represented in Senate and Assembly, do enact as follows:

Section 1. Chapter thirty-three of the laws of nineteen hundred and nine, entitled "An act in relation to insurance corporations, constituting chapter twenty-eight of the consolidated laws," is hereby amended by inserting a new section, to be one hundred and thirty-nine, and to read as follows:

§ 139. **Organizations for assisting underwriters in insurance business generally.** Every corporation, association, bureau or board which now exists or hereafter may be formed, and every person who maintains or hereafter may maintain a bureau or office, located within or without this state, for the purpose of inspecting risks, adjusting losses, testing appliances, formulating rules or establishing standards for the information or benefit of

underwriters in the transaction within this state of the business
of insurance and which corporation, association, bureau or
person receives contributions from or is financially aided
directly or indirectly, wholly or partially or in any manner
by any person, association or corporation authorized to transact
the business of insurance within this state, shall file on demand
with the superintendent of insurance a copy of the articles of
agreement, association or incorporation and the bylaws and all
amendments thereto under which such person, association, corporation, board or bureau operates or proposes to operate, together with his or its business address as well as such other information concerning such organization and its operation as may
be required by the superintendent. Every such person, corporation, association, bureau or board, whether before or after filing
of the information specified in the last preceding paragraph,
shall be subject to the visitation and examination of the
superintendent of insurance, who shall cause to be made an examination thereof whenever he deems it expedient. For this
purpose he may appoint as examiners one or more competent persons, and upon such examination, he, his deputy or any examiner
authorized by him shall have all the powers given to the superintendent, his deputy or any examiner authorized by him by section
thirty-nine[1] of this chapter, including the power to examine under
oath the officers or agents and all persons deemed to have material
information regarding the business of or manner of operation
by every such person, corporation, association, bureau or board.
No person, association or corporation authorized to transact the
business of insurance within this state shall be a member or sub-
scriber to any corporation, association, bureau, board or person
referred to in this section nor shall it contribute to or financially
aid any such corporation, association, bureau, board or person
who shall fail to comply with the provisions of this section. Upon
notice furnished by the superintendent of insurance every person, association or corporation authorized to transact the business
of insurance within this state, shall terminate immediately its
subscription or membership and shall cease to make further contributions directly or indirectly or in any manner to such corporation, association, bureau, board or person.

This section shall not apply to any contract of life insurance,
nor to any contract of insurance upon or in connection with

---

[1] As amended by L. 1910, ch. 634.

marine or transportation risks or hazards other than contracts for
automobile insurance, nor to contracts of insurance upon property or risks located without this state, nor to contracts made by
persons, partnerships, associations or corporations authorized to
do business under articles five, six, seven and nine of this chapter, but it shall apply to all other forms of insurance mentioned
in any article of this chapter.

§ 2. This act shall take effect immediately.

Chap. 24.

AN ACT to amend the general corporation law, in relation to
corporate names.

Became a law February 19, 1913, with the approval of the Governor. Passed,
three-fifths being present.

*The People of the State of New York, represented in Senate
and Assembly, do enact as follows:*

Section 1. Section six of chapter twenty-eight of the laws of
nineteen hundred and nine, entitled "An act relating to corporations generally, constituting chapter twenty-three of the consolidated laws," as amended by chapter six hundred and thirty-eight
of the laws of nineteen hundred and eleven and chapter two of
the laws of nineteen hundred and twelve, is hereby amended to
read as follows:

§ 6. **Corporate names.**   1. No certificate of incorporation of
a proposed corporation having the same name as a corporation
authorized to do business under the laws of this state, or a name
so nearly resembling it as to be calculated to deceive, shall be filed
or recorded in any office for the purpose of effecting its incorporation, or of authorizing it to do business in this state; nor shall
any corporation except a religious, charitable or benevolent corporation be authorized to do business in this state unless its name
has such word or words, abbreviation, affix or prefix, therein or
thereto, as will clearly indicate that it is a corporation as distinguished from a natural person, firm or copartnership; or unless
such corporation uses with its corporate name, in this state, such
an affix or prefix. A corporation formed by the reincorporation,
reorganization or consolidation of other corporations or upon the
sale of the property or franchises of a corporation, or a corporation

[margin note: L. 1909, ch. 28, § 6, as amended by L. 1911, ch. 638, and L. 1912, ch. 2, amended.]

acquiring or becoming possessed of all the estate, property, rights, privileges and franchises of any other corporation or corporations by merger, may have the same name as the corporation or one of the corporations to whose franchises it has succeeded. No corporation shall be hereafter organized under the laws of this state with the word "trust," "bank," "banking," "insurance," "assurance," "indemnity," "guarantee," "guaranty," "title," "casualty," "surety," "fidelity,"[1] "savings," "investment," "loan" or "benefit" as part of its name, except a corporation formed under the banking law or the insurance law.

2. No corporation, society or association, whether now existing or hereafter organized under or by virtue of the laws of this state, shall ever employ the words "Lucretia Mott" to designate, describe or name any hospital, infirmary or dispensary, or any part thereof, or any similar institution.

§ 2. This act shall take effect immediately.

Chap. 25.

AN ACT to amend the insurance law, in relation to life or casualty insurance corporations upon the co-operative or assessment plan.

Became a law February 19, 1913, with the approval of the Governor. Passed, three-fifths being present.

The People of the State of New York, represented in Senate and Assembly, do enact as follows:

L. 1909, ch. 33, § 65, as added by L. 1911, ch 416, and amended by L. 1912. ch. 225. amended.

Section 1. Section sixty-five of chapter thirty-three of the laws of nineteen hundred and nine, entitled "An act in relation to insurance corporations, constituting chapter twenty-eight of the consolidated laws," as added by chapter four hundred and sixteen of the laws of nineteen hundred and eleven, and amended by chapter two hundred and twenty-five of the laws of nineteen hundred and twelve, is hereby amended to read as follows:

§ 65. **Rebating and discriminations prohibited.** No insurance corporation, association, partnership, Lloyds or individual underwriters authorized or permitted to do any insurance business within this state, or any officer, agent, solicitor or representative

---

1 Words " " casualty," " surety," " fidelity," " new.

thereof, shall make any contract for such insurance, on property
or risk located within this state, or against liability, casualty,
accident or hazard that may arise or occur therein or agreement
as to such contract, other than as plainly expressed in the policy
issued or to be issued thereon; nor shall any such corporation,
association, partnership, Lloyds or individual underwriters, or
officer, agent, solicitor or representative thereof, directly or indirectly, in any manner whatsoever, pay or allow or offer to pay
or allow as inducement to such insurance, or after the insurance
shall have been effected, any rebate from the premium which is
specified in the policy or any special favor or advantage in the
dividends or other benefit to accrue thereon, or any valuable
consideration or inducement whatever, not specified in the policy
or contract of insurance, or give, sell or purchase, or offer to
give, sell, or purchase, as inducement to such insurance, or in
connection therewith, any stock, bonds or other securities of any
insurance company, or other corporation or association, or any
dividends or profits accrued thereon, or anything of value whatsoever, not specified in the policy, nor shall any insurance broker,
his agent or representative, or any other person, directly or
indirectly, either by sharing commissions or in any manner whatsoever pay or allow or offer to pay or allow as inducement to
such insurance, or after the insurance shall have been effected,
any rebate from the premium which is specified in the policy;
nor shall the insured, his agent or representative, directly or
indirectly accept or knowingly receive any such rebate from the
premium specified in the policy; this section shall not prevent
any corporation, person, partnership or association lawfully doing
such insurance business in this state from the distribution of
surplus and dividends to policyholders after the first year of
insurance nor prevent any member of an inter-insurance or
Lloyds association from receiving the profit of his or its underwriting; nor shall this section prevent any such corporation or
other insurer, or his or its agent, from paying commissions to
the broker who shall have negotiated for the insurance, nor shall
this section prevent any licensed broker from sharing or dividing
a commission earned or received by him with any other licensed
broker or brokers who shall have aided him in respect to the
insurance for the negotiation of which such commission shall
have been earned or paid, and nothing herein contained shall
be held to prevent the covering of risks by temporary binders

or such other memoranda as do not conflict with the provisions of this chapter. Nor shall this section prevent any such corporation or other insurer, or any agent or insurance broker, from distributing or presenting to any person or corporation any[1] article of merchandise not exceeding one dollar in value, which shall have conspicuously stamped or printed thereon the advertisement of such insurance corporation, agent or broker.

No person shall be excused from attending and, when ordered so to do, from testifying or producing any books, papers or other documents before any court or magistrate, upon any investigation, proceeding or trial for a violation of any of the provisions of this section, upon the ground or for the reason that the testimony or evidence, documentary or otherwise, required of him may tend to convict him of a crime or subject him to a penalty or forfeiture, but no person shall be prosecuted or subjected to any penalty or forfeiture for or on account of any transaction, matter or thing concerning which he may have been required so to testify or to produce evidence, documentary or otherwise, and no testimony so given or produced shall be received against him upon any criminal investigation or proceeding. Any person or corporation violating the provisions of this section shall be guilty of a misdemeanor and shall forfeit to the people of the state the sum of five hundred dollars for each such violation. This section shall not apply to any contract of life insurance nor to any contract of insurance upon or in connection with marine or transportation risks or hazards other than contracts for automobile insurance, nor to contracts made by persons, associations or corporations authorized to do business under articles five,[2] seven and nine of this chapter.

§ 2. This act shall take effect immediately.

---

[1] Formerly read: "in."
[2] Word "six" omitted.

Chap. 26.

AN ACT to amend the insurance law, in relation to rate-making associations.

Became a law February 19, 1913, with the approval of the Governor. Passed, three-fifths being present.

The People of the State of New York, represented in Senate and Assembly, do enact as follows:

Section 1. Section one hundred and forty-one of chapter thirty-three of the laws of nineteen hundred and nine, entitled "An act in relation to insurance corporations, constituting chapter twenty-eight of the consolidated laws," as added by chapter four hundred and sixty of the laws of nineteen hundred and eleven and amended by chapter one hundred and seventy-five of the laws of nineteen hundred and twelve, is hereby amended to read as follows: *L. 1909, ch. 33, § 141, as added by L. 1911, ch. 460, and amended by L. 1912, ch. 175, amended.*

§ 141. **Rate-making associations.** Every corporation, association or bureau which now exists or hereafter may be formed, and every person who maintains or hereafter may maintain a bureau or office, for the purpose of suggesting, approving or making rates to be used by more than one underwriter for insurances, including surety bonds, on property or risks of any kind located in this state, shall file with the superintendent of insurance a copy of the articles of agreement, association or incorporation and the by-laws and all amendments thereto under which such person, association or bureau operates or proposes to operate, together with his or its business address and a list of the members or insurance corporations represented or to be represented by him or it, as well as such other information concerning such rating organization and its operations as may be required by the superintendent.

Every such person, corporation, association or bureau, whether before or after the filing of the information specified in the last preceding paragraph, shall be subject to the visitation, supervision and examination of the superintendent of insurance, who shall cause to be made an examination thereof as often as he deems it expedient and at least once in three years. [1] For such purpose he may appoint as examiners one or more competent persons, and upon such examination, he, his deputy or any examiner author-

---

[1] Following sentence new.

ized by him shall have all the powers given to the superintendent, his deputy or any examiner authorized by him by section thirty-nine of this chapter, including the power to examine under oath the officers or agents and all persons deemed to have material information regarding the business of or manner of operation by every such person, corporation, association, bureau or board. The superintendent shall make public the results of such examination and shall report to the legislature in his annual report on the methods of such rating organization and the manner of its operation.

Each such person, corporation, association or bureau shall file with the superintendent of insurance whenever he may call therefor any and every schedule of rates or such other information concerning such rates as may be suggested, approved or made by any such rating organization for the purposes specified in the first paragraph of this section.

No such person, corporation, association or bureau shall fix or make any rate or schedule of rates which is to or may apply to any risk within this state, on the condition that the whole amount of insurance on such risk or any specified part thereof shall be placed at such rates, or with the members of or subscribers to such rating organization; nor shall any such person, corporation, association or bureau, or any person, association or corporation authorized to transact the business of insurance within this state, fix or make any rate or schedule of rates or charge a rate which discriminates unfairly between risks within this state of essentially the same hazard or, if such rate be a fire insurance rate. which discriminates unfairly between risks [2]in the application of like charges or credits or which discriminates unfairly between risks of essentially the same hazards and having substantially the same degree of protection against fire. Whenever it is made to appear to the satisfaction of the superintendent of insurance that such discrimination exists, he may, after a full hearing either before himself or before any salaried employee of the insurance department whose report he may adopt, order such discrimination removed; and all such persons, corporations, associations or bureaus affected thereby shall immediately comply therewith; [3]nor shall such persons, corporations, associations or bureaus remove

---

[2] Remainder of sentence formerly read: " within this state of essentially the same hazard belonging to classes having substantially the same fire class record, and which are similarly situated and protected against fire."
[3] Remainder of sentence new.

such discrimination by increasing the rates on any risk or class of risks affected by such order unless it is made to appear to the satisfaction of the superintendent of insurance that such increase is justifiable.

No such person, corporation, association or bureau or any other person, corporation, association or bureau, shall charge any licensing, registration, certification or membership fee to brokers who shall have been or hereafter may be licensed or authorized as such pursuant to the provisions of this chapter; nor shall any such rating organization or any other person, corporation, association or bureau or any two or more persons, associations or corporations authorized to transact the business of insurance within this state, acting in agreement, refuse to do business with or to pay commissions to any person who may be licensed or authorized as an insurance broker, pursuant to the provisions of this chapter, because such a broker will not agree to secure insurance only at the rates of premium fixed by such rating organization or the parties to such agreement.

Every such rating organization shall keep a careful record of its proceedings and shall furnish upon demand to any person upon whose property or risk a rate has been made, or to his authorized agent, full information as to such rate, and, if such property or risk be rated by a schedule, a copy of such schedule; it shall also provide such means as may be approved by the superintendent of insurance whereby any person or persons affected by such rate or rates may be heard, either in person or by agent, before the governing or rating committee or other proper executive of such rating organization on an application for a change in such rate or rates.

This section shall not apply to any contract of life insurance, nor to any contract of insurance upon or in connection with marine or transportation risks or hazards other than contracts for automobile insurance, nor to contracts of insurance upon property or risks located without this state, nor to contracts made by persons, partnerships, associations or corporations authorized to do business under articles five, six, seven and nine of this chapter, but it shall apply to all other forms of insurance mentioned in any article of this chapter.

§ 2. This act shall take effect immediately.

Chap. 27.

AN ACT to repeal chapter eighty-five of the laws of eighteen
hundred and ninety-nine, entitled "An act to provide the minimum capital stock required for the organization of fire or marine
insurance corporations."

Became a law February 19, 1913, with the approval of the Governor. Passed,
three-fifths being present.

*The People of the State of New York, represented in Senate
and Assembly, do enact as follows:*

L. 1899.
ch. 85
repealed.

Section 1. Chapter eighty-five of the laws of eighteen hundred
and ninety-nine, entitled "An act to provide the minimum capital
stock required for the organization of fire or marine insurance
corporations," is hereby repealed.[1]

§ 2. This act shall take effect immediately.

Chap. 28.

AN ACT to amend the insurance law, in relation to the policy or
certificate of a life or casualty insurance corporation upon the
co-operative or assessment plan.

Became a law February 19, 1913, with the approval of the Governor. Passed,
three-fifths being present.

*The People of the State of New York, represented in Senate
and Assembly, do enact as follows:*

§ 219 added
to L. 1909,
ch. 33.

Section 1. Article six of chapter thirty-three of the laws of
nineteen hundred and nine, entitled "An act in relation to insurance corporations, constituting chapter twenty-eight of the consolidated laws," is hereby amended by adding at the end a new
section to be section two hundred and nineteen, to read as follows:

§ 219. **Policy to indicate assessment plan.** Every policy or
certificate hereafter issued by any corporation, company, society,
organization or association transacting business under this article

---

[1] L. 1899, ch. 85 was specifically repealed by the consolidated insurance
law (L. 1909, ch. 33), § 360. It was intended to consolidate the act of
1899 in § 12 of the insurance law, but only part of the act seems to have
been so consolidated. Therefore doubt having arisen under the act for the
construction of the consolidated laws (L. 1909, ch. 596) as to the efficacy
of such repeal, it is here again specifically repealed.

shall have conspicuously printed on the face of such policy or
certificate and at the top thereof in capital letters not smaller than
great primer roman condensed capitals, the words " assessment
system."

§ 2. This act shall take effect immediately.

Chap. 29.

AN ACT to amend the insurance law, in relation to proceedings
against and the liquidation of delinquent insurance corporations.

**Became a law February 19, 1913, with the approval of the Governor. Passed,
three-fifths being present.**

*The People of the State of New York, represented in Senate
and Assembly, do enact as follows:*

Section 1. Section sixty-three of chapter thirty-three of the
laws of nineteen hundred and nine, entitled "An act in relation
to insurance corporations, constituting chapter twenty-eight of the
consolidated laws," as added by chapter three hundred of the laws
of nineteen hundred and nine, and amended by chapter six
hundred and thirty-four of the laws of nineteen hundred and ten,
chapter three hundred and sixty-six of the laws of nineteen hundred and eleven and chapter two hundred and seventeen of the
laws of nineteen hundred and twelve, is hereby amended by adding
thereto, at the end thereof, a new subdivision, to be subdivision
twelve, to read as follows: *[margin: Subd. 12 added to L. 1909, ch. 82. § 63, as added by L. 1909, ch. 300.]*

12. At any time after the commencement of proceedings under
an order of liquidation made pursuant to this section, the said
superintendent may remove the principal office of the corporation
in liquidation to the county of Albany. In event of such removal
the court shall, upon the application of the superintendent, direct
the clerk of the county wherein such proceeding was commenced to
transmit all of the papers filed therein with such clerk to the clerk
of the county of Albany, and the proceeding shall thereafter be
conducted in the same manner as though it had been commenced
in the county of Albany. *[margin: Removal of principal office of corporation in liquidation to Albany.]*

§ 2. This act shall take effect immediately.

Chap. 30.

AN ACT to amend the code of civil procedure, in relation to docket of judgment.

Became a law February 19, 1913, with the approval of the Governor. Passed, three-fifths being present.

The People of the State of New York, represented in Senate and Assembly, do enact as follows:

§ 1260, opening paragraph amended.

Section 1. The opening paragraph preceding subdivision one of section twelve hundred and sixty of the code of civil procedure is hereby amended to read as follows:

Docket of judgment, how canceled.

§ 1260. The docket of a judgment must be canceled and discharged by the clerk in whose office the judgment-roll is filed, or by the clerk of any county where a transcript of said judgment shall have been docketed,[1] upon filing with him a satisfaction-piece, describing the judgment, and executed as follows:

In effect Sept. 1, 1913.

§ 2. This act shall take effect September first, nineteen hundred and thirteen.

Chap. 31.

AN ACT to amend the Greater New York charter, in relation to the transfer of moneys from the general fund of the city to appropriate accounts for the purpose of adjusting deductions made under the provisions of the tax law referring to taxes upon special franchises.

Became a law February 20, 1913, with the approval of the Governor. Passed, three-fifths being present.

Accepted by the City.

The People of the State of New York, represented in Senate and Assembly, do enact as follows:

L. 1897, ch. 378, § 162, as re-enacted by L. 1901, ch. 466, amended.

Section 1. Section one hundred and sixty-two of the Greater New York charter, as re-enacted by chapter four hundred and sixty-six of the laws of nineteen hundred and one, is hereby amended to read as follows:

Application of certain moneys.

§ 162. It shall be lawful for the comptroller to apply the moneys accruing for interest on the sales of lands in said city for

---

[1] Words "or by the clerk of any county where a transcript of said judgment shall have been docketed," new.

unpaid taxes, assessments and water rents, or so much thereof as shall be required, to the account or fund designated "lands purchased for taxes and assessments," such moneys to be used for purchases by the corporation at such sales. [1] For the purpose of adjusting the reductions heretofore or hereafter made in the amount of taxes receivable by reason of the operation of the provisions of the tax law providing for the deduction from special franchise taxes of payments made in the nature of a tax, it shall also be lawful for the comptroller to transfer at any time, and from time to time, from the moneys in the general fund of the city to the credit of the appropriate account or accounts, a sum or sums equivalent to but not exceeding such deductions.

§ 2. This act shall take effect immediately.

Chap. 32.

AN ACT to authorize and empower the city of New York to acquire a site beyond its territorial limits for use of The New York City Reformatory of Misdemeanants under the jurisdiction of the department of correction of the city of New York.

Became a law February 21, 1913, with the approval of the Governor. Passed, three-fifths being present.

Accepted by the City.

The People of the State of New York, represented in Senate and Assembly, do enact as follows:

Section 1. The city of New York is authorized and empowered, upon the approval of the board of estimate and apportionment, to acquire, by purchase or condemnation, a farm site outside the territorial limits of said city, for use as a part of The New York City Reformatory of Misdemeanants under the jurisdiction of the department of correction of the city of New York. *Acquisition of site.*

§ 2. Any action which shall have been taken by the board of estimate and apportionment, and by the board of aldermen of the city of New York, at the date of the passage of this act, authorizing the acquisition of a site and the erection of buildings thereon for the use and purpose aforesaid, shall be and remain applicable to the acquisition of a site beyond the territorial limits of the city of New York under this act. *Action already taken to be applicable under this act.*

§ 3. This act shall take effect immediately.

---

[1] Remainder of section new.

Chap. 33.

AN ACT to amend the Greater New York charter, in relation to the cancellation of certain assessments for public improvements levied against property belonging to the city.

Became a law February 21, 1913, with the approval of the Governor. Passed, three-fifths being present.

Accepted by the City.

The People of the State of New York, represented in Senate and Assembly, do enact as follows:

L. 1897, ch. 378, § 215, as re-enacted by L. 1901, ch. 466, amended.

Section 1. Section two hundred and fifteen of the Greater New York charter, as re-enacted by chapter four hundred and sixty-six of the laws of nineteen hundred and one, is hereby amended to read as follows:

Disposition of certain assessments for local improvements.

§ 215. The assessments made for local improvements prior to the ninth day of June, eighteen hundred and eighty, by the corporation known as the mayor, aldermen and commonalty of the city of New York, including assessments for improvements contracted for or authorized by said corporation, prior to said date, shall, when collected, be paid over to the commissioners of the

Cancellation of such assessments levied against property of city.

sinking fund, and applied by them in accordance with law. ¹ Said commissioners may, in their discretion, upon the written request of the comptroller of the city, authorize the said comptroller to cancel and annul any or all of such assessments which may have been levied against or be a charge against any real property now owned by the city, and thereupon the said comptroller shall cause the records of all such assessments to be marked in accordance with such determination of said commissioners.

§ 2. All acts and parts of acts inconsistent with this act are hereby repealed.

§ 3. This act shall take effect immediately.

---

¹ Remainder of section new.

Chap. 34.

AN ACT to amend the Greater New York charter, in relation to the department of parks.

Became a law February 21, 1913, with the approval of the Governor. Passed, three-fifths being present.

Accepted by the City.

The People of the State of New York, represented in Senate and Assembly, do enact as follows:

Section 1. Section six hundred and twelve-b of the Greater New York charter, added thereto by chapter six hundred and eighty-one of the laws of nineteen hundred and ten is hereby amended so as to read as follows:

L. 1897, ch. 378, § 612b, as added by L. 1910, ch. 621, amended.

OCEAN BOULEVARD; RESTRICTIONS AS TO USE OF.

§ 612-b. The commissioner of parks of the borough of Brooklyn[1] is hereby authorized, in his discretion by rules and regulations, to restrict the use and occupation of the main drive of Ocean boulevard in the borough of Brooklyn, from Twenty-second avenue to King's highway, to horses and light carriages and to exclude therefrom vehicles of all other kinds, including bicycles and motor vehicles.

§ 2. Section six hundred and thirteen of the Greater New York charter, as re-enacted by chapter four hundred and sixty-six of the laws of nineteen hundred and one, is hereby amended so as to read as follows:

§ 613, as re-enacted by L. 1901, ch. 466, amended.

MAINTENANCE AND MANAGEMENT OF BUILDINGS IN PARKS.

§ 613. It shall be the duty of the commissioner for the boroughs of Manhattan and Richmond to maintain the meteorological and astronomical observatory, the museum of natural history, the metropolitan museum of art in Central park, the aquarium in Battery place, and such other buildings as now are or may hereafter be erected in such parks or in any other park, square or public place under his jurisdiction by authority of the board of aldermen. It shall be the duty of the commissioner for the borough of Brooklyn[1] to maintain the Brooklyn institute of arts and sciences, and such other buildings as now are or may here-

---

1 Formerly read: "boroughs of Brooklyn and Queens."

after be erected in any park, square or public place under his jurisdiction by authority of the board of aldermen. It shall be the duty of the commissioner for the borough of the Bronx to maintain the New York botanical garden and the buildings appurtenant thereto, and such other institutions or buildings as may be established or erected in any park, square or public place in his jurisdiction by authority of the board of aldermen. ² It shall be the duty of the commissioner for the borough of Queens to maintain such institutions and buildings as now are or may hereafter be erected in any park, square or public place under his jurisdiction by authority of the board of aldermen. It shall be the duty of the several commissioners to provide the necessary instruments, furniture and equipments for the several buildings and institutions within their respective jurisdictions, and, with the authority of the board of aldermen, to develop and improve the same, and to erect additional buildings; but the maintenance of all such buildings and institutions shall be subject to the provisions of the acts incorporating said institutions, or either of them, and the acts amendatory thereof, and to the powers of said corporations thereunder, and of the boards by such acts created or provided for; and shall also be subject to and in conformity with such contracts and agreements as have heretofore been made with such institutions respectively, and are in force and effect when this act takes effect, or as may be hereafter made by the authority of the board of aldermen, and no moneys shall be expended for such purposes unless an appropriation therefor has been made by the board of estimate and apportionment and the board of aldermen. Out of the moneys annually appropriated for the maintenance of parks each commissioner may apply such sum as shall be fixed by the board of estimate and apportionment for the keeping, preservation and exhibition of the collections placed or contained in buildings or institutions now situated or hereafter erected in the parks, squares or public places under the jurisdiction of such commissioner.

§ 617, as re-enacted by L. 1901, ch. 466, amended.

§ 3. Section six hundred and seventeen of the Greater New York charter, as re-enacted by chapter four hundred and sixty-six of the laws of nineteen hundred and one, is hereby amended so as to read as follows:

---

² Following sentence new.

ACCOUNTS; ANNUAL ESTIMATES; EXPENDITURES.

§ 617. Each commissioner shall keep accurate and detailed accounts, in a form approved by the comptroller of all moneys received and expended by him, the sources from which they are received and the purposes for which they are expended. Each commissioner shall, on or before the first day of September in each year prepare an itemized estimate of his necessary expenses for the ensuing fiscal year and present the same to the board. The* estimates so prepared, as revised by the board, shall together constitute the annual estimate of the department of parks, and shall be submitted to the board of estimate and apportionment within the time prescribed by this act for the submission of estimates for the several departments of the city. No commissioner shall incur any expense for any purpose in excess of the amount appropriated therefor; nor shall he expend any money so appropriated for any purpose other than that for which it was appropriated. It shall be the duty of the board of estimate and apportionment and of the board of aldermen to provide in the annual budget the proportionate part of the appropriation for the department of parks applicable to the administration of each commissioner.

§ 4. This act shall take effect immediately.

Chap. 35.

AN ACT to amend the Greater New York charter, in relation to the disposition of the proceeds of certain personal property sold by the board of education.

Became a law February 21, 1913, with the approval of the Governor. Passed, three-fifths being present.

Accepted by the City.

The People of the State of New York, represented in Senate and Assembly, do enact as follows:

Section 1. Section ten hundred and sixty-six of the Greater New York charter, as re-enacted by chapter four hundred and sixty-six of the laws of nineteen hundred and one, and as amended by chapter four hundred and fifty-six of the laws of nineteen hundred and ten, is hereby amended to read as follows:

L. 1897, ch. 378, § 1066, as re-enacted by L. 1901, ch. 466, and amended by L. 1910, ch. 466, amended.

---

* Word " three " omitted.

Disposition of personal property no longer required. § 1066. [1] The board of education shall have power, in the name of the city of New York and for said city, to dispose of such personal property used in the schools or other buildings under the charge of said board as shall no longer be required for use therein. **Sale of articles made in certain schools.** [2] The said board may sell at prevailing market prices such manufactured articles or other products of its vocational, trade, preparatory trade schools, and truant schools, day and evening, as may not be utilized by the board of education, and all moneys **Disposition of proceeds.** realized by the sale thereof shall be paid into the city treasury and shall at once be appropriated by the board of estimate and apportionment to a special trade school fund to be administered by the board.[3] [4]All other[5] moneys realized by the sale of personal property[6] shall be paid into the city treasury and shall at once be appropriated by the board of estimate and apportionment, to the special school fund of the board of education for use in the borough in which the property sold was situated. Said **Lease of property for school accommodations.** board shall have power to lease property required for the purpose of furnishing school accommodations, and to prepare and execute leases therefor.

§ 2. This act shall take effect immediately.

Chap. 36.

AN ACT to amend the Greater New York charter, in relation to the transfer and utilization of cash balances in corporate stock funds.

Became a law February 21, 1913, with the approval of the Governor. Passed, three-fifths being present.

Accepted by the City.

The People of the State of New York, represented in Senate and Assembly, do enact as follows:

L. 1897, ch. 378, § 237, as re-enacted Section 1. Section two hundred and thirty-seven of the Greater New York charter, as re-enacted by chapter four hundred and

---

[1] Section to words "Said board" in lines sixteen and seventeen formerly consisted of one sentence.
[2] Words "and to" omitted. Words "The said board may," new.
[3] Words "and all moneys realized by the sale thereof shall be paid into the city treasury and shall at once be appropriated by the board of estimate and apportionment to a special trade school fund to be administered by the board," new.
[4] Words "and a" omitted.
[5] Word "other" new.
[6] Words "of personal property" substituted for word "thereof."

sixty-six of the laws of nineteen hundred and one, is hereby amended to read as follows:

§ 237. The board of estimate and apportionment shall have the power at any time to transfer any appropriation for any year which may be found, by the president of a borough, the head of a department or other officer having control of such appropriation, to be in excess of the amount required or deemed to be necessary for the purposes or objects thereof, to such other purposes or objects for which the appropriations in such year are insufficient, or such as may require the same. But nothing in the power thus conferred shall authorize the transfer by said board of an appropriation made for any object or purpose, in one year, to any purpose or object, whether an appropriation has been made therefor or otherwise, in any subsequent year. And any balance of appropriations remaining unexpended at the close of any fiscal year, after allowing sufficient to satisfy all claims payable therefrom, and also any balance to the credit of any account of moneys which have been or may hereafter be paid into the treasury of the city, under existing laws, appropriated or authorized to be expended for any specific purpose, and which the said board of estimate and apportionment may determine not to be necessary, or to be in excess of the amount required therefor, may, at any time, but not less than sixty days after the expiration of the year for which such appropriations are made, or sixty days after the expiration of the year during which the moneys aforesaid were paid into the treasury of the city, after allowing sufficient to satisfy all claims payable from such appropriations, or which the comptroller shall certify should be paid from said moneys paid into the treasury, as aforesaid, be transferred by the comptroller, with the approval of the said board of estimate and apportionment, to the general fund of the city, and applied to the reduction of taxation. The approval by the board of estimate and apportionment of the certificate of the comptroller, as aforesaid, shall be an appropriation of the amounts therein stated to the object or purposes in said certificate specified. [1] Nothing hereinbefore in this section contained shall be deemed to apply to such cash balances as may remain unexpended from the sale of corporate stock issued for permanent improvements, and which are no longer required for the specific purposes for which said corporate stock was issued.

Marginal notes: by L. 1901. ch. 466, amended. — Transfer of excess of appropriation to other purposes. — Limitation. — Transfer of balances of appropriations to general fund. — Transfer of balances from sale of corporate stock issued for permanent improvements.

---

[1] Remainder of section new.

Where there remains a cash balance from the sale of corporate
stock issued for permanent improvements, which the president
of a borough, the head of a department, or other officer having
control thereof, finds to be in excess of the amount required for
the purposes for which such corporate stock was issued, after allowing sufficient sums to satisfy all claims payable therefrom, and
when certification to that effect is made by said president of a
borough, head of a department or other officer having control
thereof to the comptroller, the board of estimate and apportionment upon the recommendation of the comptroller may transfer
such unincumbered cash balance to a fund, to be known as
" moneys available for permanent improvements for which corporate stock may lawfully be issued," created for this purpose.

Application of fund. The board of estimate and apportionment may apply all or any
part of the above-mentioned fund to or toward the payment of
the cost of any permanent improvement, which may lawfully be
paid for from the proceeds of the sale of corporate stock, the disbursements from such fund to be made with the same legal force
and effect as though the expenditure was from the proceeds of a
Transfer of balances from sale of corporate stock for armory purposes. sale of corporate stock. Where there remains a cash balance from
the sale of corporate stock issued by authority of the board
of commissioners of the sinking fund for armory purposes, which
balance of cash the armory board finds to be in excess of the
amount required for the purposes for which such corporate stock
was issued, after allowing sufficient sums to satisfy all claims
payable therefrom, and when certification to that effect is made
by the armory board to the board of commissioners of the sinking
fund, the latter board may, upon the recommendations of the
comptroller, transfer such cash balance to the fund above mentioned, known as " moneys available for permanent improvements
for which corporate stock may lawfully be issued."

§ 2. This act shall take effect immediately.

Chap. 37.

AN ACT to extend the time for making the final report of the commissioners designated to consolidate, codify and revise the laws, relating to the estates of deceased persons and the procedure and practice in surrogates' courts.

Became a law February 25, 1913, with the approval of the Governor. Passed, three-fifths being present.

The People of the State of New York, represented in Senate and Assembly, do enact as follows:

Section 1. The time for making the final report to the legislature of the commissioners designated by chapter five hundred and forty-seven of the laws of nineteen hundred and twelve, to consolidate, codify and revise the laws relating to the estates of deceased persons and the procedure and practice in surrogates' courts, is hereby extended until February fifteenth, nineteen hundred and fourteen.

§ 2. This act shall take effect immediately.

Chap. 38.

AN ACT to amend the domestic relations law, in relation to the adoption of a child directly from foster parents by either of such foster parents.

Became a law February 25, 1913, with the approval of the Governor. Passed, three-fifths being present.

The People of the State of New York, represented in Senate and Assembly, do enact as follows:

Section 1. Section one hundred and sixteen of article seven of chapter nineteen of the laws of nineteen hundred and nine, entitled "An act relating to the domestic relations, constituting chapter fourteen of the consolidated laws," as amended by chapter one hundred and fifty-four of the laws of nineteen hundred and ten, is hereby amended to read as follows:

§ 116. **Abrogation of voluntary adoption.** A minor may be deprived of the rights of a voluntary adoption by the following proceedings only:

The foster parent, the minor and the persons whose consent

[marginal note: L. 1909, ch. 19, § 116, as amended by L. 1910, ch. 154, amended.]

would be necessary to an original adoption, must appear before
the county judge or surrogate of the county where the foster
parent resides, who shall conduct an examination as for an
original adoption. If he is satisfied that the abrogation of the
adoption is desired by all parties concerned, and will be for the
best interests of the minor, the foster parent, the minor, if over
the age of twelve years, and the persons whose consent would
have been necessary to an original adoption shall execute an
agreement, whereby the foster parent agrees, or whereby the
foster parent and minor, if the latter is above the age of twelve
years and thereby a necessary party as above required, agree to
relinquish the relation of parent and child and all rights acquired by such adoption, and the parents or guardian of the
child or the institution having the custody thereof agree to reassume such relation. The judge or surrogate shall indorse,
upon such agreement, his consent to the abrogation of the adoption. The agreement and consent shall be filed and recorded in
the office of the county clerk of the county where the foster
parent resides, and a copy thereof filed and recorded in the office
of the county clerk of the county where the parents or guardian
reside, or such institution is located, if they reside, or such institution is located, within this state. From the time of the filing and recording thereof, the adoption shall be abrogated, and
the child shall reassume its original name and the parents or
guardian of the child shall reassume such relation. Such child,
however, may be adopted directly from such foster parents by
another person or by either of such foster parents[1] in the same
manner as from parents, and as if such foster parents were the
parents of such child.

§ 2. This act shall take effect immediately.

---

[1] Words " or by either of such foster parents," new.

Chap. 39.

AN ACT to amend chapter two hundred and eighty-one of the laws
of nineteen hundred and twelve, entitled "An act to authorize
the city of Buffalo to issue sinking fund water bonds for the
purpose of raising money to pay and retire water bonds for
which no sinking fund is provided," authorizing the payment
and retirement also of outstanding refunding bonds issued
heretofore to pay and retire such water bonds, and relating
to the rate of interest and place of payment of such sinking
fund water bonds.

Became a law February 25, 1913, with the approval of the Governor. Passed,
three-fifths being present.

Accepted by the City.

*The People of the State of New York, represented in Senate
and Assembly, do enact as follows:*

Section 1. Section one of chapter two hundred and eighty- L. 1912, ch.
one of the laws of nineteen hundred and twelve, entitled "An 281, § 1
act to authorize the city of Buffalo to issue sinking fund water amended.
bonds for the purpose of raising money to pay and retire water
bonds for which no sinking fund is provided," is hereby amended
to read as follows:

Section 1. It shall be lawful for the city of Buffalo to issue Bond issue
what shall be known as sinking fund water bonds for the pur- authorised.
pose of raising money to pay and retire as they become due the
outstanding bonds heretofore issued for the purpose of raising
money to defray the cost of extending, enlarging and improving
the waterworks supply system of said city, and also to pay and
retire as they become due outstanding refunding bonds heretofore issued to pay and retire any such water bonds,[1] as such outstanding bonds shall become due and payable between the first
day of January, nineteen hundred and twelve, and the first day
of January, nineteen hundred and thirty-seven. Such sinking fund Interest.
bonds shall bear interest at a rate to be fixed and determined by
the common council of said city,[2] payable semi-annually at the
office of the comptroller of the city of Buffalo, or at the Hanover[3]

---

[1] Words "and also to pay and retire as they become due outstanding
refunding bonds heretofore issued to pay and retire any such water bonds,"
new.

[2] Words "to be fixed and determined by the common council of said city"
substituted for words "not exceeding four and one-half per centum per
annum."

[3] Word "Hanover" substituted for word "Gallatin."

3

national bank of[4] the city of New York, as the purchaser of
Payment of said bonds may elect, and the principal shall be payable at
principal.
the same place twenty-five years from the date of such bonds.
Sale.   Such bonds shall be issued from time to time as ordered by the
common council, by the mayor and comptroller, under the city
seal, and shall be sold or awarded as provided in section four
hundred and ninety-two of the charter of said city, being chapter one hundred and five of the laws of eighteen hundred and
Sinking   ninety-one, and the acts amendatory thereof. Such bonds shall
fund.
be paid from a fund to be known as the water bond sinking fund,
to be created by an annual payment into the fund from the receipts of the sale of water to be inserted annually in the estimate
of the bureau of water and payable to the comptroller of said
city, of the sum of two thousand, six hundred and sixty-three
dollars for each one hundred thousand dollars of bonds so issued,
and said fund shall be held and invested and reinvested by the
comptroller of said city to retire said bonds as they become due.
Provision The common council shall make provision for the payment of
in general
fund   the interest on and the principal of said bonds as the same shall
estimates.
become due in the general fund estimates for said city.

§ 2. This act shall take effect immediately.

Chap. 40.

AN ACT to amend the county law, in relation to county hospitals
for tuberculosis.

Became a law February 25, 1913, with the approval of the Governor. Passed,
three-fifths being present.

*The People of the State of New York, represented in Senate
and Assembly, do enact as follows:*

L. 1909, ch.   Section 1. Subdivision six of section forty-seven of chapter
16, § 47,
subd. 6, as sixteen of the laws of nineteen hundred and nine, entitled "An
added by
L. 1909, act in relation to counties, constituting chapter eleven of the con-
ch. 341,
amended. solidated laws," as added by chapter three hundred and forty-one
of the laws of nineteen hundred and nine, is hereby amended to
read as follows:

Payment of   6. Shall certify all bills and accounts including salaries and
accounts
and sala- wages and transmit them to the board of supervisors of the county,
ries.

4 Word " of " substituted for word " in."

who shall provide for their payment in the same manner as other charges against the county are paid. [1] The board of supervisors of a county not having a purchasing agent or auditing commission may make an appropriation for the maintenance of such hospital and direct the county treasurer to pay all bills, accounts, salaries and wages, which are approved by the board of managers, within the amount of such appropriation, subject to such regulations as to the payment and audit thereof as the board of supervisors may deem proper.

§ 2. This act shall take effect immediately.

Chap. 41.

AN ACT to amend the military law, in relation to privileges, prohibitions and penalties.

Became a law February 25, 1913, with the approval of the Governor. Passed, three-fifths being present.

The People of the State of New York, represented in Senate and Assembly, do enact as follows:

Section 1. Section two hundred and forty-one of chapter forty-one of the laws of nineteen hundred and nine, entitled "An act in relation to the militia, constituting chapter thirty-six of the consolidated laws," as amended by chapter two hundred and ten of the laws of nineteen hundred and eleven, and chapter sixty-nine of the laws of nineteen hundred and twelve, is hereby further amended so as to read as follows:

§ 241. **Military parades and organizations by unauthorized bodies prohibited.** No body of men, other than the active militia and the troops of the United States except such independent military organizations as were on the twenty-third day of April, eighteen hundred and eighty-three, and now are, in existence, shall associate themselves together as a military company or organization, or parade in public with firearms in any city or town of this state. No body of men shall be granted a certificate of incorporation under any corporate name which shall mislead, or tend to mislead, any person into believing that such corporation is connected with or attached to the National Guard or Naval Militia[2] of

Marginal note: L. 1909, ch. 41, § 241, as amended by L. 1911, ch. 210, and L. 1912, ch. 69, amended.

---

[1] Remainder of subdivision new.
[2] Words "or Naval Militia" new.

this state in any capacity or way whatsoever. In case any such
certificate has been heretofore or may hereafter be granted, which
in the judgment of the adjutant-general of the state, misleads or
tends to mislead anyone into believing that such corporation is
connected with or attached to the National Guard or Naval Militia[3]
in any capacity or way whatsoever, the adjutant-general of the
state shall notify such corporation, in writing, to forthwith discontinue the use of its said corporate name and forthwith take
the necessary steps to change its name pursuant to the statute in
such case made and provided, to some name not so calculated to
mislead.   In the event such proceedings are not forthwith taken
and completed within six months from the service of said notice,
the attorney-general is authorized and directed to bring an action
to procure a judgment vacating or annulling the act of incorporation of such corporation, or any act renewing the corporation
or continuing its corporate existence or annulling the existence
of such corporation.   No city or town shall raise or appropriate
any money toward arming or equipping, uniforming or in any
other way supporting, sustaining or providing drill rooms or
armories for any such body of men; but associations wholly composed of soldiers honorably discharged from the service of the
United States, or members of the order of Sons of Veterans, may
parade in public with firearms on Decoration day, or on May first,
known as Dewey day, or upon the reception of any regiments or
companies of soldiers returning from such service, and for the
purpose of escort duty at the burial of deceased soldiers, and
students in educational institutions where military science is a
prescribed part of the course of instruction, and cadet organizations composed of youths under eighteen years of age, under responsible instructors, may, with the consent of the governor, drill
and parade with firearms in public under the superintendence of
their instructors.   This section shall not be construed to prevent
any organization authorized to do so by law from parading with
firearms, nor to prevent parades by the National Guard or naval
militia of any other state.   The independent military organizations mentioned in this section, not regularly organized as organizations of the National Guard or Naval Militia,[3] are hereby
made subject to the orders of the governor in case of emergency or
necessity, to aid the National Guard or Naval Militia[3] in quelling

---

[3] Words " or Naval Militia " new.

invasion, insurrection, riot or breach of the peace provided the officers and members of such organization shall, when so called upon, first sign and execute and deliver through their commanding officer to the officer to whom it is ordered to report, a form of enlistment in form to be prescribed by the governor in regulations or orders for a term not less than thirty days nor more than ninety days at one time; and if the service of such organization shall not be required for the full term of their enlistment they shall be discharged by the order of the governor. All members of such independent organizations when called into service of the state, as herein provided for, shall be equipped and paid by the state, and shall be protected in the discharge of their duties, and in obeying the orders of the governor, as though a part of the National Guard or Naval Militia[4] of the state. Any person violating any provision of this section shall be deemed guilty of a misdemeanor.

§ 2. This act shall take effect immediately.

Chap. 42.

AN ACT to authorize the board of supervisors of the county of Westchester to issue temporary loan bonds for the purpose of raising money to pay certificates of indebtedness of said county, issued pursuant to the provisions of chapter three hundred and forty-two of the laws of nineteen hundred and two, entitled "An act to make the office of the supervisor in the county of Westchester a salaried office, and to regulate the sessions of the board of supervisors in said county," and acts amendatory thereof and supplemental thereto.

Became a law February 27, 1913, with the approval of the Governor. Passed, three-fifths being present.

The People of the State of New York, represented in Senate and Assembly, do enact as follows:

Section 1. It shall be lawful for the board of supervisors of the county of Westchester, to issue what shall be known as temporary loan bonds, for the purpose of raising money to pay as they become due the outstanding certificates of indebtedness of the said county

<small>Issue of bonds authorized</small>

---

[4] Words "or Naval Militia" now.

of Westchester, aggregating four hundred thousand dollars, heretofore issued for the purpose of raising money to pay the amount of
county audited bills, audited by the board of supervisors of Westchester county, between the fourth day of March, nineteen hundred
and twelve, and January twenty-seventh, nineteen hundred and
Interest, number, denomina- tion. thirteen. Said bonds shall bear date the first day of May, nineteen
hundred and thirteen, and interest at a rate not exceeding five per
centum per annum, payable semi-annually on the first day of
November and May, in each year, to be in number eighty, numbered from one to eighty inclusive, and each bond to be of the
Maturity. denomination of five thousand dollars. The principal of the first
five of said bonds to fall due on the first day of May, nineteen
hundred and eighteen, and of each five bonds thereafter on the
first day of May, and of each and every year thereafter, up to and
including the first day of May, nineteen hundred and thirty-three.
Execution. Said bonds shall be executed by the chairman of the board of
supervisors of the county of Westchester, and the treasurer of the
county of Westchester, and countersigned by the county clerk, who
shall affix the county seal thereto, and the board of supervisors of
Provision for pay- ment. the county of Westchester shall make provision for the payment
of the principal and interest on the said bonds as same shall be-
come due from time to time.

§ 2. This act shall take effect immediately.

Chap. 43.

AN ACT to amend the second class cities law, in relation to the
creation of funded indebtedness.

Became a law February 27, 1913, with the approval of the Governor. Passed,
three-fifths being present.

*The People of the State of New York, represented in Senate
and Assembly, do enact as follows:*

L. 1909, ch. 55, § 60, as amended by L. 1910, ch. 692, and L. 1911, ch. 60, amended. Section 1. Section sixty of chapter fifty-five of the laws of
nineteen hundred and nine, entitled "An act in relation to cities
of the second class, constituting chapter fifty-three of the consolidated laws," as amended by chapter six hundred and ninety-
two of the laws of nineteen hundred and ten, and chapter sixty
of the laws of nineteen hundred and eleven, is hereby amended
to read as follows:

§ 60. **Temporary and funded debts.** Temporary and funded debts of the city for the various purposes authorized or contemplated by this chapter and otherwise by law, may be created by ordinance of the common council, provided, however, that any such ordinance shall, before it takes effect, be submitted to and approved by the board of estimate and apportionment. Funded debts may be created for any municipal purpose, [1]including the raising of funds to meet any deficiency in the estimated revenues for two or more years caused by reductions in the assessed valuations of special franchises, made pursuant to the provisions of sections forty-three to forty-nine inclusive of the tax law, and any such deficiency caused by the deduction from the amount of the special franchise tax assessed and levied in such years of such percentage of the gross receipts of the corporation so taxed as such corporation may be required to pay to the city under any franchise. The creation of funded and temporary debts and the refunding of existing debts, shall be subject to the provisions of the general municipal law, except as otherwise herein provided. Every funded debt, refunded or created, except to provide for the supply of water, shall be issued in such amounts and shall fall due at such times that the principal of the same shall be fully paid in not more than twenty equal annual instalments, the last of which shall become due at the end of not more than twenty years after its issue. Every funded debt refunded or created to provide for the supply of water shall be issued in such amounts and shall fall due at such times that the principal of the same shall be fully paid in not more than forty equal instalments, the last of which shall become due at the end of not more than forty years after its issue, and may by the ordinance creating said funded debt be made payable out of water rents received by the city. Any bonds of the city heretofore issued, other than revenue bonds, and not payable in annual instalments, may be refunded. No funded debt which is payable in annual instalments shall be refunded, but provision shall be made for the payment of each instalment and accrued interest in the year in which it shall become due by the insertion of the proper sum in the annual estimate for the year in question. An ordinance creating a funded debt may provide that the bonds therein authorized shall contain a recital that they are issued pursuant to law and an ordinance of the common council, as provided by section sixty of the second class cities law.

---

[1] Remainder of sentence new.

Such recital, when so authorized, as aforesaid, shall be conclusive evidence of the regularity of the issue of said bonds and of their validity.

§ 2. This act shall take effect immediately.

Chap. 44.

AN ACT to amend chapter one hundred and eighty-two of the laws of eighteen hundred and ninety-two, entitled "An act to incorporate the city of Mount Vernon," in relation to the public school teachers' retirement fund of said city and payments therefrom.

Became a law February 27, 1913, with the approval of the Governor. Passed, three-fifths being present.

Accepted by the City.

The People of the State of New York, represented in Senate and Assembly, do enact as follows:

L. 1892,
ch. 182,
§§, 229t,
229u, as
added by
L. 1909,
ch. 92,
amended.

Section 1. Sections two hundred and twenty-nine-t and two hundred and twenty-nine-u of chapter one hundred and eighty-two of the laws of eighteen hundred and ninety-two, entitled "An act to incorporate the city of Mount Vernon," as added by chapter ninety-two of the laws of nineteen hundred and nine, are hereby amended to read, respectively, as follows:[1]

Teachers'
retirement
fund asso-
ciation
established.
Members.

§ 229-t. The Mount Vernon Public School Teachers' Retirement Fund Association is hereby established. The following shall be members: (1) any superintendent, supervisor, principal, teacher. registrar, janitor, or other employee of the board of education of the city of Mount Vernon, who shall have voluntarily joined said association within one month after the original passage of this act; (2) any of the above classes of employees of the board of education of the city of Mount Vernon, who at a subsequent period, but before the adoption of the amendment herein incorporated, voluntarily joined said association upon the payment of back dues; (3) any of the above classes, in the employment of said board of education previous to the adoption of this amendment, who shall voluntarily join said association within one month after this act takes effect, being excused from the payment of back dues; (4) any superintendent, supervisor,

---

[1] Sections materially amended.

principal, teacher, registrar, janitor, or other employee, who shall
for the first time enter into a contract with said board of education after this act takes effect; and for such person's membership
in this association shall be a stated condition in their several
contracts. All members of said teachers' retirement fund association shall be considered members of said association during
their term of employment in the public schools of the city of
Mount Vernon. The board of education shall constitute a board $\begin{smallmatrix}\text{Board of}\\\text{trustees.}\end{smallmatrix}$
of trustees who shall have the general care and management of
the public school teachers' retirement fund created by this act.
The public school teachers' retirement fund shall consist of the $\begin{smallmatrix}\text{Fund, how}\\\text{constituted.}\end{smallmatrix}$
following moneys with the interest or income therefrom.

(a) All donations, legacies and gifts which shall be made to $\begin{smallmatrix}\text{Donations,}\\\text{etc.}\end{smallmatrix}$
the said fund.

(b) One per centum per annum of the respective salaries paid $\begin{smallmatrix}\text{1 per}\\\text{centum of}\\\text{salaries.}\end{smallmatrix}$
to the employees of the board of education of the city of Mount
Vernon, who are or shall hereafter become, under any of the above
provisions, members of this association.

(c) A sum of money annually hereafter, equal to but not $\begin{smallmatrix}\text{5 per}\\\text{centum of}\\\text{excise}\\\text{moneys.}\end{smallmatrix}$
greater than five per centum of all excise moneys, (after deduct-
ing rebates or returns), received by the city of Mount Vernon
under or by virtue of any of the provisions of the liquor tax law
of the state of New York; which sum shall be paid into said
retirement fund and duly credited thereto, by the proper officials
of said city, having the legal custody thereof.

(d) All forfeitures and deductions of or from the salary of $\begin{smallmatrix}\text{Forfeitures}\\\text{of and}\\\text{deductions}\\\text{from}\\\text{salaries.}\end{smallmatrix}$
any superintendent, supervisor, principal, teacher, registrar,
janitor, or other employee employed in the public schools of said
city. Such forfeitures and deductions shall be paid into said
retirement fund and duly credited thereto by the proper officials
of said city having the legal custody thereof. The unpaid salary
of a teacher who is on leave of absence, formally granted by the
board of education, shall not be regarded as a forfeiture or deduction, and shall not be paid into the retirement fund. The
comptroller of said city shall be the custodian of said fund and $\begin{smallmatrix}\text{Custodian}\\\text{and treas-}\\\text{urer of}\\\text{fund.}\end{smallmatrix}$
the city treasurer shall be the treasurer thereof, and all orders
made payable from said fund except for moneys drawn for investment by the comptroller shall be made upon the vote of said
board of trustees. All orders except for moneys drawn for in- $\begin{smallmatrix}\text{Orders,}\\\text{how made.}\end{smallmatrix}$
vestment by the comptroller are to be signed by its president and
countersigned by the city comptroller and city treasurer.

Investment
of fund.

The comptroller of said city shall invest for the benefit of the retirement fund all moneys not necessary for the payment of annuities. Such investments shall be made only in securities in which the savings banks of the state of New York are authorized by law to invest. All orders made payable from said fund for investment by the comptroller shall be signed by the comptroller

Annual
financial
report of
comptrol-
ler.

and countersigned by the city treasurer. He shall report to the board annually in the month of January the condition and disposition of the fund, and the items of receipts and disbursements during the year ending on the thirty-first day of the December

Deductions
from
salaries,
how made.

preceding. The board of education in making the pay-rolls for October and March each year for the superintendent, supervisors, principals, teachers, registrars, janitors and other employees hereinbefore mentioned, shall deduct from the salary payable for each of such months to each of said persons who shall be members of said public school teachers' retirement fund association the sum of one-half of one per centum of his or her annual salary. The board of education shall thereupon issue a certificate to the treasurer stating the total sum of deductions and also the total amount of deductions from the salaries of any persons who are members of said association, for absence from duty during the preceding six months. Such amount shall be paid into the retirement fund and duly credited thereto by the city comptroller.

Require-
ments for
retirement
as annui-
tant.

§ 229-u. The board of education shall have power to retire from service any superintendent, supervisor, principal, teacher, registrar, janitor or other employee, who shall have served in such capacity or capacities for an aggregate period of twenty-five years for a female and thirty years for a male, and no person so retired shall become an annuitant under this act unless fifteen years of such service shall have been rendered in the public schools of Mount Vernon, and unless he or she shall have come under the provisions of this act as hereinbefore provided.

Amount of
annuity,
how deter-
mined.

Annuities paid in pursuance of this act shall be one-half of the salary of the annuitant at the time of retirement from service, except that no annuity shall exceed eight hundred dollars annually, but if the moneys in the fund and the receipts of said fund shall be found insufficient to fully carry out the provisions hereinbefore set forth, the trustees shall then determine the pro rata amount which in their judgment each annuitant shall receive in one year, and such an amount shall be deemed full payment of the annuity for that year. If, however, any person, a member of this association, after twenty years' service, ten years of which service shall have been in the public schools of Mount Vernon, shall become mentally or physically incapacitated for duty, he or she may be retired by the board of education upon an annuity of as many twenty-fifths, if a woman, and as many thirtieths, if a man, of the full annuity as said person has taught, or otherwise served, in years. If at any time any member of this association shall be refused re-employment by the board of education, or shall be discharged before he or she would become an annuitant under the provisions of this act, then such a person shall be entitled to receive from the treasurer, without interest, a sum equal to the total deductions from his or her salary in pursuance of this act other than the forfeitures and deductions specified in subdivision (d) of section two hundred and twenty-nine-t of this article. *Refund of salary deductions on discharge from employment.*

No member of this association shall be entitled to an annuity who has not contributed to the retirement fund an amount equal to at least thirty per centum of his annuity. But a person, who is otherwise entitled to retirement and an annuity under this article, may become an annuitant and entitled to an annuity by making a cash payment to the retirement fund of an amount which, when added to his previous contributions to such fund, will equal thirty per centum of his annuity. In case a member of this association, who shall retire or be retired, is unable to pay in advance the sum required to make up the said thirty per centum of the annuity, the payment of such annuity may be withheld until the portion of the annuity withheld shall equal the sum required to make up said thirty per centum of the annuity. *Amount required to have been contributed by annuitant.*

§ 2. This act shall take effect immediately.

Chap. 45.

AN ACT to amend the Greater New York charter, in relation to
the power of the city superintendent of schools to enforce the
compulsory education law.

Became a law February 27, 1913, with the approval of the Governor. Passed,
three-fifths being present.

Accepted by the City.

*The People of the State of New York, represented in Senate
and Assembly, do enact as follows:*

L. 1897,
ch. 378,
§ 1078, as
re-enacted
by L. 1901,
ch. 466,
amended.

Section 1. Section ten hundred and seventy-eight of the Greater
New York charter, as re-enacted by chapter four hundred and
sixty-six of the laws of nineteen hundred and one, is hereby
amended to read as follows:

ID.; FURTHER DUTIES; ANNUAL REPORT; CLERKS OF MAIN OFFICE.

§ 1078. The city superintendent of schools, so often as he can
consistently with his other duties, shall visit the schools of the
city as he shall see fit, and inquire into all matters relating to
the government, course of instruction, methods of teaching, management and discipline of such schools, and the condition of the
schoolhouses and of the schools generally; and shall advise and
encourage the pupils and teachers and officers thereof; subject
to the by-laws of the board of education, he shall prescribe suitable registers, blanks, forms and regulations for the making of
all reports, and for conducting all necessary business connected
with the school system and he shall cause the same, with such
information and instructions as he shall deem conducive to the
proper organization and government of the schools, and the due
execution of their duties by school officers, to be transmitted to
the officers or persons entrusted with the execution of the same.
He shall submit to the board of education an annual report containing a statement of the conditions of the schools of the city,
and all such matters relating to his office, and such plans and sug-
gestions for the improvement of the schools and the school system,
and for the advancement of public instruction in The City of
New York as he shall deem expedient, and as the by-laws of the
board of education may direct. He shall under the direction of
the board of education[1] enforce the compulsory education law,[2]

---

[1] Words " under the direction of the board of education," new.
[2] See education law (L. 1909, ch. 21), art. 23, as generally amended by L.
1910, ch. 140.

and shall nominate attendance officers to the board of education and shall direct such officers in their duties. He may appoint such clerks as he may deem necessary, and as are authorized by the board of education. He shall assign his clerks to the various duties, and may suspend or discharge them for cause, but in such case, the clerks shall have a right of appeal to the board of education. He shall report as often as the board of education shall direct upon any matter or matters, entrusted to his charge, in such detail as shall be required of him. He shall maintain his main office in the borough of Manhattan, and in such building as the board of education shall direct. He shall have power, at any time, to call together any or all of the associate city superintendents and district superintendents for consultation, and shall assign to them, subject to the by-laws of the board of education, such duties as in his judgment will be conducive to the welfare of the public schools of The City of New York. Twenty-three of the district superintendents shall be assigned by the city superintendent to the work of supervision in the local school board districts, to be constituted as hereinafter provided, in such manner that one district superintendent shall be assigned to such duty in two of such districts for the period of one school year. At the end of such period the city superintendent shall have power to change such assignments as he may deem best for the interests of the school system, but only in the manner above provided. District superintendents when not so assigned to such duty in said districts shall be assigned by the city superintendent to such other professional duties as the welfare of the school system may require. It shall further be the duty of the city superintendent to report any case of gross misconduct, insubordination, neglect of duty, or general inefficiency on the part of any associate city superintendent or district superintendent to the board of education. The city superintendent may empower an associate city superintendent to execute all the duties of the city superintendent during his absence or disability.

§ 2. This act shall take effect immediately.

Chap. 46.

AN ACT to amend chapter one hundred and ninety-five of the laws
of eighteen hundred and eighty-four, entitled "An act to amend
chapter one hundred and forty of the laws of eighteen hundred and fifty-three, entitled 'An act to consolidate and amend
the several acts relating to the village of Batavia, to alter the
bounds and to enlarge the powers of the corporation of said
village,' and the several acts amendatory thereof," in relation to providing moneys by taxation for the village sanitary
sewer system and extensions thereof.

Became a law February 27, 1913, with the approval of the Governor. Passed,
three-fifths being present.

*The People of the State of New York, represented in Senate
and Assembly, do enact as follows:*

L. 1884,
ch. 195, tit.
8, § 1, as
amended by
L. 1895, ch.
117, L. 1903,
ch. 190, and
L. 1910,
ch. 337,
amended.

Section 1. Section one of title eight of chapter one hundred
and ninety-five of the laws of eighteen hundred and eighty-four,
entitled "An act to amend chapter one hundred and forty of the
laws of eighteen hundred and fifty-three, entitled 'An act to consolidate and amend the several acts relating to the village of
Batavia, to alter the bounds and to enlarge the powers of the
corporation of said village,' and the several acts amendatory
thereof," as amended by chapter one hundred and seventeen of
the laws of eighteen hundred and ninety-five, chapter one hundred
and ninety of the laws of nineteen hundred and three and chapter
three hundred and thirty-seven of the laws of nineteen hundred
and ten, is hereby amended to read as follows:

Estimate of
proposed
expendi-
tures.

§ 1. The board of trustees shall in each year, within one month
after the annual election, make a careful estimate of expenditures
proposed to be made in said village for the ensuing year, which
estimate shall contain a statement of the several amounts, and for
what purpose they are to be expended, a copy of which shall be
delivered to the treasurer of said village, which estimate may be
amended or changed by said board of trustees at any time
before the tax-roll of said village for such year shall be completed, by adding thereto and including therein an estimate of
any expenditures then authorized by law, or by making any cor-

Aggregate
limited;
exception.

rection or alteration therein. The aggregate of such estimates
shall not exceed the sum of thirty-five thousand dollars; except
that the said trustees may expend in addition to such sum of thirty-

five thousand dollars the amount necessary to provide for the
maintenance and support of the electric lighting system of such
village, which shall not exceed in the aggregate more than one and
one-half mills per annum for every dollar of the taxable property
in such village to be ascertained from the last preceding assessment-
roll, unless a resolution therefor shall be submitted to and approved by the electors of said village as provided in section two
of this title, [1]and in addition thereto the said trustees shall raise
by taxation as hereinafter provided, moneys necessary to pay any
moneys which may become due during the ensuing year upon any
sewer bonds of the village duly issued and authorized by law and
also moneys necessary to provide for the maintenance and operation of the new sanitary sewer system of the village and to pay the
expense of installing and operating any extension thereof which
may be ordered by the board of sewer commissioners of the village
during the ensuing year, which sewer system and any extension
thereof shall be under the control and jurisdiction of the said
board, an estimate of all which moneys shall be made by said board
in a report to the trustees to be made on or before March fifteenth,
each year, but the moneys so raised to pay for the maintenance
and operation of said sewer system and the extension thereof
shall not exceed in the aggregate the sum of one mill per annum
for every dollar of the taxable property in said village to be ascertained from the last preceding assessment-roll of the village, unless
a resolution therefor shall be submitted to and approved by the
electors of such village as provided in section two of this title, and
the trustees shall have the power in anticipation of such tax to *Issue of certificates*
borrow the money necessary to defray such expense and to issue *of indebt-edness.*
certificates of indebtedness therefor, bearing interest, and all of
said sewer moneys so reported, estimated and raised by taxation *Disposition of moneys*
or thus borrowed shall be credited by the village treasurer to the *raised.*
credit of the said board of sewer commissioners and shall be drawn
therefrom only in pursuance of an order of said board signed by
the clerk thereof and countersigned by the chairman or the presiding officer for the time being of said board. In case there is
no such board in office then said moneys shall be deposited to the
credit of the sewer funds of the village and drawn therefrom as
other funds of the village are drawn therefrom[2] and all of[3] said

---

[1] Remainder of sentence new.
[2] Sentence to here new.
[3] Words " all of " new.

Poll and
property
tax.
other[4] sums of money,[5] when raised, shall be placed by the treasurer to the credit of the several funds stated in said estimate, and no other. The board of trustees shall have power, for the purpose aforesaid, to raise the sums of money above stated in each year from the taxable inhabitants and property of said village, and said sums shall be assessed as follows: Each male inhabitant of twenty-one years and upwards, and not exempt by law from payment of poll-tax, shall be assessed fifty cents, and the balance shall be assessed among and upon all persons owning property and estate, real and personal, incorporated companies, banks and banking associations in said village, according to the value of their real and personal estate in said village.

§ 2. This act shall take effect immediately.

Chap. 47.

AN ACT to amend the insurance law, in relation to misrepresentations by certain insurance corporations.

Became a law March 6, 1913, with the approval of the Governor. Passed,
three-fifths being present.

*The People of the State of New York, represented in Senate
and Assembly, do enact as follows:*

L. 1909, ch
33, § 60, as
amended by
L. 1911,
ch. 533,
amended.
Section 1. Section sixty of chapter thirty-three of the laws of nineteen hundred and nine, entitled "An act in relation to insurance corporations, constituting chapter twenty-eight of the consolidated laws," as amended by chapter five hundred and thirty-three of the laws of nineteen hundred and eleven, is hereby amended to read as follows:

§ 60. **Estimates and misrepresentations prohibited.** No life, health or casualty[1] insurance corporation, including corporations operating on the co-operative or assessment plan[2] doing business in this state and no officer, director or agent therefor or any other person, copartnership or corporation shall issue or circulate, or cause or permit to be issued or circulated, any illustration, circular or statement of any sort misrepresent-

---

4 Word " other " new.
5 Words " of money " new.
1 Words " health or casualty," new.
2 Words " including corporations operating on the co-operative or assessment plan," new.

ing the terms of any policy issued by any such corporation or the benefits or advantages promised thereby, or any misleading estimate of the dividends or share of surplus to be received thereon, or shall use any name or title of any policy or class of policies misrepresenting the true nature thereof. Nor shall any such corporation or agent thereof or any other person, copartnership or corporation make any misleading representation or incomplete comparison of policies to any person insured in any such corporation for the purpose of inducing or tending to induce such person to lapse, forfeit, or surrender his said insurance. The superintendent of insurance may in his discretion revoke the certificate of authority issued to any corporation or agent on his being satisfied that such corporation or agent has violated any of the provisions of this section. Any violation of this section shall constitute a misdemeanor, and it shall be the duty of the superintendent of insurance to revoke the certificate of authority of the corporation or agent on a conviction for so offending.

§ 2. This act shall take effect immediately.

Chap. 48.

AN ACT to amend the insurance law, in relation to reorganization of existing corporations and amendment of certificates.

Became a law March 6, 1913, with the approval of the Governor. Passed, three-fifths being present.

The People of the State of New York, represented in Senate and Assembly, do enact as follows:

Section 1. Section fifty-two of chapter thirty-three of the laws of nineteen hundred and nine, entitled "An act in relation to insurance corporations, constituting chapter twenty-eight of the consolidated laws," as amended by chapter six hundred and thirty-four of the laws of nineteen hundred and ten and by chapter forty-seven of the laws of nineteen hundred and eleven, is hereby amended to read as follows:

§ 52. **Reorganization of existing corporations and amendment of certificates.** Any domestic corporation existing or doing business on October first, eighteen hundred and ninety-two, may, by a vote of a majority of its directors or trustees, accept the provisions

of this chapter and amend its charter to conform with the same,
upon obtaining the consent of the superintendent of insurance
thereto in writing; and thereafter it shall be deemed to have been
incorporated under this chapter, and every such corporation in re-
incorporating under this provision may for that purpose so adopt in
whole or in part a new charter, in conformity herewith, and include therein any or all provisions of its existing charter, and
any or all changes from its existing charter, to cover and enjoy any
or all the privileges and provisions of existing laws which might
be so included and enjoyed if it were originally incorporated thereunder, and it shall, upon such adoption of and after obtaining the
consent, as in this section before provided, to such charter, and
filing the same and the record of adoption and consent in the office
of the superintendent of insurance, perpetually enjoy the same as
and be such corporation, which is declared to be a continuation of
such corporation which existed prior to such reincorporation; and
the offices therein which shall be continued shall be filled by the
respective incumbents for the periods for which they were elected,
and all others shall be filled in the same manner by such amended
charter provided. Every domestic insurance corporation may
amend its charter or certificate of incorporation by inserting
therein any statement or matter which might have been originally
inserted therein and may also eliminate therefrom unnecessary
words or verbiage, or any powers which have never been exercised or are not at the time being exercised, provided that proof
of the non-exercise of powers, satisfactory to the superintendent
of insurance, shall be filed in the insurance department, and, if
any business has been written under the powers proposed to be
eliminated, the fact that all liability incident to such powers has
been fully terminated shall be shown to the satisfaction of such
superintendent through an examination of such corporation or
otherwise as he may require; and may likewise amend its charter
or certificate of incorporation, by inserting therein or adding
thereto[1] any powers which at the time of such amendment, may
have been conferred by law upon domestic insurance corporations
engaged in a business of the same general character, or which
might be included in the certificate of incorporation of a domestic
insurance company organized under any general law of this state
for a business of the same general character; and the same proceedings shall be taken upon the presentation of such amended charter

---

[1] Words " or adding thereto " new.

or certificate or amendment to such charter or certificate,[2] to the superintendent of insurance, as are required by this chapter to be taken with respect to an original charter or certificate, except that no examination of the condition and affairs of such corporation shall be required unless so ordered by the superintendent, and if the amended charter or certificate or amendment[3] be appoved by the superintendent of insurance, and his certificate of authority to do business thereunder is granted, the corporation shall thereafter be deemed to possess the same powers and be subject to the same liabilities as if such [4]charter or certificates[5] as so amended[6] had been its original charter or certificate of incorporation, but without prejudice to any pending action or proceeding or any rights previously accrued. Upon the reincorporation or upon the amendment of the charter of any life insurance corporation, having a capital stock in accordance with the provisions of this section, it may by a vote of the majority of its directors confer upon its policyholders or upon such policyholders as may have a prescribed amount of insurance upon their lives the right to vote for all or any less number of the directors in such manner not inconsistent with any provision of this chapter as may be authorized by a vote of the stockholders representing at least a majority of the capital stock at a meeting of stockholders called for the purpose. Section eighteen of the stock corporation law shall not apply to such a corporation. This section shall apply to insurance corporations organized under or subject to article six of this chapter as well as to insurance corporations organized under a special act or any general law or article two of this chapter. In the case of any corporation organized under or subject to article six of this chapter, which corporation has amended its charter and is now operating under article two of this chapter, all contracts, policies and certificates issued prior to its reincorporation, shall be valued as one year term insurance at the ages attained excepting when such contracts, policies or certificates shall provide for a limited number of specified premiums or for specified surrender values, in which case they shall be valued as provided in article two, section eighty-four[7] of this chapter. But no life in-

---

[2] Words " or amendment to such charter or certificate," new.
[3] Words " or amendment " new.
[4] Word " amended " omitted.
[5] Formerly " certificate."
[6] Words " as so amended " new.
[7] As amended by L. 1909, ch. 301, L. 1910, ch. 616, and L. 1913, ch. 304, post.

surance corporation shall hereafter be permitted to avail itself of the provisions of this section unless it shall hold for all its out standing policies or certificates assets equal in value to the minimum reserve required by section eighty-four of this chapter. Whenever any domestic insurance corporation changes the number of its directors or increases or reduces the amount of its capital stock, pursuant to and in conformity with the provisions of the stock corporation law, it may file in the office of the superintendent of insurance a complete copy of its charter, duly authenticated, containing the changes of its capital stock or its directors, or both, as the case may be. Such charter shall not be filed until it has attached thereto the certificate of approval of the attorney-general, as provided in section ten of this chapter.

§ 2. This act shall take effect immediately.

Chap. 49.

AN ACT to amend the insurance law, in relation to the by-laws of title, credit guaranty and securities guaranty corporations.

Became a law March 6, 1913, with the approval of the Governor. Passed, three-fifths being present.

The People of the State of New York, represented in Senate and Assembly, do enact as follows:

L. 1909, ch. 33, § 172 amended.

Section 1. Section one hundred and seventy-two of chapter thirty-three of the laws of nineteen hundred and nine, entitled "An act in relation to insurance corporations, constituting chapter twenty-eight of the consolidated laws," is hereby amended to read as follows:

§ 172. **By-laws.** The by-laws of every corporation created under the provisions of this article shall be deemed and taken to be its law, and shall provide:

1. The number of its directors.

2.[1] Their terms of office, so arranged that at least one-fourth in number of all the directors shall be elected annually.

3. The manner of filling vacancies among directors and officers.

4. The time and place of the annual meeting.

---

[1] Subd. 2 formerly read: " 2. Their term of office which shall not exceed one year."

5. The manner of calling and holding special meetings of stockholders.

6. The number of stockholders who shall attend either in person or by proxy at every meeting to constitute a quorum.

7. The officers of the corporation and the manner of their election by the directors, and their powers and duties. Such officers shall always include a president, secretary, treasurer, and a general manager. The president must be elected from among the directors.

8. The manner of electing or appointing inspectors of election.

9. The manner of amending or repealing the by-laws.

§ 2. This act shall take effect immediately.

Chap. 50.

AN ACT to amend the penal law, in relation to acting for foreign insurance corporation which has not designated superintendent of insurance as attorney.

Became a law March 6, 1913, with the approval of the Governor. Passed, three-fifths being present.

The People of the State of New York, represented in Senate and Assembly, do enact as follows:

Section 1. Section eleven hundred and ninety-nine of chapter L. 1909, ch eighty-eight of the laws of nineteen hundred and nine, entitled amended. "An act providing for the punishment of crime, constituting chapter forty of the consolidated laws," is hereby amended to read as follows:

§ 1199. **Acting for foreign insurance corporation which has not designated superintendent of insurance as attorney.** Any person acting for himself or for others,[1] who solicits or procures, or aids in the solicitation or procurement of policies or certificates of insurance from, or adjusts losses or in any manner aids the transaction of any business for, any foreign insurance corporation, which has not executed and filed in the office of the superintendent of insurance, a written appointment of the superintendent to be the true and lawful attorney of such corporation in and

---

[1] Words "not having been specially licensed, as provided by law, by the superintendent of insurance," omitted.

for this state, upon whom all lawful process in any action or proceeding against the corporation may be served, is guilty of a misdemeanor.

In effect
Sept. 1,
1918. § 2. This act shall take effect September first, nineteen hundred and thirteen.

Chap. 51.

AN ACT to amend the insurance law, in relation to forms of policies or certificates of casualty insurance corporations upon the co-operative or assessment plan.

Became a law March 6, 1913, with the approval of the Governor. Passed, three-fifths being present.

The People of the State of New York, represented in Senate and Assembly, do enact as follows:

§ 220
added to
L. 1909,
ch. 33. Section 1. Article six of chapter thirty-three of the laws of nineteen hundred and nine, entitled "An act in relation to insurance corporations, constituting chapter twenty-eight of the consolidated laws," is hereby amended by adding at the end a new section, to be section two hundred and twenty, to read as follows:

§ 220. **Forms of policies or certificates must be filed and approved.** On and after the first day of January, nineteen hundred and fourteen, no policy or certificate of insurance against loss or damage from the sickness, or the bodily injury or death of the insured by accident, shall be issued or delivered in this state by any corporation authorized under this article, until copies of the form thereof have been filed with the superintendent of insurance and formally approved by him. On or before the first day of October, nineteen hundred and thirteen, the superintendent shall make and announce rules and regulations concerning the terms and provisions of such forms of policies and certificates, the manner in which they shall be printed, and the practice to be followed in their submission and approval. The superintendent may, in his discretion, permit any such corporation to continue to use in this state after the first day of January, nineteen hundred and fourteen, any form of policy or certificate, which, prior to October first, nineteen hundred and thirteen, has been duly approved for such corporation under section one hundred and seven of this chapter.

In effect
Oct. 1,
1913. § 2. This act shall take effect October first, nineteen hundred and thirteen.

Chap. 52.

AN ACT to amend the insurance law, in relation to the sale of the securities of insurance corporations and of corporations organized to promote or hold the capital stock of insurance corporations.

Became a law March 6, 1913, with the approval of the Governor. Passed, three-fifths being present.

The People of the State of New York, represented in Senate and Assembly, do enact as follows:

Section 1. Chapter thirty-three of the laws of nineteen hundred and nine, entitled "An act in relation to insurance corporations, constituting chapter twenty-eight of the consolidated laws," is hereby amended by adding thereto, at the end of article one thereof, a new section, to be section sixty-six, to read as follows: §66 added to L. 1909, ch. 33.

§ 66. **Promotion of insurance corporations; sale of securities.** 1. As the terms are used in this section " promoting corporation " means a corporation or joint stock association, engaged in the business of organizing or promoting or endeavoring to organize or promote the organization of an insurance corporation or corporations, or in any way assisting therein; " holding corporation " means a corporation or joint stock association, which holds or is engaged in the acquisition of the capital stock or a major portion thereof of one or more insurance corporations for the purpose of controlling the management thereof, as voting trustee or otherwise; and " securities " means the shares of capital stock, subscription certificates, debenture bonds and any and all other contracts or evidences of ownership of or interest in insurance corporations, or in promoting or holding corporations as defined in this section.

2. No individual, partnership, association or corporation, as the agent of another or as broker, shall sell or offer for sale or in any way assist in the sale in this state of the securities of any promoting or holding corporation, as defined in this section, or of any insurance corporation which is not at the time of such sale or offer of sale, lawfully engaged or authorized to engage in the transaction of the business of insurance in this state, without first procuring, as hereinafter provided, a certificate of authority from the insurance department to sell such securities; nor shall any individual, partnership, association or corporation sell or offer for

sale in this state the securities of any promoting or holding corporation as defined in this section, or of any insurance corporation which is not at the time of such sale or offer of sale, lawfully engaged or authorized to engage in the transaction of the business of insurance in this state, unless such corporation shall have first procured from the superintendent of insurance, as hereinafter provided, a certificate that said corporation has fully complied with the provisions of this section and is authorized to sell such securities. Every certificate issued by the superintendent of insurance pursuant to the provisions of this section shall state in bold type that the superintendent in no way recommends the securities thereby authorized to be sold, and shall be renewable annually, upon written application, filed on or before the first day of January of each year, and may be revoked for cause at any time by such superintendent. The superintendent shall prepare and furnish upon request suitable blank forms of application for the certificates required by this section.

3. Every individual, copartnership, association or corporation who or which desires or intends to sell or to offer for sale in this state, the securities of any insurance corporation or of any promoting or holding corporation as defined in this section, shall file with the superintendent of insurance an application for a certificate of such authority. Such application shall contain a statement, verified by oath, setting forth the name and address of the applicant, previous business experience, date and place of birth or organization, and such other and further information as the said superintendent may require. It shall be the duty of the superintendent of insurance to examine the application so filed, and to make any further inquiry or examination of any such applicant as he may deem advisable. If upon such examination the superintendent shall find that the applicant, or applicants, or if a corporation, the officers and directors thereof, is or are all trustworthy persons of good business credit, the superintendent may issue to such applicant a certificate of authority to sell or offer for sale in this state, the securities of any insurance corporation or corporations and of any promoting or holding corporation previously authorized under this section which shall be mentioned therein.

4. Every such unauthorized insurance corporation, and every promoting or holding corporation, as defined in this section, whose securities are to be offered for sale in this state, shall file with the superintendent of insurance copies of all securities to be

offered for sale, and an application for a certificate of authority under this section which shall contain a statement in detail of the plans and purposes of such corporation, the amount and par value of the securities to be offered for sale and the selling price thereof, the manner in which the moneys paid in therefor are to be spent or employed, the rate of commissions to be paid for the sale of such securities, the salaries to be paid to the officers of such corporation, and such other and further information as the said superintendent may require. No change shall thereafter be made in the form or character of the securities to be offered for sale, or in the plans or purposes of any such corporation without the approval thereof in writing by the said superintendent. It shall be the duty of the superintendent of insurance to examine the application and other documents so filed, and to make any further inquiry or examination of any such corporation as he may deem advisable. If upon such examination the superintendent shall find that the plans and purposes of any such corporation are proper, that its condition is satisfactory, that the amount of its securities is reasonable, that the price at which such securities are to be sold is adequate, and that the manner in which the moneys paid in therefor, the rate of commissions to be paid and the salaries of officers are fair, the superintendent may issue a certificate that such corporation has complied with all the provisions of this section and is authorized to sell or offer its securities for sale in this state.

5. The superintendent of insurance may refuse to issue or renew any certificate provided for by this section, if, in his judgment, such refusal will best promote the interest of the people of the state. No individual whose certificate of authority granted under this section is revoked, nor any copartnership of which he is a member, nor any corporation of which he is an officer or director, shall be entitled to any certificate of authority under this section for a period of five years after such revocation; and if any such certificate held by a copartnership or corporation is so revoked, no member of such copartnership or officer or director of such corporation shall be entitled to any such certificate for the same period of time.

6. No printed matter shall be used in connection with the sale of securities of any such promoting, holding or insurance corporation, for advertising purposes, or in the dissemination of information with reference thereto, unless such printed matter shall first be submitted to the superintendent of insurance and

approved by him in writing. No such corporation and no officer, director or agent thereof, or any other person, coparlnership, association or corporation shall issue, circulate or employ or cause or permit to be used, issued, circulated or employed any circular or statement, whether printed or oral, of any sort, misrepresenting or exaggerating the earnings of insurance corporations or the value of their corporate stock, or other securities or the profits to be derived either directly or indirectly from the organization and management of insurance corporations or of organizing or holding corporations as defined in this section. No insurance or other corporation, and no individual, copartnership or association, transacting business in this state shall place or offer to place insurance in any corporation in connection with the sale or purchase of the securities of any insurance corporation or of any promoting or holding corporation as defined in this section.

§ 2. This act shall take effect immediately.

Chap. 53.

AN ACT to amend the village law, in relation to boards of commissioners.

Became a law March 6, 1913, with the approval of the Governor. Passed, three-fifths being present.

The People of the State of New York, represented in Senate and Assembly, do enact as follows:

L. 1909, ch. 64, § 42 amended.

Section 1. Section forty-two of chapter sixty-four of the laws of nineteen hundred and nine, entitled "An act relating to villages, constituting chapter sixty-four of the consolidated laws," is hereby amended to read as follows:

§ 42. **Eligibility to office.** A president or trustee, or a fire, water, light, sewer, cemetery or police[1] commissioner must, at the time of his election, be owner of property assessed to him on the last preceding assessment roll, and must also be the owner during the term of his office of property assessed to him on the assessment roll of said village; except that a president or trustee elected at the first village election must be the owner of

---

[1] Provision for police commissioner new.

property assessed upon the last preceding town assessment roll. Any resident elector is eligible to any other village office. A resident woman, who is a citizen of the United States, and of the age of twenty-one years, is eligible to the office of village clerk or deputy clerk. A person shall not hold two village offices at the same time, except the offices of collector and police constable or water and light commissioner; and except that village trustees may also be water commissioners.

§ 2. Section sixty-three of such chapter, as amended by chapter four hundred and sixty-nine of the laws of nineteen hundred and nine, is hereby amended to read as follows:

§ 63. **Separate boards of commissioners.** A village which has no separate board of fire, water, light, sewer, park or cemetery commissioners, by adopting a proposition therefor at an annual election, may establish such a board, or may establish a municipal board, with the powers, duties and responsibilities of two or more of such separate boards. In a village of the first class a board of commissioners or a municipal board may be composed of three or five members as shall be determined by the proposition. If such proposition be adopted, the board of trustees at its next annual meeting shall appoint such commissioners, for the terms of one, two and three years, respectively, or in a village which determines to have five commissioners, for the terms of one, two, three, four and five years, respectively; and at each annual meeting thereafter the board of trustees shall appoint one commissioner for the full term of three or five years, as the case may be. [2]A village of the first class, by the adoption of a proposition therefor, at an annual election, may establish a separate board of police commissioners, composed of three members. If the proposition to establish such board be adopted, the board of trustees, at its next annual meeting, shall appoint such commissioners for the terms of one, two and three years respectively; and at each annual meeting thereafter the board of trustees shall appoint one commissioner for the full term of three years. Said board of police commissioners shall have all the powers, be subject to all the liabilities and perform all the duties of the president and board of trustees so far as the same relate to the police or police department.

§ 3. This act shall take effect immediately.

_____

[2] Remainder of section new.

§ 63, as amended by L. 1909, ch. 469, amended.

Chap. 54.

AN ACT to amend the conservation law, in relation to the taking of fish in Richmond county and Raritan bay.

Became a law March 6, 1913, with the approval of the Governor. Passed, three-fifths being present.

The People of the State of New York, represented in Senate and Assembly, do enact as follows:

L. 1911, ch. 647, § 329, as added by L. 1912, ch. 318, amended.

Section 1. Section three hundred and twenty-nine of chapter six hundred and forty-seven of the laws of nineteen hundred and eleven, entitled "An act relating to conservation of land, forests, waters, parks, hydraulic power, fish and game, constituting chapter sixty-five of the consolidated laws," as added by chapter three hundred and eighteen of the laws of nineteen hundred and twelve, is hereby amended to read as follows:

§ 329. **Richmond county and Raritan bay.** Fish, except shad, in Raritan bay or waters adjacent thereto in Richmond county shall not be taken except by angling. Shad shall not be taken except by pounds or[1] drifting shad nets from March fifteenth to June fifteenth, both inclusive.

§ 2. This act shall take effect immediately.

Chap. 55.

AN ACT to amend the real property law, in relation to creation and division of estates.

Became a law March 6, 1913, with the approval of the Governor. Passed, three-fifths being present.

The People of the State of New York, represented in Senate and Assembly, do enact as follows:

L. 1909, ch. 52, §§ 67, 68, 70 amended.

Section 1. Sections sixty-seven, sixty-eight and seventy of chapter fifty-two of the laws of nineteen hundred and nine, entitled "An act relating to real property, constituting chapter fifty of the consolidated laws," are hereby amended to read, respectively, as follows:

§ 67. **Sale or lease**[1a] **of real property held by tenant for life**

---

1 Words " pounds or " new.
1a Words " or lease " new.

with contingent remainder or remainders over to persons whose
identity is unknown. In any case where real property is devised
by will or conveyed by deed to a person for life, with contingent
remainder or remainders over, to persons the identity of whom
can not be definitely ascertained until the death of the person
entitled to the life estate, the supreme court may, by order, on
such terms and conditions as seem just and proper, authorize the
sale or lease[1] of such real property, or any part thereof, whenever
it appears to the satisfaction of the court that said real property,
or some portion thereof, has become so unproductive or such circumstances or conditions have arisen subsequent to the devise or
deed that it is for the best interest of the life tenant and of the
remaindermen that a sale or lease[1] should be had, or that for other
peculiar reasons, or on account of other peculiar circumstances,
it is for the best interest of the life tenant and the remaindermen that a sale or lease[1] should be had. The supreme court
shall not grant such an order, unless it appears to the satisfaction of such court, that a written notice, stating the time and
place of the application therefor, has been served upon the life
tenant, and upon every other person in being having an estate,
vested or contingent, in reversion or remainder in said real property at least eight days before the making thereof. If such beneficiary or other person is an adult without the state, or is a minor,
lunatic, person of unsound mind, habitual drunkard or absentee,
notice shall be served on such beneficiary or other person in such
manner as the court or a justice thereof may prescribe. Upon
the return day of the notice the court shall, upon its own motion,
appoint a special guardian for any minor and for any lunatic,
person of unsound mind or habitual drunkard who shall not be
represented by a committee duly appointed.

§ 68. **Application, how made.** The application must be made
by petition duly verified, which shall set forth the provisions of
the will or the deed creating the estate, the condition of the estate
and the particular facts which make it necessary or proper that
the application should be granted. After taking proof of the
facts either before the court or by a referee and hearing the parties and fully examining into the matter, the court must make
an order upon the application. In case the application is
granted, the order must authorize the real property described in

---

[1] Words "or lease" new.

the petition to be sold or leased[2] upon such terms and conditions as the court may prescribe, [3]but in the case of a lease the term thereof shall not exceed twenty-one years.

§ 70. **Instruments[4] upon sale or lease.[5]** A deed or lease[5] made pursuant to a final order granted as provided in the foregoing sections sixty-seven and sixty-eight shall be valid and effectual against all minors, lunatics, persons of unsound mind, habitual drunkards and persons not in being, interested in the real property aforesaid, or having estates, vested or contingent, in reversion or remainder in said real property, but before the order directing the sale or lease[5] can be made, all adult persons not under disability having an interest in said real estate, vested or contingent, in reversion or remainder, must make and file with the clerk of the court in which the proceedings have been instituted, a written instrument, duly executed and acknowledged, consenting that such an order of sale or lease[5] may be made, and in no event shall such order be made without the like written consent of the life tenant if not suffering from disability.

§ 2. This act shall take effect immediately.

Chap. 56.

AN ACT authorizing the common council and mayor of the city of Buffalo to lease or grant a right to use to abutting owners on the north side of Sienkiewicz place in said city a strip of land of said street not to exceed six feet in width.

Became a law March 6, 1913, with the approval of the Governor. Passed, three-fifths being present.

Accepted by the City.

The People of the State of New York, represented in Senate and Assembly, do enact as follows:

Section 1. The common council of the city of Buffalo is hereby authorized to lease to each owner of land abutting on the north line of Sienkiewicz place in said city and to their successors and assigns a strip of land of said street not to exceed six feet in width of the northerly part thereof and running the entire length

---

[2] Words " or leased " new.
[3] Remainder of sentence new.
[4] Word " Instruments " substituted for word " Conveyances."
[5] Words " or lease " new.

of the same, or, to grant a right to use the same, upon such terms, conditions and reservations and for such period of time as may be fixed by said common council. Upon the adoption of a resolution by the common council authorizing or directing the same, the mayor may execute and deliver to each such owner and to their successors and assigns a lease or grant containing such terms, conditions and reservations as shall be fixed by such resolution.

§ 2. This act shall take effect immediately.

Chap. 57.

AN ACT to release the interest of the state of New York in the property and estate of Margaret E. Tompkins, deceased, to the heirs and next of kin of Noah D. Tompkins, deceased.

Became a law March 6, 1913, with the approval of the Governor. Passed by a two-thirds vote.

The People of the State of New York, represented in Senate and Assembly, do enact as follows:

Section 1. All the estate, right, title, interest and property Interest of the people of this state which may have been acquired by them, released. by escheat or otherwise, in and to the property and estate, real, personal and mixed, of Margaret E. Tompkins, late of the borough of Brooklyn, county of Kings, city and state of New York, deceased, is hereby released to the heirs and next of kin of Noah D. Tompkins, deceased.

§ 2. Nothing in this act contained shall be construed to impair Rights not or affect the right in or to said property, estate, real or personal, affected. of any heir at law, devisee, grantee or of any creditor by mortgage, judgment or otherwise, nor to warrant or insure by the state Title not the title to the property so released, or to any part thereof. warranted.

§ 3. This act shall take effect immediately.

Chap. 58.

AN ACT to amend chapter one hundred and thirty-seven of the laws of nineteen hundred and eleven, entitled "An act to authorize the county of Franklin to construct and maintain a county road system in said county, and to authorize the board of supervisors thereof to issue the bonds of said county in the aggregate amount of five hundred thousand dollars for such county road system," in relation to funds applicable to the purpose of said act.

Became a law March 6, 1913, with the approval of the Governor. Passed, three-fifths being present.

The People of the State of New York, represented in Senate and Assembly, do enact as follows:

L. 1911. ch.
137, § 3
amended.

Section 1. Section three of chapter one hundred and thirty-seven of the laws of nineteen hundred and eleven, entitled "An act to authorize the county of Franklin to construct and maintain a county road system in said county, and to authorize the board of supervisors thereof to issue the bonds of said county in the aggregate amount of five hundred thousand dollars for such county road system," is hereby amended to read as follows:

§ 3. **County road commission.** A commission to consist of five members shall be created to represent the board of supervisors of said county in the management of the construction, repair and maintenance of said county road system which shall be known and designated the Franklin county road commission, three members of which shall be members of the board of supervisors designated by said board, and shall continue in office as members of said commission, only during their term of office as supervisors, the fourth shall be the county superintendent of highways, and the fifth shall be chosen by the four members above designated. Any vacancy occurring by resignation, death, termination of office of supervisor, or otherwise, in the membership of said commission shall be filled in the same manner as originally provided. Said commission shall organize as a board by choosing one of its members as a president, and one as secretary thereof. The board thus organized shall meet regularly every two weeks at least for the purpose of approving payrolls, bills and accounts for services performed and materials furnished, and all other matters, relative to said county road system. All matters coming before said board shall be acted on by motion or resolution, and the result evidenced by the certificate of the secretary thereof. All bills so approved by said commission, shall be audited by a person to be appointed by the board of supervisors, and when so approved and audited, shall be paid by the county treasurer of said county out of the funds in his hands received from the sale of county bonds, hereinafter provided for, moneys received as premiums on such bonds, at sales thereof, and moneys derived from interest upon deposits of the proceeds of such bonds, including premiums, from time to time,[1] or from moneys received from taxes levied and collected for the maintenance of said county road system. It shall be the duty of said commission to file with the state commission of highways at Albany, before the fifteenth of each month, a report of its expenditures, during the preceding month, in such form as may be prescribed by the said state commission and the books of said commission shall be subject to audit by the said state commission in the same manner that supervisors' accounts are audited by it. Said county road commission shall adopt a standard plan and standard specifications for the construction of gravel and macadam roads within said system, and all roads therein shall be constructed in accordance with such plans and specifications and it shall have the sole management of the construction, maintenance and improvement of said county road system during the recess of the board of supervisors of said county. It shall adopt a system of bookkeeping that will show the cost of construction of each section of said system and shall make an annual report to said board of supervisors of the total disbursements, mileage of road construction, and of such other facts and information as may be required by said board. Each member of said commission, except the county superintendent, shall be paid the sum of four dollars per day and necessary traveling expenses for each day while engaged in the work of said county road system.

§ 2. Section five of such chapter is hereby amended to read as follows: § § amended.

§ 5. **Issue and sale of county bonds.** The board of supervisors of said county in accordance with the provisions of the county law and general municipal law as hereinafter changed

---

[1] Words "moneys received as premiums on such bonds, at sales thereof, and moneys derived from interest upon deposits of the proceeds of such bonds, including premiums, from time to time;" new.

4

and modified, is hereby authorized to borrow such sum or sums as may be necessary, not exceeding in the aggregate five hundred thousand dollars for the purpose of paying the expense of constructing, maintaining and improving said county road system and the expenses lawfully incurred under this act, and to issue bonds as security for the payment of said sum in the name and under the seal of said county, which bonds shall be in denominations of one thousand dollars each, numbered from one to five hundred inclusive and shall be divided into five series, to wit: series A, B, C, D and E respectively. Such bonds shall be dated on the first day of March of the year of issue, and be payable in installments of ten bonds each as consecutively numbered, on the first day of March in the year nineteen hundred and twenty-one, and ten bonds on the first day of March in each year thereafter until all of said bonds are fully paid, interest thereon to be paid semi-annually on the first day of March and the first day of September in each year at a rate not to exceed five per centum per annum, and shall be signed by the chairman and clerk of the board of supervisors and attested by the county clerk under the corporate seal of said county. They shall be made payable at such bank as may be designated by the said county road commission and shall be sold by said commission at a price not less than par as money shall be required for the purposes of this act, the amount to be sold to be designated by resolution adopted by said commission. The acceptance of any proposal to purchase said bonds shall be entered upon the minutes of said commission and certified by the secretary thereof to the county treasurer, who shall cause the bonds so sold to be executed and delivered to the purchaser or purchasers thereof, upon the receipt of the money offered therefor. The county treasurer shall immediately deposit the money so received to the credit of a separate fund to be designated as the Franklin county road fund. ²Moneys representing premiums on such bonds, at sales thereof, and interest received upon deposits of the proceeds of such bonds, including premiums, from time to time, including moneys thus received and derived heretofore and now in the hands of the county treasurer, shall also constitute a part of such fund and be applicable to the construction, maintenance and improvement of said county roads.

§ 3. This act shall take effect immediately.

---

² Remainder of section new.

Chap. 59.

AN ACT to amend chapter fifty-one of the laws of nineteen hundred and nine, entitled "An act in relation to public officers, constituting chapter forty-seven of the consolidated laws," known as the public officers law.

Became a law March 6, 1913, with the approval of the Governor. Passed, three-fifths being present.

The People of the State of New York, represented in Senate and Assembly, do enact as follows:

Section 1. Section ten of chapter fifty-one of the laws of nineteen hundred and nine, constituting chapter forty-seven of the consolidated laws, known as the public officers law, is hereby amended so as to read as follows:

§ 10. **Official oaths.** Every officer shall take and file the oath of office required by law before he shall be entitled to enter upon the discharge of any of his official duties. An oath of office may be administered by a judge of the court of appeals or by[1] any officer authorized to take, within the state, the acknowledgment of the execution of a deed of real property, or by an officer in whose office the oath is required to be filed, or may be administered to any member of a body of officers, by a presiding officer or clerk, thereof, who shall have taken an oath of office. The oath of office of a notary public or commissioner of deeds shall be filed in the office of the clerk of the county in which he shall reside. The oath of office of every state officer shall be filed in the office of the secretary of state; of every officer of a municipal corporation, with the clerk thereof; and of every other officer, in the office of the clerk of the county in which he shall reside, if no place be otherwise provided by law for the filing thereof.

§ 2. This act shall take effect immediately.

L. 1909, ch 51, § 10 amended.

---

1 Words " a judge of the court of appeals or by," new.

Chap. 60.

AN ACT to amend the code of civil procedure, relating to when
a foreign corporation may be sued.

Became a law March 6, 1913, with the approval of the Governor. Passed,
three-fifths being present.

*The People of the State of New York, represented in Senate
and Assembly, do enact as follows:*

§ 1780
amended.

Section 1. Section seventeen hundred and eighty of the code
of civil procedure is hereby amended so as to read as follows:

§ 1780. **When foreign corporation may be sued.** An action
against a foreign corporation may be maintained by a resident of
the state, or by a domestic corporation, for any cause of action.
An action against a foreign corporation may be maintained by
another foreign corporation, or by a non-resident, in one of the
following cases only:

1. Where the action is brought to recover damages for the
breach of a contract made within the state, or relating to property situated within the state, at the time of the making thereof.

2. Where it is brought to recover real property situated within
the state, or a chattel, which is replevied within the state.

3. Where the cause of action arose within the state, except
where the object of the action is to affect the title to real property
situated without the state.

4.[1] Where a foreign corporation is doing business within this
state.

In effect
Sept. 1,
1913.

§ 2. This act shall take effect September first, nineteen hundred and thirteen.

---

[1] Subd. 4 new.

Chap. 61.

AN ACT to amend the village law, in relation to the compensation of collectors.

Became a law March 6, 1913, with the approval of the Governor. Passed, three-fifths being present.

The People of the State of New York, represented in Senate and Assembly, do enact as follows:

Section 1. Section eighty-six of chapter sixty-four of the laws of nineteen hundred and nine, entitled "An act relating to villages, constituting chapter sixty-four of the consolidated laws," as amended by chapter sixty-six of the laws of nineteen hundred and eleven, is hereby amended to read as follows:

§ 86. **Compensation and duties of village officers not otherwise prescribed.** Except as provided in this section the president and trustees, and the fire, water, light, sewer and cemetery commissioners, shall serve without compensation, but the members of the board of trustees shall be entitled to the compensation fixed by law for inspectors of election when acting as such, and to the same compensation as town assessors for each day actually and necessarily spent by them in making the village assessment. The board of trustees of a village incorporated under and subject to this chapter or to a special law may, upon its own motion, and shall, upon the petition of twenty-five electors of such village qualified as provided by this chapter to vote upon a proposition, cause to be submitted at a village election a proposition to fix the compensation of the president or of the trustees or of the fire, water, light, sewer or cemetery commissioners of such village at an amount specified in such proposition. Only persons who possess the qualifications prescribed in this chapter for voters upon a proposition shall be entitled to vote upon such proposition. If such proposition be adopted the salary of the officer or officers shall be deemed fixed in accordance with the amount specified therein, but a proposition may be submitted in like manner at a subsequent election either changing the amount fixed by such resolution or providing that such officer or officers shall thereafter receive no compensation for services. [1]A village may, on the adop-

Margin note: L. 1909, ch. 64, § 86, as amended by L. 1911, ch. 66, amended.

---

1 Following sentence new.

tion of a proposition therefor, determine that the compensation
of the collector of such village shall be fixed by the board of trustees; after which determination the collector in said village shall
not collect or receive fees.

The board of trustees may fix the compensation and further declare the powers and duties of all other village officers or boards
and may require any officer or board of the village to furnish reports, estimates or other information relating to any matter within
his or its jurisdiction.

§ 115
amended.

§ 2. Section one hundred and fifteen of such chapter is hereby
amended to read as follows:

§ 115. **Collection of taxes by collector.** Upon receiving the
assessment-roll and warrant the collector shall cause a notice to
be published at least once in the official paper, if any, and also in
each other newspaper published in the village, and posted conspicuously in five public places in the village, stating that on six
days specified therein, not less than nine nor more than twenty
days after the publication and posting thereof, he will attend at a
convenient place in the village, specified in the notice, for the purpose of receiving taxes. At least seven days before the first date
fixed in such notice, the collector shall serve a copy thereof upon
each corporation named in or subject to taxation upon the assessment-roll, and whose principal office is not in the village, by delivering such copy to a person designated by the corporation for
that purpose by a written designation filed with the village clerk,
or to any person in the village acting as the agent or representative
in any capacity of such corporation. If there is no such designated person or agent in the village, service of such notice upon
the corporation shall not be required. Any person or
corporation paying taxes within twenty days from the date of
the notice, shall be charged with one per centum thereon, and
thereafter with five per centum, for the fees of the collector; [2]pro-
vided that in a village in which the compensation of the collector
has been fixed by the board of trustees as provided in this act, the
taxes may be paid within the said twenty days without additional
charge and all taxes in such village remaining unpaid after the expiration of said twenty days shall be increased five per centum.
If a notice is not served upon a corporation as herein required,
the collector shall only be entitled to one per centum as his fees
upon the taxes assessed against it. After the expiration of such

---

[2] Remainder of sentence new.

twenty days the collector shall proceed to collect the taxes remaining unpaid, and for that purpose he possesses all the powers of a town collector. The laws relating to town collectors shall also, so far as consistent with this chapter, apply to the collection of village taxes.

§ 3. This act shall take effect immediately.

Chap. 62.

AN ACT to grant to the city of New York certain lands under water in Flushing bay and Flushing creek and vicinity and providing for the improvement thereof.

Became a law March 6, 1913, with the approval of the Governor. Passed by a two-thirds vote.

Accepted by the City.

The People of the State of New York, represented in Senate and Assembly, do enact as follows:

Section 1. To the end that the city of New York may co-operate with the federal government in the improvement of and straightening of Flushing creek intended for the advancement of the commercial interests of the city, state and nation there is hereby granted to the city of New York such right, title and interest as the state of New York may have in and to the lands under water in Flushing creek within the bounds of and between original high water marks upon either side thereof and in and to the lands under water of Flushing bay southerly of a line extending from Sanford Point at North Beach to College Point. *Lands granted.*

§ 2. For the purpose of enabling the city of New York to carry into effect the straightening of Flushing creek, its commissioner of docks is hereby authorized by and with the approval of its board of estimate and apportionment to adopt and determine upon a plan or plans for such improvement, and such plan or plans when approved by the board of estimate and apportionment and filed in the office of the commissioner of docks shall be the sole plan or plans for the improvement of said Flushing creek. *Plans for straightening Flushing creek*

§ 3. The board of estimate and apportionment is authorized and empowered to exchange the lands under water herein conveyed to the city of New York for lands and lands under water owned by *Exchange of lands under water for similar*

lands privately owned.
private parties required and necessary to carry into effect the improvement of Flushing creek herein provided for.

Sale of lands under water not required.
§ 4. The board of estimate and apportionment is also authorized and empowered to sell and dispose of so much of the lands under water herein conveyed to the city of New York as may not be required for the improvement of Flushing creek herein provided for to the abutting owners upon such terms and conditions as it may deem just and proper or as may be agreed upon.

Acquisition of uplands under water.
§ 5. The board of estimate and apportionment is also authorized to acquire either by purchase or by the exercise of the right of eminent domain any and all upland or uplands under water owned by private parties for which no exchange as herein provided for can be made.

Application of inconsistent acts.
§ 6. The provisions of any acts, and parts of acts, including the Greater New York charter, which are inconsistent with this act, and in so far only as they are inconsistent with this act, shall have no application to the rights, powers, grants and obligations authorized, prescribed or created by this act or to the proceedings to be had or taken under the authority of this act.

§ 7. This act shall take effect immediately.

Chap. 63.

AN ACT to amend chapter seven hundred and fifty-one of the laws of eighteen hundred and ninety-five, entitled "An act to revise and consolidate the several acts in relation to the city of Hudson; to revise the charter of said city; and to establish a city court therein and define its jurisdiction and powers," in relation to the terms of and the time and manner of the election of the elective officers in said city.

Became a law March 7, 1913, with the approval of the Governor. Passed, three-fifths being present.

Accepted by the City.

The People of the State of New York, represented in Senate and Assembly, do enact as follows:

L. 1895, ch. 751, § 7 amended.
Section 1. Section seven of chapter seven hundred and fifty-one of the laws of eighteen hundred and ninety-five, entitled "An act to revise and consolidate the several acts in relation to the city of Hudson; to revise the charter of said city; and to establish a city

court therein and define its jurisdiction and powers," is hereby
amended to read as follows:[1]

§ 7. A municipal election shall be held on the twenty-third ^{Municipal elections.}
day of April, in the year nineteen hundred and thirteen, and at
the general election in the year nineteen hundred and thirteen,
and at the general election in each year thereafter.

§ 2. Section nine of said act of eighteen hundred and ninety- ^{§ 9 amended.}
five is hereby amended to read as follows:

§ 9. The election officers in each election district of the city ^{Statement of result of election.}
shall forthwith upon its completion deliver to and file with the city
clerk a certified statement of the result of such election in each
such district respectively, and the city clerk[2] shall deliver such
certified statement to the common council at its regular meeting
next succeeding such election in each year, and the common council
shall, upon such certified statement, declare and determine what
persons have been duly elected and make and subscribe a certifi- ^{Certificates of election.}
cate thereof in a book of record provided for that purpose, where-
upon the city clerk shall serve each person so elected to office
with a written notice of his election by either serving such notice
personally or leaving the same at his place of residence.

§ 3. Section ten of said act of eighteen hundred and ninety-five ^{§ 10 amended.}
is hereby amended to read as follows:[3]

§ 10. The persons having a plurality of votes for the respective ^{Who to be declared elected.}
offices to be filled by the electors of the whole city, and those having
a plurality of votes for the offices to be filled by the electors of
the several wards, shall be declared duly elected, and shall enter
upon the discharge of the duties of their respective offices at the ^{Commencement of terms.}
times following: those elected on the twenty-third day of April,
in the year nineteen hundred and thirteen, and at the general
election in the year nineteen hundred and thirteen, on the first
day of May next following their elections, respectively, and those
thereafter elected, on the first day of January next following their
elections, respectively, unless a different time is hereinafter
specified.

§ 4. Section eleven of said act of eighteen hundred and ninety- ^{§ 11 amended.}
five is hereby amended to read as follows:[3]

§ 11. If at any election authorized by this act any officer voted ^{Appointment by common}
for thereat shall not have been chosen by reason of two or more

---

[1] Section materially amended.
[2] Section to here formerly read: " The city clerk, with whom the certified
statements of the result of such election shall be filed."
[3] Section materially amended.

council in
case of
tie vote. candidates having received an equal number of votes for the same office, the common council shall appoint a person to fill such office. If such failure to elect shall have occurred at the election held on the twenty-third day of April in the year nineteen hundred and thirteen the person so appointed shall take office on the first day of May in the year nineteen hundred and thirteen and hold office until and including the thirty-first day of December in the year nineteen hundred and thirteen, and his successor shall be elected at the general election in the year nineteen hundred and thirteen and shall take office on the first day of January next following and hold office for the unexpired portion of the term of the office to which he was elected. Such appointment shall be made at a special meeting of the common council to be called and held for that purpose; and no other business shall be transacted at such meeting. If such failure to elect shall have occurred at the election held on the twenty-third day of April in the year nineteen hundred and thirteen such appointment shall be made not less than ten days nor more than twenty days after the occurrence of such failure, and if it shall have occurred at any other election such appointment shall be made between the first day and the fifteenth day of December next following. Each such appointment shall be in writing; it shall be signed by a majority of the members of the common council; and shall be delivered by the presiding officer of the common council to the city clerk who shall file the same in his office and record it in a book of record to be kept by him for that purpose.

§ 12
amended.

§ 5. Section twelve of said act of eighteen hundred and ninety-five, is hereby amended to read as follows:[3]

Notice of
election
April 23,
1913.

§ 12. The city clerk, at least forty days before the election to be held on the twenty-third day of April, nineteen hundred and thirteen, shall make, under his hand and official seal, and deliver to the custodian of primary records in and for the county of Columbia, a notice in writing stating the day upon which such election shall be held, and stating each officer who may be lawfully voted for at such election by the electors of the city, and by the electors of each ward, respectively, and stating also which, if any,

Filing.

of said officers are to be elected to fill a vacancy. The custodian of primary records upon the receipt of such notice shall file and

Publication.

record the same in its office, and shall cause a copy of the same

---

[3] Section materially amended.

to be published once in each week thereafter until the election
therein specified, in each of the official papers of the city.

Party and independent nominations of candidates for all of the Nominations for such election.
offices to be filled at such election may be made. Party nomina-
tions of candidates for all of the offices to be voted for by the
electors of the city shall be made at a primary election to be held
at least seven days before said election, which primary election
shall be deemed in law an official primary. Independent nominations may be made in accordance with the provisions of the election law.

At least thirty-three days before such official primary day the Notice of primary election.
city clerk shall certify under his hand and official seal and deliver
to the custodian of primary records a statement of such official
primary election and the time when it is to be held. The custodian
of primary records shall prepare a notice of such official primary
election, and shall publish such notice not more than ten days nor
less than five days before such primary election in the official
papers of the city.

Such notice shall specify the day of such primary election, the Contents of notice.
hours during which it will be held, the location of the polling
places, the names of the party or parties whose primary election
will be held thereat, and the offices for which candidates will be
voted for thereat.

Designations of candidates for party nominations for offices Designations for party nominations.
to be voted for by all the electors of the city shall be made in
accordance with the provisions of section forty-six[4] of the election
law.

The provisions of section forty-seven[4] of the election law shall Conduct of city committees.
govern the conduct of the city committees of political parties in
making such designations, except that each such city committee
shall determine for itself the procedure that shall govern its meeting in case there has been no procedure prescribed by the rules
and regulations of the party to which it belongs.

Designations of party candidates for all of the offices to be Designations, how made.
voted for by the electors of each ward, respectively, shall be made
in the following manner: the member or a majority of the members of the city committee of a political party in each of the
several wards of the city, not less than fifteen days before the
primary election, shall call a primary meeting of the electors of

---

[4] As added by L. 1911, ch. 891.

the ward in which such member or members of the city committee reside, which electors shall be at the time of such primary meeting enrolled voters of the party of which the person or persons calling such primary meeting shall be members, for the purpose of designating candidates for party nominations for ward offices to be placed upon the official primary ballot. Each such primary meeting shall elect a chairman and a secretary and two tellers. At such primary meeting a majority of the enrolled voters present may designate candidates for party nominations for ward offices to be placed upon the official primary ballot. The secretary shall sign a written statement of the results of such primary meeting and, within forty-eight hours, deliver such statement to the custodian of primary records who shall receive and file such statement and cause the names of the persons so designated to be placed upon the official primary ballot for such ward.

Filing certificates of nominations. Certificates of party nominations and of independent nominations for the elections provided for by this act shall be filed with the city clerk at least six days before such elections.

Primary districts. Each election district in the city shall be a primary district for the purposes of such official primary elections.

Revision of register. The board of inspectors in each election district in the city shall hold a meeting for revising and correcting the register five days before the election to be held on the twenty-third day of April, nineteen hundred and thirteen, as provided in this act.

Expense of such primary elections, how paid. The expense of such official primary elections shall be a charge against the city. A statement of the expense incurred by the custodian of primary records, by reason of the provisions of this act, shall be delivered by it to the city clerk. Such statement shall be verified by the oaths of the commissioners of elections, and the common council shall audit, allow and cause to be paid such expense in the same manner as other claims against the city.

Definitions. The following terms, "general election," "party," "designation," "official primary," "official primary election," "primary day," "official primary ballot," "committee," "nomination," "party nominations," "independent nominations," "party candidate," "party nominee," "independent candidate," and "independent nominee," when used in this act, have the same signification in respect to the elections herein provided for as those terms have in the election law, in so far as the meaning of those terms is applicable, unless other meaning is clearly apparent in the language and context of this act or of the election law.

The provisions of the election law shall govern the elections Application of election provided for in this act in so far as they are applicable, except as law. otherwise provided in this act.

§ 6. Section thirteen of said act of eighteen hundred and § 13 amended ninety-five, is hereby amended to read as follows:

§ 13. The officers of the city to be elected by general ballot Elective officers. shall be a mayor, a recorder,[5] a city judge, a city treasurer, and three assessors.

§ 7. Section fourteen of said act of eighteen hundred and § 14 amended. ninety-five is hereby amended to read as follows:[6]

§ 14. On the twenty-third day of April in the year nineteen hun- Officers to be elected dred and thirteen shall be elected a mayor, a recorder, and an assessor April 23, 1913. who shall take office on the first day of May, nineteen hundred and thirteen, and respectively hold office as follows: the mayor until Terms. and including the thirty-first day of December, nineteen hundred and fourteen, the recorder, until and including the thirty-first day of December, nineteen hundred and fifteen, and the assessor until and including the thirty-first day of December, nineteen hundred and fifteen. At the general election in the year nineteen hundred Officers to be elected and thirteen shall be elected a city treasurer, and an assessor, who at general election, shall respectively take office on the first day of May, nineteen hun- 1913. dred and fourteen, and hold office until and including the thirty- Terms. first day of December, nineteen hundred and sixteen. At the general election in nineteen hundred and fourteen shall be elected Officers to be elected a mayor, a city judge, and an assessor who shall respectively hold at general election, office as follows: the mayor shall take office on the first day of 1914. January, nineteen hundred and fifteen, and hold office to and Terms. including the thirty-first day of December, nineteen hundred and sixteen; the city judge shall take office on the first day of May, nineteen hundred and fifteen, and shall hold office to and includ- ing the thirty-first day of December, nineteen hundred and eighteen; the assessor shall take office on the first day of May, nineteen hundred and fifteen, and shall hold office to and including the thirty-first day of December, nineteen hundred and seventeen. Thereafter the term of office of the city judge shall be four years; Terms of officers the term of office of the mayor shall be two years; and the term thereafter. of office of the recorder, city treasurer, and assessors shall be respectively three years; and until the successor of each of said several officers shall have been duly elected, have qualified and entered upon the duties of the office.

---

[5] Words "an alderman-at-large" omitted. Words "a recorder" new.
[6] Section materially amended.

§ 16
amended.

§ 8. Section sixteen of said act of eighteen hundred and ninety-five is hereby amended to read as follows:[6]

Election of
aldermen
April 23,
1913.

Terms.

§ 16. On the twenty-third day of April, nineteen hundred and thirteen, shall be elected in each of the first, second, third and fourth wards, an alderman who shall take office on the first day of May, nineteen hundred and thirteen, and who shall hold office until and including the thirty-first day of December, nineteen hundred and fourteen; and in the fifth ward there shall be elected on the twenty-third day of April, nineteen hundred and thirteen, an alderman who shall take office on the first day of May, nineteen hundred and thirteen, and who shall hold office until and including the thirty-first day of December, nineteen hundred and fourteen, and an alderman who shall take office on the first day of May, nineteen hundred and thirteen, and who shall hold office until and including the thirtieth day of April, nineteen hundred

Election of
aldermen
at general
election,
1913.

Terms.

and fourteen. At the general election in the year nineteen hundred and thirteen shall be elected in each ward of the city one alderman who shall take office on the first day of May, nineteen hundred and fourteen, and hold office until and including the thirty-first day of December, nineteen hundred and fifteen.

Election
and terms
thereafter.

Thereafter an alderman shall be elected in each ward of the city at the general election in each year who shall take office on the next following first day of January and hold office until and including the thirty-first day of December in the second year succeeding his election.

Election of
supervisors
at general
election,
1913.

Terms.

At the general election in the year nineteen hundred and thirteen shall be elected in each ward a supervisor who shall take office on the first day of May, nineteen hundred and fourteen, and hold office until and including the thirty-first day of

At general
election,
1915.

Terms.

December, nineteen hundred and fifteen. At the general election in nineteen hundred and fifteen shall be elected in each ward a supervisor who shall take office on the first day of January next following and hold office until and including the thirty-first day of December in the second year following his election.

§ 20
amended.

§ 9. Section twenty of said act of eighteen hundred and ninety-five is hereby amended to read as follows:[6]

Vacancies
in elective
offices, how
filled;
terms of
appointees.

§ 20. Vacancies occurring in any manner in any elective office, shall be filled by appointment by the common council. Such appointments, except in the cases specified in section eleven of this act, shall be made not less than ten days nor more than twenty days after the occurrence of such vacancy, at a special meeting

----

[6] Section materially amended.

of the common council to be called and held for that purpose.
Such officers so appointed to fill vacancies shall serve until and
including the thirty-first day of December next following such
appointment. In case the appointment by the common council
to fill a vacancy as herein provided cannot be made until after the
expiration of the time in which the name of the candidate for election to fill the unexpired term of the office in question can be
placed upon the ballots to be voted at the next general election,
then and in that event the common council shall proceed to fill the
vacancy by appointment; the person so appointed shall hold office
from the date of such appointment to and including the thirty-
first day of December, in the next year; and in case such term of
office does not expire on the thirty-first day of December next
following such appointment, there shall be elected at the general
election in the year next following the year in which such appointment was made a person who shall take office on the first
day of January next following, and who shall hold office for the
remainder of the unexpired term.

§ 10. Section twenty-nine of said act of eighteen hundred and § 29 amended.
ninety-five is hereby amended to read as follows:

§ 29. The city clerk shall present each ordinance, resolution Approval or disap-
and audit of the common council, with the exception of rules proval of ordinances,
adopted by that body for its own procedure, and with the further etc.
exception of appointments to be made by the common council in
cases of failure to elect elective officers and of appointments to fill
vacancies in elective office as provided for in section eleven and
section twenty of this act,[7] to the mayor within three days after
its passage; if the mayor shall approve it, he shall sign it and
return it to the city clerk within three days; if he disapprove it,
or any item or items of an audit, he shall, within three days
after its presentation to him, return it or such item or items with
a statement of his objections, in writing, to the city clerk, who
shall present the same to the common council at its next regular
meeting, and the same shall have no effect unless that body shall
then proceed to reconsider the ordinance, resolution, audit, or item Passage over veto
or items of an audit objected to. If, after such reconsideration,
two-thirds of the members elected shall agree to pass the same, it
shall take effect. In every such case the vote shall be taken by

---

[7] Words "and with the further exception of appointments to be made by
the common council in cases of failure to elect elective officers and of appointments to fill vacancies in elective office as provided for in section eleven and
section twenty of this act," new.

yeas and nays and entered in the minutes with the objection of the mayor.

§ 38 amended.

§ 11. Section thirty-eight of said act of eighteen hundred and ninety-five is hereby amended to read as follows:

Special meetings of common council.

§ 38. Special meetings may be called by the mayor, or by the recorder or by any three aldermen. Written notice of all special meetings shall be served on the mayor and each member of the common council personally, or by leaving the same at his *plcae of residence. Such notice shall contain a list of the subjects to be considered at said special meeting, and no other business shall be transacted at said special meeting except by unanimous consent of all the members elected to the common council.

Special meetings to all vacancies in elective offices.

ⁱEach special meeting of the common council for the purpose of making appointments in cases of failure to elect elective officers, and for the purpose of making appointments to vacancies in elective offices, as provided in section eleven and section twenty of this act shall be called by the mayor, or by the recorder, or by any three aldermen; and no other business shall be transacted at such

How called.

meeting. Such call shall be in writing and be signed by the officer or officers issuing it, and shall be filed in the office of the city clerk at least six days before the day of meeting. The city clerk shall indorse upon the call, when the same is filed, the day and time of filing, and if more than one call shall be so filed, that first received in order of time shall be deemed to be the official call for the meet-

Purpose.

ing. Such call shall state the purpose of the meeting and the time

Publication of call.

and place of holding the same. The city clerk shall cause the same to be published in each of the official papers once in each day for two successive days, excluding Sundays and holidays, the last of which days of publication shall be the day before the date of hold-

Service on certain officers.

ing the meeting; he shall also cause a written copy of such call to be served on the mayor, recorder, and each alderman, either personally or by leaving the same at the place of residence of each of such persons on or before the first day of publication of such call.

Mayor to appoint in case of failure of common council.

In the event of the failure of the common council to make any appointments to elective office in case such appointment is necessary under the provisions of this act, within the periods of time respectively prescribed, the mayor, or in case of his inability to act, the recorder, shall make such appointment within ten days after such failure of the common council shall have occurred.

§ 12. This act shall take effect immediately.

---

* So in original.
ⁱ Remainder of section new.

Chap. 64.

AN ACT to authorize the city of Hudson to borrow money for street improvements, and to issue bonds of the city therefor.

Became a law March 7, 1913, with the approval of the Governor. Passed, three-fifths being present.

Accepted by the City.

The People of the State of New York, represented in Senate and Assembly, do enact as follows:

Section 1. The common council of the city of Hudson, upon service upon its clerk of an application signed by the members of the commission of public works, is hereby authorized to issue bonds of said city, to be known as street improvement bonds, to the amount of twenty-seven thousand eight hundred dollars, and payable at such time or times, and at such rate of interest, not to exceed the legal rate of interest per annum, and of such denominations as said common council may determine, and to sell the same in such manner as shall be deemed by the common council as likely to secure the largest attainable price for such bonds, but not less than par, and to deposit the proceeds of such sale, including any premiums thereon, with the city treasurer, to the credit of the commission of public works, subject to its draft, to be used by it for the purpose of street improvement other than ordinary repairs. *Bond issue authorized. Sale. Disposition of proceeds.*

§ 2. The common council of said city shall raise and collect such amounts, by tax upon the taxable property of said city, as shall be sufficient to pay the principal and interest of said bonds as the same shall become due and payable, which amounts so to be levied and collected by tax shall be in addition to the amounts that are now or shall be hereafter authorized by law to be raised for other purposes. *Tax for payment.*

§ 3. This act shall take effect immediately.

Chap. 65.

'AN ACT transferring from the common council of the city of Buffalo to the board of park commissioners of said city jurisdiction and control over Kenilworth avenue in said city and providing for the improvement of said avenue.

Became a law March 10, 1913, with the approval of the Governor. Passed, three-fifths being present.

Accepted by the City.

The People of the State of New York, represented in Senate and Assembly, do enact as follows:

Jurisdiction transferred.

Section 1. All jurisdiction and control over Kenilworth avenue in the city of Buffalo, between the northerly line of said city and Main street, is hereby transferred from the common council of said city to the board of park commissioners thereof, and after

Improvement authorized.

this act takes effect said board of park commissioners shall have authority to improve said Kenilworth avenue as a parkway or public place for purposes of travel, and to embellish the same

Jurisdiction, how exercised and improvement how made.

suitably and cause the same to be widened. Such jurisdiction and control shall be exercised and all improvements of said Kenilworth avenue shall be made and the cost thereof defrayed in the manner prescribed by chapter one hundred and five of the laws of eighteen hundred and ninety-one and the acts amendatory thereof, constituting the charter of said city.

Agreements with abutting owners for conveyance of land.

§ 2. Discretionary authority is hereby conferred upon the board of park commissioners of the city of Buffalo to enter into an agreement or agreements with the owners of lands abutting on said Kenilworth avenue for the conveyance to the city of lands adjoining said Kenilworth avenue on either side, or both sides, thereof, of such width and length as said board of park commissioners

Deduction of value of such lands from sewer assessments.

may determine shall be advisable, and to deduct the actual value of said lands from the amount of local assessments that may be imposed upon lands of said owners, to defray in whole or in part the cost of constructing one or more drains or sewers in said avenue as it now exists or as it may be widened. Such agree-

Agreements, how executed and recorded.

ment or agreements shall be in writing duly executed by the board of park commissioners for the city of Buffalo and by the owners of said lands, and shall be acknowledged so that it or they may be recorded in the office of the clerk of Erie county.

The amount so deducted from the local assessment upon said lands Deductions, how paid. shall be paid out of funds appropriated therefor in the estimates of the park department, and it shall be the duty of the common council to place such amount in the annual estimate for the park department upon written request therefor from the board of park commissioners; or the common council may, in its dis- Bond issues cretion, issue the bonds of said city to such amount for such length of time and at such rate of interest and on such terms and conditions as said common council shall prescribe by resolution.

§ 3. This act shall take effect immediately.

Chap. 66.

AN ACT to authorize the grant and conveyance by the commissioners of the land office of lands under water to the city of Buffalo, and to prohibit corporations from acquiring such lands by condemnation.

Became a law March 10, 1913, with the approval of the Governor. Passed by a two-thirds vote.

Accepted by the City.

The People of the State of New York, represented in Senate and Assembly, do enact as follows:

Section 1. The commissioners of the land office are hereby Grant authorized. authorized to grant and convey to the city of Buffalo, for dock, park and recreation purposes, all the estate, right, title and interest of the people of the state of New York in and to the lands under the waters of Lake Erie and Niagara river, bounded on the north Description of lands granted. by Jersey street in said city extended to the harbor line established by the government of the United States; on the east by the present shore line of Lake Erie and of Niagara river; on the south by the south line of Georgia street extended to said harbor line, and on the west by said harbor line; or so much of said lands as has not heretofore been acquired or is not now owned by said city of Buffalo; saving and excepting from the above described premises, however, all that tract or parcel of land under water situate in the city of Buffalo, county of Erie and state of New York, more particularly described as a plot of land covered with water, beginning at the intersection of the easterly line of Black Rock harbor as established by the United States, and the northerly line of lands heretofore owned by Henry Koons, as granted to him by chapter three hundred and forty-three of the laws of eighteen hundred and ninety-four; thence northerly along the said harbor line four hundred and fifty feet; thence easterly and parallel with the lands of the said Koons three hundred and fifty feet; thence southerly and parallel to said harbor line four hundred and fifty feet to the northerly line of said lands of Koons; thence westerly along the northerly line of said lands of Koons

Improvement for certain purposes, authorized. three hundred and fifty feet to the point of beginning. Such lands may be filled in by said city or otherwise improved and used for dock, park and recreation purposes.

Corporations prohibited from condemning such lands. § 2. It shall not be lawful for any corporation to take or acquire by right of eminent domain any part of the lands described in section one of this act, or to take or acquire by right of eminent domain any right, title or interest in or to said lands and premises, **Applies to pending proceedings.** or any part thereof. This section shall apply to all proceedings pending when this act takes effect.

Inconsistent acts. § 3. All acts or parts of acts inconsistent with this act shall be deemed to have no application to the lands described in section one of this act, or to any part of such lands.

§ 4. This act shall take effect immediately.

Chap. 67.

AN ACT to amend section one hundred and one of chapter six hundred and forty-eight of the laws of nineteen hundred and eleven, entitled "An act to revise, consolidate and amend generally chapter two hundred and twenty-five of the laws of nineteen hundred and one, known as ' the charter of the city of Oneida,' and the several acts amendatory thereof, and repealing certain acts," in relation to street cleaning and sprinkling.

Became a law March 10, 1913, with the approval of the Governor. Passed, three-fifths being present.

Accepted by the City.

The People of the State of New York, represented in Senate and Assembly, do enact as follows:

L. 1911, ch. 648, § 101 amended. Section 1. Section one hundred and one of chapter six hundred and forty-eight of the laws of nineteen hundred and eleven, entitled "An act to revise, consolidate and amend generally chapter two hundred and twenty-five of the laws of nineteen hundred and one, known as 'the charter of the city of Oneida,' and the several acts amendatory thereof, and repealing certain acts," is hereby amended to read as follows:

§ 101. **Street cleaning and sprinkling.** The board of public works as soon as practicable after the first Tuesday in March of each year may, in its discretion, advertise in the official papers for proposals to clean the street crossings, intersections, junctions, crosswalks and sidewalks in front of lands of the city of Oneida and walks in the public parks and for removing snow and ice from the sidewalks; also for the cleaning of pavements in said city; also for proposals to remove ashes, garbage, sweepings or rubbish deposited in piles, boxes or barrels, as required by ordinance, by the owners or occupants of any premises in said corporation tax district; [1]also, in its discretion, to require or cause any street or highway, or streets or highways, in said city or any portion or portions thereof to be sprinkled during such time and in such manner as it may deem necessary and proper. Detailed specifications of the said work shall be prepared by the board of public works with an estimate of the expense thereof. It shall determine the manner of doing such work and whether the same shall be done by one contract for the whole work, or different contracts and specifications for different parts of such work. The notice, proposals, certified check and bonds therefor shall be in accordance with the provisions of section eighty-six of this act so far as the same may be applicable. The board of public works may direct any temporary repairs to, or defects remedied in the streets, pavements, cross and sidewalks and bridges, so that the same shall be passable and safe. Such work may be done by contract or otherwise under the direction of the board of public works as it shall determine, and the expense thereof and of the work specified in this section shall be paid out of the local improvement fund except the cleaning of pavements, which shall be paid out of the highway fund, [2]and the expenses for street sprinkling which shall be paid as herein provided. The expense of sprinkling, including the cost of advertising, making measurements and assessments shall be paid by the owners of the real estate fronting, adjoining or abutting on such street or highway,

---

[1] Remainder of sentence new.
[2] Remainder of section materially amended.

or portion thereof, in proportion as they shall own feet fronting, adjoining or abutting thereon. The assessment for such expenses shall be made in the same manner as assessments for local improvements, stating the amount assessed for "street sprinkling," and collected in the same manner and by the same authority as general taxes in said city. The city may purchase and own one or more sprinklers, for the purpose aforesaid.

§ 2. This act shall take effect immediately.

Chap. 68.

AN ACT to amend the military law, in relation to pay of officers serving on boards, commissions and courts.

Became a law March 10, 1913, with the approval of the Governor. Passed, three-fifths being present.

The People of the State of New York, represented in Senate and Assembly, do enact as follows:

L. 1909, ch. 41, § 212 amended.

Section 1. Section two hundred and twelve of chapter forty-one of the laws of nineteen hundred and nine, entitled "An act in relation to the militia, constituting chapter thirty-six of the consolidated laws," is hereby amended to read as follows:

§ 212. **Pay of officers serving on boards, commissions and courts.** Members of the militia council, and members of boards and commissions created by this chapter, and[1] all officers detailed to serve on any board or commission ordered by the governor, or under his authority by the major general, or the commanding officer of the naval militia, or on any court of inquiry, court-martial or delinquency court, ordered by proper authority in pursuance of any provision of this chapter, shall be paid for each day actually employed in such council, board, commission,[2] or court, or engaged in the business thereof, or in traveling to and from the same. Except for members of the militia council and members of boards and commissions created by this chapter,[3] the sum in no case shall exceed ten days' pay and actual traveling expenses and subsistence, unless, upon application of the judge-advocate of

---

[1] Words "members of boards and commissions created by this chapter, and," new.
[2] Word "commission" new.
[3] Words "members of boards and commissions created by this chapter," new.

a court-martial or the presiding officer of a delinquency court, or
the presiding officer of the board, the officer appointing the court or
board has authorized such court or board to sit for a longer period,
or in case of such delinquency court, the governor or the officer or-
dering such court, has authorized such court to sit for a longer period than ten days.   An officer detailed to serve on a delinquency
court for the trial of enlisted men shall be paid for each day actually employed therein, engaged in the business thereof, or in traveling to and from the same, and traveling expenses and subsistence
when such court shall be held at a place other than the city or town
of his residence. An officer to whom a warrant for the collection of
fines, dues or penalties under the sentence of a military court is
delivered shall be paid by retaining to his own use, twenty-five
per centum of the fines, dues or penalties collected by him. Said
percentage shall be taxed by the officer issuing the warrant and
indorsed thereon and added to the amount collectible to satisfy the
sentence of the court. In addition to this percentage a marshal
of a military court shall be paid two dollars for each day actually
employed in the execution of the duties required of him and
mileage or actual necessary traveling expenses while engaged in
executing any process or mandate of a military court. Mileage
shall be computed at the rate of ten cents for each mile necessarily traveled going and returning to serve any process or mandate of a military court, the distance to be computed from the
place where it is served to the place where it is returnable.

§ 2. This act shall take effect immediately.

Chap. 69.

AN ACT to amend the code of civil procedure, in relation to notices of pendency of action.

Became a law March 10, 1913, with the approval of the Governor. Passed,
three-fifths being present.

*The People of the State of New York, represented in Senate
and Assembly, do enact as follows:*

Section 1. Section one thousand six hundred and seventy-two § 1672
of the code of civil procedure is hereby amended to read as amended.
follows:

§ 1672. **Notice to be recorded and indexed.** Each county clerk
with whom such a notice is filed, must immediately record it in

a book kept in his office for that purpose, and index it to the name of each defendant, specified in a direction appended at the foot of the notice, and subscribed by the attorney for the plaintiff. [1]The notice filed in partition suits must be indexed against the name of each plaintiff and of each defendant having any interest or estate in the premises. The expense of procuring a new book, when necessary, must be paid out of the county treasury, as other county charges.

§ 2. The code of civil procedure is hereby amended by adding after section twenty-three hundred and twenty-five thereof a new section, to be numbered twenty-three hundred and twenty-five-a, and to be as follows:

§ 2325-a. **Notice to be filed, recorded and indexed.** In all proceedings taken under this title, if real property or any interest therein is intended to be affected, the petitioner shall file in the clerk's office of each county where the property is situated, a notice of the pendency of such proceeding, which shall set forth the general nature and object of the proceeding and a brief description of the real property in that county to be affected thereby, and which notice must be filed with the petition or any time thereafter and before any final adjudication in the proceeding. The clerk shall index such notice against the name of the alleged incompetent. The pendency of the proceeding is constructive notice from the time of so filing the notice only to a purchaser or incumbrancer of the property affected thereby from or against the alleged incompetent with respect to whom the notice is directed to be indexed as aforesaid. A person whose conveyance or incumbrance is subsequently executed or subsequently recorded is bound by all proceedings taken after the filing of the notice to the same extent as if he was a party to the proceeding. But this provision shall not prevent a jury in a proper proceeding, on sufficient proof, from rendering a verdict that shall over-reach any conveyance or incumbrance theretofore executed by the alleged incompetent, so as to make such conveyance or incumbrance prima facie void.

§ 3. This act shall take effect September first, nineteen hundred and thirteen.

§ 2325a added.

In effect Sept. 1, 1913.

---

[1] Following sentence new.

Chap. 70.

AN ACT to amend the second class cities law, in relation to municipal lighting.

Became a law March 10, 1913, with the approval of the Governor. Passed, three-fifths being present.

The People of the State of New York, represented in Senate and Assembly, do enact as follows:

Section 1. Section one hundred and twenty-two of chapter fifty-five of the laws of nineteen hundred and nine, entitled "An act in relation to cities of the second class, constituting chapter fifty-three of the consolidated laws," is hereby amended to read as follows: _{L. 1909, ch 55, § 122 amended.}

§ 122. Contracts for lighting. All municipal lighting shall be supplied pursuant to contract therefor, awarded by the board of contract and supply as herein provided. Such contract shall cover and include the lighting and supplying of the lamps and the oil, gas, electric current, the cleaning, repair and renewal of the lamps and all the materials required in the use and care thereof. No bid or proposal for any such contract shall be received, nor contract awarded therefor, unless the bidder shall, prior to the making of such bid or proposal, have a franchise under the authority of which the proposed contract can be performed. No contract shall be advertised for or entered into for a period exceeding five years. Each bidder shall be required to furnish with each bid or proposal a certified check, payable to the order of the city treasurer, in such sum as the board of contract and supply shall prescribe, but not less than ten thousand dollars. Such sum shall be forfeited to and become the absolute property of the city in case the bidder depositing the same shall be awarded the contract and shall not execute the same and furnish a bond for the faithful performance of such contract, in the penal sum of not less than fifty thousand dollars, within thirty days after the award of such contract. Such certified check shall be returned to the bidder if the contract be not awarded to him, or, if awarded, he shall have executed and furnished the contract and required bond.

[1]The common council may by ordinance establish a special lighting district or districts for the purpose of ornamental street

---

[1] Remainder of section new.

lighting, and from time to time may alter or extend the same. The board of contract and supply may contract for lighting any such district or districts so established or extended, as such board may deem proper or expedient. Any contract so entered into shall be in conformity with the provisions of this section, except that the bond to be given for the faithful performance of the contract shall be in such amount as the board of contract and supply shall determine. The amount of any contract that may be entered into for such special lighting pursuant to the provisions of this act, shall be assessed, levied and collected upon and between the taxable property in said city and district or districts respectively, in the same manner, at the same time and by the same officers as the city taxes, charges or expenses of said city are now assessed, levied and collected. The common council shall, by ordinance, approved by the board of estimate and apportionment, apportion the expense that shall be borne by the taxable property in such special lighting district or districts, and the city at large; but, in no event shall the taxable property in any such special lighting district or districts, be charged with less than fifty per centum of such charges or expenses.

§ 2. This act shall take effect immediately.

Chap. 71.

AN ACT to amend the public health law, in relation to the practice of undertaking and embalming and the licensing of undertakers and embalmers.

Became a law March 11, 1913, with the approval of the Governor. Passed, three-fifths being present.

The People of the State of New York, represented in Senate and Assembly, do enact as follows:

L. 1909,
ch. 49,
§ 290, as
amended
by L. 1911,
ch. 841,
amended.

Section 1. Section two hundred and ninety of chapter forty-nine of the laws of nineteen hundred and nine, entitled "An act in relation to the public health, constituting chapter forty-five of the consolidated laws," as amended by chapter eight hundred and forty-one of the laws of nineteen hundred and eleven, is hereby amended to read as follows:

§ 290. **Board of embalming examiners; compensation.** The board of embalming examiners of the state of New York is con-

tinued. The members of said board now in office shall continue in
office until the expiration of their respective terms. The board
shall consist of five members appointed by the governor, each of
whom shall serve for a term of three years. Any vacancies occurring in said board shall be filled by the governor, for the unexpired term. The governor may remove from office any member of
said board of examiners for continued neglect of any of the duties
imposed upon him by this article, or for incompetency or improper conduct. No person shall be eligible to appointment as a
member of said board unless he shall have had an experience of
at least five years as a practical embalmer, duly licensed as such.[1]
Each member of said board shall receive an annual salary of two
hundred dollars and in addition thereto all necessary expenses incurred in the performance of his duties. The secretary shall receive an annual salary of one thousand dollars in addition to his
salary as a member. The salaries provided for in this section,
however, shall be payable only from the moneys collected and received by said board as provided in this article.

§ 2. Section two hundred and ninety-one of said chapter is §291 amended
hereby amended to read as follows:

§ 291. Corporate name; powers and duties of board. Said
board shall be known by the name "Board of embalming examiners of the state of New York." Every person appointed to
serve on said board shall receive a certificate of his appointment
from the governor of the state of New York, and within
fifteen[2] days after receiving such certificate, shall take, subscribe
and file, in the office of the secretary of state, the oath prescribed
by the thirteenth[3] article of the constitution of the state of
New York. The board may adopt a common seal and shall
elect from its membership a president and secretary. Said board
shall ascertain what constitute the best tests for determining
whether life is extinct, and shall prescribe the using of such tests,
before embalming, as they may deem necessary; and all persons
thereafter embalming the dead shall apply such tests prescribed
before injecting any fluid into any body. Said board by its presiding officer may issue subpoenas and administer oaths to witnesses, and a quorum of said board, which shall consist of not less

---

[1] Words " duly licensed as such," new.
[2] Formerly " ten."
[3] Formerly read " twelfth." See art. 13, § 1, and public officers law (L.
1909, ch. 51), § 10, as amended by L. 1913, ch. 59, ante.

than three members, and any committees thereof, is hereby authorized to take testimony concerning matters within its jurisdiction. Said board shall, from time to time, make and adopt rules, regulations and by-laws not inconsistent with law, whereby the performance of the duties of said board and the transaction of the business and the practice of embalming and undertaking[4] shall be regulated and performed, subject to the approval of the state department of health. A certified copy of any of said rules and regulations, attested as true and correct by the secretary of said board of embalmers, shall be presumptive evidence of the regular making, adoption and approval thereof. The said board may investigate all alleged violations of the statutes relating to embalming and undertaking, and of all rules and regulations adopted as provided in this section. It may revoke any license upon proof that the same was procured by fraud or that the holder thereof has been guilty of a violation of any of such statutes or rules and regulations.

§ 293
amended.

§ 3. Section two hundred and ninety-three of said chapter is hereby amended to read as follows:

§ 293. **Application for license and examination.** Every person desiring to engage· in the business or practice of embalming, within the state of New York,[5] shall make a written application to the said board of embalming examiners for an examination for an[6] embalmer's license, accompanying the same with the application fee of five dollars, and with a certificate of some reputable person, that said applicant is more than twenty-one years of age, is of good moral character, and has obtained a common school education, whereupon the secretary of said board of embalming examiners shall issue to said applicant a permit to enter any examination held pursuant to the provisions of this article. At the close of every such examination, the questions submitted and the answers made thereto by the applicant, shall be forthwith delivered, by the examiner conducting such examination, to the board of embalming examiners, who shall, without unnecessary delay, transmit to the state board of health an official report thereon, signed by its president and secretary, stating in detail the result of the examination of each candidate. Such report shall embrace all the examination papers, questions and answers

---

[4] Words "and undertaking" new.
[5] Words "and not already engaged therein," omitted.
[6] Words "examination for an," new.

thereto, and shall be kept for reference and inspection among the
public records of the state board of health.

§ 4. Section two hundred and ninety-four of said chapter is § 294,
hereby amended to read as follows: amended.

§ 294. **Duty of state board of health concerning reports of
examination.** On receiving such official reports of the examination of applicants for license, the state board of health shall
examine and verify the same, and thereupon recommend for license
by the board of embalming examiners, those applicants who shall,
in their judgment, be duly qualified to practice embalming of
human dead bodies in the state of New York, upon said applicant
paying to the secretary of the board of embalming examiners an
examining and licensing fee of ten dollars. Said license, when
issued, shall be recorded by the board of embalming examiners,
and such record shall be open to public inspection.[7]

§ 5. Section two hundred and ninety-five of said chapter as § 295, as
amended by chapter eight hundred and forty-one of the laws of L. 1911,
nineteen hundred and eleven, is hereby amended to read as ch. 841,
follows:[8]   amended.

§ 295. **License to practice as undertaker.** Any person who, at
the time this section as hereby amended takes effect, shall be
actually engaged in the business of undertaking and who desires
to continue in such business shall, on or before December thirty-
first, nineteen hundred thirteen, file with the board of embalming
examiners a verified written application for authority to do business as an undertaker, stating therein the fact of his having been
so engaged in business and accompanying the same with the payment of a fee of five dollars, and said board shall thereupon issue
to said applicant a license to do business as an undertaker. Every
undertaker, who shall take into his employ an apprentice shall
report to the board of embalming examiners within three months
thereafter that fact together with such further information as
the board may by regulation require for registration. The board
shall issue to such apprentice, when his character and qualifications are satisfactory, a certificate of registration as a " registered
apprentice." The fee for such registration shall be one dollar.
An application for a license to do business as an undertaker shall
contain the name, residence and place of business of the applicant, and a statement of the times and places where he has been

---

[7] Remainder of section which provided for admission in evidence of a certified copy of such license, registration of person licensed with local board
of health, and display of license at place of business, omitted.
[8] Section materially amended.

employed as an apprentice to an undertaker, accompanied with
such proof, by affidavit or otherwise, as the board may require
showing that the applicant had served as an apprentice to an
undertaker for at least two years in the aggregate; but the application above provided for shall not be required of a person actually engaged in the business of undertaking at the time this amendment takes effect. Satisfactory proof of practical experience with
an undertaker for said period, or any portion thereof prior to the
passage of this act, may be accepted by said board in lieu of the
certificate herein provided. After June first, nineteen hundred
and fifteen no candidate shall be eligible, to enter such examinations, unless his certificate of registration shall have been filed as
herein provided. An application fee of five dollars shall accompany the application. The secretary of the board shall issue to
the applicant a permit to enter any examination for the license
provided for in this section. Upon the applicant's passing a satisfactory examination in sanitation, disinfection, preparation and
care of human dead bodies for burial or transportation, the board
shall issue to said applicant, on payment of a further fee of five dollars, a license to engage in the business of undertaking. If a firm
or corporation shall desire to engage in the business or practice of
undertaking at least one member of such firm and the manager of
each place of business conducted by a corporation shall be a
licensed undertaker; and no member of a firm whose duties
engage him in the care, preparation, disposal and burial of dead
human bodies shall discharge the duties of his employment unless
he shall be licensed in accordance with the provisions of this
article. Nor shall an undertaker firm or corporation permit an
assistant who is not a duly licensed undertaker or embalmer or
registered apprentice to assume the care or preparation for burial
or transportation of the body of any person who has died of a
communicable disease. No person shall practice or hold himself
out as an undertaker unless he has complied with the provisions
of this section or with chapter four hundred and ninety-eight of
the laws of nineteen hundred and four, as amended by chapter
five hundred and seventy-two of the laws of nineteen hundred and
five, or by chapter eight hundred and forty-one of the laws of
nineteen hundred and eleven.

§ 296
amended.

    § 6. Section two hundred and ninety-six of this chapter is hereby
amended to read as follows:[8]

---

8 Section materially amended.

§ 296. **Reciprocal licenses; license not assignable.** Any holder of a license issued by state authority in any other state maintaining a system and standard of examination for licenses to engage in the business of undertaking, or of the practice of embalming which in the judgment of the board shall be substantially equivalent to those required in this state for the issue of licenses therefor, may obtain a license from the board under the provisions of this article without examination, in the discretion of the board, upon payment of the application and license fees provided for herein. A copy of any license issued by said board or of any rules, regulations, applications or other records or files of said board duly certified as correct by the secretary of the board of embalming examiners shall be entitled to be admitted in evidence in any of the courts of this state, and shall be presumptive evidence as to the facts therein contained. Every person licensed pursuant to the provisions of this article shall register that fact in the office of the board of health of the city, town or place in which it is proposed to carry on said business, and shall display such license in a conspicuous place in the office or place of business of such licensee. No license granted or issued by said board shall be assignable, and every such license shall specify by name the person to whom it shall be issued, and not more than one person shall practice embalming under one license. This section shall not apply to any personal representative of any deceased undertaker to whom a license shall have been issued under this article, who engages in the business of undertaking and embalming with a person duly authorized to practice the same under the provisions of this article.

§ 7. This act shall take effect immediately.

Chap. 72.

AN ACT to amend the town law, in relation to the establishment
and maintenance of sewer systems outside of incorporated cities
and villages.

Became a law March 11, 1913, with the approval of the Governor. Passed,
three-fifths being present.

*The People of the State of New York, represented in Senate
and Assembly, do enact as follows:*

§§ 246-248
added to
L. 1909,
ch. 62.
     Section 1. Chapter sixty-three of the laws of nineteen hun-
dred and nine, entitled "An act relating to towns, constituting
chapter sixty-two of the consolidated laws," is hereby amended
by inserting after section two hundred forty-five, three new
sections to be known as sections two hundred forty-six, two hundred forty-seven, and two hundred forty-eight, to read as follows:
     § 246. Constructing laterals in such districts. The board of
sewer commissioners may in any town where a sewer district has
been laid out and established as hereinbefore set forth, construct
one or more laterals upon one or more streets within the sewer
district as established, from time to time, entirely at the expense
of the owners of the land fronting on said street, streets or portions thereof whereupon said lateral or laterals are constructed
provided a petition therefor be presented to the board of sewer
commissioners signed by at least a majority of the owners of
real property fronting on said street, streets or portions thereof
whereupon it is proposed to lay and construct said lateral or
laterals. The board of sewer commissioners shall upon the receipt of a petition as aforesaid give a public hearing thereon to
all persons interested on a notice of at least ten days, which
notice shall specify the time and place said hearing shall be held
and shall be served upon the owners of the land fronting upon
said street, streets or portions thereof set forth and described in
said petition by mailing the same to their last known respective
addresses or by publishing the same once each week for two
weeks in a newspaper which circulates in said district, or by
either or any of said methods. If the board of sewer commissioners shall act favorably upon said petition, they shall by
resolution direct that suitable plans be prepared, showing the
location of such lateral or laterals and such street, streets or
portions thereof it is proposed to sewer thereby, giving the

dimensions of the pipes proposed to be laid, the location of the manholes and flush tanks, and showing where the same are to be connected with the sewer system within said district, and if there be a lateral or portion thereof upon such street, streets or portions thereof, said commissioners are hereby given power and authority to repair or enlarge the same so as to conform as near as possible with the lateral to be constructed.

§ 247. **Contracts for construction of laterals.** The board of sewer commissioners may employ a suitable engineer to make a survey and prepare the plans referred to in section two hundred forty-six, and after the same has been prepared and adopted by the board of sewer commissioners they may cause specifications to be made, and to advertise for bids to construct such lateral, laterals or portions thereof referred to in such petition, and to do all things necessary in connection therewith, and to award a contract for the construction thereof to the lowest bidder, or they may reject any and all bids and readvertise.

§ 248. **Improvements; how paid for.** After the board of sewer commissioners have received the bids, they must ascertain the total cost of constructing said laterals including the fees of the engineer and inspectors. They shall then report to the town board of the town wherein said sewer system is located, to which report there shall be attached a copy of the plans and specifications for such improvement and tabulated statement of the bids received, showing the lowest bid and the estimated cost of the improvement as determined by the sewer commissioners, which shall be filed in the office of the clerk of said town, and the town board shall direct the issue and sale of bonds for the aggregate amount of the cost of said improvement as provided in section two hundred and forty-three[1] of this act, and the principal and interest on said bonds shall be apportioned upon the property fronting upon said street, streets or portion thereof referred to and mentioned in said petition in the same manner as the original cost of constructing the sewer system is directed to be apportioned upon the property within the district, and the sewer commissioners shall have the same control and make the same rules and regulations in connection with the lateral, laterals or portions thereof so constructed as they may enforce from time to time in reference to the sewer system within said district, and the cost of maintaining the same shall become a part of maintaining the

---

[1] As added by L. 1910, ch. 134.

5

entire sewer system and be apportioned in the same manner.
After the money is obtained for the construction of said lateral,
laterals or portions thereof, the commissioners shall then enter
into a contract for the construction of the same, which contract
shall be entered into in the same manner as the contract referred
to in reference to the construction of the entire system.

§ 2. This act shall take effect immediately.

Chap. 73.

AN ACT to amend the town law, in relation to the establishment
and maintenance of sewer systems outside of incorporated cities
and villages.

Became a law March 11, 1913, with the approval of the Governor. Passed,
three-fifths being present.

*The People of the State of New York, represented in Senate
and Assembly, do enact as follows:*

L. 1909,
ch. 63,
§ 236
amended.

Section 1. Section two hundred and thirty-six of chapter sixty-
three of the laws of nineteen hundred and nine, entitled "An
act relating to towns, constituting chapter sixty-two of the consolidated laws," is hereby amended to read as follows:

§ 236. **Acquisition of property by condemnation.** If sewer
commissioners are unable to agree with the owners for the purchase of real property necessary for the construction of the sewer
system, they may acquire the same by condemnation, [1]whether it
be necessary to acquire the fee or an easement for a right of way
therein, and whether the property and easements necessary to be
acquired are within the territorial limits of the sewer district
as established; said sewer commissioners may enter into an agreement with the board of trustees or other duly authorized officers
of an adjoining incorporated village, to sewer some part or portion of such incorporated village, and to lay and maintain pipes
therein, and when pipes are laid and maintained, and sewer system constructed within the limits of an adjoining incorporated
village pursuant to an agreement so made, the sewer commissioners shall have the same control and exercise the same rights and
privileges in connection with the system constructed within the

---

[1] Remainder of section new.

limits of an incorporated village as they have in connection with
the system established within the sewer district as laid out.

§ 2. This act shall take effect immediately.

Chap. 74.

AN ACT to legalize certain acts and proceedings of the town of
Harrison, its officers, agents and taxpayers, in the county of
Westchester, relating to the establishment of a sewer district
for such town and to the sale and issuance of its bonds therefor,
and the acts and proceedings of the village of Rye in said county
and of the conservation commission in connection therewith,
and to provide for the payment of such bonds.

Became a law March 11, 1913, with the approval of the Governor. Passed,
three-fifths being present.

*The People of the State of New York, represented in Senate
and Assembly, do enact as follows:*

Section 1. All acts and proceedings of the town of Harrison, in
the county of Westchester, done and performed by its taxpayers,
town board, officers, agents and sewer commissioners, leading up
to and including the issuance and proposed sale of its bonds in the
aggregate amount of two hundred and thirty thousand dollars, for
the establishment and construction of a sewer system in and for
a section of said town, in accordance with maps, plans and specifications therefor, approved by the commissioner of health of the
state of New York, and the several acts of the board of health of
the village of Rye, state conservation commission in connection
therewith, and the act of the sewer commissioners of the town of
Harrison in locating the disposal plant and certain pipe lines used
in connection with said sewer system outside of the established
district and within the incorporated limits of the village of Rye,
are hereby in all things ratified and confirmed, notwithstanding
any defect or irregularity, or omissions of any lawful requirement in such acts and proceedings or the action of such sewer commissioners in establishing said disposal plant and pipe lines, as
aforesaid.

§ 2. All, and each, of said bonds so issued consisting of four
hundred and sixty registered bonds of the denomination of five
hundred dollars each, numbered one to four hundred and sixty

inclusive, dated January first, nineteen hundred and thirteen, payable five bonds of five hundred dollars each on the first day of January, nineteen hundred and fourteen, and five bonds of five hundred dollars each on the first day of January in each succeeding year thereafter up to and including the first day of January, twenty hundred and five, the principal and interest on said bonds to be payable at the Rye National Bank, in New York exchange, the interest thereon to be the lowest rate obtainable, not to exceed five per centum per annum, which interest is to be payable semi-annually on the first day of July and January of each year, until the principal sum thereof is fully paid, said bonds to be signed by the supervisor of the town of Harrison and attested by the town clerk of said town, who shall affix the town seal thereto, are hereby declared to be valid and legal obligations of the town of Harrison, **Sale and delivery directed.** and the supervisor of said town of Harrison is hereby authorized and directed to sell said bonds, and to deliver the same to the purchaser thereof, his assignee, nominee, successor, or successors, upon the receipt of the amount for which said bonds are sold, which sum is to be not less than par and accrued interest.

Tax for payment § 3. The board of supervisors of the county of Westchester are hereby authorized and directed to annually levy such sum or sums against the property within said town liable to pay the same, and in the manner prescribed by law a sum or sums sufficient to pay principal and interest on said bonds as the same shall become due.

§ 4. This act shall take effect immediately.

Chap. 75.

AN ACT reappropriating the unexpended balance of the appropriation heretofore made to the New York interstate bridge commission, and making an additional appropriation therefor.

Became a law March 11, 1913, with the approval of the Governor. Passed by a two-thirds vote.

The People of the State of New York, represented in Senate and Assembly, do enact as follows:

Reappropriation. Section 1. The sum of twelve thousand seven hundred and two and eighty-one one-hundredths dollars ($12,702.81), being the unexpended balance of the appropriation of seventeen thousand three hundred and six and eight one-hundredths dollars

($17,306.08) made to the New York interstate bridge commission by chapter one hundred and forty-eight of the laws of one thousand nine hundred and eleven, is hereby reappropriated and made available, and in addition thereto, the sum of twelve thousand four hundred dollars ($12,400), or so much thereof as may be necessary, is hereby appropriated out of any moneys in the treasury not otherwise appropriated, for the purpose of contributing an equal proportionate share of the expense of borings and general engineering, and to provide for the share of the expenses of said commission in co-operating with the New Jersey interstate bridge and tunnel commission of the state of New Jersey. The amount so appropriated shall be payable by the state treasurer on the warrant of the comptroller on itemized vouchers certified by the chairman of the New York interstate bridge commission.

§ 2. This act shall take effect immediately.

Chap. 76.

AN ACT to amend the code of civil procedure, relating to the place of trial of actions to recover damages for injuries to real estate situated without the state.

Became a law March 13, 1913, with the approval of the Governor. Passed, three-fifths being present.

The People of the State of New York, represented in Senate and Assembly, do enact as follows:

Section 1. Article two of title one of chapter ten of the code of civil procedure is hereby amended by adding thereto a new section, to be section nine hundred and eighty-two-a, to read as follows:

§ 982-a. **Actions relating to real property situate without the state.** An action may be maintained in the courts of this state to recover damages for injuries to real estate situate without the state, or for breach of contracts or of covenants relating thereto, whenever such an action could be maintained in relation to personal property without the state. The action must be tried in the county in which the parties or some one thereof resides, or if no party resides within the state, in any county.

§ 2. This act shall take effect September first, nineteen hundred and thirteen.

Chap. 77.

AN ACT authorizing the city of Elmira to issue bonds for paving
purposes.

Became a law March 13, 1913, with the approval of the Governor. Passed,
three-fifths being present.

Accepted by the City.

*The People of the State of New York, represented in Senate
and Assembly, do enact as follows:*

Issuance
of bonds
authorized.
Section 1. The city of Elmira is hereby authorized and empowered, by resolution of its common council duly adopted, to
cause the bonds of said city in a sum not exceeding two hundred
thousand dollars, to be known as " pavement bonds " to be issued
and sold. Such bonds shall be signed by the mayor and city clerk,

Bonds,
execution,
denomina-
tions, etc.
and sealed with the seal of said city. They shall be of such denominations, and shall mature at such times as the said common
council shall determine; and shall bear interest at a rate not exceeding four and one-half per centum per annum, payable semi-
annually. They shall be sold at not less than par value.

Record of
bonds.
§ 2. The chamberlain of said city shall make and keep in his
office a record of said bonds by number, date, amount, date or
dates of maturity, and the name of payee or names of payees, if

Disposition
of proceeds.
registered. The money therefrom shall be paid to the city chamberlain and by him placed to the credit of the pavement and sidewalk fund as created by the charter of said city, and shall be used
and expended by and under the direction of the board of public
works of said city in paying the city's share of the cost of construction or improvement of city streets as state and county highways under sections one hundred and thirty-seven[1] and one hundred and thirty-eight[2] of the highway law, which streets form connecting links between highways heretofore improved by state aid
and city streets which have been paved or improved; and for any
and all of the purposes specified in chapter four hundred and
seventy-seven of the laws of nineteen hundred and six, entitled
" An act to revise the charter of the city of Elmira," as amended,
known as the charter of the city of Elmira, for which said pave-

Application
of city
charter.
ment and sidewalk fund may be used. All regulations and provisions of said chapter four hundred and seventy-seven of the laws

[1] As amended by L. 1910, ch. 233, L. 1911, ch. 88, and L. 1912, ch. 88.
[2] As amended by L. 1911, ch. 88, and L. 1912, ch. 88.

of nineteen hundred and six, entitled "An act to revise the charter of the city of Elmira," as amended, relative to the liability of
adjacent property owners, street surface railways, and the city, for
their respective shares of the cost of said work, and the payment,
assessment, collection and expenditure of the money of said pavement and sidewalk fund, in so far as applicable shall apply to the
avails of said bonds, as forming a part of said fund.

§ 3. The city of Elmira is hereby authorized to raise by tax, in Tax for payment.
addition to all other sums now authorized by law, whatever sums
may be necessary to pay the interest of said bonds, and the principal at the times of maturity.

§ 4. This act shall take effect immediately.

Chap. 78.

AN ACT to repeal chapter five hundred and sixty-five of the laws
of nineteen hundred and ten, entitled "An act to authorize the
town board and the superintendent of highways of the town of
Wales, in the county of Erie, to cancel the assessment for the
improvement of the Big Tree road in said town of Wales and
to refund all moneys heretofore paid upon said rolls."

Became a law March 13, 1913, with the approval of the Governor. Passed,
three-fifths being present.

*The People of the State of New York, represented in Senate
and Assembly, do enact as follows:*

Section 1. Chapter five hundred and sixty-five of the laws of L. 1910,
nineteen hundred and ten, entitled "An act to authorize the town ch. 565 repealed.
board and the superintendent of highways of the town of Wales,
in the county of Erie, to cancel the assessment for the improvement of the Big Tree road in said town of Wales and to refund
all moneys heretofore paid upon said rolls," is hereby repealed,
but such repeal shall not affect any action taken by the town board Saving clause.
or superintendent of highways under such act or any action or
proceeding now pending in any court.

§ 2. This act shall take effect immediately.

Chap. 79.

AN ACT to provide for existing deficit in funds available for support of the military establishment of the state and making an appropriation therefor.

Became a law March 13, 1913, with the approval of the Governor. Passed, three-fifths being present.

The People of the State of New York, represented in Senate and Assembly, do enact as follows:

Section 1. The sum of one hundred and seventy-five thousand dollars ($175,000), or so much thereof as may be necessary, is hereby appropriated out of any money in the treasury not otherwise appropriated, to be used by the adjutant-general of the state for necessary general expenses of the land and naval forces of the state.

§ 2. This act shall take effect immediately.

Chap. 80.

AN ACT to amend the highway law, generally.[1]

Became a law March 14, 1913, with the approval of the Governor. Passed, three-fifths being present.

The People of the State of New York, represented in Senate and Assembly, do enact as follows:

L. 1909, ch. 30, § 2, as amended by L. 1911, ch. 646, and L. 1912, ch. 83, amended.

Section 1. Section two of chapter thirty of the laws of nineteen hundred and nine, entitled "An act relating to highways, constituting chapter twenty-five of the consolidated laws," as amended by chapter six hundred and forty-six of the laws of nineteen hundred and eleven and chapter eighty-three of the laws of nineteen hundred and twelve, is hereby amended to read as follows:

§ 2. **Definitions.** 1. The term "department," when used in this chapter, shall mean the department of highways, as constituted herein.

2. The terms "commission," "highway commission," and "state highway commission," when so used, shall each mean the state commission of highways. The term "state superintendent of highways," when so used, shall mean the commissioner of

---

[1] The amendments effected by this chapter are so numerous and extensive that it is impracticable to indicate the changes made.

highways, and reference to powers and duties of the state superintendent of highways to be exercised subject to the commission shall mean the exercise of such powers and duties by the commissioner of highways without the concurrence of any other commission or officer.

3. The term " district superintendent " or " county superintendent," when so used, shall mean the district superintendent of highways or county superintendent of highways, respectively.

4. The term " town superintendent," when so used, shall mean the town superintendent of highways.

5. A highway within the provisions of this chapter shall be deemed to include necessary culverts, sluices, drains, ditches, waterways, embankments, retaining walls and all bridges having a span of five feet or less.

§ 2. Section eleven of such chapter, as amended by chapter six hundred and forty-six of the laws of nineteen hundred and eleven, is hereby amended to read as follows: § 11. as amended by L. 1911, ch. 646, amended.

§ 11. State commission of highways; commissioner of highways. The state commission of highways is continued. Such commission shall consist of a single commissioner, to be known as the commissioner of highways, who shall be the head of the department of highways. Such commissioner shall be appointed by the governor by and with the advice and consent of the senate for a term of five years. He shall devote all of his time to the duties of his office. The governor may remove such commissioner for inefficiency, neglect of duty or misconduct in office. A copy of the charges against him shall be served upon such superintendent and he shall have an opportunity of being publicly heard in person or by counsel in his own defense upon not less than a ten days' notice. If such commissioner shall be removed, the governor shall file in the office of the secretary of state a complete statement of all charges made against such commissioner and his findings thereon, together with a complete record of the proceedings. The commissioner of highways shall receive an annual salary to be fixed by the governor of not exceeding ten thousand dollars. Wherever by the terms of this chapter or other statute, action by the commission is required to be taken by resolution or in any manner by the concurrence of the members *of a majority, such action shall, when the commission consists of a single commissioner, be taken by a formal order of such commissioner entered in the records of the department of highways.

---

* So in original.

§ 12, as
amended by
L. 1911,
ch. 646,
amended. § 3. Section twelve of such chapter, as amended by chapter six hundred and forty-six of the laws of nineteen hundred and eleven, is hereby amended to read as follows:

§ 12. **Oath of office; undertaking.** The commissioner of highways shall, before entering upon the duties of his office, take and subscribe the constitutional oath of office and execute an undertaking in the sum of twenty-five thousand dollars, to be approved by and filed with the comptroller and renewed as often as the governor may require. Such undertaking shall be to the effect that he will faithfully discharge the duties of his office and promptly account for and pay over all moneys or property received by him as such commissioner of highways in accordance with law, or in default thereof that the parties executing such undertaking will pay all damages, costs and expenses resulting from such default.

New § 14
added. § 4. Such chapter is hereby amended by inserting therein, in place of section fourteen hereinafter renumbered, a new section fourteen, to read as follows:

§ 14. **Deputy commissioners, secretary and chief auditor of the department.** The commissioner of highways shall appoint a secretary and chief auditor of the department and three deputy commissioners. Each of the deputy commissioners shall have had practical experience in actual building, construction and maintenance of highways and be familiar with the operation and effect of state statutes relating to highways and bridges. One of such deputies shall be a practical civil engineer, to be known as the first deputy, and his duties shall relate to the plans, specifications and execution of all contracts pertaining to state and county highways; one of such deputies shall be known as the second deputy, and his duties shall relate to the maintenance of state and county highways; one of such deputies shall be known as the third deputy and his duties shall relate to the repair, improvement and maintenance of town highways and bridges, and county roads and roads and bridges on the Indian reservations. The first deputy shall receive an annual salary of six thousand dollars. The second and third deputies and the secretary shall each receive an annual salary of five thousand dollars. The chief auditor shall receive an annual salary of five thousand dollars. Each deputy, the secretary and the chief auditor shall before entering upon the duties of his office each take and subscribe the constitutional oath of office. Each deputy, the secretary and the chief auditor shall each execute an undertaking in

the sum of five thousand dollars, to be approved by and filed with
the comptroller and renewed as often as the commissioner of highways may require. The commissioner of highways, by order filed
in the office of the department, may at any time designate a
deputy to sign on behalf of the commission such papers and
documents as are specified in such order. The chief auditor shall
determine the authorization for and the accuracy of every expenditure of state funds for highway purposes and his report thereon,
after approval by the commissioner of highways, shall be transmitted to the comptroller for final audit. Each deputy, the secretary and the chief auditor shall have such other and further duties
as the commissioner of highways may determine, and shall each
be subject to his direction and control and may be removed by
him.

§ 5. Section fifteen of such chapter is hereby amended to read § 15
as follows: amended.

§ 15. General powers and duties of the commissioner of highways.
The commissioner of highways shall

1. Have general supervision of all highways and bridges which
are constructed, improved or maintained in whole or in part by
the aid of state moneys.

2. Prescribe rules and regulations not inconsistent with law,
fixing the duties of division engineers, resident engineers, district,
county and town superintendents in respect to all highways and
bridges and determining the method of the construction, improvement or maintenance of such highways and bridges. Such rules
and regulations shall, before taking effect, be printed and transmitted to the highway officers affected thereby.

3. Compel the compliance with laws, rules and regulations relating to such highways and bridges by highway officers and see
that the same are carried into full force and effect.   .

4. Aid district, county and town superintendents in establishing
grades, preparing suitable systems of drainage and advise with
them as to the construction, improvement and maintenance of
highways and bridges.

5. Cause plans, specifications and estimates to be prepared for
the repair and improvement of highways and the construction
and repair of bridges, when requested so to do by a district,
county or town superintendent.

6. Investigate and determine upon the various methods of road
construction adapted to different sections of the state, and as to

the best methods of construction and maintenance of highways and bridges.

7. Make an annual report to the legislature on or before February fifteenth, stating the condition of the highways and bridges, the progress of the improvement and maintenance of state, county and town highways, the amount of moneys received and expended during the year upon highways and bridges and in the administration of his office, and also containing such matters as in his judgment should be brought to the attention of the legislature, together with recommendations as to such measures in relation to highways as in his judgment the public interests require.

8. Compile statistics relating to the public highways throughout the state, and collect such information in regard thereto as he shall deem expedient.

9. Cause public meetings to be held at least once each year, in each district or county, for the purpose of furnishing such general information and instruction as may be necessary, regarding the construction, improvement or maintenance of the highways and bridges and the application of the highway law, and the rules and regulations of the department, and also for the purpose of hearing complaints. He shall notify the district or county superintendent of his intention to hold such meeting or meetings, specifying the date and the place thereof.

10. Aid at all times in promoting highway improvement throughout the state, and perform such other duties and have such other powers in respect to highways and bridges as may be imposed or conferred on him by law.

11. Approve and determine the final plans, specifications and estimates for state and county highways upon the receipt of the report and recommendations of the county or district superintendent, as provided herein, and transmit the same in the case of a county highway to the board of supervisors. After the approval of such plans, specifications and estimates by the board of supervisors and the return thereof to the commissioner of highways, in the case of a county highway and after his final determination in respect thereto in the case of a state highway, the commissioner of highways shall cause a contract to be let for the construction or improvement of such state or county highway after due advertisement.

12. Prepare tables showing the total number of miles of high-

ways in the state, by town and county, and file a copy of the same
in the office of the comptroller.

13. Divide the state into not more than nine divisions and assign a division engineer to the charge of each, subject to his direction, supervision and control. In making such division no county
shall be divided.

14. Make and file with the comptroller a schedule of salaries
of all officers, clerks, employees, engineers and superintendents,
appointed by him, whose salaries are not fixed by law.

15. Inquire into the official conduct of all subordinates of the
department.

16. Direct and cause to be made such repairs of state and
county highways as he deems necessary, within the estimates and
appropriations made therefor.

§ 6. Sections sixteen and seventeen of such chapter, as amended
by chapter six hundred and forty-six of the laws of nineteen hundred and eleven, are hereby amended to read, respectively, as
follows:

§ 16. **Division engineers.** The commissioner of highways shall
appoint a division engineer for each of the divisions of the state.
Each person so appointed as a division engineer shall be a practical
civil engineer having had actual experience in the construction and
maintenance of highways and bridges. The salary of such engineers shall be four thousand dollars per annum. An office may
be maintained by such division engineers at a convenient place
within each division as authorized by the commissioner of highways. The salary and expenses of such engineers shall be paid
out of moneys appropriated therefor upon the requisition of the
commissioner of highways. Each division engineer shall, before
entering upon the duties of his office, take and subscribe the constitutional oath of office and execute an official undertaking in
the sum of ten thousand dollars to be approved by and filed with
the comptroller and renewed as often as the commissioner of
highways may require. The commissioner of highways, subject
to the provisions of the civil service law, may remove such division
engineers.

§ 17. **Duties of division engineers.** Each division engineer shall
devote his entire time to the performance of his duties. He
shall, under the direction and control of the commissioner of
highways:

1. Make or cause to be made all surveys, maps, plans, specifica-

tions and estimates necessary or required for the improvement, construction and maintenance of state and county highways within the division for which he is appointed.

2. Examine, revise and approve all plans, specifications and estimates and proposals for the improvement, construction, and maintenance of highways and bridges within his division, which may be submitted by the commissioner of highways, pursuant to the provisions of this chapter, or the rules and regulations of such commissioner.

3. Examine and inspect, or cause to be examined and inspected, the work performed on any highways, and report to the commissioner of highways as to whether the work has been done in accordance with the plans and specifications and contracts made therefor.

4. Approve and certify to the monthly estimates or allowances for work being performed under any contract let for the construction, improvement or maintenance of state and county highways.

5. Inspect, or cause to be inspected, all state and county highways, and report from time to time in respect thereto, when required by the commissioner of highways.

6. Consult with district, county and town superintendents and other highway officers in respect to the proper methods of constructing, improving and maintaining highways and bridges.

7. Perform such other duties as may be prescribed by the commissioner of highways.

8. Have charge of the construction, reconstruction, maintenance and repair of state and county highways in his division, under the supervision of the deputy having jurisdiction thereof.

§ 14, as amended by L. 1911, ch. 646, renumbered § 18, and amended. § 7. Section fourteen of such chapter, as amended by chapter six hundred and forty-six of the laws of nineteen hundred and eleven, is hereby renumbered section eighteen, inserted in place of present section eighteen hereinafter renumbered, and amended to read as follows:

§ 18. Salaries and expenses. All engineers, superintendents, clerks, officers and other employees of the department shall receive the compensation fixed by the commissioner of highways except as otherwise defined and established in this chapter. In the discharge of their official duties the commissioner of highways, deputies, secretary, engineers, and the clerks, officers and other employees of the department shall have reimbursed to them their necessary traveling expenses and disbursements. Such salaries and expenses shall be paid by the state treasurer upon the warrant of the comptroller, out of moneys appropriated therefor in the same manner as the salaries and expenses of other officers, clerks and employees are paid.

§ 8. Such chapter is hereby amended by inserting therein, in place of section nineteen hereinafter renumbered, a new section nineteen, to read as follows: New § 19 added.

§ 19. **Appointment of officers, clerks and employees.** The commissioner of highways shall appoint such resident engineers, district superintendents, clerks, officers and employees as may be required to carry out the provisions of this chapter, subject to the civil service laws and the provisions of this chapter, within the amount appropriated therefor, unless the appointment of such clerks, officers or employees is otherwise provided for herein. District superintendents, appointed as provided in this chapter, shall be appointed from lists prepared from examinations which shall test their qualifications for the actual construction and maintenance of highways and their executive capacity, rather than their scientific attainments. Clerks, other than those employed in the principal office of the commissioner of highways, inspectors and other employees in the department whose duties pertain to the maintenance of highways, shall likewise be selected from lists prepared from examinations testing their general knowledge of the highway law and of the practical construction of highways. Inspectors of construction, other than engineers and levelers, shall be selected from lists similarly prepared, except that they shall be residents of the county within which the highway constructed or improved is located. To the end that the employees of the department of highways engaged in the work of constructing, improving or maintaining highways under the provisions of this chapter may be practical highway builders, the commissioner of highways is authorized to indicate to the civil service commission the relative value which should be given to experience and scientific attainments. The commissioner of highways. subject to the provisions of the civil service law, may remove the resident engineers, district superintendents, clerks, officers and employees of the department.

§ 9. Section eighteen of such chapter is hereby renumbered section twenty, inserted in place of present section twenty hereinafter renumbered, and amended to read as follows: § 18 renumbered § 20. and amended.

§ 20. **Blank forms and town accounts.** The commissioner of highways shall prescribe and furnish blank forms of orders, reports and accounts and blank books, whenever in his judgment they are required for the convenience of his office and of highway officers.

§ 10. Section nineteen of such chapter is hereby renumbered section twenty-one, inserted in place of present section twenty-one hereinafter renumbered, and amended to read as follows:

§ 21. **Examination of accounts and records.** The commissioner of highways may, at such times as may be deemed expedient, cause an examination of all accounts and records kept as required by this chapter, and it shall be the duty of all county and town officers to produce all such records and accounts for examination and inspection, at any time on demand of a representative of the commissioner of highways.

§ 11. Section twenty of such chapter is hereby renumbered section twenty-two, inserted in place of present section twenty-two hereinafter renumbered, and amended to read as follows:

§ 22. **Condemnation of bridges.** The commissioner of highways shall cause an inspection to be made of any bridge which is reported to be unsafe for public use and travel by the district or county superintendent, the town superintendent, or five residents of the town. If such bridge is found to be unsafe for public use and travel the commissioner of highways shall condemn such bridge, and notify the district or county superintendent, the town superintendent and the supervisor of the town, of that fact. The district or county superintendent shall either prepare or approve plans, specifications and estimates for the construction or repair of such bridge without delay. The town shall provide for the construction or reconstruction of such bridge, as provided for by section ninety-three of this chapter.

§ 12. Section twenty-one of such chapter, as amended by chapter eighty-three of the laws of nineteen hundred and twelve, is hereby renumbered section twenty-three, inserted at the end of article two, after section twenty-two and amended to read as follows:

§ 23. **Estimate of cost of maintenance of state and county highways.** The commissioner of highways shall annually cause to be inspected all improved state and county highways, either by the division engineer, or the district or county superintendent of the district or county in which such highways are situated and shall require a complete report of such inspection

Marginal notes:

§ 19 renumbered § 21, and amended.

§ 20 renumbered § 22, and amended.

§ 21, as amended by L. 1912, ch 83, renumbered § 23 and amended.

which shall show in detail the condition of the highway inspected, the necessary work to be performed in the repair and maintenance of such highways, and the estimated cost thereof. The commissioner of highways shall revise said estimates and annually report to the legislature his estimated cost of such repair and maintenance for the ensuing year, as so revised, in detail by counties.

§ 13. Section twenty-two of such chapter is hereby renumbered section twenty-four, inserted at the end of article two, after section twenty-three, and amended to read as follows:

§ 24. **Rules and regulations for state and county highways.** The commissioner of highways is hereby empowered to make rules and regulations from time to time for the protection of any state or county highway or section thereof. He may prescribe the width of tires to be used on such highways and he may prohibit the use of chains or armored tires by motor vehicles upon such highways, and any disobedience thereof shall be punishable by a fine of not less than ten dollars and not exceeding one hundred dollars, to be prosecuted for by the town, county or district superintendent and paid to the county treasurer to the credit of the fund for the maintenance of such highways in the town where such fine is collected.

§ 14. Such chapter is hereby amended by adding at the end of article two thereof a new section to be section twenty-five and to read as follows:

§ 25. **Patented material or articles.** In the construction, maintenance or repair of state or county highways, no patented material or article or any other material or article shall be specified, contracted for or purchased, except under such circumstances that there can be fair and reasonable opportunity for competition, the conditions to secure which shall be prescribed by the commissioner of highways.

§ 15. Section fifty-three-a of such chapter, as added by chapter five hundred and sixty-seven of the laws of nineteen hundred and ten, is hereby amended to read as follows:

§ 53-a. **Temporary obstruction of highways.** The necessary obstruction of a highway by the removal of buildings or other temporary obstruction shall only be allowed if a highway other than a state or county highway under a permit granted by the county superintendent upon the written request of the town superintendent, and if a state or county highway under a permit granted by the commissioner of highways.

§ 22 renumbered § 24. and amended.

§ 25 added.

§ 53a, as added by L. 1910. ch· 567, amended.

§ 146, as
amended by
L. 1911,
ch. 646,
amended.
§ 16. Section one hundred and forty-six of such chapter, as amended by chapter six hundred and forty-six of the laws of nineteen hundred and eleven, is hereby amended to read as follows:

§ 146. **Railroads and other works and structures in and upon highways.** No street surface or other railroad shall be constructed upon any portion of a state or county highway which has been or may be improved under the provisions of this article, nor shall any person, firm or corporation enter upon or construct any works in or upon any such highway, or construct any overhead or underground crossing thereof, or lay or maintain therein drainage, sewer or water pipes underground, except under such conditions and regulations as may be prescribed by the commissioner of highways, notwithstanding any consent or franchise granted by any town, county or district superintendent, or by the municipal authorities of any town. Any person, firm or corporation violating this section shall be liable to a fine of not less than one *hundrede dollars nor more than one thousand dollars for each day of such violation, to be recovered by the commissioner of highways and paid to the state treasurer to the credit of the fund for the maintenance and repair of state and county highways, and may also be removed therefrom as a trespasser by the commissioner of highways upon petition to the county court of the county or the supreme court of the state.

§ 170, as
amended by
L. 1911,
ch. 646, and
L. 1912,
ch. 83,
amended.
§ 17. Section one hundred and seventy of such chapter, as amended by chapter six hundred and forty-six of the laws of nineteen hundred and eleven and chapter eighty-three of the laws of nineteen hundred and twelve, is hereby amended to read as follows:

§ 170. **Commission to provide for maintenance and repair.** The maintenance and repair of improved state and county highways in towns, incorporated villages and cities of the third class. exclusive, however, of the cost of maintaining and repairing bridges having a span of five feet or over, shall be under the direct supervision and control of the commissioner of highways and he shall be responsible therefor. Such maintenance and repair may be done in the discretion of the commissioner either directly by the department of *highway or by contract awarded to the lowest responsible bidder at a public letting after due advertisement, and under such rules and regulations as the commissioner of highways may prescribe. The commissioner of highways

* So in original.

shall also have the power to adopt such system as may seem expedient so that each section of such highways, shall be under constant observation, and be effectively and economically preserved, maintained and repaired. The commissioner of highways shall have the power to purchase materials for such maintenance and repairs, except where such work is done by contract, and contract for the delivery thereof at convenient intervals along such highways.

§ 18. The state commission of highways shall continue as now constituted until the appointment and qualification of the commissioner of highways, pursuant to the highway law as hereby amended, and thereupon the term of office of the state superintendent of highways shall expire, and the superintendent of public works and state engineer shall cease to be members of such commission and all their powers and duties in respect to highways shall terminate; and thereupon the state commission of highways as constituted in pursuance of the highway law as amended by this act shall be deemed and held to constitute a continuation of the state commission of highways as now constituted and not as a new commission for the purpose of succession to all the rights, powers, duties and obligations of the state commission of highways as now constituted, except as modified by this act, with the same force and effect as if such modifications were made without any change in the membership of the present commission; and the present commission as now constituted, and the commission to be constituted in pursuance of the highway law as amended by this act, shall be deemed and held to be one continuing commission notwithstanding the changes in the membership thereof. The division engineers in office when this act takes effect shall continue in office as six of the division engineers, in pursuance of the highway law as hereby amended, in charge of the divisions to which they may be respectively assigned by the commissioner of highways. This act shall make no changes in any of the civil service positions under the highway law, and the present deputies, division engineers, resident engineers, division superintendents, clerks, officers and employees of the state commission of highways, shall continue in their respective offices and employments until the appointment and qualification of their successors in pursuance of the highway law as amended by this act, and in pursuance of the civil service law.

§ 19. This act shall take effect immediately.

Chap. 81.

AN ACT to amend the insurance law, in relation to the capital of title, credit guaranty and securities guaranty corporations.

Became a law March 15, 1913, with the approval of the Governor. Passed, three-fifths being present.

The People of the State of New York, represented in Senate and Assembly, do enact as follows:

L. 1909,
ch. 33,
§ 170, as
amended by
L. 1909,
ch. 302, and
L. 1911,
ch. 525,
amended.

Section 1. Section one hundred and seventy of chapter thirty-three of the laws of nineteen hundred and nine, entitled "An act in relation to insurance corporations, constituting chapter twenty-eight of the consolidated laws," as amended by chapter three hundred and two of the laws of nineteen hundred and nine and chapter five hundred and twenty-five of the laws of nineteen hundred and. eleven, is hereby amended to read as follows:[1]

§ 170. **Incorporation.** Five or more persons may form a corporation for one of the following purposes:

1. To examine titles to real property and chattels real, to procure and furnish information in relation thereto, make and guarantee the correctness of searches for all instruments, liens or charges affecting the same, guarantee or insure the payment of bonds and mortgages,. invest in, purchase and sell, with such guarantee or with guarantee only against loss by reason of defective title or incumbrances, such bonds and mortgages as are lawful investments for insurance companies under this act, and guarantee and insure the owners of real property and chattels real and others interested therein against the loss by reason of defective titles thereto and other incumbrances thereon, which shall be known as a title guarantee corporation; or

1-a. To guarantee the validity and legality of bonds or other evidences of indebtedness issued by any state or by any city, county, town, village, school district, municipality or other civil division of any state, or by any private or public corporation; to act as registrar or transfer agent, but not fiscal of any such corporation, and to transfer and countersign its certificates of stocks, bonds or other evidences of indebtedness. Such corporation shall be known as a securities guaranty corporation and shall be gov-

---

[1] Section 170 is further amended by L. 1913, ch. 215, post. The amendments here effected are incorporated in such section as amended by said ch. 215.

erned by and subject to the provisions of law applicable to a title guaranty corporation organized under this article; or

2. To guarantee and indemnify merchants, traders and those engaged in business and giving credit from loss and damage by reason of giving and extending credit to their customers, and those dealing with them, which shall be known as a credit guaranty corporation; by making, acknowledging and filing a certificate stating:

1. The name of the proposed corporation.
2. The kind of corporation to be formed and its purposes.
3. The amount and description of the capital stock.
4. The location of its office.
5. The duration of the corporation, not exceeding fifty years.

No credit guaranty corporation or securities guaranty corporation[2] shall be formed for the transaction of business in this state, with a smaller capital than two[3] hundred and fifty thousand dollars. No title guaranty corporation shall be formed with a smaller capital than one hundred and fifty thousand dollars,[4] which shall be divided into shares of one hundred dollars each. Such certificate shall be filed in the office of the superintendent of insurance, who shall thereupon issue a license to the persons making such certificate, empowering them as commissioners to open books of subscription to the capital stock of the corporation at such times and places as they may determine.

§ 2. This act shall take effect immediately.

Chap. 82.

AN ACT to amend the labor law, in relation to cleanliness of workrooms in factories.

Became a law March 15, 1913, with the approval of the Governor. Passed, three-fifths being present.

The People of the State of New York, represented in Senate and Assembly, do enact as follows:

Section 1. Section eighty-four of chapter thirty-six of the L. 1909, ch. 36, laws of nineteen hundred and nine, entitled "An act relating to § 84, as amended

---

[2] Words " or securities guaranty corporation," new.
[3] Formerly "one."
[4] Words " or with a larger capital than ten million dollars," omitted.

by L. 1910,
ch. 114.
amended. labor, constituting chapter thirty-one of the consolidated laws,"
as amended by chapter one hundred and fourteen of the laws of
nineteen hundred and ten, is hereby amended to read as follows:[1]

§ 84. **Cleanliness of rooms.** Every room in a factory and the
floors, walls, ceilings, windows and every other part thereof and
all fixtures therein shall at all times be kept in a clean and sanitary
condition. The walls and ceilings of each room in a factory shall
be lime washed or painted, except when properly tiled or covered
with slate or marble with a finished surface. Such lime wash or
paint shall be renewed whenever necessary as may be required by
the commissioner of labor. Floors shall, at all times, be maintained in a safe condition. No person shall spit or ex ectorate
upon the walls, floors or stairs of any building used in whole or
in part for factory purposes. Sanitary cuspidors shall be provided, in every workroom in a factory in sufficient numbers. Such
cuspidors shall be thoroughly cleaned daily. Suitable receptacles
shall be provided and used for the storage of waste and refuse;
such receptacles shall be maintained in a sanitary condition.

In effect
Oct. 1,
1913. § 2. This act shall take effect October first, nineteen hundred
and thirteen.

Chap. 83.

AN ACT to amend the labor law, in relation to protecting the
health and morals of females employed in factories by providing an adequate period of rest at night.[2]

Became a law March 15, 1913, with the approval of the Governor. Passed,
three-fifths being present.

*The People of the State of New York, represented in Senate
and Assembly, do enact as follows:*

§ 93b
added to
L. 1909,
ch. 36. Section 1. Chapter thirty-six of the laws of nineteen hundred
and nine, entitled "An act relating to labor, being chapter thirty-
one of the consolidated laws," is hereby amended by inserting
therein, after section ninety-three-a, a new section, to be section
ninety-three-b, to read as follows:

§ 93-b. **Period of rest at night for women.** In order to protect
the health and morals of females employed in factories by providing an adequate period of rest at night no woman shall be em-

---

[1] Section materially amended.
[2] See People v. Williams, 189 N. Y. 131.

ployed or permitted to work in any factory in this state before
six o'clock in the morning or after ten o'clock in the evening of
any day.

§ 2. This act shall take effect July first, nineteen hundred In effect
and thirteen.   July 1,
    1913.

Chap. 84.

AN ACT making an appropriation for the expenses incident to
the proceeding entitled "The People of the State of New York,
ex rel. Mary C. Thaw, against John W. Russell, medical
superintendent of Matteawan State Hospital."

Became a law March 15, 1913, with the approval of the Governor. Passed,
three-fifths being present.

*The People of the State of New York, represented in Senate
and Assembly, do enact as follows:*

Section 1. The sum of eighteen thousand, seven hundred and
sixty-five dollars and eighty-eight cents ($18,765.88), or so much
thereof as may be necessary, is hereby appropriated out of any
money in the treasury, not otherwise appropriated, for the payment of counsel, investigators, printing, expert witnesses and
other expenses incurred in behalf of the state of New York incident
to the proceeding entitled "The People of the State of New York,
ex rel. Mary C. Thaw, against John W. Russell, medical
superintendent of Matteawan State Hospital," the hearings of
which were held at New Rochelle and White Plains, in nineteen
hundred and twelve. The money hereby appropriated shall be
payable by the treasurer, upon the audit and warrant of the
comptroller, on vouchers approved by the attorney-general.

§ 2. This act shall take effect immediately.

Chap. 85.

AN ACT to amend the code of civil procedure, in relation to undertakings.

Became a law March 19, 1913, with the approval of the Governor. Passed, three-fifths being present.

The People of the State of New York, represented in Senate and Assembly, do enact as follows:

§ 813a added.

Section 1. After section eight hundred and thirteen of the code of civil procedure there shall be inserted a new section to be numbered eight hundred and thirteen-a and to be as follows:

§ 813-a. **Further protection for undertakings in certain cases.** Where an undertaking has been or shall be given in any action or proceeding the court may in its discretion, if justice so requires, order further or other security to be given in addition to such security. Upon cause shown the court may permit an examination or re-examination of any surety upon any such undertaking. Upon such examination or re-examination, if justice so requires, the court may require a new surety or sureties to be furnished or further or other security to be given in addition to the security already given. The court may enforce such order by any disposition of the action or proceeding that may be proper.

In effect Sept. 1, 1913.

§ 2. This act shall take effect September first, nineteen hundred and thirteen.

Chap. 86.

AN ACT to amend the code of civil procedure, in relation to discovery of books and papers by photographing the same.

Became a law March 19, 1913, with the approval of the Governor. Passed, three-fifths being present.

The People of the State of New York, represented in Senate and Assembly, do enact as follows:

§ 803 amended.

Section 1. Section eight hundred and three of the code of civil procedure is hereby amended to read as follows:

§ 803. **The court may direct discovery of books, et cetera.** A court of record, other than a justices' court in a city, has power to compel a party to an action pending therein, to produce and discover, or to give to the other party, an inspection and copy, or permission to take a copy or photograph[1] of a book, document, or other paper, or to make discovery of any article or property, in his possession or under his control, relating to the merits of the action, or of the defense therein.

§ 2. This act shall take effect September first, nineteen hundred and thirteen.

In effect Sept. 1, 1913.

Chap. 87.

AN ACT to amend chapter four hundred and fifty-two of the laws of nineteen hundred and eight, entitled "An act to supplement the general laws relating to the government of the city of Yonkers, and to revise and consolidate the local laws relating thereto," in relation to pensions for certain retired employees of such city.

Became a law March 19, 1913, with the approval of the Governor. Passed, three-fifths being present.

Accepted by the City.

The People of the State of New York, represented in Senate and Assembly, do enact as follows:

Section 1. Section one of article three of chapter four hundred and fifty-two of the laws of nineteen hundred and eight, entitled "An act to supplement the general laws relating to the government of the city of Yonkers, and to revise and consolidate the local laws relating thereto," is hereby amended by adding thereto, at the end thereof, a new subdivision, to be subdivision forty, to read as follows:

Subd. 40 added to L. 1908, ch. 452, art. 3, § 1.

40. To provide for the retirement from active service of any officer, clerk or employee of the city who shall have been in the employ of the city in one or more capacities continuously for the period of fifty years and upwards and to cause an annual pension to be paid to such retired officer, clerk or employee during his life in a sum equal to one-half of the rate of compensation received by him during the year in which he shall be retired as aforesaid; such pension to be paid from moneys to be levied and raised by the common council each year in the manner prescribed by law. In determining that such service has been continuous

Common council authorized to retire and pension certain employees.

---

[1] Words "or photograph" new.

for said period of fifty years, no change in the title, duty or
salary or any promotion, vacation, leave of absence, temporary
disability by reason of sickness or accident or any transfer from
one department or office to another or any change of any board,
bureau or department in which the service shall have been performed shall affect the continuity of such service; but this subdivision shall not apply to a person who is or may be entitled to
share in the police or fireman's pension fund of the city or in any
other similar retirement or relief fund.

§ 2. This act shall take effect immediately.

Chap. 88.

AN ACT to amend the lien law, in relation to service of copy
of notice.

Became a law March 20, 1913, with the approval of the Governor. Passed,
three-fifths being present.

*The People of the State of New York, represented in Senate
and Assembly, do enact as follows:*

L. 1909, ch.
38. § 11
amended.
Section 1. Section eleven of chapter thirty-eight of the laws
of nineteen hundred and nine, entitled "An act in relation to
liens, constituting chapter thirty-three of the consolidated laws,"
is hereby amended to read as follows:

§ 11. **Service of copy of notice.** At any time after filing the
notice of lien, the lienor may serve a copy of such notice upon
the owner, if a natural person,[1] by delivering the same to him
personally, or if the owner cannot be found, to his agent or attorney, or by leaving it as his last known place of residence in
the city or town in which the real property or some part thereof
is situated, with a person of suitable age and discretion, or by
registered letter addressed to his last known place of residence,
or, if such owner has no such residence in such city or town,
or can not be found, and he has no agent or attorney, by affixing
a copy thereof conspicuously on such property, between the hours
of nine o'clock in the forenoon and four o'clock in the afternoon;
[2]if the owner be a corporation, said service shall be made by delivering such copy to and leaving the same with the president,

---

[1] Words " if a natural person." new.
[2] Remainder of sentence new.

vice-president, secretary or clerk to the corporation, the cashier, treasurer or a director or managing agent thereof, personally, within the state, or if such officer cannot be found within the state by affixing a copy thereof conspicuously on such property between the hours of nine o'clock in the forenoon and four o'clock in the afternoon, or by registered letter addressed to its last known place of business. Until service of the notice has been made, as above provided, an owner, without knowledge of the lien, shall be protected in any payment made in good faith to any contractor or other person claiming a lien. A failure to serve the notice does not otherwise affect the validity of such lien.

§ 2. This act shall take effect immediately.

Chap. 89.

AN ACT to authorize the village of Peekskill, in Westchester county, to widen Washington street in said village between Hudson avenue and South street, to acquire title to the land necessary for such widening, and to issue bonds for said purpose.

Became a law March 20, 1913, with the approval of the Governor. Passed, three-fifths being present.

The People of the State of New York, represented in Senate and Assembly, do enact as follows:

Section 1. The board of trustees of the village of Peekskill is hereby authorized and empowered by resolution of its body, to submit to the electors of such village at a special election, called and held in the same manner as an annual village election in such village a proposition to issue and sell bonds in the name of, in behalf of and upon the credit of the said village, in an amount not exceeding the sum of forty thousand dollars for the purpose of paying the expense of widening and improving Washington street in said village between Hudson avenue and South street. If such proposition be adopted by a majority vote of the electors voting thereon, the board of trustees may cause such bonds to be issued accordingly and the proceeds of said bonds shall be used by said board of trustees to pay the expense incurred in connection with, growing out of or arising from the widening and improving of said street as aforesaid, and to acquire title to any property along said portion of Washington street, which the board of trustees of said village shall determine to be expedient, judicious or advantageous to the village for such purpose.

Bonds, execution, denomination, etc.
§ 2. Said bonds shall be issued in the name and under the seal of said village, signed by the president and treasurer thereof and attested by the village clerk, and shall be for the sum of one thousand dollars each. Said bonds shall become due fifty years from the date of issue, and shall bear such rate of interest as the board of trustees may determine, not exceeding five per centum per annum, payable semi-annually, and shall be negotiated for not **Sale.** less than their par value. They shall be sold on sealed proposals to the bidder who will take them at the lowest rate of interest, upon notice duly published in each of the newspapers printed and published in such village and in such other newspapers or manner as the board of trustees may determine, but such board shall reserve the right to reject any and all bids. They **How numbered and denominated. To cite this act.** shall be consecutively numbered from one to the highest number issued and shall be known as "street improvement bonds," and they shall contain a recital that they are issued pursuant to and in conformity with the provisions of this act. The board of trustees shall keep a record of the number of each bond, its date, the amount, rate of interest, when and where payable, and the purchaser thereof, or the person to whom they are issued, or in whose name registered.

Tax for payment.
§ 3. The board of trustees of said village shall raise by annual tax in the same manner as other village taxes are raised, an amount sufficient to pay the interest on such bonds, and the principal thereof, as they become due.

Condemnation proceedings authorized.
§ 4. The board of trustees of said village, if unable to agree with the owners for the purchase of the real property necessary for the widening and improving of said Washington street as contemplated by this act, may acquire title thereto by condemnation pursuant to the provisions of the condemnation law.[1]

§ 5. This act shall take effect immediately.

---

[1] See code of civil procedure, §§ 3357-3384.

Chap. 90.

AN ACT to amend chapter six hundred and seventy-six of the
laws of nineteen hundred and seven, entitled "An act to authorize the extension of Riverside park, in the city of New York,
by filling in certain land under water so as to permit the construction therein of a water gate and monument to Robert
Fulton, the inventor of steam navigation, by the corporation
known as The Robert Fulton Monument Association of the
City of New York," generally.

**Became a law March 20, 1913, with the approval of the Governor. Passed,
three-fifths being present.**

Accepted by the City.

*The People of the State of New York, represented in Senate
and Assembly, do enact as follows:*

Section 1. Sections one and two of chapter six hundred and _{*omitted*} L. 1907,
seventy-six of the laws of nineteen hundred and seven, entitled ch. 676,
"An act to authorize the extension of Riverside park in the city §§ 1, 2 amended.
of New York by filling in certain land under water so as to
permit the construction therein of a water gate and monument
to Robert Fulton, the inventor of steam navigation, by the corporation known as The Robert Fulton Monument Association
of the City of New York," are hereby amended to read as follows:

§ 1. The city of New York is hereby authorized to fill in and Improve-
improve all or any part of the land under water and upland front- certain land
ing upon Riverside park, in the city of New York, bounded south- under water
erly by a line fifty feet south of the southerly line of One Hundred land, au-
and Ninth street,[1] if extended westerly; northerly by a line fifty thorized.
feet north of the northerly line of One Hundred and Eleventh
street,[2] if extended westerly; easterly by the westerly line of the
route or roadway of the Hudson River Railroad Company, as laid
down upon the map of said route or roadway filed in the office of
the register of the city and county of New York on or about the
second day of September, eighteen hundred and forty-seven; and
westerly by the pierhead harbor line now established or that may

---

[1] Words "a line fifty feet south of the southerly line of One Hundred and
Ninth street," substituted for words "the northerly line of One Hundred and
Fourteenth street."

[2] Words "a line fifty feet north of the northerly line of One Hundred and
Eleventh street," substituted for words "the northerly line of One Hundred
and Sixteenth Street."

hereafter be established by the secretary of war of the United
States; provided, however, that no such filling in or improvement
shall be made under authority of this act, except in pursuance
of an agreement to be entered into as hereinafter provided.

§ 2. The board of estimate and apportionment of the city of
New York is hereby authorized and empowered in its discretion
at any time or times after the passage of this act to enter into an
agreement or agreements with the corporation known as the
Robert Fulton Monument Association of the City of New York
in reference to the filling in and improvement of the land under
water and upland within the limits specified in the first section of
this act, and the land so filled in and improved shall constitute a
part of or an extension of Riverside park. Such agreement or
agreements shall fix and define the boundaries of the proposed
extension and shall provide in what manner and by whom the
same shall be constructed and improved, and how it shall be connected with that portion of Riverside park which lies east of the
said route or roadway of the Hudson River Railroad Company,
and what alterations and improvements, if any, shall be made in
the last mentioned portion of Riverside park. In case the said
The Robert Fulton Monument Association of the City of New
York shall agree to assume the expense of constructing the said
extension and of improving the same, then the said agreement or
agreements may provide, subject to such conditions and upon such
terms as the said board of estimate and apportionment shall in its
discretion think proper, that any portion or portions of Riverside
park lying west of the said route or roadway of the Hudson
River Railroad Company may be set apart as a water gate and
basin for boat landing for public use, to be known as The Robert
Fulton Water Gate, and for the erection and maintenance of a
suitable monument to Robert Fulton, the inventor of steam navigation, whose first steamboat, the " Clermont," built in the city of
New York, made the first steam voyage up the Hudson from New
York to Albany in August, eighteen hundred and seven, and to
other distinguished Americans.[1] The said agreement or agreements shall provide that all work to be done thereunder shall be
subject to the jurisdiction and control of the department of parks
of the city of New York and shall define how and to what extent
such jurisdiction and control are to be exercised.

§ 2. This act shall take effect immediately.

―――――――――――――――――――――――

[1] Words " and to other distinguished Americans," new.

Chap. 91.

AN ACT to amend the public health law, in relation to the state institute for the study of malignant disease.

Became a law March 20, 1913, with the approval of the Governor. Passed, three-fifths being present.

The People of the State of New York, represented in Senate and Assembly, do enact as follows:

Section 1. Section three hundred and forty-six of chapter forty-nine of the laws of nineteen hundred and nine, entitled "An act in relation to the public health, constituting chapter forty-five of the consolidated laws," as added by chapter one hundred and twenty-eight of the laws of nineteen hundred and eleven, is hereby amended to read as follows:

§ 346. **Objects and purposes of the institute; gifts to institute in aid thereof.**[1] The institute shall conduct investigations into the cause, nature, mortality rate, treatment, prevention and cure of cancer and allied diseases, and may receive in its hospital for study, experimental or other treatment, cases of cancer and allied diseases free of charge. It shall publish from time to time the results of its investigations for the benefit of humanity and shall from time to time collect its publications into the form of a scientific report for distribution to scientific bodies and to medical scientists and qualified members of the medical profession. The direction of research work in whole or in part toward malignant diseases other than cancer shall not be a violation of the conditions of the grants made under the provisions of which this article is a part. [2]The institute may receive gifts, legacies and bequests, and use the same in such manner as the board of trustees may determine for the advancement of its objects and purposes.

§ 2. This act shall take effect immediately.

Marginal notes: L. 1909, ch. 49, § 346, as added by L. 1911, ch. 128, amended

---

[1] Words "gifts to institute in aid thereof," new.
[2] Following sentence new.

Chap. 92.

AN ACT to amend the insurance law, in relation to capital requirements.

Became a law March 21, 1913, with the approval of the Governor. Passed, three-fifths being present.

The People of the State of New York, represented in Senate and Assembly, do enact as follows:

L. 1909,
ch. 33,
§ 12, as
amended
by L. 1910,
ch. 634,
amended.

Section 1. Section twelve of chapter thirty-three of the laws of nineteen hundred and nine, entitled "An act in relation to insurance corporations, constituting chapter twenty-eight of the consolidated laws," as amended by chapter six hundred and thirty-four of the laws of nineteen hundred and ten, is hereby amended to read as follows:

§ 12. **Minimum capital stock.** No domestic fire or marine stock insurance corporation shall be hereafter organized with a smaller capital stock than two hundred thousand dollars fully paid in in cash, but nothing in this section contained shall be understood to relate to the class of corporations provided for in articles nine or ten of this chapter.

[1]A domestic stock insurance corporation, having the power to transact the kind of insurance business described in subdivisions one, two, five, six, seven, eight, nine and ten of section seventy of this chapter shall not be hereafter organized with a smaller capital stock than one hundred thousand dollars fully paid in in cash. [2]A domestic stock insurance corporation having the power to transact any kind of insurance business described in subdivisions three or four of section seventy of this chapter shall not be hereafter organized with a smaller capital stock than two hundred and fifty thousand dollars fully paid in in cash if authorized to transact any kind of insurance business described in one of such subdivisions or a smaller capital stock than five hundred thousand dollars fully paid in in cash if authorized to transact the kinds of insurance business described in both such subdivisions. [2]Except as to the requirements of a minimum capital stock for the transaction of the kinds of insurance business described in subdivisions three or four of section seventy of this chapter every domestic stock insurance corporation hereafter organized having power to

---

1 Following sentence materially amended.
2 Following sentence new.

transact business under more than one subdivision of such section shall, in addition to the minimum capital stock prescribed in this section, have an additional capital stock of fifty thousand dollars fully paid in in cash, for every kind of insurance business more than one which it is authorized to transact. Any corporation to which this section is applicable shall also, at the time of its organization, have a surplus equal to fifty per centum of its capital stock, which surplus shall also be fully paid in in cash; provided that this requirement shall not apply to existing corporations reincorporated.

§ 2. This act shall take effect immediately.

Chap. 93.

AN ACT to amend chapter seven of the laws of nineteen hundred and four, entitled "An act to revise, amend and consolidate the several acts relating to the village of Norwich, and to repeal certain acts and parts of acts," in relation to lighting contracts in such village and payments thereon.

Became a law March 21, 1913, with the approval of the Governor. Passed, three-fifths being present.

The People of the State of New York, represented in Senate and Assembly, do enact as follows:

Section 1. Section nine of title six of chapter seven of the laws of nineteen hundred and four, entitled "An act to revise, amend and consolidate the several acts relating to the village of Norwich, and to repeal certain acts and parts of acts," is hereby amended to read as follows:

§ 9. Neither the board of trustees nor any officer of the village shall have the power to make any contract or incur any debt or obligation against the village or impose any liability upon the village for any purpose [1]in excess of the money raised under sections one and two of title seven of this act nor beyond the end of the fiscal year in which such contract shall be made or such debt or liability incurred, except that such board of trustees may make contracts for lighting the streets, alleys and public places of the village for terms of not exceeding five years and provide by gen-

[margin notes: L. 1904, ch. 7, tit. 6, § 9 amended. Liabilities in excess of moneys raised for specific purposes not to be incurred; exceptions.]

---

1 Words "beyond the end of the fiscal year in which such contract shall be made or such debt or liability incurred, nor," omitted.

6

eral tax annually for paying the sums maturing thereon during the year;[2] nor shall said trustees or any officer of the village make any contract or incur or create any obligation, debt or liability against the village beyond or in excess of the money raised for the specific purpose which includes such debt, obligation or liability; and any such contract or obligation shall be void; except that the trustees may make such a contract or incur such debt or obligation or impose such liability as shall have been authorized by a resolution duly published, submitted and adopted at an annual or special meeting as provided by section two of title seven of this act.

§ 2. This act shall take effect immediately.

Chap. 94.

AN ACT to amend the banking law, in relation to removal of trustees of savings banks.

Became a law March 21, 1913, with the approval of the Governor. Passed, three-fifths being present.

The People of the State of New York, represented in Senate and Assembly, do enact as follows:

§ 140a added to L. 1909, ch. 10.

Section 1. Chapter ten of the laws of nineteen hundred nine, entitled "An act in relation to banks, individual bankers and corporations under the supervision of the banking department, constituting chapter two of the consolidated laws," is hereby amended by adding thereto, after section one hundred and forty, a new section, to be section one hundred and forty-a thereof, to read as follows:

§ 140-a. **Removals.** Whenever the conduct and habits of a trustee of any savings bank are, in the judgment of three-fourths of the trustees of such savings bank, of such a character as to be injurious to such savings bank, or he has been, in the judgment of three-fourths of the trustees of such savings bank, guilty of acts that are detrimental or hostile to the interests of such savings bank, he may be removed from office, at any regular meeting of the trustees of such savings bank, by the affirmative vote of three-fourths of the total number of trustees thereof, provided, however,

---

[2] Words " nor beyond the end of the fiscal year ... during the year," new.

that a written copy of the charges made against such trustee shall have been served upon him personally at least two weeks before such meeting, that the vote of such trustees by ayes and nays shall be entered in the record of the minutes of such meeting, and that such removal shall receive the written approval of the superintendent of banks, which may be given or withheld, in his discretion, which approval, if given, shall be attached to the minutes of such meeting and form a part of the record. When the written approval of the superintendent of banks has been received and attached to such record, the office of such trustee shall be vacant, and the trustees of such savings bank may proceed to fill the vacancy resulting from such removal.

§ 2. This act shall take effect immediately.

Chap. 95.

AN ACT to legalize and confirm the official acts of notaries public and commissioners of deeds.

Became a law March 22, 1913, with the approval of the Governor. Passed, three-fifths being present.

The People of the State of New York, represented in Senate and Assembly, do enact as follows:

Section 1. The official acts of every person as notary public or commissioner of deeds within the state of New York, heretofore commissioned as such, which acts have been performed since the twenty-sixth day of March, nineteen hundred and twelve[1] so far as such acts may be affected, impaired or questioned by reason of change of residence made after appointment, or by reason of misnomer or misspelling of name or other errors made in the appointment or commission of said notary public or commissioner of deeds, or by reason of omission or failure to take the prescribed oath of office within the time required by law,[2] or by reason of such persons being under the age of twenty-one years, or by reason of the expiration of the term of office of such notaries public or commissioners of deeds, where such notary public or commissioner of deeds has acted in good faith, upon payment being made by such notary public or commissioner of

Acts since March 26, 1912, notwithstanding certain irregularities, legalized.

---

[1] See L. 1912, ch. 78.
[2] See executive law (L. 1909, ch. 23), §§ 103, 106.

deeds of the legal fees for holding such office, are hereby legalized and confirmed and made effectual and valid, as the official acts of a notary public or commissioner of deeds legally qualified to perform the same, as fully as if neither of the various errors, omissions, matters and conditions hereinabove enumerated had occurred or existed.

Pending actions. § 2. Nothing in this act contained shall affect any legal action or proceeding pending at the time this act takes effect.

§ 3. This act shall take effect immediately.

Chap. 96.

AN ACT to amend the general business law, in relation to pressing and marketing hay and straw.

Became a law March 22, 1913, with the approval of the Governor. Passed, three-fifths being present.

The People of the State of New York, represented in Senate and Assembly, do enact as follows:

L. 1909, ch. 25, art. 15, title amended. Section 1. The title of article fifteen of chapter twenty-five of the laws of nineteen hundred and nine, entitled "An act relating to general business, constituting chapter twenty of the consolidated laws," is hereby amended to read as follows:

HOPS, HAY AND STRAW.[1]

§ 253 amended. § 2. Section two hundred and fifty-three of such chapter is hereby amended to read as follows:[2]

§ 253. **Presser of hay and straw defined; correct scales to be used; bales to be marked.** The term "presser" as used in this and the following sections of this article shall mean the person, firm, association or corporation owning or having possession and operating the hay press. A presser who presses hay or straw for market shall use correct scales, properly sealed. Every presser of hay or straw for market shall mark each bale of any of such commodities pressed by him with his name and business address and the correct weight of the bale. These markings shall be made upon

[1] Formerly read: "Hops and Hay."
[2] Section materially amended.

a tag, securely fastened to the bale, of not less than one and one-half inches in width and three inches in length.

A person violating this section shall forfeit to the people of the state the sum of five dollars for each such violation.

§ 3. This act shall take effect July first, nineteen hundred and thirteen. <small>In effect July 1, 1913.</small>

Chap. 97.

AN ACT to amend chapter seventy-five of the laws of nineteen hundred and ten, entitled "An act authorizing and empowering the city of Mount Vernon to acquire lands for a site and to improve the same, or a site already possessed, and to erect a municipal building or buildings thereon, and to issue bonds for the purpose of purchasing or otherwise acquiring, improving and erecting the same," in relation to the amount of such bonds.

Became a law March 22, 1913, with the approval of the Governor. Passed, three-fifths being present.

Accepted by the City.

The People of the State of New York, represented in Senate and Assembly, do enact as follows:

Section 1. Section one of chapter seventy-five of the laws of nineteen hundred and ten, entitled "An act authorizing and empowering the city of Mount Vernon to acquire lands for a site and to improve the same, or a site already possessed, and to erect a municipal building or buildings thereon, and to issue bonds for the purpose of purchasing or otherwise acquiring, improving and erecting the same," is hereby amended so as to read as follows: <small>L. 1910, ch. 75, § 1 amended.</small>

§ 1. The common council of the city of Mount Vernon is hereby authorized and empowered to borrow upon the faith and credit of the said city of Mount Vernon by the issuing of bonds of said city, such sum or sums, not exceeding in the aggregate four hundred and twenty-five thousand[1] dollars, as may in its judgment be necessary for the purpose of purchasing lands in said city for a site and of improving the same, or of improving lands already possessed by the said city, and erecting upon any site so purchased or possessed such municipal building or buildings as the said common council may determine. <small>Bond issue for site and erection of municipal building, authorized.</small>

§ 2. This act shall take effect immediately.

---

[1] Formerly "two hundred thousand."

Chap. 98.

AN ACT to amend chapter eighty-seven of the laws of nineteen hundred and five, entitled "An act to authorize the city of Mount Vernon to borrow money by the issue of bonds, for the purpose of purchasing sites and erecting buildings for the use of the fire and police departments, and to provide a sinking fund to pay principal and interest of said bonds," in relation to the amount of such bonds.

Became a law March 22, 1913, with the approval of the Governor. Passed, three-fifths being present.

Accepted by the City.

The People of the State of New York, represented in Senate and Assembly, do enact as follows:

L. 1905, ch. 87, § 1, as amended by L. 1910, ch. 390, and L. 1912, ch. 132, amended.

Section 1. Section one of chapter eighty-seven of the laws of nineteen hundred and five, entitled "An act to authorize the city of Mount Vernon to borrow money by the issue of bonds, for the purpose of purchasing sites and erecting buildings for the use of the fire and police departments, and to provide a sinking fund to pay principal and interest of said bonds," as amended by chapter three hundred and ninety of the laws of nineteen hundred and ten, and as amended by chapter one hundred and thirty-two of the laws of nineteen hundred and twelve, is hereby amended so as to read as follows:

Bond issue authorized.

§ 1. The common council of the city of Mount Vernon is hereby authorized and empowered, by resolution of its body, to issue and sell bonds in the name, in behalf of and upon the credit of said city, in an amount not exceeding in the aggregate the sum of two hundred fifty thousand[1] dollars, par value, so far as the same may be determined advisable and necessary by said common council, for the purpose of purchasing sites and erecting suitable buildings for the use of the fire and police departments of said city[2] and for no other purpose.

§ 2. This act shall take effect immediately.

---

[1] Formerly "two hundred and twenty-five thousand."
[2] Words "and for the purpose of completing such buildings as have been heretofore partially erected but not completed," omitted.

Chap. 99.

AN ACT to amend section one hundred and fifty-eight of chapter one hundred and eighty-two of the laws of eighteen hundred and ninety-two, entitled "An act to incorporate the city of Mount Vernon," in relation to the annual meeting of the common council.

Became a law March 22, 1913, with the approval of the Governor. Passed, three-fifths being present.

Accepted by the City.

The People of the State of New York, represented in Senate and Assembly, do enact as follows:

Section 1. Section one hundred and fifty-eight of chapter one hundred and eighty-two of the laws of eighteen hundred and ninety-two, entitled "An act to incorporate the city of Mount Vernon," as amended by chapter three hundred and twenty-nine of the laws of nineteen hundred and one, is hereby amended so as to read as follows:

§ 158. The aldermen shall constitute the common council of the city.[1] It must hold its annual meeting on the first Tuesday in January in each year,[2] and stated meetings at least twice in each month. Special meetings may be called by the mayor or any three aldermen, by appointment in writing to be filed with the city clerk, and notice thereof shall be served as the common council shall by ordinance prescribe. The mayor when present, shall preside at all such meetings. At its annual meeting, or as soon thereafter as practicable, the common council shall elect by ballot one of the aldermen as president of the common council, who shall preside at its meetings when the mayor is absent, and shall possess the powers, perform the duties of, and act as mayor during vacancy in the office of mayor or while the mayor is absent from the city, or is unable to act. A vacancy in the office of president of the common council shall be filled by the common council by ballot. In the common council the president shall vote as an alderman only.

§ 2. This act shall take effect immediately.

---

[1] Sentence omitted which read: "It must meet on the day next after each annual city election."

[2] Words "first Tuesday in January in each year," substituted for words "Tuesday next after the annual city election,"

Chap. 100.

AN ACT to amend chapter four of the laws of eighteen hundred and ninety-one, entitled "An act to provide for rapid transit railways in cities of over one million inhabitants," in relation to exempted parts of the borough of Brooklyn, city of New York.

Became a law March 22, 1913, with the approval of the Governor. Passed, three-fifths being present.

Accepted by the City.

The People of the State of New York, represented in Senate and Assembly, do enact as follows:

L. 1891, ch.
4. § 4, as
amended
by L. 1894,
ch., 528, L.
1896, ch.
518, L.
1900, ch.
616, L.
1904, ch.
564, L.
1909, ch.
498, L.
1910, ch.
505, and
L. 1912,
ch. 226,
amended.
Section 1. Section four of chapter four of the laws of eighteen hundred and ninety-one, entitled "An act to provide for rapid transit railways in cities of over one million inhabitants," as amended by chapter four of the laws of eighteen hundred and ninety-one,[1] chapters five hundred and twenty-eight and seven hundred and fifty-two of the laws of eighteen hundred and ninety-four,[2] chapter five hundred and nineteen of the laws of eighteen hundred and ninety-five, chapter six hundred and sixteen of the laws of nineteen hundred, chapter five hundred and sixty-four of the laws of nineteen hundred and four, chapter four hundred and ninety-eight of the laws of nineteen hundred and nine, chapter five hundred and ten[3] of the laws of nineteen hundred and ten, and chapter two hundred and twenty-six of the laws of nineteen hundred and twelve, is hereby amended to read as follows:

§ 4. **Public service commission to determine necessity for railroads; routes; plan; consents; parks and streets excepted.**

1. The public service commission of the first district upon its own motion may proceed, from time to time, to consider and determine whether it is for the interest of the public and of a city having over one million of inhabitants, according to the last preceding national or state census, that a rapid transit railroad or railroads for the conveyance and transportation of persons and property should be established therein, and upon the request in writing of the local authorities of any such city at any time, the said commission shall proceed forthwith to consider and determine

---

[1] Inclusion of L. 1891, ch. 4, error.
[2] Section 4 was not, in fact, amended by L. 1894, ch. 752.
[3] Should read: " chapter five hundred and five."

the same questions, and in each case the said commission shall
conduct such an inquest and investigation as may be deemed
necessary in the premises. If, after any such consideration and
inquest, the said commission shall determine that a rapid transit
railroad or railroads, in addition to any already existing, authorized or proposed, are necessary for the interest of the public,
and such city, it shall proceed to determine and establish the route
or routes thereof and the general plan of construction. Such
general plan shall show the general mode of operation and contain such details as to manner of construction as may be necessary
to show the extent to which any street, avenue or other public
place is to be encroached upon and the property abutting thereon
affected. The commission, from time to time, may locate the
route or routes of such railroad or railroads over, under, upon,
through and across any streets, avenues, bridges, viaducts, rivers,
waters and lands within such city, including blocks between streets
or avenues, or partly over, under, upon, through and across any
streets, avenues, bridges, viaducts, and lands within such city and
partly through blocks between streets or avenues; provided that
the consent of the owners of one-half in value of the property
bounded on and the consent also of the local authorities having
control of that portion of a street, bridge, viaduct, or highway,
upon which it is proposed to construct or operate such railroad or
railroads be first obtained, or in case the consent of such property
owners cannot be obtained, that the determination of three commissioners appointed by the appellate division of the supreme
court in the department of the proposed construction, given after
due hearing of all parties interested, and confirmed by the court,
that such railroad or railroads ought to be constructed or operated,
be taken in lieu of the consent of such property owners; except
that no public park nor any lands or places, lawfully set apart
for, or occupied by, any public building of any city or county, or
of the state of New York, or of the United States, nor those portions of Grand, Classon, Franklin, Bedford[4] avenues and Downing
street in the borough of Brooklyn, city of New York, lying between
the southerly line of Lexington avenue and northerly line of Atlantic avenue, nor that portion of the borough of Brooklyn lying
between and circumscribed by the said avenues and streets exclusive of that portion of the streets and places in the foregoing
territory upon or through which elevated railroads are now in

4 Word " Bedford," new.

operation;[5] nor that portion of Classon avenue in said borough
lying between the northerly line of Lexington avenue and
southerly line of Park avenue, nor that portion of Washington avenue in said borough lying between Park and
Atlantic avenues, nor that portion of Nostrand avenue in
said borough lying northerly of the northerly line of Eastern
parkway, nor Debevoise place, Irving place and Lefferts place, Lee
avenue, Waverly avenue, Saint James place, Cambridge
place,[6] Vanderbilt avenue and Clinton avenue in said borough of Brooklyn, nor that portion of the city of Buffalo
lying between Michigan and Main streets, nor any part of Fifth
avenue, in the borough of Manhattan, city of New York, nor
that portion of any street or avenue which is now actually occupied
by any elevated railroad structure, shall be occupied by any corporation for the purpose of constructing a railroad in or upon any
of such public parks, lands or places, or upon or along either of
the said excepted streets or avenues. It shall be lawful for said
commissioners to locate the route of a railroad or railroads by
tunnel under any such public parks, lands, places, rivers or waters
and to locate the route of any railroad to be built, under this act,
across any of the streets and avenues now occupied by an elevated
railroad structure in the city of New York, or across any of the
streets or avenues excepted in this act at any point at which, in its
discretion, the public service commission may deem necessary in
the location of any route or routes, or under, or under and along,
any of the said streets or avenues now so occupied or so excepted
in this act. Nothing in this act shall authorize the construction
of an elevated railroad on Broadway south of Thirty-third street,
nor on Madison avenue in the borough of Manhattan, city of New
York. It shall not be lawful to grant, use or occupy, for the purposes of an elevated railroad, except for the purpose of crossing
the same, any portion of the following named streets and places
in the borough of Manhattan, city of New York, that is to say:
Second avenue, below Twenty-third street; Fourteenth street, between the easterly line or side of Seventh avenue, and the westerly
side of Fourth avenue; nor Eleventh street, west of Seventh
avenue, nor any part of Bank street; Nassau street; Printing

---

[5] Words " nor that portion of the borough of Brooklyn . . . now in operation," new.
[6] Words " Saint James place, Cambridge place," new.

House square, so called, south of Franklin street; Park row, south of Tryon row; Broad street and Wall street.

2. The provisions of the said section four of the said act shall, with reference to any rapid transit railroad for which routes and a general plan have been heretofore adopted by the board of rapid transit railroad commissioners of any city, and for the municipal construction of which a contract has been heretofore made by any city, be deemed to have been in full force as hereby amended from before the time when the routes and general plan for which such railroad or railroads were so adopted by the board of rapid transit railroad commissioners.

§ 2. This act shall take effect immediately.

Chap. 101.

AN ACT to amend the educational law, in relation to school-record certificates.

Became a law March 22, 1913, with the approval of the Governor. Passed, three-fifths being present.

The People of the State of New York, represented in Senate and Assembly, do enact as follows:

Section 1. Subdivision one of section six hundred and thirty of chapter twenty-one of the laws of nineteen hundred and nine, entitled "An act relating to education, constituting chapter sixteen of the consolidated laws," as amended by chapter one hundred and forty of the laws of nineteen hundred and ten, is hereby amended to read as follows:

1. A school-record certificate shall contain a statement certifying that a child has regularly attended the public schools, or schools equivalent thereto, or parochial schools, for not less than one hundred and thirty days during the twelve months next preceding his fourteenth birthday or during the twelve months next preceding his application for such school record, and that he is able to read and write simple sentences in the English language and has received during such period instruction in reading, writing, spelling, English grammar and geography and is familiar with the fundamental operations of arithmetic up to and including fractions, [1]and has completed the work prescribed for the first six

L. 1909, ch. 21, § 630, subd. 1, as generally amended by L. 1910, ch. 140, amended.

School-record certificate, contents.

---

[1] Remainder of sentence new.

years of the public elementary school, or school equivalent thereto, or parochial school, from which such school record is issued. Such record shall also give the date of birth and residence of the child, as shown on the school records, and the name of the child's parents, guardian or custodian.

In effect
Oct. 1,
1913.

§ 2. This act shall take effect October first, nineteen hundred and thirteen.

Chap. 102.

AN ACT to amend the penal law, relative to abstraction of or willful misapplication of money, funds or property, or misapplication of credit, of any corporation subject to the banking law, by an officer, director, trustee, employee or agent thereof.

Became a law March 22, 1913, with the approval of the Governor. Passed, three-fifths being present.

The People of the State of New York, represented in Senate and Assembly, do enact as follows:

§ 305
added to
L. 1909,
ch. 88.

Section 1. Article twenty-seven of chapter eighty-eight of the laws of nineteen hundred nine, entitled " An act providing for the punishment of crime, constituting chapter forty of the consolidated laws," is hereby amended by adding thereto a new section, to be section three hundred and five, and to read as follows:

§ 305. Abstraction or misappropriation of money, funds or property, or misapplication of credit of corporations to which the banking law is applicable, by an officer, director, trustee, employee or agent thereof. Any officer, director, trustee, employee or agent of any corporation to which the banking law is applicable, who abstracts or willfully misapplies any of the money, funds or property of such corporation, or willfully misapplies its credit, is guilty of a felony. Nothing in this section shall be deemed or construed to repeal, amend or impair any existing provision of law prescribing a punishment for any such offense.

In effect
Sept. 1,
1913.

§ 2. This act shall take effect September first, nineteen hundred and thirteen.

Chap. 103.

AN ACT to amend the banking law, in relation to closing a trust company.

Became a law March 22, 1913, with the approval of the Governor. Passed, three-fifths being present.

The People of the State of New York, represented in Senate and Assembly, do enact as follows:

Section 1. Article five of chapter ten of the laws of nineteen hundred and nine, entitled "An act in relation to banks, individual bankers and corporations under the supervision of the banking department, constituting chapter two of the consolidated laws," is hereby amended by adding thereto at the end of said article a new section, to be known as section one hundred and ninety-nine, to read as follows:

§ 199. **Proceedings on closing a trust company.** The stockholders of a trust company may at any time direct that it be closed for the purpose of winding up its affairs. Such direction may be given at a stockholders' meeting by a two-thirds vote of its stock after written notice by mail to each stockholder of record at his last known place of residence, which notice shall contain a statement of the purpose for which such meeting is called. A copy of the proceedings of the stockholders' meeting duly certified by the president and secretary of the trust company must be filed in the banking department. The supreme court shall thereupon in a proper case after due notice to the superintendent of banks, make an order declaring the business of said trust company closed, and prescribing the notice to be given to creditors to present their claims to the trust company for payment. A certified copy of such order shall thereupon be filed in the banking department. Upon the granting of said order said trust company shall cease to do a banking business but may wind up its affairs, pay its debts and distribute its assets among its stockholders. Upon a petition of the trust company showing that all its debts and obligations are discharged and on notice to the attorney-general and superintendent of banks, and such further notice as the court may prescribe, the court may on such terms as justice requires, make an order declaring the said trust company dissolved and the corporate existence thereof terminated.

On filing a certified copy of said order in the banking department, said trust company shall cease to exist as a corporation.

§ 2. This act shall take effect immediately.

Chap. 104.

AN ACT to amend chapter two hundred and twenty of the laws of eighteen hundred and sixty-six, entitled "An act to amend the charter of the village of Saratoga Springs, and the several acts amendatory thereof." in relation to creating a comptroller's expense fund.

Became a law March 22, 1913, with the approval of the Governor. Passed, three-fifths being present.

The People of the State of New York, represented in Senate and Assembly, do enact as follows:

L. 1866, ch. 220, § 82, as added by L. 1901, ch. 250, amended.

Section 1. Section eighty-two of chapter two hundred and twenty of the laws of eighteen hundred and sixty-six, entitled "An act to amend the charter of the village of Saratoga Springs, and the several acts amendatory thereof," as added by chapter two hundred and fifty of the laws of nineteen hundred and one,[1] is hereby amended to read as follows:

Trustees to furnish comptroller with office.

Office expenses, how provided for.

§ 82. The board of trustees shall furnish said comptroller a suitable office, and shall furnish and maintain the same suitably, when requested in writing by said comptroller so to do, the expense of which shall be paid by the village. [2]A comptroller's expense fund is hereby created and the comptroller shall in the month of April in each year make his requisition to the board of trustees of his estimate of the necessary expenses of his office for the ensuing year. The board of trustees shall place in the annual village tax budget such sum as they deem necessary to pay the expenses of the comptroller's office for the ensuing year, the same to be collected as other village taxes and when collected to be placed by the receiver of taxes in the comptroller's expense fund and be paid out by him as other village funds.

§ 2. This act shall take effect immediately.

---

[1] A different § 82 was added by L. 1890, ch. 289.
[2] Remainder of section new.

Chap. 105.

AN ACT to amend chapter three hundred and twenty-three of the laws of eighteen hundred and seventy-two, entitled "An act authorizing the election of a receiver of taxes and assessments for the town and village of Saratoga Springs," in relation to collecting interest on village funds from the depositories of the same.

Became a law March 22, 1913, with the approval of the Governor. Passed, three-fifths being present.

The People of the State of New York, represented in Senate and Assembly, do enact as follows:

Section 1. Section five of chapter three hundred and twenty- L. 1872. ch. three of the laws of eighteen hundred and seventy-two, entitled 223. § 5 "An act authorizing the election of a receiver of taxes and assessments for the town and village of Saratoga Springs," is hereby amended to read as follows:

§ 5. It shall be the duty of the said receiver to receive and collect Duties all state, county, town and village taxes and assessments that relative to taxes and may be levied in said town or village, including excise moneys, assessments. water rents, non-resident licenses, and all moneys now provided by law to be paid either to the supervisor or collector of said town, or to the treasurer or collector of said village, or to the village trustee; and the board of trustees upon ascertaining the Duties amount to be paid by any person for any non-resident license or relative to licenses. permit shall forthwith deposit such license or permit with such receiver of taxes, and it shall be the duty of such receiver forthwith to collect the amount charged therefor; and it shall be the duty of the boards of excise of said town and village forthwith upon the granting of any license, to deposit the same with such receiver of taxes, and the person to whom such license shall be granted shall, within ten days after such deposit, due notice of which shall be given, pay to said receiver the fee charged therefor, to keep safely all assessment rolls that may be delivered to him; to enter daily in a suitable book or books the sums of money Assessment received, the names of persons from whom received, and the par- book of ticular tax or assessments, subject or department for which such moneys received. sums were paid, and the percentage, if any, paid thereon; and the said book or books shall be public records, and shall be open during office hours to public inspection to any tax-payer in said

Designation
of deposi-
tories.
town or village. [1]The said receiver of taxes and assessments shall on or before the first day of May in each year, advertise in the two official papers of said village that on the fifteenth day of May of each year at his office in the village of Saratoga Springs at ten o'clock in the forenoon of that day, he will offer at public auction to the bank or banks or trust company agreeing to pay the highest rate of interest on the daily balances for the deposits of the village funds for the ensuing year from the first day of June following. The bank or banks or trust company offering the highest rate of interest for the moneys deposited during the year shall be designated by said receiver of taxes as official depository for village funds for the ensuing year from June first. The receiver of taxes and assessments shall file a certificate of desig nation of such depository or depositories with the village clerk of the village of Saratoga Springs within ten days after such

Interest on
deposits.
designation. The accrued interest thereon shall as often as once in six months be credited by such depository or depositories to the account of such receiver of taxes and assessments for the use of the village of Saratoga Springs. Each bank or banks or trust

Undertak-
ings of de-
positories.
company so designated shall for the benefit and security of the village of Saratoga Springs and before receiving any such deposits, give to the village a good and sufficient undertaking of a solvent surety company, to be approved by the comptroller and president of the village of Saratoga Springs. Such undertaking shall be sufficient in amount to cover all village funds which would be held by such depository or depositories in any cne year. Such undertaking after being duly approved shall be filed with

Deposit of
moneys.
the village clerk. The receiver of taxes shall deposit all sums of public money received by him, by virtue of the warrant from the board of supervisors, or board of trustees or the sewer, water and street commission, in one or more of the banks of said village, as herein provided, within twenty-four hours of receiving the same, that proportion thereof constituting the state and county tax and excise moneys being deposited to the credit of the treasurer of the county of Saratoga, and the residue to his own credit, to be drawn out on his own checks, in payment of town and village audits, and to such town or village officers as by law are authorized to receive and disburse public moneys within the limits of said town or village. All other sums of money received or collected by him shall be deposited, within twenty-four hours of receiving them,

---

[1] Remainder of section materially amended.

in such bank or banks or trust company, to the joint credit of the supervisor of the town and the president of said village. And said money so deposited shall constitute a fund for payment of the salary of the said receiver and the expenses of his office.

§ 2. This act shall take effect immediately.

Chap. 106.

AN ACT to amend chapter two hundred and twenty of the laws of eighteen hundred and sixty-six, entitled "An act to amend the charter of the village of Saratoga Springs, and the several acts amendatory thereof," in relation to cemeteries and the amount of money to be raised for the care of the same.

Became a law March 22, 1913, with the approval of the Governor. Passed, three-fifths being present.

The People of the State of New York, represented in Senate and Assembly, do enact as follows:

Section 1. Subdivision eight of section fifty-four of chapter two hundred and twenty of the laws of eighteen hundred and sixty-six, entitled "An act to amend the charter of the village of Saratoga Springs, and the several acts amendatory thereof," as amended by chapter three hundred and fourteen of the laws of eighteen hundred and ninety-six, is hereby amended to read as follows:[1]

8. A cemetery fund is hereby created. The board of trustees shall annually place in the village tax budget such sum as they think necessary for the proper care and maintenance of the public cemeteries of the village, the same to be collected by the receiver of taxes and when collected to be placed in the cemetery fund and paid out as other village funds.

§ 2. This act shall take effect immediately.

[1] Subd. 8 formerly read: "8. Not exceeding five hundred dollars for the public cemeteries."

Chap. 107.

AN ACT to incorporate The Ministers and Missionaries Benefit
Board of the Northern Baptist Convention.

**Became a law March 24, 1913, with the approval of the Governor. Passed,
three-fifths being present.**

*The People of the State of New York, represented in Senate
and Assembly, do enact as follows:*

Corporators.
Section 1. William A. Davison, W. Howard Doane, George
G. Dutcher, Charles A. Eaton, Edwin P. Farnham, Clarence M.
Gallup, Frank M. Goodchild, Arthur M. Harris, Edward H.
Haskell, Luther Keller, Andrew MacLeish, Henry L. More-
house, Charles H. Prescott, Jr., Eli S. Reinhold, William S.
Shallenberger, Charles M. Thoms, Andrew K. Van Deventer,
Homer J. Vosburgh, Herbert J. White, Joseph K. Wilson and
Peter C. Wright, and their successors are hereby constituted a
Corporate name.
body corporate with the name " The Ministers and Missionaries
Benefit Board of the Northern Baptist Convention," and under
Property rights.
that name shall have perpetual succession and shall have the
right, either absolutely or in trust, to purchase or to acquire by
gift, devise, bequest or otherwise, and to sell, convey or otherwise dispose of, any real or personal property.

Objects.
§ 2. The objects of the corporation shall be to administer its
funds for the benefit of worthy Baptist ministers and Baptist
missionaries, their wives or widows, and their dependent children, either directly or through the medium of related organizations; to co-operate with such organizations in securing, so far
as practicable, uniformity in the methods for the extension of
such aid, to promote interest in the better maintenance of the
ministry, and to adopt such measures to these ends as may be
recommended by the Northern Baptist Convention.

Terms and appoint-
ment of incorpo-
rators.
§ 3. The twenty-one incorporators named in section one of
this act shall be so divided at their first meeting that seven shall
serve for three years, seven shall serve for two years and seven
shall serve for one year, and each shall serve until his successor
is chosen, and as these respective terms expire seven shall be appointed by the Northern Baptist Convention to serve for three
years, and said convention shall have also the power to fill vacancies caused by death, resignation or otherwise.

Election of officers.
§ 4. The body hereby incorporated may elect or appoint such

officers as to it may seem proper, and, subject to the confirmation
of the Northern Baptist Convention, said body may adopt such
by-laws or regulations in relation to its organization, to the By-laws.
management and disposition and sale of its real or personal
property, to the duties and powers of its officers and to the
management and conduct of its corporate affairs as it shall think
proper, provided such by-laws or regulations are not inconsistent
with the laws of the United States or of this state. It shall
present a written annual report to the Northern Baptist Con- Annual report.
vention at each of its annual meetings, and the said convention Power of convention.
shall have the power to instruct the body hereby incorporated in
respect to its general policies.

§ 5. Meetings of the corporation may be held at such time or Meetings.
times and at such place or places in the United States as the
corporation may determine, subject however to the right of the
Northern Baptist Convention to fix the time and place of any
meeting of the corporation.

§ 6. This act shall take effect immediately.

Chap. 108.

AN ACT to amend the judiciary law, in relation to the appointment of special deputy clerks in certain counties.

Became a law March 24, 1913, with the approval of the Governor. Passed,
three-fifths being present.

*The People of the State of New York, represented in Senate
and Assembly, do enact as follows:*

Section 1. Sections one hundred and fifty-nine and two hun- L. 1909,
dred and eighty of chapter thirty-five of the laws of nineteen hun- §§ 159, 280,
dred and nine, entitled "An act in relation to the administration by L. 1910,
of justice, constituting chapter thirty of the consolidated laws," as amended.
amended by chapter six hundred and ninety-five of the laws of
nineteen hundred and ten, are hereby amended to read, respectively, as follows:

§ 159. **Appointment of special deputy clerks in Queens county.**[1]
In the county of Queens[2] the justice or, if more than

---

[1] Words "Queens county" substituted for words "certain counties."
[2] Words "and in counties containing a city having a population of not less
than three hundred thousand and not more than one million, wholly within
the county," omitted.

one, the justices of the supreme court residing in the county, or a
majority of them, shall appoint and at pleasure remove a special
deputy to the county clerk for each part or term of the courts of
which he is clerk, and[3] may appoint as many assistants to such
clerk as may be necessary for the transaction of the business of
such court.

§ 280. **Duty of special deputy and other clerks in Queens county.**[4]
It shall be the duty of the special deputy clerks appointed in Queens county[5] pursuant to section one hundred and
fifty-nine of this chapter, to attend each session of the part or
term of the court to which he is assigned and keep the minutes
thereof and to perform such other duties as shall be prescribed
by the rules made by such justices; such special deputy clerks
shall be subject to the supervision of the county clerk, and shall
possess the same power and authority as the county clerk at any
sitting or term of the court which he attends, with respect to the
business transacted thereat.

§ 2. This act shall take effect immediately.

Chap. 109.

AN ACT to amend the county law, in relation to special deputy
clerks in certain counties.

Became a law March 24, 1913, with the approval of the Governor. Passed,
three-fifths being present.

*The People of the State of New York, represented in Senate
and Assembly, do enact as follows:*

L. 1909,
ch. 16,
§ 169, as
amended by
L. 1910,
ch. 694,
amended.

Section 1. Section one hundred and sixty-nine of chapter sixteen of the laws of nineteen hundred and nine, entitled "An act in
relation to counties, constituting chapter eleven of the consolidated
laws," as amended by chapter six hundred and ninety-four of the
laws of nineteen hundred and ten, is hereby amended to read as
follows:[1]

---

[3] Words " in the county of Queens such justice," omitted.
[4] Words " Queens county " substituted for words " certain counties."
[5] Words " and in counties containing a city having a population of not less
than three hundred thousand and not more than one million wholly within
the county," omitted.
[1] Section 169 is further amended by L. 1913, chaps. 367, 637, post.

§ 169. **Special deputy clerks.** 1. In every county other than the county of Queens[1a] the county clerk may, subject to the approval of the justices of the supreme court residing within the judicial district of the appointee, from time to time, by an instrument in writing, filed in his office, appoint, and at pleasure remove, one or more special deputy clerks to attend upon any or all of the terms or sittings of the courts of which he is clerk, and in any county having a population of more than sixty thousand at the last enumeration, the salary of such special deputy clerks shall be fixed by a justice of the supreme court, residing in such county, and when the said salary shall be so fixed the same shall be paid from the court funds of said county or from an appropriation made therefor. Each person so appointed must, before he enters upon the duties of his office, subscribe and file in the clerk's office the constitutional oath of office;[2] and he possesses the same power and authority as the clerk at any sitting or term of the court which he attends, with respect to the business transacted thereat. The salaries of special deputy clerks and assistants appointed in Queens county under the provisions of section one hundred and fifty-nine[3] of the judiciary law shall be fixed by the justice residing in such county and shall be a county charge. The provisions of this subdivision shall not apply to the first judicial department.

2. The minutes of the part or term of the supreme court to which any of the special deputy clerks to the clerk of the county of New York appointed pursuant to the judiciary law is assigned, kept by him, and the records kept by the supreme court jury clerk in the first judicial district shall be kept by the county clerk of New York county in his office and said county clerk shall give extracts from such minutes and records as now prescribed by law.

3. The minutes and records kept by the special deputy clerks appointed in the county of Queens[4] pursuant to the judiciary law shall be kept by the county clerk in his office and he shall give extracts from such minutes and records as now prescribed by law.

§ 2. This act shall take effect immediately.

[1a] Words "or a county containing a city having a population of not less than three hundred thousand and not more than one million wholly within the county," omitted.

[2] See constitution. art. 13, § 1; public officers law (L. 1909, ch. 51), § 10, as amended by L. 1913, ch. 59, ante.

[3] As amended by L. 1910, ch. 695, and L. 1913, ch. 108, ante.

[4] Words "and in counties containing a city having a population of not less than three hundred thousand and not more than one million wholly within the county," omitted.

Chap. 110.

AN ACT making an appropriation for the payment of compensation for services of employees required for the care and maintenance of the state education building.

Became a law March 24, 1913, with the approval of the Governor. Passed, three-fifths being present.

The People of the State of New York, represented in Senate and Assembly, do enact as follows:

Section 1. The sum of thirty thousand dollars ($30,000), or so much thereof as may be necessary, is hereby appropriated out of any money in the treasury not otherwise appropriated, for the payment of compensation for services of elevatormen, orderlies, engineers, mechanics, laborers, porters, cleaners and other necessary employees in the care and maintenance of the education building and the various offices thereof from February first, nineteen hundred and thirteen, to October first, nineteen hundred and thirteen, to be paid in the manner provided by law for the payment of compensation for services of other employees of the education department.

§ 2. This act shall take effect immediately.

Chap. 111.

AN ACT to amend the town law, in relation to fees of officers in criminal proceedings.

Became a law March 24, 1913, with the approval of the Governor. Passed, three-fifths being present.

The People of the State of New York, represented in Senate and Assembly, do enact as follows:

L. 1909.
ch. 63.
§ 171, as
amended by
L. 1909,
ch. 523,
amended.

Section 1. Section one hundred and seventy-one of chapter sixty-three of the laws of nineteen hundred and nine, entitled "An act relating to towns, constituting chapter sixty-two of the consolidated laws," as amended by chapter five hundred and twenty-three of the laws of nineteen hundred and nine, is hereby amended to read as follows:

§ 171. **Fees of officers in criminal proceedings.** The fees of magistrates and other officers for services in criminal proceedings, for or on account of an offense which a court of special sessions has not jurisdiction to try, shall be a county charge, if the magistrate had jurisdiction of the proceedings in which the services were rendered. The fees of magistrates and other officers in other criminal proceedings, or in criminal actions tried before a magistrate of the town where the offense is charged to have been committed shall be a charge against such town. The fees of a magistrate or officer in issuing or serving process for an offense committed in a town other than that in which such magistrate resides, and of which a court of special sessions has jurisdiction to try, or which a magistrate has jurisdiction to hear and determine, and the fees of a magistrate in the trial or examination of a person brought before him by reason of the absence or inability to act of the magistrate before whom he is directed by the warrant to be brought, charged with such an offense committed in a town other than that in which the magistrate before whom such person is brought resides, shall, in either case, be a charge against the town in which such offense was committed. Except as provided in this section no fees shall be allowed either as a town or county charge to a magistrate or other officer, for services in a criminal action or proceeding, before a magistrate of one town for or on account of an offense charged to have been committed in another town, and which a court of special sessions has jurisdiction to try, or which a magistrate has jurisdiction to hear and determine. The fees of a magistrate and the fees and mileage of a peace officer in connection with the arrest, examination, conviction and commitment of a tramp, or of a vagrant under subdivisions one, five or six of section eight hundred and eighty-seven of the code of criminal procedure, or of a person charged with a violation of section nineteen hundred and ninety of the penal law, and any other criminal action or proceeding of which a court of special sessions has jurisdiction to try, or which a magistrate has jurisdiction to hear and determine,[1] may be fixed by the board of town auditors, if any, and otherwise by the town board of the town, or the board of supervisors of the county, to which the same are chargeable, not exceeding the amount now allowed by law; and when so fixed, shall supersede as to such town or county any other provision of law fixing fees or mileage in such case.

§ 2. This act shall take effect immediately.

---

[1] Words "and any other criminal action or proceeding of which a court of special sessions has jurisdiction to try, or which a magistrate has jurisdiction to hear and determine," new.

Chap. 112.

AN ACT to amend the code of civil procedure, in relation to injunctions.

Became a law March 24, 1913, with the approval of the Governor. Passed, three-fifths being present.

The People of the State of New York, represented in Senate and Assembly, do enact as follows:

§ 606 amended.

Section 1. Section six hundred and six of the code of civil procedure is hereby amended so as to read as follows:

By whom injunction may be granted.

§ 606. Except where it is otherwise specially prescribed by law, an injunction order may be granted by the court in which the action is brought, or by a judge thereof, or by any county judge; and where it is granted by a judge, it may be enforced as the order of the court. [1]An injunction order which may be modified or vacated by the appellate division may also be granted or continued by the appellate division, or a justice thereof, pending appeal to that court or to the court of appeals from an order or judgment denying or vacating an injunction.

In effect Sept. 1, 1913.

§ 2. This act shall take effect September first, nineteen hundred and thirteen.

Chap. 113.

AN ACT to amend the banking law, in relation to oaths of trustees of savings banks, their qualification for a continuance in office and vacancies in the office of trustee.

Became a law March 24, 1913, with the approval of the Governor. Passed, three-fifths being present.

The People of the State of New York, represented in Senate and Assembly, do enact as follows:

L. 1909, ch. 10, § 137, as amended by L. 1912, ch. 237, amended.

Section 1. Section one hundred and thirty-seven of chapter ten of the laws of nineteen hundred and nine, entitled "An act in relation to banks, individual bankers and corporations under the supervision of the banking department, constituting chapter two of the consolidated laws," as amended by chapter two hun-

---

[1] Remainder of section new.

dred and thirty-seven of the laws of nineteen hundred and twelve, is hereby amended to read as follows:

§ 137. **Trustees and their powers.** There shall be a board of not less than thirteen trustees of every such corporation, who shall have the entire management and control of all its affairs, and who shall elect from their number, or otherwise, a president and two vice-presidents, and such other officers as they may deem fit. The persons named in the certificate of authorization shall be the first trustees. A vacancy in the board shall be filled by the board, as soon as practicable, at a regular meeting after the vacancy occurs. Each trustee, whether named in the certificate of authorization or elected to fill a vacancy, shall, when such certificate of authorization has been issued or when notified of such election, take an oath that he will, so far as it devolves on him, diligently and honestly administer the affairs of such corporation, and will not knowingly violate, or willingly permit to be violated any of the provisions of law applicable to such corporation. Such oath shall be subscribed by the trustee making it and certified by the officer before whom it is taken, and shall be immediately transmitted to the superintendent of banks and filed and preserved in his office.

[1]Every trustee of every such corporation who has not heretofore taken and filed the oath hereinbefore required shall, prior to the first day of July, nineteen hundred and thirteen, take and subscribe such oath. Such oath, duly certified by the officer before whom the same is taken, shall, before the first day of July, nineteen hundred and thirteen, be transmitted to the superintendent of banks and filed and preserved in his office.

[1]Prior to the first day of March in each year, every trustee of every such corporation shall subscribe a declaration to the effect that he is, at the date thereof, a trustee of such corporation, and that he has not resigned, become ineligible, or in any other manner vacated his office as such trustee. Such declaration shall be acknowledged in like manner as a deed to be entitled to record and shall be transmitted to the superintendent of banks and filed in his office prior to the tenth day of March in each year.

No person who is not a resident of this state or against whom a judgment for any sum of money shall have been recovered or shall hereafter be recovered and remain unsatisfied of record, or unsecured upon appeal, for a period of more than three months, or

[1] Following paragraph new.

who hereafter takes the benefit of any law of bankruptcy or insolvency, or who makes a general assignment for the benefit of creditors, shall be a trustee of any savings bank, and the office of any such trustee is hereby vacated; except that a resident of a state which adjoins the city of New York may be a trustee of a savings bank in such city, provided that not more than one-fifth of the trustees of any savings bank[2] shall be nonresidents of the state of New York. It shall be lawful for the board of trustees of every such corporation by a resolution to be incorporated in its by-laws, a copy of which shall also be filed with the superintendent of banks, to reduce the number of trustees named in the original charter of such corporation to a number not less than the minimum named in this article. Such reduction shall be effected gradually by the occurrence of vacancies by death, resignation, or forfeiture, until the number is reduced to thirteen, or to such greater number as shall be designated in the aforesaid resolution; or the number of trustees may be increased to any number designated in a resolution for that purpose, where reasons therefor are shown to the satisfaction of the superintendent and his consent in writing is obtained thereto. It shall not be lawful for a majority of the board of trustees of any savings bank to belong to the board of directors of any one bank or national banking association.

When any trustee of a savings bank shall, by becoming a director of a bank or national banking association, cause a majority of the trustees of such savings bank to be directors of any one bank or national banking association, his term of office as trustee of the savings bank shall thereupon end. Any savings bank knowingly violating this provision shall forfeit all its rights, privileges and franchises. Such violation shall be determined in the same manner as a violation of subdivision six of section twenty-seven of article two of this chapter.

§ 140
amended.

§ 2. Section one hundred and forty of said chapter is hereby amended to read as follows:

§ 140. Vacancies. Whenever a trustee of any savings bank shall become a trustee, officer, clerk or employee of any other savings bank, or when he shall borrow, directly or indirectly, any of the funds of the savings bank in which he is trustee, or become a surety or guarantor for any money borrowed of or any loan made by such savings bank, or when he shall fail to attend the

---

[2] Formerly read: "banks."

regular meetings of the board, or perform any of the duties devolved upon him as such trustee, for six successive months, without having been previously excused by the board for such failure, or when he shall fail to take and file the oath or declaration required by section one hundred and thirty-seven of this chapter,[3] the office of such trustee shall thereupon immediately become vacant; but the trustee vacating his office by failure to attend meetings, or to discharge his duties, or to take and file the oath or declaration required by section one hundred and thirty-seven of this chapter,[4] may, in the discretion of the board, be eligible to re-election.

§ 3. This act shall take effect immediately.

Chap. 114.

AN ACT to authorize the city of Buffalo and the county of Erie to provide by agreement or otherwise for the transfer and conveyance of the city and county hall in said city, and the site on which it stands, and the acquisition of lands and construction of buildings for county and courthouse purposes or for city purposes; or for the improvement, enlargement or reconstruction of said city and county hall.

Became a law March 24, 1913, with the approval of the Governor. Passed, three-fifths being present.

Accepted by the City.

The People of the State of New York, represented in Senate and Assembly, do enact as follows:

Section 1. Discretionary power is hereby conferred upon the city of Buffalo and the county of Erie to enter into an agreement or agreements with each other for the transfer and conveyance from one to the other of all title, right and interest owned or held by either said city or said county in and to the city and county hall therein, and in and to the land on which such building stands, to wit, the land bounded by Eagle, Franklin and Church streets and Delaware avenue in said city. Any agreement made pursuant to this act shall be embodied in a resolution adopted by the

City or county authorised to transfer to the other its interest in city and county hall.

---

[3] Words "or when he shall fail to take and file the oath or declaration required by section one hundred and thirty-seven of this chapter," new.
[4] Words "or to take and file the oath or declaration required by section one hundred and thirty-seven of this chapter," new.

common council of said city and by the board of supervisors of
Conveyance, how made. said county. Upon said resolution becoming of force through the
action of said common council and the board of supervisors, the
proper deeds or other instruments shall be executed by and in behalf of the party named therein as grantor and delivered to the
party named therein as grantee, conveying all the right, title and
interest of the grantor or party of the first part in said city and
county hall and the land hereinbefore described to the party of
the second part. Upon the execution and delivery of such deed
or other instrument, all of the right, title and interest of said
party of the first part in and to said land and building shall be
Value, how determined. vested in perpetuity in the party of the second part therein. The
price to be paid for the interest and title so conveyed shall be the
fair value thereof, to be fixed by agreement, or, in case the parties
Appoint- ment of commis- sioners. cannot agree, such value may be determined by three commissioners to be appointed by the supreme court at special term, upon
the application of the city through its mayor or corporation counsel, or by the county, by its attorney, which commissioners shall
appraise and determine the value of said property and the price
Duties and powers of commis- sioners. that shall be paid for the interest therein and title thereto of the
party which shall convey the same. Such commissioners having
first taken an oath to faithfully discharge their duties as commissioners and to ascertain and report the value of said property and
the price to be paid as herein provided, shall view and examine
the land and building to be appraised by them. The commissioners shall have the power to issue subpoenas, to compel the
attendance of witnesses, to administer oaths to witnesses and to
adjourn from time to time; they shall hear the proofs submitted
Report; confirma- tion. to them and report the evidence taken before them, together with
their decision of the value of such property and the price to be
Action on confirma- tion. paid as herein provided. Upon such report being filed, either
party interested may move the court for a confirmation thereof
and it may be confirmed. Upon such order of confirmation, the
party agreeing to convey its interest in such property shall execute
the proper deeds and instruments of conveyance, and the party
purchasing or acquiring the title to said property shall provide
the funds and make the payment required by such report and
Appeal from report. order. Either party to the proceedings may appeal from the report of the commissioners and from the order of the special term
confirming such report to the appellate division of the supreme
court for the fourth department. The appellate division on such

appeal shall examine the proceedings before the commissioners
and may affirm or modify the order of the special term and the
report of the commissioners, or reverse the same, and remit the
proceedings to the same commissioners or to new commissioners
to be appointed by the special term, and their report shall be
final. Except as herein otherwise provided, the provisions of the
charter of the said city shall apply to such proceeding. The said   Payment of consideration.
city or county, as the case may be, purchasing the property here-
inbefore described, shall have power to transfer and convey to
the grantor real and personal property at a price to be agreed
upon or determined, as hereinbefore provided, as a consideration
for the value of the grantor's interest in said city and county
hall and the land hereinbefore described on which it stands.

In case said city and county shall be unable to agree upon the   Enlargement of building in case of failure to agree.
transfer and conveyance from one to the other of its interest in
said property, they shall be authorized to make an agreement or
agreements for the improvement, enlargement or reconstruction
of said city and county hall and for the joint and common use and
occupation thereof by said city and county for city, county and
courthouse purposes, and to make an agreement or agreements
as to the manner of such enlargement, improvement or reconstruction, at a maximum cost to be fixed and determined in and
by such agreement. Upon such agreement being of force, by   Plans.
resolution duly adopted by the common council of said city and
the board of supervisors of said county, the board of trustees of
said city and county hall shall have authority to cause plans, specifications and drawings to be prepared for such improvement, enlargement or reconstruction, and shall enter into a contract or   Contracts.
contracts with any person or persons, firm or firms, corporation
or corporations, for furnishing the labor and materials and doing
the work of improving, enlarging or reconstructing said city and
county hall, who shall be the lowest responsible bidders for such
work or parts thereof, who shall submit sealed proposals in response to a notice to be previously published by said board of
trustees in the official paper of said city of Buffalo and two other
daily papers of the city, twice a week for two weeks, inviting
sealed proposals for such work, pursuant to the plans, specifications or other proper description of the work to be specified in said
notice; provided, however, that the aggregate of all such bids or
proposals shall not exceed the sum fixed in and by said agreement
between said city and county. One-half of the cost of such work   Division of cost.
and improvement, enlargement or reconstruction shall be borne

by and shall be a charge upon said city of Buffalo, and one-half of such cost shall be borne by and shall be a charge upon said county of Erie.

Bond issues authorised.
§ 2. Said city of Buffalo, through its common council, mayor and comptroller, and said county of Erie, through its board of supervisors, shall have power, respectively, to borrow money for the payment of all sums required to be paid in pursuance of any agreement which shall be made as hereinbefore provided, and the comptroller of said city may issue its bonds for this purpose in such amounts and payable at such times and places and bearing such rate of interest as shall be determined by the common council
By county. by resolution. The county treasurer of the county of Erie may issue the bonds of said county for this purpose in such amounts and payable at such times and places and bearing such rate of interest as shall be determined by the board of supervisors by resolution.

By city.
Money may be borrowed and bonds issued also by said city of Buffalo or said county of Erie in the manner provided by this section for the purchase or acquisition of lands and the construction and equipment of buildings for city or county and courthouse purposes by the party which shall convey its interest in and title to said city and county hall.

Care of building in case of enlargement.
§ 3. In case said city and county hall shall be improved, enlarged or reconstructed as hereinbefore provided, the management, care and control of said city and county hall shall continue to be in charge of the board of trustees which shall have charge and control of the care and management of said building at the time this act takes effect.

§ 4. All acts or parts of acts inconsistent with this act are hereby repealed.

§ 5. This act shall take effect immediately.

Chap. 115.

AN ACT to amend chapter sixty-eight of the laws of eighteen hundred and sixty, entitled "An act to consolidate and amend the several acts relating to the village of Catskill," generally.

Became a law March 25, 1913, with the approval of the Governor. Passed, three-fifths being present.

The People of the State of New York, represented in Senate and Assembly, do enact as follows:

Section 1. Section one of chapter sixty-eight of the laws of eighteen hundred and sixty, entitled "An act to consolidate and amend the several acts relating to the village of Catskill," as amended by chapter thirty-two of the laws of eighteen hundred and eighty-three, chapter two hundred and fifty-four of the laws of eighteen hundred and eighty-eight, and chapter three hundred and forty-two of the laws of eighteen hundred and ninety-eight,*" is hereby amended to read as follows:

§ 1. All that part of the town of Catskill, in the county of Greene, embraced in the following bounds, that is to say, beginning in the south of the Ramshorn creek, in north latitude forty-two degrees eleven minutes fifty-one and fifty-five one-hundredths seconds, and west longitude (from Greenwich) seventy-three degrees fifty-one minutes twenty-seven and twenty-three one-hundredths seconds, and running thence to a stone monument in latitude forty-two degrees twelve minutes forty-one and fifty-six one-hundredths seconds, longitude seventy-three degrees fifty-two minutes fifty-eight and sixty-three one-hundredths seconds; thence to a stone monument in latitude forty-two degrees twelve minutes forty-four and seventy-five one-hundredths seconds, longitude seventy-three degrees fifty-three minutes twenty-three and fifty-four one-hundredths seconds; thence to a stone monument in latitude forty-two degrees twelve minutes forty-five and twenty one-hundredths seconds, longitude seventy-three degrees fifty-three minutes twenty-four and sixty one-hundredths seconds; thence to a stone monument in latitude forty-two degrees twelve minutes fifty and twenty-three one-hundredths seconds, longitude seventy-three degrees fifty-three minutes twenty-one and eighteen one-hundredths seconds; thence in the same course fourteen and four-

Marginal notes: L. 1860, ch. 68, § 1, as amended by L. 1883, ch. 32, L. 1888, ch. 254, and L. 1898, ch. 342, amended.

Village boundaries.

* So in original.

tenths feet; thence to a stone monument in latitude forty-two
degrees twelve minutes fifty-one and five one-hundredths seconds,
longitude seventy-three degrees fifty-three minutes twenty-two
and seventy-two one-hundredths seconds; thence to a stone monument in latitude forty-two degrees twelve minutes and fifty-nine
seconds, longitude seventy-three degrees fifty-three minutes nineteen and fourteen one-hundredths seconds; thence to a stone monument in latitude forty-two degrees twelve minutes fifty-nine and
seventy-three one-hundredths seconds, longitude seventy-three degrees fifty-three minutes nine and ninety-nine one-hundredths
seconds; thence to a stone monument in latitude forty-two degrees thirteen minutes seven and one one-hundredths seconds,
longitude seventy-three degrees fifty-three minutes five and fifty-
four one-hundredths seconds; thence to a stone monument in
latitude forty-two degrees thirteen minutes fifteen and eighteen
one-hundredths seconds, longitude seventy-three degrees fifty-two
minutes fifty-nine and fifty one-hundredths seconds; thence to the
center of a fourteen-inch white oak tree at the ground, in latitude
forty-two degrees thirteen minutes seventeen and eighty-seven one-
hundredths seconds, longitude seventy-three degrees fifty-two minutes fifty-eight and eighty-two one-hundredths seconds; thence to
a stone monument in latitude forty-two degrees thirteen minutes
twenty and thirty one-hundredths seconds, longitude seventy-three
degrees fifty-three minutes two and eighty-two one-hundredths
seconds; thence to a three-quarter-inch hole in a rock on the south
side of the Catskill creek at high water mark, in latitude forty-
two degrees thirteen minutes twenty-four and thirteen one-hundredths seconds, longitude seventy-three degrees fifty-three minutes one and seven one-hundredths seconds; thence to a stone
monument in latitude forty-two degrees thirteen minutes thirty-
nine and twenty-six one-hundredths seconds, longitude seventy-
three degrees fifty-two minutes twenty and twelve one-hundredths
seconds; thence to a stone monument in latitude forty-two degrees
thirteen minutes forty and twenty one-hundredths seconds, longitude seventy-three degrees fifty-two minutes four and seven one-
hundredths seconds; thence to a hole in a rock on the north side
of the mouth of the creek called Stuck, in latitude forty-two degrees thirteen minutes forty-one and eighty-six one-hundredths
seconds, longitude seventy-three degrees fifty-one minutes thirteen and fourteen one-hundredths seconds; thence south seventy-
three degrees fifty minutes east (true), to the eastern boundary

line of the town of Catskill; thence southerly along said easterly
boundary line of the town of Catskill to a point south seventy-one
degrees eighteen minutes east (true) from the place of beginning; thence to the place of beginning, shall hereafter be known
by the name of "the village of Catskill," and the territory, together with the inhabitants therein shall be a municipal corpora-
tion by the name of "the village of Catskill," and by that name _{Corporate name and}
shall have perpetual succession, and said corporation is hereby de- _{powers.}
clared to be vested with and in possession of all the estate, real
and personal, rights, privileges and immunities, which (at the
time of the passing of this act) appertain and belong to the village of Catskill. The said corporation shall be capable of suing
and being sued, complaining and defending, in its corporate name,
in any court, make and use a common seal and alter the same at
pleasure, and shall have power to take by gift, grant or devise and
to hold, purchase and convey such real and personal estate as the
purposes of the corporation may require; and shall also have
power to hold, purchase and convey such other real estate in the
town of Catskill, outside of the boundaries of said village for
hospital and pest house purposes, as the corporation may require,
not exceeding fifteen hundred dollars in value at the time of the
acquisition thereof.[1]

§ 2. Section two of such act, as amended by chapter three _{§ 2. as amended by}
hundred and forty-two of the laws of eighteen hundred and _{L. 1898, ch. 342.}
ninety-eight, is hereby amended to read as follows: _{amended.}

§ 2. The officers of the corporation shall consist of five _{Elective officers.}
trustees,[2] one of whom shall be president of the village, who, at
the time of their election shall have been assessed and paid a village tax upon real or personal property, assessed upon the last
preceding assessment roll of said village;[3] three assessors, one
treasurer, one collector and one police justice, each to be elected
by the people of the corporation qualified to vote at the annual
state election for member of assembly; a village clerk to be ap- _{Appointive officers.}
pointed annually by the trustees for the term of one year; and the
trustees may appoint four police constables, one pound-master,
one sexton, and such other appointive officers as shall be author-

---

[1] Remainder of section which provided for division of village into districts,
omitted.
[2] Words "one only of whom shall be a resident of any of the districts
aforesaid," omitted.
[3] Words "assessed upon the last preceding assessment roll of said village,"
new.

Eligibility
to office.

ized by law. No person shall be eligible to an office unless he shall be, at the time, a resident and elector in said village; and when any officer of said village shall not have been at the time of his election, or shall afterwards cease to be a resident of said village, his office shall thereby become vacant. The trustees may, if

Extra
police
constables.

in their opinion the public good requires, appoint an extra number of police constables to serve during the pleasure of the said trustees, and who shall have no authority to serve civil process.

§ 4
amended.

§ 3. Section four of such act is hereby amended to read as follows:

Presiding
officers at
elections;
powers and
duties.

§ 4. One or more of the trustees shall preside at such elections; and in case no trustee shall be present at the hour appointed for opening the polls, the electors assembled may appoint a chairman to preside. The presiding officer or officers at all such elections are authorized and required to preserve order, judge of the qualifications of electors, canvass the ballots, and declare the persons elected by the greatest number of votes; and all the powers possessed by inspectors of elections, by the election laws of this state, are hereby conferred upon them, for the purposes of

Terms of
officers
elected.

such charter election; and the persons elected, except trustees and assessors, shall hold their offices, respectively, one year and until others shall be elected, except as hereinafter provided. The trustees shall hold their office for three years, except as herein provided; within five days after the first election they shall meet, at a time and place to be designated by the clerk of the village, of which they shall be notified, and must determine by ballot, marked one, two and three, to be drawn in the presence of the clerk, their respective terms of service. The terms of the first trustees shall be two for one year, two for two years, and one for three years, according to the ballots they shall respectively draw. If either of the trustees shall fail to attend, the clerk shall draw for him; the result must be entered in the records of the village. At the expiration of the terms so drawn, respectively, the vacancies so existing shall be filled by an election of one or more *trutees, as the case may be,⁴ and those so elected shall, respectively, hold their offices for the term of three years. The assessors shall hold their offices for three years, one to be elected each year; within eight days after the first election they shall meet, at a

---

* So in original.
⁴ Words "who shall reside in the district or districts in which those resided when elected, whose terms of office will have expired," omitted.

time and place to be designated by the president, of which they shall be notified, and must determine by ballot, numbered one, two and three, to be drawn in the presence of the clerk, their respective terms of service; the terms of the first assessors shall be, the first for one year, the second for two years, and the third for three years, according to the ballots they shall, respectively, draw. If either of the assessors shall fail to attend, the clerk shall draw for him; the result must be entered in the records of the village. If a vacancy happen, it must be filled by the trustees until the Vacancies. next annual election, and if the vacant term be not then terminated, it must then be filled for the residue of the term by election; all elections under this section shall be by ballot, and de- Conduct of termined by a plurality of votes,[5] and the candidate[6] having the greatest number of votes shall be declared to be elected.

§ 4. Section fifty of such act as amended by chapter three § 50, as amended by hundred and forty-two of the laws of eighteen hundred and L. 1898, ch. 342, ninety-eight is hereby amended to read as follows:[7] amended.

§ 50. A person shall be entitled to vote upon all propositions Eligibility to vote on to raise money by tax or assessment, or upon any proposition re- propositions. lating to the disposition of any funds or property of the corporation, or for the dissolution of the village, or for the borrowing of money upon the bonds or other obligations of the village, payable in future fiscal years, who is

1. A citizen of the United States.

2. Twenty-one years of age.

3. A resident of the village for a period of thirty days next preceding the meeting at which he or she offers to vote; and who in addition thereto is the owner of real or personal property in the village assessed upon the last preceding assessment roll thereof.

No person shall be deemed to be ineligible, by reason of sex, to vote upon the propositions enumerated in this section, who has the other qualifications required by this section.

§ 5. This act shall take effect immediately.

---

[5] Words " in the case of trustees," omitted.
[6] Words " in each district," omitted.
[7] Section materially amended.

Chap. 116.

AN ACT to amend the town law, in relation to the limitation of indebtedness of certain towns.

Became a law March 25, 1913, with the approval of the Governor. Passed, three-fifths being present.

The People of the State of New York, represented in Senate and Assembly, do enact as follows:

L. 1909, ch. 63, § 195 amended.

Section 1. Section one hundred and ninety-five of chapter sixty-three of the laws of nineteen hundred and nine, entitled "An act relating to towns, constituting chapter sixty-two of the consolidated laws," is hereby amended to read as follows:

§ 195. **Limitation of indebtedness.** No town including a portion of the Adirondack park and having state lands within the boundaries of the town[1] shall hereafter contract any debt or debts which shall exceed the sum of three thousand dollars, except upon the duly verified petition of the owners of at least sixty-five per centum of the taxable real property therein, as such real property appears on the last preceding completed assessment-roll of such town. For the purposes of this article the consent of the comptroller shall be deemed to be the consent of the state. This section shall not apply to debts contracted for the purpose of retiring or paying any existing indebtedness pursuant to law.

§ 2. This act shall take effect immediately.

Chap. 117.

AN ACT making appropriations, supplementary appropriations and reappropriations for improvements at the state hospitals for the insane.

Became a law March 25, 1913, with the approval of the Governor. Passed, three-fifths being present.

The People of the State of New York, represented in Senate and Assembly, do enact as follows:

Amounts, how expended.

Section 1. The several amounts named in this act are hereby appropriated for the several purposes indicated, to be expended under the direction of the state hospital commission.

---

[1] Words "and having state lands within the boundaries of the town," new.

For the Central Islip State Hospital, for furniture and equip- Central Islip State Hospital. ment of three new pavilions for three hundred seventy-five pa- tients, twenty thousand dollars ($20,000); to supplement original appropriation made by chapter eight hundred nineteen, laws of nineteen hundred eleven, for additions to existing buildings at such hospitals as the commission may designate, one thousand seven hundred and six dollars ($1,706).

For the Buffalo State Hospital, to supplement original appro- Buffalo State Hospital. priation for the construction of a tuberculosis pavilion for men, made by chapter five hundred thirty, laws of nineteen hundred twelve, three thousand dollars ($3,000); to supplement original appropriation made by chapter five hundred thirty, laws of nine- teen hundred twelve, for refrigerating plant, including equipment, eighteen thousand dollars ($18,000); to supplement original ap- propriation made by chapter five hundred thirty, laws of nineteen hundred twelve, for addition to bakery, five thousand dollars ($5,000).

For the Kings Park State Hospital, to supplement the original Kings Park State Hospital. appropriation made by chapter eight hundred nineteen, of the laws of nineteen hundred eleven, for extension of sewage disposal system, ten thousand dollars ($10,000); to supplement original appropriation made by chapter eight hundred nineteen, of the laws of nineteen hundred eleven, for additions to existing buildings at such hospitals as the commission may designate, four thousand seven hundred ninety-two dollars ($4,792).

For the Manhattan State Hospital, to supplement original ap- Manhattan State Hospital. propriation made by chapter five hundred thirty, of the laws of nineteen hundred twelve, for additional accommodations for two hundred patients, sixty-five thousand dollars ($65,000), such ac- commodations to provide for patients of the acute and curable class; to supplement original appropriation made by chapter five hundred thirty of the laws of nineteen hundred twelve, for the concreting of the east dock, two thousand six hundred dollars ($2,600); to supplement original appropriation made by chapter five hundred and thirty of the laws of nineteen hundred and twelve, for nurses' home, twenty thousand dollars ($20,000).

For the Middletown State Homeopathic Hospital, to supplement Middletown State Homeo- pathic Hospital. original appropriation made by chapter five hundred seven, of the laws of nineteen hundred ten, for power house and to provide coal pockets, eighteen thousand dollars ($18,000).

Reappro-
priation.

The following sums are hereby re-appropriated and made available for purposes similar to the original purposes:

Hudson
River State
Hospital.

Hudson River State Hospital: The sum of two thousand dollars (re. $2,000), being the unexpended balance of the appropriation of twenty thousand dollars ($20,000), made by chapter five hundred thirty, of the laws of nineteen hundred twelve, for finishing three-story space in main building for women nurses, is hereby re-appropriated and made available for the furnishing of these quarters.

§ 2. This act shall take effect immediately.

Chap. 118.

AN ACT to amend chapter five hundred and seventy of the laws of nineteen hundred and nine, entitled "An act to establish the city court of Buffalo, defining its powers and jurisdiction and providing for its officers," as amended by chapter three hundred and thirty-nine of the laws of nineteen hundred and ten, in relation to compensation of jurors in said court.

Became a law March 25, 1913, with the approval of the Governor. Passed, three-fifths being present.

Accepted by the City.

The People of the State of New York, represented in Senate and Assembly, do enact as follows:

L. 1909,
ch. 570,
§ 51, as
amended by
L. 1910,
ch. 339,
amended.

Section 1. Section fifty-one of chapter five hundred and seventy of the laws of nineteen hundred and nine, entitled "An act to establish the city court of Buffalo, defining its powers and jurisdiction and providing for its officers," as amended by chapter three hundred and thirty-nine of the laws of nineteen hundred and ten, is hereby further amended to read as follows:

§ 51. **List of jurors; how selected.** A list of civil and criminal[1] trial jurors for the court must be selected by the commissioner of jurors for the county of Erie and must consist of not less than one thousand persons qualified to serve. A person shall not be placed upon such jury list who does not reside or have a place where he regularly transacts business in person within the city of Buffalo. The said commissioner of jurors shall, on or before the first Monday in September of each and every year, furnish the

---

1 Words "civil and criminal" new.

clerk of the court with such list, together with the residences and occupations of the persons so selected by him. The clerk of the court shall write on separate slips of paper the name of each juror upon such list, and shall place the slips in a box to be called the undrawn jury box and no person shall serve as juror more than once in a calendar year. The contents of the drawn and undrawn jury boxes may be at any time inspected by the commissioner of jurors, or his deputy. Each juror shall be paid two dollars for each and every day or portion thereof that he actually serves upon jury, and each person summoned to attend as a juryman shall be paid two dollars for each day that he attends, unless he is excused from serving as a juryman at his own request, in which event he shall be paid as herein otherwise provided. Such payment shall be made only upon the certificate of the judge presiding at the trial of the number of days served, and the amount due each juror, and in civil cases[2] shall be made by the clerk of said court out of the fund paid for jury trials into said court so long as sufficient. [3]The common council of the city of Buffalo shall provide a fund for the payment of jurors in criminal cases and payment of such jurors shall be made by the clerk of said court out of such fund. If any person summoned hereinunder to attend as a juror does not serve by reason of the adjournment of the trial of an action in which he was to serve then the fees of such person shall be paid to the clerk of the court by the party to the action seeking such adjournment.

§ 2. This act shall take effect immediately.

Chap. 119.

AN ACT to repeal chapter three hundred and ninety of the laws of eighteen hundred and fifty-nine.

Became a law March 25, 1913, with the approval of the Governor. Passed, three-fifths being present.

The People of the State of New York, represented in Senate and Assembly, do enact as follows:

Section 1. Chapter three hundred and ninety of the laws of L. 1859, eighteen hundred and fifty-nine, entitled "An act in relation to the ch. 390 repealed.

---

[2] Words " in civil cases " new.
[3] Following sentence new.

auditing of accounts by the board of supervisors of the county of Montgomery, and the duties of certain officers of said county in connection therewith," is hereby repealed.

§ 2. This act shall take effect immediately.

Chap. 120.

AN ACT to amend chapter one hundred and eighty-five of the laws of eighteen hundred and forty-six, entitled "An act authorizing the election of trustees of public lands in the town of East-chester, and defining their duties," in relation to the election and powers of such trustees.

Became a law March 25, 1913, with the approval of the Governor. Passed, three-fifths being present.

The People of the State of New York, represented in Senate and Assembly, do enact as follows:

L. 1846, ch. 185, § 1 amended.

Section 1. Section one of chapter one hundred and eighty-five of the laws of eighteen hundred and forty-six, entitled "An act authorizing the election of trustees of public lands *of the town of Eastchester, and defining their duties," is hereby amended to read as follows:

Election of trustees of public lands.b

§ 1. The inhabitants of the town of Eastchester in the county of Westchester, may elect at the next [1]town meeting held in said town, and biennially[2] thereafter, in the same manner as other town officers are elected, three of the legal voters

To be corporation; corporate name.

of said town, who shall be a corporation, for the purposes of their office, by the name of "the trustees of the public lands" in said town; and the justices of the peace of said town of East-chester are hereby authorized to appoint three of the legal voters of said town to the office of trustees of public lands in said town, who shall hold their offices until the next [1]town meeting to be held therein, with the same force and effect as if said officers had been elected at the last [1]town meeting held in said town.

§ 2. subds. 2-5 amended.

§ 2. Subdivisions three, four and five of section three of said act are hereby amended to read, respectively, as follows:

---

* So in original.
1 Word "annual" omitted.
2 Formerly read: "annually."

3. To transfer, sell, grant, deed and convey at public or private ^{Power to convey real property.} sale, all their right, title and interest and the right, title and interest of the town of Eastchester in the county of Westchester in and to any real property and to execute, acknowledge and deliver releases, deeds and conveyances thereof in the name of the trustees of public lands of the town of Eastchester and of the town of Eastchester; [3]to lease the same for such time not ^{Power to lease.} exceeding two years, and upon such conditions as said inhabitants in such meeting may direct, or in the absence of such directions, as they may deem expedient.

4. To apply the proceeds, rents and profits of such lands, and ^{Application of proceeds.} the interest and moneys derived therefrom to such lawful purposes and in such manner as [4]the town board of the town of Eastchester may direct.

5. To render a just and true account of the proceeds, rents and ^{Rendering of accounts} profits, or income from or on account of such lands and moneys arising therefrom, and of all appropriations and expenditures on account thereof, by items, on the last Tuesday next preceding the [5]town meeting in said town[6] to the board of auditors of other town accounts.

§ 3. Section four of said act is hereby amended to read as ^{§ 4 amended.} follows:

§ 4. The board of auditors in said town shall annually report ^{Annual report of board of auditors.} the state of the accounts of the " trustees of public lands " therein, to the [7]town board of the town of Eastchester.

§ 4. This act shall take effect immediately.

---

[3] Subdivision to here, new.
[4] Remainder of subdivision formerly read: " said inhabitants so assembled in town meeting may direct."
[5] Word " annual " omitted.
[6] Words " in each year " omitted.
[7] Remainder of section formerly read: " inhabitants thereof at their annual town meeting."

Chap. 121.

AN ACT to amend the Greater New York charter, in relation to vacations of employees.

Became a law March 25, 1913, with the approval of the Governor. Passed, three-fifths being present.

Accepted by the City.

The People of the State of New York, represented in Senate and Assembly, do enact as follows:

L. 1897, ch. 378, § 1567, as added by L. 1909, ch. 559, and amended by L. 1910, ch. 679, amended.

Section 1. Section fifteen hundred and sixty-seven of title three of chapter twenty-three of the Greater New York charter, as re-enacted by chapter four hundred and sixty-six of the laws of nineteen hundred and one, as added by chapter five hundred and fifty-nine of the laws of nineteen hundred and nine and amended by chapter six hundred and seventy-nine of the laws of nineteen hundred and ten, is hereby amended to read as follows:

Vacations of employees.

§ 1567. The executive heads of the various departments are authorized and empowered to grant to every employee of the city of New York, or of any department or bureau thereof, and of the department of education, a vacation of not less than two weeks in each year and for such further period of time as the duties, length of service and other qualifications of an employee may warrant, at such time as the executive head of the department or any officer having supervision over said employee may fix, and for such time they shall be allowed the same compensation as if

Per diem employees.

actually employed, except that no such vacation shall be granted to per diem employees for longer than two weeks and only during the months of June, July, August and September.[1]

§ 2. This act shall take effect immediately.

---

[1] Inclusion of September new.

Chap. 122.

AN ACT authorizing the city of Buffalo to borrow money, by the issue and sale of bonds in sums not exceeding in the aggregate thirty thousand dollars, for the purpose of participating in the fourth international congress on school hygiene to be held in said city, and for the benefit of the public health.

Became a law March 25, 1913, with the approval of the Governor. Passed, three-fifths being present.

Accepted by the City.

The People of the State of New York, represented in Senate and Assembly, do enact as follows:

Section 1. The city of Buffalo is hereby authorized to borrow Bond issue authorized. money in a sum or sums not to exceed in the aggregate thirty thousand dollars, and to issue its bonds therefor, for the purpose of participating in the fourth international congress on school hygiene, which is to be held in said city during the last week of August in the year nineteen hundred and thirteen, and in connection therewith, for the purpose of providing instruction as to the most approved methods of conserving and promoting the health of school children and the public. Such bonds shall be Bonds; issued in such sums and for such periods of time and at such amounts, etc. rate of interest as the common council shall prescribe, and shall be issued from time to time by the mayor and comptroller, under the city seal, as ordered by the common council; and such bonds Sale. shall be sold or awarded as provided in section four hundred and ninety-two of the charter of said city, being chapter one hundred and five of the laws of eighteen hundred and ninety-one, as amended by chapter two hundred and eighty-nine of the laws of eighteen hundred and ninety-four, and chapter forty-eight of the laws of nineteen hundred and six. The interest on said bonds Payment of interest shall be paid semi-annually at the office of the comptroller of the and principal. city of Buffalo, or at the Hanover National Bank of the city of New York, as the purchaser may elect, and the principal of said bonds shall be payable at the same place at such time as shall be ordered by the common council. The common council shall make provision in the general fund estimates of said city for the payment of the interest on and the principal of said bonds as the same shall become due.

§ 2. The disbursement of the moneys received from the sale of the bonds mentioned in section one of this act shall be in charge of a commission of five citizens of Buffalo, to be appointed by its mayor on or before the first day of August, nineteen hundred and thirteen. The commissioners shall, within ten days after their appointment, qualify by taking the oath prescribed by the first section of the thirteenth article of the constitution,[1] and shall organize by electing one of their number as chairman, and another as secretary and treasurer. Two of the members of said commission shall be officers of said city. The mayor shall have power to fill vacancies on said commission. The secretary and treasurer shall give a bond to the city, with a sufficient surety or sureties, for the faithful discharge of his duties and the accounting for all the funds of the city which shall come into his hands, and for returning to the city treasurer of all moneys not disbursed for the purposes for which said moneys shall have been raised. The said city shall pay the premium on said bond, if any. Moneys shall be paid to said secretary and treasurer by the treasurer of said city, with the written consent of its comptroller, upon written requisition of said secretary and treasurer, countersigned by the chairman thereof; said requisition, after the first, shall not be honored, however, by the city treasurer and the comptroller, unless an itemized account of all expenditures by said commission of moneys previously paid by said city shall have been delivered to and approved by the auditor of the city as being reasonable and proper within the meaning and intent of this act. After the close of said congress and after all said receipts and disbursements shall have been accounted for, the accounts all approved by the auditor, and all sums unexpended returned to the city treasurer by the secretary and treasurer of said commission, the common council of the city, upon proof that there has been no breach of said bond, may by resolution order the same cancelled. The powers and duties of said commission shall thereupon cease.

§ 3. This act shall take effect immediately.

---

[1] See also public officers law (L. 1909, ch. 51), § 10, as amended by L. 1913, ch. 59, ante.

Marginal notes:
Commission for disbursement of moneys; appointment, organization, etc.
Bond of secretary and treasurer.
Payments to secretary and treasurer, how made.
Cancelation of bond.
Cessation of powers of commission.

Chap. 123.

AN ACT to amend chapter six hundred and sixty-seven of the laws of nineteen hundred and ten, entitled "An act to amend, revise and consolidate the charter of the village of Ossining," in relation to sewer assessment bonds.

Became a law March 25, 1913, with the approval of the Governor. Passed, three-fifths being present.

The People of the State of New York, represented in Senate and Assembly, do enact as follows:

Section 1. Section one hundred and thirty-three of chapter six hundred and sixty-seven of the laws of nineteen hundred and ten, entitled "An act to amend, revise and consolidate the charter of the village of Ossining," is hereby amended to read as follows: L. 1910, ch. 667, § 133 amended.

§ 133. **Assessments.** The board of trustees is hereby authorized and empowered to issue certificates of indebtedness or assessment bonds of the village of Ossining in the amount of the assessment upon individual owners, of the cost of the construction and maintenance of sewers; such certificates or bonds to draw interest not to exceed five per centum per annum, and to be issued payable in ten years, and to be signed by the president and village clerk, and to be sold at not less than par, and the proceeds thereof to be used only for the payment of the cost of construction and maintenance of sewers. Such certificates of indebtedness or assessment bonds to be and become a lien upon the taxable estate, both real and personal, within the said village, and the said board of trustees shall refund any certificate of indebtedness or assessment bond becoming due and payable pending the collection of assessments by issuing new certificates of indebtedness or assessment bonds in the place and stead of the certificates of indebtedness or assessment bonds so becoming due and payable; such new certificates of indebtedness or assessment bonds running for a period not to exceed five years and to draw interest not exceeding five per centum per annum, and to be signed by the president and village clerk, and to be sold at not less than par, and the proceeds thereof to be used only for the payment of such certificates of indebtedness or assessment bonds so becoming due and payable during the pendency of the collection of assessments; such certificates of indebtedness or assessment bonds when issued, to be a lien upon the taxable property within the village.

[1]The faith and credit of the village are pledged to the payment
of the principal and interest of all such bonds or certificates of
indebtedness, and a tax shall be levied upon all of the taxable
property in the village sufficient to meet any deficiency in the
receipts from the assessments levied upon the property benefited
applicable to the payment of said principal and interest.

§ 2. This act shall take effect immediately.

Chap. 124.

AN ACT to amend the town law, in relation to the qualification
of voters.

Became a law March 25, 1913, with the approval of the Governor. Passed,
three-fifths being present.

*The People of the State of New York, represented in Senate
and Assembly, do enact as follows:*

L. 1909,
ch. 63,
§§ 53-55
amended.

Section 1. Sections fifty-three, fifty-four and fifty-five of chapter
sixty-three of the laws of nineteen hundred and nine, entitled "An
act relating to towns, constituting chapter sixty-two of the consolidated laws," are hereby amended to read, respectively, as
follows:

§ 53. **Qualification of elector at town meeting.** An elector of a
town shall not be entitled to vote by ballot upon any proposition
for the raising or appropriation of money, or the incurring of any
town liability, unless he or his wife is the owner of property in the
town, assessed to him or her[1a] upon the last preceding assessment-
roll thereof.

§ 54. **Qualification of elector to vote for site for town house.**
An elector shall not be entitled to vote upon a proposition submitted for the purposes of section three hundred and forty of this
chapter, unless he or his wife is the owner of property in the town
assessed to him or her[1a] upon the last preceding assessment-roll
thereof.

§ 55. **When women are qualified to vote.** A woman who possesses the qualifications to vote for town officers, except the qualification of sex, and who is the owner of property in the town

---

[1] Remainder of section new.
[1a] Words " to him or her " new.

assessed to her[2] upon the last preceding assessment-roll thereof, is entitled to vote upon a proposition to raise money by tax or assessment.

§ 2. This act shall take effect immediately.

Chap. 125.

AN ACT to amend the code of criminal procedure, in relation to appeals to the supreme court from suspended sentences.

Became a law March 25, 1913, with the approval of the Governor. Passed, three-fifths being present.

The People of the State of New York, represented in Senate and Assembly, do enact as follows:

Section 1. Section five hundred and seventeen of the code of criminal procedure is hereby amended to read as follows: §517 amended.

§ 517. **In what cases appeal may be taken by defendant.** An appeal to the supreme court may be taken by the defendant from the judgment on a conviction after indictment, except that when the judgment is of death, the appeal must be taken direct to the court of appeals, and upon the appeal, any actual decision of the court in an intermediate order or proceeding forming a part of the judgment-roll, as prescribed by section four hundred and eighty-five, may be reviewed. [1]For every purpose of an appeal herein, a conviction shall be deemed a final judgment, although sentence has been or may hereafter be suspended by the court in which the trial was had, or otherwise suspended or stayed, and the supreme court upon such an appeal may review all decisions of the court upon a motion for a new trial, or in arrest of judgment. A judgment of affirmance upon any such appeal shall not operate to exclude any appellant, otherwise entitled thereto, from the right of suffrage.

§ 2. This act shall take effect September first, nineteen hundred and thirteen. In effect Sept. 1, 1913.

---

[2] Words " to her " new.
[1] Remainder of section new. See People v. Markham, 114 App. Div. 387; People v. Flaherty 126 App. Div. 65 (appeal dismissed, 198 N. Y. 602).

Chap. 126.

AN ACT to amend the village law, in relation to street improvement.

Became a law March 25, 1913, with the approval of the Governor. Passed, three-fifths being present.

The People of the State of New York, represented in Senate and Assembly, do enact as follows:

L. 1909, ch.
64, § 148
amended.

Section 1. Section one hundred and forty-eight of chapter sixty-four of the laws of nineteen hundred and nine, entitled "An act relating to villages, constituting chapter sixty-four of the consolidated laws," is hereby amended to read as follows:

§ 148. **Effect of determination.** The determination by the board has the following effect:

1. If the petition for the laying out, alteration or widening of a street be granted, the board of trustees may acquire the land for such improvement by purchase or by proceedings under this article or by proceedings under the condemnation law.[1] But no street shall be laid out through a building or any fixtures or erections for the purposes of trade or manufacture, or any yard or inclosure necessary to be used for the enjoyment thereof, without the consent of the owner, except upon the order of a justice of the supreme court residing in the judicial district in which the village or a part thereof is situated, to be granted upon an application by the board of trustees on a notice to the owner of not less than ten days.

2. If the petition for the narrowing of a street be granted, the board shall enter upon its records a description of the street after such narrowing, and the portion of the former street not included in such description is abandoned.

3. If the petition for the discontinuance of a street be granted, such street or the part thereof so discontinued is abandoned.

§ 2. This act shall take effect immediately.

---

[1] Words "or by proceedings under the condemnation law," new. See code of civil procedure, §§ 3357–3384.

Chap. 127.

AN ACT to amend the county law, in relation to fire districts.

Became a law March 25, 1913, with the approval of the Governor. Passed, three-fifths being present.

The People of the State of New York, represented in Senate and Assembly, do enact as follows:

Section 1. Section thirty-eight of chapter sixteen of the laws of nineteen hundred and nine, entitled "An act in relation to counties, constituting chapter eleven of the consolidated laws," as amended by chapter four hundred and five of the laws of nineteen hundred and nine, is hereby amended by adding thereto a new subdivision, to be subdivision eleven, to read as follows: *Subd. 11 added to L. 1909, ch. 16, § 38.*

11. Territory not in a city, village or fire district may be annexed to an adjoining fire district as provided in this subdivision. A verified petition for such annexation describing the territory and signed by taxable inhabitants whose names appear on the last preceding assessment-roll of the town wherein such proposed annexed territory is located as owning or representing more than one-half of the taxable real property of such annexed territory or as owning or representing more than one-half of the taxable real property of such annexed territory owned by the residents thereof, may be presented to the commissioners of such fire district. Each person signing the petition shall state opposite his or her name the assessed valuation of the property assessed to him or her in such territory. Such petition must be verified by at least three persons signing the same to the effect that the petition represents in value more than one-half of the assessed valuation of the property as above described or that it represents in value more than one-half of the taxable real property of such territory owned by the residents thereof. Such petition must be accompanied by a resolution of the board of supervisors of the county in which such territory is situated consenting to such annexation. Upon the presentation of such petition and consent the fire commissioners shall cause a proposition for such annexation to be submitted at a special election. If the proposition be adopted, the petition and consent and the certificate of the election shall be recorded in the book of records of the commissioners of *Annexation of territory not in city, village or fire district, to adjoining fire district. Petition. Election on proposition.*

Annexation.
in effect
when.
the district. Such annexation shall take effect upon the receipt by the fire commissioners of the certificate of the clerk of the board of supervisors, under the seal of his office, certifying that he has received and placed on file in the office of the board of supervisors an outline map and description of the corporate limits of such fire district as extended, together with the date of filing the same in his office. Such outline map and description shall plainly show and describe the territory annexed. A certificate thereof containing a description of the territory annexed shall, within ten days after such election, be filed by the fire commissioners in the offices of the clerk of the town and of the county in which such annexed territory is situated.

Map and
description
of terri-
tory.

§ 2. This act shall take effect immediately.

Chap. 128.

AN ACT to amend the religious corporation law, in relation to the sale, mortgage and lease of real property of religious corporations.

Became a law March 25, 1913, with the approval of the Governor. Passed, three-fifths being present.

The People of the State of New York, represented in Senate and Assembly, do enact as follows:

L. 1909, ch.
53, § 12, as
amended by
L. 1912,
ch. 290,
amended.

Section 1. Section twelve of article two of chapter fifty-three of the laws of nineteen hundred and nine, entitled "An act in relation to religious corporations, constituting chapter fifty-one of the consolidated laws," as amended by chapter two hundred and ninety of the laws of nineteen hundred and twelve, is hereby amended to read as follows:

§ 12. **Sale, mortgage and lease of real property of religious corporations.** A religious corporation shall not sell or mortgage any of its real property without applying for and obtaining leave of the court therefor pursuant to the provisions of article four of the general corporation law. The trustees of an incorporated Protestant Episcopal church shall not vote upon any resolution or proposition for the sale, mortgage or lease of its real property, unless the rector of such church, if it then has a rector, shall be present, and shall not make application to the court for leave to sell or mortgage any of its real property without the consent of the bishop and standing committee of the diocese to which such

church belongs; but in case the see be vacant, or the bishop be
absent or unable to act, the consent of the standing committee
with their certificate of the vacancy of the see or of the absence
or disability of the bishop shall suffice. The trustees of an incorporated Roman Catholic church shall not make application to the
court for leave to mortgage, lease or sell any of its real property
without the consent of the archbishop or bishop of the diocese to
which such church belongs or in case of their absence or inability
to act, without the consent of the vicar general or administrator of
such diocese. The petition of the trustees of an incorporated
Protestant Episcopal church or Roman Catholic church shall, in
addition to the matters required by article four of the general corporation law to be set forth therein, set forth that this section has
also been complied with. But lots, plats or burial permits in a
cemetery owned by a religious corporation may be sold without
applying for or obtaining leave of the court. No cemetery lands
of a religious corporation shall be mortgaged while used for cemetery purposes. Except as otherwise provided in this chapter in respect to a religious corporation of a specified denomination, any
solvent religious corporation may, by order of the supreme court,
obtained as above provided in proceedings to sell, mortgage or
lease real property, convey the whole or any part of its real property to another religious corporation, for a consideration of one
dollar or other nominal consideration, and for the purpose of applying the provision of article four of the general corporation law,
a proposed conveyance for such consideration shall be treated as
a sale, but it shall not be necessary to show, in the petition or
otherwise, nor for the court to find, that the pecuniary or pro-
prietary interest of the grantor corporation will be promoted
thereby; and the interests of such grantor shall be deemed to be
promoted if it appears that religious or charitable objects generally are conserved by such conveyance; provided, however, that
such an order shall not be made if tending to impair the claim
or remedy of any creditor. If a sale or mortgage of any real
property of any such religious corporation has been heretofore or
shall be hereafter made and a conveyance or mortgage executed
and delivered without the authority of a court of competent jurisdiction, obtained as required by law, or not in accordance with its
directions, the court may, thereafter, upon the application of the
corporation, or of the grantee or mortgagee in any such conveyance or mortgage or of any person claiming through or under any

such grantee or mortgagee, upon such notice to such corporation, or its successor, and such other person or persons as may be interested in such property, as the court may prescribe, confirm said previously executed conveyance or mortgage, and order and direct the execution and delivery of a confirmatory deed or mortgage, or the recording of such confirmatory order in the office where deeds and mortgages are recorded in the county in which the property is located; and upon compliance with the said order such original conveyance or mortgage shall be as valid and of the same force and effect as if it had been executed and delivered after due proceedings had in accordance with the statute and the direction of the court.[1] But no confirmatory order may be granted unless the consents required in the first part of this section for a Protestant Episcopal or Roman Catholic church have first been given by the prescribed authority thereof, either upon the original application or upon the application for the confirmatory order.

§ 2. This act shall take effect immediately.

Chap. 129.

AN ACT to amend the education law, relative to the consolidation of districts by a vote of a district meeting.

Became a law March 25, 1913, with the approval of the Governor. Passed, three-fifths being present.

The People of the State of New York, represented in Senate and Assembly, do enact as follows:

§§ 130-134 added to L. 1909, ch. 21, as generally amended by L. 1910, ch. 140.

Section 1. Article five of chapter twenty-one of the laws of nineteen hundred and nine, entitled "An act relating to education, constituting chapter sixteen of the consolidated laws," as amended by chapter one hundred and forty of the laws of nineteen hundred and ten, is hereby amended by inserting therein new sections to be known as sections one hundred and thirty, one hundred and thirty-one, one hundred and thirty-two, one hundred and thirty-three, and one hundred and thirty-four, to read as follows:

---

[1] Sentence omitted which read: " Such confirmatory order shall be granted only on proof, by petition or otherwise, satisfactory to the court granting the order, that an original proceeding was instituted and showing in what respect such original proceeding was defective, the facts applicable to the said defects and the conditions existing at the time of the application for the confirmatory order."

§ 130. Consolidation of districts by vote of qualified electors.
Two or more common school districts may be consolidated and
created as one common school district, *of two or more union free
school districts may be consolidated and created as one union free
school district, or one or more common school districts may be
consolidated with one or more union free school districts and
created as a union free school district, by a vote of the qualified
electors thereof as provided in the following sections:

§ 131. Request for meeting to consolidate districts; notices of
meeting. 1. Whenever ten or more of the qualified electors of
each of two or more districts shall sign a request for a meeting to
be held for the purpose of determining whether such districts
shall be consolidated as a common school district, and submit the
same to the trustees or board of education of each of such districts, it shall be the duty of such trustees or board of education
to give public notice that a meeting of the qualified electors of
such districts will be held at some convenient place within such
districts, as centrally located as may be, to vote upon the question
of consolidating such districts. Such notice shall specify the day
and hour when such meeting shall be held, not less than twenty
nor more than thirty days after the posting, service or publication
of such notice. If the trustees or board of education shall refuse
or neglect to give such notice within twenty days after such request is submitted the commissioner of education may authorize
and direct any qualified elector of the district to give such notice.

2. If any part of either of such districts is situated wholly or
partly within an incorporated village in which one or more newspapers are published, such notice shall be published once in each
week for three consecutive weeks before such meeting in all the
newspapers published in such village, and shall also be posted at
least twenty days prior to such meeting, in at least five conspicuous places in each district. In all other districts the trustees
or board of education of each district shall authorize and direct
a qualified elector thereof to notify each qualified elector of such
district of such meeting by delivering to him a copy of such notice,
or in case of his absence from home, by leaving a copy thereof,
or so much thereof as relates to the time, place and object of the
meeting, at the place of his abode, at least twenty days prior to
the time of such meeting.

3. The reasonable expense of the publication and service of

---

* So in original.

such notice shall be chargeable upon the districts, if the vote be
in favor of consolidation, and if not, shall be paid by the persons
signing the request for such meeting as provided by section one
hundred and forty-four.

§ 132. Proceedings at meeting for consolidation; adoption of
resolution; proceedings to be filed. Such meeting shall be organized as provided in section one hundred and forty-five. If
there are at least ten qualified electors of each of the two or more
districts joining in such request, present at such meeting, such
meeting may adopt a resolution to consolidate such districts. The
vote upon such resolution shall be by taking and recording the
ayes and noes. The clerk shall keep a poll-list upon which shall
be recorded the names of all qualified electors voting upon the
resolution, the districts in which such electors reside, and how
each elector voted. If it shall appear from the votes so recorded
that a majority of the qualified electors present and voting from
each district are in favor of such resolution it shall be declared
adopted. If a majority of the qualified electors present and voting from each district are not in favor of such resolution, all further proceedings at such meeting, except a motion to reconsider
or adjourn shall be dispensed with and no such meeting shall be
again called within one year thereafter.

Copies of such request, notice of meeting, order of the commissioner of education directing a qualified elector to call such
meeting, if any, and the minutes of the meeting, including the
record of the vote upon the resolution, duly certified by the chairman and clerk, shall be transmitted by either the chairman or
clerk, one to the commissioner of education, and one to the district
superintendent of schools in whose jurisdiction such districts are
located.

§ 133. Order creating consolidated district; effect. The district superintendent shall thereupon issue an order consolidating
such districts and creating a common school district, or union free
school district, as the case may be, designating such district by
number. Such order shall take effect at some date to be specified
therein, not more than three months after the date of the meeting. He shall file such order in the town clerk's office of the
town in which such districts are located. If such districts are
located in two or more supervisory districts such order shall be
executed jointly by the district superintendents of such districts.
Such order shall have the same effect as an order executed by a

district superintendent dissolving two or more common school districts and forming a new district therefrom, or dissolving one or
more of such districts and uniting the territory thereof to a union
free school district. But a district superintendent may, upon a
petition of at least twenty-five qualified electors of the consolidated district, where one of the districts consolidated is a union
free school district, or shall, when directed by the commissioner of
education, direct the clerk of the board of education of such union
free school district to call a special meeting of the qualified
electors thereof, for the purpose of increasing the number of members of the board of education of such new district, subject to the
limitations prescribed by section three hundred and eight of this
chapter, or for the purpose of terminating the offices of the members of the board of education in office when the consolidation
takes effect. If it be determined to increase the number of such
members, such meeting shall elect the additional number so determined upon, as provided in such section three hundred and
eight. If it be determined to elect a new board of education in
place of the board in office when the consolidation takes effect,
such meeting shall proceed with the election of a board of education as provided in sections three hundred and one and three hundred and two of this chapter.

§ 134. **District quotas of consolidated districts.** There shall
be apportioned and paid to the district created by the consolidation of districts as provided in section one hundred and thirty-
two of this article district quotas for each of the districts consolidated in the same amount and under the same conditions as though
such consolidation had not been effected. Such apportionment
shall be based upon the assessed valuation of the taxable property
within such districts as they existed at the time of the consolidation, and the trustees or board of education of the consolidated
district shall include in their report a statement of such assessed
valuation.

§ 2. Section one hundred and thirty-three of such chapter as § 133, as
amended by said chapter one hundred and forty of the laws of amended by
nineteen hundred and ten is hereby renumbered section one hun- L. 1910,
dred and thirty-four-a, and amended to read as follows: renumbered
§ 134a, and
§ 134-a. **The bonded indebtedness of certain dissolved districts.** amended.
Whenever two or more districts are dissolved pursuant to the
provisions of section one hundred and twenty-eight of this article
and annexed to adjoining districts or consolidated as provided

in section one hundred and thirty-two,[1] the bonded indebtedness of any such district shall thereupon become a charge upon the enlarged district formed by such annexation. The board of education or trustees[2] of such district shall raise by tax an amount sufficient to pay *one of the bonds and interest thereof of such district as the same shall become due.

§ 3. Sections one hundred and ninety, one hundred and ninety-five and two hundred and twenty-five of such chapter as amended by chapter one hundred and forty of the laws of nineteen hundred and ten, are hereby amended to read as follows:

§ 190. **Notice of first meeting of district.** Whenever any school district shall be formed, or two or more common school districts are consolidated as provided in section one hundred and thirty-two[3] the district superintendent of schools,[4] or any one or more of such district superintendents[5] within whose districts it may be, shall prepare a notice describing such district, and appointing a time and place for the first district meeting, and deliver such notice to a taxable inhabitant of the district.

§ 195. **Annual meetings of districts re-formed after dissolution.** The districts formed by the dissolution of a union free school district, as provided in sections one hundred and forty-six and one hundred and forty-seven[6] of this chapter shall hold their annual meetings on the first Tuesday of May[7] next after the dissolution of such union free school district, and shall elect officers as now required by law.

§ 225. **Terms of officers of newly created district.** The terms of all officers elected at the first meeting of a newly created district shall expire on the first Tuesday of May[7] next thereafter.

§ 4. This act shall take effect immediately.

---

* So in original.
[1] Words " or consolidated as provided in section one hundred and thirty-two," new.
[2] Words " or trustees " new.
[3] Words " or two or more common school districts are consolidated as provided in section one hundred and thirty-two," new.
[4] Words " district superintendent of schools," substituted for words " school commissioner."
[5] Words " district superintendents," substituted for word " commissioners."
[6] Words " one hundred and forty-six and one hundred and forty-seven," substituted for words " one hundred and twenty-nine and one hundred and thirty."
[7] Word " May " substituted for word "August."

Chap. 130.

AN ACT to amend the education law, relative to the apportionment of school moneys by district superintendents of schools.

Became a law March 25, 1913, with the approval of the Governor. Passed, three-fifths being present.

The People of the State of New York, represented in Senate and Assembly, do enact as follows:

Section 1. Sections three hundred and sixty-five and four hundred and ninety-eight of chapter twenty-one of the laws of nineteen hundred and nine, entitled "An act relative to education, constituting chapter sixteen of the consolidated laws," as amended by chapter one hundred and forty of the laws of nineteen hundred and ten, are hereby amended to read as follows:[1]

L. 1909, ch.
21, §§ 365,
488, as
generally
amended by
L. 1910,
ch. 140,
amended.

§ 365. **Report by supervisors to district superintendents.** On the first Tuesday of February in each year, each supervisor shall make a return in writing to the district superintendent of schools of the supervisory district in which the town is situated, showing the amounts of school moneys in his hands not paid on the orders of trustees for teachers' salaries, and the districts to which they stand accredited, and if such moneys remain in his hands, he shall report that fact; and thereafter he shall not pay out any of said moneys until he shall have received the certificate of the next apportionment; and the moneys so returned by him shall be reapportioned as directed in article eighteen of this chapter.

§ 498. **Apportionment of school moneys by district superintendents.** The district superintendent of schools shall, on or before the fifteenth day of February in each year, apportion the supervision, district and teachers' quotas to the several districts entitled thereto, within his supervisory district, as shown by the certificate of the commissioner of education to the said district superintendent. He shall procure from the supervisors of the towns in his district a transcript showing the unexpended moneys in their hands applicable to the payment of teachers' salaries. The amounts in each supervisor's hands shall be charged as a partial payment of the sums apportioned to the town teachers' salaries.

He shall procure from the county treasurer a full list and statement of all payments to him of moneys for or on account

---

[1] Sections materially amended.

of fines and penalties, or accruing from any other source, for the benefit of schools and of the towns or districts for whose benefit the same were received. Such of said moneys as belong to a particular district, he shall set apart and credit to it; and such as belong to the schools of a town he shall set apart and credit to the schools in that town, and shall apportion them together with such as belong to the schools of the county as hereinafter provided for the payment of teachers' salaries.

He shall sign, in duplicate, a certificate, showing the amounts apportioned and set apart to each school district and part of a district, and the towns in which they were situated, and shall forthwith deliver one of said duplicates to the treasurer of the county and transmit the other to the commissioner of education.

He shall certify to the supervisor of each town, in his supervisory district the amount of school moneys apportioned to each district or part of a district of his town for teachers' wages.

§ 2. This act shall take effect immediately.

Chap. 131.

AN ACT to amend the highway law, in relation to the construction of state and county highways in villages.

Became a law March 26, 1913, with the approval of the Governor. Passed, three-fifths being present.

The People of the State of New York, represented in Senate and Assembly, do enact as follows:

L. 1909, ch. 30, § 137, as amended by L. 1910, ch. 233, L. 1911. ch. 88, and L. 1912, ch. 88, amended.

Section 1. Section one hundred and thirty-seven of chapter thirty of the laws of nineteen hundred and nine, entitled "An act relating to highways, constituting chapter twenty-five of the consolidated laws," as amended by chapter two hundred and thirty-three of the laws of nineteen hundred and ten, chapter eighty-eight of the laws of nineteen hundred and eleven and chapter eighty-eight of the laws of nineteen hundred and twelve,[1a] is hereby amended to read as follows:

§ 137. **State and county highways in villages and cities of the second and third classes.** A state or county highway may be constructed through a city of the second or third class or a village in the same manner as outside thereof, unless the street through which it runs has, in the opinion of the commission, been so im-

---

[1a] Section 137 is further amended by L. 1913, ch. 319, post.

proved or paved as to form a continuous and improved highway of sufficient permanence as not to warrant its reconstruction, in which case such highway shall be constructed or improved to the place where such paved or improved street begins. If it is desired to construct or improve any portion of a state or county highway within such village or city of the second or third class at a width greater than that provided for in the plans and specifications therefor, or if a modification of the plans and specifications is desired by which the cost thereof is increased, the board of trustees of such village or common council of such city shall petition the commission by resolution, to so modify such plans and specifications as to provide for such construction. The commission shall thereupon cause the plans, specifications and estimate for such highway to be modified so as to provide for such additional construction, and shall provide therefor in the contract. Upon the completion of such state or county highway within the village or city of the second or third class in accordance with such modified plans and specifications the commission shall notify the board of trustees or common council, as the case may be, as provided in the case of a county highway. Such board or common council may file a written protest against the acceptance of such work with the commission who shall examine in respect thereto, and if it is sustained the commission shall delay the acceptance of the highway within the village or city until it be properly completed. Upon the proper completion thereof and the notification as above provided, the commission shall certify to the board of trustees or common council the cost of such additional construction, and such board or common council shall pay the same out of moneys raised by tax or from the issue and sale of bonds as provided in the village law,[1] if in a village, or by the general or special act governing bond issues and taxation in any such city if in a city of the second or third class. The provisions of the general village law, special village or city charters and other general or special laws relative to the pavement or improvement of streets and the assessment and payment of the cost thereof shall apply, as far as may be, to such additional construction and the assessment and payment of the cost thereof, [2]except that the provisions of section one hundred and sixty-six[3] of the village law requiring the owners,

[1] See § 128 (as amended by L. 1910, ch. 4, and L. 1911, chaps. 57, 738), §§ 129, 130; and § 131 (as amended by L. 1910, ch. 598).
[2] Remainder of section new.
[3] As amended by L. 1909, ch. 430.

or any of the owners, of the frontage on a street to consent to the improvement or pavement thereof, or requiring a hearing to be given to the persons interested shall not apply to the portion of the improvement or pavement of a state or county highway the expenses for which is required to be paid by the village.

§ 2. This act shall take effect immediately.

Chap. 132.

AN ACT to provide means for the completion and furnishing of the new Schenectady county jail and the furnishing of the new Schenectady county courthouse in the city of Schenectady, New York, for the use of the county of Schenectady.

Became a law March 26, 1913, with the approval of the Governor. Passed, three-fifths being present.

The People of the State of New York, represented in Senate and Assembly, do enact as follows:

Bond issue authoris'd.

Section 1. The board of supervisors of the county of Schenectady is hereby authorized to borrow upon the faith and credit of the said county such a sum of money as shall be sufficient to meet and pay all of the expenditures necessary to complete and furnish the new Schenectady county jail, and to complete the furnishing of the new courthouse, both of which are situated in the city of Schenectady, New York, for the use of the county of Schenectady, not exceeding the sum of one hundred thousand dollars, and to issue the bonds of the said county of Schenectady therefor, bearing interest at a rate of not exceeding four and one-half per centum per annum, payable semi-annually; the principal of such bonds shall be payable at such time and times not exceeding fifty years from the respective date of issue, and in such amount in each and every year from the date of issue, as shall be fixed and determined by the said board of supervisors of such county, excepting, however, that the sum of two thousand dollars of the principal of said bonds issued hereunder shall be made payable each and every year from the first day of January, nineteen hundred and thirteen, said bonds to bear interest from the date of issue and none of such bonds to be renewed when due. Said bonds shall be of the denomination of not less than one thousand dollars each, shall be signed by the county treasurer of

Bonds, interest, maturity, etc.

the county of Schenectady, and countersigned by the chairman
of the board of supervisors of said county, and the seal of said
board of supervisors shall be affixed to each of said bonds, by the
said county treasurer. Said bonds shall be sold by the county *When to be sold.*
treasurer of said county from time to time, as hereinafter provided, as the proceeds shall be required by the said board of
supervisors for the purpose of the completion and furnishing
of such buildings. Said bonds may be registered in the office *To be registered.*
of the county treasurer of the county of Schenectady, and shall
be in such form consistent with law, as the said board of super- *Form.*
visors shall deem proper; interest shall be payable at one or more *Interest, where payable.*
banking institutions in the county of Schenectady, New York, to
be designated in the body of said bond. The county treasurer *Account of moneys raised.*
shall keep a separate account of the moneys raised from said
bonds and shall pay therefrom upon the order of the said board *Payments.*
of supervisors, from time to time, such amounts as shall be required under this act to pay for the completion and furnishing of
the said buildings. Said bonds shall be negotiated by the county *Sale, how conducted.*
treasurer by selling the same at his office to the highest bidder at
public auction or in such other manner as he may deem for the best
interests of the said county, at not less than the par value thereof.
Said county treasurer shall give public notice of the time and
place of any sale of such bonds by public auction and of any
reception and opening of sealed proposals therefor by publishing
a notice thereof for at least fifteen days previous to each sale
or opening, in the newspapers published in the county of Schenectady designated by said board of supervisors for the publication
of official notices. The county treasurer of said county is hereby *Advances for expenditures prior to bond issue, authorized.*
authorized to make advances for the necessary expenditures for
the purposes of the completion and furnishing of said buildings
from any funds of the county in his possession prior to the issuance of said bonds herein authorized, and to be reimbursed from
the proceeds of the subsequent sale of such bonds.

§ 2. It shall be the duty of the board of supervisors of said *Tax for payment.*
county to be caused to be raised yearly, in each fiscal year from
the time said bonds shall be issued, by taxes upon the taxable
property in said county in the same manner as other taxes are
levied, a sufficient sum to pay the interest upon said bonds when
and as the same shall become due and payable, and the principal of such bonds as the same shall become due.

§ 3. The county treasurer of the county of Schenectady *Bond of county treasurer.*
shall be required before the issuance of said bonds to file with

the county clerk of the county of Schenectady a bond in the penalty of fifty thousand dollars, with sufficient surety or sureties thereon to be approved as to form and sufficiency of said surety or sureties by the county judge of Schenectady county, conditioned for the faithful performance of his duties as such county treasurer in the issuance of said bonds and the handling of the moneys received therefrom, and the expenses of such bond to be a county charge. The said board shall advertise in one or more newspapers published in Schenectady county for such time as they deem necessary for bids for the performance of the work and supplying the materials required in the completion of said new jail and for the furnishing of said jail and courthouse. The form of all contracts for which bids are so invited shall be fixed by said board and the work of completing and furnishing the said new jail and furnishing said new courthouse, may be divided into as many contracts as said board shall elect. All bids received in response to said advertisements shall be publicly opened at a meeting of the board of supervisors and said board shall award each contract as aforesaid, to the lowest responsible bidder, and the said board may accept or reject either or any of said bids, and may readvertise for bids, whenever and as often as said board of supervisors shall deem it necessary for the best interest of the county so to do. All said contracts when awarded shall be executed by said board, in the name and on behalf of said county. Each bidder to whom a contract is awarded as hereinbefore provided, must execute and deliver to said board of supervisors a good and sufficient bond to said county with surety satisfactory to said board of supervisors in such form and for such sum as said board shall direct, for the faithful and prompt performance of such contract. If such accepted bidder for any contract shall fail to execute such contract, or fail to execute and deliver the bonds herein provided, after notice that a contract has been awarded to him, he shall forfeit all right to the contract or any forfeiture deposited, and the said contract shall thereupon be readvertised and relet by said board. Said contracts, when executed, shall be carried out under the direction and supervision and subject to the inspection and approval at all times of said board of supervisors.

§ 4. This act shall take effect immediately.

[Marginal notes:]

Advertising for bids for work.

Form of contracts.

Award of contracts.

Bond of contractor.

Reletting on failure of contractor.

Supervision of board of supervisors.

Chap. 133.

AN ACT to amend the code of criminal procedure, in relation to
deposit instead of bail.

Became a law March 26, 1913, with the approval of the Governor. Passed,
three-fifths being present.

*The People of the State of New York, represented in Senate
and Assembly, do enact as follows:*

Section 1. Section five hundred and eighty-six of the code of § 586 amended.
criminal procedure is hereby amended to read as follows:

§ 586. **Deposit, when and how made.** The defendant, at any
time after an order admitting him to bail, instead of giving bail,
or a witness committed in default of an undertaking to appear
and testify, instead of entering into such an undertaking, may
deposit with the county treasurer of the county in which he is
held to answer or appear, or in the city of New York with the
chamberlain,[1] or with the magistrate by whom he is so held, or with
any other justice or magistrate of the same court or with the clerk
or deputy clerk of a court held by any such justice or magistrate, or
with the warden, deputy warden or keeper in charge of the jail in
which he so stands committed, the sum mentioned in the order
of commitment, and upon delivering to the officer in whose custody he is, a certificate of such deposit from such justice, magistrate, clerk or deputy clerk, or upon the said sum being deposited
in money with such warden, deputy warden or keeper in charge,
the defendant must forthwith be discharged from custody.

When any such deposit is so made, the justice, magistrate or
other person with whom it is deposited shall deposit the sum so
received by him in the same manner as may be by law provided
for the payment and deposit of money with the clerk of such
court.

[2]Upon the termination of the proceeding the money so deposited
shall, by order of the presiding justice or magistrate, be refunded
to such defendant or witness.

Whenever any person other than the defendant, or a witness
mentioned in this section, in behalf of the defendant, or witness,
deposits with the person authorized to receive the same, the sum
of money required to procure the discharge as aforesaid of said

---

[1] Words " or in the city of New York with the chamberlain," new.
[2] Remainder of section new.

defendant, or witness, the defendant or witness may execute a
consent that upon the termination of the proceeding in which
the deposit is made, the money so deposited be refunded to the
person depositing it. Said consent shall be filed with the clerk
of the court in which the proceeding is pending and upon the
termination of the proceeding, the presiding justice or magistrate
shall make an order directing the county treasurer, or in the city
of New York the chamberlain, to refund the money deposited
to the person making the deposit and the order directing such
refund shall contain an endorsement by the clerk to the effect
that such consent has been executed and filed.

In effect
Sept. 1,
1913.

§ 2. This act shall take effect September first, nineteen hundred
and thirteen.

Chap. 134.

AN ACT to amend the tax law, in relation to payment of expenses in certiorari proceedings.

Became a law March 26, 1913, with the approval of the Governor. Passed,
three-fifths being present.

*The People of the State of New York, represented in Senate
and Assembly, do enact as follows:*

L. 1909, ch.
62, § 47, as
amended by
L. 1911,
ch. 471,
amended.

Section 1. Section forty-seven of chapter sixty-two of the laws
of nineteen hundred and nine, entitled "An act in relation to
taxation, constituting chapter sixty of the consolidated laws," as
amended by chapter four hundred and seventy-one of the laws of
nineteen hundred and eleven, is hereby amended to read as
follows:

§ 47. **Tax commissioners to appear by counsel; employment of
experts.** In any proceeding for the review of an assessment of a
special franchise made by the state board of tax commissioners,
said state board of tax commissioners is authorized to appear
by counsel to be designated by the attorney-general. The attorney-
general or such counsel may employ experts and the compensation
of such counsel and experts and their necessary and proper expenses and disbursements, incurred or made in such proceeding,
and upon any appeals therein, shall when audited and allowed
as are other charges against such tax district, be a charge upon
the tax district upon whose rolls appears the assessment sought to
be reviewed. Where, in one proceeding, there is reviewed the

assessment of a special franchise in more than one tax district, separate accounts shall be rendered for said costs, expenses and disbursements to the proper officer of each of said tax districts and audited and allowed by him as aforesaid. For the purposes of this section, the city of New York shall be deemed one tax district. [1]If provision shall not have been made for the payment of such expense in any year, then the officers who are empowered by law to make such provision in any county, city, town or other political subdivision of the state, are hereby authorized and directed to raise money to such an amount as may be necessary, in any manner provided by law for meeting expenses in anticipation of the collection of taxes and to pay such expense therefrom. The amount so raised shall be included in the amount to be raised by tax in the ensuing year.

§ 2. This act shall take effect immediately.

Chap. 135.

AN ACT to declare the effect of the appearance by the attorney-general in a proceeding in the surrogate's court of the county of Putnam for the disposition of the real property of Caroline Palmer, deceased, for the payment of debts and funeral expenses.

Became a law March 26, 1913, with the approval of the Governor. Passed, three-fifths being present.

The People of the State of New York, represented in Senate and Assembly, do enact as follows:

Section 1. The appearance of the attorney-general of the state of New York, on or about January twenty-second, nineteen hundred and nine, in a certain proceeding pending in the surrogate's court of the county of Putnam, brought by Henry B. Stevens, as administrator of the goods, chattels and credits of Caroline Palmer, deceased, for the disposition of the real property of such decedent for the payment of debts and funeral expenses, shall be as valid and effectual as though at the time of such appearance chapter four hundred and thirty-seven of the laws of nineteen hundred and eleven, amending section twenty-seven hundred and fifty-four of the code of civil procedure, had then been in force.

§ 2. This act shall take effect immediately.

---

[1] Remainder of section new.

8

Chap. 136.

AN ACT to amend the public health law, in relation to the fees of
the health officer of the port of New York.

**Became a law March 26, 1913, with the approval of the Governor. Passed,
three-fifths being present.**

The People of the State of New York, represented in Senate
and Assembly, do enact as follows:

L. 1909,
ch. 49,
§ 144, as
amended by
L. 1909,
ch. 375,
and L. 1910,
ch. 425,
amended.

Section 1. Section one hundred and forty-four of chapter forty-
nine of the laws of nineteen hundred and nine, entitled "An act
in relation to the public health, constituting chapter forty-five
of the consolidated laws," as amended by chapter three hundred
and seventy-five of the laws of nineteen hundred and nine and
chapter four hundred and twenty-five of the laws of nineteen
hundred and ten, is hereby amended to read as follows:[1]

§ 144. **Fees of health officer, payment of salaries and expenses.**
The health officer shall receive, on behalf of the state of New
York, for services rendered by him, fees at rates not to exceed
the following, namely: For inspection of any vessel from a
foreign port, whose registered gross tonnage shall exceed five
hundred tons, the sum of ten dollars. For inspection of every
vessel from a foreign port, whose gross registered tonnage shall
not exceed five hundred tons, five dollars. For inspection of
every such other vessel, as the health officer may deem to be quar-
antinable and subject to visitation and inspection and so designate either by name or by class, three dollars. For medical inspection of third-class or steerage passengers upon all ships entering the port of New York, as follows: For the first one hundred, or fraction thereof, five dollars; for every additional one
hundred, or fraction thereof, of such passengers, three dollars.
For each special permit issued for the discharge of cargo, portion
of cargo or baggage brought as freight, one dollar. For special
sanitary inspection of every vessel before or after the discharge
of cargo or ballast, ten dollars. For fumigation and disinfection
of every vessel which, in the judgment of the health officer shall
require fumigation and disinfection at rates to be fixed in proportion to the service rendered by the health officer, but not to
exceed the following: For vessels whose gross registered tonnage
shall not exceed two thousand tons, fifty dollars. For vessels

---

[1] Section materially amended.

whose gross registered tonnage shall exceed two thousand tons, for every thousand, or fraction thereof, in excess of the said two thousand tons, twenty-five dollars. For boarding every vessel carrying passengers between sunset and sunrise and inspecting the same, at the request of the owner, consignee or master of the vessel and granting pratique when such pratique can be given without danger to the public health, fifteen dollars. For vaccination of persons on vessels, each twenty-five cents. But no charge shall be made for the vaccination of any person who shall have been successfully vaccinated by the medical officer of said vessel. For the maintenance and care of all persons removed from vessels and detained at quarantine for observation, one dollar and fifty cents per capita per diem. For the maintenance, care, medical treatment and hospital accommodation of all persons removed from vessels, whose physical condition shall make such medical treatment and hospital accommodation necessary in the judgment of the health officer, two dollars per capita per diem. He shall pay all the salaries and wages of the deputy health officers and other officers and employees as may be necessary for the performance of the duties imposed upon him by law for the carrying on of a quarantine establishment, and shall pay all the necessary expenses of maintaining such establishment and the steamboat service necessarily connected therewith. The salary of the health officer and of all persons appointed or employed by him, and all the expenses necessarily incurred by him in the performance of the duties of his office, shall be paid by the state out of the money appropriated therefor. There may be annually appropriated for the health officer a contingent fund which, notwithstanding any other provision of law, may be paid to him by the treasurer on the warrant of the comptroller. Such fund may be used by him to pay the current expenses of his office for which an immediate payment in cash is required, but he shall render to the state comptroller on or before the fifth day of each month a sworn itemized statement of all expenditures from such fund during the preceding calendar month. The health officer shall keep an account of all moneys received or disbursed by him under this section. This section shall not affect the liability of masters or owners of vessels, or consignees or agents of such masters or owners of vessels, passengers or other persons to pay for such services, labor or work as they are respectively required to pay

or discharge by law.   And the health officer shall have the power
to order to quarantine and detain therein any vessel whose master, owner, consignee or agent doing business in the city of New
York, if there be such agent of said master, owner or consignee,
or any one of such, shall refuse or neglect to pay the fees and
charges herein provided for within three days after notification
to such master, owner, consignee, or agent of the fact that such
charges have been assessed against such vessel.   Such power may
be exercised by the health officer within a period of one year after
the performance of the services for which such charges are made;
and such vessel may be released from the health officer's custody
as aforesaid only upon the filing of a bond in double the amount
of said charges, or a judicial determination with respect to the
same.   Nothing herein contained shall affect the right of the
health officer, or of the state through the health officer, to proceed
for the collection of such fees, as is otherwise by law provided.

§ 2. This act shall take effect immediately.

Chap. 137.

AN ACT to continue the commission created by chapter five hundred and sixty-one of the laws of nineteen hundred and eleven,
entitled "An act to create a commission to investigate the
conditions under which manufacture is carried on in cities of
the first and second class in this state, and making appropriation therefor," and to enlarge the scope of the investigation
of the commission and making an appropriation therefor.

Became a law March 27, 1913, with the approval of the Governor. Passed,
three-fifths being present.

*The People of the State of New York, represented in Senate
and Assembly, do enact as follows:*

Commission continued.

Section 1. The commission created by chapter five hundred and
sixty-one of the laws of nineteen hundred and eleven, entitled "An
act to create a commission to investigate the conditions under
which manufacture is carried on in cities of the first and second
class in this state, and making an appropriation therefor," is
hereby continued with all the powers conferred by said chapter, as
amended by chapter twenty-one of the laws of nineteen hundred
and twelve.

§ 2. In addition to the powers heretofore conferred upon it by such chapter, as amended, the said commission shall have power to inquire into the wages of labor in all industries and employments and the conditions under which labor is carried on throughout the state, and into the advisability of fixing minimum rates of wages or of other legislation relating to the wages or conditions of labor in general or in any industry. Said commission shall also have power to subpoena and require the attendance of witnesses and the production of books and papers pertaining to the investigation and inquiries hereby authorized and to take the testimony of all such witnesses and to examine all such books and papers. in relation to any matter which it has power to investigate.

Power to investigate wages and conditions of labor.

Powers as to obtaining testimony.

§ 3. The said commission shall make a report of its proceedings, together with its recommendations, including a revision of the labor law, to be prepared by the said commission if deemed advisable by it, to the legislature on or before the fifteenth day of February, nineteen hundred and fourteen.

Report; revision of labor law.

§ 4. The sum of fifty thousand dollars ($50,000), or so much thereof as may be needed, is hereby appropriated for the actual and necessary expenses of the commission in carrying out the provisions of chapter five hundred and sixty-one of the laws of nineteen hundred and eleven, as amended, and of this act, payable by the treasurer on the warrant of the comptroller on the order of the chairman of said commission.

Appropriation.

§ 5. This act shall take effect immediately.

Chap. 138.

AN ACT to amend chapter eight hundred and fifty-five of the laws of nineteen hundred and eleven, entitled "An act authorizing the justices of the appellate division of the supreme court in the first department to retire employees for incapacity and providing for their compensation," in relation to the services prerequisite to such retirement, and to voluntary retirement.

Became a law March 27, 1913, with the approval of the Governor. Passed, three-fifths being present.

The People of the State of New York, represented in Senate and Assembly, do enact as follows:

Section 1. Section one of chapter eight hundred and fifty-five of the laws of nineteen hundred and eleven, entitled "An act au- L. 1911, ch. 855, § 1, as amended by L. 1912, ch. 486, amended.   thorizing the justices of the appellate division of the supreme court in the first department to retire employees for incapacity and providing for their compensation," as amended by chapter four hundred and eighty-six of the laws of nineteen hundred and twelve, is hereby amended to read as follows:

Who may be retired.   § 1. The appellate division of the supreme court in the first department is hereby authorized in its discretion to retire any clerk, assistant clerk, stenographer, librarian or attendant who shall have served as such in the supreme court in and for the first judicial district or in any court which has been consolidated with the said supreme court, or who has had charge of the records of any such court in the office of the clerk of the county of New York, and who shall have become physically or mentally incapacitated for the Length of service. further performance of the duties of his position, provided such person was employed continuously for a period of twelve and one-half years[1] or more in one or more of such positions and for twelve and one-half years[2] or more prior to such service was employed continuously either in one or more of such positions or in any department or office of the state or of the county or city of Payment of annuity. New York. Any person or persons retired from service pursuant to this act shall be paid out of the funds apportioned to the supreme court of the first department an annual sum for annuity to be determined by said appellate division but not exceeding one-half of the average amount of his annual salary or compensation for a period of two years preceding the time of such retirement. Such annuity shall be paid in equal monthly instalments during the lifetime of the person or persons so retired.

§ 2 added.   § 2. Such chapter is hereby amended by adding thereto a new section, to be section two, to read as follows:

Retirement of employees having formerly been employed in other courts or departments.   § 2. Any employee mentioned in section one of this act who shall have been employed continuously for a period of twelve and one-half years or more in the supreme court in and for the first judicial district and for twelve and one-half years or more prior to such service was employed continuously in any other court, department or office of the state or of the county or city of New York, Length of aggregate service. provided however that a person desiring retirement shall have served thirty years in the aggregate, shall upon his own application in writing to the appellate division of the supreme court in the Payment of annuity. first department be retired, and shall be paid an annual sum for

---

[1] Formerly " fifteen years."
[2] Formerly " ten years."

annuity to be determined by said appellate division but not exceeding one-half of the average amount of his annual salary or compensation for a period of two years preceding the time of such retirement. Such annuity shall be paid in equal monthly instalments during the lifetime of the person or persons so retired. Any person or persons retired from service pursuant to this act shall be paid out of the funds apportioned to the supreme court of the first department, and from the contributions to the retirement fund. No employee shall be retired pursuant to this section unless he shall have signified his intention to the said appellate division that he desires to take advantage of this act, and shall at the end of each full calendar month after this act takes effect pay to the appellate division of the supreme court in the first department one per centum of his monthly salary.

§ 3. This act shall take effect immediately.

Chap. 139.

AN ACT to amend the membership corporations law, to prohibit the formation of cemetery corporations to operate in the county of Nassau, and to prohibit the acquiring, setting apart or using of land for cemetery purposes in said county except for family cemeteries.

Became a law March 27, 1913, with the approval of the Governor. Passed, three-fifths being present.

The People of the State of New York, represented in Senate and Assembly, do enact as follows:

Section 1. Article four of chapter forty of the laws of nineteen hundred and nine, entitled "An act relating to membership corporations, constituting chapter thirty-five of the consolidated laws," is hereby amended by adding a new section, to be known as section eighty-five, to read as follows:[1]

§ 85. **Cemeteries in Nassau county.** A cemetery corporation shall not hereafter be incorporated for the purpose of conducting its operations in the county of Nassau; nor shall it be lawful for any corporation, association or person, except as herein provided, hereafter to acquire or take by deed, devise or otherwise,

---

[1] Different §§ 85 were added by L. 1912, chaps. 151, 315.

or to set apart or use, any land in the said county for cemetery, burial or mausoleum purposes. Nothing herein contained shall prevent existing corporations owning in the said county cemeteries in which burials have been made prior to January first, nineteen hundred and thirteen, from acquiring contiguous land for cemetery purposes in the manner now permitted by law; nor to prohibit the dedication or use of land within the said county for a family cemetery as provided in section seventy-eight of this article.

§ 2. This act shall take effect immediately.

Chap. 140.

AN ACT to amend the code of civil procedure, in relation to evidence in actions and proceedings involving title to real property.

Became a law March 27, 1913, with the approval of the Governor. Passed, three-fifths being present.

The People of the State of New York, represented in Senate and Assembly, do enact as follows:

§§ 1688-f, 1688-g, 1688-i amended.

Section 1. Sections sixteen hundred and eighty-eight-f, sixteen hundred and eighty-eight-g and sixteen hundred and eighty-eight-i of the code of civil procedure, are hereby amended to read, respectively, as follows:

§ 1688-f. **Appointment of referee; notice to appear.** Upon the presentation of the petition, the judge shall make an order containing directions as to the persons to whom, and the manner in which, notice shall be given of the time and place at which such application will be heard; and at the time fixed in said notice for that purpose, if it shall be shown to the satisfaction of the court that the case comes within the provisions of this article, the court shall make an order appointing a referee to take such testimony and prescribing the manner in which and the persons to whom notice shall be given of the time and place at which the testimony will be taken before said referee.

¹If it shall appear from the petition that the person or persons to be examined reside without the state, the judge to whom the pe-

---

¹ Remainder of section new.

tition may be presented may direct that a commission be issued
to one or more competent persons named therein to examine the
person or persons named therein under oath upon the interroga-
tories annexed to the commission; to take and certify the deposition of each witness, and to return the same and the commission
according to the directions given in or with the commission; and
for this purpose the judge shall make an order directing that in-
terrogatories be settled on notice to persons who, from the petition it may appear, may be adversely affected by the testimony
sought to be taken. All the provisions of chapter nine, title three,
article two of the code of civil procedure shall apply to depositions taken without the state as herein provided; and a deposition taken and filed in accordance with the provisions thereof
and of this article, shall have the same force and effect as the
depositions of a witness before a referee as herein provided, if,
before it may be read in evidence, the petition and order under
which it was taken and proof of service of all the notices required
by this article, shall be filed in the office of the clerk of the county
in which the real estate is situated, and the deposition or a certified copy thereof shall be recorded in the office of the register,
or, if there be none, of the county clerk, of the county in which
the real estate is situated.

§ 1688-g. **Referee to take deposition.** Before proceeding with
the testimony, the referee shall require proof that due notice
of the hearing has been given in accordance with the directions
in said order contained, and thereupon the referee must proceed
to take the depositions of the persons proposed to be examined,
as stated in the petition, at the time and place mentioned in the
notice, and may from time to time adjourn the examination to
another day and another place within the same county. All the
provisions of sections eight hundred and fifty-four, eight hundred and fifty-five, eight hundred and fifty-six, eight hundred
and fifty-seven and eight hundred and fifty-eight of the code of
civil procedure apply to the examination of a person taken before
a referee[2] as prescribed in this article.

§ 1688-i. **Depositions as evidence.** Subject to the provisions
of this article, the depositions taken before a referee or pursuant
to a commission[3] or a certified copy thereof may be read in evidence by any party to an action or proceeding, which shall in-

---

[2] Words " before a referee," new.
[3] Words " taken before a referee or pursuant to a commission," new.

volve the title to such real property, as against the person on whose petition said depositions were taken, each person to whom notice of the taking of such depositions was given as directed in the order appointing the referee, and all persons claiming from, through or under them or any of them.

§ 2. This act shall take effect immediately.

Chap. 141.

AN ACT to amend the second class cities law, in relation to contracts for paving.

Became a law March 28, 1913, with the approval of the Governor. Passed, three-fifths being present.

The People of the State of New York, represented in Senate and Assembly, do enact as follows:

L. 1909, ch 55. § 124 amended.
Section 1. Section one hundred and twenty-four of chapter fifty-five of the laws of nineteen hundred and nine, entitled "An act in relation to cities of the second class, constituting chapter fifty-three of the consolidated laws," is hereby amended so as to read as follows:

§ 124. **Contracts for paving.** The common council shall, by general ordinance, prescribe, approve and adopt the materials to be used in paving, repaving, repairing, surfacing or resurfacing the streets and public places of the city, and fix the standard of excellence and test required for each such material. The city engineer shall prepare standard specifications, in accordance with such ordinance, for the performance of the work involved in such improvements with each kind of materials so prescribed, approved and adopted therefor. Whenever the common council shall determine to make any such improvement, and the proceedings provided by law as preliminary thereto shall have been taken, the board of contract and supply shall advertise for proposals for the furnishing of the materials and the performance of the work involved in such improvements, and specifications. shall be prepared and proposals shall be invited, pursuant to the provisions of this chapter, for the construction of such improvement with each kind of paving material so prescribed, approved and adopted by the common council. In case the expense of any such improvement is to be assessed upon the property abutting upon the street, or part thereof, to be improved and more than one kind of material is prescribed, approved or adopted therefor, the secretary of the board shall, within one week after proposals for such work have been received and opened, cause to be published in a daily official paper for four successive days, exclusive of Sunday, a notice containing a summary statement of all such proposals. A majority of said property owners, owning not less than one-third of the feet front of property abutting on such street, exclusive of city property, may present to the board of contract and supply a petition or other writing designating the general kind of pavement or material to be used in making said improvement. If no part of the expense of such improvement is to be assessed upon the property abutting upon said street, or if such expense is to be so assessed, but the property owners shall not have made a designation or shall have made more than one designation, as herein provided, the common council shall, not later than at its next regular meeting after the expiration of ten days from the service of such notice, designate the kind of pavement or material to be used in making such improvement, and the contract for such improvement shall be awarded for the kind of pavement or material so designated by the property owners or common council as aforesaid, and to the lowest bidder for doing the work with the kind of pavement or material so designated. In case, however, two-thirds of the owners of property, owning at least three-fifths of the linear feet fronting upon said street, or part thereof, shall designate a particular make, style or brand of the kind of pavement or material to be used in making such improvement, the contract therefor shall be awarded to the lowest bidder for such make, style or brand of such kind of pavement or material, although the same is not the lowest bid for such kind of pavement or material so designated. [1]Where a street surface railroad shall be laid in any street which it is determined to improve as herein provided, the proposals and contract for such improvement shall include the improvement of the space between the tracks of such street surface railroad, the rails of such tracks and two feet in width outside of such tracks, and the work of improvement in such space shall be done at the same time and under the same supervision as the work of improvement of the remainder of such street. After opportunity to be heard has been given to the company owning or operating such street surface railroad, the board

---

[1] Remainder of section new.

of contract and supply may prescribe the materials to be used in improving such street within the railroad space above described. The entire expense of the improvement within such railroad space shall be assessed and levied upon the property of the company owning or operating such railroad and shall be collected in the same manner as other expenses for local improvements are assessed, levied and collected in the city; and an action may also be maintained by the city against the company in any court of record for the collection of such expense and assessment.

§ 2. This act shall take effect immediately.

Chap. 142.

AN ACT to amend the Greater New York charter, in relation to proceedings for street openings.

Became a law March 28, 1913, with the approval of the Governor. Passed, three-fifths being present.

Accepted by the City.

The People of the State of New York, represented in Senate and Assembly, do enact as follows:

L. 1897, ch. 378, § 990, as amended by L. 1906, ch. 658, amended.

Section 1. Section nine hundred and ninety of the Greater New York charter, as re-enacted by chapter four hundred and sixty-six of the laws of nineteen hundred and one,[1] as amended by chapter six hundred and fifty-eight of the laws of nineteen hundred and six, is hereby amended to read as follows:

VESTING OF TITLE OF LAND TAKEN FOR STREETS OR PARKS OR OTHER PURPOSES.

§ 990. Should the board of estimate and apportionment at any time deem it for the public interest that the title to the lands and premises required for any improvement authorized herein should be acquired by the city of New York at a fixed or specified time, the said board of estimate and apportionment may direct, by a three-fourths vote,[1a] that upon the date of the filing of the oaths of the commissioners of estimate, as provided for in this chapter, or

---

[1] Section 990 was neither re-enacted nor repealed by L. 1901, ch. 466. Section 990 was also amended by L. 1903, ch. 418.
[1a] Words "where no buildings are upon such lands," omitted.

upon a specified date thereafter,[2] the title to any piece or parcel of
land lying within the lines of any such street or park, or of any
improvement herein authorized shall be vested in the city of New
York. Thereafter, when the said commissioners shall have taken
and filed said oath upon the date of such filing or upon such subsequent date as may be specified[3] the city of New York shall become
and be seized in fee of[4] or of the easement, in, over, upon or under,
as the board of estimate and apportionment may as herein provided determine, the said lands, tenements and hereditaments in
the said resolution mentioned, that shall or may be so required as
aforesaid, the same to be held, appropriated, converted and used to
and for such purpose accordingly. In such cases interest at the
legal rate upon the sum or sums to which the owners, lessees,
parties or persons are justly entitled upon the date of vesting of
title in the city of New York, as aforesaid, from said date to the
date of the report of the commissioners of estimate, shall be allowed
by the commissioners, as part of the compensation to which such
owners, lessees, parties or persons are entitled. In all other cases,
title as aforesaid, shall vest in the city of New York upon the
confirmation by the court of the report of the commissioners of
estimate and the reversal on appeal of[5] the order of confirmation[6]
shall not [7]divest the city of title to the real property affected by the
appeal. Upon the vesting of title the city of New York, or any
person or persons acting under its authority, may immediately, or
any time thereafter, take possession of the same, or any part or
parts thereof, without any suit or proceeding at law for that purpose. The title acquired by the city of New York to lands and
premises required for a street, shall be in trust, that the same be
appropriated and kept open for, or as part of a public street, forever, in like manner as the other streets in the city are and of
right ought to be. If any individual or corporation before the
appointment of commissioners of estimate has acquired by private

---

[2] Words "and where there are buildings upon such lands, that upon a date
not less than six months from the date of the filing of said oaths," omitted.
[3] Words "where no buildings are upon such lands, and where there are
buildings upon such lands, upon the date specified by said board of estimate
and apportionment, either before or after the filing of such oath, the same
being not less than six months from the date of said filling," omitted.
[4] Formerly " in."
[5] Words " reversal on appeal of," substituted for words " taking of an
appeal from."
[6] Words " as elsewhere provided for," omitted.
[7] Remainder of sentence formerly read: " effect such vesting of title in
the city."

grant, prescription or otherwise, any easement for the purpose of laying or maintaining, in lands to be acquired for street purposes as herein provided, underground pipes or conduits for the distribution of water, gas, steam or electricity, or for pneumatic service, such easement shall not be extinguished, but the title to the lands so to be acquired for the purposes as herein provided for, shall be taken subject to such easement; provided, however, that nothing herein contained shall be so construed as to limit the power of the city of New York to acquire by purchase or by condemnation proceedings the entire plant or service of such individual or corporation or to acquire such easement in such street in any other appropriate proceedings. The title in fee acquired by the city of New York to lands and premises required for all purposes provided for in this title, except street purposes, shall be a fee simple absolute.

Application to pending proceedings. § 2. This act shall apply to pending proceedings in which commissioners shall have been appointed and their oaths filed at the time this act takes effect.

§ 3. This act shall take effect immediately.

Chap. 143.

AN ACT to amend the code of criminal procedure, in relation to an order to compel a person to support a poor relative.

Became a law March 28, 1913, with the approval of the Governor. Passed, three-fifths being present.

The People of the State of New York, represented in Senate and Assembly, do enact as follows:

§ 915 amended. Section 1. Section nine hundred and fifteen of the code of criminal procedure is hereby amended to read as follows:

§ 915. **Order to compel a person to support a poor relative, et cetera.** If a relative of a poor person fail to relieve and maintain him, as provided in the last section, the overseers of the poor of the town where he is, or in the city of New York, the commissioners of public charities may apply to the court of general sessions of the county of New York, or to the supreme court of the state of New York,[1] or to the county court of any other county

---

[1] Words " or to the supreme court of the state of New York," new.

where the poor person dwells, for an order to compel such relief, upon at least five days' written notice, served personally, or by leaving it at the last place of residence of the person to whom it is directed, in case of his absence, with a person of suitable age and discretion. If such poor person be insane and legally committed to and confined in an institution supported in whole or in part by the state, and his relatives refuse or neglect to pay for his support and maintenance therein, application may be made by the treasurer of such institution in the manner provided in this section, for an order directing the relatives liable therefor to make such payment.

§ 2. This act shall take effect September first, nineteen hundred and thirteen.   In effect Sept. 1, 1913.

Chap. 144.

AN ACT to amend the labor law, in relation to employment certificates.

Became a law March 28, 1913, with the approval of the Governor. Passed, three-fifths being present.

The People of the State of New York, represented in Senate and Assembly, do enact as follows:

Section 1. Subdivision (e) of section one hundred and sixty-three of chapter thirty-six of the laws of nineteen hundred and nine, entitled " An act relating to labor, constituting chapter thirty-one of the consolidated laws," is hereby amended to read as follows: L. 1909, ch. 36, § 163, subd. (e) amended.

(e) Physicians' certificates. In cities of the first class only, in case application for the issuance of an employment certificate shall be made to such officer by a child's parent, guardian or custodian who alleges his inability to produce any of the evidence of age specified in the preceding subdivisions of this section, and if the child is apparently at least fourteen years of age, such officer may receive and file an application signed by the parent, guardian or custodian of such child for physicians' certificates. Such application shall contain the alleged age, place and date of birth, and present residence of such child, together with such further facts as may be of assistance in determining the age of such child. Such application shall be filed for not less than ninety days after date of such application for such physicians' certificates, for an examination to be made of the statements con-

tained therein, and in case no facts appear within such period or
by such examination tending to discredit or contradict any material statement of such application, then and not otherwise the
officer may direct such child to appear thereafter for physical
examination before two physicians officially designated by the
board of health, and in case such physicians shall certify in writing
that they have separately examined such child and that in their
opinion such child is at least fourteen years of age such officer
shall accept such certificate as sufficient proof of the age of such
child for the purposes of this section. In case the opinions of
such physicians do not concur, the child shall be examined by a
third physician and the concurring opinions shall be conclusive
for the purpose of this section as to the age of such child.

Such officer shall require the evidence of age specified in subdivision (a) in preference to that specified in any subsequent
subdivision and shall not accept the evidence of age permitted by
any subsequent subdivision unless he shall receive and file in
addition thereto an affidavit of the parent showing that no evidence
of age specified in any preceding subdivision or subdivisions of
this section can be produced. Such affidavit shall contain the age,
place and date of birth, and present residence of such child, which
affidavit must be taken before the officer issuing the employment
certificate, who is hereby authorized and required to administer
such oath and who shall not demand or receive a fee therefor.
Such employment certificate shall not be issued until such child
shall further have personally appeared before and been examined
by the officer issuing the certificate, and until such officer shall,
after making such examination, sign and file in his office a statement that the child can read and legibly write simple sentences
in the English language and that in his opinion the child is fourteen years of age or upwards and has reached the normal development of a child of its age, and is in sound health and is physically
able to perform the work which it intends to do. [1] In every case,
before an employment certificate is issued, such physical fitness
shall be determined by a medical officer of the department or board
of health, who shall make a thorough physical examination of the
child and record the result thereof on a blank to be furnished for
the purpose by the commissioner of labor and shall set forth
thereon such facts concerning the physical condition and history

---

[1] Sentence omitted which read: "In doubtful cases such physical fitness
shall be determined by a medical officer of the board or department of health."
Following sentence new.

of the child as the commissioner of labor may require. Every such employment certificate shall be signed in the presence of the officer issuing the same, by the child in whose name it is issued.

§ 2. Sections seventy-three and one hundred and sixty-five of §§ 73, 165 such chapter are hereby amended to read as follows: _amended._

§ 73. **School record, what to contain.** The school record required by this article shall be signed by the principal or chief executive officer of the school which such child has attended and shall be furnished, on demand, to a child entitled thereto or to the board, department or commissioner of health. It shall contain a statement certifying that the child has regularly attended the public schools or schools equivalent thereto, or parochial schools, for not less than one hundred and thirty days during the twelve months next preceding his fourteenth birthday, or during the twelve months next preceding his application for such school record and is able to read and write simple sentences in the English language, and has received during such period instruction in reading, spelling, writing, English grammar and geography and is familiar with the fundamental operations of arithmetic up to and including fractions [2]and has completed the work prescribed for the first six years of the public elementary school or school equivalent thereto or parochial school from which such school record is issued. Such school record shall also give the date of birth and residence of the child as shown on the records of the school and the name of its parent or guardian or custodian.

§ 165. **School record, what to contain.** The school record required by this article shall be signed by the principal or chief executive officer of the school which such child has attended and shall be furnished on demand to a child entitled thereto or to the board, department or commissioner of health. It shall contain a statement certifying that the child has regularly attended the public schools or schools equivalent thereto or parochial schools for not less than one hundred and thirty days during the twelve months next preceding his fourteenth birthday, or during the twelve months next preceding his application for such school record, and is able to read and write simple sentences in the English language, has received during such period instruction in reading, spelling, writing, English grammar and geography and is familiar with the fundamental operations of arithmetic up to and including fractions [2]and has completed the work prescribed

---

[2] Remainder of sentence new.

for the first six years of the public elementary school or school
equivalent thereto or parochial school, from which such school
record is issued. Such school record shall also give the date of
birth and residence of the child as shown on the records of the
school and the name of its parent or guardian or custodian.

§ 3. Section seventy-five of such chapter as amended by chapter
three hundred and thirty-three of the laws of nineteen hundred and
twelve is hereby amended to read as follows:

§ 75. **Supervision over issuance of certificates.**[3] The board or
department of health or health commissioner of a city, village
or town, shall transmit, between the first and tenth day of each
month, to the[4] commissioner of labor, a list of the names of all[5]
children to whom certificates have been issued[6] during the preceding month together with a duplicate of the record of every examination as to the physical fitness, including examinations resulting in rejection.

[7]In cities of the first and second class all employment certificates and school records required under the provisions of this
chapter shall be in such form as shall be approved by the commissioner of labor. In towns, villages or cities other than cities
of the first or second class, the commissioner of labor shall prepare
and furnish blank forms for such employment certificates and
school records. No school record or employment certificate required by this article, other than those approved or furnished by
the commissioner of labor as above provided, shall be used. The
commissioner of labor shall inquire into the administration and
enforcement of the provisions of this article by all public officers
charged with the duty of issuing employment certificates, and for
that purpose the commissioner of labor shall have access to all
papers and records required to be kept by all such officers.

§ 4. Such chapter is hereby amended by inserting therein,
after section one hundred and sixty-five, a new section to be known
as section one hundred and sixty-six and to read as follows:

§ 166. **Supervision over issuance of certificates.** The board
or department of health or health commissioner of a city, village
or town shall transmit between the first and tenth day of each

---

[3] Section heading formerly read: "Report of certificates issued."
[4] Words "office of the" omitted.
[5] Word "all" substituted for word "the."
[6] Remainder of sentence formerly read: "together with a duplicate of the
record of the physical examination of all such children made as hereinbefore
provided."
[7] Remainder of section new.

month to the commissioner of labor a list of the names of all
children to whom certificates have been issued during the preceding month, together with a duplicate record of all examinations
as to physical fitness, including those resulting in rejection. In
cities of the first and second class all employment certificates and
school records required under the provisions of this chapter shall
be in such form as shall be approved by the commissioner of labor.
In towns, villages or cities other than cities of the first or second
class, the commissioner of labor shall prepare and furnish blank
forms for such employment certificates and school records. No
school record or employment certificate required by this article
other than those approved or furnished by the commissioner of
labor as above provided shall be used. The commissioner of labor
shall inquire into the administration and enforcement of the provisions of this article by all public officers charged with the duty
of issuing employment certificates, and for that purpose the commissioner of labor shall have access to all papers and records
required to be kept by all such officers.

§ 5. This act shall take effect October first, nineteen hundred ^{In effect} Oct. 1, 1913.
and thirteen.

Chap. 145.

AN ACT to amend the labor law, in relation to the organization of
the department of labor and its various bureaus, the creation of
an industrial board and the extension of the department's
jurisdiction over mercantile establishments in cities of the
second class.[1]

Became a law March 28, 1913, with the approval of the Governor. Passed,
three-fifths being present.

*The People of the State of New York, represented in Senate
and Assembly, do enact as follows:*

Section 1. Article three of chapter thirty-six of the laws of L. 1909,
nineteen hundred and nine, entitled "An act relating to labor, art. 3, as
constituting chapter thirty-one of the consolidated laws," as L. 1910, ch.
amended by chapter five hundred and fourteen of the laws of ch. 729, and
nineteen hundred and ten, chapter seven hundred and twenty-nine ch. 333, amended.

---

[1] The amendments effected by this act are so numerous and extensive that
it is impracticable to indicate the changes made.

of the laws of nineteen hundred and eleven and chapter three
hundred and eighty-two of the laws of nineteen hundred and
twelve, is hereby amended to read as follows:

ARTICLE 3.

DEPARTMENT OF LABOR.

Section 40. Commissioner of labor.

　　　　41. Deputy commissioners.

　　　　42. Bureaus.

　　　　43. Powers.

　　　　44. Salaries and expenses.

　　　　45. Branch offices.

　　　　46. Reports.

　　　　47. Old records.

　　　　48. Counsel.

§ 40. **Commissioner of labor.** There shall continue to be a
department of labor, the head of which shall be the commissioner
of labor, who shall be appointed by the governor by and with the
consent of the senate, and who shall hold office for a term of
four years beginning on the first day of January of the year
in which he is appointed. He shall receive an annual salary
of eight thousand dollars. He shall appoint and may remove all
officers, clerks and other employees in the department of labor
except as in this chapter otherwise provided.

§ 41. **Deputy commissioners.** The commissioner of labor shall
forthwith upon entering upon the duties of his office, appoint and
may at pleasure remove two deputy commissioners of labor. The
first deputy commissioner shall receive a salary of five thousand
dollars a year; the second deputy commissioner shall receive a
salary of four thousand five hundred dollars a year.

The first deputy commissioner shall, during the absence or
disability of the commissioner of labor, possess all the powers and
perform all the duties of the commissioner except the power of
appointment and removal. During the absence or disability of
both the commissioner of labor and the first deputy commissioner
of labor, the second deputy commissioner shall possess all the
powers and perform all the duties of the commissioner except the
power of appointment and removal. In addition to their duties
and powers as prescribed by the provisions of this chapter, the
deputy commissioners of labor shall perform such other duties and

possess such other powers as the commissioner of labor may prescribe.

§ 42. **Bureaus.** The department of labor shall have four bureaus as follows: inspection; statistics and information; mediation and arbitration and industries and immigration. There shall be such other bureaus in the department of labor as the commissioner of labor may deem necessary.

§ 43. **Powers.** 1. The commissioner of labor, his deputies and their assistants and each agent, chief factory inspector, factory inspector, mine inspector, tunnel inspector, chief investigator, special investigator, chief mercantile inspector, and mercantile inspector may administer oaths and take affidavits in matters relating to the provisions of this chapter.

2. No person shall interfere with, obstruct or hinder by force or otherwise the commissioner of labor, any member of the industrial board, or any officer, agent or employee of the department of labor while in the performance of their duties, or refuse to properly answer questions asked by such officers or employees pertaining to the provisions of this chapter, or refuse them admittance to any place which is affected by the provisions of this chapter.

3. All notices, orders and directions of any officer, agent or employee of the department of labor other than the commissioner of labor or the industrial board given in accordance with this chapter are subject to the approval of the commissioner of labor, and may be performed or given by and in the name of the commissioner of labor and by any officer or employee of the department thereunto duly authorized by such commissioner in the name of such commissioner.

4. The commissioner of labor may procure and cause to be used badges for himself and his subordinates in the department of labor while in the performance of their duties.

§ 44. **Salaries and expenses.** All necessary expenses incurred by the commissioner of labor in the discharge of his duties shall be paid by the state treasurer upon the warrant of the comptroller issued upon proper vouchers therefor. The reasonable and necessary traveling and other expenses of the deputy commissioners, their assistants, the agents and statisticians, the chief factory inspectors, the factory inspectors, chief investigator, the special investigators, the chief mercantile inspector, mercantile inspectors, and other field officers of the department while engaged in the performance of their duties shall be paid in like manner upon vouchers approved by the commissioner of labor and audited by the comptroller.

§ 45. **Branch offices.** The commissioner of labor shall establish and maintain branch offices of the department in.the city of New York and in such other cities of the state as he may deem advisable. Such branch offices shall, subject to the supervision and direction of the commissioner of labor, be in immediate charge of such officials or employees as the commissioner of labor may designate. The reasonable and necessary expenses of such offices shall be paid as are other expenses of the commissioner of labor.

§ 46. **Reports.** The commissioner of labor shall report annually to the legislature and shall include in his annual report or make separately in each year a report of the operation of each bureau in the department.

§ 47. **Old records.** All statistics furnished to and all complaints, reports and other documentary matter received by the commissioner of labor pursuant to this chapter or any act repealed or superseded thereby may be destroyed by such commissioner after the expiration of six years from the time of the receipt thereof.

§ 48. **Counsel.** The commissioner of labor shall appoint and may at pleasure remove counsel who shall be an attorney and counsellor at law of the state of New York to represent the department of labor and to take charge of and assist in the prosecution of actions and proceedings brought by or on behalf of the commissioner of labor or the department of labor, and generally to act as legal adviser to the commissioner. Such counsel shall receive a salary of four thousand dollars a year. The commissioner of labor shall have power to appoint and at pleasure remove attorneys and counsellors at law to assist the counsel in the performance of his duties who shall receive such compensation as may be provided by law.

Art. 3a added. § 2. Such chapter is hereby further amended by inserting therein after article three, a new article to be article three-a thereof to read as follows:

ARTICLE 3-A.

INDUSTRIAL BOARD.

Section 50. Industrial board; organization.
    51. Jurisdiction of board.
    52. Rules and regulations; industrial code.

§ 50. **Industrial board; organization.** 1. There shall be an industrial board, to consist of the commissioner of labor, who shall be chairman of the board, and four associate members. The associate members shall be appointed by the governor by and with the consent and advice of the senate. Of the associate members first appointed, one shall hold office until December first, nineteen hundred and fourteen, one until December first, nineteen hundred and fifteen, one until December first, nineteen hundred and sixteen, and one until December first, nineteen hundred and seventeen. Upon the expiration of each of said terms, the term of office of each associate member thereafter appointed shall be four years from the first day of December. Vacancies shall be filled by appointment for the unexpired term. The associate members shall each receive a salary of three thousand dollars a year and each of said associate members shall be paid his reasonable and necessary traveling and other expenses while engaged in the performance of his duties in the manner provided in section forty-four of this chapter.

2. The board shall appoint and may remove a secretary who shall receive a salary to be fixed by the board. The commissioner of labor shall detail, from time to time, to the assistance of the board, such employees of the department of labor as the board may require. In aid of its work, the board is empowered to employ experts for special and occasional services, and to employ necessary clerical assistants. The counsel to the department of labor shall be counsel to the board without additional compensation.

3. The board shall hold stated meetings, at least once a month during the year at the office of the department of labor in the city of Albany or in the city of New York and shall hold other meetings at such times and places as the needs of the public service may require, which meetings shall be called by the chairman or by any two associate members of the board. All meetings of the board shall be open to the public. The board shall keep minutes of its proceedings showing the vote of each member upon every question and records of its examinations and other official action.

§ 51. **Jurisdiction of board.** The board shall have power: (1) To make investigations concerning and report upon all matters touching the enforcement and effect of the provisions of this chapter and the rules and regulations made by the board there-

under, and in the course of such investigations, each member of
the board and the secretary shall have power to administer oaths
and take affidavits. Each member of the board and the secretary
shall have power to make personal inspections of all factories,
factory buildings, mercantile establishments and other places to
which this chapter is applicable.

(2) To subpoena and require the attendance in this state of
witnesses and the production of books and papers pertinent to the
investigations and inquiries hereby authorized and to examine
them in relation to any matter which it has power to investigate,
and to issue commissions for the examination of witnesses who are
out of the state or unable to attend before the board or excused
from attendance.

(3) To make, alter, amend and repeal rules and regulations
for carrying into effect the provisions of this chapter, applying
such provisions to specific conditions and prescribing specific
means, methods or practices to effectuate such provisions.

(4) To make, alter, amend or repeal rules and regulations for
guarding against and minimizing fire hazards, personal injuries
and disease, with respect to (a) the construction, alteration, equipment and maintenance of factories, factory buildings, mercantile
establishments and other places to which this chapter is applicable,
including the conversion of structures into factories and factory
buildings; (b) the arrangement and guarding of machinery and
the storing and keeping of property and articles in factories, factory buildings and mercantile establishments; (c) the places
where and the methods and operations by which trades and occupations may be conducted and the conduct of employers, employees and other persons in and about factories, factory buildings and mercantile establishments; it being the policy and intent of this chapter that all factories, factory buildings, mercantile
establishments and other places to which this chapter is applicable,
shall be so constructed, equipped, arranged, operated and conducted in all respects as to provide reasonable and adequate protection to the lives, health and safety of all persons employed
therein and that the said board shall from time to time make
such rules and regulations as will effectuate the said policy and
intent.

§ 52. Rules and regulations; industrial code. 1. The rules
and regulations adopted by the board pursuant to the provisions
of this chapter shall have the force and effect of law and shall

be enforced in the same manner as the provisions of this chapter. Such rules and regulations may apply in whole or in part to particular kinds of factories or workshops, or to particular machines, apparatus or articles; or to particular processes, industries, trades or occupations; and they may be limited in their application to factories or workshops to be established, or to machines, apparatus or other articles to be installed or provided in the future.

2. At least three affirmative votes shall be necessary to the adoption of any rule or regulation by the board. Before any rule or regulation is adopted, altered, amended or repealed by the board there shall be a public hearing thereon, notice of which shall be published not less than ten days, in such newspapers as the board may prescribe. Every rule or regulation and every act of the board shall be promptly published in bulletins of the department of labor or in such newspapers as the board may prescribe. The rules and regulations, and alterations, amendments and changes thereof shall, unless otherwise prescribed by the board, take effect twenty days after the first publication thereof.

3. The rules and regulations which shall be in force on the first day of January, nineteen hundred and fourteen, and the amendments and alterations thereof, and the additions thereto, shall constitute the industrial code. The industrial code may embrace all matters and subjects to which and so far as the power and authority of the department of labor extends and its application need not be limited to subjects enumerated in this article. The industrial code and all amendments and alterations thereof and additions thereto shall be certified by the secretary of the board and filed with the secretary of state.

§ 3. Such chapter is hereby further amended by inserting therein after section twenty-à, a new section, to be section twenty-b,[2] to read as follows: §20b added.

§ 20-b. **Protection of employees.** All factories, factory buildings, mercantile establishments and other places to which this chapter is applicable, shall be so constructed, equipped, arranged, operated and conducted in all respects as to provide reasonable and adequate protection to the lives, health and safety of all persons employed therein. The industrial board shall, from time to time, make such rules and regulations as will carry into effect the provisions of this section.

---

[2] A different § 20b is added by L. 1913, ch. 543, post.

Art. 5, as
amended by
L. 1911, ch.
729, and L.
1912, ch.
158, re-
numbered
art. 4 and
amended. § 4. Article five of such chapter as amended by chapter seven hundred and twenty-nine of the laws of nineteen hundred and eleven and chapter one hundred and fifty-eight of the laws of nineteen hundred and twelve is hereby renumbered article four, inserted in place of present article four hereinafter renumbered and amended to read as follows:

ARTICLE 4.

BUREAU OF INSPECTION.

Section 53. Bureau of inspection; inspector general; divisions.
    54. Inspectors.
    55. Division of factory inspection; factory inspection districts; chief factory inspectors.
    56. Idem; general powers and duties.
    57. Division of homework inspection.
    58. Division of mercantile inspection.
    59. Idem; general powers and duties.
    60. Division of industrial hygiene.
    61. Section of medical inspection.

§ 53. **Bureau of inspection; inspector general; divisions.** The bureau of inspection, subject to the supervision and direction of the commissioner of labor, shall have charge of all inspections made pursuant to the provisions of this chapter, and shall perform such other duties as may be assigned to it by the commissioner of labor. The first deputy commissioner of labor shall be the inspector general of the state, and in charge of this bureau subject to the direction and supervision of the commissioner of labor, except that the division of industrial hygiene shall be under the immediate direction and supervision of the commissioner of labor. Such bureau shall have four divisions as follows: factory inspection, homework inspection, mercantile inspection and industrial hygiene. There shall be such other divisions in such bureau as the commissioner of labor may deem necessary. In addition to their respective duties as prescribed by the provisions of this chapter, such divisions shall perform such other duties as may be assigned to them by the commissioner of labor.

§ 54. **Inspectors.** 1. Factory inspectors. There shall be not less than one hundred and twenty-five factory inspectors, not more than thirty of whom shall be women. Such inspectors shall be appointed by the commissioner of labor and may be removed by him at any time. The inspectors shall be divided into seven grades. Inspectors of the first grade, of whom there shall be not more than ninety-five, shall each receive an annual salary of one thousand two hundred dollars; inspectors of the second grade, of whom there shall be not more than fifty, shall each receive an annual salary of one thousand five hundred dollars; inspectors of the third grade, of whom there shall be not more than twenty-five shall each receive an annual salary of one thousand eight hundred dollars; inspectors of the fourth grade, of whom there shall be not more than ten, shall each receive an annual salary of two thousand dollars and shall be attached to the division of industrial hygiene and act as investigators in such division; inspectors of the fifth grade, of whom there shall be not more than nine, one of whom shall be able to speak and write at least five European languages in addition to English, shall each receive an annual salary of two thousand five hundred dollars and shall act as supervising inspectors; inspectors of the sixth grade, of whom there shall be not less than three and one of whom shall be a woman, shall act as medical inspectors and shall each receive an annual salary of two thousand five hundred dollars; inspectors of the seventh grade, of whom there shall be not less than four, shall each receive an annual salary of three thousand five hundred dollars; all of the inspectors of the sixth grade shall be physicians duly licensed to practice medicine in the state of New York. Of the inspectors of the seventh grade one shall be a physician duly licensed to practice medicine in the state of New York, and he shall be the chief medical inspector; one shall be a chemical engineer; one shall be a mechanical engineer, and an expert in ventilation and accident prevention; and one shall be a civil engineer, and an expert in fire prevention and building construction.

2. Mercantile inspectors. The commissioner of labor may appoint from time to time not more than twenty mercantile inspectors not less than four of whom shall be women and who may be removed by him at any time. The mercantile inspectors may be divided into three grades but not more than five shall be of the third grade. Each mercantile inspector of the first grade shall receive an annual salary of one thousand dollars; of the second grade an annual salary of one thousand two hundred dollars; and of the third grade an annual salary of one thousand five hundred dollars.

§ 55. Division of factory inspection; factory inspection districts; chief factory inspectors. For the inspection of factories, there shall be two inspection districts to be known as the first factory inspection district and the second factory inspection district. The first factory inspection district shall include the counties of New York, Bronx, Kings, Queens, Richmond, Nassau and Suffolk. The second factory inspection district shall include all the other counties of the state. There shall be two chief factory inspectors who shall be appointed by the commissioner of labor and who may be removed by him at any time and each of whom shall receive a salary of four thousand dollars a year. The inspection of factories in each factory inspection district shall, subject to the supervision and direction of the commissioner of labor, be in charge of a chief factory inspector assigned to such district by the commissioner of labor. The commissioner of labor may designate one of the supervising inspectors as assistant chief factory inspector for the first district, and while acting as such assistant chief factory inspector he shall receive an additional salary of five hundred dollars per annum.

§ 56. Idem; general powers and duties. 1. The commissioner of labor shall, from time to time, divide the state into sub-districts, assign one factory inspector of the fifth grade to each sub-district as supervising inspector, and may in his discretion transfer such supervising inspector from one sub-district to another; he shall from time to time, assign and transfer factory inspectors to each factory inspection district and to any of the divisions of the bureau of inspection; he may assign any factory inspector to inspect any special class or classes of factories or to enforce any special provisions of this chapter; and he may assign any one or more of them to act as clerks in any office of the department.

2. The commissioner of labor may authorize any deputy commissioner or assistant and any agent or inspector in the department of labor to act as a factory inspector with the full power and authority thereof.

3. The commissioner of labor, the first deputy commissioner of labor and his assistant or assistants, and every factory inspector and every person duly authorized pursuant to sub-division two of this section may, in the discharge of his duties enter any place, building or room which is affected by the provisions of this chapter and may enter any factory whenever he may have reasonable cause to believe that any labor is being performed therein.

4. The commissioner of labor shall visit and inspect or cause to be visited and inspected the factories, during reasonable hours, as often as practicable, and shall cause the provisions of this chapter and the rules and regulations of the industrial board to be enforced therein.

5. Any lawful municipal ordinance, by-law or regulation relating to factories, in addition to the provisions of this chapter and not in conflict therewith, may be observed and enforced by the commissioner of labor.

§ 57. **Division of homework inspection.** The division of homework inspection shall be in charge of an officer or employee of the department of labor designated by the commissioner of labor and shall, subject to the supervision and direction of the commissioner of labor, have charge of all inspections of tenement houses and of labor therein and of all work done for factories at places other than such factories.

§ 58. **Division of mercantile inspection.** The division of mercantile inspection shall be under the immediate charge of the chief mercantile inspector, but subject to the direction and supervision of the commissioner of labor. The chief mercantile inspector shall be appointed and be at pleasure removed by the commissioner of labor, and shall receive such annual salary not to exceed three thousand dollars as may be appropriated therefor.

§ 59. **Id.; general powers and duties.** 1. The commissioner of labor may divide the cities of the first and second class of the state into mercantile inspection districts, assign one or more mercantile inspectors to each such district, and may in his discretion transfer them from one such district to another; he may assign any of them to inspect any special class or classes of mercantile or other establishments specified in article twelve of this chapter, situated in cities of the first and second class, or to enforce in cities of the first or second class any special provision of such article.

2. The commissioner of labor may authorize any deputy commissioner or assistant and any agent or inspector in the department of labor to act as a mercantile inspector with the full power and authority thereof.

3. The commissioner of labor, the chief mercantile inspector and his assistant or assistants and every mercantile inspector or acting mercantile inspector may in the discharge of his duties enter any place, building or room in cities of the first or second

class which is affected by the provisions of article twelve of this chapter, and may enter any mercantile or other establishment specified in said article, situated in the cities of the first or second class, whenever he may have reasonable cause to believe that it is affected by the provisions of article twelve of this chapter.

4. The commissioner of labor shall visit and inspect or cause to be visited and inspected the mercantile and other establishments specified in article twelve of this chapter situated in cities of the first and second class, as often as practicable, and shall cause the provisions of said article and the rules and regulations of the industrial board to be enforced therein.

5. Any lawful municipal ordinance, by-law or regulation relating to mercantile or other establishments specified in article twelve of this chapter, in addition to the provisions of this chapter and not in conflict therewith, may be enforced by the commissioner of labor in cities of the first and second class.

§ 60. **Division of industrial hygiene.** The inspectors of the seventh grade shall constitute the division of industrial hygiene, which shall be under the immediate charge of the commissioner of labor. The commissioner of labor may select one of the inspectors of the seventh grade to act as the director of such division, and such director while acting in that capacity shall receive an additional compensation of five hundred dollars a year. The members of the division of industrial hygiene shall make special inspections of factories, mercantile establishments and other places subject to the provisions of this chapter, throughout the state, and shall conduct special investigations of industrial processes and conditions. The commissioner of labor shall submit to the industrial board the recommendations of the division regarding proposed rules and regulations and standards to be adopted to carry into effect the provisions of this chapter and shall advise said board concerning the operation of such rules and standards and as to any changes or modifications to be made therein. The members of such division shall prepare material for leaflets and bulletins calling attention to dangers in particular industries and the precautions to be taken to avoid them; and shall perform such other duties and render such other services as may be required by the commissioner of labor. The director of such division shall make an annual report to the commissioner of labor of the operation of the division, to which may be attached the individual reports of each member of the division as above specified, and same shall be transmitted

to the legislature as part of the annual report of the commissioner
of labor.

§ 61. **Section of medical inspection.** The inspectors of the
sixth grade shall constitute the section of medical inspection which
shall, subject to the supervision and direction of the director of the
division of industrial hygiene, be under the immediate charge of
the chief medical inspector. The section of medical inspection
shall inspect factories, mercantile establishments and other places
subject to the provisions of this chapter throughout the state with
respect to conditions of work affecting the health of persons employed therein and shall have charge of the physical examination
and medical supervision of all children employed therein and shall
perform such other duties and render such other services as the
commissioner of labor may direct.

§ 5. Article four of such chapter as amended by chapter two Art. 4, as amended by L. 1911, ch. 358, re-numbered art. 5 and amended.
hundred and fifty-eight of the laws of nineteen hundred and
eleven, is hereby renumbered article five, inserted in place of
article four hereinbefore renumbered, and amended to read as
follows:

ARTICLE 5.

BUREAU OF STATISTICS AND INFORMATION.

Section 62. Bureau of statistics and information.
  63. Divisions; duties and powers.
  64. Information to be furnished upon request.
  65. Industrial poisoning to be reported.

§ 62. **Bureau of statistics and information.** The bureau of
statistics and information, shall be under the immediate charge of
a chief statistician, but subject to the direction and supervision of
the commissioner of labor.

§ 63. **Divisions; duties and powers.** 1. The bureau of
statistics and information shall have five divisions as follows:
general labor statistics; industrial directory; industrial accidents
and diseases; special investigations; and printing and publication.
There shall be such other divisions in such bureau as the commissioner of labor may deem advisable. Each of the said divisions
shall, subject to the supervision and direction of the commissioner
of labor and of the chief statistician, be in charge of an officer or
employee of the department of labor designated by the commissioner of labor; and each of the said divisions, in addition to the
duties prescribed in this chapter, shall perform such other duties
as may be assigned to it by the commissioner of labor.

2. The division of general labor statistics shall collect, and prepare statistics and general information in relation to conditions of labor and the industries of the state.

3. The division of industrial directory shall prepare annually an industrial directory for all cities and villages having a population of one thousand or more according to the last preceding federal census or state enumeration. Such directory shall contain information regarding opportunities and advantages for manufacturing in every such city or village, the factories established therein, hours of labor, housing conditions, railroad and water connections, water power, natural resources, wages and such other data regarding social, economic and industrial conditions as in the judgment of the commissioner would be of value to prospective manufacturers, and their employees. If a city is divided into boroughs the directory shall contain such information as to each borough.

4. The division of industrial accidents and diseases shall collect and prepare statistical details and general information regarding industrial accidents and occupational diseases, their causes and effects, and methods of preventing, curing and remedying them, and of providing compensation therefor.

5. The division of special investigations shall have charge of all investigations and research work relating to economic and social conditions of labor conducted by such bureau.

6. The division of printing and publication shall print, publish and disseminate in such manner and to such extent as the commissioner of labor shall direct, such information and statistics as the commissioner of labor may direct for the purpose of promoting the health, safety and well being of persons employed at labor.

7. The commissioner of labor may subpoena witnesses, take and hear testimony, take or cause to be taken depositions and administer oaths.

§ 64. **Information to be furnished upon request.** The owner, operator, manager or lessee of any mine, factory, workshop, warehouse, elevator, foundry, machine shop or other manufacturing establishment, or any agent, superintendent, subordinate, or employee thereof, and any person employing or directing any labor affected by the provisions of this chapter, shall, when requested by the commissioner of labor, furnish any information in his possession or under his control which the commissioner is authorized to require, and shall admit him or his duly authorized representative to any place which is affected by the provisions of this chapter for the purpose of inspection. A person refusing to admit such commissioner, or person authorized by him, to any such establishment, or to furnish him any information requested, or who refuses to answer or untruthfully answers questions put to him by such commissioner, in a circular or otherwise, shall forfeit to the people of the state the sum of one hundred dollars for each refusal or untruthful answer given, to be sued for and recovered by the commissioner in his name of office. The amount so recovered shall be paid into the state treasury.

§ 65. **Industrial poisonings to be reported.** 1. Every medical practitioner attending on or called in to visit a patient whom he believes to be suffering from poisoning from lead, *phosphorous, arsenic, brass, wood alcohol, mercury or their compounds, or from anthrax, or from compressed air illness, contracted as the result of the nature of the patient's employment, shall send to the commissioner of labor a notice stating the name and full postal address and place of employment of the patient and the disease from which, in the opinion of the medical practitioner, the patient is suffering, with such other and further information as may be required by the said commissioner.

2. If any medical practitioner, when required by this section to send a notice, fails forthwith to send the same, he shall be liable to a fine not exceeding ten dollars.

3. It shall be the duty of the commissioner of labor to enforce the provisions of this section, and he may call upon the state and local boards of health for assistance.

§ 6. Sections forty-nine and sixty-three of such chapter are §§ 49, 63 hereby repealed. repealed.

§ 7. Section sixty-seven of such chapter is hereby renumbered § 67 re- section twenty-two, and inserted in article two after section numbered twenty-one, to read as follows: § 22.

§ 22. **Duties relative to apprentices.** The commissioner of labor shall enforce the provisions of the domestic relations law, relative to indenture of apprentices, and prosecute employers for failure to comply with the provisions of such indentures and of such law in relation thereto.

§ 3. Section sixty-eight of such chapter is hereby renumbered § 68 re- section ninety-nine-a, inserted at the end of article six, and numbered amended to read as follows: § 99a, and amended.

---

* So in original.

9

§ 99-a. **Laws to be posted.** Copies or digests of the provisions of this chapter and of the rules and regulations of the industrial board, applicable thereto, in English and in such other languages as the commissioner of labor may require, to be prepared and furnished by the commissioner of labor, shall be kept posted by the employer in such conspicuous place or places as the commissioner of labor may direct on each floor of every factory where persons are employed who are affected by the provisions thereof.

§ 69, as added by L. 1912, ch. 335, transferred to art. 6.

§ 9. Section sixty-nine of such chapter as amended[2] by chapter three hundred and thirty-five of the laws of nineteen hundred and twelve, is hereby transferred to and inserted in article six of such chapter, instead of article five.

§ 119 added.

§ 10. Such chapter is hereby further amended by inserting therein in article nine, before section one hundred and twenty, a new section, to be section one hundred and nineteen, to read as follows:

§ 119. **Protection of employees in mines, tunnels and quarries.** Every necessary precaution shall be taken to insure the safety and health of employees employed in the mines and quarries and in the construction of tunnels in the state. The industrial board shall have power to adopt rules and regulations to carry into effect the provisions of this article and may amend or repeal rules and regulations heretofore prescribed by the commissioner of labor under the provisions of this article. The rules and regulations heretofore prescribed by the commissioner of labor under this article shall continue in force until amended or repealed by the industrial board.

§ 120 amended.

§ 11. Section one hundred and twenty of such chapter is hereby amended to read as follows:

§ 120. **Duties of commissioner of labor relating to mines, tunnels and quarries; record and report.** 1. The commissioner of labor shall enforce the provisions of this article, the rules and regulations adopted by the industrial board pursuant thereto, and the rules and regulations of the commissioner of labor continued in force by this article.

2. The commissioner of labor shall keep a record of the names and location of all mines, tunnels and quarries, and the names of the persons or corporations owning or operating the same; collect data concerning the working thereof; examine carefully into the method of timbering shafts, drifts, inclines, slopes, and tunnels,

---

[2] Should read added.

through which employees and other persons pass, in the performance of their daily labor, and see that the persons or corporations
owning and operating such mines, and quarries and constructing
tunnels comply with the provisions of this chapter; and such information shall be furnished by the person operating such mine,
tunnel or quarry, upon the demand of the commissioner of labor.
The commissioner of labor shall keep a record of all mine, tunnel
and quarry examinations, showing the date thereof, and the condition in which the mines, tunnels and quarries are found, and the
manner of working the same. He shall make an annual report to
the legislature during the month of January, containing a statement of the number of mines, tunnels and quarries visited, the
number in operation, the number of men employed, and the number and cause of accidents, fatal and nonfatal, that may have
occurred in and about the same.

§ 12. Article ten-a[3] of such chapter is hereby renumbered Art. 10a
article eleven and inserted in place of present article eleven here- renumbered
inafter renumbered.   art. 11.

§ 13. Article eleven of such chapter is hereby renumbered Art. 11
article twelve and inserted in place of present article twelve here- renumbered
inafter repealed.   art. 12.

§ 14. Sections one hundred and sixty-seven, one hundred and §§ 167-169,
sixty-eight,[4] one hundred and sixty-nine, one hundred and seventy- 171-173
one, one hundred and seventy-two and one hundred and seventy- amended.
three of such chapter are hereby amended to read as follows:

§ 167. **Registry of children employed.** The owner, manager
or agent of a mercantile or other establishment specified in section one hundred and sixty-one, employing children, shall keep
or cause to be kept in the office of such establishment, a register,
in which shall be recorded the name, birthplace, age and place
of residence of all children so employed under the age of sixteen
years. Such register and the certificate filed in such office shall
be produced for inspection, upon the demand of an officer of the
board, department or commissioner of health of the town, village
or city where such establishment is situated, or if such establishment is situated in a city of the first or second class, upon the
demand of the commissioner of labor. On termination of the
employment of the child so registered and whose certificate is so
filed, such certificate shall be forthwith surrendered by the em-

---

[3] As added by L. 1910, ch. 514.
[4] As amended by L. 1911, ch. 866.

ployer to the child or its parent or guardian or custodian. An officer of the board, department or commissioner of health of the town, village or city where a mercantile or other establishment mentioned in this article is situated, or if such establishment is situated in a city of the first or second class the commissioner of labor may make demand on an employer in whose establishment a child apparently under the age of sixteen years is employed or permitted or suffered to work, and whose employment certificate is not then filed as required by this chapter, that such employer shall either furnish him, within ten days, evidence satisfactory to him that such child is in fact over sixteen years of age, or shall cease to employ or permit or suffer such child to work in such establishment. The officer may require from such employer the same evidence of age of such child as is required on the issuance of an employment certificate and the employer furnishing such evidence shall not be required to furnish any further evidence of the age of the child. A notice embodying such demand may be served on such employer personally or may be sent by mail addressed to him at said establishment, and if served by post shall be deemed to have been served at the time when the letter containing the same would be delivered in the ordinary course of the post. When the employer is a corporation such notice may be served either personally upon an officer of such corporation or by sending it by post addressed to the office or the principal place of business of such corporation. The papers constituting such evidence of age furnished by the employer in response to such demand shall, except in cities of the first and second class, be filed with the board, department or commissioner of health, and in cities of the first and second class with the commissioner of labor, and a material false statement made in any such paper or affidavit by any person shall be a misdemeanor. In case such employer shall fail to produce and deliver to the officer of the board, department or commissioner of health, or in cities of the first and second class to the commissioner of labor, within ten days after such demand such evidence of age herein required by him, and shall thereafter continue to employ such child or permit or suffer such child to work in such mercantile or other establishment, proof of the giving of such notice and of such failure to produce and file such evidence shall be prima facie evidence in any prosecution brought for a violation of this article that such child is under sixteen years of age and is unlawfully employed.

§ 168. **Wash-rooms and water-closets.** Suitable and proper wash-rooms and water-closets shall be provided in, adjacent to or connected with mercantile establishments. Such rooms and closets shall be so located and arranged as to be easily accessible to the employees of such establishments.

Such water-closets shall be properly screened and ventilated, and, at all times, kept in a clean condition. The water-closets assigned to the female employees of such establishments shall be separate from those assigned to the male employees.

If a mercantile establishment has not provided wash-rooms and water-closets, as required by this section, the board or department of health or health commissioners of the town, village or city where such establishment is situated, unless such establishment is situated in a city of the first or second class, in which case the commissioner of labor shall cause to be served upon the owner, agent or lessee of the building occupied by such establishment a written notice of the omission and directing such owner, agent or lessee to comply with the provisions of this section respecting such wash-rooms and water-closets.

Such owner shall, within fifteen days after the receipt of such notice, cause such wash-rooms and water-closets to be provided.

§ 169. **Lunch-rooms.** If a lunch-room is provided in a mercantile establishment where females are employed, such lunch-room shall not be next to or adjoining the water-closets, unless permission is first obtained from the board or department of health or health commissioners of the town, village or city where such mercantile establishment is situated, unless such establishment is situated in a city of the first or second class in which case such permission must be obtained from the commissioner of labor. Such permission shall be granted unless it appears that proper sanitary conditions do not exist, and it may be revoked at any time by the board or department of health or health commissioners, if it appears that such lunch-room is kept in a manner or in a part of a building injurious to the health of the employees, unless such establishment is situated in a city of the first or second class, in which case said permission may be so revoked by the commissioner of labor.

§ 171. **Employment of women and children in basements.** Women or children shall not be employed or permitted to work in the basement of a mercantile establishment, unless permitted by the board or department of health, or health commissioner of the town, village or city where such mercantile establishment is

situated, unless such establishment is situated in a city of the
first or second class in which case such permission must be obtained from the commissioner of labor. Such permission shall
be granted unless it appears that such basement is not sufficiently
lighted and ventilated, and is not in good sanitary condition.

§ 172. **Enforcement of article.** Except in cities of the first
and second class the board or department of health or health commissioners of a town, village or city affected by this article shall
enforce the same and prosecute all violations thereof. Proceedings to prosecute such violations must be begun within sixty days
after the alleged offense was committed. All officers and members
of such boards or department, all health commissioners, inspectors and other persons appointed or designated by such boards,
departments or commissioners may visit and inspect, at reasonable
hours and when practicable and necessary, all mercantile or
other establishments herein specified within the town, village or
city for which they are appointed. No person shall interfere with
or prevent any such officer from making such visitations and inspections, nor shall he be obstructed or injured by force or otherwise while in the performance of his duties. All persons connected
with any such mercantile or other establishment herein specified
shall properly answer all questions asked by such officer or inspector in reference to any of the provisions of this article. In
cities of the first and second class the commissioner of labor shall
enforce the provisions of this article, and for that purpose he and
his subordinates shall possess all powers herein conferred upon
town, village, or city boards and departments of health and their
commissioners, inspectors, and other officers, except that the
board or department of health of said cities of the first and second
class shall continue to issue employment certificates as provided
in section one hundred and sixty-three of this chapter.

§ 173. **Laws to be posted.** A copy or abstract of applicable
provisions of this chapter and of the rules and regulations of the
industrial board to be prepared and furnished by the commissioner of labor shall be kept posted by the employer in a conspicuous place on each floor of every mercantile or other establishment
specified in article twelve of this chapter situated in cities of the
first or second class, wherein three or more persons are employed
who are affected by such provisions.

§ 15. Article twelve of such chapter is hereby repealed.

§ 16. This act shall take effect immediately.

Art. 12
repealed.

Chap. 146.

AN ACT to amend chapter four hundred and eighty-one of the laws of nineteen hundred and ten, being chapter forty-nine of the consolidated laws, known as the railroad law, by adding a section thereto prescribing the minimum number of employees to be employed in the operation of certain trains.

Became a law March 31, 1913, with the approval of the Governor. Passed, three-fifths being present.

The People of the State of New York, represented in Senate and Assembly, do enact as follows:

Section 1. Chapter four hundred and eighty-one of the laws of nineteen hundred and ten, constituting chapter forty-nine of the consolidated laws, known as the railroad law, is hereby amended by adding thereto, after section fifty-four, a new section, to be numbered fifty-four-a, to read as follows:

§ 54-a. **Full crews for certain trains.** No person, corporation, trustee, receiver, or other court officer, shall run or operate, or cause to be run or operated, outside of the yard limits, on any railroad of more than fifty miles in length within this state, a freight train of more than twenty-five cars, unless said train shall be manned with a crew of not less than one engineer, one fireman, one conductor and three brakemen; nor any train other than a freight train of five cars or more, without a crew of not less than one engineer, one fireman, one conductor and two brakemen, and if the train is a baggage train or a passenger train having a baggage car or baggage compartment without a baggageman in addition to said crew; nor any freight train of twenty-five cars or less without a crew of not less than one engineer, one fireman, one conductor and two brakemen; nor any light engine without a car or cars, without a crew of not less than one engineer, one fireman and one conductor or brakeman. Each separate violation of the provisions of this section shall be a misdemeanor punishable by a fine of not less than one hundred dollars nor more than five hundred dollars. Each train or light engine run in violation of the provisions of this section shall be deemed to be a separate offense.

§ 2. This act shall take effect September first, nineteen hundred and thirteen.

§ 54a added to L. 1910, ch. 481.

In effect Sept. 1, 1913.

Chap. 147.

AN ACT to amend the conservation law, in relation to the open
season for muskrat.

Became a law April 1, 1913, with the approval of the Governor. Passed,
three-fifths being present.

*The People of the State of New York, represented in Senate
and Assembly, do enact as follows:*

L. 1911,
ch. 647,
§ 201, as
added by
L. 1912,
ch. 318,
amended.

Section 1. Section two hundred and one of chapter six hundred
and forty-seven of the laws of nineteen hundred and eleven, entitled "An act relating to conservation of land, forests, waters,
parks, hydraulic power, fish and game, constituting chapter sixty-
five of the consolidated laws," as added by chapter three hundred
and eighteen of the laws of nineteen hundred and twelve, is hereby
amended to read as follows:

§ 201. **Muskrat; open season.** Muskrat may be taken in any
manner and possessed from November first to April twentieth,[1]
both inclusive. Muskrat houses shall not be molested, injured
or disturbed at any time.

§ 2. This act shall take effect immediately.

Chap. 148.

AN ACT to amend the town law, in relation to the appointment
of special constables.

Became a law April 1, 1913, with the approval of the Governor. Passed,
three-fifths being present.

*The People of the State of New York, represented in Senate
and Assembly, do enact as follows:*

L. 1909,
ch. 63,
§§ 117, 118
amended.

Section 1. Sections one hundred and seventeen and one hundred and eighteen of chapter sixty-three of the laws of nineteen
hundred and nine, entitled "An act relating to towns, constituting
chapter sixty-two of the consolidated laws," are hereby amended
to read, respectively, as follows:

§ 117. **Special constables.** The supervisor and two justices
of the peace of any town may, when in their judgment necessary for the preservation of the public peace during any period

---

[1] Formerly "November tenth to April first." Section 201 is again amended
by L. 1913, ch. 508, post. The amendment here made is incorporated in the
section as amended by ch. 508.

of ninety[1] days or less, appoint five or less special constables of such town for such period. Duplicate certificates of the appointment, signed by such supervisor and such justices of the peace as such, shall be delivered to each of such special constables, specifying the days for which he is so appointed, and one of such duplicates shall be by such special constables filed with the town clerk of said town. The supervisor of such town shall cause to be provided and furnished to each of such special constables a badge on which shall be plainly printed the words "special constable," which shall be worn conspicuously by each of such special constables while serving as such, and be delivered by him on the completion of his service to the supervisor of such town, who shall preserve the same for future use and deliver the same to his successor in office, who shall preserve the same when not in use.

§ 118. **Powers, duties and liabilities of special constables.** Each of the special constables, appointed pursuant to section one hundred and seventeen of this chapter, while in office as such, shall be a peace officer, and have all the powers and be subject to all the duties and liabilities of a constable of such town in all criminal actions and proceedings and special proceedings of a criminal nature, and shall be entitled to receive compensation from the town at the rate of [2]wages previously established by the town board for such services.

§ 2. This act shall take effect immediately.

Chap. 149.

AN ACT to incorporate the Altman Foundation.

Became a law April 1, 1913, with the approval of the Governor. Passed, three-fifths being present.

The People of the State of New York, represented in Senate and Assembly, do enact as follows:

Section 1. Benjamin Altman, Michael Friedsam, George R. Read, Bernard Sachs, Edwin J. Steiner, Edward J. Hancy, and their successors, are hereby constituted a body corporate by the name of Altman Foundation, for the purpose of receiving and maintaining a fund or funds, administering the same, and apply- Corporators. Corporate name. Purposes.

---

[1] Formerly "three."
[2] Remainder of sentence formerly read: "two dollars per day during his term of office."

ing the principal and income thereof, and either of them, to promote the social, physical or economic welfare and efficiency of the employees of B. Altman and Company, a New York corporation, and to the use and benefit of charitable, benevolent or educational institutions within the state of New York, by such agencies and means as from time to time shall be found appropriate therefor.

Powers as to property

§ 2. Said corporation hereby formed shall have power to take and hold, by bequest, devise, gift, purchase or lease, either absolutely or in trust, for any of its purposes, any property, real or personal, without limitation, as to amount or value, except such limitation, if any, as the legislature may hereafter impose, to transfer and convey the same, and to invest and reinvest the principal and income thereof, and deal with and expend the principal and income of the corporation in such manner as in the judgment of the trustees will best promote its objects. The said corporation shall have all the powers, and be subject to all restrictions, which now pertain by law to membership corporations in so far as the same are applicable thereto and are not inconsistent with the provisions of this act. The persons named in the first section of this act shall constitute the first board of trustees and members of the corporation. Such persons so named in the first section of this act, or a majority of them, shall hold a meeting and organize the corporation and adopt a constitution and by-laws not inconsistent with the constitution and laws of this state. Such constitution shall prescribe the qualifications and manner of election of members, the number of members who shall constitute a quorum for the transaction of business at meetings of the corporation, the number of trustees by whom the business and affairs of the corporation shall be managed, the qualifications, powers, and the manner of selection of the trustees and officers of the corporation, and all other provisions for the regulation of the affairs of the corporation, and the management and disposition of its property, which may be deemed expedient.

Application of membership corporation laws.

Organization; constitution and by-laws.

Pecuniary profit prohibited

§ 3. The corporation hereby formed is not established and shall not be maintained or conducted for pecuniary profit, or for the pecuniary profit of its members, and no member of the corporation shall be entitled to or shall receive any such profit; provided, however, that reasonable compensation may be paid to an officer or member for services actually rendered the corporation.

Compensation for services.

§ 4. This act shall take effect immediately.

Chap. 150.

AN ACT authorizing payments to injured or representatives of deceased volunteer firemen in the county of Westchester.

Became a law April 1, 1913, with the approval of the Governor. Passed, three-fifths being present.

The People of the State of New York, represented in Senate and Assembly, do enact as follows:

Section 1. **Payments to injured or representatives of deceased volunteer firemen in the county of Westchester:**

First. If an active member of a volunteer fire company in any city, incorporated village or in any fire district of a town outside of an incorporated village or in any part of a town protected by a volunteer fire company incorporated under the provisions of the membership corporations law, within the county of Westchester, dies from injuries incurred while in the performance of his duty as such fireman within one year thereafter, the city, village or town shall pay as follows: Payments when volunteer fireman dies from injuries incurred in performance of duty.

a. If such volunteer fireman is a member of a volunteer fire company located in any of the cities of the second or third class in which a pension fund is maintained, the relatives of such volunteer fireman shall be entitled to a pension in the same manner and at the same rates as if he were a member of the paid fire department of said cities. In city maintaining pension fund.

b. If in a city of the third class not maintaining a pension fund for the benefit of the members of the paid fire department therein, such city shall pay to the executor or administrator of such deceased volunteer fireman the sum of two thousand dollars. In city of third class not maintaining pension fund.

c. If in any other city, village, fire district or town the sum of fifteen hundred dollars shall be paid to the executor or administrator of such deceased volunteer fireman. In other municipality.

§ 2. Any such volunteer fireman in the county of Westchester who shall become permanently incapacitated for performing the full duties of a volunteer fireman by reason of disease or disability caused or induced by actual performance of the duties of his position, without fault or misconduct on his part, shall When incapacitated because of performance of duties.

a. If a member of a volunteer fire company located in any of the cities of the second or third class, in which a pension fund is maintained, be paid a pension in the same manner and at the same rates as if he were a member of the paid fire department of said city. In city maintaining pension fund.

In other place.

b. If a member of the fire department in any other place, such volunteer fireman shall be paid one-half the amount which would have been payable in case of death to his executor or administrator under the provisions of subdivision c of section one of this act.

Sums; how charged and collected.

§ 3. In cities such sum shall be a city charge and shall be audited and paid in the same manner as other city charges, except that no part of the moneys payable under this act shall be deducted from the pension funds of the paid departments therein. In villages such sum shall be a village charge and shall be audited and paid in the same manner as village charges, and shall be assessed upon the property and persons liable to taxation in said village, and levied and collected in the same manner as village taxes. If such fireman was a member of a fire company in a fire district outside of a city or an incorporated village, such sum shall be a town charge, audited and paid in the same manner as town charges, and shall be assessed upon the property and persons in such fire district liable to taxation, and levied and collected in the same manner as town charges. If such fireman was a member of a fire company incorporated under the membership corporations law, such sum shall be a town charge audited and paid as town charges and shall be assessed upon the property and persons liable to taxation in the territory protected by such fire company and levied and collected in the same manner as town charges therein.

Distribution when paid to executor or administrator.

Provided, however, that any money paid to an executor or administrator under any of the provisions of this act shall be distributed in the manner provided by law for the distribution of personal property.

Determination of controversies by county judge.

§ 4. In case any controversy shall arise at any time under the provisions of this act, the same shall be determined by the county judge of Westchester county. For that purpose, any party may present a petition to the county judge, setting forth the facts and rights which are claimed. A copy of such petition and notice of the time and place when the same will be presented shall be served on all persons interested therein, at least eight days prior to such presentation.

§ 5. This act shall take effect immediately.

Chap. 151.

AN ACT to amend the code of criminal procedure, in relation to the number of deputy clerks in the court of general sessions of the city and county of New York.

Became a law April 1, 1913, with the approval of the Governor. Passed, three-fifths being present.

The People of the State of New York, represented in Senate and Assembly, do enact as follows:

Section 1. Section fifty-five[1] of the code of criminal procedure is hereby amended to read as follows:

§ 55. **Accommodation for courts and officers, et cetera.** The courts have the same power to direct suitable provisions to be made for their accommodation as is now possessed by the supreme court. The judges of the court of general sessions of the city and county of New York must appoint a clerk, not more than fourteen[2] deputy clerks, five interpreters, six stenographers, six record clerks, six chief court attendants, a warden to the regular grand jury, and a warden to the additional grand jury, and such warden shall hold his office during the pleasure of said judges; [3]and any person who has heretofore held the office and performed the duties of a deputy clerk in said court for more than one year is eligible for appointment as deputy clerk provided for in this section.

§ 2. This act shall take effect immediately.

[margin note: § 55 amended]

Chap. 152.

AN ACT to amend the real property law, in relation to tenure of real property by aliens.

Became a law April 1, 1913, with the approval of the Governor. Passed, three-fifths being present.

The People of the State of New York, represented in Senate and Assembly, do enact as follows:

Section 1. Section ten of chapter fifty-two of the laws of nineteen hundred and nine, entitled "An act relating to real property.

[margin note: L. 1909, ch. 52, § 10 amended.]

---

[1] Section 55 is further amended by L. 1913, ch. 530, post.
[2] Formerly "thirteen."
[3] Remainder of section new.

constituting chapter fifty of the consolidated laws," is hereby amended to read as follows:

§ 10. **Capacity to hold real property.** 1. A citizen of the United States is capable of holding real property within this state, and of taking the same by descent, devise or purchase.

2.[1] Alien friends are empowered to take, hold, transmit and dispose of real property within this state in the same manner as native-born citizens and their heirs and devisees take in the same manner as citizens; provided, however, that nothing herein contained shall affect the rights of this state in any action or proceeding for escheat instituted before May nineteenth, eighteen hundred and ninety-seven.

§§ 12-14 repealed.

§ 2. Sections twelve, thirteen and fourteen of such chapter are hereby repealed.

§ 3. This act shall take effect immediately.

Chap. 153.

AN ACT to repeal section thirteen of the decedent estate law, in relation to devises of real property to aliens.

Became a law April 1, 1913, with the approval of the Governor. Passed, three-fifths being present.

The People of the State of New York, represented in Senate and Assembly, do enact as follows:

L. 1909, ch. 18, § 13 repealed.

Section 1. Section thirteen of chapter eighteen of the laws of nineteen hundred and nine, entitled "An act relating to estates of deceased persons, constituting chapter thirteen of the consolidated laws," is hereby repealed.

§ 2. This act shall take effect immediately.

---

[1] Subd. 2 materially amended.

Chap. 154.

AN ACT to amend the penal law, in relation to arson.

Became a law April 2, 1913, with the approval of the Governor. Passed, three-fifths being present.

The People of the State of New York, represented in Senate and Assembly, do enact as follows:

Section 1. Sections two hundred and twenty-two and two hundred and twenty-three of chapter eighty-eight of the laws of nineteen hundred and nine, entitled "An act providing for the punishment of crime, constituting chapter forty of the consolidated laws," are hereby amended to read, respectively, as follows:

§ 222. **Arson in second degree.** A person who:

1. Commits an act of burning in the day time, which, if committed in the night time, would be arson in the first degree; or.

2. Wilfully burns, or sets on fire, in the night time, a dwelling house, wherein, at the time, there is no human being; or,

3. Wilfully burns, or sets on fire, in the night time, a building not inhabited, but adjoining or within the curtilage of an inhabited building, in which there is, at the time, a human being, so that the inhabited building is endangered, even though it is not in fact injured by the burning; or,

4. Wilfully burns, or sets on fire, in the night time, a car, vessel, or other vehicle, or a structure or building, ordinarily occupied at night by a human being, although no person is within it at the time; or

5.[1] Wilfully burns, or sets on fire, a vessel, car, or other vehicle, or a building, structure, or other erection, which is at the time insured against loss or damage by fire, with intent to prejudice or defraud the insurer thereof,

Is guilty of arson in the second degree.

§ 223. **Arson in third degree.** [2]A person who wilfully burns, or sets on fire a vessel, car, or other vehicle, or a building, structure, or other erection, under circumstances not amounting to arson in the first or second degree,

Is guilty of arson in the third degree.

§ 2. This act shall take effect September first, nineteen hundred and thirteen.

Marginal notes: L. 1909. ch. 101. §§ 222, 223 amended. In effect Sept. 1, 1913.

---

[1] Subd. 5 new. It consists substantially of former subd. 1 of § 223. See note 2 infra.

[2] Former subd. 1 repealed. See note 1 supra.

Chap. 155.

AN ACT to amend the insurance law, in relation to standard provisions for accident and health policies and discriminations.

Became a law April 2, 1913, with the approval of the Governor. Passed, three-fifths being present.

The People of the State of New York, represented in Senate and Assembly, do enact as follows:

L. 1909. ch. 33, § 107, as added by L. 1910, ch. 636, repealed.

Section 1. Section one hundred and seven of chapter thirty-three of the laws of nineteen hundred and nine, entitled "An act in relation to insurance corporations, constituting chapter twenty-eight of the consolidated laws," as added by chapter six hundred and thirty-six of the laws of nineteen hundred and ten, is hereby repealed.

New § 107 added.

§ 2. Such chapter is hereby amended by inserting therein a new section, to be section one hundred and seven thereof, to read as follows:

§ 107. **Standard provisions for accident and health policies.**

Subdivision (a). On and after the first day of January, nineteen hundred and fourteen, no policy of insurance against loss or damage from the sickness, or the bodily injury or death of the insured by accident shall be issued or delivered to any person in this state by any corporation organized under article two of this chapter, or, if a foreign corporation, authorized to do business in this state, until a copy of the form thereof and of the classification of risks and the premium rates pertaining thereto have been filed with the superintendent of insurance; nor shall it be so issued or delivered until the expiration of thirty days after it has been so filed unless the said superintendent shall sooner give his written approval thereto. If the said superintendent shall notify, in writing, the company, corporation, association, society or other insurer which has filed such form that it does not comply with the requirements of law, specifying the reasons for his opinion, it shall be unlawful thereafter for any such insurer to issue any policy in such form. The action of the said superintendent in this regard shall be subject to review by any court of competent jurisdiction, provided, however, that nothing in this section shall be so construed as to give jurisdiction to any court not already having jurisdiction.

Subd. (b). No such policy shall be so issued or delivered

(1) unless the entire money and other considerations therefor are expressed in the policy; nor (2) unless the time at which the insurance thereunder takes effect and terminates is stated in a portion of the policy preceding its execution by the insurer; nor (3) if the policy purports to insure more than one person; nor (4) unless every printed portion thereof and of any endorsements or attached papers shall be plainly printed in type of which the face shall be not smaller than ten point; nor (5) unless a brief description thereof be printed on its first page and on its filing back in type of which the face shall be not smaller than fourteen point; nor (6) unless the exceptions of the policy be printed with the same prominence as the benefits to which they apply, provided, however, that any portion of such policy which purports, by reason of the circumstances under which a loss is incurred, to reduce any indemnity promised therein to an amount less than that provided for the same loss occurring under ordinary circumstances, shall be printed in bold face type and with greater prominence than any other portion of the text of the policy.

Subd. (c). Every such policy so issued shall contain certain standard provisions, which shall be in the words and in the order hereinafter set forth and be preceded in every policy by the caption, "Standard Provisions." In each such standard provision wherever the word "insurer" is used, there shall be substituted therefor "company" or "corporation" or "association" or "society" or such other word as will properly designate the insurer. Said standard provisions shall be:

(1) A standard provision relative to the contract which may be in either of the following two forms: Form (A) to be used in policies which do not provide for reduction of indemnity on account of change of occupation, and Form (B) to be used in policies which do so provide. If Form (B) is used and the policy provides indemnity against loss from sickness, the words "or contracts sickness" may be inserted therein immediately after the words "in the event that the insured is injured":

(A): 1. This policy includes the endorsements and attached papers, if any, and contains the entire contract of insurance. No reduction shall be made in any indemnity herein provided by reason of change in the occupation of the insured or by reason of his doing any act or thing pertaining to any other occupation.

(B): 1. This policy includes the endorsements and attached papers, if any, and contains the entire contract of insurance except as it may be modified by the insurer's classification of risks and premium rates in the event that the insured is injured after having changed his occupation to one classified by the insurer as more hazardous than that stated in the policy, or while he is doing any act or thing pertaining to any occupation so classified, except ordinary duties about his residence or while engaged in recreation, in which event the insurer will pay only such portion of the indemnities provided in the policy as the premium paid would have purchased at the rate but within the limits so fixed by the insurer for such more hazardous occupation.

If the law of the state in which the insured resides at the time this policy is issued requires that prior to its issue a statement of the premium rates and classification of risks pertaining to it shall be filed with the state official having supervision of insurance in such state, then the premium rates and classification of risks mentioned in this policy shall mean only such as have been last filed by the insurer in accordance with such law, but if such filing is not required by such law then they shall mean the insurer's premium rates and classification of risks last made effective by it in such state prior to the occurrence of the loss for which the insurer is liable.

(2) A standard provision relative to changes in the contract, which shall be in the following form:

2. No statement made by the applicant for insurance not included herein shall avoid the policy or be used in any legal proceeding hereunder. No agent has authority to change this policy or to waive any of its provisions. No change in this policy shall be valid unless approved by an executive officer of the insurer and such approval be endorsed hereon.

(3) A standard provision relative to reinstatement of policy after lapse which may be in either of the three following forms: Form (A) to be used in policies which insure only against loss from accident; Form (B) to be used in policies which insure only against loss from sickness; and Form (C) to be used in policies which insure against loss from both accident and sickness.

(A): 3. If default be made in the payment of the agreed premium for this policy, the subsequent acceptance of a premium by the insurer or by any of its duly authorized agents shall reinstate the policy, but only to cover loss resulting from accidental injury thereafter sustained.

(B): 3. If default be made in the payment of the agreed premium for this policy, the subsequent acceptance of a premium by the insurer or by any of its duly authorized agents shall reinstate the policy but only to cover such sickness as may begin more than ten days after the date of such acceptance.

(C): 3. If default be made in the payment of the agreed premium for this policy, the subsequent acceptance of a premium by the insurer or by any of its duly authorized agents shall reinstate the policy but only to cover accidental injury thereafter sustained and such sickness as may begin more than ten days after the date of such acceptance.

(4) A standard provision relative to time of notice of claim which may be in either of the three following forms: Form (A) to be used in policies which insure only against loss from accident; Form (B) to be used in policies which insure only against loss from sickness, and Form (C) to be used in policies which insure against loss from both accident and sickness. If Form (A) or Form (C) is used the insurer may at its option add thereto the following sentence, " In event of accidental death immediate notice thereof must be given to the insurer."

(A): 4. Written notice of injury on which claim may be based must be given to the insurer within twenty days after the date of the accident causing such injury.

(B): 4. Written notice of sickness on which claim may be based must be given to the insurer within ten days after the commencement of the disability from such sickness.

(C): 4. Written notice of injury or of sickness on which claim may be based must be given to the insurer within twenty days after the date of the accident causing such injury or within ten days after the commencement of disability from such sickness.

(5) A standard provision relative to sufficiency of notice of claim which shall be in the following form and in which the insurer shall insert in the blank space such office and its location as it may desire to designate for such purpose of notice:

5. Such notice given by or in behalf of the insured or beneficiary, as the case may be, to the insurer at . . . . or to any authorized agent of the insurer, with particulars sufficient to identify the insured, shall be deemed to be notice to the insurer. Failure to give notice within the time provided in this policy shall not invalidate any claim if it shall be shown not to have been reasonably possible to give such notice and that notice was given as soon as was reasonably possible.

(6) A standard provision relative to furnishing forms for the convenience of the insured in submitting proof of loss as follows:

6. The insurer upon receipt of such notice, will furnish to the claimant such forms as are usually furnished by it for filing proofs of loss. If such forms are not so furnished within fifteen days after the receipt of such notice, the claimant shall be deemed to have complied with the requirements of this policy as to proof of loss upon submitting within the time fixed in the policy for filing proofs of loss, written proof covering the occurrence, character and extent of the loss for which claim is made.

(7) A standard provision relative to filing proof of loss which shall be in such one of the following forms as may be appropriate to the indemnities provided:

(A): 7. Affirmative proof of loss must be furnished to the insurer at its said office within ninety days after the date of the loss for which claim is made.

(B): 7. Affirmative proof of loss must be furnished to the insurer at its said office within ninety days after the termination of the period of disability for which the company is liable.

(C): 7. Affirmative proof of loss must be furnished to the insurer at its said office in case of claim for loss of time from disability within ninety days after the termination of the period for which the insurer is liable, and in case of claim for any other loss, within ninety days after the date of such loss.

(8) A standard provision relative to examination of the person of the insured and relative to autopsy which shall be in the following form:

8. The insurer shall have the right and opportunity to examine the person of the insured when and so often as it may reasonably require during the pendency of claim hereunder, and also the right and opportunity to make an autopsy in case of death where it is not forbidden by law.

(9) A standard provision relative to the time within which payments other than those for loss of time on account of disability shall be made, which provision may be in either of the following two forms and which may be omitted from any policy providing only indemnity for loss of time on account of disability. The insurer shall insert in the blank space either the word "immediately" or appropriate language to designate such period of time, not more than sixty days, as it may desire; Form (A) to be used in policies which do not provide indemnity for loss of time on account of disability and Form (B) to be used in policies which do so provide.

(A): 9. All indemnities provided in this policy will be paid .... after receipt of due proof.

(B): 9. All indemnities provided in this policy for loss other than that of time on account of disability will be paid......... after receipt of due proof.

(10) A standard provision relative to periodical payments of indemnity for loss of time on account of disability, which provision shall be in the following form, and which may be omitted from any policy not providing for such indemnity. The insurer shall insert in the first blank space of the form appropriate language to designate the proportion of accrued indemnity it may desire to pay, which proportion may be all or any part not less than one-half, and in the second blank space shall insert any period of time not exceeding sixty days:

10. Upon request of the insured and subject to due proof of loss .... accrued indemnity for loss of time on account of disability will be paid at the expiration of each ...... during the continuance of the period for which the insurer is liable, and any balance remaining unpaid at the termination of such period will be paid immediately upon receipt of due proof.

(11) A standard provision relative to indemnity payments which may be in either of the two following forms: Form (A) to be used in policies which designate a beneficiary, and Form (B) to be used in policies which do not designate any beneficiary other than the insured.

(A): 11. Indemnity for loss of life of the insured is payable to the beneficiary if surviving the insured, and otherwise to the estate of the insured. All other indemnities of this policy are payable to the insured.

(B): 11. All the indemnities of this policy are payable to the insured.

(12) A standard provision providing for cancellation of the policy at the instance of the insured which shall be in the following form:

12. If the insured shall at any time change his occupation to one classified by the insurer as less hazardous than that stated in the policy, the insurer, upon written request of the insured and surrender of the policy, will cancel the same and will return to the insured the unearned premium.

(13) A standard provision relative to the rights of the beneficiary under the policy which shall be in the following form and

which may be omitted from any policy not designating a beneficiary:

13. Consent of the beneficiary shall not be requisite to surrender or assignment of this policy, or to change of beneficiary, or to any other changes in the policy.

(14) A standard provision limiting the time within which suit may be brought upon the policy as follows:

14. No action at law or in equity shall be brought to recover on this policy prior to the expiration of sixty days after proof of loss has been filed in accordance with the requirements of this policy, nor shall such action be brought at all unless brought within two years from the expiration of the time within which proof of loss is required by the policy.

(15) A standard provision relative to time limitations of the policy as follows:

15. If any time limitation of this policy with respect to giving notice of claim or furnishing proof of loss is less than that permitted by the law of the state in which the insured resides at the time this policy is issued, such limitation is hereby extended to agree with the minimum period permitted by such law.

Subd. (d). No such policy shall be so issued or delivered which contains any provision (1) relative to cancellation at the instance of the insurer; or, (2) limiting the amount of indemnity to a sum less than the amount stated in the policy and for which the premium has been paid; or, (3) providing for the deduction of any premium from the amount paid in settlement of claim; or, (4) relative to other insurance by the same insurer; or, (5) relative to the age limits of the policy; unless such provisions which are hereby designated as optional standard provisions, shall be in the words and in the order in which they are hereinafter set forth, but the insurer may at its option omit from the policy any such optional standard provision. Such optional standard provisions if inserted in the policy shall immediately succeed the standard provisions named in *subdivison (c) of this section.

(1) An optional standard provision relative to cancellation of the policy at the instance of the insurer as follows:

16. The insurer may cancel this policy at any time by written notice delivered to the insured or mailed to his last address, as shown by the records of the insurer, together with cash or the insurer's check for the unearned portion of the premiums actu-

---

* So in original.

ally paid by the insured, and such cancellation shall be without prejudice to any claim originating prior thereto.

(2) An optional standard provision relative to reduction of the amount of indemnity to a sum less than that stated in the policy as follows:

17. If the insured shall carry with another company, corporation, association or society other insurance covering the same loss without giving written notice to the insurer, then in that case the insurer shall be liable only for such portion of the indemnity promised as the said indemnity bears to the total amount of like indemnity in all policies covering such loss, and for the return of such part of the premium paid as shall exceed the pro rata for the indemnity thus determined.

(3) An optional standard provision relative to deduction of premium upon settlement of claim as follows:

18. Upon the payment of claim hereunder any premium then due and unpaid or covered by any note or written order may be deducted therefrom.

(4) An optional standard provision relative to other insurance by the same insurer which shall be in such one of the following forms as may be appropriate to the indemnities provided, and in the blank spaces of which the insurer shall insert such upward limits of indemnity as are specified by the insurers' classification of risks, filed as required by this section.

(A): 19. If a like policy or policies, previously issued by the insurer to the insured be in force concurrently herewith, making the aggregate indemnity in excess of $....................., the excess insurance shall be void and all premiums paid for such excess shall be returned to the insured.

(B): 19. If a like policy or policies, previously issued by the insurer to the insured be in force concurrently herewith, making the aggregate indemnity for loss of time on account of disability in excess of $.................... weekly, the excess insurance shall be void and all premiums paid for such excess shall be returned to the insured.

(C): 19. If a life policy or policies, previously issued by the insurer to the insured be in force concurrently herewith, making the aggregate indemnity for loss other than that of time on account of disability in excess of $......, or the aggregate indemnity for loss of time on account of disability in excess of $...... weekly, the excess insurance of either kind shall be void and all premiums paid for such excess shall be returned to the insured.

(5) An optional standard provision relative to the age limits of the policy which shall be in the following form and in the blank spaces of which the insurer shall insert such number of years as it may elect:

20. The insurance under this policy shall not cover any person under the age of .... years nor over the age of .... years. Any premium paid to the insurer for any period not covered by this policy will be returned upon request.

Subd. (e). No such policy shall be so issued or delivered if it contains any provision contradictory, in whole or part, of any of the provisions hereinbefore in this section designated as " Standard Provisions " or as " Optional Standard Provisions;" nor shall any endorsements or attached papers vary, alter, extend, be used as a substitute for, or in any way conflict with any of the said " Standard Provisions " or the said " Optional Standard Provisions;" nor shall such policy be so issued or delivered if it contains any provision purporting to make any portion of the charter, constitution or by-laws of the insurer a part of the policy unless such portion of the charter, constitution or by-laws shall be set forth in full in the policy, but this prohibition shall not be deemed to apply to any statement of rates or classification of risks filed with the superintendent of insurance in accordance with the provisions of this section.

Subd. (f). The falsity of any statement in the application for any policy covered by this section shall not bar the right to recovery thereunder unless such false statement was made with actual intent to deceive or unless it materially affected either the acceptance of the risk or the hazard assumed by the insurer.

Subd. (g). The acknowledgment by any insurer of the receipt of notice given under any policy covered by this section, or the furnishing of forms for filing proofs of loss, or the acceptance of such proofs, or the investigation of any claim thereunder shall not operate as a waiver of any of the rights of the insurer in defense of any claim arising under such policy.

Subd. (h). No alteration of any written application for insurance by erasure, insertion or otherwise, shall be made by any person other than the applicant without his written consent, and the making of any such alteration without the consent of the applicant shall be a misdemeanor. If such alteration shall be made by any officer of the insurer, or by any employee of the insurer with the insurer's knowledge or consent, then such act shall be deemed to have been performed by the insurer thereafter issuing the policy upon such altered application.

Subd. (i). A policy issued in violation of this section shall be held valid but shall be construed as provided in this section and when any provision in such a policy is in conflict with any provision of this section, the rights, duties and obligations of the insurer, the policyholder and the beneficiary shall be governed by the provisions of this section.

Subd. (j). The policies of insurance against accidental bodily injury or sickness issued by an insurer not organized under the laws of this state may contain, when issued in this state, any provision which the law of the state, territory or district of the United States under which the insurer is organized, prescribes for insertion in such policies, and the policies of insurance against accidental bodily injury or sickness issued by an insurer organized under the laws of this state may contain, when issued or delivered in any other state, territory, district or country, any provision required by the laws of the state, territory, district or country in which the same are issued, anything in this section to the contrary notwithstanding.

Subd. (k). (1) Nothing in this section, however, shall apply to or affect any policy of liability or workmen's compensation insurance or any general or blanket policy of insurance issued to any municipal corporation or department thereof, or to any corporation, copartnership, association or individual employer, police or fire department, underwriters' corps, salvage bureau, or like associations or organizations, where the officers, members or employees or classes or departments thereof are insured for their individual benefit against specified accidental bodily injuries or sickness while exposed to the hazards of the occupation or otherwise in consideration of a premium intended to cover the risks of all the persons insured under such policy.

(2) Nothing in this section shall apply to or in any way affect contracts supplemental to contracts of life or endowment insurance where such supplemental contracts contain no provisions except such as operate to safeguard such insurance against lapse or to provide a special surrender value therefor in the event that the insured shall be totally and permanently disabled by reason of accidental bodily injury or by sickness; provided that no such supplemental contract shall be issued or delivered to any person in this state unless and until a copy of the form thereof has been

submitted to and approved by the superintendent of insurance, under such reasonable rules and regulations as he shall make concerning the provisions in such contracts and their submission to and approval by him.

(3) Nothing in this section shall apply to or in any way affect fraternal benefit societies.

(4) The provisions of this section contained in clause (5) of subdivision (b) and clauses (2), (3), (8) and (12) of subdivision (c) may be omitted from railroad ticket policies sold only at railroad stations, or at railroad ticket offices by railroad employees.

Subd. (l). Any company, corporation, association, society or other insurer or any officer or agent thereof, which or who issues or delivers to any person in this state any policy in willful violation of the provisions of this section shall be punished by a fine of not more than five hundred dollars for each offense, and the superintendent of insurance may revoke the license of any company, corporation, association, society or other insurer of another state or country, or of the agent thereof, which or who willfully·violates any provision of this section.

Subd. (m). The term "indemnity" as used in this section means benefits promised.

§ 108 added. § 3. Such chapter is hereby further amended by adding thereto a new section after section one hundred and seven, to be section one hundred and eight and to read as follows:

§ 108. **Discriminations under accident or health policies prohibited.** No insurance corporation authorized to make insurance in this state under subdivision two of section seventy of this chapter, nor any agent of such corporation, shall make or permit any discrimination between individuals of the same class in the amount of premiums, policy fees, or rates charged for any policy of accident or health insurance, or in the benefits payable thereunder, or in any of the terms or conditions of such insurance contract, or in any other manner whatsoever. Any person or corporation violating any provision of this section shall be guilty of a misdemeanor, and shall forfeit to the people of the state the sum of five hundred dollars for each such violation.

In effect Oct. 1, 1913. § 4. This act shall take effect on the first day of October, nineteen hundred and thirteen. Any policy covered by this act, the form of which has received the approval of the superintendent of insurance may be issued or delivered in this state on and after the said date.

Chap. 156.

AN ACT to amend chapter one hundred and thirty-four of the
laws of eighteen hundred and ninety-one, entitled "An act to
incorporate the Church Insurance Association," generally.[1]

Became a law April 2, 1913, with the approval of the Governor. Passed,
three-fifths being present.

*The People of the State of New York, represented in Senate
and Assembly, do enact as follows:*

Section 1. Section one of chapter one hundred and thirty-four L. 1891, ch.
of the laws of eighteen hundred and ninety-one, entitled "An act 134, § 1, as
to incorporate the Church Insurance Association," as amended by amended by
chapter five hundred and fifty-four of the laws of nineteen hun- L. 1901, ch. 554,
dred and one, is hereby amended to read as follows: amended.

§ 1. The First Wesleyan Methodist Episcopal church of Roches- Corporators.
ter, New York and others, religious societies duly organized under
the laws of the state of New York, which collectively own property
of the value of four hundred thousand dollars, which they desire
to have insured and such other religious societies, and such pastors, ministers, clergymen, preachers, ordained or duly licensed,
active or retired, and such wives or widows of the same, as shall
from time to time associate themselves with them in the manner
hereinafter provided, and such other members of religious societies
as may desire the insurance of dwelling houses and their contents
only, located wholly within the state of New York, to which such
insurance shall be strictly limited, are hereby made a body corporate, by the name of the Church Insurance Association of the Corporate
state of New York, for the purpose of transacting the business of Purposes.
co-operative insurance in the state of New York against loss or
damage by fire or lightning, or windstorm, its policies to cover the
property insurable in this association located in the said state outside of New York city; and property within the boundaries of any
conference, synod, diocese, ecclesiastical association or other religious body in the state, the jurisdiction of which extends into
territory adjoining the state of New York, upon written application made at its principal office in Rochester, New York. Every
church corporation, and every individual eligible to member- Applica-
ship desiring to be insured in said association shall make to the insurance.

---

[1] The amendments effected by this act are so numerous and extensive that
it is impracticable to indicate the changes made.

secretary of the association a written application for insurance, signed by such person or persons and in such manner, and containing such agreement on the part of the applicant for himself, itself, his or its successors, heirs and assigns to pay his or its pro rata share to the association of all losses or damages caused by fire or lightning, or windstorm, to any of the property insured therein by any member or members thereof, and the expenses of conducting the business of the association as the by-laws of said

Acceptance of application. association shall prescribe; and such application, if accepted, shall be accompanied by the payment of such membership fee as said by-laws shall require; and each such application, when accepted, shall be filed by the secretary in the office of the association; and the applicant shall thereupon be and become a member thereof.

§ 2 amended. § 2. Section two of such chapter is hereby amended to read as follows:

Directors. § 2. This association shall be managed by a board of twenty-
Terms. five directors, divided into five classes, whose respective terms of office shall be five years and until their successors, respectively,
Election. shall be elected, as said board is now constituted, the successors of the class of nineteen hundred and fourteen to be elected at the next annual meeting of the association, by ballot for the full term of five years, and those of the other classes annually thereafter in the
Who entitled to vote. order in which their respective terms shall expire. At the next annual meeting of the association, each member of said association, may have a seat in said meeting, and may have one vote, and at each subsequent annual meeting for the election of directors, only members of the association shall be entitled to representation, each religious society to be represented by a delegate duly appointed therefor by its board of trustees and to have one vote, and each other member, to be entitled to a seat in said meetings and to one vote.

§§ 4, 7, as amended by L. 1901, ch. 554, amended. § 3. Sections four and seven of such chapter, as amended by chapter five hundred and fifty-four of the laws of nineteen hundred and one, are hereby amended to read, respectively, as follows:

Powers of board of directors. § 4. Said board of directors, who shall be members of the association by virtue of their office and be entitled to vote at the annual meetings of the association, shall have full management and control of the affairs and business of the association. It shall have
By-laws. power to make, adopt and enforce by-laws, not inconsistent with this act and the laws of this state, for its government and the

orderly transaction of the business of the association, and from
time to time amend the same, which by-laws shall be the by-laws
of the association and shall bind all its members. Said by-laws
shall prescribe the number and time of the meetings of said board,
the number of directors necessary to constitute a quorum for the
transaction of business, the manner of filling vacancies in office,
the manner of fixing the compensation of officers, the amount of
membership fees, the manner of placing and classification of risks,
the manner of adjustment and collection of assessments for the
payment of losses and damages sustained by members, the manner of notification of members of assessments levied, and may
embrace all other provisions, rules and regulations necessary for
transacting the business of said association and for carrying into
effect the purposes of this act. Said by-laws may provide for an
executive committee for such purposes as may be necessary, which
committee shall be elected by said board at such time as it shall
see fit and may be changed at the pleasure of said board, and may
require its officers to give such bonds as the interests of said association may demand.

§ 7. The directors of this association may issue policies of in- Issuance of
surance, signed by the president and secretary, agreeing in the thorized.
name of the association, to pay all damages not exceeding the
amount insured, done by fire or lightning or windstorm to
churches, parsonages and their contents, sheds, barns and other
property, belonging to the several religious societies and to the
pastors, clergymen and other persons eligible to membership in said
association, which the association is hereinbefore authorized to
insure, and detached at such distances from other buildings as
the by-laws of the association may prescribe, during the period of
five years from the date of the policy, or such shorter period as
the by-laws of the association may prescribe; and no risk upon a Limitation
dwelling house and contents shall exceed the sum of five thousand of risks.
dollars, and no other single risk shall exceed the sum of twenty
thousand dollars; but every such risk above five thousand dollars
in amount shall be reinsured in solvent insurance companies
authorized to do business in the state so that the net risk of this
association in such cases shall not exceed five thousand dollars;
and no policy shall be issued on any building or property except
buildings and contents owned by corporations or persons eligible to
membership in said association. This association may issue more
than one policy to one member thereof owning separate or de-

tached buildings or property, such as this act or the by-laws of
said association permit it to insure. Every policy issued by the
association shall have attached thereto or printed thereon, a copy
of the by-laws and regulations of the association, or such parts
thereof as shall be deemed necessary, which shall form a part of
the contract between the association and the insured.

By-laws as part of contract of insurance.

§ 4. Section eight of such chapter is hereby amended to read
as follows:

§ 8 amended.

§ 8. Every member of this association holding a policy thereof,
not expired or vitiated, who or which has sustained a loss or damage by fire or lightning, or windstorm, in cases where damage by
windstorm is insured against in the policy, to the building or
buildings or other property covered by said policy since the issue
of the same shall immediately notify the secretary of the association in the manner prescribed by the by-laws of the association
of his or its loss or damage, and it shall be the duty of the officers
of the association to proceed at once to ascertain and adjust such
loss or damage in the manner provided by said by-laws.

Notice of loss.

Adjustment.

§ 5. Such chapter is hereby amended by adding thereto a new
section, to be section thirteen, to read as follows:

§ 13 added.

§ 13. An exemption from taxation equivalent to that granted
to a town or county co-operative insurance corporation by subdivision three of section one hundred and eighty-seven of article nine
of chapter sixty of the consolidated laws[2] shall be allowed to this
association.

Exemption from taxation.

§ 6. This act shall take effect immediately.

[2] Tax law.

Chap. 157.

AN ACT to amend chapter five hundred and seventy of the laws
of nineteen hundred and nine, entitled "An act to establish the
city court of Buffalo, defining its powers and jurisdiction and
providing for its officers," in relation to attachment of property
and compensation of marshals.

Became a law April 2, 1913, with the approval of the Governor. Passed,
three-fifths being present.

Accepted by the City.

*The People of the State of New York, represented in Senate
and Assembly, do enact as follows:*

Section 1. Subdivision ten of section twenty of chapter five L. 1909, ch. hundred and seventy of the laws of nineteen hundred and nine, 570, § 20, subd. 10 entitled "An act to establish the city court of Buffalo, defining amended. its powers and jurisdiction and providing for its officers," is hereby amended to read as follows:

10. In an action commenced by an attachment of property as now Jurisdiction provided by statute if[1] the debt or damages claimed do not exceed in action commenced one thousand dollars, exclusive of interest and costs. [2]A warrant by attach- of attachment issued by the court may be levied by the marshal Warrant, upon any personal property of the defendant not exempt from how levied levy and sale under an execution and the procedure so far as applicable thereto shall be the same as that provided in chapter seven, title three, article two of the code of civil procedure.

§ 2. Section fifty-three of such chapter is hereby amended to § 53 read as follows: amended.

§ 53. **Jury; how summoned.** The marshal, or the person deputed, as provided in this act, must thereupon immediately
summon each person named in the above list, by giving him the
sum of ten cents and the notice above mentioned personally, or
by leaving it at his place of residence or business, with some
person of suitable age and discretion, and must return the list
to the court, at its opening, on the day for which the jury was
drawn, specifying the persons summoned, and the manner in
which each was notified. [2]The marshal or the person deputed as
provided in this act shall be entitled to a fee of twenty-five cents
for each person summoned by him as aforesaid. If a sufficient
number of competent and indifferent jurors do not attend, the

---

[1] Word " if " substituted for word " for."
[2] Following sentence new.

court must direct to be summoned from the said list so furnished by the commissioner of jurors a sufficient number to complete the jury, by a marshal or a person deputed for that purpose. The ballots containing the names of the jurors summoned and not drawn, or excused from serving must be returned by the clerk to the undrawn jury box, to be drawn as in the first instance. The ballots containing the names of the jurors who served must be placed in a box to be called the drawn jury box, containing a minute thereon of the date of their service, and left until all the other names have been drawn, and as often as that happens, the whole number must be returned to the undrawn jury box, as in the first instance. Any judge presiding in said court may impose a fine of twenty-five dollars upon each person duly drawn and notified to attend the court as trial juror, who fails to attend as required by the notice. The clerk of the court must, within ten days thereafter, issue a warrant under the seal of the court, directed to a marshal of said court, commanding him to collect from the person therein mentioned said sum and to pay over the same when collected to the treasurer of the city of Buffalo. The marshal shall execute such warrant in the same manner as provided by section two thousand two hundred and ninety-six of the code of civil procedure. A clerk who violates any one of the provisions of this section or of the two next preceding sections forfeits one hundred dollars for each offense, to be paid to said treasurer of the city of Buffalo.

§ 3. This act shall take effect immediately.

Chap. 158.

AN ACT to amend chapter seven hundred and fifty-one of the laws of nineteen hundred and seven, entitled "An act to revise the charter of the city of Binghamton," in relation to appropriations for hospital purposes.

Became a law April 2, 1913, with the approval of the Governor. Passed, three-fifths being present.

Accepted by the City.

The People of the State of New York, represented in Senate and Assembly, do enact as follows:

L. 1907, ch. 751, § 74 amended.   Section 1. Section seventy-four of chapter seven hundred and fifty-one of the laws of nineteen hundred and seven, entitled "An act to revise the charter of the city of Binghamton," is hereby amended to read as follows:

§ 74. **Appropriation for hospital purposes; pavements, sewers, sidewalks and curbs; park purposes; celebrations.** The board of estimate and apportionment may annually include in the tax budget not more than thirty[1] thousand dollars for hospital purposes; not more than twenty thousand dollars to defray the city's portion of the construction of new pavements; not more than twenty thousand dollars to defray the city's portion of the construction of sewers; not more than twenty thousand dollars to defray the city's portion of the construction of stone or concrete sidewalks and curbs; not more than eight thousand dollars for the maintenance of parks. The board of estimate and apportionment may also annually include in the tax budget a sum or sums not exceeding one thousand dollars for the decoration of public buildings and for carriage hire upon the occasion of any public celebration in which the officers of the city shall participate, or in the entertainment of guests of the city.

§ 2. This act shall take effect immediately.

Chap. 159.

AN ACT to amend the code of criminal procedure, in relation to peace officers.

Became a law April 2, 1913, with the approval of the Governor. Passed, three-fifths being present.

The People of the State of New York, represented in Senate and Assembly, do enact as follows:

Section 1. Section one hundred and fifty-four of the code of criminal procedure is hereby amended to read as follows: § 154 amended

§ 154. **Who are peace officers.** A peace officer is a sheriff of a county, or his under sheriff or deputy, or a county detective[2] appointed pursuant to chapter sixty-two of the laws of eighteen hundred and ninety-seven as amended by chapter five hundred and thirty-two of the laws of nineteen hundred and by chapter five hundred and ninety-eight of the laws of nineteen hundred

---

[1] Formerly "twenty."
[2] Inclusion of county detectives new.

10

and eleven, or a constable, marshal, police constable or policeman
of a city, town or village.

In effect
Sept. 1,
1913. § 2. This act shall take effect September first, nineteen hundred
and thirteen.

Chap. 160.

AN ACT to amend chapter eighteen of the laws of eighteen hundred and sixty-two, entitled "An act to revise the charter of the
city of Utica," relative to local improvements.

**Became a law April 2, 1913, with the approval of the Governor. Passed,
three-fifths being present.**

Accepted by the City.

*The People of the State of New York, represented in Senate
and Assembly, do enact as follows:*

L. 1862, ch. 18, § 99, as amended by L. 1868, ch. 737, L. 1870, ch. 28, L. 1872, ch. 625, L. 1876, ch. 371, L. 1882, ch. 536, L. 1886, ch. 536, L. 1887, ch. 426, L. 1890, ch. 473, L. 1892, ch. 88, L. 1893, ch. 489, L. 1894, ch. 437, L. 1901, ch. 577, L. 1903, ch. 288, and L. 1908, ch. 224, amended.

Section 1. Section ninety-nine of chapter eighteen of the laws
of eighteen hundred and sixty-two, entitled "An act to revise the
charter of the city of Utica," as amended by chapter seven hundred
and thirty-seven of the laws of eighteen hundred and sixty-eight,
chapter twenty-eight of the laws of eighteen hundred and seventy,
chapter six hundred and twenty-five of the laws of eighteen hundred and seventy-two, chapter three hundred and seventy-one of
the laws of eighteen hundred and seventy-six, chapter three hundred and fifty-eight of the laws of eighteen hundred and eighty-
two, chapter five hundred and thirty-eight of the laws of eighteen
hundred and eighty-six, chapter four hundred and twenty-six of the
laws of eighteen hundred and eighty-seven, chapter four hundred
and seventy-three of the laws of eighteen hundred and ninety,
chapter eighty-eight of the laws of eighteen hundred and ninety-
two, chapter four hundred and eighty-nine of the laws of eighteen
hundred and ninety-three, chapter four hundred and thirty-seven
of the laws of eighteen hundred and ninety-four, chapter five hundred and seventy-seven of the laws of nineteen hundred and one,
chapter two hundred and eighty-eight of the laws of nineteen
hundred and three, and chapter two hundred and twenty-four of
the laws of nineteen hundred and eight, is hereby amended to read
as follows:

Street paving materials, how adopted. § 99. The common council shall by general ordinance prescribe,
approve and adopt the materials to be used in paving, repaving, re-
pairing, surfacing or resurfacing the streets and public places of the

city, and fix the standard of excellence and test required for each such material. The city engineer shall prepare standard specifications, in accordance with such ordinance, for the performance of the work involved in such improvements with each kind of material so prescribed, approved and adopted therefor. The common council shall have power to cause any street, highway, lane or alley in said city to be graded, leveled, paved or repaved, macadamized or telfordized, and to cause such crosswalks, sidewalks, drains and sewers to be made therein as it shall deem necessary, and the same to be repaired, mended or relaid, as it shall deem necessary. At least eight days' notice shall be published by the common council of an intention to pass an ordinance for the paving of any street, specifying the time and place of hearing, and at such meeting the property owners affected may attend and be heard. After the passage of any ordinance for such purpose the city engineer, under the direction of the commissioner of public works, shall cause plans and accurate specifications of the work proposed to be constructed to be prepared and filed with the secretary of the board of contract and supply. Such specifications for the performance of any work shall be prepared and set forth with sufficient detail to inform all persons proposing to bid therefor, of the nature of the work to be done and of the materials to be supplied, and written or printed copies thereof shall be delivered to all applicants therefor. The board of contract and supply shall then cause to be published in the official newspaper, for three alternate days, a notice of the filing of said plans and specifications, which shall describe the work and materials for which a contract will be let and invite proposals for the construction of such improvement with each kind of paving material prescribed, approved and adopted by the common council, and specify the day, hour and place of the meeting of the board at which proposals therefor will be opened, and that sealed proposals for constructing the work, with bonds for the faithful performance thereof, will be received by the board of contract and supply. In case the whole expense of any improvement under this section in the opinion of the board of contract and supply will not exceed the sum of two hundred and fifty dollars, no specifications or notice need be published, except the publication in the official proceedings of the action of the common council in relation thereto at least eight days before final action shall be taken thereon. [1]The board may in its discretion require, as a condition precedent

Marginal notes: Street and sewer improvements. Hearing on ordinance. Plans and specifications. Advertising for proposals. Deposit with proposal.

---

[1] Following sentence new.

to the reception or consideration of any bid or proposal in respect
to which it has authority to award a contract, the deposit of a
certified check upon a state or national bank, drawn to the order
of the secretary of said board, or of money, in an amount not exceeding ten per centum of the amount specified in said bid or
proposal, said deposit so made to be returned to the bidders making the same, except the bidder whose bid has been accepted, and
if such bidder whose bid has been accepted shall refuse or neglect
to execute the contract within ten days after due notice that the
same has been awarded, or to give security, if any, required for
the performance thereof, the amount of the deposit made by him
shall be forfeited to and be retained by the city as liquidated damages for such neglect or refusal, but if the said bidder shall execute the contract within the time aforesaid, and give the security,
if any, required for the performance thereof, the amount of his

Bond of contractor said deposit shall be returned to him. The board may also require
in its discretion that the successful bidder must execute and
deliver to the city a bond in the sum and in the number of sureties
designated by it,[2] both to be approved by the board of contract and
supply, and conditioned for the faithful performance of the contract, and the construction of[3] the work at the price and upon the
terms proposed, according to the plans and specifications filed
with the board of contract and supply and subject to the supervision and approval of the commissioner of public works, and
that the person making the proposal will erect and maintain
suitable guards and lights to prevent injuries to such work, or to
persons or property by or in consequence of the prudent
and careful use of such street, highway, lane, alley, side
or crosswalk during the progress of such work, and will save the
city harmless and indemnified against all loss, damage or expense
that may arise by or through any neglect of such person or those
in his employ, to erect or maintain such guards or lights, or either
of them. [4]In case the work to be done is paving or repaving, the
said board shall require a bond with the above conditions, and
shall require that the surety thereon be an approved surety company. No contract shall be let, except after the receipt of sealed

---

[2] Sentence to here formerly read: " No bid or proposal will be considered
which shall not be accompanied by a bond, with sureties, and in a penalty."
[3] Words " and conditioned for the faithful performance of the contract,
and the construction of " substituted for words " conditioned that if the
proposal or bid be accepted, the person proposing will construct."
[4] Following sentence new.

bids or proposals therefor, and no bid or proposals shall be received
at any time other than at a regular meeting of said board, and unless they conform to the rules of the board and the general ordinances of the common council. All bids or proposals must be en- Receipt
dorsed with the title of the work or materials to which they relate, ing of
the name of the bidder and his residence. It shall be the duty of proposals.
each member of the board to be present at the time and place mentioned in the public notice for the receipt and opening of bids or
proposals, and such meetings shall be open to the public. After all
the bids or proposals have been presented, but not until one-half
hour after the time stated in the public notice for holding the
meeting, all bids or proposals shall be opened by some member of
the board or by its secretary, publicly and in the presence of the
bidders and other persons there present, and an abstract of all of
such bids or proposals, with the prices and security offered, shall
be transcribed in a book kept for that purpose, without any
change, correction or addition whatever. A majority of the board
need not be present when such bids or proposals are opened. The
board shall have power to reject all bids or proposals if, in its Power to
opinion, the lowest bid or proposal is excessive, and it may reject reject bids.
all bids or proposals received at any meeting and advertise again
for new bids or proposals to be received at another meeting as
above prescribed. No person submitting, or on whose behalf a Withdrawal
bid or proposal is submitted, nor the principal or sureties on any prohibited.
bond or security accompanying the same, shall have the right to
withdraw or cancel any such bid, proposal or bond until the board
shall have awarded the contract for which such bid or proposal is
made, and such contract shall have been duly executed. In case
the expense of any such improvement is to be assessed upon the Action by
property abutting upon the street, or part thereof, to be improved owners
and more than one kind of material is prescribed, approved or where more
adopted therefor, the secretary of the board shall, within one kind of
week after proposals for such work have been received and opened, approved.
cause to be published in a daily official paper for four successive
days (exclusive of Sunday) a notice containing a summary statement of all such proposals. A majority of said property owners,
owning not less than one-third of the feet front of property abutting on such street, exclusive of city property, may present to
the board of contract and supply a petition or other writing designating the general kind of pavement or material to be used in making said improvement. If no part of the expense of such improve-

Action by
board of
contract
and supply
otherwise.
ment is to be assessed upon the property abutting upon said street, or if such expense is to be so assessed, but the property owners shall not have made a designation or shall have made more than one designation, as herein provided, the board of contract and supply shall, not later than at its next regular meeting after the expiration of ten days from the service of such notice, designate the kind of pavement or material to be used in making such im-

Award of
contract for
material
designated.
provement, and the contract for such improvement shall be awarded for the kind of pavement or material so designated by the property owners or board of contract and supply as aforesaid, and to the lowest bidder for doing the work with the kind of pavement or material so designated. In case, however, two-thirds of the owners of property, owning at least three-fifths of the linear feet fronting upon said street, or part thereof, shall designate a particular make, style or brand of the kind of pavement or material to be used in making such improvement, the contract therefor shall be awarded to the lowest bidder for such make, style or brand of such kind of pavement or material, although the same is not the lowest bid for such kind of pavement or material so designated.

Right of
person
assessed to
do work.
Any power to award a contract given to the board of contract and supply, under this section, shall be subject to the right of one or more persons liable to be assessed for said work, to do the work proposed at an expense at least fifteen per centum less than the contract proposed to be awarded to a bidder; provided, that within five days after such proposed award by the board of contract and supply, he shall propose and tender bonds therefor, conditioned as aforesaid, and file the same with the secretary of the board of contract and supply, in which case the contract shall be let to said person or persons.

Ascertain-
ing front
length of
abutting
lots.
1. In case the work shall be the grading, leveling or paving, repaving, macadamizing or telfordizing a street, lane or alley, whether with or without crosswalks, sidewalks, drains or sewers at one operation, or the grading, leveling or paving a street, lane or alley, the city engineer shall ascertain the aggregate front length of lots upon both sides thereof, and the front length of each lot or parcel, with a correct description thereof, and the

Ascertain-
ing total
expense.
name of the owner so far as it can be ascertained. The board of contract and supply shall then determine the expense of the whole work, including the expense of engineering, inspection, advertising and interest if any on certificates of indebtedness, or local improvement certificates issued to provide for partial

payments to contractors during the progress of the work. [s]The board of contract and supply shall certify the same to the board of assessors who shall cause the average expense upon each foot of the lots or parcels of land on both sides of said street, lane or alley, excluding cross streets from the computation, to be ascertained, and each lot or parcel of real estate to be assessed with its portion of the expense, by multiplying its number of feet front into the average expense per foot. Except that on any street, avenue or public place where any street surface railroad corporation continues to use any of its tracks it shall pave and keep in permanent repair that portion of such street, avenue or public place between its tracks, the rails of its tracks, and two feet in width outside of its tracks at its own expense. And all of such paving constructed by such railroad companies shall be constructed in such manner and of material that shall be approved by the commissioner of public works. The common council may, whenever deemed expedient, direct such street railway corporation to pave or repave the space between its tracks and two feet in width outside of its tracks of such material as shall be prescribed by the common council; and if such street railway corporation fails or neglects to pave or repave when so directed by the common council, the city may pave or repave such streets between the tracks and two feet outside the tracks and collect the expense thereof from said railway corporation in the manner provided by law. In case the work shall be the paving, macadamizing, telfordizing or repaving a street, the sum to be assessed as aforesaid shall be two-thirds of the expense of the whole work, including the expense of engineering, inspection, advertising and interest of certificates of indebtedness or local improvement certificates as hereinbefore provided; the other one-third thereof shall be borne by and paid by the city; and upon the making and delivery to the city treasurer of the assessment list, as provided in the act creating the board of assessors of the city of Utica (chapter seven hundred and thirty-eight of the laws of eighteen hundred and ninety-seven and amendments thereto), and the giving of notice to the owners or representatives respectively of the property assessed, and upon the expiration of one month ensuing the giving of such notice, the city treasurer shall receive the assess-

Assessment of lots.

Pavement by street railroad.

Division of expense between property assessed and city.

City treasurer to receive assessments.

---

s Words omitted which read: "Such interest to be computed from the date of such certificate up to the date of filing of the assessment with the city treasurer; and."

Return of
unpaid as-
sessments.

ments upon said assessment lists for one month. Upon the expiration of said period of one month, the city treasurer shall
certify to the common council the whole amount unpaid upon
said assessment list, and thereupon the common council shall provide for the issue of local improvement bonds, to be known as
paving bonds, in amount not exceeding such unpaid local assessments, which bonds shall mature, one-sixth in one year, one-sixth
in two years, one-sixth in three years, one-sixth in four years, one-
sixth in five years and one-sixth in six years, from a date not
more than thirty days after the date of the certificate of the city
treasurer. Such bonds shall be executed by the mayor and the
city treasurer in the name of the city and countersigned by the
comptroller under the corporate seal of said city, and shall be
issued at not less than par value thereof, and shall bear interest
at a rate to be approved by the common council, not exceeding
five per centum per annum, and which interest shall be payable
on each series of bonds annually; and said bonds shall specify
the improvement for which they are issued.   In case the city
treasurer shall have certified to the common council the amount
unpaid upon several assessment lists as above provided, the common council may include more than one of such assessments in
one series of bonds or may issue a separate series of bonds for
each assessment. The proceeds of the sale of such bonds shall be
applied towards the payment of the cost of such improvement,
provided that in any case where the common council shall have
provided for the issue of such paving or improvement bonds, as
authorized herein, the payment of such tax shall become due and
payable at the time or times, and subject to the penalties hereinafter prescribed, one-sixth thereof each year for six successive
years; the time of such annual payments to be computed from
the date of filing the assessment list with the city treasurer, with
interest added at the rate of five per centum per annum to the
time of such annual payments, and such payments to be subject
to the same penalties and all provisions for the enforcement and
collection of said assessment. In case of any default in payment
of any installment within thirty days after the same becomes due
and payable as above provided, the whole amount of the tax
assessed upon such improvement against the person or persons so
in default, and their grantees or assigns, with fees as provided
in section fifty-three, computed upon such whole amount, shall
thereupon become due and payable, and the treasurer shall pro-

Issue of
local im-
provement
bonds;
maturity,
execution,
etc.

Application
of proceeds.

Payment of
assessments
in annual
install-
ments.

Default in
payment of
installment.

ceed to collect the same with the fees as provided in section fifty-three of this charter, and interest thereon at the rate of twelve per centum per annum, in the manner above provided. No action to set aside, cancel or annul any assessment made under the provisions of this subdivision shall be maintained by any person, unless such action shall have been commenced within thirty days after the delivery to the city treasurer of the city of Utica of the assessment list, and unless within said thirty days an injunction shall have been procured by such persons from a court of competent jurisdiction restraining the common council from issuing the local improvement or paving bonds hereinbefore provided to be issued for such assessment.[6]

Limitation of action to set aside assessment.

2. In case the work shall be the constructing in a street of any crosswalk, drain or sewer separate from any other work, such expense, together with the engineer's fees, expense of advertising and two dollars for the expense of such assessment, shall be assessed by the assessors, upon the certification of the amount by the city engineer, upon the real estate which they shall deem benefited thereby, as near as may be in proportion to the amount of its benefits, unless the board of estimate and apportionment shall determine that all or a portion of the expenses shall be borne by the city at large. In such case the amount so determined by said board shall be included in the budget and raised by tax the same as other general city charges, or may be borrowed and raised by the city by the issue of bonds in accordance with the provisions of the uniform charter of cities of the second class, as shall be determined by the board of estimate and apportionment. An amount sufficient to pay any such bonds with the accrued interest thereon, shall be included in the tax budget and raised by tax the same as other general city charges, and such bonds as they mature together with the interest thereon shall be paid out of moneys so raised by tax. If the sewer or drain is the continuation or extension of one previously existing the assessors in making their assessments shall take into consideration such sums as have heretofore been assessed upon the real estate benefited, in order, so far as practicable, to render the assessment equal upon each lot or parcel, considering the whole drain or sewer, as continued or extended, a single work.

Assessment for crosswalk or sewer separate from other work.

Tax or bond issue for city's share.

Assessment when sewer an extension.

---

[6] Sentence omitted which read: "This provision shall be operative in conjunction with the provisions of sections one hundred and sixty-three, one hundred and sixty-four and one hundred and sixty-five of the uniform charters of cities of the second class."

Assessment
for
sidewalk.

3. In case the work shall be the construction of a sidewalk, each lot or parcel of land fronting thereon shall be assessed with the expense of its construction in front thereof, by the assessors upon the certification of the expense by the city engineer in the manner provided in subdivision one of this section.

Repair of
sidewalk by
abutting
owner.

4. In case the work shall be the repairing of any sidewalk, such repairs shall be made by the owners of the property fronting thereon, in accordance with such rules, regulations or ordinances as the common council shall, from time to time prescribe.

Connections
with
sewers, gas
and water
pipes may
be required.

The commissioner of public works shall have authority to require that all buildings or vacant lots shall, at the expense of the owners thereof, under the supervision and to the satisfaction of the commissioner of public works, be properly connected with the public sewers, gas and water pipes in the streets in front

Work to be
done by
city on
failure of
owner.

thereof; and whenever the owners of said property shall fail to comply with the directions of the commissioner of public works, he shall cause the same to be done and collect the expense thereof from said property or the owners thereof by presenting a bill for the expenses incurred thereby to the owner personally or by leaving the same at his residence or if he be a non-resident, by mailing the same to him at his last known place of residence, or if the name of such owner or his place of residence cannot be ascertained after due diligence, by posting the same in a conspicuous place on his premises, and, if he shall fail to pay the same within ten days thereafter, the commissioner shall file each year immediately preceding the time for making the annual assessment roll his certificate of the actual cost of the work, together with a statement as to the property in front of which the connections were made, with the assessors of the city, who shall, in the preparation of the next assessment roll of general city taxes, assess such amount upon such property, and the same shall be levied, assessed, enforced and collected in the same manner, by the same proceedings, at the same time, under the same penalties and having the same lien upon the property assessed as the general

Repair and
grading of
sidewalk
and re-
moval of
snow by
abutting
owner may
be required.

city tax and as a part thereof. The commissioner of public works shall have full power and authority to require the owner of property abutting upon a street to repair any sidewalk in front thereof or bring the same to true grade, and to remove the snow and ice therefrom. Where the owner of such property shall fail or neg-

To be done
by city on
failure of
owner.

lect to repair any sidewalk or bring the same to true grade for five days after written notice so to do has been served on him,

either personally or by delivering the same at his residence, or
if he be a non-resident by mailing the same to him at his last
known place of residence, or if the name of the owner or his
place of residence cannot be ascertained after due diligence, by
posting the same in a conspicuous place upon the premises; or
where the owner of any such premises shall fail or neglect to remove snow and ice from any such sidewalk after the same has re-
mained thereon for more than twelve hours, and the commissioner
shall have repaired such sidewalk or brought the same to grade
or removed the ice or snow therefrom, the expenses thereof shall
be collected and enforced in the same manner as above provided
for the expenses of sewer connections. Whenever the owners or
occupants of property fronting on any street, lane or highway,
shall fail to keep or put the sidewalk in proper repair, in accordance with the rules, regulations or ordinances prescribed by the
common council, the commissioner of public works shall repair
the same, and the expense of such repair shall be a lien upon
said property, and be collected and enforced in the same manner
as herein provided for the expenses of sewer connections.

6. Whenever the city engineer shall certify to the common
council that more than one-third of the carriage way of any
street, highway, lane or alley is in a condition requiring repairs,
the common council may direct the repair of the same. Such
repairs shall be deemed a repaving within the provisions of this
section and the provisions of this section relative to repaving
shall be applicable to such repairs. The specifications required
by this section may provide that the persons submitting bids or
proposals shall agree to do the work and keep and maintain the
same in good repair and condition for a certain, definite period
and a contract may be entered into in accordance therewith and
a local assessment made to defray the expense thereof, anything
in this act to the contrary notwithstanding. This subdivision
shall not be construed as requiring ordinary repairs to a street,
highway, lane or alley to be paid only from the repair fund but
such ordinary repairs may be made upon such street, highway,
lane or alley by the commissioner of public works if the expense
thereof is under two hundred and fifty dollars; otherwise, by contract by the board of contract and supply and paid from the repair
fund or by local assessment as the board of contract and supply
shall determine.

7. Whenever any contract has been let for pavement or any

of indebted- other local improvement, the common council may, in anticipation
ness.
of the collection of the assessment for such improvement, provide
for the issue of certificates of indebtedness to be signed by the
mayor and treasurer, and countersigned by the comptroller and
the proceeds of such certificates of indebtedness, may be used in
payment or partial payment upon such contracts, or the com-
Issue of   mon council may provide for the issue of certificates to be known
local im-
provement   as local improvement certificates bearing interest at the rate of
certificates.
five per centum per annum. Such local improvement certificates are to be issued and paid to the contractor in payment or
partial payments upon such contracts, and such local improvement certificates shall be paid from the first moneys collected on
account of such improvements, or from moneys received from the
Payment.   sale of bonds provided for in this act. The city shall have the
right to call in and pay any local improvement certificates at any
time by advertising such call in the official papers for five consecutive days, and no interest on such local improvement certifi-
Approval   cates shall thereafter be paid. Any ordinance to such effect
of board of
estimate.   adopted by the common council must be approved by the board
of estimate and apportionment before such certificates of indebted-
Interest to   ness or local improvement certificates can be signed. If such pro-
be added to
total cost.   vision is made by the common council and approved by the board
of estimate and apportionment, the interest upon such certificates
of indebtedness or local improvement certificates shall be added
to the total cost of such pavement or other local improvement, and
assessed as a part of the expenses thereof, as hereinbefore pro-
Payments   vided. All payments made to contractors during the progress of
to con-
tractors.   the work as hereinbefore provided shall be made upon the certificate of the city engineer and the approval of the commissioner
of public works of the value of the work done from time to time
during the construction, in no case to exceed ninety per centum of
Effect of   the value of the work done; but such payment shall not be used
payments.
as evidence against the city that the work already done has been
completed according to contract nor shall it preclude the city from
contesting the claims of the contractor that such pavement or other
local improvement has been completed according to contract.
Inconsistent   § 2. Any provision of the second class cities law (chapter fifty-
provisions
of second   five of the laws of nineteen hundred and nine, and the amendments
class cities
law not   thereto) which is in conflict with this act, shall be inapplicable to
applicable.
the city of Utica.

§ 3. This act shall take effect immediately.

Chap. 161.

AN ACT to amend chapter eight hundred and fifty-one of the laws of nineteen hundred and eleven, entitled "An act to establish a state college of forestry at Syracuse University, and making an appropriation therefor," relative to the objects and purposes of the college.

Became a law April 2, 1913, with the approval of the Governor. Passed by a two-thirds vote.

The People of the State of New York, represented in Senate and Assembly, do enact as follows:

Section 1. Subdivision one of section two of chapter eight hundred and fifty-one of the laws of nineteen hundred and eleven, entitled "An act to establish a state college of forestry at Syracuse University, and making an appropriation therefor," is hereby amended to read as follows:

1. The conduct upon land acquired by purchase, gift or lease[1] for such purpose of such experiments in forestry and forestation as the board of trustees deem most advantageous to the interests of the state and the advancement of the science of forestry.

§ 2. This act shall take effect immediately.

L. 1911, ch. 851, § 2, subd. 1 amended.

Objects and purposes.

Chap. 162.

AN ACT to amend the public health law, in relation to the collection of fees and expenses of the health officer of the port of New York.

Became a law April 2, 1913, with the approval of the Governor. Passed, three-fifths being present.

The People of the State of New York, represented in Senate and Assembly, do enact as follows:

Section 1. Section one hundred and thirty-eight of chapter forty-nine of the laws of nineteen hundred and nine, entitled "An act in relation to public health, constituting chapter forty-five of the consolidated laws," as amended by chapter three hun-

L. 1909, ch. 49, § 138, as amended by L. 1909, ch. 375, amended.

---

[1] Words " by purchase, gift or lease," new.

dred and seventy-five of the laws of nineteen hundred and nine,
is hereby amended to read as follows:

§ 138. **Lien for services and expenses.** All such expenses,
services and charges shall be a lien on the vessels, merchandise
or other property in relation to which they shall have been made,
incurred or rendered, and if such master, owner, [1]consignee or
the charterer or agent of vessels where the owner does not reside within the United States,[2] shall omit to pay the same within
three days after the presentation of such account, the health
officer may proceed to enforce such lien in the manner provided
in the lien law for the enforcement of liens upon vessels; or he may
have or maintain an action against such master, owner, [1]consignee
or the charterer or agent of such vessels where the owner does
not reside within the United States[3] to recover the amount of
such expenses, services and charges, and such master, owner,
[1]consignee, charterer or agent[4] shall be deemed indebted to him in
such amount and may recover from any passenger liable
to pay the same * amount of any expense incurred on
account of such passenger. The health officer shall have the
same remedies to enforce any other lien or to recover for any
expenses, services or charges which are by law made payable to
him if they remain unpaid for three days after payment shall
have been demanded by him. The vessel, cargo or other property upon which any lien exists by virtue of any provision in this
article, shall be held in quarantine until the amount due for the
expenses, services or charges constituting such lien is paid, unless
such master, owner, [1]consignee, charterer or agent[4] shall execute
to the health officer a bond with sufficient sureties to be approved by him, conditioned for the payment thereof within ten
days thereafter.

§ 2. This act shall take effect immediately.

---

* So in original.
[1] Word "or" omitted.
[2] Words "or the charterer or agent of vessels where the owner does not
reside within the United States," new.
[3] Words "or the charterer or agent of such vessels where the owner does
not reside within the United States," new.
[4] Words "charterer or agent," new.

Chap. 163.

AN ACT to amend the town law, in relation to the powers of supervisors and assessors in certain towns to employ clerks.

Became a law April 2, 1913, with the approval of the Governor. Passed, three-fifths being present.

The People of the State of New York, represented in Senate and Assembly, do enact as follows:

Section 1. Article five of chapter sixty-three of the laws of nineteen hundred and nine, entitled " An act relating to towns, constituting chapter sixty-two of the consolidated laws," is hereby amended by adding at the end thereof a new section, to be section one hundred and twenty-five, to read as follows:

§ 125. **Powers of supervisors and assessors in certain towns to employ clerks.** The supervisor of each town having a population, as appears by the last federal census, of fifteen thousand or more and where the assessed valuation of real estate is over fifteen million dollars, may in his discretion employ a clerk at a salary to be fixed by the town board of such town. The assessors of each town having a population, as appears by the last federal census, of fifteen thousand or more and where the assessed valuation of real estate is over fifteen million dollars, may also, in their discretion, employ a clerk at a salary to be fixed by the town board of such town. The salaries of said clerks shall be paid by the supervisor of said town in equal quarterly payments and shall be a town charge and shall be levied and collected in the same manner as other town charges.

§ 2. This act shall take effect immediately.

Chap. 164.

AN ACT to amend chapter two hundred and twenty of the laws of eighteen hundred and sixty-six, entitled "An act to amend the charter of the village of Saratoga Springs, and the several acts amendatory thereof," in relation to permitting the commissioner of parks to expend the sum of money to be received from the commissioners of the state reservation at Saratoga Springs.

Became a law April 2, 1913, with the approval of the Governor. Passed, three-fifths being present.

The People of the State of New York, represented in Senate and Assembly, do enact as follows:

§ 94a added to L. 1866, ch. 220.

Section 1. Chapter two hundred and twenty of the laws of eighteen hundred and sixty-six, entitled "An act to amend the charter of the village of Saratoga Springs, and the several acts amendatory thereof," is hereby amended by adding thereto after section ninety-four as added by chapter three hundred and sixty-six of the laws of nineteen hundred and twelve, a new section to be section ninety-four-a, to read as follows:

Application of moneys received for mineral water rights.

§ 94-a. The commissioner of parks of the village of Saratoga Springs is authorized to use for the improvement and beautifying of the parks of the village and furnishing entertainment therein, such sums as the village receives for the mineral water rights in said parks from the commissioners of the state reservation at Saratoga Springs. The receiver of taxes shall place to the credit of the park fund all sums of money thus received, the same to be used for the improvement, beautifying and furnishing entertainment in the parks of said village.

§ 2. This act shall take effect immediately.

Chap. 165.

AN ACT to provide campaign badges for the officers and enlisted men who served in the army or navy of the United States during the Spanish, Philippine or China campaigns, and making an appropriation therefor.

Became a law April 2, 1913, with the approval of the Governor. Passed, three-fifths being present.

The People of the State of New York, represented in Senate and Assembly, do enact as follows:

Section 1. The adjutant-general shall cause to be prepared and shall distribute to the officers and enlisted men who served honorably in the army or navy of the United States during the Spanish, Philippine and China campaigns, and who enlisted from the state of New York, appropriate campaign badges commemorative of their services. If any such officer, soldier or sailor be deceased, the badge to which he would be entitled shall be delivered to his proper legal representatives. *Preparation and distribution of badges.*

§ 2. The sum of one thousand dollars ($1,000), or so much thereof as may be needed, is hereby appropriated for the purposes of this act, out of any money in the treasury, not otherwise appropriated, payable by the treasurer on the warrant of the comptroller, on the order of the adjutant-general. *Appropriation.*

§ 3. This act shall take effect immediately.

Chap. 166.

AN ACT to amend the county law, in relation to the establishment of county hospital for tuberculosis.

Became a law April 2, 1913, with the approval of the Governor. Passed, three-fifths being present.

The People of the State of New York, represented in Senate and Assembly, do enact as follows:

Section 1. Section forty-five[1] of chapter sixteen of the laws of nineteen hundred and nine, entitled "An act in relation to counties, constituting chapter eleven of the consolidated laws," is hereby amended to read as follows: *L. 1909, ch. 16, § 45 amended.*

---

[1] As added by L. 1909, ch. 341.

§ 45. **Establishment of county hospital for tuberculosis.** The board of supervisors of any county shall have power by a majority vote to establish a county hospital for the care and treatment of persons suffering from the disease known as tuberculosis. When the board of supervisors of any county shall have voted to establish such hospital, it shall have the following power:

1. To purchase and lease real property therefor, or acquire such real property, and easements therein, by condemnation proceedings, in the manner prescribed by the condemnation law,[2] in any town, city or village in the county. [3]After the presentation of the petition in such proceeding prescribed in section three thousand three hundred and sixty of the code of civil procedure and the filing of the notice of pendency of action prescribed in section three thousand three hundred and eighty-one thereof, said board of supervisors shall be and become seized of the whole or such part of the real property described in said petition to be acquired for carrying into effect the provisions of this act, as such board may, by resolution adopted at a regular or special session, determine to be necessary for the immediate use, and such board for and in the name of such county may enter upon, occupy and use such real property so described and required for such purposes. Such resolution shall contain a description of the real property of which possession is to be taken and the day upon which possession will be taken. Said board of supervisors shall cause a copy of such resolution to be filed in the county clerk's office of the county in which such property is situate, and notice of the adoption thereof, with a copy of the resolution and of its intention to take possession of the premises therein described on a day certain, also therein named, to be served, either personally or by mail, upon the owner or owners of, and persons interested in such real property, at least five days prior to the day fixed in such resolution for taking possession. From the time of the service of such notice, the entry upon and appropriation by the county of the real property therein described for the purposes provided for by this act, shall be deemed complete, and such notice so served shall be conclusive evidence of such entry and appropriation and of the quantity and boundaries of the lands appropriated. The board of supervisors may cause a duplicate copy of such papers so served, with an affidavit of due service thereof on such

[2] Code of civil procedure, §§ 3357–3384.
[3] Remainder of subd. 1 new.

owner or person interested, to be recorded in the books used for recording deeds in the office of the county clerk of its county, and the record of such notice and such proof of service shall be prima facie evidence of the due service thereof. Compensation for property thus acquired shall be made in such condemnation proceeding.

2.[4] To erect all necessary buildings, make all necessary improvements and repairs and alter any existing buildings, for the use of said hospital, provided that the plans for such erection, alteration or repair shall first be approved by the state commissioner of health.

3. To cause to be assessed, levied and collected such sums of money as it shall deem necessary for suitable lands, buildings and improvements for said hospital, and for the maintenance thereof, and for all other necessary expenditures therefor; and to borrow money for the erection of such hospital and for the purchase of a site therefor on the credit of the county, and issue county obligations therefor, in such manner as it may do for other county purposes.

4. To appoint a board of managers for said hospital as hereinafter provided.

5. To accept and hold in trust for the county, any grant or devise of land, or any gift or bequest of money or other personal property, or any donation to be applied, principal or income, or both, for the benefit of said hospital, and apply the same in accordance with the terms of the gift.

§ 2. This act shall take effect immediately.

---

[4] Subd. 2 is amended by L. 1913, ch. 379, post.

Chap. 167.

AN ACT to amend the public lands law, in relation to the creation of a commission to have jurisdiction and control of the Newtown Battlefield Reservation, and making an appropriation therefor.

Became a law April 3, 1913, with the approval of the Governor. Passed by a two-thirds vote.

The People of the State of New York, represented in Senate and Assembly, do enact as follows:

L. 1909,
ch. 50,
art. 11,
§§ 120-122,
as renumbered by
L. 1911,
ch. 731,
renumbered
art. 12,
§§ 140-142.

Section 1. Article eleven and sections one hundred and twenty to one hundred and twenty-two of chapter fifty of the laws of nineteen hundred and nine, entitled "An act relating to the public lands, constituting chapter forty-six of the consolidated laws," as renumbered by chapter seven hundred and thirty-one of the laws of nineteen hundred and eleven, are hereby renumbered, respectively, article twelve and sections one hundred and forty to one hundred and forty-two thereof.

New art. 11
added.

§ 2. Such chapter is hereby amended by inserting therein a new article to be article eleven, to read as follows:

ARTICLE 11.

NEWTOWN BATTLEFIELD RESERVATION.

Section 120. Jurisdiction and control.
 121. Commissioners.
 122. Officers; treasurer's undertaking.
 123. Powers and duties of the commission.
 124. Purposes of reservation.
 125. Gifts of property for purpose of the reservation.
 126. Annual report; quarterly accounts.
 127. Payment of moneys appropriated.

§ 120. **Jurisdiction and control.** The land now held by the state of New York, and known as the Newtown Battlefield Reservation land, in the town of Elmira, county of Chemung, acquired by the state during the years nineteen hundred and eleven and nineteen hundred and twelve, shall be known as the Newtown Battlefield Reservation, and jurisdiction and control thereof is hereby transferred to the board of commissioners of the Newtown Battlefield Reservation, established by this article.

§ 121. **Commissioners.** There shall be a board of commissioners of the Newtown Battlefield Reservation, consisting of five persons appointed by the governor, by and with the advice and consent of the senate, to hold office for a term of five years each; but the original appointments shall be made in such manner that the term of one commissioner shall expire annually thereafter on the first day of February in each year. No member of such board shall receive any compensation for his services as commissioner, but shall be entitled to his actual and necessary expenses in performing the duties of his office. A meeting of such board shall be held on the first day of March, June, August, October and December.

§ 122. **Officers; treasurer's undertaking.** The commissioners shall select from among their number a president, and shall appoint some person to act as secretary and treasurer. The treasurer shall give an official undertaking in such a sum as the commission shall determine.

§ 123. **Powers and duties of the commission.** Such commissioners shall

1. Have the management, supervision and custody of such premises and of all property of the state therein or thereon and shall preserve and protect the same;

2. Lay out, manage and maintain such reservation, have charge of the necessary improvements and repairs, make and enforce such rules and regulations as may be necessary to effect the purposes thereof not inconsistent with law;

3. Have the power to acquire for the state by condemnation such other lands adjoining such reservation as may be necessary and for the acquisition of which appropriation shall have been made by the legislature;

4. Fix the price to be charged by drivers of public conveyances for carrying persons for hire along the roadway and the limits of such reservation, and the price to be charged by guides for their services;

5. Employ such persons as may be needed to care for such reservation and fix their compensation.

§ 124. **Purposes of reservation.** The state reservation of Newtown Battlefield shall forever be reserved by the state for the purpose of preserving the monument and the park surrounding it, and for forestry purposes, and to keep open and free of access to all mankind, without fee, charge or expense to any person for entering upon or passing to or from any part of said reservation.

§ 125. **Gifts of property for purpose of the reservation.** Real and personal property may be granted, conveyed, bequeathed or devised to and taken by the state in aid of the purposes of such reservation or to increase the same and on such trusts and conditions as may be prescribed by the grantors or devisors thereof. provided the same be accepted and agreed to in writing by such commissioners. All such property shall be managed and controlled by the commissioners and the rents, issues and profits thereof shall be turned into the state treasury, except where such rents, issues and profits are specifically devised or bequeathed to be used for a specific and definite purpose.

§ 126. **Annual report; quarterly accounts.** The commissioners shall make an annual report of their proceedings to the legislature in the month of January, with a detailed statement of all their receipts and expenditures for the preceding fiscal year, and an estimate of the work necessary to be done and of the expenses of maintaining the reservation for the ensuing fiscal year, with such recommendations as they shall see fit. They shall, quarterly, on the first days of January, April, July and October of each year. send to the comptroller a detailed and itemized account of all receipts and expenditures with subvouchers for the items thereof, for the preceding quarter and such account shall be verified by the commissioners or their treasurer.

§ 127. **Payment of moneys appropriated.** Moneys appropriated for caring for and maintaining such reservation and carrying out the provisions of this article, shall be paid to the order of the treasurer of the commission by the state treasurer upon the warrant of the comptroller. No warrant shall be issued until amounts claimed have been audited and allowed by the comptroller, who is hereby authorized to determine the same, except that on the requisition of the treasurer of such commission the comptroller may advance out of the sum appropriated whatever moneys he deems necessary for the proper carrying out of the provisions of this article.

Appropriation for care and improvements.

§ 2. There is hereby appropriated for the care and maintenance of, for the acquisition of land adjoining said park, for grading and fencing the road leading to said park, for gateway, for the rights of way thereto, for public comfort stations, for deficiency incurred by reason of the insufficiency of former appro-

priations, for the placing of tablets on monument, for painting all
guard rails on road, for the expense of moving and implacement
of cannon and for the payment of the expenses of such commission,
the sum of ten thousand dollars ($10,000), or so much thereof
as may be necessary.

§ 3. This act shall take effect immediately.

Chap. 168.

AN ACT to amend the liquor tax law, in relation to the issuance of certificates under the provisions of subdivision two of
section eight, limitation of such certificates and transfers thereof
under abandonment notices.

Became a law April 3, 1913, with the approval of the Governor. Passed,
three-fifths being present.

*The People of the State of New York, represented in Senate
and Assembly, do enact as follows:*

Section 1. Section eight of chapter thirty-nine of the laws of subd. 10
nineteen hundred and nine, entitled "An act in relation to the L. 1909,
traffic in liquors and for taxation and regulation of the same, and ch. 39, § 8.
to provide for local option, constituting chapter thirty-four of the
consolidated laws," as amended by chapter two hundred and
eighty-one of the laws of nineteen hundred and nine, chapter four
hundred and eighty-five and chapter four hundred and ninety-
four of the laws of nineteen hundred and ten and chapter two hundred and ninety-eight of the laws of nineteen hundred and eleven,
is hereby amended by adding thereto after subdivision nine, a
new subdivision, to be subdivision ten, to read as follows:

10. Issuance of certificates under the provisions of subdivision
two of this section. No liquor tax certificates shall hereafter be
issued for traffic in liquors, under the provisions of subdivision
two of this section, for any premises in any town, village, borough
or city, unless or until the ratio of population therein, to the number of certificates issued under the provisions of said subdivision
two, shall be greater than seven thousand five hundred to one, and
then only pursuant to the provisions of this subdivision; but this
prohibition shall not apply to any premises in which traffic in liquors under the provisions of subdivision two of this section was
lawfully carried on at some time within one year immediately

preceding the passage of this act, provided such traffic was not
abandoned thereat during said period or to any premises that have
been continuously occupied for a hotel from and including the
twenty-third day of March, eighteen hundred and ninety-six; nor
shall this prohibition apply to any premises in which, during said
period of one year, or any part thereof, such traffic in liquors was
suspended because of the result of a vote on the local option questions; nor to any premises in which, during said period of one
year, or any part thereof, such traffic in liquors was prohibited because of the revocation or forfeiture of a liquor tax certificate on
the ground that the certificated premises were suffered and permitted to become disorderly, or that gambling was allowed therein,
as provided in subdivision eight of section fifteen of this chapter;
nor to any premises in which, during said period of one year, or
any part thereof, such traffic in liquors has been temporarily suspended, but not abandoned. Provided, however, that at any time
during the unexpired term of any liquor tax certificate issued for
traffic in liquors under the provisions of subdivision two of this
section in any premises in which such traffic may lawfully be carried on, a notice stating that such traffic in liquors is abandoned
at the premises named in such certificate may be filed with the
county treasurer or special deputy commissioner of excise of the
county or borough in which the certificated premises are located,
which notice shall also particularly describe some other premises
in which it is intended to carry on such traffic, which premises
shall be situated in the same city, borough, village or town as that
in which the abandoned premises are located. Such notice shall
be in writing and executed and acknowledged by the certificate
holder or by his duly authorized attorney and by any person to
whom such certificate may have been transferred or assigned as
collateral security for moneys loaned or any other obligation incurred. Such notice shall be null and void unless within *sixty-
days from the filing thereof such traffic in liquors shall be lawfully carried on at the premises described in such notice as the
premises in which it is intended to carry on such traffic, and continued thereat for a period of not less than sixty days, and the
filing of a notice that becomes null and void shall not be deemed
an abandonment of the traffic at the premises described in such
liquor tax certificate. After the filing of such notice as aforesaid,
the prohibition herein contained shall not apply to the premises

---

* So in original.

described in such notice as the premises in which it is intended to carry on such traffic, provided that an application for a certificate to carry on such traffic in liquors thereat shall be made in due form to the proper officer, within sixty days from the filing of such notice, and provided further that such traffic is continuously thereafter carried on at said premises for a period not less than sixty days. Except in a case where such notice becomes null and void as aforesaid, no liquor tax certificate for traffic in liquors under the provisions of subdivision two of this section shall thereafter be issued for, and it shall be unlawful to so traffic in liquors in the premises described in such notice as the premises in which the traffic in liquors has been abandoned, unless there shall subsequently be filed another notice of abandonment, in the manner herein provided; which notice shall describe such first abandoned premises as the premises in which it is intended to again carry on such traffic in liquors. Whenever the ratio between the population of any city, borough, village or town, and the number of such premises situated therein for such traffic in liquors to which this prohibition does not apply, shall exceed the ratio of seven thousand five hundred to one, additional certificates for traffic in liquors under the provisions of subdivision two of this section may be issued to the highest bidders therefor, in the same manner as is provided in subdivision nine of this section for the issuance of additional certificates under the provisions of subdivision one of this section.

§ 2. Subdivision three of section fifteen of said chapter, as amended by chapter four hundred and ninety-four of the laws of nineteen hundred and ten, is hereby amended to read as follows:

3. The premises where such business is to be carried on, stating the street and number, if the premises have a street and number, and otherwise such apt description as will reasonably indicate the locality thereof, and also the specific location on the premises of the bar or place at which liquors are to be sold. The applicant or applicants shall also state whether or not there has been filed with the certificate issuing officer a notice of abandonment pursuant to the provisions of subdivision nine or ten[1] of section eight of this chapter by virtue of which traffic in liquors under the provisions of subdivision one or two[2] of said section eight may lawfully be carried on at the premises described in the application statement;

§ 15, subd. 3, as amended by L. 1910, ch. 494, amended.

---

[1] Words " or ten " new.
[2] Words " or two " new.

together with the date of the filing of such notice, the name of the person or persons filing the same, and a description of each of the premises affected thereby, also whether or not the applicant or applicants claim the right to traffic in liquors at said premises by reason of being the highest bidder or bidders therefor pursuant to any of the provisions of subdivision nine or ten[3] of said section eight.

§ 17, as amended by L. 1910, ch. 494, amended.

§ 3. Section seventeen of said chapter, as amended by chapter four hundred and ninety-four of the laws of nineteen hundred and ten, is hereby amended to read as follows:

§ 17. **The payment of the tax and issuing of the tax certificate.** When the provisions of sections fifteen and sixteen of this chapter have been complied with and the application provided for in section fifteen is found to be correct in form and does not show on the face thereof that the applicant is prohibited from trafficking in liquor under the subdivision of section eight under which he applies, nor at the place where the traffic is to be carried on, and the bond required by section sixteen is found to be correct as to its form and the sureties thereon are approved as sufficient by the county treasurer, or by the special deputy commissioner of excise, if there be one, then upon the payment of the taxes levied under section eight of this chapter the county treasurer of the county, or the special deputy commissioner of excise, if there be one, or if the application be made under subdivision four or five of section eight of this chapter, the state commissioner of excise shall, at least two days before the commencement of the period for which the tax is paid, or, if the period for which the tax is paid has already commenced, at once prepare and issue to the person making such application and filing such bond and paying such tax, a liquor tax certificate in the form provided for in this chapter, unless it shall appear by a certified copy of the statement of the result of an election held on the question of local option, pursuant to section thirteen of this chapter, in and for the town where the applicant proposes to traffic in liquors under the certificate applied for, or by material facts set forth in a certificate under the hand and seal of the state commissioner of excise, on file in the office of the special deputy commissioner or county treasurer, that the liquor tax certificate applied for cannot be lawfully held by the applicant or at the premises mentioned in the application as the place where traffic in

---

[3] Words " or ten " new.

liquors is proposed to be carried on, or unless it shall appear by the report filed pursuant to section thirty-two of this chapter with the special deputy commissioner of excise or county treasurer to whom the application is made that such liquor tax certificate cannot be lawfully granted, or unless it shall appear by a notice duly filed with the certificate issuing officer pursuant to the provisions of subdivision nine or ten[2] of section eight of this chapter that such traffic has been abandoned at the premises described in the application statement, or unless the traffic is prohibited at such premises by virtue of the provisions of subdivision nine or ten[2] of said section eight, in which case the application shall be refused.

§ 4. This act shall take effect immediately.

Chap. 169.

AN ACT to amend chapter two hundred and twenty of the laws of eighteen hundred and sixty-six, entitled "An act to amend the charter of the village of Saratoga Springs, and the several acts amendatory thereof," in relation to moneys to be raised for village purposes.

Became a law April 3, 1913, with the approval of the Governor. Passed, three-fifths being present.

The People of the State of New York, represented in Senate and Assembly, do enact as follows:

Section 1. Section fifty-four of chapter two hundred and twenty of the laws of eighteen hundred and sixty-six, entitled "An act to amend the charter of the village of Saratoga Springs, and the several acts amendatory thereof," is hereby amended by adding thereto four new subdivisions, to be subdivisions four-a, nine, ten and eleven, to read, respectively, as follows: *(margin: Subds. 4a, 9-11 added to L. 1866, ch. 220, § 54.)*

4-a.[1] Such sum as the board of trustees deem necessary to meet the expenses of the office of the village attorney for the ensuing year. *(margin: Tax for office expenses of attorney.)*

9. Such sum as the board of trustees deem advisable to appropriate for Luther M. Wheeler Post, No. 92, G. A. R., for the proper observance of Memorial day which said sum the board of *(margin: G. A. R. post.)*

---

[2] Words "or ten" new.
[1] Identical subd. 4a is added by L. 1913, ch. 171, post.

trustees of the village of Saratoga Springs is hereby authorized to
appropriate.

Charter
election
fund.

10. A charter election fund is hereby created. The board of
trustees shall levy and cause to be collected such sum of money as
they deem necessary for the purpose of meeting the expenses of
the charter election or any special election for the ensuing year,
the same when collected to be placed by him in the charter election
fund and to be paid out by him as are other village funds.

Miscellane-
ous fund.

11. The board of trustees may levy and cause to be collected
such sum as they deem necessary to meet the miscellaneous expenses of the village, the same when collected to be placed in the
miscellaneous fund by the receiver of taxes and paid out by him
as are other village funds.

§ 2. This act shall take effect immediately.

Chap. 170.

AN ACT to amend chapter sixty-eight of the laws of eighteen hundred and eighty, entitled "An act to authorize the sale of lands
in the town and village of Saratoga Springs, for unpaid state,
county and municipal taxes, including water rates and special
assessments," in relation to unredeemed tax sale certificates.

Became a law April 3, 1913, with the approval of the Governor. Passed,
three-fifths being present.

*The People of the State of New York, represented in Senate
and Assembly, do enact as follows:*

§ 9 added
to L. 1880,
ch. 68.

Section 1. Chapter sixty-eight of the laws of eighteen hundred
and eighty, entitled "An act to authorize the sale of lands in the
town and village of Saratoga Springs, for unpaid state, county
and municipal taxes, including water rates and special assessments," is hereby amended by adding thereto after section eight
thereof a new section to be section nine, to read as follows:

Tax sale
certificates
held by
village
and town.

§ 9. The receiver of taxes shall after the expiration of two
years from the date of the tax sale certificate of real estate bid
in by him for the village or town, or town and village, and which
tax sale certificates remain unredeemed, proceed to take the necessary proceedings to take title to said real estate in the name of the
town or village, or town and village. The said receiver of taxes
may assign any tax sale certificate unredeemed held by the village

or town, or town and village, and execute the necessary assignment of the same on payment to him by the purchaser of said tax
sale certificate, the sum mentioned on the face of said certificate
with interest on the same as provided by this act.

§ 2. Section nine of such chapter is hereby renumbered §9 renum-
section ten.   bered § 10.

§ 3. This act shall take effect immediately.

Chap. 171.

AN ACT to amend chapter two hundred and twenty of the laws of
eighteen hundred and sixty-six, entitled "An act to amend the
charter of the village of Saratoga Springs, and the several acts
amendatory thereof," in relation to providing for a legal expense fund.

Became a law April 3, 1913, with the approval of the Governor. Passed,
three-fifths being present.

*The People of the State of New York, represented in Senate
and Assembly, do enact as follows:*

Section 1. Section twelve of chapter two hundred and twenty   L. 1866,
of the laws of eighteen hundred and sixty-six, entitled "An act to   ch. 220,
                                                                      § 12, as
amend the charter of the village of Saratoga Springs, and the sev-   amended
                                                                      by L. 1869,
eral acts amendatory thereof," as amended by chapter eight hun-   ch. 893, and
                                                                      L. 1894,
dred and ninety-three of the laws of eighteen hundred and sixty-   ch. 445,
                                                                      amended.
nine and chapter six hundred and forty-five of the laws of eighteen
hundred and ninety-four is hereby amended to read as follows:

§ 12. Said monthly meetings of the board of trustees shall be   Meetings of
                                                                  trustees.
held, and special meetings may be held when called by the president or requested by any two of the trustees. A majority of the   Quorum.
board of trustees shall constitute a board for the transaction of
business. Within ten days after each annual election the board   Village
                                                                   clerk.
of trustees shall appoint some suitable person for village clerk.
Within the same time, the president of the village shall appoint   Village
                                                                    attorney,
some practicing lawyer of at least seven years' standing at the bar   appoint-
                                                                       ment,
for village attorney. Such village attorney may be removed at   duties, etc.
any time by the president of said village. It shall be the duty of
the village attorney to prosecute and defend all actions and proceedings brought by or against said village and by or against any
board of officers of said village, and to give to the several boards

of said village, and to every village officer, not a member of one of said boards an opinion on any legal question arising in the

Compensation of attorney. performance of the duties of such board or officer. The village attorney shall receive in lieu of all other compensation a salary of twelve hundred dollars per annum, payable in monthly installments of one hundred dollars each at the end of each month of his term of office together with all necessary disbursements made by

Legal expense fund. him in the progress of any action or proceeding, which shall be paid out of the [1]legal expense fund of such village which is hereby created. [2]The village attorney shall in the month of April, in each

Estimate of expenses of attorney. year, submit to the board of trustees his estimate of the expenses of his department for the ensuing year, which are to include his office expenses, all witnesses' fees, all judgments against said village, all actions or special proceedings which have been compromised and all other expenses of said department for the ensuing

Tax for expenses of legal department. year. [2]The board of trustees shall place in the tax budget and collect the same as other village taxes, such sums as they deem necessary to meet the expenses of the legal department for the ensuing year, and all disbursements made by said village attorney to

Disposition of costs recovered. be paid out of said legal expense fund. All taxable costs [3]recovered by said village shall be paid by said attorney or the officer collecting the same, to the receiver of taxes, and by him passed to the credit of the [1]legal expense fund of said village.

Subd. 4a added to § 54. § 2. Section fifty-four of such chapter is hereby amended by inserting therein a new subdivision to be subdivision four-a, to read as follows:

Tax for office expenses of attorney. 4-a.[4] Such sum as the board of trustees deem necessary to meet the expenses of the office of the village attorney for the ensuing year.

§ 3. This act shall take effect immediately.

---

[1] Remainder of sentence formerly read: "miscellaneous department."
[2] Following sentence new.
[3] Words "of water to" omitted. Words "recovered by" new.
[4] Identical subd. 4a added by L. 1913, ch. 169, ante.

Chap. 172.

AN ACT in relation to the disposition of ten thousand dollars and accrued interest belonging to the village of Saratoga Springs now on special deposit in the Adirondack Trust Company of Saratoga Springs, and permitting the same to be applied on the village tax budget for the year nineteen hundred and thirteen.

Became a law April 3, 1913, with the approval of the Governor. Passed, three-fifths being present.

The People of the State of New York, represented in Senate and Assembly, do enact as follows:

Section 1. The receiver of taxes and assessments of the town and village of Saratoga Springs shall transfer to certain village fund or funds such part or the whole of the ten thousand dollars and accrued interest in the Adirondack Trust Company on special deposit, as the board of trustees of the village shall direct by a resolution duly passed by the board of trustees. A certified copy of said resolution shall be filed with the receiver of taxes before any transfer of the whole or any part of said fund is made. *Transfer to village funds.*

§ 2. This act shall take effect immediately.

Chap. 173.

AN ACT to amend the state charities law, in relation to the office and clerical force of the fiscal supervisor.

Became a law April 3, 1913, with the approval of the Governor. Passed, three-fifths being present.

The People of the State of New York, represented in Senate and Assembly, do enact as follows:

Section 1. Section forty-one of chapter fifty-seven of the laws of nineteen hundred and nine, entitled "An act relating to state charities, constituting chapter fifty-five of the consolidated laws," is hereby amended to read as follows: *L. 1909. ch. 57, § 41 amended.*

§ 41. Office and clerical force of fiscal supervisor. The fiscal supervisor of state charities shall be provided by the proper authorities with a suitably furnished office in the state capitol. He

may employ a first[1] deputy and a second deputy,[2] a stenographer
and such other employees as may be needed. The salaries and
reasonable expenses of the fiscal supervisor, his deputies,[3] and the
necessary clerical assistants shall be paid by the treasurer of the
state, on the warrant of the comptroller, out of any moneys appropriated therefor.

§ 2. This act shall take effect immediately.

Chap. 174.

AN ACT to amend the charter of the city of Oneida, in relation to
the payment of claims.

Became a law April 3, 1913, with the approval of the Governor. Passed,
three-fifths being present.

Accepted by the City.

*The People of the State of New York, represented in Senate
and Assembly, do enact as follows:*

§ 236
added to
L. 1911,
ch. 648.

Section 1. Title sixteen of chapter six hundred and forty-eight
of the laws of nineteen hundred and eleven, entitled "An act to
revise, consolidate and amend generally chapter two hundred and
twenty-five of the laws of nineteen hundred and one, known as
' the charter of the city of Oneida,' and the several acts amendatory thereof, and repealing certain acts," is hereby amended by
adding section two hundred and thirty-six, to read as follows:

§ 236. **Claims against city; power of common council to pay
or compromise on equitable grounds.** The common council may,
in its discretion, inquire into, hear and determine any claim
against the city of Oneida which has been certified to said common council in writing by the city attorney as an illegal or
invalid claim against the city, but which, notwithstanding, in his
judgment it is equitable and proper for the city to pay in whole
or in part, and if upon such inquiry the common council by a
unanimous vote determines that the city has received a benefit
and is justly and equitably obligated to pay such claim and that
the interest of the city will be best subserved by the payment or
compromise thereof, it may authorize the city chamberlain to

---

[1] Word "first" new.
[2] Words "and a second deputy," new.
[3] Words "his deputies" new.

pay the claim and the city chamberlain shall thereupon pay the claim in such amount as the common council shall so determine to be just, in full satisfaction of such claim, provided that the claimant shall fully release the city upon any such payment, in such form as shall be approved by the city attorney. The provisions of this section shall not authorize the audit or payment of any claim barred by the statute of limitations, nor any claim for services performed under an appointment in violation of any provision of the civil service law.

§ 2. This act shall take effect immediately.

Chap. 175.

AN ACT to amend the education law, relative to aid for blind and deaf students in colleges and universities.

Became a law April 3, 1913, with the approval of the Governor. Passed, three-fifths being present.

The People of the State of New York, represented in Senate and Assembly, do enact as follows:

Section 1. Section nine hundred and seventy-six of chapter twenty-one of the laws of nineteen hundred and nine, entitled "An act relating to education, constituting chapter sixteen of the consolidated laws," as amended by chapter one hundred and forty of the laws of nineteen hundred and ten, is hereby amended to read as follows: *L. 1909, ch. 21, § 976, as generally amended by L. 1910, ch. 140, amended.*

§ 976. **Aid for blind and deaf students.**[1] 1. Whenever a blind or deaf[2] person, who is a citizen of this state and a pupil in actual attendance at a college, university, technical or professional school located in this state and authorized by law to grant degrees, other than an institution established for the regular instruction of the blind or deaf,[2] shall be designated by the trustees thereof as a fit person to receive the aid hereinafter provided for, there shall be paid by the state for the use of such pupil the sum of three hundred dollars per annum with which to employ persons to read to such blind[3] pupil from text-books and pamphlets used by such pupil in his studies at

---

[1] Section heading formerly read: "Employment of reader for blind students."
[2] Words "or deaf" new.
[3] Word "blind" new.

11

such college, university or school, [4]or to aid a deaf student in receiving instruction in such studies.

2. Such moneys shall be paid annually, after the beginning of the school year of such institution, by the treasurer of the state on the warrant of the comptroller, to the treasurer of such institution, on his presenting an account showing the actual number of blind or deaf[5] pupils matriculated and attending the institution, which account shall be verified by the president of the institution and accompanied by his certificate that the trustees have recommended the pupils named in said account as hereinbefore provided.

3. The trustees of any of the said institutions shall recommend no blind or deaf[5] person, who is not regularly matriculated, and who is not in good and regular standing, and who is not working for a degree from the institution in which he is matriculated; and no blind or deaf[5] person shall be recommended, who is not doing the work regularly prescribed by the institution for the degree for which he is a candidate. The moneys so paid to any such institution shall be disbursed for the purposes aforesaid by and under the direction of its board of trustees.

§ 2. This act shall take effect immediately.

Chap. 176.

AN ACT to amend the education law, relative to the establishment and maintenance of temporary schools in camps and other places of temporary habitation.

Became a law April 3, 1913, with the approval of the Governor. Passed, three-fifths being present.

The People of the State of New York, represented in Senate and Assembly, do enact as follows:

Art. 6a
added to
L. 1909,
ch. 21, as
generally
amended
by L. 1910,
ch. 140. Section 1. Chapter twenty-one of the laws of nineteen hundred and nine, entitled "An act relating to education, constituting chapter sixteen of the consolidated laws," as amended by chapter one hundred and forty of the laws of nineteen hundred and ten, is hereby amended by inserting therein a new article to be known as article six-a, and to read as follows:

---

[4] Remainder of sentence new.
[5] Words " or deaf " new.

ARTICLE 6-A.

TEMPORARY SCHOOL DISTRICTS.

§ 175. **Establishment of temporary school districts.** Temporary school districts may be established outside of cities and union free school districts and public schools shall be maintained therein as hereinafter provided. Such districts may be established whenever any considerable number of persons shall have been congregated in camps or other places of temporary habitation, who are engaged in the construction of public works by, or under contract with, the state, or in the construction of public works or improvements by or under contract with any municipality. Such temporary districts shall be established by order of the district superintendent of schools of the supervisory district within which such camps or other places of temporary habitation are located, subject to the approval of the commissioner of education. Such order shall be filed in the state education department and if the public works or improvements are being constructed by a municipality, a copy thereof shall be filed in the office of the officer or board of the city under whose direction they are being constructed. When so established such districts shall be entitled to share in the apportionment of public money as in the case of other school districts, except that each district quota shall be one hundred and twenty-five dollars. The money so apportioned shall be paid to the treasurer of the district and be applied in the payment of teachers' salaries.

§ 176. **Organization of districts; officers.** Each of such districts shall have a trustee who shall be appointed by the district superintendent of schools, and a district clerk and treasurer to be appointed by the trustee. Each of such officers shall serve during the continuance of the camp or other place of temporary habitation, unless sooner removed by the district superintendent. The treasurer shall give a bond to the people of the state, in an amount to be determined by the district superintendent, and with sureties approved by him, conditioned for the proper disbursement and accounting of all moneys received by him in behalf of such district.

§ 177. **Maintenance of schools; teachers.** Such schools shall be under the supervision of the district superintendent and shall be maintained pursuant to regulations adopted by the commissioner of education. They shall be free to all children of school age residing in such camps and other places of temporary habitation, and also to all adults residing therein. They shall be open at such hours as may be prescribed by the district superintendent, subject to the approval of the commissioner of education. The trustee of each such district shall employ qualified teachers for the school therein, for such term and at such rate of compensation as may be determined upon by the district superintendent, with the approval of the commissioner of education. The said trustees shall provide suitable building or rooms for such school and shall require the same to be kept in proper condition for the maintenance thereof, and shall cause the same to be equipped and supplied with all necessary books, furniture, apparatus and appliances.

§ 178. **Payment of expenses; gifts and contributions.** The costs and expenses of maintaining such schools in temporary districts, exclusive of the amount apportioned thereto out of the public moneys, shall be paid in such districts where the public works are being constructed by the state, out of moneys appropriated for such purpose. In districts where public works or improvements are being constructed for a municipality, such costs and expenses shall be a charge upon such municipality, and shall be paid out of funds available for the payment of the cost of construction of such works or improvements.

The trustee of such district shall prepare an estimate of the amount of probable expenditures for the maintenance of the public schools in such district, which shall include a statement of the amount in the hands of the treasurer available for such maintenance, the amount received by such treasurer from gifts, contributions and other sources, and the amount to be received from the public school moneys, as herein provided, and shall also state the amount required to be raised for such school, specifying the items thereof, for the ensuing school year. The form of such estimate shall be prescribed by the district superintendent. In the districts where the public works are being constructed by a municipality the said estimate shall be executed in duplicate, one of which shall be filed with the state education department, and the other shall be filed in the office of the department or officer of the municipality under whose supervision such public works are being constructed. Upon the approval of such estimates by the state education department notice thereof shall be given to the said department or officer of the municipality, and payment of the amount specified in such estimate shall be made to the treasurer of such district. The treasurer shall preserve vouchers of all payments made by him on account of the school in his district and shall make no payments for purposes not provided for in the estimate, nor without the order of the trustee of the district accompanied with the necessary vouchers.

§ 179. **Regulations of commissioner of education.** The commissioner of education shall make regulations, not inconsistent herewith, for the purpose of providing for the establishment and maintenance of schools as herein provided, and for the purpose of carrying into effect the full intent of this article.

§ 2. This act shall take effect immediately.

Chap. 177.

AN ACT to amend the highway law, in relation to the cost of improvement of highways between the rails and tracks and outside thereof, of street surface railroads in villages and in cities of the second and third classes.

Became a law April 3, 1913, with the approval of the Governor. Passed, three-fifths being present.

The People of the State of New York, represented in Senate and Assembly, do enact as follows:

Section 1. Chapter thirty of the laws of nineteen hundred and nine, entitled "An act relating to highways, constituting chapter twenty-five of the consolidated laws," is hereby amended by adding thereto a new section, to be known as section one hundred and forty-two-a, to read as follows:

§ 142-a. Where a street surface railroad shall be laid in any street, highway or public place in any village, or in any city of the second or third classes, which it was heretofore or shall hereafter be determined to pave or improve as provided in this chapter, the proposals and contract for such improvement shall include the improvement of the space between the tracks of such street surface railroad, the rails of such tracks and two feet in width outside of such tracks, and the work of improvement in such

space shall be done at the same time and under the same supervision as the work of improvement of the remainder of such

Material
prescribed.
street, highway or public place. The commission may prescribe
the materials to be used in paving or improving such street, highway or public place within the railroad space above described,

Certification
of cost.
and upon the proper completion of the work, the commission shall
certify to the board of trustees of such village, or the common
council of cities of the second or third classes, as the case may be,
the cost of the pavement or improvement of such street, highway

Assessment
and collec-
tion of ex-
pense.
or public place within such railroad space, and the entire expense
of the pavement *of improvement within such railroad space
whether heretofore or hereafter made or ordered, shall be assessed
and levied upon the property of the company owning or operating
such railroad, and shall be collected in the same manner as other
expenses for local improvements are assessed, levied and collected
in such village or city; and an action may also be maintained
by the municipality against the company in any court of record

Certain
villages
excepted.
for the collection of such expense and assessment. This section
shall not apply to such paving or improvements in villages in
counties adjoining cities of the first class.

§ 2. This act shall take effect immediately.

Chap. 178.

AN ACT to authorize the macadamizing or paving of streets,
avenues or highways, and the construction of the necessary
drains, curbing and gutters therefor, and in connection therewith, in the village of White Plains, New York, Westchester
county, and to provide the manner and means of paying therefor.

Became a law April 3, 1913, with the approval of the Governor. Passed,
three-fifths being present.

*The People of the State of New York, represented in Senate
and Assembly, do enact as follows:*

Paving of
main
streets
authorised.
Section 1. The board of trustees of the village of White Plains,
New York, in the county of Westchester, is hereby authorized and
empowered to macadamize or pave any main street, avenue or high-

---

* So in original.

178.]   Laws of New York, 1913.   327

way in said village, and for that purpose said board of trustees is
hereby authorized and empowered by resolution to designate and
determine which of the streets, avenues or highways are main
streets, avenues or highways, and said board of trustees is hereby Change of grade;
authorized to make such change in the grade of such main streets, drains, culverts;
avenues or highways, and construct any necessary drain or cul- damage.
vert, as may be necessary for the proper macadamizing or paving
of said street, avenue or highway, and the cost of such change of
grade and the construction of any necessary drain or culvert, or
any damage occasioned thereby upon the lines of said streets, avenues or highways, shall be considered as part of the cost of such
macadamizing or paving.

§ 2. The board of trustees of the village of White Plains, in Paving of other than main streets.
addition to the power vested in said board by section one of this
act, is hereby authorized and empowered upon a petition signed
by a majority of the property owners fronting upon any street,
avenue or highway in said village not designated and determined
by the board of trustees to be a main street, avenue or highway
to macadamize or pave said street, avenue or highway, and for that
purpose, said board of trustees is hereby authorized and empow- Change of grade; damage.
ered to change or regulate the grade of such streets and highways
as may be necessary for the proper macadamizing or paving of
said streets, avenue or highway and the cost of such change of
grade, or any damage occasioned thereby upon the lines of said
street, avenue or highway shall be considered as part of the cost
of said macadamizing or paving.

§ 3. Whenever said board of trustees shall determine to macad- Division of cost between village and property benefited.
amize or pave any street, avenue or highway in said village, two
thirds of the cost and expense thereof shall be paid by bonds of
said village to be issued as provided in section six of this act, and
the remaining one-third of the cost shall be paid for by the property benefited thereby in proportion to such benefit.

§ 4. Prior to contracting for any such work, a plan and ac- Plan and specifica- tion.
curate specification of the work proposed to be constructed must
be prepared and placed in the office of the village clerk for public
inspection. The board of trustees shall then fix a district of as- District of assessment.
sessment of the property in the judgment of said board benefited
by said macadamizing or paving and beyond which district the
assessment for one-third of such cost of macadamizing or paving
shall not extend, and shall then cause to be published in one or Advertising for proposals.
more of the newspapers published in said village, a notice that

on a day therein to be named, at least two weeks from the first publication thereof, it will act in relation to the work proposed to be constructed and in the meantime sealed proposals for constructing the work will be received by the village clerk. Upon

Opening proposals. the day mentioned in the notice, or upon such subsequent day as the said board of trustees may adjourn to for that purpose, the president of the village, or in his absence the presiding officer shall in the presence of the board of trustees, open such proposals.

Deposit with proposal; bond. No proposals shall be considered unless accompanied by a certified check for ten per centum of the amount of the bid payable to the village of White Plains with a statement in writing signed by the person, firm, corporation or persons making such bid to the effect that if the bid be accepted they will furnish and deliver to the village a bond executed by two or more persons, as the board may require, who own unincumbered real estate in the county of Westchester, or the bond of a surety company in a penalty to be fixed by the board of trustees, conditioned for the construction of the work at the price and upon the terms proposed within such reasonable time as the board of trustees may limit, and subject to the supervision and approval of the said board of trustees. The said

Acceptance of most favorable bidder. board may, by a vote of the majority of all its members, to be ascertained by taking and recording the ayes and noes, direct the construction of the proposed work and accept the most favorable bidder.

Return of deposits. § 5. Upon the awarding of the contract all checks other than the check of the successful bidder shall be immediately returned to the person or persons or corporations delivering the same to the clerk, and the check of the successful bidder or the amount of the check in cash shall be held until the bond hereinbefore provided

Report of assessment of lands affected. for shall be furnished. The board of trustees shall make a report in writing of the assessment for one-third of the cost of said macadamizing or paving upon the different parcels of land affected thereby, and deposit the same with the village clerk, and cause to be published in one or more of the village newspapers, once in each week for two successive weeks, a notice that the report has been completed and so deposited, and that they will meet at a time and place therein to be specified, not less than ten days from the first publication of said notice to review their report. At such

Hearing; correct.on and filing of report. time and place the parties interested can be heard, and thereafter the said trustees shall review the report, correct the same when necessary and file it with the village clerk with all the objections in writing which have been left with them by the parties interested. And upon the filing of such report the amount of the cost of said improvement, as fixed by the said trustees in said report, shall be a first lien upon the various parcels of land described in said report, and said amount shall be collected and the lien enforced in the same manner as is provided for the collection of taxes in said village. *Lien and collection of assessment.*

§ 6. The board of trustees may from time to time issue bonds for such sums as may be necessary to pay two-thirds of the expense of macadamizing or paving the said streets and highways, provided that the aggregate amount of such bonds shall not exceed the sum of one hundred thousand dollars; said bonds shall be of such denomination as the board of trustees shall determine, shall become due at such time as the board of trustees may determine not to exceed forty years from the date thereof and shall bear interest at not exceeding five per centum per annum, and mature in sums not exceeding five thousand dollars in any one year. Said bonds shall be signed by the president and village clerk, and sealed with the village seal. The board of trustees shall convert such bonds into money at not less than their par value or may obtain temporary loans on the same, and the proceeds therefrom shall be used only for the payment of two-thirds of the. cost of such macadamizing or paving. The board of trustees of the village of White Plains is hereby authorized and directed to raise by tax from year to year such sum or sums of money as may be necessary to pay the interest on the said bonds, and the principal thereof at maturity; said bonds when so issued shall be a lien upon all of the taxable estates in the village of White Plains, both real and personal. No more than twenty thousand dollars of such bonds shall be issued or sold in any one year. *Bond issues authorized; amount limited. Bonds, denomination, maturity, etc. Sale; temporary loans on bonds; application of proceeds. Tax for payment. Lien of bonds. Limitation of bonds issued within year.*

§ 7. Pending the collection of the assessments, the board of trustees is hereby authorized and empowered to issue certificates of indebtedness, or assessment bonds of the village of White Plains, not to exceed the amount of one-third of the cost of said improvement, such certificates or bonds to draw interest not to exceed five per centum per annum, and to be signed by the president and village clerk, and to be sold at not less than par, and the proceeds thereof shall be used only for the payment of the cost of one-third of said macadamizing or paving. Such certificates of indebtedness or assessment bonds to be and become a lien upon all of the taxable estates, both real and personal, within said *Issue of certificates or bonds pending collection of assessments; amount, interest, etc. Lien.*

Tax for
payment.

village, and the board of trustees is hereby authorized and directed to raise from time to time by tax, such sum or sums of money as may be necessary to pay the interest on such certificates of indebtedness or assessment bonds and the principal thereof at maturity, providing the amount has not been collected from the real property assessed therefor.

Contracts
with and
control of
surface
railroads.

§ 8. Nothing in this act shall in any way interfere with any contract or arrangement between the village of White Plains and any surface railroad company now, or that may hereafter be authorized to operate within said village, or with the control vested by law in the board of trustees over any such surface railroad company, and the cost of macadamizing or paving between the tracks of said surface railroad company and two feet outside, shall be borne by said railroad company as provided by any contract or agreement heretofore made or that may be hereafter made between said village and said railroad company, or as now or hereafter may be provided by law.

Curbs,
gutters
and drains.

§ 9. The board of trustees may order the laying or relaying of curb and gutters and construction of such drains as may be deemed necessary on such streets, avenues or highways, as they shall determine to macadamize or pave, of such character and material as the board by resolution may determine, and the cost thereof shall be considered as part of the cost of said macadamizing or paving, and such curbing, guttering and drains may be included in any contract let by the board of trustees for the macadamizing or paving of any street, avenue or highway.

Bond issue
for 1913;
limitation.

§ 10. The board of trustees is hereby authorized and empowered to issue bonds during the year nineteen hundred and thirteen not to exceed the sum of ten thousand dollars, to pay for the resurfacing and repairing of the macadamized or paved streets, avenues or highways in said village heretofore macadamized or paved under the acts "authorizing the macadamizing or paving of streets, avenues or highways, and the construction of the necessary drains, curbing and gutters therefor and in connection therewith in the village of White Plains, Westchester county, and to provide the manner and means of paying therefor." Such bonds shall bear interest at such rates as the board of trustees may determine not exceeding the rate of six per centum per annum, payable semi-annually; the principal shall become due at such times as the board of trustees shall by resolution determine. Such bonds shall be signed by the president and clerk of the said village, and shall

Interest,
maturity,
etc.

have the corporate seal thereof affixed thereto, and shall not be sold or disposed of below par. The board of trustees of the village of White Plains is hereby authorized and directed to raise by tax, from year to year, such sum or sums of money as may be necessary to pay the interest on said bonds and principal thereof at maturity. Such bonds when so issued shall be a lien upon all taxable estates of the village of White Plains, both real and personal.

§ 11. This act shall take effect immediately.

Chap. 179.

AN ACT to amend the code of civil procedure, in relation to service of summons by publication.

Became a law April 3, 1913, with the approval of the Governor. Passed, three-fifths being present.

The People of the State of New York, represented in Senate and Assembly, do enact as follows:

Section 1. Subdivision one of section four hundred and thirty-eight of the code of civil procedure, is hereby amended to read as follows:

1. Where the defendant to be served is a foreign corporation; or, is an unincorporated association consisting of seven or more persons, having a president and treasurer, neither of whom is a resident of this state; or, being a domestic corporation, where after diligent effort, service cannot be made within the state upon the president or other head of the corporation, the secretary or clerk to the corporation, the cashier, the treasurer or a director or managing agent;[1] or, being a natural person, is not a resident of the state; or, where, after diligent inquiry, the defendant remains unknown to the plaintiff, or the plaintiff is unable to ascertain whether the defendant is or is not a resident of the state.

§ 2. This act shall take effect September first, nineteen hundred and thirteen.

---

[1] Words "or, being a domestic corporation, where after diligent effort, service cannot be made within the state upon the president or other head of the corporation, the secretary or clerk to the corporation, the cashier, the treasurer or a director or managing agent," new.

Chap. 180.

AN ACT to amend the penal law, in relation to discriminations and rebates by corporations transacting the business of life insurance on the co-operative or assessment plan.

Became a law April 3, 1913, with the approval of the Governor. Passed, three-fifths being present.

The People of the State of New York, represented in Senate and Assembly, do enact as follows:

L. 1909,
ch. 88,
§ 1191
amended.

Section 1. Section eleven hundred and ninety-one of chapter eighty-eight of the laws of nineteen hundred and nine, entitled "An act providing for the punishment of crime, constituting chapter forty of the consolidated laws," is hereby amended to read as follows:

§ 1191. **Discriminations and rebates by life insurance corporations prohibited.** Any life insurance corporation or corporation transacting the business of life insurance on the co-operative or assessment plan[1] doing business in this state, or any officer or agent thereof, who:

1. Makes any discrimination in favor of individuals of the same class or of the same expectation of life either in the amount of the premium charged or in any return of premiums, dividends or other advantages; or,

2. Makes any contract for insurance or agreement as to such contract other than that which is plainly expressed in the policy issued; or,

3. Pays or allows, or offers to pay or allow as an inducement to any person to insure, any rebate or premium, or any special favor or advantage whatever, in the dividends to accrue thereon or any inducement whatever not specified in the policy; or,

4. Makes any distinction or discrimination between white persons and colored persons, wholly or partially of African descent, as to the premiums or rates charged for policies upon the lives of such persons, or in any other manner whatever; or demands or requires a greater premium from such colored persons than is at that time required by such company from white persons of the same age, sex, general condition of health and prospect of lon-

---

[1] Words "or corporation transacting the business of life insurance on the co-operative or assessment plan," new.

gevity; or makes or requires any rebate, diminution or discount upon the amount to be paid on such policy in case of the death of such colored persons insured, or inserts in the policy any condition, or makes any stipulation whereby such person insured shall bind himself, or his heirs, executors, administrators and assigns to accept any sum less than the full value or amount of such policy in case of a claim accruing thereon by reason of the death of such person insured, other than such as are imposed upon white persons in similar cases, is guilty of a misdeameanor. [2]Nothing in this section shall be construed to require any corporation doing business under articles six or seven of the insurance law, which limits and confines its business or membership to the members of a secret or fraternal order or body, to insure or accept any individual who is not a member of such secret or fraternal order or body.

§ 2. This act shall take effect September first, nineteen hundred and thirteen. *In effect Sept. 1, 1913.*

Chap. 181.

AN ACT to amend the insurance law, in relation to the standard fire insurance policy of the state of New York and the adjustment of losses thereunder.

Became a law April 3, 1913, with the approval of the Governor. Passed, three-fifths being present.

The People of the State of New York, represented in Senate and Assembly, do enact as follows:

Section 1. Section one hundred and twenty-one of chapter thirty-three of the laws of nineteen hundred and nine, entitled "An act in relation to insurance corporations, constituting chapter twenty-eight of the consolidated laws," as amended by chapter two hundred and forty of the laws of nineteen hundred and nine, and chapters one hundred and sixty-eight, six hundred and thirty-eight and six hundred and sixty-eight of the laws of nineteen hundred and ten, is hereby amended to read as follows: *L. 1909, ch. 33, § 121, as amended by L. 1909, ch. 240, and L. 1910, chaps. 168, 638, 668, amended.*

§ 121. **Standard fire insurance policy to be prescribed and used.** The printed blank form of a contract or policy of fire insurance, with such provisions, agreements or conditions as may be indorsed thereon or added thereto and form a part of such contract or policy, heretofore filed in the office of the secretary of

[2] Remainder of section new.

state by the superintendent of insurance or by the New York board of fire underwriters pursuant to the provisions of chapter four hundred and eighty-eight of the laws of eighteen hundred and eighty-six shall be transferred by the secretary of state to the office of the superintendent of insurance and, together with such provisions, agreements or conditions as may[1] be filed by the New York board of fire underwriters in the office of the superintendent of insurance and approved by him, which provisions, agreements or conditions shall be void if they are inconsistent with the standard fire insurance policy heretofore filed in the office of the secretary of state, shall be known and designated as the " standard fire insurance policy of the state of New York." No fire insurance corporation, its officers or agents, shall make, issue, or deliver for use, any fire insurance policy or the renewal of any such policy on property in this state, other than such as shall conform in all particulars as to blanks, size of type, context, provisions, agreements and conditions with such printed blank form of contract or policy; and no other or different provision, agreement, condition or clause shall be in any manner made a part of such contract or policy or indorsed thereon or delivered therewith, except as follows, to wit:

First. The name of the corporation, its location and place of business, date of its incorporation or organization. whether it is a stock or mutual corporation, the names of its officers, the number and date of the policy, and if issued through a manager or agent the words " this policy shall not be valid until countersigned by the duly authorized manager or agent of the corporation at "................."

Second. Printed or written forms of description and specification, or schedules of the property covered by any particular policy, and any other matter necessary to clearly express all the facts and conditions of insurance on any particular risk not inconsistent with or a waiver of any of the conditions or provisions of the standard policy herein provided for.

Third. With the approval of the superintendent of insurance, if the same is not already included in such standard form, any provision which any such corporation is required by law to insert in its policies, not in conflict with the provisions of such standard form. Such provisions shall be printed apart from the

---

[1] Words " previous to the thirty-first day of December, nineteen hundred and one," omitted.

other provisions, agreements or conditions of the policy under a separate title as follows: "Provisions required by law to be stated in this policy."

After the first day of January, nineteen hundred and eleven, such policy or contract may be printed, written or typewritten with any size of type or on any size or shape of paper which shall have the written approval of the superintendent of insurance.

The name, with the word "agent" or "agents," and place of business, of any insurance agent or agents, either by writing, printing, stamping or otherwise, may be indorsed on the outside of such policies.

Two or more fire insurance corporations, authorized to transact business in this state, may issue a combination standard form of policy, using a distinctive title therefor, which title shall appear at the head of such policy followed by the titles of the several corporations obligated thereupon, and which policy shall be executed by the officers of each of such corporations; provided, that before such corporation shall issue such combination policy, they shall have received the express permission of the superintendent of insurance to issue the same, and the title of such proposed policy and the terms of the additional provisions thereof, hereby authorized, shall have been approved by him, which terms, in addition to the provisions of the standard policy and not inconsistent therewith, shall provide substantially under a separate title therein, to be known as "Provisions specially applicable to this combination policy," as follows:

(a) That each corporation executing such policy shall be liable for the full amount of any loss or damage, according to the terms of the policy, or a specific percentage thereof; (b) that service of process, or of any notices required by the said policy, upon any of the corporations executing the same shall be deemed to be service upon all; and provided, further, that the unearned premium liability on each policy so issued shall be maintained by each of such corporations on the basis of the liability of each to the insured thereunder.

§ 2. Such chapter is hereby amended by inserting therein a new section, to be section one hundred and twenty-one-a, to read as follows:

§ 121-a. **Appointment of umpire by court.** When, in the event of any loss or damage to property in this state described in any policy of fire insurance and covered thereby, the ascertainment of

the amount of any such loss or damage is, as provided in the
policy, to be determined by appraisers, one selected by the company, the other by the insured, and the two so chosen shall have
failed or neglected, for a space of ten days after both have been
chosen, to agree upon and select an umpire, it shall be lawful for
either the insured or the company to apply to any court of record
in the county in which the property is or was located, on five days'
notice in writing, to the other party of his or its intention so to
do, to appoint a competent and disinterested umpire. Any such
notice in writing, when served by the insured, may be served
upon any local agent of the company; and the said court shall, on
proof by affidavit of the failure or neglect of the said appraisers
to agree upon and select an umpire within the time aforesaid,
and of the service of notice aforesaid, forthwith appoint a competent and disinterested person to act as umpire in the ascertainment of the amount of said loss or damage; and the acts of the
umpire so appointed shall be binding upon the insured and the
company to the same extent as if such umpire had been selected
in the manner provided for in said policy of insurance.

No policy of fire insurance shall be hereafter issued on property
located in this state, unless the foregoing provisions of this section
shall be printed on or attached thereto under the following title:
" Provisions required by law to be stated in this policy."

In effect
June 30,
1913. § 3. This act shall take effect June thirtieth, nineteen hundred and thirteen.

Chap. 182.

AN ACT to amend the insurance law, in relation to surety companies.

Became a law April 3, 1913, with the approval of the Governor. Passed,
three-fifths being present.

*The People of the State of New York, represented in Senate
and Assembly, do enact as follows:*

L. 1909,
ch. 33,
§ 181
amended. Section 1. Section one hundred and eighty-one of chapter
thirty-three of the laws of nineteen hundred and nine, entitled "An
act in relation to insurance corporations, constituting chapter
twenty-eight of the consolidated laws," is hereby amended to read
as follows:[1]

---

[1] Section materially amended.

§ 181. **May execute bonds and undertakings.** Whenever a bond, undertaking, recognizance, guaranty or other obligation is required, permitted, authorized or allowed; or whenever the performance of any act, duty or obligation, or the refraining from any act, is required, permitted, authorized or allowed to be secured or guaranteed, such bond, undertaking, recognizance or other obligation, or such security or guaranty, may be executed by a corporation authorized by the laws of this state and by its charter to execute such instrument; and such corporations are authorized and empowered to execute all such instruments; and the execution by any such corporation of such bond, undertaking, recognizance, guaranty or other obligation by an officer, attorney in fact or other authorized representative shall be sufficient and be accepted as and be a full compliance with every law or other requirement now in force or that may hereafter be enacted or made that such bond, undertaking, recognizance, guaranty or like obligation be required or permitted or be executed by a surety or sureties, or that such surety or sureties be residents, householders or freeholders, or possess any other qualifications.

§ 2. Section one hundred and eighty-two of such chapter is § 182 hereby amended to read as follows:[1]   amended.

§ 182. **Issuance of certificate of solvency by superintendent of insurance.** The superintendent of insurance shall on application issue to any such corporation his certificate that it is qualified to become and be accepted, subject to the limitations specified in section twenty-four of this chapter, as surety or guarantor on all bonds, undertakings, other obligations or guaranties specified in section one hundred and eighty-one of this chapter or under any other law or requirement which certificate or a copy thereof certified to be such by the superintendent, shall be conclusive evidence of the solvency of such corporation and of its sufficiency as such surety or guarantor, and of the propriety of accepting and approving it as such, and be in lieu of any justification required of such corporation by any law or requirement. The superintendent may at any time after the issuance of a certificate of solvency, upon notice to and hearing of such corporation, revoke such certificate by filing a revocation thereof in his office and serving a copy on the corporation to which such certificate was issued. The superintendent may publish notice of such revocation in such newspapers as he deems proper.

---

[1] Section materially amended.

§ 183 re-
pealed.

§ 3. Section one hundred and eighty-three of such chapter is hereby repealed.

§ 184 re-
numbered
§ 183, and
amended.

§ 4. Section one hundred and eighty-four is hereby renumbered section one hundred and eighty-three, and amended to read as follows:[1]

§ 183. **Supreme court may require statement to be filed.** If a certificate of solvency shall not have been issued by the superintendent of insurance to any such corporation, or if such certificate shall have been revoked, the supreme court in the judicial department which includes the county in which the principal place of business in this state of any such corporation shall be located, may, at any time, and as frequently as said court shall deem requisite, require such corporation to file with the clerk of said county a sworn statement of its condition, and may also require such corporation, through one or more of its officers, to submit to an examination as to its solvency. Such statement and examination, when filed with said clerk, or a certified copy thereof filed with the clerk of any other county, may be received and considered as justification upon any and all bonds, undertakings or other instruments executed or guaranteed by such corporations, which shall thereafter be presented for approval.

In effect
July 1, 1913.

§ 5. This act shall take effect July first, nineteen hundred and thirteen.

Chap. 183.

AN ACT to amend the village law, in relation to the lien of water rents.

Became a law April 3, 1913, with the approval of the Governor. Passed, three-fifths being present.

The People of the State of New York, represented in Senate and Assembly, do enact as follows:

L. 1909, ch.
64, § 229
amended.

Section 1. Section two hundred and twenty-nine of chapter sixty-four of the laws of nineteen hundred and nine, entitled "An act relating to villages, constituting chapter sixty-four of the consolidated laws," is hereby amended to read as follows:

§ 229. **Establishment of water rents.** The board of water com-

---

[1] Section materially amended.

missioners shall establish a scale of rents for the use of water, to be called " water rents," and to be paid at such times as the board may prescribe. Such rents shall be a lien on the real property upon which the water is used, [1]and such lien is prior and superior to every other lien or claim, except the lien of an existing tax, and the board of water commissioners may bring and maintain an action in the name of the village for the foreclosure of such liens for such water rents.

§ 2. This act shall take effect immediately.

Chap. 184.

AN ACT to legalize certain acts and proceedings of the former village of Saint Regis Falls, its voters, officers and agents, dissolving such village, and to confirm and make effectual such dissolution.

Became a law April 3, 1913, with the approval of the Governor. Passed, three-fifths being present.

The People of the State of New York, represented in Senate and Assembly, do enact as follows:

Section 1. The acts and proceedings of the former village of Saint Regis Falls, in the county of Franklin, by its voters, in determining by majority vote September sixth, eighteen hundred and eighty-seven, to dissolve the incorporation of such village, and in again determining upon such dissolution pursuant to a proposition submitted March twentieth, eighteen hundred and eighty-eight, and the acts and proceedings of the officers and agents of such village leading up to and relating to the submission of each of such propositions, are hereby in all things legalized, ratified and confirmed and are hereby declared to have been effectual to dissolve such village and the incorporation thereof, notwithstanding any defect, irregularity or illegality in any of such acts or proceedings and notwithstanding a failure to certify to the secretary of state a record of such acts or proceedings or to file with the secretary of state any paper required by law relating thereto; and such village is hereby declared to have had no corporate existence as a village from and after the expiration of the time at which, under general

Proceedings to dissolve incorporation legalised.

Village declared to have had

----

[1] Remainder of section new.

no corpo-
rate exist-
ence there-
after.
laws for the dissolution of villages to which such acts and proceedings purported to comply, such dissolution would have been consummated had all legal requirements been complied with, subject only to the provisions of such laws relating to the winding up of village affairs with respect to debts, village property and the collection and apportionment of the then current taxes; it being the

Object of
this act.
object of this act, among other things, to eliminate the existence of such village for the purpose of applying any and every provision of the highway law or of any law relating to state routes which refers specially to villages.

Secretary
of state
to cancel
records.
§ 2. The secretary of state is hereby directed to cancel all records or entries in his office, or upon any list of villages kept by him, whether official or otherwise, purporting to show that Saint Regis Falls aforesaid is, or since the time above mentioned has been, an incorporated village.

§ 3. This act shall take effect immediately.

Chap. 185.

AN ACT to amend the judiciary law, in relation to the retirement of employees by the appellate division of the second department.

Became a law April 3, 1913, with the approval of the Governor. Passed, three-fifths being present.

The People of the State of New York, represented in Senate and Assembly, do enact as follows:

§ 117
added to
L. 1909,
ch. 35.
Section 1. Article four of chapter thirty-five of the laws of nineteen hundred and nine, entitled "An act in relation to the administration of justice, constituting chapter thirty of the consolidated laws," is hereby amended by adding at the end thereof a new section, to be section one hundred and seventeen,[1] to read as follows:

§ 117. **Retirement of employees by the appellate division of second department.** The appellate division of the supreme court of the second department is hereby authorized in its discretion to retire any clerk, assistant clerk, stenographer, interpreter, librarian or attendant who shall have served as such in the supreme court in and for the second or ninth judicial districts or

---

[1] A different § 117 is added by L. 1913, ch. 722, post.

in any court which has been consolidated with the said supreme
court and who shall have become physically or mentally incapacitated for the further performance of the duties of his position,
provided such service in one or more of such positions has continued for a period of twenty-five years or more. Any person
retired from service pursuant to this section shall be paid an annual sum or annuity to be determined by the appellate division
of the second department not exceeding one-half of the average
amount of his annual salary or compensation for a period of two
years preceding the time of such retirement. Such annuity shall
be paid in equal monthly instalments during the lifetime of the
person so retired, and the amount thereof shall otherwise be collected and paid in the same manner as the salary or compensation
of such person was required to be collected and paid at the time
of such retirement.

§ 2. This act shall take effect immediately.

Chap. 186.

AN ACT making an appropriation for completing the construction of new buildings for the Buffalo state normal and training
school, as provided by chapter five hundred and twenty of the
laws of nineteen hundred and ten.

Became a law April 3, 1913, with the approval of the Governor. Passed,
three-fifths being present.

*The People of the State of New York, represented in Senate
and Assembly, do enact as follows:*

Section 1. The sum of three hundred thousand dollars
($300,000), or so much thereof as may be necessary, is hereby
appropriated out of any moneys in the treasury not otherwise
appropriated, for the purpose of completing the construction of
new buildings for the Buffalo state normal and training school,
as authorized by chapter five hundred and twenty of the laws of
nineteen hundred and ten, which sum shall be expended as provided in such act, in accordance with and pursuant to contracts
let as provided by such act and chapter fourteen of the laws of
nineteen hundred and twelve. Payments on such contracts shall
be made in the manner provided by said chapter five hundred
and twenty of the laws of nineteen hundred and ten, and the

provisions of such act shall apply in all respects to the construction of such buildings, except as herein otherwise provided. The amount so appropriated shall be payable by the treasurer on the warrant of the comptroller on vouchers approved by the commissioner of education. Such new buildings shall be erected under the direction of the commissioner of education on the site in the city of Buffalo now occupied by such school.

§ 2. This act shall take effect immediately.

Chap. 187.

AN ACT to amend the executive law, relative to geographic names.

Became a law April 3, 1913, with the approval of the Governor. Passed, three-fifths being present.

The People of the State of New York, represented in Senate and Assembly, do enact as follows:

§ 110 added to L. 1909, ch. 23.

Section 1. Article ten of chapter twenty-three of the laws of nineteen hundred and nine, entitled "An act in relation to executive officers, constituting chapter eighteen of the consolidated laws," is hereby amended by adding, at the end thereof, a new section, to be known as section one hundred and ten, and to read as follows:

§ 110. **Board of geographic names; powers and duties.** A state board of geographic names is hereby created, to consist of five members, of which the commissioner of education and the state geologist shall be ex-officio members, and three of whom shall be appointed by the governor to hold for terms of two, four and six years, to be designated by him when the appointments are made. Their successors shall be appointed by the governor for terms of six years. Vacancies shall be filled by the governor for the unexpired terms of the offices vacated. The state geologist shall be the secretary and executive officer of such board. All of such members shall serve without compensation. The said board shall have power, and it shall be its duty:

1. To determine and establish the correct historical and etymological form of the place names in this state and to recommend the adoption of such correct forms for public use.

2. To determine the form and propriety of new place names proposed for general use, and no corporation, individual or community shall introduce such new place names without the consent and approval of this board.

3. To co-operate with the United States board of geographic names and with the United States post-office department in establishing a proper, correct and historically accurate form for all place names proposed as designations of new post-offices.

§ 2. This act shall take effect immediately.

Chap. 188.

AN ACT authorizing the acquisition by the United States of lands in the borough of Queens, city of New York, as a site for a life saving station.

Became a law April 3, 1913, with the approval of the Governor. Passed by a two-thirds vote.

The People of the State of New York, represented in Senate and Assembly, do enact as follows:

Section 1. The consent of the state of New York is hereby given to the acquisition by the United States of the following described tract of land, to be used as a life saving station and for other public purposes, that is to say: All that certain plot or parcel of land situated at Rockaway beach, in the fifth ward of the borough of Queens, of the city of New York, Queens county and state of New York, being parts of lots numbered nineteen, thirty-eight, thirty-nine and forty on a map filed in the office of the clerk of Queens county October the seventh, eighteen hundred and ninety-seven, as map numbered seventy-four and referred to in an action of partition in the supreme court of the state of New York, Queens county, in which Horace H. Chittenden as assignee of the real and personal property of Alfrederick S. Hatch and Frederick H. Hatch were plaintiffs and Isaac E. Gates and others were defendants, which map is entitled map of Rockaway Point in the town of Hempstead, Queens county, surveyed June, eighteen hundred and ninety-seven, by Walter M. Messerole, C. E., which plot or parcel hereby authorized to be acquired by the United States is bounded and described as follows: Beginning at a point on the shore of the Atlantic ocean

United States authorized to acquire certain described land for life saving station.

where it is intersected by the division line between lots numbered nineteen and forty on said map, which line was formerly the division line between lands of Andrew K. Van Deventer and Neponsit Realty Company, and running thence easterly along said shore sixty-eight feet and nine inches; thence north twenty-three degrees, fifty-five minutes and seven seconds west, two thousand five hundred and eighty-four feet to Jamaica bay; thence westerly along high water mark of Jamaica bay three hundred and fifty feet; thence south twenty-nine degrees, nineteen minutes and fifty seconds east, two thousand six hundred and thirty feet to the shore of the Atlantic ocean, and thence easterly along the same thirty-one feet and three inches to the point of beginning.

When jurisdiction ceded. § 2. Whenever a certified copy of record or transfer of the title of said property to the United States shall have been filed and recorded in the office of the secretary of this state, together with a map and description of such lands by metes and bounds, exclusive jurisdiction is thereupon ceded to the United States, subject to the restrictions hereinafter mentioned.

Duration of cession. § 3. The jurisdiction hereby ceded shall continue no longer than the United States shall own such lands and premises; and **Concurrent jurisdiction to execute civil or criminal process retained.** such consent is given and jurisdiction ceded on the express condition that the state of New York shall retain concurrent jurisdiction with the United States, in and over such lands, so far as may be necessary or proper, for the purpose of executing thereon any process, civil or criminal, issued under the laws or authority of this state, and such process may be executed thereon in the same manner as if such consent and jurisdiction had not been given.

Property exempted from taxation, etc. § 4. The said property shall be now and continue forever thereafter exonerated and discharged from all taxes. assessments and other charges, which have been or may be levied or imposed **Duration of jurisdiction ceded and of exemption.** upon the authority of this state; but the jurisdiction hereby ceded and the exemption from taxation hereby granted, shall continue in respect to said property so long as the same shall remain the property of the United States, and to be used for the purposes aforesaid, and no longer.

§ 5. This act shall take effect immediately.

Chap. 189.

AN ACT to amend chapter four hundred and fifty-nine of the laws of nineteen hundred and ten, entitled "An act designating the commission heretofore created to confer with the governor and the legislature of the state of New Jersey, for the purpose of developing a system of transit between the city of New York and state of New Jersey, as the New York interstate bridge commission," in relation to changing its name, and providing for fuller co-operation.

Became a law April 3, 1913, with the approval of the Governor. Passed, three-fifths being present.

The People of the State of New York, represented in Senate and Assembly, do enact as follows:

Section 1. Section one of chapter four hundred and fifty-nine of the laws of nineteen hundred and ten, entitled "An act designating the commission heretofore created to confer with the governor and the legislature of the state of New Jersey, for the purpose of developing a system of transit between the city of New York and the state of New Jersey, as the 'New York Interstate Bridge Commission,'" is hereby amended to read as follows: L. 1910. ch. 459, § 1 amended.

§ 1. The commission heretofore created to confer with the governor and legislature of the state of New Jersey, for the purpose of developing a system of transit between the city of New York and state of New Jersey, by chapter two hundred and sixty of the laws of nineteen hundred and six, as amended by chapter three hundred and nineteen of the laws of nineteen hundred and seven,[1] shall be known hereafter as the "New York State Bridge and Tunnel Commission."[2] Commission how de-nominated.

§ 2. Said commission, in co-operating with the New Jersey interstate bridge and tunnel commission, shall consider the subject of tunnel communication between the city of New York and the state of New Jersey. Tunnel communication.

§ 3. This act shall take effect immediately.

---

[1] The act of 1907 does not, in terms, amend the act of 1906. The act of 1907 has since been amended by L. 1908, ch. 218, and L. 1909, ch. 457.
[2] Formerly read: "New York Interstate Bridge Commission."

Chap. 190.

AN ACT making an appropriation to aid in the celebration of the
one hundredth anniversary of the battle of Lake Erie, fought
September tenth, eighteen hundred and thirteen, the erection
of a memorial to Commodore Perry and his men, and other expenses in connection with such celebration, and relating to
Perry's Victory Centennial Commission.

Became a law April 3, 1913, with the approval of the Governor. Passed
by a two-thirds vote.

*The People of the State of New York, represented in Senate
and Assembly, do enact as follows:*

Appro-
priation.

Section 1. The sum of one hundred and fifty thousand dollars
($150,000) is hereby appropriated out of any moneys in the treas-
ury, not otherwise appropriated, for the purpose of enabling the
state of New York to participate in the celebration of the one hundredth anniversary of the battle of Lake Erie, fought September
tenth in the year eighteen hundred and thirteen, to aid in the construction of a memorial at Put-in-Bay in Lake Erie, state of Ohio,
to the American commander, Commodore Oliver Hazard Perry,
and the officers and the men of his fleet, killed during the
battle, to aid in the celebration, including any entertainment or public function held within the state of New York
during the said celebration in connection therewith, and to
defray the expenses of the state commission, Perry's Victory
Centennial Commission, appointed pursuant to concurrent resolution number twenty-three of the legislative session of nineteen hun-

Payments
and dis-
bursements,
how made.

dred and ten and this act. The said sum of one hundred and fifty
thousand dollars ($150,000) shall be paid by warrant of the comp-
troller to the treasurer of the said state commission, Perry's Victory Centennial Commission, and be disbursed by the commission.

Use of part
of appro-
priation for
permanent
memorial.

§ 2. It shall be lawful for the said commission, at its discretion, to transfer and pay to the treasurer-general of the interstate
board of the Perry's Victory Centennial Commission, not exceeding the sum of fifty thousand dollars ($50,000) out of the said
one hundred and fifty thousand dollars ($150,000), to aid in the
erection of a suitable and permanent memorial on South
Bass island (sometimes called Put-in-Bay island), in Lake
Erie, in the state of Ohio, in commemoration of the victory
of Commodore Oliver Hazard Perry at the battle of Lake Erie.

provided that no part of the money hereby appropriated shall be ᴾʳᵒᵛⁱˢᵒ. available for said memorial until the commissioners are satisfied that a sufficient sum has been appropriated by the United States and the states participating for the completion of said memorial, and provided also that the title to all the sites and memorials constructed thereon, pursuant to the provisions of this act, shall be vested in the United States of America.

§ 3. It shall be lawful for the said Perry's Victory Centennial ᵁˢᵉ ᵒᶠ ᵖᵃʳᵗ ᵒᶠ ᵃᵖᵖʳᵒ⁻ Commission, at its discretion, to transfer and pay from the said ᵖʳⁱᵃᵗⁱᵒⁿ ᶠᵒʳ ᵉˣᵖᵉⁿˢᵉˢ ᵒᶠ one hundred and fifty thousand dollars ($150,000) to the treas- ⁱⁿᵗᵉʳˢᵗᵃᵗᵉ ᵇᵒᵃʳᵈ. urer-general of the interstate board of the Perry's Victory Centennial Commission, such amount as it may deem proper to aid in defraying the general expenses of said interstate board only in connection with the celebration of Perry's victory. The state ᵛᵒᵘᶜʰᵉʳˢ ᵗᵒ ᵇᵉ ᶠⁱˡᵉᵈ. commission shall file in the office of the comptroller, after the close of the celebration, vouchers for all sums expended, showing amounts paid, to whom and for what purpose. The term expenses "ᴱˣᵖᵉⁿˢᵉˢ" ᵗᵒ ⁱⁿᶜˡᵘᵈᵉ shall be held to include the actual and necessary expenses of the ʷʰᵃᵗ. individual members of said commission in connection with the said celebration, including expenses incurred prior to this time.

§ 4. The said Perry's Victory Centennial Commission is hereby ᴼᶠᶠⁱᶜᵉʳˢ ᵃⁿᵈ ᵉᵐᵖˡᵒʸᵉᵉˢ authorized to appoint a secretary, a stenographer, a director, ᵒᶠ ᶜᵒᵐᵐⁱˢ⁻ ˢⁱᵒⁿ; ʳᵉⁿᵗᵃˡ and such other officers and employees as it may deem necessary, ᵒᶠ ᵒᶠᶠⁱᶜᵉˢ, ᵉᵗᶜ. and it may also rent suitable office quarters and do any and all other acts for the proper discharge of its duties and the carrying on of the work entrusted to it. It shall have power to fix and determine the compensation of all such officers and employees and pay the same out of the money hereby appropriated. No salary hereby authorized shall continue after the thirty-first day of December, nineteen hundred and thirteen, and no person shall be debarred from receiving pay for services rendered by reason of membership in the said commission.

§ 5. The commission representing the state of New York in the ᴾᵉʳʳʸ'ˢ ⱽⁱᶜ⁻ ᵗᵒʳʸ ᶜᵉⁿᵗᵉⁿ⁻ celebration of the one hundredth anniversary of the battle of Lake ⁿⁱᵃˡ ᶜᵒᵐ⁻ ᵐⁱˢˢⁱᵒⁿ, Erie, as hereinbefore referred to, shall continue to be known as ʰᵒʷ ᵈᵉ⁻ ⁿᵒᵐⁱⁿᵃᵗᵉᵈ Perry's Victory Centennial Commission. Such commission ᵃⁿᵈ ᶜᵒᵐ⁻ ᵖᵒˢᵉᵈ. shall consist of the five members heretofore appointed by the governor, the lieutenant-governor, two senators to be appointed by the temporary president of the senate, and three members of assembly to be appointed by the speaker of the assembly. If a vacancy ⱽᵃᶜᵃⁿᶜⁱᵉˢ. occurs in the office of any member, it shall be filled by the officer

Annual re-
port.

Officers.

By-laws.

making the original appointment. Said commission shall make
an annual report of its expenses, with the items thereof and the
progress of the proceedings of the interstate board, to the governor
and legislature of the state of New York. Its officers shall be a
chairman, a vice-chairman and a treasurer, elected by the commission, and it may make by-laws for its own government and for
those in its employ.

§ 6. This act shall take effect immediately.

Chap. 191.

AN ACT to amend chapter five hundred and ninety-two of the
laws of nineteen hundred and ten, entitled "An act in relation
to the care and investment of the Adam Haverling school fund
belonging to Haverling union free school district number five,
town of Bath, Steuben county, and repealing certain acts in
relation thereto," in relation to bond of treasurer of board of
education of such free school district.

Became a law April 3, 1913, with the approval of the Governor. Passed,
three-fifths being present.

*The People of the State of New York, represented in Senate
and Assembly, do enact as follows:*

L. 1910, ch
592, § 2
amended.

Section 1. Section two of chapter five hundred and ninety-two
of the laws of nineteen hundred and ten, entitled "An act in
relation to the care and investment of the Adam Haverling school
fund belonging to Haverling union free school district number
five, town of Bath, Steuben county, and repealing certain acts
in relation thereto," is hereby amended to read as follows:

Treasurer's
bond.

§ 2. Every person who shall hereafter be chosen to the office
of treasurer of said board of education shall, within ten days
after his election or appointment, execute a bond to the board
of education of Haverling union free school district number five,
Bath, in the sum of fifteen thousand dollars,[1] in addition to the
bond already required of such treasurer, to be given with sufficient
sureties to be approved by said board of education, which bond
shall be conditioned for the faithful performance of his duties

---

[1] Words "the sum of fifteen thousand dollars," substituted for words
"double the amount of said Haverling fund."

required of him respecting said fund, and for the payment by him, or proper investment of all sums of money he shall receive belonging thereto or by reason thereof. Said bond shall be delivered to and kept by the clerk of said board of education.

§ 2. This act shall take effect immediately.

Chap. 192.

AN ACT to amend the insurance law, in relation to lists of officers to be furnished to the state fire marshal by county clerks.

Became a law April 3, 1913, with the approval of the Governor. Passed, three-fifths being present.

The People of the State of New York, represented in Senate and Assembly, do enact as follows:

Section 1. Article ten-a of chapter thirty-three of the laws of nineteen hundred and nine, entitled "An act in relation to insurance corporations, constituting chapter twenty-eight of the consolidated laws," as added by chapter four hundred and fifty-one of the laws of nineteen hundred and eleven and amended by chapter four hundred and fifty-three of the laws of nineteen hundred and twelve, is hereby amended by adding thereto a new section, to be section three hundred and seventy-seven, to read as follows:

§ 377. **County clerks to furnish lists.** County clerks shall on or before January fifteenth, in each year, forward to the state fire marshal for the purposes of his department full and accurate lists of all municipal fire marshals, chiefs of fire departments or like senior officers in incorporated and unincorporated cities and villages, or fire districts under the county law, presidents or like senior officers of each incorporated village and clerks of each organized town without the limits of any incorporated village or city.

§ 2. This act shall take effect immediately.

§ 377 add'd to L. 1909, ch. 33.

Chap. 193.

AN ACT to incorporate the "Mount Vernon Masonic Guild."

Became a law April 3, 1913, with the approval of the Governor. Passed, three-fifths being present.

The People of the State of New York, represented in Senate and Assembly, do enact as follows:

Section 1. **Corporators.** William A. Anderson, George C. Appell, George H. Bard, George R. Crawford, William L. Chapman, Franklin T. Davis, James Dean, Arthur Dummett, Edwin W. Fiske, Albert F. Gescheidt, Robert A. Greenfield, J. Agate House, Samuel N. Hoag, Henry B. Pruser, Jacques W. Redway, Theodore Taylor and all persons who shall hereafter be associated with them, are hereby created a body corporate under the name of Mount Vernon Masonic Guild. Such corporation is formed for and is hereby authorized to acquire, construct, maintain and manage a hall, temple, or other building within the city of Mount Vernon, Westchester county, New York, for the use of Masonic bodies and other fraternal associations and benevolent organizations, and others desiring to use the same, or parts thereof, and for social, benevolent and charitable purposes and generally to promote and cherish a spirit of brotherhood among the members thereof. Out of the funds derived from rents, or income thereof, or other sources over and above obligations and all expenses, it may acquire, construct, establish, maintain and manage or contribute to the maintenance of an asylum or asylums, a home or homes, a school or schools, for the free education of the children of masons, and for the relief, support and care of worthy and indigent masons, their wives, widows and orphans and to render direct relief to worthy and indigent masons, their wives, widows and orphans.

§ 2. **Powers.** Said corporation shall have power to take and hold real and personal estate, by purchase, gift, devise, or bequest, subject to the provisions of law regulating devises or bequests by last will and testament or otherwise, and to hold, lease, transfer and convey all or any of such real or personal property as may be necessary for attaining the objects and carrying into effect the purposes of such corporation; and for such purposes to borrow money and issue bonds therefor, and secure the same by mortgage, and it shall and may be lawful for any masonic or other fraternal body, association or organization, to purchase the bonds authorized by this act and to invest its funds in the same.

§ 3. **Trustees.** The number of trustees of the corporation hereby created shall be fifteen, who shall be designated, selected, appointed or elected in such manner and at such times as may be prescribed by the by-laws to be adopted by said corporation, which is authorized to alter, modify and change the same from time to time as shall be prescribed therein.

§ 4. **Annual meeting.** Such corporation shall hold, within the city of Mount Vernon, county of Westchester, New York, a stated annual meeting in such manner and subject to such regulations as its by-laws may provide, at which meeting a specific report shall be made of its financial condition and its operations for the preceding year. A duplicate copy of such report shall be presented to the Grand Lodge of Free and Accepted Masons of the state of New York at its annual communication.

§ 5. **Election of officers.** At the annual meeting for the election of officers or trustees of such corporation a majority of the persons entitled to vote at such meeting shall not be necessary to constitute a quorum.

§ 6. **General corporation law applicable.** This corporation shall possess the powers and be subject to the liabilities prescribed by the general corporation law, so far as the same are not inconsistent with this act.

§ 7. This act shall take effect immediately.

Chap. 194.

AN ACT to amend the labor law, in relation to fire prevention in factories.

Became a law April 3, 1913, with the approval of the Governor. Passed, three-fifths being present.

The People of the State of New York, represented in Senate and Assembly, do enact as follows:

Section 1. Section eighty-three-c of chapter thirty-six of the laws of nineteen hundred and nine, entitled "An act relating to labor, constituting chapter thirty-one of the consolidated laws," as amended[1] by chapter three hundred and twenty-nine of the

L. 1909, ch. 36, § 83c, as added by L. 1912, ch. 329, amended.

---

1 Should read "added."

laws of nineteen hundred and twelve, is hereby amended to read as follows:

§ 83-c. **Fireproof receptacles; gas jets; smoking.** 1. Every factory shall be provided with properly covered fireproof receptacles, the number, style and location of which shall be approved in the city of New York by the fire commissioner, and elsewhere, by the commissioner of labor. There shall be deposited in such receptacles all inflammable waste materials, cuttings and rubbish. No waste materials, cuttings or[2] rubbish shall be permitted to accumulate on the floors of any factory but shall be removed therefrom not less than twice each day. All such waste materials, cuttings and rubbish shall be entirely removed from a factory building at least once in each day, [3]except that baled waste material may be stored in fireproof enclosures provided that all such baled waste material shall be removed from such building at least once in each month.

2. All gas jets or lights in factories shall be properly enclosed by globes, wire cages or otherwise properly protected in a manner approved in the city of New York by the fire commissioner of such city, and elsewhere, by the commissioner of labor.

3. No person shall smoke in any factory.[4] A notice of such prohibition stating the penalty for violation thereof shall be posted in every entrance hall and every elevator car, and in every stairhall and room[5] on every floor of such factory in English and also in such other language or languages as the fire commissioner of the city of New York in such city, and elsewhere, the state fire marshal, shall direct. The fire commissioner of the city of New York in such city, and elsewhere, the state fire marshal shall enforce the provisions of this subdivision.

§ 2. This act shall take effect immediately.

---

[2] Word " or " substituted for word " and."
[3] Remainder of sentence new.
[4] Sentence formerly read: " Smoking in a factory is prohibited."
[5] Words " in every entrance hall and every elevator car, and in every stairhall and room," new.

Chap. 195.

AN ACT to amend the labor law, in relation to the housing of factory employees.

Became a law April 3, 1913, with the approval of the Governor. Passed, three-fifths being present.

The People of the State of New York, represented in Senate and Assembly, do enact as follows:

Section 1. Chapter thirty-six of the laws of nineteen hundred and nine, entitled "An act relating to labor, constituting chapter thirty-one of the consolidated laws," is hereby amended by inserting therein after section ninety-seven, a new section to be known as section ninety-eight, to read as follows: ^{§ 98 added to L. 1909, ch. 36.}

§ 98. **Labor camps.** Every employer operating a factory, and furnishing to the employees thereof any living quarters at any place outside the factory, either directly or through any third person by contract or otherwise, shall maintain such living quarters and every part thereof in a thoroughly sanitary condition. The industrial board shall have power to make rules and regulations to provide for the sanitation of such living quarters. The commissioner of labor may enter and inspect any such living quarters.

§ 2. This act shall take effect immediately.

Chap. 196.

AN ACT to amend the labor law, in relation to ventilation in factories and the removal of impurities and of excessive heat therein.

Became a law April 3, 1913, with the approval of the Governor. Passed, three-fifths being present.

The People of the State of New York, represented in Senate and Assembly, do enact as follows:

Section 1. Section eighty-six of chapter thirty-six of the laws of nineteen hundred and nine, entitled "An act relating to labor, constituting chapter thirty-one of the consolidated laws," is hereby, amended to read as follows:[1] ^{L. 1909, ch. 36, § 86 amended.}

---

[1] Section materially amended.

12

§ 86. Ventilation.　1. The owner, agent or lessee of every factory shall provide, in each workroom thereof, proper and sufficient means of ventilation by natural or mechanical means or both, as may be necessary, and shall maintain proper and sufficient ventilation and proper degrees of temperature and humidity in every workroom thereof at all times during working hours.

2. If dust, gases, fumes, vapors, fibers or other impurities are generated or released in the course of the business carried on in any workroom of a factory, in quantities tending to injure the health of the operatives, the person operating the factory, whether as owner or lessee of the whole or of a part of the building in which the same is situated, or otherwise, shall provide suction devices that shall remove said impurities from the workroom, at their point of origin where practicable, by means of proper hoods connected to conduits and exhaust fans of sufficient capacity to remove such impurities, and such fans shall be kept running constantly while such impurities are being generated or released. If, owing to the nature of the manufacturing process carried on in a factory workroom, excessive heat be created therein the person or persons operating the factory as aforesaid shall provide, maintain, use and operate such special means or appliances as may be required to reduce such excessive heat.

3. The industrial board shall have power to make rules and regulations for and fix standards of ventilation, temperature and humidity in factories and may prescribe the special means, if any, required for removing impurities or for reducing excessive heat, and the machinery, apparatus or appliances to be used for any of said purposes, and the construction, equipment, maintenance and operation thereof, in order to effectuate the purposes of this section.

4. If any requirement of this section or any rule or regulation of the industrial board made under the provisions thereof shall not be complied with, the commissioner of labor shall issue or cause to be issued an order directing compliance therewith by the person whose duty it is to comply therewith within thirty days after the service of such order. Such person shall, in case of failure to comply with the requirements of such order, forfeit to the people of the state fifteen dollars for each day during which such failure shall continue after the expiration of such thirty days, to be recovered by the commissioner of labor. The liability to such penalty

shall be in addition to the liability of such person to prosecution for a misdemeanor as provided by section twelve hundred and seventy-five of the penal law.

5. When the commissioner of labor shall issue, or cause to be issued, an order specified in subdivision four hereof, he may in such order require plans and specifications to be filed for any machinery or apparatus to be provided or altered, pursuant to the requirements of such order. In such case, before providing, or making any change or alteration in any machinery or apparatus for any of the purposes specified in this section, the person upon whom such order is served shall file with the commissioner of labor plans and specifications therefor, and shall obtain the approval of such plans and specifications by the commissioner of labor before providing or making any change or alteration in any such machinery or apparatus.

§ 2. This act shall take effect October first, nineteen hundred and thirteen. ^{In effect Oct. 1, 1913.}

Chap. 197.

AN ACT to amend the labor law, in relation to seats in factories and other establishments for female employees.

Became a law April 3, 1913, with the approval of the Governor. Passed, three-fifths being present.

The People of the State of New York, represented in Senate and Assembly, do enact as follows:

Section 1. Section seventeen of chapter thirty-six of the laws of nineteen hundred and nine, entitled "An act relating to labor, constituting chapter thirty-one of the consolidated laws," is hereby amended to read as follows: ^{L. 1909, ch. 36, § 17 amended.}

§ 17. **Seats for female employees.** Every person employing females in a factory or as waitresses in a hotel or restaurant shall provide and maintain suitable seats, with proper backs where practicable, for the use of such female employees, and permit the use thereof by such employees to such an extent as may be reasonable for the preservation of their health. [1]Where females are engaged in work which can be properly performed in a sitting posture, suitable seats, with backs where practicable, shall be

---

[1] Remainder of section new.

supplied in every factory for the use of all such female employees and permitted to be used at such work. The industrial board may determine when seats, with or without backs, are necessary and the number thereof.

In effect
Oct. 1, 1913. § 2. This act shall take effect October first, nineteen hundred and thirteen.

Chap. 198.

AN ACT to amend the labor law, in relation to the clean, sanitary and safe condition of factory buildings.

Became a law April 3, 1913, with the approval of the Governor. Passed, three-fifths being present.

The People of the State of New York, represented in Senate and Assembly, do enact as follows:

§ 84a added
to L. 1909,
ch. 36. Section 1. Article six of chapter thirty-six of the laws of nineteen hundred and nine, entitled "An act relating to labor, constituting chapter thirty-one of the consolidated laws," is hereby amended by inserting after section eighty-four, a new section, to be section eighty-four-a, to read as follows:

§ 84-a. **Cleanliness of factory buildings.** Every part of a factory building and of the premises thereof and the yards, courts, passages, areas or alleys connected with or belonging to the same, shall be kept clean, and shall be kept free from any accumulation of dirt, filth, rubbish or garbage in or on the same. The roof, passages, stairs, halls, basements, cellars, privies, water-closets, cesspools, drains and all other parts of such building and the premises thereof shall at all times be kept in a clean, sanitary and safe condition. The entire building and premises shall be well drained and the plumbing thereof at all times kept in proper repair and in a clean and sanitary condition.

In effect
Oct. 1, 1913. § 2. This act shall take effect October first, nineteen hundred and thirteen.

Chap. 199.

AN ACT to amend the labor law, in relation to protecting the lives, health and safety of employees in dangerous trades.

Became a law April 3, 1913, with the approval of the Governor. Passed, three-fifths being present.

The People of the State of New York, represented in Senate and Assembly, do enact as follows:

Section 1. Chapter thirty-six of the laws of nineteen hundred and nine, entitled "An act relating to labor, constituting chapter thirty-one of the consolidated laws," is hereby amended by inserting therein, after section ninety-eight, a new section to be section ninety-nine, to read as follows:

§ 99. **Dangerous trades.**   Whenever the industrial board shall find as a result of its investigations that any industry, trade or occupation by reason of the nature of the materials used therein or the products thereof or by reason of the methods or processes or machinery or apparatus employed therein or by reason of any other matter or thing connected with such industry, trade or occupation, contains such elements of danger to the lives, health or safety of persons employed therein as to require special regulation for the protection of such persons, said board shall have power to make such special rules and regulations as it may deem necessary to guard against such elements of danger by establishing requirements as to temperature, humidity, the removal of dusts, gases or fumes and requiring licenses to be applied for and issued by the commissioner of labor as a condition of carrying on any such industry, trade or occupation and requiring medical inspection and supervision of persons employed and applying for employment and by other appropriate means.

§ 2. This act shall take effect immediately.

Chap. 200.

AN ACT to amend the labor law, in relation to the physical examination of children employed in factories and cancellation of their employment certificates because of physical unfitness.

Became a law April 3, 1913, with the approval of the Governor. Passed, three-fifths being present.

The People of the State of New York, represented in Senate and Assembly, do enact as follows:

§ 76a added to L. 1909, ch. 36.

Section 1. Chapter thirty-six of the laws of nineteen hundred and nine, entitled " An act relating to labor, constituting chapter thirty-one of the consolidated laws," is hereby amended by inserting therein, after section seventy-six thereof, a new section, to be section seventy-six-a, to read as follows:

§ 76-a. **Physical examination of children in factories; cancellation of employment certificates.**   1. All children between fourteen and sixteen years of age employed in factories shall submit to a physical examination whenever required by a medical inspector of the state department of labor.   The result of all such physical examinations shall be recorded on blanks furnished for that purpose by the commissioner of labor, and shall be kept on file in such office or offices of the department as the commissioner of labor may designate.

2. If any such child shall fail to submit to such physical examination, the commissioner of labor may issue an order cancelling such child's employment certificate.   Such order shall be served upon the employer of such child who shall forthwith deliver to an authorized representative of the department of labor the child's employment certificate.   A certified copy of the order of cancellation shall be served on the board of health or other local authority that issued the said certificate.   No such child whose employment certificate has been cancelled, as aforesaid, shall, while said cancellation remains unrevoked, be permitted or suffered to work in any factory of the state before it attains the age of sixteen years.   If thereafter such child shall submit to the physical examination required, the commissioner of labor may issue an order revoking the cancellation of the employment certificate and may return the employment certificate to such child.   Copies of the order of revocation shall be served upon the former employer of the child and the local board of health as aforesaid.

3. If as a result of the physical examination made by a medical inspector it appears that the child is physically unfit to be employed in a factory, such medical inspector shall forthwith submit a report to that effect to the commissioner of labor which shall be kept on file in the office of the commissioner of labor, setting forth in detail his reasons therefor, and the commissioner of labor may issue an order cancelling the employment certificate of such child. Such order of cancellation shall be served, and the child's employment certificate delivered up, as provided in subdivision two hereof, and no such child while the said order of cancellation remains unrevoked shall be permitted or suffered to work in any factory of the state before it attains the age of sixteen years. If upon a subsequent physical examination of the child by a medical inspector of the department of labor it appears that the physical infirmities have been removed, such medical inspector shall certify to that effect to the commissioner of labor, and the commissioner of labor may thereupon make an order revoking the cancellation of the employment certificate and may return the certificate to such child. The order of revocation shall be served in the manner provided in subdivision two hereof.

§ 2. This act shall take effect October first, nineteen hundred and thirteen. *In effect Oct. 1, 1913.*

Chap. 201.

AN ACT to amend the labor law, in relation to foundries.

Became a law April 3, 1913, with the approval of the Governor. Passed, three-fifths being present.

The People of the State of New York, represented in Senate and Assembly, do enact as follows:

Section 1. Chapter thirty-six of the laws of nineteen hundred and nine, entitled "An act relating to labor, constituting chapter thirty-one of the consolidated laws," is hereby amended by inserting therein, after section ninety-six, a new section, to be section ninety-seven, to read as follows: *§ 97 added to L. 1909, ch. 36.*

§ 97. **Brass, iron and steel foundries.** 1. Foundries shall be subject to all the provisions of this chapter relating to factories.

2. All entrances to foundries shall be so constructed and maintained as to minimize drafts, and all windows therein shall be maintained in proper condition and repair.

3. All gangways in foundries shall be constructed and maintained of sufficient width to make the use thereof by employees reasonably safe; during the progress of casting such gangways shall not be obstructed in any manner.

4. Smoke, steam and gases generated in foundries shall be effectively removed therefrom, in accordance with such rules and regulations as may be adopted with reference thereto by the industrial board, and whenever required by the regulations of such board, exhaust fans of sufficient capacity and power, properly equipped with ducts and hoods, shall be provided and operated to remove such smoke, steam and gases. The milling and cleaning of castings, and milling of cupola cinders, shall be done under such conditions to be prescribed by the rules and regulations of the industrial board as will adequately protect the persons employed in foundries from the dust arising during the process.

5. All foundries shall be properly and thoroughly lighted during working hours and in cold weather proper and sufficient heat shall be provided and maintained therein. The use of heaters discharging smoke or gas into workrooms is prohibited. In all foundries suitable provisions shall be made and maintained for drying the working clothes of persons employed therein.

6. In every foundry in which ten or more persons are employed or engaged at labor, there shall be provided and maintained for the use of employees therein suitable and convenient washrooms of sufficient capacity adequately equipped with hot and cold water service; such washrooms shall be kept clean and sanitary and shall be properly heated during cold weather. In every such foundry lockers shall be provided for the safe-keeping of employees' clothing. In every foundry in which more than ten persons are employed or engaged at labor where water closets or privy accommodations are permitted by the commissioner of labor to remain outside of the factory under the provisions of section eighty-eight of this chapter, the passageway leading from the foundry to the said water-closets or privy accommodations shall be so protected and constructed that the employees in passing thereto or therefrom shall not be exposed to outdoor atmosphere and such water closets or privy accommodations shall be properly heated during cold weather.

7. The flasks, molding machines, ladles, cranes and apparatus for transporting molten metal in foundries shall be maintained in proper condition and repair, and any such tools or implements that are defective shall not be used until properly repaired. There shall be in every foundry, available for immediate use, an ample supply of lime water, olive oil, vaseline, bandages and absorbent cotton, to meet the needs of workmen in case of burns or other accidents; but any other equally efficacious remedy for burns may be substituted for those herein prescribed.

§ 2. This act shall take effect October first, nineteen hundred and thirteen. *In effect Oct. 1, 1913.*

Chap. 202.

AN ACT to amend the labor law, in relation to elevators and hoisting shafts in factory buildings.

Became a law April 3, 1913, with the approval of the Governor. Passed, three-fifths being present.

The People of the State of New York, represented in Senate and Assembly, do enact as follows:

Section 1. Section seventy-nine of chapter thirty-six of the laws of nineteen hundred and nine, entitled "An act relating to labor, constituting chapter thirty-one of the consolidated laws," as amended by chapter two hundred and ninety-nine of the laws of nineteen hundred and nine, is hereby amended to read as follows:[1] *L. 1909, ch. 36, § 79, as amended by L. 1909, ch. 459, amended.*

§ 79. **Elevators and hoistways.** 1. Inclosure of shafts. Every hoistway, hatchway or well-hole used for carrying passengers or employees, or for freight elevators, hoisting or other purpose, shall be protected on all sides at each floor including the basement, by substantial vertical inclosures. All openings in such inclosures shall be provided with self-closing gates not less than six feet high or with properly constructed sliding doors. In the case of elevators used for carrying passengers or employees, such inclosures shall be flush with the hatchway and shall extend from floor to ceiling on every open side of the car, and on every other side shall be at least six feet high, and such enclosures shall be free from fixed obstructions on every open side of the car. In the case of freight elevators the enclosures shall be flush with the hoistway on every open side of the car. In place of the inclosures herein required for freight elevators, every hatchway used for

---

[1] Section materially amended.

freight elevator purposes may be provided with trap doors so
constructed as to form a substantial floor surface when closed
and so arranged as to open and close by the action of the car in its
passage both ascending and descending; provided that in addition
to such trap doors, the hatchway shall be adequately protected on
all sides at all floors, including the basement, by a substantial railing or other vertical inclosure at least three feet in height.

2. Guarding of elevators and hoistways. All counter-weights of
every elevator shall be adequately protected by proper inclosures
at the top and bottom of the run. The car of all elevators used
for carrying passengers or employees shall be substantially enclosed on all sides, including the top, and such car shall at all
times be properly lighted, artificial illuminants to be provided and
used when necessary. The top of every freight elevator car or
platform shall be provided with a substantial grating or covering
for the protection of the operator thereof, in accordance with
such rules and regulations as may be adopted with reference
thereto by the industrial board.

3. Elevators and hoistways in factory buildings hereafter
erected. The provisions of subdivisions one and two of this section shall apply only to factory buildings heretofore erected. In
all factory buildings hereafter erected, every elevator and every
part thereof and all machinery connected therewith and every
hoistway, hatchway and well-hole shall be so constructed, guarded,
equipped, maintained and operated as to be safe for all persons
using the same.

4. Maintenance of elevators and hoistways in all factory buildings. In every factory building heretofore erected or hereafter
erected, all inclosures, doors and gates of hoistways, hatchways or
well-holes, and all elevators therein used for the carrying of passengers or employees or freight, and the gates and doors thereof
shall at all times be kept in good repair and in a safe condition.
All openings leading to elevators shall be kept well lighted at all
times during working hours, with artificial illumination when
necessary. The cable, gearing and other apparatus of elevators
used for carrying passengers or employees or freight shall be kept
in a safe condition.

5. Powers of industrial board. The industrial board shall have
power to make rules and regulations not inconsistent with the
provisions of this chapter regulating the construction, guarding,
equipment, maintenance and operation of elevators and all parts

thereof, and all machinery connected therewith and hoistways, hatchways and well-holes, in order to carry out the purpose and intention of this section.

§ 2. This act shall take effect October first, nineteen hundred and thirteen. In effect
Oct. 1, 1913.

Chap. 203.

AN ACT to amend the labor law, in relation to fire alarm signal systems and fire drills.

Became a law April 3, 1913, with the approval of the Governor. Passed, three-fifths being present.

The People of the State of New York, represented in Senate and Assembly, do enact as follows:

Section 1. Section eighty-three-a of chapter thirty-six of the laws of nineteen hundred and nine, entitled "An act relating to labor, constituting chapter thirty-one of the consolidated laws," as amended[1] by chapter three hundred and thirty of the laws of nineteen hundred and twelve, is hereby amended to read as follows:[2] L. 1909, ch.
36, § 83a,
as added
by L. 1912,
ch. 330,
amended.

§ 83-a. **Fire alarm signal systems and fire drills.** 1. Every factory building over two stories in height in which more than twenty-five persons are employed above the ground floor shall be equipped with a fire alarm signal system with a sufficient number of signals clearly audible to all occupants thereof. The industrial board may make rules and regulations prescribing the number and location of such signals. Such system shall be installed by the owner or lessee of the building and shall permit the sounding of all the alarms within the building whenever the alarm is sounded in any portion thereof. Such system shall be maintained in good working order. No person shall tamper with, or render ineffective any portion of said system except to repair the same. It shall be the duty of whoever discovers a fire to cause an alarm to be sounded immediately.

2. In every factory building over two stories in height in which more than twenty-five persons are employed above the ground floor, a fire drill which will conduct all the occupants of such building to a place of safety and in which all the occupants of

---

1 Should read: "added."
2 Section materially amended.

such building shall participate simultaneously shall be conducted at least once a month.

In the city of New York the fire commissioner of such city, and in all other parts of the state, the state fire marshal shall cause to be organized and shall supervise and regulate such fire drills, and shall make rules, regulations and special orders necessary or suitable to each situation and in the case of buildings containing more than one tenant, necessary or suitable to the adequate co-operation of all the tenants of such building in a fire drill of all the occupants thereof. Such rules, regulations and orders may prescribe upon whom shall rest the duty of carrying out the same. Such special orders may require posting of the same or an abstract thereof. A demonstration of such fire drill shall be given upon the request of an authorized representative of the fire department of the city, village or town in which the factory is located, and, except in the city of New York, upon the request of the state fire marshal or any of his deputies or assistants.

3. In the city of New York the fire commissioner of such city, and elsewhere, the state fire marshal is charged with the duty of enforcing this section.

In effect
Oct. 1, 1913.   § 2. This act shall take effect October first, nineteen hundred and thirteen.

Chap. 204.

AN ACT to amend the insurance law, in relation to inspecting water supply and apparatus for fire fighting purposes.

Became a law April 4, 1913, with the approval of the Governor. Passed, three-fifths being present.

The People of the State of New York, represented in Senate and Assembly, do enact as follows:

L. 1909, ch.
33, § 351,
as added
by L. 1911,
ch. 451, and
amended
by L. 1912,
ch. 453,
amended.   Section 1. Section three hundred and fifty-one of chapter thirty-three of the laws of nineteen hundred and nine, entitled "An act in relation to insurance corporations, constituting chapter twenty-eight of the consolidated laws," as added by chapter four hundred and fifty-one of the laws of nineteen hundred and eleven and amended by chapter four hundred and fifty-three of the laws of nineteen hundred and twelve, is hereby amended to read as follows:

§ 351. **Duties of the state fire marshal.**[1] It shall be the duty of the state fire marshal to enforce all laws and ordinances of the state, and the regulations made hereunder, except in cities having over one million inhabitants, as follows:

1. The prevention of fires;

2. The storage, sale or use of combustibles and explosives;

3. The installation and maintenance of automatic or other fire-alarm systems and fire extinguishing equipment;

4. The inspection of steam boilers;

5. The construction, maintenance and regulation of fire escapes;

6. The means and adequacy of exit, in case of fire, from factories, asylums, hospitals, churches, schools, halls, theatres, amphitheatres and all other places in which numbers of persons work, live, or congregate from time to time for any purpose and the institution and supervision of fire drills in such premises;

7. The suppression of arson and investigations of the cause, origin and circumstances of fires and explosions;

8.[2] The adequacy and sufficiency of water supply and fire apparatus and their inspection for fire fighting purposes.

§ 2. This act shall take effect immediately.

Chap. 205.

AN ACT to amend the insurance law, in relation to the contents of advertisements.

Became a law April 4, 1913, with the approval of the Governor. Passed, three-fifths being present.

The People of the State of New York, represented in Senate and Assembly, do enact as follows:

Section 1. Section forty-eight of chapter thirty-three of the laws of nineteen hundred and nine, entitled "An act in relation to insurance corporations, constituting chapter twenty-eight of the consolidated laws," is hereby amended to read as follows:[3]

§ 48. **Contents of advertisements.** Every advertisement or public announcement, and every sign, circular or card issued by

---

[1] Section heading new.
[2] Subd. 8 new.
[3] Section materially amended.

any insurance corporation or association incorporated by
or existing under the laws of this state or of any other state of
the United States and doing business in this state, purporting
to make known its financial standing, shall exhibit the amount of
the capital actually paid in in cash, the assets owned, the liabilities, including therein the premium and loss reserves required
by law, and the amount of net surplus of assets over all its liabilities actually available for the payment of its losses and claims, and
held for the protection of its policyholders, and shall correspond
with the verified statement made by it to the insurance department
next preceding the making or issuing of the same. Every advertisement or public announcement, and every sign, circular or
card issued by any insurance corporation or association incorporated by or existing under the government or laws of a country
outside of the United States and doing business in this state, purporting to make known its financial standing, shall exhibit as
capital and as assets only the capital and assets held by its United
States branch, the liabilities, including therein the premium and
loss reserves required by law, and the amount of net surplus of
assets over all its liabilities actually available for the payment of
its losses and claims and held for the protection of its policyholders
in the United States, and shall correspond with the verified statement made by it to the insurance department next preceding the
making or issuing of the same. For every violation of this and
the preceding section by any such corporation, it shall forfeit for
the first offense to the people of the state the sum of five hundred
dollars, and for every subsequent offense the sum of one thousand
dollars, which sums, when recovered, shall be paid into the treasury of the state. This section shall not apply to any life insurance
corporation nor to any domestic or foreign insurance corporation
or association engaged solely in the business of marine or *trans-
poration insurance or in such business in connection with the
business of automobile insurance.

§ 2. This act shall take effect immediately.

---

* So in original.

Chap. 206.

AN ACT to amend the military law, in relation to armory
employees.

Became a law April 4, 1913, with the approval of the Governor. Passed,
three-fifths being present.

*The People of the State of New York, represented in Senate
and Assembly, do enact as follows:*

Section 1. Section one hundred and eighty-seven of chapter
forty-one of the laws of nineteen hundred and nine, entitled "An
act in relation to the militia, constituting chapter thirty-six of
the consolidated laws," as amended by chapter one hundred and
two of the laws of nineteen hundred and eleven, is hereby further
amended to read as follows:[1]

§ 187. *Armories, janitors and engineers. There shall be allowed for each armory, and for the headquarters of the division,
the naval militia and of each brigade, one armorer. If an armory
be heated by steam there shall be allowed one chief engineer and
also one assistant engineer if the commanding officer of the
brigade within whose command such armory is located, and the
officer in charge of such armory shall certify to the disbursing
officer of the county in which such armory is located that the services of an assistant engineer are necessary; in an armory occupied
by a regiment and lighted by electricity produced by machinery
operated by the power of steam, if such steam is generated and
machinery operated within such armory, there shall be allowed on
like certificate an additional assistant engineer; there shall also
be allowed for an armory occupied by a regiment, by a battalion or
squadron not part of a regiment, by a battery, by a troop, by a
company of signal corps, by a field hospital, by an ambulance
company or by two or more separate batteries or companies, one
janitor; and the armorer, the engineer and the janitor thus authorized shall be appointed by the officer having control and charge
of the armory. Where a field hospital, an ambulance company, a
company of signal corps, troop, battery, separate division, or the
headquarters of the division, or a brigade, or of a regiment of field
artillery,[2] or of a battalion not part of a regiment, occupies a portion of an armory or state arsenal, each shall be entitled to an

Marginal notes: L. 1909, ch. 41, § 187, as amended by L. 1911, ch. 102, amended.

---

* So in orginal. [Should read: "armorers."]
[1] Section 187 is again amended by L. 1913, ch. 558, post. The amendment
effected here is not incorporated in § 187 as amended by said ch. 558.
[2] Words "or of a regiment of field artillery," new.

armorer, and such field hospital, ambulance company, company of signal corps, troop, battery, or separate division shall also be entitled to a janitor, who shall be appointed by its respective commanding officer, and such headquarters and quarters shall be considered an independent armory, upon the approval and certificate of the major-general or commanding officer of the brigade within whose command such armory is located. All persons appointed or employed pursuant to this or the succeeding section shall perform such duties as shall from time to time be prescribed by the officer appointing or employing them.

§ 2. This act shall take effect immediately.

Chap. 207.

AN ACT to amend the military law, in relation to allowances for brigade headquarters in certain counties.

Became a law April 4, 1913, with the approval of the Governor. Passed, three-fifths being present.

The People of the State of New York, represented in Senate and Assembly, do enact as follows:

L. 1909, ch. 41, § 218, as amended by L. 1911, ch. 101, and L. 1912, ch. 56, amended.

Section 1. Section two hundred and eighteen of chapter forty-one of the laws of nineteen hundred and nine, entitled "An act in relation to the militia, constituting chapter thirty-six of the consolidated laws," as amended by chapter one hundred and one of the laws of nineteen hundred and eleven and chapter fifty-six of the laws of nineteen hundred and twelve, is hereby amended to read as follows:

§ 218. **Allowances for headquarters.** On the certificate of the adjutant-general of the state, the comptroller shall, annually, draw his warrant upon the treasurer for the following sums, namely: twelve hundred dollars for the headquarters of the naval militia, for the chief of coast artillery, and for each brigade headquarters; fifteen hundred dollars for each regimental headquarters; five hundred dollars for each battalion and squadron headquarters, one hundred dollars additional to naval battalions for each signal division and two hundred and fifty dollars for each engineer division contained therein. For brigade headquarters in brigades covering a territory of more than ten counties, and in counties containing over two million inhabitants,[1] five hundred dollars, and in brigades

---

[1] Words "and in counties containing over two million inhabitants," new.

whose organizations are located in fifteen or more counties, eight hundred dollars additional shall be allowed. For the headquarters of each regiment whose organizations are located in more than four counties, an additional one hundred dollars shall be allowed for each county in excess of four, in which a company organization of such regiment is stationed. For the headquarters of each separate battalion whose organizations are located in more than two counties, an additional one hundred dollars shall be allowed for each county in excess of two, in which a company organization of such battalion is stationed. For the corps of engineers fifteen hundred dollars, for each artillery district containing eight or more companies fifteen hundred dollars, for each artillery district containing less than eight and more than four companies one thousand dollars, for each artillery district containing four companies five hundred dollars, the funds thus allowed shall only be expended by the respective commanding officers, the colonel of the corps of engineers and the ranking officer commanding the artillery district to which the fund is allowed on the approval of the adjutant-general of the state. Squadrons not part of a regiment if organized into a regiment shall thereby not be deprived of the allowances granted in this section.

§ 2. This act shall take effect immediately.

Chap. 208.

AN ACT to amend the executive law, in relation to the powers and duties of notary public. .

Became a law April 4, 1913, with the approval of the Governor. Passed, three-fifths being present.

The People of the State of New York, represented in Senate and Assembly, do enact as follows:

Section 1. Subdivision two of section one hundred and five of chapter twenty-three of the laws of nineteen hundred and nine, entitled "An act in relation to executive officers, constituting chapter eighteen of the consolidated laws," as amended by chapter six hundred and sixty-eight of the laws of nineteen hundred and eleven, is hereby amended to read as follows:

2. In the county in and for which he shall have been appointed and elsewhere, as provided in section one hundred and two of

L. 1909, ch. 23, § 105, subd. 2, as amended by L. 1911, ch. 668, amended.

Powers and duties within county.

this chapter, to administer oaths and affirmations, to take affidavits and certify the acknowledgment and proof of deeds and
other written instruments to be read in evidence or recorded in
this state, in all cases in which commissioners of deeds may now
take and certify the same, and under the same rules, regulations
and requirements prescribed to said last-mentioned officers, not
inconsistent with any of the provisions of this chapter; except
that a county clerk's certificate authenticating the official character and the signature of such notary shall not be necessary
to entitle any deed or other written instrument so proved and
acknowledged, to be read in evidence or recorded in a county in
which the autograph signature and certificate of appointment and
qualification of such notary shall have been filed, pursuant to
section one hundred and two of this chapter. [1]A notary public
also has authority anywhere within the state to administer oaths
and affirmations, to take affidavits and certify the acknowledgment and proof of deeds and other written instruments to be read
in evidence or recorded in this state, in all cases in which commissioners of deeds may now take and certify the same within the
state, and under the same rules, regulations and requirements
prescribed to said last-mentioned officers, not inconsistent with
any of the provisions of this chapter, provided that said deeds
or other written instruments so proved or acknowledged are to
be read in evidence or recorded only in the county for which the
notary public shall have been appointed, or in which the autograph signature and certificate of appointment and qualification
of such notary shall have been filed pursuant to section one hundred and two of this chapter. The acts authorized by this subdivision may be performed by such notary without official seal.
For any misconduct in the performance of any such powers, a
notary public shall be liable to the parties injured for all damages sustained by him. A notary public shall not, directly or
indirectly, demand or receive for the protest for the nonpayment
of any note, or for the nonacceptance or nonpayment of any bill
of exchange, check or draft, and giving the requisite notices and
certificates of such protest, including his notarial seal, if affixed
thereto, any greater fee or reward than seventy-five cents for such
protest, and ten cents for each notice. not exceeding five, on any
bill or note. He shall, except as otherwise provided, when requested, affix his seal to such protest free of expense. A notary

Powers and duties throughout state.

Seal.

Liability for misconduct.

Protest fees.

Numbers to be given to

----

[1] Following sentence new.

public **whose** oath of office is filed in the office of the clerk in the notaries in New York county of New York, must affix to each instrument acknowledged, county. in addition to his signature, his official number, as given to him by the clerk of the county when his oath of office is filed; and if the instrument is to be recorded in the office of the register of the county of New York, and the notary has been given a number by such register, he shall affix that number; the numbers to be written or stamped upon the instrument in the following form: New York County, No. ......; and New York Register No. ...... But the validity of an instrument or of an acknowledgment shall not be affected by the failure of a notary to so affix his official number.

§ 2. This act shall take effect immediately.

Chap. 209.

AN ACT to amend the real property law, in relation to the certificates of authentication of acknowledgments and proofs of deeds, mortgages or other instruments, relating to real property.

Became a law April 4, 1913, with the approval of the Governor. Passed, three-fifths being present.

The People of the State of New York, represented in Senate and Assembly, do enact as follows:

Section 1. Section three hundred and eleven of article nine of L. 1909, ch. chapter fifty-two of the laws of nineteen hundred and nine, 52, § 311 entitled "An act relating to real property, constituting chapter amended. fifty of the consolidated laws," is hereby amended to read as follows:

§ 311. **When other authentication necessary.** In the following cases a certificate of acknowledgment or proof is not entitled to be read in evidence or recorded unless authenticated by certificates[1] by the following officers, respectively:

1. Where the original certificate of acknowledgment or proof is made by a commissioner appointed by the governor, by the secretary of-state.

2. Where made by a judge of a court of record in Canada, by the clerk of the court.

3.[2] Where made by the officer of a state of the United States, or of any province or territory of the Dominion of

---
[1] Words "by certificates" new.
[2] Subd. 3 materially amended.

Canada, authorized by the laws thereof to take the acknowledgment or proof of deeds to be recorded therein, by the secretary of state of the state, the provincial secretary, deputy provincial secretary or assistant provincial secretary of the province, or commissioner of the territory of the Dominion of Canada, or by the clerk, register, recorder or prothonotary of a county, city or parish in which the certificate purports to be made, or by the clerk of any court in or of such state or dominion, county, city or parish having by law a seal. The word county shall be deemed to apply to and include the District of Columbia for the purpose of this section. All certificates authenticating such acknowledgments or proofs of deeds, mortgages or other instruments relating to real property heretofore made by any of the officers above referred to are confirmed, saving, however, the rights of purchasers in good faith and for a valuable consideration whose conveyance shall have been duly recorded before this act shall take effect; this act shall not affect any action or legal proceeding now pending.

4. All acts of the secretary of state of any state or territory of the United States in authenticating a certificate of acknowledgment or proof of a conveyance of real property within the state, performed before October first, eighteen hundred and ninety-six, are hereby confirmed, provided that the said certificate of authentication is in the form required by the laws of this state.

§ 2. This act shall take effect immediately.

Chap. 210.

AN ACT to amend the code of civil procedure, in relation to the removal of causes.

Became a law April 4, 1913, with the approval of the Governor. Passed, three-fifths being present.

The People of the State of New York, represented in Senate and Assembly, do enact as follows:

§ 319a.
added.

Section 1. After section three hundred and nineteen of the code of civil procedure there shall be inserted a new section, to be numbered three hundred and nineteen-a, to read as follows:

§ 319-a. **Removal of cause in certain cases from city court to supreme court.** The supreme court, at a term held in the first judicial district, must, on the motion of any party, by an order made at any time before the entry of judgment, remove to itself an action brought in the city court of the city of New York in the following cases:

1. An action to foreclose or enforce a lien, for a sum exceeding two thousand dollars, exclusive of interest, upon one or more chattels.

2. An action wherein the complaint demands judgment for a sum of money only, exceeding two thousand dollars, exclusive of interest and costs as taxed; except where the action is brought upon a bond or undertaking given in an action or special proceeding in the same court, or before a justice thereof; or to recover damages for a breach of promise of marriage; or where it is a marine cause, as that expression is defined in section three hundred and seventeen of this code.

3. An action to recover one or more chattels the aggregate value of which exceeds two thousand dollars.

Upon the entry of the order of removal in the office of the clerk of the county of New York, the city court shall proceed no further therein, and the clerk of the city court must forthwith deliver to the clerk of the county of New York all papers filed therein, and certified copies of all minutes and entries relating thereto, which must be filed, entered or recorded, as the case requires, in the office of the clerk of the county of New York, and thereupon the supreme court shall proceed in said action as though said action had been commenced in said supreme court, and all proceedings had in the city court prior to the entry of said order of removal shall be of like force and effect as though had in the supreme court.

§ 2. This act shall take effect immediately.

Chap. 211.

AN ACT to amend the code of civil procedure, in relation to the vacation of judgments and the removal of causes.

Became a law April 4, 1913, with the approval of the Governor. Passed, three-fifths being present.

The People of the State of New York, represented in Senate and Assembly, do enact as follows:

Section 1. After section three hundred and nineteen-a of the code of civil procedure, there shall be inserted a new section, to be numbered three hundred and nineteen-b, to read as follows:

§ 319-b. **Vacation of judgment in certain cases.** Whenever judgment has been or shall be entered in the city court of the city of New York in any one or more of the following cases, to-wit:

1. An action to foreclose or enforce a lien, for a sum exceeding two thousand dollars, exclusive of interest, upon one or more chattels;

2. An action wherein the complaint demands judgment for a sum of money only, and the judgment is in favor of the plaintiff, and exceeds two thousand dollars, exclusive of interest and costs as taxed; except where the action is brought upon a bond or undertaking given in an action or special proceeding in the same court or before a justice thereof; or to recover damages for a breach of promise of marriage; or where it is a marine cause, as that expression is defined in section three hundred and seventeen of this code.

3. An action to recover one or more chattels, and the judgment is in favor of the plaintiff for a chattel or chattels, the aggregate value of which exceeds two thousand dollars.

Any party to such action, at any time after the entry of such judgment, may apply to the said city court to have such judgment vacated, and thereupon the said city court may in its discretion vacate such judgment. Any case, wherein a judgment has been so vacated, may be removed to the supreme court in the first judicial district, as provided in section three hundred and nineteen-a.

§ 2. This act shall take effect immediately.

Chap. 212.

AN ACT to amend the code of criminal procedure, relative to the appointment of stenographers to take evidence before grand juries and at coroners' inquests and examinations and trials of criminal cases and their compensation and payment.

Became a law April 4, 1913, with the approval of the Governor. Passed, three-fifths being present.

The People of the State of New York, represented in Senate and Assembly, do enact as follows:

§ 952p amended.

Section 1. Section nine hundred and fifty-two-p of the code of criminal procedure is hereby amended to read as follows:

§ 952-p. **Appointment of stenographers.** It shall be lawful

for the district attorney of any county of this state, to appoint
a stenographer to take the testimony given before the grand juries
in said county. In the counties of Erie and Kings,[1] it shall be
lawful for the district attorney of each of such counties to appoint
two stenographers, each of whom shall have authority to take and
transcribe the testimony given before the grand juries in the said
counties of Erie and Kings[1] respectively, and such appointments
shall be in writing, under the hand and seal of such district attorney, and shall be filed in the county clerk's office of said counties
of Erie and Kings[1] respectively. In the county of New York, it
shall be lawful for the district attorney of such county to appoint
three stenographers, each of whom shall have authority to take and
transcribe the testimony given before the grand juries in said
county of New York, and such appointments shall be in writing,
under the hand and seal of such district attorney, and shall be filed
in the county clerk's office of said county of New York. In the
county of Monroe, it shall be lawful for the district attorney of
such county to appoint three stenographers, to be known as the
first, second and third stenographer, each of whom shall have
authority to take and transcribe the testimony given before the
grand juries in said county of Monroe, and each of whom shall be
considered as an assistant to the district attorney and under his
direction and control. Every stenographer so appointed whenever
directed by the district attorney, shall have authority to attend
upon and take and transcribe the testimony given at coroner's
inquests and the examination and trial of criminal cases, which
said testimony so taken and transcribed shall be for the exclusive
use and benefit of the district attorney, unless otherwise ordered
by the court, or otherwise agreed upon by the district attorney.
The appointment of a stenographer by said district attorney shall
be deemed a revocation of any prior appointment of a stenographer.

§ 2. Section nine hundred and fifty-two-v of the code of criminal
§ 952v amended.
procedure is hereby amended to read as follows:

§ 952-v. **Compensation and payment of stenographers.** Each
stenographer appointed as aforesaid shall receive such compensation for services rendered while engaged in taking testimony before a grand jury, as shall be determined by the board of supervisors of the county in which he is appointed, excepting that in
the county of New York, such compensation shall be fixed by the

---

[1] Inclusion of Kings county new.

board of estimate and apportionment of the city of New York, and such compensation shall not be less than five nor more than ten dollars per day; and in addition thereto such stenographer shall be entitled to and shall be allowed for a copy of testimony furnished to the district attorney the same rate per folio as is now allowed to the stenographers of the county court or court of common pleas, in their respective counties, and such stenographer[2] shall receive the same compensation for all copies of the evidence in excess of three copies, furnished by him to the district attorney. Such compensation shall be a county charge, and shall be paid by the treasurer of such county upon the affidavit of the stenographer and the certificate of the district attorney specifying the number of days of actual service and the number of folios furnished; excepting that in the counties of Erie and Monroe the salaries of said stenographers shall be fixed by the board of supervisors; and excepting that in the counties of Queens and Oneida said stenographers shall receive a salary of one thousand dollars per annum, and in the county of Orange, twelve hundred dollars per annum; [3]and excepting that in the county of Kings the salaries of said stenographers shall be fixed by the board of estimate and apportionment of the city of New York. Such salaries shall be a county charge and shall be paid monthly, and in Erie county semi-monthly, by the treasurer of said county in the same manner as the salaries of other county officers are paid.

In effect Sept. 1, 1913.

§ 3. This act shall take effect September first, nineteen hundred and thirteen.

Chap. 213.

AN ACT to amend the code of criminal procedure, relating to drawing grand juries.

Became a law April 4, 1913, with the approval of the Governor. Passed, three-fifths being present.

The People of the State of New York, represented in Senate and Assembly, do enact as follows:

§ 226 amended.

Section 1. Section two hundred and twenty-six of the code of criminal procedure is hereby amended to read as follows:

---

[2] Word "stenographer" substituted for word "clerk."
[3] Remainder of sentence new.

§ 226. **Idem.** A grand jury may also be drawn:

1. For every other county court, when specially ordered by the court or by the board of supervisors.

2. For the supreme court in the city and county of New York, upon the order of a justice of the supreme court, elected in the first judicial district.

3. For the supreme court, of the county of Kings, upon the order of a justice of the supreme court, elected in the second judicial district.

4. For an extraordinary term of the supreme court or a term thereof for which a trial jury is not required to be drawn, upon the order of the justice named to hold or preside at the same.

5. For any term of the court of general sessions of the city and county of New York upon the order of a judge of the court of general sessions, whenever the public interest requires such additional grand jury.

6.[1] For any term of the county court of the county of Kings, upon the order of a judge thereof whenever the public interest requires such additional grand jury.

§ 2. This act shall take effect immediately.

Chap. 214.

AN ACT to amend the insurance law, in relation to firearms.

Became a law April 4, 1913, with the approval of the Governor. Passed, three-fifths being present.

The People of the State of New York, represented in Senate and Assembly, do enact as follows:

Section 1. Section three hundred and sixty-seven of chapter thirty-three of the laws of nineteen hundred and nine, entitled "An act in relation to insurance corporations, constituting chapter twenty-eight of the consolidated laws," as added by chapter four hundred and fifty-one of the laws of nineteen hundred and eleven and amended by chapter four hundred and fifty-three of the laws of nineteen hundred and twelve, is hereby amended to read as follows:

§ 367. **Firearms.** No person shall discharge any firearms

L. 1909. ch. 33, § 367, as added by L. 1911, ch. 451, and amended by L. 1912, ch. 453, amended.

---

[1] Subd. 6 new.

within five hundred feet of any magazine or factory, [1]except that the provisions of this section shall not apply to the testing of firearms in or upon the premises of any manufacturing plant engaged in the manufacture of firearms. The method of testing all firearms in any manufacturing plant engaged in the business of manufacturing firearms shall be subject to the approval of the state fire marshal.

§ 2. This act shall take effect immediately.

Chap. 215.

AN ACT to amend the insurance law, in relation to the capital of title, credit guaranty and securities guaranty corporations.

Became a law April 4, 1913, with the approval of the Governor. Passed, three-fifths being present.

The People of the State of New York, represented in Senate and Assembly, do enact as follows:

L. 1949, ch. 33, § 170, as amended by L. 1909, ch. 302, and L. 1911, ch. 525, amended.

Section 1. Section one hundred and seventy of chapter thirty-three of the laws of nineteen hundred and nine, entitled "An act in relation to insurance corporations, constituting chapter twenty-eight of the consolidated laws," as amended by chapter three hundred and two of the laws of nineteen hundred and nine and chapter five hundred and twenty-five of the laws of nineteen hundred and eleven,[1a] is hereby amended to read as follows:

§ 170. **Incorporation.**   Five or more persons may form a corporation for one of the following purposes:

1. To examine titles to real property and chattels real, to procure and furnish information in relation thereto, make and guarantee the correctness of searches for all instruments, liens or charges affecting the same, guarantee or insure the payment of bonds and mortgages, or notes of individuals or partnerships secured by mortgages upon real property situated in this or any other state, and bonds, notes, debentures and other evidences of indebtedness of solvent corporations secured by deed of trust or mortgage upon real property situated in this or any other state,[2]

---

[1] Remainder of section new.
[1a] Section 170 was amended by L. 1913, ch. 81, ante. The amendments effected by said ch. 81 are incorporated in said section as here amended.
[2] Words " or notes of individuals . . . secured by deed of trust or mortgage upon real property situated in this or any other state," new.

invest in, purchase and sell, with such guarantee or with guarantee only against loss by reason of defective title or incumbrances, [3]bonds and mortgages,[4] and notes of individuals or partnerships secured by mortgages upon improved and unincumbered real property situated in this or any other state worth fifty per centum more than the amount loaned thereon, and bonds, notes, debentures and other evidences of indebtedness of solvent corporations secured by deed of trust or mortgages upon improved and unincumbered real property situated in this state or outside of this state worth fifty per centum more than the amount loaned thereon,[5] and guarantee and insure the owners of real property and chattels real and others interested therein against the loss by reason of defective titles thereto and other incumbrances thereon, which shall be known as a title guaranty[6] corporation; or

1-a. To guarantee the validity and legality of bonds or other evidences of indebtedness issued by any state or by any city, county, town, village, school district, municipality or other civil division of any state, or by any private or public corporation; to act as registrar or transfer agent, but not fiscal of any such corporation, and to transfer and countersign its certificates of stocks, bonds or other evidences of indebtedness. Such corporation shall be known as a securities guaranty corporation and shall be governed by and subject to the provisions of law applicable to a title guaranty corporation organized under this article; or

2. To guarantee and indemnify merchants, traders and those engaged in business and giving credit from loss and damage by reason of giving and extending credit to their customers, and those dealing with them, which shall be known as a credit guaranty corporation; by making, acknowledging and filing a certificate stating:

1. The name of the proposed corporation.

2. The kind of corporation to be formed and its purposes.

3. The amount and description of the capital stock.

4. The location of its office.

5. The duration of the corporation, not exceeding fifty years.

No credit guaranty corporation or securities guaranty corpora-

---

[3] Word "such" omitted.

[4] Words "as are lawful investments for insurance companies under this act," omitted.

[5] Words "and notes of individuals . . . situated in this state or outside of this state worth fifty per centum more than the amount loaned thereon." new.

[6] Formerly read: "guarantee."

tion shall be formed for the transaction of business in this state,
with a smaller capital than two hundred and fifty thousand dollars. No title guaranty corporation shall be formed with a
smaller capital than one hundred and fifty thousand dollars,
which shall be divided into shares of one hundred dollars each.
Such certificate shall be filed in the office of the superintendent
of insurance, who shall thereupon issue a license to the persons
making such certificate, empowering them as commissioners to
open books of subscription to the capital stock of the corporation
at such times and places as they may determine.

[7]Any corporation heretofore organized under subdivision one
of this section shall have all the powers conferred by such subdivision as amended hereby.

§ 2. This act shall take effect immediately.

Chap. 216.

AN ACT to amend the education law, in relation to the manner
of payment of school taxes by telephone, telegraph, electric
light and gas companies.

Became a law April 4, 1913, with the approval of the Governor. Passed,
three-fifths being present.

*The People of the State of New York, represented in Senate
and Assembly, do enact as follows:*

L. 1909,
ch. 21,
§§ 427-431,
as generally
amended by
L. 1910,
ch. 140,
amended.

Section 1. Sections four hundred and twenty-seven, four hundred and twenty-eight, four hundred and twenty-nine, four hundred and thirty and four hundred and thirty-one of chapter
twenty-one of the laws of nineteen hundred and nine, entitled "An
act relating to education, constituting chapter sixteen of the consolidated laws," as amended by chapter one hundred and forty
of the laws of nineteen hundred and ten, are hereby amended
to read respectively as follows:

§ 427. **Notice to railroad companies and certain other corporations**[1] **of assessment and tax.** 1. It shall be the duty of the
school collector in each school district in this state, within five
days after the receipt by such collector of any and every tax or
assessment roll of his district, to prepare and deliver to the county

---

[7] Remainder of section new.
[1] Words " and certain other corporations," new.

treasurer of the county in which such district, or the greater part thereof, is situated, a statement showing the name of each railroad, telegraph, telephone, electric light or gas[2] company, including a company engaged in the business of supplying natural gas,[3] appearing in said roll, the assessment against each of said companies for real and personal property respectively, and the tax against each of said companies.

2. It shall thereupon be the duty of such county treasurer, immediately after the receipt by him of such statement from such school collector, to notify the ticket agent or manager[4] of any such railroad, telegraph, telephone, electric light or gas[2] company, including a company engaged in the business of supplying natural gas[3] assessed for taxes at the station or office[5] nearest to the office of such county treasurer or to notify the company at its principal office within this state[6] personally or by mail, of the fact that such statement has been filed with him by such collector, at the same time specifying the amount of tax to be paid by such [7]company.

§ 2. Section four hundred and twenty-eight of such chapter is § 428 amended. hereby amended to read as follows:

§ 428. Payment of tax by railroad and certain other corporations[8] to county treasurer. Any railroad company heretofore organized, or which may hereafter be organized, under the laws of this state and any telegraph, telephone, electric light or gas company including a company engaged in the business of supplying natural gas[9] may within thirty days after the receipt of such statement by such county treasurer, pay the amount of tax so levied or assessed against it in such a district and in such statement mentioned and contained with one per centum fees thereon, to such county treasurer, who is hereby authorized and directed to receive such amount and to give proper receipt therefor.

§ 3. Section four hundred and twenty-nine of such chapter is § 429 amended. hereby amended to read as follows:

---

[2] Words " telegraph, telephone, electric light or gas," new.
[3] Words " including a company engaged in the business of supplying natural gas," new.
[4] Words " or manager " new.
[5] Words " or office " new.
[6] Words " or to notify the company at its principal office within this state," new.
[7] Word " railroad " omitted.
[8] Words " and certain other corporations," substituted for word " company."
[9] Words " and any telegraph . . . supplying natural gas," new

§ 429. **Duty of collector after failure of railroad and certain other corporations[8] to pay within thirty days.** In case any railroad company and any telegraph, telephone, electric light or gas company including a company engaged in the business of supplying natural gas[9] shall fail to pay such tax within said thirty days, it shall be the duty of such county treasurer to notify the collector of the school district in which such delinquent railroad company is assessed, of its failure to pay said tax, and upon receipt of such notice it shall be the duty of such collector to collect such unpaid tax in the manner now provided by law together with five per centum fees thereon; but no school collector shall collect by distress and sale any tax levied or assessed in his district upon the property of any such[10] company until the receipt by him of such notice from the county treasurer.

§ 430
amended.

§ 4. Section four hundred and thirty of such chapter is hereby amended to read as follows:

§ 430. **Payment of tax by county treasurer to collector.** The several amounts of tax received by any county treasurer in this state, under the provisions of the last three sections, of and from such[10] companies, shall be by such county treasurer placed to the credit of the school district for or on account of which the same was levied or assessed, and on demand paid over to the school collector thereof, and the one per centum fees received therewith shall be placed to the credit of, and on demand paid to, the school collector of such school district.

§ 431
amended.

§ 5. Section four hundred and thirty-one of such chapter is hereby amended to read as follows:

§ 431. **Such companies[11] may pay collector.** Nothing in the last four sections contained shall be construed to hinder, prevent or prohibit any railroad company or telegraph, telephone, electric light or gas company including a company engaged in the business of supplying natural gas[12] from paying its school tax to the school collector direct, as provided by law.

§ 6. This act shall take effect immediately.

---

[8] Words " and certain other corporations," substituted for word " company."
[9] Words " and any telegraph . . . supplying natural gas," new.
[10] Word " such " substituted for word " railroad."
[11] Words " Such companies " substituted for words " Railroad company."
[12] Words " or telegraph . . . supplying natural gas," new.

Chap. 217.

AN ACT to provide for the acquisition and preservation of the historic house and grounds formerly owned and occupied by General Nicholas Herkimer, in the town of Danube, in the county of Herkimer, and making an appropriation therefor.

Became a law April 5, 1913, with the approval of the Governor. Passed, three-fifths being present.

The People of the State of New York, represented in Senate and Assembly, do enact as follows:

Section 1. The commissioners of the land office may, upon the recommendation of the German American Alliance and a committee of the Daughters of the American Revolution of New York State, to be appointed by the state regents, by agreement with the owner or owners, upon such price and terms as they may deem just, not exceeding the amount hereinafter appropriated, acquire title, on behalf and in the name of the people of the state, to the farm lands and buildings owned and occupied as a home by General Nicholas Herkimer in his lifetime, now known as the Herkimer farm, situated in the town of Danube and county of Herkimer. Acquisition of Herkimer farm.

§ 2. After title to such premises shall have been acquired, as aforesaid, said German American Alliance and the committee of the Daughters of the American Revolution of New York State shall have control and jurisdiction thereof for the purpose of preserving the same for the benefit of the people of the state of New York as an historic land mark and for educational and patriotic purposes. Control and jurisdiction.

§ 3. Upon the requisition of such commissioners of the land office, and upon a voucher or vouchers certified by such commissioners, or by such officer or officers thereof as they may designate for the purpose, in form to be approved by the comptroller, the comptroller shall· pay the sum or sums that may be necessary to pay for the lands authorized to be acquired by the authority of this act, and to build, construct and repair upon the said premises such buildings as may be necessary to properly and satisfactorily carry out the intent and purposes of this act. Payments for lands and construction and repair of buildings, how made.

§ 4. The sum of fifteen thousand dollars ($15,000), or so much thereof as may be necessary, payable out of money in the treasury not otherwise appropriated, is hereby appropriated, subject to the Appropriation.

audit of the comptroller, to carry out the provisions of this act, and the same shall be payable by the treasurer on the warrant of the comptroller on the requisition of said commissioners of the land office.

§ 5. This act shall take effect immediately.

Chap. 218.

AN ACT to permit the common council of the city of Oneonta to vote extra compensation to the chamberlain, commissioner of charities and assessors, of such city for the year nineteen hundred and thirteen.

Became a law April 5, 1913, with the approval of the Governor. Passed, three-fifths being present.

Accepted by the City.

The People of the State of New York, represented in Senate and Assembly, do enact as follows:

Section 1. The common council of the city of Oneonta may in their discretion vote to the chamberlain, commissioner of charities, and assessors of said city an extra compensation for the year nineteen hundred and thirteen. The extra compensation, for the assessors shall not exceed two hundred and fifty dollars each, per annum, the commissioner of charities three hundred dollars, per annum, and the city chamberlain five hundred dollars, per annum.

§ 2. This act shall take effect immediately.

Chap. 219.

AN ACT authorizing the town board of the town of Mooers, Clinton county, to convey lands for cemetery purposes.

Became a law April 5, 1913, with the approval of the Governor. Passed, three-fifths being present.

The People of the State of New York, represented in Senate and Assembly, do enact as follows:

Section 1. The town board of the town of Mooers, Clinton county, is hereby authorized and empowered to grant, lease, sell, assign, transfer, convey and set over to any corporate body in said town engaged in the care and maintenance of a cemetery or cemeteries, any land or lands now owned by said town and devoted to cemetery purposes, and any land or lands now owned by said town which may hereafter be devoted to cemetery purposes.

§ 2. This act shall take effect immediately.

Chap. 220.

AN ACT to provide for making surveys for improving and extending the canal system of the state, and making an appropriation therefor.

Became a law April 5, 1913, with the approval of the Governor. Passed, three-fifths being present.

The People of the State of New York, represented in Senate and Assembly, do enact as follows:

. Section 1. The state engineer and surveyor shall cause surveys to be made for the improvement of the canal system of the state by the extension of the Black river canal, the reconstruction of the Chemung canal, the conversion of the Glens Falls feeder into a canal, the construction of a canal between Flushing river and Jamaica bay and the construction of a canal from Newtown creek, sometimes known as Nassau river, to connect with the proposed canal between Flushing bay and Jamaica bay. Such officer shall make a report to the legislature of nineteen hundred and fourteen, embodying the result of his investigations, together with estimates of the cost for which such work may be done. *State engineer directed to cause surveys to be made.* *Report.*

§ 2. The sum of thirty-five thousand dollars ($35,000), or so much thereof as may be necessary, is hereby appropriated for the purposes of this act, out of any money in the treasury, not otherwise appropriated, payable by the treasurer on the warrant of the comptroller, on the order of the state engineer and surveyor. *Appropriation.*

§ 3. This act shall take effect immediately.

13

Chap. 221.

AN ACT to amend the education law, relative to the powers of voters of school districts, and extending the use of school buildings.[1]

Became a law April 5, 1913, with the approval of the Governor. Passed, three-fifths being present.

The People of the State of New York, represented in Senate and Assembly, do enact as follows:

L. 1909, ch. 21, § 206, subds. 7, 8, as generally amended by L. 1910, ch. 140, amended.

Section 1. Subdivisions seven and eight of section two hundred and six of chapter twenty-one of the laws of nineteen hundred and nine, entitled "An act relating to education, constituting chapter sixteen of the consolidated laws," as amended by chapter one hundred and forty of the laws of nineteen hundred and ten, is hereby amended to read as follows:

Designation of sites for school-houses and of grounds for other purposes in school districts.

7. To designate a site for a schoolhouse, or for grounds to be used for playgrounds, or for agricultural, athletic center and social center purposes, or, with the consent of the district superintendent of schools within whose district the school district lies, to designate sites for two or more schoolhouses for the district. Such designation of a site for a schoolhouse, or for such grounds, can be made only at a special meeting of the district, duly called for such purpose by a written resolution in which the proposed site shall be described by metes and bounds, and which resolution must receive the assent of a majority of the qualified voters present and voting, to be ascertained by taking and recording the ayes and noes, or by ballot.

Tax for sites, school-houses and grounds in school districts.

8. To vote a tax upon the taxable property of the district, to purchase, lease and improve such sites or an addition to such sites; and grounds for the purposes specified in the preceding subdivision, to hire or purchase rooms or buildings for school rooms or schoolhouses, or to build schoolhouses; to keep in repair and furnish the same with necessary fuel, furniture and appurtenances, and to purchase such implements, apparatus and supplies as may be necessary to provide instruction in agriculture and other subjects, and for the organization and conduct of athletic, playground and other social center work.

§ 275, subds. 4, 8, 18, as generally

§ 2. Subdivisions four, eight and eighteen of section two hundred and seventy-five of the said chapter, as so amended by chapter

---

[1] The amendments effected by this act are so numerous and extensive that it is impracticable to indicate the changes made.

one hundred and forty of the laws of nineteen hundred and ten, are hereby further amended to read as follows:

amended by L. 1910, ch. 140, amended.

4. To purchase or lease such schoolhouse sites and other grounds to be used for playgrounds, or for agriculture, athletic center and social center purposes, and to purchase or build such schoolhouses, as a district meeting may authorize; to hire temporarily such rooms or buildings as may be necessary for school purposes; and to purchase such implements, supplies and apparatus as may be necessary to provide instruction in agriculture, or to equip and maintain playgrounds, and to conduct athletic and social center activities in the district, when authorized by a vote of a district meeting.

Purchase or lease of sites for schoolhouses, grounds, buildings, etc., in school districts.

8. To contract with and employ as many legally qualified teachers as the schools of the district require; to determine the rate of compensation and the term of the employment of each teacher and to determine the terms of school to be held during each school year, and to employ persons to supervise, organize, conduct and maintain athletic, playground and social center activities when they are authorized by a vote of a district meeting as provided by law. The regular teachers of the school may be employed at an increased compensation or otherwise, and by separate agreement, written or oral, for one or more of such purposes.

Employment of teachers and supervisors of athletic, playground and social center activities in school districts.

18. To expend in the purchase of a dictionary, books, maps, globes or other school apparatus, including implements, apparatus and supplies for instruction in agriculture, or for conducting athletic playgrounds and social center activities, a sum not exceeding twenty-five dollars in any one year, without a vote of the district.

Expenditures for certain purposes in school districts.

§ 3. Subdivisions six and fifteen of section three hundred and ten of said chapter, as so amended by said chapter one hundred and forty of the laws of nineteen hundred and ten, are hereby further amended to read as follows:

§ 310, subds. 6, 15, as generally amended by L. 1910, ch. 140, amended.

6. To purchase sites, or additions thereto, for recreation grounds, for agricultural purposes, and for schoolhouses for the district, when designated by a meeting of the district; and to construct such schoolhouses and additions thereto as may be so designated; to purchase furniture and apparatus for such schoolhouses, and to keep the furniture and apparatus therein in repair; and, when authorized by such meeting, to purchase implements, supplies, and apparatus for agricultural, athletic, playground, and social center purposes.

Purchase of sites, erection of buildings and purchase of furniture, supplies, etc., in union free school districts.

Employ-
ment of
teachers and
supervisors
of athletic,
playground
and social
center ac-
tivities in
union free
school
districts.
15. To contract with and employ such persons as by the provisions of this chapter are qualified teachers, to determine the
number of teachers to be employed in the several departments
of instruction in said school, and at the time of such employment,
to make and deliver to each teacher a written contract as required
by section five hundred and sixty-one of this chapter; and employ
such persons as may be necessary to supervise, organize, conduct
and maintain athletic, playground and social center activities, or
for any one or more of such purposes. The regular teachers of
the school may be employed at an increased compensation or otherwise, and by separate agreement, written or oral, for one or more
of such purposes.

§ 455, as
generally
amended
by L. 1910,
ch. 140,
amended.
§ 4. Section four hundred and fifty-five of said chapter, as so
amended by chapter one hundred and forty of the laws of nineteen
hundred and ten, is hereby further amended to read as follows:

§ 455. Use of schoolhouse and grounds out of school hours.
Schoolhouses and the grounds connected therewith and all property belonging to the district shall be in the custody and under
the control and supervision of the trustees or board of education
of the district. The trustees or board of education may adopt
reasonable regulations for the use of such schoolhouses, grounds
or other property, when not in use for school purposes. Such
regulations shall not conflict with the provisions of this chapter
and shall conform to the purposes and intent of this section and
shall be subject to review on appeal to the commissioner of education as provided by law. The trustees or board of education of
each district may, subject to regulations adopted as above provided, permit the use of the schoolhouse and rooms therein, and
the grounds and other property of the district, when not in use
for school purposes, for any of the following purposes:

1. By persons assembling therein for the purpose of giving and
receiving instruction in any branch of education, learning or the
arts.

2. For public library purposes, subject to the provisions of this
chapter, or as stations of public libraries.

3. For holding social, civic and recreational meetings and entertainments, and other uses pertaining to the welfare of the community; but such meetings, entertainment and uses shall be non-
exclusive and shall be open to the general public.

4. For meetings, entertainments and occasions where admission
fees are charged, when the proceeds thereof are to be expended

for an educational or charitable purpose; but such use shall not
be permitted if such meetings, entertainments and occasions are
under the exclusive control, and the said proceeds are to be applied
for the benefit of a society, association or organization of a religious sect or denomination, or of a fraternal, secret or other
exclusive society or organization.

5. For polling places for holding primaries and elections, and
for the registration of voters, and for holding political meetings.
But no such use shall be permitted unless authorized by a vote of
a district meeting, held as provided by law. It shall be the duty
of the trustees or board of education to call a special meeting for
such purpose upon the petition of at least ten per centum of the
qualified electors of the district. If such authority be granted by
a district meeting it shall be the duty of such trustees or board
of education to permit such use, under reasonable regulations to
be adopted by such trustees or board until another meeting held
in like manner shall have revoked such authority.

§ 5. Section four hundred and sixty-three of said chapter, as $^{§ 463. as}_{generally}$
so amended by chapter one hundred and forty of the laws of $^{amended}_{by L. 1910,}$
nineteen hundred and ten, is hereby amended to read as follows: $^{ch. 140,}_{amended.}$

§ 463. **Acquisition of real property.** Real property may be
acquired in any school district and in any city except a city of the
first or second class, for school purposes and for any other purpose for which such property may be acquired as provided in
this chapter, as follows:

1. By gift, grant, devise or purchase.

2. By condemnation, if an agreement cannot be made with the
owner for the purchase thereof. Such proceedings shall be instituted and conducted by the trustee or board of education, in the
name of the district under the provisions of the condemnation law.

3. This section does not permit the acquisition by condemnation
of less than the whole of a city or village lot with the erections
and improvements thereon.

§ 6. Subdivisions one and three of section four hundred and $^{§ 467, subds-}_{1, 3, as}$
sixty-seven of said chapter as so amended by chapter one hundred $^{generally}_{amended}$
and forty of the laws of nineteen hundred and ten, are hereby $^{by L. 1910,}_{ch. 140,}$
amended to read as follows: $^{amended.}$

1. A majority of the voters of any school district, present at $^{Tax for}_{certain}$
any annual or special district meeting, duly convened, may author- $^{purposes in}_{school}$
ize such acts and vote such taxes as they shall deem expedient for $^{districts.}$
making additions, alterations, repairs or improvements, to the

sites or buildings belonging to the district, or for the purchase of other sites or buildings, or for a change of sites, or for the purchase of land and buildings for agricultural, athletic, playground or social center purposes, or for the erection of new buildings, or for buying apparatus, implements, or fixtures, or for paying the wages of teachers, and the necessary expenses of the school, or for such other purpose relating to the support and welfare of the school as they may, by resolution, approve.

Notice of special meeting to levy such tax.

3. No addition to or change of site or purchase of a new site or tax for the purchase of any new site or structure, or for the purchase of an addition to the site of any schoolhouse, or for the purchase of lands and buildings for agricultural, athletic, playground or social center purposes, or for building any new schoolhouse or for the erection of an addition to any schoolhouse already built, shall be voted at any such meeting in a union free school district unless a notice by the board of education stating that such tax will be proposed, and specifying the object thereof and the amount to be expended therefor, shall have been given in the manner provided herein for the notice of an annual meeting. In a common school district the notice of a special meeting to authorize any of the improvements enumerated in this section shall be given as provided in section one hundred and ninety-seven.

§ 480, subd. 1, as generally amended by L. 1910, ch. 140, amended. Issuance of school district bonds.

§ 7. Subdivision one of section four hundred and eighty of such chapter as amended by chapter one hundred and forty of the laws of nineteen hundred and ten, is hereby amended to read as follows:

1. For the purpose of giving effect to the provisions of section four hundred and sixty-seven of this chapter, trustees or boards of education are hereby authorized, whenever a tax shall have been voted to be collected in instalments, for the purpose of building a new schoolhouse, or building an addition to a schoolhouse, or making additions, alterations or improvements to buildings or structures belonging to the district or city, or for the purchase of a new site or for an addition to a site. or for the purchase of land or buildings for agricultural, athletic, playground, or social center purposes, to borrow so much of the sum voted as may be necessary, at a rate of interest not exceeding six per centum, and to issue bonds or other evidences of indebtedness therefor, which shall be a charge upon the district, and be paid at maturity, and which shall not be sold below par.

§ 8. This act shall take effect immediately.

Chap. 222.

AN ACT to amend chapter one hundred and seven of the laws of eighteen hundred and eighty-seven, entitled "An act to incorporate the Nyack fire department, and to exempt its property from taxation," in relation to the funds of such department and the distribution thereof.

Became a law April 7, 1913, with the approval of the Governor. Passed, three-fifths being present.

The People of the State of New York, represented in Senate and Assembly, do enact as follows:

Section 1. Section eight of chapter one hundred and seven of L. 1887, ch. 107, § 8 amended. the laws of eighteen hundred and eighty-seven, entitled "An act to incorporate the Nyack fire department, and to exempt its property from taxation," is hereby amended to read as follows:[1]

§ 8. The funds of said corporation which shall be derived Funds to be paid to treasurer. from the tax on insurance companies, subscriptions, fines and membership dues from the various companies of the department, donations, bequests or income from any and all sources, shall be paid to the treasurer of the department and shall be expended How expended. and disbursed by said board of fire commissioners in the manner and for the purposes hereinbefore provided, except the amount payable to the Firemen's Association of the state of New York under the provisions of the insurance law, which amount shall be paid to said Firemen's Association. If at the time for holding Distribution of surplus. the meeting of the said board of fire commissioners in July of each year the accumulated funds of said corporation shall then exceed the sum of five thousand dollars, the surplus or excess over and above such sum, may by a two-thirds vote of all of said fire commissioners, be distributed by paying to each company of said department a sum equal to the amount paid into the said fund by the respective companies for membership since the previous distribution hereby authorized, as evidenced by the records of the said department. If after disbursing to each of said companies the amount of said fund to which said company is entitled there shall remain in said funds, an amount in excess of said five thousand dollars, the balance of said surplus shall thereupon be divided among the several companies equally share and share alike.

§ 2. This act shall take effect immediately.

---

[1] Section materially amended.

Chap. 223.

AN ACT to amend the public health law, in relation to violations of the provisions relating to pharmacy.

Became a law April 7, 1913, with the approval of the Governor. Passed, three-fifths being present.

The People of the State of New York, represented in Senate and Assembly, do enact as follows:

§ 240a added to L. 1909, ch. 49.
Section 1. Article eleven of chapter forty-nine of the laws of nineteen hundred and nine, entitled "An act in relation to the public health, constituting chapter forty-five of the consolidated laws," as amended by chapter four hundred and twenty-two of the laws of nineteen hundred and ten, is hereby amended by inserting therein after section two hundred and forty, a new section, to be section two hundred and forty-a, to read as follows:

§ 240-a. **Proof required in prosecuting for certain violations.** In an action or proceeding, civil or criminal, against any person for violating any provision of this article relating to retailing or dispensing drugs, chemicals, medicines, prescriptions and poisons, or to misbranding or substituting, it shall be necessary to prove at the trial or hearing that at the time and place of the taking of any sample of drugs, chemicals, medicines, or poisons, to be analyzed, the person taking the same divided it into two substantially equal parts, hermetically or otherwise effectively and completely sealed, delivered one such sealed part to the pharmacist, druggist or store-keeper from whose premises such sample was taken and delivered the other part so sealed to the chemist designated by the state board of pharmacy; and the facts herein required to be proven shall be alleged in the complaint or information by which such action or proceeding was begun.

§ 2. This act shall take effect immediately.

Chap. 224.

AN ACT to authorize the commissioners of the home of the city and town of Newburgh to purchase lands adjoining the premises owned by them.

Became a law April 7, 1913, with the approval of the Governor. Passed, three-fifths being present.

Accepted by the City.

The People of the State of New York, represented in Senate and Assembly, do enact as follows:

Section 1. The corporation created by chapter forty-four of the laws of eighteen hundred and fifty-three, entitled "An act for the better support of the poor in the town of Newburgh in the county of Orange," the name of which corporation was changed by chapter four hundred and sixty-seven of the laws of nineteen hundred and five to the commissioners of the home of the city and town of Newburgh is hereby authorized in its discretion to purchase in fee simple and take a deed of conveyance to the said commissioners, in their corporate name, of a farm of land situate in the town of New Windsor, and owned by Henry Spengler, and adjoining on the south the premises of the said commissioners, and to pay for said farm not exceeding the sum of seven thousand dollars. *Purchase of Spengler farm authorized.*

§ 2. The said corporation shall and it is hereby authorized to raise the said sum of seven thousand dollars, or as much thereof as may be necessary, in the same manner as are taxes raised to meet other audits of the said commissioners. *Money for payment, how raised*

§ 3. This act shall take effect immediately.

Chap. 225.

AN ACT to amend chapter five hundred and fifty-nine of the laws of nineteen hundred and ten, entitled "An act to provide a charter for the city of New Rochelle," in relation to the board of public works of the city of New Rochelle.

Became a law April 7, 1913, with the approval of the Governor. Passed, three-fifths being present.

Accepted by the City.

The People of the State of New York, represented in Senate and Assembly, do enact as follows:

L. 1910, ch. 559, § 12 amended.

Section 1. Section twelve of chapter five hundred and fifty-nine of the laws of nineteen hundred and ten, entitled "An act to provide a charter for the city of New Rochelle," is hereby amended so as to read as follows:

§ 12. **Appointive officers.** The mayor shall appoint and may at pleasure remove: a city clerk, three civil service commissioners, a corporation counsel, and a commissioner of streets. He shall appoint a commissioner of public works,[1] a commissioner of assessment and taxation,[2] three commissioners of parks, docks, and harbors, three police commissioners, three fire commissioners, nine trustees who shall constitute the board of education, three commissioners of health, an inspector of buildings, a commissioner of charities, a sealer of weights and measures, and such other officers as the mayor is authorized to appoint by law, and for the appointment of whom provision is not in other manner made.

§§ 271-273 amended.

§ 2. Sections two hundred and seventy-one, two hundred and seventy-two and two hundred and seventy-three of chapter five hundred and fifty-nine of the laws of nineteen hundred and ten, entitled "An act to provide a charter for the city of New Rochelle," are hereby amended so as to read as follows:

§ 271.[3] **Commissioner.** The terms of office of the members of the board of public works who are in office when this act takes effect, shall forthwith cease and determine. After this act shall take effect the mayor shall appoint a commissioner of public works, who shall succeed to all the powers and rights, obligations and duties of the former board of public works, and all proceedings and matters pending before the said board shall in no wise be

---

[1] Words "a commissioner of public works," new.
[2] Words "three commissioners of public works," omitted.
[3] Section 271 materially amended.

affected by said change. The term of office of the commissioner of public works shall be three years and until the appointment and qualification of his successor, and his compensation shall be fixed by the board of estimate and apportionment.

§ 272. **Powers and duties.** He[4] shall have charge of all public sewers and sewer disposal works, and of the maintenance of the same. He[4] shall also have charge of the construction, widening, grading, paving, repaving, flagging, curbing, and improving of the streets and sidewalks, and of the construction of all gutters and sewers. He[4] shall also have charge of the[5] construction of surface drains and culverts when so directed by the council.

§ 273. **Engineers, inspectors and other employees.** He[4] shall also have power to appoint and for cause remove a secretary, engineers, inspectors and such other employees as he[6] may deem necessary, provided that the position has been authorized and the salary thereof fixed by the board of estimate and apportionment. He[6] may also employ a consulting engineer from time to time as occasion may require, whose compensation shall be fixed by the board of estimate and apportionment.

§ 3. This act shall take effect immediately.

Chap. 226.

AN ACT to amend chapter six hundred and ninety-six of the laws of eighteen hundred and eighty-seven, entitled "An act to provide hospitals, orphan asylums and other charitable institutions in the city of New York with water, and remitting assessments therefor," in relation to exempting real estate owned or leased by a religious society and devoted to social settlement work.

Became a law April 7, 1913, with the approval of the Governor. Passed, three-fifths being present.

Accepted by the City.

The People of the State of New York, represented in Senate and Assembly, do enact as follows:

Section 1. Section one of chapter six hundred and ninety-six of the laws of eighteen hundred and eighty-seven, entitled "An act

L. 1887,
ch. 696,
§ 1, as
amended by

---

[4] Word " He " substituted for words " The board."
[5] Words " macadamizing of streets and the," omitted.
[6] Word " he " substituted for word " it."

L. 1890,
ch. 492;
L. 1894,
ch. 672;
L. 1896,
ch. 459;
L. 1896,
ch. 852;
L. 1902,
ch. 605;
L. 1906,
ch. 440;
L. 1907,
ch. 135,
and L. 1911,
ch. 636,
amended.

to provide hospitals, orphan asylums and other charitable institutions in the city of New York with water, and remitting assessments therefor," as amended by chapter four hundred and ninety-
two of the laws of eighteen hundred and ninety, chapter six hundred and seventy-two of the laws of eighteen hundred and ninety-
four, chapter four hundred and fifty-nine of the laws of eighteen
hundred and ninety-five, chapter eight hundred and fifty-two of
the laws of eighteen hundred and ninety-six, chapter six hundred
and five of the laws of nineteen hundred and two, chapter four
hundred and forty of the laws of nineteen hundred and six, chapter one hundred and thirty-five of the laws of nineteen hundred
and seven and chapter six hundred and eighty-six of the laws of
nineteen hundred and eleven,[1] is hereby amended to read as follows:

Certain
hospitals,
asylums,
etc., ex-
empt from
payment
for city
water.

§ 1. The several hospitals, dispensaries, orphan asylums,
homes for the aged, houses or homes for the reformation, protection or shelter of females, day nurseries or corporations or societies for the care and instruction of poor babies and needy children, and industrial homes, and any benevolent or charitable corporation owning or maintaining an institution for medical research, public baths, for free school societies or free circulating
libraries or veteran firemen's associations, and any social settlement, whether incorporated or unincorporated, which shall own
or lease for a term not less than three years a building or buildings
devoted exclusively to the purposes of such social settlement or
any religious society owning or leasing for a period of not less
than three years a building devoted exclusively to social settlement work,[2] now existing or hereafter established in the city of
New York, or the real estate owned by any religious corporation
located in the city of New York as now constituted, actually dedicated and used by such corporation exclusively as a place of public worship, are hereby exempted from the payment of any sum of
money whatever to said city, for the use of water taken by same
from said city, and water shall be supplied to the same by
said city, in sufficient quantity for all purposes for which it is
now used by said corporations, societies and institutions, or which
may be necessary to be used by the same, free of all charge what-

---

1 Section 1 was also amended by L. 1903, ch. 386.
2 Words "any religious society owning or leasing for a period of not less
than three years a building devoted exclusively to social settlement work,"
new.

soever, and the real estate necessarily used for any hospital, dis- _{Release
from liens
for unpaid
water rates.}
pensary, institution for medical research, orphan asylum, home
for the aged, free school or free circulating library, veteran firemen's association, house or home for reformation, protection or
shelter of females, day nurseries or corporations or societies for
the care and instruction of poor babies and needy children, or industrial homes, or social settlements maintained or conducted by
any incorporated or unincorporated social settlement, church or religious society,[3] or occupied for such public bath, owned or leased
for a term of not less than three years, or held under any renewal
or extension of such lease by any such corporation, societies and
institutions aforesaid, or the real estate owned by any religious
corporation located in the city of New York, as now constituted,
actually dedicated and used by such corporation exclusively as a
place of public worship, is hereby released, discharged and exempted from all lien and charge for water heretofore used or
which may hereafter be used by any such institutions, society
or corporation.

§ 2. Section two of such act as amended by chapter four hun- _{§ 2. as
amended by
L. 1890,
ch. 492;
L. 1895,
ch. 459;
L. 1896,
ch. 852;
L. 1902,
ch. 605;
L. 1906,
ch. 440;
L. 1907,
ch. 135, and
L. 1911,
ch. 686,
amended.}
dred and ninety-two of the laws of eighteen hundred and ninety,
chapter four hundred and fifty-nine of the laws of eighteen hundred and ninety-five, chapter eight hundred and fifty-two of the
laws of eighteen hundred and ninety-six, chapter six hundred and
five of the laws of nineteen hundred and two, chapter four hundred and forty of the laws of nineteen hundred and six, chapter
one hundred and thirty-five of the laws of nineteen hundred and
seven and chapter six hundred and eighty-six of the laws of nineteen hundred and eleven,[4] is hereby amended to read as follows:

§ 2. The real property situated in the city of New York, neces- _{Real estate
of cer-
tain insti-
tutions ex-
empt from
water as-
sessments.}
sarily now in use, or which may hereafter necessarily be used and
devoted to any hospital, dispensary, institution for medical research, orphan asylum, home for the aged, house or home for the
reformation, protection or shelter of females, day nurseries or
corporations or societies for the care and instruction of poor babies
and needy children, industrial home, public baths, free school or
free circulating library, or veteran firemen's association, or society which has among its objects either the care, support or education of orphans, or of the sick, the infirm or aged, free educa-

---

[3] Words "maintained or conducted by any incorporated or unincorporated
social settlement, church or religious society," new.
[4] Section 2 was also amended by L. 1903, ch. 386.

tion or free circulation of books, or social settlement maintained
or conducted by any incorporated or unincorporated social settlement, church or religious society,[5] or the real estate owned by any
religious corporation located in the city of New York, as now constituted, actually dedicated and used by such corporation exclusively as a place of public worship, shall be and hereby is declared discharged and exempt from all assessments laid or made
for use of water and sales thereunder, and from all such assessments hereafter, so long as the same shall be owned or leased for
a term of not less than three years, or held under any renewal or extension of such lease, by any such corporation, society or institution aforesaid, and used for the purposes herein mentioned, and
Exemption to cease upon sale. whenever a sale and conveyance thereof shall be made to any person, association or corporation, other than those mentioned in this
act, or the same shall cease to be held under lease as herein provided, thereupon the real estate so sold and conveyed, or ceasing
to be so held, and not so used, shall be thereafter subject to assessment in the same manner as other real estate situated in the city
of New York.

§ 3. This act shall take effect immediately.

Chap. 227.

AN ACT to regulate and restrain the practice of midwifery in
the city of Syracuse by others than legally authorized
physicians.

Became a law April 7, 1913, with the approval of the Governor. Passed,
three-fifths being present.

Accepted by the City.

*The People of the State of New York, represented in Senate
and Assembly, do enact as follows:*

Board of examiners in mid-wifery. Section 1. On or before the first day of September, nineteen
hundred and thirteen, the mayor of the city of Syracuse shall
appoint a board of examiners in midwifery to consist of three
members, two of whom shall be regularly qualified physicians
and surgeons of at least five years' practice who, together with
the health officer of said city, ex-officio, shall constitute such board

---

[5] Words "maintained or conducted by any incorporated or unincorporated
social settlement, church or religious society," new.

and thereafter as often as any vacancy shall occur in said board, said mayor shall fill such vacancy. The members of such board shall serve without compensation, but shall be paid their neces- sary expenses incurred in the performance of their duties. Such expenses shall be paid by the city treasurer, out of the general fund from moneys set apart for the contingent expenses of said city, by order of the common council, upon proper vouchers or other proofs of such expenses. The terms of office of the members of such board, other than the health officer, shall be for three years.

§ 2. Immediately after appointment such board shall organize by the selection of one of its members as president and of an- other as secretary and treasurer, who shall hold their offices for one year, and be thereafter annually elected, and shall adopt and have power to enforce such rules and regulations as are necessary to carry out the provisions of this act.

§ 3. Such board of examiners shall meet on the first Tuesday of October and April in each year, and on such other days as it may appoint, in the city of Syracuse, after due notice thereof is publicly given, and shall then examine as to their moral char- acter and qualifications to practice midwifery, all candidates of the age of twenty-one years and upwards who shall present them- selves to be examined, and shall, upon receipt of ten dollars, issue its certificate to any person, so examined, who shall be found by it to be qualified, which certificate shall set forth that such board has found the person to whom it is issued, qualified to practice midwifery in the city of Syracuse, and such certifi- cate shall be recorded by the clerk of said city in a book to be kept for that purpose. All moneys going into the treasury of such board shall be turned over to the city treasurer and by him credited to the contingent fund of said city.

§ 4. Any person who shall have received and recorded such certificate shall thereupon be designated as a midwife and au- thorized and entitled, within the city of Syracuse, to practice midwifery in cases of normal labor and in no others; but such persons shall not, in any case of labor, use instruments of any kind, nor assist labor by any artificial, forcible or mechanical means, nor perform version, nor attempt to remove adherent placentae, nor administer, prescribe, advise or employ any poison- ous or dangerous drug, herb or medicine, nor attempt the treat- ment of disease except where the attendance of a physician can- not be speedily procured, and in such cases, such person shall

Margin notes: No compensation; expenses. Terms. Organiza- tion. Rules and regulations. Meetings. Examina- tion and certification of candi- dates to practice midwifery. Disposi- tion of moneys re- ceived. Person receiving certificate may prac- tice what; prohibi- tions.

at once and in the most speedy way procure the attendance of a physician.

Revocation of certificate. § 5. Such board of examiners shall have power, on proper cause shown, and after giving hearing to the person holding its certificate, to recommend to the mayor of the city of Syracuse the revoking of the same and said mayor shall have power to revoke such certificate and license.

Penalties for violations. § 6. Any person who shall practice or, without the attendance of a physician where one can be procured, attend a case of obstetrics within the city of Syracuse, after the first day of November, nineteen hundred and thirteen, without being duly authorized so to do under existing laws of this state, or without having received and recorded the certificate provided for by this act, and any person who shall violate any of the provisions of this act shall be guilty of a misdemeanor and on conviction thereof shall be fined not less than fifty dollars nor more than one hundred dollars, and shall forfeit any certificate granted under the provisions of this act.

§ 7. This act shall take effect immediately.

Chap. 228.

AN ACT to amend the code of civil procedure, in relation to the burden of proof of contributory negligence in an action to recover damages for causing death.

Became a law April 7, 1913, with the approval of the Governor. Passed, three-fifths being present.

The People of the State of New York, represented in Senate and Assembly, do enact as follows:

§ 841b added. Section 1. The code of civil procedure is hereby amended by adding thereto after section eight hundred and forty-one-a thereof, a new section, to be section eight hundred and forty-one-b, to read as follows:[1]

§ 841-b. **Trial and burden of proof of contributory negligence.** On the trial of any action to recover damages for causing death the contributory negligence of the person killed shall be a defense, to be pleaded and proven by the defendant.

In effect Sept. 1, 1913. § 2. This act shall take effect September first, nineteen hundred and thirteen.

---

[1] A different § 841b is added by L. 1913, ch. 395, post.

Chap. 229.

AN ACT to amend the canal law, in relation to the Shinnecock and Peconic canal.

Became a law April 8, 1913, with the approval of the Governor. Passed, three-fifths being present.

The People of the State of New York, represented in Senate and Assembly, do enact as follows:

Section 1. Section thirty-three of chapter thirteen of the laws of nineteen hundred and nine, entitled "An act relating to canals, constituting chapter five of the consolidated laws," is hereby amended by inserting therein, after subdivision fourteen, a new subdivision, to be subdivision fourteen-a, to read as follows: _{Subd. 14a added to L. 1909, ch. 13, § 33.}

14-a. Have charge of and exercise the same powers that he has as to other canals, over the waterway connecting Shinnecock and Peconic bays in the county of Suffolk, known as the Shinnecock and Peconic canal, and to remove such obstructions therefrom, from time to time, and make such improvements, as may be necessary to keep the channel of such canal of sufficient depth and capacity to admit the free passage of boats or water craft between such bays. _{Superintendent of public works to have charge of Shinnecock and Peconic canal.}

§ 2. This act shall take effect immediately.

Chap. 230.

AN ACT to amend the code of civil procedure, in relation to substituted service of the summons.

Became a law April 8, 1913, with the approval of the Governor. Passed, three-fifths being present.

The People of the State of New York, represented in Senate and Assembly, do enact as follows:

Section 1. Sections four hundred and thirty-five and four hundred and thirty-six of the code of civil procedure are hereby amended to read as follows: _{§§ 435, 436 amended.}

§ 435. Where a summons is issued in any court of record, an order for the service thereof upon a defendant, whether a domestic corporation, other than a municipal corporation, a joint-

Order for
substituted
service of
summons
on defen-
dant re-
siding in
state. stock or other unincorporated association or a natural person,[1] residing within the state may be made by the court, or a judge
thereof, or the county judge of the county where the action is tri-
able upon satisfactory proof, by the affidavit of a person, not a
party to the action, or by the return of the sheriff of the county
where such[2] defendant resides, or has its principal office or place of
business,[3] that proper and diligent effort has been made to serve
the summons upon the defendant and that none of the persons
mentioned in subdivision three of section four hundred and thirty-
one, nor the president or treasurer of such association, can be
found, or if the defendant is a natural person,[4] that the place of
his sojourn cannot be ascertained, or if he is within the state, that
he avoids service, so that personal service cannot be made.

Service,
how made. § 436. The order must direct that the service of the summons
be made, by leaving a copy thereof, and of the order, if the defendant is a domestic corporation or joint-stock or other unincorporated association at its principal office or place of business, or
if a natural person[5] at the residence of the defendant, with a person of proper age, if upon reasonable application, admittance can be obtained, and such person found who will receive
it; or, if admittance cannot be so obtained, nor such a person
found, by affixing the same to the outer or other door of the defendant's said place of business or office, or of his[6] residence, and by depositing another copy thereof, properly enclosed in a post-paid wrapper, addressed to the defendant at
its said principal office or place of business, or[7] to him at his
place of residence, in the post-office at the place where he resides,
or where said office, place of business or residence is located,[8] or
upon proof being made by affidavit[9] that no such residence can be

---

[1] Words " whether a domestic corporation, other than a municipal corporation, a joint-stock or other unincorporated association or a natural
person," new.
[2] Word " such " substituted for word " the."
[3] Words " or has its principal office or place of business," new.
[4] Words " and that none of the persons mentioned in subdivision three of
section four hundred and thirty-one, nor the president or treasurer of such
association, can be found, or if the defendant is a natural person," new.
[5] Words " if the defendant is a domestic corporation or joint-stock or other
unincorporated association at its principal office or place of business, or if a
natural person," new.
[6] Words " said place of business or office, or of his," new.
[7] Words " to the defendant at its said principal office or place of business,"
new.
[8] Words " or where said office, place of business or residence is located,"
new.
[9] Formerly " affidavits."

found, service of the summons may be made in such manner as the court may direct.

§ 2. This act shall take effect September first, nineteen hundred and thirteen. In effect Sept. 1, 1913.

Chap. 231.

AN ACT to amend the town law, in relation to biennial town meetings and the election and terms of office of town officers.

Became a law April 8, 1913, with the approval of the Governor. Passed, three-fifths being present.

The People of the State of New York, represented in Senate and Assembly, do enact as follows:

Section 1. Section eighty-two of chapter sixty-three of the laws of nineteen hundred and nine, entitled "An act relating to towns, constituting chapter sixty-two of the consolidated laws," as amended by chapters four hundred and ninety-one of the laws of nineteen hundred and nine and two hundred and seventy-one of the laws of nineteen hundred and ten, is hereby amended to read as follows: L. 1909, ch. 63, § 82, as amended by L. 1909, ch. 491, and L. 1910, ch. 271, amended.

§ 82. **Term of office.** Supervisors, town clerks, town superintendents of highways, collectors, overseers of the poor, inspectors of election and constables, when elected, shall hold their respective offices for two years. The terms of office of assessors shall be two years for one assessor and four years each for two assessors. But whenever there is or shall be a change in the time of holding town meetings in any town, persons elected to such offices at the first[1] biennial town meeting held after such change has been authorized as provided by law,[2] shall enter upon the discharge of their duties at the expiration of the term of their predecessors, and serve until the next biennial town meeting thereafter or until their successors are elected and have qualified, except that the assessor elected for four years shall serve until the second biennial town meeting thereafter, or until his successor is elected and has qualified. Whenever the time of holding town meetings in any town is changed to the first Tuesday after the first Monday in November, except

---

[1] Word "first" substituted for word "next."

[2] Words "held after such change has been authorized as provided by law," substituted for words "after such change shall take effect."

when changed as provided in section forty-one of this chapter, the
town officers elected thereat shall take office on the first day of
January succeeding their election. Except that the collector
elected at such town meeting shall take office immediately upon
his election and qualification as prescribed by law. The term of
a town superintendent of highways, if such superintendent be
elected at a town meeting held at the time of a general election,
shall begin on the Thursday succeeding his election, or as soon
thereafter as he shall have been officially notified of his election
and shall have duly qualified, and if elected at a town meeting held
at any other time his term of office shall begin on the first day of
November succeeding his election. Except as otherwise provided
in this section, [3]in case the time of the holding of town meetings
in any county is changed by resolution of the board of supervisors of the county to the first Tuesday after the first Monday in
November, all town officers in any town of such county elected at
the first biennial town meeting held after the adoption of such
resolution shall hold office until the first day of January succeeding the biennial town meeting first held pursuant to such resolution. [4]No resolution changing the time of holding town meetings
to the first Tuesday after the first Monday in November shall be
effectual to dispense with the holding of the first biennial town
meeting after the adoption of such resolution at the time fixed
when such resolution was adopted. But the collector in each
town shall complete the duties of his office in respect to the collection of taxes, and the payment and return thereof, upon any
warrant received by him during his term of office, notwithstanding
the[5] fact that his successor has entered upon the duties of his
office.

§ 2. This act shall take effect immediately.

---

[3] Remainder of sentence materially amended.
[4] Following sentence new.
[5] Remainder of sentence formerly read: "election of his successor."

Chap. 232.

AN ACT to amend the code of civil procedure, in relation to the compensation of condemnation commissioners.

Became a law April 8, 1913, with the approval of the Governor. Passed, three-fifths being present.

The People of the State of New York, represented in Senate and Assembly, do enact as follows:

Section 1. Section thirty-three hundred and seventy of the code of civil procedure is hereby amended to read as follows:

§ 3370. **Duties and powers of commissioners.** The commissioners shall take and subscribe the constitutional oath of office. Any of them may issue subpœnas and administer oaths to witnesses; a majority of them may adjourn the proceeding before them, from time to time in their discretion. Whenever they meet, except by appointment of the court or pursuant to adjournment, they shall cause at least eight days' notice of such meeting to be given to the defendants who have appeared, or their agents or attorneys. They shall view the premises described in the petition, and hear the proof and allegations of the parties, and reduce the testimony taken by them, if any, to writing, and after the testimony in each case is closed, they, or a majority of them, all being present, shall, without unnecessary delay ascertain and determine the compensation which ought justly to be made by the plaintiff to the owners of the property appraised by them; and, in fixing the amount of such compensation, they shall not make any allowance or deduction on account of any real or supposed benefits which the owners may derive from the public use for which the property is to be taken, or the construction of any proposed improvement connected with such public use. But in case the plaintiff is a railroad corporation and such real property shall belong to any other railroad corporation, the commissioners on fixing the amount of such compensation, shall fix the same at its fair value for railroad purposes. They shall make a report of their proceedings to the supreme court with the minutes of the testimony taken by them, if any; and they shall each be entitled to six dollars for services for every day they are actually engaged in the performance of their duties, and their necessary expenses to be paid by the plaintiff; provided, that in proceedings within the counties of New York and Kings such commissioners shall be entitled to such additional compensation not exceeding twenty-five dollars for every such day, as may be awarded by the court. [1]and provided that in proceedings instituted by a village or any board thereof under this title such commissioners shall be entitled to such additional compensation, not exceeding five dollars for every such day, as may be awarded by the court.

In effect
Sept. 1,
1913.
§ 2. This act shall take effect September first, nineteen hundred and thirteen.

Chap. 233.

AN ACT to amend the conservation law in respect to water supply to provide for union water districts and conservation water works.

Became a law April 8, 1913, with the approval of the Governor. Passed, three-fifths being present.

The People of the State of New York, represented in Senate and Assembly, do enact as follows:

Art. 9a
added to
L. 1911,
ch. 647.
Section 1. Chapter six hundred and forty-seven of the laws of nineteen hundred and eleven, entitled "An act relating to conservation of land, forests, waters, parks, hydraulic power, fish and game, constituting chapter sixty-five of the consolidated laws," is hereby amended by adding thereto a new article to be known as article nine-a and to read as follows:

ARTICLE 9-A.
UNION WATER DISTRICTS.

Section 530. Union water districts; formation.
    531. Petition to conservation commission; hearing.
    532. Submission of proposition.
    533. Acquiring of lands.
    534. Letting of contracts; construction work.
    535. Maintenance and operation of works.
    536. Cost and expenses.
    537. When other municipalities may participate; regulations.
    538. Sale of water by commission.
    539. Definitions.

§ 530. **Union water districts; formation.** Any number of municipalities, including water districts, within contiguous coun-

---

[1] Remainder of section new.

ties may join in the formation of a union water district, and
three or more such municipalities may meet and confer for that
purpose. The subject for consideration at any such meeting shall
be the proposition that the municipalities thus conferring shall
join in the formation of a union water district. Municipalities
not represented at the first meeting may participate in adjourned
meetings and each municipality represented at any such meeting
shall have one vote, which shall be cast by the chief executive
officer thereof. The officers so attending shall choose a chairman,
who shall preside over the meeting and a clerk whose duty it shall
be to keep minutes of the proceedings. Whenever ten or more municipalities so attending shall vote in the affirmative on said proposition, those so voting shall thereupon become a union water district, except that if less than ten municipalities shall vote in the
affirmative, they shall become a union water district provided
they shall have a combined population of at least twenty-five
thousand inhabitants, according to the last preceding federal
census or state enumeration, and the census or enumeration last
taken shall control. Whenever such meeting shall result in the
formation of a union water district, a report in writing of such
meeting shall be made and subscribed by the chairman and the
clerk of the meeting, and such report shall set forth the attendance at such meeting, the vote taken, and the name adopted for
such district, which shall consist of one word to precede the
words " union water district " and shall not be a name previously
adopted by any other such district, and the same shall, within five
days after such meeting, be filed in the office of the clerk of each
county wherein any municipality becoming a member of such
union water district shall be situated.

There shall be a board, to be known as the trustees of such
union water district, consisting of the chief executive officer of
each municipality becoming a member thereof. A majority of
all the members of such board of trustees shall constitute a
quorum for the transaction of business, and they shall choose one
of their number chairman, whose duty it shall be to preside at
meetings of the board, and they shall choose a clerk, whose duty
it shall be to keep the records of its proceedings. Within ten
days after the filing of such a report in the offices of the county
clerks, the said trustees shall meet and each shall take and file
with the said clerk the constitutional oath of office.[1]

---

[1] See constitution, art. 13, § 1; public officers law (L. 1909, ch. 51), § 10,
as amended by L. 1913, ch. 59, ante.

The said board of trustees shall have power and it shall be their duty to adopt by-laws and rules to govern the conduct of its business. Meetings, in addition to any meetings otherwise provided for in this article, may be called by at least three trustees who shall file said call with the clerk, and it shall be the duty of the clerk to give written notice of such meeting by mail to each member at least two days prior to the time fixed therefor, stating in such notice the time and place of the meeting. All meetings shall be held at a convenient place within one of said municipalities.

§ 531. Petition to conservation commission; hearing. The board of trustees of such union water district may apply in writing to the conservation commission to investigate the proposition and to cause surveys, maps, plans and estimates to be made and such further or other information supplied as may be deemed advisable by the conservation commission to be made. Such petition shall set forth the formation of such union water district and state the population thereof determined in the manner hereinbefore specified, and shall contain an estimate of the probable population of each municipality at the end of ten years next succeeding and an estimate of the consumption of water per capita per diem which such municipality will require, and a statement in detail of all water supplies and works then owned by any such municipality and of the water works of any water works company or of any person supplying water to them or any of them and such other matters, if any, as may be prescribed by the rules and regulations of the commission. The petition shall also state at what location or point in or for each municipality it is desired to have water supplied by works to be constructed.

Upon the receipt of such petition, the conservation commission may in its discretion, and if it has funds available for such purpose, cause preliminary investigations, surveys, maps and plans to be prepared under direction of the chief engineer of said commission. If the commission thereupon finds that the physical conditions are unfavorable for the acquisition of a water supply and the construction of works for the supply of such union water district, or that the same would be excessively expensive, it shall so report, and in that case may in its discretion decline to take further action on such petition. If the commission shall deem it advisable so to do, it may make final investigations of the proposition and cause final surveys, plans, estimates of cost and specifications to be made and take any other steps incidental thereto. Upon completion thereof the commission shall furnish the board of trustees of said union water district with copies of its report therein. Thereupon the commission shall set a time and place for a public hearing upon the petition and on such report and shall hear allegations and proofs for or against the same and after such hearing the commission shall determine whether an adequate supply of pure and wholesome water is obtainable at reasonable cost for serving all the municipalities within such union water district. In making such determination the commission shall consider the present and future necessities of municipalities and the inhabitants thereof not parties to the petition but whose sources of water supply might be affected or impaired by the project under consideration. The determination so arrived at shall be reported by the commission to each such municipality.

The purpose of such project shall be to supply water to central distributing points for each municipality. All reservoirs, stand pipes, mains, pipes, valves, hydrants and appurtenances for the storage and distribution of water from such central points to consumers shall be such as may have been heretofore or may be hereafter constructed by or for each municipality as otherwise provided by law. The ownership, construction and maintenance of such municipal works, and the distribution and sale of water after the same leaves such central points shall be and remain under the duly constituted officers of each municipality as is now provided by law. All water shall be metered at such central points under the direction and control of the commission. The report of the commission if in favor of the project shall determine what proportion of the whole original cost of establishing conservation water works for such union water district for delivery of water at such central points shall be borne by each municipality.

The pendency of a proceeding on the part of any municipality or water district for procuring an independent supply of water under any statute, shall not prevent such municipality or water district from taking part in the formation of a union water district as herein provided.

§ 532. **Submission of proposition.** Upon receiving from the commission the report, maps, plans, estimates of cost, and other information aforesaid, the board of trustees shall consider and either adopt or reject the same. If the board adopts the same, such adoption shall be certified by the board to each municipality included within such union water district, and thereupon there shall be submitted to the electors of each such municipality a proposition for issuing its bonds for its proportion of the estimated cost aforesaid. Such proposition shall be submitted within thirty days after receiving such certification from the board of trustees.

In case of a city, except as herein otherwise provided, such elections shall be conducted according to the statutes applicable to the submission of a proposition for the establishment of an independent water supply for such city or for authorization of a bonded debt. In case of a village, except as herein otherwise provided, such election shall be conducted in the manner provided by article nine of the village law. In case of a water district, except as herein otherwise provided, such election shall be conducted as provided in article thirteen of the town law, but only electors resident within the water district shall participate in the election. Such proposition shall be deemed adopted by a municipality if a majority of all the votes cast at said election shall be cast in favor of the proposition. Except as otherwise provided herein, a municipality, when the issuance of such bonds has been authorized as herein provided, shall issue and sell the same in the manner now provided by law for the issuance and sale of bonds, except that the limitations now provided by law upon indebtedness of municipalities shall not apply to a debt incurred under the provisions of this section except as otherwise provided by the constitution of the state.

It shall be the duty of the proper authorities of such municipality to levy annually, in the manner now provided by law in case of bonds authorized to be issued by such a municipality, such sum or sums as shall be necessary to meet the principal and interest upon the bonds issued as provided herein, or for the establishment of a sinking fund on account of the bonds so issued.

An affirmative vote in any municipality at an election held as aforesaid shall be binding for a period of two years. A negative vote in any municipality shall not be final as to said municipality, but the same proposition may be resubmitted not more than three times to the electors thereof and in such case not more than four months shall elapse between such resubmission unless an affirmative vote shall result. If the vote of any such municipality shall be in the negative four times, then such union water district shall cease to exist, except that in such case the municipalities voting in the affirmative may through the said board of trustees apply to the commission to certify the proportion of cost which each such municipality should bear of such project, as the same should be modified by reason of the elimination of the municipalities voting in the negative, and on a report by the commission of such estimate, a proposition based thereon shall be submitted to each such municipality in the manner herein provided for the submission of an original proposition and in that case the provision aforesaid as to the issuance and sale of bonds shall apply as so modified. If in such case any municipality shall vote in the negative, no further proceeding shall be had upon such petition and said union water district shall cease to exist.

Upon the issuance and sale by a municipality of bonds as herein provided, the proceeds shall be deposited in a national or state bank or in a trust company by each municipality separately, but to the credit of the conservation commission, and such moneys shall be used and paid out by the commission for the purposes herein provided. Such municipality shall select the depositories which shall agree to pay the highest rate of interest upon such deposit and the deposit shall be secured by bonds to the municipality approved by the commission. The interest accumulating upon such deposit shall be credited to the municipality making the same and shall be used by it in paying interest on its bonds issued as above provided. In withdrawing such deposits, the commission shall withdraw not more than one-half of the amount so deposited by any one municipality until one-half of the separate deposits of other municipalities shall have been withdrawn.

Upon concurrence of a sufficient number of municipalities by affirmative votes on submission of the proposition aforesaid and the deposit of an aggregate amount of money equal to the estimate of the cost reported as herein provided, the commission shall proceed to construct water works, as described in its report or as the same may after such hearing be modified, subject only to such minor changes in the design as circumstances may from time to time in the opinion of the commission require. Such works shall be known as conservation water-works.

§ 533. Acquiring of lands. The commission or its agents, engineers, and such other persons as may be necessary for the execution of the powers and duties herein provided, may enter upon any land or water for the purpose of making surveys, examinations and investigations for preparing the maps, plans, specifications and reports herein provided for, and the persons damaged thereby shall be entitled to file claims therefor with the board of claims and recover against the state such damages.

The commission shall have the power to purchase and take possession of in the name of the people of the state of New York and to be held by said people for the purposes authorized by this article or to acquire in the same name by condemnation as hereinafter provided for such purposes, all lands above or under water and structures and to acquire and take in the same name and manner and divert and use waters, public or private, deemed by the commission to be necessary for said purposes. If the commission shall be unable to agree with the private owner of lands and properties for the purchase thereof or with the private owner of frontage along waters for acquiring of the right to divert such waters or to agree with the private owner of lands for acquiring of easements in, over or against such lands, the same may be acquired by the commission by condemnation as follows:

An accurate survey of the lands so acquired or of lands in, over or against which any easement is so required shall be made and a map thereof shall be prepared accompanied with an accurate description of the said lands, rights and easements so required, which description shall state the volume of water to be taken or diverted where less than the whole flow of any stream or water is to be taken or diverted and of the period during which such lands are to be held or such waters used or diverted and a sufficient description of any other easements in, over or against such lands, so as to describe with common certainty the lands, rights or easements to be taken, and the same shall be certified by the commission and filed in its office and a duplicate thereof made and recorded in the office of the clerk of the county within which any lands taken or affected are situated. Thereupon the commission may apply to the supreme court within the judicial district containing such lands for the appointment of commissioners of appraisal to determine the amount of compensation to be paid by the conservation commission for the property to be so appropriated and, except as otherwise provided in this article, the provisions of title one of chapter twenty-three of the code of civil procedure known as the condemnation law shall apply to and govern the procedure on such application and regulate the fixing and payment of the compensation to be made. The commission may in its discretion unite in one petition to said court, applications to acquire several such properties or all the separate properties sought to be taken for any one project carried on under this article.

Such petition shall be accompanied by a duplicate of the map and descriptions of the properties to be taken and required to be filed as aforesaid.

On the appointment of commissioners of appraisal and the taking and filing of official oaths by them as required by the condemnation law in case of such application, the conservation commission may enter upon and take possession of and use, for the purposes herein authorized, the lands' and properties described in such petition and the said maps and statements accompanying the same. Said petition and the said duplicate map and statements filed therewith shall be conclusive evidence of the boundaries of the lands to be appropriated and of the extent and nature of any rights and easements described therein to be taken. This provision for compensation shall not be construed to require payment of compensation except to the extent of the legal rights of such private owners and according to the legal measure of damages and there shall be no presumption that the lands and property rights so described are privately owned.

In case any lands or rights as hereinbefore described are owned by the public not including the lands and waters of the canals and lands within the forest preserve, and the acquisition thereof for the purposes herein described shall be necessary, the same may be entered upon and used by the conservation commission and if the same were at the time of such taking the separate property or under the jurisdiction of any county or other municipality or other civil division of the state or contain improvements made by them, a just and fair sum on account of such taking may be agreed upon by the conservation commission and the governing board or body of such county, municipality or civil division and the amount thereof shall be paid over by the conservation commission to the proper officers of such county, municipality or civil division on the execution and delivery to the commission of an appropriate conveyance describing the lands and rights so taken and in case such amount cannot be agreed upon the same shall be fixed and determined by three commissioners to be appointed by the supreme court within the judicial district where said lands affected are located on application either by the commission or the proper authorities of such county, municipality or civil division on notice to the other and when the determination of such commissioners shall be confirmed by said court the sum so affixed and determined upon shall be paid by the conservation commission.

Any diversion right now exercised for private purposes and under which public waters are diverted under any gratuitous franchise, express or implied, or franchise terminable at will as against the user, shall be and be deemed to be revoked when and to the extent that the waters subject to diversion are in the opinion of the commission, to be so certified by order to be made by it, needed for public water supply as herein provided.

The commission shall have the right subject, in case of state improved highways, to the approval of the state commission of highways, to relocate highways which are within lands to be flowed by works constructed hereunder and shall have the right to lay pipes or conduits for conveyance of water along or across any highway or other public place and across any railroad, canal, transmission or other way devoted to public use, but the same shall be restored to its former condition of usefulness. The commission shall have power to apply in behalf of the state under any law of congress for permission to divert waters from any Indian lands when required for furnishing public water supply for a union water district.

Whenever it shall be necessary to appropriate lands occupied by graves, burial places, cemeteries or other places of interment of human remains, the same may be acquired in the same manner as other lands as herein provided and where the same is to be acquired by condemnation, service of notice of the time and place of presentation of the petition upon a person, corporation or other governing board, body or officer having possession, ownership or exercising control thereover, or service thereof in such manner or upon such other persons as shall be specially directed by the court, shall be sufficient. But such lands shall not be entered upon by the conservation commission in such case until after judgment adjudging that the condemnation thereof is necessary for the purposes herein specified shall be rendered, nor until the special provisions of such judgment as to the removal and reinterment of the human remains in said lands shall be complied with by the commission and the judgment shall require that such remains be removed to some other appropriate lands or places to be specified in said judgment including the removal and replacing of all marks distinguishing the per-

sons so interred and the removal, transportation and reinterment
of such remains shall be made in accordance with the provisions of
the public health law and the local rules or ordinances of any city,
village or town wherein the lands containing such remains or lands
in which they shall be reinterred are located. Upon completing
the work of reinterment the commission shall convey an appropriate right and title in the lands acquired by it for such reinterment, to the person, corporation or governing board or officer, if
any, formerly owning, possessing or controlling the property from
which said remains were removed. If there be no such person,
corporation or other governing board or officer, the commission
shall, as part of the expense of the project prosecuted by it, maintain the property acquired for such reinterment as a cemetery.
The lands required for such reinterment shall be deemed to be
required for the purposes of the project authorized by this article.

Before any lands are acquired by purchase or any condemnation
proceedings instituted or any expenditure made for excavation or
construction hereunder, the commission shall cause a general map
to be made and filed in its office and furnish a certified copy thereof
to each municipality a member of a union water district, which
map shall show the lands necessary to be acquired and waters
necessary to be diverted, and shall show the lands needed for rights
of way and for the location of reservoirs and central points of delivery of water, and the commission shall cause general plans of
all construction and excavation work to be made and filed, and
copies thereof furnished in the same manner.

§ 534. **Letting of contracts; construction work.** All excavation and construction work shall be performed under contracts
based upon maps, plans and specifications and estimates of quantities made by the commission as hereinbefore provided, and any
contract for performance of the whole work to be done or material, based upon any one petition or any contract for any part of
such work or materials shall be let to the lowest responsible bidder
after public notice of such letting, to be given by advertising the
same once in each week for four weeks immediately preceding the
day fixed for the receiving of bids and one such notice shall be
published in a newspaper printed within each of the counties
wherein any part of such work is to be performed. The requirements of the state finance law and the labor law as to the form and
contents of public contracts in respect to the requirements of bonds
from contractors to secure faithful performance and completion

of the work shall apply to all contracts let under the provisions of this article.

If in the judgment of the chief engineer any work is not being performed according to the contract or for the best interests of the public, he shall so certify to the commission and the commission shall thereupon have power to suspend or stop the work under such contract while it is in progress, and to provide for completion of the same in such manner as will accord with the contract specifications and for the best interests of the public, or the contract may be cancelled and readvertised and relet in the manner herein prescribed and any excess in the cost of completing the work beyond the price charged for which the same was originally awarded, shall be charged to and paid by the contractor failing to perform the work.

If at any time in the conduct of the work under any contract it shall become apparent to the chief engineer that any item in the contract will exceed in quantity the engineer's estimate by more than fifteen per centum, he shall so certify to the commission and the commission shall thereupon determine whether the work in excess thereof shall be completed by the contractor under the terms and at the prices specified in the contract or whether it shall be done by the commission or whether a special contract shall be made for such excess in the manner above prescribed. Every contract made hereunder shall reserve to the commission the right to suspend or cancel the contract as above provided and to complete the work or readvertise or re-let the same as the commission may determine and reserve to the commission the right to enter and complete any item of the contract which shall exceed in quantity the engineer's estimate by more than fifteen per centum or to make a special contract for such excess as the commission may determine.

All excavation and construction work shall be performed under the supervision of the conservation commission through its chief engineer and all payments upon contracts shall be made upon estimates to be made by said chief engineer. All works to be constructed hereunder shall be designed for delivery of water by gravity and all such water shall, before it is delivered to any municipality, be properly filtered under direction of the commission.

§ 535. Maintenance and operation of works. Upon completion of any conservation water works as provided hereunder, the commission shall maintain and shall operate the same and shall guard the waters from contamination. The commission shall cause records to be kept of the quantity of water delivered to the central points and the same shall be measured by meter to each municipality and the commission shall render to each municipality in a union water district annually as of the first day of January a statement of the quantity so delivered for the calendar year last preceding.

If the quantity of water so delivered exceeds the aggregate quantity due to a municipality based on the rate of one hundred and twenty-five gallons per diem to each actual inhabitant thereof as shown in the petition herein provided, then a charge shall be made to such municipality for such excess and at such rate per million gallons as the commission shall determine. Payment for such excess by such municipality shall be made on or before July first of each calendar year to the commission. The commission shall annually apportion the whole sum so received among the municipalities in proportion to the amount which each has contributed to the cost of the conservation water works and shall promptly pay to each municipality its share thereof. Upon the completion and placing in operation of such water works, the commission shall employ such superintendent and assistants as it deems necessary for the proper and economical operation and administration thereof, and shall purchase and supply such materials and labor as are necessary in the maintenance, repair and operation. The commission shall cause an accurate account of all such expenses to be made and kept and shall report the same annually in the month of January for the calendar year last past.

The commission may from time to time, upon temporary loan certificates to be issued by it, borrow such sums as may be necessary to carry on such operation and maintenance. Such certificates shall bear interest at the rate of six per centum and shall be sold at not less than par and each municipality within a union water district shall be liable for its share of such expense in the proportion which it contributed to the original cost of the works. The annual amounts for such expenses, as apportioned by the commission, shall be paid by each municipality on the first day of March following the calendar year in which the said expenses were incurred. Interest to March first shall be included in the sum annually reported by the commission for such expense. A member of the board of trustees of a union water district shall be reimbursed by his municipality for his actual and necessary expenses and disbursements paid or incurred by him in the performance of

14

his duties, upon vouchers audited and approved in the manner
provided by law for other claims against such municipality.

§ 536. **Cost and expenses.** If the cost of a conservation water
works exceeds the original estimate of the commission, the excess
shall be borne among the municipalities according to the proportion which each contributed to the estimated cost and the same
shall be raised by each municipality in a manner to be determined
by it and the said sum paid over to the conservation commission.
If the total cost of such construction shall be less than the cost as
estimated and as raised by the municipalities, such excess shall be
refunded to said municipalities by the conservation commission
ratably as the same was contributed, and when so refunded, the
same shall be used by said municipalities to retire the bonds issued
by them or paid into the sinking fund for the retirement of said
bonds.

All cost and expenses on the part of the state of New York,
including the expense of engineering or other professional services
incurred on account of the construction of conservation water
works or the acquiring of lands and diversion rights shall be
deemed a part of the cost thereof to be borne by the municipalities in a union water district, and shall be estimated as part of
the expense and shall be paid from the funds raised by said
municipalities for said purpose.

§ 537. **When other municipalities may participate; regulations.** Any municipality originally eligible to membership in a
union water district and not a member thereof, may on a majority
vote of the governing board or body of such municipality, or in
case of a water district, the town board may apply by petition to
the conservation commission and to the trustees of such union
water district to become a member of such union water district.
If the commission and the board of trustees approve the petition
the commission shall estimate and determine the cost of additional construction to provide for service of water to such municipality from the conservation water works, and shall likewise estimate and determine what share of the original cost thereof should
be paid by such petitioning municipality and shall report the
same to it and to the board of trustees. Such municipality shall
thereupon in the manner hereinbefore provided in the original
formation of a union water district determine whether it will issue bonds to cover the aggregate amount so reported and if the
same is determined in the affirmative, bonds shall be issued and

sold by such municipality and the proceeds raised and deposited and taxes imposed for the retirement of such bonds issued, in the same manner as in case of the original organization of a union water district. The proceeds of such bonds issued shall be deposited to the credit of the commission for the purposes of this act in the manner hereinbefore provided. Upon the deposit of such funds, such municipality shall thereupon become a member of such union water district and shall be supplied with water from such conservation water works.

The funds so deposited by said municipality shall be disposed of as follows: The estimated cost of the additional construction due to each municipality becoming a member of a union water district shall be deducted; the remainder shall be apportioned to each municipality in the district including the municipality thus last added thereto, in the proportion in which each has contributed to the cost of the conservation water works, and the commission shall as soon as possible pay to each municipality its share thereof. All sums so received by each municipality shall be applied by it to the payment of the principal of any outstanding bonds which it may have issued for the construction of conservation water works.

§ 538. Sale of water by commission. The commission, with the unanimous consent of the board of trustees of a union water district, may sell water by meter to water works companies or others, exclusive of municipal corporations, provided such water is for use or resale in territory outside that of any municipality in such district and provided that no additional construction connected with the conservation water works shall be necessitated by reason of such sale, except for the installation of meters to measure water so sold and for meter houses and for not exceeding five hundred feet of pipe lines for connections to each of such meters.

Contracts for such sale shall be limited to periods of five years from the time of making the same, and upon the expiration thereof, new contracts so limited may be made in like manner.

The receipts from such sales shall be applied, first, to the installation of meters and appurtenances above named, and the remainder shall be distributed among the municipalities which are members of the union water district, and in the proportion in which each has contributed to the cost of the conservation water works.

§ 539. Definitions. The term " chief executive officer of a municipality" as used in this article shall in the case of a city be deemed to refer to the mayor thereof; in case of a village, the village president; in case of a town, the supervisor; in case of a water district, the supervisor of the town within which such district or the major part thereof is located.

§ 2. This act shall take effect immediately.

Chap. 234.

AN ACT to amend the village law, in relation to providing an additional remedy for purchasers of land at village tax sales of certain villages.

Became a law April 9, 1913, with the approval of the Governor. Passed, three-fifths being present.

The People of the State of New York, represented in Senate and Assembly, do enact as follows:

§§ 124-135 added to L. 1909, ch. 64.

Section 1. Article five of chapter sixty-four of the laws of nineteen hundred and nine, entitled "An act relating to villages, constituting chapter sixty-four of the consolidated laws," is hereby amended by adding thereto the following sections:

Action by holder of tax sale certificate for amount paid.

§ 134. In each village in this state adjoining a city having a population of over three hundred thousand inhabitants situate within a county having a population of four hundred thousand or upwards, excluding New York and Kings counties, the number of such inhabitants in each instance to be ascertained by reference to the latest state enumeration, the holder, including such village, of any certificate of sale heretofore or hereafter executed by the village treasurer, may recover the amount paid, stated in said certificate, with all interest, additions and expenses allowed by law, and for that purpose may maintain an action in the supreme court or in the county court of the county in which such village is situate. Jurisdiction of such action is hereby conferred upon said county court.

Jurisdiction of county court.

Limitation, law and practice applicable.

§ 135. The action provided for in the last section may be commenced at any time after two years from the date that the tax or assessment on account of which the sale was had was payable and all the provisions of law and the rules of practice relating to actions for the foreclosure of mortgages shall apply to the action thereby authorized so far as practicable, except as herein otherwise specially provided. It shall be sufficient for the plaintiff to set *Sufficiency of complaint.* forth in his complaint in such action a copy of or the substance of his certificate of sale and the interest, additions and expense claimed by him, with a statement that the same have not been paid and that the plaintiff elects to recover as herein provided, also that the defendants have or claim to have or may have some interest in or lien upon the property affected by the action. The plaintiff in such action shall include and join therein and may likewise *What certificates to be included.* recover upon all prior and subsequent certificates of sale held by him, executed by the village treasurer, relating to the same real property in whole or in part. He may include and join in one action all such certificates of sale relating to two or more separate and *district parcels of real property belonging to the same person or persons, notwithstanding the fact that other defendants in said action may not be interested or have liens upon all of the parcels included and joined in said action. He shall make parties to the *Parties to action.* action the owner or owners of and all other persons interested in the real property affected, or any part thereof, including the holders of all prior and subsequent certificates of sale as shown by the records in the village treasurer's office. He may make parties thereto any municipal corporation which claims an interest in or lien upon the premises described in the complaint or any part thereof, by reason of any tax or assessment levied by said municipal corporation or on account of any other claim which said municipal corporation may have or claim to have against said real property.

The defendants in said action who are the holders of certificates *Defendant holders of certificates, how paid.* of sale, shall be paid from the proceeds of sale the several amounts paid for the real estate as mentioned and described in the certificates of sale held by them, with all interest, additions and expenses allowed by law, so far as the said proceeds shall suffice to pay the same, in the order of the lawful priority of the liens and the interests of the respective parties in and against the premises as the same may be determined in the action. It shall be sufficient for *Sufficiency of answer of such defendants.* any such defendant to set forth in his answer the certificate of sale or the substance thereof, with the other allegations in effect as therein provided, with regard to the complaint in the action. A defendant alleging irregularity or invalidity in any tax, assess- *Invalidity of tax, how pleaded.* ment or sale shall particularly specify in his answer such irregu- larity or invalidity.

---

* So in original.

Power of court to determine and enforce rights. The court shall have full power to determine and enforce in all respects the rights, claims and demands of the several parties to said action, including the rights, claims and demands of the defendants as between themselves, to direct a sale of such property and the distribution or other disposition of the proceeds of such **Parties may become purchasers.** sale. Any party to the action may become the purchaser on any such sale.

Validity of certificate, sale and taxes. § 136. Every certificate of sale on which the holder shall elect to recover, as herein provided, shall presumptively be valid and shall be presumptive evidence that the sale was regular and valid and that all previous steps and proceedings required by law were duly had and taken. No such certificate of sale and no tax or assessment for the nonpayment of which the same was executed shall be deemed invalid or impaired on account of any irregularity or illegality therein or in the proceedings relating thereto, unless it is shown that the person complaining thereof has suffered actual injury and damage therefrom and then only to the extent of such injury and damage, and no such tax, assessment or certificate of sale shall be deemed invalid or impaired on account of any error or omission in the description of the property assessed or sold if the description is sufficient to identify such property with reasonable certainty.

Remedy provided additional to other remedies. § 137. The remedy herein provided shall be in addition to all other remedies allowed by law, with regard to certificates of sale, and shall not be dependent upon them or any of them, and may be had whether notice to redeem has been given or not.

Title vested by conveyance made pursuant to judgment in action herein provided. A conveyance made pursuant to a judgment in any such action brought as herein provided shall vest in the purchaser all right, title, interest, claim, lien and equity of redemption in or against the premises sold of all the parties to the action and of all persons claiming under them or any or either of them, subsequent to the filing of the notice of the pendency of the action, or whose conveyance or encumbrance is subsequent or is subsequently recorded, except subsequent taxes and assessments and sales on account thereof and except taxes and assessments which were liens on the premises at the time of the filing of a notice of the pendency of the action, but for the nonpayment of which no sale had been had prior thereto and any sales on account of such taxes and of such parties and persons shall be barred and forever foreclosed by the judgment in said action of all right, title, interest, lien and equity of redemption in and to the premises sold or any part thereof, except as aforesaid.

§ 138. The judgment in said action shall designate the village *Sale to be made by* treasurer of such village as the officer to make sale of real property *village* in any action brought as herein provided and said village treasurer *treasurer;* for conducting said sale shall receive the same fees as are allowed *fees.* by law to a referee appointed by a judgment in an action to foreclose a mortgage upon real estate. Unless the judgment otherwise *Payment of* directs, the village treasurer making the sale must, out of the pro- *taxes and assessments* ceeds, first pay as a part of the expenses of the sale all taxes and *from proceeds.* assessments which are liens upon the property sold, but which have become such subsequent to the filing of notice of pendency of the action or for the nonpayment of which no sale had been had prior thereto and redeem the property sold from any sales for unpaid taxes and assessments which were had subsequent to the filing of such notice of pendency and shall pay all unpaid taxes and assessments assessed against said property by any other municipal corporation and redeem such property from any sales for unpaid taxes and assessments made by any other municipal corporation. The plaintiff's costs and allowances, exclusive of disbursements, shall *Amount of plaintiff's* not exceed fifteen dollars if he recovers less than fifty dollars, or *costs.* twenty-five dollars if he recovers more than fifty dollars and less than five hundred dollars, unless in such a case the court shall, in its discretion, otherwise direct. If the plaintiff recovers more than five hundred dollars, his costs shall be at the rate allowed by law in actions to foreclose mortgages upon real estate. The village treasurer may have made such tax and title searches of each *Tax and* parcel of land involved in any action brought as hereinbefore pro- *title searches.* vided, to which the village is a party, as he deems best in the interest of the village. Whenever the village is the owner and *When* holder of tax liens against the certificates of sale of premises di- *village may bid* rected in or by a judgment in any such action to be sold, the village *at sale.* treasurer may attend such sale and bid thereat such an amount as he deems best in the interest of the village not exceeding, however, the aggregate amount due upon the liens and certificates of sale held by the village, plus the amount of all prior liens and the legal costs and expenses of the action and sale.

Actions instituted hereunder on account of tax sale certificates *Actions on* held by any village shall be commenced by the village treasurer in *behalf of village,* his discretion or whenever instructed to do so by the village board *how instituted.* of trustees. For the purpose of instituting such action, the vil- *Attorney.* lage treasurer is authorized to employ an attorney, whose compensation shall be limited to the costs recoverable in each action instituted by him.

§ 2. This act shall take effect immediately.

Chap. 235.

AN ACT to amend the agricultural law, in relation to the creation
of a bureau of supervision of co-operative associations.

Became a law April 9, 1913, with the approval of the Governor. Passed,
three-fifths being present.

*The People of the State of New York, represented in Senate
and Assembly, do enact as follows:*

§ 319
added to
L. 1909,
ch. 9.

Section 1. Article fourteen of chapter nine of the laws of nineteen hundred and nine, entitled "An act in relation to agriculture,
constituting chapter one of the consolidated laws," is hereby
amended by adding thereto a new section, to be section three
hundred and nineteen, to read as follows:

§ 319. **Bureau of supervision of co-operative associations.**
There is hereby established in the department of agriculture a
bureau of supervision of co-operative associations. The bureau
shall be in charge of the superintendent who shall be appointed
by the commissioner of agriculture. He shall receive an annual
salary of three thousand dollars, and all necessary traveling and
other expenses incurred in the performance of his duties. The
superintendent of co-operative associations shall under the direction of the commissioner of agriculture have general charge of the
development of agricultural co-operative associations, for the buying and selling of farm produce throughout the state; shall assist
at the organization of such associations at points where they can
be developed; shall issue such information as shall be necessary
and desirable for the increase of co-operative associations of this
class, and shall collect and disseminate through farmers' institutes
or otherwise, as the commissioner may direct, information, statistics and other assistance leading to the development of co-operative associations. Such superintendent shall also visit from time
to time co-operative associations formed in this state and assist
them with aid and advice in the management and conduct of
their affairs. He shall report quarterly to the commissioner of
agriculture the results of his endeavors and the conditions of co-operative associations within the state.

§ 2. This act shall take effect immediately.

Chap. 236.

AN ACT to amend the penal law, in relation to bucket shops.

Became a law April 9, 1913, with the approval of the Governor. Passed, three-fifths being present.

The People of the State of New York, represented in Senate and Assembly, do enact as follows:

Section 1. Section three hundred and ninety of chapter eighty-eight of the laws of nineteen hundred and nine, entitled "An act providing for the punishment of crime, constituting chapter forty of the consolidated laws," is hereby amended to read as follows: _{L. 1909, ch. 88, § 390 amended.}

§ 390. **Acts prohibited; penalty for violation.** Any person, co-partnership, firm, association or corporation, whether acting in his, their or its own right, or as the officer, agent, servant, correspondent or representative of another, who shall,

1. Make or offer to make, or assist in making or offering to make any contract respecting the purchase or sale, either upon credit or margin, of any securities or commodities, including all evidences of debt or property and options for the purchase thereof, shares in any corporation or association, bonds, coupons, scrip, rights, choses in action and other evidences of debt or property and options for the purchase thereof or anything movable that is bought and sold,[1] intending[2] that such contract shall be[3] terminated, closed or settled according to, or upon the basis of the public market quotations of prices made on any board of trade or exchange upon which such commodities or securities are dealt in, and without intending a bona fide purchase or sale of the same; or,

2. Makes or offers to make or assists in making or offering to make any contract respecting the purchase or sale, either upon credit or margin, of any such securities or commodities[4] intending[2] that such contract shall[5] be deemed terminated, closed and settled when such market quotations of prices for such securities or commodities named in such contract shall reach a certain figure, without intending a bona fide purchase or sale of the same; or,

3. Makes or offers to make, or assists in making or offering to

---

[1] Words "wherein both the parties thereto," omitted.
[2] Formerly "intend."
[3] Words "or may be," omitted.
[4] Words "wherein both parties," omitted.
[5] Words "or may" omitted.

make any contract respecting the purchase or sale, either upon
credit or margin of any such securities or commodities,[6] not intending[2] the actual bona fide receipt or delivery of any such securities or commodities, but[7] intending[2] a settlement of such contract
based upon the difference in such public market quotations of
prices at which said securities or commodities are, or are asserted
to be, bought or sold; or,

4. Shall, as owner, keeper, proprietor or person in charge of,
or as officer, director, stockholder, agent, servant, correspondent
or representative of such owner, keeper, proprietor or person in
charge, or of any other person, keep, conduct or operate any
bucket shop, as hereinafter defined; or knowingly permit or
allow or induce any person, copartnership, firm, association or
corporation whether acting in his, their or its own right, or as
the officer, agent, servant, correspondent or representative of
another to make or offer to make therein, or to assist in making
therein, or in offering to make therein, any of the contracts
specified in any of the three preceding subdivisions of this section,

Shall be guilty of a felony and on conviction thereof shall,
if a corporation, be punished by a fine of not more than five thousand dollars for each offense and all other persons so convicted
shall be punished by a fine of not more than one thousand dollars or by imprisonment for not more than five years, or by
both such fine and imprisonment. The prosecution, conviction
and punishment of a corporation hereunder shall not be deemed
to be a prosecution, conviction or punishment of any of its officers, directors or stockholders.

§ 395 added. § 2. Article thirty-six of such chapter is hereby amended by
adding at the end thereof a new section, to be section three hundred and ninety-five, to read as follows:

§ 395. **Witnesses.** No person shall be excused from attending
and testifying, or producing any book, paper, or other document
before any court or magistrate, upon any trial, investigation, or
proceeding initiated by the district attorney, grand jury or court
for a violation of any of the provisions of this article, upon the
ground or for the reason that the testimony or evidence, documentary or otherwise, required of him may tend to convict him
of a crime or to subject him to a penalty or forfeiture; but no

---

[2] Formerly " intend."
[6] Words "wherein both parties do," omitted.
[7] Word "do " omitted.

person shall be prosecuted or subjected to any penalty or forfeiture for or on account of any transaction, matter or thing
concerning which he may so testify or produce evidence, documentary or otherwise, and no testimony so given or produced
shall be received against him upon any criminal action, suit or
proceeding, investigation, inquisition or inquiry.

§ 3. This act shall take effect immediately.

Chap. 237.

AN ACT to authorize the board of supervisors of the county of
Westchester to pay, as a county charge, a sum of money deposited with the county treasurer of said county by order of
the supreme court.

Became a law April 9, 1913, with the approval of the Governor. Passed,
three-fifths being present.

*The People of the State of New York, represented in Senate
and Assembly, do enact as follows:*

Section 1. The board of supervisors of the county of Westchester is hereby authorized and empowered to audit and pay, as a
county charge against said county, the amount that said board may
determine to be due as the balance of a certain fund of eight
hundred and eighty-nine dollars and forty-two cents, deposited
with the county treasurer of the county of Westchester on or about
November four, eighteen hundred and seventy-five, in an action
in the supreme court of the state of New York, brought in the
county of Westchester, between Sarah Embree, plaintiff, against
Margaret Embree, Hannah Embree, Araminta Embree, Alma
Embree and Albert Embree, defendants, for the determination of
their interests in real property situated in said county, and for a
sale thereof, which fund was invested by the county treasurer of
the county of Westchester in a bond and mortgage of George W.
King and others in the year eighteen hundred and seventy-eight,
and upon which bond and mortgage, after foreclosure, there was
realized but the sum of eighty-eight dollars. Said board of supervisors is hereby empowered to investigate the investment made
by the county treasurer of said county as aforesaid, and to pay to
the persons entitled to receive the moneys so deposited with said
county treasurer, the difference between the amount in the hands

of the said county treasurer as realized upon the aforesaid foreclosure and the amount deposited with said official, to wit: the
sum of eight hundred and one dollars and forty-two cents, together
with the interest thereon at the rate of three per centum per
annum, provided, however, that it is determined by said board of
supervisors that the persons entitled to receive the fund herein
referred to, were infants or were not entitled to demand or receive
said moneys within six years prior to the passage of this act.

§ 2. This act shall take effect immediately.

Chap. 238.

AN ACT to amend the code of criminal procedure, in relation to
compensation of witnesses committed.

Became a law April 9, 1913, with the approval of the Governor. Passed,
three-fifths being present.

*The People of the State of New York, represented in Senate
and Assembly, do enact as follows:*

§ 618-b
amended.

Section 1. Section six hundred and eighteen-b of the code of
criminal procedure is hereby amended to read as follows:

§ 618-b. **Judge may order witness to enter into an undertaking
for appearance or be committed on refusal to comply therewith.**
Whenever a judge of a court of record in this state is satisfied,
by proof on oath, that a person residing or being in this state is a
necessary and material witness for the people in a criminal action
or proceeding pending in any of the courts of this state, he may,
after an opportunity has been given to such person to appear
before such judge and be heard in opposition thereto, order such
person to enter into a written undertaking, with such sureties
and in such sum as he may deem proper, to the effect that he will
appear and testify at the court in which such action or proceeding
may be heard or tried, and upon his neglect or refusal to comply
with the order for that purpose, the judge must commit him to
such place, other than a state prison, as he may deem proper,
until he comply or be legally discharged. [1]Said judge shall also
in said order fix an amount in his discretion not exceeding the
sum of three dollars per day, to be paid to said witness for com-

---
[1] Remainder of section new.

pensation during the time of his detention; said sum to be paid by the county treasurer of the county, upon filing with him a certified copy of the order of commitment and the order discharging such witness from custody.

§ 2. This act shall take effect September first, nineteen hundred and thirteen.

In effect
Sept. 1,
1913.

Chap. 239.

AN ACT reappropriating an unexpended balance for the Saratoga Springs state reservation.

Became a law April 9, 1913, with the approval of the Governor. Passed by a two-thirds vote.

The People of the State of New York, represented in Senate and Assembly, do enact as follows:

Section 1. The sum of four hundred sixty-two thousand eight hundred twenty-five dollars and fifty-one cents ($462,825.51), being the unexpended balance of the appropriation made by chapter three hundred and ninety-four of the laws of nineteen hundred and eleven for the selection, location and appropriation of certain lands in the town of Saratoga Springs, for the said reservation, is hereby reappropriated from the same funds and for the same purpose as provided by said act.

§ 2. This act shall take effect immediately.

Chap. 240.

AN ACT to reappropriate certain unexpended balances of former appropriations.

Became a law April 9, 1913, with the approval of the Governor. Passed by a two-thirds vote.

The People of the State of New York, represented in Senate and Assembly, do enact as follows:

Section 1. The following unexpended balances of former appropriations are hereby re-appropriated for the same objects and purposes and to be expended in the same manner, as provided in the acts making the original appropriations: the sum of eighteen thousand, five hundred and fifteen dollars and seven cents, ($18,515.07), for the improvement of the Black River canal north of Boonville and for the repair of the structures thereof, as provided by chapter eight hundred and six of the laws of nineteen hundred and eleven; the sum of two hundred and twenty-one dollars and ninety-six cents ($221.96), for the improvement of the Cayuga inlet in the city of Ithaca and the repair and reconstruction of the bridges over the same, as provided in chapter eight hundred and eleven of the laws of nineteen hundred and eleven; the sum of four thousand dollars ($4,000) for the salary and necessary traveling expenses of an engineer to be employed by the superintendent of public works to act in an advisory capacity, as provided by chapter eight hundred and eleven of the laws of nineteen hundred and eleven; the sum of three hundred and eighty-eight dollars and fifty-three cents ($388.53), for repairing and reconstructing the dikes and repairing the banks of the Chemung river in the city of Elmira, as provided by chapter two hundred and sixty-two of the laws of nineteen hundred and eleven; the sum of six hundred and eighty dollars and seventy-six cents ($680.76) for traveling expenses of the inspectors of steam vessels and for the supplies necessary for the performance·of their official duties, as provided by chapter eight hundred and ten of the laws of nineteen hundred and eleven; the sum of thirteen thousand, eight hundred and seventy-five dollars and two cents ($13,875.02), for the construction of a new bridge over the Black River canal at East Dominick street in the city of Rome, as provided by chapter eight hundred and seventy-seven of the laws of nineteen hundred and eleven; the sum of three hundred and ten dollars and thirty-four cents ($310.34), for the repair and maintenance of the two state dams and the locks therein situated on state land on the Saranac river between Middle Saranac lake and Oseetah lake, as provided by chapter eight hundred and eleven of the laws of nineteen hundred and eleven; the sum of one thousand and fourteen dollars and sixty-eight cents ($1,014.68), for the improvement and removing of obstructions of Senix river and Aersconk creek, Suffolk county, as provided by chapter eight hundred and eighty-nine of the laws of nineteen hundred and eleven; the sum of thirteen thousand three hundred and seventy-nine dollars and fifty cents ($13,379.50), for certain improvements in the channel and banks of the Mohawk river and West Canada creek, made necessary by the building of the barge canal, as provided by chapter one hundred and thirty-two of the laws of nineteen hundred and eleven; the sum of thirty thousand dollars ($30,000), for the construction of a bridge over a portion of the Oswego river at Phoenix, as provided by chapter seven hundred and ninety-two of the laws of nineteen hundred and eleven; the sum of fifty thousand dollars ($50,000), for the construction of a bridge over the barge canal in the city of Fulton, as provided by chapter seven hundred and ninety-three of the laws of nineteen hundred and eleven.

§ 2. This act shall take effect immediately.

Chap. 241.

AN ACT to amend the canal law, in relation to advances of moneys to division engineers, and drafts of money by the superintendent of public works.

Became a law April 9, 1913, with the approval of the Governor. Passed, three-fifths being present.

The People of the State of New York, represented in Senate and Assembly, do enact as follows:

Section 1. Sections sixty-four and one hundred and fifty-three of chapter thirteen of the laws of nineteen hundred and nine, entitled "An act relating to canals, constituting chapter five of the consolidated laws," as amended[1] by chapter one hundred and thirteen of the laws of nineteen hundred and ten, are hereby amended to read as follows: L. 1909, ch. 13, § 64, as amended by L. 1910, ch. 113, amended; § 153 amended.

§ 64. **Advances to division engineers.** If a division engineer has filed his official undertaking, he may draw on the comptroller for advances to meet the expenses of the engineer department upon his division. If such draft be countersigned by the state engineer, and a receipt for the amount thereof be filed with the comptroller, the comptroller shall pay the same by warrant on the treasurer in favor of such division engineer. But the advances unaccounted for to a division engineer shall, at no time, exceed sixty thousand[2] dollars, and no money shall be drawn from

---

[1] Section 153 was not amended by L. 1910, ch. 113.
[2] Formerly "fifty thousand."

the treasury to meet the expenses of the engineer department of the canals, other than those pertaining to the office of the state engineer, in any other manner.

§ 153. **Drafts of money by the superintendent for the payment of contracts.** The superintendent of public works may draw on the comptroller for any sum to be paid to a contractor on his contract, and if a copy of the contract shall have been duly filed in the office of the comptroller, and a receipt of the contractor for such drafts filed in the same office, the comptroller shall draw a warrant on the treasury for the amount of such draft. The superintendent of public works shall not be allowed to have in his hands at any one time more than one hundred and fifty thousand[3] dollars, and every sum advanced to or received by him shall be deemed to remain in his hands until its application shall have been properly accounted for to the comptroller.

§ 2. This act shall take effect immediately.

Chap. 242.

AN ACT to expedite the work of improving the Oswego canal by providing for the suspension of navigation on a portion thereof during the season of nineteen hundred and thirteen.

Became a law April 9, 1913, with the approval of the Governor. Passed, three-fifths being present.

The People of the State of New York, represented in Senate and Assembly, do enact as follows:

Section 1. The superintendent of public works is hereby authorized to close to navigation such portion or portions of the Oswego canal between barge canal lock number two on said canal and Lake Ontario, during the year nineteen hundred and thirteen, as in his judgment may result in expediting the progress of the improvement work on said canal; provided that nothing herein contained shall be deemed to authorize the closing of said canal during any other year than that herein named.

§ 2. All conflicting acts or parts of acts are hereby repealed to an extent that they may not conflict herewith.

§ 3. This act shall take effect immediately.

---

[3] Formerly " one hundred thousand."

Chap. 243.

AN ACT to provide for the retention and maintenance of portions of the present Champlain and Erie canals in the counties of Saratoga and Albany for navigation purposes after the completion of the barge canal.

Became a law April 9, 1913, with the approval of the Governor. Passed, three-fifths being present.

The People of the State of New York, represented in Senate and Assembly, do enact as follows:

Section 1. On and after the completion of the improvement of the Erie and Champlain canals, as authorized by chapter one hundred and forty-seven of the laws of nineteen hundred and three as amended, that portion of the present unimproved Champlain canal from its junction with the improved Erie canal at Waterford southerly to its junction with the present unimproved Erie canal, and that portion of the present unimproved Erie canal from its said junction with the said Champlain canal southerly to lock number two, Erie canal, together with the so-called Watervliet basin and the so-called Watervliet and Port Schuyler side-cuts in addition to their use as canal feeders shall be retained as part of the canal system of the state and shall be maintained together with the towing-path and other necessary structures in a condition for navigation on the same by craft of the dimensions now making use of said portions of the canals. Retention of portions of present Champlain and Erie canals as part of canal system.

§ 2. The cost of maintaining said portions of the Erie and Champlain canals referred to in section one of this act shall be paid from any funds provided for the repair, operation and maintenance of the improved system of canals, when the same shall have been completed and placed in commission. On and after the completion of the canal improvement, as authorized by said chapter one hundred and forty-seven of the laws of nineteen hundred and three, the superintendent of public works may fix and determine the hours of the day during which the portions of the unimproved Champlain and Erie canals described in section one of this act shall be open to navigation. Cost of maintenance, how paid. Hours when open to navigation.

§ 3. This act shall take effect immediately.

Chap. 244.

AN ACT reappropriating an unexpended balance for the purpose of furnishing proper terminals and facilities for barge canal traffic.

Became a law April 9, 1913, with the approval of the Governor. Passed by a two-thirds vote.

The People of the State of New York, represented in Senate and Assembly, do enact as follows:

Section 1. The sum of seven hundred fifty-eight thousand seven hundred forty-six dollars and seventeen cents ($758,746.17), being the unexpended balance of the appropriation made by chapter seven hundred forty-six of the laws of nineteen hundred and eleven, to be expended in carrying out the purposes of the act for furnishing proper terminals and facilities for barge canal traffic, is hereby reappropriated from the same funds and for the same purpose as provided in said act.

§ 2. This act shall take effect immediately.

Chap. 245.

AN ACT to amend chapter one hundred and thirty-two of the laws of nineteen hundred and eleven, entitled "An act to provide for certain improvements in the channel and banks of the Mohawk river and West Canada creek, made necessary by the building of the barge canal, and making an appropriation therefor."

Became a law April 9, 1913, with the approval of the Governor. Passed, three-fifths being present.

The People of the State of New York, represented in Senate and Assembly, do enact as follows:

§ 3a added to L. 1911, ch. 132.

Section 1. Chapter one hundred and thirty-two of the laws of nineteen hundred and eleven, entitled "An act to provide for certain improvements in the channel and banks of the Mohawk river and West Canada creek, made necessary by the building of the barge canal, and making an appropriation therefor," is hereby amended by adding thereto a new section, to be known as section three-a, to read as follows:

§ 3-a. The additional sum of sixty thousand dollars ($60,000), **Additional appropriation.** or so much thereof as may be necessary, is hereby appropriated out of any moneys in the state treasury, not otherwise appropriated, for carrying out to completion the purposes expressed in the foregoing provisions of this act, payable by the state treasurer on the warrant of the comptroller upon vouchers audited by the superintendent of public works.

§ 2. This act shall take effect immediately.

Chap. 246.

AN ACT to provide for the construction of a bridge over the Black river and Moose river at Lyons Falls, in the county of Lewis, and making appropriations and reappropriations therefor.

Became a law April 9, 1913, with the approval of the Governor. Passed, three-fifths being present.

The People of the State of New York, represented in Senate and Assembly, do enact as follows:

Section 1. The superintendent of public works is hereby author- **Construction of bridge authorized** ized to construct a reinforced concrete arch bridge over the Black river and Moose river at Lyons Falls, in the county of Lewis, on the street or highway crossing the bridge over the Black River canal constructed or to be constructed pursuant to chapter five hundred and ten of the laws of nineteen hundred and twelve, according to plans and specifications to be prepared by the state engineer and surveyor and approved by the canal board.

§ 2. Of the moneys appropriated by chapter five hundred and **Appropriation.** ten of the laws of nineteen hundred and twelve for the construction of a bridge over the Black River canal at Lyons Falls the sum of thirty thousand dollars ($30,000), or so much thereof as may be necessary, is hereby reappropriated for the construction of the bridge provided for in section one of this act; and the additional sum of twenty thousand dollars ($20,000), or so much thereof as may be necessary, is hereby appropriated out of any moneys in the state treasury not otherwise appropriated, for the same purpose. The moneys appropriated or reappropriated by **Moneys appropriated, how paid.** this act shall be paid out by the state treasurer on the warrant of the comptroller to the order of the superintendent of public works, and no part of said moneys shall be available except for necessary surveys, plans, specifications and advertising until a contract or contracts shall have been executed for the completion of such bridge within the aggregate amount herein appropriated and re-appropriated.

§ *2. This act shall take effect immediately.

Chap. 247.

AN ACT to amend the general city law, in relation to the powers of cities.

Became a law April 10, 1913, with the approval of the Governor. Passed, three-fifths being present.

The People of the State of New York, represented in Senate and Assembly, do enact as follows:

Art. 2a added to L. 1909, ch. 26.

Section 1. Chapter twenty-six of the laws of nineteen hundred and nine, entitled "An act in relation to cities, constituting chapter twenty-one of the consolidated laws," is hereby amended by inserting therein after article two a new article, to be two-a thereof, to read as follows:

ARTICLE 2-A.
POWERS OF CITIES.

Section 19. General grant of powers.
20. Grant of specific powers.
21. Public or municipal purpose defined.
22. This grant in addition to existing powers.
23. Powers hereby granted, how to be exercised.
24. Construction of this article.

§ 19. **General grant of powers.** Every city is granted power to regulate, manage and control its property and local affairs and is granted all the rights, privileges and jurisdiction necessary and proper for carrying such power into execution. No enumeration of powers in this or any other law shall operate to restrict the meaning of this general grant of power, or to exclude other powers comprehended within this general grant.

§ 20. **Grant of specific powers.** Subject to the constitution and general laws of this state, every city is empowered:

---

* So in original.

1. To contract and be contracted with and to institute, maintain and defend any action or proceeding in any court.

2. To take, purchase, hold and lease real and personal property within and without the limits of the city, and acquire by condemnation real and personal property within the limits of the city, for any public or municipal purpose, and to sell and convey the same, but the rights of a city in and to its water front, ferries, bridges, wharf property, land under water, public landings, wharves, docks, streets, avenues, parks, and all other public places, are hereby declared to be inalienable, except in the cases provided for by subdivision seven of this section.

3. To take by gift, grant, bequest or devise and to hold and administer real and personal property within and without the limits of the city, absolutely or in trust for any public or municipal purpose, upon such terms and conditions as may be prescribed by the grantor or donor and accepted by the city.

4. To levy and collect taxes on real and personal property for any public or municipal purpose.

5. To become indebted for any public or municipal purpose and to issue therefor the obligations of the city, to determine upon the form and the terms and conditions thereof, and to pledge the faith and credit of the city for payment of principal and interest thereof, or to make the same payable out of or a charge or lien upon specific property or revenues; to pay or compromise claims equitably payable by the city, though not constituting obligations legally binding on it, but it shall have no power to waive the defense of the statute of limitations or to grant extra compensation to any public officer, servant or contractor.

6. To establish and maintain sinking funds for the liquidation of principal and interest of any indebtedness, and to provide for the refunding of any indebtedness other than certificates of indebtedness or revenue bonds issued in anticipation of the collection of taxes for amounts actually contained or to be contained in the taxes for the year when such certificates or revenue bonds are issued or in the taxes for the year next succeeding, and payable out of such taxes.

7. To lay out, establish, construct, maintain, operate, alter and discontinue streets, sewers and drainage systems, water supply systems, and lighting systems, for lighting streets, public buildings and public places, and to lay out, establish, construct, main-

tain and operate markets, parks, playgrounds and public places, and upon the discontinuance thereof to sell and convey the same.

8. To control and administer the water front and waterways of the city and to establish, maintain, operate and regulate docks, piers, wharves, warehouses and all adjuncts and facilities for navigation and commerce and for the utilization of the water front and waterways and adjacent property.

9. To establish, construct and maintain, operate, alter and discontinue bridges, tunnels and ferries, and approaches thereto.

10. To grant franchises or rights to use the streets, waters, water front, public ways and public places of the city.

11. To construct and maintain public buildings, public works and public improvements, including local improvements, and assess and levy upon the property benefited thereby the cost thereof, in whole or in part.

12. To prevent and extinguish fires and to protect the inhabitants of the city and property within the city from loss or damage by fire or other casualty.

13. To maintain order, enforce the laws, protect property and preserve and care for the safety, health, comfort and general welfare of the inhabitants of the city and visitors thereto; and for any of said purposes to regulate and license occupations and businesses.

14. To create, maintain and administer a system or systems for the enumeration, identification and registration, or either, of the inhabitants of the city and visitors thereto, or such classes thereof as may be deemed advisable.

15. To establish, maintain, manage and administer hospitals, sanitaria, dispensaries, public baths, almshouses, workhouses, reformatories, jails and other charitable and correctional institutions; to relieve, instruct and care for children and poor, sick, infirm, defective, insane or inebriate persons; to provide for the burial of indigent persons; to contribute to and supervise charitable, eleemosynary, correctional or reformatory institutions wholly or partly under private control.

16. To establish and maintain such institutions and instrumentalities for the instruction, enlightenment, improvement, entertainment, recreation and welfare of its inhabitants as it may deem appropriate or necessary for the public interest or advantage.

17. To determine and regulate the number, mode of selection, terms of employment, qualifications, powers and duties and compensation of all employees of the city and the relations of

all officers and employees of the city to each other, to the city
and to the inhabitants.

18. To create a municipal civil service; to make rules for the
classification of the offices and employments in the city's service,
for appointments, promotions and examinations, and for the
registration and selection of laborers.

19. To regulate the manner of transacting the city's business
and affairs and the reporting of and accounting for all transactions of or concerning the city.

20. To provide methods and provide, manage and administer
funds for pensions and annuities for and retirement of city
officers and employees.

21. To investigate and inquire into all matters of concern to
the city or its inhabitants, and to require and enforce by subpoena the attendance of witnesses at such investigations.

22. To regulate by ordinance any matter within the powers of
the city, and to provide for the enforcement of ordinances by
legal proceedings, to compel compliance therewith, and by penalties, forfeitures and imprisonment to punish violations thereof.

23. To exercise all powers necessary and proper for carrying
into execution the powers granted to the city.

§ 21. **Public or municipal purpose and general welfare defined.**
The terms "public or municipal purpose," and "general welfare," as used in this article, shall each include the promotion
of education, art, beauty, charity, amusement, recreation, health,
safety, comfort and convenience, and all of the purposes enumerated in the last preceding section.

§ 22. **This grant in addition to existing powers.** The powers
granted by this article shall be in addition to and not in substitution for, all the powers, rights, privileges and functions existing in any city pursuant to any other provision of law.

§ 23. **Powers hereby granted, how to be exercised.** 1. The
powers granted by this act are to be exercised by the officer,
officers or official body vested with such powers by any other provision of law or ordinance (subject to amendment or repeal of
any such ordinance) and in the manner and subject to the conditions prescribed by law or ordinance (subject to amendment
or repeal of any such ordinance), but no provision of any special
or local law shall operate to defeat or limit in extent the grant
of powers contained in this act; and any provision of any special
or local law which in any city operates, in terms or in effect, to

prevent the exercise or limit the extent of any power granted
by this article, shall be superseded. Where any such provision
of special or local law is superseded under the provisions of this
subdivision, such power, freed from the limitations imposed by
such provision, shall be exercised by the same officer, officers or
official body that would be vested with the same under the provisions of this subdivision, if such provision had not been superseded, but the exercise thereof shall be subject to the limitations
provided for in subdivision two of this section.

2. In the absence of any provision of law or ordinance determining by whom or in what manner or subject to what conditions any
power granted by this act shall be exercised, the common council
or board of aldermen or corresponding legislative body of the city
shall, subject to the provisions of this section, have power by
ordinance to determine by whom and in what manner and subject to what conditions said power shall be exercised. The exercise
by any city of any power granted by this article not now vested in
such city or now vested in such city subject to provisions which
are superseded by the provisions of subdivision one of this section, shall be subject to the following limitations:

a. No city shall issue any obligations for expenses for maintenance, repairs or current operation or administration of the property or government of the city or otherwise than for betterments,
improvements and acquisitions of property of a permanent nature,
or for the purpose of refunding obligations of the city. No city
shall issue obligations until there shall first have been filed in the
office of the city clerk a certificate of the comptroller or other
chief financial officer of the city under his hand and seal, stating
(1) the then existing indebtedness of the city; (2) how much,
if any, thereof consists of certificates of indebtedness or revenue
bonds issued in anticipation of the collection of taxes, and how
much, if any, of such certificates or revenue bonds has not been
paid out of the taxes for the year when such certificates or revenue
bonds were issued or for the year next succeeding; (3) the amount
of the assessed valuation of the real estate of the city subject to
taxation, as shown by the assessment-rolls of said city on the last
previous assessment for state or county taxes; (4) a description
of the property or improvement for the acquisition or making of
which the debt is to be created; and (5) the probable life of such
property or improvement. Such certificate shall be a public
record. The term of payment of any obligations issued to secure

such debt shall not exceed the probable life of such property or improvement as stated in such certificate and shall in no case exceed fifty years. This subdivision shall not apply to certificates of indebtedness or revenue bonds issued in anticipation of the collection of taxes for amounts actually contained or to be contained in the taxes for the year when such certificates or revenue bonds are issued and payable out of such taxes. This subdivision shall not apply to certificates of indebtedness or revenue bonds issued in anticipation of the collection of taxes for amounts to be contained in the taxes for the year next succeeding the year when such certificates or revenue bonds are issued and payable out of such taxes, except that a certificate shall be filed as required by this subdivision before any such certificates or revenue bonds shall be issued.

b. No sale or lease of city real estate or of any franchise belonging to or under the control of the city shall be made or authorized except by vote of three-fourths of all the members of the common council or corresponding legislative body of the city. In case of a proposed sale or lease of real estate or of a franchise, the ordinance must provide for a disposition of the same at public auction to the highest bidder, under proper regulations as to the giving of security and after public notice to be published at least once each week for three weeks in the official paper or papers. A sale or lease of real estate or a franchise shall not be valid or take effect unless made as aforesaid and subsequently approved by a resolution of the board of estimate and apportionment in any city having such a board, and also approved by the mayor. No franchise shall be granted or be operated for a period longer than fifty years. The common council or corresponding legislative body of the city may, however, grant to the owner or lessees of an existing franchise, under which operations are being actually carried on, such additional rights or extensions in the street or streets in which the said franchise exists, upon such terms as the interests of the city may require, with or without any advertisement, as the common council may determine, provided, however, that no such grant shall be operative unless approved by the board of estimate and apportionment in any city having such a board, and also by the mayor.

In any city the question whether any proposed sale or lease of city real estate or of any franchise belonging to or under the control of the city shall be approved shall, upon a demand being filed, as hereinafter provided, be submitted to the voters of such city at a general or special election, after public notice to be published at least once each week for three weeks in the official paper or papers. Such demand shall be subscribed and acknowledged by voters of the city equal in number to at least ten per centum of the total number of votes cast in such city at the last preceding general election and shall be filed in the office of the clerk of such city before the adoption of an ordinance or resolution making or authorizing such sale or lease. If such demand is filed, as aforesaid, such sale or lease of real estate or such franchise shall not take effect unless in addition to the foregoing requirements a majority of the electors voting thereon at such election shall vote in the affirmative.

The foregoing limitations shall not apply to the exercise by any city of any power now vested in it, where the existing provisions of law determining by whom or in what manner or subject to what conditions such power shall be exercised are not superseded by the provisions of subdivision one of this section; but in such case the exercise of such power shall be subject only to such existing provisions of law, and shall not be limited or restricted by any provision of this section.

§ 24. **Construction of this act.** This article shall be construed, not as an act in derogation of the powers of the state, but as one intended to aid the state in the execution of its duties, by providing adequate power of local government for the cities of the state.

§ 2. This act shall take effect immediately.

Chap. 248.

AN ACT to amend the executive law, in relation to powers of notaries public in New York county residing in Bronx county, ratifying their acts and continuing their powers in the new county of Bronx.

Became a law April 10, 1913, with the approval of the Governor. Passed, three-fifths being present.

The People of the State of New York, represented in Senate and Assembly, do enact as follows:

Subd. 1 added to L. 1909, ch. 23, § 105.

Section 1. Section one hundred and five of chapter twenty-three of the laws of nineteen hundred and nine, entitled "An act in relation to executive officers, constituting chapter eighteen of the consolidated laws," as amended by chapter six hundred and sixty-eight of the laws of nineteen hundred and eleven, is hereby amended by adding thereto, at the end thereof, a new subdivision, to be subdivision three, to read as follows:

3. All notaries public, appointed for the county of New York prior to January first, nineteen hundred and fourteen, shall have power, and shall be deemed to have had the power, to administer oaths and affirmations, to take affidavits and acknowledgments and proofs of deeds and other written instruments to be read in evidence or to be recorded in this state, in all cases in which commissioners of deeds may now take and certify the same, within the county of New York, including the territory embraced within the newly created county of Bronx, up to January first, nineteen hundred and fourteen; their official acts subsequent to the passage of the act creating Bronx county are hereby ratified and confirmed; and such notaries public residing in said county of Bronx on January first, nineteen hundred and fourteen, shall also have the power to exercise their functions as such notaries public in said county of Bronx for the full term for which they have been appointed; provided that, on or before January tenth, nineteen hundred and fourteen, they shall have filed in the clerk's office of the county of Bronx the certificate and signature provided for in section one hundred and two of this chapter.

§ 2. This act shall take effect immediately.

Chap. 249.

AN ACT to amend the general business law, in relation to regulating the profession of shorthand reporters.

Became a law April 10, 1913, with the approval of the Governor. Passed, three-fifths being present.

The People of the State of New York, represented in Senate and Assembly, do enact as follows:

Section 1. Article eight-a of chapter twenty-five of the laws of nineteen hundred and nine, entitled "An act relating to general business, constituting chapter twenty of the consolidated laws," as added by chapter five hundred and eighty-seven of the laws of nineteen hundred and eleven, is hereby amended to read as follows:

L. 1909, ch.
25, art. 8a,
as added by
L. 1911,
ch. 587,
amended.

ARTICLE 8-A.

CERTIFIED SHORTHAND REPORTERS.

§ 85.[2] **Certified shorthand *reported; defined.** A certified short-hand reporter is one who has been adjudged competent to report court proceedings, references, commissions, conventions, delibera-tive assemblies or meetings of like character.

§ 86.[3] **Qualifications.** Any citizen of the United States, or per-son who has duly declared his intention of becoming such citizen, residing or having a place for the regular transaction of business in this state, being over the age of twenty-one years, and of good moral character, and who shall have received from the regents of the university a certificate of his qualifications to practice as a public shorthand reporter as hereinafter provided, shall be styled and known as a certified short hand *reported, and no other person shall assume such title or use the abbreviation C. S. R., or any other words, letters or figures to indicate that the person using the same is such certified shorthand reporter.

§ 87.[4] **Idem; examination and certification; revocation.**[5] The regents of the university[6] shall appoint a board of three examiners,[7] which board shall after the year nineteen hundred and fourteen be composed of certified shorthand reporters. The term of office of the members of such board of examiners shall be three years, except that of the first board appointed under this article, one member shall hold office for one year, one member for two years, and one member for three years, such respective terms to be determined by the regents of the university, who shall also fill any vacancies which may occur in such board   [8]Said board of examiners shall,

---

* So in original.
[1] Schedule of sections materially amended.
[2] Section 85 new.
[3] Formerly § 85. Section heading formerly read: "Certified shorthand reporters; qualifications."
[4] Formerly § 86.
[5] Word "revocation" new.
[6] Words "shall make rules for the examination of persons applying for cer-tificates under this article and," omitted.
[7] Words "for the purpose," omitted.
[8] Following sentence new.

subject to the approval of the regents, make such rules and regulations, not inconsistent with the law, as may be necessary for the
proper performance of its duties. [8]Any member of the board may,
upon being duly designated by the board or a majority thereof,
administer oaths or take testimony concerning any matter within
the jurisdiction of the board. The regents shall charge for examination and certificates such fee as may be necessary to meet
the actual expenses of such examinations, and they shall report
annually their receipts and expenses under the provisions of this
article to the state comptroller, and pay the balance of the receipts over expenditures to the state treasurer. The regents may
revoke any such certificate for sufficient cause after written notice
to the holder thereof, and a hearing thereon.

§ 88.[9] **Exceptions.** Any person who shall submit to said board
of examiners satisfactory proof as to his character, competency
and qualifications, and that he has been actively engaged in the
practice of shorthand reporting for more than three years before
the enactment of this article, as hereby amended, or who is at the
time this article, as amended, takes effect a shorthand reporter duly
appointed as an official in any court of this state, and who
shall apply for such certificate on or before January first,
nineteen hundred and fourteen, may, upon the recommendation
of said board of examiners, receive from the board of regents a
certificate of exemption from such examination, which certificate
shall be registered and entitle him to practice as a certified shorthand reporter under this article.

§ 89.[10] **Extension of waiver.** Any person who was on the
thirtieth day of June, nineteen hundred and eleven, entitled to a
certificate of exemption as formerly provided by this article, but
who failed or neglected to make application therefor and to present evidence to entitle him thereto on or before June thirtieth,
nineteen hundred and twelve, must make such application and
present such evidence on or before January first, nineteen hundred
and fourteen, or he shall be deemed to have waived his right to
such certificate.

§ 89-a.[11] **Violations.** Any violation of the provisions of this
article shall be a misdemeanor.

§ 2. This act shall take effect immediately.

---

[8] Following sentence new.
[9] Formerly § 87. Section materially amended.
[10] Section 89, new.
[11] Formerly § 88.

Chap. 250.

AN ACT to amend the benevolent orders law, in relation to the National Order of the Daughters of Isabella.

Became a law April 10, 1913, with the approval of the Governor. Passed, three-fifths being present.

The People of the State of New York, represented in Senate and Assembly, do enact as follows:

L. 1909, ch. 11, § 2, subd. 21, as added by L. 1912, ch. 213 renumbered subd. 22; subd. 23 added.

Section 1. Subdivision twenty-one of section two of chapter eleven of the laws of nineteen hundred and nine, entitled "An act relating to benevolent orders, constituting chapter three of the consolidated laws," as added by chapter two hundred and thirteen of the laws of nineteen hundred and twelve, is hereby renumbered subdivision twenty-two, and such chapter is hereby amended by adding after subdivision twenty-two, as thus renumbered, and before the final unnumbered paragraph, a new subdivision, to be subdivision twenty-three, to read as follows:

23. The National Order of the Daughters of Isabella, or any subordinate court thereof, which is duly chartered and instituted in accordance with the constitution and laws of said National Order of the Daughters of Isabella.

§ 2. This act shall take effect immediately.

Chap. 251.

AN ACT to amend the poor law, in relation to almshouse construction and administration.

Became a law April 10, 1913, with the approval of the Governor. Passed, three-fifths being present.

Accepted by the City.

The People of the State of New York, represented in Senate and Assembly, do enact as follows:

L. 1909, ch. 46, § 118 amended.

Section 1. Section one hundred and eighteen of chapter forty-six of the laws of nineteen hundred and nine, entitled "An act in relation to the poor, constituting chapter forty-two of the consolidated laws," is hereby amended to read as follows:

§ 118. **Almshouse construction and administration.** No almshouse shall be built or reconstructed, in whole or in part, except on
plans and designs approved in writing by the state board of
charities, [1]provided, however, that such approval in writing as to
almshouses to be constructed by the city of New York shall be by
the board of estimate and apportionment of said city. It shall be
the duty of such board to call the attention, in writing or otherwise, of the board of supervisors and the superintendent of the
poor, or other proper officer, in any county, of any abuses, defects
or evils, which, on inspection, it may find in the almshouse of such
county, or in the administration thereof, and such county officer
shall take proper action thereon, with a view to proper remedies,
in accordance with the advice of such board.

§ 2. This act shall take effect immediately.

Chap. 252.

AN ACT to amend chapter one hundred and thirty-eight of the
laws of eighteen hundred and fifty-eight, entitled "An act to
amend an act entitled 'An act to authorize the improving and
keeping in repair a certain highway, in the county of Putnam,
and to assess certain non-resident lands along the line of said
road, and to pay the expenses of keeping the same in repair,'
passed March twenty-fourth, eighteen hundred and fifty-seven,"
in relation to the amount to be raised annually for the maintenance thereof.

**Became a law April 10, 1913, with the approval of the Governor. Passed,
three-fifths being present.**

*The People of the State of New York, represented in Senate
and Assembly, do enact as follows:*

Section 1. Section two[1a] of chapter one hundred and thirty-eight
of the laws of eighteen hundred and fifty-eight, entitled "An act
to amend an act entitled 'An act to authorize the improving and
keeping in repair a certain highway, in the county of Putnam,
and to assess certain non-resident lands along the line of said road,
and to pay the expenses of keeping the same in repair,' passed
March twenty-fourth, eighteen hundred and fifty-seven," as

L. 1858, ch.
138, § 2, as
amended by
L. 1875,
ch. 455,
amended.

---

[1] Remainder of sentence new.
[1a] L. 1858, ch. 138, § 2 amended L. 1857, ch. 179, § 8.

amended by chapter four hundred and fifty-five of the laws of eighteen hundred and seventy-five, is hereby amended to read as follows:

Annual expenditure for repair. § 2. The board of supervisors of the said county, at their annual meeting the present year, and in each and every year hereafter, shall cause to be raised, and in the same manner as other county expenses are raised and provided, the sum of one thousand dollars² to be expended by or under the direction of the commissioners appointed by this act each year in putting and keeping the said highway in proper order and repair. No part of said sum of one thousand dollars² shall be retained by said commissioners or either of them, for services as such commissioners, but the board of supervisors shall audit their accounts in addition to the sum of one thousand dollars² as herein provided.

§ 2. This act shall take effect immediately.

Chap. 253.

AN ACT to amend the penal law, in relation to the manipulation of prices of securities and conspiring movements to deceive the public.

Became a law April 10, 1913, with the approval of the Governor. Passed, three-fifths being present.

The People of the State of New York, represented in Senate and Assembly, do enact as follows:

§ 953 added to L. 1909, ch. 88. Section 1. Article eighty-six of chapter eighty-eight of the laws of nineteen hundred and nine, entitled "An act providing for the punishment of crime, constituting chapter forty of the consolidated laws," is hereby amended by adding at the end a new section, to be section nine hundred and fifty-three thereof, to read as follows:

§ 953. **Manipulation of prices of securities.** Any person, who inflates, depresses, or causes fluctuations in, or *attempts to inflate, depress or cause fluctuations in, or combines or conspires with any other person or persons to inflate, depress or cause fluctuations in, the market prices of the stocks, bonds or other evidences

---

* So in original.
² Formerly " five hundred dollars."

of debt of a corporation, company or association, or of an issue or any part of an issue of the stock, bonds or evidences of debt of a corporation, company or association, by means of pretended purchases and sales thereof, or by any other fictitious transactions or devices, for or on account of such person or of any other person, or for or on account of the persons so combining or conspiring, whereby either in whole or in part a simultaneous change of ownership of or interest in such stocks, bonds or evidences of debt, or of such issue or part of an issue thereof, is not effected, is guilty of a felony, punishable by a fine of not more than five thousand dollars or by imprisonment for not more than two years, or by both.

A pretended purchase or sale of any such stocks, bonds or other evidences of debt whereby, in whole or in part, no simultaneous change of ownership or interest therein is effected, shall be prima facie evidence of the violation of this section by the person or persons taking part in the transaction of such pretended purchase or sale.

§ 2. This act shall take effect immediately.

Chap. 254.

AN ACT to amend the county law, in relation to compensation of supervisors in Niagara county.

Became a law April 10, 1913, with the approval of the Governor. Passed, three-fifths being present.

The People of the State of New York, represented in Senate and Assembly, do enact as follows:

Section 1. Section twenty-three of chapter sixteen of the laws of nineteen hundred and nine, entitled "An act in relation to counties, constituting chapter eleven of the consolidated laws," as amended by chapter two hundred and seventy-nine of the laws of nineteen hundred and ten, chapter five hundred and fifty-four of the laws of nineteen hundred and eleven and chapter thirty-four of the laws of nineteen hundred and twelve, is hereby amended to read as follows:[1]

§ 23. **Compensation of supervisors.** For the services of supervisors, except in the counties of Albany, Columbia, Dutchess, Erie,

[marginal note:] L. 1909, ch. 16, § 23, as amended by L. 1910, ch. 279, L. 1911, ch. 554, and L. 1912, ch. 34, amended.

------

[1] Section 23 is again amended by L. 1913, ch. 355, post. The amendment here effected is not incorporated in the section as amended by ch. 355.

15

Herkimer, Montgomery, Niagara, Oneida, Onondaga, Rensselaer, Rockland, Schenectady, Steuben and Westchester, each supervisor shall receive from the county compensation at the rate of four dollars per day for each calendar day's actual attendance at the sessions of their respective boards, and mileage at the rate of eight cents per mile, for once going and returning from his residence to the place where the sessions of the board shall be held, by the most usual route, for each regular and special session. In the counties of Herkimer, Niagara, Rockland, Schenectady and Steuben each supervisor shall receive an annual salary, in the county of Herkimer of one hundred and twenty dollars and the mileage hereinabove prescribed, in the county of Niagara of three hundred dollars, and in addition compensation at the rate of four dollars per day and mileage at the rate of ten cents per mile for going and returning when the board is sitting as a board of county canvassers,[2] in the county of Rockland of four hundred dollars, in the county of Schenectady of five hundred dollars and in the county of Steuben of one hundred and fifty dollars, in lieu of any per diem compensation. In the county of Dutchess each supervisor shall receive an annual salary from the county of one hundred and fifty dollars and also mileage at the rate of ten cents per mile for going and returning, once in each week during the annual session of the board of supervisors and when the board is sitting as a board of county canvassers, by the most usually traveled route, from his residence to the place where the sessions of the board shall be held, and in addition thereto compensation at the rate of four dollars per day and mileage as hereinabove provided for each special session of the board which he attends; such compensation and mileage to be paid by the county treasurer on the last day of the annual session in each year. Each supervisor, except in the counties of Albany, Columbia, Dutchess, Erie, Montgomery, Niagara, Oneida, Onondaga, Rensselaer, Schenectady and Westchester, may also receive compensation from the county at the rate of four dollars per day while actually engaged in any investigation or other duty, which may be lawfully committed to him by the board, except for services rendered when the board is in session and, if such investigation or duty require his attendance at a place away from his residence, and five miles or more distant

---

[2] Words "and in addition compensation ·at the rate of four dollars per day and mileage at the rate of ten cents per mile for going and returning when the board is sitting as a board of county canvassers," new.

from the place where the board shall hold its sessions, his actual
expenses. incurred therein.   Each supervisor in the county of
Dutchess shall also be entitled to receive in addition to the compensation hereinabove provided, to be paid in the same time and
manner, compensation at the rate of four dollars per day while
actually engaged in any investigation or other duty which may
be lawfully committed to him by the board together with his
actual expenses incurred therein.   No other compensation or allowance shall be made to any supervisor for his services, except
such as shall be by law a town charge, except that in the counties
of Niagara and Herkimer each supervisor, while heretofore or
hereafter actually engaged in any investigation, or in the performance of any other duty, which shall have been legally delegated
to him by the board of supervisors, except when the board is in
session, shall be entitled to receive in addition to the compensation hereinbefore provided, his actual expenses incurred therein.
The board of supervisors of any county may also allow to each
member of the board for his services in making a copy of the
assessment-roll, three cents for each written line for the first one
hundred lines, two cents per line for the second hundred written
lines, and one cent per line for all written lines in excess of two
hundred, and one cent for each line of the tax roll actually extended by him.

§ 2. This act shall take effect immediately.

Chap. 255.

AN ACT to amend chapter one hundred and fifty-seven of the
laws of eighteen hundred and forty-four, entitled "An act to
incorporate the village of Mohawk," in relation to the Weller
library of such village.

Became a law April 10, 1913, with the approval of the Governor.   Passed,
three-fifths being present.

*The People of the State of New York, represented in Senate
and Assembly, do enact as follows:*

Section 1. Subdivision twenty-five of section seventeen of L. 1844, ch.
chapter one hundred and fifty-seven of the laws of eighteen subd. 25, as
hundred and forty-four, entitled "An act to incorporate the L. 1911,

ch. 20.
amended
village of Mohawk," as amended[1] by chapter twenty of the laws of nineteen hundred and thirteen, is hereby amended to read as follows:

Village
trustees to
appoint
Weller
library
commis-
sion.
25. (a) To appoint twelve[2] commissioners, six men and six women[3] who shall constitute a separate board of commissioners, vested with the care, management and control of the real and personal property devised and bequeathed to the village of Mohawk by the last will and testament of Frederick U. Weller and Helen Weller, both deceased, late of Mohawk, New York, which board so created shall be hereafter styled " Weller library com-

Qualifica-
tions of
commis-
sioners.
mission." Each of the male[4] commissioners so appointed shall be at the time of his appointment and during his term of office a resident of the village and a taxpayer and qualified elector therein and no person shall be eligible to such office who is the incumbent of any village office;[5] and they shall be so appointed that not more than three of such male[4] commissioners in office at any one time shall be members of the same political party. They

Terms.
shall hold office from the date of their appointment, or as soon thereafter as they shall have qualified, respectively, until the first day of January next ensuing and one man and one woman[6] for one, two, three, four, and five years thereafter, and their respective terms of office shall be designated by the board of trustees at

Appoint-
ment of
successors.
the time of making such appointments. Thereafter it shall be the duty of the board of trustees of the village of Mohawk[7] to appoint, during the month of December of each year, a man and also a woman[8] commissioner to succeed the ones whose terms of office expire[9] on the first day of January following, and such appointees[10] shall hold office for the term of five years from the first day of

Holdovers.
January next ensuing their[11] appointment; provided, however, that if such[12] board[13] fail to so appoint before the first day of January,

---

1 Should read: " added."
2 Formerly " six."
3 Words " six men and six women," new.
4 Word " male " new.
5 Words " and no person shall be eligible to such office who is the incumbent of any village office," new.
6 Words " one man and one woman," new.
7 Words " trustees of the village of Mohawk," substituted for words " the Weller library commission."
8 Words " man and also a women," new.
9 Formerly " the one whose term of office expires."
10 Formerly " appointee."
11 Formerly " his."
12 Word " such " substituted for word " the."
13 Words " of the Weller library commission," omitted.

the commissioner whose term of office then expires shall continue
to hold office until his or her[14] successor is appointed and has qualified, but the office shall be deemed vacant for the purpose of appointing his or her[14] successor, and such appointment may be made
at any time thereafter for the balance of the unexpired term.

(b) Every commissioner, before entering upon the duties of
his or her[14] office, shall take and file with the village clerk the oath
of office prescribed by the constitution[15] of the state.

Oath of office.

(c) Within thirty days after their appointment as hereinbefore
provided, such commissioners shall meet at the Weller library in
said village and proceed to organize as the Weller library commission. They shall, at such meeting, designate one of their
number to be president of the commission whose duty it shall
be to preside at the meetings at which he or she[16] is present, to call
special meetings of the commission upon the request of any two
other commissioners, or of his or her[14] own motion whenever in
[17]his or her discretion it may be deemed necessary. In the absence of the president, the commissioner having the shortest term to serve shall preside. Any eight[18] of said commissioners shall constitute a quorum for the transaction of business, and the concurrence of at least seven[18] commissioners
shall be necessary for the transaction of any business, and no
resolution shall be adopted or other action taken unless seven[18]
commissioners present at the meeting shall vote affirmatively
therefor. They shall also designate at such first meeting one of
their number to be secretary of the commission whose duty it
shall be to keep accurate and correct minutes of all the proceedings of the commission, to keep in his or her[19] custody and properly preserve all books, records, maps and papers appertaining to
the business and proceedings of the commission. They shall also
designate at said first meeting one of their number to be the
treasurer of the commission to receive and collect all moneys
paid, turned over or to be paid or turned over to said commission
and to keep an accurate statement of all receipts and disbursements of the commission. Said Weller library commission shall

Organiza-
tion.

President.

Quorum.

Secretary.

Treasurer.

Annual
financial
report.

---

[14] Words " or her " new.

[15] See constitution, art. 13, § 1; public officers law (L. 1909, ch. 51), § 10,
as amended by L. 1913, ch. 59, ante.

[16] Words " or she " new.

[17] Remainder of sentence formerly read: " his discretion he may deem
necessary."

[18] Formerly " four."

[19] Words " or her " new.

on December thirty-first of each year make and file with the
village clerk of Mohawk a report of its receipts and disbursements which shall be published in the official newspaper in con-

Bond of treasurer. junction with the annual village report. The treasurer shall,
before entering upon the duties of his or her[19] office, execute and
file with the village clerk a bond with one or two sureties
approved by the board of trustees of the village, in the sum of
fifty thousand dollars and conditioned upon his or her[19] promptly
turning over all village funds which shall come into his or her[19]
hands and faithfully performing the duties of the office.[20]

Powers of commissioners as to property. The commissioners so appointed, when they shall have organized
as the Weller library commission, shall be vested with the control,
management and supervision of the property, real and personal
devised and bequeathed to the village of Mohawk by the last will
and testament of Frederick U. Weller and Helen Weller, respectively, and they shall hold legal title to all such property in trust
for said village for the uses and purposes as set forth and described in said wills of Frederick U. Weller and Helen Weller.

Acceptance and maintenance of house as library. (d) The Weller library commission shall accept, receive and
maintain in trust as aforesaid, the house and grounds surround-
ing and connected with said house situate in the village of
Mohawk which was occupied by Frederick U. Weller at the time
of his death for the sole purposes and to be used solely for a free

Name of library; when open; free to inhabitants. public library for said village to be named and known as the
"Weller Library." Said library shall be open at least two days
in each week and more if deemed necessary or beneficial and
shall be free to all of the inhabitants of said village; all as pre-

Acceptance in trust of property under will of Frederick U. Weller. scribed in the fourth clause of said will. The Weller library
commission shall accept and receive in trust all the rest and
residue of the property which passed to said village under the ·
sixth clause of said will of Frederick U. Weller to be collected
and sold and converted into money and the proceeds thereof to be
invested in United States government bonds and the interest and

Purposes to which devoted. income therefrom to be used and devoted as follows: To keep and
maintain in good repair and order the burial lot and vault of
Weller and Morgan in the cemetery at Mohawk; to keep in order
the grounds devised for the use of the library and to rebuild and
remodel the buildings on said grounds making them suitable for
a library and to keep the same in proper repair; and to purchase

---

[19] Words " or her " new.
[20] Formerly read: " his office."

books for and to care for, support and maintain the library in a proper manner. If, at any time, it shall be deemed necessary by the Weller library commission for the benefit and the proper support and maintenance of said library to have more income than above provided, the commission is hereby authorized and directed, as provided in the seventh clause of said will, to dispose of, sell and convey so much of the grounds devised for the purposes of a library, as shall not be necessary for the proper use and convenience of such library, provided, however such sale shall first be authorized by the adoption of a proposition therefor submitted in the manner provided in the village law, to the resident electors entitled to vote upon a proposition to raise money by tax or assessment,[21] and in case of such sale of any of said grounds, the proceeds thereof shall be invested in United States government bonds, the income therefrom to be used and devoted the same as the interest and income from the other property devised and bequeathed to the said village as provided in said will. The Weller library commission shall accept and receive in trust for said village all the property, bequeathed and devised to the village of Mohawk by the third clause of the will of Helen Weller, to be invested in United States government bonds and the interest and income therefrom to be used and devoted as follows: To keep and maintain in good repair and order the burial lot and vault of Weller and Morgan in the cemetery at Mohawk; pursuant to the second subdivision of the third clause of said will, to rebuild and remodel the buildings suitable for a library and keep the same in repair; to purchase books and support and maintain the public library for the village of Mohawk as provided for in the last will and testament of her husband Frederick U. Weller. The said commission may receive and hold in trust for said village any gift, devise or bequest of money or other property for the purpose of using the avails and earnings thereof in caring for and maintaining said Weller library and grounds or fulfilling the purpose of said gift, devise or bequest. Any vacancy which may at any time occur in said board of commissioners through death, resignation or any other cause shall be filled by the board of trustees of the village.[22] The commissioners may make and adopt all necessary and reasonable rules

Sidenotes: Sale of surplus grounds to increase income. Acceptance in trust of property under will of Helen Weller. Purposes to which devoted. Acceptance of gifts, etc. Vacancies in commission. Rules for care and management of library.

---

[21] Words "provided, however such sale . . . tax or assessment," new.
[22] Words "board of trustees of the village," substituted for words "remaining commissioners."

and regulations for the use, care, management and protection of said Weller library, and to provide for the conduct of persons while within the said library building and grounds and the exclusion therefrom of improper persons or assemblages, and jointly to enact all such rules, by-laws and regulations, and to alter the same, as may be reasonable and essential to the proper conduct and care of said Weller library and grounds. All such rules and regulations shall be plainly printed and posted in conspicuous places throughout the library building and grounds and when so posted shall be deemed to be brought to the notice of all persons and to become forthwith in full force and effect, and the commission may prescribe penalties for the violation of any rule, regulation or ordinance not to exceed twenty-five dollars for each violation to be recovered in an action brought by them in the name of the village against the persons who have been guilty of such violations. No commission appointed hereunder shall be interested directly or indirectly in any contract, claim or account for or relating to any work done or material furnished for or on account of any matter under the control of the commission; nor shall any commissioner receive any compensation for his or her[23] services except for actual disbursements made or expenses incurred by him or her[23] by the express direction of the commission. It shall be the duty of the board of trustees of the village of Mohawk to appoint said commissioners within thirty[24] days after this act as hereby amended[25] goes into effect. Upon the organization of the Weller library commission it shall be the duty of the board of village trustees to immediately turn over to said commissioners all property of every description pertaining and relating to the Weller library. All funds received by the treasurer of said commission shall be kept and set aside as a separate and distinct Weller library fund which shall thereafter be withdrawn and paid out only by said treasurer upon the audit and order of said commissioners, certified to him by a written order signed by the secretary of the commission and countersigned by its president, which shall specify the names of the persons to whom and the amount of money to be paid, together with a statement of the purposes for which such payment is made, and it shall be the duty of said treasurer upon the audit

(marginal notes:)
Posting of rules.
Penalties for violations.
Commissioners not to be interested in work done or material furnished. No compensation.
Commission, when to be appointed.
Property, when to be turned over.
Weller library fund.
Payments therefrom, how made.

---

[23] Words "or her" new.
[24] Formerly "twenty."
[25] Words "as hereby amended," new.

and order of said commissioners to pay to the persons as in the order directed the sum of money specified. All moneys in any Deposi-tories. way acquired by said commission for the purposes of said Weller library shall be deposited by the treasurer of the commission in such bank or place of deposit as the Weller library commissioners shall direct. The commission shall provide suitable books for the Books for secretary secretary and treasurer for the entry of all items of receipts and and treasurer. disbursements and for the recording of all transactions affecting the powers and duties of the commission. The commission shall Employees. have power to appoint, employ and discharge agents or subordi-nates and other employees and to fix their compensation. The by-laws shall prescribe regular meetings for the commission, and Amend-ment of the by-laws, rules and regulations shall be subject to alteration, by-laws and rules. revision or amendment only at regular meetings or at a meeting called for such purpose, provided that ten days' written notice be given either personally or by mail, of the proposed change. [26]A husband and wife shall not hold office on the commission.

§ 2. This act shall take effect immediately.

·Chap. 256.

AN ACT to amend the county law, in relation to the printing and distribution of the proceedings of the board of supervisors in certain counties.

Became a law April 10, 1913, with the approval of the Governor. Passed, three-fifths being present.

The People of the State of New York, represented in Senate and Assembly, do enact as follows:

Section 1. Section nineteen of chapter sixteen of the laws of L. 1909. ch. 16, § 19 nineteen hundred and nine, entitled "An act in relation to coun- amended. ties, constituting chapter eleven of the consolidated laws," is hereby amended to read as follows:

§ 19. **Printing and distribution of proceedings of board.** Each board of supervisors shall cause as many copies of the proceed-ings of its sessions as it may deem necessary, certified by its chairman and clerk, to be printed as a county charge, in a pamphlet volume, as soon as may be after each session, for exchange with other boards, and for the members of the board

[26] Following sentence new.

and other town and county officers. At least three copies of such printed volume shall be forwarded to and filed in each town clerk's office and in the county clerk's office. In counties containing cities of the first class and in counties containing three cities of the third class,[1] the publication of the proceedings of the board of supervisors may be ordered to be made in a daily newspaper, the work to be done by contract, let to the lowest bidder, after an opportunity to bid therefor has been given to the proprietors of all the daily newspapers printed in the English language in said county; such bid may include the printing and binding in pamphlet volumes of such number of copies of the proceedings of such board as may be required, and also the printing of pamphlet copies thereof for the use of the members of said board at its sessions. Such printed proceedings shall contain a summary statement of all bills against the county, presented to the board and audited and allowed or disallowed, indicating the amount allowed or disallowed. The board of supervisors may as often as it shall deem necessary, cause to be printed and distributed in like manner, in the same volume or otherwise, its county laws, combined with suitable forms and instructions thereunder. Whenever the proceedings of the board of supervisors of any county are printed in a volume by authority of the board of supervisors, the volume so printed, and duly certified by the chairman and clerk of the said board of supervisors to be a true record of such proceedings, shall be and constitute the book of records of the said board.

§ 2. This act shall take effect immediately.

---

[1] Words " and in counties containing three cities of the third class," new.

Chap. 257.

AN ACT to amend the code of civil procedure, in relation to the compensation of constables, deputy sheriffs and jurors.

Became a law April 10, 1913, with the approval of the Governor. Passed, three-fifths being present.

The People of the State of New York, represented in Senate and Assembly, do enact as follows:

Section 1. Sections thirty-three hundred and twelve and thirty-three hundred and fourteen of the code of civil procedure are hereby amended to read, respectively, as follows: §§ 3312, 3314 amended.

§ 3312. **Compensation of deputy sheriffs and constables attending courts.** A constable or a deputy sheriff is entitled, for attending a sitting of a court of record, pursuant to a notice from the sheriff, to a fee for each day's actual attendance, in any county in the state, to be fixed by the board of supervisors thereof, and mileage as allowed by law to trial jurors in courts of record. Such fees must be paid by the county treasurer, upon the production of the certificate of the clerk, stating the number of days that the constable or deputy sheriff attended. [1]If a constable or deputy sheriff attending a sitting of a court of record pursuant to a notice from the sheriff is unable to reach his home upon the day he is excused from attendance, he shall be entitled to compensation for an additional day, and the clerk shall certify accordingly upon satisfactory proof of such fact by affidavit. But the provisions of this section shall not be applicable to the counties of Kings, New York and Erie. All other acts or section of acts conflicting herewith are hereby repealed.

§ 3314. **Supervisors may make allowance to grand and trial jurors.** In the counties within the city of New York the board of aldermen, and in any other county the board of supervisors, may direct that a sum, not exceeding three dollars in addition to the fees prescribed in the last section, or in any other statutory provision, be allowed to each grand juror, and each trial juror for each day's attendance at a term of a court of record, of civil or criminal jurisdiction, held within their county. If a different rate is not otherwise established as herein provided, each juror is entitled to five cents for each mile necessarily traveled by him in going to

---

[1] Following sentence new.

and returning from the term; but such board of aldermen or board of supervisors may establish a lower rate. A juror is entitled to mileage for actual travel once in each calendar week during the term, except that in the counties of Queens, Rockland and Orange, grand and trial jurors may be paid four cents a mile for each mile necessarily traveled in going to and returning for each day of actual travel during the term in lieu of any other mileage. The sum so established or allowed must be paid by the county treasurer upon the certificate of the clerk of the court, stating the number of days that the juror actually attended, and the number of miles traveled by him in order to attend. [2]If a juror in attendance at a term of a court of record cannot reach his home upon the day he is excused from attendance, he shall be entitled to compensation for an additional day, and the clerk shall certify accordingly upon satisfactory proof of such fact by affidavit. The amount so paid must be raised in the same manner as other county charges are raised.

In effect
Sept. 1,
1913.

§ 2. This act shall take effect September first, nineteen hundred and thirteen.

Chap. 258.

AN ACT to provide for the excavation and construction of a shaft and the erection, installation and operation of an elevator connecting Fort Washington avenue and a tunnel street from Bennett avenue at One Hundred and Ninetieth street to Riverside Drive, and for assessing the cost and expense thereof upon the property benefited.

Became a law April 10, 1913, with the approval of the Governor. Passed, three-fifths being present.

Accepted by the City.

The People of the State of New York, represented in Senate and Assembly, do enact as follows:

Construction of shaft and erection of elevator authorized.

Section 1. The president of the borough of Manhattan in the city of New York, when thereto directed by the board of estimate and apportionment of the city of New York, is hereby authorized, in the manner now provided by law for the improvement of public streets in the city of New York, to excavate and construct a vertical shaft between Fort Washington avenue and a tunnel

---

[2] Following sentence new.

street from Bennett avenue at One Hundred and Ninetieth street
to Riverside Drive, in the borough of Manhattan, city of New
York, and to erect and install therein an elevator connecting Fort
Washington avenue and said tunnel street.

§ 2. The plans and specifications of said shaft and elevator Plans and specifica-
shall be prepared under the direction of the president of the tions.
borough of Manhattan and shall be approved by the board of
estimate and apportionment of the city of New York.

§ 3. The board of estimate and apportionment of the city of Portion to be paid for
New York shall determine whether any, and, if any, what pro- by city.
portion of the cost and expense of excavating and constructing
said shaft and erecting and installing said elevator shall be borne
and paid by the city of New York, and the remainder of said Assessment of re-
cost and expense shall be assessed upon the property deemed to mainder on property
be benefited thereby, and the assessment shall be laid and con- benefited.
firmed and collected in accordance with the provisions of chapter
seventeen of the Greater New York charter. The determination
or decision of such board as to the proportion of cost and expense
to be borne and paid by the city of New York and as to the proportion to be borne by the property benefited, after it shall have
been made and announced, shall be final, and such determination
or decision shall not be reopened or reconsidered by said board.

§ 4. The president of the borough of Manhattan shall care for, Mainte-
maintain and operate said elevator and the cost of such care, operation of
maintenance and operation shall be paid for out of the annual elevator.
appropriation for the maintenance of streets in the borough of
Manhattan.

§ 5. This act shall take effect immediately.

Chap. 259.

AN ACT to amend the Greater New York charter, in relation to
the powers of the commissioners of the sinking fund.

Became a law April 10, 1913, with the approval of the Governor. Passed,
three-fifths being present.

Accepted by the City.

*The People of the State of New York, represented in Senate
and Assembly, do enact as follows:*

Section 1. Section two hundred and five of the Greater New L. 1897, ch.
York charter, as re-enacted by chapter four hundred and sixty- 378, § 205, as re-

enacted
by L. 1901,
ch. 466, and
as amended
by L. 1902,
ch. 279, L.
1906, ch.
659, L.
1907, ch.
439, L.
1909, ch.
398, L. 1910,
ch. 683, and
L. 1911, ch.
684,
amended.
six of the laws of nineteen hundred and one, as amended by chapters three hundred and seventy-nine of the laws of nineteen hundred and three, six hundred and fifty-nine of the laws of nineteen hundred and six, four hundred and thirty-nine of the laws of nineteen hundred and seven, three hundred and ninety-eight of the laws of nineteen hundred and nine, six hundred and eighty-three of the laws of nineteen hundred and ten, six hundred and ninety-four of the laws of nineteen hundred and eleven, is hereby further amended to read as follows:

POWERS OF COMMISSIONERS OF SINKING FUND.

§ 205. The said board shall, except as in this act otherwise specifically provided, have power to sell or lease for the highest marketable price or rental at public auction or by sealed bids, and always after public advertisement for a period of at least fifteen days in the City Record, and after appraisal under the direction of said board made within three months of the date of sale, any city property except parks, wharves and piers and land under water, except as hereinafter provided, but no such lease shall run for a term longer than ten years nor a renewal for a longer period than ten years. If such property be market property it shall be sold only pursuant to a resolution adopted by an unanimous vote of the commissioners of the sinking fund, concurred in by the board of aldermen. The commissioners of the sinking fund shall have power to assign to use for any public purposes any city property, for whatsoever purpose originally acquired, which may be found by the department having control thereof to be no longer required for such purpose. The proceeds of said sale or leasing shall on receipt thereof, after paying necessary charges, be immediately paid to the credit of the sinking fund for the redemption of the city debt; [1]except that the commissioners of the sinking fund shall have power to provide, that the proceeds derived from any sale of real estate, or interest therein, remaining after the payment therefrom of the necessary charges of the sale and of any liens and charges upon the property sold, be paid to the credit of an appropriately designated fund, hereby created, and applied to the purchase of other real estate deemed necessary for public purposes when and as authorized, pursuant to the provisions of this act, with the same force and effect as though such disburse-

---

[1] Remainder of sentence new.

ment was from the proceeds of the sale of corporate stock authorized to be issued for the purchase of real estate. ²The fund hereby
created shall be under the control of the said commissioners of the
sinking fund, and the monies therein not disposed of in the purchase of real estate, shall when and as directed by the commissioners of the sinking fund, with the concurrence of the board
of estimate and apportionment, be paid to the credit of the sinking fund for the redemption of the city debt. ²All the provisions of this act, relative to the purchase of real estate by the city,
shall be made applicable to the acquisition of such real estate,
purchased through the medium of the fund hereby created. Said
commissioners of the sinking fund shall have power, by unanimous vote, to settle and adjust by mutual conveyances or otherwise, and upon such terms and conditions as may seem to them
proper, disputes existing between the city and private owners of
property, in respect to boundary lines, and to release such interests
of the city in real estate as the corporation counsel shall certify
in writing to be mere clouds upon titles of private owners, in
such manner and upon such terms and conditions as in their
judgment shall seem proper.

The commissioners of the sinking fund are hereby authorized to
approve agreements, submitted by the commissioner of docks,
fixing, determining upon and establishing the line of high water
as provided for in section eight hundred and eighteen-a and are
further authorized to sell and convey to the upland owner lands
under water inside of such line, to purchase from the upland owner
any lands outside of such line and to exchange lands under water
inside of such line for lands outside of such line upon such terms
and conditions as in their judgment shall seem proper.

Said commissioners of the sinking fund shall also have power to
sell and convey the right, title and interest of the city in and to
lands lying within any street, avenue, road, highway, alley, lane
or public place or square that has been discontinued and closed,
in whole or in part, by lawful authority, to the owner of lands
fronting on such street, avenue, road, highway, alley, lane or public
place or square so discontinued and closed, on such terms and
conditions and for such consideration as in the judgment of the
said commissioners of the sinking fund shall seem proper, provided the said commissioners of the sinking fund shall first determine that the said lands or the part thereof so sold and conveyed,

---

² Following sentence new.

are not needed for any public use. Said commissioners of the sinking fund shall have discretion to direct the demolition or removal of all buildings or other structures, the title to which has been acquired by the city in condemnation proceedings or by purchase, and not needed for any public purposes, in the same manner as now provided by law for the demolition and removal of unsafe buildings, and in such cases the expense of such demolition and removal shall be paid in the same manner as is now provided for the demolition and removal of unsafe buildings. They may also, prior to the confirmation of the report of commissioners of estimate and[3] appraisal, or prior to the purchase of the premises upon which said buildings or parts of buildings or other structures are erected, or prior to the vesting of title therein, agree with the owner or owners thereof, or any person having a beneficial interest therein, in case title has not vested in the city, and in the case the title has vested in the city, with the person or persons entitled to the award or awards therefor, as to the cost and compensation to be allowed and paid to said owner or owners, or other persons for the removal of said buildings or parts of buildings or other structures, as the compensation to be awarded by said commissioners or allowed for the damage done said *buildings or buildings or other structures in the acquisition of title thereto, and it may also, as a condition of the sale by the city at private sale of its interest therein after vesting of title in said building or parts of buildings or other structures to the owner or owners of the award or awards therefor, or other persons having an interest therein, agree that damages to be awarded by the commissioners shall be the agreed compensation for the purpose of the removal thereof, provided, however, that such buildings or parts of buildings or other structures shall not, in any case, be relocated or re-erected within the lines of any proposed street or other public improvement.

Commissioners of estimate and appraisal shall accept such agreed amounts of compensation for the removal of buildings or parts of buildings or other structures as the amounts to be awarded as such compensation and include the same in their reports. Said commissioners of the sinking fund shall prescribe such conditions in the terms of sale which, if broken, shall entitle the city to a resale of said property, and which shall revest title to same in the city.

---

* So in original.
[3] Word "and" substituted for word "of."

Said commissioners of the sinking fund shall also have power to lease all or any part of the right, title and interest heretofore or hereafter acquired by the city in and to any lands outside the limits of said city for the sanitary protection of the water supply, and to grant in perpetuity, or for shorter periods, rights, easements, or rights of way in, over or across any such lands, for highway purposes, or for the improvement of the facilities and public service of railroads heretofore located thereon upon such terms and conditions, for such consideration, and subject to such restrictions as in the judgment of said commissioners shall seem proper; provided that no such lease or grant shall be made unless the said commissioners shall first determine that the said lands or interests therein, so granted or conveyed, are to be used or enjoyed for a purpose which is consistent with the sanitary protection of the water supply of said city, and provided that every such grant or lease shall contain covenants restricting the use of such lands, or interests therein, in accordance with the determination of said commissioners and providing for the forfeiture to the city of the lands or interests therein upon breach of any of said covenants. The provisions of existing laws or ordinances relative to the investment of moneys and assets of the several sinking funds hereby made subject to the control of the commissioners of the sinking fund as hereby constituted, in bonds, stocks, or obligations of the municipal or public corporations or parts thereof hereby consolidated into The city of New York, including the counties of Kings and Richmond, shall hereafter apply to investments thereof in the bonds and stock of the corporation of The city of New York, issued on and after January first, eighteen hundred and ninety-eight, provided, however, that such bonds or stock shall not thereupon or thereafter be canceled except as herein otherwise specifically provided, but the same shall upon their maturity be paid off, liquidated or discharged in the same manner as they would be if held by private creditors. It shall be lawful for the commissioners of the sinking fund in their discretion, and they are hereby empowered in such discretion to cancel from time to time, but not before maturity, bonds and stock of any of the municipal and public corporations or parts thereof forming part of the corporation of The city of New York, as hereby constituted, and of the counties of Kings and Richmond, which may be held by any of said sinking funds on December thirty-first, eighteen hundred and ninety-seven, providing said bonds and stocks are

by law redeemable from the sinking funds in which the same are
held.   It shall also be lawful for the commissioners of the sinking
fund in their discretion and they are hereby empowered in such
discretion, to cancel from time to time but not before maturity,
any portion of the indebtedness of The city of New York, as
hereby constituted, incurred on or after January first, eighteen
hundred and ninety-eight, which may be held by them in the
sinking fund of The city of New York, as hereinafter constituted,
and which may by law be redeemable from said sinking fund as
herein or elsewhere provided, and all such similar indebtedness
incurred to provide for the supply of water, which may be held
by them and redeemable from the water sinking fund of The city
of New York as hereinafter constituted.   The funds to be known
as the sinking fund of The city of New York as hereinafter constituted, shall be administered by the commissioners of the sinking
fund, in like manner as provided by the ordinance of the mayor,
aldermen and commonalty of The city of New York, approved by
the mayor, February twenty-second, eighteen hundred and forty-
four, so far as the same may be applicable; provided, however,
that nothing contained in said ordinance shall affect or alter the
composition of the board of commissioners of the sinking fund,
as by this act constituted.   The rate of interest on all corporate
stock, bonds or other obligations for the payment of money of
whatsoever kind or description issued by The city of New York
except certificates of indebtedness or other evidences of indebtedness, issued pursuant to the provisions of section one hundred and
eighty-seven of this act, shall be prescribed by the commissioners
of the sinking fund.   The commissioners of the sinking fund may
by resolution assign the places where the several municipal courts
shall be held within their respective districts and may assign
such place in said city as may to it seem most conducive to the
public convenience for the holding of the courts of general and
special sessions, and, upon the application of the board of city
magistrates, may designate additional places for the holding of
magistrates' or police courts and jail delivery to be held in and for
the city; notice of any change of the places of holding such courts
shall, before the same takes effect, be published in the City Record
and the corporation newspapers for a period of not less than two
weeks.   Said publication shall be made under the direction of the
comptroller.   The commissioners of the sinking fund may by resolution designate from time to time any building or buildings

within the city to be the common jails of said city or of any of the counties contained within its territorial limits, for all the purposes for which common jails may by law be used, and such building or buildings so designated shall be such common jails until changed by a like resolution of the commissioners of the sinking fund. The sinking fund commissioners of the city of New York shall not have the power in any event to compromise or release any existing liability or obligation to The city of New York or to the mayor, aldermen or commonalty of the city of New York, or to any of the municipalities or parts of municipalities consolidated with the former city of New York, under the provisions of chapter six hundred and forty-two of the laws of eighteen hundred and eighty-six or under chapter four hundred and thirty-four of the laws of eighteen hundred and ninety-three, but such liabilities and obligations shall be and remain inviolable.

§ 2. This act shall take effect immediately.

Chap. 260.

AN ACT to amend the labor law, in relation to the manufacture of articles in tenement houses.[1]

Became a law April 10, 1913, with the approval of the Governor. Passed, three-fifths being present.

The People of the State of New York, represented in Senate and Assembly, do enact as follows:

Section 1. Article seven of chapter thirty-six of the laws of nineteen hundred and nine, entitled "An act relating to labor, constituting chapter thirty-one of the consolidated laws," is hereby amended to read as follows: L. 1909, ch. 36, art. 7 amended.

ARTICLE 7.

TENEMENT-MADE ARTICLES.

Section 100. Manufacturing, altering, repairing or finishing articles in tenements.

101. Register of persons to whom work is given; identification label.

102. Goods unlawfully manufactured to be labelled.

---

[1] The amendments effected by this chapter are so numerous and extensive that it is impracticable to indicate the changes made.

§ 100. **Manufacturing, altering, repairing or finishing articles
in tenements.** 1. No tenement house nor any part thereof shall
be used for the purpose of manufacturing, altering, repairing or
finishing therein, any articles whatsoever except for the
sole and exclusive use of the person so using any part of such
tenement house or the members of his household, without a license
therefor as provided in this article. But nothing herein contained
shall apply to collars, cuffs, shirts or shirt waists made of cotton or
linen fabrics that are subjected to the laundrying process before
being offered for sale.

2. Application for such a license shall be made to the commissioner of labor by the owner of such tenement house, or by his
duly authorized agent. Such application shall describe the house
by street number or otherwise, as the case may be, in such manner
as will enable the commissioner of labor easily to find the same;
it shall also state the number of apartments in such house;
it shall contain the full name and address of the owner of the said
house, and shall be in such form as the commissioner of labor may
determine. Blank applications shall be prepared and furnished
by the commissioner of labor.

3. Upon receipt of such application the commissioner of labor
shall consult the records of the local health department or board,
or other appropriate local authority charged with the duty of sanitary inspection of such houses; if such records show the presence of any infectious, contagious or communicable disease, or the
existence of any uncomplied-with order or violations which indicate the presence of unsanitary conditions in such house, the commissioner of labor may, without making an inspection of the building, deny such application for a license, and may continue to deny
such application until such time as the records of said department,
board or other local authority show that the said tenement house
is free from the presence of infectious, contagious or communicable
disease, and from all unsanitary conditions. Before, however,

any such license is granted, an inspection of the building sought to be licensed must be made by the commissioner of labor, and a statement must be filed by him as a matter of public record, to the effect that the records of the local health department or board or other appropriate authority charged with the duty of sanitary inspection of such houses show the existence of no infectious, contagious or communicable disease nor of any unsanitary conditions in the said house; such statement must be dated and signed in ink with the full name of the employee responsible therefor. A similar statement similarly signed, showing the results of the inspection of the said building, must also be filed in the office of the commissioner of labor before any license is granted. If the commissioner of labor ascertain that such building is free from infectious, contagious or communicable disease, that there are no defects of plumbing that will permit the entrance of sewer air, that such building is in a clean and proper sanitary condition and that articles may be manufactured therein under clean and healthful conditions, he shall grant a license permitting the use of such building, for the purpose of manufacturing.

4. Such license may be revoked by the commissioner of labor if the health of the community or of the employees requires it, or if the owner of the said tenement house, or his duly authorized agent, fails to comply with the orders of the commissioner of labor within ten days after the receipt of such orders, or if it appears that the building to which such license relates is not in a healthy and proper sanitary condition, or if children are employed therein in violation of section seventy of this chapter. In every case where a license is revoked or denied by the commissioner of labor the reasons therefor shall be stated in writing, and the records of such revocation or denial shall be deemed public records. Where a license is revoked, before such tenement house can again be used for the purposes specified in this section, a new license must be obtained, as if no license had previously existed.

5. Every tenement house and all the parts thereof in which any articles are manufactured, altered, repaired or finished shall be kept in a clean and sanitary condition and shall be subject to inspection and examination by the commissioner of labor, for the purpose of ascertaining whether said garments or articles, or part or parts thereof, are clean and free from vermin and every matter of an infectious or contagious nature. An inspection shall be made by the commissioner of labor

of each licensed tenement house not less than once in every six
months, to determine its sanitary condition, and shall include all
parts of such house and the plumbing thereof. Before making
such inspection the commissioner of labor may consult the records
of the local department or board charged with the duty of sanitary inspection of tenement houses, to determine the frequency
of orders issued by such department or board in relation to the
said tenement house, since the last inspection of such building was
made by the commissioner of labor. Whenever the commissioner
of labor finds any unsanitary condition in a tenement house for
which a license has been issued as provided in this section, he shall
at once issue an order to the owner thereof directing him to remedy such condition forthwith. Whenever the commissioner of
labor finds any articles manufactured, altered, repaired
or finished, or in process thereof, in a room or apartment of a tenement house, and such room or apart-
ment is in a filthy condition, he shall notify the tenants thereof to
immediately clean the same, and to maintain it in a cleanly condition at all times; where the commissioner of labor finds such
room or apartment to be habitually kept in a filthy condition, he
may in his discretion cause to be affixed to the entrance door of
such apartment a placard calling attention to such facts and prohibiting the manufacture, alteration, repair or finishing of any
articles therein. No person, except the commissioner of labor,
shall remove or deface any such placard so affixed.

6. No articles shall be manufactured, altered, repaired
or finished in any room or apartment of a tenement
house where there is or has been a case of infectious,
contagious or communicable disease in such room or
apartment, until such time as the local department or board of
health shall certify to the commissioner of labor that such disease
has terminated, and that said room or apartment has been properly disinfected, if disinfection after such disease is required by
the local ordinances, or by the rules or regulations of such department or board. No articles shall be manufactured, altered, repaired or finished in a part of a cellar or basement of a tenement
house, which is more than one-half of its height below the level
of the curb or ground outside of or adjoining the same; but this
prohibition shall not apply to the use for a bakery of a cellar
for which a certificate of exemption is issued under section one
hundred and sixteen of this chapter. No person shall hire, em-

ploy or contract with any person to manufacture, alter, repair
or finish any articles in any room or apartment in any tenement
house not having a license therefor issued as aforesaid.   No
articles shall be manufactured, altered, repaired or finished in any room or apartment of a tenement house
unless said room or apartment shall be well lighted and ventilated
and shall contain at least five hundred cubic feet of air space for
every person working therein, or by any person other than the
members of the family living therein; except that in licensed tenement houses persons not members of the family may be employed
in apartments on the ground floor or second floor, used only for
shops of dressmakers who deal solely in the custom trade direct to
the consumer, provided that such apartments shall be in the opinion of the commissioner of labor in the highest degree sanitary,
well lighted, well ventilated and plumbed, and provided further
that the whole number of persons therein shall not exceed one to
each one thousand cubic feet of air space, and that there shall be
no children under fourteen years of age living or working therein;
before any such room or apartment can be so used a special permit
therefor shall be issued by the commissioner of labor, a copy of
which shall be entered in his public records with a statement of
the reasons therefor.   Nothing in this section contained shall prevent the employment of a tailor or seamstress by any person or
family for the purpose of making, altering, repairing or finishing
any article of wearing apparel for the use of such person or family.   Nor shall this article apply to a house if the only manufacturing therein be carried on in a shop on the main or ground floor
thereof with a separate entrance to the street, unconnected with
living rooms and entirely separate from the rest of the building
by closed partitions without any openings whatsoever and not
used for sleeping or cooking.

§ 101. **Register of persons to whom work is given; identification label.**   Every employer in any factory contracting for the
manufacturing, altering, repairing or finishing of any articles in
a tenement house or giving out material from which they or any
part of them are to be manufactured, altered, repaired or finished,
in a tenement house, shall keep a register of the names and addresses plainly written in English of the persons to whom such
articles or materials are given to be so manufactured, altered, repaired or finished or with whom they have contracted to do the
same, and shall issue with all such articles or materials a label

bearing the name and place of business of such factory written or
printed legibly in English. It shall be incumbent upon every
employer and upon all persons contracting for the manufacturing,
altering, repairing or finishing of any articles or giving out material from which they or any part of them are to be manufactured, altered, repaired or finished, before giving out any such
articles or materials to ascertain from the office of the
commissioner of labor whether the tenement house in
which such articles or materials are to be manufactured,
altered, repaired or finished, is licensed as provided in
this article, and also to ascertain from the local department or board of health the names and addresses of all persons
then sick of any infectious, contagious or communicable disease,
and residing in tenement houses; and none of the said articles nor
any material from which they or any part of them are to be manufactured, altered, repaired or finished shall be given out or sent
to any person residing in a tenement house that is not licensed as
provided in this article, or to any person residing in a room or
apartment in which there exists any infectious, contagious or communicable disease. The register mentioned in this section shall
be subject to inspection by the commissioner of labor, and a copy
thereof shall be furnished on his demand as well as such other information as he may require. The label mentioned in this section
shall be exhibited on the demand of the commissioner of labor at
any time while said articles or materials remain in the tenement
house.

§ 102. **Goods unlawfully manufactured to be labeled.** Articles
manufactured, altered, repaired or finished in a tenement house contrary to the provisions of this chapter shall not be sold or exposed for sale by any person. The commissioner of labor may conspicuously affix to any such article
found to be unlawfully manufactured, altered, repaired or finished, a label containing the words "tenement made"
printed in small pica capital letters on a tag not less than four
inches in length, or may seize and hold such article until the same
shall be disinfected or cleaned at the owner's expense, or until all
provisions of this chapter are complied with. The commissioner
of labor shall notify the person stated by the person in possession
of said article to be the owner thereof, that he has so labeled or
seized it. No person except the commissioner of labor, or a local
board of health in a case provided for in section one hundred and

three, shall remove or deface any tag or label so affixed. Unless the owner or person entitled to the possession of an article so seized shall provide for the disinfection or cleaning thereof within one month thereafter it may be destroyed.

§ 103. **Powers and duties of boards of health relative to tenement-made articles.** If the commissioner of labor finds evidence of disease present in a room or apartment in a tenement house in which any articles are manufactured, altered, repaired or finished or in process thereof, he shall affix to such article the label prescribed in the preceding section, and immediately report to the local board of health, who shall disinfect such articles, if necessary, and thereupon remove such label. If the commissioner of labor finds that infectious, contagious or communicable diseases exist in a room or apartment of a tenement house in which any articles are being manufactured, altered, repaired or finished, or that articles manufactured or in process of manufacture therein are infected or that goods used therein are unfit for use, he shall report to the local board of health. The local health department or board in every city, town and village whenever there is any infectious, contagious or communicable disease in a tenement house shall cause an inspection of such tenement house to be made within forty-eight hours. If any articles are found to be manufactured, altered, repaired or finished, or in process thereof in an apartment in which such disease exists, such board shall issue such order as the public health may require, and shall at once report such facts to the commissioner of labor, furnishing such further information as he may require. Such board may condemn and destroy all such infected article or articles manufactured or in the process of manufacture under unclean or unhealthful conditions. The local health department or board or other appropriate authority charged with the duty of sanitary inspection of such houses in every city, town and village shall, when so requested by the commissioner of labor, furnish copies of its records as to the presence of infectious, contagious or communicable disease, or of unsanitary conditions in said houses; and shall furnish such other information as may be necessary to enable the commissioner of labor to carry out the provisions of this article.

§ 104. **Manufacturing of certain articles in tenements prohibited.** No article of food, no dolls or dolls' clothing and no article of children's or infants' wearing apparel shall be manufactured, altered, repaired or finished, in whole or in part, for a factory, either directly or through the instrumentality of one or more contractors or other third person, in a tenement house, in any portion of an apartment, any part of which is used for living purposes.

§ 105. **Owners of tenement houses not to permit the unlawful use thereof.** The owner or agent of a tenement house shall not permit the use thereof for the manufacture, repair, alteration or finishing of any article contrary to the provisions of this chapter. If a room or apartment in such tenement house be so unlawfully used, the commissioner of labor shall serve a notice thereof upon such owner or agent. Unless such owner or agent shall cause such unlawful manufacture to be discontinued within ten days after the service of such notice, or within fifteen days thereafter institutes and faithfully prosecutes proceedings for dispossession of the occupant of a tenement house, who unlawfully manufactures, repairs, alters or finishes any articles therein, he shall be deemed guilty of a violation of this chapter as if he, himself, was engaged in such unlawful manufacture, repair, alteration or finishing. The unlawful manufacture, repair, alteration or finishing of any articles by the occupant of a room or apartment of a tenement house shall be a cause for dispossessing such occupant by summary proceedings to recover possession of real property, as provided in the code of civil procedure.

§ 106.[2] **Factory permits.** The owner of every factory for which any articles are manufactured in any tenement house shall secure a permit therefor from the commissioner of labor who shall issue such permit to any such owner applying therefor. Such permit may be revoked or suspended by the commissioner of labor whenever any provision of this article or of section seventy of this chapter is violated in connection with any work for such factory. Such permit may be reissued or reinstated in the discretion of the commissioner when such violation has ceased. No articles shall be manufactured in any tenement house for any factory for which no permit has been issued or for any factory whose permit is suspended or revoked. A complete list of all factories holding such permits, together with the name of the owner of each such factory, the address of the business and the name under which it is carried on, and of all tenement houses holding licenses, and a list of all permits and licenses revoked or suspended shall be published from time to time by the department of labor.

In effect
Oct. 1, 1913.
§ 2. This act shall take effect October first, nineteen hundred and thirteen.

---

[2] Section 106 new.

Chap. 261.

AN ACT to provide for the repair and improvement of existing mechanical and other structures and works on and connected with the canals of the state.

Became a law April 10, 1913, with the approval of the Governor. Passed, three-fifths being present.

The People of the State of New York, represented in Senate and Assembly, do enact as follows:

Section 1. The sum of one hundred and fifty thousand dollars ($150,000), or so much thereof as may be necessary, is hereby appropriated out of any moneys in the treasury not otherwise appropriated, for the repairs and improvements of existing mechanical and other structures and works on, and connected with the canals of this state, the same to be in addition and supplemental to the fund appropriated for the ordinary repairs of the said canals, and to be expended by the superintendent of public works for said purposes, on plans prepared by the state engineer and surveyor where such may be deemed to be necessary by the superintendent of public works and approved by him. *Appropriation.*

§ 2. The state comptroller is hereby authorized to borrow on the credit of the state, by the issue of emergency bonds therefor, the said sum of one hundred and fifty thousand dollars provided for by section one of this act, so that said sum may be made available for the purposes named therein; the said bonds to be paid from the avails of the state tax when collected for the fiscal year beginning October first, nineteen hundred and thirteen. *Issue of emergency bonds.*

§ 3. This act shall take effect immediately.

Chap. 262.

AN ACT making an appropriation for the state's proportion of the amounts appropriated for the repair of highways, pursuant to sections ninety and ninety-three of the highway law, and to provide funds for complying with the requirements of section one hundred and fifty-nine of the highway law.

Became a law April 11, 1913, with the approval of the Governor. Passed, by a two-thirds vote.

The People of the State of New York, represented in Senate and Assembly, do enact as follows:

Section 1. The sum of one million seven hundred and ninety-six thousand six hundred and fifty-five dollars ($1,796,655) is hereby appropriated from any moneys in the treasury not otherwise appropriated, payable by the treasurer on the warrant of the comptroller. Of the money hereby appropriated, the sum of one million seven hundred and twenty thousand dollars or so much thereof as may be necessary, shall be available for the purpose of paying the state's proportion of the amounts appropriated for the repair of highways pursuant to sections ninety and ninety-three of the highway law; the sum of seventy-six thousand six hundred and fifty-five dollars, or so much thereof as may be necessary shall be available for complying with the requirements of section one hundred and fifty-nine[1] of said law.

§ 2. This act shall take effect immediately.

---

[1] As added by L. 1910, ch. 46, and amended by L. 1911, ch. 646, and L. 1913, ch. 474, post.

Chap. 263.

AN ACT to amend chapter forty-five of the laws of nineteen hundred and one, entitled "An act to establish a public park in the
village of Mechanicville, in the county of Saratoga; to create
a commission for the improvement, management and control of
such park; to define the powers and duties of such commission,
and to provide for raising an annual tax in said village for the
improvement of such park, in relation to moneys to be raised
for park purposes and extending the power of such commission.

Became a law April 11, 1913, with the approval of the Governor. Passed,
three-fifths being present.

*The People of the State of New York, represented in Senate
and Assembly, do enact as follows:*

Section 1. The title of chapter forty-five of the laws of nine- L. 1901,
teen hundred and one, entitled "An act to establish a public park amended.
in the village of Mechanicville, in the county of Saratoga; to
create a commission for the improvement, management and control of such park," is hereby amended to read as follows:

An act to establish a public park in the village of Mechanicville, in the county of Saratoga; to create a commission for the
improvement, management and control of such park; to define
the powers and duties of such commission and extend its jurisdiction to other parks,[1] and to provide for raising an annual tax
in said village for the improvement of such park or parks.[2]

§ 2. Sections four and five of such chapter are hereby amended §§ 4, 5
to read, respectively, as follows: amended.

§ 4. Said commission shall have power and it shall be its duty, Powers
subject, as to Talmadge park,[3] to the provisions contained in of commis-
said deed: sion.

1. To meet between the first and tenth days of April in each Meetings,
year and choose a president and secretary from its members, books, etc.
to serve until their successors are chosen, which officers shall
have and possess the authority and discharge the duties usually
appertaining to such offices; and to meet as often as, and whenever, the commission shall direct or two members thereof shall
request, all which meetings shall be held at some convenient

---

1 Words "and extend its jurisdiction to other parks," new.
2 Words "or parks" new.
3 Words "as to Talmadge park," new.

place in said village and shall be public; and all books, records, maps, surveys, drawings and proceedings, of the commission shall at all reasonable times be open to the inspection of any taxpayer of said village;

Improvement and maintenance of parks.

2. To map, lay out, grade and complete roads, walks and drives in and through village parks;[4] to construct and maintain fountains, ponds and streams therein, and to embellish, improve and ornament said parks,[5] in such manner as such commission shall deem best for the benefit and enjoyment of the public;

Regulations for use of parks.

3. To adopt reasonable rules and regulations relative to the use of village parks[6] by the public, and for the preservation of the same and every part thereof; to prescribe fines and penalties for a violation of such rules and regulations, not to exceed one hundred dollars or imprisonment in the county jail of said county not to *exceeed thirty days, for each offense, and in case of violation, to prosecute therefor in the name of said village; all of which rules and regulations shall be conspicuously posted in at least ten public places in each of said parks[7] five days before the same shall take effect;

Annual expenditure.

4. For the purposes of this act[8] to expend annually the sum raised for the [9]park fund as hereinafter provided, or such part thereof as the commission shall determine; provided, that if in any year a balance shall remain after paying and discharging all indebtedness theretofore incurred, such balance may be expended for such purposes or any of them, in any succeeding year. No debt or liability beyond the income of the current year shall be incurred or created.

Control of parks.

5. To have the exclusive management, supervision and control of[10] Talmadge park and all other public parks of the village,[11] and any and all additions made thereto, subject to the reasonable use and enjoyment thereof by the public.

Tax for park fund.

§ 5. The board of trustees of said village is empowered and directed to raise annually, by tax to be assessed upon the taxable property in said village, at the same time and in the same manner

---

* So in original.
4 Formerly read: "through said park."
5 Formerly "park."
6 Formerly read: "use of the park."
7 Formerly read: "in said park."
8 Words "of this act" substituted for word "aforesaid."
9 Word "Talmadge" omitted.
10 Words "the park" omitted.
11 Words "Talmadge park and all other public parks of the village," new.

that general taxes are raised therein, such sum as it may determine necessary, to be known as the "park fund," [12] which fund shall be paid by the collector of said village to the treasurer thereof and by him kept separate and apart from all other village moneys; and no part thereof shall be transferred to any village fund nor used for any purpose except the purposes mentioned and intended in the last preceding section.

§ 3. This act shall take effect immediately.

Chap. 264.

AN ACT to amend chapter one hundred and six of the laws of eighteen hundred and ninety-one, entitled "An act to revise, consolidate and amend the several acts relating to the village of Mechanicville, and to repeal certain acts," in relation to village funds and obligations.

Became a law April 11, 1913, with the approval of the Governor. Passed, three-fifths being present.

The People of the State of New York, represented in Senate and Assembly, do enact as follows:

Section 1. Subdivision thirty of section three of title five of chapter one hundred and six of the laws of eighteen hundred and ninety-one, entitled "An act to revise, consolidate and amend the several acts relating to the village of Mechanicville, and to repeal certain acts," as amended by chapter one hundred and forty of the laws of eighteen hundred and ninety-seven, and chapter two hundred and seventy-three of the laws of nineteen hundred and two, and chapter eighty-four of the laws of nineteen hundred and six, is hereby amended to read as follows:

30. To raise annually by tax, to be assessed upon the estates, real and personal, within said village, such an amount of money, denominated highway tax, as they shall deem advisable;[1] and also to annually assess a poll tax of one dollar on each male inhabitant of the village, of the age of twenty-one years, and upward, which

[margin notes:] L. 1891, ch. 106, tit. 5, § 3, subd. 30, as amended by L. 1897, ch. 140, L. 1902, ch. 273, and L. 1906, ch. 84, amended.

[margin notes:] Trustees authorized to assess tax for highway fund.

---

[12] Words "such sum as it may determine necessary, to be known as the "park fund,"" substituted for words "the sum of not less than two hundred dollars nor more than five hundred dollars, to be known as the "Talmadge park fund.""

[1] Words "not exceeding the sum of three thousand five hundred dollars," omitted.

poll tax shall be collected as in this act provided. The highway tax and poll tax shall be paid to the treasurer and by him kept separate from all other moneys, and shall be denominated the highway fund.

Tit. 5, § 2, subd 31, as amended by L. 1897, ch. 140, L. 1900, ch. 459, L. 1902, ch. 273, L 1905, ch. 161, and L. 1906, ch. 84, amended. § 2. Subdivision thirty-one of section three of title five of such act, as amended by chapter one hundred and forty of the laws of eighteen hundred and ninety-seven, chapter four hundred and fifty-nine of the laws of nineteen hundred, chapter two hundred and seventy-three of the laws of nineteen hundred and two, and chapter one hundred and one of the laws of nineteen hundred and five, and chapter eighty-four of the laws of nineteen hundred and six, is hereby amended to read as follows:

Tax for general fund. 31. To raise annually by tax, to be assessed upon the real and personal estate within said village, such an amount of money as they shall deem necessary,[2] which sum shall be expended by said board of trustees in liquidating the general expenses of said village. Such money shall be denominated the general fund. **Tax for garbage fund.** And also to raise annually by tax to be assessed upon the real and personal estate in said village such an amount of money as they shall deem necessary,[3] which sum, or so much thereof as may be necessary, shall be expended by said board of trustees in the removal or destruction of garbage and refuse matter in said village. Such money shall be denomi- **Provision for garbage removal.** nated the garbage fund. The board of trustees may provide for such removal or destruction by contract or otherwise in its discretion; if by contract it shall be let to the lowest responsible bidder after due notice of the letting of such contract, published once a week for two consecutive weeks in a newspaper published in such village.

Tit. 7, § 15 amended. § 3. Section fifteen of title seven of such act is hereby amended to read as follows:

Liability beyond income not to be incurred. § 15. No debt or liability beyond the income of the current year shall be incurred or created by said village, or by any board or officer thereof. A wilful violation of this section is hereby de- **Raising money when authorized by vote of electors.** clared a misdemeanor. When the raising of any money by vote of the qualified electors as provided by law has been voted, the amount may be borrowed, or a liability by contract for the purpose for which such money has been voted may be incurred, not exceeding the sum so voted, until the amount can be raised by tax. [4]But

---

[2] Words " not exceeding the sum of four thousand dollars," omitted.
[3] Words " not exceeding the sum of two thousand dollars," omitted.
[4] Remainder of section new.

this section shall not be construed to prevent, nor shall it prevent, Issuance of bonds. the issue and sale of bonds by the board of trustees of said village when authorized by village election for any of the purposes mentioned and stated in section one hundred and twenty-eight[5] of the village law.

§ 4. This act shall take effect immediately.

Chap. 265.

AN ACT to amend the civil rights law, in relation to equal rights in places of public accommodation and providing penalty for violation thereof.

Became a law April 11, 1913, with the approval of the Governor. Passed, three-fifths being present.

The People of the State of New York, represented in Senate and Assembly, do enact as follows:

Section 1. Section forty of chapter fourteen of the laws of nineteen hundred and nine, entitled "An act relating to civil rights, constituting chapter six of the consolidated laws," is hereby amended to read as follows:[1] L. 1909, ch. 14, § 40 amended.

§ 40. **Equal rights in places of public accommodation, resort or amusement.** All persons within the jurisdiction of this state shall be entitled to the full and equal accommodations, advantages and privileges of any place of public accommodation, resort or amusement, subject only to the conditions and limitations established by law and applicable alike to all persons. No person, being the owner, lessee, proprietor, manager, superintendent, agent or employee of any such place, shall directly or indirectly refuse, withhold from or deny to any person any of the accommodations, advantages or privileges thereof, or directly or indirectly publish, circulate, issue, display, post or mail any written or printed communication, notice or advertisement, to the effect that any of the accommodations, advantages and privileges of any such place shall be refused, withheld from or denied to any person on account of race, creed or color, or that the patronage or custom thereat, of any person belonging to or purporting to be of any particular race, creed or color is unwelcome, objectionable or not acceptable, de-

---

[5] As amended by L. 1910, ch. 4, and L. 1911, chaps. 57, 738.
[1] Section materially amended.

16

sired or solicited. The production of any such written or printed communication, notice or advertisement, purporting to relate to any such place and to be made by any person being the owner, lessee, proprietor, superintendent or manager thereof, shall be presumptive evidence in any civil or criminal action that the same was authorized by such person. A place of public accommodation, resort or amusement within the meaning of this article, shall be deemed to include any inn, tavern or hotel, whether conducted for the entertainment of transient guests, or for the accommodation of those seeking health, recreation or rest, any restaurant, eating-house, public conveyance on land or water, bathhouse, barber-shop, theater and music hall. Nothing herein contained shall be construed to prohibit the mailing of a private communication in writing sent in response to a specific written inquiry.

§ 41 amended. § 2. Section forty-one of said act is hereby amended to read as follows:[2]

§ 41. **Penalty for violation.** Any person who shall violate any of the provisions of the foregoing section, or who shall aid or incite the violation of any of said provisions shall for each and every violation thereof be liable to a penalty of not less than one hundred dollars nor more than five hundred dollars, to be recovered by the person aggrieved thereby or by any resident of this state, to whom such person shall assign his cause of action, in any court of competent jurisdiction in the county in which the plaintiff or the defendant shall reside; and shall, also, for every such offense be deemed guilty of a misdemeanor, and upon conviction thereof shall be fined not less than one hundred dollars nor more than five hundred dollars, or shall be imprisoned not less than thirty days nor more than ninety days, or both such fine and imprisonment.

In effect Sept. 1, 1913. § 3. This act shall take effect September first, nineteen hundred and thirteen.

---

[2] Section materially amended.

Chap. 266.

AN ACT to amend chapter five hundred and forty-eight of the laws of nineteen hundred and twelve, entitled "An act to erect the county of Bronx from the territory now comprised within the limits of the borough of Bronx, in the city of New York, as constituted by chapter three hundred and seventy-eight of the laws of eighteen hundred and ninety-seven and all acts amendatory thereof and supplemental thereto," in relation to the commissioner of jurors of such county, and providing for the raising of money to pay the immediate expenses of such office.

Became a law April 11, 1913, with the approval of the Governor. Passed by a two-thirds vote.

The People of the State of New York, represented in Senate and Assembly, do enact as follows:

Section 1. Sections four and eight of chapter five hundred and forty-eight of the laws of nineteen hundred and twelve, entitled "An act to erect the county of Bronx from the territory now comprised within the limits of the borough of Bronx, in the city of New York, as constituted by chapter three hundred and seventy-eight of the laws of eighteen hundred and ninety-seven and all acts amendatory thereof and supplemental thereto," are hereby amended to read, respectively, as follows: L. 1912, ch. 548, §§ 4, 8 amended.

§ 4. The salary of the county judge shall be ten thousand dollars per annum; the salary of the surrogate shall be ten thousand dollars per annum; the salary of the district-attorney shall be ten thousand dollars per annum; the salary of the sheriff shall be ten thousand dollars per annum; the salary of the county clerk shall be ten thousand dollars per annum; the salary of the register of deeds shall be ten thousand dollars per annum,[1] and except as herein otherwise provided the positions, terms, grades, salaries, and compensation of all persons who may be appointed under the provision of law by any of the officers above mentioned or who may be required to carry on the public business as contemplated by this act shall be fixed by the board of estimate and apportionment of the city of New York, and such Salaries of county officers. Positions, terms, grades, salaries, etc. how fixed.

[1] Words " and the salary of the commissioner of jurors shall be five thousand dollars per annum," omitted.

salaries or other compensation and all other county charges and expenses of the county of Bronx shall be audited and paid by the department of finance in the manner provided for the audit and payment of the salaries of all county officers and the charges and expenses of the counties now included within the city of New York by chapter three hundred and seventy-eight of the laws of eighteen hundred and ninety-seven, and all acts amendatory thereof and supplemental thereto. All fees, statutory or otherwise, which under any provision of law may be paid to any of the officials above pro-vided for in this act or for rendering any services whatever of a public nature within the scope of the duties and powers of the said officials shall be paid into the treasury of the city of New York, except as herein otherwise provided. Any moneys payable into court under the provisions of title three, chapter eight of the code of civil procedure or otherwise shall be paid to the chamber-lain of the city of New York.

Commis-
s'oner of
jurors con-
tinued.
Appoint-
ment of
successor. § 8.[2] The commissioner of jurors for the county of Bronx now in office is continued in office. Whenever a vacancy shall occur in such office, the justice of the appellate division of the supreme court of the department in which such county is situated or a majority of them, shall appoint a successor to such commissioner. Such appointment shall be in writing, signed by the justices making the same, and filed in the office of the clerk of the appel-late division, and a copy thereof duly certified by the clerk of the appellate division shall be filed in the office of the clerk of
the county. A commissioner of jurors of the county of Bronx may be removed for cause upon notice and an opportunity to be heard by the justices of the appellate division of the supreme court of the department in which such county is situated. Such
commissioner of jurors shall receive an annual salary of six
Assistant
commis-
sioners,
secretary,
clerks, etc.,
compen-
sation. thousand dollars. Such commissioner shall appoint two assistant commissioners, a secretary, and such clerks, stenographers and messengers as may be necessary for the proper discharge of the duties of the office. Each assistant commissioner and the secre-tary shall receive an annual salary of three thousand dollars. The number and compensation of the clerks, stenographers and messengers shall be fixed by the justices of the appellate division,
or a majority of them. The commissioner of jurors may, with the written consent of the justices of the appellate division of the supreme court of the department in which such county is

---

[2] Section 8 materially amended.

situated, or a majority of them, secure a suitable office, properly furnished and equipped, and all books, stationery, blanks, postal cards and postage stamps as shall be required for the proper performance of the duties of the office. The rent of such office and the cost of the furniture and equipment thereof, and of all books, stationery, printing, blanks, postal cards and postage stamps to be so provided shall, with the salary paid to the commissioner, his assistants, secretary, clerks, stenographers and messengers, be a county charge, and shall be audited and paid as are the compensation and expenses of county officers. If the office of commissioner of jurors shall become vacant or such commissioner shall be unable to act by reason of sickness, absence or any other cause, while such vacancy or inability exists, all the powers of such commissioner shall be possessed and exercised by and all the duties of such commissioner shall devolve upon and be performed by such one of the assistant commissioners as shall have been designated by him for such purpose. The commissioner of jurors shall make such designation and may from time to time revoke the same and make a new designation by filing a certificate thereof in the office of the clerk of the county. The commissioner of jurors within said county of Bronx shall exercise all the powers and possess all the authority as to the selecting, returning and summoning of grand and trial jurors for the said county of Bronx as now provided by chapter four hundred and forty-one of the laws of eighteen hundred and ninety-nine, and all acts amendatory thereof and supplemental thereto. The president and commissioners of the department of taxes and assessments in the city of New York, must render to the commissioner of jurors of the county of Bronx such assistance as they are now required to render to the commissioners of jurors of each of the counties of Richmond and Queens.

§ 2. If money be not available for the payment of the salary of the commissioner of jurors from the time of his appointment until this act takes effect, and for the payment of the salaries, compensation and expenses authorized or required by this act, the comptroller of the city of New York shall cause special revenue bonds or certificates of indebtedness to be issued to provide the necessary money therefor; and such bonds or certificates of indebtedness shall be a charge upon the county of Bronx.

§ 3. This act shall take effect immediately.

Chap. 267.

AN ACT to amend the state finance law, in relation to the powers
and duties of the state comptroller.

Became a law April 11, 1913, with the approval of the Governor. Passed,
three-fifths being present.

*The People of the State of New York, represented in Senate
and Assembly, do enact as follows:*

L. 1909,
ch. 58, § 63
amended.

Section 1. Section sixty-three of chapter fifty-eight of the laws
of nineteen hundred and nine, entitled "An act in relation to state
finances, constituting chapter fifty-six of the consolidated laws,"
is hereby amended to read as follows:

§ 63. **Charges on the canal fund.** All moneys expended in the
construction, repair or improvement of the canals now authorized
by law, or allowed or expended by the commissioners of the canal
fund, or the superintendent of public works or other officer or assistant employed on such canals pursuant to law, with the compensation of such officers respectively, including the salary of the
superintendent of public works, shall be charged to the canal fund
unless otherwise expressly provided by law.[1] The comptroller
shall also charge to such fund from time to time so much for the
services of the clerks in his office, devoted to the accounts and revenues of the canals, as in his opinion is just, [2]and he is hereby
authorized in his discretion to transfer from time to time such
amounts of the surplus of canal fund to the general fund as may
not be needed to meet the expenses incident to the maintenance
and repair of canals.

§ 2. This act shall take effect immediately.

---

[1] Word " and " omitted. Section formerly consisted of one sentence.
[2] Remainder of section new.

Chap. 268.

AN ACT in relation to the board of trustees of foreign parishes of the Protestant Episcopal Church in the United States of America.

Became a law April 11, 1913, with the approval of the Governor. Passed, three-fifths being present.

The People of the State of New York, represented in Senate and Assembly, do enact as follows:

Section 1. The majority duly convened of the trustees of the body corporate created by chapter two hundred and fifty-seven of the laws of eighteen hundred and eighty-three, under the name and title of "The Board of Trustees of Foreign Parishes of the Protestant Episcopal Church in the United States of America," or, if less than a majority survive, the survivors or the survivor of said board of trustees, when duly convened, shall have power to fill any vacancy or vacancies which may be created in the number of said trustees by death, resignations or otherwise; provided, however, that no person shall be eligible to succeed to the office of such trustee who is not a communicant member of said Protestant Episcopal Church. *(margin: Vacancies in board authorized to be filled. Eligibility.)*

§ 2. From time to time the said board of trustees shall have power to increase the number of trustees to nine. *(margin: Increase of trustees authorized.)*

§ 3. This act shall take effect immediately.

Chap. 269.

AN ACT conferring jurisdiction upon the county court of Ontario county over cases involving offenses against children under sixteen years of age, as defined in article forty-four of the penal law, and regulating the procedure therein.

Became a law April 11, 1913, with the approval of the Governor. Passed, three-fifths being present.

The People of the State of New York, represented in Senate and Assembly, do enact as follows:

Section 1. Jurisdiction is hereby conferred upon the county court of Ontario county to hear, try and determine all cases arising in said county under article forty-four of the penal law. *(margin: Jurisdiction conferred.)*

§ 2. The prosecution of a person charged with any offense under said article forty-four less than the grade of felony may be instituted by the filing of an information, no indictment being necessary, and a warrant may be issued by the court or the judge thereof, and all subsequent proceedings shall be carried on in the same way as if the person were prosecuted upon an indictment for said offense, except that the trial shall be had before the court without a jury unless the court, in its discretion, grants a jury trial. The said county court and the judge thereof shall have all the power exercised by magistrates in regard to the issuing of subpoenas, the examination of witnesses and taking of depositions prior to the issuing of a warrant in such cases. This section shall not apply to cases under section four hundred and eighty-six[1] of said penal law.

§ 3. Nothing in this act shall be held to deprive police courts, courts of special sessions and the magistrates holding the same of concurrent jurisdiction to hear and dispose of cases embraced within section two of this act, not pending in the county court.

§ 4. This act shall take effect September first, nineteen hundred and thirteen.

Chap. 270.

AN ACT conferring jurisdiction upon the county court of Ontario county in matters relating to children; and regulating the procedure in such cases, including the temporary detention of children, a probation system and the appointment of guardians.

Became a law April 11, 1913, with the approval of the Governor. Passed, three-fifths being present.

The People of the State of New York, represented in Senate and Assembly, do enact as follows:

Section 1. **Jurisdiction.** The county court of Ontario county shall have original and exclusive jurisdiction of all cases coming within the terms and provisions of this act. This act shall be construed liberally and as remedial in character; and the powers hereby conferred are intended to be general to effect the beneficial purposes herein set forth.

§ 2. **Definitions of children.** This act shall apply to any child

---

[1] As amended by L. 1912, ch. 169.

less than sixteen years of age residing or being at the time in Ontario county:

(a) who violates any penal law or any municipal ordinance, or who commits any act or offense for which he could be prosecuted in a method partaking of the nature of a criminal action or proceeding (except a crime punishable by death or life imprisonment), or

(b) who engages in any occupation, calling or exhibition or is found in any place for permitting which an adult may be punished by law, or who so deports himself or is in such condition or surroundings or under such improper or insufficient guardianship or control, as to endanger the morals, health or general welfare of said child.

§ 3. **Petition.** Any person having knowledge or information that a child residing in or actually within the county is within the provisions of the preceding section may file with said county court a verified petition stating the facts that bring such child within said provisions. The petition may be upon information and belief. The title of the proceeding shall be " Children's Part, County Court, County of Ontario. In the Matter of (inserting name), a Child under Sixteen Years of Age." The petition shall set forth the name and residence of the child and of the parents, if known to the petitioner, and the name and residence of the person having the guardianship, custody, control and supervision of such child, if the same be known or ascertained by the petitioner, or the petition shall state that they are unknown, if that be the fact.

§ 4. **Issuance of summons.** Upon the filing of the petition, the court or the judge thereof may forthwith, or after first causing an investigation by a probation officer or other person, cause a summons to be issued signed by the judge or the special clerk of the children's part of said court, requiring the child to appear before the court and the parents, or the guardian, or the person having the custody, control or supervision of the child, or the person with whom the child may be, to appear with the child, at a place and time stated in the summons, to show cause why the child should not be dealt with according to the provisions of this act.

§ 5. **Custody of child; bail.** If it appears from the petition that the child is embraced within subdivision a of section two, or is in such condition that the welfare of the child requires that

its custody be immediately assumed, the court may indorse upon
the summons a direction that the officer serving the same shall
at once take said child into his custody. Such child may thereafter be admitted to bail or released in the custody of a probation
officer or other person by the judge of said court, the clerk or the
chief probation officer; but when not so released, the child shall
be detained, pending the hearing of the case, in such place of
detention as is hereinafter provided for. In no case arising
under this act shall any child be placed in a jail, common lock-up
or other place used for the confinement of adults charged with
or convicted of crime or other offenses.

§ 6. Service of summons. Service of summons within the
county of Ontario shall be made personally by delivering to and
leaving with the person summoned a true copy thereof. If it
shall be made to appear, by affidavit, that reasonable but unsuc-
cessful effort has been made to serve the summons personally upon
the parties named therein, other than said child, the court or the
judge thereof at any stage of the proceedings may make an order
for substituted service of the summons or of a supplemental
summons in the manner provided for substituted service of civil
process in courts of record, and if such parties are without said
county, service may be made by mail, by publication or personally
without the county in such manner and at such time before the
hearing as in said order directed. It shall be sufficient to confer
jurisdiction if service is effected at any time before the time
fixed in the summons for the return thereof, but the court, if requested by the child or parent or such other person as is mentioned in section four, shall not proceed with the hearing earlier
than the third day after the date of the service. Proof of service
shall be made substantially as in courts of record. Failure to
serve summons upon any person other than said child shall not
impair the jurisdiction of the court to proceed in cases arising
under subdivision a of section two, provided that, for good cause
shown, the court make an order dispensing with such service.
The summons shall be considered a mandate of the court, and
wilful failure to obey its requirements shall subject any person
guilty thereof to liability for punishment as for a criminal contempt. At any stage of the case, the court may, in its discretion,
appoint an attorney or other suitable person to be the guardian
ad litem of the said child for the purposes of the proceeding, and
the court may call upon the district attorney of said county to

appear in any proceeding under this act. The sheriff of said county shall serve or cause to be served all papers which are directed by the court to be served by him, and a suitable allowance shall be made by the board of supervisors for his actual disbursements in effecting such service; but all papers may be served by any person delegated by the court for that purpose. The expense incurred in making substituted service or service by publication or personally without the county shall be a county charge.

§ 7. Hearing; judgment; records. Upon the return of the summons, or at the time set for the hearing, the court shall proceed to hear and determine the case. The court may conduct the examination of the witnesses without the assistance of counsel, and may take testimony and inquire into the habits, surroundings, condition and tendencies of said child, to enable the court to render such order or judgment as shall best conserve the welfare of said child and carry out the objects of this act. The court, if satisfied that the child is in need of the care or discipline and protection of the state, may so adjudicate, and may in addition find said child to be delinquent or neglected, or in need of more suitable guardianship, as the case may be; and in addition to the powers granted by this act, may render such judgment and make such order or commitment, according to the circumstances of the case, as any court or magistrate is now or may hereafter be authorized by law to render or make in any of the cases coming within section two of this act. It is the intention of this act that in all proceedings coming under its provisions the court shall proceed upon the theory that said child is the ward of the state, and is subject to the discipline and entitled to the protection which the court should give such child under the conditions disclosed in the case; and when once jurisdiction has been obtained in the case of any such child, it shall, unless a court order shall be issued to the contrary, continue for the purposes of this act during the minority of said child. The court shall have power, upon the hearing of any case involving any child, to exclude the general public from the room wherein said hearing is held, admitting thereto only such persons as may have a direct interest in the case. The hearings may be conducted in the judge's chambers or in such other room or apartment in any place in the county as the supervisors may provide or as the judge without the action of the supervisors and without expenses to the county may secure. As far as practicable such cases shall not be heard in conjunction with the other business of the court. The records of all cases may be withheld from indiscriminate public inspection in the discretion of the court; but such records shall be open to inspection by such child, his parents or guardians, or his attorneys, at all times. No adjudication under the provisions of this act shall operate as a disqualification of the child for any office under any state or municipal civil service; and such child shall not be denominated a criminal by reason of any such adjudication; nor shall such adjudication be denominated a conviction.

§ 8. **Arrest; transfer from other courts.** Nothing in this act shall be construed as forbidding the arrest, with or without warrant, of any child as now or hereafter may be provided by law, or as forbidding the issuing of warrants by magistrates, as provided by law. Whenever a child less than sixteen years of age is brought before a magistrate in said county, such magistrate should transfer the case to the county court by an order directing that said child be taken forthwith to the shelter; such magistrate may, however, by order admit such child to bail, or release said child in the custody of some suitable person as now provided by law, to appear before said county court at a time designated in the said order. All informations, depositions, warrants and other process in the hands of such magistrate shall be forthwith transmitted to the county court, and shall become part of its records. The county court shall thereupon proceed to hear and dispose of such case in the same manner as if the proceeding had been instituted in said county court upon petition, as hereinbefore provided. In all cases the nature of the proceeding shall be explained to said child, and if they appear, to the parents, custodian or guardian; and between the time of the arrest of such child and its appearance before the county court, he shall, if not bailed or otherwise released, be detained as provided in section five.

§ 9. **Appeals.** An appeal may be taken from any final order or judgment of said court to the appellate division of the supreme court within sixty days after the entry of said order, and if any such appeal is taken by the guardian ad litem appointed for said child by said court, said court may, in its discretion, grant an order auditing and allowing the actual disbursements of said guardian ad litem in printing his papers on appeal; whereupon said disbursements shall become a claim against the county of Ontario, to be paid as a county charge.

§ 10. **Place of detention.** The county judge may arrange with any incorporated society or association maintaining a suitable place for the detention of children in said county for the use thereof or of a part thereof as a temporary detention home for children coming within the provisions of this act, and may enter an order which shall be effectual for that purpose; and a reasonable sum shall be appropriated by the board of supervisors for the compensation of said society or association for the care of such children. If, however, the county judge shall certify that a suitable arrangement for such use cannot be made, or continued, the board of supervisors may establish, equip and maintain a temporary detention home for such children entirely separated from any place of confinement of adults, to be called "the county shelter," which shall be conducted as an agency of the county court for the purposes of this act and, so far as possible, shall be furnished and carried on as a family home and shall be in charge of a superintendent or matron who shall reside therein. The board of supervisors may authorize the county judge to appoint a superintendent, matron and other necessary employees of said county shelter in the same manner in which probation officers are appointed under this act, their salaries to be fixed and paid in the same manner as the salaries of probation officers. The county judge may appoint as such superintendent or matron a probation officer. The necessary expenses incurred in maintaining said county shelter shall be paid by the county.

§ 11. Clerk; probation officer; co-operation. The county judge may appoint a chief probation officer, whose duty it shall be to act under the direction of said court in the cases arising under this act to keep the records and act as clerk of the children's part of the county court and who shall be appointed, and perform all of the duties of, county probation officer by virtue of and according to the provisions of section eleven-a of the code of criminal procedure; and said chief probation officer shall be paid such reasonable compensation as the board of supervisors may determine. The court is authorized to seek the co-operation of all societies or organizations, public or private, having for their object the protection or aid of indigent or neglected children, to the end that the court may be assisted in every reasonable way to give to all of such children the care, protection and assistance which will conserve the welfare of such children. And it is hereby made the duty of every county, town or municipal official or department, in said county, to render such assistance and co-operation within his or its jurisdictional power to further the objects of this act; and all institutions, associations or other custodial agencies in which any child may be, coming within the provisions of this act, are hereby required to give such information to the court or any of said officers appointed by it as said court or officers may require for the purposes of this act.

§ 12. **Probation; commitments.** All provisions of law applicable to probation of children brought before any court or magistrate are made applicable to cases coming within the provisions of this act, except that the period of probation may be extended by the court during the minority of said child. If it becomes necessary to commit any such child over sixteen years of age who is on probation the order of commitment, nunc pro tunc, shall be entered as of the date of judgment, and any institution to which commitment originally could be made is authorized to receive such child and have payment therefor as if under sixteen. The times and places for the appearance of said child during said probationary period shall be entirely within the discretion of the court, and during said probationary period and during the time when said child may be committed to any institution or to the care of any association or person for custodial or disciplinary purposes, said child shall always be subject to the friendly visitation of such probation officers or other agents of the court as may be appointed for that purpose. And any final order or judgment made by the court in the case of any such child shall be subject to such modifications from time to time as the court may consider to be for the welfare of said child; and no commitment of any child to any institution or other custodial agency shall deprive the court of the jurisdiction to change the form of the commitment or transfer the custody of said child to some other institution or agency on such conditions as the court may see fit to impose, the duty being constant upon the court to give to all children subject to its jurisdiction such oversight and control in the premises as will conduce to the welfare of said child and the best interests of the state.

§ 13. **Support of children in institutions.** Whenever any child is found to be in such condition, surroundings or under such improper or insufficient guardianship as to lead the court, in its discretion, to take the custody of said child away from its parents and place it in some institution or under some other custodial agency, the court may, after the issuance and service of an order to show cause upon the parents or other person having the duty under the law to support said child, adjudge that the expense of caring for said child by said custodial agency or institution as fixed by the court shall be paid by the person or persons bound by law to support said child; in which event such person or persons shall be liable to pay to such custodial agency or institution and in .such manner as the court may direct the money so adjudged to be payable by him or them; and willful failure to pay said sum may be punished as a contempt of court and the order of the court for the payment of said money may be also enforced as money judgments of courts of record are enforced.

§ 14. Medical care.　Whenever a child within the jurisdiction of said court and under the provisions of this act appears to the court to be in need of medical care, a suitable order may be made for the treatment of such child in a hospital, and the expense thereof shall be a county charge; provided that the county may recover the said expense in a suitable action from the person or persons liable for the furnishing of necessaries for said child, and that for that. purpose the court may cause any such child to be examined by any health officer within the jurisdiction of the court, or by any duly licensed physician.

§ 15. Return of child to parents; selection of institution.　Whenever it shall appear to the court, in the case of any neglected child or of any child in need of more suitable guardianship that has been taken from its home or the custody of its parents, that conditions have so changed that it is consistent with the public good and the welfare of said child that the parents again have the custody of said child the court may make a suitable order in the premises.　In committing any child to any custodial agency or placing it under any guardianship other than that of its natural guardians, the court shall, as far as practicable, select as the custodial agency some individual holding the same religious belief as the parents of said child, or some institution or association governed by persons of like religious faith, unless said institution is a state or municipal institution.

§ 16. Guardian.　Whenever, in the course of a proceeding instituted under this act, it shall appear to the said court that the welfare of said child will be promoted by the appointment of an individual as general guardian of its property, and of his person, when such child is not committed to any institution or to the custody of any incorporated society, the court shall have jurisdiction to make such appointment either upon the application of the child or some relative or friend, or upon the court's own motion, and in that event an order to show cause may be made by the court, to be served upon the parent or parents of said child in such manner and for such time prior to the hearing as the court may deem reasonable. In any case arising under this act, the court may determine as between parents whether the father or mother shall have the custody, tuition and direction of said child.

§ 17. **Power of other courts.** Nothing herein contained shall be construed as abridging the general chancery power and jurisdiction exercised by the supreme court over the persons and estates of minors, nor as abridging the authority of the surrogate to appoint guardians for infants as now provided by law.

§ 18. **Visitation of institutions.** It shall be the duty of the judge, so far as practicable, to visit at least once a year each institution in which there shall be at the time any child under commitment pursuant to this act, and the managers and officers of said institution shall accord to said judge full opportunity to inspect the said institution in all its departments. Said judge may examine witnesses under oath within the county where said institution is located, or appoint a referee for the purpose of obtaining any information as to the efficiency and character of such institution.

§ 19. **Rules; substitute judge.** The court shall have power to devise and publish rules to regulate the procedure for cases coming within the provisions of this act, and for the conduct of all probation and other officers of the court in such cases, and such rules shall be enforced and construed beneficially for the remedial purposes embraced herein. The court may devise and cause to be printed for public use such forms for records and for the various petitions, orders, process and other papers in the cases coming under this act and shall meet the requirements thereof; and all the expenses incurred by the court in complying with the provisions of this act shall be a county charge. In the absence or disability of the county judge the surrogate of the county shall preside over the children's part.

§ 20. **Other provisions of law.** All provisions of the penal law or code of criminal procedure or other statute inconsistent with or repugnant to this act shall be considered inapplicable to the cases arising under this act.

In effect
Sept. 1,
1913.   § 21. This act shall take effect September first, nineteen hundred and thirteen.

Chap. 271.

AN ACT to revive and extend the corporate existence of the German American Brewing Company of Buffalo, New York.

Became a law April 11, 1913, with the approval of the Governor. Passed, three-fifths being present.

The People of the State of New York, represented in Senate and Assembly, do enact as follows:

Section 1. The corporate existence of the German American Brewing Company of Buffalo, New York, is hereby revived, and the said German American Brewing Company is hereby declared to be a valid corporation, with the same force and effect as the same existed on the twenty-fourth day of July, nineteen hundred and ten, and prior to the expiration of the period for which said corporation was created; and with all the powers, privileges, franchises and subject to the same duties, obligations and restrictions in respect to such powers under the laws of this state in force on and before the said twenty-fourth day of July, nineteen hundred and ten, which were conferred and imposed in respect of said corporation and with the same force and effect as if the said corporate existence and organization had been extended according to law prior to the said twenty-fourth day of July, nineteen hundred and ten, and before the expiration of the period of time for which said corporation was created. *Corporate existence revived.*

§ 2. The said corporation shall continue for a period of twenty-five years after this act takes effect, to be possessed and seized of all the property and be vested with all the rights and privileges had, possessed, seized and enjoyed by the said German American Brewing Company, at any time prior to the twenty-fourth day of July, nineteen hundred and ten, and subject to the same liabilities and restrictions provided by law. *Corporation continued.*

§ 3. This act shall take effect immediately.

Chap. 272.

AN ACT to amend the military law, in relation to uniforms.

Became a law April 11, 1913, with the approval of the Governor. Passed, three-fifths being present.

The People of the State of New York, represented in Senate and Assembly, do enact as follows:

L. 1909, ch. 41, § 168, as amended by L. 1912, ch. 67, amended.

Section 1. Section one hundred and sixty-eight of chapter forty-one of the laws of nineteen hundred and nine, entitled "An act in relation to the militia, constituting chapter thirty-six of the consolidated laws," as amended by chapter sixty-seven of the laws of nineteen hundred and twelve, is hereby amended to read as follows:

§ 168. **Full-dress uniform.** Any command may, with the consent of the governor, adopt a full-dress uniform of its own and at its own expense. To such command such portions of the state uniform may be issued as the governor may direct. A squadron of cavalry which has adopted a full-dress uniform of its own under this section shall have the right to continue its use upon becoming part of a regiment [1]and any additional troop or troops of the same regiment that may be permanently quartered in the armory of such squadron shall with the consent of the commanding officers of the regiment and squadron have the right to adopt the same full-dress uniform for such time as they are so quartered.

§ 2. This act shall take effect immediately.

Chap. 273.

AN ACT to amend the military law, in relation to the formation of associations by squadrons and troops.

Became a law April 11, 1913, with the approval of the Governor. Passed, three-fifths being present.

The People of the State of New York, represented in Senate and Assembly, do enact as follows:

L. 1909, ch. 41, § 252, as amended by L. 1909,

Section 1. Section two hundred and fifty-two of chapter forty-one of the laws of nineteen hundred and nine, entitled "An act in relation to the militia, constituting chapter thirty-six of the

---

1 Remainder of section new.

consolidated laws," as amended by chapter three hundred and eleven of the laws of nineteen hundred and nine and by chapter one hundred and four of the laws of nineteen hundred and eleven, is hereby amended to read as follows: ch. 311, and L. 1911, ch. 104, amended.

§ 252. **Formation of associations; by-laws.** The officers of any regiment or battalion or squadron not a part of a regiment, the officers of the corps of engineers serving with the engineer troops, and the officers of the coast artillery corps serving in the same artillery district, and the members of any squadron, troop, battery, company, division, company of signal corps, field hospital, ambulance company or detachment of hospital corps, may organize themselves into an association of which the commanding officer shall be president; provided, however, that such associations shall by an affirmative vote of two-thirds of all their members adopt by-laws, rules and regulations not inconsistent with this chapter, and which shall conform to the system prescribed in general regulations, and be submitted to the major-general or the commanding officer of the naval militia, as the case may be, for his approval; and which by-laws shall provide that the treasurer of such association shall furnish proper security for the faithful performance of his duties; that all funds of the association shall be kept in a bank of deposit in a separate account in the name of the association; that checks upon such funds shall be signed both by the treasurer and the commanding officer of such association; and that the books and accounts of such association shall at all times be open to the inspection of any official whose duty it is to inspect the organized militia of the state or of any member of the association. Such by-laws may contain such other provisions as are not inconsistent with the limitations herein set forth, and when approved by the major-general or the commanding officer of the naval militia, as the case may be, such by-laws, rules and regulations shall be binding upon all commissioned officers and enlisted men therein; but they may be altered in the manner provided for their adoption from time to time as may be found necessary, provided, however, that the essential provisions hereinabove set forth shall in no case be omitted or qualified. Every association already formed which has not adopted by-laws under the regulations and limitations hereinabove set forth; and every association heretofore formed which has adopted by-laws that do not contain the essential requirements hereinabove set forth, shall adopt revised by-laws containing such requirements and submit the same for approval

to their respective commanding officers as above set forth. [1]A
squadron of cavalry which has formed an association under this
section shall, upon becoming part of a regiment, have the right
upon the application of a majority of the members of the field and
staff or non-commissioned staff or hospital corps or troop or troops
of the same regiment permanently quartered in the armory of that
squadron to extend the membership of such association by a majority vote of its members so as to embrace such members of such
field and staff or non-commissioned staff or hospital corps or
troop or troops, who shall when such extensions are made and
while so quartered become and be members of such association for
all purposes.

§ 2. This act shall take effect immediately.

Chap. 274.

AN ACT to amend chapter one hundred and sixty of the laws of
nineteen hundred and twelve, entitled "An act providing for
the erection of a boathouse, shelters, wharves and retaining
walls at the city of Buffalo, for the third division of the third
battalion of the naval militia, upon lands of the state in the city
of Buffalo, and making an appropriation therefor," in relation
to the location of such lands and powers of the commissioners
of the land office relative thereto.

Became a law April 11, 1913, with the approval of the Governor. Passed,
three-fifths being present.

*The People of the State of New York, represented in Senate
and Assembly, do enact as follows:*

L. 1912,
ch. 160, §§
amended.
Section 1. Section two of chapter one hundred and sixty of
the laws of nineteen hundred and twelve, entitled "An act providing for the erection of a boathouse, shelters, wharves and retaining walls at the city of Buffalo, for the third division of the
third battalion of the naval militia, upon lands of the state in
the city of Buffalo, and making an appropriation therefor," is
hereby amended to read as follows:[2]

Location of
site on
lands owned
by state.
§ 2. Said boathouse, shelters for boats, gear and equipment,
wharves, runways, retaining walls, slips, boat landings, piling and

---

[1] Remainder of section new.
[2] Section materially amended.

other necessary structures, shall be erected and constructed upon land owned by the state of New York, described as follows: All that tract or parcel of land under water situate in the city of Buffalo, county of Erie and state of New York, more particularly described as a plot of land covered with water, beginning at the intersection of the easterly line of Black Rock harbor as established by the United States, and the northerly line of the most northerly plot heretofore owned by Henry Koons, as granted to him by chapter three hundred and forty-three of the laws of eighteen hundred and ninety-four between Carolina and Virginia streets extended; thence northerly along the said harbor line four hundred and fifty feet; thence easterly and parallel with the northerly line of the lands of the said Koons three hundred and fifty feet; thence southerly and parallel to said harbor line four hundred and fifty feet to the northerly line of said lands of Koons; thence westerly along the northerly line of said lands of Koons three hundred and fifty feet to the place of beginning. The commissioners of the land office are hereby directed to set aside the above described lands and lands under water in said city of Buffalo belonging to the state for the purposes of this act so long as such lands shall be used for the purpose herein stated.

Description of lands.

Commissioners of land office directed to set aside lands described.

§ 2. This act shall take effect immediately.

Chap. 275.

AN ACT to amend the military law, in relation to the militia council.

Became a law April 11, 1913, with the approval of the Governor. Passed, three-fifths being present.

The People of the State of New York, represented in Senate and Assembly, do enact as follows:

Section 1. Section fifteen of chapter forty-one of the laws of nineteen hundred and nine, entitled "An act in relation to the militia, constituting chapter thirty-six of the consolidated laws," as amended by chapter three hundred and seventy-three of the laws of nineteen hundred and nine and chapter eight hundred and eight of the laws of nineteen hundred and eleven, is hereby amended to read as follows:

L. 1909, ch. 41, § 15, as amended by L. 1909, ch. 373, and L. 1911, ch. 808, amended.

§ 15. **Militia council.** There shall be for the state a militia council composed of the major-general of the national guard, who shall be chief of the council, the commanding officer of the naval militia, the adjutant-general of the state and seven officers of the national guard in active service detailed by the governor and comprising three field officers of infantry, one field officer of the coast artillery corps, one field officer of the corps of engineers serving with the organized battalions, one field officer of cavalry and one [1]field officer of field artillery. In the first instance three of the details shall be made for one year, two for two years and two for three years, but thereafter all details shall be made for three years. An officer who has served on the council shall not be again detailed until the expiration of three years from the completion of his former term. In anticipation of vacancies the militia council shall submit to the governor the names of officers recommended for detail, these having been selected by a committee of five officers of the active militia appointed by the militia council and of which two may be already serving as detailed members of the council. The militia council shall be advisory in its function. It shall recommend to the governor from time to time such action as it may deem advisable relating to the military law, regulations, organization, equipment, duty and discipline of the militia, and it shall report on matters referred to it by the governor, or by the legislature of the state, or by any committee thereof. The militia council shall make an annual report to the governor. The militia council shall hold stated sessions in Albany or elsewhere in the state as the governor or the council may direct in February, September and December in each year and extraordinary sessions shall be held at the call of the governor, the chief of the council or a majority of the members of the council.

§ 2. This act shall take effect immediately.

---

[1] Remainder of sentence formerly read: "commanding officer of a battalion or of a battery of field artillery."

Chap. 276;

AN ACT to amend chapter three hundred and fifty-one of the laws of nineteen hundred and seven, entitled "An act to provide a park board in and for the city of Utica," relative to the powers of said board.

Became a law April 14, 1913, with the approval of the Governor. Passed, three-fifths being present.

Accepted by the City.

The People of the State of New York, represented in Senate and Assembly, do enact as follows:

Section 1. Chapter three hundred and fifty-one of the laws of nineteen hundred and seven, entitled "An act to provide a park board in and for the city of Utica," is hereby amended by adding thereto a new section to be section three-a, to read as follows: §§ is added to L. 1907, ch. 351.

§ 3-a. Said board shall have the power, anything in the railroad law notwithstanding, in its discretion, to grant a revocable license to a street surface railroad corporation to construct its tracks into any of the outer parks of said city, and to operate cars thereon by means of electricity as a motive power; such license shall not be effective until it has been approved by the public service commission. License to street railroads to operate in outer parks.

§ 2. This act shall take effect immediately.

Chap. 277.

AN ACT to amend the code of civil procedure, in relation to service of petition in summary proceedings.

Became a law April 14, 1913, with the approval of the Governor. Passed, three-fifths being present.

The People of the State of New York, represented in Senate and Assembly, do enact as follows:

Section 1. Section twenty-two hundred and forty of the code of civil procedure is hereby amended to read as follows: § 2240 amended.

§ 2240. Idem; how served. The precept must be served as follows:

1. By delivering, to the person to whom it is directed, or, if it is directed to a corporation, to an officer of the corporation, upon

whom a summons, issued out of the supreme court, in an action against the corporation, might be served, a copy of the precept, together with a copy of the petition,[1] and at the same time showing him the original precept.[2]

2. If the person, to whom the precept is directed, resides in the city or town in which the property is situated, but is absent from his dwelling-house, service may be made by delivering a copy thereof, together with a copy of the petition,[1] at his dwelling-house, to a person of suitable age and discretion, who resides there; or, if no such person can, with reasonable diligence, be found there, upon whom to make service, then by delivering a copy of the precept and petition,[3] at the property sought to be recovered, either to some person of suitable age and discretion residing there, or if no such person can be found there, to any person of suitable age and discretion employed there.

3. Where service cannot, with reasonable diligence, be made, as prescribed in either of the foregoing subdivisions of this section, by affixing a copy of the precept and petition[3] upon a conspicuous part of the property.

If the precept is returnable on the day on which it is issued, it must be served at least two hours before the hour at which it is returnable; in every other case, it must be served at least two days before the day on which it is returnable.

In effect
Sept. 1,
1913.

§ 2. This act shall take effect September first, nineteen hundred and thirteen.

Chap. 278.

AN ACT to amend the code of civil procedure, in relation to depositions taken and to be used within the state.

Became a law April 14, 1913, with the approval of the Governor. Passed, three-fifths being present.

The People of the State of New York, represented in Senate and Assembly, do enact as follows:

§ 872,
subd. 7
amended.

Section 1. Subdivision seven of section eight hundred and seventy-two of the code of civil procedure is hereby amended to read as follows:

---

[1] Words " together with a copy of the petition," new.
[2] Word " precept " new.
[3] Words " and petition " new.

7. Any other fact necessary to show that the case comes within _{Application to take deposition; contents.} one of the two last sections. And if the party sought to be examined is a corporation, joint-stock or other unincorporated association,[1] the affidavit shall state the name of the officers, [2]directors, or managing agents[3] thereof, or any of them whose testimony is necessary and material, or the books and papers as to the contents of which an examination or inspection is desired, and the order to be made in respect thereto shall direct the examination of such persons and the production of such books and papers, and on such examination the books or papers, or any part or parts thereof, may be offered and received in evidence in addition to the use thereof by the witness to refresh his memory.

§ 2. This act shall take effect September first, nineteen hundred and thirteen. _{In effect Sept. 1, 1913.}

Chap. 279.

AN ACT to amend the code of civil procedure, in relation to personal service of summons.

Became a law April 14, 1913, with the approval of the Governor. Passed, three-fifths being present.

The People of the State of New York, represented in Senate and Assembly, do enact as follows:

Section 1. Subdivision one of section four hundred and twenty-six of the code of civil procedure is hereby amended to read as follows: _{§ 426. subd. 1 amended.}

§ 426. Personal service of the summons upon a defendant, being a natural person, must be made by delivering a copy thereof, within the state, as follows: _{Personal service of summons on natural person.}

1. If the defendant is an infant, under the age of fourteen years,[1] to his father, mother or guardian; or, if there is none within the state, to the person having the care and control of him, or with whom he resides, or in whose service he is employed. [2]If the defendant is an infant over the age of fourteen years, to the infant in person, and also to his father, mother or guardian; or, if there is none within the state, to the person having the _{When infant.}

---

[1] Words " joint-stock or other unincorporated association," new.
[2] Word " or " omitted.
[3] Words " or managing agents," new.
[1] Words " to the infant in person and also," omitted.
[2] Remainder of section new.

care and control of him, or with whom he resides, or in whose service he is employed. Where the defendant is an infant under the age of fourteen years, the court shall, in the defendant's interest, make an order, requiring a copy of the summons to be also delivered, in behalf of the defendant, to a person designated in the order, and that service of the summons shall not be deemed complete until it is so delivered. Where the defendant is an infant over the age of fourteen years a similar order may be made by the court in its discretion, with or without application therefor.

§ 427
amended.

§ 2. Section four hundred and twenty-seven of the code of civil procedure is hereby amended to read as follows:

Personal
service of
summons
on incompe-
tent not
judicially
declared.

§ 427. [3]If the court has, in its opinion, reasonable ground to believe, that the defendant, by reason of habitual drunkenness, or for any other cause, is mentally incapable adequately to protect his rights, although not judicially declared to be incompetent to manage his affairs, the court may, in its discretion, with or without an application therefor, and, in the defendant's interest, make an order, requiring a copy of the summons to be also delivered, in behalf of the defendant, to a person designated in the order, and that service of the summons shall not be deemed complete, until it is so delivered.

In effect
Sept. 1,
1913.

§ 3. This act shall take effect September first, nineteen hundred and thirteen.

Chap. 280.

AN ACT to promote efficiency and economy in the public service and to create a department of efficiency and economy and to authorize the appointment of a commissioner of efficiency and economy as the head of such department.

Became a law April 14, 1913, with the approval of the Governor. Passed, three-fifths being present.

The People of the State of New York, represented in Senate and Assembly, do enact as follows:

Department
established.

Section 1. A department of efficiency and economy for the state is hereby established and shall be known as the state department of efficiency and economy. Within ten days after this act

---

[3] Words " If the defendant is an infant of the age of fourteen years, or upwards, or," omitted.

shall take effect, the governor, by and with the advice and con- ^{Appoint-} sent of the senate, shall appoint a commissioner of efficiency and economy who shall be the head of said department of efficiency and economy. Said commissioner of efficiency and economy shall receive an annual salary of twelve thousand dollars. His term of office shall be five years. He may appoint and employ such depu- ties, clerks, assistants, experts and employees as may be neces- sary for the conduct of the business of said department and he shall, upon such appointment or employment, fix the salaries or compensation of all such clerks, assistants, experts and employees at such reasonable sums as shall fairly compensate them for the service to be rendered.

§ 2. The trustees of public buildings shall provide suitable offices for the said department of efficiency and economy at the state capitol, and said offices shall be kept open by said commis- sioner during business hours on each secular day of the year, holidays excepted.

§ 3. The commissioner of efficiency and economy shall make a careful and thorough study of each office, institution and de- partment maintained by the state and shall from time to time make recommendations to the governor and to the officer, board or commission in charge of said office, institution or department touching the efficiency and economy of the work, business and service therein. He is hereby empowered, and it shall be his duty to examine the accounts, and the methods of business, accounting and administration of the several offices, institutions and depart- ments supported by the state, for the conduct and maintenance of which any appropriation of moneys is made by law, and for the purpose of such examination, he shall have the power, and he is hereby authorized to subpoena witnesses and compel their at- tendance before him and to subpoena and compel the production before him of books, papers, accounts and documents of every kind, and to administer oaths to all persons subpoenaed or ap- pearing as witnesses before him and to examine, take the testi- mony of and require answers from all such persons upon all sub- jects pertinent to any examination being conducted by him. He shall have the power and he is hereby authorized to require the several officers, institutions and departments of the state to fur- nish to him, upon forms prescribed by him, all such detailed in- formation touching the business, accounts, affairs and administra- tion of such officers, institutions or departments as he may demand, and it is hereby made the duty of all the officers, institutions and departments of the state to furnish such information in such form to the said commissioner of efficiency and economy.

Institutions and departments to file statement of desired appropriations.

§ 4. On or before the first day of November in each year, each officer, institution and department of the state, for the support and maintenance of which appropriations of money are made by law, shall present to and file with said commissioner of efficiency and economy, upon forms prescribed by him, a detailed statement of all moneys which said officer, institution or department desires to have appropriated by law for the support and maintenance of said officer, institution or department for the fiscal year for which said appropriations are asked. The said commissioner

Recommendations thereon by commissioner.

of efficiency and economy shall examine said statements and make such recommendations thereon as shall, in his opinion, contribute to promote efficiency and economy in the conduct of the business of the state.

§ 5. This act shall take effect immediately.

Chap. 281.

AN ACT to establish a state board of estimate and to prescribe its powers and duties.

Became a law April 14, 1913, with the approval of the Governor. Passed, three-fifths being present.

The People of the State of New York, represented in Senate and Assembly, do enact as follows:

Board established; how composed.

Section 1. There shall be and there is hereby constituted and established a state board of estimate which shall be composed of nine members, to wit: The governor, the lieutenant-governor, the president pro tempore of the senate, the chairman of the finance committee of the senate, the speaker of the assembly, the chairman of the ways and means committee of the assembly, the comptroller, the attorney-general and the commissioner of efficiency

Organization; officers.

and economy. The board shall meet and organize within ten days after this act shall take effect. The governor shall be the president of the board and the commissioner of efficiency and

Minutes; record open to inspection.

economy shall be its secretary. The secretary shall keep the minutes of each meeting of the board and shall record them in a

minute book to be kept for that purpose. The minutes of the
board shall be a public record and shall be at all times open to
public inspection.

§ 2. The said board shall annually, on or before the first day **Preparation of annual budget.**
of January in each year, meet and prepare an estimate for a
budget of the amounts required to be appropriated by the legislature for the conduct of the public business of the state in all
its offices, institutions and departments for the fiscal year next
ensuing. Such estimate shall be prepared in such detail, as said
board shall deem sufficient to advise the legislature, as to the
aggregate sum and the items thereof estimated to be necessary
for the maintenance of each office, institution and department
in the state for such fiscal year. Before finally making up such **Examination of requests for appropriations.**
estimate, the state board of estimate shall have power, and it is
hereby made its duty, to examine into all requests for appropriations made by each officer, institution and department of the state,
and it may hold such public hearings as shall in its judgment
be advantageous for such purpose. When said estimate shall be **Transmission of estimate to legislature.**
made up, it shall be transmitted to the legislature with such
recommendations, reasons and explanations with regard thereto
as shall be determined by said board.

§ 3. Within sixty days and not less than thirty days **Presentation by institutions and departments of statements of needed appropriations.**
before the beginning of each fiscal year, each officer, in-
stitution and department of the state, for the support and
maintenance of which appropriations of money are made by law,
shall present to and file with the secretary of said board of estimate, upon forms prescribed by said board, a detailed statement of all moneys which said officer, institution or department
deems it necessary to have appropriated by law for the support
and maintenance of said officer, institution and department for
the fiscal year for which said appropriations are asked, together
with such reasons and explanations with regard thereto as the
said officer, institution or department may desire to present.
The said board shall, in connection with its estimate, transmit **Transmission to legislature.**
all such statements, or copies thereof, to the legislature. The
said board shall examine all said statements and all requests for **Examination of statements and requests for appropriations.**
appropriations presented to it, and shall afford to the several
officers, institutions and departments of the state presenting such
statements and making such requests, reasonable opportunity for
explanation in regard thereto and, whenever necessary, shall
grant to such officer, institution or department a hearing thereon.

Estimate
of moneys
required for
interest on
state debt
and for
sinking
funds. § 4. The said board, in making up the estimate to be trans-mitted by it as aforesaid to the legislature, shall, in connection therewith, and as a part thereof, make an estimate of all moneys required to be raised or appropriated for the payment of interest upon the funded debts of the state and its other obligations bearing interest, and shall also make an estimate of the several sums of money required to be contributed in said fiscal year to the several sinking funds maintained for the redemption and payment of Comptroller
to furnish
detailed
statement. the debts of the state. For the purpose of such estimates, the comptroller of the state is hereby required to furnish to the said board, a detailed statement of the moneys which he deems neces-sary for such purposes.

Estimate of
revenues to
be received
during fis-
cal year. § 5. In connection with and as a part of the said estimate to be presented by said board to the legislature, the said board shall make an estimate of the revenues of the state expected to be re-ceived during said fiscal year and shall make such recommenda-tions with regard thereto as it shall deem appropriate for the Report as
to unex-
pended
balances. disposition of said revenues. The said board shall also, in con-nection with and as a part of said estimate, ascertain and report the amounts of all unexpended balances under appropriations theretofore made by law and shall make such recommendations to the legislature as it deems appropriate for the disposition thereof.

§ 6. This act shall take effect immediately.

Chap. 282.

AN ACT to amend chapter three hundred and ninety-four of the laws of eighteen hundred and ninety-five, entitled "An act to revise the charter of the city of Oswego," in relation to the construction of sewers and sewage disposal plants and other necessary construction incidental thereto and to the issuance of bonds therefor.

Became a law April 14, 1913, with the approval of the Governor. Passed, three-fifths being present.

Accepted by the City.

The People of the State of New York, represented in Senate and Assembly, do enact as follows:

L. 1895,
ch. 394,
§ 230a, as
added by Section 1. Section three hundred and thirty-a of chapter three hundred and ninety-four of the laws of eighteen hundred and ·

ninety-five, entitled "An act to revise the charter of the city of Oswego," as added by chapter three hundred and seventy of the laws of nineteen hundred and eleven, and amended by chapter four hundred and eleven of the laws of nineteen hundred and twelve, is hereby amended to read as follows:

§ 330-a. In addition to all the rights, powers and authority hereinbefore and hereinafter by this chapter conferred upon the common council and the department of works, or either of them, or upon any other department or officer of said city of Oswego, with reference to the construction of sewers, the city of Oswego is hereby fully authorized and empowered, without limitation or restriction by any provision hereinbefore or hereinafter in this act contained, acting through the department of works and the common council, to construct in the city of Oswego, in addition to its present sewer system, the additional sewers herein provided for and two sewage disposal plants, one upon each side of the Oswego river at such places as shall be most suitable and convenient, as follows: a trunk sewer for sanitary purposes only on the east side of the Oswego river commencing at a point near the junction of the Hall road and East Tenth street, and running thence in a general northerly direction toward and to Lake Ontario and to connect with one of said sewage disposal plants hereinbefore specified; a trunk sewer for sanitary purposes only on the west side of the Oswego river commencing at a point near the corner of Erie and Singleton streets, and running thence in a general northerly direction toward and to Lake Ontario and to connect with the other of said sewage disposal plants hereinbefore specified, together with such lateral sanitary sewers connecting with said trunk sanitary sewers or with said sewage disposal plants, or either of them, as it may deem proper and necessary, together with such drains or sewers for storm and surface water as it may deem proper and necessary, and it is further fully authorized and empowered in connection with such sewer construction to do and perform such other needful and necessary improvement of the two creeks, or either of them, lying and being in its easterly and westerly confines and into which the said drains or sewers for storm and surface water may discharge as it may deem proper,[1] and such further improvement in the raising and grading of West Bridge street, Turrell street and West Schuyler street

Margin notes:
L. 1911, ch. 370, and amended by L. 1912, ch. 411, amended.

Construction of additional sewers and sewage disposal plants, authorized.

Location of sanitary trunk sewers.

Improvement of creeks.

Grading of streets.

---

[1] Words "but neither of said creeks shall be inclosed," omitted.

as shall be necessary and proper for the purposes of sewer construction therein.

§ 330k, as
added by
L. 1913,
ch. 411,
amended.

Section 2. Section three hundred and thirty-k of such chapter, as added by chapter four hundred and eleven of the laws of nineteen hundred and twelve, is hereby amended to read as follows:

Construc-
tion to be
through
city prop-
erty where
practicable.

§ 330-k. The said sewers[2] by this act authorized to be constructed shall, so far as practicable, be constructed in the public streets of the city of Oswego or through other public property of said city.

§ 330l
added.

Section 3. Such chapter is hereby amended by adding thereto, after section three hundred and thirty-k, a new section, to be section three hundred and thirty-l, to read as follows:

Application
of moneys
heretofore
raised.

§ 330-l. Any moneys heretofore raised for the purposes mentioned in section three hundred and thirty-a of said chapter, including all bonds heretofore authorized or sold under section three hundred and thirty-b, shall be used and applied for the purposes mentioned in section three hundred and thirty-a as amended hereby.

Section 4. This act shall take effect immediately.

Chap. 283.

AN ACT to authorize the corporation known as Christ Church, Rochester, to take and hold real and personal property, as an endowment fund, and to restrict the use and investment of the same.

Became a law April 14, 1913, with the approval of the Governor. Passed, three-fifths being present.

The People of the State of New York, represented in Senate and Assembly, do enact as follows:

Endowment
fund.

Section 1. The corporation known as Christ Church, Rochester, having its place of worship in the city of Rochester, New York, is hereby empowered to take and hold real and personal property heretofore or hereafter given, devised or bequeathed to it absolutely or in trust, thereby establishing and maintaining an endowment fund, and all property given, devised or bequeathed to it in trust, unless otherwise specified in such gift, devise or bequest,

---

[2] Words " and drains " omitted.

together with the trust funds heretofore transferred to the endowment fund by resolution of said corporation duly adopted and
entered in its minutes, and now so held by it, and also all such
funds or sums as shall hereafter be so transferred, shall constitute
a fund to be known as the permanent endowment fund, the income Application
of which only shall be subject to expenditure for parish and of income.
church uses and purposes. No resolution of said corporation Transfers to
heretofore or hereafter duly adopted and entered in its minutes, vocable.
transferring any gift, bequest, fund, sum or property whatsoever,
to the endowment fund or to the permanent fund above mentioned,
shall be revocable or repealable by said corporation. No part of
such fund, either principal or income, shall be liable, either at Exemptions
law or in equity, to the claims of the future creditors of said cor- of fund.
poration, or subject to any mortgage or lien hereafter executed
or created by it.

§ 2. Said permanent endowment fund shall be under the con- Control and
trol of the vestry of the said church, and the laws of this state, of fund.
as the same now exist, or shall hereafter be enacted, relating to
the securities in which trust funds may be invested, shall apply
to and govern the said vestry in the investment of the said fund.

§ 3. This act shall take effect immediately.

Chap. 284.

AN ACT to amend the railroad law, in relation to the acquisition
of title to real property.

Became a law April 15, 1913, with the approval of the Governor. Passed,
three-fifths being present.

*The People of the State of New York, represented in Senate
and Assembly, do enact as follows:*

Section 1. Section seventeen of chapter four hundred and L. 1910,
eighty-one of the laws of nineteen hundred and ten, entitled "An ch. 481, § 17
act in relation to railroads, constituting chapter forty-nine of the amended.
consolidated laws," is hereby amended to read as follows:

§ 17. **Acquisition of title to real property; additions, betterments and facilities.** All real property required by any railroad
corporation for the purpose of its incorporation or for any purpose stated in this chapter shall be deemed to be required for a
public use, and may be acquired by such corporation. If the

17

corporation is unable to agree for the purchase of any such real property, or of any right, interest or easement therein, required for any such purpose, or if the owner thereof shall be incapable of selling the same, or if after diligent search and inquiry the name and residence of any such owner cannot be ascertained, it shall have the right to acquire title thereto by condemnation. Every railroad corporation shall have the power from time to time to make and use upon or in connection with any railroad either owned or operated by it, such additions, betterments and facilities as may be necessary or convenient for the better management, maintenance or operation of any such railroad, and shall have the right by purchase or by condemnation, to acquire any real property required therefor, and it shall also have the right of condemnation in the following additional cases:

1. Where title to real property has been acquired, or attempted to be acquired, and has been found to be invalid or defective.

2. Where its railroad shall be lawfully in possession of a lessee, mortgagee, trustee or receiver, and additional real property shall be required for the purpose of running or operating such railroad.

3. Where it shall require for any railroad owned or operated by it any further rights to lands or the use of lands for additional main tracks or for branches, sidings, switches, or turn-outs or for connections or for cut-offs or for shortening or straightening or improving the line or grade of its road or any part thereof. Also where it shall require any further rights to lands or the use of lands for filling any structures of its road, or for constructing, widening or completing any of its embankments or roadbeds, by means of which greater safety or permanency may be secured, and such land shall be contiguous to such railroad and reasonably accessible.

4. Where it shall require any further right to lands or to the use of lands for the flow of water occasioned by railroad embankments or structures now in use, or hereafter rendered necessary, or for any other purpose necessary for the operation of such railroad, or for any right to take and convey water from any spring, pond, creek or river to such railroad, for the uses and purposes thereof, together with the right to build or lay aqueducts or pipes for the purpose of conveying such water, and to take up, relay and repair the same, or for any right of way required for carrying away or diverting any water, stream or floods from such railroad for the purpose of protecting its road or for the purpose of pre-

venting any embankment, excavation or structure of such railroad from injuring the property of any person who may be rendered liable to injury thereby.

Waters commonly used for domestic, agricultural or manufacturing purposes, shall not be taken by condemnation to such an extent as to injuriously interfere with such use in future. No railroad corporation shall have the right to acquire by condemnation any right or easement in or to any real property owned or occupied by any other railroad corporation, except the right to intersect or cross the tracks and lands owned or held for right of way by such other corporation, without appropriating or affecting any lands owned or held for depots or gravel-beds.

[1]Whenever any real property is required by any steam surface railroad corporation, the lines of which within this state are situated wholly within a city of over one million inhabitants, for the purposes mentioned in this section, it shall be a condition precedent to the bringing, or, if heretofore brought, to the continuing of condemnation proceedings by any railroad corporation to acquire said real property that it procure the consent of the public service commission having jurisdiction of the district within which the land is situated, to acquire such real property, and unless such consent is given and procured the said property shall not be condemned. The last preceding requirement shall apply to all proceedings pending at the time this amendment takes effect.

§ 2. This act shall take effect immediately.

Chap. 285.

AN ACT to authorize the city of Troy to provide funds to pay its contract obligations and expenses for public improvements in said city.

Became a law April 15, 1913, with the approval of the Governor. Passed, three-fifths being present.

Accepted by the City.

The People of the State of New York, represented in Senate and Assembly, do enact as follows:

Section 1. Whenever a contract for any public improvement shall be let by the city of Troy, the expense of which is to be Temporary loans to pay for

---

[1] Remainder of section new.

public im-
provements. assessed in whole or in part upon the property benefited, it shall
be lawful for the comptroller of said city, from time to time,
when authorized by an ordinance of the common council, which
shall be approved by the board of estimate and apportionment,
to borrow money temporarily, to the extent required to pay the
cost or any part of the cost of any such improvement, or to repay
any money borrowed under this section with interest thereon.
Certificates
of indebt-
edness, ma-
turity, exe-
cution, etc. The comptroller shall issue obligations of the city to be known as
certificates of indebtedness for public improvements, for such loan
or loans payable either on demand or at a fixed time not more than
nine months from the date thereof. Such certificates of indebtedness shall be signed by the mayor and treasurer and countersigned
by the comptroller and the corporate seal shall be attached thereto.
They shall be dated and issued in such amounts and at such times
and shall bear interest at such a rate not exceeding five per centum
Sale. per annum, and shall be sold at public or private sale, but for not
less than par, all as shall be determined by the comptroller. The
Application
of proceeds. proceeds of the sale of such certificates of indebtedness shall be
deposited with the treasurer of the city and shall be used toward
the payment of all costs and expenses incurred or to be incurred
on account of any public improvement for which they shall have
been issued.

Issue of
assessment
bonds.   § 2. The entire cost and expense of any such improvement
including the interest on any temporary indebtedness incurred
under the authority of this act, shall be included in the assessment for such improvement and shall be raised as follows: The
cost and expense thereof which is to be assessed upon the property
benefited, or any part thereof, shall be raised by the issue and sale
of assessment bonds, as authorized and provided by chapter six
hundred and seventy of the laws of eighteen hundred and ninety-
Issue of
bonds for
city's share. two, and the laws amendatory thereof. The cost and expense
thereof which is to be borne by the city at large, shall be raised by
incurring a funded debt by the issue and sale, in the manner provided by law, of the bonds of the city, or may be included in the
tax budget and raised by tax.

Payment of
temporary
indebted-
ness.   § 3. Any temporary indebtedness incurred under the authority
of this act, with the interest thereon, shall be paid out of the
moneys raised as provided in section two of this act, or from the
moneys received from the assessments upon the property benefited,
or both.

     § 4. This act shall take effect immediately.

Chap. 286.

AN ACT to amend the labor law, in relation to the protection of employees operating machinery, dust creating machinery, and the lighting of factories and workrooms.

Became a law April 16, 1913, with the approval of the Governor. Passed, three-fifths being present.

The People of the State of New York, represented in Senate and Assembly, do enact as follows:

Section 1. Section eighty-one of chapter thirty-six of the laws of nineteen hundred and nine, entitled "An act relating to labor, constituting chapter thirty-one of the consolidated laws," as amended by chapter one hundred and six of the laws of nineteen hundred and ten,[1] is hereby amended to read as follows:[2]

§ 81. **Protection of employees operating machinery; dust-creating machinery; lighting of factories and workrooms.** 1. The owner or person in charge of a factory where machinery is used, shall provide, as may be required by the rules and regulations of the industrial board, belt shifters or other mechanical contrivances for the purpose of throwing on or off belts on pulleys. Whenever practicable, all machinery shall be provided with loose pulleys. Every vat and pan wherever set so that the opening or top thereof is at a lower level than the elbow of the operator or operators at work about the same shall be protected by a cover which shall be maintained over the same while in use in such manner as effectually to prevent such operators or other persons falling therein or coming in contact with the contents thereof, except that where it is necessary to remove such cover while any such vat or pan is in use, such vat or pan shall be protected by an adequate railing around the same. Every hydro-extractor shall be covered or otherwise properly guarded while in motion. Every saw shall be provided with a proper and effective guard. Every planer shall be protected by a substantial hood or covering. Every hand-planer or jointer shall be provided with a proper and effective guard. All cogs and gearing shall be boxed or cased either with metal or wood. All belting within seven feet of the floors shall be properly guarded. All revolving shafting within seven feet of the floors shall be protected on its exposed surface by being encased in such

In margin: L. 1909, ch. 36, § 81, as amended by L. 1910, ch. 106, amended.

---

[1] Section 81 was also amended by L. 1909, ch. 299.
[2] Section materially amended.

a manner as to effectively prevent any part of the body, hair or
clothing of the operators or other persons from coming in contact
with such shafting. All set-screws, keys, bolts and all parts projecting beyond the surface of revolving shafting shall be counter-
sunk or provided with suitable covering, and machinery of every
description shall be properly guarded and provided with proper
safety appliances or devices. All machines, machinery, apparatus,
furniture and fixtures shall be so placed and guarded in relation to one another as to be safe for all persons. Whenever any
danger exists which requires any special care as to the character
and condition of the clothing of the persons employed there-
abouts, or which requires the use of special clothing or guards,
the industrial board may make rules and regulations prescribing
what shall be used or worn for the purpose of guarding against
such danger and regulating the provision, maintenance and use
thereof. No person shall remove or make ineffective any safeguard or safety appliance or device around or attached to machinery, vats or pans, unless for the purpose of immediately making repairs thereto or adjustment thereof, and any person who
removes or makes ineffective any such safeguard, safety appliance or device for a permitted purpose shall immediately replace
the same when such purpose is accomplished. It shall be the duty
of the employer and of every person exercising direction or control over the person who removes such safeguard, safety appliance
or device, or over any person for whose protection it is designed
to see that a safeguard or safety appliance or device that has been
removed is promptly and properly replaced. All fencing, safeguards, safety appliances and devices must be constantly maintained in proper condition. When in the opinion of the commissioner of labor a machine or any part thereof is in a dangerous
condition or is not properly guarded or is dangerously placed, the
use thereof shall be prohibited by the commissioner of labor and
a notice to that effect shall be attached thereto. Such notice shall
not be removed except by an authorized representative of the department of labor, nor until the machinery is made safe and the
required safeguards or safety appliances or devices are provided,
and in the meantime such unsafe or dangerous machinery shall
not be used. The industrial board may make rules and regulations regulating the installation, position, operation, guarding and
use of machines and machinery in operation in factories, the furnishing and use of safety devices and safety appliances for ma-

chines and machinery and of guards to be worn upon the person,
and other cognate matters, whenever it finds such regulations
necessary in order to provide for the prevention of accidents in
factories.

2. All grinding, polishing or buffing wheels used in the course
of the manufacture of articles of the baser metals shall be
equipped with proper hoods and pipes and such pipes shall be connected to an exhaust fan of sufficient capacity and power to remove all matter thrown off such wheels in the course of their
use. Such fan shall be kept running constantly while such grinding, polishing or buffing wheels are in operation; except that in
case of wet-grinding it is unnecessary to comply with this provision unless required by the rules and regulations of the industrial board. All machinery creating dust or impurities shall
be equipped with proper hoods and pipes and such pipes shall be
connected to an exhaust fan of sufficient capacity and power to
remove such dust or impurities; such fan shall be kept running
constantly while such machinery is in use; except where, in case
of wood-working machinery, the industrial board shall decide
that it is unnecessary for the health and welfare of the operatives.

3. All passageways and other portions of a factory, and all
moving parts of machinery which are not so guarded as to prevent
accidents, where, on or about which persons work or pass or may
have to work or pass in emergencies, shall be kept properly and
*and sufficiently lighted during working hours. The halls and
stairs leading to the workrooms shall be properly and adequately
lighted, and a proper and adequate light shall be kept burning by
the owner or lessee in the public hallways near the stairs, upon
the entrance floor and upon the other floors on every workday in
the year, from the time when the building is open for use in the
morning until the time it is closed in the evening, except at times
when the influx of natural light shall make artificial light unnecessary. Such lights shall be so arranged as to insure their reliable
operation when through accident or other cause the regular factory lighting is extinguished.

4. All workrooms shall be properly and adequately lighted during working hours. Artificial illuminants in every workroom
shall be installed, arranged and used so that the light furnished
will at all times be sufficient and adequate for the work carried on
therein, and so as to prevent unnecessary strain on the vision or

---

* So in original.

glare in the eyes of the workers. The industrial board may make rules and regulations to provide for adequate and sufficient natural and artificial lighting facilities in all factories.

In effect
Oct. 1, 1913.   § 2. This act shall take effect October first, nineteen hundred and thirteen.

Chap. 287.

AN ACT to amend chapter six hundred and fifty-nine of the laws of eighteen hundred and sixty-five, entitled "An act in relation to the collection of taxes in the city of Utica."

Became a law April 16, 1913, with the approval of the Governor. Passed, three-fifths being present.

Accepted by the City.

The People of the State of New York, represented in Senate and Assembly, do enact as follows:

L. 1905, ch. 659, § 2 amended.   Section 1. Section two of chapter six hundred and fifty-nine of the laws of eighteen hundred and sixty-five, entitled "An act in relation to the collection of taxes in the city of Utica," is hereby amended so as to read as follows:[1]

Bond of city treasurer.   § 2. The treasurer of the city of Utica before he receives the assessment rolls mentioned in the first section of this act, and within eight days after he receives notice of the amount of taxes thereon, shall execute to the county treasurer of the county of Oneida, a bond, with one or more sureties, to be approved of, by such treasurer in double the amount of the taxes on the said assessment rolls of the wards, conditioned for the faithful execution of his duties in the receipt and payment of said taxes.

§ 4, as amended by L. 1868, ch. 592, amended.   § 2. Section four of such chapter, as amended by chapter five hundred and ninety-two of the laws of eighteen hundred and sixty-eight, is hereby amended so as to read as follows:[1]

Delivery of tax lists to ward collectors.   § 4. The said treasurer of the city of Utica, shall, within five days after the expiration of the month mentioned in the preceding section deliver the tax list in his hands of each ward of said city to the collector of such ward, in the same manner as provided by sections fifty-one, fifty-two and fifty-three of the revised charter of the city of Utica, in reference to the collection of city taxes, and the said collectors shall furnish an undertaking, and perform

Undertakings and

[1] Section materially amended.

such duties and have the same power in the collection of said duties of collectors.
taxes and in making return and paying over the same as in the
collection of the city taxes of said city. Within five days after Amounts returned
the return to him of said tax list, the city treasurer shall certify unpaid to be raised
to the comptroller and city clerk of said city the amount remain- by bonds.
ing unpaid upon the assessment rolls of the various wards of
said city, and thereupon the said city shall cause to be raised by
bonds, under the provisions of section sixty of the revised charter
of the city of Utica, as amended by chapter two hundred and
seventy-one of the laws of nineteen hundred and seven, sufficient
money to meet the sum so certified to be due and unpaid, and
upon receipt of the same the city treasurer shall pay over Payment over of
to the county treasurer of Oneida county the entire sum levied state and county
upon the city or town of Utica for state or county purposes and the taxes.
said county treasurer shall give to such city treasurer a receipt
therefor, and thereupon the said sums as set forth upon said assess- Unpaid taxes
ment rolls of the various wards, as due and unpaid, shall be due deemed
and owing to said city, shall be deemed city taxes, and shall be a city taxes.
lien upon the real estate assessed therefor in case of real estate Lien and collection
assessment, and the said city shall have the right to collect same thereof.
in accordance with the charter of said city in reference to the collection of city taxes by tax sale or otherwise, and all the revisions
of the revised charter of said city, as amended, as to ordinary city
taxes, shall apply to every tax or assessment under this act, and the
said city shall have the right to add to such tax the same penalties
in the same manner as for city taxes.

§ 3. Sections five and six of such act are hereby repealed. §§ 5, 6 repealed.

§ 4. Section seven of such act, as amended by chapter forty- § 7, as amended
seven of the laws of eighteen hundred and eighty-seven, is hereby by L. 1887, ch. 47, amended.
amended so as to read as follows :[2]

§ 7. The treasurer of the city of Utica may expend such sums Expenses of collection
of money for extra clerk hire and for postage and printing for the of county taxes.
collection of the county taxes in said city as shall be allowed in
the annual budget of said city, the expenses thereof to be audited
and paid in the same manner as other city expenses.

§ 5. The repeal of the sections referred to in section three of Present rights,
this act and the amendments contained in sections two, four and remedies and pro-
seven of this act, shall not be construed to impair or affect any ceedings not affected.
right or remedy acquired or given by an act or part of act hereby

---

[2] Section materially amended.

repealed or amended, and all proceedings or actions commenced
under any such prior act or acts may be carried out and completed
or provided in such prior acts, unrepealed and unamended, except
Unpaid town, county and state taxes of 1912. that the county treasurer of Oneida county shall certify to the city
clerk and comptroller of the city of Utica, within five days after
the books or tax rolls of the various wards of the city of Utica for
the town, county and state taxes of the year nineteen hundred
and twelve are returned to him, the amount of such taxes which
are unpaid thereon, and thereupon the said city may raise and
pay to said county treasurer the said amounts unpaid in the same
manner as provided in section four of chapter six hundred and
fifty-nine of the laws of eighteen hundred and sixty-five, as herein
amended, and upon such payment the said taxes shall be deemed
city taxes and may be collected by said city in the same manner
and with the same force and effect as provided in said section four.

§ 6. This act shall take effect immediately.

Chap. 288.

AN ACT to authorize the city of Troy to borrow moneys and to
issue bonds therefor, for the water works department of said
city, and to provide for the payment of said bonds.

Became a law April 16, 1913, with the approval of the Governor. Passed,
three-fifths being present.

Accepted by the City.

*The People of the State of New York, represented in Senate
and Assembly, do enact as follows:*

Borrowing of money to supply deficiencies, authorized. Section 1. The city of Troy is hereby empowered to borrow
money not to exceed in the aggregate two hundred and five thou-
sand dollars, or so much thereof as may be necessary, and to pay
over the same to the treasurer of said city to be by him placed to
the credit of the water works department, for the purpose of supplying the differences and deficiencies arising between the
revenues of said department and its expenditures in the period
between the twelfth day of April, nineteen hundred and six, and
the first day of January, nineteen hundred and twelve.

Bond issues authorized. § 2. To secure the payment of the sums so borrowed, with interest thereon, the said city is hereby authorized to issue its
bonds from time to time, which bonds shall be duly sealed and

signed, and shall be considered as a funded debt of said city. The issuing of said bonds shall be made in conformity with the _{How issued.} provisions of the general municipal law and of the second class cities law in so far as the same are applicable thereto. The said bonds shall be issued in such amounts and shall be made payable _{when payable.} at such times that the principal of the same shall be fully paid in twenty equal annual payments, the last of which shall become due at the end of twenty years after its issue. They shall bear _{Interest.} a rate of interest not exceeding the legal rate per annum. They shall be advertised for sale and sold by the comptroller of said _{Sale.} city as required by law. A sinking fund shall be created on the _{Sinking fund.} issuing of said bonds for their redemption, by raising annually a sum which will produce an amount equal to the sum of the principal and interest of said bonds at their maturity. The water rents and rates hereafter fixed must be at such amounts as will produce said sinking fund in addition to the sinking funds of other bond issues heretofore provided for and established as required by law.

§ 3. The said city is also hereby empowered to borrow money _{Bond issue for construction and renewals, authorized.} and to issue its bonds therefor from time to time, for the purpose of renewing or replacing any structures or pipe lines which were built or laid under the provisions of chapter five hundred and seventy-six of the laws of eighteen hundred and ninety-three, entitled "An act relative to the water works department of the city of Troy, and to provide for an increased supply of water in the said city," as amended by chapter four hundred and thirty-five of the laws of eighteen hundred and ninety-four, and as further amended by chapter three hundred and seventy of the laws of nineteen hundred; and also for the purpose of meeting the expenses of new construction work, consisting of the renewal, enlargement, or extension of water mains in said city, and the construction of a culvert from a point at or near the Oakwood avenue reservoir to the Hudson river.

§ 4. To secure the payment of the sums under the provisions _{Bonds, how issued.} of section three of this act, borrowed, with interest thereon, the said city is hereby authorized to issue its bonds from time to time, which bonds shall be duly sealed and signed, and shall be considered as a funded debt of said city. The issuing of said bonds shall be made in conformity with the provisions of the general municipal law and of the second class cities law in so far as the same are applicable thereto. The said bonds shall be issued in _{When payable.}

Interest.

Sale.

Sinking fund.

such amounts and shall be made payable at such times that the principal of the same shall be fully paid in twenty equal annual payments the last of which shall become due at the end of twenty years after its issue. They shall bear a rate of interest not exceeding the legal rate per annum. They shall be advertised for sale and sold by the comptroller of said city as required by law. A sinking fund shall be created on the issuing of said bonds for their redemption by raising annually a sum which will produce an amount equal to the sum of the principal and interest of said bonds at their maturity. The water rents and rates hereafter fixed must be at such amounts as will produce said sinking fund in addition to the sinking funds of other bond issues heretofore provided for and established as required by law.

§ 5. This act shall take effect immediately.

Chap. 289.

AN ACT providing for the relief of William Shanley.

Became a law April 16, 1913, with the approval of the Governor. Passed, three-fifths being present.

Accepted by the City.

The People of the State of New York, represented in Senate and Assembly, do enact as follows:

Vacation of sale of building to William Shanley, authorized.

Section 1. The comptroller of the city of New York is hereby authorized and directed in his discretion to vacate and set aside the sale of the building purchased by William Shanley on October nine, nineteen hundred and twelve, and known as parcel number four of the Malbone street proceeding, in the borough of Brooklyn, city of New York.

Refund of moneys, authorized.

§ 2. The comptroller of the city of New York is hereby authorized and directed in his discretion to refund to William Shanley the sum of eighteen hundred dollars, which included the sum of twelve hundred dollars paid by William Shanley for the said building and the sum of six hundred dollars paid by William Shanley to the said comptroller as security.

§ 3. This act shall take effect immediately.

Chap. 290.

AN ACT making an appropriation for surveys, field notes and manuscript maps affecting various canals and canal lands.

Became a law April 16, 1913, with the approval of the Governor. Passed, three-fifths being present.

The People of the State of New York, represented in Senate and Assembly, do enact as follows:

Section 1. The state engineer and surveyor is hereby directed to continue the work authorized by chapter one hundred and ninety-nine of the laws of nineteen hundred and ten, and chapter five hundred and eleven of the laws of nineteen hundred and twelve in making necessary surveys, field notes and manuscript maps of all of such portions of the Erie, Oswego, Champlain, and Cayuga and Seneca canals as are within the lines of the improved Erie, Oswego, Champlain, and Cayuga and Seneca canals and of all the lands belonging to the state or adjacent thereto or connected therewith on which the boundary line or "blue line" of any parcel of state land to which the state shall have a separate title shall be designated, together with the names of the adjoining owners. The sum of twenty-five thousand dollars ($25,-000), or so much thereof as may be necessary, is hereby appropriated from any moneys in the treasury not otherwise appropriated for the purpose of making all necessary surveys, field notes, maps and obtaining any other necessary data, payment of salaries, compensation, wages and expenses, traveling or otherwise, of engineers, laborers and other employees and for necessary supplies and materials to carry into effect the provisions of this act, payable from the treasury upon the warrant of the comptroller on the order of the state engineer and surveyor.

§ 2. This act shall take effect immediately.

Chap. 291.

AN ACT to authorize the county treasurer of the county of Steuben, to extend the time for the collection of taxes in the city of Hornell.

Became a law April 16, 1913, with the approval of the Governor. Passed, three-fifths being present.

Accepted by the City.

The People of the State of New York, represented in Senate and Assembly, do enact as follows:

Section 1. The treasurer of the county of Steuben is hereby authorized to extend the time for the collection of taxes in the city of Hornell, for a period of sixty days, upon the chamberlain of such city, filing his bond in a penal sum of double the amount of taxes to be collected by him approved in the manner provided by law; that such extension shall have the same force and effect as if made before the time for such extension had expired and as if the said chamberlain had proceeded and collected taxes by virtue of his warrant and properly accounted for the same to said treasurer; and such warrant so extended by said treasurer shall be a valid legal warrant for the collection of taxes in and for the city of Hornell for said period of sixty days and the said warrant and the time for collection thereunder may thereafter be extended by said treasurer in the same manner as like warrants may be extended by him, but nothing herein contained shall be construed as extending the time for the payment of state taxes or any part thereof by the county treasurer of said county to the comptroller as now provided by law.

§ 2. This act shall take effect immediately.

Chap. 292.

AN ACT to amend the education law, relative to the establishment of scholarships for the aid of students in colleges.

Became a law April 16, 1913, with the approval of the Governor. Passed, three-fifths being present.

The People of the State of New York, represented in Senate and Assembly, do enact as follows:

Section 1. Article three of chapter one hundred and forty of the laws of nineteen hundred and ten,[1] entitled "An act to amend the education law, generally," is hereby amended by adding at the end thereof the following new sections, to be known as sections seventy, seventy-one, seventy-two, seventy-three, seventy-four, seventy-five, seventy-six and seventy-seven, and to read as follows: §§ 70-77 added to L. 1910, ch. 140.

§ 70. **State scholarships established.** 1. State scholarships are hereby established in the several counties of the state, to be maintained by the state and awarded as provided by this act.

2. Five such scholarships shall be awarded each county annually for each assembly district therein.

3. Each such scholarship shall entitle the holder thereof to the sum of one hundred dollars for each year which he is in attendance upon an approved college in this state during a period of four years, to be paid to or for the benefit of such holder as hereinafter provided, and out of a fund which is hereinafter created.

§ 71. **Scholarship fund of the University of the State of New York.** 1. The scholarship fund of the University of the State of New York is hereby created. Such fund shall consist:

a. Of all money appropriated therefor by the legislature;

b. Of all money and property hereafter received by the state, the regents of the university or the commissioner of education by gift, grant, devise or bequest for the purpose of providing funds for the payment of such scholarships and of all income or revenue derived from any trust created for such purpose.

2. Such fund shall be kept separate and distinct from the other state funds by the state treasurer, and payment shall be made therefrom to the persons entitled thereto in the same manner as from other state funds, except as otherwise provided by this act.

3. Whenever any such gift, grant, devise or bequest shall have

---

[1] L. 1910, ch. 140 amends generally the consolidated education law (L. 1909, ch. 21).

been made or any trust shall have been created for the purpose of providing funds for such scholarships, the incomes or revenues derived therefrom shall be applied in maintaining scholarships in addition to those to be maintained by appropriations made by the state legislature, as provided herein, and no part of such income or revenue shall be applied for the maintenance of state scholarships hereinbefore established for each county. Such additional scholarships shall be equitably apportioned by the commissioner of education among the several counties, unless it be provided in the will, deed or other instrument making such gift, grant, devise or bequest, or creating such trust, that the incomes or revenues derived therefrom be applied to the establishment and maintenance of additional scholarships in a specified county.

§ 72. **Regents to make rules.** The regents shall make rules governing the award of such scholarships, the issuance and cancellation of certificates entitling persons to the benefits thereof, the use of such scholarships by the persons entitled thereto, and the rights and duties of such state scholars, and the colleges which they attend, in respect to such scholarships, and providing generally for carrying into effect the provisions of this act. Such rules shall be in conformity with this act and shall have the force and effect of a statute.

§ 73. **List of candidates, award of scholarships.** 1. The commissioner of education shall cause to be prepared for each county of the state, annually, during the month of August, from the records of the education department, a list of the names of all pupils residing therein who became entitled to college entrance diplomas under regents' rules, during the preceding school year. Such list shall also show the average standing of the pupils in the several subjects on which each of such diplomas was issued.

2. The commissioner of education shall also cause the names of all pupils on the foregoing lists of the several counties, who are not appointed to scholarships in the county of their residence, to be arranged upon a state list in the order of their merit, as shown by their average standings on the several county lists, from which unclaimed vacant scholarships shall be filled as hereinafter provided.

3. The scholarships to which each county is entitled shall be awarded by the commissioner of education annually in the month of August to those pupils residing therein who became entitled to college entrance diplomas, under regents' rules, during the pre-

ceding school year and in the order of their merit as shown by the list prepared as provided in subdivision one of this section.

4. In case a pupil who is entitled to a scholarship shall fail to apply for such scholarship within thirty days after being notified that he is entitled thereto or shall fail to comply with the rules of the regents as to such scholarships and the same shall have been revoked or cancelled on account thereof, or, if for any other reason such scholarship shall become vacant, then the pupil standing next highest to those pupils on such list for such county who have received scholarships, shall be entitled to receive appointment to such vacant scholarship.

5. In case a scholarship belonging to a county shall not be claimed by a resident of such county or if there be no resident of the county entitled to appointment to the vacant scholarship in such county, the commissioner of education shall fill such vacancy by appointing from the state list the person entitled to such vacancy as provided in subdivision two of this section.

6. The commissioner of education shall cause such person entitled to receive appointment to a scholarship to be notified of his rights thereto and of his forfeiture of such rights by failure to make the application for such scholarship required under section seventy-four of this act.

§ 74. Issuance of scholarship certificate. Upon the application of a pupil duly notified of his right to a scholarship, the commissioner of education shall issue to such pupil a scholarship certificate. Such application and such certificate shall be in the form prescribed by the commissioner of education and such certificate shall specify the college for which it is valid. Said commissioner may also require such additional statements and information to accompany such application as he may deem necessary.

§ 75.[2] Effect of certificate; payments thereon. The certificate issued as provided in the preceding section shall entitle the person named therein to receive the sum of one hundred dollars each year for a period of four years to be applied in partial or entire payment of the annual tuition fee charged by the college named in such certificate for instruction in the course specified therein. Such sum shall be paid by the state treasurer in two equal payments, one on October first and the other on March first out of the scholarship fund of the University of the State of New York, upon the warrant of the comptroller issued with the approval of

---

[2] Section 75 is amended by L. 1913, ch. 437, post.

the commissioner of education. Such approval shall be given
upon vouchers or other evidence showing that the person named
therein is entitled to receive the sum specified, either directly or
for his or her benefit. The rules of the regents may prescribe
conditions under which payments may be made direct to the college attended by the person named in such certificate, in behalf
and for the benefit of such person.

§ 76. Revocation of scholarship. If a person holding a state
scholarship shall fail to comply with the rules of the regents in respect to the use of such scholarship, or shall fail to observe the
rules, regulations or conditions prescribed or imposed by such college on students therein, or shall for any reason be expelled or suspended from such college, or shall absent himself therefrom without leave, the commissioner of education may, upon evidence of
such fact deemed by him sufficient, make an order under the seal
of the education department revoking such scholarship and thereupon such scholarship shall become vacant and the person holding
such scholarship shall not thereafter be entitled to further payment or benefits under the provisions of this act and the vacancy
caused thereby shall be filled as provided in section seventy-three
of this act.

§ 77. Limitation as to number of scholarships; courses of
study. At no time shall there be more than twenty scholarships
established and maintained for each assembly district and at no
time shall there be more than three thousand such scholarships
so established and maintained for the entire state not including
scholarships maintained from the revenues or income of trust
funds, or gifts, devises or bequests created or made as provided
in this act for the maintenance of such scholarships. A person
entitled to such scholarship shall not be restricted as to the choice
of the college which he desires to attend, or the course of study
which he proposes to pursue; provided that no such scholarship
shall include professional instruction in law, medicine, dentistry,
veterinary medicine or theology, except so far as such instruction
is within a regularly prescribed course of study leading to a degree other than in the above-named professions; and provided further, that the college selected by the person entitled to such
scholarship is situated within the state of New York, and is incorporated as a college and authorized under the laws of this state
and the rules of the regents of the university to confer degrees.

In effect
Aug. 1,
1913.
§ 2. This act shall take effect August first, nineteen hundred
and thirteen.

Chap. 293.

AN ACT to create the office of commissioner of charities and
correction of the county of Erie, and to prescribe the powers
and duties of such office.

Became a law April 16, 1913, with the approval of the Governor. Passed,
three-fifths being present.

*The People of the State of New York, represented in Senate
and Assembly, do enact as follows:*

Section 1. There is hereby created in and for Erie county, the office
office of commissioner of charities and correction. The term of
office shall be six years, and the salary thereof shall be five thousand dollars per annum. In case of a vacancy occurring during
a term the same shall be filled by appointment by the board of
supervisors until the first day of January next following the
ensuing general election, except that if such vacancy occurs
within thirty days prior to the general election, a commissioner
shall not be elected until the general election in the year following, and the commissioner appointed by the board of supervisors
shall continue in office until the first day of January following
such election. A commissioner elected at a general election shall
hold his office for the full term of six years. A commissioner
shall give a bond in the penal sum of five thousand dollars for the
faithful discharge of the duties of his office. A commissioner
shall be elected at the general election in the year nineteen hundred and thirteen.

§ 2. Upon the taking of office by the commissioner elected in
the year nineteen hundred and thirteen all the rights, powers,
authority and jurisdiction now possessed by, and all duties devolving upon the superintendent or keeper of the penitentiary,
the superintendent of the county home and hospital, otherwise
called keeper of the almshouse or poor house, the superintendent
of poor, the medical examiner and assistant medical examiner,
the superintendent of the county lodging house, and the keeper
of the morgue shall devolve upon, and be possessed, exercised
and performed by such commissioner in person or by deputy.

§ 3. The commissioner shall have the power to appoint and at
pleasure remove all officers and employees serving in or connected
with the penitentiary, the almshouse or county home, the county
hospital, the office of the medical examiner, the county lodging

County
physician.

house and the morgue. The commissioner shall appoint a deputy to be known as the county physician, who, under the commissioner, shall have charge and control of the county hospital, and of the physicians, nurses and employees employed thereat or serving therein; of the care of the sick, confined in the penitentiary; of the physicians, medical attendants, and nurses employed or serving at the penitentiary and at the county lodging house; of the morgue, and of the keepers and employees serving in the morgue. The said county physician, under the commissioner, and in person, or by an assistant, or by assistants, lawfully appointed or employed, shall exercise the powers and perform the duties now exercised and performed by the medical examiner and the deputy medical examiner, save as herein otherwise especially provided. In addition to the powers conferred upon the commissioner by existing law or by this act, he may appoint and at pleasure remove such deputies, subordinates, clerks and employees as may be authorized by the board of supervisors, and at such salaries or compensation as may be fixed by said board. The commissioner shall have such other powers and perform such other duties as the said board may prescribe.

Additional
appointees.

Additional
powers.

Continua-
tion of
certain
officers
until éx-
piration of
terms.

§ 4. Notwithstanding the provisions hereof, a superintendent of the poor and a superintendent of the county home and hospital, otherwise called the keeper of the almshouse, or poor house, heretofore elected, and in office on January first, nineteen hundred and fourteen, shall continue to be such superintendents respectively, with such powers· and duties as the commissioner may prescribe, until the expiration of the terms for which they were severally elected; and at the expiration of the terms of said incumbents said offices shall cease and determine.

§ 5. This act shall take effect immediately.

Chap. 294.

AN ACT to amend chapter two hundred and sixty-one of the laws of nineteen hundred and two, entitled "An act to authorize the county of Albany to provide for the temporary detention of juvenile delinquents with the Mohawk and Hudson River Humane Society and make compensation therefor," by authorizing said society to receive and detain in its houses of detention minors after arrest, before trial, and pending their reception into some other institution.

Became a law April 16, 1913, with the approval of the Governor. Passed, three-fifths being present.

The People of the State of New York, represented in Senate and Assembly, do enact as follows:

Section 1. Section one of chapter two hundred and sixty-one of the laws of nineteen hundred and two, entitled "An act to authorize the county of Albany to provide for the temporary detention of juvenile delinquents with the Mohawk and Hudson River Humane Society and make compensation therefor," as amended by chapter two hundred and twenty-seven of the laws of nineteen hundred and four and by chapter two hundred and forty-one of the laws of nineteen hundred and eight, is hereby amended to read as follows:

§ 1. The Mohawk and Hudson River Humane Society is hereby authorized to receive and detain temporarily in its houses of detention any minors[1] who may be received by it over night after arrest by a peace officer or who may be temporarily committed to its charge before trial or pending a decision by any magistrate or court, or the superintendents of almshouses, or superintendents or overseers of the poor within the jurisdiction of said society before whom such minors[2] may be brought as to the disposition or judgment which may be made in the particular case, or pending their reception into some other institution to which they may have been committed by final commitment. All magistrates, courts, superintendents of almshouses, and superintendents and overseers of the poor within the jurisdiction of said society are authorized

(margin notes): L. 1902, ch. 261, § 1, as amended by L. 1904, ch. 227, and L. 1908, ch. 241, amended.

Detention of minors in houses of society.

Commitment of minors to houses of detention of society

---

[1] Words "any minors" substituted for words "juvenile delinquents or dependents."

[2] Word "minors" substituted for words "delinquents or dependents."

to commit such minors[3] temporarily to the houses of detention
of said society, and any magistrate within said jurisdiction
may commit any minor held as a witness to appear in trial
in criminal cases to the custody of said society, while being
held as a witness, and the said society is authorized to receive
and detain such witness when committed by such magistrate.

Notification of proper poor officers of commitments and discharges. Immediately upon the commitment of any minor[4] or witness, to it
for the purposes aforesaid, the Mohawk and Hudson River Hu-
mane Society shall notify the superintendent of the almshouse, or
superintendent, or overseer of the poor, of the county from which
such minor[5] shall have been received of the fact of such commitment stating the name of such minor,[5] its sex, its age, the offense
charged or the cause of commitment, and the date of the commitment and by whom. Immediately upon the discharge of such
minor[5] or its commitment to and receipt by some other institution,
it shall be the duty of the society to advise the proper officer of

Statements of poor officers to supervisors; latter authorised to audit claims of society. the poor before mentioned to that effect. Each of such superintendents of almshouses or superintendents or overseers of the
poor shall include within his statement to the board of supervisors of his county each year a statement of minors[6] who may have
been committed within the year to the care and custody of said
society, and all boards of supervisors within the jurisdiction of
said society are authorized to audit the claim of said society for
the care of said minors[6] during the time that they shall remain
under its custody and control and for such services as shall be rendered and such disbursements as shall be made by the society in
connection therewith.

§ 2. This act shall take effect immediately.

---

[3] Word "minors" substituted for words "juvenile delinquents or dependents."

[4] Word "minor" substituted for words "juvenile delinquent, or dependent."

[5] Word "minor" substituted for word "child."

[6] Word "minors" substituted for word "children."

Chap. 295.

AN ACT to provide for the construction of a boulevard and viaduct in the county of Albany, connecting state route three, trunk
line (the so-called " stone road "), in the town of Bethlehem
in said county with Delaware avenue in the city of Albany
and making an appropriation therefor.

Became a law April 16, 1913, with the approval of the Governor. Passed,
three-fifths being present.

*The People of the State of New York, represented in Senate
and Assembly, do enact as follows:*

Section 1. The sum of one hundred thousand dollars ($100,- Appropria-
000), or so much thereof as may be necessary, is hereby appropri- tion.
ated for the purpose of a boulevard in the county of Albany, connecting state route three, trunk line (the so-called " stone road "),
in the town of Bethlehem in said county with Delaware avenue in
the city of Albany, and for the construction of a viaduct across
the *Norman'skill, in said county as part thereof, no portion of
such appropriation to become available, however, until the property within the lines of the proposed boulevard shall have been
conveyed for highway purposes to the county of Albany.

§ 2. The state commission of highways is hereby directed to Survey.
survey said proposed boulevard from a point in the stone road
near the *Norman'skill aforesaid and running from thence northwesterly across said *Norman'skill to Delaware avenue in the city
of Albany, and to submit the preliminary survey for such improvement to the board of supervisors of Albany county for its
approval and acceptance. Upon the acceptance of such plans by Plans and
the board of supervisors the state engineer and surveyor is hereby estimates.
directed to prepare plans and submit estimates for the construction of the viaduct across the *Norman'skill, as aforesaid, which
plans shall also receive the approval of the said board of supervisors. Title having been acquired to the lands within the lines Advertising
of the proposed boulevard and plans for the viaduct and roadway letting
having been approved by the board of supervisors, the state engi- of bids.
neer is hereby directed to advertise for bids for the construction
of the said viaduct and empowered to let the construction of the
same to the lowest responsible bidder. The state commission of Expense,
highways shall thereupon build the portion of the said boulevard divided.

---

* So in original.

not included in the viaduct in the same manner and with the same proportionate expense to the state, county, town and city, as provided in and under the county highway system of the highway law.

§ 3. This act shall take effect immediately.

Chap. 296.

AN ACT to amend the insurance law, in relation to the incorporation of fire insurance corporations.

Became a law April 16, 1913, with the approval of the Governor. Passed, three-fifths being present.

The People of the State of New York, represented in Senate and Assembly, do enact as follows:

L. 1909, ch. 33, § 110, as amended by L. 1910, ch. 168, and L. 1911, ch. 126, amended.

Section 1. Section one hundred and ten of chapter thirty-three of the laws of nineteen hundred and nine, entitled "An act in relation to insurance corporations, constituting chapter twenty-eight of the consolidated laws," as amended by chapter one hundred and sixty-eight of the laws of nineteen hundred and ten and chapter one hundred and twenty-six of the laws of nineteen hundred and eleven, is hereby amended to read as follows:

§ 110. **Incorporation.** Thirteen or more persons may become a corporation for the purpose of making insurances on dwelling houses, stores and all kinds of buildings and household furniture, and other property against loss or damage, including loss of use or occupancy, by fire, lightning, windstorm, tornado, cyclone, earthquake,[1] hail, frost or snow, and by explosion whether fire ensues or not, except explosion on risks specified in subdivision seven of section seventy of this chapter,[2] and also against loss or damage by water to any goods or premises arising from the breakage or leakage of sprinklers, pumps or other apparatus erected for extinguishing fires, and of water pipes, and against accidental injury to such sprinklers, pumps or other apparatus, and upon vessels, boats, cargoes, goods, merchandise, freights and other property against loss or damage by all or any of the risks

---

[1] Formerly read: "by fire, lightning, windstorms, tornadoes or earthquakes." Word "cyclone" new.

[2] Words "hail, frost or snow, and by explosion whether fire ensues or not, except explosion on risks specified in subdivision seven of section seventy of this chapter," new.

of lake, river, canal and inland navigation and transportation, as well as by any or all of the risks specified in section one hundred and fifty of this chapter, including insurances upon automobiles, whether stationary or being operated under their own power, which shall include all or any of the hazards of fire, explosion, transportation, collision, loss by legal liability for damage to property resulting from the maintenance and use of automobiles, and loss by burglary or theft or both, but shall not include insurance against loss by reason of bodily injury to the person, and to effect reinsurances of any risks taken by it, by filing in the office of the superintendent of insurance a declaration signed by all of them, of their intention to form a corporation for the purpose of transacting the business of making any or all of such insurances, which shall comprise a copy of the charter proposed to be adopted by them, setting forth the name of the corporation, the place of location of its office, the mode in which its corporate powers are to be exercised and its directors elected, a majority of whom shall be citizens of this state, and if a stock corporation, the owner in his own right of at least five hundred dollars of the stock of the corporation at its par value, the mode of filling vacancies in the office of director, the period for the commencement and termination of its fiscal year and the amount of capital to be employed in the transaction of its business; provided that a corporation including in its charter a provision to assume any of the risks of ocean marine insurance as specified in section one hundred and fifty of this chapter must have a capital, paid in in cash, of at least four hundred thousand dollars.

No such declaration shall be filed, unless the persons signing the same shall have previously published for at least two weeks successively a notice of their intention to form such a corporation in a public newspaper in the county where its office is to be located.

Every such corporation shall be known as a fire insurance corporation. No such corporation shall directly or indirectly deal or trade in buying or selling any goods, wares, merchandise or other commodities whatever, except such articles as may be insured by it and are claimed to be damaged by any cause so insured against.

§ 2. This act shall take effect immediately.

Chap. 297.

AN ACT authorizing the city of Buffalo to establish and maintain a fund for the insurance of buildings and other property owned by said city, and authorizing said city to borrow money by the issuance and sale of bonds for such purpose.

Became a law April 16, 1913, with the approval of the Governor. Passed, three-fifths being present.

Accepted by the City.

The People of the State of New York, represented in Senate and Assembly, do enact as follows:

Bond issue.

Section 1. It shall be lawful for the city of Buffalo to issue its bonds in a sum or sums not to exceed in the aggregate one million dollars, for the purpose of raising money to establish a fund with which to provide insurance against loss through the destruction or injury from any cause of buildings, structures, machinery or other property owned by the city wheresoever situated. Such bonds shall be issued under the city seal by the mayor and comptroller from time to time as they may be ordered by the common council. They shall be sold or awarded as provided by the charter of said city and shall bear interest at a rate to be fixed by the common council, payable semi-annually at the office of the comptroller of the city of Buffalo or at the Hanover National Bank of the city of New York, as the purchaser may elect, the principal to be payable at the same place at the end of a term of fifty years from date of issue. Such bonds shall be paid from a fund to be known as the insurance bond sinking fund, to be created by an annual payment of eight hundred and sixty and fifty one-hundredths dollars for each one hundred thousand dollars of said bonds issued, which sum shall be inserted annually in the general fund estimates for the city. The common council shall make provision for the payment of the interest on and the principal of said bonds as the same shall become due in the general fund estimates for said city, counting the accumulation of said insurance bond sinking fund as a resource. Such sinking fund shall be held and invested and reinvested by the comptroller of the city of Buffalo to retire said bonds when due. The proceeds of the issue and sale of the bonds hereby authorized to be issued and sold shall be held and invested and reinvested by the comptroller of the city of Buffalo as a fund for the

Sale, interest, etc.

Insurance bond sinking fund.

Payment of interest and principal.

Investment of sinking fund.

Disposition of proceeds of bonds.

insurance of buildings, structures, machinery and other property
owned by the city, as hereinbefore provided. Said city shall *Establishment of system of insurance, authorized.*
have authority by ordinance to establish a system for the safe
and adequate insurance of buildings, structures, machinery and
other property owned by the city; for the regulation of such insurance and the reimbursement from said fund of all losses.

§ 2. This act shall take effect immediately.

Chap. 298.

AN ACT to amend chapter three hundred and twenty-one of the
laws of eighteen hundred and ninety-eight, entitled "An act
to make the office of sheriff of Oneida county a salaried office,
and to regulate the management thereof," in relation to the
salary of the sheriff, and the care and maintenance of jails and
prisoners.

Became a law April 16, 1913, with the approval of the Governor. Passed,
three-fifths being present.

*The People of the State of New York, represented in Senate
and Assembly, do enact as follows:*

Section 1. Section one of chapter three hundred and twenty- *L. 1898, ch. 321, § 1, as amended by L. 1901, ch. 666, and L. 1907, chaps. 39, 702, amended.*
one of the laws of eighteen hundred and ninety-eight, entitled "An
act to make the office of sheriff of Oneida county a salaried office,
and to regulate the management thereof," as amended by chapter
six hundred and sixty-six of the laws of nineteen hundred and
one, chapters thirty-nine and seven hundred and two of the laws
of nineteen hundred and seven, is hereby amended to read as
follows:

§ 1. The sheriff of the county of Oneida shall receive as com- *Salary.*
pensation for all his services which are now or may by law be
made a county charge upon the said county of Oneida, an annual
salary of six thousand dollars;[1] he shall also be entitled to receive *Other compensation.*
and retain to his own use, his fees and perquisites in all actions and
proceedings in which the same are to be paid by private persons
or corporations other than the county of Oneida; and he shall perform the duties in connection therewith without expense to the
county of Oneida. He shall also be reimbursed for his actual *Expenses.*
and necessary expenses incurred in the performance of his duties,

---

[1] Formerly " twelve hundred dollars."

or in the performance of any duty which he is required by law
to perform and which is now or may be made a county charge upon
the county of Oneida, which said expenses and disbursements shall
be presented in the form of an itemized account, and shall be
audited and allowed by the board of supervisors the same as other
claims against the county are audited and allowed. [2]The sheriff
shall pay from his salary[3] all such assistants other than those whose
salaries are herein specifically provided for, as shall be necessary
for him to properly[4] exercise the duties of his office, and in consideration of which he shall do or perform all duties which
now are, or may hereafter be imposed upon him by law, unless thereby otherwise provided for, and which are now or shall
be made a county charge. There shall be one under sheriff who
shall be appointed by the sheriff and may be removed by him at
any time. The under sheriff of the county of Oneida shall receive
an annual salary of twelve hundred dollars. There shall be a
jailer at Utica and a jailer at Rome, each of whom shall be
appointed by the sheriff and may[5] be removed by him at any
time, and each of whom shall receive an annual salary of
eight hundred dollars. The jailers shall also be appointed
deputy sheriffs and shall act in that capacity and perform the
duties in connection therewith. The sheriff may also appoint and
may remove at any time a deputy sheriff and turnkey for the safe
conduct of prisoners to and from court and institutions and for
the performance of such other duties as may be required by the
sheriff, and who shall receive an annual salary to. be fixed
by the board of supervisors. The sheriff shall appoint
and may remove at any time at least seven other deputies
who shall not be residents of the cities of Utica or Rome and not
more than one of whom shall be a resident of any of the towns
adjoining the city of Utica, and no two of whom shall be residents
of the same town. The said seven, or more deputies appointed as
above provided shall each receive an annual salary, which shall be
fixed[6] and apportioned by the sheriff, but the aggregate of said
salaries shall not exceed the sum of two thousand dollars in
any one year. The sheriff shall also appoint and may remove

Marginal notes: Compensation of assistants. Under sheriff. Jailers. Deputy sheriff and turnkey. Other deputies. Clerk or counsel.

---

[2] Words "The salary shall not be increased or diminished during his term
of office, and from it he," omitted. Words "The sheriff" new.
[3] Words "from his salary" new.
[4] Word "properly" substituted for word "conveniently."
[5] Word "may" new.
[6] Formerly read: "affixed."

at any time a clerk or counsel. The clerk or counsel shall receive an annual salary of twelve hundred dollars. Whenever any of the prisoners confined in the jails of said county are employed at hard labor of any kind the sheriff shall appoint such number of additional deputies, or designate such number of deputies already appointed, as he shall deem necessary to properly guard said prisoners while so employed, not exceeding in number, however, two deputies to guard all prisoners employed within said jails or jail yards; and not exceeding one deputy for each eight prisoners employed outside of said jails or jail yards; said deputies shall receive a compensation of two dollars per day for each day they are actually employed in guarding said prisoners, and their compensation shall be a county charge upon the county of Oneida, and shall be audited and allowed by the board of supervisors of said county, as other claims against the county are audited and allowed. The under sheriff, jailers, deputies, turnkey and clerk or counsel appointed as herein provided, shall be paid all necessary expenses incurred by them in the performance of their duties in criminal actions and proceedings, or in the performance of any duty which they are by law required to perform for the county of Oneida, and said disbursements shall be presented to the board of supervisors of said county in the form of an itemized account, and shall be audited and allowed by said board the same as other claims against the county are audited and allowed. The sheriff may appoint as many more deputies or assistants as he may deem necessary, all of whom shall serve without any expense to the county.

§ 2. Section four of such chapter, as amended by chapter six hundred and sixty-six of the laws of nineteen hundred and one, is hereby amended to read as follows:[7]

§ 4. The jails in the county shall be kept by the sheriff of the county as required by law. All books, records, furniture, implements, tools, materials and supplies of whatever nature necessary for the custody, care and maintenance of the prisoners and persons detained within said jails and all implements, materials and supplies necessary to maintain the said jails in a proper and sanitary condition; such drugs and medicine as are provided for the prisoners in said jails under the direction

Marginal notes: Deputies to guard prisoners employed at hard labor. — Expenses of under sheriff, jailers, etc. — Additional deputies and assistants. — § 4, as amended by L. 1901, ch. 666, amended. — Sheriff to keep jails and furnish supplies: latter a county charge.

---

[7] Section materially amended.

in writing of the respective jail physicians; and such clothing as shall be necessary for the prisoners confined in such jails shall be provided by the sheriff subject to the approval of the county comptroller, and actual and necessary disbursements of the sheriff in providing for the same and as approved by the county comptroller, shall be a county charge and shall be paid by the county. The

Food, how provided; to be a county charge. sheriff shall also provide the food for the prisoners in said jails at cost including the cost of preparing the same, it being the intent of this act that the feeding of prisoners shall not be a source of profit to the sheriff. The expenditures for such food and for preparing the same for use and as approved by the county comptroller shall be a county charge and shall be paid by the county. The

Account of disbursements. sheriff shall keep a correct and itemized account of all of said disbursements in a book or books provided for that purpose at the expense of the county and each item of such account shall specify the date on which it was incurred, to whom paid, the place where

Expenditures for food to be kept separate. paid and the purpose for which it was incurred. The expenditures for food of such prisoners and for preparing the same for use shall be kept in a separate place in said book or books and

Audit of accounts. separately stated in the sheriff's report. The accounts for all said disbursements shall be audited by the county comptroller of Oneida county and the board of supervisors of said county in the same manner as other claims against the county are required by law to be audited.

Statement of sheriff as to prisoners confined. At such times as the sheriff presents to the county comptroller and to the board of supervisors an account of said disbursements, he shall also present therewith a statement showing the names of all prisoners confined in either of said jails during the time, or any part thereof, for which such account is rendered, and showing the actual time each prisoner was confined in either of said jails as a county charge, and whether employed or unemployed, and the actual time, place and the kind of labor at which each was employed.

§ 3. This act shall take effect immediately.

Chap. 299.

AN ACT to amend the Greater New York charter, in relation to
expenditures for the relief of the blind.

Became a law April 16, 1913, with the approval of the Governor. Passed,
three-fifths being present.

Accepted by the City.

*The People of the State of New York, represented in Senate
and Assembly, do enact as follows:*

Section 1. Subdivision third of section two hundred and thirty
of the Greater New York charter, as re-enacted by chapter four
hundred and sixty-six of the laws of nineteen hundred and one, is
hereby amended to read as follows:

Third. Such sum, not exceeding one hundred and fifty thousand dollars,[1] as is included in the departmental estimates
submitted to it by the department of public charities, to be applied
to the relief of poor adult blind persons.

§ 2. Section six hundred and seventy-six of said charter is
hereby amended to read as follows:

EXPENDITURES FOR THE RELIEF OF THE BLIND.

§ 676. The commissioner is hereby authorized and empowered
to insert in his annual estimate of expenditures an item of expenditure for the relief of the poor adult blind not to exceed in all one
hundred and fifty thousand dollars.[1] The commissioner shall
distribute the sum so appropriated each year in uniform sums
not to exceed one hundred dollars to each[2] person, to such poor
adult blind persons, not inmates of any of the public or private
institutions in the city of New York, who shall be in need of
relief and who shall be citizens of the United States, and shall
have been residents of said city continuously for two years previous to the date of application for such relief. [3]Such distribution shall be made in semi-annual payments within ten days after
the first day of July and December, respectively.

§ 3. To provide the commissioner of public charities with additional funds, if any are needed, for paying during the current year

Marginal notes: L. 1897, ch. 378, § 230, subd. 3, as re-enacted by L. 1901, ch. 466, amended. Item to be included in annual estimate. § 676 amended. Issue of certificates of indebtedness.

---

[1] Formerly " seventy-five thousand dollars."
[2] Word " each " substituted for words " any one."
[3] Following sentence new.

the increased allowances created by this act, the comptroller of
said city may, when so directed by the board of estimate and apportionment of said city, issue and sell certificates of indebtedness.

§ 4. This act shall take effect immediately.

Chap. 300.

AN ACT to amend chapter five hundred and eighteen of the laws
of eighteen hundred and sixty-seven, entitled "An act to amend
an act, entitled 'An act to incorporate the village of White
Plains,'" passed April third, eighteen hundred and sixty-six,
in relation to the powers and duties of the village trustees, et
cetera, and the acts amendatory thereof.

Became a law April 16, 1913, with the approval of the Governor. Passed,
three-fifths being present.

*The People of the State of New York, represented in Senate
and Assembly, do enact as follows:*

L. 1867,
ch. 518,
tit. 4, § 8,
as added by
L. 1878, ch.
179, and
amended by
L. 1884,
ch. 493,
1896, ch.
768, L.
1902, ch.
201, and L.
1912, ch.
126,
amended.

Section 1. Section eight of title four of chapter five hundred
and eighteen of the laws of eighteen hundred and sixty-seven, entitled "An act to amend an act, entitled 'An act to incorporate the
village of White Plains,' passed April third, eighteen hundred and
sixty-six, in relation to the powers and duties of the village trustees, et cetera, and the acts amendatory thereof," as added thereto
by chapter one hundred and seventy-nine of the laws of eighteen
hundred and seventy-eight, as amended by chapter four hundred
and ninety-three of the laws of eighteen hundred and eighty-four,
chapter seven hundred and sixty-eight of the laws of eighteen
hundred and ninety-six, chapter two hundred and one of the laws
of nineteen hundred and two, and by chapter one hundred and
twenty-six of the laws of nineteen hundred and twelve, is hereby
amended so as to read as follows:

Bond
issues to
meet de-
ficiencies.

§ 8. The board of trustees is hereby authorized and empowered
by resolution to issue the bonds of said village to raise moneys to
meet deficiencies which may arise in the collection of taxes or
assessments for local improvements which have been heretofore
or may hereafter be levied, assessed or imposed in accordance
with provisions of the existing charter of said village or of this
act, and to pay outstanding, existing and unpaid certificates of
indebtedness heretofore issued to meet deficiencies arising in col-

lection of taxes and assessments for local improvements, such bonds shall be issued in such amounts as may be authorized by such resolution, not in excess of the amount of taxes or assessments uncollected[1] for which no provision has been made by the issue of bonds, and certificates of indebtedness remaining outstanding, existing and unpaid, and payable during the follow-. ing year, and shall bear interest, at such rate as the board of trustees may determine,[2] not exceeding the rate of six per centum per annum, payable semi-annually, the principal payable at such times as the board of trustees shall by resolution determine. All moneys received from arrears of taxes or assessments shall be used for the purpose of paying the interest and principal of the said bonds issued by the board of trustees under the provisions of this section and for no other purpose. Such bonds shall be signed by the president and clerk of said village and shall have the corporate seal thereof affixed thereto and shall not be sold or disposed of below par. A record shall be kept of the number, date and amount of each bond issued as aforesaid, and of the time when the same becomes due or payable, by the clerk of said village. If at the time of the maturing of any bond or bonds there shall not be in the village treasury sufficient moneys arising from the collection of the arrears of taxes and assessments to pay the same or the interest due thereon, the board shall cause the amount of any deficiency there may be to be levied and assessed upon all of the taxable property, real and personal, in said village, and collected in the same manner and at the same time as other taxes are collected, to pay such deficiency.

§ 2. Section eighteen of title two of such chapter as added by chapter seven hundred and thirteen of the laws of nineteen hundred and eleven is hereby amended so as to read as follows:

§ 18. The village engineer appointed, as provided by this act, subject to the provisions of law and the ordinances of the board of trustees, shall have [3]the direction, supervision and inspection[4] of the construction, maintenance, alterations, repairs and care of all public sewers and drains in the village [5]and of the construction, grading, alterations, repairing, paving, re- paving, resurfacing and flagging the streets, highways, sidewalks

Marginal notes: Interest. Principal, when payable. Application of moneys received from arrears. Execution and sale of bonds. Record. Tax for payment of deficiency. Tit. 2, § 18, as added by L. 1911, ch. 713, amended. Duties of village engineer.

---

1 Word " and " omitted.
2 Words "at such rate as the board of trustees may determine," new.
3 Words " cognizance and " omitted. Word " the " new.
4 Words " supervision and inspection," new.
5 Remainder of sentence new.

18

and public places in the village, in all cases where the work of such improvements is done under contract. It shall be his duty to perform all the ordinary engineering and surveying services needed in the affairs and business of the village,[6] in which the skill of the profession may be required or useful. He shall act as .the superintendent of public buildings and bridges under such regulations as may be prescribed by the ordinances of the board

Subordinates.

of trustees, and under the direction of the president. He shall employ such subordinates to serve during his pleasure as the board

Compensation.

of trustees shall prescribe. The village engineer and his subordinates, if any, shall receive no fees or compensation of any kind, other than their salaries, as fixed by the board of trustees.

Tit. 2,
§ 19, as
added by
L. 1911, ch.
713,
amended.

§ 3. Section nineteen of title two of such chapter as added by chapter seven hundred and thirteen of the laws of nineteen hundred and eleven is hereby amended so as to read as follows:[7]

Duties of
superin-
tendent of
highways.

§ 19. The superintendent of highways appointed as provided by this act, subject to the provisions of law and the ordinances of the board of trustees shall have the direction, supervision, and inspection of the maintenance, repairing, care and cleaning, of the streets, highways, sidewalks and public places of the village, in all cases where the work of such improvements is not done under contract, and of the lighting of streets, highways and public places. He shall procure such materials and employ such laborers as shall be authorized and prescribed by the board of trustees for the doing of any work which he is authorized to do under this act, and shall have the direction, supervision and control of all contracts of the village for lighting, sprinkling, watering or flushing of the streets, highways or public places and shall cause the same to be performed in full compliance with the provisions of any con-

Subordi-
nates.

tract therefor. He shall employ such subordinates to serve during his pleasure as the board of trustees shall prescribe. The super-

Compen-
sation.

intendent of highways and his subordinates, if any, shall receive no fees or compensation of any kind, other than their salaries as fixed by the board of trustees.

Tit. 4, § 1,
as amended
by L. 1873,
ch. 409;
L. 1878,
ch. 179;
L. 1884,
ch. 493;
L. 1890,
ch. 215;
L. 1895,

§ 4. Section one of title four of such chapter as amended by chapter four hundred and nine of the laws of eighteen hundred and seventy-three and by chapter one hundred and seventy-nine of the laws of eighteen hundred and seventy-eight, and chapter four hundred and ninety-three of the

---

[6] Words "and to supervise all the work done by the village," omitted.
[7] Section materially amended.

laws of eighteen hundred and eighty-four, and by chapter three hundred and fifteen of the laws of eighteen hundred and ninety and by chapter one hundred and nine of the laws of eighteen hundred and ninety-five and by chapter seven hundred and sixty-eight of the laws of eighteen hundred and ninety-six and by chapter two hundred and one of the laws of nineteen hundred and two and by chapter ninety-four of the laws of nineteen hundred and six, and by chapter six hundred and four of the laws of nineteen hundred and seven, and by chapter seven hundred and thirteen of the laws of nineteen hundred and eleven, and by chapter four hundred and ninety-three of the laws of nineteen hundred and twelve, is hereby amended to read as follows:

ch. 189; L. 1894, ch. 768; L. 1902, ch. 201; L. 1906, ch. 94; L. 1907, ch. 604; L. 1911, ch. 713, and L. 1912, ch. 493, amended.

§ 1. The board of trustees is authorized and empowered without any vote of the taxable inhabitants of said village to raise every year by tax, to be assessed upon the estate and property, real and personal, within said village and to be collected from the several owners and occupants thereof the following sums for the following purposes, namely:

Purposes for which tax may be levied.

1. For the purchase of any real estate or personal property for the use of said village or for the hiring of suitable rooms for the use of said village, and to defray the ordinary, necessary or contingent expenses of the village a sum not to exceed twenty thousand dollars.

2. For making, working, repairing and improving roads and bridges and for laying and maintaining crosswalks a sum not exceeding thirty thousand dollars[8] in any one year; which amount shall be denominated the highway tax or fund, and when raised twenty thousand dollars,[9] or so much thereof as may be necessary, shall be devoted exclusively to the working, maintenance and repair of roads, avenues, streets, lanes, crosswalks and bridges of the village, and the balance of the sum so raised shall be devoted to the permanent improvement of such roads, avenues, streets, lanes, crosswalks and bridges and to no other purpose whatsoever, and the treasurer shall keep such sums as separate and distinct funds.

3. For lighting the streets as hereinafter provided an amount not exceeding twenty thousand dollars.[10] The existing contract made and entered into by the board for lighting the streets and public places in the village shall be and continue in full force and effect until the expiration thereof.

---

[8] Formerly "twenty thousand dollars."
[9] Formerly "ten thousand dollars."
[10] Formerly "eighteen thousand dollars."

4. For the payment of any judgment which may hereafter be recovered against the said village, such sum as may be necessary to discharge the same.

5. For the care, maintenance, improvement and beautifying the parks and public places of the village a sum not to exceed three thousand dollars.

6. For the salary of the police justice an amount not exceeding one thousand five hundred dollars.

7. For the salary of the village clerk an amount not to exceed two thousand dollars.

8. For the salary of the village treasurer, an amount not to exceed five hundred dollars.

9. For the salary of the superintendent of highways an amount not exceeding one thousand five hundred dollars.

10. For the cleaning of crosswalks and the removal and disposal of ashes and of garbage, dead animals and general refuse matter an amount not exceeding ten thousand dollars.

11. For the salaries of health officers, secretary to the board of health, and the ordinary expenses incurred by said board, an amount not to exceed five thousand dollars.

12. For the salary of the corporation counsel an amount not to exceed three thousand five hundred dollars.

13. For the salary of the village engineer an amount not to exceed three thousand five hundred dollars.

14. For the salary of the building inspector an amount not exceeding the sum of one thousand dollars.

15. For the expenses of the police commissioners and the salary and maintenance of the police force established and existing under the provisions of an act, entitled "An act to organize and establish a police department for the village of White Plains, in the county of Westchester and state of New York," being chapter three hundred and six of the laws of nineteen hundred and four, as amended by chapter one hundred and sixty-five of the laws of nineteen hundred and six, and chapter three hundred and thirty-seven of the laws of nineteen hundred and seven, and all other acts amendatory thereof and supplemental thereto, an amount not to exceed the sum of twenty-five thousand dollars.[11]

16. For the purpose of paying any existing indebtedness of said village incurred during the year nineteen hundred and eleven and arising by reason of the current expenses of said village for

---

[11] Formerly " twenty thousand dollars."

the said year nineteen hundred and eleven, exceeding the amount provided by law for the payment thereof on the first day of May, nineteen hundred and eleven, an amount not to exceed the sum of twenty-five thousand dollars.

17. For the salary of the assessor an amount not to exceed the sum of two thousand five hundred dollars.

§ 5. This act shall take effect immediately.

Chap. 301.

AN ACT to amend chapter eight hundred and fifty-eight of the laws of eighteen hundred and sixty-seven, entitled "An act to amend the statutes in reference to the collection of taxes in the county of Onondaga," relative to the time of filing statement of unpaid taxes by the county treasurer of Onondaga county.

Became a law April 16, 1913, with the approval of the Governor. Passed, three-fifths being present.

The People of the State of New York, represented in Senate and Assembly, do enact as follows:

Section 1. Section one of chapter eight hundred and fifty-eight of the laws of eighteen hundred and sixty-seven, entitled "An act to amend the statutes in reference to the collection of taxes in the county of Onondaga," as amended by chapter two hundred and sixty-three of the laws of eighteen hundred and ninety-nine, and chapter three hundred and thirty-two of the laws of nineteen hundred and four and by chapter two hundred and fifty-three of the laws of nineteen hundred and five, is hereby amended to read as follows: *L. 1867, ch. 858, § 1, as amended by L. 1899, ch. 263, L. 1904, ch. 332, and L. 1905, ch. 253, amended.*

§ 1. It shall be the duty of the treasurer of the city of Syracuse, to pay to the county treasurer of Onondaga county, on the first Tuesday of each January, February, March and April, respectively, next succeeding the delivery of the annual tax rolls of state and county taxes to him by the board of supervisors of Onondaga county, all moneys collected by him for state and county taxes in accordance with said tax rolls and annexed warrants, and on the first Tuesday of May next succeeding the delivery of said rolls to him, to return to the county treasurer an account of all state and county taxes remaining unpaid in manner and form required by law, and pay over to said county treasurer all moneys then remain- *Payment to county treasurer of moneys received for taxes.*

Statement of unpaid taxes. ing in his hands, received by him for said taxes. Neither the city treasurer nor any collector shall enforce the payment of any such taxes assessed upon real estate in said county by levy upon the sale of personal property, but an account of all such taxes remaining unpaid at the expiration of the period for payment to the city treasurer and collectors shall be returned by them to the county treasurer as provided by law and the collection thereof shall be enforced by him in the manner hereinafter provided.

Statement to be filed with county clerk. On or before the first day of January, nineteen hundred and five, and on the first day of July, of each and every year thereafter the county treasurer shall prepare and file with the county clerk a certified statement containing a list of all unpaid taxes returned to him by the collectors of the several towns and the treasurer of the city of Syracuse,[1] which remain unpaid and a statement of which has not previously been filed with said clerk. The county clerk shall cause the same to be entered of record and properly indexed. [2]The county treasurer shall add to each one of such unpaid taxes and

Discharge to be filed with county clerk. collect the sum of twenty-five cents for filing. Upon the payment to the county treasurer of any unpaid tax appearing upon any such statement, together with the accumulated fees, interest, expenses and charges thereon, he shall deliver to the person paying the same a discharge thereof, which may be filed with the county clerk and when so filed shall be entered upon and shall operate to discharge said tax of record. A transcript of the record of every such tax, remaining undischarged of record, shall be noted upon every subsequent abstract of title of the premises affected thereby. The expense of preparing such statement shall be a county charge. The county clerk shall be entitled to charge and receive a fee of twenty-five cents for each parcel of land described in any such statement or discharge, for filing, entering and indexing the same. When such fees shall be paid by the county treasurer, he shall add to and collect the same as a part of the expense charged against the property affected thereby.

§ 2. This act shall take effect immediately.

---

[1] Words " and the treasurer of the city of Syracuse," new.
[2] Following sentence new.

Chap. 302.

AN ACT to amend the Greater New York charter, in relation to the rehearing of charges against, and reinstatement of persons dismissed.

Became a law April 17, 1913, with the approval of the Governor. Passed, three-fifths being present.

Accepted by the City.

The People of the State of New York, represented in Senate and Assembly, do enact as follows:

Section 1. The Greater New York charter, as re-enacted by chapter four hundred and sixty-six of the laws of nineteen hundred and one, is hereby amended by adding thereto a new section, to be known as section fifteen hundred and forty-three-b and to read as follows:

§ 1543b added to L. 1897, ch. 378, as re-enacted by L. 1901, ch. 466.

HEADS OF DEPARTMENTS, OTHER THAN THE POLICE AND FIRE COMMISSIONER, MAY REHEAR CHARGES AGAINST AND REINSTATE PERSONS DISMISSED.

§ 1543-b. The head of a city department or any other officer, board or body of the city, or of a borough, or of a county, vested with the power of appointment and employment, except the police commissioner and the fire commissioner, upon written application by the person aggrieved, setting forth the reasons for demanding an opportunity of making a further explanation, shall have the power, in his discretion, to rehear the explanation and any new matter offered in further reply to the charges or complaint upon which such person was dismissed from the service, provided that such person shall waive, in writing, all claim against the city of New York for back pay. Such application for another opportunity to explain shall only be presented to, and granted by the officer who made the removal or to the immediate successor of the removing official when the applicant for the further explanation makes it appear, by affidavit, that on a further chance to explain he can produce evidence such as if before received would probably have changed the decision; if such evidence has been discovered since the previous explanation; is not cumulative; and the failure to produce it at the first explanation was not owing to want of diligence. No reinstatement by a successor shall be made where the applicant has been removed more than two years, nor without the consent of the mayor. If upon the further ex-

planation such head of department or other officer, board or
body determine that such person has been illegally or unjustly
dismissed, such head of department or other officer, board or
body, in his discretion, may, upon the approval in writing of the
municipal civil service commission, reinstate such person.

§ 2. This act shall take effect immediately.

Chap. 303.

AN ACT to amend the insurance law, in relation to regulations by the state fire marshal.

Became a law April 17, 1913, with the approval of the Governor. Passed,
three-fifths being present.

*The People of the State of New York, represented in Senate
and Assembly, do enact as follows:*

§ 379 added
to L. 1909,
ch. 33.

Section 1. Article ten-a of chapter thirty-three of the laws of
nineteen hundred and nine, entitled "An act in relation to insurance corporations, constituting chapter twenty-eight of the consolidated laws," as added by chapter four hundred and fifty-one
of the laws of nineteen hundred and eleven and amended by chapter four hundred and fifty-three of the laws of nineteen hundred and twelve, is hereby amended by adding thereto a new section to be section three hundred and seventy-nine, to read as
follows:

§ 379. State fire marshal to make regulations. The state
fire marshal is hereby authorized and empowered to formulate
and adopt suitable regulations upon each of the subjects enumerated in section three hundred and fifty-one of this article, and
from time to time to make amendments thereto. He shall cause
a copy of such regulations to be filed with the clerk of each
county, town or village, and it shall be the duty of members
of the fire and police departments and of the legally constituted
law officers of each city, town or village to assist the state fire
marshal in the enforcement of this article and the regulations
made thereunder, provided, however, that nothing herein contained shall be construed to confer on the state fire marshal any
authority or power to adopt such regulations upon the subjects
covered in sections three hundred and fifty-eight to three hundred
and sixty-seven both inclusive.

§ 2. This act shall take effect immediately.

Chap. 304.

AN ACT to amend the insurance law, generally.

Became a law April 17, 1913, with the approval of the Governor. Passed, three-fifths being present.

The People of the State of New York, represented in Senate and Assembly, do enact as follows:

Section 1. Section six of chapter thirty-three of the laws of nineteen hundred and nine, entitled "An act in relation to insurance corporations, constituting chapter twenty-eight of the consolidated laws," as amended by chapter six hundred and thirty-four of the laws of nineteen hundred and ten, is hereby amended to read as follows:

§ 6. **Fees.** Every corporation or person to whom this chapter shall be applicable shall pay the following fees to the superintendent, unless remitted by him. For filing the declaration and certified copy of the charter required by law, thirty dollars. For filing the annual report required by law, twenty dollars. For each certificate of authority and certified copy thereof, and for each certificate of deposit, valuation or compliance, not exceeding five dollars. For every copy of any paper filed in his office, ten cents per folio; and for affixing the official seal on such copy and certifying the same, one dollar. All fees, perquisites and moneys received by the insurance department, or any officer thereof, [1]shall be paid into the state treasury as required by the state finance law.

§ 2. Section sixteen of such chapter as amended by chapters two hundred and forty and three hundred and two of the laws of nineteen hundred and nine, chapter six hundred and thirty-four of the laws of nineteen hundred and ten, chapter one hundred and fifty of the laws of nineteen hundred and eleven and chapter two hundred and thirty-three of the laws of nineteen hundred and twelve, is hereby amended to read as follows:

§ 16. **Investment of capital and surplus.** The cash capital of every domestic insurance corporation required to have a capital, to the extent of the minimum capital required by law, shall be invested and kept invested in the stocks or bonds of the United States or of this state, not estimated above their current market value, or in the bonds of a county or incorporated city in this

Margin notes: L. 1909, ch. 33, § 6, as amended by L. 1910, ch. 634, amended.

Margin notes: § 16, as amended by L. 1909, chaps. 240, 302, L. 1910, ch. 634, L. 1911, ch. 150, and L. 1912, ch. 233, amended.

---

[1] Remainder of sentence formerly read: "from or on account of any insurance corporation, shall be paid into the state treasury monthly."

state authorized to be issued by the legislature, not estimated
above their par value or their current market value, or in bonds
and mortgages on improved unencumbered real property in this
state worth fifty per centum more than the amount loaned
thereon. The cash capital of every foreign insurance corporation
to the extent of the minimum capital required of a like domestic
corporation shall be invested and kept invested in the same class
of securities specified for domestic insurance corporations, except
that like securities of the home state or foreign country shall be
recognized as legal investments for the amount of the minimum
capital required. The residue of the capital and the surplus
money and funds of every domestic insurance corporation over
and above its capital, and the deposit that it may be required to
make with the superintendent, may be invested in or loaned on
the pledge of any of the securities in which deposits are required
to be invested or in the public stocks or bonds of any one of the
United States, or in bonds and mortgages on improved unencumbered real property in this state worth fifty per centum more than
the amount loaned thereon, or except as in this chapter otherwise
provided, in the stocks, bonds or other evidence of indebtedness
of any solvent institution incorporated under the laws of the
United States or of any state thereof, or in such real estate as it
is authorized by this chapter to hold; but no such funds shall be invested in or loaned on its own stock or the stock of any other insurance corporation carrying on the same kind of insurance business, except that any such company organized under section seventy of this chapter for the purpose of engaging in business
principally[2] as a surety company[3] may, subject to the consent of
the superintendent of insurance,[4] invest such funds in or loan such
funds on the stock of any other corporation carrying on
[5]the same kind of business outside of but not within the United
States; provided, however, that the superintendent in determining the condition of any such corporation so loaning or investing
such funds shall not allow it as an asset the amount of the funds
so loaned or invested; and, provided that, if a stock life insurance corporation shall determine to become a mutual life insurance corporation, it may, in carrying out any plan to that end

---

[2] Word "principally" substituted for word "solely."
[3] Words "as provided in subdivision four of that section," omitted.
[4] Words "may, subject to the consent of the superintendent of insurance,"
new.
[5] Word "solely" omitted.

under the provisions of section ninety-five of this chapter, acquire
any shares of its own stock by gift, bequest or purchase. Any
domestic insurance corporation may, by the direction and consent of two-thirds of its board of directors, managers or finance
committee, invest, by loan or otherwise, any such surplus moneys
or funds in the bonds issued by any city, county, town, village or
school district of this state, pursuant to any law of this state.
Any corporation organized under subdivision one-a, section one
hundred and seventy of this chapter, for guaranteeing the validity
and legality of bonds issued by any state, or by any city, county,
town, village, school district, municipality or other civil division
of any state, may invest by loan or otherwise any of such surplus
moneys or funds [6]as provided in section one hundred of this chapter. Every such domestic corporation doing business in other
states of the United States or in foreign countries, may invest
[7]its funds in the same kind of securities in such other states or
foreign countries as[8] such corporation is by law allowed to invest
in, in this state. [9]Any life insurance company may lend to any
policyholder upon the security of the value of his policy a sum
not exceeding the lawful reserve which it holds thereon, and such
loan shall become due and payable and be satisfied as provided
in the loan agreement or policy. But nothing in this section
shall be held to authorize one insurance corporation to obtain, by
purchase or otherwise, the control of any other insurance
corporation.

§ 3. Section thirty-nine of such chapter, as amended by chapter
six hundred and thirty-four of the laws of nineteen hundred and
ten, is hereby amended to read as follows:

§ 39. **Examiners and examinations.** The superintendent of insurance shall, as often as he deems it expedient, and, if a domestic
life or casualty[10] insurance corporation, at least once in three years,
or, if any other domestic insurance corporation, association, society
or order, at least once in five years, examine into the affairs of any
insurance corporation doing business in this state, and into the

§ 39, as
amended by
L. 1910,
ch. 634,
amended.

---

[6] Remainder of sentence formerly read: "in the bonds which they are authorized to guarantee."
[7] Words "the funds required to meet its obligation incurred in such other
states or foreign countries and in conformity to the laws thereof," omitted.
Words "its funds" new.
[8] Word "as" substituted for word "that."
[9] Following sentence formerly read: "Any life insurance company may lend
a sum not exceeding the lawful reserve which it holds upon any policy, on
the pledge to it of such policy and its accumulations as collateral security."
[10] Words "or casualty" new.

affairs of any corporation organized under any law of this state or having an office in this state, which corporation is engaged in or is claiming or advertising that it is engaged in organizing or receiving subscriptions for or disposing of stock of, or in any manner aiding or taking part in the formation or business of, an insurance corporation or corporations, or which is holding the capital stock of one or more insurance corporations for the purpose of controlling the management thereof as voting trustee or otherwise. For such purpose he may appoint as examiners one or more competent persons not officers of or connected with or interested in any insurance corporation other than as policyholders; and upon such examination he, his deputy or any examiner authorized by him may examine under oath the officers and agents of such corporation and all persons deemed to have material information regarding the company's property or business. Every such corporation, its officers and agents, shall produce its books and all papers in its or their possession relating to its business or affairs, and any other person may be required to produce any book or paper in his custody deemed to be relevant to the examination, for the inspection of the superintendent, his deputies or examiners whenever required; and the officers and agents of such corporation shall facilitate such examination and aid the examiners in making the same so far as it is in their power to do so. Every such examiner shall make a full and true report of every examination made by him, verified by his oath, which shall comprise only facts appearing upon the books, papers, records or documents of such corporation, or ascertained from the testimony, sworn to, of its officers or agents or other persons examined under oath concerning its affairs, and such conclusions and recommendations as may reasonably be warranted from such facts so disclosed, and said report so verified shall when filed[11] be presumptive evidence in any action or proceeding in the name of the people against the corporation, its officers or agents, of the facts stated therein. The superintendent shall grant a hearing to the corporation examined before filing any such report; and may withhold any such report from public inspection for such time as he may deem proper and may, if he deems it for the interest of the public to do so, publish any such report or the result of any such examination as contained therein, in one or more newspapers of the state.

---

[11] Words " when filed " new.

§ 4. Section seventy of such chapter, as amended by chapter three hundred and two of the laws of nineteen hundred and nine, chapter six hundred and thirty-seven of the laws of nineteen hundred and ten, chapter three hundred and twenty-four of the laws of nineteen hundred and eleven and chapters two hundred and thirty-one and two hundred and thirty-two of the laws of nineteen hundred and twelve, is hereby amended to read as follows:

§ 70. **Incorporation.** Thirteen or more persons may become a corporation for the purpose of making any of the following kinds of insurance:

1. Upon the lives or the health of persons and every insurance appertaining thereto, and to grant, purchase or dispose of annuities.

2. Against injury, disablement or death resulting from traveling or general accident, and against disablement resulting from sickness and every insurance appertaining thereto.

3. Insuring any one (a) against loss or damage resulting from accident to or injury suffered by an employee or other person, and for which the person insured is liable, and (b) against loss or damage to property caused by horses or by any vehicle drawn by animal power, and for which loss or damage the person insured is liable.

4. Guaranteeing the fidelity of persons holding places of public or private trust. Guaranteeing the performance of contracts other than insurance policies; guaranteeing the performance of insurance contracts where surety bonds are accepted by states or municipalities;[12] and executing or guaranteeing bonds and undertakings required or permitted in all actions or proceedings or by law allowed.[13]

4-a.[14] Guaranteeing and indemnifying merchants, traders and those engaged in business and giving credit from loss and damage by reason of giving and extending credit to their customers and those dealing with them; and corporations authorized to do such last named business in this subdivision mentioned shall have all the powers conferred by section one hundred and seventy-eight of this chapter.

5.[15] Against loss by burglary, theft or forgery or any one or more of such hazards.

Marginal note: § 70, as amended by L. 1909, ch. 302, L. 1910, ch. 637, L. 1911, ch. 324, and L. 1912, chaps. 231, 232, amended.

---

[12] Words " in lieu of actual deposits," omitted.
[13] Word " allowed " substituted for word " required."
[14] Subd. 4a new.
[15] Subd. 5 formerly read: " 5. Against loss by burglary or theft, or both."

6. Upon glass against breakage.

7. Upon steam boilers and pipes, fly-wheels, engines and machinery connected therewith or operated thereby, against explosion and accident and against loss or damage to life or property resulting therefrom and against loss of use and occupancy caused thereby, and to make inspection of and to issue certificates of inspection upon such boilers, pipes, fly-wheels, engines and machinery.

8. Upon the lives of horses, cattle and other live stock or against loss by the theft of any of such property or both.[16]

9. Against loss or damage to automobiles (except loss or damage by fire, or while being transported in any conveyance by land or water), including loss by legal liability for damage to property resulting from the maintenance and use of automobiles.

10. Against loss or damage by water to any goods or premises, arising from the breakage or leakage of sprinklers, pumps or other apparatus erected for extinguishing fires, and of water pipes, and against accidental injury to such sprinklers, pumps or other apparatus.

By making and filing in the office of the superintendent of insurance a certificate signed by each of them, stating their intention to form a corporation for the purpose or purposes named in some one of the foregoing subdivisions specifying the subdivisions; and setting forth a copy of the charter which they propose to adopt, which shall state the name of the proposed corporation, the place where it is to be located, the kind of insurance to be undertaken, and under which of the foregoing subdivisions it is authorized, the mode and manner in which its corporate powers are to be exercised, the manner of electing its directors and officers, a majority of whom shall be citizens and residents of this state, the time of such elections, the manner of filling vacancies, the amount of its capital, if any, and such other particulars as may be necessary to explain and make manifest the objects and purposes of the corporation.

Such certificate shall be proved or acknowledged and recorded in a book to be kept for that purpose, and a certified copy thereof delivered to the persons executing the same. A mutual company. without capital stock, may be organized for the purposes either separately or taken together, specified in the first and second subdivisions of this section. Except as above provided, no such

---

[16] Words " or against loss by the theft of any such property or both," new.

corporation shall be formed under this article for the purpose of undertaking any other kind of insurance than that specified in some one of the foregoing subdivisions, or more kinds of insurance than are specified in a single subdivision; but a corporation other than a mutual corporation may be formed for all the purposes combined, or any two or more of them, specified in the first and second subdivision and clause (a) of the third subdivision, or for all the purposes combined, or any two or more of them specified in the second, third, fourth, fifth, sixth, seventh, eighth, ninth and tenth[17] subdivisions; provided, however, that policies under subdivision nine shall be issued only by companies authorized to issue policies under subdivision two, three or five. No corporation or association shall transact, in connection with any other kind of insurance mentioned in the foregoing subdivisions, the business of guaranteeing and indemnifying merchants, traders and those engaged in business and giving credit from loss and damage by reason of giving and extending credit to their customers and those dealing with them, except such corporation or association as was authorized to transact such business before June first, nineteen hundred and five; but such corporation or association may continue to transact such business with all the powers and privileges theretofore possessed or enjoyed by it. No one policy issued by any one corporation shall embrace more kinds of insurance than are specified in one of such subdivisions, except that a policy may embrace risks specified in subdivisions one and two, and in subdivision two and clause (a) of subdivision three, and also that companies electing to issue policies under subdivision nine may embrace in one policy risks under subdivision two, clause (a) of subdivision three, and subdivisions five and nine, or either of them.

§ 5. Section eighty-four of such chapter, as amended by chapter three hundred and one of the laws of nineteen hundred and nine and chapter six hundred and sixteen of the laws of nineteen hundred and ten, is hereby amended to read as follows: § 84, as amended by L. 1909, ch. 301, and L. 1910, ch. 616, amended.

§ 84. **Valuation of policies.** The superintendent of insurance shall annually make valuations of all outstanding policies, additions thereto, unpaid dividends, and all other obligations of every life insurance corporation doing business in this state. All valuations made by him or by his authority shall be made upon the

---

[17] Inclusion of tenth subdivision, new.

net premium basis. The legal minimum standard for contracts issued before the first day of January, nineteen hundred and one, shall be the actuaries' or combined experience table of mortality with interest at four per centum per annum, and for contracts issued on or after said day shall be the American experience table of mortality with interest at three and one-half per centum per annum; provided that the legal minimum valuation of all contracts issued on or after the first day of January, nineteen hundred and seven, shall be in accordance with the select and ultimate method, and on the basis that the rate of mortality during the first five years after the issuance of said contracts respectively shall be calculated according to the following percentages of the rates shown by the American experience table of mortality, to wit: first insurance year fifty per centum thereof, second insurance year sixty-five per centum thereof, third insurance year seventy-five per centum thereof, fourth insurance year eighty-five per centum thereof, and fifth insurance year ninety-five per centum thereof. The superintendent may vary the standards of interest and mortality in the case of corporations from foreign countries as to contracts issued by such corporations in other countries than the United States; and in particular cases of invalid lives and other extra hazards, and value policies in groups, use approximate averages for fractions of a year and otherwise, and accept the valuation of the department of insurance of any other state or country if made upon the basis and according to the standards herein required in place of the valuation herein required.[18] No policy issued after the thirty-first day of December, nineteen hundred and six, shall be valued as term insurance unless premiums are based upon net term rates; and no policy with level premiums issued after said date shall be valued as term insurance for the first policy year. The legal minimum standard for the valuation of annuities issued after January first, nineteen hundred and seven, shall be McClintock's " Tables of Mortality among Annuitants " with interest at three and one-half per centum per annum, but annuities deferred ten or more years and written in connection with life or term insurances shall be valued on the same mortality table from which the consideration or premiums were computed, with interest not higher than three and one-half per centum per annum. The

---

[18] Words " if the insurance officer of such state or country accepts as sufficient and valid for all purposes the certificate of valuation of the superintendent of insurance of this state," omitted.

legal minimum standard for the valuation of industrial policies issued after the first day of January, nineteen hundred and seven,
shall be the American experience table of mortality with interest at
three and one-half per centum per annum, provided, that any life
insurance corporation may voluntarily value its industrial policies
written on the weekly premium payment plan according to the
standard industrial mortality table or the substandard industrial
mortality table.   Any life insurance corporation may voluntarily
value its policies, or any class thereof, according to the American
experience table of mortality, or if industrial, at its option, according to the standard industrial mortality table or substandard
industrial mortality table, at a lower rate of interest than that
above prescribed, but not lower than three per centum per annum.
and with or without reference to the select and ultimate method
of valuation, and in every such case shall report[19] the standards
used by it in making the same to the superintendent of insurance
in its annual statement, provided that no such standards, if
adopted, shall be abandoned without the consent of the superintendent of insurance first obtained in writing.

§ 6. Subdivision one of section eighty-six of such chapter as
amended by chapter one hundred and eighty-three of the laws of
nineteen hundred and eleven, is hereby amended to read as follows:

1. In estimating the condition of any life insurance corporation, under the provisions of this chapter, or in any examination
made by him, or by an examiner appointed by him, the superintendent shall allow as assets only such investments as are
authorized by the laws of this state,[20] and shall charge as
liabilities, in addition to the capital stock, all outstanding
indebtedness of the corporation, and the premium reserve
on policies, and additions thereto in force computed according to the table of mortality and rate of interest prescribed in this
article.   Any assets or securities lawfully held or acquired for
the satisfaction, reduction or guaranty of any indebtedness to the
corporation shall be allowed as assets at their just value in the
judgment of the superintendent, but the total assets, invested and
otherwise, of every domestic life insurance corporation shall be
held to be accumulations for the exclusive benefit of policyholders,
and no payment to stockholders shall be made therefrom until all

Marginal notes: § 86, subd. 1, as amended by L. 1911, ch. 183, amended.   Assets and liabilities of life and casualty insurance corporations; method of computation.

---

[19] Words " any excess of its valuations over those computed by the said legal
minimum standard and also," omitted.
[20] Words " at the date of examination," new.

obligations to policyholders and creditors have been fully provided for, including the reserve required by section eighty-four of this chapter to be determined by the superintendent of insurance.

Procedure in case of impair- ment of capital stock. Whenever it shall appear to the said superintendent from the statement of any life insurance corporation made to the insurance department, or from an examination of the affairs of any such corporation, if a stock corporation, that its capital stock is impaired to the extent of fifty per centum thereof upon the basis of such reserve liability for policies and annuities in force as may be the standard used within this state at the time of ascertaining such impairment, it shall be the duty of said superintendent, if the corporation is organized under the laws of any other state or country, to revoke the certificate of authority issued to the agent or agents of such corporation, and cause a notice thereof to be published in the state paper for four weeks, and the agent or agents of such corporation are, after such notice, required to discontinue the issuing of any new policies. If the corporation so impaired is organized under the laws of this state, it shall be the duty of said superintendent to direct the officers thereof to require the stockholders to make good in cash the amount of such deficiency within ninety days after the date of his requisition. And upon the failure of the stockholders to make good such deficiency within the time specified in such requisition, the corporation shall then be subject to the provisions of section twenty-one of this chapter. Provided, that any corporation organized under the laws of this state, whose capital is impaired as above fifty per centum, may by a vote of a majority of its directors at a meeting called for that purpose reduce its capital stock to an amount not less than one hundred thousand dollars; and the said directors are hereby empowered to issue new certificates of stock to the stockholders for the amount of the reduced capital, and require in return all certificates previously issued.

§ 96, as amended by L. 1910, ch. 697, and L. 1911, ch. 369, amended. § 7. Section ninety-six of such chapter, as amended by chapter six hundred and ninety-seven of the laws of nineteen hundred and ten and chapter three hundred and sixty-nine of the laws of nineteen hundred and eleven, is hereby amended to read as follows:

§ 96. **Limitation of new business.** No domestic life insurance corporation shall issue in any year new policies for a larger amount in the aggregate than as follows, to wit: If the total amount of insurance by said corporation in force on the thirty-first day of December of the preceding year is more than fifty million dollars, and not in excess of one hundred million dollars, not more than thirty per centum thereof; if more than one hundred million dollars, and not in excess of three hundred million dollars, not more than twenty-five per centum thereof, or thirty million dollars, whichever is the larger; if more than three hundred million dollars, and not in excess of six hundred million dollars, not more than twenty per centum thereof, or seventy-five million dollars, whichever is the larger; if more than six hundred million dollars, not more than one hundred and fifty million dollars, or it may increase its new business over the largest amount issued in any one of the three years immediately preceding in the proportion in respect to said amount which the difference between twenty-five per centum of its net renewal premiums computed according to the bases of mortality and interest assumed in calculating its liabilities, and its total expenses for such preceding year, after deducting from said total expenses, (1) the items of the first year expenditure specified in the first sentence of section ninety-seven of this chapter, (2) its actual investment expenses (not exceeding one-fourth of one per centum of the mean invested assets) and (3) taxes on real estate and other outlays exclusively in connection with real estate, bears to said net renewal premiums; provided, that in determining the amount of insurance in force and the amount of new insurance issued, policies of reinsurance and industrial policies issued upon the weekly premium plan and all premiums on such policies and the expenses in connection with such policies, shall be excluded and there shall be included only that insurance upon which the first premium or installment thereof has actually been received. [21]If it appear that in the ordinary course of its business for any calendar year the amount of insurance issued by any corporation will probably exceed the limitation imposed by this section, the superintendent of insurance may before the expiration of such year authorize such corporation in writing to issue additional insurance not to exceed ten per centum of the limitation for such year; but such additional insurance shall be charged as a part of the new policies for the next succeeding year, in accordance with the limitations of this section. A foreign life insurance corporation, which shall not conduct its business within the limitation and in accordance with the requirements imposed by this section upon domestic corporations, shall not be permitted to do business within this state.

---

[21] Following sentence new.

§ 97, as amended by L. 1909, ch. 301, and L. 1910, ch. 697, amended.

§ 8. Section ninety-seven of such chapter as amended by chapter three hundred and one of the laws of nineteen hundred and nine, and chapter six hundred and ninety-seven of the laws of nineteen hundred and ten, is hereby amended to read as follows:

§ 97. **Limitation of expenses.** No domestic life insurance corporation shall in any calendar year, after the year nineteen hundred and six, expend or become liable for, including any and all amounts which any person, firm or corporation is permitted to expend on its behalf or under any agreement with it (1) for commissions on first year's premiums, (2) for compensation, not paid by commission, for services in obtaining new insurance exclusive of salaries paid in good faith for agency supervision either at the home office or at branch offices, (3) for medical examinations and inspections of proposed risks, and (4) for advances to agents, a total amount exceeding in the aggregate (a) the loadings upon the premiums for the first year of insurance received in said calendar year (calculated on the basis of the American experience table of mortality with interest at the rate of three and one-half per centum per annum) and (b) the present values of the assumed mortality gains for the first five years of insurance on policies in force at the end of said calendar year on which the first premium, or instalment thereof, has been received during said calendar year, as ascertained by the select and ultimate method of valuation as provided in section eighty-four of this chapter; and (c) on policies issued and terminated in said calendar year the full gross premiums received, less the net cost of insurance for the time the insurance was in force, computed by the American experience select and ultimate table, three and one-half per centum. No such corporation shall make or incur any expense or permit any expense to be made or incurred upon its behalf or under any agreement with it, except actual investment expenses (not exceeding one-fourth of one per centum of the mean invested assets) and also except taxes on real estate and other outlays exclusively in connection with real estate, in excess of the aggregate amount of the actual loadings upon premiums received in said year calculated according to the standards adopted by the company under section eighty-four of this chapter, and the present values of the assumed mortality gains hereinbefore mentioned. No such corporation, nor any person, firm or corporation on its behalf or under any agreement with it shall pay

or allow to any agent, broker or other person, firm or corporation
for procuring an application for life insurance, for collecting any
premium thereon or for any other service performed in connection
therewith any compensation other than that which has been determined in advance. Except as hereinafter provided[22] all
bonuses, prizes and rewards, and all increased or additional commissions or compensation of any sort based upon the volume of
any new or renewed business or the aggregate of policies written
or paid for, are prohibited. [23]Nothing herein contained is to be
construed as prohibiting the institution of contests or competitions
among agents, and the recognition of success in such competitions
by the awarding of ribbon decorations, medals, pins, buttons or
other tokens of small intrinsic value, given not as compensation
but as a bona fide recognition of merit. No such corporation
shall pay commissions upon renewal premiums received upon policies issued after the year nineteen hundred and six, in excess of
five per centum of the premium annually for fourteen years after
the first year of insurance in the case of endowment policies providing for less than twenty annual premiums, nor in excess of
seven and one-half per centum of the premium annually for the
first nine years after the first year of insurance and five per
centum of the premium annually for the next ensuing five years
in the case of other forms of policies; provided that an amount
found to be equivalent to the aggregate amount so payable by a
calculation approved by the superintendent of insurance and
based upon mortality, interest and lapse rates, may be distributed
through three or more years, or through a period exceeding fourteen years, but not more than two-fifths of such amount shall be
payable for any one year; provided further that in any agency
district subject to the supervision of a local salaried representative the renewal commission payable to agents of such district
shall not exceed two-thirds of the foregoing rates annually for
fourteen years, subject to the calculation as aforesaid; provided
further that any such corporation may condition the allowance or
payment in whole or in part of any of the renewal commissions
allowed to be paid as aforesaid upon the efficiency of service of
the agent receiving the same or upon the amount and quality of
the business renewed under his supervision; and also provided that
a fee not exceeding three per centum may be paid for the collec-

---

[22] Words " Except as hereinafter provided," new.
[23] Following sentence new.

tion of premiums which shall be received for any year after the
fifteenth year of insurance. If any such corporation shall compensate its agents, or any of them, after the first insurance year,
in whole or in part, upon any other plan than commissions and
collection fees, the aggregate sum so paid shall in no year exceed
the limitations herein imposed and the schedule and plan of such
compensation shall be submitted to and approved by the superintendent of insurance. No such corporation, nor any person, firm
or corporation on its behalf or under any agreement with it, shall
make any loan or advance to any person, firm or corporation so-
liciting or undertaking to solicit applications for insurance without adequate collateral security, nor shall any such loan or advance be made upon the security of renewal commissions, or of
other compensation earned or to be earned by the borrower except
advances against compensation for the first year of insurance. A
foreign life insurance corporation which shall not conduct its business within the limitations and in accordance with the requirements
imposed by this section upon domestic corporations shall not be
permitted to do business within the state. This section shall not
apply to expenses made or incurred in the business of industrial
insurance nor, except as to the limitation of expenses for the first
year of insurance and as to compensation of and loans and advances to agents or solicitors, to stock corporations issuing and
representing themselves as issuing non-participating policies
exclusively.

§ 134
amended.

§ 9. Section one hundred and thirty-four of such chapter is
hereby amended to read as follows:

§ 134. Undertaking of agent. No person shall, as agent for
any such foreign insurance corporation, association or individuals, effect any insurance upon any property situate in any city
or village of this state upon which the sums specified in the preceding section are required to be paid; or as such agent procure
such insurance to be effected, until he shall have executed and
delivered to the officer to whom such account is to be rendered
and such payments to be made, a bond to such fire department in
the penal sum of five hundred dollars, with such sureties as such
treasurer, supervisor or other fiscal officer shall approve, with a
condition that he will annually render to such treasurer, supervisor or other fiscal officer, on the first day of February in each
year a just and true account, verified by his oath that the same
is true, of all premiums which, during the year ending on the

thirty-first day of December preceding such report, shall have been received by him or any other person for him, for any insurance against loss or injury by fire upon property situated in such city or village, which shall have been effected or procured by him to have been effected by any such corporation, association or individuals, and that he will annually, on the first day of February in each year, pay to such treasurer or supervisor or other fiscal officer two dollars upon every hundred dollars, and at that rate upon the amount of such premiums. [24]If any such agent shall desire to transact business in more than one city, town or village, he may, instead of executing and delivering a separate bond for each such city, town or village, as required by this section, execute and file with the superintendent of insurance a bond in the penal sum of fifteen hundred dollars, with such sureties as the superintendent shall approve, conditioned that he will make his account and pay the sums so required to be paid in each city, town or village in which he shall effect insurance. Any such corporation, association or individual, having authority to transact business in this state, on filing a bond in the penal sum of two thousand five hundred dollars with the superintendent of insurance that it will make its account and pay the sum so required to be paid, may effect such insurance in any city, town or village wherein it has no agent.

§ 10. This act shall take effect immediately.

Chap. 305.

AN ACT to amend the stock corporation law, in relation to the certificate of increase or reduction of capital stock of a banking or insurance corporation.

Became a law April 17, 1913, with the approval of the Governor. Passed, three-fifths being present.

The People of the State of New York, represented in Senate and Assembly, do enact as follows:

Section 1. Section sixty-four of chapter sixty-one of the laws of nineteen hundred and nine, entitled " An act relating to stock

---

[24] Following sentence new.

corporations, constituting chapter fifty-nine of the consolidated laws," is hereby amended to read as follows:

§ 64. **Conduct of such meeting; certificate of increase or reduction.** If, at the time and place specified in the notice, the stockholders shall appear in person or by proxy in numbers representing at least a majority of all the shares of stock, they shall organize by choosing from their number a chairman and secretary, and take a vote of those present in person or by proxy, and if a sufficient number of votes shall be given in favor of such increase or reduction, or if the same shall have been authorized by the unanimous consent of stockholders expressed in writing signed by them or their duly authorized proxies, a certificate of the proceedings showing a compliance with the provisions of this chapter, the amount of capital theretofore authorized, and the proportion thereof actually issued, and the amount of the increased or reduced capital stock, and in case of the reduction of capital stock the whole amount of the ascertained debts and liabilities of the corporation, shall be made, signed, verified and acknowledged by the chairman and secretary of the meeting, and filed in the office of the clerk of the county where its principal place of business shall be located, [1]a duplicate thereof in the office of the secretary of state, [2]and, if a corporation formed under or subject to the banking law, a triplicate thereof in the office of the superintendent of banks, and if an insurance corporation, a triplicate thereof in the office of the superintendent of insurance. In case of a reduction of the capital stock, except of a railroad corporation or a moneyed corporation, such certificate or consent hereinafter provided for shall have indorsed thereon the approval of the comptroller, to the effect that the reduced capital is sufficient for the proper purposes of the corporation, and is in excess of its ascertained debts and liabilities; and in case of the increase or reduction of the capital stock of a railroad corporation or a moneyed corporation, the certificate or the unanimous consent of stockholders, as the case may be, shall have indorsed thereon the approval of the public service commission having jurisdiction thereof, if a railroad corporation; of the superintendent of banks, if a corporation formed under or subject to the banking law, and of the superintendent of insurance, if an insurance corporation. When the certificate herein provided for, or the unanimous consent of stockholders in writing, signed by

---

[1] Word " and " omitted.
[2] Remainder of sentence new.

them or their duly authorized proxies, approved as aforesaid, has been filed, the capital stock of such corporation shall be increased or reduced, as the case may be, to the amount specified in such certificate or consent. The proceedings of the meeting at which such increase or reduction is voted, or, if such increase or reduction shall have been authorized by unanimous consent without a meeting, then a copy of such consent shall be entered upon the minutes of the corporation. If the capital stock is reduced, the amount of capital over and above the amount of the reduced capital shall, if the meeting or consents so determine or provide, be returned to the stockholders pro rata, at such times and in such manner as the directors shall determine, except in the case of the reduction of the capital stock of an insurance corporation, as an alternative to make good an existing impairment.

§ 2. This act shall take effect immediately.

Chap. 306.

AN ACT to amend the general corporation law, in relation to the extension of corporate existence of insurance and banking corporations.

Became a law April 17, 1913, with the approval of the Governor. Passed, three-fifths being present.

The People of the State of New York, represented in Senate and Assembly, do enact as follows:

Section 1. Section thirty-seven of chapter twenty-eight of the laws of nineteen hundred and nine, entitled "An act relating to corporations generally, constituting chapter twenty-three of the consolidated laws," is hereby amended to read as follows: L. 1909, ch. 28, § 37 amended.

§ 37. **Extension of corporate existence.** Any domestic corporation at any time before the expiration thereof, may extend the term of its existence beyond the time specified in its original certificate of incorporation, or by law, or in any certificate of extension of corporate existence, by the consent of the stockholders owning two-thirds in amount of its capital stock, or if not a stock corporation, by the consent of two-thirds of its members, which consent shall be given either in writing or by vote at a special meeting of the stockholders called for that purpose, upon the same notice as that required for the annual meetings of the corporation;

and a certificate under the seal of the corporation that such consent was given by the stockholders in writing, or that it was given by vote at a meeting as aforesaid, shall be subscribed and acknowledged by the president or a vice-president, and by the secretary or an assistant secretary of the corporation, and if a corporation formed under or subject to the banking law[1] shall be filed in the office of the superintendent of banks, if an insurance corporation, in the office of the superintendent of insurance, and otherwise[2] in the office of the secretary of state, and shall by such officer[3] be duly recorded and indexed in a book specially provided therefor, and a certified copy of such certificate, with a certificate of such officer[4] of such filing and record, or a duplicate original of such certificate, shall be filed and similarly recorded and indexed in the office of the clerk of the county wherein the corporation has its principal place of business, and shall be noted in the margin of the record of the original certificates of such corporation, if any, in such offices, and thereafter the term of the existence of such corporation shall be extended as designated in such certificate.

The certificate of incorporation of any corporation whose duration is limited by such certificate or by law, may require that the consent of the stockholders owning a greater percentage than two-thirds of the stock, if a stock corporation, or of more than two-thirds of the members, if a non-stock corporation, shall be requisite to effect an extension of corporate existence as authorized by this section.

§ 2. This act shall take effect immediately.

---

[1] Words " if a corporation formed under or subject to the banking law," new.

[2] Words " in the office of the superintendent of banks, if an insurance corporation, in the office of the superintendent of insurance, and otherwise," new.

[3] Words " such officer " substituted for word " him."

[4] Words " such officer " substituted for words " the secretary of state."

Chap. 307.

AN ACT to extend the boundaries of the city of Utica by annexing thereto a part of the town of New Hartford, and to provide. for the government of the territory so annexed.

Became a law April 17, 1913, with the approval of the Governor. Passed, three-fifths being present.

Accepted by the City.

The People of the State of New York, represented in Senate and Assembly, do enact as follows:

Section 1. All that part of the town of New Hartford hereinafter bounded and described, is annexed to and shall form a part of the city of Utica, to wit: Beginning at an iron pipe in the boundary line between the city of Utica and the town of New Hartford, said point being located in the easterly line of Churchill avenue, and nine hundred and fifty and five tenths feet southerly from the northwest corner of the state hospital grounds, as fenced; thence north eighty-six degrees and two minutes west, along the boundary line between the city of Utica and the town of New Hartford, one thousand four hundred and eleven feet to an iron pipe; thence south forty-two degrees and thirty minutes west, four thousand one hundred and eight feet to an iron pipe in the southerly line of the Burrstone road; thence along the southerly line of the Burrstone road south sixty-three degrees and thirty-six minutes east, one thousand and seven feet to an iron pipe; thence continuing along the southerly line of the Burrstone road, south eighty-one degrees and forty-one minutes east, two hundred and seventy feet to a stone monument in the city line; thence along said boundary line between the city of Utica and the town of New Hartford, north forty-two degrees and thirty-eight minutes east, about four thousand five hundred and twenty-seven and five-tenths feet to the place of beginning. *Territory annexed. Description.*

§ 2. All that part of the town of New Hartford, hereinafter bounded and described, is hereby annexed to and shall form a part of the city of Utica, to wit: Beginning at a point on the easterly line of Tilden avenue two hundred feet from the northeasterly corner of Tilden avenue and Pleasant street; running thence north forty-three degrees thirty minutes east, along the easterly line of Tilden avenue two thousand nine hundred and forty feet to a monument in the easterly side of Tilden avenue, *Territory annexed. Description.*

forming the present line between the city of Utica and the town
of New Hartford; thence south forty-six degrees twenty minutes
east, four thousand and fifty-six feet to the Herkimer county
line; thence south forty-three degrees thirty minutes west, along
the Herkimer county line two thousand four hundred and ten feet
to a point in the Herkimer county line; thence north forty-six
degrees thirty minutes west, one thousand two hundred and fourteen feet; thence north forty-three degrees forty-two minutes east,
one hundred and sixty-five feet; thence north thirty-seven degrees
six minutes west, seven hundred and thirty-nine feet; thence
north fifty-four degrees twelve minutes west, eight hundred and
eighteen feet; thence south fifty-three degrees twenty-three
minutes west, one hundred and eighty-four feet; thence south
forty-six degrees fifty-three minutes west, three hundred and
ninety-two feet to a point two hundred feet northerly of the
northerly line of Pleasant street; thence north thirty-seven degrees twelve minutes west, one thousand three hundred and forty-
five feet to the place of beginning.

Made part of certain wards.

§ 3. All the territory described in the first section of this act,
hereby annexed to said city, shall be a part of. the seventh ward
of said city, and all that part described in the second section of
this act, shall be a part of the twelfth ward of said city.

Application of laws relating to Utica.

§ 4. All the laws applicable to the city of Utica, not inconsistent with the provisions of this act, shall be deemed to apply
and shall apply to the territory annexed to the city of Utica by
the provisions of this act, and described in the first and second
sections hereof.

Property to belong to city.

§ 5. All the property belonging to the town of New Hartford
or to any school district situated in the territory hereby annexed
to said city, shall hereafter belong to the city of Utica. All the
bonded indebtedness, including principal and interest, of any
school district, the whole or any part of whose territory is by this
act annexed to the city of Utica, and such portion of the bonded
indebtedness of the town of New Hartford, including principal
and interest, as shall be a charge upon the territory hereby annexed, shall be a charge upon, and shall be paid by the city of
Utica, as the same shall become due and payable, and in the same
proportion to the whole debt of such town or school district as the
assessed valuation of the part of such school district or town
hereby annexed to said city, bears to the whole valuation of said
school district or of said town, as shown by the last assessment roll

Apportion-
ment of
bonded in-
debtedness.

of the town of New Hartford, made prior to the passage of this act. All unpaid taxes heretofore levied against said annexed territory, shall be due and payable and collected in all respects the same as if this law had not been enacted. Unpaid taxes.

§ 6. All acts and parts of acts inconsistent with the provisions of this act, are hereby repealed. Inconsistent acts.

§ 7. This act shall take effect immediately.

Chap. 308.

AN ACT to amend the general business law, in relation to the operation of the cinematograph or any other apparatus for projecting moving pictures.

Became a law April 17, 1913, with the approval of the Governor. Passed, three-fifths being present.

The People of the State of New York, represented in Senate and Assembly, do enact as follows:

Section 1. Article twelve-a of chapter twenty-five of the laws of nineteen hundred and nine, entitled "An act relating to general business, constituting chapter twenty of the consolidated laws," as added by chapter seven hundred and fifty-six of the laws of nineteen hundred and eleven, is hereby amended to read as follows: L. 1909. ch. 25, art. 12a, as added by L. 1911, ch. 756, amended.

ARTICLE 12-A.

PUBLIC ENTERTAINMENTS OR EXHIBITIONS BY CINEMATOGRAPH OR ANY OTHER APPARATUS FOR PROJECTING MOVING PICTURES.

Section 209. Fireproof booth for cinematograph or any other apparatus for projecting moving pictures.

210. Construction of booth; approval of plans and specifications.

211.[1] This article not retroactive under certain conditions.

212.[2] Inspection; certificate for permanent booths.

213.[3] Portable booth for temporary exhibitions.

---

[1] Section 211 new.
[2] Formerly § 211. Words "for permanent booths," new.
[3] Section 213 new.

§ 209. **Fireproof booth for cinematograph or any other apparatus for projecting moving pictures.** No cinematograph or any
other apparatus for projecting moving pictures, save as excepted
in sections two hundred and eleven and two hundred and thirteen
of this article, which apparatus uses combustible films of more
than ten inches in length, shall be set up for use or used in any
building, place of public assemblage or entertainment, unless such
apparatus for the projecting of moving pictures shall be inclosed
therein in a booth or inclosure constructed of concrete, brick, hollow
tile or other approved fireproof material or any approved fireproof framework[7] covered or lined with asbestos board, or with
some other approved[8] fire resisting material, and unless such
booth shall have been constructed as provided in section two
hundred and ten of this article and the certificate provided in
section two hundred and twelve[9] of this article shall have been
issued to the owner or lessee of the premises wherein such booth
is situated.

§ 210. **Construction of booth; approval of plans and specifications.** The booths provided for in section two hundred and nine
of this article shall be constructed according to plans and specifications which shall have been first approved, in a city, by the mayor
or chief executive officer of the city department having supervision
of the erection of buildings in such city; in a village, by the president of such village; in a town outside the boundaries of a city or
village, by the supervisor of such town. Provided, however, that
no plans and specifications for the construction of such booths
shall be approved by any public official, unless the following requirements are substantially provided for in such plans and
specifications:

---

[4] Section 214 new.
[5] Section 215 new.
[6] Formerly § 212.
[7] Words "concrete, brick, hollow tile or other approved fireproof material or
any approved fireproof framework " substituted for words " iron frame work."
[8] Words "other approved" substituted for words " equally strong and."
[9] Formerly read: " two hundred and eleven."

1. Dimensions. Such booths shall be at least six[10] feet in height. If one machine is to be operated in such booth the floor space shall be not less than forty-eight square feet. If more than one machine is to be operated therein, an additional twenty-four square feet shall be provided for each such additional machine.

2.[11] General specifications. In case such booth is not constructed of concrete, brick, hollow tile or other approved fireproof material than asbestos, such booth shall be constructed with an angle framework of approved fireproof material, the angles to be not less than one and one quarter inches by three-sixteenths of an inch thick, the adjacent members being joined firmly with angle plates of metal. The angle members of the framework shall be spaced not more than four feet apart on the sides and not more than three feet apart on the front and back and top of such booth. The sheets of asbestos board or other approved fire-resisting material shall be at least one-quarter of an inch in thickness and shall be securely attached to the framework by means of metal bolts and rivets. The fire-resisting material shall completely cover the sides, top and all joints of such booth. The floor space occupied by the booth shall be covered with fire-resisting material not less than three-eighths of an inch in thickness. The booth shall be insulated so that it will not conduct electricity to any other portion of the building. There shall be provided for the booth a door not less than two feet wide and five feet ten inches high, consisting of an angle frame of approved fireproof material covered with sheets of approved fireproof material one-quarter of an inch thick, and attached to the framework of the booth by hinges, in such a manner that the door shall be kept closed at all times, when not used for ingress or egress.

The operating windows, one for each machine to be operated therein and one for the operator thereof, shall be no larger than reasonably necessary, to secure the desired service, and shutters of approved fireproof material shall be provided for each window. When the windows are open, the shutters shall be so suspended and arranged that they will automatically close the window openings, upon the operating of some suitable fusible or mechanical releasing device.

Where a booth is so built that it may be constructed to open directly on the outside of the building through a window, such

---

10 Formerly "seven."
11 Subd. 2 materially amended.

window shall be permitted for the comfort of the operator, but such booth shall not be exempted from the requirement of the installation of a vent flue as hereinafter prescribed. Said booth shall contain an approved fireproof box for the storage of films not on the projecting machine. Films shall not be stored in any other place on the premises; they shall be rewound and repaired either in the booth or in some other fireproof inclosure. The booth in which the picture machine is operated shall be provided with an opening or vent flue in its roof or upper part of its side wall leading to the outdoor air. The vent-flue shall have a minimum cross-sectional area of fifty square inches and shall be fireproof. When the booth is in use there shall be a constant current of air passing outward through said opening or vent flue at the rate of not less than thirty cubic feet per minute.

§ 211.[12] **This article not retroactive under certain conditions.** Sections two hundred and nine and two hundred and ten of this article shall not be retroactive for any booth approved by the appropriate public authority or official prior to this article taking effect, provided such booth have or be so reconstructed of the same material as to have dimensions as specified in section two hundred and ten of this article; provided such booth conform to the specification of section two hundred and ten as regards vent flue, box for storage of films, specifications for rewinding and repairing films and specifications for windows and doors, and provided such booth be of rigid fireproof material, and be insulated so as not to conduct electricity to any other part of the building and be so separated from any adjacent combustible material as not to communicate fire through intense heat in case of combustion within the booth.

§ 212.[13] **Inspection; certificate for permanent booths.** After the construction of such booth shall have been completed, the public officer charged herein with the duty of passing upon the plans and specifications therefor shall within three days after receipt of notice in writing that such booth has been completed cause such booth to be inspected. If the provisions of sections two hundred and nine, and two hundred and ten of this article have been complied with,[14] such public officer shall issue to the

---

[12] Section 211 new.
[13] Formerly § 211.
[14] Words "and if, in the judgment of such public officer such booth is otherwise constructed in a manner so as to render safe the operation of apparatus for projecting moving pictures," omitted.

owner or lessee of the premises wherein such booth is situated a certificate stating that the provisions of sections two hundred and nine and two hundred and ten of this article have been complied with.

§ 213.[15] **Portable booth for temporary exhibitions.** Where motion pictures are exhibited daily for not more than one month, or not oftener than three times a week, in educational or religious institutions or bona fide social, scientific, political or athletic clubs, a portable booth may be substituted for the booth required in sections two hundred and nine and two hundred and ten of this article. Such booth shall have a height of not less than six feet and an area of not less than twenty square feet and shall be constructed of asbestos board, sheet steel of no less gauge than twenty-four; or some other approved fireproof material. Such portable booth shall conform to the specifications of section two hundred and ten of this article with reference to windows and door, but not with reference to vent flues. The floor of such booth shall be elevated above the permanent support on which it is placed by a space of at least one-half inch, sufficient to allow the passage of air between the floor of the booth and the platform on which the booth rests, and the booth shall be insulated so that it will not conduct electricity to any other portion of the building.

§ 214.[16] **Exemption and requirements for miniature cinematograph machines.** The above sections, two hundred and nine, two hundred and ten, two hundred and eleven, two hundred and twelve and two hundred and thirteen, referring to permanent and portable booths, shall not apply to any miniature motion picture machine in which the maximum electric current used for the light shall be three hundred and fifty watts. Such miniature machine shall be operated in an approved box of fireproof material constructed with a fusible link or other approved releasing device to close instantaneously and completely in case of combustion within the box. The light in said miniature machine shall be completely inclosed in a metal lantern box covered with an unremovable roof.

§ 215.[17] **Inspection; certificate for portable booths and * miniature cinematograph machines.** Before moving pictures shall be exhibited with a portable booth, under section two hundred and thirteen of this article, and before a miniature machine without a

---

booth shall be used as prescribed in section two hundred and fourteen of this article, there shall be obtained from the appropriate
authority, as defined in section two hundred and ten of this article,
a certificate of approval.

§ 216.[18] **Penalty for violating this article.** The violation of
any of the provisions of this article shall constitute a misdemeanor. This act shall not apply to cities which have local laws
or ordinances now in force which provide for fireproof booths of
any kind for moving picture machines or apparatus.

§ 2. This act shall take effect immediately.

Chap. 309.

AN ACT to amend chapter five hundred and seventy of the laws
of nineteen hundred and nine, entitled "An act to establish
the city court of Buffalo, defining its powers and jurisdiction
and providing for its officers," in relation to the compensation
and lien of attorneys and counsellors in said court.

Became a law April 17, 1913, with the approval of the Governor. Passed,
three-fifths being present.

Accepted by the City.

*The People of the State of New York, represented in Senate
and Assembly, do enact as follows:*

§ 57 added
to L. 1909,
ch. 570.

Section 1. Chapter five hundred and seventy of the laws of
nineteen hundred and nine, entitled "An act to establish the city
court of Buffalo, defining its powers and jurisdiction and providing for its officers," is hereby amended by inserting therein, at
the end of article two, a new section, to be section fifty-seven, to
read as follows:

§ 57. **Attorney or counsel's compensation.** From the commencement of an action in this court, or the service of an answer
containing a counter-claim, the attorney who appears for a party
has a lien upon his client's cause of action, claim or counter-claim,
which attaches to a verdict, decision, judgment or final order in
his client's favor, and the proceeds thereof, in whosesoever hands
they may come; and the lien cannot be affected by any settlement
between the parties before or after judgment or final order. The

---

[18] Formerly § 212.

court upon the petition of the client or attorney may determine and enforce the lien. The provisions of this section shall apply to claims and accounts of attorneys in respect of services hereafter rendered in actions now pending, as well as to actions hereafter brought.

§ 2. This act shall take effect immediately.

Chap. 310.

AN ACT to amend chapter five hundred and forty-seven of the laws of eighteen hundred and ninety, entitled "An act to make the office of county clerk of Chautauqua county a salaried office, and regulating the management of said office," generally.

Became a law April 17, 1913, with the approval of the Governor. Passed, three-fifths being present.

The People of the State of New York, represented in Senate and Assembly, do enact as follows:

Section 1. Section five of chapter five hundred and forty- L. 1890, ch. seven of the laws of eighteen hundred and ninety, entitled 547, § 5 "An act to make the office of county clerk of Chautauqua county amended. a salaried office, and regulating the management of said office," is hereby amended to read as follows:

§ 5. Such clerk shall make a full and true statement for each Monthly calendar month of all moneys received each day by him or by his statement of fees. assistants, for fees, perquisites and emoluments, for all services rendered by him or them in his or their official capacity, and shall transmit and deliver such statement to the county treasurer of said county within ten[1] days from the expiration thereof. Such statement shall specify, in the following order, the amount so What to received for the calendar month: specify.

For recording deeds,
For recording mortgages,
For recording other documents and papers,
For docketing judgments and canceling dockets,
For searches and certificate thereof,
For copies and exemplification of papers and records,
For filing papers, and for any and all other services,

---

[1] Formerly "five."

Affidavit
thereto. and shall also show the total receipts for said month. Every such statement shall have attached thereto an affidavit of said county clerk in effect that the same is in all respects a full and true statement of all moneys by him received as herein required.

§ 2. This act shall take effect immediately.

Chap. 311.

AN ACT making an appropriation for the protection of the forests from fire and the enforcement of the fire provisions of the conservation law.

Became a law April 17, 1913, with the approval of the Governor. Passed by a two-thirds vote.

The People of the State of New York, represented in Senate and Assembly, do enact as follows:

Section 1. The sum of twenty-five thousand dollars ($25,000), is hereby appropriated from any moneys in the treasury, not otherwise appropriated, for the use of the conservation commission in paying traveling expenses, services, supplies and equipment for the enforcement of the fire provisions of the conservation law to be paid by the treasurer on the warrant of the comptroller upon vouchers approved by the said commission.

§ 2. This act shall take effect immediately.

Chap. 312.

AN ACT providing for the erection of a state armory and stable in the city of Buffalo, the acquisition of a site therefor, authorizing the board of supervisors of Erie county to convey county lands for such site, and making an appropriation for building said armory and stable.

Became a law April 17, 1913, with the approval of the Governor. Passed, three-fifths being present.

The People of the State of New York, represented in Senate and Assembly, do enact as follows:

Appropriation. Section 1. The treasurer shall pay on the warrant of the comptroller the sum of twenty-five thousand dollars ($25,000), which sum is hereby appropriated out of any of the moneys in the

treasury not otherwise appropriated, for the erection of an
armory and stable in the city of Buffalo, Erie county, for the
use of troop I, first cavalry of the national guard of the state of
New York, there stationed, to be expended under the direction
of the armory commission of this state. But no part of this ap- Site to be
propriation, except for plans and expenses of the commission, to state.
shall be expended by the said commission until an indefeasible
title, to be approved by the attorney-general, to a suitable site
for such armory, to be approved by said commission, free from
all incumbrances, without expense to the state, shall be vested in
the people of the state, nor until, upon plans and specifications Limitation
of said building or buildings submitted by the state architect to
such commission, they shall be satisfied that the buildings, including necessary sewerage, and necessary expense of the commission and for superintendence and inspection of the work, can
and will be completed within the sum of one hundred and fifty
thousand dollars. Upon the vesting of such title in the state Contracts
and approval thereof, the commission may enter into a struction.
contract or contracts for the construction of such armory and
stable in an amount not exceeding the difference between said
sum of one hundred and fifty thousand dollars and the estimated
expenditure for necessary sewerage and the necessary expense of
the commission and for superintendence and inspection of the
work.

§ 2. Whenever any sum or sums shall become due under any Audit and
contract authorized by this act, the commission shall make and of sums
file with the comptroller a statement thereof and the comptroller
shall thereupon examine and audit the same and draw his warrant
upon the treasurer for the sum he shall find to be due, and such
sum shall be payable out of any moneys theretofore appropriated
and available therefor.

§ 3. The title of said land shall be vested in the people of the Title to
state of New York, and in case the land or any part thereof can- vested in
not be obtained by agreement with the owner or owners thereof, right of
the said commission shall acquire title thereto by the exercise of domain.
the right of eminent domain in proceedings duly taken and had
under and in accordance with the provisions and requirements of
the condemnation law.[1]

§ 4. The site selected for said armory and stable shall not be Dimen-
less than four hundred feet broad and two hundred and fifty feet tion and

---

[1] See code of civil procedure, §§ 3357–3384.

deep, and shall be prominently and conveniently located, and the
cost of said land shall not exceed twenty-five thousand dol-
Plans and specifications. lars.   Plans and specifications of said armory shall be prepared in detail and shall receive the approval of the armory com-
Work to be done by contract. mission, and all work upon said armory structure, except the interior finishing and furnishing, shall be done by contract, exe-
cuted by and between the contractor or contractors and said ar-
Award of contracts. mory commission, which contract or contracts shall be awarded
to the lowest responsible bidder or bidders after due publication
and advertisement based upon said plans and specifications.

Bond of contractor.   § 5. Contractor or contractors for such construction shall, before commencing the same, make and execute to the state a bond
in such sum and with such surety as said armory commission
shall prescribe, conditioned for the faithful performance of such
work of construction.

Issue of certificates of indebtedness by county for purchase of site, etc.   § 6. The county treasurer of the county of Erie, whenever a
written notice shall be served upon him by the said commission
that such land has been contracted for or purchased, or the title
thereto has been acquired as above directed shall execute in behalf of and in the name of the county of Erie a certificate or certificates of indebtedness for the moneys required to purchase such
site, pay the cost of acquiring the title thereto and to pay for the
cost of grading, filling, excavating, draining, paving of the streets,
paving of the sidewalks, and fencing of such lands, and shall after
Sale of certificates. ten days' notice *specify the time and place where bids shall be
received for the purchase of such certificate or certificates, sell
the same to the highest bidder; such notice shall be published
for ten days in two newspapers in the county of Erie.   The afore-
Interest; when payable. said certificate or certificates shall bear interest at the rate of
not to exceed five per centum per annum, and shall be made pay-
able on the first day of February, following the expiration of two
Tax for payment. months from its or their issue, and the amount thereof and the
interest thereon shall be raised in the next tax budget of said
county succeeding its issue, and applied to the payment of such
Issue of bonds in lieu of certificates. certificate; provided, however, that if in the judgment of the
board of supervisors of said county of Erie it shall be deemed for
the best interest of said county not to raise all the funds necessary to pay such certificate or certificates from the tax levy next
succeeding the issuance thereof by the treasurer of said county
as aforesaid, they are hereby authorized and empowered to raise

---

* So in original.

the whole or any portion of the amount of such certificate or certificates by issuing and disposing of bonds of said county in denominations, for such time and in such manner as they may determine, the interest thereof not to exceed five per centum per annum. The proceeds of the sale of such certificate or certificates *Application of proceeds of certificates.* shall be retained by the county treasurer and shall be by him paid out upon written requisition of the aforesaid commission, by which it shall be applied to the payment of the amount of the purchase price or cost of acquiring site, together with the cost of the title thereto, and the grading, excavating, draining, paving of streets, flagging of sidewalks, and fencing of such lands. In case the board of supervisors of the county of Erie shall deem it for the *Appropriation for cost of site, etc.* best interests of said county to pay the amount of the purchase price or cost of such property, together with the cost of acquiring the title thereto and the grading, excavating, draining, paving of streets, flagging of sidewalks and fencing of such lands, they are authorized to appropriate such sums of money as required for such purpose.

§ 7. The board of supervisors of Erie county are hereby author- *Appropriation of land belonging to county for site.* ized and empowered to appropriate such plot or plots of land belonging to said county of Erie or hereafter to be acquired by said county, as a site on which said armory and stable may be erected, as shall receive the approval of the armory commission. Said lands shall be conveyed by said board of supervisors to the state by a good and sufficient deed, the title of said property to be approved by the attorney-general.

§ 8. This act shall take effect immediately.

Chap. 313.

AN ACT to establish the New York commercial tercentenary commission and to prescribe the powers and duties thereof.

Became a law April 17, 1913, with the approval of the Governor. Passed, three-fifths being present.

Accepted by the City.

The People of the State of New York, represented in Senate and Assembly, do enact as follows:

Section 1. Cornelius Vanderbilt, Herman Ridder, Louis Annin *Corporators.* Ames, August Belmont, Union N. Bethell, Henry L. Bogert,

Elmer Ellsworth Brown, Jacob A. Cantor, Andrew Carnegie, Howard Carroll, Joseph H. Choate, Thomas W. Churchill, Cesare Conti, George B. Cortelyou, Fred B. Dalzell, John H. Finley, George J. Gould, Edward Hagaman Hall, Ernest Harvier, Franklin W. Hooper, William A. Johnston, Lucien Jouvard, George F. Kunz, Henry M. Leipziger, A. E. MacKinnon, William A. Marble, J. Pierpont Morgan, William C. Muschenheim, Morgan J. O'Brien, Eben E. Olcott, Henry Fairfield Osborn, Alton B. Parker, N. Taylor Phillips, William C. Reick, Edward V. P. Ritter, John D. Rockefeller, Jr., Henry W. Sackett, Jacob H. Schiff, Isaac N. Seligman, Theodore P. Shonts, Robert A. C. Smith, James Speyer, Charles Steckler, Henry R. Towne, Theodore N. Vail, William R. Willcox, Arthur Williams, William Ziegler, Junior, Berthold Flesch, M. J. Cummings, George R. Dyer, and all such persons as may now or hereafter be associated with them by appointment by the governor of the state of New York or the mayor of the city of New York, together with such persons, not to exceed fifty in number, who may be elected by the trustees of the commission created by this act; the mayors of all of the cities of the state ex-officio, and the presidents of the villages of Athens, Castleton, Catskill, Cold Spring, Corinth, Cornwall, Coxsackie, Croton-on-Hudson, Dobbs Ferry, Fishkill, Fishkill Landing, Fort Edward, Green Island, Hastings-on-Hudson, Haverstraw, Hudson Falls, Irvington, Matteawan, Mechanicville, North Tarrytown, Nyack, Ossining, Peekskill, Piermont, Red Hook, Rhinebeck, Saugerties, Schuylerville, South Glens Falls, South Nyack, Stillwater, Tarrytown, Tivoli, Upper Nyack, Victory Mills, Wappingers Falls, Waterford and West Haverstraw, ex-officio, shall be and are hereby constituted a body politic and corporate by the name of the New York Commercial Tercentenary Commission, which corporation shall be a public corporation, with all the powers specified in the eleventh section of the general corporation law, except as otherwise provided by this act. It shall have no capital stock.

§ 2. The object of said corporation shall be the public celebration or commemoration, in such manner and form either permanent or temporary as may be found appropriate by such commission, of the three hundredth anniversary of the beginning of the regularly chartered commerce of what is now the state of New York under the auspices of the states general of the United Netherlands in the year sixteen hundred and fourteen,

Corporate name.

Powers.

No capital stock.

Object.

§ 3. The said commission shall have power to acquire, hold and ^{Powers as to property.} possess for the purposes of its incorporation real or personal estate within the state of New York in fee or for a term of years or any easement therein, by gift, devise, bequest, grant, lease or purchase; and in case such commission should be unable to agree with the ^{Acquisition of real estate by condemnation.} owners thereof for the purchase or lease of any real estate required for the purposes of its incorporation, it shall have the right to acquire the same, by condemnation, in the manner provided by the condemnation law, being chapter twenty-three of the code of civil procedure; provided, however, that no real property shall be acquired by condemnation within the city of New York until after the approval of the board of estimate and apportionment of that city.

§ 4. The affairs and business of said commission shall be conducted by a board of not less than twenty-five nor more than one ^{Board of trustees; quorum.} hundred trustees a quorum of whom for the transaction of business shall be fixed by the by-laws. The trustees for the first year ^{Trustees for first year.} shall be Cornelius Vanderbilt, Herman Ridder, Louis Annin Ames, August Belmont, Union N. Bethell, Henry L. Bogert, Elmer Ellsworth Brown, Jacob A. Cantor, Andrew Carnegie, Howard Carroll, Joseph H. Choate, Thomas W. Churchill, Cesare Conti, George B. Cortelyou, Fred B. Dalzell, John H. Finley, George J. Gould, Edward Hagaman Hall, Ernest Harvier, Franklin W. Hooper, William A. Johnston, Lucien Jouvard, George F. Kunz, Henry M. Leipziger, A. E. MacKinnon, William A. Marble, J. Pierpont Morgan, William C. Muschenheim, Morgan J. O'Brien, Eben E. Olcott, Henry Fairfield Osborn, Alton B. Parker, N. Taylor Phillips, William C. Reick, Edward V. P. Ritter, John D. Rockefeller, Jr., Henry W. Sackett, Jacob H. Schiff, Isaac N. Seligman, Theodore P. Shonts, Robert A. C. Smith, James Speyer, Charles Steckler, Henry R. Towne, Theodore N. Vail, William R. Willcox, Arthur Williams, William Ziegler, Junior, Berthold Flesch, M. J. Cummings, George R. Dyer, and such others as may be added thereto in accordance with the by-laws. Such trustees shall make the by-laws of ^{By-laws.} the commission, providing among other things for the election of ^{Election of trustees and officers} their successors within thirteen months from the passage of this act, and for the election of officers, as therein specified, to hold office until the succeeding annual election of trustees, and until their successors are elected, and for the filling of vacancies in ^{Vacancies.} any office. They shall continue to hold office until the succeeding ^{Terms of trustees.}

election of trustees to the number and in the manner provided by the said by-laws.

Compensation. § 5. None of the trustees or members of said commission, except the secretary and one or more assistants to the secretary. **Pecuniary interest.** shall receive any compensation for services, nor shall any of them be pecuniarily interested directly or indirectly in any contract relating to the affairs of said commission; nor shall said **No dividends.** commission make any dividend or division of its property among **No individual liability.** its members, managers or officers; nor shall any member of the commission nor any trustee be liable individually for any of its debts or liabilities.

Reports to legislature. § 6. Said commission shall annually make to the legislature a statement of its affairs, and from time to time report to the legislature such recommendations as are pertinent to the objects for **Joint action with persons appointed by another state.** which it is created, and may act jointly or otherwise with any persons appointed by any other state for purposes similar to those intended to be accomplished by this act.

Final disposition of property. § 7. Whenever the commission shall report to the legislature that the purposes for which the commission is created have been attained and all its debts and obligations have been paid, its remaining real and personal property shall be disposed of as the legislature may direct.

Subscriptions. § 8. The commission shall have power to receive subscriptions from parties who may desire to contribute to the object of the said commission.

Reports to governor. § 9. The commission shall, as requested by the governor, from time to time render to him reports of its proceedings.

City of New York may provide money. § 10. The city of New York may provide for the said commission such sums of money as the city shall deem expedient, and in such a manner as it shall deem proper for the purpose of carrying out the objects of the commission.

Duration of corporation. § 11. The duration of the corporation shall be five years.
§ 12. This act shall take effect immediately.

Chap. 314.

AN ACT to amend chapter seven hundred and fifty-one of the laws of eighteen hundred and ninety-five, entitled "An act to revise and consolidate the several acts in relation to the city of Hudson; to revise the charter of said city; and to establish a city court therein and define its jurisdiction and powers," in relation to the issue and sale of bonds for the purpose of building, rebuilding, enlarging and repairing school buildings in said city, and purchasing furniture, equipment and sites therefor.

Became a law April 17, 1913, with the approval of the Governor. Passed, three-fifths being present.

Accepted by the City.

The People of the State of New York, represented in Senate and Assembly, do enact as follows:

Section 1. Section one hundred and fifty-one of chapter seven L. 1895, hundred and fifty-one of the laws of eighteen hundred and ninety- ch. 751, § 151 five, entitled "An act to revise and consolidate the several acts in amended. relation to the city of Hudson; to revise the charter of said city; and to establish a city court therein and define its jurisdiction and powers," is hereby amended to read as follows:[1]

§ 151. Whenever it shall be necessary, in the opinion of the Bond issues board of education, to build, enlarge, rebuild or repair any school for school buildings, building, or buildings, their outhouses or appurtenances, or to pur- furniture chase a site or sites or furniture or equipment therefor, then, upon and equipment. the recommendation in writing of three-fourths of the members of said board, filed in the office of the city clerk, the common council may, by a vote of two-thirds of all the members thereof, raise the amount necessary for such *purposes or purposes on the credit of the city, said amount not to exceed ten thousand dollars in any one year, by issuing bonds of said city, of such form as said council shall prescribe, at a rate of interest not to exceed five Interest. per centum per annum, and payable at the rate of two thousand When payable. dollars a year.

In the year nineteen hundred and thirteen the board of educa- Bond issue tion may, by a certificate in writing signed by four-fifths of its high members and filed in the office of the city clerk, certify to the school, furniture and equipment.

---

* So in original.
[1] Section materially amended.

common council that the erection of a new high school building
in said city and the purchase of a site, furniture and equipment
therefor, are necessary, which certificate shall further certify the
sum or sums of money required, in the opinion of the board of
education, for such purposes. Said certificate shall be presented
by the city clerk to the common council at its next meeting after
such filing, and shall be recorded at length in the record of the
proceedings of the common council. The common council shall
thereupon, and within thirty days after the filing of such certificate, raise upon the credit of the city such sum or sums of money
as shall be stated in said certificate and for the purpose or purposes therein stated, but not exceeding the sum of seventy-five
thousand dollars, by the issue and sale of bonds of the city in
such form and of such denominations as the common council shall
prescribe, and at a rate of interest not exceeding five per
centum per annum and payable at such times and in such instalments as the common council shall prescribe. Such bonds
shall be known and described as " high school bonds " and shall
be signed by the mayor and city clerk and shall be sealed with
the seal of the city, and shall be sold in such manner as shall be
deemed by the common council as likely to secure the greatest
attainable price for such bonds, but not less than par. The proceeds of the sale of such bonds shall be deposited with the city
treasurer to the credit of the board of education, subject to its
draft, to be used for the purpose or purposes stated in said certificate of the board of education.

Any and all bonds provided for in this section and the interest
thereon shall be paid and discharged by tax on the taxable property within the city, and the common council shall cause the
amount falling due each year on such bonds to be assessed, levied
and collected at the same time and in the same manner as other
taxes are collected and paid in said city, and in addition thereto.

§ 2. This act shall take effect immediately.

Chap. 315.

AN ACT to amend chapter three hundred and thirty-six of the laws of nineteen hundred and three, entitled "An act to provide for the erection of a court house in the county of New York and authorizing the acquisition of a site therefor," in relation to the compensation of commissioners of estimate and appraisal appointed in pursuance of said act.

Became a law April 17, 1913, with the approval of the Governor. Passed, three-fifths being present.

Accepted by the City.

The People of the State of New York, represented in Senate and Assembly, do enact as follows:

Section 1. Section seven of chapter three hundred and thirty-six of the laws of nineteen hundred and three, entitled "An act to provide for the erection of a court house in the county of New York, and authorizing the acquisition of a site therefor," is hereby amended to read as follows:

§ 7. Sections fourteen hundred and thirty-eight, fourteen hundred and thirty-eight-a, fourteen hundred and thirty-eight-b and sections fourteen hundred and forty to fourteen hundred and forty-five inclusive, of the Greater New York charter, shall, in so far as the same are consistent with the provisions of this act, apply to the regulation and procedure upon all proceedings instituted to acquire real estate or any interest therein, pursuant to the provisions in this act contained; [1]provided that, in lieu and instead of the compensation prescribed by section fourteen hundred and forty-four of the Greater New York charter, the commissioners of estimate and appraisal, appointed in pursuance of this act, shall receive as compensation for their services such fees and expenses as may be taxed by the court, upon eight days' notice to the corporation counsel of the city of New York.

§ 2. This act shall take effect immediately.

L. 1903, ch. 336, § 7 amended.

Acquisition of real estate.

Compensation of commissioners.

---

[1] Remainder of section new.

Chap. 316.

AN ACT to authorize the village of Weedsport and the president and board of trustees of said village to remove the remains of deceased persons from the old cemetery or burial ground in said village.

Became a law April 17, 1913, with the approval of the Governor. Passed, three-fifths being present.

The People of the State of New York, represented in Senate and Assembly, do enact as follows:

Removal of remains authorized.

Section 1. The president and board of trustees of the village of Weedsport are hereby authorized and empowered to remove all the remains of deceased persons from the old cemetery or burial ground in said village, located and lying on the east side of Seneca street, in said village of Weedsport.

Burials hereafter forbidden.

§ 2. All interments or burials of human bodies or remains in said old cemetery or burying ground are forbidden, and shall hereafter be unlawful.

Publicat'on of notice of removal of remains.

§ 3. No removal of remains, as herein provided, shall be made until the president and board of trustees of said village of Weedsport shall have published, once in each week for four successive weeks in a newspaper published in said village known and designated by said board of trustees as the official newspaper, a notice that on or after a day specified in said notice said president and board of trustees of said village of Weedsport will commence to remove the bodies interred in such cemetery, which day shall be at least thirty days after the last or final publication of said

Removal of bodies by personal representatives and next of kin.

notice. If the personal representatives or next of kin of any person now interred in said cemetery are known, and they or any of them are residents of this state, such notice shall be personally served upon them, and no body of such deceased person shall be removed until after the lapse of thirty days from the personal service of said notice, and the said representatives and next of kin shall be allowed to have and remove, and it shall be lawful for them to have and remove, the body or bodies of such deceased person or persons from said cemetery during said last

Reburial of other bodies.

mentioned thirty days. Bodies not claimed by representatives or next of kin must be reburied by such village in a place or places to be acquired and selected by the president and board of trustees.

§ 4. All bodies removed by said president and board of trus- Method of reinterment; monuments, etc. tees under the provisions of this act shall, when distinguishable, be encased in a separate box or coffin, and every monument, head-stone, footstone, slab, board or other designation or distinguishing mark shall be carefully removed and properly set at the grave of each body at the time of said reinterment. Members of the same family shall be placed in contiguous graves.

§ 5. The expenses of such removal and reinterment, not de- Expenses, how defrayed. frayed by private subscription or individual enterprise, includ-ing the expense of procuring a place or places for said reinter-ment, shall be a village charge or indebtedness, to be levied and collected as the other indebtedness of said village is raised, levied and collected and in the manner provided by the charter of said village. But no obligation shall be made or indebtedness incurred Payment, how authorized. upon or against said village as herein provided, except when au-thorized by a vote of the taxpayers of said village therefor, at a regular or special election at which said question shall have been submitted, as provided by law for the submission of any proposi-tion for the expenditure of money, and the majority of the votes cast shall be in favor of such expenditure.

§ 6. This act shall take effect immediately.

Chap. 317.

AN ACT to amend the banking law, in relation to the enforce-ment of certain corporate mortgages.

Became a law April 17, 1913, with the approval of the Governor. Passed, three-fifths being present.

The People of the State of New York, represented in Senate and Assembly, do enact as follows:

Section 1. Subdivision eleven of section one hundred and L. 1909, ch. 10, § 186, eighty-six of chapter ten of the laws of nineteen hundred and subd. 11, as amended nine, entitled "An act in relation to banks, individual bankers by L. 1911, ch. 687, and corporations under the supervision of the banking depart amended. ment, constituting chapter two of the consolidated laws," as amended by chapter six hundred and eighty-seven of the laws of nineteen hundred and eleven, is hereby further amended to read as follows:

Loans.

11. To exercise the powers and possess the privileges conferred on banks and individual bankers by sections seventy-four and seventy-five of this chapter, subject to the restrictions contained in said sections. No such corporation shall have any right or power to make any contract, or to accept or to execute any trust whatever, which it would not be lawful for any individual to make, accept or execute. No loan exceeding in amount one-tenth of its capital stock, shall be made by any such corporation, directly or indirectly, to any director or officer thereof and no loan to such director or officer shall be made without the consent of a majority of the directors. No such corporation shall receive funds and moneys paid or brought into court, except it be designated by the comptroller of the state of New York a depositary thereof. No such corporation shall transact its ordinary business by branch office in any city not named in its certificate of incorporation or charter as the place where its business is to be transacted except that a trust company having a combined capital and surplus of at least two million dollars[1] may open and maintain a branch office or branch offices in one or more places located without the state of New York either in the United States of America or in foreign countries. No trust company shall open a branch office within or without the state of New York without first having obtained the written approval of the superintendent of banks to the opening of such branch office, which written approval may be given or withheld in his discretion, and shall not be given by him until he has ascertained to his satisfaction that the public convenience and advantage will be promoted by the opening of such branch office within the state or that the convenience and advantage of citizens of this state would be promoted by the opening of such branch offices without the state either in the United States of America or in foreign countries; and, provided further, that no trust company in this state, or any officer or director thereof, shall open or maintain a branch office, unless the capital of such trust company actually paid in cash shall exceed the amount required by the law under which it was incorporated by the sum of one hundred thousand dollars for each branch office so opened or maintained. Every trust company and every such officer or director opening a branch office without such written approval shall

Court funds.

Branch officers.

---

1 Formerly " five million dollars."

forfeit to the people of the state the sum of one thousand dollars for every week during which any branch office shall be maintained without such written approval. No foreign corporation shall have or exercise in this state the power to receive deposits o. trust moneys, securities and other personal property from any person or corporation or any of the powers specified in subdivisions one, four, five, six, seven, eight, ten and eleven of this section, nor have or maintain an office in this state for the transaction of, or transact directly or indirectly, any such or similar business. Except that a trust company incorporated in another state may be appointed and may accept appointment and may act as executor of or trustee under the last will and testament of any deceased person provided that similar corporations of this state are permitted to act as such executors or trustees in the state where such foreign corporation was organized, and provided that the superintendent of banks, for the time being, shall be the attorney of such foreign corporation qualifying or acting as such executor or trustee, upon whom process against such corporation may be served in any action or other legal proceeding against such executor or trustee affecting or relating to the estate represented or held by such executor or trustee, or the acts or defaults of such corporation in reference to such estate, and it shall be the duty of any such foreign corporation so qualifying or acting to file in the office of said superintendent of banks a copy of its charter, certified by its secretary under its corporate seal, together with the post-office address of its home office, and a duly executed appointment of said superintendent of banks as its attorney to accept service of process as above provided, and said superintendent of banks, when any such process is served upon him, shall at once mail the paper so served to the home office of such corporation; and provided further, that no foreign corporation having authority to act as executor of or trustee under the last will and testament of any deceased person shall establish or maintain, directly or indirectly, any branch office or agency in this state, or shall in any way solicit, directly or indirectly, any business as executor or trustee therein, and that for any violation of this proviso, the superintendent of banks may, in his discretion, revoke the right of such foreign corporation thereafter to act as executor or trustee in this state. [2]Except also that the validity of any mortgage heretofore given by a foreign corporation to a trust company

Powers of foreign corporations.

---

[2] Remainder of section new.

doing business within the foreign domicile of such mortgagor, to secure the payment of an issue of bonds, shall not be affected by any of the provisions of this section, and such mortgage shall be enforceable in accordance with the laws of this state against any property covered thereby within the state of New York.

§ 2. This act shall take effect immediately.

Chap. 318.

AN ACT to amend the highway law, in relation to the construction of new highways, alteration of highways and the payment of expenses therefor by town obligations.

Became a law April 17, 1913, with the approval of the Governor. Passed, three-fifths being present.

The People of the State of New York, represented in Senate and Assembly, do enact as follows:

L. 1909, ch. 30, § 208 amended.
Section 1. Section two hundred and eight of chapter thirty of the laws of nineteen hundred and nine, entitled "An act relating to highways, constituting chapter twenty-five of the consolidated laws," is hereby amended to read as follows:

§ 208. **Final determination, how carried out.** The final determination of commissioners appointed by any court, relating to laying out, altering or discontinuing a highway, and all orders and other papers filed or entered in the proceedings, or certified copies thereof from the court where such determination, order and papers are filed and entered, shall be forthwith filed and recorded in the town clerk's office of the town where the highway is located; and every such decision shall be carried out by the town superintendent of the town, the same as if they had made an order to that effect. [1]The said town superintendent shall thereupon proceed to construct the highway so laid out, and construct any alteration so provided for, and put same in good condition for public travel. The expense of such construction of such new highway or alteration of an existing highway, shall be a charge upon and against the town in which such highway is constructed or any existing highway is altered, and when same is completed the town board of such town may issue certificates of indebtedness for such ex-

---

[1] Remainder of section new.

pense, to draw interest at the rate of not to exceed five per centum per annum until paid, and shall at the next annual meeting for auditing accounts, after such work is done, and after such certificates may have been issued, audit such claims against the town, including interest, if any, and include same in the annual tax budget to be collected from the taxpayers of said town to pay said indebtedness; such money to be paid over to the supervisor of the town and by him paid and applied to the purposes aforesaid. This amendment is made subject to the provisions of section forty-eight, relating to contracts for construction.

§ 2. This act shall take effect immediately.

Chap. 319.

AN ACT to amend the highway law, in relation to the construction of state and county highways in cities and villages.

Became a law April 17, 1913, with the approval of the Governor. Passed, three-fifths being present.

The People of the State of New York, represented in Senate and Assembly, do enact as follows:

Section 1. Section one hundred and thirty-seven of chapter thirty of the laws of nineteen hundred and nine, entitled "An act relating to highways, constituting chapter twenty-five of the consolidated laws," as amended by chapter two hundred and thirty-three of the laws of nineteen hundred and ten, chapter eighty-eight of the laws of nineteen hundred and eleven and chapter eighty-eight of the laws of nineteen hundred and twelve,[1] is hereby amended to read as follows: L. 1909, ch. 30, § 137, as amended by L. 1910, ch. 233, L. 1911, ch. 88, and L. 1912, ch. 88, amended.

§ 137. **State and county highways in villages and cities of the second and third classes.** A state or county highway may be constructed through a city of the second or third class or a village in the same manner as outside thereof, unless the street through which it runs has, in the opinion of the commission, been so improved or paved as to form a continuous and improved highway of sufficient permanence as not to warrant its reconstruction, in which case such highway shall be constructed or improved to the place where such paved or improved street begins. If it is

---

1 Section 137 was amended by L. 1913, ch. 131, ante.

desired to construct or improve any portion of a state or county
highway within such village or city of the second or third class
at a width greater than that provided for in the plans and specifications therefor, or if a modification of the plans and specifications is desired by which the cost thereof is increased, the
board of trustees of such village or common council of such city
shall petition the commission by resolution, to so modify such
plans and specifications as to provide for such construction. The
commission shall thereupon cause the plans, specifications and
estimate for such highway to be modified so as to provide for
such additional construction, and shall provide therefor in the
contract. Upon the completion of such state or county highway
within the village or city of the second or third class in accordance with such modified plans and specifications the commission
shall notify the board of trustees or common council, as the case
may be, as provided in the case of a county highway. Such board
or common council may file a written protest against the acceptance of such work with the commission who shall examine in
respect thereto, and if it is sustained the commission shall delay
the acceptance of the highway within the village or city until it
be properly completed. Upon the proper completion thereof and
the notification as above provided, the commission shall certify
to the board of trustees or common council the cost of such additional construction, and such board or common council shall pay
the same out of moneys raised by tax or from the issue and sale
of bonds as provided in the village law, if in a village, or by the
general or special act governing bond issues and taxation in any
such city if in a city of the second or third class. The provisions
of the general village law, special village or city charters and
other general or special laws relative to the pavement or improvement of streets and the assessment and payment of the cost
thereof shall apply, as far as may be, to such additional construction and the assessment and payment of the cost thereof,
except that the provisions of any general or local act affecting the
pavement or improvement of streets or avenues in any city or
village and[2] requiring the owners, or any of the owners, of the
frontage on a street to consent to the improvement or pavement
thereof, or requiring a hearing to be given to the persons who,

---

[2] Words "any general or local act affecting the pavement or improvement
of streets or avenues in any city or village and," substituted for words "section one hundred and sixty-six of the village law."

or whose premises, are subject to assessment, upon the question of doing such paving or making such improvement[3] shall not apply to the portion of the improvement or pavement of a state or county highway the expense[4] for which is required to be paid by the city or village to the state.[5]

§ 2. This act shall take effect immediately.

Chap. 320.

AN ACT to amend the labor law, in relation to physical examination of employees.

Became a law April 17, 1913, with the approval of the Governor. Passed, three-fifths being present.

The People of the State of New York, represented in Senate and Assembly, do enact as follows:

Section 1. Article two of chapter thirty-six of the laws of nineteen hundred and nine, entitled "An act relating to labor, constituting chapter thirty-one of the consolidated laws," is hereby amended by adding at the end thereof a new section, to be section twenty-two, to read as follows: [§ 22 added to L. 1909, ch. 36.]

§ 22. **Physical examination of employees.** Whenever an employer shall require a physical examination by a physician or surgeon as a condition of employment, the party to be examined, if a female, shall be entitled to have such examination before a physician or surgeon of her own sex. If an employer shall require or attempt to require a female applicant for employment to submit to an examination in violation of the provisions of this section, he shall be guilty of a misdemeanor.

§ 2. This act shall take effect immediately.

---

[3] Words " who, or whose premises, are subject to assessment, upon the question of doing such paving or making such improvement," substituted for word "interested."

[4] Formerly "expenses."

[5] Formerly read: " to be paid by the village."

Chap. 321.

AN ACT to amend the Greater New York charter, in relation to a nautical school.

Became a law April 17, 1913, with the approval of the Governor. Passed, three-fifths being present.

Accepted by the City.

The People of the State of New York, represented in Senate and Assembly, do enact as follows:

L. 1897,
ch. 378,
§ 1157, as
re-enacted
by L. 1901,
ch. 466,
amended.
Section 1. Section eleven hundred and fifty-seven of the Greater New York charter, as re-enacted by chapter four hundred and sixty-six of the laws of nineteen hundred and one, is hereby amended to read as follows:

NAUTICAL SCHOOL MAY BE ESTABLISHED AND MAINTAINED.[1]

§ 1157. The board of education may, in its discretion,[2] provide and maintain a nautical school in said city, for the education and training of pupils in the science and practice of navigation; to furnish accommodations for said school, and make all needful rules and regulations therefor, and for the number and compensation of instructors and others employed therein; to prescribe the government and discipline thereof, and the terms and conditions upon which pupils shall be received and instructed therein, and discharged therefrom, and provide in all things for the good management of said nautical school. And said board shall have power to purchase the books, apparatus, stationery, and other things necessary or expedient to enable said school to be properly and successfully conducted, and may cause the said school or the pupils, or part of the pupils, thereof to go on board vessels in the harbor of New York, and take cruises in or from said harbor for the purpose of obtaining a practical knowledge in navigation and of the duties of mariners. And the said board are hereby authorized to apply to the United States government for the requisite use of vessels and supplies for the purpose above mentioned.

§ 2. This act shall take effect immediately.

---

[1] Section heading formerly read: "Nautical school to be established."
[2] Words "may, in its discretion," substituted for words "is authorized and directed to."

Chap. 322.

AN ACT to provide for the maintenance and government of a
school for the education and training of pupils from the various counties of this state in the science and practice of navigation, seamanship, steam and electrical engineering.

**Became a law April 17, 1913, with the approval of the Governor. Passed,
three-fifths being present.**

*The People of the State of New York, represented in Senate
and Assembly, do enact as follows:*

Section 1. A nautical school shall be maintained at the city Nautical
of New York for the purpose of giving instruction in the science school to be main-
and practice of navigation, seamanship, steam and electrical tained.
engineering to male pupils from the several counties of this
state who shall have the qualifications of good moral character,
elementary education, and physical fitness which may be required
by the board of governors of said school.

§ 2. It is not the purpose of this act to duplicate the New Relation
York Nautical School now conducted under the management of to nautical school
the board of education of the city of New York, but to perpetuate maintained by city of
and insure the continuance of that institution and to extend its New York.
privileges to young men throughout this state who shall have
the requisite qualifications and who shall apply for admission
with the approval of their parents or guardian. It is, therefore,
provided that in the event of the board of education of the city
of New York deciding to discontinue the New York Nautical
School and notifying the governor of such intention and of the
purpose of the city of New York to transfer to the state the
present training ship and the equipment consisting of books,
charts, instruments, apparatus and supplies now used by said
school, the governor shall within thirty days after the receipt of
such notice appoint a board of governors of the New York State
Nautical School which is hereby authorized.

§ 3. The board of governors of the New York State Nautical Board of governors
School shall consist of the commissioner of education of the state
of New York, and eight appointive members, to be appointed as follows: One shall be a member of the chamber of commerce of the
state of New York; one shall be a member of the maritime association of the port of New York; one shall be a member of the
marine society; one shall be a member of the New York board

of trade and transportation; one shall be an alumnus of the
New York Nautical School; one shall be a member of the Buffalo
chamber of commerce; one shall be a member of the Albany
chamber of commerce; one shall be a New York state member
of the national board of steam navigation.

Terms.   § 4. Three of the members of the board of governors shall be
appointed for one year; three shall be appointed for two years;
and three shall be appointed for three years. At the expiration
of any such terms and each year three members of the board
of governors shall be appointed as in the first instance from
among the members of the organization named in section three
Vacancies. of this act and for a full term of three years. In the case of a
vacancy from any cause such vacancy shall be filled by the
governor for the unexpired term from among the members of
the organization represented by the member whose unexpired
term is to be filled.

No compensation; allowance of expenses.   § 5. The members of the board of governors shall serve without pay, but they shall be allowed their actual expenses in-
curred in attending any regular or called meeting of the board
of governors, or in attending the sessions of any duly appointed
subcommittee of said board, for any purpose authorized by said
board, which allowance shall be paid from any appropriations
which may be provided for the purposes of said nautical school.

Chairman.   § 6. The board at its first meeting shall elect one of its members as chairman and such chairman under the instructions of
the board shall have the general supervision and control of the
school and of all its property, and shall have the direction of
its work and that of the instructors and others engaged in the
school. The chairman so elected shall serve as such for one
year or until his successor is elected. His successor as chairman
shall be elected by a vote of the members of the board at a
regular meeting thereof after one month's notice that the chair-
Oaths of office.   man is to be elected at such meeting. The chairman of the board,
as well as the members of the board before entering upon their
duties as such, respectively, shall take the oath prescribed for
state officers by the constitution of the state.[1]

First meeting.   § 7. Within two weeks after their appointment in the first
instance the members of the board of governors of the State
Nautical School shall meet in the office of the department of
education in the city of Albany upon a notice calling such meet-

---

[1] See constitution, art. 13, § 1; public officers law (L. 1909, ch. 51), § 10,
as amended by L. 1913, ch. 59, ante.

ing issued by the state superintendent of education.[2] The board of governors shall provide and maintain a nautical training school pursuant to the provisions of this act, aboard a proper vessel which shall be stationed at the port of New York; they shall purchase and provide the necessary books, charts, instruments, apparatus and supplies required in the work of the school and for the proper accommodation and keep of the superintendent, instructors and pupils aboard such vessel; they shall appoint and remove the superintendent, who shall also be commander, the instructors and the necessary employees; determine their number, duties and compensation; fix the terms and conditions upon which pupils shall be received and instructed in the school and be graduated, discharged or suspended; they shall establish all rules and regulations necessary for the proper management of the school and from time to time shall arrange for cruises from and to the harbor of New York. Provided that admission as a pupil, tuition and keep shall be free on board such vessel to any male resident of the state of New York having the required qualifications prescribed by the board of governors, excepting an initial fee of fifty dollars for part cost of uniforms, equipment, et cetera.

Duties as to maintenance of nautical training school.

Tuition.

§ 8. The board of governors of the State Nautical School may take over for the purposes of the school the United States ship "Newport," when the governor shall have been notified by the board of education of the city of New York of its purpose to discontinue the New York Nautical School, or the said board of governors may apply for and receive from the United States government or any other source any more suitable vessel or vessels as conditions may require and the secretary of the navy may detail. They may annually expend for the purposes of such school any sum which the legislature may appropriate, and shall annually submit a budget or estimate of the sum required for the maintenance of the school and for its cruises. They shall keep full and detailed accounts of all such expenditures and shall make a complete report thereof with a report of all the work of the school annually to the legislature. They shall appoint a secretary to the board, determine his duties and fix his compensation and who shall be removable at the discretion of the board.

Acquisition of ship.

Annual expenditure.

Accounts and financial report.

Secretary to board.

§ 9. The sum of one hundred thousand dollars ($100,000).

Appropriation.

---

[2] Should read " state commissioner of education."

or so much thereof as may be necessary, is hereby appropriated from moneys in the treasury not otherwise appropriated for the expenses of the New York Nautical School for the first year; said appropriation to become available when the governor shall have appointed the board of governors as provided in this act.

§ 10. This act shall take effect immediately.

Chap. 323.

AN ACT making an appropriation for the construction of a poultry building on the state fair grounds at Syracuse, and for the improvement of said grounds.

Became a law April 18, 1913, with the approval of the Governor. Passed by a two-thirds vote.

The People of the State of New York, represented in Senate and Assembly, do enact as follows:

Appropria-
tion.
Section 1. The sum of eighty thousand dollars ($80,000), or so much thereof as may be necessary, is hereby appropriated out of any money in the treasury, not otherwise appropriated, for the construction and equipment on the state fair grounds at Syracuse, New York, of a poultry building, and for the permanent improvement of such grounds. Such moneys shall be payable by the treasurer, on the warrant of the comptroller and the certificate of the state fair commission.

Employ-
ment of
architect.
§ 2. The state fair commission may employ an architect to prepare the plans and specifications for, and supervise the construction of said building and improvements, and the compensation for such architect shall be fixed by the commission and payable from the money hereby appropriated.

Contracts.
No part of such appropriation shall be available for the construction of said poultry building, except for plans and specifications and necessary advertising, until contracts have been let to responsible bidders for the completion of such building within the amount of the above appropriation.

Approval
of plans
and specifi-
cations and
payments.
The plans and specifications for the construction of said poultry building shall be approved by the state architect prior to the letting of said contract, and estimates for the payment of all of the cost of the construction of said building shall be approved by him prior to their audit by the comptroller.

§ 3. This act shall take effect immediately.

Chap. 324.

AN ACT to amend the Greater New York charter, in relation to the duties and powers of the department of taxes and assessments.

Became a law April 18, 1913, with the approval of the Governor. Passed, three-fifths being present.

Accepted by the City.

The People of the State of New York, represented in Senate and Assembly, do enact as follows:

Section 1. The Greater New York charter, as re-enacted by chapter four hundred and sixty-six of the laws of nineteen hundred and one, is hereby amended by adding a new section, to be known as section eight hundred and eighty-eight-a to follow section eight hundred and eighty-eight and to read as follows: §888a added to L. 1897, ch. 378, as re-enacted by L. 1901, ch. 466.

§ 888-a. **Right of entry.** The department may, by its officers and employees or others acting in its behalf, enter upon real property and into buildings and structures at all reasonable times to ascertain the character of the property.

§ 2. The said Greater New York charter is hereby amended by inserting a new section to be known as section eight hundred and eighty-nine-a to follow section eight hundred and eighty-nine and to read as follows: §889a added.

§ 889-a. A building in course of construction, commenced since the preceding first day of October and not ready for occupancy, shall not be assessed.

§ 3. The said Greater New York charter is hereby amended by inserting a new section to be known as section eight hundred and ninety-one-a to follow section eight hundred and ninety-one and to read as follows: §891a added.

§ 891-a. **Tax maps.** The department shall maintain maps showing each separately assessed parcel of real property. Each separately assessed parcel shall be indicated either by a parcel number or by an identification number. Parcel numbers shall designate each parcel by the use of three or more numbers, of which one shall be a section or ward number, another a block, district or plot number, and another a lot number.

The parcel numbering upon the tax maps shall be in such sequence as the department determines.

Each separately assessed parcel indicated by an identification number shall be shown by a separate map, or by a description or

by a map and description. A separate identification number shall
be entered upon the tax maps in such manner as clearly to indicate each separately assessed parcel of real property not indicated
by parcel numbering. Real property indicated by a single identification number shall be deemed to be a separately assessed parcel.

The department may maintain as tax maps the maps established
or maintained by law so far as the same apply. The tax maps
may be altered by the department except as otherwise provided by
law.

§ 895, as
amended
by L. 1911,
ch. 455,
amended. § 4. Section eight hundred and ninety-five of said Greater
New York charter, as amended by chapter four hundred and
fifty-five of the laws of nineteen hundred and eleven, is hereby
amended to read as follows:

§ 895. **Applications for correction of assessment.** During the
time that books shall be open to public inspection as aforesaid
application may be made by any person or corporation claiming
to be aggrieved by the assessed valuation of real or personal estate,
to have the same corrected. If such application be made in relation to the assessed valuation of real estate, it must be made in
writing, stating the ground of objection thereto. The board of
taxes and assessments shall examine into the complaint, as herein
provided, and if in their judgment the assessment is erroneous
they shall cause the same to be corrected. If such application be
made in relation to the assessed valuation of personal estate, the
applicant shall be examined under oath by a commissioner of taxes
and assessments or by an assistant commissioner or assistant to a
commissioner,[1] or by a deputy tax commissioner, as herein provided, who are hereby authorized to administer such oath, and if
the assessment as hereinafter provided be determined by the board
of taxes and assessments to be erroneous, it shall cause the same
to be corrected and fix the amount of such assessment as the board
of taxes and assessments may believe to be just, and declare its
decision upon and application within the time and in the manner
hereinafter provided. But the commissioners of taxes and assessments may, during the last fifteen days of the month of November
and during the months of December and January in any year,
act upon applications, examine applicants under oath and take
other testimony thereon, for the reduction of assessments upon
either real or personal property filed in their offices on or before

---

[1] Words " or by an assistant commissioner or assistant to a commissiouer."
new.

the fifteenth day of November preceding as to real estate, and on or before the thirtieth day of November preceding as to personal estate, and cause the amount of any assessment as corrected by the board of taxes and assessments to be entered upon the assessment rolls for the year for which such correction is made.

§ 5. Section eight hundred and ninety-seven of the said Greater New York charter, as amended by chapter one hundred and ninety-two of the laws of nineteen hundred and two, and by chapter sixty-four of the laws of nineteen hundred and eight, is hereby amended to read as follows:

§ 897. **Power of board of taxes and assessments to remit or reduce taxes.** The board of taxes and assessments is hereby invested with power to remit or reduce where[2] lawful cause therefor is shown. It may remit or reduce if found excessive or erroneous a tax imposed upon real or personal property. It shall require a majority of the commissioners of taxes and assessments to remit or reduce the assessed valuation of personal property, and no tax on personal property shall be remitted, canceled or reduced, except to correct clerical errors, unless the person aggrieved shall satisfy the board of taxes and assessments that illness or absence from the city had prevented the filing of the complaint or making the application to the said board within the time allowed by law for the correction of taxes. Any remission or reduction of taxes upon the real estate of individuals or corporations must be made within one year after the delivery of the books to the receiver of taxes for the collection of such tax.

§ 6. This act shall take effect immediately.

§ 897, as amended by L. 1902, ch. 192, and L. 1908, ch. 64, amended.

Chap. 325.

AN ACT to amend the public officers law, in relation to official undertakings.

Became a law April 19, 1913, with the approval of the Governor. Passed, three-fifths being present.

The People of the State of New York, represented in Senate and Assembly, do enact as follows:

Section 1. Section eleven of chapter fifty-one of the laws of nineteen hundred and nine, entitled "An act in relation to public

L. 1909, ch. 51, § 11, as amended by L. 1911.

---

[2] Words " in the opinion of the corporation counsel," omitted.

ch. 424, and
L. 1912,
ch. 481,
amended.

officers, constituting chapter forty-seven of the consolidated laws,"
as amended by chapter four hundred and twenty-four of the laws
of nineteen hundred and eleven and chapter four hundred and
eighty-one of the laws of nineteen hundred and twelve, is hereby
amended to read as follows:

Official un-
dertakings.

§ 11. Every official undertaking, when required by or in pursuance of law to be hereafter executed or filed by any officer, shall
be to the effect that he will faithfully discharge the duties of his
office and promptly account for and pay over all moneys or property received by him as such officer, in accordance with law, or in
default thereof, that the parties executing such undertaking will
pay all damages, costs and expenses resulting from such default,
not exceeding a sum, if any, specified in such undertaking. The
undertaking of a state officer shall be approved by the comptroller
both as to its form and as to the sufficiency of the sureties and be
filed in the comptroller's office. The undertaking of a municipal
officer shall, if not otherwise provided by law, be approved as to
its form and the sufficiency of the sureties by the chief executive
officer or by the governing body of the municipality and be filed
with the clerk thereof. The approval by such governing body
may be by resolution, a certified copy of which shall be attached

Approval.

Sum to
be speci-
fied.

to the undertaking. The sum specified in an official undertaking
shall be the sum for which such undertaking shall be required by
or in pursuance of law to be given. If no sum, or a different sum
from that required by or in pursuance of law, be specified in the
undertaking, it shall be deemed to be an undertaking for the
amount so required. If no sum be required by or in pursuance
of law to be so specified, and a sum be specified in the undertaking, the sum so specified shall not limit the liability of the

Execution
of under-
taking.

sureties therein. Every official undertaking shall be executed and
duly acknowledged by at least two sureties, each of whom shall
add thereto his affidavit that he is a freeholder or householder
within the state, stating his occupation and residence and the
street number of his residence and place of business if in a city,
and a sum which he is worth over and above his just debts and
liabilities and property exempt from execution. The aggregate
of the sums so stated in such affidavits must be at least double

Payment of
premium.

the amount specified in the undertaking. If the surety on an official undertaking of a state or local officer, clerk, or employee of
the state or political subdivision thereof or of a municipal corpo-

ration[1] be a *fiedlity or surety corporation, the reasonable expense of procuring such surety, not exceeding one per centum per annum upon the amount of such undertaking, shall be a charge against the state or political subdivision or municipal corporation respectively in and for which he is elected or appointed.   The failure to execute an official undertaking in the form or by the number of sureties required by or in pursuance of law, or of a surety thereto to make an affidavit required by or in pursuance of law, or in the form so required, or the omission from such an undertaking of the approval required by or in pursuance of law, shall not affect the liability of the sureties therein. *Liability of sureties not affected by certain irregularities.*

§ 2. This act shall take effect immediately.

Chap. 326.

AN ACT to amend the Greater New York charter, in relation to tax liens.

Became a law April 19, 1913, with the approval of the Governor. Passed, three-fifths being present.

Accepted by the City.

The People of the State of New York, represented in Senate and Assembly, do enact as follows:

Section 1. Section ten hundred and twenty-seven of the Greater New York charter, as re-enacted by chapter four hundred and sixty-six of the laws of nineteen hundred and one, and amended by chapter four hundred and ninety of the laws of nineteen hundred and eight, is hereby amended to read as follows: *L. 1897, ch. 378, § 1027, as re-enacted by L. 1901, ch. 466, amended.*

SALES OF TAX LIENS FOR TAXES AND ASSESSMENTS; PROCEEDINGS.

§ 1027. The right of the city to receive taxes, assessments and water rents and the lien thereof, may be sold by the city, and after such sale, shall be transferred, in the manner provided by this title.   The right and lien so sold shall be called " tax lien " and the instrument by which it is assigned shall be called " transfer of tax lien."   Whenever any tax on lands or tenements,

---

* So in original.
[1] Words " clerk, or employee of the state or political subdivision thereof or of a municipal corporation," new.

or any assessments on lands or tenements for local improvements,
shall remain unpaid for the term of three years from the time the
same shall have been fully confirmed, so as to be due and payable
and also whenever any water rents in said city shall have been
due and unpaid for the term of four years from the time the
same shall have been due, it shall and may be lawful, for the
collector of assessments and arrears, under the direction of the
comptroller, to advertise the tax liens on the said lands and tenements or any of them for sale, including in such advertisement
the tax lien for all items up to a day named in the advertisement,
and by such advertisement the owner or owners of such lands and
tenements respectively shall be required to pay the amount of
such tax, assessment, or water rents, with the said penalties
thereon so remaining unpaid, together with the interest thereon
at the rate of seven per centum per annum to the time of payment, with the charges of such notice and advertisement, to the
said collector, and notice shall be given by such advertisement that
if default shall be made in such payment the tax lien on such
lands and tenements will be sold at public auction at a day and
place therein to be specified, for the lowest rate of interest, not
exceeding twelve per centum per annum, at which any person or
persons shall offer to take the same in consideration of advancing
the said tax, assessment and water rents and penalties, as the case
may be, the interest thereon as aforesaid to the time of sale, the
charges of the above mentioned notices and advertisement and all
other costs and charges accrued thereon; and if, notwithstanding
such notice, the owner or owners shall refuse or neglect to pay
such tax, assessment, water rents and penalties, with the interests
as aforesaid, and the charges attending such notice and advertisement, then it shall and may be lawful for the said collector under
the direction of the said comptroller, to cause such tax lien on
such lands and tenements to be sold at public auction, for the
purpose and in the manner expressed in the said advertisement.
and such sale shall be made on the day and at the place for that
purpose mentioned in the said advertisement, and shall be continued from time to time, if necessary, until all the tax liens on
the lands and tenements so advertised shall be sold. But the tax
lien on houses or lots, or improved or unimproved lands, in the
city of New York, shall not be hereafter sold at public auction
for the non-payment of any tax, assessment or water rents which
may be due thereon, unless notice of such sale shall have been

published once in each week successively for three months in the City Record and the corporation newspapers, which advertisement shall contain, appended to said notice, a particular and detailed statement of the property the tax lien on which is to be sold. Or the said detailed statement and description, instead of being published in the City Record and the corporation newspapers, shall, at the option of the said comptroller, be printed in a pamphlet, in which case copies of the pamphlet shall be deposited in the office of the said collector, and shall be delivered to any person applying therefor. And the notice provided for in this section to be given of the sale of tax liens on houses and lots and improved and unimproved lands, shall also state that the detailed statement of the taxes, assessments, or water rents, and the property taxed, assessed, or on which the water rents are unpaid, is published in the City Record and the corporation newspapers, or in a pamphlet, as the case may be, and that copies of the pamphlet are deposited in the office of the said collector, and will be delivered to any person applying for the same. No other notice or demand of the tax, assessment or water rent shall be required to authorize the sale of tax liens on any lands and tenements as hereinbefore provided. The collector of assessments and arrears may, with the written approval of the comptroller, cancel any certificate or lease or transfer of tax lien[1] for unpaid taxes, assessments and water rents, held by the city of New York, or to which the city has acquired the right, and upon such cancellation, the lien of such tax, assessment or water rent shall be and remain the same as if no sale for such unpaid tax, assessment or water rent had been made.

§ 2. This act shall take effect immediately.

---

1 Words " or transfer of tax lien," new.

20

Chap. 327.

AN ACT to amend the Greater New York charter, in relation
to plans for water fronts.

Became a law April 19, 1913, with the approval of the Governor. Passed,
three-fifths being present.

Accepted by the City.

*The People of the State of New York, represented in Senate
and Assembly, do enact as follows:*

L. 1897,
ch. 378,
§ 819, as re-
enacted by
L. 1901,
ch. 466,
amended.

Section 1. Section eight hundred and nineteen of the Greater
New York charter, as re-enacted by chapter four hundred and
sixty-six of the laws of nineteen hundred and one, is hereby
amended so as to read as follows:

Plans for
water front
continued.

§ 819. The plan or plans for the whole or any part of the water
front of the city of New York, as constituted by this act, including the water front on the westerly side of the Harlem river from
the easterly line of the Third avenue where said line strikes said
river along the water front from said line to the northerly side
of Eighty-sixth street on the East river determined upon by the
department of docks, of the city of New York, as heretofore
known and bounded, adopted and certified to by the commissioners
of the sinking fund, and filed in the office of said department of
docks, in accordance with the provision of the third sub-division
of section ninety-nine of chapter one hundred and thirty-seven
of the laws of eighteen hundred and seventy as amended by section
six of chapter five hundred and seventy-four of the laws of
eighteen hundred and seventy-one and such plan or plans as may be
determined upon pursuant to section eight hundred and seventeen
of this act, adopted and certified to by the commissioners of the
sinking fund and filed, or that may be filed in the office of said
commissioner of docks shall be and continue to be the sole plan or
plans. according to which any wharf, pier, bulkhead, basin, dock,
slip or any wharf structure or superstructure shall be laid out
or constructed within the territory or district embraced, or that
may hereafter be embraced in and specified upon said plan or plans,
and shall be the sole plan or plans and authority for solid filling in
the waters surrounding the city of New York, and on said Harlem
river, and for extending piers into said waters and erecting
bulkheads around said city, and on the westerly side of the

Inconsis-
tent laws
deemed
repealed.

Harlem river, and all other provisions of law regulating solid filling and pier and bulkhead lines in said waters, are to be deemed to

be repealed whenever said plan or plans is or are inconsistent with such provisions of law and all laws giving any power or authority as to said water front in the territory embraced in this section, to any other department of the city of New York, as heretofore known and bounded, or to any department of any municipal or public corporation which, or part of which, is consolidated by this act with the mayor, aldermen and commonalty of the city of New York, are hereby repealed. No wharf, pier, bulkhead, basin, dock, slip, exterior street or any wharf, structure or super- structure shall be laid out, built or rebuilt, within such territory or district except in accordance with such plan or plans, provided that said commissioner of docks, with the consent and approval of the commissioners of the sinking fund, may, from time to time, change the width or location of the piers laid down on said plan or plans; and provided, also, that said commissioner of docks may build, or rebuild, or license, or permit the building or rebuilding, of temporary wharf structures, and said commissioner may lease land covered with water belonging to the city of New York for the purpose thereof, such lease, or permit to continue and remain at the will and pleasure of said commissioner, or for a time not longer than until the wharves, piers, bulkheads, basins, docks, or slips to be built or constructed according to such plan or plans, shall in the judgment of said commissioner, require and need to be built or constructed; and provided, further, that the commis- sioner of docks with the consent and approval of the commissioners of the sinking fund may alter and extend the present pier head line, as now established on the Hudson river, between Battery place and Seventieth street, and establish a new pier head line between these points, and may authorize the construction of new piers out to said pier head line, and may extend those piers already built out to said line; and may build new piers or extend piers already built, out to such pier head lines as are now or may hereafter be established by the secretary of war under act of congress. The commissioner of docks is hereby authorized and empowered, with the consent and approval of the commissioners of the sinking fund, [1]after a public hearing shall have been given by said commis- sioners, of which hearing and its purposes at least seven days' notice shall be published in the City Record, to alter, amend and modify any and all existing plans for the improve- ment of the water front hereinbefore recited or which may have

Marginal notes: Wharves, etc., to be built according to such plans. Temporary wharf structures. Alteration of pier head line on Hudson river. Modification of existing plans for improvement of water front.

---

[1] Remainder of sentence materially amended.

been determined upon or adopted in pursuance hereof notwithstanding that any or all of such plans may have been wholly or partially physically perfected and improvements made in conformity therewith. [2]And any such alteration, amendment or modification may include the elimination and closing of any marginal wharf, street or place shown on any plan, whether or not such marginal wharf, street or place has been physically constructed, and any such altered, amended, or modified plan or any new plan determined upon or adopted in pursuance of the provisions of this section need not provide for or show any such marginal wharf, street or place. Whenever the plan so determined upon and adopted, or hereafter to be determined upon and adopted, shall include the widening of an exterior street or avenue, or the opening and construction of a new exterior street or exterior avenue, or the abandonment or closing of such street or avenue already in existence, the power to widen, open, construct, abandon or close the same shall exclusively reside with the said commissioner of docks, who is hereby authorized to take such steps as may be necessary in that regard, and after the same shall have been so widened or opened, the right to maintain the widened portion of a street or avenue already opened, and such new street or avenue shall also reside with the said commissioner of docks; but the street or avenue so widened to the extent of the part so widened, or such new street or avenue opened under this plan shall not be a public street, but shall be a marginal wharf, and shall be used in that regard in such manner from time to time as the commissioner of docks shall, by resolution, determine. The commissioner of docks shall have exclusive power to regulate the use of marginal streets so that the land and buildings upon all such marginal streets may be used to the best advantage in connection with the wharves and bulkheads; and the commissioner of docks shall have the power to regulate, by license or by any other suitable means, the transfer of goods and merchandise upon, over or under all such marginal streets; except that the said commissioner of docks shall not, under this section, have any power in respect to, or jurisdiction over, the public driveway authorized by and constructed under chapter one hundred and two of the laws of eighteen hundred and ninety-three and acts amendatory thereof.

§ 2. This act shall take effect immediately.

---

[2] Following sentence new.

Marginal notes:
Elimination of marginal wharves, etc.
Widening, construction or abandonment of exterior streets.
Regulation of use of marginal streets.

Chap. 328.

AN ACT to amend the Greater New York charter, relative to
the acquisition of wharf property by the city of New York.

Became a law April 19, 1913, with the approval of the Governor. Passed,
three-fifths being present.

Accepted by the City.

*The People of the State of New York, represented in Senate
and Assembly, do enact as follows:*

Section 1. Section eight hundred and twenty-two of the Greater
New York charter, as re-enacted by chapter four hundred and
sixty-six of the laws of nineteen hundred and one and amended by
chapter six hundred and twenty-four of the laws of nineteen hundred and three, is hereby amended to read as follows:[1]

§ 822. **Acquisition of wharf property by The City of New
York; proceedings to acquire.** The commissioner of docks, with
the approval of the commissioners of the sinking fund, is authorized to acquire in the name and for the benefit of The City of New
York any and all wharf property or any rights, terms, easements
and privileges pertaining to any wharf property in said city that
is not owned by the city or to which it has no right or title;
and the said commissioner may acquire the same either by
purchase or by process of law, as herein provided. He
may agree with the owners of any such property, rights, terms,
easements or privileges upon a price for the same and shall certify
such agreement to the commissioners of the sinking fund, and
if the said commissioners approve of such agreement the
commissioner of docks shall take from the owners, at such
price, the necessary conveyances and covenants for vesting said
property, rights, terms, easements or privileges in, and assuring
the same to The City of New York forever, and said owners shall
be paid such price from the city treasury as provided in this act.
If, however, the commissioner of docks shall deem it proper
and expedient that The City of New York should acquire possession of such wharf property, rights, terms, easements or privileges
by process of law, as herein provided, without having first attempted to agree with the owners thereof for the purchase of
such wharf property, rights, terms, easements or privileges,

L. 1897,
ch. 378,
§ 822, as
re-enacted
by L. 1901.
ch. 466, and
amended
by L. 1903,
ch. 624,
amended.

---

[1] Section materially amended.

he may, with the approval of the commissioners of the sinking fund, direct the corporation counsel to take legal proceedings to acquire the same for the city. Thereupon, the corporation counsel shall take the same proceedings to acquire such wharf property, rights, terms, easements or privileges as are by law provided for the taking of private property in said city for public streets or places, and the provisions of law relating to the taking of private property for public streets or places in said city are hereby made applicable, as far as may be necessary, in any legal proceeding taken under this section. In a proceeding hereafter brought for the acquirement of any such wharf property, rights, terms, easements or privileges, or uplands, or lands under water, it shall not be necessary for the commissioner of docks to make any attempt to agree with the owners of the same upon a price for its acquisition, before commencing the proceedings authorized by this section, and, if the commissioners of the sinking fund shall by resolution so direct, the title to the same shall vest in The City of New York at such time as said resolution shall direct, after the filing, in the office of the clerk of the county where such proceedings are pending, of the oaths of the commissioners of estimate in said proceeding appointed; and all of the rights, title and interest of any and all of the owners or persons interested in the said wharf property, rights, terms, easements and privileges, lands under water or uplands, shall cease and determine and be extinguished at such time. All the awards made in such proceedings for the value of property acquired or interests extinguished shall draw interest from the time of the vesting of the title in The City of New York.

The commissioner of docks is also empowered to acquire by purchase or by process of law, as provided in this section, the title to such lands under water and uplands, or any rights, terms or easements appertaining thereto, within The City of New York, as he shall deem necessary to be taken for the improvement of the waterfront or for the equipment, maintenance or operation of a ferry, or for the acquirement of terminal facilities therefor or approaches thereto upon the water-front of the borough of Richmond or upon the water-front of the borough of Brooklyn. Provided that said commissioner of docks, with the approval of the commissioners of the sinking fund, hereby is empowered to agree, license and permit private owners of any bulkheads, piers or water rights, to make the necessary improvements upon their bulkheads, piers or water rights, so as to conform to the plan already adopted by the department of docks, and approved by the commissioners of the sinking fund of The City of New York, as heretofore known and bounded, or to be hereafter adopted and approved, pursuant to this chapter, during the period which shall intervene prior to the extinguishment of such private ownership by The City of New York, such improvements to be made by such owners under the supervision of or by the commissioner of docks, as may be agreed upon, at the cost and expense of such private owners, in the first instance, and upon such reasonable terms as to reimbursing said private owners for such improvements, and as to wharfage and other riparian rights thereon and therefrom, as may be agreed upon. All agreements, and licenses or permits heretofore made or entered into between the mayor, aldermen and commonalty of The City of New York and any private owners, as to the making of like improvements upon their property, are hereby ratified, confirmed and made valid. The provisions of this section shall apply to any wharf property, lands under water, uplands, rights, terms, easements or privileges, when required for the equipment, maintenance or operation of a ferry or the acquirement of terminal facilities therefor, or approaches thereto, upon the waterfront of The City of New York, whether such wharf property, lands under water, uplands, rights, terms, easements or privileges have been previously taken for a public use or not.

§ 2. This act shall take effect immediately.

Chap. 329.

AN ACT to amend the Greater New York charter, in relation to playgrounds.

Became a law April 19, 1913, with the approval of the Governor. Passed, three-fifths being present.

Accepted by the City.

The People of the State of New York, represented in Senate and Assembly, do enact as follows:

Section 1. Section four hundred and thirty-nine of the Greater New York charter,[1] as amended by chapter six hundred and sev-

L. 1897,
ch. 378,
§ 439, as

---

[1] As re-enacted by L. 1901, ch. 466

amended
by L. 1911,
ch. 675.
amended. enty-five of the laws of nineteen hundred and eleven[2] is hereby amended to read as follows:

MAP TO BE COMPLETED.

§ 439. It shall be the duty of the president of each borough comprised within the city of New York, as constituted by this act, subject to the limitations hereinafter provided, to prepare a map of that part of the territory embraced within the borough of which he is president, of which a map or plan has not heretofore been finally established and adopted, as set forth in section four hundred and thirty-eight of this act, locating and laying out all parks, playgrounds,[3] streets, bridges, tunnels and approaches to bridges and tunnels, and indicating the width and grades of all such streets so located and laid out. It shall be the duty of the president of each borough under the direction of the mayor to continue and complete the system of exact triangulation inaugurated in the borough of the Bronx, over that part of the borough of which he shall be president, of which no map or plan has heretofore been established and approved, provided that such system of triangulation, after the most approved and exact method, shall be finished before the first day of January, nineteen hundred and seven. The duty of conducting such system of triangulation shall be entrusted only to a civil engineer who shall have had at least five years' experience in the method and manner of precise surveying, and whose fitness and competency shall have been determined in a civil service examination, or, with the consent of the mayor, to such civil engineer or other expert as may be designated by the superintendent of the United States coast and geodetic survey, or other proper officer of the United States. The mayor with the approval of the board of estimate and apportionment shall have power to enter into a contract or agreement with the proper representative of the United States so that the city of New York may be able to avail itself of the aid and assistance of the United States coast and geodetic survey in making an exact triangulation of the territory embraced within the boundaries of the city of New York. The mayor with the approval of the board of estimate and apportionment shall have power to employ such persons to assist in the work as they may deem necessary and to pay such sums as may be reasonable and necessary for their

---

[2] Section 439 was also amended by L. 1903, ch. 406.
[3] Word " playgrounds " new.

services and subsistence and for reasonable and necessary expenses, but not to exceed the sum of fifteen thousand dollars in any one year. The comptroller is authorized and directed to issue special revenue bonds not to exceed said amount in any one year upon the request of the board of estimate and apportionment in order to provide the means to make the payments thus authorized. The said civil engineer or other expert shall prepare and furnish, for primary stations, the latitude and longitude determined in conformity with the method used by the United States coast and geodetic survey; for secondary stations, the rectangular spherical co-ordinates; and for all stations, rectangular co-ordinates referred to a given fixed central meridian, or assumed meridian. Such co-ordinates shall be official and binding upon all officers making any map or plan relating to any borough or part thereof. Whenever and as often as the president of any borough shall have completed the map of a part of the territory aforesaid, he shall report the same together with the surveys, maps and profiles, showing the parks, playgrounds,[4] streets, bridges, tunnels, and approaches to bridges and tunnels located and laid out by him, and the grades thereof, to the board of estimate and apportionment for its concurrence and approval, subject, nevertheless, to such corrections or modifications as in the judgment of the majority of said board may be advisable; and the said board thereafter shall cause such map or plan, and such profiles, as finally adopted by it, to be certified by the secretary of said board, and filed as follows: One copy thereof in the office in which conveyances of real estate are required to be recorded in the county in which the territory shown upon such map is located; one copy thereof in the office of the corporation counsel; and one copy thereof in the office of the president of the borough, who shall have prepared such map. Such map and profiles, when so adopted and filed, shall become a part of the map or plan of the city of New York, and shall be deemed to be final and conclusive with respect to the location, width and grades of the streets shown thereon, and the same shall not be subject to any further change or modification except as provided in section four hundred and forty-two of this act; provided, however, that local boards at a joint meeting of all the boards comprised within the borough for which said map was adopted, within three months after the opening of a street, shall have the power to alter the grade of

---

[4] Word " playgrounds " new.

such street, and to alter the grades of intersecting streets, so far as it may be necessary to conform the same to new grades of the street opened.

§ 442, as amended by L. 1908, ch. 409, amended.

§ 2. Section four hundred and forty-two of said charter, as amended by chapter four hundred and nine of the laws of nineteen hundred and three, is hereby amended to read as follows:

AUTHORITY OF BOARD OF ESTIMATE TO CHANGE MAP OR PLAN OF CITY OR TO CHANGE GRADES.

§ 442. The board of estimate and apportionment is authorized and empowered, whenever and as often as it may deem it for the public interest so to do, to change the map or plan of the city of New York, so as to lay out new streets, parks, playgrounds,[5] bridges, tunnels and approaches to bridges and tunnels and parks and playgrounds,[6] and to widen, straighten, extend, alter and close existing streets, and to change the grade of existing streets shown upon such map or plan, by publishing notice of its proposed action for ten days, in the City Record and the corporation newspapers, and giving an opportunity for all persons interested in such change to be heard, at a time and place to be specified in such notice, such time to be not less than ten days after the first publication of such notice. After the due publication of such notice, and after hearing protests and objections, if any there be, against the proposed change, if the said board shall favor such change, notwithstanding such protests and objections, and the same receives the approval of the mayor, such change in the map or plan of the city of New York, or in the grade of any street or streets shown thereon, shall be deemed to have been made.

§ 970, as amended by L. 1910, ch. 336, amended.

§ 3. Section nine hundred and seventy of said charter, as amended by chapter three hundred and thirty-six of the laws of nineteen hundred and ten,[7] is amended to read as follows:

AUTHORITY TO OPEN STREETS, ET CETERA.

§ 970. The city of New York is authorized to acquire title either in fee or to an easement, as may be determined by the board of estimate and apportionment, for the use of the public to all or any of the lands required for streets, parks, playgrounds,[8]

---

[5] Word " playgrounds " new.
[6] Words " and playgrounds " new.
[7] Section 970 was also amended by L. 1906, ch. 658, and L. 1909, ch. 394.
[8] Word " playgrounds " new.

approaches to bridges and tunnels, sites or lands above or under
water for bridges and tunnels, and sites or lands above or under
water, for all improvements of the navigation of waters within
or separating portions of the city of New York, or of the water
fronts of the city of New York, or part or parts thereof, heretofore duly laid out upon the map or plan of the city of New York,
of the city of Brooklyn, or Long Island City, or of any of the
territory consolidated with the corporation heretofore known as
the mayor, aldermen and commonalty of the city of New York,
or hereafter duly laid out upon the map or plan of the city of
New York, as herein constituted, and to cause the same to be
opened, or to acquire title as above stated to such interests in
lands as will promote public utility, comfort, health, enjoyment,[s]
or adornment, the acquisition of which is not elsewhere provided
for. The board of estimate and apportionment is authorized
to specify what use is required of the lands which it may determine to be acquired for public use, and the extent of such use,
and it is hereby authorized to change the map or plan of the city
of New York in accordance with the provisions of this act, on
this subject, and to direct the same to be acquired whenever and
as often as it shall deem it for the public interest so to do. The
lands, tenements and hereditaments that may be required for such
purposes may be taken therefor, and compensation and recompense made to the parties and persons, if any such there shall be,
to whom the loss and damage thereby shall be deemed to exceed
the benefit and advantage thereof, for the excess of the damage over
and above the value of said benefit. The city of New York is
authorized to make application, or to cause application to be made,
to the supreme court of this state in the first judicial department,
when the lands to be taken are situated within New York county,
and in the second judicial department, when the lands to be
taken are situated in the counties of Kings, Queens or Richmond
for the appointment of commissioners of estimate to ascertain
and determine the compensation and recompense which should
justly be made to the respective owners, lessees, parties and persons respectively entitled unto or interested in the lands, tenements, hereditaments and premises proposed to be taken for any
of the purposes aforesaid, and, in a proper case, for the appointment of one of such commissioners of estimate as a commissioner
of assessment to assess the cost of such improvement or such pro-

---

[s] Word "enjoyment" new.

portion thereof as the board of estimate and apportionment directs, upon such parties and persons, lands and tenements as may be deemed to be benefited thereby. The board of estimate and apportionment may authorize as many proceedings to be joined in one application for the appointment of commissioners of estimate or commissioner of assessment as it may deem advisable for the public interest. In the latter proceedings, whether now pending or hereafter authorized, it may determine upon a partial or separate area or areas of benefit for the opening of a street or streets joined in one application or for as many streets as it may see fit, and authorize that a partial or separate report or reports containing both the awards for damage and the assessments for benefit be made by the commissioners of estimate and the commissioner of assessment and presented together for confirmation. Notice of a hearing upon such partial or separate area or areas of assessment may be given, as herein provided either before the application for the appointment of the commissioners of estimate and assessment or during the pendency of the proceeding. It may also include in a single proceeding contiguous premises to be acquired in more than one borough of the city of New York, and authorize the appointment of commissioners of estimate and a commissioner of assessment therefor, to be selected from any of the boroughs embracing the premises sought to be acquired, and it may make and determine upon an area of assessment covering more than one borough, in such and all other proceedings, and all the provisions of this title as amended shall be applicable thereto. The moneys collected upon the assessment of the commissioner of assessment shall be paid into the city treasury. The damages awarded by the commissioners of estimate shall become due and payable immediately upon the confirmation of the report of said commissioners of estimate.

§ 4. This act shall take effect immediately.

Chap. 330.

AN ACT to ratify and confirm an agreement made under date of July twenty-first, nineteen hundred and eleven, between the city of New York and The Long Island Rail Road Company, providing for the elimination of grade crossings and for a payment by the city towards the expense thereof and to enable the city of New York to carry out all of the provisions and conditions thereof.

Became a law April 19, 1913, with the approval of the Governor. Passed, three-fifths being present.

Accepted by the City.

The People of the State of New York, represented in Senate and Assembly, do enact as follows:

Section 1. The agreement between the city of New York and The Long Island Rail Road Company, providing for the elimination of grade crossings on a number of streets in the borough of Queens and for a payment by the city toward the expense thereof, executed under date of July twenty-one, nineteen hundred and eleven, by the said city and railroad company is hereby ratified and confirmed and all the terms and provisions of such agreement shall be binding and effective upon the said city and the said railroad company, their successors and assigns, and shall inure to the benefits of the parties thereto, without any further consent, approval, act, or proceeding by or on the part of the public service commission, or by or on the part of said city, or any officer, board or department thereof.

§ 2. This act shall take effect immediately.

Chap. 331.

AN ACT to amend the Greater New York charter. in relation to the transfer of jurisdiction and control of streets.

Became a law April 19, 1913. with the approval of the Governor. Passed, three-fifths being present.

Accepted by the City.

The People of the State of New York, represented in Senate and Assembly, do enact as follows:

§ 242a. added to L. 1897, ch. 278, as re-enacted by L. 1901, ch. 466.

Section 1. The Greater New York charter, as re-enacted by chapter four hundred and sixty-six of the laws of nineteen hundred and one, is hereby amended by adding thereto after section two hundred and forty-three thereof, a new section to be known as section two hundred and forty-three-a, and to read as follows.

STREETS; TRANSFERS OF JURISDICTION AND CONTROL OF.

§ 243-a. The board of estimate and apportionment, with the concurrence of the board of aldermen, may transfer the jurisdiction and control of any street from any department, board or office to another department, board or office.

§ 2. This act shall take effect immediately.

Chap. 332.

AN ACT to amend "An act to provide for a commission to investigate and consider means for protecting the waters of New York bay and vicinity against pollution and authorizing the city of New York to pay the expenses thereof." in relation to the term of said commission.

Became a law April 19, 1913, with the approval of the Governor. Passed, three-fifths being present.

Accepted by the City.

The People of the State of New York, represented in Senate and Assembly, do enact as follows:

L. 1906, ch. 639, § 5, as amended by L. 1908. ch. 422,

Section 1. Section five of chapter six hundred and thirty-nine of the laws of nineteen hundred and six, entitled "An act to provide for a commission to investigate and consider means for protecting the waters of New York bay and vicinity against pollution and authorizing the city of New York to pay the expenses thereof," and L. 1910, as amended by chapter four hundred and twenty-two of the laws ch. 200, amended. of nineteen hundred and eight and chapter two hundred of the laws of nineteen hundred and ten, is hereby amended to read as follows:

§ 5. The commission shall terminate May first, nineteen hundred and sixteen,[1] and all maps, results or surveys and examinations, estimates and other papers and matter acquired by the New York commission shall be properly indexed and labeled and turned over to the board of estimate and apportionment of New York city. Termination of commission. Disposition of maps, etc.

§ 2. This act shall take effect immediately.

Chap. 333.

AN ACT to amend the Greater New York charter, in relation to the powers of the board of aldermen.

Became a law April 19, 1913, with the approval of the Governor. Passed, three-fifths being present.

Accepted by the City.

The People of the State of New York, represented in Senate and Assembly, do enact as follows:

Section 1. Section six hundred and ten of the Greater New York charter, as re-enacted by chapter four hundred and sixty-six of the laws of nineteen hundred and one, and as amended by chapter six hundred and twenty-eight of the laws of nineteen hundred and four, is hereby further amended to read as follows: L. 1897, ch. 378, § 610, as re-enacted by L. 1901, ch. 466, and amended by L. 1904, ch. 628, amended.

§ 610. General powers of the board; ordinances. The board of aldermen shall by general ordinances from time to time establish all needful rules and regulations for the government and protection of the public parks and of all property placed in charge of the park board and under its control by the provisions of this chapter, and the same shall at all times be subject to all such ordinances as to the use and occupation thereof and in respect to any erections or encumbrances thereon. [2]The board of aldermen shall have power to name or rename parks, parkways and all public places under the jurisdiction of the park board. The park

---

[1] Formerly " thirteen."
[2] Following sentence new.

board shall have power to establish and enforce general rules and regulations for the administration of the department, and, subject to the ordinances of the board of aldermen, to establish and enforce rules and regulations for the government and protection of the public parks and of all property in charge of said board or under its control, which rules and regulations so far as practicable shall be uniform in all the boroughs. All ordinances, rules and regulations of the park board which on the first day of January, nineteen hundred and two, shall be in force in the city of New York, are hereby continued in full force and effect until modified or repealed by the establishment of new ordinances, rules or regulations as herein provided. The rules and regulations for the government and protection of the public parks and of all property in charge of the said board or under its control, which are in force May first, nineteen hundred and four, shall, together with the ordinances adopted by the board of aldermen, constitute a chapter of the code of ordinances of the city of New York. On or before the fifteenth day of May, nineteen hundred and four, the secretary of the park board shall file with the city clerk all such rules and regulations which were in force on May first, nineteen hundred and four, and upon the filing of the same, they shall thereby become general ordinances of the city of New York. No such rule or regulation adopted by the park board subsequent to May first, nineteen hundred and four, shall become valid and effectual until a copy of such rule or regulation, duly certified to be a correct copy by the secretary of the park board, be filed with the city clerk. Upon so filing such rule or regulation shall become a general ordinance of the city of New York. Any person violating any ordinances relating to the parks or other property mentioned in this section shall be guilty of a misdemeanor and shall on conviction before a city magistrate be punished by a fine not exceeding fifty dollars, or in default of payment of such fine by imprisonment not exceeding thirty days.

§ 2. This act shall take effect immediately.

Chap. 334.

AN ACT to amend the executive law, in relation to the powers of notaries public who are stockholders, directors, officers or employees of banks or other corporations.

Became a law April 19, 1913, with the approval of the Governor. Passed, three-fifths being present.

The People of the State of New York, represented in Senate and Assembly, do enact as follows:

Section 1. Chapter twenty-three of the laws of nineteen hundred and nine, entitled "An act in relation to executive officers, constituting chapter eighteen of the consolidated laws," is hereby amended by inserting therein a new section, to be section one hundred and five-a thereof, to read as follows:

§ 105-a. **Powers of notaries who are stockholders, directors, officers or employees of banks or other corporations.** A notary public, who is a stockholder, director, officer or employee of a bank or other corporation may take the acknowledgment of any party to a written instrument executed to or by such corporation, or administer an oath to any other stockholder, director, officer, employee or agent of such corporation, or protest for nonacceptance or nonpayment, bills of exchange, drafts, checks, notes and other negotiable instruments owned or held for collection by such corporation; but a notary public shall not take the acknowledgment of an instrument by or to a bank or other corporation of which he is a stockholder, director, officer or employee, if such notary be a party executing such instrument, either individually or as representative of such corporation, or protest any negotiable instrument owned or held for collection by such corporation, if such notary be individually a party to such instrument.

§ 2. This act shall take effect immediately.

(margin note) § 105a added to L. 1909, ch. 2.

Chap. 335.

AN ACT to amend the public health law. in relation to cadavers for medical and surgical study.

Became a law April 19, 1913, with the approval of the Governor. Passed, three-fifths being present.

The People of the State of New York, represented in Senate and Assembly, do enact as follows:

L 1909,
ch 49,
§ 316
amended.

Section 1. Section three hundred and sixteen of chapter forty-nine of the laws of nineteen hundred and nine. entitled "An act in relation to the public health, constituting chapter forty-five of the consolidated laws," is hereby amended to read as follows:

§ 316. **Cadavers.** The persons having lawful control and management of any hospital, prison, asylum. morgue or other receptacle for corpses not interred, and every undertaker or other person having in his lawful possession any such corpse for keeping or burial may deliver and he is required to deliver, under the conditions specified in this section, every such corpse in their or his possession, charge, custody or control, not placed therein by relatives or friends in the usual manner for keeping or burial, to the medical colleges and universities[1] of the state authorized by law to confer the degree of doctor of medicine and to all other colleges or schools incorporated under the laws of the state for the purpose of teaching medicine, anatomy or surgery to those on whom the degree of doctor of medicine has been conferred,[2] and to any university of the state having a medical preparatory or medical post-graduate course of instruction.[3] No corpse shall be so delivered or received if desired for interment by relatives or friends within forty-eight hours after death, or if known to have relatives or friends without the assent of such relatives or friends; or of a person who shall have expressed a desire in his last illness that his body be interred, but the same shall be buried in the usual manner. If the remains of any person so delivered or received shall be subsequently claimed by any relative or friend, they shall be given up to such relative or friend for interment. Any person claiming any corpse or

---

[1] Words " and universities " new.
[2] Words " and to all other colleges or schools . . . conferred," new.
[3] Words " and the professors and teachers in every such college, or university may receive any such corpse and use it for the purpose of medical study," omitted.

remains for interment as provided in this section, may be required by the persons, college, school or university or officer or agent thereof, in whose possession, charge or custody the same may be, to present an affidavit stating that he is such relative or friend, and the facts and circumstances upon which the claim that he is such relative or friend is based, the expense of which affidavit shall be paid by the persons requiring it. If such person shall refuse to make such affidavit, such corpse or remains shall not be delivered to him but he shall forfeit his claim and right to the same. Any such medical college, school[4] or university desiring to avail itself of the provisions of this section shall notify such persons having the control and management of the institutions and places heretofore specified, and such undertakers and other persons having any such corpse in their possession, custody or control in the county where such college, school[4] or university is situated, and in any other[5] county in the state. in which no medical college, school or university is situated, or in which[6] no such medical college, school or university desires to avail itself of the provisions of this section,[7] of such desire, and thereafter all such persons shall notify the proper officers of such college, school[4] or university whenever there is any corpse in their possession, custody or control, which may be delivered to a medical college, school[4] or university under this section, and shall deliver the same to such college, school[4] or university. [8]If two or more medical colleges, schools or universities are entitled to receive corpses under the provisions of this act and shall have given notice as aforesaid, they shall receive the same in proportion to the number of matriculated students in each college, school or university who are pursuing courses of anatomy and surgery at the time of making the apportionment. The professors and teachers in every college, school[4] or university receiving any corpse under this section shall dispose of the remains thereof, after they have served the purposes of medical science and study, in accordance with the regulations of the local board of health where the college, school[4] or university is situated. Every person neglect-

[4] Word "school" new.
[5] Word "other" substituted for word "adjoining."
[6] Words "school or university is situated, or in which," new.
[7] Words "medical college, school or university desires to avail itself of the provisions of this section," new.
[8] Following sentence formerly read: "If two or more medical colleges located in one county are entitled to receive corpses from the same county or adjoining counties, they shall receive the same in proportion to the number of matriculated students in each college."

ing to comply with or violating any provision of this section, shall
forfeit to the local board of health where such non-compliance or
violation occurred, the sum of twenty-five dollars for every such
non-compliance or violation, to be sued for by the health officer of
such place, and when recovered to be paid over, less the costs and
expenses of the action, to such board for its use and benefit.

§ 2. This act shall take effect immediately.

Chap. 336.

AN ACT to authorize the village of Peekskill to construct a
building to be used as a jail, police court and police headquarters, and to acquire necessary lands therefor, and to issue
bonds for such purpose; and repealing chapter seven hundred
and thirty-five of the laws of nineteen hundred and eleven,
and ratifying and confirming the bonds issued thereunder;
and directing the use of the proceeds of such bonds.

Became a law April 19, 1913, with the approval of the Governor. Passed,
three-fifths being present.

*The People of the State of New York, represented in Senate
and Assembly, do enact as follows:*

Bond issue and acquisition of lands, etc., authorized.
Section 1. The board of trustees of the village of Peekskill is
hereby authorized and empowered to issue bonds for the construction of a building to be used as a jail, police court and police
headquarters in such village, and to contract for the purchase
and acquire by deed or by proceedings under the condemnation
law of the state of New York, in the name of the board of trustees of the village of Peekskill, lands, tenements or easements
necessary for the acquisition and construction of the said building contemplated by this act.

Cost and amount of bonds limited.
§ 2. The cost of the construction of such building and the
acquisition by purchase or otherwise, as aforesaid, of the lands
and easements necessary for such purpose under this act, shall in
no event exceed the sum of seventy thousand dollars, and the
bonds issued under the provisions of this act shall not exceed the
sum of forty thousand dollars in addition to the bonds heretofore
issued under the provisions of chapter seven hundred and thirty-
five of the laws of nineteen hundred and eleven.

Bonds to be issued; how desig-
§ 3. The board of trustees shall cause such bonds to be issued
upon the credit of such village, to an amount not exceeding the

sum provided by section two of this act, which bonds shall be nated; execution, etc.
designated as " jail bonds of the village of Peekskill, New York."
Such bonds shall be signed by the president and treasurer of such
village, and shall bear the corporate seal of said village of Peekskill. Said bonds shall be of the denomination of one thousand
dollars each, and shall be payable in installments; the first of said
bonds to be due and payable five years from the date of issue,
and one of such bonds shall become due and payable in each succeeding year thereafter; and such bonds shall bear such rate of
interest as the board of trustees shall determine, not exceeding
five per centum per annum, payable semi-annually, and shall not
be negotiated for less than their par value. They shall be sold Sale.
on sealed proposals to the bidder who will take them at the lowest
rate of interest, upon notice duly published in each of the newspapers printed and published in such village, and in such other
newspapers or manner as the board of trustees may determine,
but such board shall reserve the right to reject any and all bids.
They shall be consecutively numbered from one to the highest Record.
issued, and the board of trustees shall keep a record of the number
of each bond, its date, the amount, rate of interest, when and
where payable, and the purchaser thereof or the person to whom
they are issued. The board of trustees shall raise by annual tax Tax for payment.
in the same manner as other taxes are raised, an amount sufficient
to pay the interest on such bonds, and the principal thereof as
they may become due.

§ 4. Chapter seven hundred and thirty-five of the laws of L. 1911, ch. 735
nineteen hundred and eleven is hereby repealed, but all proceed- repealed; proceedings had or taken by the board of trustees of the village of Peeks- ings thereunder
kill thereunder, including all bonds issued by such board under legalized.
the powers conferred thereby, are hereby ratified and confirmed.

§ 5. The board of trustees of the village of Peekskill is hereby Expenditure of
authorized to expend the amount realized from the sale of such proceeds of bond
bonds, together with any sum heretofore realized from the sale issues, authorised.
of bonds issued under and in pursuance of chapter seven hundred
and thirty-five of the laws of nineteen hundred and eleven, for
the purposes specified in section one of this act.

§ 6. This act shall take effect immediately.

Chap. 337.

AN ACT to amend the code of civil procedure, in relation to the powers of the surrogate respecting the construction or effect of dispositions of property by will.

Became a law April 19, 1913, with the approval of the Governor. Passed, three-fifths being present.

The People of the State of New York, represented in Senate and Assembly, do enact as follows:

§ 2624 amended.

Section 1. Section twenty-six hundred and twenty-four of the code of civil procedure is hereby amended to read as follows:

Validity and construction of testamentary provisions.

§ 2624. But if a party expressly puts in issue, before the surrogate, the validity, construction, or effect of any disposition of property, contained in a will of a resident of the state, executed within the state, the surrogate may[1] determine the question upon rendering a decree; or,[2] unless the decree refuses to admit the will to probate, by reason of a failure to prove any of the matters specified in the last section, [3]may admit the will to probate and reserve the question of construction *of *efforts for future consideration and decree.

In effect Sept. 1, 1913.

§ 2. This act shall take effect September first, nineteen hundred and thirteen.

Chap. 338.

AN ACT relating to the management and investment of the moneys and property constituting any endowment fund of " The Rector and Inhabitants of the City of Albany, in Communion of the Protestant Episcopal Church in the State of New York," generally known as Saint Peter's church of the city of Albany.

Became a law April 19, 1913, with the approval of the Governor. Passed, three-fifths being present.

The People of the State of New York, represented in Senate and Assembly, do enact as follows:

Transfer of endowment fund to trust

Section 1. The corporation " The Rector and Inhabitants of the City of Albany, in Communion of the Protestant Episcopal

---

* So in original.
[1] Word " may " substituted for word " must."
[2] Word " or " new.
[3] Remainder of section new.

Church in the State of New York," generally known as Saint company in trust to be invested, authorised. Peter's church of the city of Albany, created and existing by virtue of a charter under the great seal of the then colony, now state of New York, bearing date the twenty-fifth day of April, in the year of our Lord one thousand seven hundred and sixty-nine, is hereby authorized to transfer, convey and assign such moneys and property as it may now have constituting an endowment fund of or for the uses of Saint Peter's church in the city of Albany, and such as it may hereafter acquire for the same purpose, to such trust company, organized and existing under the laws of this state, as may be designated by such corporation; such moneys and property to be held by such trust company in trust to invest and reinvest in such manner as trust funds are allowed to be invested under the laws of this state, existing at the time of such investment, for the benefit and support of such corporation; and the income from said moneys and property shall be paid and ap- Payment of income. portioned by such trust company to that purpose according to the directions to be from time to time given by the vestry of such corporation.

§ 2. In case the trust company appointed by such corpora- Other trust company, how substituted. tion shall resign its trust, or in case such company shall become insolvent, or such corporation for any cause may deem it advisable to designate another trust company, such corporation may present a petition to the supreme court for the substitution of another trust company, and the supreme court is hereby authorized to appoint another trust company, as trustee.

§ 3. The trust company, having custody of such moneys and Reports by trust company. property shall at least annually, and as often as may be required by the vestry of such corporation, make a full and true report to it of the condition of the funds and property, and the receipts and disbursements thereof.

§ 4. This act shall take effect immediately.

Chap. 339.

AN ACT to amend chapter eight hundred and fifty-one of the laws of nineteen hundred and eleven, in relation to the management and control of the state college of forestry at Syracuse University.

Became a law April 19, 1913, with the approval of the Governor. Passed, three-fifths being present.

The People of the State of New York, represented in Senate and Assembly, do enact as follows:

L. 1911,
ch. 851,
§ 3, as
amended by
L. 1912,
ch. 16,
amended.

Section 1. Section three of chapter eight hundred and fifty-one of the laws of nineteen hundred and eleven, entitled "An act to establish a state college of forestry at Syracuse University, and making an appropriation therefor," as amended by chapter fifteen of the laws of nineteen hundred and twelve, is hereby amended to read as follows:[1]

§ 3. **Management and control of college.** The care, management and control of such college and the property and premises required therefor shall be exercised by a board of thirteen trustees. The chairman of the state conservation commission, the temporary president of the senate, the state commissioner of education and the chancellor of Syracuse University, shall be ex-officio members of the board of trustees. The remaining nine members of the board of trustees shall be appointed by the governor, by and with the advice and consent of the senate, immediately after this act takes effect and shall be divided into three classes, so that the terms of one-third thereof shall expire on June thirtieth, nineteen hundred and fifteen, and one-third thereof on the thirtieth day of June of each second year thereafter. Successors to such trustees shall be appointed for full terms of six years. In case of any vacancy in the office of any appointive trustee his successor shall be appointed for the unexpired term for which he was appointed. The members of the board of trustees shall serve without compensation, but shall be entitled to their actual necessary expenses incurred in the performance of their duties.

§ 2. This act shall take effect immediately.

---

[1] Section materially amended.

Chap. 340.

AN ACT to amend the labor law, in relation to washrooms, dressing rooms and water closets in factories.

Became a law April 19, 1913, with the approval of the Governor. Passed, three-fifths being present.

The People of the State of New York, represented in Senate and Assembly, do enact as follows:

Section 1. Section eighty-eight of chapter thirty-six of the laws of nineteen hundred and nine, entitled "An act relating to labor, constituting chapter thirty-one of the consolidated laws," as amended by chapter three hundred and thirty-six of the laws of nineteen hundred and twelve,[1] is hereby amended to read as follows:[2]

§ 88. **Drinking water, washrooms and dressing rooms.** 1. In every factory there shall be provided at all times for the use of employees, a sufficient supply of clean and pure drinking water. Such water shall be supplied through proper pipe connections with water mains through which is conveyed the water used for domestic purposes, or, from a spring or well or body of pure water; if such drinking water be placed in receptacles in the factory, such receptacles shall be properly covered to prevent contamination and shall be thoroughly cleaned at frequent intervals.

2. In every factory there shall be provided and maintained for the use of employees suitable and convenient washrooms, separate for each sex, adequately equipped with washing facilities consisting of sinks or stationary basins provided with running water or with tanks holding an adequate supply of clean water. Every washroom shall be provided with means for artificial illumination and with adequate means of ventilation. All washrooms and washing facilities shall be constructed, lighted, heated, ventilated, arranged and maintained according to rules and regulations adopted with reference thereto by the industrial board. In all factories where lead, arsenic or other poisonous substances or injurious or noxious fumes, dust or gases are present as an incident or result of the business or processes conducted by such factory there shall be provided washing

_____
[1] Section 88 was also amended by L. 1910, ch. 229.
[2] Section materially amended.

facilities which shall include hot water and soap and individual towels.

3. Where females are employed, dressing or emergency rooms shall be provided for their use; each such room shall have at least one window opening to the outer air and shall be enclosed by means of solid partitions or walls. In every factory in which more than ten women are employed, there shall be provided one or more separate dressing rooms in such numbers as required by the rules and regulations of the industrial board and located in such place or places as required by such rules and regulations. having an adequate floor space in proportion to the number of employees, to be fixed by the rules and regulations of the industrial board, but the floor space of every such dressing room shall in no event be less than sixty square feet; each dressing room shall be separated from any water closet compartment by adequate partitions and shall be provided with adequate means for artificial illumination; each dressing room shall be provided with suitable means for hanging clothes and with a suitable number of seats. All dressing rooms shall be enclosed by means of solid partitions or walls, and shall be constructed, heated, ventilated, lighted and maintained in accordance with such rules and regulations as may be adopted by the industrial board with reference thereto.

§ 88a added.

§ 2. Such chapter is hereby amended by inserting after section eighty-eight a new section, to be section eighty-eight-a, to read as follows:

§ 88-a. **Water closets.** 1. In every factory there shall be provided suitable and convenient water closets separate for each sex. in such number and located in such place or places as required by the rules and regulations of the industrial board. All water closets shall be maintained inside the factory except where, in the opinion of the commissioner of labor, it is impracticable to do so.

2. There shall be separate water closet compartments for females, to be used by them exclusively, and notice to that effect shall be painted on the outside of such compartments. The entrance to every water closet used by females shall be effectively screened by a partition or vestibule. Where water closets for males and females are in adjoining compartments, there shall be solid plastered or metal covered partitions between the compartments extending from the floor to the ceiling. Whenever any water closet compartments open directly into the workroom ex-

posing the interior, they shall be screened from view by a partition or a vestibule. The use of curtains for screening purposes is prohibited.

3. The use of any form of trough water closet, latrine or school sink within any factory is prohibited. All such trough water closets, latrines or school sinks shall, before the first of October, nineteen hundred and fourteen, be completely removed and the place where they were located properly disinfected under the direction of the department of labor. Such appliances shall be replaced by proper individual water closets, placed in water closet compartments, all of which shall be constructed and installed in accordance with rules and regulations to be adopted by the industrial board.

4. Every existing water closet and urinal inside any factory shall have a basin of enameled iron or earthenware, and shall be flushed from a separate water-supplied cistern or through a flushometer valve connected in such manner as to keep the water supply of the factory free from contamination. All woodwork enclosing water closet fixtures shall be removed from the front of the closet and the space underneath the seat shall be left open. The floor or other surface beneath and around the closet shall be maintained in good order and repair and all the woodwork shall be kept well painted with a light-color paint. All existing water closet compartments shall have windows leading to the outer air and shall be otherwise ventilated in accordance with rules and regulations adopted for that purpose by the industrial board. Such compartments shall be provided with means for artificial illumination and the enclosure of each compartment shall be kept free from all obscene writing or marking.

5. All water closets, urinals and water closet compartments hereafter installed in a factory, including those provided to replace existing fixtures, shall be properly constructed, installed, ventilated, lighted and maintained in accordance with such rules and regulations as may be adopted by the industrial board.

6. All water closet compartments, and the floors, walls, ceilings and surface thereof, and all fixtures therein, and all water closets and urinals shall at all times be kept and maintained in a clean and sanitary condition. Where the water supply to water closets or urinals is liable to freeze, the water closet compartment shall be properly heated so as to prevent freezing, or the supply and flush pipes, cisterns and traps and valves shall be effectively covered with wool felt or hair felt, or other adequate covering.

7. All water closets shall be constructed, lighted, ventilated, arranged and maintained according to rules and regulations adopted with reference thereto by the industrial board.

§ 3. This act shall take effect October first, nineteen hundred and thirteen.

Chap. 341.

AN ACT to amend the general municipal law, in relation to the establishment of workshops in connection with tuberculosis hospitals or sanatoriums.

Became a law April 19, 1913, with the approval of the Governor. Passed, three-fifths being present.

The People of the State of New York, represented in Senate and Assembly, do enact as follows:

Section 1. Chapter twenty-nine of the laws of nineteen hundred and nine, entitled "An act relating to municipal corporations, constituting chapter twenty-four of the consolidated laws," is hereby amended by inserting therein a new section, to be section one hundred and thirty-five-a, to read as follows:

§ 135-a. **Workshops in connection with tuberculosis hospitals.** Any municipal corporation maintaining a hospital or a sanatorium for the treatment of tuberculosis may establish and maintain workshops in connection therewith for the production of articles or supplies required by such hospital or sanatorium, or by any other institution or department of such municipality. Except in a supervisory capacity no person shall be employed in such workshop or workshops unless he is or shall have been a patient suffering from tuberculosis in such hospital or sanatorium. The appropriate municipal authorities may appropriate or provide funds for the establishment and maintenance of the said workshops in the same manner as for the establishment and maintenance of such hospitals or sanatoria. Notwithstanding the provisions of the prison law in relation to the sale of articles manufactured in the state prisons, the products of such workshop may be used in such hospital or sanatorium or by any other institution or department of such municipality. Such workshops shall be under the direction and control of the municipal authority having direction and control of the hospital or sanatorium to which they may be attached.

§ 2. This act shall take effect immediately.

Chap. 342.

AN ACT to amend the state finance law, in relation to the powers
and duties of the state comptroller.

Became a law April 21, 1913, with the approval of the Governor. Passed,
three-fifths being present.

*The People of the State of New York, represented in Senate
and Assembly, do enact as follows:*

Section 1. Subdivision five of section four of chapter fifty- L. 1909, eight of the laws of nineteen hundred and nine, entitled "An act § 4, subd. in relation to state finance, constituting chapter fifty-six of the consolidated laws," is hereby amended to read as follows:

5. Draw warrants on the treasury for the payment of the Duty of moneys directed by law to be paid out of the treasury, but no such ler to warrant shall be drawn unless authorized by law, and every such rants. warrant shall refer to the law under which it is drawn.[1]

§ 2. Section sixteen of such chapter is hereby amended to read § 16 as follows: amended.

§ 16. **Accounts and contracts.**[2] The comptroller shall prepare a form of accounts to be observed in every state charitable institution, reformatory, house of refuge, industrial school, department, board or commission, which shall be accepted and followed by them respectively, after thirty days' notice thereof. Such forms shall include such a uniform method of bookkeeping, filing and rendering of accounts as may insure a uniform statement of purchase of like articles, whether by the pound, measure or otherwise, as the interests of the public service may require, and a uniform method of reporting in such institutions and departments, the amount and value of all produce and other articles of maintenance raised upon the lands of the state, or manufactured in such institution, and which may enter into the maintenance of such institution or department. All purchases for the use of any department, office or work of the state government shall be for cash. Each voucher, whether for a purchase or for services or other charge shall be filled up at the time it

---

[1] Remainder of subdivision omitted which read: "Whenever the comptroller shall be satisfied that moneys have been paid into the treasury through mistake, he may draw his warrant therefor on the treasurer, in favor of the person who may have made such payment; but this provision shall not extend to payments on account of taxes, nor to payments on bonds and mortgages."
[2] Section heading formerly read: "Forms of state accounts."

is taken. Where payment is not made directly by the state treasurer, proof in some proper form shall be furnished on oath that the voucher was so filled up at the time it was taken, and that the money stated therein to have been paid, was in fact paid in cash or by check or draft on some specified bank.

[2]Before any contract made for or by any state charitable institution, reformatory, house of refuge, industrial school, officer, department, board or commission, shall be executed or become effective, when such contract exceeds one thousand dollars in amount, it shall first be approved by the comptroller and filed in his office. Whenever any liability of any nature shall be incurred by or for any state charitable institution, reformatory, house of refuge, industrial school, officer, department, board or commission, notice that such liability has been incurred shall be immediately given in writing to the state comptroller. Whenever any supplies or materials are furnished to any state charitable institution, reformatory, house of refuge, industrial school, officer, department, board or commission, a duplicate of the invoice shall be delivered to the comptroller at the same time that it is delivered to the officer, department or institution receiving the supplies or materials.

This section, as amended, shall be deemed to supersede any other provision of this chapter or of any other general or special law inconsistent therewith.

§ 3. This act shall take effect immediately.

---

[2] Remainder of section new.

Chap. 343.

AN ACT authorizing the city of Buffalo to construct improvements along Scajaquada creek in said city for the abatement of floods or freshets, to construct a sewer or drain and a highway along the line of said creek, to purchase or acquire the fee of the necessary lands and real property and to borrow money by the issue and sale of bonds, for any or all of said improvements, or the acquisition of real property therefor.

Became a law April 22, 1913, with the approval of the Governor. Passed, three-fifths being present.

Accepted by the City.

The People of the State of New York, represented in Senate and Assembly, do enact as follows:

Section 1. Discretionary power is hereby conferred upon the city of Buffalo to make and construct such improvements in or along that part of Scajaquada creek which is situated in the nineteenth ward of said city and the territory adjacent thereto, as shall be required for the effectual abatement of the periodical floods or freshets caused by the overflow of the banks of said creek; to construct a sewer or drain in or adjacent to the bed of said creek in and adjacent to said nineteenth ward; and to open, establish, fill and grade a street or highway over, along or adjacent to said creek in the same district. Said city shall also have power to purchase the fee of such lands and real property, or to acquire such lands and real property, in fee, by proceedings in eminent domain pursuant to the provisions of the charter of said city, being chapter one hundred and five of the laws of eighteen hundred and ninety-one and the acts amendatory thereof, as shall be required for the construction of any or all of said improvements; provided, however, that the assessors shall not be required to certify the district that will be benefited by or assessed for the appropriation of real property for said improvements, but the cost thereof, and of the proceedings, may be defrayed wholly from the general fund, as herein provided.

§ 2. Said city of Buffalo is hereby authorized to issue its bonds from time to time, in a sum not to exceed in the aggregate, one hundred and eighty-five thousand dollars, for the purpose of providing funds to defray the cost of the improvements mentioned in the foregoing section and the purchase or acquisition of lands and real property therefor; provided, however, that the cost of

[marginal notes: Improvements to abate floods authorized. Sewer. Highway. Acquisition of lands for improvements. Cost may be defrayed from general fund. Issue of bonds authorized. Cost may be defrayed]

from proceeds of trunk sewer bonds. constructing the sewer or drain hereby authorized, including excavation and refilling, may be defrayed from the proceeds of the sale of bonds issued pursuant to chapter three hundred and seventy-three of the laws of nineteen hundred and twelve, entitled "An act to authorize the city of Buffalo to issue its bonds for the purpose of providing funds for the construction, reconstruction and enlargement of public trunk sewers." The bonds authorized hereby shall be issued under the city seal by the mayor and comptroller, as ordered by the common council, and shall be sold or awarded in the manner provided by the charter of said city, being chapter one hundred and five of the laws of eighteen hundred and ninety-one, and the acts amendatory thereof, and shall bear interest at such rate, not exceeding the legal rate, as shall be fixed by the common council, payable semi-annually at the office of the comptroller of the city of Buffalo or at the Hanover national bank of the city of New York, as the purchaser may elect, the principal to be payable at the same place at the end of a term to be designated by the common council, not more than fifty years from the date of issue. The common council shall make provision in the general fund estimates of said city for the payment of the interest on and the principal of said bonds as the same shall become due.

Bonds, execution, sale, interest, etc.

Provision for payment.

§ 3. This act shall take effect immediately.

Chap. 344.

AN ACT to amend the public service commissions law, in relation to common carriers and extending the jurisdiction of the public service commissions to baggage companies and transfer companies.

Became a law April 22, 1913, with the approval of the Governor. Passed, three-fifths being present.

The People of the State of New York, represented in Senate and Assembly, do enact as follows:

L. 1910, ch. 480, § 2, subd. 9 amended. Section 1. Subdivision nine of section two of chapter four hundred and eighty of the laws of nineteen hundred and ten, entitled "An act in relation to public service commissions, constituting chapter forty-eight of the consolidated laws," is hereby amended to read as follows:

9. The term "common carrier," when used in this chapter, includes all railroad corporations, street railroad corporations, express companies, car companies, sleeping-car companies, freight companies, freight-line companies, baggage companies and transfer companies,[1] and every corporation, company, association, joint-stock association, partnership and person, their lessees, trustees or receivers appointed by any court whatsoever, owning, operating or managing any such agency for public use in the conveyance of persons, or property within this state; but the said term common carrier when used in this chapter shall not include an express company, baggage company or transfer company[2] unless the same is operated wholly or in part upon or in connection with a railroad or street railroad.

§ 2. Section two of said chapter is hereby amended by adding thereto, after subdivision nine thereof, a new subdivision, to be subdivision nine-a, to read as follows:

9-a. The term "baggage company" shall apply to those companies engaged under contract or agreement with a railroad company or street railroad company in the checking of baggage, or in the collection and delivery of baggage between railroad stations, or between railroad stations and hotels, residences, business places or steamer docks; and the term "transfer company" shall apply to companies engaged under contract or agreement with a railroad company or street railroad company in the transfer of passengers or property between railroad stations, or between railroad stations and hotels, residences, business places or steamer docks.

§ 3. Section thirty-eight of said chapter is hereby amended to read as follows:

§ 38. **Liability for damage to property in transit.** Every common carrier, baggage company, transfer company,[3] [4]railroad corporation and street railroad corporation shall, upon demand, issue either a receipt or bill of lading for all property delivered to it for transportation. No contract, stipulation or clause in any receipt or bill of lading shall exempt or be held to exempt any common carrier, baggage company, transfer company,[3] railroad corporation or street railroad corporation from any liability for loss, damage or injury caused by it to property from

Marginal notes: Term common carrier to include what. § 2, subd. 9a added. Application of terms baggage company and transfer company. § 38 amended.

---

[1] Words " baggage companies and transfer companies," new.
[2] Words " baggage company or transfer company," new.
[3] Words " baggage company, transfer company," new.
[4] Words " and every " omitted.

21

the time of its delivery for transportation until the same shall have been received at its destination and a reasonable time shall have elapsed after notice to consignee of such arrival to permit of the removal of such property. Every common carrier, baggage company, transfer company,[3] railroad corporation and street railroad corporation shall be liable for all loss, damage or injury to property caused by delay in transit due to negligence while the same is being carried by it, but in any action to recover for damages sustained by delay in transit the burden of proof shall be upon the defendant to show that such delay was not due to negligence. Every common carrier, baggage company, transfer company,[3] and railroad corporation shall be liable for loss, damage and injury to property carried as baggage whether in connection with the transportation of the owner or not,[5] up to the full value and regardless of the character thereof, but the value in excess of one hundred and fifty dollars shall be stated upon delivery to the carrier, and a written receipt stating the value shall be issued by the carrier, who may make a reasonable charge for the assumption of such liability in excess of one hundred and fifty dollars and for the carriage of baggage exceeding one hundred and fifty pounds in weight upon a single ticket or receipt.[6] Nothing in this section shall deprive any holder of such receipt or bill of lading of any remedy or right of action which he has under existing law.

§ 4. This act shall take effect immediately.

Chap. 345.

AN ACT to amend the agricultural law, in relation to the commissioner of agriculture.

Became a law April 22, 1913, with the approval of the Governor. Passed, three-fifths being present.

The People of the State of New York, represented in Senate and Assembly, do enact as follows:

L. 1909,
ch. 9,
§§ 2, 3
amended.

Section 1. Sections two[1] and three of chapter nine of the laws of nineteen hundred and nine, entitled " An act in relation to

---

3 Words " baggage company, transfer company," new.
5 Words " whether in connection with the transportation of the owner or not," new.
6 Words " or receipt " new.
1 Section 2 as amended by L. 1909, ch. 580.

agriculture, constituting chapter one of the consolidated laws," are hereby amended to read as follows:

§ 2.[2] **Commissioner of agriculture.** There shall be a department of the state government known as the department of agriculture, which shall be charged with the execution of the laws relating to agriculture and agricultural products. The commissioner of agriculture shall be the chief of the department. The commissioner of agriculture shall be appointed by the governor, by and with the advice and consent of the senate. His term of office shall be three years. He shall be paid an annual salary of not to exceed six thousand dollars and his necessary expenses incurred in the discharge of his official duties. He may appoint four deputy commissioners of agriculture, a director of farmers' institutes and appoint or employ such clerks, chemists, agents, counsel and other employees as he may deem necessary for the proper enforcement of such laws and the proper administration of the department, who shall receive such compensation as may be fixed by him, in cases where it is not otherwise fixed, and their necessary expenses. The compensation of his deputies, clerks, and other persons appointed or employed by him and such necessary expenses shall be paid on his certificate by the treasurer on the warrant of the comptroller. All other charges, accounts and expenses of the department authorized by law shall be paid by the treasurer on the warrant of the comptroller, after they have been audited and allowed by the comptroller. The trustees of public buildings shall furnish suitable rooms for the use of the department.

§ 3.[3] **Power of commissioner, his deputies and employees.** The commissioner of agriculture, his deputies, clerks, experts, chemists, agents and counsel employed by him, shall have full access to all places of business, factories, farms, buildings, carriages, cars and vessels used in the manufacture, sale or transportation within the state of any dairy products or any imitation thereof, or of any article or product with respect to which any authority is conferred by this chapter on such commissioner. They may examine and open any package, can or vessel containing or believed to contain any article or product, which may be manufactured, sold or exposed for sale in violation of the provisions of this chapter, and may inspect the contents

[2] Section materially amended.
[3] In the following section wherever the words " deputy " or " deputies " occur they are substituted for words " assistant " or " assistants."

therein, and take therefrom samples for analysis. The commissioner of agriculture shall have the power by subpoena or subpoena duces tecum, issued and attested by him in his official capacity to require the attendance and testimony before him, or any of his deputy commissioners or other persons designated· by him for that purpose,[4] of any person whom he may have reason to believe has knowledge of any alleged violation of this chapter, and the production, before him or any of his deputy commissioners of agriculture of any records, books, papers and documents for the purpose of investigating any alleged violation of this chapter. Such subpoenas or subpoena duces tecum may be served by any person over the age of twenty-one years. No person shall be excused from attending and testifying or producing any records, books, papers or other documents before said commissioner of agriculture or any of his deputy commissioners of agriculture or other person designated by him for that purpose[6] upon such investigation upon the ground or for the reason that the testimony or evidence, documentary or otherwise, required of him may tend to convict him of a crime or subject him to a penalty or forfeiture, but no person shall be prosecuted or subjected to any penalty or forfeiture for or on account of any transaction, matter or thing concerning which he may so testify or produce evidence, documentary or otherwise, and no testimony so given or produced shall be received against him upon any criminal action, investigation or proceeding. Any person who shall omit, neglect or refuse to attend and testify or to produce any records, books, papers or documents, if in his power so to do, in obedience to such subpoena or subpoena duces tecum shall be guilty of a misdemeanor. Any person who shall wilfully and knowingly make any false statement under oath before the commissioner of agriculture, a deputy commissioner of agriculture or other person designated, as provided herein,[6] concerning a material matter, shall be guilty of perjury. The commissioner of agriculture and his deputy commissioners of agriculture and other persons designated, as provided herein,[7] are hereby authorized and empowered to administer oaths and affirmations in the usual appropriate forms to any person in any matter or proceedings authorized as aforesaid and in all

---

[4] Words " or other persons designated by him for that purpose," new.
[5] Words " or other person designated by him for that purpose," new.
[6] Words " or other person designated, as provided herein," new.
[7] Words " and other persons designated, as provided herein," new.

matters pertaining or relating to this chapter and to take and
administer oaths and affirmations in the usual appropriate forms,
in taking any affidavit or deposition, which may be necessary or
required by law or by any order, rule or regulation of the commissioner of agriculture for or in connection with the official
purposes, affairs, powers, duties or proceedings of said commissioner of agriculture or his deputy commissioners of agriculture or for any official purpose lawfully authorized by said
commissioner of agriculture.

§ 2. This act shall take effect immediately.

Chap. 346.

AN ACT to amend the penal law, in relation to public traffic on
Sunday.

Became a law April 22, 1913, with the approval of the Governor. Passed,
three-fifths being present.

*The People of the State of New York, represented in Senate
and Assembly, do enact as follows:*

Section 1. Section twenty-one hundred and forty-seven of chapter eighty-eight of the laws of nineteen hundred and nine, entitled
"An act providing for the punishment of crime, constituting chapter forty of the consolidated laws," is hereby amended to read as
follows:[1]

§ 2147. **Public traffic on Sunday.** All manner of public selling
or offering for sale of any property upon Sunday is prohibited, except as follows:

1. Articles of food may be sold, served, supplied and delivered
at any time before ten o'clock in the morning;

2. Meals may be sold to be eaten on the premises where sold at
any time of the day;

3. Caterers may serve meals to their patrons at any time of the
day;

4. Prepared tobacco, milk, eggs, ice, soda-water, fruit, flowers,
confectionery, newspapers, drugs, medicines and surgical instruments, may be sold in places other than a room where spirituous
or malt liquors or wines are kept or offered for sale and may be
delivered at any time of the day:

---

[1] Section materially amended.

5. Delicatessen dealers may sell, supply, serve and deliver cooked and prepared foods, between the hours of four o'clock in the afternoon and half past seven o'clock in the evening, in addition to the time provided for in subdivision one hereof.

The provisions of this section, however, shall not be construed to allow or permit the public sale or exposing for sale or delivery of uncooked flesh foods, or meats, fresh or salt, at any hour or time of the day. Delicatessen dealers shall not be considered as caterers within subdivision three hereof.

§ 2. This act shall take effect immediately.

Chap. 347.

AN ACT making an appropriation for the Panama-Pacific exposition commission.

Became a law April 22, 1913, with the approval of the Governor. Passed, three-fifths being present.

The People of the State of New York, represented in Senate and Assembly, do enact as follows:

Section 1. The sum of two hundred and fifty thousand dollars ($250,000), or so much thereof as may be necessary, is hereby appropriated out of any money in the treasury, not otherwise appropriated, for the Panama-Pacific exposition commission, in accordance with the provisions of chapter five hundred and forty-one of the laws of nineteen hundred and twelve. The money hereby appropriated shall be payable for the purposes, in the manner and subject to the provisions of such act.

§ 2. This act shall take effect immediately.

Chap. 348.

AN ACT to amend the judiciary law, in relation to the power of the justices of the appellate division in the first department to appoint interpreters for the supreme court.

Became a law April 22, 1913, with the approval of the Governor. Passed, three-fifths being present.

The People of the State of New York, represented in Senate and Assembly, do enact as follows:

Section 1. Section one hundred and thirteen of chapter thirty-five of the laws of nineteen hundred and nine, entitled "An act in relation to the administration of justice, constituting chapter thirty of the consolidated laws," is hereby amended to read as follows:

§ 113. **Appointment of interpreters for supreme court by justices of appellate division.** The justices of the appellate division in the first department, or a majority of them, may appoint and at pleasure remove [1]such number of interpreters for the supreme court as in their opinion shall be necessary.

§ 2. This act shall take effect immediately.

Margin note: L. 1909, ch. 35, § 113 amended.

Chap. 349.

AN ACT to amend the penal law, in relation to violations of provisions of the labor law, the industrial code, the rules and regulations of the industrial board of the department of labor and the orders of the commissioner of labor.

Became a law April 22, 1913, with the approval of the Governor. Passed, three-fifths being present.

The People of the State of New York, represented in Senate and Assembly, do enact as follows:

Section 1. Section twelve hundred and seventy-five of chapter eighty-eight of the laws of nineteen hundred and nine, entitled "An act to provide for the punishment of crime, constituting chapter forty of the consolidated laws," as amended by chapter

Margin note: L. 1909, ch. 88, § 1275, as amended by L. 1911, ch. 749, amended.

---

[1] Remainder of sentence formerly read: "four interpreters for the supreme court."

seven hundred and forty-nine of the laws of nineteen hundred and eleven,[1] is hereby amended to read as follows:[2]

§ 1275. **Violations of provisions of labor law; the industrial code; the rules and regulations of the industrial board of the department of labor; orders of the commissioner of labor.** Any person who violates or does not comply with any provision of the labor law, any provision of the industrial code, any rule or regulation of the industrial board of the department of labor, or any lawful order of the commissioner of labor: and any person who knowingly makes a false statement in or in relation to any application made for an employment certificate as to any matter required by articles six and eleven of the labor law to appear in any affidavit, record, transcript or certificate therein provided for, is guilty of a misdemeanor and upon conviction shall be punished, except as in this chapter otherwise provided, for a first offense by a fine of not less than twenty nor more than fifty dollars; for a second offense by a fine of not less than fifty nor more than two hundred and fifty dollars, or by imprisonment for not more than thirty days or by both such fine and imprisonment; for a third offense by a fine of not less than two hundred and fifty dollars, or by imprisonment for not more than sixty days, or by both such fine and imprisonment.

§ 1273 repealed.

§ 2. Section twelve hundred and seventy-three of such chapter is hereby repealed.

§ 3. This act shall take effect immediately.

Chap. 350.

AN ACT to provide for the acquisition and equipment of land for military and naval purposes, and making an appropriation therefor.

Became a law April 23, 1913, with the approval of the Governor. Passed by a two-thirds vote.

The People of the State of New York, represented in Senate and Assembly, do enact as follows:

Authority to acquire lands.

Section 1. The armory commission is hereby authorized to acquire by purchase or condemnation such lands within the state

---

[1] Section 1275 was also amended by L. 1912, ch. 383.
[2] Section materially amended.

as it may select, for rifle practice and other military or naval purposes.

§ 2. The sum of fifty thousand dollars ($50,000), or so much thereof as may be necessary, is hereby appropriated for the acquisition of said lands out of any moneys in the state treasury not otherwise appropriated, payable by the state treasurer on the warrant of the comptroller on the certificate of the armory commission; but no part of the money hereby appropriated shall be available for any purpose until the title to the lands embraced in such purchase shall be approved by the attorney-general and a certificate of such approval filed with the comptroller.

§ 3. This act shall take effect immediately.

Appropriation.

Chap. 351.

AN ACT to amend the county law, in relation to the power of the board of supervisors to authorize municipalities and districts to borrow money.

Became a law April 23, 1913, with the approval of the Governor. Passed, three-fifths being present.

The People of the State of New York, represented in Senate and Assembly, do enact as follows:

Section 1. Subdivision twenty-six[1] of chapter sixteen of the laws of nineteen hundred and nine, entitled "An act in relation to counties, constituting chapter eleven of the consolidated laws," as added by chapter one hundred and forty-one of the laws of nineteen hundred and ten, is hereby amended to read as follows:

L. 1909, ch. 16. § 12, subd. 26, as added by L. 1910, ch. 141, amended.

26. The board of supervisors of any county may, on the application of any [2]city of the third class, village, town, school district, water district, lighting district or fire district in the county, authorize such municipality or district by referendum vote thereon, to raise moneys or issue the bonds or other obligations of such municipality or district, to run for such period of time not exceeding fifty years, as the board of supervisors may prescribe, for paving the streets, roads and highways and constructing side-

Supervisors may authorize municipalities to borrow money for certain purposes.

---

[1] Should read: "Subdivision twenty-six of section twelve."
[2] Remainder of subdivision formerly read: "town, authorize such town to borrow such sum of money, for or on the credit of such town, as may be necessary to pay any debt lawfully incurred by it in behalf of such town."

walks within such municipality, and any public municipal or district improvement, and to raise moneys by local taxation for the
redemption of such bonds or obligations; to extend or diminish
municipal or district boundary lines; to widen, extend, limit or
diminish the area occupied by streets, roads and highways; and
to establish, increase or lower stated salaries of local officials.

Present powers of municipalities not abridged. Nothing in this subdivision, however, shall operate to abridge the
right or power now possessed by any such municipality or district,
under any general or special law, whether heretofore or hereafter
enacted, to perform any of the acts which such municipality or
district might perform without authority from such board; but

Subdivision to be liberally construed. the provisions of this subdivision shall be liberally construed to
enable municipalities and districts, with the authority of the board
of supervisors, to exercise their legitimate municipal or district
functions without special recourse to the legislature.

§ 2. This act shall take effect immediately.

Chap. 352.

AN ACT to amend the civil service law with respect to the appointment, term of office and salary of the state civil service
commissioners and as to positions to be included in the exempt class and providing for the carrying out of such amendment.

Became a law April 24, 1913, with the approval of the Governor. Passed,
three-fifths being present.

*The People of the State of New York, represented in Senate
and Assembly, do enact as follows:*

L. 1909, ch. 15, § 3 amended. Section 1. Section three of chapter fifteen of the laws of nineteen hundred and nine, entitled "An act in relation to the civil
service of the state of New York and the civil divisions and cities
thereof, constituting chapter seven of the consolidated laws as
amended," is hereby amended to read as follows:

§ 3. **State civil service commission.** The governor is authorized to appoint, by and with the advice and consent of the senate,
three persons, not more than two of whom shall be adherents of
the same political party, as civil service commissioners, and said
three commissioners shall constitute the state civil service commission. They shall hold no other political place under the state

of New York. [1]On or before the first day of May, in the year
one thousand nine hundred and thirteen the governor shall designate one member of the present state civil service commission
to serve as a member of the commission until the first day of
February, one thousand nine hundred and fifteen; one until the
first day of February, one thousand nine hundred and seventeen;
and one until the first day of February, one thousand nine hundred and nineteen. Upon the expiration of each of said terms,
the term of office of each commissioner hereafter appointed shall
be six years from the first day of February of the year in which
he shall be appointed. Vacancies shall be filled by appointment
of the governor for the unexpired term. Each of the three commissioners shall receive a salary of five thousand dollars a year,
and each of said commissioners shall be paid his necessary expenses incurred in the discharge of his duties as a commissioner.

§ 2. Section four of chapter fifteen of the laws of nineteen §4
hundred and nine, entitled "An act in relation to the civil service amended.
of the state of New York and the civil divisions and
cities thereof, constituting chapter seven of the consolidated laws
as amended," is hereby amended to read as follows:

§ 4. **Officers and employees of the commission.** The commission shall[2] elect one of its members to be president, and may
employ a chief examiner, a secretary, and such other officers,
clerks and examiners as it may deem necessary or proper to carry
out the purposes of this chapter, and such employees shall hold
office during the pleasure of the commission. The chief examiner shall be entitled to receive a salary at the rate of three
thousand six hundred dollars a year, and he shall be paid his
necessary traveling expenses incurred in the discharge of his duty.
The secretary, and other officers, clerks and examiners shall receive salaries to be fixed by the commission, and the secretary
shall also be paid his necessary traveling expenses incurred in the
discharge of his duty. The commission may select suitable persons in the official service of the state or any of its civil divisions,
after consulting the head of the department or office in which such
persons serve, to act as examiners under its direction. Persons
so selected shall be entitled to compensation from the commission
for their necessary expenses occasioned by the service actually
rendered, in addition to the regular service required in the de-

---

[1] Remainder of section materially amended.
[2] Word "shall" substituted for word "may."

partment or office where they are regularly employed. The compensation of examiners shall not exceed five dollars per day, except in case of special and expert examiners employed in the preparation of questions and rating of candidates; the commission shall not expend or authorize the expenditure of moneys for any purpose in excess of the sums appropriated therefor by law.

§ 3. Section thirteen[3] of chapter fifteen of the laws of nineteen hundred and nine, entitled "An act in relation to the civil-service of the state of New York and the civil divisions and cities thereof, constituting chapter seven of the consolidated laws as amended," is hereby amended to read as follows:

§ 13. **The exempt class.** The following positions shall be included in the exempt class:

1. The deputies of principal executive officers authorized by law to act generally for and in place of their principals;

2. One secretary of each officer, board and commission,[4] authorized by law to appoint a secretary;

3. One clerk, and one deputy clerk if authorized by law, of each court, and one clerk of each elective judicial officer;

4. In the state service, all unskilled laborers and such skilled laborers, as are not included in the competitive class or the non-competitive class; and in addition thereto there may be included in the exempt class all other subordinate officers for the filling of which competitive or non-competitive examination may be found to be not practicable. But no office or position shall be deemed to be in the exempt class unless it is specifically named in such class in the rules, and the reasons for each such exemption shall be stated separately in the annual reports of the commission. Not more than one appointment shall be made to or under the title of any such office or position, unless a different number is specifically mentioned in such rules. Appointments to positions in the exempt class may be made without examination.

§ 4. All acts or parts of acts inconsistent herewith, are hereby repealed.

§ 5. This act shall take effect immediately.

---

[3] As amended by L. 1912, ch. 170.
[4] Words "except civil service commissions," omitted.

§ 13
amended.

Chap. 353.

AN ACT granting permission for the laying out and opening of
a public street in the village of Sidney, in the county of
Delaware, through certain cemetery lands therein.

Became a law April 24, 1913, with the approval of the Governor. Passed,
three-fifths being present.

*The People of the State of New York, represented in Senate
and Assembly, do enact as follows:*

Section 1. Subject to the general or special laws governing the Opening of
laying out and opening of streets and avenues in the village of thorized.
Sidney, in the county of Delaware, such village may, through its
proper authorities, lay out and open a village street along the
following course, through the Prospect Hill cemetery, controlled
by the Prospect Hill Cemetery Association: Beginning at the Course.
southeast corner of a lot of land owned by such association, at
the corner of a lot of land owned by Arthur Delos Griswold, in
the line of the river road leading from the village of Sidney to
Unadilla; and running thence in a northerly direction along the ·
east line of such cemetery lands about thirty rods, more or less,
to a point on the brink of the hill as it dips towards the railroad,
near the end of the evergreen hedge; then in a circular direction,
on the cemetery lands at about the course of one-half of a circle
until it will be opposite the end of the evergreen hedge or nearly
so; thence in a westerly direction on a slight curve, until the line
of the street will intersect the Woods Mill road, so-called, which
road has been heretofore preserved for highway purposes, which
road will intersect the east main street between the cemetery
house and the Curtis property.

Such permission, however, is subject to the condition, hereby Consents of
imposed, that the trustees of Prospect Hill Cemetery Association, trustees
and all of the lot owners whose lots, or any part thereof, are in- owners.
cluded wholly or partly, within the boundaries of the proposed
street, shall have consented to the laying out of such street through
such cemetery; but if such consent be given, it shall not be necessary for two-thirds or any other percentage of the lot owners of
such cemetery to consent thereto, anything in the membership
corporations law to the contrary notwithstanding.

The provisions of this act granting permission to lay out and Applica-
open a street along the above described course shall apply to the to prior st

subsequent
proceed-
ings.laying out of such street under any petition heretofore presented
to the trustees of such village, or proceedings heretofore instituted
therefor, or to a subsequent petition or proceedings, as the case
may be.

§ 2. This act shall take effect immediately.

Chap. 354.

AN ACT to amend the railroad law, in relation to the alteration
of existing crossings of highways and steam surface railroads.

Became a law April 24, 1913, with the approval of the Governor. Passed,
three-fifths being present.

*The People of the State of New York, represented in Senate
and Assembly, do enact as follows:*

L. 1910,
ch. 481,
§§ 91, 94,
as amended
by L. 1911,
ch. 141,
amended.Section 1. Sections ninety-one and ninety-four of chapter four
hundred and eighty-one of the laws of nineteen hundred and ten,
entitled "An act in relation to railroads, constituting chapter
forty-nine of the consolidated laws," as amended by chapter one
hundred and forty-one of the laws of nineteen hundred and
eleven, are hereby amended to read, respectively, as follows:

§ 91.[1] **Petition for alteration of existing crossings.** The mayor
and common council of any city, the president and trustees
of any village, the town board of any town within which a street,
avenue or highway crosses or is crossed by a steam surface railroad at grade, below or above grade by structures heretofore constructed,[2] or any steam surface railroad company, whose road
crosses or is crossed by a street, avenue or highway at grade,
below or above grade,[3] may bring their petition in writing to the
public service commission, therein alleging that public safety
requires an alteration in the manner of such crossing, its approaches, the method of crossing, the location of the highway or
crossing, a change in the existing structures,[4] the closing and discontinuance of a highway crossing and the diversion of the travel
thereon to another highway or crossing, or if not practicable to
change such crossing from grade or to close and discontinue the

---

[1] Section 91 is again amended by L. 1913, ch. 744, post. The amendments
effected here are not incorporated in § 91 as amended by said ch. 744.
[2] Words "below or above grade by structures heretofore constructed," new.
[3] Words "below or above grade," new.
[4] Words "a change in the existing structures," new.

same, the opening of an additional crossing for the partial diversion of travel from the grade crossing, and praying that the same may be ordered. Where a street, avenue or highway in a city, village or town, which crosses or is crossed by a steam surface railroad at grade, below or above grade,[4a] is a part of a highway which the state commission of highways shall have determined to construct or improve as a state or county highway, as provided in article six of the highway law, such commission of highways may bring a petition containing any of the allegations above specified and praying for a like order. Upon any such petition being brought the public service commission shall appoint a time and place for hearing the petition, and shall give such personal notice thereof as it shall judge reasonable, of not less than ten days, however, to said petitioner, the railroad company, the municipality in which such crossing is situated, and if such crossing is in whole or in part in an incorporated village having not to exceed twelve hundred inhabitants, also to the supervisor or supervisors of the town or towns in which such crossing is situated; and in all cases to the owners of the lands adjoining such crossing and adjoining that part of the highway to be changed in grade or location, or the land to be opened for a new crossing, and to the state commission of highways in case of a state or county highway. The public service commission shall cause notice of said hearing to be advertised in at least two newspapers published in the locality affected by the application. Upon such notice and after a hearing the public service commission shall determine what alterations or changes, if any, shall be made. If the application be made by the state commission of highways in respect to a street, avenue or highway proposed to be constructed or improved as a part of a state highway, the decision shall state whether such highway shall cross such railroad above or below the grade of the highway; in case of a county highway, such decision shall state whether such highway shall cross such railroad at grade, or above or below the grade of the highway. The decision of said public service commission rendered in any proceeding under this section shall be communicated within twenty days after final hearing to all parties to whom notice of the hearing in said proceeding was given, or who appeared at said hearing by counsel or in person. Any person aggrieved by such decision, or by a decision made pursuant to sections eighty-nine and ninety hereof, and who was a

---

[4a] Words " below or above grade," new.

party to said proceeding, may within sixty days appeal therefrom
to the appellate division of the supreme court in the department
in which such grade crossing is situated, and to the court of appeals, in the same manner and with like effect as is provided in
the case of appeals from an order of the supreme court.

§ 94.[5] **Expense of constructing new crossings.** Whenever under
the provisions of section eighty-nine of this chapter, new railroads
are constructed across existing highways, the expense of crossing
above or below the grade of the highway shall be paid entirely by
the railroad corporations. Whenever under the provisions of section ninety of this chapter a new street, avenue or highway is constructed across an existing railroad, the railroad corporation shall
pay one-half and the municipal corporation wherein such street,
avenue or highway is located shall pay the remaining one-half of
the expense of making such crossing above or below grade; and
whenever a change is made as to an existing crossing or structure[6]
in accordance with the provisions of section ninety-one of this
chapter, fifty per centum of the expense thereof shall be borne by
the railroad corporation, twenty-five per centum by the municipal
corporation, and twenty-five per centum by the state; except that
whenever an existing crossing, in which a change is made under
the provisions of said section ninety-one, is located wholly or partly
within an incorporated village having not to exceed twelve hundred
inhabitants, the portion of expense herein required to be borne by
the municipal corporation shall be borne by the town or towns in
which such crossing is situated. Whenever under the provisions
of sections ninety and ninety-one of this chapter a highway is constructed across an existing railroad and is a part of a state or
county highway constructed or improved as provided in the highway law, one-half of the expense of making such crossing above or
below grade or changing the existing structure by which such crossing is made[7] shall be paid by the railroad corporation, and the remaining one-half of such expense shall be paid by the state in the
case of a state highway, and jointly by the state, county and town
in the case of a county highway, in the same proportion and in the
same manner as the cost of the construction or improvement of

---

[5] Section 94 is again amended by L. 1913, chaps. 425, 744, post. The amendments effected here are not incorporated in § 94 as amended by said chaps.
425, 744.
[6] Words " or structure " new.
[7] Words " or changing the existing structure by which such crossing is
made," new.

such state or county highway is paid. Whenever in carrying out the provisions of sections ninety or ninety-one of this chapter two or more lines of steam surface railroad, owned and operated by different corporations, cross a highway at a point where a change in grade is made, each corporation shall pay such proportion of fifty per centum of the expense thereof as shall be determined by the public service commission. In carrying out the provisions of sections eighty-nine, ninety and ninety-one of this chapter the work shall be done by the railroad corporation or corporations affected thereby, subject to the supervision and approval of the public service commission, and in all cases, except where the entire expense is paid by the railroad corporation, the expense of construction shall be paid primarily by the railroad company, and the expense of acquiring additional lands, rights or easements shall be paid primarily by the municipal corporation wherein such highway crossings are located, or, in case of a state or county highway, upon the order of the state commission of highways out of moneys available therefor. Plans and specifications of all changes proposed under sections ninety and ninety-one of this chapter, and an estimate of the expense thereof shall be submitted to the public service commission for its approval before the letting of any contract. If such changes are proposed in a highway which is to be constructed or improved as a state or county highway, such plans and specifications shall also be submitted to the state commission of highways for its approval before the letting of any contract. In case the work is done by contract the proposals of contractors shall be submitted to the public service commission, and if the commission shall determine that the bids are excessive it shall have the power to require the submission of new proposals. The commission may employ temporarily such experts and engineers as may be necessary to properly supervise any work that may be undertaken under sections eighty-nine, ninety and ninety-one of this chapter, the expense thereof to be paid by the comptroller upon the requisition and certificate of the commission, said expense to be included in the cost of the particular change in grade or in the structure above or below grade[8] on account of which it is incurred and finally apportioned in the manner provided in this section. Upon the completion of the work and its approval by the public service commission an accounting shall be had between the railroad corporation and the municipal corporation, or the state commission of high-

---

[8] Words " or in the structure above or below grade," new.

ways, of the amounts expended by each with interest, and if it
shall appear that the railroad corporation or the municipal corporation, or the state commission of highways has expended more
than its proportion of the expense of the crossing as herein provided, a settlement shall be forthwith made in accordance with the
provisions of this section. All items of expenditure shall be verified under oath, and, in case of a dispute between the railroad corporation and the municipal corporation or the state commission of
highways as to the amount expended, any judge of the supreme
court in the judicial district in which the municipality, or the
state or county highway, is situated may appoint a referee to take
testimony as to the amount expended, and the confirmation of the
report of the referee shall be final. In the event of the failure or
refusal of the railroad corporation to pay its proportion of the expense, the same, with interest from the date of such accounting,
may be levied and assessed upon the railroad corporation and collected in the same manner that taxes and assessments are now collected by the municipal corporation within which the work is done;
and in the event of the failure or refusal of the municipal corporation to pay its proportion of the expense, suit may be instituted by
the railroad corporation for the collection of the same with
interest from the date of such accounting, or the railroad corporation may offset such amount with interest against any taxes levied
or assessed against it or its property by such municipal corporation. The legislature shall annually appropriate out of any
moneys not otherwise appropriated the sum of one hundred thousand dollars for the purpose of paying the state's proportion of
the expense of a change in an existing grade crossing or of the
structure of any existing crossing above or below grade[9] other than
that required to be paid by the state from funds appropriated for
the construction of state and county highways as above provided.
If in any year any less sum than one hundred thousand dollars is
expended by the state for the purpose aforesaid the balance remaining unexpended shall be applied to reduce the amount appropriated by the state in the next succeeding year, except that no
such deduction shall be made in case there are outstanding and
unadjusted obligations on account of a change in an existing grade
crossing or the structure above or below grade[10] for a proportion of

---

[9] Words " or of the structure of any existing crossing above or below
grade," new.
[10] Words " or the structure above or below grade," new.

which the state is liable under the provisions of this section. In the event of the appropriation made by the state in any one year being insufficient to pay the state's proportion of the expense of any change that may be ordered the first payment from the appropriation of the succeeding year shall be on account of said change, and no payment shall be made on account of any subsequent change that may be ordered, nor shall any subsequent change be ordered until the obligation of the state on account of the first named change in grade has been fully discharged, unless the same shall be provided for by an additional appropriation to be made by the legislature. The state's proportion of the expense of changing any existing grade crossing or the structure of any existing crossing above or below grade[11] shall be paid by the state treasurer on the warrant of the comptroller, to which shall be appended the certificate of the public service commission to the effect that the work has been properly performed and a statement showing the situation of the crossing or structure[12] that has been changed, the total cost and the proportionate expense thereof, and the money shall be paid in whole or in part to the railroad corporation or to · the municipal corporation as the public service commission may direct, subject, however, to the rights of the respective parties as they appear from the accounting to be had as hereinbefore provided for. No claim for damages to property on account of the change or abolishment of any crossing or change in structure[13] under the provisions of this article shall be allowed unless notice of such claim is filed with the public service commission within six months after completion of the work necessary for such change or abolishment.

§ 2. Section ninety-five of such chapter is hereby amended to § 95 amended read as follows:

§ 95. **Proceedings by public service commission for alteration of grade crossings.** The public service commission may, in the absence of any application therefor, when in its opinion public safety requires an alteration in an existing grade crossing or a change in any existing structure above or below grade,[14] institute proceedings on its own motion for an alteration in such grade

---

[11] Words "or the structure of any existing crossing above or below grade," new.
[12] Words "or structure" new.
[13] Words "or change in structure," new.
[14] Words "or a change in any existing structure above or below grade," new.

crossing or structure,[14a] upon such notice as it shall deem reasonable, of not less than ten days however, to the railroad company, the municipal corporation and the person or persons interested, and proceedings shall be conducted as provided in section ninety-one of this chapter. The changes in existing grade crossings or structures[15] authorized or required by the commission in any one year shall be so distributed and apportioned over and among the railroads and the municipalities of the state as to produce such equality of burden upon them for their proportionate part of the expenses as herein provided for as the nature and circumstances of the cases before it will permit.

§ 3. This act shall take effect immediately.

Chap. 355.

AN ACT to amend the county law, in relation to expenses of the supervisors of the county of Saint Lawrence.

Became a law April 24, 1913, with the approval of the Governor. Passed, three-fifths being present.

The People of the State of New York, represented in Senate and Assembly, do enact as follows:

L. 1909, ch. 16, § 23, as amended by L. 1910, ch. 279, L. 1911, ch. 554, and L. 1912, ch. 34, amended. Section 1. Section twenty-three of chapter sixteen of the laws of nineteen hundred and nine, entitled "An act in relation to counties, constituting chapter eleven of the consolidated laws," as amended by chapter two hundred and seventy-nine of the laws of nineteen hundred and ten, chapter five hundred and fifty-four of the laws of nineteen hundred and eleven, and chapter thirty-four of the laws of nineteen hundred and twelve, is hereby amended to read as follows:[1]

§ 23. **Compensation of supervisors.** For the services of supervisors, except in the counties of Albany, Columbia, Dutchess, Erie, Herkimer, Montgomery, Niagara, Oneida, Onondaga, Rensselaer, Rockland, Schenectady, Steuben and Westchester, each supervisor shall receive from the county compensation at the rate of four dollars per day for each calendar day's actual

[14a] Words "or structure" new.
[15] Words "or structures" new.
[1] Section 23 was amended by L. 1913, ch. 254, ante. The amendments effected by said ch. 254 are not incorporated in § 23 as here amended.

attendance at the sessions of their respective boards, and mileage at the rate of eight cents per mile, for once going and returning from his residence to the place where the sessions of the board shall be held, by the most usual route, for each regular and special session. In the counties of Herkimer, Niagara, Rockland, Schenectady and Steuben each supervisor shall receive an annual salary, in the county of Herkimer of one hundred and twenty dollars and the mileage hereinabove prescribed, in the county of Niagara of three hundred dollars, in the county of Rockland of four hundred dollars, in the county of Schenectady of five hundred dollars and in the county of Steuben of one hundred and fifty dollars, in lieu of any per diem compensation. In the county of Dutchess each supervisor shall receive an annual salary from the county of one hundred and fifty dollars and also mileage at the rate of ten cents per mile for going and returning, once in each week during the annual session of the board of supervisors and when the board is sitting as a board of county canvassers, by the most usually traveled route, from his residence to the place where the sessions of the board shall be held, and in addition thereto compensation at the rate of four dollars per day and mileage as hereinabove provided for each special session of the board which he attends; such compensation and mileage to be paid by the county treasurer on the last day of the annual session in each year. Each supervisor, except in the counties of Albany, Columbia, Dutchess, Erie, Montgomery, Niagara, Oneida, Onondaga, Rensselaer, Schenectady and Westchester, may also receive compensation from the county at the rate of four dollars per day while actually engaged in any investigation or other duty, which may be lawfully committed to him by the board, except for services rendered when the board is in session and, if such investigation or duty require his attendance at a place away from his residence, and five miles or more distant from the place where the board shall hold its sessions,. his actual expenses incurred therein. Each supervisor in the county of Dutchess shall also be entitled to receive in addition to the compensation hereinabove provided, to be paid in the same time and manner, compensation at the rate of four dollars per day while actually engaged in any investigation or other duty which may be lawfully committed to him by the board together with his actual expenses incurred therein. No other compensation or allowance shall be made to any supervisor for his services, except such as shall be by law a town charge, except that in the counties of Niagara, Herkimer and Saint Lawrence[2] each supervisor, while heretofore or hereafter actually engaged in any investigation, or in the performance of any other duty, which shall have been legally delegated to him by the board of supervisors, except when the board is in session, shall be entitled to receive in addition to the compensation hereinbefore provided, his actual expenses incurred therein. The board of supervisors of any county may also allow to each member of the board for his services in making a copy of the assessment-roll, three cents for each written line for the first one hundred lines, two cents per line for the second hundred written lines, and one cent per line for all written lines in excess of two hundred, and one cent for each line of the tax-roll actually extended by him.

§ 2. This act shall take effect immediately.

Chap. 356.

AN ACT to amend the tax law, in relation to exceptions and limitations on taxable transfers.

Became a law April 24, 1913, with the approval of the Governor. **Passed**, three-fifths being present.

The People of the State of New York, represented in Senate and Assembly, do enact as follows:

L. 1909,
ch. 62,
§ 221, as
amended by
L. 1910,
chaps. 600,
706,
L. 1911,
ch. 732,
and
L. 1912,
ch. 206,
amended.

Section 1. Section two hundred and twenty-one of chapter sixty-two of the laws of nineteen hundred and nine, entitled "An act in relation to taxation, constituting chapter sixty of the consolidated laws," as amended by chapters six hundred and seven hundred and six of the laws of nineteen hundred and ten, seven hundred and thirty-two of the laws of nineteen hundred and eleven, and two hundred and six of the laws of nineteen hundred and twelve,[1] is hereby amended to read as follows:

§ 221. **Exceptions and limitations.** Any property devised or bequeathed for religious ceremonies, observances or commemorative services of or for the deceased donor, or to any person who is a bishop or to any religious, educational, charitable, missionary, benevolent, hospital or infirmary corporation, wherever incorporated, including corporations organized exclusively for bible

---

[2] Inclusion of Saint Lawrence county new.
[1] Section 221 is further amended by L. 1913, ch. 795, post, by which the amendments here effected are nullified.

or tract purposes and corporations organized for the enforcement of laws relating to children or animals, shall be exempted from and not subject to the provisions of this article. [2]There shall also be exempted from and not subject to the provisions of this article bonds or other obligations issued by the state of New York, provided, however, that such bonds or other obligations are registered in the name of the decedent at the time of death, or in the name of one or more persons or corporations in trust for such decedent at the time of such decedent's death. There shall also be exempted from and not subject to the provisions of this article personal property other than money or securities bequeathed to a corporation or association wherever incorporated or located, organized exclusively for the moral or mental improvement of men or women or for scientific, literary, library, patriotic, cemetery or historical purposes or for two or more of such purposes and used exclusively for carrying out one or more of such purposes. But no such corporation or association shall be entitled to such exemption if any officer, member or employee thereof shall receive or may be lawfully entitled to receive any pecuniary profit from the operations thereof except reasonable compensation for services in effecting one or more of such purposes or as proper beneficiaries of its strictly charitable purposes; or if the organization thereof for any such avowed purpose be a guise or pretense for directly or indirectly making any other pecuniary profit for such corporation or association or for any of its members or employees or if it be not in good faith organized or conducted exclusively for one or more of such purposes.

§ 2. This act shall take effect immediately.

Chap. 357.

AN ACT to amend the tax law, in relation to franchise tax and credit to be given on account of purchase of state bonds.

Became a law April 24, 1913, with the approval of the Governor. Passed, three-fifths being present.

The People of the State of New York, represented in Senate and Assembly, do enact as follows:

Section 1. Section one hundred and ninety of chapter sixty-two of the laws of nineteen hundred and nine, entitled "An act in re-

L. 1909, ch. 62, § 190 amended.

---

[2] Following sentence new.

lation to taxation, constituting chapter sixty of the consolidated laws," is hereby amended to read as follows:[1]

§ 190. **Purchase of state bonds; credit to be given.** Every corporation, company or association required by section one hundred and eighty-seven, one hundred and eighty-eight, or one hundred and eighty-nine of this chapter, to pay to the state an annual tax equal to a percentage of its gross premiums, capital stock, surplus, undivided profits or undivided earnings, or one or more, for the privilege of exercising its corporate franchise or carrying on its business in such corporate or organized capacity, which shall own any of the bonds of the state of New York, shall have credited to it annually to apply upon or in lieu of the payment of such tax an amount equal to one and one-half[2] per centum of the par value of all such bonds of the state, bearing interest at a rate not exceeding three per centum per annum, and an amount equal to one-half of one per centum of the par value of all such bonds of the state, bearing interest at a rate exceeding three per centum per annum but not exceeding four per centum per annum,[3] owned by such corporation, company or association, and registered in its name or registered in the name of a public department, a public officer or officers of this state, or of any other state, or of the United States, in trust for such corporation, company or association, on the thirtieth day of June prior to the date when such tax shall become due and payable; provided, however, that there shall in no case be credited to any such corporation, company or association an amount in excess of the amount due to the state from such corporation, company or association for taxes payable to the state under this chapter for the fiscal year for which such credit is given; and further provided that any such credit so allowed under this section shall not bear interest.

§ 2. This act shall take effect immediately.

---

[1] Section 190 is further amended by L. 1913, ch. 794, post, by which the amendments here effected are nullified.
[2] Words " and one-half " new.
[3] Words " and an amount equal to one-half of one per centum of the par value of all such bonds of the state, bearing interest at a rate exceeding three per centum per annum but not exceeding four per centum per annum," new.

Chap. 358.

AN ACT reappropriating an unexpended balance for the purpose of furnishing proper terminals and facilities for barge canal traffic.

Became a law April 24, 1913, with the approval of the Governor. Passed, three-fifths being present.

The People of the State of New York, represented in Senate and Assembly, do enact as follows:

Section 1. The sum of seven hundred and fifty-eight thousand seven hundred and forty-six dollars and seventeen cents ($758,-746.17), being the unexpended balance of the appropriation made by chapter seven hundred and forty-six of the laws of nineteen hundred and eleven, to be expended in carrying out the purposes of the act for furnishing proper terminals and facilities for barge canal traffic, is hereby reappropriated from the same funds and for the same purpose as provided in said act.

§ 2. This act shall take effect immediately.

Chap. 359.

AN ACT reappropriating an unexpended balance for the purpose of the construction or improvement of public highways.

Became a law April 24, 1913, with the approval of the Governor. Passed, three-fifths being present.

The People of the State of New York, represented in Senate and Assembly, do enact as follows:

Section 1. The sum of six million six hundred thousand eight hundred nine dollars and three cents ($6,600,809.03), being the unexpended balance of the appropriation made by chapter seven hundred and fifty of the laws of nineteen hundred and eleven, to be expended for the construction or improvement of public highways in accordance with the provisions of article six of chapter thirty of the laws of nineteen hundred and nine, entitled "An act relating to highways, constituting chapter twenty-five of the consolidated laws," is hereby reappropriated from the same funds and for the same purpose as provided in said act.

§ 2. This act shall take effect immediately.

Chap. 360.

AN ACT reappropriating an unexpended balance for the purpose of the construction or improvement of public highways.

Became a law April 24, 1913, with the approval of the Governor. Passed, three-fifths being present.

The People of the State of New York, represented in Senate and Assembly, do enact as follows:

Section 1. The sum of four hundred fifty-nine thousand ninety-four dollars and seven cents ($459,094.07), being the unexpended balance of the appropriation made by chapter five hundred and thirty-two of the laws of nineteen hundred and ten, to be expended for the construction and improvement of portions of state routes numbers two and six as defined by section one hundred and twenty of chapter thirty of the laws of nineteen hundred and nine, so as to complete the connections between stone roads already built and those to be built under the equitable apportionment in nineteen hundred and ten and nineteen hundred and eleven, as defined by the highway law, is hereby reappropriated from the same funds and for the purpose of the construction or improvement of public highways in accordance with the provision of article six of chapter thirty of the laws of nineteen hundred and nine, entitled "An act relating to highways, constituting chapter twenty-five of the consolidated laws."

§ 2. This act shall take effect immediately.

Chap. 361.

AN ACT reappropriating an unexpended balance for the Saratoga Springs state reservation.

Became a law April 24, 1913, with the approval of the Governor. Passed, three-fifths being present.

The People of the State of New York, represented in Senate and Assembly, do enact as follows:

Section 1. The sum of four hundred and sixty-two thousand eight hundred twenty-five dollars and fifty-one cents ($462,-825.51), being the unexpended balance of the appropriation made by chapter three hundred and ninety-four of the laws of nineteen hundred and eleven for the selection, location and appropriation of certain lands in the town of Saratoga Springs, for the said reservation, is hereby reappropriated from the same funds and for the same purpose as provided by said act.

§ 2. This act shall take effect immediately.

Chap. 362.

AN ACT reappropriating unexpended balances for the purpose of the construction and improvement of portions of state routes within several counties of the state.

Became a law April 24, 1913, with the approval of the Governor. Passed, three-fifths being present.

The People of the State of New York, represented in Senate and Assembly, do enact as follows:

Section 1. The sum of eight hundred fifty-six thousand one hundred twenty-eight dollars and one cent ($856,128.01), being the unexpended balance of the appropriation made by chapter ninety-two of the laws of nineteen hundred and eleven;

And the sum of one million twenty-five thousand two hundred seventy-eight dollars and thirty-six cents ($1,025,278.36), being the unexpended balance of the appropriation made by chapter one hundred and thirty-three of the laws of nineteen hundred and eleven;

And the sum of four hundred eighty-two thousand five hundred ninety-five dollars and sixty-eight cents ($482,595.68), being the unexpended balance of the appropriation made by chapter one hundred and thirty-four of the laws of nineteen hundred and eleven;

And the sum of four hundred ninety-two thousand nine hundred fifty-seven dollars and seventy cents ($492,957.70), being the unexpended balance of the appropriation made by chapter one hundred and thirty-five of the laws of nineteen hundred and eleven;

And the sum of one million twenty-four thousand thirty-nine dollars and two cents ($1,024,039.02), being the unexpended balance of the appropriation made by chapter one hundred and thirty-six of the laws of nineteen hundred and eleven;

And the sum of eight hundred seventy thousand eight hundred

forty dollars and seventeen cents ($870,840.17), being the unexpended balance of the appropriation made by chapter one hundred and fifty-four of the laws of nineteen hundred and eleven;

And the sum of forty thousand five hundred thirty-eight dollars and forty-eight cents ($40,538.48), being the unexpended balance of the appropriation made by chapter one hundred and fifty-five of the laws of nineteen hundred and eleven;

And the sum of four hundred seventy-seven thousand ten dollars and fifty cents ($477,010.50), being the unexpended balance of the appropriation made by chapter three hundred and forty-eight of the laws of nineteen hundred and eleven;·

And the sum of six hundred eighty-six thousand eight hundred seven dollars and thirty-two cents ($686,807.32), being the unexpended balance of the appropriation made by chapter four hundred and twenty-six of the laws of nineteen hundred and eleven;

And the sum of nine hundred ninety-four thousand three hundred fifty-four dollars and eighty-nine cents ($994,354.89), being the unexpended balance of the appropriation made by chapter four hundred and sixty-three of the laws of nineteen hundred and eleven;

And the sum of two hundred forty-four thousand one hundred twenty-two dollars and forty-one cents ($244,122.41), being the unexpended balance of the appropriation made by chapter four hundred and sixty-seven of the laws of nineteen hundred and eleven;

And the sum of five hundred sixty thousand five hundred thirty dollars and sixty-seven cents ($560,530.67), being the unexpended balance of the appropriation made by chapter four hundred and ninety-six of the laws of nineteen hundred and eleven;

And the sum of six hundred fifty-two thousand three hundred thirty-nine dollars and forty-four cents ($652,339.44), being the unexpended balance of the appropriation made by chapter five hundred and fifty-nine of the laws of nineteen hundred and eleven;

And the sum of one hundred twenty-three thousand eight hundred twenty-eight dollars and sixty-nine cents ($123,828.69), being the unexpended balance of the appropriation made by chapter six hundred and fourteen of the laws of nineteen hundred and eleven;

And the sum of six hundred seventy-five thousand five

hundred eighty-eight dollars and two cents ($675,588.02), being the unexpended balance of the appropriation made by chapter six hundred and fifty-seven of the laws of nineteen hundred and eleven;

And the sum of three hundred one thousand forty-five dollars and forty-eight cents ($301,045.48), being the unexpended balance of the appropriation made by chapter seven hundred and fifteen of the laws of nineteen hundred and eleven;

And the sum of sixty thousand two hundred sixty-seven dollars and seventy-two cents ($60,267.72), being the unexpended balance of the appropriation made by chapter seven hundred and twenty-six of the laws of nineteen hundred and eleven;

And the sum of seven hundred seventy-eight thousand six hundred thirty-seven dollars and five cents ($778,637.05), being the unexpended balance of the appropriation made by chapter seven hundred and thirty-three of the laws of nineteen hundred and eleven;

And the sum of three hundred eighty-three thousand three hundred ninety-one dollars and sixty-seven cents ($383,391.67), being the unexpended balance of the appropriation made by chapter seven hundred and forty-one of the laws of nineteen hundred and eleven;

And the sum of two hundred thousand five hundred ninety-five dollars and fifty-six cents ($200,595.56), being the unexpended balance of the appropriation made by chapter seven hundred and forty-two of the laws of nineteen hundred and eleven;

And the sum of three hundred fifty-three thousand two hundred ten dollars and forty-eight cents ($353,210.48), being the unexpended balance of the appropriation made by chapter seven hundred and forty-three of the laws of nineteen hundred and eleven;

And the sum of one hundred eighty-nine thousand ninety-five dollars and eighty-six cents ($189,095.86), being the unexpended balance of the appropriation made by chapter seven hundred and fifty-three of the laws of nineteen hundred and eleven;

And the sum of ninety-three thousand seven hundred twenty dollars and fifty-three cents ($93,720.53), being the unexpended balance of the appropriation made by chapter seven hundred and fifty-four of the laws of nineteen hundred and eleven;

To be expended in carrying out the purpose of the acts for the construction and improvement of portions of state routes desig-

forty dollars and seventeen cents ($870,840.17), being the un-
expended balance of the appropriation made by chapter one hundred and fifty-four of the laws of nineteen hundred and eleven;

And the sum of forty thousand five hundred thirty-eight dollars and forty-eight cents ($40,538.48), being the unexpended
balance of the appropriation made by chapter one hundred and
fifty-five of the laws of nineteen hundred and eleven;

And the sum of four hundred seventy-seven thousand ten dollars and fifty cents ($477,010.50), being the unexpended balance
of the appropriation made by chapter three hundred and forty-
eight of the laws of nineteen hundred and eleven; ·

And the sum of six hundred eighty-six thousand eight hundred
seven dollars and thirty-two cents ($686,807.32), being the un-
expended balance of the appropriation made by chapter four
hundred and twenty-six of the laws of nineteen hundred and
eleven;

And the sum of nine hundred ninety-four thousand three hundred fifty-four dollars and eighty-nine cents ($994,354.89), being
the unexpended balance of the appropriation made by chapter
four hundred and sixty-three of the laws of nineteen hundred
and eleven;

And the sum of two hundred forty-four thousand one hundred
twenty-two dollars and forty-one cents ($244,122.41), being the
unexpended balance of the appropriation made by chapter four
hundred and sixty-seven of the laws of nineteen hundred and
eleven;

And the sum of five hundred sixty thousand five hundred thirty
dollars and sixty-seven cents ($560,530.67), being the unex-
pended balance of the appropriation made by chapter four hundred and ninety-six of the laws of nineteen hundred and eleven;

And the sum of six hundred fifty-two thousand three hundred
thirty-nine dollars and forty-four cents ($652,339.44), being the
unexpended balance of the appropriation made by chapter five
hundred and fifty-nine of the laws of nineteen hundred and
eleven;

And the sum of one hundred twenty-three thousand eight hundred twenty-eight dollars and sixty-nine cents ($123,828.69), be-
ing the unexpended balance of the appropriation made by chapter
six hundred and fourteen of the laws of nineteen hundred and
eleven;

And the sum of six hundred seventy-five thousand five

hundred eighty-eight dollars and two cents ($675,588.02), being
the unexpended balance of the appropriation made by chapter
six hundred and fifty-seven of the laws of nineteen hundred and
eleven;

And the sum of three hundred one thousand forty-five dollars
and forty-eight cents ($301,045.48), being the unexpended bal-
ance of the appropriation made by chapter seven hundred and
fifteen of the laws of nineteen hundred and eleven;

And the sum of sixty thousand two hundred sixty-seven dollars
and seventy-two cents ($60,267.72), being the unexpended bal-
ance of the appropriation made by chapter seven hundred and
twenty-six of the laws of nineteen hundred and eleven;

And the sum of seven hundred seventy-eight thousand six
hundred thirty-seven dollars and five cents ($778,637.05), being
the unexpended balance of the appropriation made by chapter
seven hundred and thirty-three of the laws of nineteen hundred
and eleven;

And the sum of three hundred eighty-three thousand three
hundred ninety-one dollars and sixty-seven cents ($383,391.67),
being the unexpended balance of the appropriation made by
chapter seven hundred and forty-one of the laws of nineteen hundred and eleven;

And the sum of two hundred thousand five hundred ninety-five
dollars and fifty-six cents ($200,595.56), being the unexpended
balance of the appropriation made by chapter seven hundred and
forty-two of the laws of nineteen hundred and eleven;

And the sum of three hundred fifty-three thousand two hundred ten dollars and forty-eight cents ($353,210.48), being the
unexpended balance of the appropriation made by chapter seven
hundred and forty-three of the laws of nineteen hundred and
eleven;

And the sum of one hundred eighty-nine thousand ninety-five
dollars and eighty-six cents ($189,095.86), being the unexpended
balance of the appropriation made by chapter seven hundred
and fifty-three of the laws of nineteen hundred and eleven;

And the sum of ninety-three thousand seven hundred twenty
dollars and fifty-three cents ($93,720.53), being the unexpended
balance of the appropriation made by chapter seven hundred and
fifty-four of the laws of nineteen hundred and eleven;

To be expended in carrying out the purpose of the acts for the
construction and improvement of portions of state routes desig-

nated therein within the several counties of the state, is hereby reappropriated from the same fund and for the same purpose as provided in said acts.

§ 2. This act shall take effect immediately.

Chap. 363.

AN ACT reappropriating an unexpended balance for the purpose of the construction of a bridge in the Allegany Indian reservation.

Became a law April 24, 1913, with the approval of the Governor. Passed, three-fifths being present.

The People of the State of New York, represented in Senate and Assembly, do enact as follows:

Section 1. The sum of fifty-three thousand three hundred eighty dollars and twenty cents ($53,380.20), being the unexpended balance of the appropriation made by chapter eight hundred and eleven of the laws of nineteen hundred and eleven, to be expended in carrying out the purposes of the act for the construction of a bridge in the Allegany Indian reservation across the Allegany river in the village of Salamanca, is hereby reappropriated from the same funds and for the same purpose as provided in said act.

§ 2. This act shall take effect immediately.

Chap. 364.

AN ACT to provide for the submission of a proposition to the electors of the county of Jefferson authorizing the board of supervisors to expend not more than one hundred thousand dollars for acquiring a site and erecting a soldiers and sailors' memorial hall in the city of Watertown, and for the erection and jurisdiction thereof if so authorized.

Became a law April 24, 1913, with the approval of the Governor. Passed, three-fifths being present.

The People of the State of New York, represented in Senate and Assembly, do enact as follows:

Submission of proposi-

Section 1. The board of supervisors of Jefferson county shall submit to the electors thereof at the general election to be held in

such county on the fourth day of November, nineteen hundred and ^{tlon directed.}
thirteen, a proposition to authorize the board of supervisors of
such county to expend not more than one hundred thousand dollars
in acquiring a site in the city of Watertown, and erecting thereon
a soldiers and sailors' memorial hall. If for any reason such submission shall not be made at the general election to be held on the
fourth day of November, nineteen hundred and thirteen, it shall
be made at the next general election thereof, to be held in said
county. Such proposition shall be in the following form: Shall ^{Form of proposi-tion.}
the board of supervisors be authorized to expend not more than
one hundred thousand dollars in acquiring a site and erecting a
soldiers and sailors' memorial hall? The provisions of the elec- ^{Applica-tion of election law.}
tion law in relation to the submission of propositions and the form
of ballots therefor shall apply to the submission of such proposi-
tion. If a majority of the votes upon such proposition shall be in ^{Action in case of affirma-tive vote.}
the affirmative, the board of supervisors of such county may ac-
quire a site for such memorial hall in the city of Watertown and
may cause to be erected thereon a soldiers and sailors' memorial
hall at an expense not exceeding in the aggregate for the acquisition of the site and the construction and equipment of the building one hundred thousand dollars.

§ 2. Such building when completed shall be deemed a memorial ^{Nature of memorial.}
to the soldiers and sailors who enlisted from the county of Jeffer-
son and served in any war in which the United States as a nation
has ever been engaged, including so much of the revolutionary war
as was carried on previous to the signing and promulgation of the
declaration of independence by the continental congress, and such
purposes shall be properly indicated by tablet or otherwise. The ^{Manage-ment and use of hall.}
soldiers and sailors' memorial hall and historical association of
Jefferson county shall have the management of such memorial hall,
and shall authorize the use thereof for military drills by a camp
or camps of the Sons of Veterans of such county; and as a headquarters and place of meeting of such Sons of Veterans and any
auxiliary society of such Sons of Veterans; and as a place of meeting by the Historical Society of Jefferson county; and as a place
for the proper displaying and storing of such property in the way
of relics as belongs to the said Historical Society and such as may
hereafter be donated to it for preservation and for safe keeping.
Conveniences for such purposes will be provided for in said building. It shall also be used as a place of meeting for the LeRay de
Chaumont Chapter of the Daughters of the American Revolution;

as a place of meeting for the Julia Dent Grant Circle of the
G. A. R., for a place of meeting of the Northern Frontier Chapter
of the Daughters of the War of 1812; as a place of meeting for
Joe Spratt Post, No. 323, G. A. R., for a place of meeting for the
Relief Corps Auxiliary to said post and for the storage and preservation of such personal property owned by these organizations as
they may have in their possession, respectively. The said hall
when completed and so erected to be used so far as may be for
meetings for the assemblage of the people at different times to promote patriotic objects but not to be used to the exclusion of the
proper use of the societies whose names are given herein. Rules
and regulations for the occupancy of said building not inconsistent
with the purposes of this act may be made from time to time by
the board of supervisors of Jefferson county.

§ 3. This act shall take effect immediately.

Chap. 365.

AN ACT reappropriating unexpended balances for the improvement of the Cayuga and Seneca canals.

Became a law April 24, 1913, with the approval of the Governor. Passed,
three-fifths being present.

*The People of the State of New York, represented in Senate
and Assembly, do enact as follows:*

Section 1. The sum of seven hundred and seventy-four thousand eight hundred and fifty dollars and twenty-eight cents
($774,850.28), being the unexpended balance of an appropria-
tion made by chapter two hundred and fourteen of the laws of
nineteen hundred and eleven, to be expended in carrying out the
purposes of the act for the improvement of the Cayuga and Seneca
canals, as provided by chapter three hundred and ninety-one of
the laws of nineteen hundred and nine, is hereby reappropriated
from the same funds and for the same purpose as provided by said
act.

§ 2. This act shall take effect immediately.

Chap. 366.

AN ACT to amend the tax law, in relation to the appointment of transfer tax appraisers, stenographers and clerks.

Became a law April 24, 1913, with the approval of the Governor. Passed, three-fifths being present.

The People of the State of New York, represented in Senate and Assembly, do enact as follows:

Section 1. Section two hundred and twenty-nine of chapter sixty-two of the laws of nineteen hundred and nine, entitled "An act in relation to taxation, constituting chapter sixty of the consolidated laws," as amended by chapter two hundred and eighty-three of the laws of nineteen hundred and nine, chapter seven hundred and six of the laws of nineteen hundred and ten, chapter eight hundred and three of the laws of nineteen hundred and eleven, and chapter two hundred and fourteen of the laws of nineteen hundred and twelve, is hereby amended to read as follows:[1]

§ 229. **Appointment of appraisers, stenographers and clerks.** The state comptroller shall appoint and may at pleasure remove not to exceed six persons in the county of New York, four persons in the counties of Kings, and Bronx, and one person in the counties of Albany, Dutchess, Erie, Monroe, Nassau. Niagara, Oneida, Onondaga, Orange, Queens, Rensselaer, Richmond, Suffolk and Westchester, to act as appraisers therein. The state comptroller, from time to time and whenever in his opinion it is necessary, may also appoint and at pleasure remove not to exceed two additional persons to act as transfer tax appraisers in the county of New York, to whom shall be referred the appraisal of delinquent estates pending before the transfer tax appraisers in New York county, where more than eighteen months have elapsed since the death of such decedents, respectively, and also to act as appraiser of other estates whenever it shall appear to the comptroller that the services of such additional appraiser is necessary. The appraiser so appointed shall receive an annual salary to be fixed by the state comptroller, together with their actual and necessary traveling expenses and witness fees, as hereinafter provided, pay-

Marginal notes: L. 1909, ch. 62, § 229, as amended by L. 1909, ch. 283, L. 1910, ch. 706, L. 1911, ch. 803, and L. 1912, ch. 214, amen"d"d.

---

[1] Section materially amended.

22

able monthly by the state comptroller out of any funds in his hands or custody on account of transfer tax. The salaries of each of the appraisers so appointed shall not exceed the following amounts: In New York county, four thousand dollars; in Kings and Bronx counties, four thousand dollars; in Albany, Erie, Queens and Westchester counties, three thousand dollars; in Nassau, Orange and Rensselaer counties, two thousand dollars; in Monroe, Oneida and Onondaga counties, one thousand five hundred dollars; in Dutchess, Niagara, Richmond and Suffolk counties, one thousand dollars. Each of the said appraisers shall file with the state comptroller his oath of office and his official bond in the penal sum of not less than one thousand dollars, in the discretion of the state comptroller, conditioned for the faithful performance of his duties as such appraiser, which bond shall be approved by the attorney-general and the state comptroller. The state comptroller shall retain out of any funds in his hands on account of said tax the following amounts: First, a sum sufficient to provide the appraisers of New York county with one managing clerk, at a salary not to exceed four thousand dollars a year, whose duties shall be prescribed by the state comptroller, nine stenographers, three clerks, one examiner of values, and one assistant examiner of values, whose salaries shall not exceed two thousand dollars a year each, and one junior clerk, whose salary shall not exceed six hundred dollars a year; the appraisers of Kings and Bronx counties, with four stenographers, whose salaries shall not exceed two thousand dollars a year each, one clerk, whose salary shall not exceed seven hundred and twenty dollars a year; one page, whose salary shall not exceed four hundred and eighty dollars a year, and the appraiser of Erie county with one clerk, whose salary shall not exceed fifteen hundred dollars a year, and the appraiser of Westchester county with one clerk, whose salary shall not exceed the sum of twelve hundred dollars a year, and the appraiser of Queens county with one clerk, whose salary shall not exceed the sum of twelve hundred dollars a year, and the appraiser of Oneida county with one stenographer, whose salary shall not exceed the sum of nine hundred dollars a year, such employees to be appointed by the state comptroller. The state comptroller shall also retain out of any funds in his hands on account of said tax a sum sufficient to provide each of the additional transfer tax appraisers in New York county, whenever appointed as hereinbefore provided, with a stenographer, whose salary shall not exceed the rate of two thousand dollars a year each, such employees to be appointed by the state comptroller. Second, a sum to be used in defraying the expenses for office rent, stationery, postage, process serving and other similar expenses necessarily incurred in the appraisal of estates, not exceeding fifteen thousand dollars a year in New York county and five thousand dollars a year in Kings, and Bronx counties.

§ 2. This act shall take effect immediately.

___

Chap. 367.

AN ACT to amend the county law, in relation to special deputy clerks in certain counties.

Became a law April 24, 1913, with the approval of the Governor. Passed, three-fifths being present.

The People of the State of New York, represented in Senate and Assembly, do enact as follows:

Section 1. Section one hundred and sixty-nine of chapter six- teen of the laws of nineteen hundred and nine, entitled "An act in relation to counties, constituting chapter eleven of the con- solidated laws," as amended by chapter six hundred and ninety- four of the laws of nineteen hundred and ten, and by chapter one hundred and nine of the laws of nineteen hundred and thirteen,[1] is hereby amended to read as follows:

§ 169. **Special deputy clerks.** 1. In every county other than the county of Queens the county clerk may,[2] from time to time, by an instrument in writing, filed in his office, appoint, and at pleasure remove, one or more special deputy clerks to attend upon any or all of the terms or sittings of the courts of which he is clerk, and in any county having a population of more than sixty thousand at the last enumeration, the salary of such special deputy clerks shall be fixed by the board of supervisors of[3] such county, and when the said salary shall be so fixed

Margin note: L. 1909, ch. 16, § 169, as amended by L. 1910, ch. 694, and L. 1913, ch. 109, amended.

___

[1] Section 169 is further amended by L. 1913, ch. 637, post.
[2] Words "subject to the approval of the justices of the supreme court residing within the judicial district of the appointee," omitted.
[3] Words "the board of supervisors of," substituted for words "a justice of the supreme court, residing in."

the same shall be paid from the court funds of said county or from an appropriation made therefor. Each person so appointed must, before he enters upon the duties of his office, subscribe and file in the clerk's office the constitutional oath of office; and he possesses the same power and authority as the clerk at any sitting or term of the court which he attends, with respect to the business transacted thereat. The salaries of special deputy clerks and assistants appointed in Queens county under the provisions of section one hundred and fifty-nine of the judiciary law shall be fixed by the justice residing in such county and shall be a county charge. The provisions of this subdivision shall not apply to the first judicial department.

. 2. The minutes of the part or term of the supreme court to which any of the special deputy clerks to the clerk of the county of New York appointed pursuant to the judiciary law is assigned. kept by him, and the records kept by the supreme court jury clerk in the first judicial district shall be kept by the county clerk of New York county in his office and said county clerk shall give extracts from such minutes and records as now prescribed by law.

3. The minutes and records kept by the special deputy clerks appointed in the county of Queens pursuant to the judiciary law shall be kept by the county clerk in his office and he shall give extracts from such minutes and records as now prescribed by law.

§ 2. This act shall take effect immediately.

Chap. 368.

AN ACT to amend the county law, in relation to the powers and duties of assistants to clerks in counties.

Became a law April 24, 1913, with the approval of the Governor. Passed, three-fifths being present.

The People of the State of New York, represented in Senate and Assembly, do enact as follows:

§ 163a
added to
L. 1909,
ch. 16.

Section 1. Chapter sixteen of the laws of nineteen hundred and nine, entitled "An act in relation to counties, constituting chapter eleven of the consolidated laws," is hereby amended by adding thereto a new section, to be section one hundred and sixty-three-a, to read as follows:

§ 163-a. **Duties of assistant clerks in counties.** The clerk of any county may designate one of his assistants to be the calendar clerk of such county who may in the absence of any deputy clerk or for the purpose of assisting any deputy clerk, and after taking the required oath, perform such duties of the clerk as may be assigned to him by an order of the county clerk to be entered in his office. The compensation of any such assistant of the clerk shall be fixed by the county clerk, and when so fixed, no additional compensation shall be paid to any such assistant of the clerk for the performance of any duties whatsoever which the county clerk may assign to him.

§ 2. This act shall take effect immediately.

Chap. 369.

AN ACT to amend the tax law, in relation to the issuance of a new certificate on the setting aside of a tax sale.

Became a law April 24, 1913, with the approval of the Governor. Passed, three-fifths being present.

The People of the State of New York, represented in Senate and Assembly, do enact as follows:

Section 1. Chapter sixty-two of the laws of nineteen hundred and nine, entitled "An act in relation to taxation, constituting chapter sixty of the consolidated laws," is hereby amended by inserting therein a new section to be section one hundred and fifty-one-a, to read as follows:

§ 151-a. **New certificate upon setting aside sale.** If a purchaser shall not have paid his bid, or the same shall not have been collected from him at the expiration of one month from the conclusion of the sale at which the bid was made, the county treasurer may set aside the sale of land for which the bid is made and all rights of the purchaser under such bid shall thereby be extinguished. A certificate of such sale may thereupon be issued by the county treasurer to any person who will pay the same amount as would have been payable by the original purchaser if the sale had not been set aside. If such certificate shall not have been sold within three months from the date of such sale the county treasurer shall transfer the same to the county, in which case the whole quantity of land liable to sale for the purchase money mentioned in the certificate shall be covered by such purchase, the same as if

no person had offered to bid therefor at the sale. The change of
purchaser made pursuant to this section and the time when made
shall be noted in the sales book, and the certificate issued shall confer upon the county the same rights as it would have acquired
had the land been bid in for it at the sale.

§ 2. This act shall take effect immediately.

Chap. 370.

AN ACT restricting the filing and effect of certain maps of
lands in and near the city of Syracuse, unless such maps are
approved by the city engineer of the city of Syracuse.

Became a law April 24, 1913, with the approval of the Governor. Passed,
three-fifths being present.

Accepted by the City.

*The People of the State of New York, represented in Senate
and Assembly, do enact as follows:*

Section 1. A map of the subdivision of lands, or the platting
thereof into streets, in the city of Syracuse, or outside of and
within three miles of the limits of said city, but not within
the limits of an incorporated village, shall not be filed in
the clerk's office of Onondaga county, or become effectual and
binding as a dedication thereof, unless said map shall have thereon
the written approval of the city engineer of the city of Syracuse.

§ 2. This act shall take effect immediately.

Chap. 371.

AN ACT to incorporate the city of Canandaigua.

Became a law April 28, 1913, with the approval of the Governor. Passed,
three-fifths being present.

*The People of the State of New York, represented in Senate
and Assembly, do enact as follows:*

THE CHARTER OF THE CITY OF CANANDAIGUA.

Title   I. Incorporation, boundaries, civil divisions. (§§ 1–8.)
        II. City officers. (§§ 9–19.)
       III. General powers and duties of officers. (§§ 20–39.)

TITLE I.

INCORPORATION, BOUNDARIES, CIVIL DIVISIONS.

Section 1. Short title; public act.
     2. Corporate capacity and name.
     3. Corporate powers.
     4. City boundaries.
     5. Boundaries of town of Canandaigua.
     6. Ward boundaries.
     7. City regarded as a town for certain purposes.
     8. Wards and election districts.

§ 1. **Short title; public act.** This act is a public act, and shall be known as the charter of the " City of Canandaigua." This act shall be liberally construed.

§ 2. **Corporate capacity and name.** Sub. 1. The citizens of the state of New York from time to time inhabitants of the territory now known as the village of Canandaigua, which is hereinafter bounded and described, are continued a municipal corporation in perpetuity under the name of the " City of Canandaigua."

Sub. 2. Succession of liabilities. The corporation now known as the village of Canandaigua is hereby dissolved, subject to the provisions of this act. The city of Canandaigua shall succeed to and be vested with all the rights and property of the said village of Canandaigua, which shall succeed to and be liable for all the liabilities of said village of Canandaigua, of whatsoever name or nature, except as herein otherwise specially provided. And every suit, action or proceeding commenced by or against said village, and pending at the passage of this act, may be continued by or 'against and in the name of said village, or at the option of the parties thereto, the name of said city may be substituted in the place of the name of said village, and in the name of the said city all suits, actions or proceedings may be continued. The ownership and control of all property and effects pertaining to or connected with the fire departments of said village, shall, by virtue of this act, vest in the said city of Canandaigua and in the fire departments, in the same manner and to the same extent in all respects as the same are now vested in said village of Canandaigua and the said fire departments.

§ 3. **Corporate powers.** The city has power to receive by gift, grant, devise, bequest, purchase or condemnation proceedings, and to hold and convey such personal property and such real estate within or without the limits of the said city as the purposes of the corporation may require, and it may receive by gift, grant, bequest or devise, and hold real and personal property in trust for any purposes of education, art, charity, health or amusement, for parks or gardens, for the erection of statues, monuments, public buildings, or for any other public use or purpose, upon such terms as may be prescribed by the grantor or donor, and accepted by said corporation, and may provide for the proper execution of said trust; to contract and be contracted with; to sue and defend; and to be sued in any court; to make, have, use and alter at pleasure a common seal; to have and exercise all other rights and privileges conferred upon it by law or necessary to carry out its corporate functions and duties.

§ 4. **City boundaries.** All that portion of the territory of this state comprising a part of the town of Canandaigua, in the county of Ontario, included within the following boundaries, is hereby constituted a city, which shall be known as the " City of Canandaigua," to wit: Beginning at a point in the northern terminus of the western boundary line of West street in the present village of Canandaigua and continuing northerly in a straight line extending in the same course as said western boundary line of West street until it intersects a line extending westerly from, and in the same course as, the northern boundary line of the North road, so called; thence extending easterly from said intersection along the said westerly extension of the northern boundary line of said North road, and continuing in a straight line along the said northern boundary line of North road until it intersects the eastern boundary line of East street in said village of Canandaigua;

thence southerly in a straight line along the eastern boundary line
of East street and continuing southerly in a straight line in the
same course as the said eastern boundary line of said East street
to a point in the southern boundary line of the Canandaigua-
Geneva state road (formerly called the "Seneca Turnpike");
thence westerly in a straight line across the northern end of
Canandaigua lake to a point formed by the northeast corner of
back lot number ten, west of Main street, on the west shore of said
lake, thence extending westerly along the northern boundary line
of said back lot number ten, and a continuation thereof, until it
intersects a line extending southerly from, and in the same course
as, the western boundary line of the said West street; thence
northerly in a straight line from said intersection along the said
southerly extension of the western boundary line of the said West
street to the place of beginning, being the same and all of that
territory now contained within the corporate limits of the present
village of Canandaigua, in the county of Ontario and state of
New York.

§ 5. **Boundaries of town of Canandaigua.** The town of Canandaigua, shall, on and after the passage of this act, consist of all
that portion of said town not included within the boundaries of
the city of Canandaigua, and the territory embraced within the
boundaries of the city of Canandaigua as hereinbefore described
shall not constitute or be a part of the town of Canandaigua.

§ 6. **Ward boundaries.** The city shall be divided into four
wards, bounded respectively as follows:

First Ward. The first ward shall include all that part of said
city bounded on the north and east by the north and east lines of
the city; on the west by the center of Main street, and on the south
by a line running from Main to East street, between Gibson and
Gorham streets, so as to include all of the residents of Catherine,
Wood and Charlotte streets north of Gorham street, and all the
residents of the east side of Main street north of Gorham street.

Second Ward. The second ward shall include all that part of
said city bounded on the north by the south line of ward number
one, so as to include all of the residents of Gorham street; on the
east by the east line of said city; on the south by the center of
Phoenix street and the continuation of a line through the center of
Phoenix street to the east line of said city; and on the west by
the center of Main street.

Third Ward. The third ward shall include all that part of

said city bounded on the north by the center of Phoenix street and a continuation of a line through the center of Phoenix street to the east line of said city, and by a line running from Main street to the west line of said city south of the south line of Bristol street, so as not to include any of the residents of Bristol street; on the east and south by the east and south lines of said city; and on the west by the west line of said city and the center line of Main street from the center of Phoenix to the said south line of Bristol street.

Fourth Ward. The fourth ward shall include all that part of said city bounded on the north and west by the north and west lines of said city; on the east by the center of Main street; on the south by said line south of the south line of Bristol street and running from Main street to the west line of said city, so as to include all of the residents of Bristol street.

§ 7. City regarded as a town for certain purposes. The said city of Canandaigua shall be considered a town for the purposes specified in the judiciary law, article sixteen, chapter thirty of the consolidated laws, being chapter thirty-five of the laws of nineteen hundred and nine, and the acts amendatory thereof and supplementary thereto, respecting the selecting, drawing and procuring of jurors, and the supervisors and the assessors together with the city clerk of said city shall execute the duties of the supervisor. town clerk and assessors of the town, as prescribed by said article and a duplicate list of jurors selected by them shall be filed in the office of the clerk of said city. The said city of Canandaigua shall also be considered a town for the purposes specified in the " poor law," chapter forty-two of the consolidated laws, being chapter forty-six of the laws of nineteen hundred and nine and the acts amendatory thereof and supplementary thereto. And the poor of said city shall be received and cared for in the county almshouse in the same manner and on the same terms and conditions as the poor of other towns in the county of Ontario.

§ 8. Wards and election districts. The wards hereinbefore described shall until otherwise lawfully changed constitute the election districts for holding all elections held in the city. The inspectors of election shall be appointed by the mayor as provided by the election law of this state, and shall in said city possess the powers and qualifications and discharge the duties as prescribed by said election law.

TITLE II.

City Officers.

§ 9. **Title and number.** The officers of the city shall be a mayor; city judge; an acting city judge; a city court stenographer; a city treasurer; a city clerk; a deputy city clerk; a city attorney; a superintendent of public works; three commissioners of public works; three commissioners of health and public safety; three commissioners of civil service; two assessors; a commissioner of charity; a city physician; a chief of police; an assistant chief of police, and such number of policemen and special policemen as may be determined as provided by this act; a chief engineer; a first assistant and second assistant engineer of the fire department; a sealer of weights and measures; a cemetery sexton; two aldermen from each ward; two supervisors, one to be elected by the electors of the first and fourth wards, and one to be elected by the electors of the second and third wards as provided in this act.

§ 10. **Eligibility of city officers.** No person shall be elected to any city office, nor appointed to the office of assessor, superintendent of public works, commissioner of public works, or commissioner of health and public safety, unless he shall at the time be a resident elector, and shall be, and for one year immediately prior thereto, he shall have been a taxpayer either on real or personal property within the limits of said city. Nor shall any person be elected to any ward office unless he shall at the time be a resident elector of the ward for which he is elected, and shall be, and for one year immediately prior thereto, shall have been a taxpayer, either on real or personal property within the limits of said city. Nor shall any person be elected to the office of supervisor unless he shall be at the time a resident elector of the ward or one of the wards from which he is elected, and possess the qualifications as to a taxpayer as hereinbefore provided. No person shall be elected or appointed to the office of city judge unless he shall have been for at least two years previous to his election or appointment duly admitted to practice as an attorney and counsellor in the courts of record of this state. Whenever any officer of this city shall cease to be a resident of said city or of the district or wards for which he was elected or appointed, his office shall thereby become vacant.

§ 11. **Elective city officers enumerated.** The elective city officers to be elected by the city at large shall be a mayor, a city judge and a city treasurer. The elective officers of the city to be elected by each ward shall be two aldermen. The elective officers of the city to be elected by a district composed of the first and fourth wards shall be one supervisor. The elective officers of the city to be elected by the district composed of the second and third wards shall be one supervisor.

Other than as provided by the terms of this act, the term of office of the mayor shall be two years; city judge four years; city treasurer two years; aldermen two years; supervisors two years.

§ 12. **Appointive officers; term of office.** The appointive officers of the city of Canandaigua to be appointed by the common council shall be three commissioners of health and public safety; three commissioners of public works; a sealer of weights and measures, and one assessor.

The appointive officers of the city of Canandaigua to be appointed by the board of health and public safety, with the approval of the common council shall be, one chief of police, one assistant chief of police, and such policemen and special policemen as may be determined by said board as provided by this act; one city physician.

The appointive officers of the city of Canandaigua to be appointed by the fire companies as provided by this act shall be one chief engineer, one first and one second assistant engineer of the fire department.

The appointive officers of the city of Canandaigua to be appointed by the board of public works, subject to the approval of the common council, shall be one superintendent of public works, and a cemetery sexton.

The appointive officers of the city of Canandaigua to be appointed by the mayor shall be one city attorney, one city clerk, one assessor, one commissioner of charities, an acting city judge, and three civil service commissioners who shall have such powers and perform such duties as are prescribed by the civil service law of this state.

The appointive officer of the city of Canandaigua to be appointed by the city clerk shall be a deputy city clerk.

The appointive officer of the city of Canandaigua to be appointed by the city judge shall be a court stenographer when required as herein provided.

The term of office of the superintendent of public works shall be one year.

The term of office of the city clerk, deputy city clerk, city attorney, acting city judge, city physician, commissioner of public charities, cemetery sexton and assessors shall be two years each.

The term of office of the sealer of weights and measures shall be four years.

§ 13. Salary and compensation of officers.   The mayor, aldermen, commissioners of health and public safety, commissioners of public works, and commissioners of civil service shall not receive any compensation for their services.   The annual salary of the city judge shall be twelve hundred dollars; of the city treasurer, eight hundred dollars; of the city clerk, nine hundred dollars; of the city physician, four hundred dollars; of the assessors, one hundred and twenty-five dollars each; of the city attorney, eight hundred dollars; of the superintendent of public works, twelve hundred dollars; of the city court stenographer, four dollars per day for each day actually occupied in reporting trials; of the city sealer of weights and measures, two hundred dollars; of the cemetery sexton, three hundred dollars; of the deputy city clerk, one hundred dollars; of the chief of police, the assistant chief of police and of the policemen and special policemen, such compensation as may be determined by the provisions of section one hundred and fifty-eight of article four of title seven of this act.   The common council shall have the power to fix and change the salaries of all officers of the city, including such as are fixed by this act, except such as are otherwise provided by law, and except as provided in title seven of this act, but every such salary, except for the year nineteen hundred and thirteen, shall be fixed by resolution at least four months before the beginning of the term of office to which it belongs, and shall not be increased or diminished during the continuance of such term of office. Every resolution fixing or changing a salary shall be published, after its introduction and before being finally acted upon, in one or more newspapers in the city once a week for four successive weeks. The common council shall not have the power to provide for any salary or compensation whatsoever for any officer who by the provisions of this act is required to serve without pay.

The commissioner of charities shall receive no compensation for his services from the city, but shall be governed by the laws relating to the compensation paid to overseers of the poor in towns wherein the county system of poor is established. The supervisors shall receive the same compensation for their services as supervisors of the towns of Ontario county are entitled to receive for like services, to be paid in like manner. The acting city judge shall be paid four dollars per day for each calendar day actually occupied in discharging the duties of city judge, claims therefor to be presented to the common council and audited as provided by this act. Such claims shall, however, be certified in writing by the city judge before presentation of the same to the common council for audit. No other appointive officer of the city shall receive from the city any compensation for his services unless provided by this act or by a general law.

§ 14. Commencement and expiration of term. The term of office of each officer elected at a general city election, and of each officer appointed as provided by this act shall, except as otherwise herein provided, begin with the first day of January following his election or, if he is an appointive officer, on the date of his appointment, and the term of office of all officers shall be computed by the political year, so that such term shall terminate at the end of a municipal year, although the officer may not have been appointed until after the year shall have begun. Except as otherwise herein provided, the term of office of the majority of commissioners of public works, appointed herein, shall expire at the end of each odd numbered year, and one such commissioner shall be appointed for a term of four years and one for a term of two years; and the term of office of the majority of the commissioners of health and public safety shall likewise expire at the end of each odd numbered year, and one such commissioner shall be appointed for a term of four years and one for a term of two years; and the term of office of the majority of the commissioners of civil service shall expire at the end of each odd numbered year, and one of such commissioners shall be appointed for a term of four years and one for a term of two years, excepting that upon the taking effect of this act, the mayor shall appoint three commissioners of health and public safety, three commissioners of public works and three commissioners of civil service, who shall serve until the thirty-first day of December, nineteen hundred and thirteen, inclusive. Provided, however, that the mayor elected to take office on the first day of January, nineteen hundred and fourteen, shall appoint three commissioners of civil service, one for a term of four years and two for a term of two years; and provided further that the common council composed of the aldermen elected to take office on the first day of January, nineteen hundred and fourteen, shall appoint three commissioners of public works, one for a term of four years and two for a term of two years, and three commissioners of health and public safety, one for a term of four years and two for a term of two years.

§ 15. City election. The general city election shall be held at the same time as the general election, and special city elections at such times as herein prescribed. The common council shall provide polling places, ballot boxes and all other necessary material in each election district in said city for all elections in said city, and the manner of conducting such election shall in all respects conform to and be governed by the general laws of this state in respect to elections, not inconsistent with this act. At such general city election a successor shall be elected to each elective city officer whose term of office shall expire with the year in which such election is held. Public notice of every election under this act except as herein otherwise provided, shall be given by the common council, the notice thereof to be published in the newspaper or newspapers designated for that purpose by the common council of said city, at least once in each week for four consecutive weeks immediately preceding the holding of such election, which notice shall designate the officers to be voted for at such election and the location for each polling place, or by such notice and in such manner as may be required by the general election laws of the state. The polls at each general election and at each special election in said city in which one or more officials are to be elected, shall be open and kept open and closed in each district as provided by the general laws of the state for general elections, and the inspectors shall canvass all votes cast for the city officers and declare and make a statement of the result in the same manner as required by the general laws of the state and file the same immediately with the city clerk, unless otherwise provided by this act.

The city clerk shall at least one week before the date fixed by law for the first meeting of the board of registry for a city election, notify each inspector of election in writing of his appointment as such inspector, and of each day for the meeting of registry in each election district of the city and of the date of such election. Every inhabitant of the city who shall at the time and place of offering his vote be qualified to vote for state and county officers, shall be entitled to vote for all officers of the city at large and for all ward officers to be elected in his ward and for all officers to be elected in any district larger than a ward, provided he be a resident of such district. To entitle any elector or voter to vote upon a proposition to raise money by tax or by bonds, he must be entitled to vote for a city officer and he must be the owner of property in the city assessed upon the last preceding assessment roll thereof, and every woman who has the qualifications to vote for city officers, except that of sex, who is the owner of property in the city of Canandaigua assessed upon the last preceding assessment roll thereof, may also vote upon a proposition to raise money by tax on bonds. No elector of said city shall vote, except at special elections in any election district, except that in which he shall reside at the time he offers his vote and shall have so resided at least thirty days immediately prior to the election at which he offers his vote.

§ 16. **Canvass of vote of city elections.** The common council of said city shall meet as a board of city canvassers on the Thursday following each general city election. The city clerk shall present to the common council at said meeting the certified statements of the results of such election in the several election districts of the city as delivered to him by the inspectors of election of such districts. The common council shall canvass such certified statements and determine and declare the whole number of votes cast for each office to be filled at such election under this act; the number of votes cast for each such candidate and what person was elected thereto. The person having the greatest number of votes for the respective offices to be filled for the whole city, and those having the greatest number of votes for the offices to be filled in the several wards, and in the districts in which supervisors are elected as herein provided, shall be declared duly elected. In case of a tie vote, the common council shall fill such office by appointment.

The term of such appointment shall end on the thirty-first day of December succeeding the next general election held in the city, at which election a successor to such appointee shall be elected for the remainder of the term. The city clerk shall enter such determinations and declarations in the minutes of the meetings of the common council.

§ 17. **Official salaries; when payable; fees and perquisites.** The salaries of the city officials shall be payable in monthly installments or at such times as the common council shall determine. The compensation fixed by this act or by the general law for the several officers, shall be in full for all services which they shall respectively perform for said city in any and all capacities other than as herein provided; all fees and perquisites received by such officers shall, unless otherwise specifically provided by this act, or in pursuance of general laws, be paid into the treasury to the credit of the general city fund. The common council and each city board or officer having appointive powers may remove any city officer appointed by him or it for dishonesty, incompetency, neglect of duties or other irregularities, giving such officer reasonable notice thereof and a reasonable opportunity to be heard, and such officer may be suspended, pending such investigation.

·§ 18. **Filling vacancies.** Other than as provided in this act, if a vacancy shall occur in any elective office of the city otherwise than by expiration of term, the common council shall appoint a person to fill such vacancy, who shall hold office until the first day of January, succeeding the next general election held in the city, at which election a successor to such appointee shall be elected for the remainder of the term. A vacancy occurring in an appointive office of the city, otherwise than by expiration of term, shall be filled for the balance of the unexpired term by the same authorities and in the same manner as when appointed for a full term.

§ 19. **Suspension and removal of officers.** The mayor of the city may be removed from office by the governor in the same manner as sheriffs; the governor may direct the inquiry required by law to be conducted by the attorney-general; and after charges have been received by the governor he may, pending the investigation, suspend the mayor for a period of not exceeding thirty days. All other elective officers may be removed in the same manner as town and village officers as provided by the public officers law. Any appointive officer may be removed by a resolution adopted by the affirmative vote of seven members of the common council at

a regular meeting of said council, or a special meeting called for
that purpose.

TITLE III.

GENERAL POWERS AND DUTIES OF OFFICERS.

§ 20. **Official oath of officers.** Each officer of the city shall, before he enters upon the duties of his office, take and file his official
oath in accordance with article thirteen of the constitution, and
section ten of the public officers law, and for omission so to do,
he shall be subject to all the liabilities and penalties prescribed
by section eighteen hundred and twenty of the penal law and
sections thirteen, fifteen and thirty of the public officers law.
Each mayor, city clerk, deputy city clerk, city treasurer, acting
city judge and city judge shall, forthwith upon his election or
appointment, file a certificate with the clerk of Ontario county of
his election or appointment to act, and also take and subscribe the
constitutional oath of office and file the same with the clerk of
the county of Ontario.

§ 21. **Bonds of officers.** Each city clerk, city treasurer, superintendent of public works, commissioner of charities and city judge, shall, before he enters upon the duties of his office, execute and file an official bond in accordance with the provisions of the statutory construction law, and sections eleven, twelve and thirteen of the public officers law, and for omission so to do shall be subject to the penalties and liabilities prescribed in section eighteen hundred and twenty of the penal law, and sections thirteen, fifteen and thirty of the public officers law; otherwise than as herein provided, the penal sum named in any such bond, or the sum specified in any such undertaking as the maximum amount of liability thereon, shall be fixed by the common council. All such bonds shall be executed by the principal and by one or more sufficient sureties, and shall be approved by the common council.

§ 22. **Officers authorized to administer oaths and take acknowledgments.** Each mayor, city clerk, deputy city clerk, city judge and acting city judge of the city shall have the same power and authority to administer oaths and take and certify affidavits and acknowledgments as justices of the peace of towns in the county of Ontario.

§ 23. **When contract to be let to lowest bidder.** Whenever any expenditure to be made or incurred by the common council or any city board or officer in behalf of the city for work to be done, or materials or supplies to be furnished, except ordinary repairing and macadamizing of streets, shall exceed one hundred dollars, the city clerk shall advertise for and receive proposals therefor, in such manner as the common council, or the board or officer charged with making such contract shall prescribe, and the contract therefor shall be let to the lowest bidder, who shall execute a bond to said city for the faithful performance of the contract. All such bonds shall be executed by the principal and by a solvent surety company authorized to do business in this state as surety and shall be approved by the common council. When the lowest bid, in the opinion of the common council, board or officer charged with making the contract, is too high, it shall have the right to reject it, and may discontinue or abandon the work, or may direct the clerk to advertise for new proposals. If, however, the estimated expenditure by any board or officer does not exceed three hundred dollars, the work may be done without a public letting, if the common council consent thereto. All contracts wherein or whereby a sum of one hundred dollars or more is to be expended, shall be in writing and executed in duplicate, one of which shall be filed with the city treasurer and one with the city clerk.

§ 24. **Liability of officers for unauthorized expenditures and other official misconduct.** No officer of said city or other person shall have power or authority to make any purchase in behalf of, or on the credit of, or to contract any debts or liabilities against the city, unless authorized so to do, by or in pursuance of the provisions of this act or general law; and no account, claim or demand of any kind shall be allowed or paid unless so authorized. If any officer of the city shall vote for any appropriation or for the payment or expenditure of any moneys not authorized by this act or in pursuance of a special act or a general law, such officer shall be liable to a penalty of one hundred dollars, to be recovered by the city in a civil action and shall be guilty of a misdemeanor. If the common council or any city board shall pass any resolution authorizing or purporting to authorize any expenditure of money by the city for any purpose, exceeding the amount authorized by or in pursuance of law, to be expended in any one year by the common council, each officer voting for such resolution shall be personally liable for the amount thereof, and each officer present at the meeting at the passage of the resolution shall be deemed as voting for the resolution unless his dissent is entered upon the minutes of the meeting at which such resolution was passed, but the city of Canandaigua shall not be liable therefor, and neither the common council nor any city board or city officer shall pay any debt or expenditure so contracted or made. If any officer of the city authorized to make any contract in his official capacity, or to take part in making any such contract, becomes voluntarily interested in such contract, he shall be liable to the penalty prescribed by section eighteen hundred and sixty-eight of the penal law. If any person having been an officer of said city, whose term of office has expired, shall not within five days after notification and request deliver to his successor in office all property, papers and effects of every description in his possession or under his control belonging to said city, or appertaining to such office, he shall be liable to a penalty of one hundred dollars to be recovered by the city in a civil action, together with all damages caused by his neglect or refusal, and he may also be proceeded against, as provided in section twenty-four hundred and seventy-one-a of the code of civil procedure and section eighteen hundred and thirty-six of the penal law.

§ 25. **The aldermen.** It shall be the duty of every alderman
to attend the regular and special meetings of the common council;
to act upon committees when thereunto appointed by the mayor
or common council; to arrest or cause to be arrested all persons
violating the laws of the state or ordinances, by-laws or police
regulations of the city, when such violations are committed in
his presence; to report to the mayor all subordinate officers who
are guilty of any official misconduct or neglect of duty; to aid
in maintaining peace and good order in the city, and to perform or
assist in performing such duties as are by this act enjoined upon
the aldermen of said city separately, or upon the common council thereof. The aldermen of each ward shall be fence viewers,
and shall possess all the powers and authority in respect to division fences, and shall be entitled to receive the same fees as fence
viewers of towns.

§ 26. **General powers and duties of the mayor.** The mayor
shall be the chief executive officer of the city and shall have and
exercise all the powers conferred upon him and perform all the
duties required of him by this act or by the general statutes of this
state, not inconsistent with this act. It shall be his duty to see
that the laws of this state and the ordinances and by-laws passed
by the common council are faithfully executed within the city.
He shall sign, on behalf of the city, all written contracts made by
it or any board or officer thereof, and cause the seal of the city
to be affixed thereto. He shall be the presiding officer of the common council with a casting vote in case of a tie. He shall have
power and authority to call out and command the police and firemen whenever in his discretion he shall deem it necessary, and
such command shall be in all respects obeyed. Whenever necessary for the prevention or suppression of public disturbances, mobs
or riots, it shall be his duty to take such action as is authorized by
chapters three and four of title two, part second, of the code of
criminal procedure, section one hundred and sixty-two of the military code, and section twenty-one of the general municipal law.
It shall be his duty to exercise a constant supervision and control
over the conduct of all city officers, and he shall have power and
authority to examine at all times the books, vouchers and papers
of any officer or employee of said city, and to take and hear testimony and proof in pursuance of sections eight hundred and forty-
two to eight hundred and sixty-nine, both inclusive, of the code
of civil procedure. He may designate, from time to time, the

place in said city where he will keep his office. It shall be the duty of the mayor to communicate to the common council as soon after his election as practicable, and as soon thereafter as he may deem expedient, a general statement of the affairs of the city in relation to its finances, government and improvement, with such recommendations as he may deem proper.

§ 27. **Appointments to be made by the mayor.** The mayor shall appoint the city clerk, the city attorney, the acting city judge, a commissioner of charities, one assessor and three civil service commissioners. Such appointments shall be made in the month of January, nineteen hundred and fourteen, and in January of each alternate year thereafter, except as herein otherwise provided.

§ 28. **Acting mayor.** Whenever there shall be a vacancy in the office of mayor, or whenever the mayor by reason of sickness or absence from the city shall be prevented from attending to the duties of his office, the president of the common council shall act as mayor during such disability or absence; but he shall not, while acting mayor, during such disability or absence of the mayor, make any appointment or removal from office. In case of a vacancy in the office of mayor, until a mayor shall have been elected and qualified, he shall exercise all the powers of mayor and perform all his duties.

§ 29. **Consultation with heads of departments.** The mayor may at any time in his discretion call together the heads of the different boards and departments of the city government for consultation and advice in regard to the affairs of the city; and at such meetings he may call upon the heads of boards and departments for reports in writing in regard to the transactions of the respective departments, and it shall be the duty of such heads of boards and departments to attend such meetings and submit such reports to the mayor without delay. The city clerk shall attend such meetings and make and file a record of the transactions thereof.

§ 30. **General powers and duties of the city treasurer.** The city treasurer shall be the fiscal officer of the city and shall perform such duties incident to his office as the common council may require. He shall keep an office at such place as the common council shall provide and designate, which shall be kept open each day in the year, except Sundays and legal holidays, from nine-thirty o'clock in the forenoon until three o'clock in the afternoon. He shall keep separate accounts of the different funds of the city, and shall not pay out any money chargeable to any fund in excess of the amount standing on his books to the credit of such fund and shall not knowingly pay money from any fund which is not properly chargeable thereto. The city treasurer shall, before the first meeting of the common council in each month, file with the city clerk a report showing in detail the total expenditures and receipts of city moneys during the next preceding calendar month, a summary statement of that portion of the current fiscal year expiring with the last day of such preceding month, and the balance at the end of such month standing to the credit of each of the city funds. Such statement shall be in such form as shall be prescribed, from time to time, by the common council. An abstract of such report shall be published at least once semi-annually in the newspapers of the city as designated by the common council. Before entering upon the duties of his office, the city treasurer shall execute and file an official bond with two or more sureties, or of some solvent surety company, in such penal sum as may be fixed by the common council, not less, however, than the amount of money estimated by the common council as likely to be received by him for all purposes during the fiscal year, in accordance with section fourteen of the general construction law and sections eleven, twelve and thirteen of the public officers law; and for omission so to do he shall be subject to the penalties and liabilities prescribed by section eighteen hundred and twenty of the penal law, and sections thirteen, fifteen and thirty of the public officers law. Such bond shall be approved by the common council. A certificate of the city clerk of such approval shall be endorsed thereon and the bond so endorsed shall be filed and recorded in the clerk's office of the county of Ontario in the same manner as the official bond of town collectors, and such bond shall be a lien on all property of such treasurer and of each of such sureties in the county of Ontario, until the condition of such bond, together with all the costs and charges which may accrue upon the prosecution thereof, shall be fully satisfied, whereupon the common council shall, by resolution, declare that such bond is satisfied and a copy of such resolution may be filed and recorded in the office of the said county clerk and shall operate to discharge the same and the lien thereof from record. A true copy of such bond and certificate shall be filed in the city clerk's office. It shall be the duty of the treasurer personally to receive all state, county, city and local taxes, assessments and water rents which may be paid at such office and to retain there and not elsewhere, the possession of the warrants and assessment rolls which may from time to time be delivered to him by the clerk of the city. He shall enter daily in suitable books all sums of money received by him for taxes or otherwise, with the name of the person or corporation on whose account the same shall be paid, and shall at the expiration of each month exhibit the same in his office to the mayor and finance committee of the common council for inspection. The treasurer shall also enter in a column in the assessment rolls in his posses sion opposite the names of the persons who shall pay their taxes or assessments the fact of the payment, the amount thereof and the date when paid. He shall also keep a record of all persons, and their respective addresses, who may pay taxes for non-residents of said city, and the residences of such non-residents, so far as he can ascertain the same. The treasurer shall be the custodian of all moneys, securities, obligations and other evidences of debt belonging to the city. He shall annually, during the month of December, settle with the common council, and as much oftener as it may require, for all tax rolls and warrants issued to him. and for all moneys received or collected by him for school or other purposes and produce the proper vouchers of all officers for all moneys paid upon the warrants, drafts or orders of said officers. At the time of the annual settlement and immediately preceding the expiration of his term of office, or within such time after the annual settlement as the common council may fix, he shall pay to his successor in office all such moneys remaining in his hands, and deliver to such successor in office all assessment rolls, books, papers. securities and property belonging to said city or pertaining to the affairs of the city in connection with the duties of his office. The city treasurer shall make such arrangements as directed by the common council, with the banks or trust companies in which the money of the city is deposited by him, for the payment of interest computed as provided by this act.

§ 31. City clerk, his powers and duties. The city clerk of said city shall be clerk of the common council, and clerk of all boards and commissions provided by this act, and shall be registrar of vital statistics of the said city. He shall perform such other duties incident to his office as may be required by the common council or by any such board or by law. He shall keep the minutes of the meetings of the common council and of each board of which he is clerk, and shall record in books to be kept for that purpose all proceedings of the common council and of each board and commission, and index the same. He shall keep an office at such place as the common council shall provide and designate. He shall have charge, custody and control of the corporate seal, books, papers, documents and official minutes of the city, except as otherwise provided or in pursuance of law. He shall, upon request and the payment of fees therefor, make certified copies of records and documents in his possession or under his control, as such clerk and affix the corporate seal of the city to any such certificate, and such seal shall be deemed to be his official seal, and any such certified copy shall be received in evidence as provided in section nine hundred and thirty-three of the code of civil procedure. He shall be entitled to demand and receive fees for such certified copies at the rate of ten cents per folio, from each person other than a city officer, upon whose request any such certified copy is made and delivered. . He shall keep an accurate account of all fees and moneys received by him as such clerk, other than his salary, including fees received by him as registrar of vital statistics and shall, on or before the tenth day of each month, pay over all such fees and moneys received by him during the month immediately preceding, to the city treasurer to the credit of the contingent fund, for which he shall take a receipt and file the same in his office. Such receipts shall at all times be subject to examination by the common council or any member thereof. His office is hereby declared a town clerk's office for the purpose of depositing and filing therein all books and papers required by law to be filed in a town clerk's office and he shall possess all the powers and discharge all the duties of a town clerk not inconsistent with this act. The deputy clerk shall, during the absence from the city of the clerk, or in case of his inability by reason of sickness or disability to act, possess all the powers and perform all the duties of city clerk, and shall otherwise assist the clerk when required. Such deputy clerk shall receive for his services the compensation prescribed by this act.

§ 32. **The city attorney; his powers and duties.** The city attorney shall be and act as the sole legal adviser of the mayor, the common council and all the boards and all other officers of the city. He shall, when directed by the common council, prosecute and defend all actions and proceedings by and against the city and every department thereof, and perform such other professional services relating to said city as the mayor or common council may direct. He shall, when required, prepare all legal papers, contracts, deeds and other instruments for the city and the different departments thereof. The city attorney shall, at the expiration of his office deliver to his successor in office, as soon as qualified, the record or register of all suits or proceedings in which the city or any of its departments may be a party, and also all papers on the part of its departments and also sign stipulations substituting said successor as attorney for the city in such suits or proceedings to the end that a substitution order may be entered. All taxable costs and disbursements in cases wherein the city is successful shall belong to the city and when collected, shall be paid to the treasurer and credited to and form a part of the general fund of the city. He shall receive no fees or other compensation of any kind whatsoever from the city except his salary and his actual expenses while away from the city of Canandaigua attending to legal business of said city. He shall appear for and protect the rights and interests of the city in all actions, suits and proceedings, brought by and against any city officer, board or department; and such officers, board or departments shall not employ other counsel; and he shall attend to all the law business of the city and discharge such other duties as may be prescribed by the common council.

§ 33. **Payment of moneys by city attorney.** He shall pay over at once to the treasurer all moneys collected by him, for and on behalf of the city, including fines and penalties, and he shall annually on the thirty-first day of December, file with the mayor of the city and with the city clerk, an inventory of all the books and property belonging to the city in his custody.

§ 34. **Compromise of suits by city attorney.** He shall, whenever he considers that the best interests of the city will be subserved thereby, enter into an agreement in writing, subject to the approval of the common council, to compromise and settle any claim against the city, which agreement shall be reported to the common council at its next meeting and when so approved it shall be and constitute a valid obligation against the city; and the amount therein provided to be paid shall, with interest thereon at six per centum from its date, be included in the next city budget; and when raised by tax be paid to the claimant. If, however, before the adoption of the city tax budget, there shall be received by the treasurer from any source, any moneys not otherwise appropriated, the amount in the agreement provided to be paid shall be paid out of such moneys so received so far as they will satisfy the same.

§ 35. **Employment of counsel by city attorney.** The city attorney, when authorized by the common council, may employ counsel to assist him in the argument and conduct of important cases or proceedings in which the city is interested or a party.

§ 36. **Supervisors, their powers and duties.** The supervisors of the city of Canandaigua shall have the same powers and duties as the supervisors of the towns of Ontario county, and shall be members of the board of supervisors of the county of Ontario. They shall receive the same compensation and fees allowed by law in the same manner as supervisors of towns. The supervisors elected, appointed or qualified under this act shall be recognized by the board of supervisors of Ontario county and be allowed to take their seats as members of said board and participate in all deliberations and proceedings of said board during their term of office. Other than as provided by this act, their term of office shall begin the first day of January next after their election. They shall also discharge all other duties imposed upon them by this act. Each of the districts of the city from which a supervisor is elected shall be regarded as a town of Ontario county for the purposes specified in title three, chapter ten, article second of the code of civil procedure respecting the selection, drawing and procuring the attendance of trial jurors. The supervisor of the first and fourth wards together, and the supervisor from the second and third wards together, each supervisor acting only for the wards in which he was elected, and the city clerk and assessors of said city, shall perform for said wards, respectively, the duties prescribed in said article. A duplicate of each list of jurors selected by them respectively shall be filed in the office of the clerk of said city, which shall be deemed a town clerk's office for that purpose. The supervisors and the clerk and assessors of said city shall meet in the clerk's office at the time provided by law, and proceed to discharge the duties imposed upon them by the code of civil procedure, as aforesaid, and by this act; and the list made by them shall constitute the list of persons to serve as trial jurors for the ensuing three years. The supervisors elected under this act and the clerk and assessors of said city shall meet every third year thereafter for the same purpose and make and file lists so required of them. The clerk shall furnish to the city judge certified copies of all such lists and from the names of all such jurors in the city shall be drawn the trial jurors in actions and proceedings in the city court, and before the city judge.

§ 37. **Other city officers; their powers and duties.** The powers and duties of all other city officers shall be such as are prescribed in this act, or when not so prescribed, as provided by existing general laws or ordinances of the common council applicable to such officers.

§ 38. **Officers not to be interested, et cetera.** No officer or servant of the city, or any department thereof, shall in any manner be interested directly or indirectly in any contract to which the city or any department thereof shall be a party, for the sale or hire of any property, merchandise or materials, or for furnishing or performing any work, labor or service (except in respect of his own compensation from the city or a department thereof), or for the granting of any franchise or privilege; and no officer elected or appointed shall receive any perquisite, emolument, fee or compensation, except his salary or pay from the city or a department thereof, for any act done or service rendered by him in his official capacity, nor shall he accept or receive any sum of money or other valuable thing, fee or commission upon or derive any advantage from the sale or hiring of any property to or by the city or any department thereof. The violation of any provision of this section shall be a misdemeanor, and upon conviction thereof, in addition to the penalties provided by law, such officer shall forfeit his office.

§ 39. **Common council; powers to compel meetings of boards, et cetera; removal for misconduct.** It shall be the duty of all commissions and boards to meet at any time upon the request of the mayor or if the common council shall so require by resolution, and all boards and commissions shall carry out and execute the provisions of any resolution adopted by the common council, requiring or requesting the performance of any duty imposed upon such board or commission by the provisions of this act, or if in the judgment of a majority of the common council such board or commission should be required to do, perform or carry out any lawful act not specially provided for by this act. Any neglect, failure or refusal of such board or commission to comply with the provisions of any such resolution within a reasonable time, shall be deemed misconduct in office, and render the members of such board or commission so neglecting, failing or refusing, liable to removal from office in the manner provided for removal of city officers in section nineteen of title two of this act.

TITLE IV.

LEGISLATIVE DEPARTMENT, COMMON COUNCIL.

§ 40. **Common council; the legislative body of the city.** Except as otherwise provided in this act, the legislative and governing powers of the city shall be vested in the common council.

§ 41. **How constituted.** The mayor and the aldermen of the city shall constitute and be the members of the common council thereof.

§ 42. **Organization.** The members of the common council shall meet on the first Monday of each year, or, if that day is a public holiday, on the next day thereafter. They shall elect a president of the common council from their number, who shall, until the following first day of January, preside over all meetings of the common council in the absence of the mayor, and have a voice therein. At all meetings of the common council, the mayor, when present, shall preside.

§ 43. **Members of departments to give information.** Whenever required by the common council every member of a department or city officer shall attend its meetings and answer all questions by any member of the common council, or by the city attorney, relating to the affairs of his department or office, provided that at least forty-eight hours before the meeting he has had written notice thereof.

§ 44. **Clerk of the council.** The city clerk shall be the clerk of the council.

§ 45. **Meetings.** The council shall hold regular meetings at least once each month, and shall hold adjourned or special meetings at its chambers at such times as it shall designate, and such other times as it shall determine. The mayor, or in his absence, the president of the common council, or a majority of its members may call a special meeting by causing a written notice thereof, specifying the time and the object thereof, to be served by the city clerk upon each member personally at least three hours before the time specified in such notice for such meeting, or by mail directed to him at his place of residence or place of business at least twelve hours before the time specified in such notice for said meeting.

§ 46. **Rules of procedure.** The common council shall determine the rules of its own procedure. A majority of all its members shall constitute a quorum to do business, or a smaller number may effect a legal adjournment. The attendance of absent members may be compelled at a meeting thereof at which less than a quorum is present, and it may punish a member for disorderly conduct, for violation of its rules, or for official misconduct. The ayes and noes shall be called and recorded on all ordinances and resolutions involving the expenditure of money. All meetings and proceedings of the council shall be public. No ordinance shall be passed by the council on the same day on which it is introduced, except by unanimous consent and all members being present thereat. No resolution shall be passed authorizing or involving the expenditure of money or the collection of money by a tax or assessment unless it shall receive the assent of a majority of all the members of the council.

§ 47. **Powers and duties.** The powers of the common council shall be legislative only, except as otherwise provided by this act and any other provision of law not inconsistent therewith. The common council shall have the power to pass any ordinance or resolution not repugnant to the constitution and laws of this state for any local purpose, pertaining to the government of the city, and the management of its business, the protection of the business and property interests of the citizens, the preservation of order, peace and health and the safety and welfare of the city and the inhabitants thereof; and shall have such powers of legislation by ordinance or resolution as are conferred upon it by this act, or any other provision of law affecting the city, not inconsistent with this act or the laws of this state, except such as are especially conferred by this act upon any separate department of the city government, including the power to regulate or prohibit, by ordinance, the erection and maintenance of docks, piers, and wharves, or of any building or structure thereon or to be built thereon, in that portion of Canandaigua lake within the city limits and to regulate and prescribe the manner or form of construction of any such dock, pier or wharf, and materials used in such construction, or of any boat house, building, buildings or other structure which shall be built or constructed on or adjoining such dock, wharf or pier. Said common council shall also have the power to prohibit the erection or construction of any building or other structure anywhere in, upon or adjacent to the waters of said Canandaigua lake, within the limits of said city; including the power to prohibit and regulate the erection or construction of any building or other structure in front of or upon any street, lane or alley leading to said Canandaigua lake, or in front of or upon any public park, place or shores of said Canandaigua lake, within said city limits. In case of a violation of said ordinance or ordinances the said common council shall have the power to enter by its duly authorized officers or agents upon the premises in question and without process summarily remove all said buildings and structures found thereon.

§ 48. **Public utilities may be established.** The common council shall have power when authorized by a vote of the taxpayers at a special election as provided in this act, to establish a lighting system for said city independent of any existing plant, for the purpose of supplying light by means of electricity, gas or other approved system to said city, and the inhabitants thereof.

§ 49. **Control of finances.** The council shall have the management and control of the finances and all of the property, real and personal, belonging to the city, except as otherwise provided by this act, or by other provisions of law not inconsistent herewith, and shall have the power to contract, for a period of not exceeding five years, with any person, persons or corporation, to furnish light for the city by means of electricity, gas or other approved system. The common council shall have the management and control of the sinking fund received for the payment of bonds of the city of Canandaigua and shall direct the investment and reinvestment thereof. The common council may invest all moneys belonging to said fund in any securities allowed by law to savings banks of this state at the time of such investment, subject to the same restrictions and limitations, and for the purpose of investing said fund, may purchase or subscribe for bonds of the city of Canandaigua and hold the same as other investments. The bonds so purchased by said city shall have plainly written or printed thereon when purchased, the following words, namely, " Purchased by the City of Canandaigua. Not transferable except by resolution of the common council."

§ 50. **Bonds to be issued when; restrictions.** The common council shall not issue any bonds or other obligations which shall be a liability against the city of Canandaigua, except as provided in this act, or a special or general law of this state, or except such as shall be authorized by a vote of the taxpayers of said city at a special election held as provided in this act; and all bonds issued under the provisions of this act shall be issued and negotiated by the common council of the city of Canandaigua and shall conform to and meet with all the conditions and requirements of the general municipal law of the state of New York.

§ 51. **Penalties for violation of ordinances.** In any and all ordinances, rules and regulations ordained or adopted by the common council, except as otherwise provided in this act, said council may prescribe and impose for every violation thereof a penalty of not exceeding fifty dollars, or a fine of not exceeding fifty dollars and imprisonment in the county jail of Ontario county until such fine be paid, not exceeding one day for each dollar of the fine imposed. The common council shall have power by ordinance or resolution whenever it shall determine that public safety and protection against fire so requires, to compel the removal and regulate the erection and maintenance of all telegraph, telephone or electric light wires or cables, or other appliances for conducting electricity, and the poles connected therewith in any place within the corporate limits of the city of Canandaigua. For violation of such ordinance or resolution made pursuant to the provisions of this section, the common council may prescribe penalties and fines to the amount of two hundred fifty dollars and imprisonment in the county jail of Ontario county not exceeding one hundred days; and that such penalties, fines and imprisonments may be again imposed in case of continuing the building and repairing in such ordinance or resolution prohibited. And the common council shall also have the power to pass such ordinances for the government and discipline of the fire department as the board of health and public safety may request. The common council shall also have power to enforce and enact ordinances necessary or expedient for the prevention, summary abatement, or removal of nuisances therein, or for the establishment, or preservation of good government and order, or the security of the inhabitants of the city, or for the suppression of vice.

§ 52. **Certification of ordinances, et cetera, approval or veto of mayor.** After adoption by the common council, each bill, order, ordinance or by-law, or any resolution for the appropriation of money for any purpose, shall be duly certified by the clerk and presented to the mayor for his action thereon. Within ten days after any bill, order, ordinance or by-law, or any resolution for the appropriation of money for any purpose, shall have been certified to the mayor, he may return the same to the city clerk with his approval or disapproval written thereon. And if he shall so approve, the same shall thereupon become a law. And if he shall fail to approve or disapprove as above provided, the same shall become a law at the expiration of thirty days from the date of such certification. If the mayor shall return the same with his disapproval in writing thereon, the common council may pass the same over his veto by a two-thirds vote of all its members, where upon the same shall become a law.

§ 53. **Present ordinances to remain in force.** The ordinances, by-laws, rules, resolutions and regulations in force in the village of Canandaigua on the date on which this act takes effect, shall, in so far as they are not inconsistent with this act, continue in full force and effect, subject to modification, amendment or repeal by the council, and the council is authorized to re-enact ordinances upon the same subjects, and with the same force and effect as those in force as aforesaid when this act takes effect.

23 .

§ 54. **Ordinances to be published.** The ordinances in force in the village of Canandaigua when this act takes effect, as heretofore published in pamphlet form, shall be the code or ordinances of the city until the same shall be revised. The code of ordinances of the city shall be revised by the common council and published in pamphlet form in the year nineteen hundred and fourteen. All ordinances thereafter enacted during each calendar year shall be compiled and published on or before the first day of March of the succeeding year. Every ordinance shall, within thirty days after it has become a law as herein provided, be recorded by the city clerk in a book provided for that purpose. Such record shall contain the attestation of the city clerk and the mayor's written approval, or, in case of his disapproval, a memorandum of its passage over his veto, or, in case the ordinance took effect because he failed to approve or disapprove and return it within ten days, then a memorandum to that effect, and the date when such ordinance took effect. Such record or a certified copy thereof shall be presumptive evidence of the passage of such ordinance.

§ 55. **Examining committee.** The council may at any time appoint a special committee of its members to inquire as to whether the law and ordinances relating to any matter or department of the city are being faithfully observed, and whether the duties of any of the officers and employees are being faithfully discharged, and to examine and report whether there are unnecessary, inefficient or unfit employees, or whether there are excessive salaries, wages, or compensation paid, and to inquire generally in respect to any and all matters which will conduce to the orderly and economical conduct of the business of the city, and for such purposes such committee, so appointed, may take or hear testimony, hear or receive affidavits and take depositions, and examine witnesses before them. Such committee shall have access to any of the records of the city, and for the purposes of any such inquiries, shall have the powers conferred upon any officer, person, board or committee, as provided in sections eight hundred and forty-three and eight hundred and forty-five of the code of civil procedure.

§ 56. **Prohibitions.** No member or committee of the common council shall have power to employ any person, incur any expense, or purchase any materials for or on behalf of the city or any of its officers, members or departments, except as expressly provided for in this act. The council shall not audit or allow any claim against the city unless the same is presented in the form and manner prescribed by this act. Nor shall the common council enter into any contract for supplies or services for a longer period than one year, except as herein otherwise provided. The common council shall not change the salaries of the officers of the city as fixed by this act, nor shall it have the power to provide for any salary or compensation whatsoever for any officer, who, by the provisions of this act is required to serve without pay. No appropriation of money shall be made for any purpose except by an ordinance or resolution passed by a two-thirds affirmative vote of all the members of the common council specifying by items the amount thereof and the department or specific purpose for which the appropriation is made.

§ 57. Franchises. The common council shall have power to grant all franchises or permits granted on behalf of the city, and no person, persons, association or corporation shall erect any wires, poles, tracks, or any obstruction in, over or upon any street, bridge, sidewalk or public place in said city or in, over or upon any land owned by said city unless a franchise or permit therefor shall be granted by the common council of said city. No franchise shall be granted hereafter for a period exceeding fifty years, and in such franchise it shall specifically prohibit any sub-lease, assignment or other transfer of all or part of the rights obtained under such franchise without the consent of the common council, signified by a resolution thereof adopted by at least seven members voting therefor. The grant of any franchise by said common council shall not become valid and take effect unless made as aforesaid, and no grant of a new franchise, or for an extension of a franchise now existing, shall become valid without a resolution by said common council adopted by at least seven members voting therefor. No ordinance shall be passed making or authorizing a sale or lease of city real estate except by a resolution of said common council adopted by at least seven members voting therefor; and in case of the sale of real estate, or the sale or lease of a franchise, the ordinance must provide for a disposition under proper regulations, for the protection of the city, at public auction, after at least two weeks' public notice, and to the highest bidder.

§ 58. Depositories of city funds. The common council must at its first meeting in January or as soon thereafter as practicable, designate one or more national banks or trust companies within this state, as the depository or depositories of all moneys received

by the city treasurer, and shall agree with such bank, banks, or.
trust companies, upon a rate of interest per annum to be paid on
moneys so deposited, but on sinking funds provided for the retirement of bonds, and on any other funds, none of which are to be
expended during any one year, the rate of interest shall not be
less than two per centum.   Each depository so designated shall
for the benefit and security of the city, before receiving any such
deposits, execute to the city a good and sufficient bond with two or
more sureties, or a surety company, to be approved by the common
council.   Such bond shall be conditioned for the safe keeping and
payment on the lawful order of the city, of all such deposits and
the agreed interest thereon, and it shall be the duty of the city
clerk to file and record such bond in the office of the county clerk
of Ontario county.   It shall be the duty of the city treasurer to
deposit all funds belonging to the city that may come into his
hands in such depository or depositories pursuant to the direction
of the common council, and his failure so to do shall be a misdemeanor.

§ 59. Action to restrain violation.   The city may maintain an
action to restrain by injunction the violation of any ordinance of
the common council, the department of public works, and the board
of health and public safety, in addition to any other remedy.

§ 60. Newspapers to be designated to publish notices, et cetera.
All notices, reports and other matters required by this act to be
published shall be published in two newspapers published in the
city to be designated by the common council, one of which newspapers shall fairly represent the principles of the political party
which at the last election preceding such designation, polled the
highest number of votes for governor and the other of which said
newspapers shall fairly represent the principles of the political
party which polled the next highest number of votes for governor
at such last preceding general election.

§ 61. Common council; power to regulate freight cars on street.
The common council shall have power to regulate or prohibit
any street surface railway company from running, drawing
or propelling any railroad freight car or cars through or along
any street or section thereof within the corporate limits of the
city.

§ 62. Railroads to conform to grades, et cetera.   If any street,
section of a street, public place or square in which a street surface
railroad is now, or shall be hereafter operated, shall be paved,

repaired or macadamized, or any such street straightened, widened
or altered, the common council shall have power to require the
railroad corporation operating such street surface railroad to
change its grade and line and location of its track, tracks or parts
thereof to conform to such alteration or improvement in such
manner as said council shall designate, and the corporation operating such street surface railroad shall, at its own expense, change
its lines and grade, and location of its track, or tracks, or parts
thereof to conform to such direction as the common council may
make. Nothing herein contained shall be held to relieve any such
railroad corporation from paying its share of the cost of such
improvements, as provided by this act.

TITLE V.

Auditing and Payment of Debts, Accounts and Claims.

§ 63. **Claims not to be paid without audit and tax for same
raised.** The common council shall audit and pass upon all claims
and demands against the city corporation, and may allow the
whole or part of any claim, or disallow it entirely, as herein provided. No claim or demand shall be allowed or audited unless
the money to pay the same shall have been voted at a tax meeting
or unless the common council shall have provided for the same in
the tax budget, and raised the same by a tax for such purpose
prior to such audit, as provided by this act, and no claim or
demand shall be paid unless audited and allowed as by this
charter provided.

§ 64. **Presentation of claims and payment.** Upon the auditing
of claims against said city by the common council, a warrant for
the amount thereof shall be drawn upon the treasurer, to be signed
by the mayor, and countersigned by the city clerk, and shall there-

upon be paid by the treasurer, and filed in his office, but no account or claim against said city shall be paid until it shall have been presented to the common council, and audited and allowed by them; and when any such account or claim shall be so audited, the common council auditing the same shall endorse thereon, or annex thereto, a certificate subscribed by them, of said auditing, and of the allowing or disallowing of the same, in which the sum allowed, if any, and the charges for which the same is allowed, shall be specified.

§ 65. **Requirements for presentation of claims.** No such account or claim shall be audited or allowed by the common council unless it shall be made out in items and shall be accompanied with an affidavit of the person claiming to have performed the services, or made the disbursements therein charged, stating that the several items of such account or claim are correct; that the services therein charged have been rendered; that the disbursements therein charged have been made; that no part thereof has been paid; and that such claim has not been theretofore presented to said common council. Such affidavit shall be endorsed on, or annexed to such account or claim, and presented and preserved therewith. The mayor, or other officer then presiding, when such account or claim shall be presented to the common council, may administer the oath required by this section; and the common council may examine the claimant on oath as to any items embraced in such account or claim.

§ 66. **May allow or disallow.** Nothing in the last preceding section shall be construed to prevent the common council from disallowing any account or claim in whole or in part when so made out and verified, nor from requiring other or further evidence of the correctness and reasonableness thereof.

§ 67. **Number and record.** Every account or claim against said city, presented to the common council in any year shall be filed with the city clerk and by him numbered from number one upwards, in the order in which presented, and a memorandum made thereon of the time of presenting the same, the name of the person in whose favor it shall be made out, and of the person by whom it shall be presented and the amount allowed thereon, all of which shall be entered in the proceedings of the common council.

§ 68. **To specify fund from which paid.** Every warrant drawn by the common council to pay any account or claim shall specify the fund from which it is payable, and said warrant shall refer to

such account by its number, the name of the person in whose favor
it was made out, and the time when it was presented, and a memorandum of such reference, and of the amount of the warrant shall
be entered in the records of the common council before the warrant shall be delivered to the claimant.

§ 69. **Treasurer not to pay except on warrant, et cetera.** No
payment shall be made by the city treasurer from any money belonging to said city except upon the warrant of the common council as hereinbefore provided, endorsed on, or annexed to, the account or the claim together with attached carbon copy as provided by section seventy of this act, for which it shall be drawn,
and specifying the fund from which it is payable; and when such
warrant shall be paid, the city treasurer shall file and keep the
same together with the papers presented to him therewith, as
required by this act.

§ 70. **Requisition to purchase or employ.** No account or claim
for labor, material or supplies furnished shall be audited, allowed
and paid by the common council until a requisition shall have
been issued in triplicate by the purchasing committee which shall
consist of three members, the mayor, the chairman of the board
of public works and the chairman of the board of health and
public safety, directing such expenditure, with the items and
amount thereof, and the original filed with the mayor and a carbon
copy thereof attached to such account or claim, before its presentation to said common council, and a carbon copy thereof filed
with the city treasurer, which said requisition shall be signed by
the mayor and at least one other member of said committee.

§ 71. **Liability for violation.** If any member of the common
council, or other officer of this city, shall in any way assume to
create a debt, or incur any liability on account of, or against said
city, or to appropriate or pay any money, or use or apply any
property, or thing of value belonging to said city, for any purpose, or in any manner, whatsoever, contrary to the provisions of
this charter, he shall be deemed guilty of a misdemeanor, and he
shall also be personally liable to any person injured for such debt,
or property, or thing of value thus misapplied, or for any debt or
liability thus attempted to be incurred, and he shall in like manner
be personally liable to said city for any amount of such debt or
liability that it shall for any reason pay or assume to pay, and for
any property or thing of value thus misapplied, or for any damages
that may accrue to said city. Any person thus injured or said

city may prosecute for any violation of this section in any court of civil jurisdiction in this state.

TITLE VI.

DEPARTMENT OF PUBLIC WORKS.

§ 72. **Board of public works; how constituted.** The commissioners of public works appointed as provided in this act shall constitute the board of public works and shall receive no compensation for their services. Within ten days after the appointment of said commissioners in the year nineteen hundred and thirteen and annually thereafter within the first week in January they shall meet and organize. They shall elect a president of the board of public works from their number who shall until the following first day of January preside over all meetings of the board of public works, and have a voice and vote therein. At any meeting of the board two members present shall constitute a quorum to transact business, but a less number may regularly adjourn from time to time. The board shall have regular times and places of meeting not less than once in each calendar month. Its meetings shall be open to the public. Special meetings may be called by the mayor or by any two members of the board or by a majority of the common council by causing a written notice thereof specifying the time and object thereof to be served by the city clerk upon each member personally at least three hours before the time specified in such notice for such meeting, or by mail directed to him at his place of residence or place of business at least twelve hours before the time specified in such notice for said meeting.

§ 73. City departments in charge of the board. The board of public works shall take charge and subject to the limitations herein contained have the management and control of the following departments of the city government, and of the property belonging thereto.

1. Streets, alleys, lanes and sidewalks.
2. Sewers and drains.
3. Creeks, ditches and bridges.
4. Street and other lighting.
5. Parks, cemeteries.
6. Water works, reservoirs, pipes and hydrants.
7. Public buildings and property.
8. Such other departments as may be assigned to the board under the provisions of this act.

§ 74. Assignment of other departments. The board of public works shall take charge of and have management and control over such other department or departments as may from time to time be assigned to it by the common council of the city of Canandaigua and thereupon shall pass such rules and regulations as may be necessary for the proper management of the department or departments so assigned, subject to the approval, however, of the common council.

§ 75. Appointment of superintendent. The board of public works shall within ten days after their appointment in the year nineteen hundred and thirteen and annually thereafter within the first week of January appoint a superintendent of public works who shall receive a salary as herein provided, whose term of office shall expire on the thirty-first day of December following his appointment, unless sooner removed as herein provided.

§ 76. Engineers and other employees. The board of public works may employ such engineers and employees as may be necessary, subject, however, to the restrictions and limitations contained in this act.

It may also employ such other employees and laborers as may be necessary to carry out the provisions of this act. It shall fix the salaries and prescribe the duties of said superintendents, engineers, assistants and employees, subject to the approval of the common council.

All clerical work of the board shall be performed by the city clerk or his deputy.

§ 77. **Superintendent; powers and duties as to highways.** The board of public works shall be commissioners of highways in and for the city and shall have all the powers and perform all the duties of the town superintendents of highways in the towns, subject to the provisions of this act, and shall have power to lay out, alter, discontinue, regulate, straighten, widen, pave, curb, clean and sprinkle the streets, highways, alleys, bridges and crosswalks and to prevent the encumbering and obstruction of the same in any manner, and to protect them from encroachment and injury; and to construct sidewalks or to cause the same to be constructed. and to alter, repair, regulate, straighten, raise and lower the same, to cause the same to be kept free and clean from ice, snow and dirt, and to prevent the encumbering, encroaching upon or obstruction of the same as herein provided.

Before laying out any highway or street requiring condemnation proceedings, and before altering or discontinuing any highway or street, a public hearing shall be had after notice thereof has been given by publication at least once in the newspaper published in the city, designated for such purpose by the common council, and by mailing a copy of such notice to all owners of lands through which said new highway or street is to extend, or adjacent to the portion of any highway or street that is to be altered or discontinued.

§ 78. **Water rates; powers and duties as water commissioners.** All the powers and duties now vested in or imposed upon the water commissioners of the village of Canandaigua, under and by virtue of any general or special statute of the state, shall vest in and devolve upon the common council, and the common council may delegate to the board of public works such powers and duties as they shall determine.

All moneys that might otherwise come into the hands of said water commissioners by virtue of the statute or statutes authorizing or directing the creation of a sinking fund for the payment of the principal or interest on the water bonds of the village of Canandaigua, shall be paid over to the treasurer of the city of Canandaigua to be by him from time to time invested in interest bearing securities under the direction of the common council. The office of water commissioners and the board of water commissioners is hereby abolished and the term of office of each of said water commissioners shall expire on the date when this act takes effect. Within ten days thereafter they shall account for and turn over to the treasurer of the city of Canandaigua all moneys, evidences of debt, securities and other property in their hands. The income derived from payments for water used shall, so far as necessary, be applied to the cost of maintaining, operating and extending the system of water works and the payment of the principal and interest falling due on the water bonds now outstanding or hereafter issued.

The water rates paid by the consumers of water in the village of Canandaigua when this act takes effect shall be the schedule of water rates until changed or modified as provided in this act. The board of public works shall as soon as practicable after this act takes effect, and not later than its first meeting in January, nineteen hundred and fourteen, and at such other times as is deemed advisable, prepare a schedule of water rates to be paid by the consumers of water, and submit the same to the common council for its approval, and if approved, the same shall be the water rates to be paid by all consumers of water. The said board shall also from time to time cause bills for water to be presented to all consumers thereof either personally or by mail or left at the building or place where the water is used, and such bills shall contain a notice that they are payable at the office of the city treasurer at or before a time specified therein. At the time of the presentation of such bills to consumers the board shall deliver to the city treasurer a duplicate of such bills and file a duplicate thereof with the city clerk. The said board shall also provide rules, regulations and penalties for the collection thereof by the city treasurer.

§ 79. **Water meters.** Within two months after this act takes effect, the board of public works shall cause a written inventory of all machinery, tools, appliances, materials and water meters used in connection with the water works system of the city of Canandaigua to be made in duplicate, one to be filed in the office of the city treasurer and one in the office of the city clerk. Each water meter now in use shall be numbered and those hereafter placed in any building or other place for use shall be numbered in consecutive order, and the said board shall cause a receipt to be signed in duplicate by all persons, associations and corporations now in possession of a meter or meters, and shall require a receipt to be signed in duplicate by all persons, associations and corporations who or which shall have installed by said board a meter or meters and such receipts shall be filed one in the office of the said city treasurer and one in the office of the city clerk. The said board shall cause at the time of making such inventory all water meters to be read and the readings thereof to be recorded in duplicate and filed, one in the office of the city treasurer and one in the office of the city clerk. The said board shall cause readings of all meters in use ·to be made and such readings to be recorded in duplicate quarterly, one of said duplicates to be filed in the office of the said city treasurer and one in the office of· the city clerk. All bills for water used shall be due and payable quarterly and if not paid within sixty days after such bills become due, said board shall cause the use of water at all places where such bills have arisen to be discontinued.

§ 80. **Charge of public works; adoption of rules and regulations governing the same; prevent injury to trees, et cetera.** The board of public works shall have the power to adopt and execute plans for the laying out *of improvement and maintenance of the parks, and provide additional parks and play grounds either within or without the city of Canandaigua, and for such purpose to acquire by gift, purchase or condemnation lands for that purpose, subject to the approval thereof by the common council, and to regulate, manage, control and maintain the public parks and play grounds now established or hereafter laid out and established by said board; to preserve, beautify and protect the same: to prohibit and prevent encroachments thereon or injury to the trees, shrubs and adornments thereof; to adopt rules and regulations governing the purposes for which the parks and play grounds or any of them may be used or enjoyed; to determine the place for planting, and the relative location of, shade or ornamental trees in the parks, play grounds and other public places; to determine the methods and manner of beautifying the parks and play grounds and in all things to have complete control and authority thereover, subject only to the approval of the common council. The words " parks and play grounds " are hereby defined to include all public grounds and places except cemeteries, which at the time this act takes effect are under the control and supervision of the village of Canandaigua or any of its officers, and all public grounds and places hereafter acquired by the city of Canandaigua under the provisions of this act.

§ 81. **Sidewalks to be kept free from snow, ice, et cetera; board may do work and assess cost.** The board shall have power

---

* So in original.

to require all persons owning or occupying property in the city, and the owners of unoccupied property therein, to remove all snow, ice and dirt from the sidewalks in front of the premises so owned or occupied by them, and to keep the same free therefrom, and from any encroachment or obstruction; and in case of neglect or refusal on the part of such owner or occupant to remove the same, the board may perform the labor and thereupon make out and deliver to the city clerk a statement of the expense and description of the property and the amount of such expense with ten per centum added thereto, which shall be a lien or charge upon the lot, land or plot so described and the same shall be assessed to the owner of the property and added to the amount of the next annual city tax and collected in the same manner provided for the collection of taxes.

§ 82. **Right to use streets for laying water pipes, et cetera.** The board of public works and all acting under its authority shall have the right to use the ground or soil under any street or highway in the city, for the purpose of introducing water and through any and all portions of the city, and such right shall be continued for the purpose of repairing and relaying water pipes. Said board shall cause the surface of such street, highway or road to be restored to its normal condition.

§ 83. **Power to sell water to outside consumers.** Said board of public works may, in behalf of the city and with the approval of the common council, sell to a corporation or individual outside the city the right to make connections with the water mains for the purpose of drawing water therefrom, and shall fix the prices and conditions therefor; but the board shall not sell nor permit the use of water under this section if or when thereby the supply or pressure for the city or any of its inhabitants will be insufficient.

§ 84. **Public lighting.** The board of public works shall have power to provide for the lighting of the streets, highways, alleys, public places and municipal buildings in the city, but no contract therefor shall be made for a longer period than five years nor without the approval of the common council; and for the protection and safety of the public lamps to prevent the same from being lighted or extinguished by persons not authorized to do so, and to provide rules and regulations concerning same, and penalties for wilful violation of the rules and regulations so prescribed or wilful injury of lighting appliances.

§ 85. **Certain work to be advertised for bids.** The board of public works shall have power in all of its departments to make improvements and perform any labor contemplated within said departments by the aid of its own servants and employees or by contract. If the board shall determine to have any work performed or materials furnished by contract, except street lighting as hereinbefore provided, in excess of one hundred dollars it shall direct the city clerk, and it shall be his duty to advertise for bids upon the work to be performed and materials to be furnished, for at least twice a week for two successive weeks in one or more of the newspapers published in the city of Canandaigua designated for such purpose by the common council, and upon the receipt of the bids and the opening thereof at the time specified, the board may, if in its judgment it is deemed best, reject any or all bids submitted, or may let the contract for the particular work desired to the lowest responsible bidder, subject to the approval of the common council. The board may require security or certified check to accompany the bids, assuring the execution and faithful performance of the particular contract upon which the bid is made.

§ 86. **Moneys not to be transferred; commissioners personally liable.** Each separate department shall be credited with the amount that shall be appropriated by the common council therefor and charged with the expense thereof. Moneys appropriated for maintenance or for permanent improvements in one department may not be transferred to or used for any other purpose or in any other department until the board has certified to the common council the transfer desired and the occasion therefor, and the common council has approved of such transfer. No contract shall be made or expense incurred in any department in excess of the amount appropriated to that department, as shown in its annual estimate submitted to the common council, and the members of the board shall be personally liable for all expenses or indebtedness incurred in excess of any item of the appropriations made by the common council to said board.

§ 87. **Quarterly statement to be rendered.** The board of public works shall quarterly, and at such times as may be required either by the mayor or by the common council, render to the common council an itemized statement of all its receipts and disbursements, properly classified, and showing the balance on hand at the beginning and at the close of the period specified and covered; and at the close of each fiscal year it shall submit an annual statement, showing by suitable items and summaries the cost and income of

each department. Whenever requested by either the mayor or the
common council the board shall also furnish any additional information in regard to its work and the cost thereof.

§ 88. **Manner of paying of bills.** All bills incurred by the board
of public works and all amounts payable out of the moneys appropriated to the use of the board shall be, upon the requisition of the
purchasing committee as herein provided, and when audited by
the common council, paid by the city treasurer on such audit and
order of the common council.

§ 89. **Condemnation proceedings.** Whenever the board shall
have determined to take and appropriate any lands, interests or
easements, deemed by it necessary in the execution of any plan or
improvement adopted by the board, or in the execution of any part
of any plan or improvement in any of the departments under the
control and supervision of the board, which lands and rights
shall have been otherwise acquired, the board may in the name of
the city upon the consent of the common council, as herein provided, proceed to the condemnation of the same pursuant to the
provisions of titles one and two of chapter twenty-three of the
code of civil procedure.

§ 90. **Assessment on lands benefited by certain improvements.**
Whenever any improvement or any portion thereof in any of the
departments within the power and under the control of the board,
or of any board of which this board is the successor, shall have
been completed or partially completed, or when any section thereof
deemed sufficient for assessment purposes shall have been completed, and it shall appear to the board that real property in the
locality, whether immediately adjacent or more remote, is especially benefited thereby, the board shall thereupon determine what
portion,. if any, of the expense of such improvements, including
the damages, award or cost of acquiring lands and rights, not exceeding in its judgment the amount of the benefit, shall be assessed
upon the property benefited thereby, and what portion, if any.
shall be paid by the city at large; determine the area, district or
territory benefited, and forthwith assess in proportion as nearly as
may be to the benefits, the expense and damage that are to be paid
by local assessment upon the lots and parcels of lands to be
benefited thereby, to the several owners or occupants thereof when
known, and when unknown to the " unknown owner " of any such
lots or parcels of land to be benefited thereby. describing the same.
and shall make a written statement of such assessment and file

with the city clerk, who shall give public notice in the newspapers
designated for that purpose by the common council that the same
has been left with him, and that the common council will on a
certain day therein specified, which shall be at least ten days after
the first day of the publication of such notice, proceed to confirm
such assessments. Before the day specified said notice shall be
published at least three times in said newspapers. At the time so
specified any person interested may appear before the common
council and apply to have any such assessment altered or corrected as justice shall require. The common council may thereupon alter, correct or confirm such assessments without further
notice, and when so altered, corrected or confirmed the amount of
each assessment shall be a lien upon the real property upon which
it is assessed. The common council may prescribe and proportion
deferred payments, make such regulations therefor as may be
deemed advisable and provide for adding to the deferred payments the same percentages, fees and expense as in this act provided in the assessment, levy and collection of the city tax. This
section shall not apply to improvements in the water works system, street or other lighting, parks, cemeteries, public buildings
or sewers and drains.

§ 91. **Proportion of paving, et cetera, assessments charged to
owners of adjoining lands.** The expenses of grading, paving or
re-paving any street shall be paid, one-third by the city of Canandaigua out of the highway fund or by the issue and sale of bonds
as provided herein, two-thirds thereof exclusive, however, of the
part to be done or paid for by any railroad company as provided
by this act or by the general laws of this state, by the owners or occupants of property fronting or adjoining the street thus improved
in proportion to the frontage thereon. Expense of building, laying
or resetting curbs, storm sewers and gutters shall be paid one-third
by the city of Canandaigua out of the highway fund, and two-thirds
by the owner or owners of the property fronting or adjoining the
side of the street upon which the improvement is made in proportion to the frontage thereon. The expense of constructing, repairing, relaying, raising, lowering or changing the location of any
sidewalk shall be paid by the owner or owners of the property in
front of which the improvement is made. .

§ 92. **May make rules and regulations.** The board of public
works may make, alter and modify, publish and enforce from
time to time such rules and regulations, not inconsistent with

any provision of this act, for the employment, dismissal, discipline and government of the persons employed by it, and for the government of its superintendent of public works and his assistants, and for the performance of all work authorized by it, subject to the approval of the common council.

§ 93. **May provide penalties for injury to its property.** With the approval of the common council, the board may prescribe penalties for willful and malicious acts by any person or persons whereby any of the property or rights under the control of the board in any of its departments shall be interfered with, impaired, obstructed or injured, and may enforce the penalties and recover the actual damages sustained thereby in the manner provided for by this act, paying the money so recovered to the city treasurer to be credited to the general fund, and may also prescribe penalties, not exceeding fifty dollars for the violation of any of the rules and regulations adopted by it in any of its departments, which rules and regulations, when regularly adopted, may be enforced by action brought in the name of the city of Canandaigua. and the amount so recovered shall be paid to the city treasurer. No action shall be brought to recover any penalty for violation of any rule or regulation unless the same shall have been published prior to such violation at least once a week for two successive weeks in the newspapers. as provided in title four of this act.

§ 94. **Certain acts to be misdemeanors.** An act whereby any property, apparatus or appliances pertaining thereto, which shall be under the power and control of the board in any of its departments, shall be willfully or maliciously injured, impaired or obstructed, or the water supply shall be rendered less pure, shall be deemed a misdemeanor and the person or persons, corporation or corporations convicted thereof shall be punished accordingly.

§ 95. **Repairing and rebuilding sidewalks; notice to owner or occupant.** The power of the board to repair or rebuild sidewalks adjoining private real property shall be exercised only after the failure and neglect of the owner or occupant to repair or rebuild the same after service of a written notice as follows: ten days notice to repair and fifteen days notice to rebuild. Service of such notice must be made as provided in section two thousand two hundred and forty of the code of civil procedure for the service of a precept in summary proceedings. If the real property has no buildings thereon and service cannot be made as provided in subdivisions one and two of said section, then service shall be made by mail enclosing the notice in a postpaid wrapper addressed to the owner at his address, if known to the board, or if unknown, then to him at Canandaigua, New York. Such notice shall be addressed to the owner or occupant, if known, and shall describe the location of the walk and, if to be repaired, the repairs to be made, and if to be built, the width of the walk, the materials to be used therein and how it shall be constructed. This section shall apply to the building of a walk where none exists as well as to the rebuilding of any walk.

§ 96. **Paving, et cetera.** Whenever the board of public works contemplates causing any street or other way or part of street or other way to be paved or macadamized, or graded or paved or macadamized it shall submit to the common council a petition signed by the owners of at least a majority in value as shown by the last preceding assessment-roll of the city of the real property abutting on that portion of the street or other way to be paved, macadamized or graded, together with such proposed paving, grading or macadamizing, in writing, describing the location thereof, the terms and conditions under which it is proposed to have the work done and the maximum cost thereof. Said writing shall contain the names of all the owners of land adjacent or contiguous to that part of the street or other way proposed to be paved or macadamized, or graded, or both, and the name of every railway operated on such street or other way. Said writing shall contain the number of lineal feet front of real estate adjacent and contiguous to said part of the street or other way. The common council shall thereupon, at its next regular meeting or at a special meeting called for that purpose, have a public hearing thereon. It shall cause notice of such public meeting and the purpose thereof to be published once each week for two successive weeks in the newspapers, as provided in section sixty of title four of this act, prior to such public meeting. At such public meeting the same shall be discussed and considered. The proposition in order to be carried, must receive the affirmative votes of two-thirds of all the members of the common council. No such work shall be done by the board of public works without such vote in favor thereof. This section shall apply to all repaving, remacadamizing or regrading.

§ 97. **Acquiring land by purchase or condemnation.** Whenever the board of public works shall determine to acquire by purchase or condemnation any lands or interest in lands for the pur-

poses of any of the departments under its control or to regrade
any street or other way, requiring payment or compensation therefor, it shall submit to the common council a written statement
thereof, setting forth particularly a description of the lands or
rights to be acquired and the estimated cost thereof or the estimated
damage liable to be paid, with the names of the owners of said
lands and other persons interested therein and any other facts of
importance relating thereto. The common council at its next regular meeting or at a special meeting called for that purpose shall
consider the same. Unless the same shall receive the favorable
votes of two-thirds of all the members of the common council the
same shall be returned with the disapproval of the common council, otherwise with its approval.

§ 98. **Regrading; compensation.** When the grade of any
street or other way has been established by usage or otherwise the
grade thereof shall not be changed unless compensation be made
to all persons damaged by such regrading. Such damage to be
ascertained and determined in the same manner as herein provided for lands taken for public use by condemnation proceedings.
The board of public works, subject to the approval thereof by the
common council, is authorized and empowered to adjust all compensations to be paid without such proceedings, provided satisfactory adjustments can be effected with the persons entitled thereto.

§ 99. **Paving; sidewalks; curbs, installments.** The common
council may provide that assessments for paving, sidewalks, curbs
and gutters may be paid in such equal annual installments, not
exceeding ten, as it may prescribe, provided the person against
whom the assessment is made, files with the city clerk within
ten days after the assessment is confirmed, his election and agreement to pay the same in that manner, with interest thereon payable annually. Every assessment, to which such agreement is
made and filed, shall be collected in such installments, with annual
interest thereon, in the manner as in this title provided and every
installment with accrued interest shall be a lien upon the real
estate against which the same is assessed as provided in this
title. For the purposes of anticipating the payment of such installments the common council may issue bonds or certificates of
indebtedness of the city for such part thereof as is to be paid in
such installments.

§ 100. **Power to construct conduits, et cetera.** Subject to the
approval of the common council, said board shall have the power:

to construct conduits for carrying telegraph, telephone or electric wire or cables, or other appliances for conducting electricity in any street, section of a street or place within said city, and the expense thereof shall be paid out of the highway fund. If there shall not be sufficient money in the highway fund for that purpose, and to meet the necessary street expenses until the taxes for the next year are paid in, the board of public works shall report the deficiency to the common council which shall borrow the necessary amount and pay it into the highway fund, and include it in the next tax levy, and the amount so borrowed shall be repaid within one year from the proceeds of such tax. But the common council may in its discretion, instead of including the amount in the next tax levy, issue bonds for the amount so borrowed, or any part thereof. in such amounts and for such times as it shall deem advisable. Any bonds, however, so issued shall not be sold for a sum less than the par value thereof, and shall bear interest at a rate not exceeding five per centum per annum, and the provisions of subdivision eight of section one hundred and sixty-five of title eight of this act shall apply to the payment of the principal and interest of said bonds. Whenever the board of public works shall by resolution determine that public safety requires the removal of any telephone, telegraph or electric wires or cable, or electric feed cables of any street railway company, or other appliances for conducting electricity, or the poles connected therewith from any street or public place in said city in which conduits shall have been constructed, it shall have power by ordinance or resolution, to require any company, corporation or individual to take down and remove the same and place all such telephone, telegraph or electric wires, cables and appliances for conducting electricity, in conduits under the surface of the ground, in such manner as shall be directed by said board of public works and subject to such reasonable regula· tions and restrictions as such board may make and impose in respect thereto for the benefit of the public, the city or its citizens, and compliance with such ordinance or resolution may be enforced by mandamus by any court of competent jurisdiction upon the application of the city as relator. Any company, corporation or individual using any such conduit shall be charged for the space occupied therein a reasonable rental to be fixed by the board of public works, and the amount so charged shall be paid to the city treasurer and by him placed in the highway fund. If any company, corporation or individual shall refuse or neglect to pay the

amount of such rental at such time and in such manner as the
board of public works may direct, the city may sue for the same
and recover the amount thereof in any court of competent jurisdiction. Nothing herein contained shall be construed as authorizing the board of public works to require that any particular
patent or appliance shall be used in the construction of any such
conduits nor as preventing such board of public works from
authorizing any company to construct its own conduits in any
street in said city.

§ 101. **Power to make contracts.** Subject to the approval of
the common council, the board of public works shall have power to
make all contracts relating to construction, paving and repairs of
the streets, sidewalks, and lighting plant and other public buildings owned by the city, water works, reservoirs, water pipes, hydrants and sewers, the cleaning of the streets, sprinkling and removal of dirt therefrom, the grading, paving and repaving and macadamizing of all streets, public places and public squares, the laying and extension of water pipes, and the extension of sewers and
the provision of all materials, machinery, implements and utensils
necessary therefor.

§ 102. **Sewers; construction and extension.** Whenever the
board of public works shall recommend to the common council the
building or extension of any sewer within the city, it shall require
the superintendent of public works to cause plans of the construction and estimates of the cost thereof to be prepared, which plans
and estimates shall remain on file in the office of the board. If
the common council shall approve the same, it shall then publish a
notice in one or more newspapers of the city once a week for two
weeks stating the time when it will hear all persons interested in
the construction of the sewer, and such notice shall contain a brief
description of the character, location and extent of the proposed
improvement. After such hearing the common council shall determine whether the contemplated sewer shall be constructed; and
in case it shall determine that the same shall be constructed, it
shall record an order to that effect in its minutes and shall immediately thereafter transmit to the board of public works copies
of such order. The board of public works shall cause such improvement to be made and any expenses incurred in the construction or extension of any such sewer shall be a charge upon the
city. The amount of any expense so incurred shall be paid out of
the sewer fund, and if there shall not be sufficient money in said

fund for that purpose and to meet necessary sewer expenses until taxes for the next year are paid in, the board of public works shall report the deficiency to the common council. The common council shall thereupon borrow the necessary amount and pay it into the sewer fund and include it in the next tax levy, and the amount so borrowed shall be repaid within one year from the proceeds of such tax. But the common council may, in its discretion, instead of including the amount so borrowed in the next tax levy, issue bonds for the amounts so borrowed, or any part thereof, in such amounts and for such time as it shall deem advisable. Any bonds however, so issued, shall not be sold for a sum less than the par value thereof and shall bear interest at a rate not exceeding five per centum per annum. Said bonds shall be sold under the direction of the common council of said city and the same procedure shall be had with respect to such sales, as near as may be, as on the sale of bonds issued on account of street improvements under this act. All moneys realized from the sale of bonds shall be paid into the sewer fund and paid out only for the purpose for which the expenditure was authorized. Nothing herein contained shall be deemed to repeal any existing provision of law with respect to the building of lateral sewers for the convenience of private property or the expense of the construction thereof.

§ 103. **Estimate to be submitted to council.** The fiscal year of the board shall begin on the first day of January in each year. The board shall, prior to the first day of December in each year, submit to the common council a statement of all salaries, wages and compensation paid by said board for that year and an estimate of the amount in items, which, in its judgment, is required for the maintenance during the ensuing year of each department and also the estimated amount needed for any permanent improvements, specifying the nature of such improvements.

The written estimate of the expenses of said board for the ensuing year shall, among other things, contain the following:

1. For cleaning the streets of the city.

2. For ordinary repairs of streets, sidewalks and crosswalks of the city.

3. For the portion of the expense of paving, macadamizing, grading or curbing, or any other new work which should be borne by the city at large.

4. For the maintenance and care of the bridges or the building of new bridges.

5. For the maintenance, ornamentation and improvement of the public parks and playgrounds of the city.

6. For the care and ordinary repairs of the sewers of the city.

7. For building new sewers.

8. For the purchase or repair of machinery, implements and utensils for the use of the board.

9. For public lighting.

10. For other expenses of said board not above specifically mentioned.

The common council shall have power to modify or ratify said estimates as herein provided, and the said board shall not have the right to expend any greater sum for each purpose specified than is authorized by the common council.

§ 104. **Manner of assessing special taxes.** The two-thirds part of the expenses of grading, regrading, paving, repaving, macadamizing, remacadamizing, building, laying or resetting curbs and gutters, to be borne by the owners or occupants of property fronting or adjoining the sides of the streets upon which the improvements are made shall be assessed as follows: Whenever any such improvement or any portion thereof shall have been completed or partially completed or when any section thereof deemed sufficient for assessment purposes shall have been completed, the two-thirds amount of the expense of such improvement to be paid by the owners or occupants of the adjoining lands shall be assessed thereon by the board of public works, making a written statement containing therein the names of all owners of lands fronting or adjoining the sides of the streets upon which the improvements are made and the name of every railway operated upon such street or other way, distinguishing therein the parcels of such lands owned by non-residents according to the best knowledge and belief of the board and, in case the names of the owners of any lots are unknown, then so stating, and it shall make a just and equitable assessment of the said expenses against said lands and owners and against such railways, assessing upon the several parcels of real estate fronting or adjoining the sides of the streets upon which the improvements are made and upon the respective owners thereof such portion of such expense as shall be proportioned to the frontage thereof and shall assess upon any railway company its share of the cost of said improvement, which said share shall be the cost of that portion of the improvement between its tracks, the rails of its tracks and two feet in width on each side of the rails outside its tracks, but shall not include the cost of curbs, gutters or storm sewers or any part thereof, and its portion shall be assessed against any railway company in the same manner as other assessments for local improvements, and the amount so assessed shall be a first lien upon all the property and franchises of such railway company within the corporate limits of said city, until fully paid, and shall enter in such certificate a brief and careful description of each parcel assessed with its frontage upon the street and the sum assessed upon it and shall file such certificate with the city clerk, who shall give public notice in the newspapers that the same has been left with him and that the common council on a certain day therein specified, which shall be at least ten days after the first publication of said notice, will proceed to confirm the same. Before the day specified said notice shall be published at least twice in said newspapers.

At the time specified any person interested may appear before the common council and apply to have any such assessment altered or corrected as justice may require and as herein provided. The common council may thereupon alter, correct or confirm such assessment so as to make the same comply with the provisions hereof without further notice, and when so altered, corrected, or confirmed, the amount of each assessment shall be a lien upon the real property upon which it is assessed. When any such assessment shall be confirmed by the common council the duplicate certificate thereof hereinbefore mentioned shall be thereupon filed with the clerk and shall be both considered originals, to one of which shall be annexed a warrant for the collection of said tax and to the other a copy of said warrant with the receipt of the city treasurer for such certificate and warrant. If there be not sufficient money in the highway fund to pay the city's share of the cost of such improvement for which the city is liable and to meet the necessary street expenses until taxes for the next year are paid in, the board of public works shall make and file a report to that effect with the common council, which shall borrow the necessary amount, and pay it into the highway fund, and include it in the next tax levy and the amount so borrowed shall be repaid within one year from the proceeds of said tax. But the common council may, in its discretion, instead of including the amount so borrowed in the next tax levy, issue bonds for the amount it so borrowed, or any part thereof, in such amounts and for such time as they shall deem advisable. Any bonds, however, so issued, shall not be sold for a sum less than the par value thereof and shall bear interest at a rate not exceeding five per centum per annum. The provisions of subdivision eight of section one hundred and sixty-five of title eight of this act shall apply as to the payment of the principal and interest of said bonds.

§ 105. **Property owners to connect drains, gas and water pipes.** Subject to the approval of the common council, the board of public works is hereby authorized and empowered at any time upon any paved or unpaved street upon which improvement is contemplated to compel the residents of any such streets and the property owners whose lots front or abut thereon to lay house connecting drains, gas and water pipes, in the manner they shall provide, from the line of curbing in front of their property on any street to the sewer, gas and water mains or pipes or either connecting them therewith, and whenever the residents or owners of said property fail to comply with the regulations of the board of public works, pursuant to the authority hereby conferred, the same may be done by the board of public works at the expense of such owners. Such expense shall be assessed upon the real property so connected and added as a separate item to the assessment for local improvement and collected by distress and sale as herein provided.

§ 106. **Control of public cemeteries; protect from injury.** Subject to the direction of the common council, the board of public works shall take charge and have control of all public cemeteries now or hereafter owned by said city, with power to preserve, adorn and protect the same; to establish such rules and regulations governing the care, maintenance, adornment and uses thereof; to prohibit injury to, or mutilation of, any of the adornments or monuments therein, and to prescribe penalties for the violation thereof, and in all things to have control and authority thereover and the disposition thereof.

§ 107. **Majority vote for expenditure of money.** No contract involving the expenditure of moneys shall be made by said board except by a vote of a majority of the members of the board, and no obligation shall be incurred, money expended, or issue of bonds recommended by the board, except by resolution duly passed by a majority of the members thereof. In every case the resolution and vote thereon shall be recorded in full in the minutes of the board, and no resolution involving the expenditure of moneys shall

be made unless the amount to be expended has been appropriated
by the common council, and any expenditure made or incurred
by said board in any instance shall not exceed the amount of the
appropriation made for that purpose by the common council.

§ 108. **Lands or rights; purchasing from member of board.**
No lands or rights shall be purchased by any member of the said
board for any of the purposes over which the board shall have
control.

§ 109. **Other powers of the board.** The board, or its duly authorized agents or employees may enter upon any lands for the
purpose of survey and examination, and with the approval of the
common council may contract for, purchase and acquire by grant,
gift, condemnation or otherwise, in the name of the city of Canandaigua, all lands, water rights, easements, privileges and other
real and personal property whatsoever in whole or in part, for
such purposes, either within or outside of the corporate limits of
the city of Canandaigua, which is necessary for any of the purposes herein set forth, and shall have the right to enter upon,
take possession of and appropriate all such property, and to do any
and every act or thing that may be necessary to carry out the full
intent and purposes of all the provisions of this act.

§ 110. **Drainage, sewers, water system.** The board shall have
power to adopt and execute plans for the drainage of the city,
and for the extension and improvement of its sewer and water
systems, and for providing any additional water supply and sewer
and water systems that may be deemed necessary, subject to the
provisions of the general laws of the state, and the approval of
the common council.

§ 111. **Permits to be issued; expenses to be a lien, and to be
collected.** The board shall have the power to permit excavating in
any public street or place in said city upon execution and delivery to the city of a bond approved by the mayor and city
attorney, conditioned that the excavation so made will be
promptly filled and properly graded; that any pavement or
curbing removed shall be relaid with all convenient speed; and
that the city shall be held harmless from all claims,
demands, suits, costs and damages that may result by
reason of the excavation, and shall be so maintained
for a period of one year without expense to the city; that the excavation made shall be made at such time and in such manner,
and under such superintendence as the board may prescribe in the

order granting permission in addition to the above requirements.
Any expense incurred by the board in such superintendence,
restoration or repair, shall be a lien until paid, on the premises or
lot for which the work was done, to be enforced the same as unpaid claims in the construction of sidewalks, as in this act provided; and the city shall have a lawful demand against the claimant to whom such permission may have been given, and may sue
and collect the same in the name of the city, and which, when so
collected, shall be paid to the city treasurer, and by him credited
to the fund against which the expense is properly charged.   No
person, association or corporation shall make any excavation in
or under any street, lane or public ground, or under any sidewalk,
without first obtaining such permit in writing.

§ 112. **Permission to build, rebuild or repair sidewalks.**   The
owner or owners of property along or in front of which a sidewalk
is to be built or rebuilt, shall, upon request in writing to the superintendent of public works, be given permission to build, repair and
rebuild such sidewalk without expense to the city, in conformity,
however, with all the requirements of the board as to the time of
building and repairing or rebuilding, the material to be used therefor, grade and location thereof, and the manner and method of
construction.   If such requirements are not complied with, the
board of public works shall make such sidewalk conform therewith
at the expense of the owner or owners, to be collected in the manner provided in the next preceding section.

§ 113. **Supervision of public buildings.**   Subject to the approval of the common council, the board of public works shall have
supervision over all public buildings now owned by the village of
Canandaigua, or hereafter acquired by the city of Canandaigua,
and shall provide heat and light therefor, superintend the making
of repairs and all alterations thereto, supervise the construction
of all buildings that may be required for city purposes. and procure necessary equipment for, and have the general supervision
and control over all matters pertaining to such buildings and
equipment, except the buildings occupied by the fire department
and school buildings and their equipment.

§ 114. **Inventories to be filed.**   On or before the first day of
December in every year, said board of public works shall cause
to be made and filed in the city clerk's office an inventor. of all
personal property, equipment and material on hand. of whatsoever
name or nature belonging to its various departments, and shall

specify therein to which department such personal property, equipment and material on hand belongs.

TITLE VII.

DEPARTMENT OF HEALTH AND PUBLIC SAFETY.

ARTICLE I.

GENERAL POWERS AND DUTIES.

§ 115. **The board of health and public safety; how constituted.** The commissioners of health and public safety, appointed as provided by this act, shall constitute the board of health and public safety, and shall receive no compensation for their services. Within ten days after the appointment of said commissioners, and annually thereafter within the first week in January, they shall meet and organize. They shall elect a president of the board of health and public safety from their number, who shall preside over all meetings of the board of health and public safety and have a voice and vote therein. At any meeting of the board, two members shall constitute a quorum to transact business, but a less number may regularly adjourn from time to time. Its meetings shall be open to the public. Special meetings may be called by the mayor, or by any two members of the board, or by a majority of the common council, by causing a written notice thereof, to be served by the city clerk upon each member personally at least three hours before the time specified in such notice for said meeting, or by mail, directed to him at his place of residence, or place of business at least twelve hours before the time specified in such notice for said meeting.

§ 116. **City departments in charge of the board of health and public safety.** The board of health and public safety shall take charge and have control, subject to the approval and direction of the common council, of the following departments of city government:

1. The health department.
2. The fire department.
3. The police department.

§ 117. **Assignment of other departments.** The board of health and public safety shall take charge and have the management and control over such other departments and work as may from time to time be assigned to it by the common council of the city of Canandaigua, and thereupon shall pass such rules and regulations as may be necessary for the proper management of such department, departments or work so assigned, subject to the approval and direction of the common council.

§ 118. **May make rules and regulations.** The board of health and public safety may make, alter and modify, publish and enforce from time to time, such rules and regulations, not inconsistent with law, as may be deemed necessary for the conduct of all its departments; for the employment, dismissal, discipline and government of the persons employed by it; for the government of all its officers and their assistants; for the performance of all work authorized by it, subject to the approval of the common council.

§ 119. **May provide penalties for injury to its property.** With the approval of the common council, the board may prescribe penalties for wilful and malicious acts committed by any *persons or persons, corporation or corporations, whereby any of the property or rights under the control of the board in any of its departments shall be interfered with, impaired, obstructed, or injured, and may enforce the penalties and recover the actual damages sustained thereby in the manner provided for in this act, paying the money so recovered to the city treasurer, to be credited to the general fund; and may also prescribe penalties, not exceeding fifty dollars for the violation of any of the rules and regulations adopted by it in any of its departments, which rules and regulations, when regularly adopted, may be enforced by an action brought in the name of the city of Canandaigua, and the amount so recovered shall be paid to the city treasurer. No action shall be brought to recover any penalty for violation of any rule or regulation, unless the same shall have been published prior to such

---

* So in original.

violation, at least once a week for two successive weeks in the newspapers, as provided in section sixty of title four of this act.

§ 120. **Certain acts to be misdemeanors.** An act whereby any property, apparatus, or appliances pertaining thereto which shall be under the power and control of the board in any of its departments, shall be wilfully or maliciously injured, impaired or obstructed, shall be deemed a misdemeanor, and the person, persons, association or corporation convicted thereof shall be punished accordingly.

§ 121. **Annual estimate to be submitted to common council.** The fiscal year of the board of health and public safety shall begin on the first day of January in each year. The board shall, prior to the first day of December in each year, submit to the common council a statement of all salaries, wages and compensation paid by said board for that year, and an estimate of the amount in items, which, in its judgment, is required for the maintenance during the ensuing year of each department, and also the estimated amount needed for any permanent improvements, specifying the nature of such improvements. The written estimate of the expense of said board for the ensuing year, shall, among other things, contain the following:

1. For maintaining the police department of the city.

2. For maintaining the health department of the city.

3. For maintaining the fire department of the city.

4. For the purchase or repair of any equipment or equipments belonging to any of its departments.

5. For all other expenses of said board not above specifically mentioned.

The common council shall have power to modify or ratify said estimates as herein provided, and the said board of health and public safety shall not have the right to expend any greater sum for each purpose specified, than is authorized by the common council.

§ 122. **Inventory to be filed.** On or before the first day of December in every year, said board of health and public safety shall cause to be made and filed in the city clerk's office an inventory of all personal property, equipment and material on hand, of whatsoever name or nature belonging to its various departments, and shall specify therein to which department such personal property, equipment and material on hand belongs.

ARTICLE II.

HEALTH DEPARTMENT.

Section 123. Board of health; how constituted.
      124. Powers and duties.
      125. Existing rules continued.
      126. Registrar and records.
      127. Plumbing plans to be filed.
      128. Rules and regulations for control of plumbing.
      129. Owners to have copy of plumbing plans.
      130. Board of health may prescribe penalties.

§ 123. **Board of health; how constituted.** The board of health and public safety shall constitute the board of health. Said board shall meet regularly at least once in each calendar month. The said board shall appoint a competent physician, not one of its members, health officer of the city, who shall be under the direction of the said board of health, and shall perform such duties as may be required by it and by the provisions of the public health law of the state, not inconsistent with the provisions of this act, and the general laws of the state. Such health officer shall be appointed for a term of two years and be entitled to receive four hundred dollars annually for all his services as such officer.

§ 124. **Powers and duties.** The board of health and public safety and the members thereof shall have all the powers and be charged with all the duties and responsibilities conferred and imposed upon the board of health and the members thereof by the general laws of the state, so far as the same pertain to cities, except as herein otherwise provided.

§ 125. **Existing rules continued.** The existing rules and regulations of the board of health of the village of Canandaigua shall continue in force in said city of Canandaigua the same as if duly adopted and published by the board of health and public safety of said city, subject to the provisions of this act and of the general law, until modified or repealed.

§ 126. **Registrar and records.** The city clerk, as registrar of vital statistics in and for the city of Canandaigua, shall keep a book for that purpose and record therein all vital statistics, and shall, on or before the tenth day of each month, make out and file with the city treasurer, a report of the deaths, births and marriages occurring in the city during the previous month, together with a statement of all fees received by him as such registrar of vital statistics, as hereinafter provided; he shall also make in triplicate an annual report on the thirty-first day of December in each year, and file the original in the city clerk's office and one copy thereof with the city treasurer, and one copy thereof with the board of health and public safety, and shall perform all other duties required by the general laws of the state; he shall receive and pay over to the city treasurer for the use of the city of Canandaigua all fees which, by general law, the registrar of vital statistics is entitled to demand and receive.

§ 127. **Plumbing plans to be filed.** No plumbing shall be placed in any house, business structure, or dwelling until the plans for the same shall have been filed with and approved by the board of health. Such plans shall be kept by said board of health and be accessible to the owner or occupant of said building or structure affected by this section at all reasonable times. The plumbing in said building or structure shall be constructed according to said plans. If any alteration is desired, new plans showing the alteration shall be filed with said board of health and approved in like manner as the original plans.

§ 128. **Rules and regulations for** control of plumbing. Said board of health, as soon as possible after their appointment, shall formulate rules and regulations for the better control and sanitary arrangement of plumbing in the city of Canandaigua. Any plumber or contractor who shall put in any plumbing in the city of Canandaigua before his plans shall have been approved by the board of health as herein provided, shall forfeit to the city a sum not to exceed one hundred dollars for each offense, and the said board of health may ordain that such offense shall constitute disorderly conduct, and the party so offending a disorderly person.

§ 129. **Owners to have copy of plumbing plans.** Architects or plumbers who shall hereafter draw plans for or construct buildings, business structures or dwellings in the city of Canandaigua, shall make and leave permanently with the owner or occupant of said building, structure or dwelling, a copy of the plumbing specifications and blue print, showing the location of all drain pipes, sewer pipes, waste pipes, traps and other connections throughout the buildings, structures or dwellings herein referred to. After the passage of this act the provisions of this article shall apply and refer to any extension, alterations or additions to the plumbing in any building, structure or dwelling within the city limits.

§ 130. **Board of health may prescribe penalties.** The board of

24

health may enforce obedience to the foregoing section and to its ordinances by prescribing therefor and therein penalties for each violation thereof, not exceeding one hundred dollars for any one offense.   In addition to the penalty the board may also ordain that a violation thereof shall constitute disorderly conduct, and that the person violating the same shall be a disorderly person.

ARTICLE III.
FIRE DEPARTMENT.

§ 131. **Board of health and public safety; powers of.** The board of health and public safety, subject to the approval of the common council, shall have the power:

1. To establish and ordain the fire limits of said city, except that the fire limits for the said city of Canandaigua shall remain and be the same as the fire limits now are for the village of Canandaigua until they shall be changed or modified by the said board of health and public safety as hereinbefore provided.

2. To organize a fire department consisting of a chief engineer, first and second assistant engineers, secretary, treasurer, collector and fire wardens, to be designated and appointed as hereinafter provided, and as many hook and ladder, hose, engine and protective police companies as the common council may authorize, and to control and manage the officers and members of such fire department, and prescribe their powers and duties.

3. To procure fire engines, hose, hose carts, hooks, ladders, buckets, and other apparatus necessary for the extinguishment of fires and the protection of property; to regulate the use and management thereof; and to provide proper places for keeping the same.

4. To adopt such rules and regulations to constitute the fire department, a paid or partially paid department as the best interests of the city may demand, and to fix and regulate the pay of said department.

5. To remove or demolish any building or structure, which by reason of fire or other cause may become dangerous to life or property.

6. To make such other rules and ordinances as may be necessary and proper for the prevention and extinguishment of fires, and to enforce the same by fines and penalties.

§ 132. **Regulation of buildings and structures within fire limits.** Within any extension of the fire limits as may hereafter be ordained by the board of health and public safety of said city as provided by this act, no buildings or structure of wood shall be erected, or extension, addition or repairs of wood be made to any buildings now erected, or cornices or roofs of wood or other material liable to take fire be built. The term "wooden building," as used in this section, shall be construed to include wooden buildings covered with corrugated iron or other metal. The board of health and public safety shall have power to regulate the erection, extension and repair of buildings within said limits; to require iron

shutters to be placed on the outer doors and windows of such
buildings now erected, and upon such as shall be erected within
said limits, and to direct and determine the materials of partition
walls, and the construction of chimneys within said limits.

§ 133. **Violation to be misdemeanors.** Any person, persons,
firm, or corporation violating the provisions of this title, or the
resolutions or ordinances adopted by the board of health and
public safety pursuant to the provisions of this act, shall be guilty
of a misdemeanor, and in addition thereto shall be liable to such
penalty or penalties as the board of health and public safety may
have prescribed in any such resolution or ordinance. And every
building or structure erected, extended or repaired in violation of
the provisions of this title, or in violation of the resolutions or
ordinances adopted by the common council pursuant to the provisions of this act, is hereby declared to be a common nuisance and
may be abated and removed as such by the board of health and
public safety.

§ 134. **Mayor and other officers members of fire department.
Power to inspect buildings.** The mayor, each member of the board
of health and public safety and the chief engineer shall be members ex-officio of the fire department, and shall have power to enter
into and examine all stores, shops, factories, dwelling-houses,
offices, outhouses, barns, buildings, lots and yards in the day time;
to inspect places therein where fires are used; to ascertain how
ashes are kept; to direct and compel the owner or occupant to put
the premises inspected in a safe condition, and in default to appoint any person to do the same at the expense of such owner or
occupant.

§ 135. **Control of fire department.** The chief engineer and his
assistant engineers shall have the immediate control of the
fire department and apparatus, subject to the regulations
and requirements of the common council. It shall be
the duty of the chief engineer, and in his absence or inability,
of the first assistant engineer, and in his absence or inability, of
the second assistant engineer, to be present at fires within said city;
to take command of the fire companies and general control of the
apparatus for extinguishing and preventing such fires; and to perform such other duties and exercise such other powers as the common council in the by-laws or ordinances may require or confer.

§ 136. **Suspension of officers or members.** The mayor of the
city or any two of the members of the board of health and public

safety, at any time, upon charges being preferred, or upon finding any officer or member of the fire department guilty of misconduct, may suspend such officer or member from service until the common council shall convene and take action in the matter; but no such officer or member shall remain so suspended for a period longer than thirty days without an opportunity of being heard in his defense. After such hearing the common council may, by a majority vote, restore or remove such officer or member.

§ 137. **Present officers and members continued; registration of members.** The officers and members of the present fire department of said city shall continue to be such officers and members, subject to the provisions of this act. The name of each member of the fire department shall be registered with the city clerk, to whom the officers of each company shall report the name of every member expelled from, or who shall have resigned from such company, with the date of such expulsion or resignation.

§ 138. **Powers exercised at fires.** The mayor of the city, an alderman or member of the board of health and public safety, the policemen, the chief engineer and his assistants, and the protective police, and each one of them, shall have power to keep away from the vicinity of any fire all idle or suspicious persons, and compel all persons to aid in the extinguishment of fires and the preservation and protection of property exposed to danger thereat. For such purposes, the chief engineer, his assistants, and the members of the protective police shall have the powers conferred upon policemen by this act, and any person who shall disobey the reasonable order of any one of said officers shall incur a penalty of twenty-five dollars, to be recovered as other penalties imposed by this act.

§ 139. **Duties of members; violations of rules or orders. Members exempt from prosecution and indictment in certain cases.** It shall be the duty of the members of the fire department to turn out promptly upon every alarm of fire; to aid in the extinguishment thereof, as directed by the chief engineer or assistant engineer; and whenever called upon by the mayor or an alderman, to aid in the suppression of riots and riotous assemblages in said city. Any member or other person who shall during the time of any fire neglect or refuse to obey the orders of the chief engineer or any assistant engineer shall incur such penalty as the by-laws or ordinances of the board of health and public safety may provide not exceeding five dollars for each offense. Every member of the fire department is hereby declared to be exempt from prosecution or indictment for any act done in the reasonable and proper discharge of his duties at riots and riotous assemblages.

§ 140. **Number of members to a company; fire department to be body corporate and politic and may purchase and hold real estate.** All persons who now are or who hereafter shall become members of hose, hook and ladder, engine, or protective police companies, not exceeding fifty members to each hose company, and fifty members to each hook and ladder, engine or protective police company of said city, after being duly elected by their respective companies, and confirmed by the common council of said city, shall be, and are hereby ordained, constituted and declared to be a body corporate and politic, in fact and in name, by name and style of "The Fire Department of Canandaigua," and by that name they and their successors shall and may have perpetual succession and shall be persons in law capable of suing and being sued in all courts and in all actions within the jurisdiction of the state of New York, and that they and their successors may have a common seal and may change and alter the same at their pleasure, and also that they and their successors by the name of "The Fire Department of Canandaigua," shall be in law capable of purchasing, holding and conveying any estate, real or personal, for the use of said corporation, provided the amount of real and personal estate so held shall not exceed at any time the sum of twenty thousand dollars.

§ 141. **Companies to elect delegates; chief engineer and assistants to be recommended.** The several hose, hook and ladder, engine and protective police companies, constituting this corporation shall, at their regular meeting to be held on the first Tuesday in April in each year, elect by ballot three delegates from each of their respective companies to meet in convention at the council rooms of the department on the Thursday following, at eight o'clock in the evening, and after choosing one of their members as chairman, and another as secretary, shall elect separately, by ballot, suitable persons, electors of such city, for chief engineer, first and second assistant engineers and the individuals receiving the majority of votes for those offices shall be recommended to the common council of said city for their appointment.

§ 142. **Chief engineer and assistants appointed by common council.** The common council of said city, upon such recommendation shall appoint a chief engineer, and two assistant engineers, who shall be electors of said city, and who shall hold their offices during the pleasure of the common council.

§ 143. **Chief engineer; powers and duties.** The chief engineer, and in his absence his assistants in their order, shall preside over all meetings of the council and of the department, both regular and special; shall have the immediate control of the department at fires, inspections and review, shall have charge of the hose and engine houses, and all apparatus entrusted to the care of or belonging to the department; shall have authority over all employees of the department; shall hold them strictly to account for neglect of duty, and may suspend or discharge the same at any time, subject to the approval of two-thirds of the council at the next meeting; shall issue through the secretary, upon application, a certificate of the time of service of any member of the department, provided such time shall have been granted by the council; and shall give to the officers of the council immediately after their election at the annual meeting of the council, or at any special election, a certified warrant of their election countersigned by the secretary.

§ 144. **Organization of fire council.** The different hose, hook and ladder, engine and protective police companies shall at the regular meeting to be held on the first Tuesday in April in each year, elect by ballot two of their number to be known and designated as wardens, who are electors of such city, who, with the chief engineer as president, and his assistants as vice-presidents, shall constitute a "fire council" and shall exercise such powers as are hereinafter committed to them; which appointment shall not exempt them from their other duties as firemen.

§ 145. **Fire council; powers and duties of.** The said fire council shall meet on the third Tuesday in April of each year, and choose out of their own body a secretary, treasurer and collector, to hold their respective offices until others are appointed in their stead, agreeably to the provisions of this act, and in the case of any vacancy in the office of warden, such vacancy shall be filled by the company in which it occurs, at a special election held for that purpose; and in case of a vacancy occurring in the office of secretary, treasurer, or collector, such vacancy shall be filled by the fire council at their next meeting.

Two-thirds of the said fire council shall constitute a quorum and shall have full power to make and prescribe such laws, ordinances and regulations not inconsistent with the laws of this state or ordi-

nances of said city, as shall be by them deemed necessary for the
proper management of the affairs and the disposition of the
funds of the said corporation, and shall have power to appoint
all meetings, both regular and special, (except the one hereafter
provided for,) and shall also designate one or more days in each
and every year as days of public exercise, inspection and review,
and all such other matters as appertain to the business and purposes for which the said corporation is by this act constituted and
no other.

§ 146. **Failure to hold elections.** And in case any election
shall not be held on the day when pursuant to this act it ought
to have been held, the said corporation shall not on that account
be deemed dissolved, but it may be lawful to hold such election
on any subsequent day agreeable to the ordinances and regulations of such corporation.

§ 147. **General meeting of firemen. Report of council.** The
firemen constituting the several hose, hook and ladder, engine
and protective police companies of this corporation, shall hold
a general meeting at the council room or such other place as the
council may direct, on the first Friday following the first Tuesday of April of each and every year, at seven o'clock in the afternoon, to hear the report of the secretary and treasurer, and to
transact such other business as may be deemed for the interest of
this corporation.

§ 148. **Constitution and by-laws of each company.** Each hose,
hook and ladder, engine, and protective police company may
adopt a constitution and by-laws, for the government and regulation of its own affairs, subject to the approval of the council,
and of the common council of the city, and not inconsistent with
the laws of this state, or the ordinances of the said common
council. And when so adopted and approved, such constitution
and by-laws shall be valid and enforceable against any member
or officer of the company as to all discipline, regulations, fines,
penalties or forfeitures therein provided.

§ 149. **Privileges and exemptions.** A member of the fire department of any other village, or city, within this state shall,
upon his removal to the city of Canandaigua, and his attain-
ment to membership in the fire department of Canandaigua be
allowed the time he has served as a fireman in such village or
city in the fire department of the city of Canandaigua, provided he shall produce a certificate of such previous service.

signed by the chief engineer and secretary and bearing the seal of such other corporation, and when such fireman shall have served for so long a time thereafter as shall make his whole term of service the same as required by the statute laws of this state, he shall be entitled to all the privileges and exemptions secured to firemen in this state for such service.

§ 150. **Certificate of exemption.** A certificate signed by the chief engineer and secretary bearing the seal of this corporation declaring the term of service of said member to have been fully completed as required by the laws of this state, shall be sufficient evidence to entitle him to the final certificate of exemption provided in the next section.

§ 151. **Exemption of firemen from jury duty and military duty.** Every member of the fire department shall so long as he shall remain such member be exempt from serving on juries in any court, and from paying any poll tax and from serving in the militia excepting in case of invasion or insurrection, and every member who shall serve in such fire department five years successively, including the time he shall have continually served as fireman in said village of Canandaigua before this act shall take effect, also including the time he shall have duly served as fireman in any other fire department in this state, certified to, and continued in the fire department of Canandaigua, as in this title provided, shall thereafter be entitled to the like exemption of military service and jury duty and a certificate of such service in the fire department with a copy of this section, authenticated by the signature of the mayor and seal of the corporation, shall be legal evidence before all courts and officers, civil, or military, of such exemption.

§ 152. **Rules and regulations continued.** All rules and regulations pertaining to the organization and government of the fire department of the "trustees of the village of Canandaigua," in force at the time when this act takes effect, shall, except as hereinafter in this act provided, remain, be and continue the same under said city of Canandaigua, until the repeal thereof and the adoption of other or further rules and regulations in relation thereto, as provided by this act, and all officers and members of the fire department of the village of Canandaigua shall perform all duties devolving upon them as such firemen, and have and retain all their rights and privileges in the same manner and in all respects as if this act had not been passed, subject, however, to the further provisions of the act.

ARTICLE IV.

POLICE DEPARTMENT.

§ 153. **Rules and regulations.** The board of health and public safety shall keep a record of all appointments and removals made by it in the police department, as hereinafter provided, and also a record of its acts, and of the rules and regulations adopted by it pertaining to said department of police, which said records shall at all times be open to the public. And the said board of health and public safety is hereby empowered, in its discretion, to enact, adopt, modify and repeal, from time to time, subject to the approval of the common council and other provisions of this act, rules and regulations for the management and discipline of the policemen appointed by it, and may fine or suspend from pay or duty, or both, any of said policemen. All such rules and regulations, when duly made, enacted, or adopted by said board of health and public safety, shall have the same force and effect as if herein specially enacted; provided that the same rules and regulations shall not be in conflict with the provisions of this act or with the laws of this state, or of the United States.

§ 154. **Policemen; special police constables; manner of appointment.** The board of health and public safety shall appoint such number of policemen as shall from time to time be fixed by the common council of the said city, which number as fixed by said common council may be, but shall not exceed one policeman for each one thousand or major fraction of one thousand of inhabitants, as appearing from the latest census of said city, and may appoint at any time such number of special policemen from among the citizens of said city as the common council of said city may direct. Such policemen and said special policemen together with the said board of health and public safety, shall constitute the police force of said city. And the said board of health and public safety may, upon application of any person or persons, or corporation, showing the necessity thereof, appoint special police constables to do special duty as required by the applicant, but such last named police constables shall not be entitled to any compensation for their services from either the town or city of Canandaigua, or the county of Ontario. Nor shall any appointment of special police constables be made upon application of any person or persons or corporation as herein provided, until after the applicant or applicants shall have secured and indemnified the said city of Canandaigua with a good and sufficient bond, to be approved by the common council of said city, conditioned that the said city will be saved harmless from all costs, salaries, expenses or damages by reason of such appointment. Any person appointed either as policeman, special policeman or special police constable, shall take and file with the clerk of the city of Canandaigua the constitutional oath of office before entering upon the duties of his office. A certificate of the appointment of such policeman shall be duly filed with the clerk of the said city of Canandaigua and a copy thereof duly certified by said clerk shall be filed in the office of the clerk of Ontario county.

§ 156.* **Chief of police; assistant chief of police.** One of such policemen shall be designated by the board of health and public safety as "chief of police," who shall wear a uniform and be on duty at the police office, within call of the telephone from the hours of six o'clock in the morning to six o'clock in the afternoon, and perform such other duties as shall be prescribed by law, or by the rules and regulations of the common council of the city and of the board of health and public safety. And the board of health and public safety shall designate another of said policemen, assistant chief of police who shall perform the same duties as the "chief of police" as herein provided, during the hours from six o'clock in the evening to six o'clock of the following morning.

§ 156. **Vacancies; how filled.** In case of a vacancy in said police force from any cause, the said board of health and public safety shall appoint to fill the vacancy, and they shall remove any

---

* So in original.

of said policemen upon being convinced of their incompetency, or
their being guilty of illegal, corrupt or other improper conduct,
after the preferring of charges and an opportunity to be heard
thereon having been granted.

§ 157. **Powers and duties of policemen; assistant chief of
police to fix bail in certain cases; assistant chief may be required to give bond.**   The said policemen shall have the full
powers and duties of constables of the towns in regard to criminal
and civil process and proceedings, and in addition thereto, all the
powers and duties conferred by this act, and they shall perform
such other duties as shall be lawfully prescribed by the rules and
regulations of the common council of the city, and the board of
health and public safety, and it shall be the duty of such policemen
to serve any and all process papers, both civil and criminal, issued
by the city judge of said city, and no other officer or person shall
have the authority to serve such process and papers, except where
in the opinion of the city judge the service can be more efficiently
performed by the sheriff of Ontario county, and this discretion
shall apply only to those cases arising without the corporate limits
of said city or in cases of felony, and it shall not be competent
for any constable, sheriff, or deputy sheriff to make arrests within
the limits of the said city of Canandaigua without a warrant, except in cases of felony, or in case of a breach of peace, while actually occurring.   But no limitations of the powers of constables,
sheriffs or deputy sheriffs shall apply to any special police or
those special deputy sheriffs appointed under an act passed April
twelve, eighteen hundred and sixty-seven (being chapter three
hundred and seventy-five of the laws of eighteen hundred and
sixty-seven), or to any violations of the game laws of the state.
Between the hours of six o'clock in the evening and six o'clock of
the following morning, the chief of police, or the assistant chief of
police shall have the power to fix and accept bail temporarily in
all cases of misdemeanor, upon and with the consent and advice
of the city judge.   And such police officer, upon fixing and receiving such bail as herein provided, shall pay the same into the city
court upon the convening of the same the next following morning,
and report to the presiding judge thereof the name of the person or
persons, charged with having committed such misdemeanor or
misdemeanors charged.

The common council may require the policemen fixing and receiving bail as herein provided, to execute and file a bond in the

same manner as other officers mentioned in section twenty-one of title three of this act.

§ 158. **Compensation; manner of payment; actual expenses paid in certain cases; vacations.** The pay of said policemen and special policemen shall be fixed by said board of health and public safety, subject to the approval of the common council and when so fixed shall not thereafter be changed except after notice given as provided in section fourteen, title two of this act.

The salaries of such policemen shall be paid monthly upon the warrant of the common council, drawn upon the city treasurer, and the money to pay the same and the money to pay said special policemen shall be taken from the fund which is designated as police fund; whenever there shall not be sufficient money to the credit of that fund, with which to pay such salary, then and in that case, the common council of the city of Canandaigua are hereby authorized to borrow money sufficient for that purpose, and the amount so borrowed shall be in addition to and collected with the amount annually raised by taxation in said city as now authorized by law. Such policemen shall not receive any other compensation, except when traveling in the discharge of their duty in conveying persons to prison or by direction of the board of health and public safety in the discharge of their duties, or by the direction of the city judge upon warrant issued by him, when their actual expenses shall be paid upon a verified statement of the items of such expenses in detail, to be certified by the board of health and public safety and audited and paid out of the police fund and in the same manner as other claims against the city as herein provided, out of the police fund. The board of health and public safety may, by resolution, give to any such policemen, including the policeman designated as the "chief of police" a vacation or vacations, not exceeding in the aggregate, two weeks in any one year, and the period or periods of such vacation or vacations shall be included as a part of the time for which such policeman shall be entitled to pay as time actually served by him.

§ 159. **Policemen to keep records of accounts chargeable to town or county; how paid.** Each of such policemen shall keep a correct account of such services rendered by him as have heretofore been a town or county charge, and such accounts duly verified and sworn to by such policemen shall be presented by the board of health and public safety at least once a year to the proper town

and county auditing boards, which accounts shall be a charge
against the town or county as if made by a town constable as heretofore. The amount allowed by the county auditing board and
charged to the county, shall be paid by the supervisors of said
county to the treasurer of the city of Canandaigua, and the amount
thereof charged to and allowed by the town of Canandaigua shall
be paid by the supervisor of said town, when collected, to the
treasurer of the said city to the credit of said police fund.

TITLE VIII.

Assessment and Taxation.

§ 160. **Powers and duties of assessors.** The assessors shall
constitute the board of assessors and shall possess all the powers

conferred, be subject to all the obligations imposed and perform all the duties appertaining to the office of assessors in the towns of the state in reference to the assessment of property within the city, except as otherwise provided by law. They shall perform all the duties now provided by law in reference to the assessment of property for the purpose of levying taxes and assessments for local improvements, imposed according to law except as herein otherwise provided.

§ 161. **Assessment of taxes.** The assessors shall in each year prepare an assessment roll of the persons and property taxable within the city in the same manner and form as is required by law for the preparation of town assessment rolls, except as modified by this act. The said assessment roll shall be so prepared as to show separately the taxable persons and property within the city and the same shall be footed by the assessors. In the assessment of any land in said city for any purpose, it shall be sufficient to state the name of any one of the owners or occupants of said land and also the street and number of any building thereon; but if the land be vacant or if the buildings thereon be not numbered, then the name of the street upon which it fronts, shall be given. In case no inhabited building is on the land, the owner may be designated as " unknown." In all cases the assessment of real property shall be deemed as against the real property itself and the property itself shall be holden and liable to sale for any tax levied upon it, and no error in the name of the owner or occupant, nor in the description, if sufficient to identify the same, shall invalidate the assessment. Only one assessment shall be made in each year for all the taxes levied within the city during that year.

§ 162. **Completion of the roll.** The assessors between the first day of January and the first day of July in each year shall prepare such assessment roll and shall complete the same by the first day of July in each year and shall file the same with the city clerk, and shall give notice for thirty days by posting such notice in three public places in the city and by publication thereof in the newspapers designated to publish notices, as provided in this act. once in each week for four weeks, that such roll is completed and filed, and that all persons interested may examine the same at the city clerk's office, and that also on the first Tuesday in September next ensuing, at a place specified in such notice, the assessors will sit as a board of review to review the same.

§ 163. **Review of assessment.** The board of assessors shall

meet at the time and place specified in the notice mentioned in
section one hundred and sixty-two of this act and review the
assessment.   Their sessions shall not aggregate more than
four days, nor be continued beyond the fifteenth day of
September in each year. During the time the assessors review
any tax or assessment, they shall have power to add or insert
in such assessment roll any property liable to assessment, and
the valuation thereof which may have been omitted from such
roll upon giving notice either personally or by mail to the
owner of such property or to his agent at least two days
prior to adding the same to said assessment roll, and in case
the owner is unknown or had no known agent within the city,
they shall post such notice in three public places in said city at
least two days prior to adding the same to the assessment roll.
Except as modified by this act, the board of assessors shall have
all the powers given by the tax law of the state of New York to
assessors sitting to hear complaints in relation to assessments,
and the proceedings in relation thereto shall be the same as provided by the tax law of the state. Any person assessed upon assessment roll claiming to be aggrieved by any assessment for property therein may review the same in the manner provided by
article thirteen of the tax law. On or before the first day of
October the corrected assessment roll together with their minutes
shall be filed in the office of the city clerk.

§ 164. **Equalization and levy; county taxes.** The city clerk
shall immediately thereupon proceed to prepare the roll for the
ensuing year. He shall upon the written direction of the assessors
correct all clerical errors appearing therein, make a true copy of
the assessment roll as corrected, certify it under the seal of the
city and deliver it to the chairman or clerk of the board of supervisors of the county of Ontario on or before the fifteenth day of
October in each year. The board of supervisors of Ontario county
shall in each year equalize the assessments within the city of Canandaigua with the assessments in the towns of said county in the
same manner as the assessments are required by law to be equalized between such towns. The board of supervisors shall not
cause the state and county tax apportioned to said city to be spread
upon any tax roll of property within the city, but shall by resolution ascertain and direct the amount of tax to be levied in the
city for state and county purposes and shall on or before the
thirty-first day of December in each year transmit to the common

council of the city of Canandaigua a copy of such resolution certified under the hand of the clerk of the board of supervisors and the seal of said board. Such certified resolution shall be filed with the city clerk and the city clerk shall thereupon extend and apportion such tax on the assessment roll together with the city taxes levied as hereinafter provided and no other extension and apportionment of such state and county taxes need be made. The amount of state and county tax apportioned to the city of *Canandiagua shall be ascertained and apportioned upon the equalized value of real estate within said city and the assessed value of personal property including the assessed value of banks within the city of Canandaigua.

§ 165. **Amount of annual tax levy.** The common council must annually cause to be levied and raised by general tax upon all taxable property, real, personal and franchise, in the city, except in case of taxation by districts less in area than the city for lighting, water supply, sewerage and other purposes as provided by law, and then upon all the taxable property, real, personal and franchise, in the proper district, according to the valuation upon the assessment roll for the current year, corrected as aforesaid, for the following purposes:

1. The amount of taxes certified to the common council by the board of supervisors apportioned to the city for state and county taxes.

2. The payment of expenses of a police department including the salary of the city judge and the salary of the officers of the said department, to be designated the " Police Fund."

3. For paying the expense of paving streets and curbing gutters pursuant to this act and for repairing and keeping in order the streets, highways, alleys, cross-walks, parks, play grounds, and other public places, lands and squares of the city; for cleaning snow and ice from the walks; for defraying the salary and expenses of the superintendent of public works, his assistants and employees, the erection and maintenance of bridges and culverts and other expenses relating to the streets and highways to be designated the " Highway Fund."

4. A sum necessary to defray the payment of the general and contingent expenses of the city at large, the expenses of elections and for the payment of all salaries and wages of officers and servants of the city, and other sums not otherwise provided for,

---

* So in original.

which with all of the moneys received by the city treasurer, not belonging to any other fund specified by this act, shall be kept as a separate fund, to be designated the " Contingent Fund."

5. For defraying the expenses of repairing and keeping in order the sewers and defraying the cost of constructing sewers and for the services of engineers employed therefor by the city, to be designated the " Sewer Fund."

6. A sum necessary for defraying the expenses of the fire department to be designated the " Fire Fund."

7. A sum necessary for lighting the streets and public buildings and places of the city and the expenses of maintaining all necessary apparatus and fixtures connected therewith, to be designated the " Lighting Fund."

8. A sum necessary to meet the principal and interest falling due during the fiscal year, for which the tax is levied upon the bonds or other permanent debt of the city, to be designated the " Public Debt Fund."

9. A sum necessary for defraying the expenses of the board of health and public safety, and the expenses of enforcing the public health law rules, regulations and ordinances of said board and other matters within said board's jurisdiction as provided by this act, to be designated the " Public Health Fund."

10. Such other sums as shall have been voted at a regular city election or a special city election, called for that purpose, and also such sums as may be necessary to meet all indebtedness remaining unpaid on all judgments against the city, and also for such other sums as the common council is authorized to spend for the purposes specified in this act, to be designated as the Special Fund.

§ 166. **Extraordinary expenditures; special election for.** If the board of public works, or the board of health and public safety recommend, or if the owners of ten per centum of the value of the property appearing upon the last preceding assessment roll of the city shall petition for an extraordinary expenditure to be made for any purpose for the benefit of the city, or if, upon its own motion, the common council shall resolve by an affirmative vote of two-thirds of its members, that an extraordinary expenditure, including the paving or improving of a street, ought for the benefit of the city, to be made for any specific purpose set forth in the resolution, it shall make an estimate of the sum necessary therefor and for all such purposes, if there

be more than one, and publish such resolution and estimate
for at least three weeks in one or more newspapers printed
in the city, together with a notice that at a time and place
therein specified a special election of the taxpayers of the
city will be held to decide whether the amount of such expenditure shall be raised by tax. The common council shall appoint
four inspectors of such election and shall fill all vacancies occur-
ing among them. All provisions of law prescribing the duties of
inspectors of election and their powers and with reference to
preserving order at elections and false swearing and fraudulent
voting thereat, shall, so far as applicable, apply to the special
elections held hereunder. Every person, male or female, who
owns any real or personal property, which shall have been
assessed and taxed upon the last assessment roll of the city before
such special election, and no other person, shall be entitled to vote
at such election. The election shall be by ballot, and each ballot
shall contain a brief statement of each purpose for which such
expenditure is required and the amount thereof, and be in the
form required by the election law for voting upon questions submitted. The inspectors shall, at the time and place designated
as aforesaid, sit without intermission from nine o'clock in the
morning until four o'clock in the afternoon, to receive the ballots cast at such special election, and shall deposit the same in
a suitable ballot-box to be provided by the city. If the right to
vote of any person offering to vote at such special election be
challenged by any other person entitled to vote thereat, an inspector of the election shall administer to him the following
oath: "You do swear that you are the owner of property
assessed upon the last assessment roll of the city of Canandaigua,
and that you have not voted at this election?" After he shall take
such oath, and if he owns property assessed upon the assessment
roll aforesaid, his vote shall be received. The inspectors shall
canvass the votes received immediately after closing the polls,
and immediately make a certificate, signed by them or two of
them, stating the whole number of ballots voted at such election,
the whole number for each special tax, and the whole number
against each special tax, and deliver the same forthwith to the
city clerk. The city clerk shall deliver the same to the common
council at its next meeting, and it shall cause the result of the
said election thus certified to be entered in its minutes, and if
the whole number of votes received at such election for any such

special tax exceeds the whole number of votes against the same,
the common council shall, except as hereinafter otherwise provided, cause the sum or sums of money thus voted to be
assessed, levied and raised with and in addition to other
taxes in and upon the next assessment roll.   But the sum
or sums of money so voted to be assessed shall not with the other
taxes above mentioned, exceed the limit of one per centum upon
the assessed valuation of the real and personal property of the city,
except for the purposes herein provided, to wit: the amount of
taxes certified to the city by the board of supervisors to be assessed
upon said city, and also the special assessments on property benefited by street improvements as set forth in section ninety of title
six of this act. No more than one such election in the city
shall be held in any one year, except by the unanimous vote of the
common council. After such special tax or taxes shall have been
authorized as herein provided, the common council may proceed to
authorize the expenditure of the amount thereof for the purpose or
purposes specified in its published statement aforesaid and sanctioned by such election. The common council may borrow, if
necessary, the amount so voted in anticipation of the collection of
said tax, and the amount so raised or borrowed shall be expended
only for the purpose or purposes for which the special tax was
voted, and shall be repaid within one year from the proceeds of
the tax, or at the option of the common council not less than two-
thirds of the entire council voting in the affirmative, the city may
issue its bonds for the whole or any part of the sum or sums voted
at said special election. Said bonds shall be paid in yearly installments during a term of years not to exceed twenty, with interest at
a rate not to exceed five per centum per annum, payable yearly or
half yearly, as the council may determine. The annual installment of principal and interest on said bonds, falling due each year,
shall be part of the one per centum maximum city taxes as provided in section one hundred and eighty-five of this act. The
common council shall, prior to the publication of the resolution
and estimate, as provided in this section, determine whether the
money to be raised shall be included in the next annual tax
levy, or whether bonds as hereinbefore provided shall be
issued therefor, and if the latter then the number of years
said bonds shall run, and it shall publish such determination
as a part of the notice of the special election, and said determination shall not be changed by the common council after said special

election is had. Any bonds issued hereunder shall be designated
as "special appropriation bonds," shall be signed by the mayor and
treasurer, and shall be sold by the treasurer under the direction,
and with the approval of the common council at public or private
sale for the highest attainable price, but not less than par, and the
avails of said bonds shall be kept by the treasurer in a separate
fund, and be applied only to the payment of the object or objects.
stated in the published notice of the special election, and shall
be paid out only upon warrants drawn on the treasurer by
the common council as herein provided, for expenditures
hereunder, audited by the common council. If it shall at
any time appear that the object or objects for which said
bonds were issued is accomplished, and that there is an
unexpended balance in the hands of the treasurer to the credit of
the aforesaid fund, not required for the specific purpose for which
said money was raised, said balance shall not be used for any other
purpose, except to apply on the principal or interest of said bonds
as they fall due. All moneys received by the city treasurer from
this or any other source shall, as soon as may be, and not later than
twenty-four hours after its receipt, be deposited by said treasurer
in one or more national banks or trust companies as herein provided for the deposit of city funds, to be drawn out only for payments made in accordance with the provisions of this act. All
municipal plants, buildings, or other undertakings, whether for
electric lighting or otherwise, sanctioned by the taxpayers under
and by virtue of this section, shall be bought, or built and operated
by the board of public works in the same manner as provided for
other public works herein.

§ 167. **Issue of tax-roll and warrant to treasurer.** The city
clerk under the direction of the common council, shall extend
the city tax together with the state and county taxes, on the
assessment roll delivered to him in each year, and shall make
a copy thereof and file the same in his office. The original roll
with the taxes extended therein as aforesaid, shall then and on or
before the first day of February, or as soon thereafter as practicable, be delivered by the city clerk to the treasurer of the city
with a warrant annexed thereto signed by the mayor and the
city clerk under the seal of the city, commanding him to
receive and collect the several sums in the tax-roll specified as
assessed against the person or property therein mentioned or described, with such percentage, or penalty and interest as is in this

act provided, in the manner provided by law for the collection
of town and county taxes by town collectors except that said tax-
roll and warrant shall be kept on file in the city treasurer's office,
and that said taxes shall be collected within thirty days after the
date of the warrant; but the time to collect taxes under said warrant may be extended or said warrant may be renewed by the
common council from time to time. From the time of the receipt of the tax-roll and warrant by the city treasurer all taxes
assessed and levied upon any real estate shall be a lien upon such
real estate for the amount thereof with the percentages and interest herein provided, until the same be fully paid.

§ 168. **Notice of receiving taxes.** Immediately on the delivery
of the city tax-roll and warrant to the treasurer, he shall publish
a notice in such newspaper or newspapers of the city as the common council shall designate, once each week for two consecutive
weeks, that he will attend at his office with the said tax-roll and
warrant for thirty days next after the first publication of said
notice, Sundays, legal holidays and half holidays excepted, from
nine o'clock in the morning to three o'clock in the afternoon to
receive city, county and state taxes, and it shall be his duty to
attend accordingly. All taxes or assessments paid within thirty
days after the first publication of the treasurer's notice aforesaid,
shall be payable without fee, percentage or interest thereon. On
all taxes or assessments remaining unpaid after the expiration of
such thirty days and within sixty days, the treasurer shall collect
one per centum additional; on all remaining taxes unpaid after
the expiration of sixty days and within ninety days he shall collect
three per centum additional; and all remaining taxes unpaid
after the expiration of ninety days from such first publication
shall bear and there shall be collected thereon five per centum
additional and interest at the rate of one per centum per month
from the expiration of said ninety days, and the same shall belong
to the city.

§ 169. **Tax receipts.** Immediately upon receiving any tax, the
city treasurer shall enter in a column prepared for the purpose and
opposite the name of the person, persons, association or corporation
paying the same, the fact of payment and the date thereof, and
shall give the person paying the same a receipt therefor and retain
a copy of said receipt in his office. Any person may pay any one
or more taxes or assessments upon his property and leave others
unpaid to be enforced in the manner provided by this act. All re-

ceipts issued by the treasurer for taxes paid to him shall be numbered consecutively, commencing with number one on the first receipt issued for taxes for any one year, and he shall not receipt for more than one year's taxes on the same property in one tax receipt; but shall use a separate and distinct series of numbers of receipts, issued for the taxes for each year for which the same is levied and assessed. The city clerk shall cause all tax receipts to be printed and numbered and firmly bound together in book form and to be in duplicate, and each duplicate to bear the same number as the original.

§ 170. **Notice of unpaid taxes; demand of payment.** If any such tax shall remain unpaid after the expiration of sixty days from the first publication of the notice specified in section one hundred and sixty-nine of this act, the city treasurer shall forthwith serve or cause to be served upon the person, persons, association or corporation against whom such tax remains charged, a written notice requiring him to pay the same to the city treasurer within ten days from the service of such notice. Such notice may be served upon such person, persons, association or corporation personally, or by leaving it at his residence or his or its place of business, in said city, or by depositing it in the post office in said city, properly enclosed in a postpaid wrapper, directed to such person, persons, association or corporation at his or its reputed place of residence or business. It shall not be necessary to make any other demand for the payment of said tax.

§ 171. **Collection of tax by sale of personal property.** If any person, persons, association or corporation shall neglect or refuse to pay any tax against him or it within the ten days above prescribed, the city treasurer shall forthwith issue his warrant under his hand and the seal of the city, and addressed to any police officer of the city, commanding such officer to levy upon any personal property in the city of Canandaigua or county of Ontario belonging to or in possession of the person, persons, association or corporation, whose or which tax so remains unpaid; cause the same to be sold at public auction for the payment of such tax, and the fees and expenses of the collection thereof; and no claim of property to be made thereto by any other person shall be available to prevent such sale. The officer to whom such warrant shall be delivered shall proceed immediately as therein directed. Public notice of the time and place of sale of the property to be sold shall be given by posting the same in at least three public places in the city at least

six days previous thereto. The officer conducting such sale shall
return the proceeds thereof, together with his warrant, to the city
treasurer within fifteen days after the same shall have been issued
and delivered to him. He shall be entitled to charge the same
fee as constables are entitled to receive for collecting money by
virtue of execution. If the proceeds of such sale be more than the
amount of such tax, the fees of collection and the expenses of the
sale, the surplus shall be paid to the person, persons, association
or corporation against whom or which the tax is assessed unless
the right thereto is disputed by some other person, persons, association or corporation, in which case such surplus shall remain
in the hands of the city treasurer, without any liability on his
part, or that of the city for costs, or damages, until the rights of
the parties thereto shall be determined, by due course of law.

§ 172. Collection of taxes by action. The city treasurer is
hereby authorized and empowered to recover, by action in any
court of competent jurisdiction, and in the corporate name of the
city, the amount of any tax remaining unpaid after the expiration
of ninety days with the additions and fees unpaid thereon, and
to recover judgment therefor, with ten per centum interest
thereon, with cost and expense of such action. The city judge
shall have exclusive jurisdiction to try such action when the sum
claimed does not exceed five hundred dollars. A transcript of the
judgment obtained in such action may be filed and such judgment
docketed in the office of the clerk of the county of Ontario, and it
shall, however small the amount, thereupon become a judgment
of the county court of said county and a lien to the amount of said
judgment upon all real estate of the judgment debtor situate in
said county, and shall have the same priority over any other lien
or encumbrance thereon or transfer of the property charged with
the tax sought to be recovered in said action. Upon any judgment
recovered for said unpaid taxes and docketed in said county clerk's
office, execution may be issued and collected as provided by law,
and all the provisions of law in reference to sale and redemption
of real estate on execution, or to proceedings supplementary to
executions, shall apply to sales, redemptions or such proceedings
which may be had under this act. A judgment in such action in
favor of the city shall not operate to release any lien of such tax
or assessment until satisfied.

§ 173. Lien of taxes and water rates. Every tax for county
and state purposes, and every tax assessment or other lien on real

estate under this act for whatever purpose imposed or charged
upon any real estate within the city shall be a lien upon such real
estate from the time of the adoption of the resolution imposing
the same until paid.   Water rates shall be a lien until paid, and
every assessment upon real estate, or water rate imposed under this
act may, when due, be collected in the same manner as herein
provided for the collection of taxes, except that the warrant for
the collection of water rates shall be issued by the board of public
works.

§ 174. **Proceedings in case of failure to collect tax on warrant.**
On or before the first day of July next after tax shall have been
imposed upon any real estate in said county, the city treasurer shall
make and deliver to the board of assessors a transcript of any
and all such taxes which remain unpaid, and it shall be the duty
of the board of assessors on or before the fifteenth day of July
thereafter to make and deliver to the city treasurer a statement
containing a brief general description of the location, boundary
and estimated quantity of each parcel of said lands, and in case
any such lands shall have been erroneously assessed, then it shall
be the duty of such officers to make and include in such statement
a corrected assessment at the same valuation as before, and such
corrected assessment and amount of tax levied upon said land shall
be as valid and effectual for all purposes as though they had
originally been corrected.

§ 175. **Sale of land for unpaid taxes.** Whenever any such tax,
penalty, or interest or any part of either of them, shall remain unpaid on the first day of August following the assessment and levy
of such tax, the city treasurer shall proceed to advertise and sell
the lands upon which the same was imposed for the payment of
such tax, penalty or interest, or the part remaining unpaid, and
the expense of such sale, as hereinafter prescribed, shall also be
a charge upon such lands.

§ 176. **Notice of sale of land for taxes.** The city treasurer
shall cause to be published a notice of such sale containing a description of the lands to be sold, specifying the same by street and
number if any, and the approximate dimensions and quantity
thereof, or, if there be an official tax map of said city, then by
specifying the description given on said map of the lands to be
sold, and also specifying the time and place of sale, which notice
shall be published in a newspaper or newspapers of the city, designated for that purpose by the common council, once a week
for at least six successive weeks immediately prior to the day of

sale, and shall also post such notice of sale in at least three public
places of the city at least forty-two days before the day of sale.
On the day named the city treasurer shall commence the sale of
such lands and shall continue such sale from day to day until the
whole thereof be sold. At any time before the sale the owner or
any purchaser of land, or his representative, or any person interested therein, may avoid the sale thereof by paying the tax or
taxes to the treasurer with all accrued interest, fees, additions and
expenses.

§ 177. **Manner of conducting sale of land for taxes.** Each
parcel shall be sold at public auction to the highest bidder. The
purchaser or purchasers on such sale shall pay the amounts of
their respective bids to the city treasurer immediately after each
parcel shall be struck off. In case the purchaser shall fail to pay
the amount of his bid as herein prescribed, the city treasurer shall
forthwith offer the parcel for sale again and proceed as though it
had not been struck off. Should there be no bid of the amount
due on any lot or parcel of land to be sold, then the city treasurer
shall bid in the same for the city, and the city is hereby authorized
to acquire said parcels, and the common council shall have the
care, management and control of all such parcels and may lease
or sell and convey the same. As soon as practicable after the sale,
the city treasurer shall prepare and execute in duplicate, as to
each parcel sold, a certificate of such sale, describing the parcel
purchased by brief general description of the location, approximate dimensions, estimated quantity thereof, stating the fact of
the sale, the name of the purchaser, the sum paid therefor, the
amount due thereon, the time of the sale, the name of the person,
persons, association or corporation against whom or which such
tax was assessed and the name of the reputed owner thereof. One
of said duplicates shall be delivered to the purchaser, or, in case
the parcel was struck off to the city, then it shall be retained and
filed in the office of the city treasurer. The city treasurer shall
deliver the other duplicate certificate to the clerk of the county of
Ontario, who shall file said certificate in his office and record the
same in a book to be kept in said clerk's office for that purpose,
and shall index the certificate in the name of the person, persons,
association or corporation to whom or to which the parcel was
assessed, the name of the reputed owner thereof, and the name
of the purchaser, in the same book and manner as deeds are required by law to be indexed. The county clerk shall be entitled to

receive a fee of fifty cents for each certificate so filed and recorded, which fee shall be paid by the city treasurer, and shall be a part of the expenses of the sale of the parcel. The city clerk of said city may conduct the sale with the same force and effect as though made by the city treasurer.

§ 178. **Disposition of proceeds of sale.** The proceeds of the sale of each parcel, other than those struck off to the city, shall be applied to the payment of the expenses of the sale as herein provided, and the extinguishment of the tax, penalty or interest for which it was sold, and if there shall be any residue, the city treasurer shall hold the same until the owner of the premises at the time of the sale shall redeem them from the sale as herein provided, and the city treasurer shall pay such owner the said surplus. In all such other cases the city treasurer shall hold the same until after the period of redemption shall have expired and then he shall pay such surplus, and the person, persons, association, or corporation entitled thereto shall be ascertained in the same manner and by the same proceedings as in the case of surplus on statutory foreclosure of a mortgage on real estate. In case any taxes shall be assessed and levied on real estate which has been sold for taxes, subsequent to such sale, and before the redemption thereof or the conveyance thereof to the purchaser and the same shall be unpaid, the city treasurer may deduct the amount thereof from any surplus in his hands of the sum bid for the same, if there be any surplus; if there shall be no surplus or the same shall be insufficient to pay such taxes, the person redeeming shall pay the same, otherwise the purchaser shall pay the same before he shall receive his conveyance of the same.

§ 179. **Redemption of lands.** The owner of, or any person interested in or having a lien upon any parcel or lot so sold, may redeem the same from such sale at any time within fifteen months by paying to the city treasurer for the use of the purchaser or his assigns or, if they shall have been redeemed by any person other than the owner thereof, then for the use of such person, the sum mentioned in the certificate as having been bid for the premises, with interest thereon at the rate of ten per centum per annum from the day of the sale, together with any tax or assessment upon any parcel or any part thereof, that the said purchaser or assigns before redeeming shall have been paid between the day of sale and the day of the redemption, with interest at the rate of ten per centum upon such tax or assessment from the time of payment.

The time during which such redemption may be made shall not commence to run against infants or incompetent persons, until the termination of their disability. In case of the redemption of any land sold for taxes as herein provided, by the person who was the owner thereof at the time of the sale, the city treasurer shall give such owner a receipt for the amount paid by him to effect . such redemption, and on the production thereof by the owner to him, the county clerk shall cancel the certificate of sale by a proper entry at the foot of the record of such certificate in his office.

§ 180. **Notice of redemption.** At least three months before the expiration of the time for the final redemption of any parcels or lots so sold, the city treasurer shall commence the publication of a notice of redemption from such sales, which shall show the year when the sale took place, and the last day for the redemption of the lands not already redeemed by the owners, without other or further description, and such notice shall be published at least twice in each of said three months, in the newspaper or newspapers designated for that purpose by the common council. A copy of such notice shall be served personally on the owner or the occupant of the lands, or, if unoccupied, posted on the premises. at least twenty days before the expiration of such time for final redemption. The publication and service of such notice shall bar and preclude any and all persons except the purchaser on such sale, or his assigns, or the person finally redeeming, from claiming any interest in or lien upon such lands or any part thereof, in case the said lands shall not be redeemed from such sale as hereinbefore provided.

§ 181. **Conveyance of land sold for taxes.** If any parcel or lot so sold shall not be redeemed as herein provided, the city treasurer, immediately after the expiration of the said fifteen months, shall execute and deliver to the purchaser, his heirs or assigns, or to the city or its assigns, or to the person finally redeeming, as the case may be, a conveyance of the real estate so sold, which conveyance shall vest in the grantee an estate in fee. subject only to the liens, if any, of unpaid taxes or assessments thereon. The city treasurer executing such conveyance shall be entitled to demand and receive from the grantee two dollars for preparing every such conveyance, but all purchases made for the city in any year, shall be included in one conveyance, and no fee shall be charged therefor. Every such conveyance shall be executed by the city treasurer and the execution thereof shall be acknowledged before some officer authorized to take and certify acknowledgments of instruments for record in said county, and such conveyance shall be conclusive evidence that the sale and subsequent proceedings were regular and presumptive evidence that all the previous proceedings were regular and according to law. Any such conveyance may be recorded in like manner and with like effect as any other conveyance of real estate. The said grantee or his assigns, or the city or its assigns, as the case may be, shall be entitled to have and to possess the granted lands from and after the execution of such conveyance, and may cause the occupants of such lands to be removed therefrom and the possession thereof delivered to them in the same manner and by the same proceedings and by and before the same officers as in the case of a tenant holding over after the expiration of his term without permission of his landlord.

§ 182. Settlement by city treasurer for taxes collected. It shall be the duty of the city treasurer to pay over to the treasurer of the county of Ontario at the end of each month during the period that the tax roll and warrant is in his hands all moneys received by him for county and state taxes. He shall take duplicate receipts for each payment, one of which shall be immediately filed with the city clerk. Except as otherwise provided in this act, the city treasurer shall settle with the county treasurer for state and county taxes in the manner required by law of town collectors, and with the common council for city taxes and assessments in the same manner. Upon the final settlement with the county treasurer, the city treasurer may pay from the general fund of the city the amount of the uncollected state and county taxes in his hands for collection, and thereupon such taxes shall belong to the city of Canandaigua. At the time of the delivering to him of the city roll and tax warrant, the city treasurer shall receipt for the same, and shall then be charged with the whole amount which he is hereby authorized to collect. He shall not be authorized to credit himself with any amount as unpaid on any warrant until he shall make and file with the city clerk an affidavit stating the amount paid, and setting forth the reason in each case why such tax or assessment is not or has not been collected. The common council may thereupon order and authorize said city treasurer to credit himself with the whole or any part of said tax or assessment unpaid, and the city treasurer shall be credited only with such amount as the common council shall so order.

Upon settling with the common council the city treasurer must show that he has duly settled with the county treasurer for state and county funds. The city clerk shall, on the delivery of the blank tax receipts to the city treasurer, charge the city treasurer with the number of receipts delivered, and the city treasurer shall immediately examine the numbering of the receipts and report to the city clerk any irregularity found therein. The city treasurer shall receipt to the city clerk therefor and shall be held strictly accountable for all receipts found missing at regular assessments; also for all the detached receipts, including receipts the duplicates of which do not show the entry of taxes. All irregularities in the issuance of receipts that render them worthless must be shown on the face of the original, which must in no case be detached from the duplicate. At the time of the annual settlement the city treasurer shall deliver to the city clerk all duplicates of receipts issued by him, and other receipts delivered and charged by the city clerk to him.

§ 183. **Power of common council as to void and erroneous assessments.** The common council of the city may in its discretion, release, discharge, remit or commute any portion of the taxes assessed or levied against any person or property for any error, irregularity or omission in the levying of said taxes, or in any of the proceedings relating to the same. In case any assessment shall remain unpaid on account of any irregularity, omission or error in any assessment authorized by this act or the laws in force when such tax is levied, or in case of error in the description of lands or in the description of the owner or occupants, the common council may in its discretion, or upon the application of any person interested, proceed to correct such irregularity, mistake or inadvertence in levying or assessing the same, and shall have the power, and it shall be its duty to cause the same to be reassessed in a proper manner. Any sum paid thereon shall be credited upon the tax so reassessed, and if the sum paid shall exceed the amount so reassessed, the excess shall be refunded to the person entitled thereto.

§ 184. **Collection of local assessments.** Whenever an assessment shall be ordered for local improvements, the assessment shall be made to resemble in form as nearly as practicable the tax list, and be provided with a column in which payments can be entered by the city treasurer. All provisions relating to the collection of taxes in this act shall be applicable to the collection of assessments mentioned in this act, and the amount of all assessments for local improvements in default at the time of the annual tax levy shall be added to the amount assessed against the same land for general city taxes, and shall be collected and enforced in the same manner as in this act provided.   At the annual tax levy all interest and principal to become due during the fiscal year upon bonds for local improvements issued by the village of Canandaigua or the city of Canandaigua, shall be levied by the common council upon the several lots or parcels assessed therefor, as provided in said bonds and pursuant to the law under which said bonds were issued.

§ 185. **Taxes limited to one per centum of assessed value.**   The amount of tax raised in any year for all the expenses provided for in this act shall not exceed one per centum of the assessed value of the real, franchise and personal property, not including the assessed value of banks, within the city as the same shall appear on the assessment roll for the last preceding year, exclusive, however, of the taxes certified to the common council by the board of supervisors as provided herein for the payment of state and county taxes to be paid by the city, and exclusive also of assessments made for street improvements which under this act may be made a lien on the property benefited and not on the city at large.

TITLE IX.
CITY COURT.

ARTICLE I.
CITY COURT.   GENERAL PROVISIONS.

Section 186. City court of Canandaigua created.
     187. City judge shall be an attorney.
     188. Common council shall provide rooms.
     189. Stenographer city court.
     190. City court to remain open; vacation of city judge; disability of city judge.
     191. Reduction of city judge's salary; moneys collected to be paid to city treasurer.
     192. Acting city judge.
     193. Removal of city judge.

§ 186. **City court of Canandaigua created.**   There is hereby constituted in said city a court to be denominated " city court of

Canandaigua," which shall be a court of civil and criminal proceedings. The city judge shall be the judge of the court and shall be denominated " city judge " with all the jurisdiction and powers of the justices' court and of ·the justices of the peace, and such additional powers and jurisdiction as are herein and otherwise by law conferred upon said court and judge.

§ 187. **City judge shall be an attorney.** The city judge shall be an attorney and counselor of the supreme court of the state of New York and shall have been admitted to practice at least two years prior to election to the office of city judge.

§ 188. **Common council shall provide rooms.** The common council shall provide suitable rooms, light, furniture, necessary books, stationery and other necessary articles for the use of said court and judge, and shall provide for the payment of all the necessary expenses of said court and judge.

§ 189. **Stenographer city court.** The city judge shall appoint a stenographer to take minutes of testimony in each trial held in the city court. The compensation of such stenographer shall be four dollars per day for each day actually occupied in reporting such trials, and shall be a general city charge, to be audited monthly by the common council in the same manner as other claims against the city, upon certification by the city judge. Such stenographer shall deliver, upon receipt of his fees, not exceeding five cents per folio, to any party to a trial or to his attorney, a full copy of all the testimony taken by him in such trial, and at the same time deliver a copy thereof to the city judge without charge. The term " trial " as used in this section shall mean a trial wherein both parties appear, issue is joined, witnesses are sworn and evidence taken.

§ 190. **City court to remain open; vacation of city judge; disability of city judge.** The city court shall be open for the transaction of business each day, except Sundays and legal holidays. It shall be the duty of the city judge to attend his office at the place provided therefor by the common council at all reasonable times, and to hear all matters, issue all processes and institute such proceedings as the proper administration of justice shall require. He shall be entitled, without deduction of his salary, to a vacation of fourteen days in each year. In case of sickness, absence from the city, or disability of the city judge, or disqualification to act in any case, the duties of such city judge shall be performed by the acting city judge appointed as hereinafter provided.

§ 191. **Reduction of city judge's salary; moneys collected to be paid to city treasurer.** There shall be deducted from the annual salary of the city judge the pro rata deduction for each day the said court is by the next preceding section of this act, required to be kept open, on which he shall fail from any other cause than illness and his fourteen days' vacation, to attend the same. Pro rata deduction from his salary shall be made for all absence on account of illness in excess of ten days in each year; all costs and fees and all fines and penalties together with all other moneys collected by him or by the acting city judge during any month shall be paid to the city treasurer on or before the regular meeting of the common council of the next succeeding month, and the city judge and acting city judge shall file with the city clerk at or before the time of the first regular meeting of the common council in each month a complete and detailed statement, verified by his oath to be true, of all moneys payable to the city treasurer by virtue of the provisions of this article, which were received by him during the next preceding month, with the receipt of the city treasurer attached to said statement. Any failure or omission to so pay over such costs, fees, fines, penalties and other moneys shall be sufficient cause for removal of said city judge or acting city judge.

§ 192. **Acting city judge.** Within thirty days after this act takes effect and thereafter within the first week of January in each of the odd numbered years, it shall be the duty of the mayor to appoint some suitable person who shall possess the qualifications of the city judge, as in this act provided, to act as judge of the city court in case of the sickness, absence from the city, disability or disqualification of the city judge, and who may be removed by the mayor as herein provided. While so acting, the said acting city judge shall sign all papers as "Acting City Judge" and shall have all the powers and perform all the duties incumbent upon the city judge. The compensation of said acting city judge shall be four dollars for every day or portion thereof actually spent in the discharge of the duties provided for in this act, to be audited, allowed and paid by the common council upon the presentation by such acting city judge of a claim showing the items of his services and duly verified. Claims for such services, if any, shall be presented to the common council monthly.

§ 193. **Removal of city judge.** A city judge elected as provided in this act may be removed from office in the same manner as a justice of the peace as provided by section seventeen of ar-

25

ticle six of the constitution of the state of New York, and by section one hundred and thirty-two of the code of criminal procedure;
and all provisions of the code of civil procedure applicable to justices of the peace, so far as the same are not in conflict or inconsistent with the provisions of this act, shall apply to the city judge.

ARTICLE II.

CIVIL AND CRIMINAL JURISDICTION; PRACTICE, ET CETERA.

Section 194. Civil jurisdiction of city court.
    195. No jurisdiction in certain cases.
    196. Summary proceedings.
    197. Transfer of proceedings to acting city judge.
    198. Seal.
    199. City judge to administer oaths, et cetera.
    200. Jurisdiction over person of defendant.
    201. Judgment; how rendered.
    202. Failure to interpose counterclaim.
    203. Counterclaim.
    204. Code of civil procedure; certain sections to apply.
    205. Discontinuance of action.
    206. Summons and practice; process, et cetera; how
        signed.
    207. Attorney's authority; how conferred.
    208. Adjournments.
    209. By whom summons must be served.
    210. Pleadings; verification, how made.
    211. Appeals in civil cases.
    212. Defaults.
    213. Fees of policemen.
    214. Costs and fees.
    215. Costs in certain actions.
    216. Other costs and disbursements.
    217. Civil court docket.
    218. Jurisdiction in case of absence, et cetera.
    219. Jurisdiction in criminal cases.
    220. Jurisdiction as court of special sessions.
    221. Jurisdiction of misdemeanors committed partly in
        city.
    222. No jurisdiction of misdemeanors committed outside
        of city.

223. In jurisdiction of offenses beyond ordinary court of special sessions, sentences as in court of sessions.
224. All powers subject to provisions relating to courts of special sessions.
225. May let to bail.
226. Hearing and jurisdiction by acting city judge.
227. Processes and mandates; by whom served; fees.
228. Criminal court docket.
229. Process, et cetera; how signed.
230. Power to punish for contempt.
231. Appeals in criminal cases.
232. Fees, fines and penalties, for use of city.

§ 194. Civil jurisdiction of city court. Said city court shall have jurisdiction of the following civil actions and proceedings:

a. An action to recover damages upon or for breach of a contract, expressed or implied, other than a promise to marry, where the sum claimed does not exceed five hundred dollars.

b. An action to recover damages for a personal injury or an injury to property, where the sum claimed does not exceed five hundred dollars.

c. An action or proceeding to recover a fine or a penalty not exceeding five hundred dollars, or to recover one or more fines or penalties for a violation of an ordinance of the city of Canandaigua, or of any of the provisions of the other titles of this act, where the amount claimed does not exceed five hundred dollars.

d. An action upon a bond conditioned for the payment of money, where the sum claimed to be due or sought to be recovered in the action does not exceed five hundred dollars.

e. An action upon a surety bond taken in city court or by any justice of the peace.

f. An action upon a judgment rendered in said court, or in a court of a justice of the peace, or in a district court of the city of New York, or in a justice's court of a city, being a court not of record.

g. An action to recover one or more chattels, without or with damages for the taking, withholding or detention thereof, where the value of the chattel or of all the chattels as stated in the affidavit made on the part of the plaintiff does not exceed five hundred dollars.

h. To render and enter judgment upon the confession of a defendant or defendants, as prescribed in title six, chapter nineteen of the code of civil procedure, where the sum confessed does not exceed one thousand dollars.

i. In an action for damages for fraud in the sale, purchase or exchange of personal property, if the damage claimed does not exceed five hundred dollars.

j. In an action commenced by. attachment pursuant to the provisions of article four of title two of chapter nineteen of the code of civil procedure, if the debt or damages claimed do not exceed five hundred dollars.

k. In summary proceedings under title two of chapter seventeen of the code of civil procedure to recover possession of real property and to remove tenants and others therefrom, provided such real property or some portion thereof be in the city of Canandaigua.

l. In any other action or civil proceeding of such character that a justice of the peace of a town would have jurisdiction thereof, wherein the sum sought to be recovered does not exceed five hundred dollars.

m. In any action to recover a tax, assessment or other charge imposed by this act.

§ 195. No jurisdiction in certain cases. The city court cannot take cognizance of a civil action in either of the following cases:

a. Where neither the plaintiff nor the defendant, nor one or more of the plaintiffs or defendants, resides in the city of Canandaigua. For the purpose of this limitation, however, a corporation having an office or agency established within the city of Canandaigua for the transaction of its business, shall be deemed a resident of the city of Canandaigua.

b. Where the title to real property comes in question as prescribed in title three of chapter nineteen of the code of civil procedure. But when such question arises the pleadings and practice shall be the same as are now provided by law for justice's court in regard thereto.

c. When the action is to recover damages for false imprisonment, libel, slander, criminal conversation, seduction or malicious prosecution.

d. Where, in a matter of account, the sum total of the accounts of both parties, proved to the satisfaction of the court, exceeds one thousand dollars.

e. Where an action is brought against an administrator or executor as such, except where the amount of the claim is less than the sum of two hundred and fifty dollars, and the claim has been duly presented to the executor or administrator and rejected by him.

§ 196. **Summary proceedings.** Summary proceedings may be commenced by petition addressed either to said judge or to said court, and in said proceedings and in all actions the jurisdiction of said judge shall be exercised by and in the name of the said court only, and all processes from said court shall be made returnable thereto by its proper title. In the solemnization of marriages, and in all other matters not otherwise by this act provided for, said city judge shall have the same powers as justices of the peace in towns now have.

§ 197. **Transfer of proceedings to acting city judge.** In any action or proceeding pending before the city judge in which he may determine that he is disqualified from acting he shall have power and it shall be his duty to adjourn the same for a period not exceeding ten days to a day certain for the purpose of procuring the attendance of the acting city judge who shall thereupon proceed with the case.

§ 198. **Seal.** Said court shall have an official seal consisting of a circle within which shall be engrossed the words " City Court of Canandaigua, New York."

§ 199. **City judge to administer oaths, et cetera.** The city judge may in the city of Canandaigua by virtue of his office administer oaths, take depositions and acknowledgments and certify the same in the manner and with the same effect as justices of courts of record.

§ 200. **Jurisdiction over person of defendant.** Said court shall have the same jurisdiction over the person of defendants as is now possessed by justices' courts of towns pursuant to the provisions of section twenty-eight hundred and sixty-nine of the code of civil procedure, and for the purpose of conferring jurisdiction of the person the said city of Canandaigua shall be deemed a town and said court a justice's court thereof.

§ 201. **Judgment; how rendered.** A judgment of said court shall be in all respects the same as a judgment rendered by a justice of the peace of towns, except as herein provided, and all provisions of the code of civil procedure in relation to filing transcripts of such judgments and docketing the same in the office of the clerk of Ontario county, or of any other county, and the effect of such judgment when so docketed, shall in all respects be

the same as if said judgment was recovered before a justice of the
peace of a town, and when so docketed shall be a lien and remain
in force for the same length of time as a judgment originally recovered in the county court. In any case in which by law a justice
of the peace is required to render judgment and enter the same
in his docket, within four days, the city court of Canandaigua, or
the judge thereof, is required to render judgment, and it must be
entered in the docket of said court within ten days after the case
shall have been submitted for final decision, anything to the contrary herein notwithstanding.

§ 202. **Failure to interpose counterclaim.** The prohibition
contained in section twenty-nine hundred and forty-seven of the
code of civil procedure relating to the failure of the defendant
in an action in justice's court to interpose a counterclaim applies
to an action in city court, but it does not apply to an action or
case in said court where the amount of the counterclaim is more
than five hundred dollars.

§ 203. **Counterclaim.** In the case provided for in section
twenty-nine hundred and forty-nine of the code of civil procedure
for justice's court, if the amount of the counterclaim established
exceeds the plaintiff's demand, the defendant must have judgment
for the excess, or so much thereof as is due from the plaintiff,
unless it is more than the sum of five hundred dollars, and if it be
more than five hundred dollars, the city court must pursue the
same course in reference to the same as in the said section provided for a case in which it is more than two hundred dollars.

§ 204. **Code of civil procedure; certain sections to apply.** Sections five hundred and five and five hundred and six of the code
of civil procedure shall apply to a counterclaim in an action
against a person sued in a representative capacity, or in favor of
an executor or an administrator, except that the defendant cannot take judgment against the plaintiff upon a counterclaim for
a sum exceeding five hundred dollars and costs, and section
twenty-nine hundred and forty-six of the code of civil procedure
shall not apply to actions in the city court.

§ 205. **Discontinuance of action.** Where, upon the trial of an
action, the sum total of the accounts of both parties proved to the
satisfaction of the court exceeds one thousand dollars, judgment
of discontinuance must be rendered against the plaintiff, with
costs, and section twenty-nine hundred and fifty of the code of
civil procedure shall not be applicable to the city court.

§ 206. Summons and practice; process, et cetera, how signed.
Except as otherwise herein specially prescribed, the summons, the form thereof and the time within which the same shall be returnable, and all other process, the. service of process, appearances, practice, pleadings, exhibiting account or demand, amendments, adjournments, trial by court or jury, obtaining jury, offers of compromise, offers of judgment and the effect thereof, judgments by confession or otherwise, and the rendering and docketing of the same; appeals, fees, costs and disbursements, shall in all matters, except as herein otherwise provided, be governed by the code of civil procedure for justices' courts as said provisions now exist or may hereafter be amended by the legislature of the state of New York, except that section two thousand eight hundred and ninety-three of the code of civil procedure shall not apply to or govern proceedings in the city court. The said judge and the said court shall have the same duties, powers and jurisdiction as justices of the peace in towns and their courts, together with the further powers and jurisdiction by this act conferred, except as herein otherwise provided. All summonses, precepts, orders and all other process or documents made or issued by the city judge shall be signed, in addition to his signature, " City Judge." When made or issued by the acting city judge, the same shall be signed, in addition to his name, "Acting City Judge."

§ 207. Attorney's authority; how conferred. The attorney's authority may be conferred orally or in writing, but the city judge shall not suffer a person who is not an attorney admitted to practice in the supreme court of this state to appear as an attorney, unless his authority is admitted by the adverse party, or proved by the affidavit or oral testimony of himself and another.

§ 208. Adjournments. The court must, upon the application of the plaintiff, grant a second or subsequent adjournment of the trial of the action, or hearing of the proceeding, upon proof, by his own oath or otherwise, to the satisfaction of the court, that he cannot safely proceed for want of some material testimony or witness, and that he has used due diligence to obtain the testimony *of witness. But the court may, as a condition of granting such adjournment, require that the plaintiff pay to the defendant the legal fees of defendant's witnesses duly subpoenaed for that day.

§ 209. By whom summons must be served. The summons, or summons and complaint and all other processes issued by the city court or city judge shall be served by a police officer of said

---

* So in original

city, and the officer so serving shall make and file his return with
the city judge in the same manner as a constable of the town in
justice's court.

§ 210. **Pleadings; verification, how made.** The complaint
may be verified in the manner provided by the code of civil procedure for the verification of pleadings in courts of record, and
in an action commenced by summons may, at the option of the
plaintiff or his attorney, be served therewith. When the complaint is so verified, the subsequent pleadings, excepting a demurrer, shall be likewise verified in all cases in which such
pleadings would be required to be verified in a court of record:
and in default thereof they shall be disregarded. In an action
arising on contract for the recovery of money only, or on an account, where the complaint is so verified and a copy of the same
is served with the summons, and the defendant fails to answer
said complaint as hereinbefore provided at the time of the return
of said summons, he shall be deemed to have admitted the allegations of the complaint as true, and the court shall, upon filing the
summons and complaint, with due proof of the service thereof,
enter judgment for the said plaintiff and against the defendant
or defendants, for the amount demanded in such complaint, with
costs, without further proof. The city judge may, by general
rule, or otherwise, require any pleading made orally to be reduced
to writing, and every pleading in writing shall be subscribed by
the party making the same or his attorney, and shall be filed
forthwith, or within such time as the city judge may designate.

§ 211. **Appeals in civil cases.** Appeals may be taken to the
county court from judgments rendered in said city court the same
as from judgments rendered by justices of the peace. Appeals
may also be taken to the county court from an order of the city
judge or court on an application to open a default made as in the
next section provided, and the time within which such appeal may
be taken and the practice thereon shall be the same as apply to
appeals from a judgment of a justice of the peace, the affidavits
read on such application constituting, for the purpose of such
appeal, a part of the return of the city judge.

§ 212. **Defaults.** In actions in the city court the city judge
shall have power to open defaults and set aside judgments rendered
and entered therein, and executions issued thereon, upon such
terms as may be just, in a case where either party shall fail to
appear on the return day of the process, or on any adjourned day,

and the party in default satisfactorily excuses his default, but no further terms shall be imposed than the payment of the costs included in the judgment, and the sum of two dollars for opposing the motion. The application therefor shall be founded upon affidavits and shall be made within twenty days from the entry of such judgment. Upon presentation of such application the city judge shall issue an order returnable in not less than five days nor more than eight days, requiring the party in whose favor judgment was rendered to show cause, if any, why said judgment or execution, as the case may be, should not be set aside. A copy of said order, and of the papers upon which the same is granted, shall be served upon the party in whose favor judgment was rendered, or upon his attorney, if one shall have appeared in the action, not less than three days prior to the return day thereof. Pending such application and the determination thereof, the city judge may stay proceedings upon such judgment or any execution which shall have been issued. When a judgment shall be set aside the action shall proceed as though no judgment had been rendered. The judgment, or an execution issued thereon by the city judge, and levy made thereunder, may, in the discretion of the city judge, be allowed to stand as a security for the satisfaction of any judgment which may be finally recovered in favor of the same party. Parties moving in the county court to open default or to obtain a new trial in said city court, in cases where a motion might have been made in said city court, as in this section provided, shall show that no such application was made in said city court.

§ 213. Fees of policemen. Policemen who lawfully serve papers or execute mandates in any action or proceeding in said court shall receive and be entitled to the same fees as are allowed to constables in like actions and proceedings in justices' courts in towns. But such fees shall be paid into city court and shall belong to the city and be paid to the city treasurer as herein provided.

§ 214. Costs and fees. In all civil actions and proceedings brought in the city court the same costs and fees shall be paid, taxed and recovered as in actions and proceedings before justices of the peace. In addition thereto there shall be allowed to the prevailing party, as an indemnity, in case he has appeared by an attorney admitted to practice in courts of record of this state, and not otherwise, the following sums as costs:

a. On judgment for the plaintiff by default, to the plaintiff, two dollars and an additional sum equal to three per centum of the amount for which judgment is rendered.

b. On judgment for plaintiff otherwise than upon a default to the plaintiff, three dollars, and an additional sum equal to five per centum of the recovery.

c. If the plaintiff recovers judgment in any action in said court for the recovery of one or more chattels the sum allowed as additional costs therein shall be estimated upon the value of said chattels as assessed by the said court or jury.

d. If judgment of nonsuit is rendered for the defendant, to the defendant, two dollars.

e. If a judgment is rendered for the defendant upon the merits after a trial, to the defendant, five dollars. And the court, in a case where the sum demanded in the complaint exceeds two hundred dollars, shall allow the defendant an additional sum, not exceeding, however, five dollars.

f. A defendant who recovers in said court a judgment upon a counterclaim therein, or obtains a judgment for the possession or recovery of chattels sued for therein, is entitled, in addition to costs heretofore allowed said defendant, to recover a sum equal to five per centum upon said recovery, or upon the value of said chattels.

g. No costs or fees shall be allowed or recovered in an action brought upon a judgment of this court, unless such action be brought more than five years after the recovery of the judgment sued on.

§ 215. Costs in certain actions. In an action in which the complaint demands the recovery of property of the value of fifty dollars or more, or in an action in which the complaint or answer demands judgment for fifty dollars or more, exclusive of costs and disbursements, when an issue of law is raised by demurrer, the party in whose favor such issue may be decided shall be entitled to a sum, in the discretion of the court, not exceeding five dollars. which shall, in case final judgment is awarded against him, be deducted therefrom.

§ 216. Other costs and disbursements. All costs and disbursements allowed to be taxed in any action or proceeding before justices of the peace in towns up to but not exceeding fifteen dollars, shall be included in the judgment as disbursements in addition to the costs herein provided, but in actions within the jurisdiction of justices of the peace in towns such disbursements included in the judgment shall not exceed the limits prescribed by section three thousand and seventy-six of the code of civil procedure for justices' courts.

§ 217. Civil court docket. The city judge shall keep an account of all his proceedings, and in his docket a complete and accurate record of all process issued from and returned to said court, and of all proceedings in every civil action, and of all proceedings brought therein or before him, and shall enter therein the judgment and decision of said court and judge. Such docket shall have the same force as evidence in courts of this state as dockets of justices of the peace in towns, and may be proved and certified in the same manner.

§ 218. Jurisdiction in case of absence, et cetera. The acting city judge, prior to trial, in any action or proceeding already instituted, shall have and retain jurisdiction only during the absence from the city, sickness or disability of the city judge. The city judge, or acting city judge, as the case may be, before whom the trial has actually commenced in any action or proceeding, shall retain power, control and jurisdiction therein until final determination in the city court; but in any such case either may adjourn the action or proceeding from time to time, in case of the absence of the other from the city or in case of the sickness of the other, but each adjournment hereby authorized shall not be for a longer period than one week.

§ 219. Jurisdiction in criminal cases. The city judge in all criminal actions and proceedings and special proceedings of a criminal nature, for or on account of offenses committed or charged to have been committed within the city, shall have jurisdiction and authority to try all persons brought before him accused of any crime of the grade of misdemeanor or of a less degree, and shall have all the jurisdiction and authority which a justice of the peace of a town would have if such offense were committed or charged to have been committed in the town, including bastardy proceedings. The city judge shall have all the power and jurisdiction in proceedings respecting bastardy conferred upon one or more magistrates by chapter one of title five of the code of criminal procedure, and it shall not be necessary for the city judge to associate with himself another magistrate in such proceedings. And the city court shall possess and exercise all the powers conferred upon courts of special sessions, and shall be subject, in the exercise of such powers, to all provisions of law relating to courts of special sessions, except as herein otherwise provided, and upon a conviction in said court for any misdemeanor the same sentence may be imposed as might be imposed were such conviction had in a county court. The city judge and the city court shall also have jurisdiction to try and determine all questions of violation of any and all city ordinances, rules and regulations and upon conviction to impose the punishment provided by law. The city judge of said city shall, in all criminal actions and proceedings and special proceedings of a criminal nature for or on account of offenses committed or charged to have been committed within said city, have all the jurisdiction and authority which a justice of the peace of any town would have if such offense were committed or charged to have been committed in such town. The said city judge shall have exclusive jurisdiction and authority to hear, try and determine, summarily and without a jury, all charges and complaints against persons of disorderly conduct in said city, as defined by this act, or of such conduct in said city as constitutes such persons tramps, vagrants or disorderly persons as defined either by this act or by the statutes of this state. Whenever any person shall be brought before said city judge, either with or without warrant, charged with being such tramp, if such city judge is satisfied by the confession of such person or by competent evidence upon such summary trial that such person is such tramp, the said city judge shall thereupon have jurisdiction and authority to render judgment convicting such person thereof, and imposing such sentence therefor as is provided by section one of chapter four hundred and ninety of the laws of eighteen hundred and eighty-five for such offense. Whenever any person is brought before such city judge either with or without warrant charged with disorderly conduct or with being either such tramp, such vagrant or such disorderly person, if said city judge shall be satisfied by the confession of such person or by competent evidence upon such summary trial that such person has been guilty of such disorderly conduct, or is such vagrant. or such disorderly person, the said city judge may thereupon take such further proceedings thereon as a magistrate is authorized by the code of criminal procedure to take in such case, or the city judge may instead render judgment convicting such person of such disorderly conduct or of being a vagrant or disorderly person as the case may be, and that he may pay a fine not exceeding fifty dollars or be imprisoned not exceeding six months, or both, as the case may require, which judgment shall be enforced in the same manner, in all respects, as judgments of courts of special sessions are enforced. And in case of the conviction of any person for disorderly conduct, or as a vagrant or disorderly person, either upon summary trial or in the manner prescribed by the code of criminal procedure, the said city judge may commit such person to be imprisoned in the county jail or in such other place of confinement as may be designated by the board of supervisors of Ontario county.

§ 220. **Jurisdiction as court of special sessions.** The said city judge is hereby empowered to hold courts of special sessions in said city, and subject to the power of removal provided for in sections fifty-seven and fifty-eight of the code of criminal procedure, courts of special sessions held by said city judge shall have, in the first instance, exclusive jurisdiction to hear, try and determine all charges of misdemeanor committed within said city, which are enumerated in section fifty-six of the code of criminal procedure. Subject to the power of removal provided by section two hundred and eleven of the code of criminal procedure, courts of special sessions held by said city judge shall also have, in the first instance, exclusive jurisdiction to hear, try and determine all other charges of misdemeanors, committed within said city.

§ 221. **Jurisdiction of misdemeanors committed partly in city.** Courts of special sessions held by said city judge shall also (subject to the power of removal as provided by sections fifty-seven and fifty-eight of the code of criminal procedure, if the misdemeanor is one of those enumerated in section fifty-six of said code, and otherwise subject to removal as provided by section two hundred and eleven of said code) have jurisdiction to hear, try and determine charges of misdemeanors committed partly within and partly without said city, or when the acts, omissions or effect thereof which constitute or are requisite to the consummation of such misdemeanor occur partly within and partly without said city.

§ 222. **No jurisdiction of misdemeanors committed outside of city.** Otherwise than as hereinbefore provided, courts of special sessions held by said city judge shall not have jurisdiction to hear, try or determine charges of misdemeanors not committed within said city.

§ 223. **In jurisdiction of offenses beyond ordinary court of special sessions, sentences as in court of special sessions.** When a person shall be convicted by a court of special sessions, held by said city judge, of any misdemeanor of which such court has jurisdiction, but jurisdiction of which is not conferred upon courts of special sessions by the code of criminal procedure, the court of special sessions held by said city judge may render such judgment imposing such sentence therefor as a court of special sessions might lawfully render and impose in case a conviction of such crime were had in a court of special sessions.

§ 224. **All powers subject to provisions relating to courts of special sessions.** Except as hereinbefore provided, courts of special sessions held by said city judge shall have the powers and jurisdiction conferred upon courts of special sessions by the code of criminal procedure, and shall be subject to all the provisions of said code relating to courts of special sessions.

§ 225. **May let to bail.** The said city judge shall have power to let to bail all persons charged with crime before him in all cases of felony when imprisonment in the state prison, on conviction for such felony, cannot exceed five years.

§ 226. **Hearing and jurisdiction by acting city judge.** In case the warrant issued by the city judge shall be returned during his absence from the city or during his inability to attend to the duties of his office, any further proceedings may be had on such warrant before the acting city judge, herein provided for; and having once obtained jurisdiction over any matter, he may retain jurisdiction thereof and proceed to the determination of the matter.

§ 227. **Processes and mandates; by whom served; fees.** All processes and mandates in criminal proceedings issued by the city judge or the acting city judge requiring service, shall be served by the city police or by officers authorized by the law of this state to serve such processes and mandates, and when served by the city police they shall be served without fees for their own benefit, but they shall demand and receive for all process served by them properly chargeable to the county the same fees as are provided by law for constables, sheriffs and deputy sheriffs, for like services. And they shall keep a correct account thereof, and the same shall be presented in the name of the said city to, and audited by, the board of supervisors of Ontario county for the benefit of the city.

§ 228. **Criminal court docket.** The city judge and acting city judge shall keep a docket of all business done by either of them, with full items and dates, and with proper and convenient index; and such docket shall contain a record or brief statement of all convictions, acquittals and judgments before either of them, and the same shall be open during office hours to public inspection when not in use.

§ 229. **Process, et cetera, how signed.** All process, mandates, orders, commitments or other documents made or issued by the city judge, shall be signed, in addition to his signature, " City Judge." When made or issued by the acting city judge, the same shall be signed, in addition to his name, "Acting City Judge."

§ 230. **Power to punish for contempt.** The judge holding such court, while in session, shall have the same powers to preserve order and to punish for contempt committed in his presence as are possessed by judges of courts of record, provided, however, that an appeal may be taken from an order adjudging a person in contempt, to the county court in the same manner as an appeal from a judgment; pending the determination of such an appeal the person adjudged in contempt, if he be imprisoned, may be admitted to bail by the judge of said court or the county judge, in such an amount and in such form as shall be approved by such judge.

§ 231. **Appeals in criminal cases.** Appeals may be taken from final orders and judgments rendered by the city judge, and by the courts of special sessions held by the said city judge, as provided by the code of criminal procedure.

§ 232. **Fees, fines and penalties; for use of city.** In all civil actions and proceedings in the city court, the city judge shall demand and receive for the use of the city for each service rendered by him the same fees as justices of the peace in towns are or may be entitled to receive for a like service, and he shall likewise require the payment from the party liable therefor for services of policemen, the same fees to which constables in towns are or may be entitled for like services; and no such service shall be rendered by him, the acting city judge, or any police officer, until such fees shall have been paid therefor, and the city judge shall pay all such fees received each month to the city treasurer at the end of each month and take his receipt therefor, which shall be filed by him in the office of the said city judge. In the case provided for in section thirty hundred and eighty-one of the code of civil procedure recovery shall be had from the city of Canandaigua instead

of the city judge. All fines and penalties received under this act,
except penalties which by law belong to the person, firm or corporation enforcing the payment thereof, in all proceedings before
the said city judge or city court or before the said acting city
judge, shall belong to the city and shall be accounted for and paid
over to the city treasurer by said city judge as herein provided in
civil cases.   The city judge and acting city judge shall keep an
account of all such fees and fines in both civil and criminal cases.
and all civil and criminal business done by either of them; and
such portion of criminal business as is by law chargeable to the
county of Ontario shall be made out by the city judge in an itemized bill as is required by law, and he shall at the time for presentation of bills against the county of Ontario present, in the
name of the city, said account, properly made and verified, to the
board of supervisors of said county, and said board shall audit
said account to the city of Canandaigua and provide for the payment thereof in the same manner as other county charges.

TITLE X.
ACTIONS BY AND AGAINST THE CITY.

Section 233. Limitation of actions against the city.
     234. No disqualification as judge or juror because of resi-
        dence in the city.
     235. Civil actions to recover penalties.

§ 233. Limitation of actions against the city. No action or
proceeding to recover or enforce any claim, debt or demand against
the city shall be brought until the expiration of thirty days after
the claim, debt or demand shall have been presented to the common council for audit. All actions brought against the city upon
any contract liability, expressed or implied, must be commenced
within one year from the time that the cause of action accrued.
or if for injuries to the person or property, caused by negligence,
within one year from the time of receiving the injuries, and in
other cases within six months after the refusal of the common
council to allow the claim; and no action or proceeding shall be
maintained against the city for personal injuries unless notice
in writing of the intention to claim damages and of the time and
place at which such injuries were received and the nature and
extent of such injuries, shall have been filed with the city attorney within two months after such injury shall have been received,

and an omission to present such notice within the time as above
provided shall be a bar to an action thereon against the city. An
action shall not be maintained for damages or injuries to the person sustained in consequence of the existence of snow or ice upon
any sidewalk, crosswalk or street, unless written notice thereof
relating to the particular place was actually given to the common
council and there was a failure or neglect to cause such snow or
ice to be removed, or the place otherwise made reasonably safe,
within a reasonable time after the receipt of such notice.

§ 234. No disqualification of judge or juror because of residence
in the city. No person shall be disqualified from acting as
judge or juror by reason of being an inhabitant or freeholder in
the city of Canandaigua, and in any action or proceeding in which
the city is a party or interested.

§ 235. Civil actions to recover penalties. Civil actions to
recover any penalties or forfeiture incurred under this act may
be brought in the corporate name of said city, and, in any action
brought in the city court, it shall be lawful to complain generally
for the amount of such penalty or forfeiture stating the section
of this act or of the ordinance under which the penalty is claimed
and to give the special matter in evidence, and the defendant may
answer by simply denying the truth of the complaint and give the
special matter in evidence. If such action be brought in the city
court against an alleged owner of real property, the fact that title
·to real property comes in question ·on the pleadings, or appears
on the trial, shall not deprive the court of jurisdiction, but may
be litigated and determined by the judge as the right of the case
may appear; but such judgment shall not be evidence concerning
the title of real property in any other action or proceeding. The
first process, in any such action, brought in the city court shall
be by summons, which may be made returnable forthwith, and an
execution may be issued immediately on the rendition of judgment. All penalties and forfeitures shall be forthwith, upon
collection, paid to the city treasurer to the credit of the city contingent fund; when any judgment shall be rendered in the city
court in favor of or against the city of Canandaigua in any action
brought for the recovery of any penalty or forfeiture or in
any other action in which the city of Canandaigua shall be a
party, the city judge shall within ten days thereafter file with the
city clerk a transcript of such judgment for which he shall be
entitled to charge the sum of twenty-five cents and include the

same in the costs of said judgment; and in case the said judge
shall omit to file such transcript or to do any of the acts above
described, he shall forfeit the sum of twenty-five dollars for each
and every of such omission, to be recovered in an action by the
city against said city judge. Whenever a judgment in favor of
the city shall be recovered for twenty-five dollars or upward, exclusive of costs, a transcript thereof may be filed in the office of
the clerk of Ontario county, and thereupon the same shall become
a lien upon the property of the defendant in such judgment to
the same extent, and may be collected and enforced in the same
manner as other judgments recovered before justices of the peace
and transcripts filed in pursuance of the laws of the state of
New York.

TITLE XI.

MISCELLANEOUS.

§ 236. **Adjustment of property and liabilities of town of Canandaigua.** The city of Canandaigua shall be liable for its proportionate share of the debts, demands and claims existing at the time
of the passage of this act against the town of Canandaigua to be
ascertained and adjusted as provided in this act. The present
town board of the town of Canandaigua shall, within thirty days

after the passage of this act, meet and ascertain and audit all debts, claims and demands against said town and adjust the amounts or proportion thereof to be paid by the city of Canandaigua and by the town of Canandaigua respectively, according to the respective valuations of the village of Canandaigua and the town of Canandaigua on the assessment-roll of said town of Canandaigua for the year nineteen hundred and twelve. The said town board shall make a statement in triplicate showing the amount of such indebtedness and the items thereof and the proportional amount thereof, and of each item to be paid by, the said city and said town, respectively, and shall file one copy thereof with the town clerk of the town of Canandaigua, one copy with the county clerk of the county of Ontario and the other with the city clerk of the city of Canandaigua, and the debt of said city and said town, so adjusted, shall be paid in accordance with such apportionment the same as other debts existing against the said city and said town respectively. All unexpended moneys belonging to the town of Canandaigua and remaining in the hands of the supervisor of said town, except the amount raised for highways under subdivision one of section ninety of the highway law, on the date when this act shall go into effect, shall thereupon be apportioned by said town board of the town of Canandaigua, between the city of Canandaigua and said town of Canandaigua in the manner and on the basis as hereinbefore provided. All unexpended moneys belonging to the town of Canandaigua remaining in the hands of any official of said town on said date, except the highway moneys hereinbefore mentioned, shall thereupon be apportioned by said town board between the city of Canandaigua and said town of Canandaigua in the manner and on the basis hereinbefore provided. The amount apportioned to the city of Canandaigua shall be paid by the supervisor of said town to the treasurer of said city to the credit of the city contingent fund, and the amount apportioned to the town shall be paid to the supervisor of said town, and receipts taken therefor. And the said supervisor shall be relieved from all further responsibility for the amount so paid to the city treasurer of the city. The said town board shall also apportion in the same manner all securities, evidences of debt, property and effects, except buildings and real estate, as the same may be valued by it, the said property to be retained by said town, at the valuation placed upon it by the said town board, and said town charged on said settlement with the

amount of the city's proportionate share therein. as determined
in the manner hereinbefore provided. Within thirty days after
the passage of this act, the county treasurer of the county of
Ontario shall open new accounts for the city of Canandaigua and
the town of Canandaigua respectively, and shall in like manner
as hereinabove stated, apportion the amounts due the city of
Canandaigua and the town of Canandaigua respectively. Said
county treasurer shall certify to the city treasurer of the city of
Canandaigua the amount in the county treasury to the credit of
the city of Canandaigua.

§ 237. Continuation of village officers. The president of the
village of Canandaigua shall be the mayor of the city of Canandaigua from the time of the passage of this act until and including the thirty-first day of December, nineteen hundred and
thirteen. The trustees of the village of Canandaigua shall be the
aldermen of the city representing the several wards in which they
respectively reside from the time of the passage of this act until
and including the thirty-first day of December, nineteen hundred
and thirteen. The collector-treasurer of the village of Canandaigua shall be the city treasurer from the time of the passage
of this act until and including the thirty-first day of December,
nineteen hundred and thirteen. The police justice of the village
of Canandaigua shall be the city judge of the city from the time
of the passage of this act until and including the thirty-first day
of December, nineteen hundred and fifteen. Each of the officers
hereinabove mentioned shall, before entering upon the duties of
his office as such city officer, qualify in accordance with the provisions of this act. The following appointive officers of said
village shall respectively be the officers of said city performing
corresponding duties and with corresponding powers until their
successors are appointed and have qualified, to wit:

The clerk of said village shall be the city clerk of the city.

The chief of police, assistant chief of police and policemen of
said village shall be respectively the chief of police, assistant
chief of police and policemen of the city.

The chief engineer and first and second assistant engineers of
the fire department of said village shall be respectively the chief
engineer and first and second assistant engineers of the fire department of the city.

The firemen and fire companies of the village shall be the
firemen and fire companies of the city.

The village attorney of said village shall be the city attorney of said city.

The health officer of said village shall be the city physician of said city.

The sexton of the cemetery in said village shall be the sexton of the cemeteries of said city.

The assessors of said village shall be the assessors of said city from the time of the passage of this act until and including the thirty-first day of December, nineteen hundred and thirteen.

On the first Monday after the passage of this act at seven o'clock in the afternoon, the mayor and aldermen of said city hereinbefore mentioned shall meet in the office of the city clerk and organize as a common council. Within twenty days thereafter said common council shall meet and audit all debts, demands and claims existing at that time against the village of Canandaigua and any of its departments, and for that purpose shall direct all officers and boards to file with said common council a statement properly itemized showing all securities, evidences of debt, property and effects in their hands or under their control, belonging to the village of Canandaigua, prior to the time this act takes effect, and it shall be the duty of all officers, boards and commissions to make such statements and file the same with the common council on or before ten days after demand is made therefor by the common council. And it shall also be the duty of each officer, board or commission of the village of Canandaigua to pay over and deliver to such city officers, as the common council shall direct, and as are entitled thereto by the provisions of this act, all such securities, evidences of debt, money, property and effects.

§ 238. Offices and courts abolished. The police court and the office of police justice in and for the village of Canandaigua, except as otherwise provided, together with all courts of special sessions within that portion of the town of Canandaigua which constituted the village of Canandaigua at the time of the passage of this act and all offices created by the village charter of Canandaigua, except as herein otherwise provided, shall be and are hereby abolished, and shall cease to exist after the date when this act takes effect. This act, however, shall not affect the jurisdiction of the police court and the police justice, nor the courts of special sessions in any action or proceeding pending before

either of them at the time this act takes effect, but all such proceedings and actions so pending in which the taking of evidence
upon the trial thereof shall not have been actually commenced are
hereby transferred to the city judge and city court of the
city of Canandaigua to be disposed of according to law, as if
instituted in said city court or before said city judge. The
justices of the peace of the town of Canandaigua who reside
within the limits of said city at the time this act takes effect, shall
be and continue as justices of the peace of said town of Canandaigua, but shall not have jurisdiction over the territory or inhabitants thereof within the limits of said city, except as herein otherwise provided. All other officers of the town of Canandaigua
residing within the limits of said city at the time this act takes
effect shall be and continue as such officers of said town until the
thirty-first day of December, nineteen hundred and fourteen, except that the constables of said town of Canandaigua residing
within the limits of said city shall not serve process issued by
the city judge or out of the city court of said city. All processes,
pleadings, bonds, undertakings, records, moneys and papers in
the actions, examinations and proceedings hereby transferred,
then in the custody of the officers of the courts, which are hereby
abolished or the powers of which are hereby limited, shall, at the
time of such transfer, be delivered to the city judge.

All trials, examinations or proceedings actually commenced by
the taking of evidence, when this title takes effect, in any court
hereby abolished, or the powers or jurisdiction of which are
hereby limited, or before any officer whose court or office is hereby
abolished, or the powers of which are hereby limited, shall be
decided by said courts or officers respectively and judgment
therein shall be entered or determination made by such courts or
judges thereof as though this act had not been passed. Such judgments or determinations shall be enforced by execution, commitment, or other proper process, the same as if this act had not been
passed. And said officers and each of them shall make return of
such actions, examinations or proceedings before them respectively, as if his office had not been abolished or his powers limited.

§ 239. First election of elective city officers. At the first city
election held under the provisions of this act on the first Tuesday
after the first Monday in November, nineteen hundred and
thirteen, there shall be elected by the city at large a mayor and

a city treasurer, for the term of office provided in this act; there shall also at the same time be elected by the electors of the first and fourth wards a supervisor for the term of office provided in this act, and by the electors of the second and third wards a supervisor for the term of office provided in this act; there shall also at the same time be elected by the electors of each ward two aldermen for the term of office provided in this act.

§ 240. **Election of officers in the town of Canandaigua.** That portion of the present town of Canandaigua which at the time of the passage of this act, lies without the limits of the present village of Canandaigua, and which after this act goes into effect, is to constitute the whole town of Canandaigua, shall, at the election of town officers to be held in nineteen hundred and thirteen, elect town officers to take the place of said officers whose terms expire on the thirty-first day of December, nineteen hundred and thirteen, and no person shall then be nominated or elected to any of said offices who shall at the time of such election be a resident of the city of Canandaigua. If any town officer of the town of Canandaigua at the time of the passage of this act, shall be a resident of the village of Canandaigua, he shall serve out the unexpired term of his office as said officer of the town of Canandaigua, except as herein otherwise provided, and his successor shall be a resident of the town of Canandaigua as the same shall be constituted on and after the passage of this act. As soon as practicable after the passage of this act, and prior to the first day of registration for the year nineteen hundred and thirteen, the town board of the town of Canandaigua as constituted at the time of the passage of this act, shall meet and re-district for election purposes that portion of the town which lies outside the limits of the city of Canandaigua. The town board of the town of Canandaigua may designate a place within the limits of the city of Canandaigua as a polling place for the electors of the said town of Canandaigua and it shall be lawful for the town of Canandaigua to hold town caucuses, primaries, conventions and elections at such polling place, and for electors of said town to vote at general elections or special town elections, caucuses, primaries and conventions at such place. The town officers of the town of Canandaigua, except as otherwise specially provided herein, are continued in office and shall have jurisdiction according to their respective offices, but only in that portion of the town hereby set apart and created as the town of Canandaigua.

The supervisor of the town of Canandaigua in office when this act takes effect, shall represent the city of Canandaigua in the Ontario county board of supervisors until and including the thirty-first day of December, nineteen hundred and thirteen, and until the supervisors of the city, provided for by this act, have duly qualified as such officers.

The town of Canandaigua may keep its town clerk's office in the city of Canandaigua if it deems the same desirable.

§ 241. **Limitation of city indebtedness.** The city of Canandaigua shall not incur indebtedness if thereby its total contract indebtedness, exclusive of liabilities, for which taxes have already been levied, shall exceed eight per centum of the assessed valuation of the real property of said city, subject to taxation, as it appears on the last preceding city assessment roll.

§ 242. **First official and fiscal year.** The first official and fiscal year of said city shall commence upon the date of the taking effect of this act and shall end with the thirty-first day of December, nineteen hundred and thirteen, but for the purpose of computing the compensation to which the city officers shall be entitled during said first official year, the time of actual service shall be the basis.

§ 243. **Reading of charter, ordinances, records, et cetera, in evidence.** The charter of the city of Canandaigua may be read in evidence from the volume of session laws of the state of New York, containing said charter, from the volume printed by the authority of the common council or from a certified copy made by the city clerk or from the volume of ordinances and by-laws provided by authority of the common council; and all records of the city which the city officers are required by law to keep shall be presumptive evidence of the truth of their contents in any court.

§ 244. **Ordinance, rules, et cetera, to have same effect as a statute and as if expressly provided in this act.** All ordinances, by-laws, resolutions, rules and regulations of any board or commission now existing in the village of Canandaigua and all ordinances, by-laws, resolutions, rules and regulations hereafter lawfully adopted by any board or commission, provided the same shall be approved by the common council as provided in this act, or any ordinance, by-law, resolution, rule or regulation, lawfully adopted by the common council, shall be and the same are hereby made, and shall have the same force and effect of, a statute, as if expressly prescribed in this act.

§ 245. **Existing rights preserved.** All property, both real and personal, franchises, rights and privileges now belonging to, held or controlled by the village of Canandaigua and all easements, water rights, water privileges in, to or connected with Canandaigua lake, including the so-called feeder and the Canandaigua lake outlet, together with all property, both real and personal and franchises, rights, privileges and interest in the water works system of the village of Canandaigua outside the corporate limits of said village, together with all other property rights and privileges of every name and nature now owned by or under the control of the village of Canandaigua under any general law or special law of this state, are hereby preserved to the city of Canandaigua to be owned, held, controlled and enjoyed by the said city in the same manner and to the full extent as if this act had not been passed.

§ 246. **Definitions.** The word "person" as used in this act shall be construed to include all persons, firms, corporations and associations. The term "resolution" as used in this act includes all motions, orders, rules, regulations and by-laws other than ordinances. The term "street" as used in this act includes highways, roads, avenues, lanes or alleys, or any section thereof, which the public have a right to use.

The term "pavement" includes macadam, telford, asphalt, brick or other similarly improved roadbed and also curbs, gutters, drains and storm sewers.

The term "his" includes the words "her," "its" or "their." The word "materials" shall be held to include supplies, stationery, books, tools and furniture.

§ 247. **Service of papers, et cetera.** When corporations, associations or co-partners are to be served with a notice under any provision of this act, or under direction of the common council, it shall be deemed a sufficient valid and legal service of such notice, to serve a copy thereof upon the president, cashier, treasurer, managing agent or local agent of such corporation or association, or upon one of such co-partners.

§ 248. **Resignations.** All resignations of any officers under this act shall be made to the common council, subject to its acceptance.

§ 249. **Powers and duties retained.** All the powers and duties, except as herein otherwise provided, which are vested in or imposed upon, any board or commission of the village of Canandaigua shall, when this act takes effect, vest in and be imposed upon the common council of the city of Canandaigua, with full power to carry out and execute any or all of such powers and duties.

§ 250. This act shall take effect immediately.

§ 251. Schedule of laws repealed.

Laws of	Chapter.	Sections.
1893	666	All.
1894	131	All.
1902	264	All.
1904	42	All.
1904	469	All.
1905	6	All.
1905	371	All.
1906	229	All.
1906	633	All.
1907	619	All.
1909	364	All.
1912	279	All.

TABLES OF LAWS AND CODES AMENDED OR REPEALED.

TABLE OF LEGALIZING ACTS.

TABLES

OF

LAWS AND CODES AMENDED OR REPEALED.

I. Changes in the Consolidated Laws, 1909–1913.*

(Sections, etc., are amended unless it is otherwise indicated.)

Section.	SUBJECT.	Year.	Chapter.	Page.
	AGRICULTURAL LAW: (L. 1909, ch. 9, constituting cons. laws, ch. 1.)			
2	Salary of commissioner...........................	1909	580	1771
2	Commissioner....................................	1913	345	642
3	Commissioner, deputies and employees.............	1913	345	643
4	Expert butter and cheese makers.................	1910	112	174
12, added	Examination of food for state institutions..........	1910	434	812
12a, added	Almshouse farms................................	1913	460	950
13, added	Decisions of department to be furnished to corporations, etc., dealing in products regulated..........	1911	313	729
30	Adulterated cream...............................	1909	186	297
30	Butter and cheese defined........................	1911	59	79
30	Adulterated milk defined.........................	1911	608	1374
30	Adulterated milk defined.........................	1913	455	938
30, subd. 2	Adulterated milk defined.........................	1910	341	604
31	Care of cows and produce therefrom...............	1910	216	398
35	Inspection of milk...............................	1911	608	1376
37	Regulations as to condensed milk.................	1911	608	1377
40	Oleaginous substances..........................	1909	357	683
41	Coloring matter, etc.............................	1909	357	684
45	Receptacles for milk; milk gathering stations.......	1911	608	1378
45	Receptacles for milk; milk gathering stations.......	1913	408	853
47	Receptacles for milk; milk can inspectors..........	1911	608	1381
48	Branding or labeling cheese......................	1910	207	387
49	Branding skim-milk cheese.......................	1913	456	940
55–61, added	Milk gathering stations; licenses..................	1913	408	856
64a, added	Tuberculous animals............................	1909	588	1783
70	Vinegar..	1909	210	330
70	Vinegar..	1912	26	42
72	Vinegar..	1909	210	330
72	Vinegar..	1911	228	505
73	Vinegar..	1909	210	330
73	Penalties for violation of art. 4..................	1910	156	280
90	Diseases of domestic animals.....................	1909	240	374
90	Diseases of domestic animals.....................	1909	312	580
91	Quarantines....................................	1909	313	582
92	Quarantined farms..............................	1909	315	585
93	Detention and destruction of animals..............	1909	315	586
95	Destruction of diseased animals	1909	316	587

* It is important to notice that the following table for the consolidated laws gives the amendments and repeals of 1909, 1910, 1911 and 1912, as well as those of 1913.

I. CHANGES IN THE CONSOLIDATED LAWS, 1909–1913 — (*Continued*).

Section.	SUBJECT.	Year.	Chap-ter.	Page.
	AGRICULTURAL LAW — (*Continued*).			
96	Regulations...	1909	352	666
96	Penalty for violation of quarantine................	1910	437	818
96	Expense of enforcing regulations..................	1911	255	641
97	Penalties...	1909	352	667
99	Appraisal of condemned animals...................	1909	314	583
99	Appraisal of condemned animals...................	1910	670	1927
101	Post-mortem examination of animals..............	1909	314	584
102	Compensation for animals destroyed..............	1909	314	584
104, repealed	Federal regulations, diseases of animals..........	1909	232	362
105, repealed	Rights of federal inspectors......................	1909	232	362
106	Veal..	1910	561	1393
160	Commercial feeding stuffs.........................	1909	317	588
160	Commercial feeding stuffs.........................	1910	436	817
160	Commercial feeding stuffs.........................	1912	277	505
161	Statements on package............................	1909	317	588
161	Statements on package............................	1911	314	730
162	Statements filed with commissioner...............	1909	317	589
162	Statements to be filed............................	1911	314	731
163	License fee...	1909	317	590
165	Adulterated meal..................................	1909	317	591
220–224	Commercial fertilizers............................	1910	435	813
240	Turpentine; linseed or flaxseed oil...............	1911	816	2313
242	Turpentine; linseed or flaxseed oil...............	1911	816	2314
262	Sale of apples, pears and peaches.................	1911	511	1168
263, repealed	Barrels; apples, pears and quinces................	1912	81	137
Art. 12a (§§ 282–289), added	Sale of farm produce on commission..............	1913	457	941
291, 293	State fair commission.............................	1910	366	658
304	Plant diseases; insect pests.......................	1909	222	347
304	Plant diseases; insect pests.......................	1911	798	2106
305	Infected nursery stock............................	1909	222	350
305	Infected nursery stock............................	1911	798	2109
307a, added	Reports of experiment station at Geneva..........	1913	458	945
310	Apportionment of moneys for promotion of agriculture	1912	73	113
310	Apportionment of moneys for promotion of agriculture	1913	459	946
319, added	Bureau of supervision of co-operative associations...	1913	235	424
Art. 15 (§§ 340, 341) renumbered art. 16 (§§ 360, 361)	Laws repealed; when to take effect...............	1912	297	544
Art. 15 (§§ 340, 341), added	Inspection and sale of seeds......................	1912	297	544
	BANKING LAW: (L. 1909, ch. 10, constituting cons. laws, ch. 2.)			
Preamble	Savings and loan associations.....................	1910	126	188
2	Savings and loan associations.....................	1910	126	189
2, ¶, added	Credit unions......................................	1913	582	1571
5a, added	Retirement of employees in banking department....	1912	212	378
8	Powers of superintendent of banks................	1912	104	179
8	Powers of superintendent of banks................	1913	482	1161

I. Changes in the Consolidated Laws, 1909–1913 — (Continued).

Section.	SUBJECT.	Year.	Chap- ter.	Page.
	BANKING LAW — (Continued).			
14	Savings and loan associations......................	1910	126	191
19	Delinquent corporations and individual bankers.....	1910	452	875
21	Reports of savings and loan associations...........	1910	126	193
21	Reports to superintendent of banks...............	1911	707	1906
23	Examination by directors; reports.................	1913	451	929
27, subd. 3	Loans upon real estate..........................	1909	410	888
27, subd. 3	Savings and loan associations....................	1910	126	195
27, subd. 4	Purchase of evidences of debt by officers, etc.......	1909	402	865
27, subd. 7	Loans to officers, etc., of money corporation.......	1911	585	1343
27, subd. 8	Savings and loan associations....................	1910	126	196
27, subd. 8	Savings and loan associations....................	1913	670	1764
27, subd. 9	Loans by banking corporations...................	1909	240	375
33a, added	Foreign banking corporations....................	1911	772	2051
33a	Foreign banking corporations....................	1913	484	1163
33b, added	Foreign banking corporations....................	1911	772	2052
38	Savings and loan associations....................	1910	126	196
42	Meetings of directors or trustees.................	1911	708	1909
44	Security by depositaries of court funds............	1911	709	1910
66	General powers of banks........................	1912	101	174
67	Deposit of bank reserves........................	1909	223	353
67	Lawful money reserve; certificates of deposit.......	1910	399	731
67	Lawful money reserve...........................	1911	200	468
104	Certificates of deposit..........................	1910	399	733
137	Trustees of savings banks.......................	1912	237	452
137	Trustees of savings banks.......................	1913	113	184
140	Trustees of savings banks, vacancies..............	1913	113	186
140a, added	Removal of trustees of savings banks.............	1913	94	162
146, subd. 3	Investment of savings bank deposits..............	1913	416	879
146, subd. 4	Investment of savings bank deposits..............	1912	100	173
159	Savings and loan associations....................	1910	126	197
160	School savings funds............................	1909	497	1199
160	Savings and loan associations....................	1910	126	197
186, subd. 11	Powers of trust companies.......................	1911	687	1809
186, subd. 11	Enforcement of corporate mortgages..............	1913	317	591
190	Security of trust company, trust fund debts preferred	1909	240	375
193	Trust company investments......................	1909	294	532
198	Lawful money reserve, trust companies...........	1911	200	471
198	Lawful money reserve, trust companies............	1912	49	74
199, added	Proceedings on closing trust company............	1913	103	173
Art. 6, preamble	Savings and loan associations....................	1910	126	198
210	Savings and loan associations....................	1910	126	200
211	Savings and loan associations....................	1910	126	200
211, subd. k	Savings and loan associations, fines...............	1912	192	339
212–214	Savings and loan associations....................	1910	126	203
215	Savings and loan associations....................	1910	126	204
215, first ¶	Savings and loan associations....................	1912	103	178
216–218	Savings and loan associations....................	1910	126	206
219	Savings and loan associations....................	1910	126	198
219	Savings and loan associations....................	1911	861	2403
219	Savings and loan associations....................	1912	102	176
220–238	Savings and loan associations....................	1910	126	198
282	Loan and investment corporations................	1913	628	1679
304	Safe deposit companies..........................	1911	371	851
305, added	Lien of safe deposit companies...................	1911	382	868

I. CHANGES IN THE CONSOLIDATED LAWS, 1909–1913 — (*Continued*).

Section.	SUBJECT.	Year.	Chapter.	Page.
	BANKING LAW— (*Continued*).			
310–313	Personal loan associations........................	1910	127	221
Art. 11 (§§ 330, 331), renumbered art. 12				
(§§ 360, 361)	Schedule of laws repealed........................	1913	582	1571
Art. 11 (§§ 330–358), added	Credit unions...................................	1913	582	1572
	BENEVOLENT ORDERS LAW: (L. 1909, ch. 11, constituting cons. laws, ch. 3.)			
2, subd. 7	Mystic Shrine for North America................	1910	145	266
2, subd. 18, added	Junior Order of United American Mechanics........	1909	420	902
2, subd. 19, added	Modern Woodmen of America....................	1910	420	761
2, subd. 20, added	Brotherhood of the Commonwealth...............	1910	297	537
2, subd. 21, added	Maccabees of the World.........................	1912	65	102
2, subd. 21, added	Loyal Order of Moose...........................	1912	213	373
2, subd. 21, renumbered subd. 22	Loyal Order of Moose...........................	1913	250	446
2, subd. 23, added	National Order of Daughters of Isabella...........	1913	250	446
2, last ¶	Organization....................................	1909	240	376
2, last ¶	Organization....................................	1910	420	761
2, last ¶	Organization....................................	1912	65	102
3	Powers...	1910	420	762
3	Powers...	1912	65	103
4	Terms of trustees...............................	1912	65	104
5	Powers of trustees..............................	1912	65	105
7	Mystic Shrine for North America................	1910	145	266
9	Powers of joint corporation......................	1913	11	16
10	Mortgaging property............................	1911	307	722
	BUSINESS CORPORATIONS LAW: (L. 1909, ch. 12, constituting cons. laws, ch. 4.)			
2, opening ¶	Incorporation...................................	1909	484	1172
2a, added	Corporation for practice of law prohibited.........	1909	484	1172
15	Water companies................................	1909	240	377
Art. 3 (§§ 25, 26) renumbered art. 4 (§§ 50, 51)	Schedule of laws repealed........................	1913	454	934
Art. 3 (§§ 25–38), added	Co-operative corporations........................	1913	454	934

Section.	SUBJECT.	Year.	Chapter.	Page.
	CANAL LAW:			
	(L. 1909, ch. 13, constituting cons. laws, ch. 5.)			
15, subd. 3	Sale or exchange of canal lands..................	1910	350	624
21	Bureau of canal affairs.........................	1913	772	1926
33, subd. 14a, added	Jurisdiction of Shinnecock and Peconic canal.......	1913	229	401
37	Advances to superintendent of repairs.............	1909	240	377
61	Undertakings of division and resident engineers.....	1910	113	174
64	Undertakings of division and resident engineers.....	1910	113	174
64	Advances to division engineers...................	1913	241	431
106	Purchasers of surplus water.....................	1909	240	377
126a, added	Expense of operating lift or swing bridge...........	1911	677	1770
153	Drafts for payment of contracts..................	1913	241	432
178	Changing names of mortgaged canal boats..........	1910	181	377
	CIVIL RIGHTS LAW:			
	(L. 1909, ch. 14, constituting cons. laws, ch. 6.)			
40, 41	Equal rights in places of public accommodation......	1913	265	481
51	Exhibition of photographs.......................	1911	226	504
	CIVIL SERVICE LAW:			
	(L. 1909, ch. 15, constituting cons. laws, ch. 7.)			
3	State civil service commission....................	1913	352	650
4	Officers and employees of commission..............	1913	352	651
13	Exempt class.................................	1913	352	652
13, subd. 2	Exempt class.................................	1912	170	307
14	Competitive class.............................	1911	547	1230
20	Disbursing officers............................	1909	240	378
22	Removal of Spanish war veterans.................	1910	264	468
29, added	Examination pamphlet and civil list..............	1910	590	1428
	CONSERVATION LAW:			
	(L. 1911, ch. 647, constituting cons. laws, ch. 65.)			
3	Office force..................................	1912	444	883
9	Suits and prosecutions.........................	1912	444	885
12	Reports.....................................	1912	444	885
22	Structures for impounding waters; penalties........	1913	736	1855
26–35, added	Actions for penalties..........................	1912	444	886
Art. 4 (§§ 50, 51), repealed	Lands and forests.............................	1912	444	888
Art. 4 (§§ 50–112), added	Lands, forests and public parks..................	1912	444	888
50–62, added	Lands and forests.............................	1912	444	888
63, added	Trespass on state lands.........................	1912	444	898
63	Trespass on state lands.........................	1913	723	1839
64, added	Determination of title to land in forest preserve.....	1912	444	898
64	Determination of title to land in forest preserve.....	1913	527	1394
64, subd. 1, ¶ b	Title to lands claimed by state..................	1913	719	1834

I. CHANGES IN THE CONSOLIDATED LAWS, 1909–1913 — (Continued).

Section.	SUBJECT.	Year	Chapter.	Page.
	CONSERVATION LAW— (Continued).			
65–89, added	Lands and forests....................	1912	444	900
90, added	Limbs and branches to be lopped.................	1912	444	910
90	Limbs to be cut off.............................	1913	723	1840
91–93, added	Lands and forests.............................	1912	444	910
94, added	Expenses of fighting fires; how paid..............	1912	444	912
94	Expenses of fighting fires; how paid..............	1913	723	1840
95–97, added	Lands and forests.............................	1912	444	913
98, added	Setting fires without permission.................	1912	444	915
98	Setting fires without permission.................	1913	723	1842
99–102, added	Lands and forests.............................	1912	444	916
103, added	Fire precautions by railroads....................	1912	444	918
103	Fire precautions by railroads....................	1913	723	1842
104–112, added	Lands and forests.............................	1912	444	920
Art. 5 (§§ 150–178), repealed	Fish and game................................	1912	318	576
Art. 5, added	Fish and game................................	1912	318	576
Art. 5, schedule of parts	Fish and game................................	1913	508	1315
Art. 5, pt. 1, schedule of sections	Powers and duties of commission..................	1913	508	1316
150, repealed	General powers of commission; fish and game.......	1912	318	576
150, added	General powers of commission; fish and game......	1912	318	577
150	General powers of commission; fish and game.......	1913	508	1316
151, repealed	Superintendent of marine fisheries................	1912	318	576
151, added	Fish culturist.................................	1912	318	577
152, repealed	Duties of superintendent of marine fisheries........	1912	318	576
152, added	Additional protection of fish and game............	1912	318	577
152	Additional protection of fish and game............	1913	508	1317
153, repealed	Reports relating to shellfish.....................	1912	318	576
153, added	Close season established; penalties................	1912	318	579
153	Fish and game closes...........................	1913	508	1318
154, repealed	Leases for cultivation of shellfish; limitations......	1912	318	576
154, added	Disposal of game and fish seized..................	1912	318	579
155, repealed	Collection of rents............................	1912	318	576
155, added	Power to take fish.............................	1912	318	580
156, repealed	Settlement of disputes as to shellfish leases........	1912	318	576
156, added	Power to purchase fish eggs......................	1912	318	580
157, repealed	Provisions for taxation.........................	1912	318	576
157, added	Power to acquire beaver. deer. moose. elk..........	1912	318	580
158, repealed	Levy and payment of tax........................	1912	318	576
158, added	Power to take birds and quadrupeds...............	1912	318	580
159, repealed	Collection of tax..............................	1912	318	576
159, added	Certificate to collect for certain purposes..........	1912	318	581
159	License for propagation and scientific purposes......	1913	508	1318
160, repealed	Sanitary inspection of oyster beds................	1912	318	576
160, added	Compilation of forest, fish and game law..........	1912	318	581
160	Publication of fish and game laws................	1913	508	1319
161, repealed	Duties of state commissioner of health............	1912	318	576
161, added	Observance of rules and regulations, penalty........	1912	318	581
162, repealed	Sale of shellfish..............................	1912	318	576
163, repealed	Close season for oysters, Harlem river.............	1912	318	576
164, repealed	Replanting Hudson river oysters..................	1912	318	576

I. CHANGES IN THE CONSOLIDATED LAWS, 1909–1913 — (*Continued*).

Section.	SUBJECT.	Year.	Chapter.	Page.
	CONSERVATION LAW— (*Continued*).			
Art. 5, pt. 2. schedule of sections	Game protectors	1913	508	1319
165, repealed	Taking oysters in South bay	1012	318	576
165, added	Game protectors; number and designation	1912	318	582
165	Game protectors; number and designation	1913	508	1320
166, repealed	Bluepoint oysters	1912	318	576
166, added	Rating of game protectors	1912	318	582
167, repealed	Oyster beds protected	1912	318	576
167, added	Game protectors' bonds	1912	318	582
168, repealed	Dredging and raking for shellfish	1912	318	576
168, added	Compensation of game protectors	1912	318	583
169, repealed	Clams and oysters about Staten Island	1912	318	576
169, added	Powers of game protectors	1912	318	583
170, repealed	Resident only to take shellfish	1912	318	576
170, added	Records and reports	1912	318	584
171, repealed	Polluting waters	1912	318	576
171, added	Special game protectors	1912	318	584
171	Special game protectors	1913	508	1320
172, repealed	Garbage; Long Island sound	1912	318	576
172, added	Powers of sheriffs and constables	1912	318	584
173, repealed	Recording and fees	1912	318	576
173, added	Suits against protectors	1913	508	1350
174, repealed	Penalties	1912	318	576
Art. 5, pt. 3. schedule of sections	Fish and game; taking, etc	1913	508	1320
175, repealed	Criminal jurisdiction of courts	1912	318	576
175, added	Ownership of fish and game	1912	318	585
176, repealed	Provisions of penal or civil code not affected	1912	318	576
176, added	Taking etc., of game and fish restricted	1912	318	585
176	Taking etc.. of fish and game restricted	1913	508	1320
177, repealed	Definitions; fish and game	1912	318	576
177, added	Manner of taking fish and game	1912	318	586
177	Manner of taking fish and game	1913	508	1321
178, repealed	Codification of laws relating to fish and game	1912	318	576
178, added	Transportation of fish and game	1912	318	586
178	Transportation of fish and game	1913	508	1321
179, added	Transportation of fish and game, special	1912	318	587
179	Transportation, sale; special	1913	508	1323
180, added	Prohibited; sale of certain birds	1912	318	587
181, added	Presumptive evidence; possession	1912	318	588
181	Presumptive evidence; possession	1913	508	1323
182, added	Penalties; fish and game	1912	318	588
182	Penalties; fish and game	1913	508	1323
Art. 5, pt. 4. schedule of sections	Licenses; hunting and trapping	1913	508	1324
185, added	Hunting and trapping license	1912	318	588
185	Hunting and trapping license	1913	508	1324
186, added	Non-resident trapping licenses	1912	318	592
186, repealed	Non-resident trapping licenses	1913	508	1350
187, added	Penalties; licenses	1912	318	592

I. CHANGES IN THE CONSOLIDATED LAWS, 1909–1913 — (*Continued*).

Section.	SUBJECT.	Year.	Chapter.	Page.
	CONSERVATION LAW— (*Continued*).			
187 renumbered 186, and amended	Penalties; licenses...............................	1913	508	1327
Art. 5, pt. 5, schedule of sections	Quadrupeds..	1913	508	1327
190, added	Wild deer; open season, etc.......................	1912	318	593
190	Wild deer; open season, etc.......................	1913	508	1328
191, added	Possession of wild deer or venison...............	1912	318	593
191	Possession of wild deer or venison...............	1913	508	1328
192, added	Deer; open season, special.......................	1912	318	594
192	Deer; open season, special.......................	1913	508	1328
193, added	Dogs in forest preserve to be killed..............	1912	318	594
194, added	Wild moose; elk; caribou and antelope...........	1912	318	594
195, added	Squirrels; open season; limit.....................	1912	318	594
195	Squirrels; open season; limit.....................	1913	508	1329
196, added	Hares and rabbits; open season, etc..............	1912	318	594
196	Hares and rabbits; open season, etc..............	1913	508	1329
197, added	Beaver; closed season............................	1912	318	595
198, added	Mink, raccoon and sable; open season............	1912	318	595
198	Mink, raccoon and sable; open season............	1913	508	1329
199, added	Skunk..	1912	318	595
199	Skunk..	1913	508	1330
200, added	Propagation of skunks permitted..................	1912	318	595
200	Propagation of skunks permitted..................	1913	508	1330
201, added	Muskrat; open season............................	1912	318	595
201	Muskrat; open season............................	1913	147	264
201	Muskrat; open season............................	1913	508	1330
202, added	Land turtles......................................	1912	318	595
203, added	Penalties; quadrupeds............................	1912	318	595
203	Penalties; quadrupeds............................	1913	508	1330
Art. 5, pt. 6, schedule of sections	Birds...	1913	508	1331
210, added	Game birds defined...............................	1912	318	596
211, added	Water fowl; open season, etc......................	1912	318	597
211	Water fowl; open season, etc......................	1913	508	1331
212, added	Water fowl; open season; taking; special..........	1912	318	597
213, added	Rallidae; open season; limit......................	1912	318	597
214, added	Upland game birds; open season...................	1912	318	598
214	Upland game birds; open season, etc..............	1913	508	1331
215, added	Upland game birds; open season; limit; special....	1912	318	598
215	Upland game birds; open season; limit; special.....	1913	508	1332
216, added	Shore birds; open season; limit...................	1912	318	598
216	Shore birds; open season; limit...................	1913	508	1332
217, added	Shore birds; open season; special.................	1912	318	598
218, added	Antwerp or homing pigeons......................	1912	318	599
219, added	Certain wild birds protected......................	1912	318	599
220, added	Destroying or robbing nests......................	1912	318	599
221, added	Snares, nets and traps...........................	1912	318	599
221	Snares, nets and traps...........................	1913	508	1332
222, added	Game shall not be taken; certain public lands.......	1912	318	599
223, added	Penalties; birds..................................	1912	318	600
223	Penalties; birds..................................	1913	508	1332

I. CHANGES IN THE CONSOLIDATED LAWS, 1909–1913 — (*Continued*).

Section.	SUBJECT.	Year.	Chap-ter.	Page.
	CONSERVATION LAW— (*Continued*).			
Art. 5, pt. 7, schedule of sections	Fish................................	1913	508	1333
230, added	Sale of minnows for bait..................	1912	318	601
231, added	Bass; open season; limit..................	1912	318	601
232, added	Trout; open season; limit.................	1912	318	601
232	Trout; open season; limit.................	1913	508	1333
233, added	Trout; open season; special...............	1912	318	601
233, repealed	Trout; open season; special...............	1913	508	1351
234, added	Lake trout and whitefish..................	1912	318	601
234	Lake trout and whitefish..................	1913	508	1334
235, added	Lake trout and whitefish..................	1912	318	602
235	Lake trout and whitefish..................	1913	508	1334
236, added	Pike perch; open season, etc..............	1912	318	602
237, added	Pickerel and pike; open season, etc........	1912	318	602
238, added	Sturgeon; open season; size limit; sale of...	1912	318	602
239, added	Maskalonge; open season; size limit; sale of...	1912	318	602
240, added	Striped bass; size limit; sale of...........	1912	318	602
241, added	Smelt or icefish; open season, etc.........	1912	318	603
241	Smelt or icefish; open season, etc.........	1913	508	1334
241a, added	Lake George, open seasons, special........	1913	583	1585
242, added	Stocking private waters prohibited.........	1912	318	603
242	Stocking private waters prohibited.........	1913	508	1335
243, added	Prohibited; disturbing certain fish while spawning...	1912	318	603
244, added	Prohibited; thumping.....................	1912	318	603
245, added	Prohibited; explosives....................	1912	318	603
246, added	Obstructing streams prohibited............	1912	318	604
246	Obstructing streams prohibited............	1913	508	1335
247, added	Polluting streams........................	1912	318	604
247	Polluting streams; prohibited.............	1913	508	1335
248, added	Polluting waters of fish hatcheries prohibited.......	1912	318	604
249, added	Drawing off water prohibited.............	1912	318	604
249	Drawing off water prohibited.............	1913	508	1335
250, added	Placing fish in certain waters prohibited...	1912	318	604
251, added	Fishing near fishways prohibited..........	1912	318	605
252, added	Fishing through ice, certain waters, prohibited.....	1912	318	605
252	Fishing through ice, certain waters, prohibited.....	1913	508	1336
253, added	Tip-ups.................................	1912	318	605
253	Tip-ups.................................	1913	508	1336
254, added	Set and trap lines.......................	1912	318	605
254	Set and trap lines.......................	1913	508	1336
255, added	Spearing...............................	1912	318	605
255	Spearing...............................	1913	508	1336
256, added	Eel weirs and eel pots....................	1912	318	605
257, added	Frogs..................................	1912	318	605
258, added	Penalties; fish..........................	1912	318	606
258	Penalties; fish..........................	1913	508	1336
Art. 5, pt. 8 schedule of sections	Nets and netting........................	1913	508	1337
270, added	Nets to be licensed......................	1912	318	607
270	Nets to be licensed......................	1913	508	1337
271, added	Fish taken with nets.....................	1912	318	607
271	Fish taken with nets.....................	1913	508	1337

I. CHANGES IN THE CONSOLIDATED LAWS, 1909-1913 — (*Continued*).

Section.	SUBJECT.	Year.	Chapter.	Page.
	CONSERVATION LAW — (*Continued*).			
272, added	Size of mesh....................	1912	318	607
273, added	Hauling of nets regulated................	1912	318	607
273	Hauling of nets regulated................	1913	508	1338
274, added	Nets to be tagged and buoyed.............	1912	318	608
275, added	Use of nets in certain waters prohibited...........	1912	318	608
276, added	Nets in Lakes Erie and Ontario..........	1912	318	608
276	Nets in Lakes Erie and Ontario..........	1913	664	1752
277, added	Niagara river; nets....................	1912	318	608
278, added	Nets in Chaumont bay and adjacent waters.........	1912	318	608
278	Nets in Chaumont bay and adjacent waters.........	1913	664	1753
279, added	Nets; Hudson and Delaware rivers, adjacent waters..	1912	318	609
280, added	Application of part 8...................	1912	318	609
281, added	Vessels to carry employees of commission...........	1912	318	609
282, added	Nets to be destroyed...................	1912	318	609
282	Nets to be destroyed...................	1913	508	1338
283, added	Seizure of nets; regulations in certain counties.......	1912	318	609
284, added	Penalties; nets and netting..............	1912	318	610
284	Penalties; nets and netting..............	1913	508	1338
Art. 5, pt. 9, schedule of sections	Fishways.........................	1913	508	1338
290, added	Notice of construction of dam..............	1912	318	610
291, added	Fishways ordered...................	1912	318	610
291	Fishways; penalties..................	1913	508	1339
292, added	Power of commission to construct fishways.......	1912	318	610
292, repealed	Power of commission to construct fishways.........	1913	508	1351
293, added	Penalties; fishways..................	1912	318	611
293, repealed	Penalties; fishways..................	1913	508	1351
Art. 5, pt. 10, schedule of sections	Marine fisheries...................	1913	508	1339
300, added	Marine district described..............	1912	318	612
301, added	Bureau of marine fisheries..............	1912	318	612
301	Bureau of marine fisheries..............	1913	508	1340
302, added	Office and clerical force...............	1912	318	612
302	Office and clerical force...............	1913	508	1340
303, added	Reports relating to shellfish.............	1912	318	613
304, added	Leases for cultivation of shellfish; limitations........	1912	318	613
305, added	Collection of rents..................	1912	318	615
306, added	Settlement of disputes as to shellfish leases..........	1912	318	615
307, added	Provisions for taxation................	1912	318	615
308, added	Shell fisheries; levy of tax, etc............	1912	318	616
308	Shell fisheries; levy of tax, etc............	1913	508	1341
309, added	Collection of tax...................	1912	318	617
310, added	Sanitary inspection of shellfish grounds, etc.........	1912	318	618
310	Sanitary inspection of shellfish grounds, etc.........	1913	508	1342
310, subd. 1	Sanitary inspection of shellfish grounds.............	1913	796	2204
311, added	Duties of state commissioner of health.............	1912	318	619
312, added	Shellfish grounds, inspection, etc................	1912	318	619
312	Shellfish grounds, inspection, etc................	1913	508	1343
313, added	Prohibited sale of shellfish; conditions certified......	1912	318	620
314, added	Taking oysters in South bay....................	1912	318	620
315, added	Blue point oysters...........................	1912	318	621

I. CHANGES IN THE CONSOLIDATED LAWS, 1909–1913 — (Continued).

Section.	SUBJECT.	Year.	Chap-ter.	Page.
	CONSERVATION LAW — (Continued).			
316, added	Shellfish beds protected...........................	1912	318	621
317, added	Dredging and raking for shellfish.................	1912	318	621
318, added	Scallops; size limit.............................	1912	318	621
318	Scallops; size limit.............................	1913	508	1344
319, added	Resident only to take shellfish...................	1912	318	621
320, added	Starfish to be destroyed..........................	1912	318	621
321, added	Prohibited; taking lobsters under certain size.......	1912	318	621
322, added	Size of openings in lobster traps..................	1912	318	622
323, added	Residents only to take lobsters; certain waters......	1912	318	622
324, added	Licenses for vessels, etc.........................	1912	318	622
325, added	Polluting waters................................	1912	318	623
326, added	Garbage not to be thrown in certain waters........	1912	318	623
327, added	Prohibited use of nets in inlets...................	1912	318	623
328, added	Prohibited; nets in Harlem river, adjacent waters..	1912	318	624
329, added	Richmond county and Raritan bay................	1912	318	624
329	Richmond county and Raritan bay..............	1913	54	92
330, added	Jamaica bay and adjacent waters.................	1912	318	624
331, added	Size of mesh in Coney Island creek...............	1912	318	624
332, added	Nets in Far Rockaway bay; Jones' Inlet and adjacent waters......................	1912	318	625
332	Nets in Rockaway bay, Jones' inlet and adjacent waters...........................	1913	508	1344
333, added	Recording and fees..............................	1912	318	625
334, added	Supervisors of Nassau and Suffolk counties........	1912	318	625
335, added	Penalties; marine fisheries.......................	1912	318	625
335 renumbered 355, and amended	Penalties; marine fisheries.......................	1913	508	1344
Art. 5, pt. 11, schedule of sections	Private parks....................................	1913	508	1345
360, added	Laying out private parks.........................	1912	318	626
360	Laying out private parks.........................	1913	508	1345
361, added	Notices in private parks.........................	1912	318	626
361	Notices in private parks.........................	1913	508	1345
361	Notices in private parks.........................	1913	746	1877
362, added	Protection of private lands not parks..............	1912	318	627
362	Protection of private lands not parks..............	1913	508	1345
363, added	Private parks; notices furnished..................	1912	318	627
363, repealed	Private parks; notices furnished..................	1913	508	1351
364, added	Signs not to be defaced..........................	1912	318	627
364	Signs not to be defaced..........................	1913	508	1346
365, added	Fish and game protected.........................	1912	318	627
365	Fish and game protected.........................	1913	508	1346
366, added	Penalties; private parks..........................	1912	318	627
366	Penalties; private parks..........................	1913	508	1346
Art. 5, pt. 12, schedule of sections	Breeding, importation and sale of fish and game.....	1913	508	1346
370, added	Fish; transportation, sale, etc..................	1912	318	628
370	Fish; transportation, sale, etc...................	1913	508	1346
371, added	Sale of trout raised in private hatcheries........	1912	318	628

I. CHANGES IN THE CONSOLIDATED LAWS, 1909–1913 — *(Continued)*.

Section.	SUBJECT.	Year.	Chapter.	Page.
	CONSERVATION LAW— *(Continued)*.			
372, added	Breeding of elk, deer, pheasants, ducks............	1912	318	629
372	Breeding of elk, deer, pheasants, ducks............	1913	508	1347
373, added	Mammals and birds; importation and sale.........	1912	318	631
373	Mammals and birds; importation and sale.........	1913	508	1349
374, added	Fees..	1912	318	632
375, added	Storage of fish..............................	1912	318	632
376, added	Penalties; breeding, etc., of fish and game.........	1912	318	633
376	Penalties; breeding, etc., of fish and game.........	1913	508	1350
380. added	Defintions.................................	1912	318	633
380, subd. 7	Game defined...............................	1913	508	1350
380, subd. 8	Wild game and game protected by law.............	1913	508	1350
380, subd. 17	Pikeperch defined...........................	1913	508	1350
381, added	Application of art. 5.........................	1912	318	635
381	Application of art. 5.........................	1913	508	1350
382, added	Construction of art. 5........................	1912	318	635
382	Construction of art. 5........................	1913	508	1350
383, added	Schedule of laws repealed.....................	1912	318	636
383 renumbered L. 1912, ch. 318, § 2	Schedule of laws repealed.....................	1913	508	1351
384, added	Laws repealed; time of taking effect..............	1912	318	636
384, renumbered L. 1912, ch. 318, § 3	Laws repealed; time of taking effect..............	1913	508	1351
524	Water supply used in other states................	1913	469	
Art. 9a, (§§ 530–539), added	Union water districts.........................	1913	233	983 406
	COUNTY LAW: (L. 1909, ch. 16, constituting cons. laws, ch. 11.)			
10	County clerks, certain counties..................	1910	279	505
10	Board of supervisors, chairman..................	1911	250	635
10	Board of supervisors, chairman..................	1912	193	340
12, subd. 5	Powers of boards of supervisors.................	1911	359	827
12, subd. 5	Powers of board of supervisors..................	1913	742	1863
12, subd. 16	Supervisors in Erie county.....................	1909	477	1162
12, subd. 26, added	Authorizing town to borrow money..............	1910	141	254
12, subd. 26	Authorizing municipalities and districts to borrow money....................................	1913	351	649
12, subd. 27, added	Societies for the prevention of cruelty to children....	1911	545	1225
12, subd. 27, added	Societies for the prevention of cruelty to animals....	1911	663	1747
12, subd. 27, re-numbered subd. 28	Societies for prevention of cruelty to animals.......	1912	148	271
12, subd. 28, added	Appropriation and tax for agricultural purposes.....	1912	35	54
12, subd. 28, added	Side-path funds..............................	1912	194	341

I. CHANGES IN THE CONSOLIDATED LAWS, 1909–1913 — (*Continued*).

Section.	SUBJECT.	Year.	Chapter.	Page.
	COUNTY LAW — (*Continued*).			
12, subd. 29, added	Maintenance of persons in state charitable institution.	1912	148	271
12, subd. 29, added	Expenses of district attorney......................	1912	235	450
12, subd. 30, added	Maintenance of county buildings...................	1912	235	450
19	Printing and distribution of proceedings of supervisors	1913	256	457
23	Compensation of supervisors, certain counties.......	1910	279	508
23	Compensation of supervisors, Rockland county......	1911	554	1258
23	Compensation of supervisors, Dutchess county......	1912	34	52
23	Compensation of supervisors, Niagara county......	1913	254	449
23	Expenses of supervisors, Saint Lawrence county.....	1913	355	660
35	Alteration and erection of towns..................	1911	250	635
38	Fire districts in two or more counties..............	1909	405	869
38, subds. 8, 9	Fire districts..................................	1910	115	176
38, subd. 11, added	Fire districts..................................	1913	127	209
42	Expenses of courts of record....................	1913	394	834
45, added	Establishment of hospitals for tuberculosis..........	1909	341	641
45	County hospitals for tuberculosis, establishment.....	1913	166	305
45, subd. 2	County hospitals for tuberculosis, buildings.........	1913	379	815
46, added	Appointments, terms of office of managers..........	1909	341	642
47, added	General duties and powers of managers.............	1909	341	642
47, subd. 6	County hospitals for tuberculosis.................	1913	40	66
47, subd. 8, added	County hospitals for tuberculosis; buildings........	1913	379	815
48, added	County hospitals for tuberculosis.................	1909	341	643
48, subd. 5	County hospitals for tuberculosis; superintendent...	1912	149	272
48, subd. 5	County hospitals for tuberculosis; superintendent...	1912	239	456
48, subd. 5	County hospitals for tuberculosis; superintendent...	1913	379	815
49, added	County hospitals for tuberculosis.................	1909	341	645
49a, added	County hospitals for tuberculosis.................	1909	341	646
49a	County hospitals for tuberculosis.................	1912	149	272
49a	County hospitals for tuberculosis.................	1912	239	456
49a	County hospitals for tuberculosis; patients........	1913	397	816
49b–49e, added	County hospitals for tuberculosis.................	1909	341	646
49e	County hospitals for tuberculosis; almshouses.......	1913	379	816
61	County highways and bridges....................	1909	240	379
117	Injuries to sheep, etc., by dogs..................	1912	200	362
133	Seizure of dogs................................	1913	629	1680
162	Special deputy county clerks.....................	1911	727	1950
163a, added	Duties of assistants to county clerks..............	1913	368	676
165	Hours, Westchester county offices.................	1909	199	316
168	Register of moneys paid into court...............	1910	160	283
169	Special deputy clerks, Queens county.............	1910	694	2007
169	Special deputy clerks, certain counties............	1913	109	180
169	Special deputy clerks, certain couunties...........	1913	367	675
169	Special deputy clerks, certain counties............	1913	637	1690
180, subd. 1	Reduction of number of coroners.................	1912	91	163
194	Employment of stenographers by coroners.........	1910	158	282
195, subd. 4	Sheriffs.......................................	1910	418	759
203	District attorney, Niagara county................	1911	95	139
203	Assistant district attorney; district attorney's stenographer, Niagara county......................	1912	544	1120

I. CHANGES IN THE CONSOLIDATED LAWS, 1909-1913 — (*Continued*).

Section.	SUBJECT.	Year.	Chapter.	Page.
	COUNTY LAW — (*Continued*).			
215, added	Appointment of county auditors..................	1910	152	275
216, added	Duties of county auditors.......................	1910	152	275
216	Duties of county auditors.......................	1913	384	822
232, subd. 1	Salaries of county judge and surrogate, Albany county.	1912	549	1360
232, subd. 14	Salaries of county judge and surrogate, Erie county.	1912	37	57
232, subd. 16	Salary of county judge, Franklin county...........	1913	436	913
232, subd. 22	Salary of surrogate, Jefferson county.............	1910	281	509
232, subd. 23	Salary of surrogate, Kings county...............	1911	413	941
232, subd. 27	Salary of county judge and surrogate, Monroe county	1912	549	1360
232, subd. 29	Salaries of county judge and surrogate, Nassau county.	1910	300	539
232, subd. 31	Salary of surrogate, Oneida county...............	1911	203	476
232, subd. 41	Salary of county judge, Richmond county..........	1911	413	941
232, subd. 58	Salary of surrogate, Westchester county...........	1912	549	1360
232, subd. 61	Salaries of county judge and surrogate, Nassau county	1910	300	539
232, subd 62, added	Salary of surrogate, Kings county................	1911	413	941
232, subd. 63, added	Salary of county judge, Richmond county..........	1911	413	941
232, subd. 64, added	Salaries of county judge and surrogate, Erie county..	1912	37	58
232, subd. 64, added	Expenses of surrogate, Chautauqua county.........	1912	92	163
232, subd. 65, added	Salaries of certain county judges and surrogates....	1912	549	1371
232, subd. 66	Salary of county judge, Franklin county..........	1913	436	914
233	Salaries and expenses of county judges...........	1909	122	193
233	Salaries and expenses of county judges............	1909	228	358
234, added	County comptroller............................	1909	466	1116
235, added	County comptroller............................	1909	466	1117
235	County comptroller............................	1910	8	12
236-239, 239a, added	County comptroller............................	1909	466	1119
240, subd. 4	Compensation of court criers....................	1910	34	51
241a, added	Compensation of supervisors and assessors attending tax meetings................................	1911	51	72
250, added	Expenses of peace officers for injuries.............	1912	95	165
	DEBTOR AND CREDITOR LAW: (L. 1909, ch. 17, constituting cons. laws, ch. 12.)			
Art. 2	Schedule of sections...........................	1909	240	379
189	Distribution of moneys.........................	1909	240	379
	DECEDENT ESTATE LAW: (L. 1909, ch. 18, constituting cons. laws, ch. 13.)			
Art. 2	Schedule of sections...........................	1909	240	380
13, repealed	Devises of real property to aliens...............	1913	153	270
18-20, repealed	Devise or bequest to certain corporations..........	1911	857	2399
29	Devise or bequest not to lapse...................	1912	384	739

I. CHANGES IN THE CONSOLIDATED LAWS, 1909–1913 — (*Continued*).

Section.	SUBJECT.	Year.	Chapter.	Page.
	DECEDENT ESTATE LAW—(*Continued*).			
44	Recording foreign will..........................	1909	240	380
45	Authentication of foreign wills...................	1909	304	571
47	Validity and effect of testamentary disposition.....	1911	244	614
48, added	Application of certain sections....................	1909	240	381
98, subd. 12	Representation among collaterals..................	1909	240	380
98, subd. 15a, added	Distribution of personal property.................	1913	489	1169
98, subd. 16	Distribution of personal property.................	1913	489	1169
103	Action against husband for debts of deceased wife...	1909	240	381
104, added	Application of certain sections...................	1909	240	381
120 renumbered 122	Appraisal of estate.............................	1909	240	382
120, added	Actions by or against executors, etc..............	1909	240	381
121, added	Action by executor of executor...................	1909	240	382
Schedule of repeals	R. S., pt. 3, ch. 8, tit. 3, §§ 1, 2, 11, inserted........	1909	240	422
Schedule of repeals	L. 1904, ch. 106, inserted.......................	1909	240	424
	DOMESTIC RELATIONS LAW: (L. 1909, ch. 19, constituting cons. laws, ch. 14.)			
11	Solemnization of marriages.......................	1911	610	1384
11	Solemnization of marriages.......................	1912	166	302
11	Solemnization of marriages.......................	1913	490	1170
14	Marriage licenses...............................	1912	216	382
15	Marriage licenses; consents of parents.............	1912	241	458
19	Marriage licenses; search of records..............	1912	241	460
111, subd. 3	Necessary consent for adoption of minors	1913	569	1549
116	Abrogation of voluntary adoption................	1910	154	277
116	Abrogation of voluntary adoption................	1913	38	63
	DRAINAGE LAW: (L. 1909, ch. 20, constituting cons. laws, ch. 15.)			
Art. 2	Title...	1910	624	1596
2	Petition for drainage...........................	1910	624	1592
4	Proceedings on petition.........................	1910	624	1593
10	Commissioners.................................	1910	624	1593
12	Survey and maps..............................	1910	624	1594
12	Survey and maps..............................	1913	613	1636
18	Condemnation of land..........................	1910	624	1595
19	Application of art. 2...........................	1910	624	1595
40	Nonpayment of assessments.....................	1909	240	382
67	Notice of assessments..........................	1909	240	382

I. CHANGES IN THE CONSOLIDATED LAWS, 1909–1913 — (*Continued*).

Section.	SUBJECT.	Year.	Chapter.	Page.
	EDUCATION LAW: (L. 1909, ch. 21, constituting cons. laws, ch. 16.)			
2	Definitions............................	1909	240	384
381	Property to be assessed for school taxes............	1909	415	899
383	Determination of values....................	1909	415	899
387a, added	School taxes, Rockland county..............	1909	263	460
462, added	Moneys for training of teachers................	1909	406	874
530, repealed	Compulsory education..................	1909	409	880
531–538 renumbered 530–538, and amended	Compulsory education..................	1909	409	880
641	Regulations for training classes..........	1909	406	875
962, added	Sewers through lands of State School for Blind.....	1910	53	91
1061	Librarian, Barnard Memorial Library.............	1909	141	218
1121, subds. 1, 2	Trustees, Cornell University..................	1909	404	867
1182	State School of Agriculture at Morrisville..........	1909	252	443
Schedule of repeals	L. 1909, ch. 1, inserted....................	1909	240	425
All	Generally revised and amended............. (*Section numbers, etc., hereafter given are those of this amendatory act.*)	1910	140	254
63, repealed	Dissolution of educational corporations............	1911	860	2402
63, added	Dissolution of educational corporations............	1911	860	2402
69, subd. 1	Water-works and sewer systems of colleges........	1913	422	887
70–74, added	Scholarships for students in colleges................	1913	292	527
75, added	Scholarships for students in colleges................	1913	292	529
75	Scholarships for students in colleges................	1913	437	914
76, 77, added	Scholarships for students in colleges................	1913	292	529
99, added	Reports, etc., filed with commissioner of education....	·1911	159	252
121	Formation of new school district..................	1912	294	534
130, repealed	Division of school district; two villages............	1911	334	774
130, added	Consolidation of districts.........................	1913	129	212
131, repealed	Method and result of election....................	1911	334	774
131, added	Request for meeting to consolidate; notices........	1913	129	213
132, repealed	Apportionment of indebtedness....................	1911	334	774
132, added	Proceedings at meeting to consolidate..............	1913	129	214
133 renumbered 134a, and amended	Bonded indebtedness of certain dissolved districts...	1913	129	215
133, added	Order creating consolidated district................	1913	129	214
134, repealed	Temporary attendance of pupils..................	1911	334	774
134, added	District quotas of consolidated districts............	1913	129	215
Art. 6a (§§ 175–179), added	Temporary school districts........................	1913	176	322
190	Notice of first meeting of district..................	1913	129	216
194	Time of school district meetings..................	1910	442	825
194	Time of school district meetings..................	1913	440	917
195	Annual meetings of reformed districts..............	1913	129	216
206, subd. 5	School district treasurer........................	1910	442	836
206, subds. 7, 8	Use of school buildings and grounds..............	1913	221	386
224, subd. 4	School year defined.............................	1910	442	837

I. CHANGES IN THE CONSOLIDATED LAWS, 1909–1913 — (*Continued*).

Section.	SUBJECT.	Year.	Chapter.	Page.
	EDUCATION LAW — (*Continued*).			
225	Terms of officers of newly created district.........	1913	129	216
275, subds. 4, 8, 18	Use of school buildings and grounds.................	1913	221	386
301, subd. 2	Union free school district trustees.................	1910	442	827
303, subd. 6	School district meetings...........................	1910	442	825
306	Boards of education, annual meetings..............	1911	830	2337
310, subds. 6, 15	Use of school buildings and grounds................	1913	221	387
310, subd. 21, added	Medical inspection of children....................	1910	602	1445
310, subd. 21	Medical inspection of children....................	1912	215	381
321	Records and reports of boards of education.........	1910	442	827
365	Report by supervisors to district superintendents....	1913	130	217
Art. 14	District superintendents..........................	1910	607	1545
380–394	District superintendents..........................	1910	607	1545
395	Powers and duties of district superintendents.......	1910	607	1551
395, subd. 2	Conferences for teachers..........................	1913	511	1354
396–398	District superintendents..........................	1910	607	1545
410	Assessment of school taxes........................	1911	830	2338
427–431	Payment of school taxes by certain corporations.....	1913	216	380
435	Unpaid school taxes..............................	1910	284	512
440, subd. 2	School tax on state lands, Dutchess county........	1911	593	1357
455	Use of school buildings and grounds................	1913	221	388
463	Use of school buildings and grounds................	1913	221	389
464	Acquisition of sites for schoolhouses...............	1911	782	2088
467, subds. 1, 3	Use of school buildings and grounds................	1913	221	389
480, subd. 1	Use of school buildings and grounds................	1913	221	390
492, subd. 2	Apportionment of funds; common schools..........	1913	511	1354
492, subd. 4, re-numbered 3, and amended	Time, how computed.............................	1913	511	1354
493, subd. 6	Apportionment of funds for non-resident pupils.....	1912	276	505
493, subd. 6	Apportionment of funds for non-resident pupils.....	1913	399	842
494	Apportionment and payment of school moneys......	1912	77	121
496	Certificate of apportionment of school moneys.....	1912	77	122
498	Apportionment of school moneys..................	1913	130	217
561, subd. 2, amended; subd. 3, added	Contracts for employment of teachers..............	1910	442	826
Art. 20a (§§ 570–577), added	Medical inspection...............................	1913	627	1675
600, 601, 603–606	Vocational instruction............................	1913	747	1878
621	Compulsory education, blind children..............	1911	710	1911
621, subd. 2	Compulsory education............................	1913	511	1355
622	Attendance at evening school......................	1913	748	1882
627	Display of certificates............................	1913	748	1884
628	Unlawful employment of children..................	1913	748	1885
630, subd. 1	School-record certificates.........................	1913	101	171
631	Evening, part-time or continuation school certificate.	1913	748	1884
832, subd. 2	State Normal College.............................	1913	511	1357
972	Kindergarten training of blind children.............	1912	60	96
973, subd. 2	Terms of instruction for blind children.............	1912	60	97
973, subd. 2	Terms of instruction for blind children.............	1912	223	405

I. CHANGES IN THE CONSOLIDATED LAWS, 1909-1913 — (*Continued*).

Section.	SUBJECT.	Year.	Chap-ter.	Page.
	EDUCATION LAW — (*Continued*).			
976	Aid for blind and deaf students....................	1913	175	321
979, 980	Tuition and maintenance of deaf-mute children.....	1910	322	565
1031, subd. 2	Cornell University trustees......................	1912	248	467
1031, subd. 2	Cornell University trustees......................	1913	423	888
1031, subd. 3	Cornell University trustees......................	1912	248	468
1050, 1052, amended; 1053, added	St. Lawrence University..........................	1910	433	828
Art. 41a (§§ 1055-1060), added	State school of agriculture, Delhi.................	1913	675	1770
1075-1078, added	State school of agriculture, Cobleskill.............	1911	852	2385
1094, added	Morrisville agricultural school, condemnation proceedings authorized....................	1912	27	43
1095, added	Retirement fund for teachers in state institutions....	1910	441	823
1095	Retirement fund for teachers in state institutions....	1912	293	533
1096, added	Retirement fund for teachers in state institutions....	1910	441	823
1097, added	Retirement fund for teachers in state institutions....	1910	441	824
1097	Retirement fund for teachers in state institutions....	1912	293	533
1098, added	Retirement fund for teachers in state institutions....	1910	441	824
1098	Retirement fund for teachers in state institutions....	1912	293	534
1099, added	Retirement fund for teachers in state institutions....	1910	441	824
1099a, added	Employment of retired teachers..................	1913	631	1663
1100, added	Definitions....................................	1911	449	1060
1100	Definitions....................................	1913	511	1355
1101-1107, added	State teachers' retirement fund..................	1911	449	1006
1108, added	State teachers' retirement fund..................	1911	449	1010
1108	State teachers' retirement fund..................	1913	511	1356
1108a, 1109, 1109a, 1109b, added	State teachers' retirement fund..................	1911	449	1010
1109c, added	Annuities from teachers' retirement fund..........	1913	509	1351
1118	Establishment of county libraries.................	1911	815	2311
1163	Appellate division, first department, law library.....	1911	832	2340
1166	Supreme court library, New York city.............	1911	832	2340
1166	Supreme court library, New York city.............	1913	512	1357
1177	Supreme court library, Buffalo...................	1911	58	78
1180, added	Supreme court library, Queens county.............	1911	557	1262
1180, added	New York city court, law library.................	1911	824	2330
Art. 45a (§§ 1185-1188), added	State school of agriculture on Long Island..........	1912	319	637
Art. 46 (§§ 1190-1192), renumbered art. 47 (§§ 1200-1202)	Schedule of laws repealed........................	1913	424	893
Art. 46 (§§ 1190-1198), added	Divisions of history and public records.............	1913	424	889
Art. 46, renumbered art. 47	Laws repealed; when to take effect................	1913	676	1774
Art. 46 (§§ 1190-1193), added	New York-American Veterinary College............	1913	676	1774
1190 renumbered 200	Laws repealed (*See foot note, L.* 1913, p. 1774).......	1913	676	1774

I. CHANGES IN THE CONSOLIDATED LAWS, 1909–1913 — (*Continued*).

Section.	SUBJECT.	Year.	Chapter.	Page.
	EDUCATION LAW—(*Continued*).			
1190, added	New York-American Veterinary College...........	1913	676	1774
1191 renumbered 201	Saving clause (*See foot note, L.* 1913, p. 1774)......	1913	676	1774
1191, added	New York-American Veterinary College...........	1913	676	1775
1192 renumbered 202	When to take effect (*See foot note, L.* 1913, p. 1774)..	1913	676	1774
1192, added	New York-American Veterinary College...........	1913	676	1775
1193, added	New York-American Veterinary College...........	1913	676	1775
	ELECTION LAW: (L. 1909, ch. 22, constituting cons. laws, ch. 17.)			
Schedule of articles	Generally.....................................	1911	891	2657
Schedule of articles	Generally.....................................	1913	800	2211
Art. 1, schedule of sections	Generally.....................................	1911	891	2658
Art. 2, tit.	Definitions...................................	1911	649	1666
2	Definitions...................................	1911	649	1666
2, added	Application of certain articles....................	1911	891	2658
2 renumbered 3, and amended	Definitions...................................	1911	891	2658
2, subd. 8	Party, defined................................	1911	872	2576
2, subd. 13	" Independent body " defined....................	1911	872	2576
3, repealed	Notice of primary.............................	1911	891	2726
Art. 2, schedule of sections	Enrollment of voters..........................	1911	891	2661
4, repealed	Organization and conduct of primaries.............	1911	891	2726
5, repealed	Qualifications of voters at primaries...............	1911	891	2726
6, repealed	Duties of chairman of primary	1911	891	2726
7, repealed	Watchers; canvass of votes at primary............	1911	891	2726
9, added	Delivery of enrollment blanks, registration not personal........	1911	891	2666
13, added	Certification and secrecy of enrollment, registration not personal...............	1911	891	2668
14a, added	Correction of enrollment lists.....................	1912	52	80
15, added	Enrollment in 1911............................	1911	891	2670
15	Enrollment for new political party.................	1913	587	1590
20, repealed	Application of art. 3............................	1911	891	2726
21, repealed	Definitions and construction	1911	649	1724
22 renumbered 4, and amended	Delivery of enrollment books.....................	1911	891	2661
22	Publication of enrollment........................	1913	587	1592
22	Publication of enrollment........................	1913	800	2212
23 renumbered 5, and amended	Enrollment books...............................	1911	891	2662
24, repealed	Enrollment books, certain cities..................	1911	891	2726
25 renumbered 6, and amended	Voting booths and enrollment boxes...............	1911	891	2662
26 renumbered 7, and amended	Enrollment blanks, and envelopes.................	1911	891	2663
27 renumbered 8, and amended	Delivery of enrollment blanks....................	1911	891	2665

I. CHANGES IN THE CONSOLIDATED LAWS, 1909–1913 — (*Continued*).

Section.	SUBJECT.	Year.	Chapter.	Page.
	ELECTION LAW — (*Continued*).			
28 renumbered 10, and amended	Enrollment...............................	1911	891	2666
29 renumbered 11, and amended	Enrollment boxes..........................	1911	891	2667
30 renumbered 12, and amended	Certification and secrecy of enrollment, registration personal...............................	1911	891	2667
31 renumbered 14, and amended	Opening of enrollment box..................	1911	891	2669
32, repealed	Special enrollment........................	1911	891	2726
33, repealed	Special enrollment for annexed territory..........	1911	891	2726
34, repealed	Special enrollment upon becoming of age..........	1911	891	2726
Art. 3, schedule of sections	Party organization.........................	1911	891	2677
35, repealed	Special enrollment after moving..............	1911	891	2726
35, added	Party committees..........................	1911	891	2677
36 renumbered 16, and amended	Duplicate enrollment books.................	1911	891	2671
36, added	State committee...........................	1911	891	2673
36	State committee...........................	1912	4	8
37 renumbered 17, and amended	Duplicate enrollment books at unofficial primaries....	1911	891	2671
37, added	Election of committees.....................	1911	891	2679
37	Election of committees.....................	1912	4	9
38 renumbered 18, and amended	Original enrollment books at official primaries......	1911	891	2671
38, added	Organization and rules of committees..............	1911	891	2680
39 renumbered 19, and amended	Right to enroll and vote at primaries..............	1911	891	2672
39, added	Review of election of committees..............	1911	891	2680
39	Review of election of committees..............	1912	4	10
40 renumbered 20	New enrollment books for changed districts.........	1911	891	2672
40, added	Removal of member of committee.................	1911	891	2681
41 renumbered 21, and amended	Transcripts of enrollment..........................	1911	891	2673
42 renumbered 22 and amended	Publication of enrollment....................	1911	891	2673
43 renumbered 23, and amended	Judicial review of enrollment....................	1911	891	2674
44 renumbered 24, and amended	Correction of enrollment..........................	1911	891	2676
Art. 4, schedule of sections	Generally..........................	1911	891	2681
45, repealed	Times and purposes of official primaries...........	1911	891	2726
45, added	Direct nominations, election of delegates...........	1911	891	2681
45, subd. 4	Official primary elections	1909	240	385
46, repealed	Congressional primaries.........................	1911	891	2726
46, added	Designations by party committees.................	1911	891	2682
47 renumbered 73, and amended	Expense of official primaries......................	1911	891	2696
47, added	Meetings of committees for designations............	1911	891	2683

I. CHANGES IN THE CONSOLIDATED LAWS, 1909-1913 — (*Continued*).

Section.	SUBJECT.	Year.	Chapter.	Page.
	ELECTION LAW — (*Continued*).			
48 renumbered				
74, and amended	Primary districts, officers and polling places.........	1911	891	2697
48, added	Designation by petition.......................	1911	891	2684
49 renumbered				
75, and amended	Notice of official primary.......................	1911	891	2698
49, added	Filing of designations...........................	1911	891	2686
50 renumbered				
92, and amended	Unofficial primaries...........................	1911	891	2712
50, added	Declinations................................	1911	891	2687
51 renumbered 76	Restrictions as to place of primaries............	1911	891	2699
51, added	Certification by secretary of state.............	1911	891	2687
52, repealed	Primary election officers.......................	1911	891	2726
52, added	Vacancies how filled.......	1911	891	2687
53, repealed	Appointment and removal, primary election officers..	1911	891	2726
53, added	Delegates to national conventions..............	1911	891	2689
53	Delegates to national conventions..............	1912	4	10
54, repealed	Chairman; inspectors; oath....................	1911	891	2726
54, added	Presidential electors..........................	1911	891	2689
55, repealed	Ballots, booths and supplies...................	1911	891	2726
55, added	Existing committees continued..................	1911	891	2690
55	Existing committees continued..................	1912	4	11
55	Existing committees continued..................	1913	587	1593
56, repealed	Voting at official primary elections.............	1911	891	2726
56, added	Contest; judicial review.......................	1911	891	2690
57 renumbered 72	Challenges at primaries.......................	1911	891	2696
57, added	Emblems....................................	1911	891	2691
58 renumbered				
83, and amended	Persons within guard-rail......................	1911	891	2704
58, added	Official primary ballot........................	1911	891	2692
58	Official primary ballot........................	1913	800	2212
59 renumbered				
84, and amended	Watchers; challengers; electioneering...........	1911	891	2704
60 renumbered				
85, and amended	Canvass of votes.............................	1911	891	2705
61	Proclamation of result........................	1909	240	385
61 renumbered				
87, and amended	Proclamation of result........................	1911	891	2709
62 renumbered				
88, and amended	Certificates of election; preservation of ballots......	1911	891	2709
63, repealed	Canvass, statement of result...................	1911	891	2726
64, repealed	Committees; rules and regulations of parties.......	1911	891	2726
65, repealed	Organisation of committees....................	1911	891	2726
66 renumbered				
111, and amended	Apportionment of delegates....................	1911	891	2714
67 renumbered				
112, and amended	Organisation of conventions...................	1911	891	2715
68, repealed	Contested seats..............................	1911	891	2726
69, repealed	Substitution of delegates......................	1911	891	2726
Art. 4a, schedule of sections, added	Conduct of primary elections....................	1911	891	2695
70, repealed	Jurisdiction of courts.........................	1911	891	2726
70, added	Organization and conduct of official primaries.......	1911	891	2695
71, repealed	Direct nomination at primary elections............	1911	891	2726
71, added	Qualifications of voters at official primaries.........	1911	891	2696

I. CHANGES IN THE CONSOLIDATED LAWS, 1909-1913 — (Continued).

Section.	SUBJECT.	Year.	Chap-ter.	Page.
	ELECTION LAW — (Continued).			
72, repealed	Application of art. 3 to political parties.............	1911	891	2726
73, repealed	Application of art. 3 to certain cities................	1911	891	2726
74 renumbered 94, and amended	Perjury	1911	891	2713
77, added	Vacancies, boards of primary election officers.......	1911	891	2699
78, added	Primary poll-clerks.................................	1911	891	2699
79, added	Ballots, booths and supplies........................	1911	891	2700
80, added	Delivery of ballots and manner of voting............	1911	891	2702
81, added	Unofficial ballots at primary elections...............	1911	891	2703
82, added	Preparation of ballots by voters....................	1911	891	2703
86, added	Intent of voters.....................................	1911	891	2706
89, added	Canvass; certificates of nomination or election......	1911	891	2710
90, repealed	Territory excepted from art. 4......................	1911	891	2726
90, added	Vacancies; determination of tie vote................	1911	891	2711
91, repealed	Application of art. 4................................	1911	891	2726
91, added	Party nominations for special elections and vacancies.	1911	891	2712
92, repealed	Enrollment books...................................	1911	891	2726
93, repealed	Entries in enrollment books........................	1911	891	2726
93, added	Penalty for violation of certain provisions...........	1911	891	2713
94, repealed	Special enrollments	1911	891	2726
95, repealed	Special enrollment upon becoming of age............	1911	891	2726
96, repealed	Special enrollment after moving....................	1911	891	2726
97, repealed	County clerks to compile enrollment lists...........	1911	891	2726
98, repealed	Enrollment lists, when to take effect...............	1911	891	2726
99, repealed	Who may be enrolled...............................	1911	891	2726
100, repealed	Enrollment lists and statements to be public records.	1911	891	2726
101, repealed	Conduct of primary elections.......................	1911	891	2726
102, repealed	Judicial review.....................................	1911	891	2726
103, repealed	Expenses of enrollment lists.......................	1911	891	2726
104, repealed	Penalty...	1911	891	2726
Art. 4b, schedule of sections, added	Conventions...	1911	891	2714
110, added	Vacancy, delegate to convention at official primary.	1911	891	2714
111, subd. 2	Election of delegates...............................	1912	4	11
113, added	State conventions; credentials of delegates.........	1911	891	2715
114, added	Voting at state conventions........................	1911	891	2716
120, repealed	Party nominations..................................	1911	891	2726
121	Party certificates of nominations...................	1911	891	2716
122	Independent nominations...........................	1911	891	2717
122	Independent nominations.	1913	800	2216
123	Independent certificates of nomination.............	1911	649	1668
125	Conflict in names or emblems......................	1911	649	1670
127	Places of filing certificates of nomination...........	1911	891	2718
128	Times of filing certificates of nomination...........	1911	891	2719
129	Certification of nominations by secretary of state....	1911	891	2719
130	Publication of nominations	1911	891	2720
131	Lists for town clerks and aldermen.................	1911	891	2721
133	Declination of nomination..........................	1911	891	2721
134	Objections to certificates of nomination.............	1911	649	1670
135	Filling vacancies in nominations....................	1911	891	2722
136	Certificates of new nominations....................	1911	891	2723
137	Death of candidate; official pasters................	1911	891	2723

I. CHANGES IN THE CONSOLIDATED LAWS, 1909–1913 — (*Continued*).

Section.	SUBJECT.	Year.	Chapter.	Page.
	ELECTION LAW — (*Continued*).			
150	Meetings for registration..........................	1911	649	1671
150	Meetings for registration..	1913	800	2216
151, repealed	Additional meetings for registration................	1911	649	1724
152	Registration......................................	1910	428	790
152	Registration......................................	1911	649	1671
153	Registration......................................	1911	649	1672
153	Registration......................................	1911	740	1974
155	Registration......................................	1910	428	790
155	Registration......................................	1911	649	1673
156, repealed	Registration.. :	1911	649	1724
157	Registration......................................	1911	649	1676
157	Registration......................................	1913	800	2217
158–160	Registration......................................	1911	649	1677
161	Registration for village elections..................	1910	424	784
169	Challenging applicants for registration.............	1910	428	795
169	Challenging applicants for registration.............	1911	649	1680
170, 171	Challenging applicants for registration.............	1911	649	1681
180	Custody of registers after election.................	1911	649	1682
181	Certifying number of registered electors............	1911	649	1682
184	Penalties...	1913	587	1593
Art. 7, tit.	Boards of elections................................	1911	649	1683
190	Boards of elections................................	1911	649	1683
190	Boards of elections................................	1911	740	1976
190	Boards of elections................................	1912	406	789
190	Boards of elections................................	1913	800	2218
191	Boards of elections, appointment, etc..............	1911	649	1683
192	Boards of elections, organization; reports.........	1911	649	1684
193	Salaries, commissioners of elections...............	1911	649	1685
193	Salaries, commissioners of elections...............	1912	406	789
193	Salaries, commissioners of elections...............	1913	800	2220
194	Commissioners of elections, appointment..........	1911	649	1685
195	Boards of elections, vacancies.....................	1911	649	1686
196	Boards of elections, bi-partisan...................	1911	649	1686
197	Boards of elections, employees....................	1911	649	1687
197	Boards of elections, employees....................	1912	406	790
197	Boards of elections, employees....................	1913	800	2220
198	Boards of elections, offices.......................	1911	649	1687
200	Boards of elections, expenses.....................	1911	649	1687
202, added	Custodian of primary records......................	1911	649	1688
203, added	Official seal of board of election..................	1911	649	1688
204, added	Filing statements of canvass, etc.................	1911	649	1688
205, added	Notices of elections..............................	1911	649	1689
206, added	Transfer of records...............................	1911	649	1689
207, added	Boards of elections, rules and regulations..........	1911	649	1689
208, added	Records...	1911	649	1689
210–215, repealed	Commissioner of elections, Erie county............	1911	649	1724
216	Seal for commissioner of elections, Erie county......	1910	433	811
216, repealed	Commissioner of elections, Erie county............	1911	649	1724
217, repealed	Commissioner of elections, Erie county............	1911	649	1724
218	Commissioner of elections, Erie county............	1910	431	807
218, repealed	Commissioner of elections, Erie county............	1911	649	1724

I. CHANGES IN THE CONSOLIDATED LAWS, 1909–1913 — (*Continued*).

Section.	SUBJECT.	Year.	Chapter.	Page.
	ELECTION LAW — (*Continued*).			
219	Commissioner of elections, Erie county............	1910	431	807
219, repealed	Commissioner of elections, Erie county............	1911	649	1724
220, repealed	Commissioner of elections, Erie county............	1911	649	1724
221	Commissioner of elections, Erie county............	1910	431	807
221, repealed	Commissioner of elections, Erie county............	1911	649	1724
230–242. repealed	Commissioner of elections, Monroe county..........	1911	649	1724
250–252, repealed	Commissioner of elections, Onondaga county........	1911	649	1724
253	Official seal of commissioner of elections, Onondaga county......................................	1910	172	320
253, repealed	Commissioner of elections, Onondaga county........	1911	649	1724
254–260, repealed	Commissioner of elections, Onondaga county........	1911	649	1724
270–281, repealed	Commissioner of elections, Westchester county......	1911	649	1724
Art. 12 renumbered art. 8	Times, places, notices, officers and expenses of elections....................................	1913	800	2230
291	Time of opening and closing polls.................	1911	649	1690
292	Vacancies in elective offices......................	1911	891	2725
293	Notices of elections.............................	1911	649	1690
294	Notice of submission of proposed constitutional amendments and propositions....................	1910	446	833
299	Designation of places for registry and voting........	1910	428	796
300a, added	Display of American flag at polling places..........	1913	783	1960
301	Publication of registration lists and polling places....	1913	587	1594
305	Election officers, examination as to qualifications.....	1911	649	1691
316	Ballot boxes....................................	1911	649	1691
Art. 13 renumbered art. 9	Ballots and stationery...........................	1913	800	2230
331	Form of general ballots..........................	1911	649	1692
331	Form of general ballots..........................	1911	872	2576
341	Providing ballots and stationery...................	1911	649	1697
Art. 14 renum- art. 10	Conduct of elections and canvass.................	1913	800	2230
352	Watchers..	1910	428	797
352	Watchers; challengers; electioneering..............	1911	649	1698
355	Poll clerks, general duties........................	1911	649	1699
355, subd. 2	Comparison of signatures........................	1910	428	798
358	Preparation of ballots by voters...................	1911	296	700
361	Challenges......................................	1910	428	801
361	Challenges......................................	1911	649	1701
362	Challenges......................................	1910	428	801
362	Preliminary oath................................	1911	649	1702
368	Intent of voters.................................	1911	296	701
368	Intent of electors................................	1911	649	1703
372	Statement of canvass, delivery to police............	1911	649	1706
377	Filing election papers............................	1911	649	1706
378	Filing of papers, New York city...................	1911	274	670
378	Filing of papers, New York city...................	1911	649	1707
379, repealed	Metropolitan district, additional requirements.......	1911	649	1724

I. CHANGES IN THE CONSOLIDATED LAWS, 1909–1913 — (Continued).

Section.	SUBJECT.	Year.	Chapter.	Page.
	ELECTION LAW—(Continued).			
Art. 15 renumbered art. 11	Voting machines................................	1913	800	2220
392	Voting machines, requirements..................	1911	649	1708
397	Voting machines, form of ballots................	1911	649	1709
400	Preparation of voting machine..................	1911	649	1709
401	Voting machines, instruction of election officers.....	1911	649	1711
413	Canvass and proclamation of vote...............	1909	240	386
413	Voting machines, canvass of vote...............	1911	649	1711
415	Voting machines..............................	1909	465	1115
419	Change in boundaries of election districts..........	1911	542	1222
Art. 16 renumbered art. 12	Boards of canvassers............................	1913	800	2220
430	County board of canvassers......................	1910	432	809
Art. 17 renumbered art. 13	United States senators, etc.......................	1913	800	2220
Art. 18, tit.	State superintendents of elections.................	1911	649	1713
Art. 18 renumbered art. 14	State superintendents of elections................	1913	800	2220
470, repealed	Metropolitan elections district.......... ˙.......	1911	649	1724
471	State superintendent of elections.................	1909	240	388
471	State superintendents of elections................	1911	649	1713
472–479	State superintendents of elections, deputies; powers and duties......................	1911	649	1174
480	Reports by hotel keepers.......................	1911	649	1718
481, 482	Affidavits by hotel keepers holding liquor licenses ..	1911	649	1719
483	Reports by police and certain departments..........	1911	649	1720
484	Lists of voters in lodging-houses, etc..............	1911	649	1721
485	Card lists of registered electors...................	1911	649	1722
486	Removal of deputies...........................	1911	649	1723
487	Salaries and expenses, superintendents and employees.	1911	649	1723
488	Annual report, state superintendents of elections.....	1911	649	1724
489, added	Authority of state superintendent of elections.......	1911	891	2725
Art. 19 renumbered art. 15	Soldiers' and sailors' elections.....................	1913	800	2220
518	Application of provisions of penal law.............	1909	240	388
Art. 20 renumbered art. 16	Corrupt practices..............................	1913	800	2220
540–542, 544, 546	Expenditure of money at primary elections........	1910	429	803
548	Statements of campaign receipts and expenses......	1910	438	820
562, added	Party funds not to be expended for primary purposes.	1911	891	2726
Art. 21 renumbered art. 17	Laws repealed; when to take effect...............	1913	800	2220
	EXECUTIVE LAW: (L. 1909, ch. 23, constituting cons. laws, ch. 18.)			
20	Salary of secretary of state.....................	1910	691	2003
34, repealed	Publication of statement of names changed........	1913	617	1643
40	Salary of comptroller..........................	1910	691	2004
41	Deputies to the comptroller.....................	1910	189	357
41	Deputies to the comptroller.....................	1911	568	1294

I. CHANGES IN THE CONSOLIDATED LAWS, 1909–1913 — (*Continued*).

Section.	SUBJECT.	Year.	Chapter.	Page.
	EXECUTIVE LAW — (*Continued*).			
43	Supervision of money paid into court..............	1910	193	364
45, added	Posting of bulletins by comptroller................	1910	159	282
45, added	Examiners appointed by comptroller..............	1911	213	488
50	Salary of state treasurer.........................	1910	691	2004
52	Deputy state treasurer..........................	1909	268	469
54	State treasurer, employee to sign receipts.........	1913	441	918
60	Salary of attorney-general.......................	1910	691	2004
60	Clerk hire and expenses of attorney-general........	1911	204	477
61	Attorney-general, deputies.......................	1911	204	477
62, subd. 2	Attorney-general, expenses.......................	1911	14	17
65	Counsel employed by attorney-general...........	1911	791	2098
68, added	Attorney-general; duty in actions where constitutionality of statute involved......................	1913	442	919
70	Salary of state engineer.........................	1910	691	2005
84	No fees by or to state officers in certain cases.......	1913	570	1549
100	State superintendent of weights and measures.......	1910	608	2016
104	Fees paid by notaries public......................	1909	240	388
105	Notaries public................................	1911	668	1756
105, subd. 2	Notaries public................................	1913	208	369
105, subd. 3, added	Notaries, Bronx county..........................	1913	248	442
105a added	Notaries who are stockholders, etc., of corporations..	1913	334	625
110, added	Board of geographic names.......................	1913	187	342
	FOREST, FISH AND GAME LAW: (L. 1909, ch. 24, constituting cons. laws, ch. 19.)			
	(*All parts of the forest, fish and game law, not heretofore repealed, with the exception of § 113, were repealed by L. 1912, chaps. 318 and 444. For status of § 113 see foot note, L. 1909, p. 1136.*)			
2	Commissioner..................................	1909	474	1136
4	Office force....................................	1909	474	1137
6	Disposal of game and fish seized..................	1911	438	976
8	Summary of law................................	1909	533	1336
8	Compilation and distribution of law................	1911	423	957
11	Game protectors...............................	1909	474	1137
11	Number of game protectors......................	1910	675	1951
13	Compensation of protectors......................	1909	474	1138
13	Compensation of protectors......................	1910	657	1753
14	Powers of protectors............................	1909	474	1139
19	Actions for penalties............................	1911	835	2343
20	Costs, actions by the people.....................	1911	835	2344
21	Moneys recovered, actions by the people..........	1911	835	2344
32a, added	Game and bird refuges..........................	1910	657	1754
37	Boundaries of Saint Lawrence reservation.........	1910	313	557
40	Powers of commissioner..........................	1909	474	1139
40	Powers of commissioner..........................	1910	657	1755
40, subd. 6	Compromise of actions, approval by governor.......	1911	835	2344

I. CHANGES IN THE CONSOLIDATED LAWS, 1909–1913 — (*Continued*).

Section.	SUBJECT.	Year.	Chapter.	Page.
	FOREST, FISH AND GAME LAW — (*Continued*).			
47	Description of land appropriated for forest preserve..	1911	835	2345
56	Cutting timber...................................	1909	474	1141
67	Auditor of fire accounts and fire inspections.........	1909	474	1141
68	Fire patrol by railroads...........................	1909	474	1141
69	Fire districts and patrols..........................	1909	474	1142
69	Fire districts and patrols..........................	1910	657	1756
70	Superintendents of fire............................	1909	474	1143
71	Compensation of fire patrolmen and fire fighters.....	1909	474	1145
72	Railroads in forest lands..........................	1910	476	916
73	Fires to clear land...............................	1909	474	1146
73	Fires to clear land...............................	1910	657	1757
73	Fires to clear land...............................	1911	529	1202
74	Forest fires prohibited............................	1909	474	1146
74	Forest fires prohibited............................	1910	657	1758
75a, added	Suspension of open season.........................	1909	474	1147
75b, added	Statistics of forest products.......................	1909	474	1148
76	Deer; open season................................	1909	474	1148
76	Deer; open season................................	1910	657	1759
76	Deer; open season................................	1911	583	1341
77	Possession of deer or venison......................	1909	474	1149
77	Possession of deer or venison......................	1910	657	1760
77	Possession of deer or venison......................	1911	438	976
78	Transportation of deer............................	1909	474	1149
78	Transportation of deer............................	1910	657	1760
78a, added	Breeding and sale of elk and deer..................	1911	438	977
80	Wild moose, elk, caribou and antelope..............	1911	438	976
81	Black and gray squirrels...........................	1910	657	1761
81	Black and gray squirrels...........................	1911	438	977
81	Black and gray squirrels...........................	1911	592	1354
82	Hares and rabbits................................	1909	240	389
82	Hares and rabbits................................	1909	474	1150
82	Hares and rabbits................................	1910	657	1761
82	Hares and rabbits................................	1911	438	977
82	Hares and rabbits................................	1911	635	1439
84	Mink, skunk, muskrat and sable....................	1909	474	1150
84	Mink, skunk, muskrat and sable....................	1910	657	1761
84	Mink, skunk, muskrat and sable....................	1911	238	517
84a, added	Propagation of skunks............................	1911	238	517
85a, added	Sale of game prohibited...........................	1911	438	980
86	Penalties..	1911	438	980
87	Wild fowl; open season............................	1910	657	1762
87	Wild fowl; open season............................	1911	438	981
88	Ducks, geese, brant and swan......................	1909	474	1150
88	Manner of killing wild fowl........................	1910	657	1763
88	Manner of killing wild fowl........................	1911	438	981
89	Quail; open season................................	1911	438	981
90	Woodcock; open season............................	1911	438	981
91	Grouse; open season..............................	1909	474	1150
91	Grouse; open season..............................	1911	438	982
92	Grouse, woodcock and quail, sale prohibited........	1909	474	1150
92	Grouse, woodcock and quail not to be bought.......	1910	657	1763
92, repealed	Grouse, woodcock and quail not to be sold or bought.	1911	438	982

I.   CHANGES IN THE CONSOLIDATED LAWS, 1909–1913 — (Continued).

Section.	SUBJECT.	Year.	Chapter.	Page.
	FOREST, FISH AND GAME LAW — (Continued).			
92, added	Sale of dead game and song birds prohibited........	1911	438	982
93	Woodcock, grouse and quail not to be possessed	1910	657	1764
93	Woodcock, grouse and quail not to be possessed....	1910	664	1862
93	Woodcock, grouse and quail not to be possessed	1911	438	982
96	Pheasants..................................	1910	657	1764
96	Pheasants..................................	1911	170	269
96	Pheasants..................................	1911	627	1422
96a, added	Breeding of pheasants, mallard and black ducks....	1911	438	983
96b, added	Mammals and birds, importation and sale.........	1911	438	985
96c, added	Fees for affixing tags............................	1911	438	985
98	Wild birds protected...........................	1909	474	1151
98	Sale of plumage of birds........................	1910	256	459
103	Birds and game not to be transported.............	1910	657	1765
104	Hunting license................................	1911	854	2302
105	Penalties.....................	1910	657	1765
106	Trout; open season............................	1909	474	1152
106	Trout; open season............................	1910	657	1766
106	Trout; open season............................	1911	188	426
106	Trout; open season............................	1911	592	1354
109	Lake trout and whitefish; open season.............	1909	474	1152
109	Lake trout and whitefish; open season.............	1910	657	1766
109	Lake trout and whitefish; open season.............	1910	663	1861
109	Lake trout and whitefish; open season.............	1911	582	1339
113, repealed	Salmon. (See note, L. 1909, p. 1136)...........	1909	474	1136
115	Black bass....................................	1910	657	1767
117	Pickerel and pike..............................	1909	474	1153
117	Blue pike, Lake Ontario........................	1911	312	728
122	Tip-ups.......................................	1910	657	1767
123	Eel weirs and pots.............................	1910	657	1767
124	Taking minnows for bait........................	1909	474	1153
124	Taking minnows for bait........................	1911	592	1355
126	Frostfish and whitefish.........................	1909	474	1153
126	Frostfish and whitefish taken with nets............	1910	657	1768
128	Thumping, Dutchess county.....................	1911	591	1353
134	Obstruction of streams.........................	1909	474	1154
135	Explosives prohibited...........................	1910	657	1768
143	Penalties.....................................	1910	657	1769
146	Nets in Chaumont bay and adjacent waters	1909	474	1154
147	Nets in Wappinger's creek......................	1910	657	1769
147	Nets in Hudson and Delaware rivers..............	1911	591	1353
150	Fishing in Seneca and Cayuga lakes..............	1909	474	1154
150	Spearing in Cayuga lake........................	1911	299	710
150	Fishing in Seneca and Cayuga lakes..............	1911	582	1340
151	Fishing in Otsego lake..........................	1910	657	1770
152	Fishing in Chautauqua and Cattaraugus counties....	1909	474	1155
152	Fishing in Chautauqua and Cattaraugus counties....	1911	592	1356
153	Spearing, hooking and set lines..................	1909	474	1155
153	Spearing, hooking and set lines..................	1910	657	1770
153	Spearing, hooking and set lines..................	1911	580	1336
153	Spearing, hooking and set lines..................	1911	590	1351
154	Warren, Essex, Washington and Saratoga counties, certain waters.................................	1910	657	1772

I. Changes in the Consolidated Laws, 1909–1913 — (*Continued*).

Section.	SUBJECT.	Year.	Chapter.	Page.
	FOREST, FISH AND GAME LAW— (*Continued*).			
154	Pike-perch and pike and perch, Lake George........	1911	530	1204
154	Fishing in Lake George..........................	1911	636	1440
154a, added	Open season, certain fish, Schuyler county.........	1911	377	860
154b, added	Spearing suckers, Schuyler and Chemung counties....	1911	378	861
154b, added	Fishing with set lines, Schuyler county............	1911	589	1350
157	Suckers, Sullivan county.........................	1910	655	1752
157	Suckers, Ulster county..........................	1911	508	1165
168	Deer, Long Island district.......................	1910	657	1772
170	Wild fowl, Long Island district...................	1910	657	1772
170a, repealed	Brant, Long Island district......................	1910	657	1773
174a	Pheasants and woodcock on Robbins and Gardners islands...	1910	656	1753
184	Superintendent of marine fisheries................	1909	240	390
187, repealed	Duties of superintendent of marine fisheries........	1911	647	1550
188, repealed	Reports of superintendent of marine fisheries.......	1911	647	1550
195–204, repealed	Shellfish.......................................	1911	647	1550
207, repealed	Polluting waters................................	1911	647	1550
208, repealed	Garbage, Long Island sound......................	1911	647	1550
210–215, repealed	Shellfish grounds; oyster beds....................	1911	647	1550
224	Leases of land for shellfish culture................	1909	240	390
224, repealed	Lands for shellfish culture.......................	1911	647	1550
240	Definitions.....................................	1909	474	1156
240, subd. 14	Open season, defined............................	1911	171	270
240, subd. 18, added	Plumage of birds, defined........................	1910	256	459
241	Storage in close season..........................	1911	438	985
	GENERAL BUSINESS LAW: (L. 1909, ch. 25, constituting cons. laws, ch. 20.)			
2–4	Standards of weights and measures................	1910	187	351
5	Units of capacity of measure......................	1909	414	898
5a, 5b, added	Milk and cream bottles..........................	1910	470	909
8	Number of pounds to the bushel..................	1910	187	353
9, repealed	Barrels of apples, quinces, pears and potatoes.......	1912	81	137
11	State superintendent of weights and measures, duties....................................	1910	187	353
13	County sealers..................................	1910	187	354
14, repealed	Town sealers...................................	1910	187	356
15 renumbered 14, and amended	City sealers....................................	1910	187	355
16 renumbered 15, and amended	Weights and measures to be sealed................	1910	187	356
16, added	Methods of sale of certain commodities............	1912	81	134
16a, added	Prescribed sizes of containers....................	1912	81	135
16b, added	Standard grape basket...........................	1913	426	898
17, repealed	Standards in possession of state superintendent......	1910	187	356
17, added	Net contents of containers to be indicated..........	1912	81	135
17a, added	Sections not applicable to certain containers........	1912	81	135
17a	Sections not applicable to certain containers........	1913	514	1360

I. CHANGES IN THE CONSOLIDATED LAWS, 1909–1913 — (*Continued*).

Section.	SUBJECT.	Year.	Chapter.	Page.
	GENERAL BUSINESS LAW — (*Continued*).			
17b, added	Guaranty of container by wholesaler...............	1912	81	136
17c, added	Definitions...........................	1912	81	136
18, added	Examination of containers; prosecution of violation..	1912	81	136
18a, added	Penalties............................	1912	81	137
18a	Penalties; sale of certain commodities..............	1913	426	899
20, repealed	Conduct of auction sales......................	1911	571	1326
25, added	Private banking.............................	1910	348	614
25	Private banking............................	1911	393	896
25, added	Books to be kept by auctioneers.................	1910	640	1712
26, added	Private banking............................	1910	348	617
26, added	Books to be kept by auctioneers.................	1910	640	1713
27, added	Private banking............................	1910	348	618
27	Private banking............................	1911	393	900
27, added	Books to be kept by auctioneers.................	1910	640	1713
28, added	Private banking............................	1910	348	618
28	Private banking............................	1911	393	900
28, added	Books to be kept by auctioneers.................	1910	640	1713
29, added	Private banking............................	1910	348	618
29a, added	Private banking............................	1910	348	618
29a	Private banking............................	1911	393	900
29b, 29c, added	Private banking............................	1910	348	618
29d, added	Private banking............................	1910	348	618
29d	Private banking............................	1911	393	901
29e, added	Private banking............................	1910	348	618
29e	Private banking............................	1911	393	902
29f, 29g, added	Private banking............................	1910	348	618
40	Pawnbroker's license, certain cities..............	1909	240	391
41	Licenses, how obtained; penalty.................	1909	240	391
Art. 5a (§§ 55–59.				
59a–59k), added	Licensing small loan brokers.................	1913	579	1563
70	Private detectives..........................	1909	529	1323
70	Private detectives..........................	1910	515	1190
71	Private detectives..........................	1909	529	1323
71	Private detectives..........................	1910	515	1191
72	Private detectives..........................	1909	529	1325
72	Private detectives..........................	1910	515	1193
73	Private detectives..........................	1909	529	1325
73	Private detectives..........................	1910	515	1194
73a–73c, added	Private detectives..........................	1910	515	1195
74	Private detectives..........................	1909	529	1325
74	Private detectives..........................	1910	515	1196
74a, 74b, added	Private detectives..........................	1910	515	1197
75	Private detectives..........................	1909	529	1325
75	Private detectives..........................	1910	515	1197
76, added	Private detectives..........................	1910	515	1198
80	Certified public accountants..................	1913	443	930
Art. 8a	Certified shorthand reporters..................	1913	249	443
Art. 8a, schedule of sections	Certified shorthand reporters..................	1913	249	444
85, added	Certified shorthand reporters; qualifications.........	1911	587	1346
85 renumbered 86, and amended	Certified shorthand reporters; qualifications.........	1913	249	444

I. CHANGES IN THE CONSOLIDATED LAWS, 1909–1913 — (*Continued*).

Section.	SUBJECT.	Year.	Chapter.	Page.
	GENERAL BUSINESS LAW — (*Continued*).			
85, added	Certified shorthand reporters; defined............	1913	249	444
86, added	Certified shorthand reporters; examination.........	1911	587	1347
86 renumbered 87, and amended	Certified shorthand reporters; examination and cer-			
	tification.....................................	1913	249	444
87, added	Certified shorthand reporters; exceptions..........	1911	587	1347
87 renumbered 88, and amended	Certified shorthand reporters; exceptions..........	1913	249	445
88, added	Certified shorthand reporters; violations...........	1911	587	1347
88 renumbered 89a	Certified shorthand reporters; violations...........	1913	249	445
89, added	Certified shorthand reporters; extension of waiver..	1913	249	445
150, repealed	Ticket agents...................................	1910	348	621
150, repealed	Ticket agents...................................	1910	349	622
150, added	Ticket agents...................................	1910	349	622
150	License to sell transportation tickets..............	1911	578	1334
151, repealed	Ticket agents...................................	1910	348	621
151, repealed	Ticket agents...................................	1910	349	622
151, added	Ticket agents...................................	1910	349	622
152, repealed	Ticket agents...................................	1910	348	621
152, repealed	Ticket agents...................................	1910	349	622
152, added	Ticket agents...................................	1910	349	622
153, repealed	Ticket agents...................................	1910	348	621
153, repealed	Ticket agents...................................	1910	349	622
153, added	Ticket agents...................................	1910	349	622
154, repealed	Ticket agents...................................	1910	348	621
154, repealed	Ticket agents...................................	1910	349	622
154, added	Ticket agents...................................	1910	349	622
Art. 11	Employment agencies............................	1910	700	2021
191, subd. 3	Relicensing of employment agencies................	1912	261	487
207	Inn-keeper's lien................................	1910	215	395
208	Inn-keeper's lien................................	1910	215	395
209, added	Inn-keeper's lien................................	1910	215	397
Art. 12a	Exhibitions of moving pictures....................	1913	308	573
209, added	Exhibitions of moving pictures....................	1911	756	2018
209	Exhibitions of moving pictures....................	1913	308	574
210, added	Exhibitions of moving pictures....................	1911	756	2018
210	Exhibitions of moving pictures....................	1913	308	574
211, added	Exhibitions of moving pictures....................	1911	756	2020
211 renumbered 212, and amended	Exhibitions of moving pictures....................	1913	308	576
211, added	Exhibitions of moving pictures....................	1913	308	576
212, added	Exhibitions of moving pictures....................	1911	756	2021
212 renumbered 216	Exhibitions of moving pictures....................	1913	308	578
213–215, added	Exhibitions of moving pictures....................	1913	308	577
Art. 15, tit.	Hops, hay and straw............................	1913	96	164
253	Pressing of hay and straw........................	1913	96	164
341	Monopolies.....................................	1910	633	1672
345	Monopolies.....................................	1910	394	724
367, added	Trademarks....................................	1909	475	1157

2

I. CHANGES IN THE CONSOLIDATED LAWS, 1909–1913 — (*Continued*).

Section.	SUBJECT.	Year.	Chapter.	Page.
	GENERAL BUSINESS LAW — (*Continued*).			
383–389, 389a, added	Sale of coal, coke and charcoal....................	1911	825	2331
391	Small fruit packages or baskets....................	1909	414	898
392a, added	Marking mattresses..............................	1913	503	1188
	GENERAL CITY LAW: (L. 1909, ch. 26, constituting cons. laws, ch. 21.)			
4, repealed	Filing financial reports with secretary of state.......	1910	217	399
4, added	Removal of officers in third-class cities.............	1913	770	1924
12	Money for Memorial day, cities of third class.......	1909	288	522
13	Moneys, how expended...........................	1909	288	522
13a, added	Moneys for annual conference of city officials.......	1911	622	1417
17	Crematories for disposal of garbage...............	1910	467	907
18, added	License to operate moving picture apparatus........	1911	252	637
Art. 2a (§§ 19–24), added	Powers of cities.................................	1913	247	436
57	Article limited..................................	1913	753	1899
60–68, added	Regulation of plastering..........................	1911	156	249
Art. 8 (§§ 120–122) renumbered art. 11a (§§ 165–167)	Art commission.................................	1911	718	1937
Art. 8 (§§ 120–129, 129a–129c), added	Dog license, third class cities......................	1911	718	1937
150–160, repealed	Protection of purchasers of coal...................	1911	825	2334
	GENERAL CONSTRUCTION LAW: (L. 1909, ch. 27, constituting cons. laws, ch. 22.)			
20	Method of computing time........................	1910	347	613
24	Columbus day..................................	1909	112	174
	GENERAL CORPORATION LAW: (L. 1909, ch. 28, constituting cons. laws, ch. 23.)			
Schedule of articles	Receivers......................................	1909	240	392
5	Corporate names or titles.........................	1913	479	1001
6	Corporate names................................	1911	638	1444
6	Corporate names................................	1912	2	5
6	Corporate names................................	1913	24	45
12	Property of nonstock corporations.................	1909	276	483
12	Property of nonstock corporations.................	1911	581	1339
20	Real estate of foreign corporations................	1910	68	112
22	Prohibition of banking powers....................	1911	771	2050
37	Extension of corporate existence..................	1913	306	509

I. CHANGES IN THE CONSOLIDATED LAWS, 1909-1913 — (*Continued*).

Section.	SUBJECT.	Year.	Chap-ter.	Page.
	GENERAL CORPORATION LAW—(*Continued*).			
38	Revival of corporate existence.....................	1911	63	87
60, 62, 63	Change of names of certain kinds of corporations....	1910	296	534
64	Change of name of corporation....................	1913	721	1836
91a, added	Actions against officers.........................	1913	633	1685
102	Service of summons in action to dissolve corporation.	1912	204	367
106	Permanent receiver.............................	1909	240	392
155	Notice to creditors by receiver...................	1909	240	392
158	Notice of accounting by receiver.................	1909	240	393
160	Claims, when barred...........................	1909	240	394
174	Petition for voluntary dissolution................	1909	240	394
178	Action upon petition...........................	1909	240	395
191	Permanent receiver.............................	1909	240	396
225, added	Security of receiver............................	1909	240	396
226, added	Removal of receiver; new bond...................	1909	240	397
227, added	Notice to sureties upon accounting...............	1909	240	397
232	Receiver's title................................	1909	240	397
232	Receiver's title to property......................	1913	766	1920
239, subd. 1	General powers of receivers......................	1913	766	1920
269	Notice of final accounting.......................	1909	240	397
	GENERAL MUNICIPAL LAW:			
	(L. 1909, ch. 29, constituting cons. laws, ch. 24.)			
6	Funded debts..................................	1910	677	1965
10	Registry of municipal bonds.....................	1910	129	228
21, added	Maximum rate of interest on municipal bonds.......	1911	573	1327
22-29, added	Legalizing bonds or proceedings for issuance........	1911	769	2044
30	Financial reports of municipal corporations........	1911	544	1224
34	Compensation of examiners of municipal accounts...	1910	301	540
72a, added	Acquisition and development of forest lands........	1912	·74	117
76	Water rights, certain counties....................	1909	240	398
88, added	Separate specifications for certain contract work....	1912	514	1043
126-135, added	Public general hospitals.........................	1910	558	1277
135a, added	Workshop in connection with tuberculosis hospitals..	1913	341	636
136-139, 139a, 139b, added	Colonies for inebriates; boards of inebriety.........	1911	700	1881
140-143, 145	Trusts for aiding and instructing children..........	1910	163	299
200a, added	Volunteer firemen..............................	1910	119	182
202	Certificate of exempt volunteer fireman...........	1909	240	398
Art. 12a (§§ 234-239, 239a), added	City and village planning commissions.............	1913	699	1809
	HIGHWAY LAW:			
	(L. 1909, ch. 30, constituting cons. laws, ch. 25.)			
2	Definition of construction.......................	1911	646	1482
2	Definition of construction.......................	1912	83	138
2	Definitions...................................	1913	80	136

I. CHANGES IN THE CONSOLIDATED LAWS, 1909-1913 — *(Continued)*.

Section.	SUBJECT.	Year.	Chapter.	Page.
	HIGHWAY LAW — *(Continued)*.			
3	Classification of highways.........................	1910	567	1400
3	Classification of highways.........................	1912	83	139
11	State commission of highways......................	1911	646	1483
11	State commission; commissioner of highways........	1913	80	137
12	State superintendent of highways, oath of office, undertaking....................................	1911	646	1484
12	Commissioner of highways; oath; undertaking.......	1913	80	138
14	Salaries and expenses.............................	1911	646	1484
14 renumbered 18, and amended	Salaries and expenses.............................	1913	80	142
14, added	Deputies, secretary, chief auditor.................	1913	80	138
15	Powers and duties of commissioner.................	1913	80	139
16	Division of state; division engineers...............	1911	646	1485
16	Division engineers................................	1913	80	141
17	Duties of division engineers.......................	1911	646	1485
17	Duties of division engineers.......................	1913	80	141
18 renumbered 20, and amended	Blank forms and town accounts....................	1913	80	143
19 renumbered 21, and amended	Examination of accounts and records..............	1913	80	144
19, added	Appointment of officers, clerks and employees.......	1913	80	143
20 renumbered 22, and amended	Condemnation of bridges..........................	1913	80	144
21	Estimate of cost of maintenance of highways........	1912	83	139
21 renumbered 23, and amended	Estimate of cost of maintenance....................	1913	80	144
22 renumbered 24, and amended	Rules and regulations for highways................	1913	80	145
25, added	Patented material or articles......................	1913	80	145
30	Expenses of county superintendent.................	1910	567	1401
31	County superintendent............................	1910	224	409
33	Duties of district or county superintendent.........	1911	646	1486
33, subd. 2a, added	Statements of amounts necessary for county roads...	1910	567	1401
47, subd. 7	Removal of weeds and brush.......................	1910	567	1402
48	Contracts; construction of highways and bridges....	1913	621	1665
53, repealed	Removal of obstruction from ditches, culverts, etc...	1912	83	147
53a, added	Temporary obstruction of highways...............	1910	567	1402
53a	Temporary obstruction of highways...............	1913	80	145
54	Weeds and obstructions...........................	1911	151	243
59a, added	Interest on damages for change of grade............	1910	701	2035
74	Liability of town for defective highways............	1913	389	829
77	Closing highways for repair........................	1911	646	1487
78, added	Labor system for removing snow...................	1909	488	1176
78	Labor system for removing snow...................	1910	136	243
79, added	Assessment of labor for removal of snow...........	1909	488	1176
79	Assessment of labor for removal of snow...........	1910	136	243
80, added	Lists of persons assessed for removal of snow.......	1909	488	1177
81, added	Appeals by non-resident; separate assessments; tenants....................................	1909	488	1177
81, added	District foremen; levy of unworked taxes...........	1910	136	245

I. CHANGES IN THE CONSOLIDATED LAWS, 1909-1913 — (Continued).

Section.	SUBJECT.	Year.	Chapter.	Page.
	HIGHWAY LAW — (Continued).			
81 renumbered 82, and amended	Appeals by non-resident; separate assessments; tenants................................... ...	1910	136	245
93	Extraordinary repairs; highways and bridges........	1913	621	1668
101, subd. 7, added	Amount of state aid in certain cases..............	1913	375	800
120, subd. 1	State highway, route 1............................	1911	570	1297
120, subd. 2	State highway, route 2............................	1910	648	1744
120, subd. 3	State highway, route 3............................	1912	157	288
120, subd. 3a, added	State highway, route 3a...........................	1911	260	647
120, subd. 4	State highway, route 4............................	1911	96	142
120, subd. 4	State highway, route 4............................	1911	747	2007
120, subd. 4a, added	State highway, route 4a...........................	1911	807	2132
120, subd. 4b, added	State highway, route 4b...........................	1912	474	993
120, subd. 5	State highway, route 5............................	1910	573	1409
120, subd. 5a, added	State highway, route 5a...........................	1911	616	1392
120, subd. 5b, added	State highway, route 5b...........................	1911	784	2089
120, subd. 5c, added	State highway, route 5c...........................	1913	784	1981
120, subd. 6	State highway, route 6............................	1910	573	1409
120, subd. 6	State highway, route 6............................	1911	472	1076
120, subd. 6a, added	State highway, route 6a...........................	1911	660	1744
120, subd. 7	State highway, route 7............................	1911	261	648
120, subd. 7	State highway, route 7............................	1911	751	2014
120, subd. 7a, added	State highway, route 7a...........................	1912	183	326
120, subd. 14	State highway, route 14...........................	1910	648	1745
120, subd. 15	State highway, route 15...........................	1911	752	2015
120, subd. 15	State highway, route 15...........................	1912	473	991
120, subd. 18	State highway, route 18...........................	1911	89	127
120, subd. 22a, added	State highway, route 22a..........................	1913	785	1981
120, subd. 22b, added	State highway, route 22b..........................	1913	785	1982
120, subd. 22c, added	State highway, route 22c..........................	1913	785	1982
120, subd. 23	State highway, route 23...........................	1910	573	1411
120, subd. 23a, added	State highway route, 23a..........................	1912	535	1099
120, subd. 26	State highway, route 26...........................	1910	573	1411
120, subd. 30	State highway, route 30...........................	1910	648	1745
120, subd. 30	State highway, route 30...........................	1911	716	1935
120, subd. 30	State highway, route 30...........................	1912	51	78
120, subd. 30	State highway, route 30...........................	1912	477	995
120, subd. 30a, added	State highway, route 30a..........................	1910	650	1748
120, subd. 32	State highway, route 32...........................	1910	648	1746

I. Changes in the Consolidated Laws, 1909–1913 — (*Continued*).

Section.	SUBJECT.	Year.	Chapter.	Page.
	HIGHWAY LAW—(*Continued*).			
120, subd. 32	State highway, route 32.........................	1911	179	280
120, subd. 37	State highway, route 37.........................	1910	648	1746
120, subd. 37	State highway, route 37.........................	1912	475	993
120, subd. 37a, added	State highway, route 37a........................	1912	476	994
120, subd. 37a, added	State highway, route 37a........................	1912	542	1112
120, subd. 37b, added	State highway, route 37b........................	1912	542	1113
120, subd. 38, added	State highway, route 38.........................	1909	504	1280
120, subd. 38a, added	State highway, route 38a........................	1912	179	323
120, subd. 39, added	State highway, route 39.........................	1910	649	1747
120, subd. 39a, added	State highway, route 39a........................	1911	531	1205
120, subd. 39b, added	State highway, route 39b........................	1911	662	1746
120, subd. 41, added	State highway, route 41.........................	1911	395	908
120, subd. 42, added	State highway, route 42.'........................	1911	614	1390
120, subd. 43, added	State highway, route 43.........................	1911	166	264
120, subd. 43, added	State highway, route 43.........................	1911	259	647
120, subd. 45, added	State highway, route 45.........................	1911	356	810
120, subd. 45	State highway, route 45.........................	1912	57	87
120, subd. 46, added	State highway, route 46.........................	1911	320	741
121	Apportionment of mileage.......................	1911	646	1488
122	Construction or improvement of county highways...	1912	83	140
123	Preliminary resolution of supervisors..............	1909	487	1175
125	Maps and plans................................	1911	646	1489
126	Maps and plans................................	1911	646	1490
128	Final resolution of supervisors...................	1909	240	399
129	Cost of county highways........................	1910	247	437
129	Order of construction of county highways..........	1911	646	1490
129	Order of construction of county highways..........	1912	83	140
132	Contracts for construction or improvement of highways.........	1911	646	1491
132	Contracts for work on highways.................	1913	517	1362
133	Acceptance of state highway....................	1911	646	1491
134	Acceptance of county highway..................	1911	646	1492
137	State roads through cities of third class...........	1910	233	421
137	County highways through cities of third class.......	1911	88	125
137	Highways through cities of second class...........	1912	88	155
137	Highways in villages and cities..................	1913	131	218
137	Highways in municipalities......................	1913	319	595
138	Connecting highways in cities of third class........	1911	88	126

I. CHANGES IN THE CONSOLIDATED LAWS, 1909–1913 — (*Continued*).

Section.	SUBJECT.	Year.	Chap-ter.	Page.
	HIGHWAY LAW — (*Continued*).			
138	Connecting highways in cities of second class.......	1912	88	156
138a, added	State and county highways of additional width......	1911	375	857
139	Cost of county highways.........................	1910	247	438
139	Cost of county highways.........................	1912	83	141
140	Cost of county highways.........................	1910	247	438
141	Cost of county highways.........................	1912	83	141
142	County or town may borrow money...............	1909	486	1174
142	Share of counties and towns for highway improve-ment....................................	1910	580	1418
142	County or town may borrow money...............	1912	83	142
142	County or town may borrow money...............	1913	538	1411
142	County or town may borrow money...............	1913	623	1670
142a, added	Pavement about rails of street surface railroads.....	1913	177	325
143, repealed	Cost of county highways.........................	1910	247	438
143, added	Expense of constructing highways, cities of second and third class............................	1912	88	157
146	Railroads on highways..........................	1911	646	1492
146	Railroads and other works on highways...........	1913	80	146
150	Petition to acquire lands for highways............	1911	503	1157
152	Duties of commissioners appointed to condemn lands	1911	503	1158
153	Awards for lands condemned.....................	1911	503	1159
154	Commissioners' fees............................	1912	182	325
155	Sale of unnecessary portion of highway...........	1911	552	1253
158, added	Superintendents of highways for Indian reservations.	1910	46	73
158	Superintendents of highways for Indian reservations.	1913	474	994
159, added	Moneys for highways on Indian reservations.......	1910	46	73
159	Highways within Indian reservations..............	1911	646	1493
159	Highways within Indian reservations..............	1913	474	995
160, added	Maintenance of detours during construction.......	1912	83	143
170	Maintenance of state and county highways........	1911	646	1494
170	Maintenance of state and county highways........	1912	83	143
170	Maintenance of state and county highways........	1913	80	146
171–175	Maintenance of state and county highways........	1912	83	144
176	Liability of state for damages....................	1910	570	1406
176	Liability of state for damages....................	1912	83	147
177	Maintenance of highways in villages..............	1911	646	1495
177, repealed	Maintenance of highways in villages..............	1912	83	148
178	State's share of maintaining certain county roads....	1910	165	304
178	State's share of maintenance of county roads.......	1910	567	1402
178	County roads when to become state or county high-ways....................................	1911	362	833
192	Application to alter, discontinue or lay out highway.	1913	472	993
193	Application for condemnation commissioners........	1910	344	606
195	Notice of meeting for laying out highway...........	1912	246	466
200	Laying out highways............................	1911	624	1419
203	Towns may borrow money for highways...........	1911	498	1119
208	Construction and alteration of highways..........	1913	318	594
263, added	Abolition of toll bridges........................	1909	146	225
263	Resolution for abolition of toll bridges............	1910	569	1404
264, added	Investigation by state commission.................	1909	146	225
264	Investigation by state commission.................	1910	569	1405
265, added	Acquisition by attorney-general..................	1909	146	226

I. CHANGES IN THE CONSOLIDATED LAWS, 1909–1913 — (*Continued*).

Section.	SUBJECT.	Year.	Chapter.	Page.
	HIGHWAY LAW — (*Continued*).			
266, added	Expense of acquisition........................	1909	146	226
267, added	Maintenance of bridge......................	1909	146	227
268, added	Use of toll bridge by public service corporations.....	1910	569	1405
Art. 11, schedule				
of sections	License of chauffeurs........................	1911	491	1106
280, repealed	Motor vehicles..............................	1910	374	673
280, added	Motor vehicles..............................	1910	374	673
281, repealed	Motor vehicles..............................	1910	374	673
281, added	Motor vehicles..............................	1910	374	674
281	Motor vehicles; definitions..................	1911	491	1106
282, repealed	Motor vehicles..............................	1910	374	673
282, added	Motor vehicles..............................	1910	374	675
282	Registration of motor vehicles..............	1911	491	1107
283, repealed	Motor vehicles..............................	1910	374	673
283, added	Motor vehicles..............................	1910	374	677
283	Motor vehicle number plates................	1911	491	1110
284, repealed	Motor vehicles..............................	1910	374	673
284, added	Motor vehicles..............................	1910	374	678
284	Registration of motor vehicles by manufacturers and dealers......................	1911	491	1110
285, repealed	Motor vehicles..............................	1910	374	673
285, added	Motor vehicles..............................	1910	374	679
286, repealed	Motor vehicles..............................	1910	374	673
286, added	Motor vehicles..............................	1910	374	679
287, repealed	Motor vehicles..............................	1910	374	673
287, added	Motor vehicles..............................	1910	374	681
288, repealed	Motor vehicles..............................	1910	374	673
288, added	Motor vehicles..............................	1910	374	681
289, repealed	Motor vehicles..............................	1910	374	673
289, added	Motor vehicles..............................	1910	374	682
289	License of chauffeurs........................	1911	491	1111
290, repealed	Motor vehicles..............................	1910	374	673
290, added	Punishment for violations of motor vehicle law......	1910	374	684
290, subd. 9	Punishment for violations of motor vehicle law......	1913	1	1
290, subd. 11	Violations of motor vehicle law..............	1913	1	1
291–310, repealed	Motor vehicles..............................	1910	374	673
291–293, added	Motor vehicles..............................	1910	374	684
320	Construction or improvement of highways; expense..	1912	534	1097
330	Injuries to highways........................	1910	568	1403
343	Albany post road............................	1910	658	1773
	HOUSING LAW FOR SECOND CLASS CITIES (L. 1913, ch. 774, constituting cons. laws, ch. 66.)			
Title	Housing law made consolidated law..................	1913	798	2207
159	When to take effect............................	1913	798	2207

I. CHANGES IN THE CONSOLIDATED LAWS, 1909–1913 — *(Continued)*.

Section.	SUBJECT.	Year.	Chapter.	Page.
	INDIAN LAW: (L. 1909, ch. 31, constituting cons. laws, ch. 26.)			
10	Licenses for clergymen to reside on tribal lands......	1910	237	425
	INSANITY LAW: (L. 1909, ch. 32, constituting cons. laws, ch. 27.)			
2	Definitions.......................................	1912	121	196
Art. 2, tit.	State hospital commission.......................	1912	121	197
3	Members of state hospital commission.............	1912	121	197
4	Medical inspector................................	1909	157	259
4	Engineers and inspectors.........................	1911	768	2037
4	State hospital commission office force............	1912	121	198
9	Visitation and inspection of certain institutions....	1912	121	196
11	Annual reports of lunacy commission.............	1910	111	173
12	Mohansic State Hospital, commitment to..........	1910	310	552
17	Provision for prospective wants of insane.........	1912	121	199
18, repealed	State hospital attorneys (*See note,* L. 1911, p. 2037.)...	1911	768	2037
18, repealed	State hospital attorneys.........................	1912	121	200
19	Board of alienists...............................	1910	604	1542
19	Bureau of deportation...........................	1912	121	200
40	Mohansic State Hospital included.................	1910	310	553
40	State hospitals for indigent persons..............	1912	121	202
40, subd. 14, added	Mohansic State Hospital for Insane, established.....	1910	57	95
40a, added	Mohansic State Hospital for Insane, established.....	1910	57	95
43	Boards of managers, state hospitals...............	1912	121	203
45	Superintendents of state hospitals................	1912	121	204
45, subd. 11a, added	Out-patient departments in state hospitals.........	1913	626	1674
47	Purchasing steward, certain hospitals, abolished.....	1911	719	1941
48	Superintendents of state hospitals, meetings........	1912	121	207
49	Salaries of officers and employees of state hospitals...	1912	121	207
50	Salaries of employees of state hospitals...........	1912	43	64
51	Quarterly estimates of expenditures...............	1911	768	2038
54	Action to recover moneys due state hospital........	1910	389	715
56	Purchases and contracts.........................	1911	768	2039
58	Actions against state hospital commissioners, managers, etc..................................	1912	121	208
59	Private institutions..............................	1910	329	583
64	State hospitals, condemnation proceedings..........	1912	121	208
65	State hospital buildings..........................	1911	768	2040
82	Proceedings to determine question of insanity......	1912	121	208
83	Review of proceedings and order of commitment....	1909	155	256
84	Costs of medical care and nursing................	1910	608	1554
85	Liability for support of indigent insane............	1910	389	716
85	Poor and indigent insane........................	1911	768	2043
86	Liability for support of insane....................	1910	608	1556
87	Duties of local officers..........................	1910	608	1556
87	Duties of local officers........	1912	121	211

I. CHANGES IN THE CONSOLIDATED LAWS, 1909–1913 — (*Continued*).

Section.	SUBJECT.	Year.	Chapter.	Page.
	INSANITY LAW—(*Continued*).			
88	Duty to care for insane; apprehension of insane persons..	1910	608	1558
88	Duty to care for insane; apprehension of insane persons..	1912	121	215
89	Patients in state hospitals under special agreement..	1912	121	216
93	Habeas corpus...	1913	542	1465
94	Discharge of patients from state hospitals..........	1912	121	217
99	Voluntary patients in state hospitals, etc..........	1912	121	218
Art. 5 renumbered art. 6	Matteawan State Hospital.........................	1912	59	95
110 renumbered 130	Matteawan State Hospital, establishment, etc.......	1912	59	95
110, added	Retirement of state hospital employees............	1912	59	90
110	Matteawan State Hospital, establishment, etc........	1912	121	219
111 renumbered 131	Matteawan State Hospital, rules and regulations....	1912	59	95
111, added	Retirement of state hospital employees............	1912	59	91
112 renumbered 132	Matteawan State Hospital, medical superintendent..	1912	59	95
112, added	Retirement of state hospital employees............	1912	59	92
113 renumbered 133	Matteawan State Hospital, treasurer................	1912	59	95
113, added	Retirement of state hospital employees............	1912	59	92
114 renumbered 134	Matteawan State Hospital, salaries.................	1912	59	95
114, added	Retirement of state hospital employees............	1912	59	93
114	Matteawan State Hospital, salaries.................	1912	121	220
115 renumbered 135	Matteawan State Hospital, medical superintendent, powers...	1912	59	95
115, added	Retirement of state hospital employees............	1912	59	93
115	Matteawan State Hospital, medical superintendent, powers...	1912	121	220
116 renumbered 136	Matteawan State Hospital, monthly estimates......	1912	59	95
116, added	Retirement of state hospital employees............	1912	59	94
117 renumbered 137	Matteawan State Hospital, medical superintendent, removal.......................................	1912	59	95
117, added	Retirement of state hospital employees............	1912	59	94
118 renumbered 138	Matteawan State Hospital, transfer of insane convicts.	1912	59	95
118, added	Retirement of state hospital employees............	1912	59	94
119 renumbered 139	Matteawan State Hospital, expiration term of imprisonment....................................	1912	59	95
119, added	Retirement of state hospital employees............	1912	59	95
119	Matteawan State Hospital, expiration term of imprisonment....................................	1912	121	221
119	Retirement board.............................	1912	283	515
120 renumbered 140	Matteawan State Hospital, recovery of insane.......	1912	59	95

I. Changes in the Consolidated Laws, 1909–1913 — *(Continued)*.

Section.	SUBJECT.	Year.	Chapter.	Page.
	INSANITY LAW— *(Continued)*.			
120, added	Retirement of state hospital employees............	1912	59	95
121 renumbered 141	Matteawan State Hospital, certificate of conviction..	1912	59	95
121, added	Retirement of state hospital employees............	1912	59	95
122 renumbered 142	Matteawan State Hospital, transfer to............	1912	59	95
122, added	Retirement of state hospital employees............	1912	59	95
122	Matteawan State Hospital, transfer to............	1912	121	222
123	Recovery for support of patients.................	1909	240	400
123 renumbered 143	Matteawan State Hospital, recovery for support....	1912	59	95
123, repealed	Matteawan State Hospital, recovery for support.....	1912	121	227
124 renumbered 144	Matteawan State Hospital, tenure of office........	1912	59	95
125 renumbered 145	Matteawan State Hospital, communications with patients..................................	1912	59	95
Art. 6 renumbered art. 7	Dannemora State Hospital......................	1912	59	95
140 renumbered 150	Dannemora State Hospital, purposes, etc..........	1912	59	95
140	Dannemora State Hospital, purposes, etc..........	1912	121	222
141 renumbered 151	Dannemora State Hospital, rules and regulations....	1912	59	95
142 renumbered 152	Dannemora State Hospital, medical superintendent.	1912	59	95
142	Dannemora State Hospital, medical superintendent..	1912	121	222
143 renumbered 153	Dannemora State Hospital, treasurer..............	1912	59	95
144 renumbered 154	Dannemora State Hospital, salaries...............	1912	59	95
144	Dannemora State Hospital, salaries...............	1912	121	222
145 renumbered 155	Dannemora State Hospital, medical superintendent, powers.................................	1912	59	95
145	Dannemora State Hospital, medical superintendent, powers.................................	1912	121	223
146 renumbered 156	Dannemora State Hospital, monthly estimates......	1912	59	95
147 renumbered 157	Dannemora State Hospital, medical superintendent, removal.................................	1912	59	95
148 renumbered 158	Dannemora State Hospital, transfer to............	1912	59	95
148	Dannemora State Hospital, transfer to............	1912	121	224
149 renumbered 159	Dannemora State Hospital, retention of insane convicts...............................	1912	59	95
149	Dannemora State Hospital, retention of insane convicts...............................	1912	121	224
150 renumbered 160	Dannemora State Hospital, expiration of term......	1912	59	95

I. CHANGES IN THE CONSOLIDATED LAWS, 1909-1913 — (*Continued*).

Section.	SUBJECT.	Year.	Chap-ter.	Page.
	INSANITY LAW—(*Continued*).			
150	Dannemora State Hospital, expiration of term......	1912	121	225
151 renumbered 161	Dannemora State Hospital, recovery of insane......	1912	59	95
152 renumbered 162	Dannemora State Hospital, certificate of conviction..	1912	59	95
152	Dannemora State Hospital, certificate of conviction..	1912	121	225
153 renumbered 163	Dannemora State Hospital, communications with patients..	1912	59	95
153	Dannemora State Hospital, communications with patients..	1912	121	226
Art. 7 renum-bered art. 8	Psychiatric Institute............................	1912	59	95
170	Psychiatric Institute............................	1910	289	534
171	Psychiatric Institute............................	1910	289	534
171	Psychiatric Institute............................	1912	121	226
172	Psychiatric Institute............................	1910	289	534
172	Psychiatric Institute............................	1912	121	226
173-176, added	Commitment of inebriates to institutions for insane..	1913	526	1391
Art. 8 renum-bered art. 9	Laws repealed; when to take effect................	1912	59	95
	INSURANCE LAW: (L. 1909, ch. 33, constituting cons. laws, ch. 28.)			
1	Short title and application......................	1912	265	491
2	Superintendent of insurance.....................	1912	265	492
6	Fees...	1910	634	1672
6	Fees...	1913	304	553
7	Expenses of examinations........................	1909	301	552
7	Expenses of examinations........................	1910	634	1673
8, repealed	Expenses of department..........................	1909	301	552
9	Certificate of authorization.....................	1910	634	1674
12	Minimum capital stock..........................	1910	634	1674
12	Minimum capital stock..........................	1913	92	160
13	Deposit of securities............................	1910	634	1675
16	Investments....................................	1909	240	400
16	Securities guaranty corporations.................	1909	302	565
16	Investment of capital and surplus................	1910	634	1676
16	Investments....................................	1911	150	240
16	Investment of capital and surplus................	1912	233	447
16	Investment of capital and surplus................	1913	304	553
18	Investments....................................	1909	301	553
18	Investments....................................	1910	634	1677
22	Reinsurance....................................	1909	301	553
22	Reinsurance, fire and marine companies...........	1910	307	307
22	Reinsurance, life insurance companies............	1911	369	843
24	Limitation of risk..............................	1910	634	1678
24	Limitation of risk..............................	1911	595	1359
25	Foreign fire and marine companies................	1910	168	308

I. CHANGES IN THE CONSOLIDATED LAWS, 1909–1913 — (*Continued*).

Section.	SUBJECT.	Year.	Chap-ter.	Page.
	INSURANCE LAW — (*Continued*).			
26	Deposits by corporations of other states............	1910	634	1679
27	Funds and capital of corporations from outside United States..	1910	634	1680
28	Special deposits...............................	1910	634	1682
30	Removal of cause to federal courts................	1910	634	1682
32	Renewal of certificate of authority................	1909	301	554
32	Renewal of certificate of authority; revocation......	1913	9	13
34	Taxation of foreign corporations..................	1910	634	1683
34	Taxation of foreign corporations..................	1911	766	2033
35	Service of process by superintendent of insurance....	1911	502	1149
37	Corporations exempted..........................	1910	634	1684
39	Examiners and examinations.....................	1910	634	1685
39	Examiners and examinations.....................	1913	304	555
44	Reports of corporations.........................	1910	634	1686
46	Annual report of superintendent.................	1910	634	1687
46	Annual report of superintendent.................	1912	89	158
46, subd. 4	Annual report of superintendent.................	1909	301	555
48	Contents of advertisements......................	1913	205	365
50	Agent's certificate of authority..................	1909	301	555
52	Reorganisation of existing corporations...........	1910	634	1687
52	Reorganisation of existing corporations...........	1911	47	65
52	Reorganisation of existing corporations...........	1913	48	81
55	Insurance without consent of insured, prohibited....	1910	634	1689
55	Insurance without consent of insured, prohibited....	1913	519	1385
56	Foreign fire and marine companies................	1910	168	309
57	Application of art. 1...........................	1909	240	402
57	Application of art. 1...........................	1910	634	1691
57, repealed	Application of art. 1...........................	1910	638	1709
60	Misrepresentations prohibited...................	1911	533	1208
60	Misrepresentations prohibited...................	1913	47	80
63, added	Delinquent corporations........................	1909	300	549
63	Delinquent corporations........................	1910	634	1692
63	Delinquent corporations........................	1911	366	838
63	Delinquent corporations........................	1912	217	384
63, subd. 12, added	Delinquent insurance corporations................	1913	29	53
64, added	Religious orders...............................	1910	615	1582
65, added	Rebating and discriminations prohibited...........	1911	416	945
65	Rebating and discriminations prohibited...........	1912	225	406
65	Rebating and discriminations prohibited...........	1913	25	46
66, added	Promotion of insurance corporations; sale of securities	1913	52	87
70	Securities guaranty corporations.................	1909	302	566
70	Incorporation.................................	1910	637	1701
70	Incorporation of casualty corporations............	1911	324	757
70	Incorporation.................................	1912	232	444
70	Incorporation.................................	1913	304	557
70, subd. 8	Incorporation of casualty corporations............	1912	231	444
73	Special deposits to secure registered policies and annuity bonds.............................	1910	697	2011
74	Annual report of registered policies and annuity bonds	1911	325	760
84	Valuation of policies...........................	1909	301	555
84	Valuation of industrial life insurance policies........	1910	616	1582

I. CHANGES IN THE CONSOLIDATED LAWS, 1909–1913 — *(Continued)*.

Section.	SUBJECT.	Year.	Chapter.	Page.
	INSURANCE LAW — *(Continued)*.			
84	Valuation of policies..........................	1913	304	559
86	Assets of employers' liability casualty companies....	1911	183	285
86, subd. 1	Assets of life and casualty corporations.............	1913	304	561
88	Surrender values...............................	1909	301	557
88	Surrender values...............................	1909	595	1794
88	Surrender values...............................	1910	614	1579
89	Discriminations, industrial insurance................	1911	249	633
91	Agent's certificate of authority...................	1909	301	559
95	Conversion of stock life insurance company into mutual......................................	1911	150	241
96	Limitation of new business........................	1910	697	2012
96	Limitation of new business........................	1911	369	845
96	Limitation of new business........................	1913	304	562
97	Limitation of expenses..........................	1909	301	560
97	Limitation of expenses..........................	1910	697	2013
97	Limitation of expenses..........................	1913	304	564
100	Investments by domestic life insurance companies...	1911	767	2035
100	Investments by domestic life insurance companies...	1913	596	1607
101, repealed	Standard forms of life insurance policies............	1909	301	562
101, added	Standard forms of life insurance policies............	1909	301	562
101	Standard forms of life insurance policies............	1911	369	846
102	Life insurance companies issuing participating policies.	1911	369	848
107, added	Standard provisions for accident and health policies..	1910	636	1696
107, repealed	Standard provisions for accident and health policies.	1913	155	272
107, added	Standard provisions for accident and health policies.	1913	155	272
108, added	Discriminations under accident or health policies....	1913	155	282
110	Purposes of insurance...........................	1910	168	309
110	Automobile insurance............................	1911	126	189
110	Incorporation of fire insurance corporations.........	1913	296	536
121	Standard fire insurance policy.....................	1909	240	403
121	Standard fire insurance policy.....................	1910	168	311
121	Lloyds..	1910	638	1708
121	Standard fire insurance policy.....................	1910	668	1923
121	Standard fire insurance policy.....................	1913	181	333
121a, added	Fire insurance, appointment of umpire.............	1913	181	335
134	Undertaking of agent............................	1913	304	566
137	Licensed agents for surplus line fire insurance.......	1911	322	743
138, repealed	Tax on unauthorized foreign fire insurance companies.	1909	286	520
138, added	License to issue fire insurance policies in excepted cases	1911	322	745
138a, added	Public adjusters; certificate of authority...........	1913	22	39
· 138a	Public adjusters; certificate of authority...........	1913	522	1377
139, repealed	Agents of unauthorized foreign fire insurance companies......................................	1909	286	520
139, added	Organizations for assisting underwriters.............	1913	23	43
140, repealed	Distribution of tax.............................	1909	286	520
140, added	Organizations for assisting in establishing rates......	1913	21	38
141, repealed	Collector of such tax............................	1909	286	520
141, added	Rate making associations.........................	1911	460	1062
141	Rate making associations.........................	1912	175	317
141	Rate making associations.........................	1913	26	49
142, repealed	Reserve funds of Lloyds, etc......................	1910	638	1709
142, added	Agents' and brokers' certificates of authority........	1911	748	2008

I. CHANGES IN THE CONSOLIDATED LAWS, 1909–1913 — (*Continued*).

Section.	SUBJECT.	Year.	Chapter.	Page.
	INSURANCE LAW — (*Continued*).			
142	Agents' and brokers' certificates of authority........	1912	1	1
142	Agents' and brokers' certificates of authority........	1912	172	308
142, repealed	Agents' and brokers' certificates of authority........	1913	7	9
142, added	Agents' certificates of authority..................	1913	7	9
143, repealed	Change of name of Lloyds, etc....................	1910	638	1709
143, added	Brokers' certificates of authority..................	1913	12	17
149, added	Foreign mutual fire insurance companies...........	1909	286	517
149	Foreign mutual fire insurance companies...........	1911	161	254
149	Foreign mutual fire insurance companies...........	1911	765	2030
149a, added	Tax.......................................	1909	286	519
149a	Premium or assessment tax.......................	1911	161	256
149b, added	Agents...................................	1909	286	519
149c, added	Distribution of tax...........................	1909	286	520
150	Marine insurance corporations....................	1909	240	404
150	Marine risks..............................	1910	168	312
150	Automobile insurance..........................	1911	126	190
162, repealed	Lloyds, etc................................	1910	638	1709
170	Securities guaranty corporations..................	1909	302	568
170	Powers of title guaranty corporations.............	1911	525	1198
170	Capital of guaranty corporations.................	1913	81	148
170	Capital of guaranty corporations.................	1913	215	378
172	By-laws of guaranty corporations.................	1913	49	84
181	Surety companies may execute undertakings........	1913	182	336
182	Surety companies, certificates of solvency..........	1913	182	337
183, repealed	Title and credit guaranty corporations, deficiencies..	1913	182	338
184 renumbered 183, and amended	Surety companies, filing statement.................	1913	182	338
210	Agreements for benefits.......................	1911	536	1212
214	Exemption of Odd Fellows and Masons............	1911	536	1213
215, repealed	Deposit of securities with superintendent of insurance	1911	536	1214
218, added	Admission of minors to certain kinds of insurance....	1911	176	275
219, added	Policy to indicate assessment plan.................	1913	28	52
220, added	Forms of policies or certificates to be approved.....	1913	51	86
230–240, repealed	Fraternal beneficiary societies....................	1911	198	448
230–240, added	Fraternal beneficiary societies....................	1911	198	448
241, added	Fraternal beneficiary societies....................	1909	589	1786
241, repealed	Fraternal beneficiary societies....................	1911	198	448
241, added	Fraternal beneficiary societies....................	1911	198	448
242, added	Fraternal beneficiary societies....................	1911	198	459
242	Fraternal beneficiary societies....................	1913	410	862
243–244, added	Fraternal beneficiary societies....................	1911	198	462
245, added	Fraternal beneficiary societies....................	1911	198	464
245	Fraternal beneficiary societies....................	1913	410	867
246–249, added	Fraternal beneficiary societies....................	1911	198	465
250	Insurance of lives of domestic animals on co-operative or assessment plan...........................	1910	318	564
260, repealed	Town and county co-operative insurance corporations.	1910	328	583
260, added	Co-operative fire insurance companies..............	1910	328	574
260	Co-operative fire insurance companies..............	1911	323	747
261, repealed	Town and county co-operative insurance corporations.	1910	328	583
261, added	Co-operative fire insurance companies..............	1910	328	575
261	Co-operative fire insurance companies..............	1911	323	749

I. CHANGES IN THE CONSOLIDATED LAWS, 1909-1913 — (*Continued*).

Section.	SUBJECT.	Year.	Chapter.	Page.
	INSURANCE LAW — (*Continued*).			
262, repealed	Town and county co-operative insurance corporations.	1910	328	553
262, added	Co-operative fire insurance companies...............	1910	328	576
262	Co-operative fire insurance companies...............	1911	323	750
263, repealed	Town and county co-operative insurance corporations.	1910	328	563
263, added	Co-operative fire insurance companies...............	1910	328	577
264, repealed	Town and county co-operative insurance corporations.	1910	328	563
264, added	Co-operative fire insurance companies...............	1910	328	578
264	Co-operative fire insurance companies...............	1911	323	752
265, repealed	Town and county co-operative insurance corporations.	1910	328	563
265, added	Co-operative fire insurance companies...............	1910	328	580
266, repealed	Town and county co-operative insurance corporations.	1910	328	563
266, added	Co-operative fire insurance companies...............	1910	328	581
266	Co-operative fire insurance companies...............	1911	303	715
267, repealed	Town and county co-operative insurance corporations.	1910	328	563
267, added	Co-operative fire insurance companies...............	1910	328	581
267	Co-operative fire insurance companies...............	1911	323	754
267	Co-operative fire insurance companies...............	1912	90	159
268, repealed	Town and county co-operative insurance corporations.	1910	328	563
268, added	Co-operative fire insurance companies...............	1910	328	583
269, repealed	Town and county co-operative insurance corporations.	1910	328	563
269, added	Co-operative fire insurance companies...............	1910	328	563
270-280, repealed	Town and county co-operative insurance corporations.	1910	328	563
300, added	Lloyds and inter-insurers.......................	1910	638	1704
300	Lloyds and inter-insurers.......................	1911	502	1150
301, added	Lloyds and inter-insurers.......................	1910	638	1704
302, added	Lloyds and inter-insurers.......................	1910	638	1704
302	Lloyds and inter-insurers.......................	1911	502	1151
303, added	Lloyds and inter-insurers.......................	1910	638	1704
304, added	Lloyds and inter-insurers.......................	1911	502	1152
305, added	Lloyds and inter-insurers.......................	1911	502	1155
330-346, repealed	Certain town insurance companies.................	1910	328	563
Art. 10a, added	State fire marshal.............................	1911	451	1018
350, added	State fire marshal.............................	1911	451	1018
350	State fire marshal.............................	1912	453	936
351, added	Duties of state fire marshal.....................	1911	451	1019
351	Duties of state fire marshal.....................	1912	453	937
351	Duties of state fire marshal.....................	1913	204	364
352, added	Deputies of state fire marshal...................	1911	451	1019
352	Deputies of state fire marshal...................	1912	453	937
353, added	Assistants to state fire marshal..................	1911	451	1020
353	Assistants to state fire marshal..................	1912	453	938
353	Assistants to state fire marshal..................	1913	432	907
354, added	Investigation of fires..........................	1911	451	1020
354	Investigation of fires and explosions..............	1912	453	938
354	State fire marshal, reports of insurance companies....	1913	433	908
355, added	Inspection of property.........................	1911	451	1021
355	Inspection of public buildings...................	1912	453	939
356, added	Powers of state fire marshal, deputies, assistants.....	1911	451	1022
356	Inspection of property.........................	1912	453	939
356	State fire marshal, service of orders..............	1913	434	910
357, added	Records.......................................	1911	451	1023
357	Inspection of steam boilers......................	1912	453	941

I. CHANGES IN THE CONSOLIDATED LAWS, 1909–1913 — (*Continued*).

Section.	SUBJECT.	Year.	Chapter.	Page.
	INSURANCE LAW — (*Continued*).			
357	State fire marshal; boiler inspection................	1913	523	1381
358, added	Annual report...........................	1911	451	1023
358	Definition of explosives..........................	1912	453	941
359, added	Witnesses........................	1911	451	1023
359	Regulations as to explosives......................	1912	453	943
360, added	Duties of district attorney....................	1911	451	1024
360	Explosives kept in suitable retainers..............	1912	453	944
361, added	Compensation of assistants...................	1911	451	1024
361	Magazines for storage of explosives..............	1912	453	945
362, added	Penalties............................	1911	451	1024
362	Caps not kept in magazine....................	1912	453	946
363, added	Reports of inspection; certificate of compliance......	1912	453	946
364, added	Transportation of explosives.....................	1912	453	947
364	Transportation of explosives....................	1913	393	833
365, added	Records of sale of explosives....................	1912	453	947
366, added	Explosives; exceptions....................	1912	453	948
367, added	Firearms........................	1912	453	948
367	Discharge of firearms near magazine or factory.....	1913	214	377
368, added	Penalties........................	1912	453	948
369, added	Powers of fire marshal, deputies, assistants.........	1912	453	948
369	State fire marshal; investigations..................	1913	405	849
369	State fire marshal; investigations..................	1913	520	1367
370, added	Records......................	1912	453	949
371, added	Annual report........................	1912	453	949
372, added	Witnesses........................	1912	453	950
373, added	Duties of district attorney....................	1912	453	950
374, added	Compensation of assistants...................	1912	453	950
375, added	Penalties..........................	1912	453	950
377, added	List of officers to be furnished state fire marshal.....	1913	192	349
378, added	State fire marshal, assistants' reports..............	1913	431	906
379, added	Regulations by state fire marshal..................	1913	303	552
Schedule of repeals	L. 1907, ch. 397, omitted.......................	1909	240	421
Schedule of repeals	L. 1898, ch. 171, inserted.......................	1909	240	424
Schedule of repeals	L. 1901, ch. 397, inserted.......................	1909	240	424
	JUDICIARY LAW: (L. 1909, ch 35, constituting cons. laws, ch. 30.)			
87	Destruction of papers by county clerk..............	1911	275	671
87	Destruction of papers by county clerk..............	1912	252	475
87	Destruction of papers by county clerk..............	1913	402	845
88, bd. 1	Attorneys; admission to practice..................	1912	253	476
88, subd. 2	Attorneys; control of supreme court over..........	1912	253	476
88, subd. 2	Attorneys, control of supreme court over..........	1913	720	1835
109	Confidential clerks, appellate division, certain departments...................................	1912	173	314
111, subd. 2	Appointment of court attendants, second department.	1910	325	571

I. CHANGES IN THE CONSOLIDATED LAWS, 1909–1913 — (*Continued*).

Section.	SUBJECT.	Year.	Chapter.	Page.
	JUDICIARY LAW — (*Continued.*)			
113	Supreme court, first judicial district, interpreters....	1913	348	647
114	Confidential attendants, first department..........	1911	611	1385
115	Appellate division, first department, official referees. .	1911	844	2369
115	Appellate division, first department, official referees. .	1912	62	99
115	Appellate division, first and second departments, official referees......................	1912	323	642
116	Appellate division, first department, official referees. .	1911	844	2369
116	Appellate division, first and second departments, official referees......................	1912	323	643
117, added	Retirement of employees, appellate division, second department......................	1913	185	340
117, added	Ex-justices of city court of New York as official referees......................	1913	722	1837
148	Special and trial terms of supreme court............	1913	561	1538
159	Special deputy clerk, Queens county...............	1910	695	2009
159	Special deputy clerk, Queens county...............	1913	108	179
160, subd. 1	Appointment of clerks in certain judicial districts....	1911	404	923
160, subd. 4	Confidential clerks to justices, fifth district........	1912	118	194
160, subd. 5, repealed	Confidential clerks to justices, fifth district........	1912	118	194
160, subd. 6, repealed	Confidential clerk to trial justice, fifth district, residing in Jefferson county..........................	1912	118	194
161	Number of stenographers, eighth judicial district....	1910	60	97
161, subd. 3	Stenographers in certain counties..................	1909	202	319
161, subd. 3a, added	Typewriter operator, second judicial department....	1909	401	865
164	Stenographers' expenses..........................	1909	240	405
165	Stenographers' compensation, certain districts.......	1909	240	405
168	Appointment of court officers, Nassau and Suffolk counties..........................	1911	182	284
169	Appointment of criers for courts of record, Erie county..........................	1910	128	228
195	Chief clerk and assistants, Kings county court......	1911	640	1449
195	Chief clerk and assistants, Kings county court......	1911	826	2334
196	Confidential clerks to county judges...............	1909	562	1602
196	Confidential clerks to county judges...............	1913	563	1540
197, subd. 2	Stenographer, county court, Jefferson county.......	1909	561	1601
202, added	Special deputy clerk, Queens county...............	1910	695	2009
233	Salaries of court officers, Erie county..............	1910	14	22
251	Court clerks, first and second districts, not to be referees..........................	1912	154	277
262	Clerks to judges of court of appeals, compensation..	1912	156	287
271, subd. 2	Clerk, appellate division, second department, salary.	1911	828	2336
271, subd. 5	Deputy clerk, appellate division, second department, salary..........................	1911	828	2336
271, subd. 6	Compensation of deputy clerk, fourth department...	1912	377	729
271, subd. 6	Compensation of deputy clerk, fourth department...	1913	632	1694
271, subd. 9	Consultation clerk, appellate division, fourth department, salary..........................	1912	119	195
271, subd. 9	Consultation clerk, fourth department, salary.......	1913	632	1685
274, subd. 2	Salary of clerks, appellate division, second department	1911	365	836

I. Changes in the Consolidated Laws, 1909–1913 — (*Continued*).

Section.	SUBJECT.	Year.	Chapter.	Page.
	JUDICIARY LAW — (*Continued*).			
275	Special deputy clerks, appellate division, first department.......................	1911	363	834
279, subd. 1	Salary of clerks to justices, first district............	1911	404	924
279, subd. 2	Salaries of confidential clerks, second district........	1911	365	837
279, subd. 3	Salaries of clerks supreme court, Kings county......	1911	365	837
279, subd. 4	Salaries of confidential clerks, fifth district..........	1912	118	194
279, subd. 5, repealed	Salaries of clerks to justices, fifth district..........	1912	118	194
279, subd. 5, added	Salaries of clerks to justices, sixth district..........	1913	554	1490
279, subd. 6, repealed	Salary of clerk to trial justice, fifth district, residing in Jefferson county...........................	1912	118	194
279, subd. 7	Salaries of clerks to justices, seventh district........	1913	554	1490
279, subd. 9	Confidential clerks to justices, ninth district........	1909	572	1660
280	Special deputy clerk, Queens county...............	1910	695	2009
280	Special deputy clerk, Queens county...............	1913	108	180
282	Chief clerk, Kings county court....................	1911	640	1449
283	Chief clerk and assistants, Kings county court......	1911	640	1450
284	Chief clerk and assistants, Kings county court......	1911	640	1451
284	Chief clerk and assistants, Kings county court......	1911	826	2334
285	Confidential clerks to county judges...............	1909	563	1603
285	Confidential clerks to county judges, salaries........	1913	563	1540
286, 287, added	Special deputy clerk, Queens county...............	1910	695	2010
288, added	Record clerks, court of general sessions, New York county..	1912	538	1102
303	Stenographers to furnish copies of proceedings to parties...	1912	202	364
307	Stenographers, appellate division, certain departments	1911	543	1223
307	Compensation, confidential clerks, appellate division, certain departments...........................	1912	173	314
307	Compensation of stenographers and confidential clerks, appellate division.....................	1913	491	1171
308	Typewriter operators, appellate division, first and second departments............................	1913	387	827
313	Stenographers; except first and second district.......	1910	180	335
313	Compensation of supreme court stenographers.......	1913	491	1172
314	Expenses of stenographers of supreme court.........	1910	180	336
316	Salary of stenographers of supreme court...........	1910	180	336
316	Compensation of stenographers, second judicial district...	1913	491	1173
316, subd. 1	Stenographers, court of general sessions............	1913	599	1613
317	Stenographers, third and fourth judicial districts.....	1911	543	1224
318, subd. 1	Stenographer, county court, Jefferson county.......	1909	561	1602
319, subd. 2	Compensation of stenographer, Albany county court.	1910	27	42
319, subd. 5	Stenographer, county court, Monroe county........	1909	560	1601
319, subd. 8	Stenographer, county court, Jefferson county.......	1909	561	1602
319, subd. 8	Stenographer, Rensselaer county court.............	1910	625	1596
347	Compensation of attendants, third and fourth departments..	1910	304	547
347	Compensation of attendants, third and fourth departments..	1912	376	728

I. CHANGES IN THE CONSOLIDATED LAWS, 1909–1913 — (*Continued*).

Section.	SUBJECT.	Year.	Chapter.	Page.
	JUDICIARY LAW — (*Continued*).			
348	Salaries of court attendants, first department and first judicial district................................	1910	261	464
348	Salaries of attendants of court of general sessions, New York county................................	1910	696	2011
348a, added	Salaries of messengers and attendants, surrogates' court, New York county....................	1911	267	662
349	Duties of court attendants, Nassau and Suffolk counties....................................	1911	182	284
351	Salaries of court attendants, Nassau and Suffolk counties....................................	1911	182	285
351	Salaries of court attendants, Queens county.........	1911	566	1277
365	Compensation of court criers....................	1910	34	52
365	Salaries of court criers, Queens county...........	1911	566	1277
366	Compensation of court criers, Erie county..........	1910	15	23
380	Salaries of interpreters, court of general sessions, New York county............................	1911	396	909
386	Salaries of court interpreters, Queens county.......	1911	566	1278
387	Court interpreters.............................	1909	259	457
388, added	Temporary appointment of interpreters............	1912	120	195
389, added	Interpreters for Erie county.....................	1913	562	1539
474	Compensation of attorney or counsellor............	1912	229	441
480, added	Settlement; actions for personal injury............	1913	603	1622
502, subd. 3	Qualifications of trial jurors, Richmond county......	1910	96	147
513	Drawing trial jurors, Richmond county............	1910	95	146
513a, added	Sheriff's jurors for Queens county................	1913	565	1543
610	Jurors in New York county......................	1911	29	40
631	Jurors in New York county......................	1913	537	1411
649	Nonattendance of jurors.......................	1909	240	406
	LABOR LAW: (L. 1909, ch. 36, constituting cons. laws, ch. 31.)			
Syllabus	Bureau of industries and immigration..............	1910	514	1184
Syllabus	Bakeries and confectioneries....................	1911	637	1441
2	Definitions..................................	1913	529	1400
3	Hours constituting day's work...................	1909	292	530
3	Hours constituting day's work...................	1913	467	980
3	Hours constituting day's work...................	1913	494	1177
7	Hours of labor on certain railroads..............	1913	462	966
8	Hours of labor, certain railroad employees........	1913	466	978
8a, added	One day of rest in seven.......................	1913	740	1861
12	Payment of wages by corporations................	1909	206	322
17	Seats for female employees.....................	1913	197	355
18	Scaffolding..................................	1911	693	1830
20	Protection of employees on buildings..............	1911	693	1830
20	Protection of employees on buildings..............	1913	492	1173
20a, added	Accidents to be reported.......................	1910	155	278
20b, added	Protection of employees........................	1913	145	249
20b, added	Switchboards to be protected...................	1913	543	1466
22, added	Physical examination of employees...............	1913	320	597

I. CHANGES IN THE CONSOLIDATED LAWS, 1909–1913 — (Continued).

Section.	SUBJECT.	Year.	Chapter.	Page.
	LABOR LAW — (Continued).			
Art. 3	Department of labor............................	1913	145	243
40	Commissioner of labor.........................	1911	729	1953
40	Commissioner of labor. .,.....................	1913	145	244
41	Deputy commissioners.........................	1911	729	1953
41	Deputy commissioners.........................	1913	145	244
42	Bureau of industries and immigration............	1910	514	1185
42	Bureaus.......................................	1913	145	245
43	Investigators..................................	1910	514	1185
43	Powers..	1913	145	245
43, subd. 1	Commissioner of labor and assistants; powers.......	1912	382	738
44	Investigators..................................	1910	514	1186
44	Salaries and expenses..........................	1913	145	245
45	Sub-offices....................................	1911	729	1953
45	Branch offices.................................	1913	145	246
46	Reports.......................................	1913	145	246
47	Old records...................................	1913	145	246
48	Counsel.......................................	1913	145	247
49, added	Industrial directory...........................	1911	565	1276
49, repealed	Industrial directory...........................	1913	145	257
Art. 3a (§§ 50–52), added	Industrial board..............................	1913	145	246
Art. 4 (§§ 60–68) renumbered art. 5 (§§ 53–61), and amended	Bureau of statistics and information..............	1913	145	255
55 renumbered 62, and amended	Bureau of statistics and information..............	1913	145	255
56 renumbered 63, and amended	Bureau of statistics and information..............	1913	145	255
57 renumbered 64, and amended	Information to be furnished upon request..........	1913	145	256
58, added	Industrial poisonings to be reported..............	1911	258	646
58 renumbered 65, and amended	Industrial poisonings to be reported..............	1913	145	257
60	Chief factory inspector.........................	1911	729	1954
Art. 5 (§§ 60–68) renumbered art. 4 (§§ 53–61), and amended	Bureau of inspection...........................	1913	145	250
61	Factory inspectors.............................	1911	729	1954
61	Factory inspectors.............................	1912	158	289
62, subds. 1, 3	Commissioner of labor, powers and duties..........	1911	729	1954
63, repealed	Reports.......................................	1913	145	257
67 renumbered 22	Duties relative to apprentices...................	1913	145	257
68 renumbered 99a and amended	Laws to be posted.............................	1913	145	257
69, added	Registration of factories........................	1912	335	665
69, transferred to art. 6	Registration of factories........................	1913	145	258
70	Employment of minors..........................	1913	529	1401
71, subd. (e) and final ¶	Employment of minors, physicians' certificates......	1912	333	662

I. CHANGES IN THE CONSOLIDATED LAWS, 1909–1913 — (*Continued*).

Section.	SUBJECT.	Year.	Chapter.	Page.
	LABOR LAW — (*Continued*).			
73	Employment certificates, school record.............	1913	144	241
75	Employment of minors, report of certificates........	1912	333	663
75	Employment certificates, supervision over issuance..	1913	144	242
76a, added	Physical examination of children in factories........	1913	200	358
77	Hours of labor; minors and women................	1912	539	1103
77, subd. 3	Hours of labor of females.......................	1913	465	977
78	Exceptions....................................	1912	539	1104
78, subd. 2	Employment of male minors in canning establishments..	1913	465	977
78, subd. 3	Employment of females in canning establishments..	1913	465	977
78, subd. 3 renumbered subd. 4	Burden of proving permit or exception.............	1913	465	978
79	Elevator and hoisting shafts.....................	1909	299	545
79	Elevators and hoistways.........................	1913	202	361
79a–79f, added	Factory buildings..............................	1913	461	951
80	Doors and windows in factories..................	1910	461	895
80, repealed	Stairs, doors and windows in factories............	1913	461	966
81	Protection of employees operating machinery.......	1909	299	546
81	Protection of employees operating machinery.......	1910	106	161
81	Protection of employees operating machinery.......	1913	286	517
82, repealed	Fire escapes on factories........................	1913	461	966
83	Doors and windows in factories..................	1910	461	895
83, repealed	Fire escapes, doors and windows of factories.......	1913	461	966
83a, added	Fire drills in factories..........................	1912	330	659
83a	Fire alarm signal systems and fire drills...........	1913	203	363
83b, added	Automatic sprinklers...........................	1912	332	661
83c, added	Fire prevention in factories......................	1912	329	656
83c	Fire prevention in factories......................	1913	194	351
84	Sanitation of factories..........................	1910	114	175
84	Cleanliness of rooms in factories.................	1913	82	149
84a, added	Sanitation of factory buildings...................	1913	198	356
86	Ventilation of factories.........................	1913	196	353
87	Accidents to be reported........................	1910	155	279
88	Sanitary conveniences in factories................	1910	229	416
88	Sanitary conveniences in factories................	1912	336	665
88	Sanitary conveniences in factories................	1913	340	633
88a, added	Water closets in factories.......................	1913	340	634
89a, added	Eating meals in workrooms prohibited.............	1912	336	666
91, repealed	Boiler inspection in factories....................	1913	523	1383
93	Employment of women and children..............	1909	299	547
93	Employment of women and children..............	1910	107	160
93	Prohibited employment of women and children......	1913	464	974
93a, added	Employment of females after childbirth prohibited..	1912	331	663
93b, added	Rest at night for women in factories..............	1913	83	150
95	Unclean factories..............................	1912	334	664
97, added	Foundries.....................................	1913	201	359
98, added	Housing of factory employees....................	1913	195	353
99, added	Dangerous trades..............................	1913	199	357
Art. 7 (§§ 100–105)	Tenement-made articles.........................	1913	260	467
106, added	Tenement-made articles.........................	1913	260	474

I. CHANGES IN THE CONSOLIDATED LAWS, 1909–1913 — (*Continued*).

Section.	SUBJECT.	Year.	Chapter.	Page.
	LABOR LAW — (*Continued*).			
Art. 8	Bakeries and confectioneries.....................	1913	463	967
110	Bakeries, enforcement of article..................	1913	463	968
111	Bakeries, definitions...........................	1911	637	1441
111	Bakeries, definitions.......................	1913	463	968
112	Bakeries, general requirements...................	1911	637	1442
112	Bakeries, general requirements...................	1913	463	969
113	Bakeries, maintenance..........................	1911	637	1443
113	Bakeries, maintenance..........................	1913	463	969
113a, added	Prohibited employment of diseased bakers.........	1913	463	970
114	Bakeries, inspection...........................	1911	637	1443
114	Bakeries, inspection (*See note* 17, *L.* 1913, p. 970.)...	1913	463	970
115, repealed	Notice requiring alterations in bakeries...........	1911	637	1444
115, added	Bakeries, sanitary certificates..................	1913	463	971
116, added	Prohibition of future cellar bakeries.............	1913	463	973
116	Prohibition of future cellar bakeries.............	1913	797	2205
117, added	Sanitary code for bakeries and confectioneries......	1913	463	974
119, added	Protection of employees in mines and tunnels.......	1913	145	258
120	Mines, tunnels and quarries.....................	1913	145	258
126	Report of accidents...........................	1910	155	279
134a, added	Hours of labor in compressed air................	1909	291	527
134a	Hours of labor in compressed air................	1912	219	394
134a	Hours of labor in compressed air................	1913	528	1396
134b, added	Work in compressed air, medical attendance.......	1909	291	528
134b	Work in compressed air, medical attendance.......	1912	219	396
134b	Work in compressed air, medical attendance........	1913	528	1398
134c, added	Penalties...................................	1909	291	529
134d, added	Work in compressed air, air pipes required........	1912	219	398
134e, added	Lighting apparatus for work in tunnels............	1912	219	398
Art. 10a renumbered art. 11	Bureau of industries and immigration..............	1913	145	259
151, added	Bureau of industries and immigration..............	1910	514	1186
152, added	Bureau of industries and immigration....	1910	514	1186
152	Bureau of industries and immigration..............	1912	543	1113
153, added	Bureau of industries and immigration..............	1910	514	1187
153	Bureau of industries and immigration..............	1912	543	1113
154, added	Bureau of industries and immigration..............	1910	514	1188
154	Bureau of industries and immigration..............	1912	543	1116
155, added	Bureau of industries and immigration..............	1910	514	1189
156, added	Bureau of industries and immigration..............	1910	514	1190
156 renumbered 156a	Bureau of industries and immigration..............	1912	543	1119
156a, added	Licensing of immigrant lodging places..............	1911	845	2370
156a renumbered 156, and amended	Licensing of immigrant lodging places.............	1912	543	1117
156a, subd. 1	Bonds of immigrant lodging places.................	1912	337	667
Art. 11 renumbered art. 12	Women and children in mercantile establishments...	1913	145	259
161	Hours of labor of minors.........................	1910	387	714
161	Hours of labor of minors.........................	1911	866	2412
161	Hours of labor, minors and females................	1913	493	1175
161a, added	Hours of labor of messengers.....................	1910	342	605

I. CHANGES IN THE CONSOLIDATED LAWS, 1909–1913 — (*Continued*).

Section.	SUBJECT.	Year.	Chapter.	Page.
	LABOR LAW — (*Continued*).			
162	Employment of children.........................	1909	293	531
162	Employment of children.........................	1911	866	2413
163, subd. (e)	Employment certificates, physicians' certificates.....	1913	144	239
165	Employment certificates, school record.............	1913	144	241
166, repealed	Summer vacation certificate.....................	1911	866	2413
166, added	Employment certificates, supervision over issuance..	1913	144	242
167	Registry of children employed...................	1913	145	259
168	Wash-rooms and water-closets...................	1911	866	2413
168	Wash-rooms and water-closets...................	1913	145	261
169	Lunch-rooms..................................	1913	145	261
171	Employment of women and children in basements...	1913	145	261
172	Enforcement of article..........................	1913	145	262
173	Laws to be posted..............................	1913	145	262
180	Mercantile inspector............................	1910	516	1198
Art. 12 (§§ 180–184), repealed	Bureau of mercantile inspection..................	1913	145	262
200–202, amended; 202a, 205–212, added 215–219, 219a–	Employer's liability.............................	1910	352	625
219g, added	Workmen's compensation in dangerous employments.	1910	674	1945
Art. 15	Employment of children; street trades.............	1913	618	1644
220	Prohibited employment, children in street trades....	1913	618	1644
221	Permit and badge; children in street trades.........	1913	618	1644
222	Contents of permit; badge.......................	1913	618	1645
223	Regulations; badge and permit...................	1913	618	1646
224	Limit of hours, children in street trades............	1913	618	1646
225	Enforcement of article..........................	1913	618	1646
226	Violations of article; how punished................	1913	618	1646
227, added	Punishment of parent; delinquency of children......	1913	618	1647
	LEGISLATIVE LAW: (L. 1909, ch. 37, constituting cons. laws, ch. 32.)			
5	Members of legislature, salaries when payable.......	1911	618	1414
10	Compensation of sergeants-at-arms................	1911	45	63
45	Publication of constitutional amendments..........	1911	272	667
46, subd. 3	Distribution of bound volumes of session laws......	1910	393	724
48, subd. 1	Publication of session laws, New York county......	1911	97	144
49, repealed	Forwarding session law slips to county clerks.......	1913	764	1908
	LIEN LAW: (L. 1909, ch. 38, constituting cons. laws, ch. 33.)			
5, repealed	Public improvement; liens.......................	1911	450	1017
5, added	Public improvement; liens.......................	1911	873	2582
11	Service of copy of notice........................	1913	88	154
12, repealed	Public improvement; notice of lien................	1911	450	1017

I. CHANGES IN THE CONSOLIDATED LAWS, 1909–1913 — (Continued).

Section.	SUBJECT.	Year.	Chapter.	Page.
	LIEN LAW — (Continued).			
12, added	Public improvement; notice of lien	1911	873	2582
16, repealed	Public improvement; assignment of contract	1911	450	1017
16, added	Public improvement; assignment of contract	1911	873	2583
18, repealed	Public improvement; duration of lien	1911	450	1017
18, added	Public improvement; duration of lien	1911	873	2584
19, subd. 3	Discharge of lien	1909	240	406
19, subd. 3	Discharge of lien	1909	427	909
21, repealed	Public improvement; discharge of lien	1911	450	1017
21, added	Public improvement; discharge of lien	1911	873	2585
25, repealed	Public improvement; priority of liens	1911	450	1017
25, added	Public improvement; priority of liens	1911	873	2586
42, repealed	Public improvement; enforcement of lien	1911	450	1017
42, added	Public improvement; enforcement of lien	1911	873	2586
60, repealed	Public improvement; judgment in action to foreclose lien	1911	450	1017
60, added	Public improvement; judgment in action to foreclose lien	1911	873	2587
62, added	Public contracts; laborers and material men to be secured	1911	450	1015
62, repealed	Public contracts; laborers and material men to be secured	1911	873	2587
63, added	Public contracts; lien of laborer or material man	1911	450	1016
63, repealed	Public contracts; lien of laborer or material man	1911	873	2587
64, added	Public contracts; enforcement of lien	1911	450	1016
64, repealed	Public contracts; enforcement of lien	1911	873	2587
65, added	Public contracts; complaint in action to enforce lien	1911	450	1017
65, repealed	Public contracts; complaint in action to enforce lien	1911	873	2587
66, added	Public contracts; costs in action to enforce lien	1911	450	1017
66, repealed	Public contracts; costs in action to enforce lien	1911	873	2587
81, 82, 90	Liens on canal boats	1910	182	338
200	Inn-keeper's lien	1910	214	395
230	Chattel mortgages	1911	326	764
232–234	Liens on canal boats	1910	182	340
	LIQUOR TAX LAW: (L. 1909, ch. 39, constituting cons. laws, ch. 34.)			
2	Definitions	1909	281	487
2	Definitions	1910	485	929
3	State commissioner of excise. (See note 2, L. 1910, p. 988.)	1910	503	986
6	Orange county, special deputy commissioner	1913	782	1978
7	Special agents; attorneys	1909	281	488
8	Excise taxes	1909	281	490
8, subd. 3	Tax upon traffic by pharmacist	1910	485	930
8, subd. 8	Enumeration	1910	485	931
8, subd. 9, added	Issuance of certificates	1910	494	952
8, subd. 9	Issuance of certificate	1911	298	705
8, subd. 10, added	Issuance of certificate	1913	168	311
12, subd. 17	Account of excise moneys	1909	240	406

I. CHANGES IN THE CONSOLIDATED LAWS, 1909–1913 — (*Continued*).

Section.	SUBJECT.	Year.	Chapter.	Page.
	LIQUOR TAX LAW — (*Continued*).			
12, subd. 17	Account of excise moneys.........................	1909	281	496
12a, added	Filing assignments of certificates as collateral security	1912	263	480
13	Local option.................................	1910	485	932
15, ¶ 3	Statement by applicant for certificate.............	1910	494	956
15, ¶ 3	Statement by applicant for certificate.............	1913	168	313
15, ¶ 5	Statement by applicant for certificate.............	1909	281	496
15, ¶ 5	Statement by applicant for certificate.............	1911	643	1456
15, ¶ 8	Consents.....................................	1909	281	497
15, ¶ 8	Effect of revocation of certificate.................	1910	485	935
15, ¶ 8	Consents; effect of cancellation of certificate.......	1910	503	988
15, ¶ 8	Consents.....................................	1911	643	1457
15, ¶ 8	Cancellation of certificate, disuse of premises........	1912	378	730
16	Bonds.......................................	1910	484	925
16	Bonds.......................................	1911	223	498
17	Payment of tax and issuing of certificate..........	1910	494	956
17	Payment of tax and issuing of certificate...... ...	1913	168	314
19	Posting liquor tax certificate.....................	1911	407	930
21	Who not to traffic in liquors.....................	1909	281	499
21, subd. 1, clauses d, e	Who not to traffic in liquors.....................	1910	503	990
23, subd. 1	Places in which traffic not permitted..............	1910	704	2033
23, subd. 2	Places in which traffic not permitted..............	1911	643	1459
24, subd. 1	Surrender of certificates........................	1910	503	990
24, subd. 1	Surrender of certificates........................	1911	408	934
24, subd. 2	Surrender of certificates........................	1910	503	990
25	Changing place of traffic........................	1911	407	931
26	Changing place of traffic........................	1911	407	932
27, subd. 2	Revocation of certificate........................	1909	281	500
27, subd. 2	Revocation of certificate........................	1910	503	993
28	Injunction...................................	1909	281	505
29	Persons to whom liquor not to be furnished........	1910	307	549
30	Illegal sales..................................	1910	494	957
30, subd. F	Illegal sales..................................	1912	264	491
30, subd. J	Illegal sales..................................	1910	485	937
30a, added	Sale of liquors to West Point cadets..............	1911	762	2026
31	Lists of lodgers...............................	1909	281	507
33	Liquors kept for unlawful traffic.................	1913	614	1637
33, ¶ 2	Search warrant...............................	1909	281	507
33, ¶ 2	Liquors kept for unlawful traffic.................	1910	485	938
33, ¶ 4	Prima facie evidence of violation.................	1909	281	510
35	Persons liable for violations.....................	1909	281	510
36	Penalties....................................	1910	485	940
43	Penalties; actions to recover. (*See note* 17, *L.* 1910, p. 999.)...................................	1910	503	998
	MEMBERSHIP CORPORATIONS LAW: (L. 1909, ch. 40, constituting cons. laws, ch. 35.)			
18, 19, repealed	Societies taking property by will..................	1911	857	2399
48, added	Place of annual meeting.........................	1909	169	277

I. CHANGES IN THE CONSOLIDATED LAWS, 1909–1913 — (*Continued*).

Section.	SUBJECT.	Year.	Chapter.	Page.
	MEMBERSHIP CORPORATIONS LAW — (*Cont'd*).			
62	Acquisition of lands for cemetery purposes..........	1909	274	478
62	Cemetery corporations, various counties...........	1911	706	1905
64	Directors of cemetery corporation................	1912	301	550
65	Acquisition of lands for cemetery purposes.........	1909	274	478
69a, added	Cemetery lots held in inalienable form............	1913	649	1703
72	Taxation of lot owners by cemetery corporation.....	1912	301	552
85, added	Cemetery corporations; record of inscriptions on monuments..................................	1912	151	274
85, added	Perpetual care of cemetery lots..................	1912	315	571
85, added	Cemeteries in Nassau county....................	1913	139	231
86, added	Exchange and cancellation of certificates..........	1913	648	1703
121	City of Yonkers, certain corporations..............	1911	623	1418
144, added	Young Men's Christian Associations, county committees.................................	1911	207	479
291, repealed	Trustees of corporations for breeding horses.........	1910	486	943
292–295, 298, repealed	Tax on race meetings...........................	1910	489	946
Schedule of repeals	L. 1898, ch. 543, in part, inserted.................	1909	240	424
Schedule of repeals	L. 1897, ch. 129, omitted.......................	1909	240	425
	MILITARY LAW: (L. 1909, ch. 41, constituting cons. laws, ch. 36.)			
7	Governor's military secretary....................	1911	796	2104
11	Reserve militia................................	1911	98	145
15	Militia council................................	1909	373	769
15	Militia council................................	1911	808	2133
15	Militia council................................	1913	275	501
16	Adjutant-general..............................	1909	373	770
16, subd. 12, repealed	Stands of arms for G. A. R......................	1909	240	407
18	Adjutant-general..............................	1911	281	678
18	Adjutant-general, assistants and employees........	1913	3	4
20	Armory commissions...........................	1913	558	1495
22	Audit and payment of accounts..................	1913	558	1498
30	Composition of national guard...................	1909	370	756
31	Division and brigades..........................	1909	370	757
32	Staff departments.............................	1909	370	758
32	Staff departments.............................	1911	167	265
33	Corps of engineers.............................	1909	370	759
38	Coast artillery corps...........................	1909	370	760
38	Coast artillery corps...........................	1911	795	2103
40, added	Aides..	1911	285	686
40, added	Colored regiment of infantry....................	1913	793	2201
51	Staff of commodore............................	1911	282	680
53	Battalion of naval militia.......................	1911	282	680
54	Division of naval militia........................	1911	282	681
56	Civilian cooks................................	1911	282	682

I. CHANGES IN THE CONSOLIDATED LAWS, 1909–1913 — (*Continued*).

Section.	SUBJECT.	Year.	Chapter.	Page.
	MILITARY LAW — (*Continued*).			
57	Retirement of officers of naval militia.............	1909	233	363
59	Appointed officers of naval militia................	1911	282	682
Art. 4, tit.	Commissioned officers.....................	1911	99	145
71	Eligibility for commission...................	1909	371	761
74	Appointed officers......................	1909	371	763
74	Appointed officers......................	1911	99	145
79	Brevet commissions.....................	1909	371	766
80	Supernumerary and retired officers.............	1909	371	766
80	Supernumerary and retired officers.............	1911	285	685
82	National guard, retirement and discharge.........	1911	464	1066
82	Retirement and discharge of officers.............	1911	770	2043
95	Enlistments...........................	1909	369	754
95	Enlistments...........................	1911	100	149
95	Enlistments...........................	1912	68	107
96	Re-enlistments.........................	1911	100	150
96	Re-enlistments.........................	1913	567	1545
97	Enlistment papers......................	1911	283	683
99	Non-commissioned officers.................	1909	372	767
101	Taking up from dropped..................	1909	369	755
101	Taking up from dropped..................	1912	161	293
101	Taking up from dropped..................	1913	567	1546
102	Retirement...........................	1913	567	1547
103	Discharges............................	1912	161	294
113, 114	Service without the state.................	1910	241	430
121, added	Organization when aiding civil authorities.........	1911	284	684
130	Military courts........................	1910	108	164
134	Punishment of officers...................	1913	566	1544
135	Offenses of enlisted men; penalties.............	1910	108	165
136	Delinquency courts for officers...............	1910	242	431
137, 139, 142	Military courts........................	1910	108	165
143	Discharge for failure to pay fine..............	1913	419	884
151–153, 158	Military courts........................	1910	108	169
168	Full-dress uniform......................	1912	267	107
168	Full-dress uniform......................	1913	272	498
175–179, added	Armories............................	1913	558	1498
180	Armories, headquarters; provision for or construction	1913	558	1502
181	Armories, altered, etc., by armory commission.....	1913	558	1503
182	Headquarters for regiments and battalions.........	1913	558	1503
183	Armories in New York city..................	1911	102	154
183	Armories in New York city..................	1912	165	299
184	New sites for armories, New York city............	1911	381	866
185	Acquisition of sites for armories..............	1912	296	542
185	Acquisition of sites for armories..............	1913	558	1504
186	Control of armories.....................	1911	102	1156
186	Control of armories.....................	1913	558	1505
187	Armories, janitors and engineers..............	1911	102	157
187	Armories, janitors and engineers..............	1913	206	367
187	Armories, janitors, engineers and electricians........	1913	558	1506
188	Laborers in armories.....................	1910	19	28
188	Laborers in armories.....................	1911	102	158
188	Laborers in armories.....................	1913	558	1507
189	Compensation of employees in armories...........	1911	102	159

I. Changes in the Consolidated Laws, 1909–1913 — (Continued).

Section.	SUBJECT.	Year.	Chapter.	Page.
	MILITARY LAW — (Continued).			
189	Compensation of employees in armories............	1912	242	461
189	Compensation of employees in armories............	1913	558	1508
192, subd. (b)	Use of armories.................................	1909	240	407
192, subd. (d)	Use of armories for national conventions..........	1911	462	1065
193	Annual estimate for maintenance.................	1913	558	1509
194	Emergency expenditures..........................	1913	558	1511
195	Inventory of property; accountability therefor......	1913	558	1512
196, added	Disposal of useless property......................	1913	558	1512
197, added	First estimate for maintenance...................	1913	558	1512
210	Pay and allowances..............................	1909	308	576
210	Pay and allowances..............................	1912	278	508
212	Pay of officers serving on boards and courts........	1913	68	118
215	Pay and allowances..............................	1909	309	577
216	Allowances for organizations.....................	1911	101	151
216	Allowances for organizations.....................	1912	56	84
216	Allowances for organizations.....................	1913	568	1547
217	Pay and allowances..............................	1909	307	575
217	Pay and allowances..............................	1912	56	85
218	Allowances for headquarters......................	1911	101	152
218	Allowances for headquarters......................	1912	56	86
218	Allowances for headquarters......................	1913	207	368
219	Allowance for salaries...........................	1913	374	808
223	Pay and allowances for injury in service...........	1912	174	315
226	Interest on military funds........................	1913	558	1514
238	Exemption from jury duty........................	1911	100	150
241	Military parades by unauthorized bodies prohibited..	1911	210	484
241	Parades and organisation by unauthorized bodies....	1912	69	109
241	Parades and organisation by unauthorized bodies....	1913	41	67
244, added	Devises and bequests............................	1909	536	1338
244	Devises and bequests............................	1911	101	153
245, added	Employees of state or municipality on military duty..	1911	103	161
246, added	Oaths..	1911	103	161
252	Associations....................................	1909	311	579
252	Formation of associations........................	1911	104	162
252	Formation of associations........................	1913	273	498

Section.	**NAVIGATION LAW:** (L. 1909, ch. 42, constituting cons. laws, ch. 37.)	Year.	Chapter.	Page.
6	Inspection of boilers............................	1913	765	1908
8	Number of passengers carried....................	1913	765	1909
11, repealed	Sailing rules....................................	1913	765	1910
11, added	Sailing rules....................................	1913	765	1910
12, repealed	Lights on vessels................................	1913	765	1910
12, added	Lights on vessels................................	1913	765	1912
17	Licenses..	1913	765	1913
19	Names of vessels................................	1913	765	1914
26	Copy of law to be posted.........................	1913	765	1914
32	Vessel owners to notify inspectors.................	1913	765	1914
33	Penalties.......................................	1913	765	1914

I. CHANGES IN THE CONSOLIDATED LAWS, 1909–1913 — (*Continued*).

Section.	SUBJECT.	Year.	Chap-ter.	Page.
37–39, 39a–39f, added	**NAVIGATION LAW** — (*Continued*).			
	Motor boats........................	1913	765	1916
40a, added	Removal of ice gorges in Hudson river.............	1910	312	557
47, added	Harbor masters along Hudson river...............	1911	620	1415
50a, added	Buoys and beacons...........................	1910	421	764
86	Claim for salvage...........................	1909	240	407
100	Application of chapter......................	1913	765	1919
Schedule of re-peals	L. 1890, ch. 569, §§ 137–150, inserted.............	1909	240	422
	PENAL LAW: (L. 1909, ch. 88, constituting cons. laws, ch. 40.)			
71	Abduction or compulsory marriage................	1909	524	1317
190	Poisoning domestic animals....................	1910	81	127
222	Arson in second degree.......................	1913	154	271
223	Arson in third degree.......................	1913	154	271
271	None but attorneys to practice in cities of first and second-class.....................	1910	327	573
280, added	Corporations not to practice law................	1909	483	1170
280	Voluntary associations not to practice law..........	1911	317	738
290, 298	Issue of certificates of deposit...................	1910	398	729
303, added	False statements or rumors as to banking institutions.	1912	211	377
304, added	Falsification of books and reports of corporations....	1912	208	373
305, added	Property and credit of banking corporation........	1913	102	172
390	Bucket shops.............................	1913	236	425
395, added	Bucket shops.............................	1913	236	426
421	False statements, sale of real estate..............	1911	759	2023
421	False advertisements, sale of real estate...........	1912	321	640
421	False advertisements.......................	1913	590	1596
443, added	Tickets issued by People's Institute not transferable.	1909	424	905
444, added	Discriminations by exchanges or members..........	1913	477	998
444, added	Manufacture and sale of mattresses...............	1913	503	1189
483, subd. 3, re-pealed	Contributing to juvenile delinquency..............	1910	699	2021
484, subd. 1	Admitting children to moving-picture shows........	1909	278	485
484, subd. 1	Admitting children to pool or billiard rooms........	1910	383	710
484, subd. 1	Permitting children to attend certain resorts........	1910	475	915
484, subd. 1	Admitting children to pool rooms and bowling alleys.	1911	243	613
486, subd. 5	Transfer of incorrigible children.................	1912	169	306
494, added	Contributing to juvenile delinquency..............	1910	699	2017
517, added	Discrimination against United States uniform.......	1911	410	938
584, added	Conspiracies.............................	1910	395	725
611, repealed	Testimony in seduction, abduction, etc.............	1909	524	1317
670, added	Misconduct by officers and directors of certain in-surance corporations and societies...............	1910	620	1589
750	Candidates at primary elections..................	1910	430	806
752	Crimes against elective franchise.................	1909	306	574
760a, added	Misconduct respecting designation petitions........	1912	207	371
776	Filing candidate's statement of expenses............	1910	439	820

I. CHANGES IN THE CONSOLIDATED LAWS, 1909–1913 — (*Continued*).

Section.	SUBJECT.	Year.	Chapter.	Page.
	PENAL LAW — (*Continued*).			
851	Threats constituting extortion.....................	1911	121	183
851	Threats constituting extortion.....................	1911	602	1368
852	Punishment for extortion.........................	1909	368	753
852	Punishment for extortion.........................	1911	602	1368
856	Blackmail.....................................	1909	368	754
857	Attemped extortion by oral threats...............	1911	121	183
889, subd. 4	Forgery, third degree...........................	1912	342	673
936a, added	Unlawful dues of secret fraternities..............	1911	837	2347
950, added	False statements as to employment...............	1911	575	1331
951, added	Reporting fictitious transactions in securities.......	1913	476	997
952, added	False statement or advertisement as to securities....	1913	475	997
953, added	Manipulation of prices of securities..............	1913	253	448
954, added	Trading by brokers against customers' orders.......	1913	592	1601
955, added	Transactions by brokers after insolvency..........	1913	500	1184
956, added	Hypothecation of customers' securities by brokers..	1913	500	1184
957, added	Brokers to give customer memoranda of transactions.	1913	593	1602
973	Gaming and betting establishments................	1910	487	944
986	Book-making..................................	1910	488	945
1140a, added	Immoral plays and exhibitions....................	1909	279	485
1141a, added	Indecent prints and pictures.....................	1909	280	486
1146	Disorderly houses..............................	1910	619	1588
1146	Disorderly houses..............................	1913	591	1600
1148, added	Male persons living on earnings of prostitution.....	1910	382	709
1191	Discrimination by life insurance corporations......	1913	180	332
1199	Acting for foreign corporation not having designated superintendent of insurance as attorney..........	1913	50	85
1203, added	Issue of false literature by insurance corporations....	1913	483	1163
1221	Intoxication in a public place....................	1911	700	1890
1250	Penalty for kidnapping..........................	1909	246	435
1250	Kidnapping....................................	1911	625	1420
1272	Payment of wages by corporations................	1909	205	322
1273, repealed	Seats for women employees.......................	1913	349	648
1275	Violations of labor law..........................	1911	749	2012
1275	Violations of labor laws.........................	1913	349	647
1275, subd. 7a, added	Violation of provisions of labor law..............	1912	383	739
1293a, added	Unauthorized use of vehicles.....................	1909	514	1305
1293a	Unauthorized use of vehicles.....................	1910	621	1590
1293b, added	Obtaining property or credit by false statement.....	1912	340	671
1296	Grand larceny, second degree....................	1912	164	298
1421	Burning crops or timber.........................	1910	474	914
1423	Injury to mile-boards, etc., on highways...........	1911	316	736
1425, subd. 11a, added	Damaging motor vehicle.........................	1909	525	1318
1433	Injury to property; how punished.................	1912	163	297
1460 renumbered 1092	Husband and wife..............................	1909	524	1316
Art. 138, heading, repealed	Married women................................	1909	524	1317
1484	Converting military property; wearing uniform, etc..	1913	555	1491
1500a, added	Mufflers for motor boats, Lake George............	1911	758	2022
1510, added	Mufflers for motor boats, tidal waters.............	1911	840	2355

I. CHANGES IN THE CONSOLIDATED LAWS, 1909–1913 — (*Continued*).

Section.	SUBJECT.	Year.	Chapter.	Page.
	PENAL LAW — (*Continued*).			
1563	Advertising as ticket agents; false information......	1911	415	944
1566	Sale of railway transfers..........................	1909	204	321
1572, added	Soliciting surrender of tickets from immigrants......	1911	540	1218
1620	Perjury..	1909	240	407
1746	Sale of cocaine or eucaine.........................	1910	131	231
1746, repealed	Sale of cocaine or eucaine.........................	1913	470	984
1746, added	Sale of cocaine or eucaine.........................	1913	470	984
1820a, added	Notaries public and commissioners of deeds.........	1910	471	911
1896	Making and disposing of dangerous weapons........	1911	195	442
1897	Carrying and use of dangerous weapons.............	1911	195	443
1897	Carrying and use of dangerous weapons.............	1913	608	1627
1899	Destruction of dangerous weapons..................	1911	195	443
1914, added	Sale of pistols and other firearms..................	1911	195	444
1914	Sale of pistols and other firearms..................	1913	608	1630
1943, renumbered				
2461	Concealment of birth of issue......................	1909	524	1317
1988	Railroads; guard posts, automatic couplers........	1913	398	841
2052, added	Stealing or destruction of will.....................	1910	357	639
2074, added	Theatrical presentations of the Divinity, prohibited..	1911	319	740
2147	Public traffic on Sunday...........................	1913	346	645
2151	Parades on Sunday.................................	1911	147	227
2151	Parades on Sunday.................................	1913	16	25
2175–2177, added	Seduction...	1909	524	1317
2184	Sentence of minors to certain institutions..........	1913	607	1636
2186	Sentence of minors................................	1909	478	1163
2189	Indeterminate sentences...........................	1909	282	511
2197, repealed	Commitments for five years or less.................	1909	467	1122
2198, added	Sentence to state prisons..........................	1909	240	408
2221, added	Burials on canal lands prohibited..................	1910	144	265
2354, subd. 5	Offenses against trade marks.......................	1909	240	408
2414a, added	False weights and measures, presumption of knowledge....	1911	53	73
2444	Convict competent witness.........................	1909	240	408
2446, added	Waiver of immunity by witness....................	1912	312	568
2460	Compulsory prostitution of women.................	1910	618	1585
2461, repealed	Seduction...	1909	524	1317
Schedule of repeals	L. 1888, ch. 490, § 6, inserted....................	1909	240	423
Schedule of repeals	L. 1894, ch. 426, § 3, inserted....................	1909	240	423
	PERSONAL PROPERTY LAW: (L. 1909, ch. 45, constituting cons. laws, ch. 41.)			
12, subd. 2	Gift for charitable, etc., purposes.................	1909	144	222
12, subd. 4, added	Application of funds collected for charitable purposes.	1911	220	494
13a, added	Trusts for care of cemetery lots...................	1909	218	343
13a	Trusts for care of cemetery lots...................	1911	430	967

I. CHANGES IN THE CONSOLIDATED LAWS, 1909–1913 — (Continued).

Section.	SUBJECT.	Year.	Chapter.	Page.
	PERSONAL PROPERTY LAW — (Continued).			
15	When proceeds of life insurance policy not alienable..	1911	327	765
20	Commissions of trustee appointed by supreme court.	1911	217	491
23, added	Revocation of trusts..............................	1909	247	436
31, subd. 6, ¶ 1, repealed	Statute of frauds, sale of goods...................	1911	571	1326
36, repealed	Sale without delivery and change of possession......	1911	571	1326
42	Loans on salaries................................	1911	626	1421
45, added	Notice of liens to secure loans....................	1911	326	762
Art. 5 (§§ 80, 81), renumbered art. 6 (§§ 165, 166)	Laws repealed; when to take effect................	1911	571	1298
Art. 5 (§§ 82–158), added	Sales of goods..................................	1911	571	1298
Art. 6 (§§ 162–185), added	Stock transfers.................................	1913	600	1614
187–241, added	Bills of lading.................................	1911	248	619

POOR LAW:
(L. 1909, ch. 46, constituting cons. laws, ch. 42.)

Section.	SUBJECT.	Year.	Chapter.	Page.
3, subd. 14	Payments of money by county superintendents......	1912	75	119
27	Taxation in towns for support of poor..............	1909	429	913
29	Support of poor in cities.........................	1909	380	792
30, subd. 2	Indigent persons, Westchester county..............	1912	309	563
56	Poor children...................................	1909	347	657
80	Relief of soldiers, sailors and marines..............	1910	102	154
81	Post or camp; notice that it assumes charge........	1910	102	155
81	Relief of veterans and families....................	1913	594	1603
82, 83	Relief of Spanish war veterans....................	1910	102	157
84	Burial of soldiers, sailors or marines...............	1912	306	560
85	Relief of Spanish war veterans....................	1910	102	158
Art. 6a (§§ 86, 87), added	Relief for women nurses..........................	1913	595	1605
118	Almshouse construction and administration.........	1913	251	446

PRISON LAW:
(L. 1909, ch. 47, constituting cons. laws, ch. 43.)

Section.	SUBJECT.	Year.	Chapter.	Page.
21	Bertillon system................................	1912	106	182
21	Bertillon system................................	1913	501	1185
70	Names and locations of state prisons..............	1909	479	1164
94	State Prison for Women; salaries..................	1912	105	181
95	Physician and chaplain, State Prison for Women....	1909	527	1320
97	Commitment of women..........................	1909	240	409
114	Compensation of officers in state prisons...........	1912	50	77
115	Principal keeper at Sing Sing Prison..............	1912	107	183
119	Bonds of certain officers.........................	1910	631	1627
210	Salaries of members of board of parole.............	1910	703	2037

3

I.   CHANGES IN THE CONSOLIDATED LAWS, 1909–1913 — (*Continued*).)

Section.	SUBJECT.	Year.	Chapter.	Page.
	PUBLIC HEALTH LAW — (*Continued*).			
230–235	Practice of pharmacy.........................	1910	422	764
236	Practice of pharmacy.........................	1910	422	764
236	Working hours and sleeping rooms in pharmacies....	1911	630	1428
237–240	Practice of pharmacy.........................	1910	422	764
240, subd. 9	Pharmacies, violations of regulations............	1911	630	1429
240a, added	Prosecution for violation of pharmacy provisions....	1913	223	302
241, added	Practice of pharmacy.........................	1910	422	764
252	Registration of nurses, waiver of examination......	1913	390	830
271	Chiropody, eligibility to certificate without examination......	1912	199	356
271	Chiropody; eligibility to certificate without examination......	1913	499	1183
272, 273	Chiropody; examination for license; expenses......	1912	199	356
277	Falsely claiming to be member of pedic society......	1912	199	358
278–281	Chiropody; registration of license; penalties.......	1912	199	358
290	Board of embalming examiners....................	1911	841	2356
290	Board of embalming examiners....................	1913	71	122
291	Board of embalming examiners....................	1913	71	122
293	Examination for embalmer's license.............	1913	71	124
294	Embalmer's license..........................	1913	71	125
295	Certified undertakers........................	1911	841	2356
295	Undertaker's license..........................	1913	71	125
296	Reciprocal licenses; license not assignable........	1913	71	126
298	Embalming without a license....................	1911	841	2358
299, added	Violations of art. 14........................	1911	841	2358
303	Optometry, exemption from examination..........	1909	134	211
307	Optometry, violations of law....................	1913	498	1182
316	Cadavers for medical and surgical study..........	1913	335	626
318, repealed	Prescriptions of opium, etc....................	1910	422	780
318a, added	Sale of hypodermic syringes....................	1911	278	674
319	Hospitals for tuberculosis....................	1909	171	278
320	Tuberculosis, reports by physicians and others......	1913	559	1530
322	Protection of records of tuberculosis............	1913	559	1531
324	Disinfection of premises infected with tuberculosis....	1909	240	411
324	Disinfection by health authorities................	1910	427	789
324	Disinfection, etc., by health authorities..........	1913	559	1532
326a, added	Control of dangerous and careless patients........	1913	559	1533
328	Reports of tuberculosis cases....................	1909	426	907
328	Reports of tuberculosis cases....................	1911	490	1103
328	Reports of tuberculosis cases....................	1913	559	1534
329	Penalty imposed on physicians....................	1913	559	1536
332	Application of provisions........................	1909	240	411
335, added	Cold storage; definitions........................	1911	335	775
336, added	Cold storage food to be marked..................	1911	335	775
336a, added	Cold storage; license..........................	1913	560	1537
337, added	Time cold storage foods may be kept..............	1911	335	775
338, added	Cold storage; powers of commissioner of health.....	1911	335	775
338a, added	Cold storage; food to be condemned..............	1913	560	1538
339, 339a–339d, added	Cold storage.................................	1911	335	776
Art. 17a (§§ 343a–343c), added	Cleanliness in preparation and service of food.......	1913	552	1488

I. CHANGES IN THE CONSOLIDATED LAWS, 1909–1913 — (*Continued*).

Section.	SUBJECT.	Year.	Chapter.	Page.
	PUBLIC HEALTH LAW — (*Continued*).			
344, 345, added	State institute for study of malignant disease.......	1911	128	205
346, added	State institute for study of malignant disease......	1911	128	206
346	State institute for study of malignant disease.......	1913	91	159
347, added	State institute for study of malignant disease......	1911	128	206
Art. 18 renumbered art. 19	Laws repealed; when to take effect................	1911	128	208
Art. 19 (§§ 350, 351) renumbered art. 20 (§§ 360, 361)	Laws repealed; when to take effect..............	1912	445	924
Art. 19 (§§ 350–353), added	Operation for prevention of procreation...........	1912	445	924
Art. 20 (§§ 360, 361) renumbered art. 21, (§§ 450, 451)	Laws repealed; when to take effect..............	1913	619	1647
Art. 20 (§§ 370–394), added	Vital statistics.................................	1913	619	1648
Art. 20 renumbered art. 21	Laws repealed; when to take effect..............	1913	630	1681
Art. 20 (§§ 354–356), added	Sanitary conditions in hotels.....................	1913	630	1682
	PUBLIC LANDS LAW:			
	(L. 1909, ch. 50, constituting cons. laws, ch. 46.)			
	Sale of unappropriated state lands................	1909	240	411
32	Escheats..	1911	399	912
60	Escheats..	1912	272	500
60, subd. 3	Escheats..	1909	240	412
60, subd. 3	Escheats..	1909	509	1286
60, subd. 7	Escheats..	1909	240	412
102, subd. 8, added	State reservation at Niagara, powers of commissioners	1912	236	451
Art. 10 (§§ 110–112) renumbered art. 11 (§§ 120–122)	Construction; laws repealed; when to take effect....	1911	731	1955
Art. 10 (§§ 110–117), added	Watkins Glen, board of commissioners.............	1911	731	1956
Art 11 renumbered art. 12	Construction; laws repealed; when to take effect.....	1913	167	308
Art. 11, added	Newtown battlefield reservation...................	1913	167	308
120 renumbered 140	Construction.....................................	1913	167	308
120, added	Newtown battlefield reservation...................	1913	167	308
121 renumbered 141	Laws repealed...................................	1913	167	308
121, added	Newtown battlefield reservation...................	1913	167	309

I. CHANGES IN THE CONSOLIDATED LAWS, 1909–1913 — (*Continued*).

Section.	SUBJECT.	Year.	Chapter.	Page.
	PUBLIC LANDS LAW — (*Continued*).			
122 renumbered 142	When to take effect..............................	1913	167	308
122, added	Newtown battlefield reservation..................	1913	167	309
123–127, added	Newtown battlefield reservation..................	1913	167	309
	PUBLIC OFFICERS LAW: (L. 1909, ch. 51, constituting cons. laws, ch. 47.)			
10	Official oaths...................................	1913	59	99
11	Official undertakings............................	1911	424	958
11	Official undertakings............................	1912	481	1001
11	Official undertakings............................	1913	325	605
16, added	Qualifications of certain judicial officers.........	1913	586	1580
63	Leaves of absence to veterans on Memorial day.....	1910	335	591
71, added	Vacations of employees of state and civil divisions..	1910	680	1908
	PUBLIC SERVICE COMMISSIONS LAW (L. 1910, ch. 480, constituting cons. laws, ch. 48.) (*See note* L. 1910, p. 923.)			
2, subd. 9	Common carriers..............................	1913	344	640
2, subd. 9a, added	Baggage companies.............................	1913	344	641
2, subds. 17–20, added	Telegraph and telephone lines and companies......	1910	673	1929
2, subd. 21, added	Steam plant defined............................	1913	505	1192
2, subd. 21, added	Stock yards...................................	1913	506	1206
2, subd. 22, added	Steam corporation defined......................	1913	505	1192
5, subd. 1, subd. h, added	Steam corporations............................	1913	505	1192
5, subds. 5–7, added	Telegraph and telephone lines and companies......	1910	673	1929
5, subd. 8, added	Stock yards...................................	1913	506	1207
7	Proceedings as evidence........................	1913	597	1609
33, subd. 3	Free or reduced transportation..................	1911	546	1226
33, subd. 4	Power of commission as to reduced rates..........	1911	546	1227
38	Liability for damage to property in transit........	1913	344	641
49, subd. 1	Power of commission to fix rates.................	1911	546	1228
54	Transfer of franchises or stocks.................	1911	788	2094
55a, added	Reorganization of railroad corporations, etc.......	1912	289	522
66, subd. 3	Standards for measurement of gas...............	1913	504	1190
69a, added	Reorganization of gas and electrical companies.....	1912	289	523
70	Transfer of franchises, approved................	1911	788	2096
Art. 4a (§§ 78–82, 82a, 83–89, 89a), added	Steam heating corporations.....................	1913	505	1193
80–87 renumbered 120–127	Telegraph and telephone lines and companies......	1910		1929
90–92, added	Telegraph and telephone lines and companies......	1910	673	1929
92, subd. 3	Free passes, telephone and telegraph companies....	1911	632	187

I. CHANGES IN THE CONSOLIDATED LAWS, 1909–1913 — *(Continued)*.

Section.	SUBJECT.	Year.	Chapter.	Page.
	PUBLIC SERVICE COMMISSIONS LAW — *(Con'd)*.			
93–101, added	Telegraph and telephone lines and companies.......	1910	673	1929
101a, added	Reorganisation of telegraph and telephone companies	1912	289	523
102, 103, added	Telegraph and telephone lines and companies.......	1910	673	1443
Art. 5 renumbered art. 6	Telegraph and telephone lines and companies.......	1910	673	1929
	RAILROAD LAW:			
	(L. 1910, ch. 481, constituting cons. laws, ch. 49. *See notes. L. 1910, pp. 917, 923, and amendments to former railroad law (L. 1890, ch. 565) in table of laws, other than consolidated laws, amended. L. 1910, appendix, p. 39.*)			
17	Acquisition of real property......................	1913	284	513
21	Railroads along highways........................	1913	743	1864
54a, added	Full crews for certain trains.....................	1913	146	263
78	Coal jimmies and caboose cars....................	1913	497	1180
88	Conductors and brakemen as policemen............	1911	817	2315
89	New railroads across streets.....................	1913	425	893
89	Alteration of crossings at county roads............	1913	744	1866
90	Alteration of crossings at county roads............	1913	744	1867
91	Petition for alteration of crossing................	1911	141	226
91	Petition for alteration of existing crossings........	1913	354	654
91	Alteration of crossings at county roads............	1913	744	1868
92	Alteration of crossings at county roads............	1913	744	1870
93	Alteration of crossings at county roads............	1913	744	1870
94	Expense of constructing new crossings............	1911	141	228
94	Expense of constructing new crossings............	1913	354	656
94	Expense of constructing new crossings............	1913	425	894
94	Alteration of crossings at county roads............	1913	744	1871
95	Proceedings for alteration of grade crossings.......	1913	354	659
97	Alteration of crossings at county roads............	1913	744	1875
99	Alteration of crossings at county roads............	1913	744	1875
140, subd. 1	Powers of consolidated corporations owning continuous lines................................	1911	506	1161
170	Condemnation by street surface railroads..........	1911	418	949
178	Repair of streets..............................	1912	368	719
191	Construction of street railroads in parks, etc........	1912	482	1003
	REAL PROPERTY LAW:			
	(L. 1909, ch. 52, constituting cons. laws, ch. 50.)			
10	Tenure of real property by aliens.................	1913	152	269
12–14, repealed	Tenure of real property by aliens.................	1913	152	270
67, 68, 70	Lease of real property held by certain life tenants...	1913	55	92
111	Commissions of trustee appointed by supreme court..	1911	216	490
113, subd. 2	Gifts for charitable, etc., purposes...............	1909	144	222
114a, added	Trusts for care of cemetery lots..................	1909	218	344

I. CHANGES IN THE CONSOLIDATED LAWS, 1909–1913 — *(Continued)*.

Section.	SUBJECT.	Year.	Chapter.	Page.
	REAL PROPERTY LAW — *(Continued)*.			
260	Grant or mortgage of real property adversely possessed	1909	481	1167
260	Grant or mortgage of real property adversely possessed	1910	628	1604
301, subd. 9, added	Acknowledgment and proofs in Austria-Hungary....	1912	70	111
310	Authentication of certificate of acknowledgment.....	1911	196	445
311	Authentication of acknowledgments................	1913	209	371
322	Discharge of mortgage, in certain counties.........	1912	254	477
333, added	Recording instruments affecting real property.......	1910	227	414
333, added	Execution of satisfaction of mortgage..............	1911	574	1328
334, added	Filing of maps.................................	1910	415	736
362	Notice to persons interested in title................	1909	240	413
370	Application to register title......................	1910	627	1602
374	Assistant deputy register........................	1909	305	573
379, 380, 382, 383, 385–387, amended; 388, repealed; 388, added; 390, 391, 393, 398, amended; 404, repealed; 404, added; 406, 410, 416, 432, amended; 434, repealed; 434, added	Registering titles to real property.................	1910	627	1603
451, added	Acquisition of lands for cemetery purposes.........	1909	274	477
451	Acquisition of lands for cemetery purposes.........	1912	300	550
Schedule of repeals	R. S., pt. 2, ch. 1, tit. 1, §§ 1–4, 8–20, inserted......	1909	240	422
Schedule of repeals	L. 1794, ch. 1, §§ 1, 3–7, inserted.................	1909	240	422
	RELIGIOUS CORPORATIONS LAW: (L. 1909, ch. 53, constituting cons. laws, ch. 51.)			
12	Real property of religious corporations.............	1912	290	534
12	Real property of religious corporations.............	1913	128	210
16	Property of extinct churches.....................	1909	408	878
16	Property of extinct churches.....................	1910	185	343
47, added	Free churches in communion with Episcopal church..	1913	487	1166
131	Baptist churches; meetings for incorporation........	1913	397	839
136	Baptist churches; number of trustees..............	1913	397	840
195	Corporate meetings.............................	1911	711	1912
197	Number of trustees of an incorporated church.......	1910	249	443

I. CHANGES IN THE CONSOLIDATED LAWS, 1909-1913 — (*Continued*).

Section.	SUBJECT.	Year.	Chapter.	Page.
	SALT SPRINGS LAW: (L. 1909, ch. 54, constituting cons. laws, ch. 52.)			
5	Superintendent of Onondaga salt springs, office abolished.................................	1911	458	1060
40, repealed	Superintendent of Onondaga salt springs..........	1911	458	1061
Schedule of repeals	L. 1867, ch. 261, omitted.........................	1909	240	421
Schedule of repeals	L. 1897, ch. 261, inserted........................	1909	240	423
	SECOND CLASS CITIES LAW: (L. 1909, ch. 55, constituting cons. laws, ch. 53.)			
60	Temporary and funded debts......................	1910	692	2005
60	Temporary and funded debts......................	1911	60	81
60	Temporary and funded debts......................	1913	43	70
79	Contracts and expenditures prohibited.............	1912	195	342
81, added	Appropriations for band concerts..................	1911	493	1115
91	Commissioner of public works.....................	1912	189	335
122	Contracts for lighting............................	1913	70	121
124	Contracts for paving.............................	1913	141	234
130, 131	Buildings department created.....................	1909	573	1661
137, 138	Appeals from commissioner of public safety........	1910	266	477
149, 152, 155–157, added	Buildings department created.....................	1909	573	1662
	STATE BOARDS AND COMMISSIONS LAW: (L. 1909, ch. 56, constituting cons. laws, ch. 54.)			
1–4, repealed	State water supply commission....................	1911	647	1550
5	State water supply commission....................	1910	285	513
5, repealed	State water supply commission....................	1911	647	1550
6	State water supply commission....................	1910	285	513
6, repealed	State water supply commission....................	1911	647	1550
7	State water supply commission....................	1910	285	513
7, repealed	State water supply commission....................	1911	647	1550
8–11, repealed	State water supply commission....................	1911	647	1550
12	Proceedings for river improvement.................	1911	36	48
12	Proceedings for river improvement.................	1911	420	951
12, repealed	State water supply commission....................	1911	647	1550
12a, added	Creation of river improvement districts............	1909	464	1106
12a	Creation of river improvement districts............	1911	142	231
12a, repealed	State water supply commission....................	1911	647	1550
13, repealed	State water supply commission....................	1911	647	1550
14	Entry upon lands................................	1909	464	1107
14, repealed	State water supply commission....................	1911	647	1550
15, 16, repealed	State water supply commission....................	1911	647	1550
17	Bonds for river improvement.....................	1909	464	1108
17, repealed	State water supply commission....................	1911	647	1550

I. CHANGES IN THE CONSOLIDATED LAWS, 1909–1913 — (*Continued*).

Section.	SUBJECT.	Year.	Chapter.	Page.
	STATE BOARDS AND COMMISSIONS LAW (*Continued*).			
18	Apportionment of cost..................	1909	464	1109
18, repealed	State water supply commission.........	1911	647	1550
19	Assessment and collection of cost......	1909	464	1111
19, repealed	State water supply commission.........	1911	647	1550
20	River improvement certificates........	1909	464	1113
20, repealed	State water supply commission.........	1911	647	1550
21	Operation and expenses...............	1909	464	1113
21, repealed	State water supply commission.........	1911	647	1550
22, repealed	State water supply commission.........	1911	647	1550
22a, added	Collectors and other officers..........	1909	464	1113
22a, repealed	State water supply commission.........	1911	647	1550
22b, added	Ratification of proceedings............	1909	464	1114
22b, repealed	State water supply commission.........	1911	647	1550
23, 24, repealed	State water supply commission.........	1911	647	1550
25, added	Improvement of water courses at private expense....	1909	284	513
25, repealed	State water supply commission.........	1911	647	1550
26, added	Refund of expenses...................	1909	284	515
26, repealed	State water supply commission.........	1911	647	1550
30	State probation commission...........	1910	613	1577
41	Term and expenses of commissioners..............	1909	240	413
Schedule of repeals	L. 1894, ch. 349, inserted.............	1909	240	423
	STATE CHARITIES LAW: (L. 1909, ch. 57, constituting cons. laws, ch. 55.)			
Analysis of articles	Generally............................	1909	258	453
41	Office and clerical force of fiscal supervisor..........	1913	173	319
42	Powers and duties of fiscal supervisor.............	1909	149	229
42	Powers and duties of fiscal supervisor.............	1911	405	924
44	Fiscal year..........................	1909	149	230
44	Fiscal year..........................	1911	405	925
45	Expenses; contingent fund............	1909	149	230
45	Expenses; contingent fund............	1911	9	10
45	Expenses; contingent fund............	1911	405	926
45	Expenses; contingent fund............	1913	663	1751
46	Receipts and expenditures............	1909	149	231
47	Affidavit of steward; vouchers........	1911	405	927
48	Purchases...........................	1909	149	232
48	Purchases...........................	1911	305	718
48	Purchases...........................	1913	662	1748
49	Erection, repairs, etc................	1909	149	233
49	Contracts in connection with state institutions......	1910	47	75
50	Visitations and reports...............	1909	149	235
50	Visitations and reports by managers.................	1911	405	928
51	Managers and trustees...............	1909	149	236
52, added	Admission to state charitable institutions..........	1911	843	2368
60–62, 66–69	Managers and officers, Syracuse State Institution for Feeble-Minded Children....................	1910	449	846

I. CHANGES IN THE CONSOLIDATED LAWS, 1909-1913 — (*Continued*).

Section.	SUBJECT.	Year.	Chapter.	Page.
	STATE CHARITIES LAW — (*Continued*).			
70	Syracuse Institution for Feeble-Minded Children, clothing for pupils..........................	1911	609	1382
71, added	Syracuse Institution for . Feeble-Minded Children, sewer system..........................	1910	376	694
81	Managers, State Custodial Asylum for Feeble-Minded Women..................................	1910	449	848
91, 92	Managers, Rome State Custodial Asylum...........	1910	449	849
95, added	Rome State Custodial Asylum....................	1909	339	637
95, subds. 9, 10, added	Rome State Custodial Asylum....................	1912	448	929
101	Managers, Craig Colony for Epileptics.............	1910	449	849
102	Buildings and improvements, Craig Colony.........	1909	149	237
102	Buildings and improvements, Craig Colony.........	1910	449	850
103	Managers, Craig Colony.........................	1910	449	850
103, subd. 3	Managers, Craig Colony.........................	1909	149	238
104	Annual report, Craig Colony.....................	1909	149	238
104	Annual report of managers, Craig Colony..........	1910	449	851
107, 108	Duties of superintendent and of agent as treasurer, Craig Colony..................................	1910	449	851
110	Support of state patients, Craig Colony...........	1909	149	238
114, repealed	Notice of opening of Craig Colony................	1910	449	854
114, added	Craig Colony, detention and discharge of inmates....	1911	588	1348
115 renumbered 114	Maintenance expenses, Craig Colony..............	1910	449	854
116	Sale of products, Craig Colony...................	1909	149	239
116 renumbered 115	Sale of products, Craig Colony...................	1910	449	854
117, added	Designation of special policemen at Craig Colony....	1910	260	463
Art. 9 renumbered art. 18	Care of inebriate women........................	1909	258	452
120-128 renumbered 340-348	Care of inebriate women........................	1909	258	452
Art. 10 renumbered art. 9	Hospital for Crippled and Deformed Children.......	1909	258	452
130	Hospital for Crippled and Deformed Children.......	1909	149	239
130	Hospital for Crippled and Deformed Children......	1909	240	413
131	Managers, Hospital for Crippled and Deformed Children...................................	1910	449	854
132	Managers, Hospital for Crippled and Deformed Children...................................	1910	449	854
132, subd. 2	Book of proceedings, Hospital for Crippled and Deformed Children.............................	1909	149	239
132, subd. 3	Report, Hospital for Crippled and Deformed Children	1909	149	239
133	Surgeon in chief, Hospital for Crippled and Deformed Children...................................	1910	449	856
133, subd. 3	Estimates for Hospital for Crippled and Deformed Children...................................	1909	149	240
134, repealed	Salaries, Hospital for Crippled and Deformed Children	1910	449	856
135, 136 renumbered 134, 135	Hospital for Crippled and Deformed Children.......	1910	449	856
136	Hospital for Crippled and Deformed Children.......	1911	172	271
137,138 renumbered 136, 137	Hospital for Crippled and Deformed Children.......	1910	449	856

I. CHANGES IN THE CONSOLIDATED LAWS, 1909-1913 — (*Continued*).

Section.	SUBJECT.	Year.	Chapter.	Page.
	STATE CHARITIES LAW — (*Continued*).			
139	Managers' report, Hospital for Crippled and Deformed Children..............................	1909	149	240
Art. 11 renumbered art. 10	Raybrook Hospital..............................	1909	258	452
151	Trustees, Raybrook Hospital......................	1910	449	856
153	Trustees, Raybrook Hospital......................	1910	449	857
153, subd. 4	Proceedings of trustees, Raybrook Hospital.........	1909	149	240
154	Report of trustees, Raybrook Hospital.............	1909	149	240
154	Report of trustees, Raybrook Hospital.............	1910	449	858
157, 158, 162	Superintendent, treasurer, and free patients, Raybrook Hospital..............................	1910	449	858
Art. 12 renumbered art. 17	Aged, decrepit and mentally enfeebled persons......	1909	258	452
170-174 renumbered 320-324	Aged, decrepit and mentally enfeebled persons......	1909	258	452
Art. 13 renumbered art. 11	Institutions for juvenile delinquents..............	1909	258	452
180	State Agricultural and Industrial School..........	1910	449	861
182, 184, 191	State Agricultural School and House of Refuge for Juvenile Delinquents...........................	1910	449	861
199, 200	State Training School for Girls..................	1910	449	863
200	Managers, State Training School for Girls..........	1911	447	1003
201	State Training School for Girls..................	1910	449	863
204	State Training School for Girls, commitments.......	1910	449	864
204	State Training School for Girls, commitments.......	1911	486	1090
204, subd. 1	State Training School for Girls..................	1909	340	639
206	State Training School for Girls, children of inmates..	1911	555	1250
213	United States female juvenile delinquents..........	1910	449	865
214	Effect of art. 11...............................	1909	240	413
Art. 14 renumbered art. 12	House of refuge and reformatory for women........	1909	258	452
220	House of refuge and reformatory for women........	1909	258	454
220	House of refuge and reformatory for women........	1910	449	866
221	Managers, house of refuge and reformatory for women....................................	1910	449	867
223	Officers and employees of certain institutions for women....................................	1909	149	241
226	Commitments, house of refuge and reformatory for women....................................	1910	449	867
226	Commitments of females.........................	1913	605	1623
Art. 15 renumbered art. 21	Anchorage at Elmira............................	1909	258	452
250 renumbered 400	Anchorage at Elmira............................	1909	258	452
251 renumbered 401	Anchorage at Elmira............................	1909	258	452
251	Managers, Woman's Relief Corps Home............	1910	449	868
252 renumbered 402	Anchorage at Elmira............................	1909	258	452
253 renumbered 403	Anchorage at Elmira............................	1909	258	452
253, repealed	Managers, Woman's Relief Corps Home............	1910	449	868

I. CHANGES IN THE CONSOLIDATED LAWS, 1909-1913 — (*Continued*).

Section.	SUBJECT.	Year.	Chapter.	Page.
	STATE CHARITIES LAW — (*Continued*).			
254 renumbered 404	Anchorage at Elmira..............................	1909	258	452
254 renumbered 253	Managers, Woman's Relief Corps Home...........	1910	449	869
255	Commitments to Anchorage at Elmira.............	1909	240	413
255 renumbered 405	Anchorage at Elmira..............................	1909	258	452
255 renumbered 254	Report, Woman's Relief Corps Home..............	1910	449	869
255	Admission to Woman's Relief Corps Home.........	1911	601	1366
255	Admission to Woman's Relief Corps Home.........	1912	310	564
256 renumbered 406	Anchorage at Elmira..............................	1909	258	452
256	Inmates, Woman's Relief Corps Home.............	1910	133	234
256 renumbered 255	Admission to Woman's Relief Corps Home.........	1910	449	869
257 renumbered 407	Anchorage at Elmira..............................	1909	258	452
257 renumbered 256	Managers, Woman's Relief Corps Home...........	1910	449	869
258 renumbered 408	Anchorage at Elmira..............................	1909	258	452
258 renumbered 257	Record, Woman's Relief Corps Home..............	1910	449	869
259-269 renumbered 409-419	Anchorage at Elmira..............................	1909	258	452
271	Managers, Thomas Indian School.................	1910	449	869
272	Managers, Thomas Indian School.................	1910	449	869
274	Superintendent, Thomas Indian School.............	1910	449	870
Art. 16 renumbered art. 19	Burnham Industrial Farm........................	1909	258	452
280-292 renumbered 360-372	Burnham Industrial Farm........................	1909	258	452
Art. 17 renumbered art. 20	Shelter for Unprotected Girls.....................	1909	258	452
300 renumbered 380	Shelter for Unprotected Girls.....................	1909	258	452
301 renumbered 381	Shelter for Unprotected Girls.....................	1909	258	452
301	Placing out destitute children....................	1910	449	871
302, 303 renumbered 382, 383	Shelter for Unprotected Girls.....................	1909	258	452
304 renumbered 384	Shelter for Unprotected Girls.....................	1909	258	452
304	Visitation of destitute children...................	1909	258	454
305, 306 renumbered 385, 386	Shelter for Unprotected Girls.....................	1909	258	452
307 renumbered 387	Shelter for Unprotected Girls.....................	1909	258	452
307	Placing out destitute children....................	1909	258	455
308 renumbered 388	Shelter for Unprotected Girls.....................	1909	258	452
308	Placing out destitute children....................	1909	258	455

I. CHANGES IN THE CONSOLIDATED LAWS, 1909-1913 — *(Continued)*.

Section.	SUBJECT.	Year.	Chap-ter.	Page.
	STATE CHARITIES LAW — *(Continued)*.			
309-311 renumbered 389-391	Shelter for Unprotected Girls.....................	1909	258	
Art. 18 renumbered art. 13	Woman's Relief Corps Home.....................	1909	258	
320-325 renumbered 250-255	Woman's Relief Corps Home.....................	1909	258	452 453
326	Admission to Woman's Relief Corps Home.........	1909	240	414
326 renumbered 256	Woman's Relief Corps Home.....................	1909	258	
327, 328 renumbered 257, 258	Woman's Relief Corps Home.....................	1909	258	
Art. 19 renumbered art. 14	Thomas Indian School...........................	1909	258	
340, 341 renumbered 270, 271	Thomas Indian School...........................	1909	258	
342 renumbered 272	Thomas Indian School...........................	1909	258	453
342, subd. 3	Proceedings of managers, Thomas Indian School....	1909	149	
343 renumbered 273	Thomas Indian School...........................	1909	258	
343, subd. 2	Duties of officers, Thomas Indian School..........	1909	149	
344-346 renumbered 274-276	Thomas Indian School...........................	1909	258	
Art. 20 renumbered art. 15	Licensing dispensaries...........................	1909	258	
350-356 renumbered 290-296	Licensing dispensaries...........................	1909	258	
Art. 21 renumbered art. 16	Licenses for placing out destitute children.........	1909	258	
360-367 renumbered 300-307	Licenses for placing out destitute children.........	1909	258	453
368 renumbered 308	Licenses for placing out destitute children.........	1909	258	453
368	Burnham Industrial Farm.........................	1909	258	455
372	Powers and liabilities, Burnham Industrial Farm....	1910	449	872
380-386 renumbered 450-456	General provisions..............................	1909	258	453
387 renumbered 457	Fees of witnesses at investigations................	1909	258	453
387	Shelter for Unprotected Girls.....................	1909	258	456
388, 389 renumbered 458, 459	General provisions..............................	1909	258	453
400, 401 renumbered 470, 471	Laws repealed; when to take effect................	1909	258	453
	STATE FINANCE LAW: (L. 1909, ch. 58, constituting cons. laws, ch. 56.)			
2a, added	Payment of salaries of state employees.............	1910	317	563
4, subd. 5	Comptroller's warrants...........................	1913	342	637
10	Deposit of moneys by state officers................	1911	294	698

I. CHANGES IN THE CONSOLIDATED LAWS, 1909-1913 — (*Continued*).

Section.	SUBJECT.	Year.	Chapter.	Page.
	STATE FINANCE LAW — (*Continued*).			
11	Deposit of moneys by charitable institutions........	1911	295	699
14	Temporary loans and revenue bonds..............	1913	645	1699
16	Accounts and contracts........................	1913	342	637
19	Securities of depositories of state institutions........	1910	77	122
19	Deposit of funds by state institutions.............	1911	293	697
37	Payments to treasurer by health officer, port of New York..	1910	440	822
37	Payments to state treasurer....................	1912	162	296
48, 49, added	Statements of desired appropriations to be filed with comptroller...........................	1910	149	270
50, added	Separate specifications for certain contract work....	1912	514	1043
63	Charges on canal fund.........................	1913	267	486
Art. 5, schedule of sections	Education funds................................	1911	634	1432
81	Education funds................................	1910	201	371
82	Education funds................................	1911	634	1432
83, repealed 84 renumbered	Education funds................................	1911	634	1432
83, and amended	Education funds................................	1911	634	1432
85, repealed 86 renumbered	Education funds................................	1911	634	1432
84, and amended	Education funds................................	1911	634	1432
87 87 renumbered	Education funds................................	1910	201	371
85, and amended 88 renumbered	Education funds................................	1911	634	1432
86, and amended 89 renumbered	Education funds................................	1911	634	1432
87, and amended	Education funds................................	1911	634	1432
90 90 renumbered	Education funds................................	1910	201	371
88, and amended	Education funds................................	1911	634	1432
91 91 renumbered	Education funds................................	1910	201	371
89, and amended	Education funds................................	1911	634	1432
92 92 renumbered	Education funds................................	1909	520	1312
90, and amended 93 renumbered	Education funds................................	1911	634	1432
91, and amended 94 renumbered	Education funds................................	1911	634	1432
92, and amended	Education funds................................	1911	634	1432
95, repealed	Education funds................................	1911	634	1432
96, repealed 97 renumbered	Education funds................................	1911	634	1432
93	Education funds................................	1911	634	1432
Schedule of repeals	L. 1864, ch. 185, § 4, omitted....................	1909	240	421

I. CHANGES IN THE CONSOLIDATED LAWS, 1909–1913 — (*Continued*).

Section.	SUBJECT.	Year.	Chapter.	Page.
	STATE LAW: (L. 1909, ch. 59, constituting cons. laws, ch. 57.)			
2	Connecticut boundary line........................	1912	352	692
2	Connecticut boundary line........................	1913	18	27
3	Massachusetts boundary line......................	1910	447	835
50	Acquisition by United States of lands for parade grounds...........................	1910	109	171
50	Purchase of lands by United States for naval purposes	1911	527	1201
51	Acquisition by United States of lands for parade grounds...........................	1910	109	171
55	Deeds of land acquired by United States..........	1909	240	414
Schedule of repeals	L. 1828, ch. 20, § 15, ¶¶ 1, 2, omitted.............	1909	240	420
	STATE PRINTING LAW: (L. 1909, ch. 60, constituting cons. laws, ch. 58.)			
11	Publication of reports...........................	1909	413	804
11	Extra copies of reports..........................	1910	392	720
	STOCK CORPORATION LAW: (L. 1909, ch. 61, constituting cons. laws, ch. 59.)			
10	Reorganization of corporation, plan or agreement...	1911	858	2399
19–23, added	Corporations having stock without par value........	1912	351	687
26	Change of number of directors....................	1909	421	903
64	Increase or reduction of capital stock.............	1913	305	567
	· **TAX LAW:** (L. 1909, ch. 62, constituting cons. laws, ch. 60.)			
4, subd. 21, added	Exemption of household furniture and personal effects	1912	267	495
9	Place of taxation of real property.................	1911	315	732
16, added	Taxation of lands used for forestry purposes........	1912	249	469
17, added	Taxation of lands maintained as wood lots..........	1912	363	710
20	Ascertaining facts for assessment.................	1911	116	179
20	Ascertaining facts for assessment.................	1911	805	2131
20	Ascertaining facts for assessment.................	1912	270	497
21	Preparation of assessment-roll....................	1911	315	732
21	Preparation of assessment-roll....................	1912	266	493
21a, added	Assessment-rolls in cities........................	1911	315	732
21b, added	Assessment of real property, Suffolk county........	1912	269	495
22	Assessment of state lands........................	1912	245	464
30–32, repealed	Real property of nonresidents and corporations.....	1911	315	734
30, added	Tax maps in each tax district.....................	1911	315	734
36	Notice of completion of assessment-roll............	1909	403	806
40	Apportionment of assessments of special franchises, etc.	1912	271	498

I. Changes in the Consolidated Laws, 1909–1913 — (Continued).

Section.	SUBJECT.	Year.	Chapter.	Page.
	TAX LAW — (Continued).			
40	Apportionment of assessments of special franchises, etc.	1913	556	1492
43	Special franchise valuations.	1909	275	480
43	Assessment of special franchises.	1910	7	9
43	Assessment of special franchises.	1910	458	890
43	Assessment of special franchise.	1911	804	2127
45	Special franchise assessment, hearings.	1911	804	2127
45a, added	Special franchise assessment, final valuation, etc.	1911	804	2128
46	Special franchise assessments, review.	1911	804	2130
46a, added	Special franchise valuations.	1911	875	2589
47	Employment of experts in certiorari proceedings.	1911	471	1075
47	Expenses of certiorari proceedings.	1913	134	224
50	Equalization by board of supervisors.	1911	801	2119
54	Description of real property.	1911	315	735
60	Statement of taxes.	1913	556	1494
61	Statement of valuation.	1911	118	180
63	Errors in assessment-rolls.	1911	315	735
64, added	Statistics of taxation, revenue and debt.	1911	119	181
70	Notice to nonresidents.	1909	207	323
73	Payment of taxes by gas corporations.	1912	221	401
81	Fees of collector.	1909	240	415
85	Extension of time for collection.	1910	332	586
88a, added	Reassessment of taxes.	1913	666	1758
89	Unpaid taxes on resident property; reassessed.	1913	666	1759
94	Receipt for taxes.	1911	579	1335
100	Return of unpaid nonresident taxes.	1913	377	811
100	Return of unpaid nonresident taxes.	1913	642	1695
150	When lands to be sold for unpaid taxes.	1913	377	812
150	When lands sold for unpaid taxes.	1913	642	1695
151	Advertisement and sale.	1913	377	813
151	Advertisement and sale.	1913	642	1696
151a, added	New certificate on setting aside tax sale.	1913	369	677
156	Refund of purchase money at tax sales.	1912	268	496
170	State board of tax commissioners.	1913	502	1187
173	Tax commissioners to visit counties.	1911	120	182
180	Organization tax.	1910	472	911
180	Organization tax.	1911	91	129
181	License tax on foreign corporations.	1910	340	603
190	Purchase of state bonds; credit given.	1913	357	663
190	Purchase of state bonds; credit given.	1913	794	2201
220	Taxable transfers.	1910	706	2041
220	Taxable transfers.	1911	732	1958
221	Exemptions from taxable transfers.	1910	600	1440
221	Exceptions and limitations of transfer tax.	1910	706	2043
221	Exceptions and limitations of transfer tax.	1911	732	1959
221	Exceptions and limitations of transfer tax.	1912	206	370
221	Exceptions and limitations of transfer tax.	1913	356	662
221	Exceptions and limitations of transfer tax.	1913	795	2203
221a, added	Rate of transfer tax.	1911	732	1960
221b, added	Exemptions from transfer tax.	1913	639	1693
225	Refund of transfer tax.	1911	308	723
229	Taxable transfers.	1909	283	512

I. CHANGES IN THE CONSOLIDATED LAWS, 1909–1913 — (Continued).

Section.	SUBJECT.	Year.	Chapter.	Page.
	TAX LAW — (Continued).			
229	Transfer tax appraisers, etc.	1910	706	2045
229	Transfer tax appraisers, appointment	1911	803	2124
229	Transfer tax appraiser, Rensselaer county	1912	214	379
229	Transfer tax appraisers, etc., appointment	1913	366	673
230	Transfer tax appraisers, proceedings	1911	800	2113
234	Salary of transfer tax clerk, Albany county	1910	70	113
234	Salaries of transfer tax clerks, various counties	1911	681	1776
234	Salary of transfer tax clerk, Albany county	1912	45	70
234, subd. 6	Salary of transfer tax clerk, Queens county	1911	160	253
234, subd. 8	Salary of transfer tax clerk, Monroe county	1913	429	905
234, subd. 14, added	Transfer tax clerk, Nassau county	1911	744	1979
240	Transfer tax reports of county treasurer	1911	800	2116
241	Transfer tax, report of comptroller; payments; refunds	1911	800	2117
243	Transfer tax, definitions	1910	706	2046
243	Transfer tax, definitions	1911	732	1961
256	Tax on mortgages	1913	665	1754
258	Effect of nonpayment of taxes on mortgages	1913	665	1755
259	Tax on trust mortgage	1909	412	890
259	Tax on trust mortgage	1913	665	1755
264	Optional tax on prior advanced mortgages	1910	601	1441
265, added	Tax a lien	1909	412	892
266, added	Enforcement:	1909	412	893
267, added	Recovery against trust mortgagee	1909	412	894
270, L. 1905, ch. 241, § 315 reenacted as	Stock transfer tax, amount, stamps	1910	38	64
270	Stock transfer tax, amount, stamps	1911	352	801
270	Stock transfer tax, amount, stamps	1912	292	528
270	Amount of stock transfer tax	1913	779	1968
271a, added	Sale of transfer tax stamps	1911	12	14
272	Failure to pay stock transfer tax	1911	352	802
272	Failure to pay stock transfer tax	1912	292	529
273	Canceling stamps; penalty for failure	1911	352	802
275	Illegal use of stock transfer tax stamps	1911	12	14
275	Illegal use of stock transfer tax stamps	1912	292	530
275a, added	Stock transfer tax; registration	1913	779	1970
276	Determination of tax on transfers of stock	1910	453	882
276	Determination of tax on transfers of stock	1911	352	803
276	Determination of tax on transfers of stock	1912	292	530
276	Stock transfer tax; power of state comptroller	1913	779	1971
277	Penalties for violation of stock transfer tax	1912	292	532
280, added	Refunds of taxes on stock transfers	1910	186	350
293	Return to writ of certiorari	1909	330	618
293	Return to writ of certiorari	1911	302	713
301	Personal tax	1909	374	773
330–337, added	Taxation of secured debts	1911	802	2121

I. CHANGES IN THE CONSOLIDATED LAWS, 1909–1913 — *(Continued)*.

Section.	SUBJECT.	Year.	Chapter.	Page.
	TENEMENT HOUSE LAW: (L. 1909, ch. 99, constituting cons. laws, ch. 61.)			
2, subd. 1	Definitions..............................	1912	13	26
2, subds. 4, 12	Definitions..............................	1912	454	966
3	Buildings converted or altered...........	1912	454	951
7	Houses located at corner of two streets....	1913	551	1475
15, renumbered 14	Fire proof tenement; when required........	1913	551	1475
15, added	Egress, means of.......................	1913	551	1475
16	Fire-escapes...........................	1909	354	671
16	Fire-escapes...........................	1913	551	1476
16, subd. 1	Fire-escapes...........................	1912	454	951
17	Bulkheads..............................	1910	445	832
18	Stairs and public halls..................	1912	454	953
21	Stairways and stairs....................	1912	454	954
22	Stair halls..............................	1912	454	954
22, subd. 1	Stair halls..............................	1913	551	1479
22a, added	Tower fire-escapes......................	1912	454	966
24	First tier of beams.....................	1913	551	1480
25	Partitions..............................	1912	454	956
27	Cellar and basement stairs..............	1912	454	956
28	Closet under first story stairs...........	1912	454	956
30	Fire stops..............................	1912	454	956
32	Scuttles, etc...........................	1909	354	674
33	Alterations; buildings moved............	1912	454	957
36	Shafts.................................	1912	454	957
37	Plastering behind wainscoting...........	1912	454	957
38	Wooden buildings on same lot...........	1912	454	957
50	Percentage of lot occupied..............	1913	551	1481
51	Height of tenement.....................	1912	454	958
52	Yards..................................	1912	454	959
54	Yards of corner lots....................	1913	551	1481
54a, added	Retaining walls in yards and courts......	1913	551	1482
55	Yard spaces............................	1912	454	959
56	Courts.................................	1913	551	1482
57	Outer courts...........................	1913	551	1483
57, subd. 1	Outer courts...........................	1912	454	953
59	Outer and inner courts.................	1912	454	960
59	Outer and inner courts.................	1913	551	1485
62	Rooms, lighting and ventilation.........	1912	454	961
63	Windows in rooms......................	1912	454	961
64	Size of rooms..........................	1912	454	962
66	Public halls............................	1912	454	962
66a, added	Elevator-vestibules.....................	1912	454	966
68	Windows for stair halls.................	1912	454	963
68	Windows for stair halls, size of.........	1913	551	1486
70	Percentage of lot occupied..............	1912	454	963
73	Rooms.................................	1909	354	675
75	New light shafts in existing buildings....	1912	454	963
76	Lights in halls.........................	1911	388	886
77	Skylights and ventilators...............	1909	354	676
78	Chimneys and fireplaces................	1912	168	305
78	Chimneys and fireplaces................	1912	454	964

I. CHANGES IN THE CONSOLIDATED LAWS, 1909-1913 — (*Continued*).

Section.	SUBJECT.	Year.	Chapter.	Page.
	TENEMENT HOUSE LAW.— (*Continued*).			
79	Vent flues.	1912	454	984
90	Basements and cellars.	1913	551	1486
93	Water-closet accommodations.	1912	454	984
95	Basement rooms.	1909	354	677
100	Basements and cellars.	1909	354	678
109	Prohibited uses.	1913	598	1610
121	Certificate of compliance.	1909	354	678
122	Unlawful occupation.	1909	354	679
140	Registry of owner's name.	1913	598	1610
150	Vagrancy.	1913	598	1611
153	Permission of owner for certain uses.	1913	598	1612
154	Rules of evidence in actions.	1913	598	1612
170	Application of chapter to second class cities.	1911	388	886
	TOWN LAW: (L. 1909, ch. 63, constituting cons. laws, ch. 62.)			
41	Terms of assessors.	1910	271	483
43, subd. 13, added	Town records.	1909	422	904
46	Special town meetings.	1910	188	356
53-55	Qualification of voters.	1913	124	206
64	Canvass of votes.	1909	240	415
80	Town officers.	1909	491	1181
80	Election and terms of assessors.	1910	271	484
82	Term of office.	1909	491	1181
82	Terms of assessors.	1910	271	485
82	Terms of town officers.	1913	231	401
85	Compensation of town officers.	1909	491	1182
89	Fires in woods.	1909	491	1183
89	Forest fires.	1910	630	1626
89, repealed	Forest fires.	1912	371	722
91	Delivery of books, etc., by officer to successor.	1909	491	1183
92a, added	Town clerks' undertakings.	1912	136	252
98, subd. 1	Supervisor to receive moneys.	1909	491	1184
98, subd. 1	General duties of supervisors.	1913	606	1625
98, subd. 8, added	Forest fires.	1910	630	1626
98, subd. 8	Forest fires.	1912	371	722
109, repealed	Commissioners of highways.	1909	491	1184
110	Pound master.	1909	491	1184
111	Town superintendent of highways.	1909	491	1184
112	Overseers of poor.	1912	203	365
117	Special constables.	1913	148	264
118	Special constables.	1913	148	265
119, 120, repealed	Tree warden.	1909	491	1185
121	Fence viewers.	1909	491	1185
122, added	Peace officers in certain towns.	1909	491	227
122-124, added	Police justice.	1909	528	1320
125, added	Clerks to supervisors and collectors.	1913	163	303

I. CHANGES IN THE CONSOLIDATED LAWS, 1909-1913 — (Continued).

Section.	SUBJECT.	Year.	Chapter.	Page.
	TOWN LAW — (Continued).			
131	Town boards, special meetings	1909	140	217
131	Town boards, regular and special meetings	1913	571	1551
133	Lists of accounts against town	1910	316	560
136a, added	Appropriations for Memorial day	1912	185	329
137	Grand army posts, Greene county	1911	465	1068
138a, added	Town board, power to borrow money	1913	571	1552
141, added	Power of town boards to borrow money	1912	258	483
153	Lists of accounts against town	1910	316	561
154	Compensation of town auditors	1910	24	38
154	Compensation of town auditors	1912	72	112
154	Meetings and compensation of town auditors	1912	258	484
154	Compensation of town auditors	1913	17	26
155	Lists of accounts against town	1910	316	562
170, subd. 8, repealed	Maintenance of watering trough	1909	491	1185
171	Fees in criminal proceedings	1909	523	1315
171	Fees in criminal proceedings	1913	111	182
177	Appeals from audit of town board	1910	61	98
195	Limitation of indebtedness	1913	116	196
215	Licensing public vehicles and entertainments	1913	496	1179
230	Sewer systems outside of cities and villages	1910	134	235
230	Petition for establishment of sewer system	1911	507	1162
230a, added	Construction of portion of sewer system	1912	205	368
231	Sewer systems outside of cities and villages	1910	134	237
231	Sewer commissioners	1911	507	1164
233	Sewer systems outside of cities and villages	1910	134	237
234	Sewer systems outside of cities and villages	1910	134	237
235	Sewer systems outside of cities and villages	1910	134	238
236	Sewer systems outside of cities and villages	1913	73	130
237	Sewer systems outside of cities and villages	1910	134	238
240	Reapportionment of assessments for sewers	1911	251	636
241-244	Sewer systems outside of cities and villages	1910	134	240
245, repealed	Lien of sewer assessment	1910	134	242
245, added	Sewer connections	1913	421	886
246-248, added	Sewer systems outside of cities and villages	1913	72	128
250-252, added	Sidewalks	1910	183	342
253, added	Sidewalks	1910	183	342
253	Sidewalk tax	1911	139	223
254, added	Sidewalks	1910	183	342
261	Lighting districts, Westchester county	1910	671	1928
288a, added	Refunding of indebtedness, water supply districts	1912	22	37
298, added	Water districts	1909	356	681
299, added	Enlarging water supply system	1912	275	504
310	Town fire companies	1910	408	747
310	Town fire companies	1912	238	453
313	Appropriations for fire companies	1910	408	747
313	Appropriations for fire company	1912	238	454
314	Assessments for maintaining fire company	1910	408	748
314	Assessments for maintaining fire company	1912	238	455
314a, added	Fire companies in incorporated cities and villages	1912	238	455
314b, added	Incorporated fire companies	1913	392	832
315, added	Fire ordinances	1910	408	748

I. CHANGES IN THE CONSOLIDATED LAWS, 1909–1913 — (*Continued*).

Section.	SUBJECT.	Year.	Chapter.	Page.
	TOWN LAW — (*Continued*).			
315	Fire ordinances..	1912	238	455
332	Care of cemeteries...............................	1909	473	1135
360, 361, 369	Division fences...............................	1911	86	121
460	Town boards in certain towns....................	1909	491	1185
460	Town boards in certain towns....................	1909	511	1289
461	Town boards in certain towns....................	1909	491	1185
461	Town boards in certain towns....................	1909	511	1290
462	Town boards in certain towns....................	1909	491	1186
462	Town boards in certain towns....................	1909	511	1290
468, 470, 472	Government of certain towns.....................	1909	511	1290
474	Acquisition of land for town purposes.............	1911	671	1760
477	Lighting streets...............................	1910	283	510
482	Sidewalks; sewer and water connections in certain towns......................................	1909	511	1292
483	Maps of proposed sewer district.................	1911	564	1274
484	Hearing objections to proposed sewer.............	1911	564	1274
486	Laying new highways; lighting highways..........	1910	283	511
501, 502	Assessment roll in certain towns.................	1909	511	1293
523	Officers in certain towns........................	1909	491	1186
530	Town meetings in certain towns.................	1909	240	416
533	Officers in certain towns........................	1909	240	416
533	Officers in certain towns........................	1909	491	1187
534	Accounting by officers of certain towns..........	1909	240	417
543, 563, 573, 583, 584	Officers in certain towns........................	1909	491	1187
586, added	Compensation of town officers, Orange and Rockland counties...........................	1911	230	507
590	Laws repealed...............................	1909	240	417
Schedule of repeals	L. 1901, ch. 34, §§ 6–8, omitted.................	1909	240	421
Schedule of repeals	L. 1866, ch. 30, §§ 2, 3, inserted.................	1909	240	422
Schedule of repeals	L. 1908, ch. 432, inserted.......................	1909	240	424
	TRANSPORTATION CORPORATIONS LAW: (L. 1909, ch. 219, constituting cons. laws, ch. 63.)			
25, added	Stage coach lines...............................	1913	495	1178
153–159, added	Freight terminal corporations....................	1911	778	2075
	VILLAGE LAW: (L. 1909, ch. 64, constituting cons. laws, ch. 64.)			
2	Requisite population............................	1909	555	1591
3	Proposition for incorporation....................	1909	555	1591
5, subd. 3	Area of territory...............................	1909	555	1592
10	Time of holding elections........................	1910	416	757

I. CHANGES IN THE CONSOLIDATED LAWS, 1909-1913 — (*Continued*).

Section.	SUBJECT.	Year.	Chapter.	Page.
	VILLAGE LAW — (*Continued*).			
14	Election to incorporate....................	1911	114	177
33, added	Incorporation in certain cases.....................	1910	258	461
33	Incorporation in certain cases...................	1913	658	1714
40a, added	Change of classification of villages.................	1910	321	567
41, subd. 2	Eligibility of women to vote on certain propositions..	1910	135	242
42	Eligibility to office.......................	1913	53	90
51	Registration of voters.......................	1910	423	781
51a, added	Registration of voters.......................	1910	423	781
51a, added	Registration of voters.......................	1911	427	963
52	Annual elections.......................	1909	472	1130
56	Borrowing money for highways...................	1910	4	5
63	Boards of park commissioners....................	1909	469	1123
63	Boards of police commissioners....................	1913	53	91
80	Filing maps of village.......................	1911	205	477
86	Compensation and duties of village officers.........	1911	66	91
86	Compensation of collectors.....................	1913	61	101
88, subd. 22a, added	Band concerts.................................	1911	519	1192
88, subd. 22a renumbered 89, subd. 22a, and amended	Band concerts.................................	1913	19	32
89, subd. 7	Fire limits.........................	1910	651	1748
89, subd. 15	Drains.........................	1910	454	·884
89, subd. 24	Contracts for fire protection....................	1911	495	1117
90, subd. 5a, added	Barbed wire fences........................	1910	69	113
90a, added	Building and sanitary codes.....................	1910	202	376
100	Fiscal year.........................	1909	472	1131
104	Annual assessment roll.......................	1909	472	1131
105	Hearing of complaints as to assessment rolls........	1909	472	1132
106	Completion and verification of assessment rolls......	1909	472	1133
107	Failure of assessors to meet...................	1909	472	1133
108	Notice of completion of assessment roll..........	1909	472	1134
108	Notice of completion of assessment-roll....:	1913	378	814
110, subd. 6, added	Special tax where June election adopted............	1909	472	1134
115	Collection of taxes..........................	1913	61	102
128	Borrowing money generally......................	1911	57	76
128	Borrowing money generally......................	1911	738	1972
128, subd. 13, added	Borrowing money for highways...................	1910	4	7
131	Second election to raise money...............	1910	598	1438
134–138, added	Purchases of land at tax sales, certain villages.......	1913	234	420
145	Petition for street improvement..................	1911	310	726
145a, added	Street improvements in villages of second class......	1911	403	923
146, subd. 5, added	Notice to railroad company of laying out street.....	1912	224	406
148	Street improvement.........................	1913	126	208
162	Credit for flagging sidewalks.........	1911	515	1175
165	Sprinkling streets..................	1912	125	231
166	Construction of sidewalks.. ,,,.......	1909	430	915

I. CHANGES IN THE CONSOLIDATED LAWS, 1909–1913 — (*Concluded*).

Section.	SUBJECT.	Year.	Chap-ter.	Page.
	VILLAGE LAW — (*Continued*).			
169	Acquisition of land for parks, etc..................	1909	469	1124
186	Civil jurisdiction of police justices..............	1911	501	1149
224	Waterworks system, supervision and extension......	1913	557	1494
229	Establishment of water rents......................	1913	183	338
244	Supervision and extension of lighting system........	1912	364	713
276	Sewers...	1909	212	334
276	Sewers...	1912	122	227
278, added	Powers of sewer commissioners....................	1910	259	462
278–283, added	Board of public works............................	1910	626	1597
290	Acquisition of lands for parks or cemeteries.........	1909	469	1124
292	Ordinances of park or cemetery commissioners......	1909	469	1125
295	Property in trust for park or cemetery.............	1909	469	1125
296	Reports of park and cemetery commissioners........	1909	469	1125
297, added	Control and maintenance of parks.................	1909	469	1126
348a, added	Annexation of territory belonging to village.........	1912	124	230
359, added	Establishment of uncertain boundaries.............	1912	123	228
390	Laws repealed. (*See note, L.* 1909, p. 418.).........	1909	240	418

II. CHANGES IN THE CODE OF CIVIL PROCEDURE, 1913.

(Sections, etc., are amended unless it is otherwise indicated.)

Section.	SUBJECT.	Chap-ter.	Page.
65	Proceedings after death or disability of attorney...........	741	1862
319a, added	Removal of causes.................................	210	372
319b, added	Vacation of judgment in certain cases....................	211	373
426, subd. 1	Personal service of summons...........................	279	505
427	Personal service of summons...........................	279	506
435, 436	Substituted service of summons........................	230	401
438, subd. 1	Service of summons by publication.....................	179	331
606	Injunctions, by whom granted.........................	112	184
803	Discovery of books, etc., by photographing.............	86	152
813a, added	Further protection for undertakings............. :	85	152
841b, added	Burden of proof of contributory negligence..............	228	400
841b, added	Recitals of heirship in deeds.........................	395	836
872, subd. 7	Depositions within the state..........................	278	504
952a, added	Actions relating to real property situate without state......	76	133
990	Issues triable by court; place of trial.................	446	923
1237	Judgment roll to be filed; contents....................	545	1468
1260, opening ¶	Cancellation of docket of judgment..................	30	54
1356	Appeal from orders in special proceedings..............	572	1553
1569	Dower; gross sum in lieu of..........................	450	928
1598	Defendants in actions for dower.......................	773	1926

II. CHANGES IN THE CODE OF CIVIL PROCEDURE, 1913 —(Concluded).

Section.	SUBJECT.	Chapter.	Page.
1672	Notice of pendency of action...........................	69	119
1688f, 1688g, 1688i	Proceedings involving title to real property..............	140	232
1745	Annulled marriage; legitimacy of children...........	444	921
1761, added	Divorce, effect on insurance policy......................	536	1410
1780	When foreign corporation may be sued..................	60	100
1904, 1905	Actions for death by negligence.........................	756	1894
2043	Discharge of prisoner unlawfully detained...............	544	1467
2067	Kinds of writs of mandamus, how granted..............	574	1554
2087	Appeals, orders relating to writs of mandamus...........	574	1555
2088	When relator to recover damages......................	574	1555
2091	Kinds of writs of prohibition, how granted..............	573	1553
2101	Appeals, writs of prohibition..........................	573	1554
2231, subd. 5	Summary proceedings; illegal use of house..............	448	925
2235	Summary proceedings; who may maintain................	448	925
2237	Petition in case of bawdy-houses, etc..................	448	926
2240	Service of petition in summary proceedings..............	277	503
2325a, added	Notices of pendency of action.........................	69	120
2387	Foreclosure of mortgages.............................	486	1165
2471	Receivers, proceedings supplementary to execution........	480	1002
2510	Surrogates' courts; powers of clerks....................	439	916
2520	Citation; service in state............................	535	1409
2558, subd. 3	Costs of an executor on a contest.....................	447	924
2618	Examination of witness to will........................	412	871
2624	Validity and construction of testamentary provisions......	337	630
2660	Letters of administration; preference in application.......	403	846
2746	Distributive shares of infants.........................	10	14
2842	Guardian to file annual inventory and account..........	533	1406
3047	Notice of appeal; service on justice....................	445	922
3048	Notice of appeal; service on respondent..	445	922
3312	Compensation of deputy sheriffs and constables attending court....	257	459
3314	Allowances to grand and trial jurors...................	257	459
3347, subd. 3	Application of certain provisions......................	485	1165
3347, subd. 4	Application of certain provisions......................	485	1165
3370	Compensation of condemnation commissioners...........	232	405

III. CHANGES IN THE CODE OF CRIMINAL PROCEDURE, 1913.

(Sections, etc., are amended unless it is otherwise indicated.)

Section.	SUBJECT.	Chap-ter.	Page.
39, subd. 2	County courts; jurisdiction............................	428	905
55	Court of general sessions, New York....................	151	269
55	Court of general sessions; accommodations; clerks, etc......	530	1402
154	Peace officers......................................	159	289
226	Drawing grand juries...............................	213	376
517	Appeals from suspended sentences......................	125	207
586	Deposit instead of bail..............................	133	223
595	Forfeiture of bail; how enforced......................	400	843
618b	Compensation of witnesses committed...................	238	423
915	Support of poor relative............................	143	238
952p	Appointment of stenographers........................	212	374
952v	Compensation of stenographers.......................	212	375

IV. CHANGES IN LAWS, OTHER THAN THE CONSOLIDATED LAWS AND CODES, 1912-13.*

(Sections, etc., are amended unless it is otherwise indicated.)

Laws of.	Chap-ter.	SUBJECTS AND SECTIONS.	Year.	Chap-ter.	Page.
		Adam Haverling school fund:			
1910	592	Care and investment, § 2............................	1913	191	348
		Albany:			
1850	86	Assessment and collection of taxes, § 48................	1912	347	683
1883	298	Charter, tit. 2, § 1, last sentence.....................	1913	584	1585
1883	298	Charter, tit. 9, §§ 56-65, repealed....................	1912	358	707
1883	298	Charter, tit. 21, § 7, repealed........................	1912	359	708
1886	77	Amends charter. All repealed........................	1912	358	707
1886	256	Amends charter. All repealed........................	1912	358	707
1891	286	Amends charter, § 27, repealed.......................	1912	358	707
1904	466	Street improvements, § 5............................	1912	196	343
1907	212	Young Men's Association for Mutual Improvement, § 3..	1913	564	1541
		Albany county:			
1893	429	Clerk's office, indexes and records, §§ 1, 3..............	1912	288	520
		Albion:			
1879	142	Charter, tit. 2, §§ 2, 5, amended; tit. 5, § 5, amended, § 14, added.....	1912	30	47
1879	142	Charter, tit. 9, § 2.................................	1913	575	1556
1879	142	Charter, tit. 10, §§ 5, 7............................	1912	30	47

*It is important to notice that the following table for laws, other than the consolidated laws and codes, gives the amendments and repeals of 1912, as well as those of 1913.

IV. CHANGES IN LAWS, OTHER THAN THE CONSOLIDATED LAWS AND CODES, 1912–13 — (Continued).

Laws of.	Chapter.	SUBJECTS AND SECTIONS.	Year.	Chapter.	Page.
		Appellate division, first department:			
1911	855	Retirement of employees, § 1........................	1912	486	1009
1911	855	Retirement of employees, § 1, amended; § 2, added......	1913	138	229
		Barge canal bonds:			
1910	66	Issue and sale, § 2................................	1912	186	331
		Batavia:			
1884	195	Charter, tit. 4, § 10...............................	1912	76	120
1884	195	Charter, tit. 8, § 1...............................	1913	46	78
		Bath:			
1895	785	Charter, tit. 5, § 9...............................	1912	365	714
		Beacon:			
....	...	Charter..	1913	539	1413
		Binghamton:			
1869	294	Incorporating fire department. All repealed...........	1912	494	1023
1907	751	Charter, § 74.....................................	1913	158	288
1907	751	Charter, § 204....................................	1912	402	775
		Bronx county:			
1912	548	Erection, §§ 4, 8.................................	1913	266	483
		Bronx river:			
1907	594	Preserving waters from pollution, §§ 10, 15, subd. b, amended; § 18a, added; § 19, amended..............	1913	757	1895
		Brooklyn:			
1861	299	Fourth avenue improvement, § 7......................	1912	450	931
1896	372	Elevated railways, Adams street. All repealed........	1913	525	1390
1907	120	Children's museum building, § 1.....................	1912	130	242
		Buffalo:			
1859	239	Grosvenor library; trustees, § 2.....................	1913	391	831
1891	105	Charter, § 27.....................................	1912	374	726
1891	105	Charter, § 115....................................	1912	25	41
1891	105	Charter, §§ 137, 138, 140..........................	1912	140	259
1891	105	Charter, § 187....................................	1912	552	1372
1891	105	Charter, §§ 187, 188, 190, 191, 211.................	1912	198	345
1891	105	Charter, § 250....................................	1912	367	718
1891	105	Charter, § 323c...................................	1912	369	720
1891	105	Charter, § 329....................................	1913	13	22
1891	105	Charter, § 395....................................	1912	412	801
1891	105	Charter, § 401....................................	1912	146	268
1891	105	Charter, § 474....................................	1912	63	100
1898	76	Abandonment of Jubliee water system, §§ 3, 4.........	1912	551	1370
1903	240	Waterworks system. All repealed....................	1912	381	737
1909	115	Tuberculosis hospital, § 2.........................	1912	138	254
1909	570	City court, § 10..................................	1913	585	1587
1909	570	City court, § 20, subd. 10.........................	1913	157	287

IV. CHANGES IN LAWS, OTHER THAN THE CONSOLIDATED LAWS AND CODES,
1912–13 — (Continued).

Laws of.	Chapter..	SUBJECTS AND SECTIONS.	Year.	Chapter.	Page.
		Buffalo — (Continued).			
1909	570	City court, § 41..........................	1913	580	1500
1909	570	City court, § 51..........................	1913	118	196
1909	570	City court, § 52..........................	1913	601	1630
1909	570	City court, § 53..........................	1913	157	287
1909	570	City court, § 55..........................	1913	581	1570
1909	570	City court, § 57, added..................	1913	309	573
1909	570	City court, § 74..........................	1913	601	1632
1910	26	Tuberculosis hospital, §§ 1, 2...........	1912	553	1574
1911	76	Waterworks system. All repealed.......	1912	381	737
1912	160	Naval militia boathouse, etc., § 2.......	1913	274	500
1912	281	Sinking fund water bonds, § 1...........	1913	39	65
		Canandaigua:			
1893	666	Charter, tit. 6, §§ 20, 22, 24, 25........	1912	279	509
1893	666	Charter. All repealed..................	1913	371	794
1894	131	Amends charter. All repealed..........	1913	371	794
1902	264	Police department. All repealed........	1913	371	794
1904	42	Amends charter. All repealed..........	1913	371	794
1904	469	Amends charter. All repealed..........	1913	371	794
1905	6	Amends charter. All repealed..........	1913	371	794
1905	371	Amends charter. All repealed..........	1913	371	794
1906	229	Police department. All repealed........	1913	371	794
1906	633	Amends charter. All repealed..........	1913	371	794
1907	619	Amends charter. All repealed..........	1913	371	794
1909	364	Amends charter. All repealed..........	1913	371	794
1912	279	Amends charter. All repealed	1913	371	794
....	...	Charter...............................	1913	371	673
		Canterbury Fire Company:			
1830	272	Charter, § 4a, added....................	1912	176	319
		Catskill:			
1860	68	Charter, §§ 1, 2, 4, 50..................	1913	115	191
		Chautauqua county:			
1890	547	County clerk, § 5.......................	1913	310	579
		Church Insurance Association:			
1891	134	Charter, §§ 1, 2, 4, 7, 8, amended; § 13, added..........	1913	156	283
		Cohoes:			
1892	671	Charter, tit. 5, § 59....................	1912	350	686
		Conrad Poppenhusen Association:			
1868	667	Charter, §§ 1, 3, 9, 10, 12.............	1913	669	1762
		Consolidated laws amended to correct errors:			
1909	240	Forest, fish and game law, §§ 28–30, repealed	1912	318	636
		Corning:			
1905	142	Charter, § 110a, added.................	1912	425	832

IV. CHANGES IN LAWS, OTHER THAN THE CONSOLIDATED LAWS AND CODES, 1912–13 — (Continued).

Laws of.	Chapter.	SUBJECTS AND SECTIONS.	Year.	Chapter.	Page.
		Cortland:			
1900	160	Charter, § 67, added...............................	1912	385	740
1900	160	Charter, § 74.......................................	1912	437	864
		Cortlandt:			
1905	263	Appropriation to Helping Hand Hospital Association of Peekskill, § 1.................................	1912	142	263
		County roads, certain counties:			
1910	564	Acquisition of land for certain purposes, § 4, added; § 4 renumbered § 5.................................	1913	473	993
		Eastchester:			
1846	185	Trustees of public lands, §§ 1, 3, subds. 3–5; § 4.........	1913	120	200
		Elmira:			
1900	525	Police pension fund, § 2.............................	1912	529	1064
1906	477	Charter, § 32, subd. h..............................	1913	8	12
1906	477	Charter, § 33......................................	1912	523	1054
		Enterprise Land Company:			
1911	289	Extension of corporate existence, § 1....................	1913	655	1711
		Erie county:			
1883	496	Salary of county treasurer, § 2, repealed...............	1913	406	852
		Factory investigating commission:			
1911	561	Time of report, § 3.................................	1912	21	36
		Fire or marine insurance corporations:			
1899	85	Minimum capital stock. All repealed.................	1913	27	52
		Food investigating commission:			
1911	787	Time extension, § 3................................	1912	177	320
		Forest, fish and game law amendments:			
1909	474	That part of § 1 adding or amending §§ 2, 4, 11, 13, 14 76–78, 82, 84, 88, 91, 92, 98, 106, 109, 117, 124, 126, 134, 146, 150, 152, 153, 240, repealed.....................	1912	318	636
1909	474	That part of § 1 adding or amending §§ 2, 4, 40, 56, 67–71, 73, 74, 75a, 75b, repealed...........................	1912	444	923
1909	533	All. Compilation and digest of law, § 8, repealed......	1912	318	636
1910	72	Reforesting lands, § 1, repealed.....................	1912	444	923
1910	256	Sale of plumage of birds, §§ 1, 2, repealed............	1912	318	636
1910	313	Saint Lawrence reservation. All repealed.............	1912	444	923
1910	476	Railroads in forest lands. All repealed..............	1912	444	923
1910	655	Suckers in Dutchess and Sullivan counties, § 157. All repealed...	1912	318	636
1910	656	Robbins and Gardiners islands, § 174a. All repealed....	1912	318	636
1910	657	Amends generally, §§ 1, 2, 4, repealed................	1912	318	636
1910	657	Section 3, amending §§ 40, 69, 73, 74, repealed..........	1912	444	923

IV. CHANGES IN LAWS, OTHER THAN THE CONSOLIDATED LAWS AND CODES, 1912–13 — (Continued).

Laws of.	Chap-ter.	SUBJECTS AND SECTIONS.	Year.	Chap-ter.	Page.
		Forest, fish and game law amendments — (Continued).			
1910	663	Lake trout and whitefish, open season, § 109. All repealed......	1912	318	636
1910	664	Grouse and quail, Dutchess county, § 93. All repealed..	1912	318	636
1910	675	Game protectors, § 11. All repealed.................	1912	318	636
1911	170	Pheasants, § 96. All repealed......................	1912	318	636
1911	171	Open season defined, § 14, subd. 14. All repealed.......	1912	318	636
1911	188	Trout; open season, § 106. All repealed..............	1912	318	636
1911	238	Skunk farms, §§ 84, 84a. All repealed...............	1912	318	636
1911	299	Fishing in Seneca and Cayuga lakes, § 150. All repealed.	1912	318	636
1911	312	Pickerel and pike, § 117. All repealed................	1912	318	636
1911	377	Open season for fish, Schuyler county, § 154a. All repealed......	1912	318	636
1911	378	Spearing suckers, Schuyler and Chemung counties, § 154b. All repealed......	1912	318	636
1911	423	Compilation of forest, fish and game law, § 8. All repealed......	1912	318	636
1911	438	Breeding and sale of game, §§ 6, 77, 78a, 80–82, 85a, 86–93, 96a–96c, 241. All repealed....................	1912	318	636
1911	508	Suckers; Dutchess, Sullivan and Ulster counties, § 157. All repealed......	1912	318	637
1911	529	Clearing lands, certain counties. All repealed.........	1912	444	923
1911	530	Fishing in Lake George, § 154. All repealed...........	1912	318	637
1911	580	Spearing, hooking and set lines, § 153. All repealed.....	1912	318	637
1911	582	Open season lake trout; nets in Seneca lake, §§ 109, 150. All repealed......	1912	318	637
1911	583	Deer; open season, § 76. All repealed................	1912	318	637
1911	589	Schuyler county; set lines in certain waters, § 154b. All repealed......	1912	318	637
1911	590	Spearing, hooking and set lines, § 153. All repealed.....	1912	318	637
1911	591	Thumping; nets in Hudson and Delaware rivers, §§ 128, 147......	1912	318	637
1911	592	Amends generally, §§ 81, 106, 124, 152. All repealed....	1912	318	637
1911	627	Close season for pheasants, § 96. All repealed..........	1912	318	637
1911	635	Hares and rabbits, § 82. All repealed................	1912	318	637
1911	636	Warren, Essex, Washington and Saratoga counties, certain waters, § 154. All repealed......	1912	318	637
1911	647	Lands and forests, §§ 50, 51, repealed................	1912	444	923
1911	647	Fish and game, §§ 150–178, repealed..................	1912	318	637
1911	835	Penalties, etc. All repealed.........................	1912	444	923
1911	854	Hunting license, § 104. All repealed.................	1912	318	637
		Franklin county:			
1911	137	County road system, §§ 3, 5.........................	1913	58	96
		Fulton monument:			
1907	676	Extension of Riverside park, §§ 1, 2..................	1913	90	157
		Harlem river and Spuyten Duyvil creek:			
1876	147	Improvement by United States, §§ 13–16, added........	1913	414	873

IV. CHANGES IN LAWS, OTHER THAN THE CONSOLIDATED LAWS AND CODES, 1912–13 — (*Continued*).

Laws of.	Chapter.	SUBJECTS AND SECTIONS.	Year.	Chapter.	Page.
		Highways:			
1911	154	Appropriation for expediting building of state routes, § 2..	1912	325	651
1911	741	Appropriation for expediting building of state routes, § 1..	1912	439	874
		Hoosick Falls:			
1909	541	Street improvement, § 14...........................	1912	184	327
1909	541	Street improvement, § 16........................	1912	8	20
		Hornell:			
1906	288	Charter, § 71, amended; § 193a, added; § 194, amended..	1912	128	237
		Hudson:			
1895	751	Charter, §§ 7, 9–14, 16, 20, 29, 38...................	1913	63	104
1895	751	Charter, § 151.................................	1913	314	587
		Ithaca:			
1908	503	Charter, §§ 6, 20, amended; § 20a, added; § 44, amended.	1912	139	255
1908	503	Charter, §§ 180, 188, subd. 3; §§ 181, 195.............	1912	438	871
		Jamestown:			
1902	274	Special terms of supreme court, § 1..................	1913	449	927
1907	387	Charter, §§ 25, 28, 31, 34, 64, 116, 137, 173, 178, amended.	1912	80	125
		Jurors, Commissioners of:			
1895	369	Qualifications of jurors, § 20........................	1912	147	269
		Kings county:			
1896	772	District attorney's office; clerks, § 3...................	1913	401	844
1901	706	Register, § 2...	1913	776	1964
1909	390	Court house, §§ 6–8..............................	1912	357	704
		Lackawanna:			
1909	574	Charter, §§ 16, 86................................	1912	355	699
1909	574	Charter, § 197...................................	1912	129	240
		Lake Champlain tercentenary commission:			
1908	149	Permanent memorials to Samuel Champlain; report, § 4..	1912	273	502
		Little Falls:			
1895	565	Charter, § 17...................................	1912	197	344
		Lockport:			
1911	870	Charter, §§ 69, 281................................	1912	416	808
		Long Sault Development Company:			
1907	355	Charter. All repealed..............................	1913	452	931
		Lyons:			
1907	459	School district number 6, § 1.........................	1913	376	810
1907	750	Charter, §§ 4, 35..................................	1912	133	246

IV. CHANGES IN LAWS, OTHER THAN THE CONSOLIDATED LAWS AND CODES, 1912–13 — (Continued).

Laws of.	Chapter.	SUBJECTS AND SECTIONS.	Year.	Chapter.	Page.
		Mechanicville:			
1891	106	Charter, tit. 3, § 5, added..........................	1913	409	800
1891	106	Charter, tit. 5, § 3, subds. 30, 31; tit. 7, § 15..........	1913	264	479
1901	45	Public-park, title, §§ 4, 5...........................	1913	263	477
		Medina:			
1909	545	Charter, §§ 7, 11, 50................................	1912	7	18
		Middletown:			
1902	572	Charter, § 107, subd. 8, added; § 112a, added; § 119, subd. 1, amended......................................	1912	415	805
		Mohawk:			
1844	157	Charter, § 17, subd. 25, added.......................	1913	20	33
1844	157	Charter, § 17, subd. 25..............................	1913	255	451
		Mohawk and Hudson River Humane Society:			
1902	261	Detention of minors, § 1............................	1913	294	533
		Mohawk river and West Canada creek improvements:			
1911	132	Appropriation, § 3a, added...........................	1913	245	434
		Monroe county:			
1864	368	Special county judge, § 3............................	1912	339	670
		Montgomery county:			
1859	390	Auditing of accounts. All repealed...................	1913	119	199
		Mount Vernon:			
1892	182	Charter, §§ 11, 23, repealed.........................	1912	430	853
1892	182	Charter, new §§ 11, 23, added........................	1912	430	853
1892	182	Charter, § 128......................................	1912	410	796
1892	182	Charter, § 158......................................	1913	99	167
1892	182	Charter, §§ 229t, 229u..............................	1913	44	72
1905	87	Buildings for fire and police departments, § 1..........	1912	132	245
1905	87	Buildings for fire and police departments, § 1..........	1913	98	166
1909	361	Repaving streets, § 1...............................	1912	159	290
1910	75	Municipal building, § 1..............................	1913	97	165
1911	127	Water supply, §§ 15, 16.............................	1912	478	996
		Newburgh:			
1907	203	Charter, tit. 3, § 9, subd. 37........................	1912	414	804
1907	203	Charter, tit. 4, § 7.................................	1912	395	762
		New Rochelle:			
1910	559	Charter, §§ 12, 271–273.............................	1913	225	394
		New York city:			
1882	410	Consolidation act, § 1503...........................	1912	191	338
1887	696	Charitable institutions exempt from water rents, §§ 1, 2..	1913	226	395
1890	523	Sheriff, § 1..	1912	500	1028
1890	523	Sheriff, § 1..	1913	373	807

IV. CHANGES IN LAWS, OTHER THAN THE CONSOLIDATED LAWS AND CODES,
1912–13 — (*Continued*).

Laws of.	Chapter.	SUBJECTS AND SECTIONS.	Year.	Chapter.	Page.
		New York city — (*Continued*).			
1891	4	Rapid transit act, § 4................................	1912	226	408
1891	4	Rapid transit act, § 4................................	1913	100	168
1891	4	Rapid transit act, § 10...............................	1912	226	411
1891	4	Rapid transit act, § 20...............................	1913	510	1352
1891	4	Rapid transit act, § 24, subds. 1, 6..................	1912	226	412
1891	4	Rapid transit act, § 24a, added......................	1913	524	1383
1891	4	Rapid transit act, § 26, subd. 2, § 27, subd. 1, amended; § 27, subd. 2, added; § 27, subds. 2–4 renumbered subds. 3–5, and amended; § 27, subd. 5, renumbered subd. 6; § 27, subds. 6–8 renumbered subds. 7–9, and amended; § 27, subd. 9 renumbered subd. 10; § 29, subd. 3, §§ 33, 34, subd. 2........................	1912	226	417
1891	4	Rapid transit act, § 36...............................	1913	540	1456
1891	4	Rapid transit act, § 37, subds. 1, 2..................	1913	540	1457
1891	4	Rapid transit act, § 38...............................	1912	226	438
1891	4	Rapid transit act, § 39, subd. 1......................	1912	226	438
1891	4	Rapid transit act, § 39, subd. 1......................	1913	524	1389
1891	4	Rapid transit act, § 39, subd. 2, amended; § 39, subd. 2a, added; § 39, subd. 4, amended....................	1913	540	1459
1896	803	Plumbing. All repealed..............................	1913	752	1889
1897	378	Charter, § 18...	1912	131	243
1897	378	Charter, § 58...	1913	418	881
1897	378	Charter, § 149..	1912	398	766
1897	378	Charter, § 162..	1913	31	54
1897	378	Charter, § 163..	1912	396	764
1897	378	Charter, § 165..	1912	479	998
1897	378	Charter, § 181..	1912	492	1015
1897	378	Charter, § 188..	1912	457	972
1897	378	Charter, § 205..	1913	259	461
1897	378	Charter, § 205b, added...............................	1912	400	771
1897	378	Charter, § 215..	1913	33	56
1897	378	Charter, § 222..	1912	6	13
1897	378	Charter, § 230, subd. 3..............................	1913	299	543
1897	378	Charter, § 231..	1912	501	1029
1897	378	Charter, § 237..	1913	36	60
1897	378	Charter, § 243a, added...............................	1913	331	622
1897	378	Charter, § 258a, added...............................	1912	435	862
1897	378	Charter, § 261..	1912	452	934
1897	378	Charter, § 276..	1912	449	930
1897	378	Charter, § 284..	1912	480	1000
1897	378	Charter, § 348, repealed.............................	1912	429	852
1897	378	Charter, § 395, subd. 3, added.......................	1912	433	858
1897	378	Charter, §§ 415, 416, added..........................	1913	754	1890
1897	378	Charter, § 420..	1912	528	1062
1897	378	Charter, § 422..	1912	527	1061
1897	378	Charter, §§ 439, 442.................................	1913	329	615
1897	378	Charter, § 476..	1912	108	184
1897	378	Charter, § 610..	1913	333	623
1897	378	Charter, §§ 612b, 613, 617...........................	1913	34	57
1897	378	Charter, § 663..	1912	446	926

4

IV. Changes in Laws, Other Than the Consolidated Laws and Codes, 1912–13 — (*Continued*).

Laws of.	Chapter.	SUBJECTS AND SECTIONS.	Year.	Chapter.	Page.
		New York city — (*Continued*).			
1897	378	Charter, § 676...............................	1913	299	542
1897	378	Charter, § 685...............................	1912	420	816
1897	378	Charter, § 686...............................	1912	419	814
1897	378	Charter, § 687...............................	1912	451	932
1897	378	Charter, § 688...............................	1912	418	813
1897	378	Charter, § 689...............................	1912	401	772
1897	378	Charter, § 690...............................	1912	421	818
1897	378	Charter, § 695...............................	1912	456	970
1897	378	Charter, § 727...............................	1912	458	974
1897	378	Charter, § 727...............................	1913	698	1808
1897	378	Charter, § 734...............................	1912	462	981
1897	378	Charter, § 740...............................	1912	328	656
1897	378	Charter, § 774, 775, subds. 2, 3............	1913	695	1803
1897	378	Charter, §.775a, added.....................	1912	458	975
1897	378	Charter, § 775a, repealed..................	1913	695	1805
1897	378	Charter, § 776.............................	1912	458	975
1897	378	Charter, § 777.............................	1913	695	1804
1897	378	Charter, § 777a............................	1912	458	977
1897	378	Charter, § 819.............................	1913	327	610
1897	378	Charter, § 821.............................	1912	434	860
1897	378	Charter, § 821.............................	1913	411	808
1897	378	Charter, § 821a, added.....................	1913	411	808
1897	378	Charter, § 822.............................	1913	328	613
1897	378	Charter, §§ 888a, 889a, 891a, added; §§ 895, 897, amended.	1913	324	603
1897	378	Charter, § 900.............................	1912	6	16
1897	378	Charter, § 910.............................	1913	690	1781
1897	378	Charter, § 937.............................	1912	461	980
1897	378	Charter, § 948.............................	1912	484	1006
1897	378	Charter, § 951.............................	1912	483	1004
1897	378	Charter, § 970.............................	1913	329	618
1897	378	Charter, § 990.............................	1913	142	236
1897	378	Charter, § 1019............................	1912	372	723
1897	378	Charter, § 1019............................	1913	685	1790
1897	378	Charter, § 1019a, added....................	1912	399	770
1897	378	Charter, § 1019a...........................	1913	684	1788
1897	378	Charter, § 1022............................	1912	108	185
1897	378	Charter, § 1023a...........................	1913	683	1786
1897	378	Charter, § 1027............................	1913	326	607
1897	378	Charter, § 1030............................	1913	682	1785
1897	378	Charter, §§ 1038, 1043, 1044...............	1913	681	1782
1897	378	Charter, § 1066............................	1913	35	59
1897	378	Charter, § 1078............................	1913	45	76
1897	378	Charter, § 1084............................	1913	749	1885
1897	378	Charter, § 1089............................	1912	455	967
1897	378	Charter, § 1091............................	1912	450	973
1897	378	Charter, § 1091............................	1913	534	1407
1897	378	Charter, § 1093............................	1913	688	1795
1897	378	Charter, § 1157............................	1913	321	598
1897	378	Charter, § 1264............................	1913	687	1794
1897	378	Charter, § 1458, repealed..................	1913	769	1923

IV. CHANGES IN LAWS, OTHER THAN THE CONSOLIDATED LAWS AND CODES, 1912–13 — (Continued).

Laws of.	Chapter.	SUBJECTS AND SECTIONS.	Year.	Chapter.	Page.
		New York city — (Continued).			
1897	378	Charter, § 1458, added..	1913	769	1923
1897	378	Charter, §§ 1459–1461, repealed.........................	1913	769	1923
1897	378	Charter, § 1526..	1913	686	1791
1897	378	Charter, § 1539a..	1912	463	982
1897	378	Charter, § 1543b, added..................................	1913	302	551
1897	378	Charter, § 1545a, added..................................	1913	697	1807
1897	378	Charter, § 1553..	1912	436	863
1897	378	Charter, § 1567..	1913	121	202
1897	378	Charter, § 1568, added....................................	1912	353	697
1897	378	Charter, § 1569, added....................................	1912	432	857
1897	378	Charter, § 1569a, added...................................	1913	694	1802
1897	378	Charter, § 1569b, added..................................	1912	251	474
1897	378	Charter, ch. 23, tit. 5 (§§ 1572–1574), added...........	1913	755	1892
1902	580	Municipal court act, § 231b, added......................	1913	690	1798
1902	580	Municipal court act, § 310...............................	1913	386	826
1902	580	Municipal court act, § 340...............................	1912	468	986
1902	580	Municipal court act, § 351a, added......................	1913	692	1801
1906	639	New York bay pollution commission, § 5.................	1913	332	622
1907	164	Queens Borough public library, § 3......................	1913	541	1464
1908	139	Lease of Ward's island to state, § 1.....................	1913	696	1806
1910	659	Inferior criminal courts act, § 31, subd. 5, added........	1913	679	1780
1910	659	Inferior criminal courts act, § 39a, added..............	1913	691	1799
1910	659	Inferior criminal courts act, § 52........................	1912	464	983
1910	659	Inferior criminal courts act, § 52........................	1913	372	795
1910	659	Inferior criminal courts act, § 60........................	1913	372	795
1910	659	Inferior criminal courts act, § 71........................	1912	469	987
1910	659	Inferior criminal courts act, § 72........................	1913	372	796
1910	659	Inferior criminal courts act, § 72a, added...............	1912	467	986
1910	659	Inferior criminal courts act, § 72a.......................	1913	372	796
1910	659	Inferior criminal courts act, § 74........................	1913	689	1797
1910	659	Inferior criminal courts act, § 75........................	1913	372	797
1910	659	Inferior criminal courts act, § 75a, added...............	1913	372	797
1910	659	Inferior criminal courts act, § 77........................	1913	372	798
1910	659	Inferior criminal courts act, § 78........................	1913	372	799
1910	659	Inferior criminal courts act, § 82........................	1913	372	799
1910	659	Inferior criminal courts act, § 84........................	1913	372	801
1910	659	Inferior criminal courts act, § 88........................	1913	372	801
1910	659	Inferior criminal courts act, § 88a, added...............	1913	372	803
1910	659	Inferior criminal courts act, § 89........................	1912	460	980
1910	659	Inferior criminal courts act, § 89........................	1913	372	804
1910	659	Inferior criminal courts act, § 90, amended; § 91, repealed; § 92, amended; §§ 92a, 98a, added..................	1913	372	805
1911	737	Manhattan bridge damages, § 1..........................	1913	577	1560
1911	776	Water-front facilities, § 2, subds. (d), (e), (f), (g), (i), (j), (l); §§ 4, 5, amended; § 6 renumbered § 8c, and amended; § 6, added; § 7, amended; § 8 renumbered § 8d, and amended; §§ 8, 8a, 8b, added........................	1913	521	1369
1911	846	Retirement of justices of municipal court, § 1............	1913	724	1844
1911	898	Sale of state arsenal lands and building, §§ 2, 3..........	1912	387	743
		New York City Baptist Mission Society:			
1893	410	Charter, § 1...	1912	304	557

IV. CHANGES IN LAWS, OTHER THAN THE CONSOLIDATED LAWS AND CODES, 1912–13 — (Continued).

Laws of.	Chap-ter.	SUBJECTS AND SECTIONS.	Year.	Chap-ter.	Page.
		New York City Society of the Methodist Episcopal Church:			
1866	581	Charter, §§ 1–4......................................	1912	317	573
		New York Commercial Association:			
1862	359	Charter, § 5..	1912	291	526
		New York County:			
1890	523	Sheriff, § 1..	1912	500	1028
1890	523	Sheriff, § 1..	1913	373	807
1903	336	Courthouse, § 7....................................	1913	315	589
1903	336	Courthouse, § 15c, added............................	1912	250	473
1906	661	Records in county clerk's office, § 4c................	1912	167	303
1907	712	Hall of records, § 1................................	1912	311	566
1910	682	Records in register's office, § 1.....................	1912	220	399
		New York state bridge and tunnel commission:			
1910	459	Name, § 1..	1913	189	345
		New York State Training School for Boys:			
1904	718	Acquisition of site, § 7.............................	1913	762	1904
1904	718	Acquisition of site, § 7.............................	1913	799	2208
		Niagara county:			
1899	151	Election of county treasurer. All repealed...........	1912	234	449
		Niagara Falls:			
1904	300	Charter, § 15, subd. 3; § 16, first ¶ and subds. 1–4......	1912	324	644
1904	300	Charter. § 16, subd. 5, repealed....................	1912	324	
1904	300	Charter, § 16, subd. 6 renumbered subd. 5, and amended; § 16, subd. 7 renumbered subd. 6; § 16, subds. 8, 9 renumbered subds. 7, 8, and amended; § 16, subds. 10–15 renumbered 9–14; § 16, new subd. 15, added; §§ 163, 211, amended; art. 7, title amended; art. 7 new sub-title, added; §§ 330–334, added; §§ 362, 363, amended......	1912	324	645
		North Tonawanda:			
1907	752	Charter, tit. 3, §§ 3, 6, 8, 10, 14....................	1912	417	810
1907	752	Charter, tit. 24, § 1...............................	1912	394	761
		Norwich:			
1904	7	Charter, tit. 6, § 9................................	1913	93	161
		Nyack fire department:			
1887	107	Charter, § 8.......................................	1913	222	391
		Ogdensburg:			
1893	87	Charter, § 19, subd. 14.............................	1912	85	152
1893	87	Charter, § 19, subd. 15, repealed....................	1912	85	153
1893	87	Charter, § 118, added..............................	1912	85	152
		Olean:			
1902	274	Special terms of supreme court, § 1	1913	449	927

IV. Changes in Laws, Other Than the Consolidated Laws and Codes, 1912–13 — (Continued).

Laws of.	Chapter.	SUBJECTS AND SECTIONS.	Year.	Chapter.	Page.
		Oneida:			
1911	648	Charter, § 101....................................	1913	67	110
1911	648	Charter, § 236, added.............................	1913	174	320
		Oneida county:			
1898	321	Sheriff, §§ 1, 4..................................	1913	298	539
		Onondaga county:			
1867	858	Collection of taxes, § 1...........................	1913	301	549
1893	520	County clerk, § 3.................................	1912	244	463
		Orange county:			
1911	876	Poor district number one, § 2....	1913	407	852
		Ossining:			
1910	667	Charter, § 114....................................	1912	24	40
1910	667	Charter, § 133....................................	1913	123	205
		Oswego:			
1895	394	Charter, § 330a...................................	1912	411	797
1895	394	Charter, § 330a...................................	1913	282	510
1895	394	Charter, §§ 330b–330j, added......................	1912	411	798
1895	394	Charter, § 330k, added............................	1912	411	801
1895	394	Charter, § 330k...................................	1913	282	512
1895	394	Charter, § 330l, added............................	1913	282	512
		Oswego Normal and Training School:			
1909	592	Sale of site; disposition of proceeds, § 4...............	1912	·487	1010
		Peekskill:			
1883	117	Charter, tit. 7, § 2, subd. 3, amended; tit. 7, § 2, subd. 3 (as added by L. 1905, ch. 511), renumbered subd. 4....	1912	326	651
1883	117	Charter, tit. 9, § 2...............................	1912	23	38
1911	735	Jail and police court and headquarters. All repealed....	1913	336	629
		Plattsburgh:			
1902	269	Charter, §§ 7, 10, 11, 24, 26, 31, 39, subd. 8, amended; § 45, subd. 18, amended, subds. 27–30, added; § 60, amended; § 60a, added; §§ 72, 73, 115, 147, 148, 157, 158, 165, amended..............................	1912	428	838
		Port Chester:			
1868	818	Charter, tit. 5, § 29..............................	1912	19	33
1868	818	Charter, tit. 5, § 50..............................	1912	18	31
1899	517	Paving streets, § 3...............................	1912	17	30
1903	285	Police department, §§ 1, 2, amended; §§ 16–19, added...	1912	295	535
1906	28	Bonds and certificates of indebtedness, § 1..............	1912	16	29
		Public records and history division in education department:			
1911	380	Created; functions. All repealed......................	1913	424	893

IV. CHANGES IN LAWS, OTHER THAN THE CONSOLIDATED LAWS AND CODES,
1912–13 — (*Continued*).

Laws of.	Chap-ter.	SUBJECTS AND SECTIONS.	Year.	Chap-ter.	Page.
		Putnam county:			
1857	179	Improvement and repair of highway, § 8. (*See note, L.* 1913, *p.* 447)...............................	1913	252	447
1858	138	Improvement and repair of highway, § 2. (*See note, L.* 1913, *p.* 447)...............................	1913	252	447
		Queens Borough Public Library:			
1907	164	Charter, § 3...	1913	541	1464
		Queens county:			
1899	441	Commissioner of jurors, § 9.........................	1913	438	915
		Rensselaer:			
1897	359	Charter. All repealed...............................	1913	481	1159
1898	326	Amends charter. All repealed.......................	1913	481	1159
1901	294	Amends charter. All repealed except § 259...........	1913	481	1159
1902	92	Amends charter. All repealed.......................	1913	481	1159
1902	446	Amends charter. All repealed.......................	1913	481	1159
1903	56	Amends charter. All repealed.......................	1913	481	1159
1905	580	Amends charter. All repealed.......................	1913	481	1159
1907	308	Amends charter. All repealed.......................	1913	481	1159
1907	309	Amends charter. All repealed.......................	1913	481	1159
1908	258	Amends charter. All repealed.......................	1913	481	1159
1910	596	Amends charter. All repealed.......................	1913	481	1159
1910	597	Amends charter. All repealed.......................	1913	481	1159
....	....	Charter revised.....................................	1913	481	1003
		Rochester:			
1907	755	Charter, § 3, subds. 10, 17–19, 21, 22..............	1913	659	1715
1907	755	Charter, § 96.......................................	1912	55	83
1907	755	Charter, § 188, subd. 4, added......................	1912	354	698
1907	755	Charter, § 273......................................	1912	370	721
1907	755	Charter, § 336, subd. 1, ¶ (f)......................	1912	54	82
1907	755	Charter, § 353, added...............................	1912	58	88
1907	755	Charter, § 383, subd. 7; §§ 631, 636................	1913	659	1730
		Rockland county:			
1905	265	Sheriff, §§ 2, 4, 8, 9..............................	1913	396	837
		Rome:			
1904	650	Charter, § 42.......................................	1912	442	879
1904	650	Charter, § 92.......................................	1912	327	654
1904	650	Charter, § 175......................................	1912	443	880
		Saint Lawrence county:			
1900	324	Sheriff, §§ 8, 11...................................	1913	383	820
		Salamanca:			
....	....	Charter...	1913	507	1207
		Saratoga Springs:			
1866	220	Charter, § 12; § 54, subd. 4a, added................	1913	171	317
1866	220	Charter, § 54, subds. 4a, 9–11, added...............	1913	169	315

IV. CHANGES IN LAWS, OTHER THAN THE CONSOLIDATED LAWS AND CODES, 1912-13 — (*Continued*).

Laws of.	Chapter.	SUBJECTS AND SECTIONS.	Year.	Chapter.	Page.
		Saratoga Springs — (*Continued*).			
1866	220	Charter, § 54, subd. 8..........................	1913	106	177
1866	220	Charter, § 82 (as added by L. 1901, ch. 250)...........	1913	104	174
1866	220	Charter, § 86..........................	1913	576	1557
1866	220	Charter, § 87..........................	1913	576	1558
1866	220	Charter, § 90, added..........................	1912	127	233
1866	220	Charter, § 91, added..........................	1912	127	234
1866	220	Charter, § 91, added..........................	1912	366	716
1866	220	Charter, § 92, added..........................	1912	127	234
1866	220	Charter, § 92, added..........................	1912	366	716
1866	220	Charter, § 93, added..........................	1912	127	235
1866	220	Charter, § 93, added..........................	1912	366	717
1866	220	Charter, § 93..........................	1913	576	1559
1866	220	Charter, § 94, added..........................	1912	127	235
1866	220	Charter, § 94, added..........................	1912	366	717
1866	220	Charter, § 94a, added..........................	1913	164	304
1866	220	Charter, §§ 95-102, added..........................	1912	127	235
1872	323	Receiver of taxes, § 5..........................	1913	105	175
1873	670	Sewers, § 4. (*See foot note, L.* 1912, p. 1059.)...........	1912	526	1059
1874	256	Roads and avenues, § 4. (*See foot note, L.* 1912, p. 1059.)	1912	526	1059
1880	68	Tax sales, § 9, added..........................	1912	525	1056
1880	68	Tax sales, § 9 renumbered § 10..........................	1913	170	317
1880	68	Tax sales, § 9, added..........................	1913	170	316
1880	68	Tax sales, §§ 10-13, added..........................	1912	525	1056
		Seneca:			
1853	252	School district number one in town of Seneca, Ontario county. All repealed..........................	1913	427	904
1855	357	School district number one in town of Seneca, Ontario county. All repealed..........................	1913	427	904
1869	43	School district number one in town of Seneca, Ontario county. All repealed..........................	1913	427	904
1870	9	School district number one in town of Seneca, Ontario county. All repealed..........................	1913	427	904
		Society of War of 1812:			
1895	91	Charter, §§ 16-18, added..........................	1913	513	1358
		State institutions:			
1911	822	Appropriation; institution at Newark, § 1..............	1913	604	1623
		Supreme court:			
1902	274	Special terms in Jamestown and Olean, § 1............	1913	449	927
		Syracuse:			
1906	75	Department of assessment and taxation, § 7a, added.....	1912	137	253
1906	75	Department of assessment and taxation, §§ 18-20.......	1912	409	794
1906	75	Department of assessment and taxation, §§ 23-27.......	1912	408	792
		Syracuse University:			
1911	851	State college of forestry, § 2, subd. 1..................	1913	161	301
1911	851	State college of forestry, § 3.........................	1912	15	27
1911	851	State college of forestry, § 3.........................	1913	339	632
1911	851	State college of forestry, § 6.........................	1912	15	28

IV. CHANGES IN LAWS, OTHER THAN THE CONSOLIDATED LAWS AND CODES,
1912–13 — (*Concluded*).

Laws of.	Chap-ter.	SUBJECTS AND SECTIONS.	Year.	Chap-ter.	Page.
		Troy:			
1892	670	Charter, tit. 4, § 14................................	1913	671	1765
		Troy Academy:			
1834	295	Charter (not amended in terms)......................	1912	143	264
1839	4	Amends charter. All repealed........................	1912	143	266
		Utica:			
1862	18	Charter, § 99......................................	1913	160	290
1865	659	Collection of taxes, §§ 2, 4, 7, amended; §§ 5, 6, repealed..	1913	287	520
1907	161	Firemen's pension fund, § 5, subd. 1, amended, subd. 4, added...	1912	345	660
1907	351	Park board, § 3a, added.............................	1913	276	503
		Wales:			
1910	565	Cancellation of Big Tree road assessment. All repealed..	1913	78	135
		Washington county:			
1819	66	Jury districts. All repealed.........................	1913	15	24
		Watervliet:			
1911	184	Charter, § 17.......................................	1912	423	820
		Watkins:			
1861	125	Charter, tit. 8, § 2.................................	1912	210	375
		Westchester county:			
1905	137	Publication of official notices by county clerk. All repealed..	1912	94	165
1905	138	Publication of official notices by board of supervisors. All repealed......................................	1912	93	164
1905	646	Sewer system, §§ 3, 4, 14............................	1912	550	1361
1905	646	Sewer system, § 17..................................	1913	417	880
		West Seneca:			
1911	459	High school bonds, title, §§ 1–3.....................	1912	41	62
		White Plains:			
1867	518	Charter, tit. 2, §§ 4, 8.............................	1912	493	1017
1867	518	Charter, tit. 2, §§ 18, 19...........................	1913	300	544
1867	518	Charter, tit. 4, § 1.................................	1912	493	1020
1867	518	Charter, tit. 4, § 1.................................	1913	300	546
1867	518	Charter, tit. 4, § 8.................................	1912	126	232
1867	518	Charter, tit. 4, § 8.................................	1913	300	544
1867	518	Charter, tit. 7, § 20................................	1912	493	1022
1905	148	Public library, § 3..................................	1913	14	23
1911	666	Police pension fund, § 2, subd. 8, added.............	1913	661	1747
		Yonkers:			
1908	452	Charter, art. 3, § 1, subd. 40, added.................	1913	87	153
1908	452	Charter, art. 4, § 1; art. 5, §§ 14, 19–21; art. 6, §§ 5–8, 10–14, 17...	1912	424	821

TABLE OF LEGALIZING ACTS.

TABLE OF LEGALIZING ACTS OF 1913.

INDEX.

INDEX.

5

6

166   INDEX.

Conservation department: *See also* Conservation commission; Conservation
    law headings; Fires; Forest headings; Lands of state; Parks and
    reservations, state; Water headings.

INDEX.

INDEX.

Letters: *See* Administrators and executors.

License fees: *See* Taxes and assessments.

Prisons, state, local laws affecting: *See* Public buildings headings; Prison
headings preceding and following; Names of following institutions:

Auburn Prison
Clinton Prison
Dannemora State Hospital
Great Meadow Prison
Harlem Prison

Matteawan State Hospital
Sing Sing Prison
State Farm for Women
State Prison for Women

12

State boards and commissions: *See* Commissions, state. created or reorganized; State boards and commissions law amended: State departments, boards, bureaus and commissions.

State boards and commissions law amended: (*See Table of amendments preceding index, p. 73.*)

State capitol: *See* Capitol.

Albany Home School for the Oral Instruction of the Deaf.
Catholic Institution for the Blind.
Central New York Institution for Deaf-Mutes, Rome.
Craig Colony for Epileptics, Sonyea.
Eastern New York Reformatory, Napanoch.
Firemen's Association Home, Hudson.

State charitable institutions, local — Continued:

Hoffman Island quarantine station; *See* Health officer of the Port of New York.

Institution for the Improved Instruction of Deaf-Mutes, New York City.

International Sunshine Society.

Le Couteulx Saint Mary's Institution for Improved Instruction of Deaf-Mutes, Buffalo.

Letchworth Village for Epileptics, Theills.

New York House of Refuge for Juvenile Delinquents, Randall's Island.

New York Institute for the Education of the Blind.

New York Institution for the Instruction of the Deaf and Dumb.

New York State Custodial Asylum for Feeble-Minded Women.

New York State Hospital for Care of Crippled and Deformed Children, West Haverstraw.

New York State Hospital for Treatment of Incipient Pulmonary Tuberculosis, Raybrook.

New York State Reformatory, Elmira.

New York State Reformatory for Women, Bedford.

New York State School for the Blind, Batavia.

New York State Soldiers and Sailors Home, Bath.

New York State Training School for Boys, Yorktown Heights.

New York State Training School for Girls, Hudson.

New York State Women's Relief Corps Home, Oxford.

Northern New York Institution for Deaf-Mutes, Malone.

Rome State Custodial Asylum for Feeble-Minded Persons, Rome.

Saint Joseph's Institution for Improved Instruction of Deaf-Mutes, West Chester.

State Agricultural and Industrial School, Industry.

State Industrial Farm Colony for Tramps and Vagrants.

State Institute for the Study of Malignant Diseases, Buffalo.

State Farm for Women.

State Reformatory for Misdemeanants.

Swinburne Island Quarantine Hospital: *See* Health officer of the Port of New York.

Syracuse State Institution for Feeble-Minded Children.

Thomas Indian School, Iroquois.

Western House of Refuge for Women, Albion.

Western New York Institution for Improved Instruction of Deaf-Mutes, Rochester.

13